UNIVERSITY CASEBOOK SERIES®

LAW OF MASS COMMUNICATIONS

FREEDOM AND CONTROL OF PRINT AND BROADCAST MEDIA

FIFTEENTH EDITION

BILL LOVING, J.D.
Professor of Journalism
San Luis Obispo, California

MICHAEL T. MARTÍNEZ, PH.D.
Asst. Professor of Journalism
University of Tennessee
Knoxville, Tennessee

FOUNDATION PRESS

444 Cedar Street, Suite 700
St. Paul, MN 55101
1-877-888-1330

Printed in the United States of America

ISBN: 978-1-68467-687-3

To Dwight L. Teeter, Jr.

PREFACE TO THE FIFTEENTH EDITION

The Fourteenth and Fifteenth editions of *"Law of Mass Communications"* marks the passage of Dwight Leland Teeter, Jr., one of the founding authors of the text. He died Feb. 27, 2015 in heart surgery. He is and will be greatly be missed. A brief recounting of Dwight's life follows, drawn from any number of obituaries and remembrances published by friends and colleagues.

Dwight was born in Avenal, California, a small town in the heart of the state's oil country in 1935. His father worked for Standard Oil in the Kettleman Oil Fields. His mother kept the household. He grew up with the families and children of other oil field workers. Teeter told of meeting then-California Gov. Earl Warren. Warren had gone to Avenal to dedicate a community hospital. Ten-year-old Dwight got an introduction and the chance to shake Warren's hand. "I haven't washed this hand, since," he would say with pride.

He was admitted the University of California, Berkeley. In order to pay for school, he worked as a roustabout for Standard Oil in the oil fields near his boyhood home. He studied journalism and continued his studies earning a master's degree in journalism. As he worked on his master's thesis, Dwight went to the Boalt Hall law library. When Law Dean William Prosser learned that Dwight was looking for information on the *Roth v. United States* obscenity case, he had him thrown out saying the library was only for law students.

Dwight later invited Jake Ehrlich to speak to the student chapter of the Society of Professional Journalists. Ehrlich was lead attorney for Lawrence Ferlinghetti, proprietor of City Lights Books along with L. Speiser and A. Bendich, defending the sale of Allen Ginsberg's book *"Howl and Other Poems"* in the obscenity trial. When Dwight told Ehrlich about being tossed out of the law library by Dean Prosser, the famed lawyer reportedly made a dismissive sound and said, "The problem with Cal's law faculty was that the professors do not know the difference between Blackstone, the legal authority, and the Blackstone Hotel in Chicago where you used to be able to get laid for $5." Ehrlich invited Dwight to do his research in his law office library.

While, at Berkley, Dwight met Letitia (Tish) Thoreson of Bismarck, North Dakota. She was an English major at Mills College. They married and carried on a love affair that spanned more than five decades. Tish was gracious and warm. She would die in 2009.

Dwight and Tish Teeter left California and traveled to Wisconsin where he earned his Ph.D. in mass communications with specializations in American history and law. He studied with Harold L. "Bud" Nelson and worked with him on the first edition of *"Law of Mass Communications"* in 1969.

Dwight was dean of the University of Tennessee's College of Communications from 1991 to 2002 and returned to full-time teaching in

2003. Before arriving at UT, Knoxville, he was a professor at the University of Wisconsin-Milwaukee; the William P. Hobby Centennial Professor of Communication and chair of the Department of Journalism at the University of Texas at Austin; professor and acting chair of the School of Journalism at the University of Kentucky; associate professor at the University of Wisconsin; visiting associate professor at the University of Washington; and assistant professor at Iowa State University.

He was a prolific researcher and academic writer and generous with his time and support for young academics. He would read a draft of an academic paper by a new assistant professor and suggest that it become a book. He shared his expertise and encyclopedic knowledge of the law and history. In some circles, he was known almost exclusively as a historian and he helped found the Symposium on the 19th Century Press, the Civil War and Free Expression. Dwight pursued his own family history and conducted extensive research on his great-grandfather Jacob "Jake" Teeter, sheriff of Truckee, California.

In addition to his teaching at American universities, Dwight lectured at the Norwegian Institute of Journalism in Fredrikstad, the Dutch School of Journalism at Utrecht, the Danish School of Journalism in Aarhus and the Napier University School of Journalism in Edinburgh. He traveled to the Soviet Union with colleague and friend Donald M. Gilmore of the University of Minnesota to talk about press freedoms at a time when press freedoms were nonexistent.

Dwight was a modest, self-effacing man with a wicked sense of humor and a stronger sense of justice. He was incensed by the words and actions of those in government whose primary concerns were amassing power and prestige and less about service to the public. He believed in the people, their rights to know what government does and their right to express themselves.

He expressed great disgust and anger with the Supreme Court's decisions in *Citizens United v. Federal Election Commission*, that overturned two important Supreme Court precedents restricting corporate contributions supporting or opposing political candidates; *McCutcheon et al. v. Federal Election Commission*, striking limits on campaign contributions; and *McBurney, et al v. Young, Deputy Commissioner and Director, Virginia Division of Child Support Enforcement,* et. al., in which the Court rejected the idea of a general citizen right to information about their own government. Some of his comments about sitting members of the court cannot be recorded here because the textbook is not printed on asbestos paper.

Dwight enjoyed the respect of his peers. He was president of the Association for Education in Journalism and Mass Communication (AEJMC) from 1986 to 1987. In 1973, he co-founded the Law Division with Don Gillmore. As clerk of the division, he started the newsletter now known as *Media Law Notes*. In 1968, he started the history division newsletter, *Clio Among the Media*.

He served on the editorial boards of *Journalism and Mass Communication Quarterly*, *Communication Law and Policy*, *Mass Communication Review*, and *Journalism Monographs*. He was the associate editor of *American National Biography*. He was a founding member and served on the editorial board of *Critical Studies in Mass Communication*.

In 1991, Dwight received the Society of Professional Journalists Distinguished Teaching Award. In 2006, he received the Hazel Dicken-Garcia Distinguished Journalism Historian Award, presented at UT Chattanooga during the Symposium on the 19th Century Press, the Civil War and Free Expression. In 2001, he received the Distinguished Service Award from AEJMC.

Dwight taught six Pulitzer Prize winners over the years. He sent Associated Press photographer Neal Ulevich a congratulatory note after his Pulitzer Prize award, jokingly taking credit for Ulevich's success. Ulevich, ever the quick wit, responded that he had to settle for a Pulitzer, saying that knowing Teeter cost him the Nobel Prize.

Dwight was a good friend, colleague and mentor.

BILL LOVING
MICHAEL T. MARTÍNEZ

May 2020

SUMMARY OF CONTENTS

TABLE OF CONTENTS

TABLE OF CASES

UNIVERSITY CASEBOOK SERIES®

LAW OF MASS COMMUNICATIONS

FREEDOM AND CONTROL OF PRINT AND BROADCAST MEDIA

FIFTEENTH EDITION

PART 1

Philosophical and Constitutional Foundations of Free Expression

CHAPTER 1

FOUNDATIONS FOR FREEDOM

Sec.

1. The Worth of Freedom.
2. The Constitutional Guarantees.
3. "The Intent of the Framers."

A major test of a nation's freedom is the degree of liberty its people have in speaking, writing, and publishing. The hand of authority rests lightly on speech and press at some places and times, heavily at others. But its presence is felt everywhere, including the nations of the Western World which generally consider themselves the most freedom-loving of all.

Throughout history, some degree of legal control over expression has been in force even in the most free societies. Although values of free speech and press may be considered paramount and exalted, there are circumstances where other values may take priority. For example, the individual's right to a good reputation limits verbal attacks through the law of civil libel. In wartime, assertions of national security may take precedence over press freedom. Laws regulating business, industry and trade apply fully to the commercial press, to advertising, to public relations, and to broadcasting, the Web and to newer communication technologies.

The goal of this textbook is to serve students in a first or survey course in communication law. A major reason for this book is to help communicators try to "stay out of trouble," to learn something about the pitfalls of libel and slander, invasion of privacy, and copyright infringement. Perhaps the examples and discussion offered here can serve, as legal historian James Willard Hurst suggested of his field, like training for wrestlers: to help keep their balance, to avoid being upset by sudden and unexpected onslaughts.[1] And on many occasions, of course, trying to behave ethically will prevent legal questions from arising at all.

The spread of social media, unknown when this book was first published in the 1960s, has meant that individual communication also is mass communication. This means that Topics that once would be considered strictly personal are now matters of societal interest as once-private conversations are delivered to a vast audience through ubiquitous social and news media.

This book will provide students with some "how to" information, especially in chapters dealing with access to information.[2] It also tries to

---

[1] James Willard Hurst, Introductory Lecture, course on Legal History, University of Wisconsin-Madison, Spring, 1961.

[2] See Chaps. 8 and 9 dealing with access to government information and the courts.

give students some understanding of the legal systems of the United States, especially as they interact with the sweeping field vaguely called "communications law." The law of mass communications can *not* be taught as if it is some compartmentalized area marked off by logical boundaries. Of necessity, this book cuts across most areas covered in a law school curriculum:

Types of Law

Constitutional Law deals with the basic governmental framework, as with a state constitution or the federal Constitution. The federal Constitution—the highest law of the land—divides government powers into the legislative, executive and judicial branches. Powers of government are apportioned among those branches, and the document also lists, in its first ten amendments, powers that the U.S. government may *not* use against its citizens.

The federal Constitution is one of many constitutions in the United States. There are, after all, fifty-one legal systems: the federal system plus fifty state systems. In addition, there are charters governing the organization and operation of cities and counties. Keep in mind that the federal Constitution is the highest law of the land: state constitutional provisions in conflict with it are not enforceable.[3]

By their nature, as basic or "organic" law, written constitutions are not easily changed. As spelled out in the federal Constitution, it takes the vote of three-fourths of the states (via states' legislatures or called constitutional conventions) to amend the Constitution.

If a state or lower federal court decision conflicts with the federal Constitution, that law or decision may be found unconstitutional and thus null and void. Constitutional law involving the First Amendment guarantees of free speech and press is central to this book.

Most of the nation's law is *statutory*: made by legislative bodies, from Congress to state legislatures to county boards and city councils. If the meaning of a statute is at issue in a legal case or controversy, the meaning of the statute can be interpreted by courts. This search for meaning, called *statutory construction*, tries to define vague terms in the statute, often by digging back into the statute's *legislative history*. What did the legislature intend to do when it passed the measure?

There are plentiful examples of statutes directly affecting the communication media. Consider, for example, the basic federal anti-obscenity law, 18 U.S.C.A. § 1461 [Title or Volume 18, United States Code, at Sec. 1461]. That statute, passed in 1872, forbids sending obscene material through the mails or in interstate commerce. But what is

---

[3] "This Constitution, and the laws of the United States which shall be made in pursuance thereof; and all treaties made, or which shall be made, under the authority of the United States, shall be the supreme law of the land; and the judges in every state shall be bound thereby, anything in the Constitution or laws of any State to the contrary notwithstanding." U.S. Constitution, Article VI.

obscene? The statute is unclear. As discussed in Chap. 3, U.S. courts have devoted much energy trying to define "the obscene."

Statutory Law was not always the most important branch of law in the United States. Well into the Nineteenth Century, *common law* was the most important point of growth. *Common law* was law that was "found" or "discovered" by judges, based on the way particular disputes or transgressions were handled by prior judges or courts. It was a tradition of the law. *Common law* is distinct from *civil law*.[4] As Winston Churchill explained in his A History of the English Speaking Peoples,[5] "The law was already there, in the customs of the land, and it was only a matter of discovering it by diligent study and comparison of recorded decisions in earlier cases, and applying it to the particular dispute before the court." Judges, in other words, made law, using earlier decisions as *precedent* to guide them.

Although the United States began its legal order on the *common law* system derived from the English tradition, actual judge-made law-making has been rare during the past century. It has been suggested that the rarity of common-law creation during the Twentieth Century spurred considerable scholarly fascination with the law of privacy. Much of privacy law has common-law origins, as described in Chap. 6, for it was created by courts instead of legislatures, at least initially.

Equity is an area which originated in England centuries ago. An officer of the Crown called the Chancellor devised a court—called a Court of Chancery or a Court of Equity (based on what was fair or equitable)—to decide disputes which did not fit into the ordinary framework of the regular or "law" courts[6]. Courts in the United States have combined the functions, and now are said to "sit in both law and equity." Pieces of "equity" remain and are sometimes in the news. For example, in some situations the monetary award remedy available by winning a lawsuit would not be appropriate. In such instances, what is "equitable" is to have a court order someone to do something (as in a writ of "mandamus," which is Latin for "we demand"), or not to do something (as by a court granting an injunction or "cease and desist" order).

One of the most famous First Amendment decisions featured in this book—the "Pentagon Papers" case discussed in Chap. 2—involved an

---

[4] *Civil law* also is the term applied to civil lawsuits where one party sues another party to protect private rights. It can be confusing but for all intents and purposes, when you are dealing with law in the United States, the term *civil law* will refer to civil lawsuits. The exception is Louisiana which continued its *civil law* tradition from its French legal antecedents.

[5] Winston S. Churchill, *A History of the English Speaking Peoples* (New York: Barnes & Noble, 1993), p. 224.

[6] Say that a church in your neighborhood has decided to provide a public service by using its bells to chime the hour, every hour, 24 hours a day. A civil suit needs an injury. You didn't sleep well but what is the measure of damages? Money will not restore your sleep. A suit in equity that results in an injunction against the church to stop the ringing from midnight to 6 a.m. would solve your problem. That is the difference between a suit for damages and a suit to achieve fairness. See *Terhune v. Trustees of Methodist Episcopal Church of Matawan, Court of Chancery of New Jersey*, March 7, 1917, 87 N.J. Eq. 1952 B.Stockton 195, 100 A. 342.

injunction ordering *The New York Times* not to publish stories based on secret documents on the history of the Vietnam War. In 1971, the Supreme Court of the United States overturned the injunction to allow publication of the "Vietnam Archive" stories to continue.

Administrative Law has grown rapidly in the past century. As the nation grew more complex, Congress found itself overmatched by commercial and industrial growth involved in the industrial revolution and the nation's westward expansion. Beginning in 1890 with the Interstate Commerce Commission (to regulate railroads), Congress delegated some of its power to an administrative agency. Similar agencies followed; two having particular applicability to the mass media are the prime federal regulator of advertising, the Federal Trade Commission (FTC), established in 1914, and the Federal Communications Commission (FCC), established in 1934 but actually following a pattern set by the Federal Radio Commission Act of 1927. Additionally, the federal Executive branch has the power to make a kind of law through *executive orders*. For example, "Confidential," "Secret" and "Top Secret" document classifications were established in 1951 by a presidential executive order by Harry S Truman, and remain in effect today. President Donald Trump issued 117 executive orders between the start of his administration and the beginning of 2019.[7]

Another way of classifying legal actions is as *criminal* and *civil* actions. "*Black's Law Dictionary*" (Seventh Ed.) defines a crime as "A social harm that the law makes punishable." A crime can be accomplished by *omission*, failing to perform a legally commanded duty (e.g. failure to notify the authorities if a person has knowledge of a terrorist plot) or *commission* (e.g. killing someone on purpose with a blunt instrument). The latter example could lead to a charge of murder, or wrongful taking of another's life. Crimes are variously classified as *misdemeanors* (minor crimes, usually carrying a jail term of less than a year) and *felonies* (major crimes, generally defined as carrying a jail term of more than a year). Crimes to be taken up in this book include obscenity, seditious libel and some aspects of copyright infringement.

Civil Law includes personal damage actions ("lawsuits") in which a person asks for "the establishment, recovery, or redress of private and civil rights." If a publication hurts your reputation by printing a false and harmful statement about you, you could bring a legal action ("sue"), asking for "damages" ("money") in order to be made whole (restored to the position or condition that you occupied before the defendant committed her tortious conduct). Much of this book is taken up with discussion of damage actions in the areas of libel, invasion of privacy, and copyright infringement.

---

[7] https://www.federalregister.gov/presidential-documents/executive-orders. His orders included the repeal of the Affordable Care Act, blocking reversal of a ban on Arctic oil drilling, reducing federal regulations and establishing a commission to investigate voter fraud.

Another term which is basic in law school curricula is *tort*. It is a French word meaning "wrong," and the law assumes that if persons have serious wrongs done to them, they ought to be able to sue for compensation, in other words, to be restored to the position or state of existence they occupied before the defendant committed her tort. Libel is a tort. Invasion of privacy is a tort.

For a further exposure to legal terminology, please see Appendices B and C of this book.

1. THE WORTH OF FREEDOM

Major values underlying free speech and press include society's need for maximum flow of information and opinion and the individual's right to fulfillment.

Freedom to speak, to write, to travel—and to criticize governments and government officials—now seems as natural as breathing to most residents of the United States. Early in the Twenty-First Century, Americans generally take for granted systems of representative self-government, with legislative and executive officials—and some judges as well—selected at regular intervals via secret ballots.

Taking freedoms for granted can be the world's most dangerous complacency. Particular concern should be directed at official efforts to discourage dissent or to push for some particular orthodoxy.

If dissenters' freedoms are not protected, then all freedoms are in danger. Sometimes, individuals will find that they hold views that are widely despised, and will take risks in speaking out, especially in times of great social or political tension.[8] And if there is no dissent, the results may be disastrous. Consider the words of Martin Niemoeller, haunted by the millions of Jews killed in Hitler's Holocaust:[9]

---

8 Consider Colin Kaepernick, an NFL quarterback. In 2016, Kaepernick began a quiet protest of the deaths of black Americans at the hands of police. He began by sitting down during the national anthem during the first two preseason games of the San Francisco 49ers in 2016. In the third game, he knelt. A former Seahawks player and Green Beret Nate Boyer talked Kaepernick into kneeling. [Will Brinson, "Here's how Nate Boyer got Colin Kaepernick to go from sitting to kneeling HBO's 'Real Sports' spoke to the former Green Beret," *CBS Sports*, Sept. 27, 2016] "Boyer wrote an open letter to Kaepernick earlier this season, and it caused the two to meet up and discuss America and honoring the anthem." 'We sorta came to a middle ground where he would take a knee alongside his teammates,' Boyer says. 'Soldiers take a knee in front of a fallen brother's grave, you know, to show respect. When we're on a patrol, you know, and we go into a security halt, we take a knee, and we pull security.' * * * He said, 'I think that would be—I think—I think that would be really powerful,' Boyer recalls."

President Donald Trump seized on the protest to condemn Kaepernick and other players who chose to protest. "Wouldn't you love to see one of these NFL owners, when somebody disrespects our flag, to say, 'Get that son of a bitch off the field right now. Out! He's fired. He's fired!' " [Bryan Armen Graham, "Donald Trump blasts NFL anthem protesters: 'Get that son of a bitch off the field', *The Guardian*, Sept. 22, 2017.] Trump said the protests were an affront to the anthem, the flag, the military and America itself. P.R. Lockhard, "Trump's reaction to the NFL protests shows how he fights the culture war," *Vox*, Feb. 4, 2018.

9 Martin Niemoeller, *Exile in the Fatherland*, ed. by H.G. Locke (Grand Rapids, MI: Eerdmans, 1986), p. viii.

> First they came for the socialists, and I did not speak out—because I was not a socialist. Then they came for the trade unionists, and I did not speak out—because I was not a trade unionist. Then they came for the Jews, and I did not speak out—because I was not a Jew. Then they came for me—and there was no one left to speak for me.

Challenges to free expression reach every conceivable topic of discussion and actual and symbolic speech. Laws have been passed and enforced protecting particular religions,[10] flags of both individual states and the United States[11] and even foods.[12] One crucial test of freedom is the ability to go unpunished after venting severe criticism of those holding political power. Another is whether a government official can check over what you've written and deny you the right to publish it, that's pre-publication censorship. More than 350 years ago, the now-legendary poet John Milton argued in his "*Areopagitica*" against pre-publication censorship by the English government and church authorities, who then had power inseparable from government. Writing in 1644, Milton declared that because religious truth was so essential to the fate of mankind the authorities should open up the arena for debate. Truth was the only safe basis for a society's life, he wrote in 1644:[13]

> And though all the winds of doctrine were let loose to play upon the earth, so truth be in the field, we do injuriously, by licensing and prohibiting, to misdoubt her strength. Let her and falsehood grapple; who ever knew Truth put to the worse, in a free and open encounter?

Those words from John Milton—expressing what is often called the "diversity principle"—still resound in key American court decisions on

---

[10] New York once had a statute denying motion picture exhibitors the ability to show their films if a part of the movie was "immoral, inhuman" or "sacrilegious." Similarly, Tennessee had a statute making it a crime for persons to engage in disorderly conduct which was defined to include the use of "blasphemous" language.

[11] Examples include a Massachusetts statute that made it a crime punishable by fine and imprisonment for "Whoever publicly mutilates, tramples upon, defaces or treats contemptuously the flag of the United States or of Massachusetts * * *" and an Arizona Law that declared that "a person who publicly mutilates, defaces, defiles, tramples upon, or by word or act casts contempt upon a flag is guilty of a misdemeanor." "Flag" was defined as including "any flag, standard, color, ensign or shield, or any copy, picture or representation thereof, made of any substance or of any size, purporting to be the flag, standard, color, ensign or shield of the United States or of this state."

[12] Talk show host Oprah Winfrey was sued under a Texas food disparagement law for more than $1 million after she broadcast a program in which she declared, after learning about bovine spongiform encephalopathy or "mad cow" disease, "It has just stopped me cold from eating another burger." She won the lawsuit. More than a dozen states enacted laws allowing suits over comments critical of particular foods. See Marianne Lavelle, "Food Abuse: Basis for Suits," *The National Law Journal*, May 5, 1997, p. A1.

[13] John Milton, *Areopagitica* (Chicago, 1953). See Thomas I. Emerson, *The System of Freedom of Expression* (New York: Random House, 1970), Chap. 1, for discussion of social and individual values of free expression. See also Vincent Blasi, "The Checking Value in First Amendment Theory," 1977 *Am.Bar Found.Res.J.* 523.

the scope of freedom.[14] Legal scholars generally look to four philosophical bases for freedom of expression. All but one came after the First Amendment was created and even Milton's ideas really began to be accepted by American courts almost 400 years after he wrote in defense of free expression. Each has been advanced in arguments for free expression.

I. Marketplace of Ideas

II. Individual Fulfillment

III. Safety Valve

IV. Self-Governance

I. Marketplace of Ideas—This philosophy began with that great Seventeenth Century English author and poet, John Milton, as quoted above at footnote 13. Strictly speaking, however, the "marketplace" phrasing should be thought of as a modern re-wording of Milton's arguments to make a judicial argument in Twentieth Century America. The "marketplace of ideas" wording came from a passionate dissent by Justice Oliver Wendell Holmes, Jr., denouncing the World War I-era conviction of Jacob Abrams for violating the Espionage Act of 1917 and its 1918 "sedition" amendment. [The case of *Abrams v. U.S.* (1918) is discussed in more detail later in this chapter.] In his dissent, Justice Holmes declared that "the best test of truth is the power of the thought to get itself accepted in the competition of the market * * *"[15] Milton's anti-censorship ideas echo in decisions of the Supreme Court. And in some cases, a majority of the Supreme Court of the United States has adopted Milton's belief that a clash of ideas is needed to produce truth.[16]

Milton wrote "*Areopagitica*" in response to an act of the English Parliament giving exclusive permission to print to the Stationers' Company, a guild of government-approved printers operating in and around London, where censors could keep close watch on what was being printed. It should be noted that although Milton argued that truth was more likely to emerge from open discussion than from repression, he had his own limits. Milton opposed giving Roman Catholics religious freedom.

Even if Milton was not a model of consistency, his ringing words against censorship still echoed in the Supreme Court in the Twentieth

---

[14] See, e.g., the dissent by Justice O.W. Holmes, Jr., in *Abrams v. United States*, 250 U.S. 616, 40 S.Ct. 17 (1919) and Justice Hugo L. Black's opinion for the Court in *Associated Press v. United States*, 326 U.S. 1, 65 S.Ct. 1416 (1945). See also discussion in Zechariah Chafee, Jr., *Free Speech in the United States* (Cambridge, Mass., 1964 [6th printing of 1941 ed.]), pp. 3, 29, 298, 316, 325, 559–561.

[15] *Abrams v. United States*, 250 U.S. 616, 629, 40 S.Ct. 17, 22 (1919).

[16] See, e.g., *Associated Press v. United States*, 326 U.S. 1, 28, 65 S.Ct. 1416, 1428 (1945), quoting Judge Learned Hand, *United States v. Associated Press*, 52 F.Supp. 362, 372 (S.D.N.Y.1943). The Supreme Court approvingly quoted Judge Hand's declaration that the First Amendment " '* * * presupposes that right conclusions are more likely to be gathered out of a multitude of tongues than through any kind of authoritative selection.' " That language bears great similarity to John Milton's arguments against licensing and pre-publication censorship made three centuries earlier. A direct use of "marketplace of ideas" is found in *Reno v. ACLU*, 521 U.S. 844, 117 S.Ct. 2329, 2351 (1997) discussed on page 9.

Century. Consider Supreme Court Justice Robert H. Jackson's downright Miltonian words in a 1943 opinion. After referring to the United States as a country of "individualism and rich cultural diversities," Justice Jackson wrote for the Court in support of a freedom to differ.[17]

> If there is any fixed star in our constitutional constellation, it is that no official, high or petty, can prescribe what shall be orthodox in politics, nationalism, religion or other matters of opinion * * *

Justice Jackson's words amounted to an invocation of the "marketplace of ideas" philosophy at least in terms of the ability of government to decide what goods should be allowed in the marketplace. This extension was very much in line with the ideas of the Nineteenth Century British philosopher John Stuart Mill. In "*On Liberty*", Mill wrote that members of society needed access to many kinds of ideas, false as well as true, to discern the truth. Mill declared that government had no legitimate power to suppress opinions:[18]

> If all mankind minus one were of one opinion, and only one person were of the contrary opinion, mankind would be no more justified in silencing that one person, than he, if he had the power, would be justified in silencing mankind.

It is not always easy to separate society's need from the individual's right as the reason for freedom of expression. If the individual's right is thoroughly protected, the social good in the confrontation of ideas presumably follows. The English writer John Locke, often called the philosophical father of the American Revolution, argued persuasively late in the Seventeenth Century in favor of the individual's rights. In words which later echoed in the Declaration of Independence, Locke wrote of the "natural right" of every person to life, liberty, and property. His ideological descendants included speech and press as among those liberties, equally applicable to all men in all times and situations.[19]

In the Twentieth and Twenty-First Century, social-good arguments have been more compelling than natural rights as a basis for freedom of expression. Society's stake in free speech and press is plain in the structure and functioning of a self-governing people. Only through a "clash of ideas in the open marketplace"[20] can working truths be reached. The social good argument runs that the widest diversity of opinion and information must flow through channels of debate and discussion to arrive at worthwhile solutions to problems adding up to sound public policy. Although Milton's pleas for freer debate were couched in terms of

---

[17] *West Virginia State Board of Education v. Barnette*, 319 U.S. 624, 63 S.Ct. 1178 (1943). Justice Jackson wrote for the Court in a 7–2 decision that children of Jehovah's Witnesses could not be compelled to salute the flag because this ceremony conflicted with their religious beliefs.

[18] John Stuart Mill, *On Liberty* (New York: Appleton-Century, 1947), p. 16.

[19] John Locke, *Second Treatise of Government*, ed. Thomas P. Peardon (N.Y., 1952); Leo Strauss, *Natural Right and History* (Chicago, 1953).

[20] Cf. Holmes, supra note 15.

seeking religious truth, Twentieth Century theorists and judges found the confrontation of idea against idea and fact against fact essential to all kinds of "truth," whether in social relations, politics, religion, economics or art.

The marketplace of ideas got a strong endorsement in *Reno v. ACLU*, 521 U.S. 844, 117 S.Ct. 2329 (1997). A coalition of Internet service providers, website operators, free speech advocates and the ACLU successfully challenged the Communications Decency Act (CDA), a part of the Telecommunications Act of 1996. The CDA made it illegal for persons knowingly to transmit "indecent" or "obscene" material to minors through the Internet. The challengers did not oppose the obscenity provisions but rather focused on the indecency ban.

A part of the argument advanced by the U.S. Department of Justice in support of the CDA was that the amount of indecent material on the Internet was keeping many adults from going online. This was a secondary argument to the government's main contention that minors need protection from indecent material. By protecting minors through the exclusion of indecency, the government would encourage more adults to go online. But the Supreme Court disagreed with the Justice Department.[21]

> We find this argument singularly unpersuasive. The dramatic expansion of this new marketplace of ideas contradicts the growth of the Internet has been and continues to be phenomenal. As a matter of constitutional tradition, in the absence of evidence to the contrary, we assume that governmental regulation of the content of speech is more likely to interfere with the free exchange of ideas than to encourage democratic society outweighs any theoretical but unproven benefit of censorship.

That reliance on the marketplace of ideas philosophy was extended early in 1999 in a different *ACLU v. Reno* case.[22] This newer case was a challenge to the Child Online Protection Act, known as COPA and sometimes referred to as "Son of CDA." COPA was passed by Congress in the wake of the defeat of the CDA in the Supreme Court. COPA's intent was to prevent Internet and Web content providers from knowingly allowing minors access to harmful materials. U.S. District Court Judge Lowell P. Reed, Jr., restrained enforcement of the statute declaring it unconstitutional. Judge Reed began his opinion with reference to the First Amendment and to the marketplace of ideas. Judge Reed wrote:[23]

> Although there is no complete consensus on the issue, most courts and commentators theorize that the importance of protecting freedom of speech is to foster the marketplace of

---

[21] *Reno v. ACLU*, 521 U.S. 844, 884, 117 S.Ct. 2329, 2351 (1997).

[22] *ACLU v. Reno*, 31 F.Supp.2d 473 (E.D.Pa.1999).

[23] Ibid. at 475.

> unrestricted in the marketplace of ideas, truth will be discovered. * * * Despite the protection of the First Amendment, unconventional speakers are often limited in their ability to promote such speech in the marketplace by the costs or logistics of reaching the masses, hence the adage that freedom of the press is limited to those who own one. In the medium of cyberspace, however, anyone can build a soap box out of Web pages and speak her mind in the virtual village green to an audience larger and more diverse than any the Framers could have imagined. In many respects, unconventional messages compete equally with the speech of mainstream speakers in the marketplace of ideas that is the Internet, certainly more than in most other media.

And so this philosophy continues to find support as technology increases the ability of anyone to express himself or to seek information and ideas. In point of historical fact, however, Judge Reed may have given the creators of the First Amendment too much credit. The First Amendment, as discussed near the end of this chapter, was a political compromise, not worship of Milton's argument that truth will win out in a contest with falsehood. Judge Reed's constitutional faith, however, may be might have been seen as an important effort to make the First Amendment work as the United States began the Twenty-First Century. This offers vibrant support for the idea that the Constitution is, indeed, a living and changing document.[24]

II. Individual Fulfillment—A great free press theorist—the late Yale law professor Thomas I. Emerson—argued that the proper goal for people is to realize their character and potential as human beings. To do that, minds must be free. Therefore, if any ideas, opinions or beliefs are suppressed, that is negating human nature. So free expression is an essential part of a good society that would maximize the goals of its members. Part of Professor Emerson's formulation for freedom was expressed in this way:[25]

> The root purpose of the First Amendment is to assure an effective system of freedom of expression in a democratic society. * * * [F]reedom of expression can flourish, and the goals of the system can be realized only if expression receives full protection * * * against governmental curtailment at all points.

---

[24] Judge Reed's decision was upheld by a three-judge panel of the Third Circuit Court of Appeals. But the appellate court did so on completely different grounds, finding that the use of "community standards" to determine whether material was harmful to minors made the statute unconstitutional. The U.S. Supreme Court reversed, while still maintaining the injunction against the enforcement of the statute, and sent the case back to the Third Circuit for reconsideration. The Third Circuit panel once again found the statute unconstitutional, but this time it focused on other grounds. The case is discussed in more detail in Chap. 3.

[25] Thomas I. Emerson, *The System of Freedom of Expression* (New York: Random House, 1970), p. 17.

One element of Professor Emerson's philosophy holds that while expression must be protected, conduct can be regulated. So, expressive conduct, say carrying a protest sign against American involvement in a military conflict, or blowing up a munitions dump would signal disagreement with a war. The first would be protected while the second would constitute a punishable crime.[26]

Another aspect of the Individual Fulfillment basis for free expression comes from Professor C. Edwin Baker, the Nicholas F. Gallicchio Professor of Law and Communication at the University of Pennsylvania Law School, who wrote that allowing people to engage in free expression is a way of letting them define themselves. After the Jan. 7, 2015, terrorist attack on the offices of the French satire magazine *Charlie Hebdo*, people started wearing "Je Suis Charlie"[27] on t-shirts or posting the words online. Almost as the Nov. 13, 2015 terrorist attacks in Paris were taking place, many people began to use #Prayers4Paris in their social media. That protester is participating to *define* herself publicly. The use of the phrases show the user's commitment to the ideas without expecting terrorists to lay down their guns and bombs because someone made the declaration. This is what would be, in Professor Baker's terms, self-realization or self-fulfillment through expression.[28] More commonplace examples of such self-definition can be found as consumers wear caps and clothing proclaiming their allegiance to particular athletic teams, institutions of higher education and musical groups.

III. Safety Valve—A third contention for free expression is the Safety Valve argument. That is, if you allow free speech such as in the demonstration against the use of American military power in Desert Storm, it allows people to make their statements, to vent pressure that might otherwise be diverted into violence such as the bombing of ROTC buildings which happened during the Vietnam War. One of the dangers even of peaceful protest, of course, is that it can reap violence. That is what happened, for example, on a spring day in 1970 at Kent State University, when the National Guard fired on students protesting the Vietnam conflict, killing four and wounding nine.[29] Perhaps the lesson

---

[26] Emerson, *The System of Freedom of Expression*, p. 17.

[27] "I am Charlie too, and if you attack the magazine Charlie Hebdo you attack me," or as simply "I follow Charlie." Eugene Volokh, "The two French meanings of 'Je suis Charlie'," *The Washington Post*, Jan. 9, 2015. https://www.washingtonpost.com/news/volokh-conspiracy/wp/2015/01/09/the-two-french-meanings-of-je-suis-charlie/. Two gunmen attacked the editorial offices of the magazine killing 12 people. Another 5 persons were killed before police killed the attackers. The magazine had, over the years, published satire about politics and religion including Catholicism, Judaism and Islam. The magazine published cartoons depicting Mohammed naked some years earlier.

[28] C. Edwin Baker, *Human Liberty & Freedom of Speech* (New York: Oxford University Press, 1989), pp. 48–52.

[29] Three of those killed were not protesting. Two of the students killed were walking to class when they were shot. A third student was a member of the campus ROTC and reportedly was watching the demonstration because he was curious about the protest. See, "My God! They're Killing Us" Newsweek's Coverage of the Kent State Shooting" *Newsweek*, May 4, 2015. https://www.newsweek.com/my-god-theyre-killing-us-our-1970-coverage-kent-state-328108.

here is that freedom is a risk, and that even a "safety valve" isn't absolutely safe. That risk of freedom, however, carries great rewards with it. As legal historian James Willard Hurst noted, freedom releases creative energies and makes for a productive and livable society.[30]

The importance of freedom to the individual and to society often is challenged. Freedom is always a risk, and in any society, many persons hate and fear the expression of ideas contrary to their own. Is it permissible to denigrate races, nationalities or religions? Should pornographers be allowed to subordinate women in demeaning or violent depictions? Should a socialist newspaper be allowed to publish in times of threat from "alien ideologies?" Even today, after more than two centuries under the First Amendment to the Constitution proclaiming freedom of speech and press, many Americans would answer that *true freedom* protects only virtuous or responsible communication. But who is to say what is responsible?

There is also the related view that true liberation of societies is not possible as long as toleration of aggression in national policies is practiced, or if racial, religious, or class hatred may be stirred up. Following this position, some ideas and policies may call for them to be forbidden, for to permit them to be expressed is to tolerate conditions that perpetuate servitude and misery.[31]

Ironically, the right to challenge the very principle of free expression is an indicator of the extent of freedom in a society. In John B. Wolfe's words, "* * * Man can *seem* to be free in any society, no matter how authoritarian, as long as he accepts the postulates of the society, but he can only *be* free in a society that is willing to allow its basic postulates to be questioned."[32]

Selective views of freedom seem insipid when one considers eloquent words from the legendary Justice Louis D. Brandeis from *Whitney v. California*.[33] The case involved the conviction of a woman from California's social elite on charges of "syndicalism." Charlotte Anita Whitney, known as Anita Whitney was the niece of U.S. Supreme Court Justice Stephen J. Field and financier Cyrus Field. She was convicted on those charges for having participated in the founding of the California Chapter of the Communist Party, a crime worth years in prison.

In a concurring opinion, Justice Brandeis said the Founding Fathers recognized the hazards of discouraging[34]

> thought, hope and imagination; [seeing clearly that] that fear breeds repression; that repression breeds hate; that hate

---

30 James Willard Hurst, *Law and Conditions of Freedom*, passim.

31 Robert P. Wolff, Barrington Moore, Jr., and Herbert Marcuse, *A Critique of Pure Tolerance* (Boston, 1965), p. 87ff.

32 John B. Wolfe, in Wilbur Schramm, *Responsibility in Mass Communication* (New York, 1957), p. 106.

33 *Whitney v. People of the State of California*, 274 U.S. 357, 47 S.Ct. 641 (1927).

34 Ibid. at 375–376, 648.

> menaces stable government; that the path of safety lies in the opportunity to discuss freely supposed grievances and proposed remedies, and that the fitting remedy for evil counsels is good ones * * *

As Justice Brandeis suggested, fear is a devil. "Men feared witches and burnt women." Although Justice Brandeis' opinion concurred in the unanimous decision by the Court to uphold her conviction, it became a telling argument for those who opposed the repression of speech and ideas.

IV. Self-Governance—The guarantee of free expression under this theory put forth by constitutional law scholar Alexander Meiklejohn is that speech must be absolutely protected when it deals with issues with which voters will have to deal. If it has to do with public issues, it should be protected. Testifying before a Senate committee in 1955, when rabid anti-Communism known as McCarthyism caught few if any Communists but smeared the reputations of many loyal Americans, Meiklejohn declared:[35]

> The First Amendment * * * admits of no exceptions. It tells us that the Congress, and by implication, all other agencies of Government are denied any authority whatever to limit the political freedom of the citizens of the United States.

On the other hand, does expression have to be about public issues—about government or politics—to be valuable and protected? Who decides what is public and what is private? What standards will courts and legislatures and prosecutors apply? What about poetry or art? Such expression can inspire, can uplift, and can cause shocked efforts to suppress art or words which energize censors to "do their thing." Under the Meiklejohn self-governance approach, political speech is protected and nonpolitical or commercial speech is in a "second tier." It may or may not find constitutional protection.

In the Twenty-First Century, it seemed that self-governance has the greatest support of the four bases for expression discussed above.

2. THE CONSTITUTIONAL GUARANTEES

Federal and State Constitutions all guarantee freedom of expression but some State Constitutions declare that citizens are responsible for the abuse of that right.

Protection for the dissenters as well as the advocates of the status quo is part of the basic, organic law of the United States. The Federal and state constitutions unanimously give free expression a position of prime value.

[35] Alexander Meiklejohn, Testimony of November 14, 1955, U.S. Senate Committee on the Judiciary, Sub-Committee on Constitutional Rights, "Security and Constitutional Rights," pp. 14–15.

The Americans who wrote and in 1791 adopted the Bill of Rights of the United States Constitution followed a theme in Anglo-American liberty. Those Americans who had seen the breaking of the ties connecting them to Britain in 1776 with the Declaration of Independence drew on a long history of struggle against arbitrary power. With their lively knowledge of their past, they knew of the Englishmen who in 1215 forced King John to sign the Magna Carta—the "great charter" of rights promising lawful rule by duly constituted authority and trial by jury. They knew also of the Englishmen who passed the Habeas Corpus Act in 1679 saying that persons could not be imprisoned except by lawful authority, and of the English Bill of Rights of 1689.[36]

This sense of history doubtless impelled Americans, after the War for Independence, to set down frameworks of government *in writing*, first in the emerging states after the Declaration of Independence, and later in the Articles of Confederation and in the Constitution. Government's powers were to be made explicit.[37]

The Constitution of 1787, adopted after weeks of meetings *in secret* by the Constitutional Convention in Philadelphia, proposed much more centralization of power in the national government than did the nation's first constitution, the Articles of Confederation. Although the Constitution of 1787 is much revered today, and was elevated virtually to the level of Divine inspiration by the 1987 Bicentennial Celebration, it should be kept in mind that the Constitution was—and is—a practical political "frame of government" document.[38]

Although much rhetoric has flowed over the Bill of Rights and the First Amendment, the practical political fact remains that the Bill of Rights and the First Amendment were political afterthoughts, compromises. Strong Antifederalist opposition led supporters of the Constitution to conclude that the required nine (of thirteen) states would never ratify the Constitution as written.[39] The Antifederalists pushed a boisterous campaign to prevent adoption of the Constitution, claiming it would create a tyrannical, monolithic national government that would trample liberties then enjoyed by the people under the Articles of Confederation. Supporters of the Constitution defused their opposition enough to secure ratification in the states by pledging to add a Bill of Rights to place explicit limits on the national government, providing a list of rights that the United States could not infringe.[40]

After initial reluctance to see a Bill of Rights added, James Madison—as a representative to the First Congress from Virginia—

---

[36] Winston Churchill, *The Birth of Britain* (New York, 1956), pp. 252–254; Leonard W. Levy, *Emergence of a Free Press* (Oxford, 1985), Chs. 1 and 2.

[37] Sanford Levinson, *Constitutional Faith* (Princeton, N.J., 1988), pp. 30–31.

[38] Jackson Turner Main, *The Antifederalists: Critics of the Constitution* (Chapel Hill, 1961), *passim*.

[39] Ibid. at 158–161.

[40] Ibid.

served as a major draftsman and the prime mover in getting the Bill of Rights passed for submission to the states. Madison, although staunchly for civil liberties, had questioned whether a national Bill of Rights would be effective. Later, evidently seeing both substance and political usefulness, Madison finally managed—after several months—to get Congress to consider drafting proposed amendments. Such delay suggests that Congress found other matters more pressing than the promised Bill of Rights. (Although some cheerleading renditions of journalism history of the after-dinner speech variety claim the First Amendment was listed first because it was considered most important, it became the first merely because a couple of early draft amendments on election and pay of congressmen were edited out.) On December 15, 1791, state ratification of the Bill of Rights gave force to these words making up the First Amendment:[41]

> Congress shall make no law respecting an establishment of religion, or prohibiting the free exercise thereof; or abridging the freedom of speech, or of the press; or the right of the people peaceably to assemble, and to petition the Government for a redress of grievances.

The meaning of the First Amendment was by no means clear. The noted constitutional historian Leonard Levy once contended that a long and bitter civil war—called by Americans the War for Independence—was hardly a good time for the birth or nurturing of civil liberties. In an inspired phrase, Levy asserted in 1960, "There is even reason to believe that the Bill of Rights was more the chance product of political expediency on all sides than of principled commitment to personal liberties."[42]

In the late Eighteenth Century, and even today, "freedom of speech and press" was an ill-defined and much-debated phrase. But however unsettled the nation's founders were about expanding the reach of free expression beyond that in England, they stated a broad principle in firmly protective terms, and left it to future generations to interpret.[43]

The states adopted their own constitutions, some beginning as early as 1776 and then revised those documents over the years. Freedoms of speech and press evidently were not seen as "absolutes;" this was recognized, over time, by most states' constitutions. Nearly all agreed that freedom of expression could be "abused," although that "abuse" was not defined. Typically, the sentence in the state constitution that started with the guarantee of free expression ended with a qualification. The Constitution of Pennsylvania of 1790 said: "The free communication of thoughts and opinions is one of the invaluable rights of man, and every

---

[41] U.S. Constitution, Amendment 1.

[42] Levy, *Legacy of Suppression* (Cambridge, Mass., 1960), pp. vii–viii.

[43] Levy, *Emergence*, pp. 348–349.

citizen may freely speak, write and print on any subject, being responsible for the abuse of that liberty."[44]

As the Federal Constitution's First Amendment left the "freedom of speech and press" to future interpretation, the state constitutions tended to leave "abuse" to later definition. The principle resembled that expressed by Sir William Blackstone, prestigious English legal authority whose famed "*Commentaries*", published in 1765–1769, amounted to a kind of legal bible for the lawyers of the emerging United States. Blackstone's definition of press freedom declared:[45]

> The liberty of the press is indeed essential to the nature of a free state: but this consists in laying no *previous* restraints upon publications, and not in freedom from censure for criminal matter when published. Every freeman has an undoubted right to lay what sentiments he pleases before the public: to forbid this, is to destroy the freedom of the press: but if he publishes what is improper, mischievous, or illegal, he must take the consequences of his own temerity.

Blackstone's formulation had great force as state legal systems emerged. In times before law schools, when would-be lawyers "read law" as assistants to experienced lawyers, a law practice would often be started with a library of just two books: the Bible and a copy of "*Blackstone*". Note that Blackstone's definition of freedom guaranteed little beyond no pre-publication censorship. As will be discussed in later sections, criticism of government which Blackstone likely would have considered illegal "abuse" of press freedom now is fully protected as courts interpret the Constitution. And although pre-publication censorship is more devastating than after-publication punishment, if it is against the law to criticize government, going to jail or being executed after publication is highly likely to discourage other dissident speakers or writers.

GITLOW V. NEW YORK (1925)

Each state's power to define what it considered abuse of free expression long went unchallenged before the Federal courts. But in 1925, the United States Supreme Court in effect enabled the *nationalizing* of the First Amendment.[46]

A hapless radical, Benjamin Gitlow, had been charged with violating the criminal anarchy law of the state of New York. That statute defined criminal anarchy as the doctrine " '* * * that organized government should be overthrown by force or violence, or by assassination of the executive head or of any of the officials of government, or by any other means.' " The state's statute also made it a crime to advocate, advise or

---

44 Constitution of Pennsylvania, Art. 1, § 7.

45 4 *Blackstone Commentaries* 151, 152.

46 *Gitlow v. New York*, 268 U.S. 652, 666, 45 S.Ct. 625, 630 (1925).

teach such a doctrine. Gitlow and friends had circulated "The Left Wing Manifesto," which advocated "revolutionary mass action" to establish Communist Socialism.[47]

Ironically, even though the Supreme Court of the United States found that a New York jury was warranted in finding Gitlow guilty of advocating governmental overthrow, it also held that the protections of the First Amendment were applicable to the states through the Fourteenth Amendment, which had been adopted in 1868 to protect the rights of slaves freed by the Civil War. The Fourteenth Amendment declares that *no state* shall "deprive any person of life, liberty or property, without due process of law * * *."[48] In the *Gitlow* case, the Supreme Court broadened the "liberty" mentioned in the Fourteenth Amendment. Until *Gitlow v. New York* (1925), state courts' rulings on freedom of expression cases were allowed to stand without review by the U.S. Supreme Court. In the *Gitlow* decision, however, Justice Sanford wrote for the seven-man majority of the Court that:[49]

> * * * we may and do assume that freedom of speech and of the press—which are protected by the First Amendment from abridgment by Congress—are among the fundamental rights and "liberties" protected by the due process clause of the Fourteenth Amendment from impairment by the States.

These words did not help Ben Gitlow; since the Supreme Court had upheld his conviction, he remained in prison. But two members of the Supreme Court—Justices Oliver Wendell Holmes and Louis D. Brandeis—dissented, saying that the "Manifesto" posed little threat of doing harm, let alone a "clear and present danger"[50] from the small minority who shared Gitlow's views. In later years, when the Supreme Court of the United States tended to be more tolerant and supportive of expression than many state courts, the 1925 decision in *Gitlow v. New York* proved to be the case which opened the door to the Supreme Court review of state courts' actions involving speech and press. After the *Gitlow* case, the Fourteenth Amendment took its place with the First Amendment as a major protection for expression. By helping to "bring the First Amendment home to the states," the *Gitlow* decision made possible the landmark case limiting pre-publication censorship, *Near v. Minnesota ex rel. Olson* (1931),[51] and the famous decision protecting the news media against libel suits by public officials, *New York Times Co. v. Sullivan* (1964).[52]

---

[47] Chafee, op. cit., pp. 318–325.

[48] U.S. Constitution, Amendment 14.

[49] *Gitlow v. New York*, 268 U.S. 652, 45 S.Ct. 625 (1925).

[50] Ibid.

[51] *Near v. Minnesota ex rel. Olson*, 283 U.S. 697, 51 S.Ct. 625 (1931).

[52] *New York Times v. Sullivan*, 376 U.S. 254, 84 S.Ct. 710 (1964).

THE FIFTH AMENDMENT

One other amendment to the Federal Constitution also applies to expression. This is the Fifth Amendment, which has language similar to part of the Fourteenth Amendment.[53] The Fifth Amendment says "No person shall be compelled in any criminal case to be a witness against himself, nor be deprived of life, liberty, or property, without due process of law."[54]

When those words are taken together with the First Amendment's command protecting "the freedom of speech, or of the press," the Fifth Amendment may be read as helping guarantee the liberty to speak or write.

This protection means that the government cannot freely restrain or remove or punish words it doesn't like. A procedure must be followed and that procedure can be a brake on government. In *Fort Wayne Books v. Indiana*, 489 U.S. 46, 109 S.Ct. 916 (1989), the Supreme Court held that the seizure of allegedly obscene books violated the First Amendment because there had been no judicial determination that the books fell outside of First Amendment protection. "[T]his Court has repeatedly held that rigorous procedural safeguards must be employed before expressive materials can be seized as 'obscene,' "[55] Justice White wrote for the Court.

In *Southeastern Promotions, Ltd. v. Conrad*, 420 U.S. 546, 95 S.Ct. 1239 (1975), the Court dealt with city officials' refusal to allow a theatrical company to produce the play "Hair" in a municipal auditorium. The directors of the auditorium rejected the company's request to use the theater because they understood the play contained nudity and obscenity on stage.[56] The Supreme Court, in an opinion written by Justice Harry Blackmun, ruled in favor of the production company and against the city officials. "We hold that respondent's rejection of petitioner's application to use this public forum accomplished a prior restraint under a system lacking in constitutionally required minimal procedural safeguards. Accordingly, on this narrow ground, we reverse."[57]

Justice Blackmun's opinion spoke eloquently in the defense of free expression in public forums over censorship imposed by those in authority. "Invariably, the Court has felt obligated to condemn systems in which the exercise of such authority was not bounded by precise and clear standards."[58]

---

[53] U.S. Constitution, Amendment 14.

[54] Ibid., Amendment 5.

[55] *Fort Wayne Books v. Indiana*, 489 U.S. 46, 63, 109 S.Ct. 916, 927 (1989).

[56] The play features full frontal nudity by the entire cast at the end of Act I. The play scandalized many because of its depiction of hippies and others in the peace movement during the Vietnam War and because of its unflattering portrayal of President Richard Nixon.

[57] *Southeastern Promotions, Ltd. v. Conrad*, 420 U.S. 546, 552, 95 S.Ct. 1239, 1243 (1975).

[58] Ibid. at 553, 1244.

But due process is not a shield for expression. It is merely the requirement that government dot all the i's and cross all the t's. Think again about the wording of the First, Fifth and Fourteenth Amendments to the Constitution as discussed in the preceding pages. The First Amendment says, with no limiting words, that "Congress shall make no law * * * abridging the freedom of speech, or of the press * * *." On the other hand, both the Fifth and the Fourteenth Amendments say that persons *can* be deprived of life, liberty, or property through due process of law. Further, many state constitutions say that although there is freedom of speech and press, those freedoms can be abused, and the abusers of those freedoms held responsible.

Even in a Constitution granting freedoms, certain boundaries for speech and press were suggested.

FIFTH AMENDMENT PREVENTS PRESIDENT TRUMP FROM TAKING REPORTER'S PRESS PASS

In November, 2018, a federal judge ordered the Trump Administration to restore the White House press pass for CNN reporter Jim Acosta holding that the revocation did not satisfy the requirements of Fifth Amendment due process.

The case arose when someone (the who was not made clear in the hearing conducted by U.S. District Judge Timothy J. Kelly) in the White House revoked Acosta's press pass after a contentious White House news conference. Acosta, who has a history of aggressive questioning from both the Obama and Trump administrations, surrendered his White House press pass to a Secret Service agent when he tried to enter the White House grounds later.

President Trump has had a difficult relation with the press. Candidate Trump denied press credentials to *The Washington Post*, *Huffington Post*, *Buzzfeed*, *Politico*, the *Daily Beast* and the *Des Moines Register*. The media organizations were allowed to send reporters to the events but as members of the public and without the access that press credentials would allow. The reporters also were not allowed into press conferences.[59] President Trump also has repeatedly said the "Fake News Media" were the "enemy of the people."

The first exchange between Acosta and President Trump came when Acosta challenged the president's claim that a migrant caravan coming from Central America was "an invasion."[60]

"I consider it to be an invasion," Trump said.

---

[59] Tom Kludt and Brian Stelter, " 'The Blacklist': Here are the media outlets banned by Donald Trump," *CNN Money*, June 14, 2016.

[60] William Cummings, "President Trump calls media 'hostile,' says of CNN reporter Jim Acosta: 'You are a rude, terrible person'," *USA Today*, Nov. 7, 2018.

> "As you know, Mr. President, the caravan was not an invasion," Acosta replied.
>
> "Thank you for telling me that. I appreciate it," Trump said sardonically.
>
> When Acosta continued to tell Trump the caravan was not an invasion, the president told the reporter: "I think you should let me run the country, you run CNN. And if you did it well, your ratings would be much better."
>
> Acosta asked a follow-up question about the Russia investigation, but President Trump rebuffed him.[61]
>
> "That's enough," Trump said repeatedly as Acosta continued to try to ask his question.
>
> When a White House aide tried to take the mic from him, Acosta yanked it back.
>
> "On the Russia investigation, are you concerned that you may . . .?" Acosta managed to get out before Trump interrupted him: "I'm not concerned about anything with the Russia investigation because it's a hoax."
>
> Trump stepped away from the lectern for a moment before returning to the microphone.
>
> "I tell you what: CNN should be ashamed of itself, having you working for them," the president said, shaking a finger at Acosta. "You are a rude, terrible person."

CNN sent a letter to the White House asking for Acosta's press pass to be returned but the Trump Administration refused. CNN then sued in federal court seeking a temporary restraining order to force the return of Acosta's pass and a ruling by the court on the constitutionality of the White House action citing both the First and Fifth Amendments.

Judge Kelly issued the order after a hearing in which attorneys from both sides argued that the revocation was, alternatively, an act that was legal in that it was prompted by an assault on a White House intern and also Acosta's behavior, or, an act taken because President Trump did not like Acosta's questions and his efforts to get answers from the president. A 1977 case involving the denial of a White House press pass by the Secret Service, *Sherill v Knight*, 569 F.2d 124 (D.C. Cir. 1977), was key in Judge Kelly's order, Briefly, Judge Kelly said that once the White House opened itself to the press corps, it created a First Amendment right of access and that the access could only be taken away after the holder of a press pass had been afforded due process.

Briefly, Judge Kelly said that once the White House opened itself to the press corps, it created a First Amendment right of access and that the access could only be taken away after the holder of a press pass had

[61] Ibid.

been afforded due process.[62] "[T]his process must include notice, an opportunity to rebut the government's reasons and a written decision."

That, Judge Kelly wrote, did not appear to have happened.[63]

> [W]hatever process occurred within the government is still so shrouded in mystery that the Government could not tell me at oral argument who made the initial decision to revoke Mr. Acosta's press pass—his hard pass.
>
> On the notice, as for notice, the Government only points to one statement that could possibly constitute prior notice to Mr. Acosta that his pass would be revoked, the President's statements to him during the exchange at the press conference on November 7th, but the President's statement did not revoke—did not reference Mr. Acosta's hard pass at all, let alone that it would be revoked; therefore, that statement can not have put him on notice of the government's intention to revoke it.

Judge Kelly also dealt with the White House attempt to show that Acosta was afforded due process, addressing the explanation offered by Press Secretary Sarah Sanders that Acosta had "laid his hands" on a White House intern who was trying to get the microphone from him in the exchange with President Trump.[64] Sanders shared a video that had been doctored to suggest that Acosta had chopped down on the intern's arm.[65]

> The edited video looks authentic: Acosta appeared to swiftly chop down on the arm of an aide as he held onto a microphone while questioning President Trump. But in the original video, Acosta's arm appears to move only as a response to a tussle for the microphone. His statement, "Pardon me, ma'am," is not included in the video Sanders shared.
>
> Critics said that video—which sped up the movement of Acosta's arms in a way that dramatically changed the journalist's response—was deceptively edited to score political points. That edited video was first shared by Paul Joseph Watson, known for his conspiracy-theory videos on the far-right website *Infowars*.

Judge Kelly said that the rationale offered by the White House came too late to give Acosta a chance to make arguments against losing his press pass.[66]

> The need for the opportunity to be heard seems especially important in this case when the record strongly suggests that one of the initial specific reasons for the revocation cited by the

---

[62] *CNN v. Donald J. Trump*, No.-18-cv-2610 (D.C.) Nov. 16, 2018.

[63] Ibid.

[64] Ibid.

[65] Drew Harwell, "White House shares doctored video to support punishment of journalist Jim Acosta," *The Washington Post*, Nov. 8, 2018.

[66] *CNN v. Donald J. Trump*, No.-18-cv-2610 (D.C.) Nov. 16, 2018.

government—that Mr. Acosta laid his hands on the White House intern—was likely untrue and was at least partly based on evidence that was of questionable accuracy.

Due Process also required that Acosta get the chance to rebut the government's claims in revoking his press pass, Judge Kelly said. The White House pointed to a letter that CNN sent the day after Acosta's pass was revoked as evidence that he had been given that chance. Judge Kelly was not convinced.[67]

> [T]his does not reflect a meaningful opportunity to rebut the government's reason for the revocation or to challenge the appropriateness of the government's action. Indeed, anyone can avail themselves of the mail, and there's nothing in the record that demonstrates that whoever the decisionmaker—the initial decisionmaker was in this case read or considered the letter.

Judge Kelly concluded that Acosta's Fifth Amendment right to due process had been denied, that he had suffered irreparable damage by being excluded from the White House and denied the opportunity to report in person.

The White House restored Acosta's press pass and CNN ended its suit.[68] The White House also instituted new rules that appeared to target reporting like Acosta's. The new rules include a single question per reporter and follow-ups at the discretion of the president. Failure to follow the rules could mean a loss of a reporter's press pass, the White House said.

PROTECTIONS FOR CORE FIRST AMENDMENT VALUES ALSO LIE IN STATUTES

The contraceptive coverage requirement for corporations under the Patient Protection and Affordable Care Act, known popularly as Obamacare, was struck down by the Supreme Court as an infringement of the religious rights of closely held corporations. But although religion is a major component of the First Amendment, the case turned on a prior federal statute to protect First Amendment rights.

In *Burwell v. Hobby Lobby Stores, Inc.*,[69] five members of the Court applied the Religious Freedom Restoration Act of 1993 granting three for-profit corporations the right to be exempted from a portion of the Affordable Care Act.

The *Hobby Lobby* case dealt with a challenge to a requirement that employers provide preventive care and health screenings for female employees. Congress authorized the Department of Health and Human

---

[67] Ibid.

[68] Michael M. Grynbaum, "CNN's Jim Acosta Has Press Pass Restored by White House," *New York Times*, Nov. 19, 2018.

[69] *Burwell v. Hobby Lobby Stores, Inc.*, 134 S.Ct. 2751 (2014).

Services to create regulations establishing what would be covered. A part of the regulations required that employers cover the cost of 20 methods of contraception that had been approved by the Food and Drug Administration. The Affordable Care Act exempted some groups.[70]

> "Religious employers, such as churches, are exempt from this contraceptive mandate. HHS has also effectively exempted religious nonprofit organizations with religious objections to providing coverage for contraceptive services."

Three closely held corporations[71] objected to being required to support some of the contraceptive methods. Hobby Lobby, a chain of 500 arts and crafts stores with 13,000 employees, Mardel, a chain of 35 Christian bookstores with 400 employees, and Conestoga Wood Specialties, a custom wood cabinetmaker with 950 employees, all claimed that their religious beliefs would be violated if they had to provide contraception methods that they sincerely believed would cause abortions. They filed lawsuits under the Religious Freedom Restoration Act[72]

The Supreme Court held in its 5–4 decision that the three corporations were entitled to assert the religious beliefs of their owners and were entitled, as corporations, to assert corporate religious beliefs. Justice Samuel Alito, writing for the majority said the Religious Freedom Restoration Act included corporations.[73]

> RFRA's text shows that Congress designed the statute to provide very broad protection for religious liberty and did not intend to put merchants to such a choice. It employed the familiar legal fiction of including corporations within RFRA's definition of "persons," but the purpose of extending rights to corporations is to protect the rights of people associated with the corporation, including shareholders, officers, and employees. Protecting the free-exercise rights of closely held corporations thus protects the religious liberty of the humans who own and control them.

A vigorous dissent by Justice Ruth Bader Ginsburg argued that the majority decision employed an incorrect view of the RFRA to create the religious exemption from the Affordable Care Act for the three

[70] Ibid. at 2755–2756.

[71] A closely held corporation is one in which all shares are held, either by a single shareholder or a close-knit group of shareholders. *Black's Law Dictionary* 308 (5th Ed. 1979).

[72] The Religious Freedom Restoration Act of 1993 (RFRA) prohibits the "Government [from] substantially burden[ing] a person's exercise of religion even if the burden results from a rule of general applicability" unless the Government "demonstrates that application of the burden to the person—(1) is in furtherance of a compelling governmental interest; and (2) is the least restrictive means of furthering that compelling governmental interest." 42 U.S.C. §§ 2000bb–1(a), (b).

[73] *Burwell v. Hobby Lobby Stores, Inc.*, 573 U.S. 682, 683, 134 S.Ct. 2751, 2756 (2014).

corporations. She criticized the extension of religious rights by the majority.[74]

> Until this litigation, no decision of this Court recognized a for-profit corporation's qualification for a religious exemption from a generally applicable law, whether under the Free Exercise Clause or RFRA. The absence of such precedent is just what one would expect, for the exercise of religion is characteristic of natural persons, not artificial legal entities.

The majority used the RFRA in ways it was not intended, Ginsburg said.[75] Still, additional protections for First Amendment rights have been found in federal statutes.

SUPREME COURT AVOIDS QUESTION OF A RELIGIOUS RIGHT TO REFUSE SERVICE

The decision in the *Hobby Lobby* case raised the question of whether other private business owners could assert First Amendment-protected religious beliefs in running their shops. While the *Hobby Lobby* case was decided under the Religious Freedom Restoration Act, Jack Phillips, owner of the Masterpiece Cakeshop, invoked his First Amendment right to free speech and the free exercise of his religion.[76]

The Supreme Court declined to rule on the question, opting instead to reverse an order by the Colorado Civil Rights Commission that Phillips violated the Colorado Anti-Discrimination Act. The 7–2 decision was based on the conclusion of the Court that the Commission had acted with hostility toward a baker's religious beliefs.

The case began in 2012 before Colorado recognized same-sex weddings or the Supreme Court decision in *Obergefell v. Hodges*.[77] David Mullins and Charlie Craig planned a wedding in Massachusetts with a later reception in Colorado. They went to Phillips' shop and tried to order a cake. Phillips told them that he did not make wedding cakes for same-sex couples. He said he would make cakes for birthdays and showers and would sell them cookies and brownies. The couple left and filed a complaint with the Colorado Civil Rights Commission.

---

[74] Ibid.

[75] The RFRA was passed to overturn a Supreme Court decision in a case involving the right to engage in religious practices. *Employment Div., Dept. of Human Resources of Ore. v. Smith*, 494 U.S. 872, 110 S.Ct. 1595, 108 L.Ed.2d 876 (1990). In *Smith*, two members of the Native American Church were fired and denied unemployment benefits because they ingested peyote in a religious ceremony. The Supreme Court upheld the firings and denial of benefits because they were based on Oregon state law. The First Amendment is not offended, *Smith* held, when "prohibiting the exercise of religion . . . is not the object of [governmental regulation] but merely the incidental effect of a generally applicable and otherwise valid provision." At 878–879. The purpose of the RFRA was "only to overturn the Supreme Court's decision in *Smith*," not to "unsettle other areas of the law." 139 Cong. Rec. 26178 (1993) (statement of Sen. Kennedy) (RFRA was "designed to restore the compelling interest test for deciding free exercise claims.").

[76] *Masterpiece Cakeshop, Ltd. v. Colorado Civil Rights Commission*, 2018 WL 2465172 (June 4, 2018).

[77] *Obergefell v. Hodges*, 135 S.Ct. 2584, 192 L.Ed.2d 609 (2015).

The Commission investigated and found probable cause that Phillips had violated the state's anti-discrimination law. Its investigators found that Phillips had refused to sell custom wedding cakes to some six other same-sex couples. The Commission sent the case to an administrative law judge. Phillips raised two constitutional issues. First, he argued that creating[78] "a cake for a same-sex wedding would violate his First Amendment right to free speech by compelling him to exercise his artistic talents to express a message with which he disagreed." Phillips also claimed that "requiring him to create cakes for same-sex weddings would violate his right to the free exercise of religion, also protected by the First Amendment."

The judge said that because the anti-discrimination law was a law of general applicability[79] and content neutral, applying it to Phillips would not violate the First Amendment. The judge also disagreed with Phillips; contention that preparing a wedding cake is a form of protected speech and did not agree that creating Craig and Mullins' cake would force Phillips to adhere to "an ideological point of view."

The case then went back to the Commission which affirmed the judge's conclusions. The Commission ordered Phillips to stop discriminating. It also ordered staff training on the public accommodation section of the anti-discrimination law as well as changes to his store's policies and two years of quarterly compliance reports that would include all instances where customers were denied service along with statements about "remedial actions."

Phillips appealed to the Colorado Court of Appeals. The court affirmed the Commission's orders. The Colorado Supreme Court declined to hear the case. Phillips appealed to the Supreme Court. The Court ruled against the Commission and court of appeals decision. But, rather than endorsing a position that religious beliefs could justify denial of services, Justice Kennedy's opinion based the holding on narrow and case-specific grounds. The Commission had not approached Phillips' case in a neutral fashion and, instead, had shown hostility to his religious beliefs.

Justice Kennedy quoted from transcripts of the Commission hearings on Phillips's business decisions. In the course of two days, several commissioners made what could be interpreted as dismissive of Phillips's position.[80]

> At several points during its meeting, commissioners endorsed the view that religious beliefs cannot legitimately be carried into the public sphere or commercial domain, implying that religious beliefs and persons are less than fully welcome in Colorado's business community. One commissioner suggested that Phillips

78 *Masterpiece Cakeshop, Ltd. v. Colorado Civil Rights Commission*, 2018 WL 2465172, at 6 (June 4, 2018).

79 For a clear explanation of laws of general applicability, see page 78 of the text.

80 *Masterpiece Cakeshop, Ltd. v. Colorado Civil Rights Commission*, 2018 WL 2465172, at 6 (June 4, 2018).

can believe "what he wants to believe," but cannot act on his religious beliefs "if he decides to do business in the state." Tr. 23.

Justice Kennedy singled out a comment made on the second day.

The commissioner stated:

"I would also like to reiterate what we said in the hearing or the last meeting. Freedom of religion and religion has been used to justify all kinds of discrimination throughout history, whether it be slavery, whether it be the holocaust, whether it be—I mean, we—we can list hundreds of situations where freedom of religion has been used to justify discrimination. And to me it is one of the most despicable pieces of rhetoric that people can use to—to use their religion to hurt others." Tr. 11–12.

To describe a man's faith as "one of the most despicable pieces of rhetoric that people can use" is to disparage his religion in at least two distinct ways: by describing it as despicable, and also by characterizing it as merely rhetorical—something insubstantial and even insincere.

The Commission appeared to use a different standard in other complaints regarding bakers. Three bakeries refused to make cakes that would have featured images showing disapproval of same-sex marriages.[81] A man named William Jack asked several bakeries to make him custom cakes in the shape of open Bibles. Jack asked the bakeries to superimpose a red X on an image of two groomsmen holding hands in front of a cross. In at least two instances, Jack asked the baker to put the statement, "Homosexuality is a detestable sin. Leviticus 18:2."

Justice Kennedy noted the different treatment the bakers received from the Commission.[82]

Each time, the Division found that the baker acted lawfully in refusing service. It made these determinations because, in the words of the Division, the requested cake included "wording and images [the baker] deemed derogatory," Jack v. Gateaux, Ltd., Charge No. P20140071X, at 4; featured "language and images [the baker] deemed hateful," Jack v. Le Bakery Sensual, Inc., Charge No. P20140070X, at 4; or displayed a message the baker "deemed as discriminatory, Jack v. Azucar Bakery, Charge No. P20140069X, at 4.

At the court of appeals, Phillips raised objections to what he saw as his disparate treatment. The other three bakers were treated as taking a principled stand—he was not, Phillips argued. But the court said the

---

[81] Andrew Kenney, "How three other bakeries—and a Colorado commissioner's comments—helped decide the Masterpiece case, Colorado's legal process treated a Christian baker unfairly, according to the U.S. Supreme Court," *Denverite*, June 4, 2018.

[82] *Masterpiece Cakeshop, Ltd. v. Colorado Civil Rights Commission*, 2018 WL 2465172, at 6 (June 4, 2018).

cases were different. The three bakeries that refused to make cakes did so because of the offensive nature of the requested messages, the court held.

It was the hostility to Phillips' religious beliefs that translated into a rationale that one message was offensive that doomed Colorado's position. As Justice Kennedy wrote:[83]

> A principled rationale for the difference in treatment of these two instances cannot be based on the government's own assessment of offensiveness. Just as "no official, high or petty, can prescribe what shall be orthodox in politics, nationalism, religion, or other matters of opinion," *West Virginia Bd. of Ed. v. Barnette,* 319 U.S. 624, 642, 63 S.Ct. 1178, 87 L.Ed. 1628 (1943), it is not, as the Court has repeatedly held, the role of the State or its officials to prescribe what shall be offensive. See *Matal v. Tam,* 582 U.S. ___, ___–___, 137 S.Ct. 1744, 1762–1764, 198 L.Ed.2d 366 (2017) (opinion of ALITO, J.). The Colorado court's attempt to account for the difference in treatment elevates one view of what is offensive over another and itself sends a signal of official disapproval of Phillips' religious beliefs.

Justice Kennedy quoted from an opinion he authored in a case where a city tried to use a newly created ordinance to stop the ritual slaughter of animals by a church.[84]

> In *Church of Lukumi Babalu Aye,* supra, the Court made clear that the government, if it is to respect the Constitution's guarantee of free exercise, cannot impose regulations that are hostile to the religious beliefs of affected citizens and cannot act in a manner that passes judgment upon or presupposes the illegitimacy of religious beliefs and practices. The Free Exercise Clause bars even "subtle departures from neutrality" on matters of religion.

The attitudes of the Commission and court of appeal showed that they were not neutral on the matter of Phillips' religion, Justice Kennedy wrote.

> The official expressions of hostility to religion in some of the commissioners' comments—comments that were not disavowed at the Commission or by the State at any point in the proceedings that led to affirmance of the order—were inconsistent with what the Free Exercise Clause requires. The Commission's disparate consideration of Phillips' case compared to the cases of the other bakers suggests the same. For these reasons, the order must be set aside.

---

[83] Ibid.

[84] *Church of the Lukumi Babalu Aye v. City of Hialeah,* 508 U.S. 520, 113 S.Ct. 2217 (1993).

The narrow grounds the case was decided on is therefore unlikely to set a general precedent on the issue of the use of religion to justify the denial of service to gay customers.

Phillips and his bake shop were back in the news after he sued the Colorado Civil Rights Commission.[85] The body ruled that Phillips had discriminated against a Colorado attorney who ordered a cake for a gender transition celebration. Autumn Scardina asked for Phillips' bakery for a cake with a pink interior and blue exterior. The commission found that Scardina was discriminated against by Phillips and ordered the two to go to mediation to settle the dispute.

Phillips then sued the commission, the state's civil rights division, the head of the division, then-Gov. John Hickenlooper and the Colorado attorney general. He is asking for a reversal of the commission finding and damages of at least $100,000. As before, Phillips asserted his religious beliefs in refusing to make the cake.[86]

> "Phillips sued in response, citing his belief that 'the status of being male or female . . . is given by God, is biologically determined, is not determined by perceptions or feelings, and cannot be chosen or changed,' according to his lawsuit."

REFUSAL OF SERVICE REMAINS UNRESOLVED

Several instances of businesses refusing service to same-sex couples have been addressed in lower courts. The Arizona Supreme Court, in a 4–3 decision, ruled that businesses have the right to refuse to provide custom wedding invitations for same-sex weddings.[87]

Chelsey Nelson, a photographer in Kentucky sued the city of Louisville over an ordinance banning local businesses from discriminating against gay customers. She argued that the ordinance violates her First Amendment rights to free speech and free exercise of religion. Her Christian belief is that "God created marriage to be an exclusive covenant between on man and one woman" and that this belief shapes "every aspect of her life," including "her business, her art, and her creativity."[88]

The Washington Supreme Court ruled against a florist who was fined for refusing to provide services for a gay couple's wedding finding

---

[85] James Anderson, "Colorado baker who refused to make cake for gay couple won't create one for gender transition," *Associated Press*, Aug. 15, 2018.

[86] Ibid.

[87] *Brush & Nib Studios, LC v. City of Phoenix*, 448 P.3d 890, 2019 Ariz. LEXIS 280, 2019 WL 4400328 (Supreme Court of Arizona, September 16, 2019, Filed), *available at* https://advance-lexis-com.proxy.lib.utk.edu/api/document?collection=cases&id=urn:contentItem:5X2H-3V71-F8SS-62K4-00000-00&context=1516831.

[88] Brooke Sopelsa, "DOJ Backs Kentucky Photographer Who Won't Do Gay Weddings," *nbcnews.com*, Feb. 27, 2020, https://www.nbcnews.com/feature/nbc-out/doj-backs-kentucky-photographer-who-won-t-do-gay-weddings-n1144516.

that the florist violated the Washington Law Against Discrimination (WLAD).[89]

The Supreme Court may finally resolve the issue of whether religious beliefs and free speech trump nondiscrimination policies. The Court agreed to decide whether the city of Philadelphia may exclude a Catholic agency that does not work with same-sex couples from the city's foster-care system. Catholic Social Services and several foster parents sued the city saying the decision violate their First Amendment rights to religious freedom and free speech. This case, *Fulton v. City of Philadelphia*, No. 19-123, is before the Supreme Court, as of the printing of this edition.[90]

BOUNDARIES FOR FREEDOM

As the final authority on what the Constitution means, it has fallen to the Supreme Court of the United States to say what expression is protected—or "constitutional"—and what is not protected. Although the First Amendment says "Congress shall make no law * * * abridging freedom of speech, or of the press * * *," the nation's courts have been unable to draw an exact, ruler-straight line between the permissible and the punishable. American theorists, courts, legislatures, and laymen have stated the boundaries of expression in various ways. If a scale could be made with "freedom" at one end and "restraint" at the other, many Americans would cluster toward "freedom."

Of all American spokesmen, the late Justice Hugo L. Black most flatly stated the position for a right of unlimited expression, interpreting the First Amendment as an "absolute" command forbidding any restraint on speech and press:[91]

> I believe when our Founding Fathers * * * wrote this [First] Amendment they * * * knew what history was behind them and they wanted to ordain in this country that Congress * * * should not tell the people what religion they should have or what they should believe or say or publish, and that is about it.
>
> It [the First Amendment] says "no law," and that is what I believe it means.
>
> * * *

---

[89] Ronn Blitzer and Bill Mears, "Washington Supreme Court Rules Against Florist Who Refused Service for Gay Couple's Wedding", *foxnews.com*, June 6, 2019, https://www.foxnews.com/politics/washington-supreme-court-rules-against-florist-who-refused-service-for-gay-couples-wedding.

[90] Adam Liptak, "Supreme Court to Hear Case on Gay Rights and Foster Care", *The New York Times*, Feb. 24, 2020, https://www.nytimes.com/2020/02/24/us/supreme-court-gay-rights-foster-care.html.

[91] Edmond N. Cahn, "Justice Black and First Amendment 'Absolutes': A Public Interview," 37 *N.Y.U.L.Rev*. 548 (1962).

> I have no doubt myself that the provision, as written and adopted, intended that there should be no libel or defamation law in the United States.

Although such ringing statements made Justice Black a hero to many journalists and civil libertarians, such words also caused consternation among legal historians. Many legal scholars, writing before and after Justice Black, have contended that such historical assertions were flawed by one-sidedness, ignoring abundant contrary evidence of libel actions brought by the generation that adopted the First Amendment.[92]

Such "absolute" positions, however, although theoretically appealing to some, have never found official acceptance or support in the United States. Ever since John Milton wrote "*Areopagitica*" in 1644, the case for freedom of expression has been qualified and limited in various ways as efforts are made to define the boundaries of legal control.

Briefly, here are some other concepts to keep in mind as you consider efforts to define freedom of expression. Please keep in mind that these are ways of justifying restrictions on free expression. They do not constitute statutory law though some have been employed by courts to justify restrictions on expression:

Liberty v. License: This often-heard old distinction rolls easily off the tongue but contains little operational content. Simply put, it means, "We have given you your liberty that you may behave as we believe you should. We did not give you a license to do as you please." The Minnesota Supreme Court applied this approach in the case of *State v. Guilford.*[93] (This case is more familiar because it was overturned as *Near v. Minnesota* (1931), a case discussed in greater detail in the section on prior restraint in Chap. 2.) The case dealt with a Minnesota district court's use of an injunction to stop the publication of a newspaper that a judge had ruled to be a "public nuisance." The owners of the newspaper, *The Saturday Press*, appealed to the Minnesota Supreme Court. That court upheld the injunction, saying approvingly, "the constitutional liberty of the press means the right to publish the truth with impunity, with good motives, and for justifiable ends; liberty to publish with complete immunity from legal censure and punishment for the publication so long as it is not harmful. * * * It was never the intent of the Constitution to afford protection to a publication devoted to scandal and defamation. It protects use and not abuse of the press."[94]

---

[92] See, e.g., Paul Murphy, "Time to Reclaim: The Current Challenge of American Constitutional History," 69 *Amer.Hist.Rev.* 64–654 (1963); Dwight L. Teeter and MaryAnn Yodelis Smith, "Mr. Justice Black's Absolutism: Notes on His Use of History to Support Free Expression," in Everette Dennis, et al., eds., *Justice Hugo Black and the First Amendment* Ames, Iowa, 1978, pp. 19–40.

[93] *State v. Guilford*, 174 Minn. 457, 219 N.W. 770 (1928).

[94] Ibid.

Bad Tendency: Under this theory supporting restrictions on expression, the utterance of a bad idea will bring about a bad occurrence: "If you say it, people will do it." The issue of sex education and the prevention of unwanted pregnancies provides an example.

Many objections to providing information about sex teaching young people about sex are founded in the belief by some people that placing the information before young people would plant wrong ideas and would, in fact, encourage them to have sex. Teens having sex would be the bad result stemming from Bad Tendency created by talking about sex.

The first Bush Administration became embroiled in a controversy over its approach to public health, specifically sex and safe sex education. In 1992, National Public Radio reported on criticism of the Administration over its decision to delete a chapter from a book on children's health problems because the chapter dealt with contraception and the use of contraceptives to prevent sexually transmitted diseases and teen pregnancies. Critics also cited the Administration's reluctance to use the word condom in AIDS prevention advertising. The National Centers for Disease Control and Prevention had, at the time, some 92 different television ads dealing with AIDS. Only four of them dealt with condoms. Only one of the agency's 75 radio ads mentioned them. National Public Radio's *Morning Edition* reported that Bush Administration officials were afraid that emphasis on condoms and other safe sex techniques could encourage young people to have sex and make the problem worse.[95] A few years later the New York City school system found itself embroiled in a controversy over the mandatory teaching of condom use to teens in a required AIDS and HIV curriculum.[96]

Presumed Intent: This legal presumption has been used to justify the suppression of speech and to punish speech that threatened orthodox views. One requirement of most criminal laws is that the defendant must have intended to commit the illegal act. In addition to the *actus reus*, the act itself, the defendant must also have *mens rea*, the mental or intent component. In theft cases, the defendant must have intended to deprive the lawful owner of the property in question. Few, if any, defendants will declare in court that they intended theft. Prosecutors point to the conduct of the defendant, leaving the store with the property without paying, as evidence of that intent.

In prosecutions using the bad tendency theory, governments had to come up with a way to tie the expression of an idea to the encouragement of the bad result. The solution was the creation of a new form of "presumed intent," in which the courts would presume that the defendant speaker had intended to bring about the bad act that would

---

[95] Michael Skoler, "Bush Evades Sex Issues Say Critics," *National Public Radio Morning Edition*, April 16, 1992.

[96] Maria Newman, "Schools Chancellor is Proposing Limits to Condom Lessons," *New York Times*, Dec. 9, 1995.

result from uttering a bad idea. That would make the speaker responsible for anyone else's subsequent action.

For example, individuals accused of opposing or disrupting the United States war effort during World War I often were convicted and jailed for words which in more recent years would be regarded as innocent expression.

Consider the case of Jacob Abrams. He and some other Russian immigrants were convicted of violating the Espionage Act of 1917, as amended in 1918. The 1918 amendment, since repealed, made punishable (among other things) any false statements harmful to the war effort. The statute went further, forbidding[97]

> "* * * any disloyal, profane, scurrilous or abusive language about the form of government of the United States, or the Constitution * * * or the military or naval forces of the United States, or the flag * * * or the uniform of the United States * * *"

Abrams and his friends were convicted of violating that statute by throwing leaflets out of a manufacturing building in New York. One leaflet, headlined "THE HYPOCRISY OF THE UNITED STATES AND HER ALLIES" did not criticize the war efforts of the U.S. against Germany. Instead, it protested the United States taking part with other nations in sending an expeditionary force into Russia, calling for workers in munitions factories to strike so bullets made by them would not strike down Russians.[98] There was no proof that such pamphleteering had any harmful effect or caused one less bullet to be made in a munitions factory. But World War I was a time of war hysteria and freedoms taken for granted in peacetime were cast aside. The pamphlet's fervent language, denouncing President Woodrow Wilson and "the plutocratic gang in Washington" was then enough to convince a jury to convict Abrams and three others.[99]

The U.S. Supreme Court upheld the conviction, basing its decision not on any demonstrable harm from the pamphlets, but on their "presumed intent." Writing for the Court, Justice Clarke declared that[100]

> It will not do to say, as is now argued, that the only intent of these defendants was to prevent injury to the Russian cause. Men must be held to have intended, and to be accountable for, the effects their acts were likely to produce.

That prosecutor's delight, the "presumed intent" test, was enough for a majority of the Supreme Court to uphold Abrams' conviction. In dissent, Justice Oliver Wendell Holmes presented a moving expression of the "marketplace of ideas" philosophy, declaring:

---

[97] U.S. Stats. at Large, vol. XL, p. 553ff.

[98] *Abrams v. United States*, 250 U.S. 616, 40 S.Ct. 17 (1919); see also Zechariah Chafee, Jr., *Free Speech in the United States* (Cambridge, 1941 ed.) p. 114ff.

[99] Chafee, p. 109ff.

[100] *Abrams v. United States*, 250 U.S. 616, 621, 40 S.Ct. 17, 19 (1919).

> In this case sentences of twenty years imprisonment have been imposed for the publishing of two leaflets that I believe the defendants had as much right to publish as the Government has to publish the Constitution now vainly invoked by them.
>
> * * *
>
> Persecution for the expression of opinions seems to me perfectly logical. If you have no doubt of your premises or your power and want a certain result with all your heart you naturally express your wishes in law and sweep away all opposition. * * * But when men have realized that time has upset many fighting faiths, they may come to believe even more than they believe the very foundations of their own beliefs that the ultimate good desired is better reached by free trade in ideas—that the best test of truth is the power of the thought to get itself accepted in the competition of the market, and that truth is the only ground upon which their wishes safely can be carried out. That at any rate is the theory of our constitution. It is an experiment, as all life is an experiment. Every year if not every day we have to wager our salvation upon some prophecy based upon imperfect knowledge.

The final concept is one that has been used for and against the suppression of ideas and punishment of speakers. It is a test to determine the constitutionality of punishment by the state.

Clear and Present Danger: In 1919, shortly before the *Abrams* case, Justice Holmes wrote for the Court's majority in *Schenck v. United States*. Schenck and his co-defendants had mailed circulars in violation of the Espionage Act of 1917, urging men who had been called to military service to resist the draft. Writing for a unanimous Court, Holmes created some famous, flashing phrases which seemed to offer promise to protect some kinds of anti-government expression, even in wartime. Justice Holmes then stated the famous *clear and present test*[101]

> We admit that in many places and in ordinary times the defendants in saying all that was said in the circular would have been within their constitutional rights. But the character of every act depends upon the circumstances in which it is done. The most stringent protection of free speech would not protect a man in falsely shouting fire in a theatre and causing a panic. * * * The question in every case is whether the words used are used in such circumstances and are of such a nature as to create a clear and present danger that they will bring about the substantive evils that Congress has a right to prevent. It is a question of proximity and degree. When a nation is at war many things that might be said in time of peace are such a hindrance to the effort that their utterance will not be endured. * * *

---

[101] *Schenck v. United States*, 249 U.S. 47, 52, 39 S.Ct. 247, 249 (1919).

The clear and present danger test did not free Schenck, nor was it to be used by Supreme Court majorities in support of free expression for two decades to come.[102] Although this helped few defendants at the time, its development by Justices Holmes and Brandeis in later dissents—as in *Abrams v. United States* (1919)—served as a rallying point for libertarians for years.[103]

3. "THE INTENT OF THE FRAMERS"

"Law office history"—assertions by judges, lawyers and politicians that they know the "intent of the Framers"—sometimes makes First Amendment law.

Statements continue to be heard about the "intent of the Founding Fathers" or the "Framers" on the true meaning of the national constitutional provision on freedom of the press. This is a cautionary note for readers of court decisions or legal arguments which purport to offer *the* meaning of The First Amendment or some other facet of the Constitution of the United States. If you believe such legal arguments, the authors of this book have some real estate and a bridge they would like to sell you.[104]

First, there's what might be called the journalistic fallacy, talking about the First Amendment as if it contained only guarantees for freedom of speech and press. But read again what that Amendment says: it is a group of rights protecting religion, speech, press, assembly, and petition * * * mentioned in that order, for whatever order of mention is worth. The exact words say:

AMENDMENT I

> Congress shall make no Law respecting an establishment of religion, or prohibiting the free exercise thereof; or abridging the freedom of speech, or of the press; or the right of the people peaceably to assemble, and to petition the Government for a redress of grievances.

Obviously, the First Amendment is not just about speech and press. As civil libertarians frequently observe, it is a bundle of rights, and whatever affects one part of that Amendment almost certainly will have repercussions for the other rights it lists.

When you hear a politician assert that "all history proves," brace yourself for a whopper. And be similarly skeptical about lawyers' and judges' use of history-as-argument or history-as-precedent. The legal process in this nation, after all, is an adversary system, and selective

---

[102] *Bridges v. California*, 314 U.S. 252, 62 S.Ct. 190 (1941), for use of that test in a contempt case.

[103] See Chaffe, *passim*.

[104] See, Levy, *Original Intent and the Framers' Constitution* (New York: 1988), pp. xii–xiii, 377.

perception of and selective presentation of evidence—especially historical evidence—is not infrequent in the judicial system.[105]

Many of the following pages will contain assertions made by judges, lawyers, and journalists about the intent underlying the First Amendment as it applies—to name just a few examples—to criticism of government, or prior restraint, access to information, defamation, or invasion of privacy.

If communicators, lawyers, judges or scholars talk about "the First Amendment intent of the Framers," regard their words skeptically. Face it, the Framers were men who met in secret, behind closed doors—so much for their intent concerning access to information?—in Philadelphia during the spring and summer of 1787. If someone insisted that their true intent on free speech or press or religion could be found in that document, then what? The body of the Constitution mentioned nothing at all about the rights guaranteed by the First Amendment. Members of the Constitutional Convention signed the document they produced in 1787. Although the Constitution was ratified by the necessary nine states in 1788, and although the new government began in the spring of 1789 the Bill of Rights was not adopted by the states until the end of 1791.

It has been said that the War for Independence and the troubled early years of the struggling new United States of America, instead of securing rights for speech and press, came close to eradicating them.[106] The Bill of Rights, indeed, was created to overcome the objections of the Antifederalists who were seeking another constitutional convention to undo the draft Constitution of 1787 aiming toward a centralized, truly national government. Under that analysis, the Bill of Rights was drafted out of pragmatism, to overcome Antifederalist charges that freedom of speech, press, assembly, and religion would be taken away under a monolithic new government. Other charges included taking away of right to trial by jury and that a heartless national government would torture people until they confessed to crimes they had not committed. Pay specific attention to the language of the First Amendment: it does *not* say that freedoms of speech and press shall not be abridged. It says that Congress (not the states) "shall make no law."

True, the Federalists argued that the various states had their own free speech and press guarantees, but the Antifederalists anti-ratification arguments dealt with what the new national government *might* do. As John Adams said so well, "the Constitution was 'a game at leapfrog.' "[107]

---

[105] Charles Miller, *The Supreme Court and the Uses of History* (Cambridge, Mass. Belknap Press, 1969).

[106] Levy, *Legacy of Suppression* (Cambridge: Belknap/Harvard, 1960) p. 182; Jackson Turner Main, op. cit., pp. 160–161.

[107] John Adams quoted in Merrill Jensen, review of "Legacy of Suppression", 75 *Harvard Law Rev. No.* 1 (Dec.1961) at p. 458.

Anthony Lewis has written that a meaningful understanding of "original intent" would have to include posthumous reading of the minds of the different groups of men who drafted the Constitution, and the men who were voting in the ratifying conventions of each state. The intent behind the Bill of Rights is even harder to discern: there is hardly any record of the legislative history of what members of the First Congress meant in offering the Amendments in 1789.[108]

It took some time and there is virtually no record of how the First Amendment developed. James Madison wrote a version and then the House select committee wrote a version and incorporated Madison's clauses about right of assembly and petition and freedom of speech and press. The Senate prepared its own version, rejecting a proposal to protect free speech based on common law principles. The Senate version included the first five words, "Congress shall make no law." Considering the politics of the time, this phrasing evidently was aimed at defusing Antifederalist fears of a too-powerful central government. The House and Senate versions went to conference committee where differences were hammered out, including deleting a Senate clause prohibiting establishment of "articles of faith, or a mode of worship."[109]

The Constitution and the Bill of Rights have not remained frozen in time. It is likely that this nation was able to celebrate 200 years under its Constitution because it is a brief, broadly stated "frame of government." And it may be asserted with safety that the First Amendment has been changed, over time, as courts—however haltingly or imperfectly—interpreted new meanings into the document. And the Framers' intent? As David A. Anderson has argued, "* * * [M]ost of the Framers perceived, however dimly, naively, or incompletely, that freedom of the press was inextricably related to the new republican form of government and would have to be protected if their vision of government by the people was to succeed."[110]

A SIGNIFICANT DEVELOPMENT IN THE EVOLUTION OF THE FIRST AMENDMENT

CITIZENS UNITED V. FEDERAL ELECTION COMMISSION (U.S. S.CT. 2010)

In a major political speech decision early in 2010, the Supreme Court of the United States gutted the 2002 McCain-Feingold Act's prohibitions against political spending for candidates in elections. *Citizens United v.*

---

[108] Anthony Lewis, review of Leonard W. Levy's "Original Intent and the Framers' Constitution" (New York: Macmillan, 1989), *New York Times Book Review*, Nov. 6, 1988, p. 11.

[109] See, e.g., Jackson Turner Main, *The Antifederalists: Critics of the Constitution* (Chapel Hill: University of North Carolina, 1961), pp. 158–161; Merrill Jensen, *The Making of the Constitution* (New York: Van Nostrand, 1964), pp. 147–150, and Irving Brant, *The Bill of Rights: Its Origin and Meaning* (Indianapolis: Bobbs Merrill, 1967), pp. 48–52, 58–74.

[110] David A. Anderson, "The Origins of the Press Clause," 30 *UCLA L.Rev No.* 3 (February, 1983), p. 537.

Federal Election Commission, found a federal election contribution law unconstitutional. It also overturned two important Supreme Court precedents restricting corporate contributions supporting or opposing political candidates.[111]

The legal controversy arose over a non-profit corporation's Citizens United-funded political attack video titled "Hillary: the Movie," released before the presidential primaries in 2008 while Senator Hillary Rodham Clinton was considered a serious candidate. Citizens United wished to distribute the video during the 30 days before the 2008 primaries. Citizens United sought an injunction against the Federal Election Commission to prevent it from enforcing statutes forbidding distribution of such communications during specified periods before elections. A federal district court, however, refused to issue the injunction, finding that § 441(b) of the McCain Feingold Act was constitutional as applied to "Hillary: the Movie."[112] The district court found that there was no reasonable interpretation of this video except appealing for votes against Sen. Clinton. Subsec. § 441(b) forbade corporations and unions from using their general treasury funds to pay for "electioneering communications" or for speech expressly advocating the election or defeat of a candidate.

The Bipartisan Campaign Reform Act (BCRA) of 2002 forbade corporations and unions from using general treasury funds to make direct contributions to candidates or independent expenditures that expressly advocate election or defeat of a candidate, through any media in connection with any specified federal elections. The BCRA amended 2 U.S.C. 441(b) to add a provision against "electioneering communication." An electioneering communication was defined as[113] "any broadcast, cable or satellite communication 'that refers to a clearly identified candidate for Federal office' made within 30 days of a primary or 60 days of a general election."

The U.S. Supreme Court, however, ruled in favor of Citizens United, with Justice Anthony M. Kennedy writing the opinion of the Court. He wrote, "The Government may regulate political speech through disclaimers and disclosure requirements, but not suppress that speech altogether." Justice Kennedy declared, "If the First Amendment has any force, it prohibits Congress from fining or jailing citizens, or associations

---

[111] *Citizens United v. Federal Election Commission*, 558 U.S. 310, 130 S.Ct. 876 (2010); Adam Liptak, "Justices, 5–4, Reject Corporate Campaign Spending Limits," *The New York Times*, Jan. 22, 2010, pp. A1, A16. The precedents reversed were *Austin v. Michigan Chamber of Commerce*, 494 U.S. 652, 110 S.Ct. 1391 (1990), upholding restrictions on corporate spending for or against political candidates, and *McConnell v. F.E.C.*, 540 U.S. 93, 124 S.Ct. 619 (2003), supporting the Bipartisan Campaign Reform Act of 2002 in restricting corporations' and unions' campaign spending.

[112] *Citizens United v. Federal Election Commission*, 530 F.Supp2d 274 (D.C.D.C. 2008), discussing 2 U.S.C. § 441(b) and its prohibition against certain "electioneering communications."

[113] *Citizens United v. Federal Election Commission*, 558 U.S. 310, 319, 130 S.Ct. 876, 887 (2010).

of citizens, from simply engaging in political speech."[114] He was joined in the majority opinion by Chief Justice John Roberts and Justices Samuel Alito, Antonin Scalia, and Clarence Thomas.

Justice Kennedy's opinion rejected the idea that unregulated political contributions, some of which run into the hundreds of millions of dollars, could lead to corruption or the appearance of corruption in the federal election system.[115]

> * * * this Court now concludes that independent expenditures, including those made by corporations, do not give rise to corruption or the appearance of corruption. That speakers may have influence over or access to elected officials does not mean that those officials are corrupt. And the appearance of influence or access will not cause the electorate to lose faith in this democracy.

One legislative shred remained, to the effect that corporations must disclose their contributions and run disclaimers with their ads. Eight Justices agreed on this point, with the exception of Justice Thomas. Justice Kennedy stated, "Disclosure permits citizens and shareholders to react to the speech of corporate entities in a proper way."[116]

The *Citizens United* decision reflected deep and irritable divisions on the Court. The document ran to 180 pages, including an 88-page dissent by Justice John Paul Stevens. Stevens, who retired from the Court later in 2010, argued at length that the Court majority made a grave error by equating corporate speech with speech by human beings.

President Barack Obama termed the *Citizens United* decision " 'a major victory for big oil, Wall Street banks, health insurance companies and the other powerful interests that marshal their power every day in Washington to drown out the voices of everyday Americans.' "[117] Others, however, including the *Wall Street Journal*, applauded the decision. In an editorial, the *Wall Street Journal* declared, "Freedom has had its best week in many years. * * * The Supreme Court issued a landmark decision supporting free political speech by overturning some of Congress's more intrusive limits on campaign spending."[118]

MONTANA SUPREME COURT SAYS MONEY CORRUPTS; REBUFFS CITIZEN UNITED DECISION (2011)

On December 30, 2011, the Montana Supreme Court ruled that *Citizens United* did not apply to Montana campaign finance law in *Western Tradition Partnership, Inc. v. Attorney General of State Supreme*

[114] Ibid. at 904.

[115] Ibid. at 884, 314.

[116] Ibid.

[117] Liptak, op. cit.

[118] "A Free Speech Landmark," *The Wall Street Journal*, January 22, 2010.

Court of Montana, 363 Mont. 220, 271 P.3d 1 (Montana 2011).[119] The Montana Corrupt Practices Act limiting campaign contributions was constitutional because it did not involve the restrictions of federal campaign contributions, for one, and, secondly, that Montana had overwhelming evidence of the corruption of unregulated political spending, Montana's supreme court held.[120]

Chief Justice Mike McGrath's opinion laid out the state's history and the influence of wealthy corporations and individuals on the election of its judges, the selection of its U.S. senators and its legislature.[121]

Examples of well-financed corruption abound. In the fight over mineral rights between entrepreneur F. Augustus Heinze and the Anaconda Company, then controlled by Standard Oil, Heinze managed to control the two State judges in Butte, who routinely decided cases in his favor. K. Ross Toole, "*Montana, An Uncommon Land*", 196–99 (Univ. of Okla. Press 1959) the Butte judges denied being bribed, but one of them admitted that Anaconda representatives had offered him $250,000 cash to sign an affidavit that Heinze had bribed him. Toole, "*Montana, An Uncommon Land*", 204.

In response to the legal conflicts with Heinze, in 1903 Anaconda/ Standard closed down all its industrial and mining operations (but not the many newspapers it controlled), throwing 4/5 of the labor force of Montana out of work. Toole, "*Montana, An Uncommon Land*", 206. Its price for sending its employees back to work was that the Governor call a special session of the Legislature to enact a measure that would allow Anaconda to avoid having to litigate in front of the Butte judges. The Governor and Legislature capitulated and the statute survives. See, e.g., *Patrick v. State,* 2011 MT 169, ¶¶ 17–23, 361 Mont. 204, 257 P.3d 365.

And Chief Justice McGrath pointed to how the corrupting influence of money could mean a seat in the U.S. Senate.[122] at a time when U.S. senators were chosen by state legislatures.[123] W.A. Clark became rich in copper mining in Butte, Mont. He decided he wanted to be a United States senator. He and tried and failed in 1890 to get the Montana Legislature to select him.[124] He tried again in 1899 and was selected by the Montana Legislature. The U.S. Senate admitted him. On the same day that Clark was allowed to enter the Senate, a complaint was lodged alleging that Clark had violated Montana state law limiting spending on political contributions. The law, aimed at political corruption, allowed

---

119 *Western Tradition Partnership, Inc. v. Attorney General of State Supreme Court of Montana*, 363 Mont. 220, 271 P.3d 1 (Montana 2011).

120 Ibid.

121 Ibid. at 230–231, 8.

122 Until 1913, state legislatures picked U.S. senators.

123 The 17th Amendment, passed in 1912 and ratified in 1913, allowed people to vote directly for senators.

124 "The Election Case of William A. Clark of Montana (1900)," History of the Senate, https://www.senate.gov/artandhistory/history/common/contested_elections/089William_Clark.html.

spending up to $2,000 in state elections. Clark admitted spending $272,000 on Montana senate races and grateful senators sent him to the U.S. Senate.[125] The U.S. Senate referred the complaint to the Committee on Privileges and Elections.[126]

> On April 23, 1900, after hearing extensive testimony from ninety-six witnesses, the committee returned a report unanimously concluding that William Clark was not entitled to his seat. The testimony detailed a dazzling list of bribes ranging from $240 to $100,000. In a high-pressure, well-organized scheme coordinated by Clark's son, Clark's agents had paid mortgages, purchased ranches, paid debts, financed banks, and blatantly presented envelopes of cash to legislators. In addition, the winning margin in Clark's election had been secured by the votes of eleven Republican legislators under suspicious circumstances. Clark did not enhance his position when he admitted that he had destroyed all his personal checks that dealt with campaign transactions.

The Senate prepared to vote to deny Clark his seat but he resigned before the Senate took action. But Clark's wealth and determination to win was not to be denied. He returned to Montana and was appointed by the Lt. Governor[127] to the Senate seat he resigned from. Clark resigned again after the Senate threatened a new investigation into the circumstances of his appointment.

But Clark did not stop. He spent lavishly on the 1900 Montana legislative elections.[128] "In January 1901 a newly elected Montana legislature—in which most of the winning candidates had received financial support from William Clark—elected him to the Senate for the same term he had filled earlier." There was no complaint and the Senate seated him. Clark served one term and then returned to copper mining.

Mark Twain wrote in 1907 that Clark "is said to have bought legislatures and judges as other men buy food and raiment. By his example he has so excused and so sweetened corruption that in Montana it no longer has an offensive smell." Mark Twain, "*Mark Twain in Eruption*", 72 (Harper & Bros. 1940).[129]

Chief Justice McGrath had laid out a record demonstrating the corrupting power of money in politics. It was then up to the U.S. Supreme

---

125 *Western Tradition Partnership, Inc. v. Attorney General of State Supreme Court of Montana*, 363 Mont. 220, 231, 271 P.3d 1, 8 (Montana 2011).

126 Ibid.

127 The governor had been called out of the state allowing the lieutenant governor to act in his absence.

128 "The Election Case of William A. Clark of Montana (1900)," History of the Senate, https://www.senate.gov/artandhistory/history/common/contested_elections/089William_Clark.html.

129 Quoted in *Western Tradition Partnership, Inc. v. Attorney General of State Supreme Court of Montana*, 363 Mont. 220, 235, 271 P.3d 1, 11 (Montana 2011).

Court to decide whether Montana's law, as a regulation by a state, could co-exist with *Citizens United.*

U.S. SUPREME COURT OVERRULES MONTANA COURT

The U.S. Supreme Court declined the opportunity to reconsider *Citizens United* in light of the record presented in *Western Tradition Partnership*. Instead of looking at corruption, the Court summarily reversed the Montana supreme court's decision.[130] The Supreme Court decision, which was not signed, held 5–4 that Montana was bound by the case.[131]

> The question presented in this case is whether the holding of *Citizens United* applies to the Montana state law. There can be no serious doubt that it does. See U.S. Const., Art. VI, cl. 2. Montana's arguments in support of the judgment below either were already rejected in Citizens United, or fail to meaningfully distinguish that case.
>
> The petition for certiorari is granted. The judgment of the Supreme Court of Montana is reversed.

Justice Breyer dissented joined by Justices Ginsburg, Sotomayor and Kagan. Breyer, who dissented in *Citizens United,* continued his argument against that case and said that the record in *Western Tradition* supported the Montana Supreme Court's holding.[132]

> * * * Montana's experience, like considerable experience elsewhere since the Court's decision in Citizens United, casts grave doubt on the Court's supposition that independent expenditures do not corrupt or appear to do so.

Then again, the majority in *Citizens United* found little evidence of the corrupting influence of money in any of the cases in which they ruled against limits on campaign contributions. The majority defined corruption as quid pro quo corruption in which money was directly exchanged for a commitment to take official action.

Direct action[133] seems a very narrow definition of the ability of money to influence politicians. Take the example of then-New Jersey Gov. Chris Christie, a candidate for the Republican presidential nomination. Christie spoke to the Republican Jewish Coalition in 2014. In his speech, he mentioned taking, "a helicopter ride from the occupied

---

[130] Adam Liptak, "Supreme Court Declines to Revisit Citizens United," *New York Times*, June 25, 2012.

[131] *American Tradition Partnership, Inc. v. Bullock*, 567 U.S. 516, 132 S.Ct. 2490 (2012).

[132] *American Tradition Partnership, Inc. v. Bullock*, 567 U.S. 516, 517, 132 S.Ct. 2490, 2491–2492 (2012).

[133] Or, as it can be described, taking the money with one hand and signing a new law with the other.

territories," and realizing risks to Israel's continued existence.[134] "Occupied territories" refers to Palestinian territory occupied by the Israeli military. Its use is objectionable to conservative supporters of the Jewish state, including GOP mega-donor Sheldon Adelson, who has given more than $200 million to Republican candidates. Christie met with Adelson not long after his speech to apologize. A source,[135]

> told POLITICO that Christie "clarified in the strongest terms possible that his remarks today were not meant to be a statement of policy."
>
> Instead, the source said, Christie made clear "that he misspoke when he referred to the 'occupied territories.' And he conveyed that he is an unwavering friend and committed supporter of Israel, and was sorry for any confusion that came across as a result of the misstatement."
>
> Adelson accepted Christie's explanation, the source said.

And, Donald Trump chimed in on Adelson's influence in a tweet about competitor Florida Sen. Marco Rubio (R) before he claimed going on to win the Republican nomination in 2016.[136]

> Trump alluded to a report this week that casino mogul Sheldon Adelson, a top Republican mega-donor, was leaning toward supporting Rubio's 2016 bid.
>
> "Sheldon Adelson is looking to give big dollars to Rubio because he feels he can mold him into his perfect little puppet. I agree!" Trump tweeted.

MCCUTCHEON V. F.E.C. (2014): SUPREME COURT FURTHER EVISCERATES CAMPAIGN FINANCE LAWS

Given the opportunity, a partisan Supreme Court of the United States disemboweled an historic bipartisan Congressional effort to regulate excessive campaign spending. An Arkansas energy magnate, Shaun McCutcheon challenged spending limits imposed on direct contributions by individuals to national political parties and to federal candidates in an election year. The limits were imposed by the Federal Election Campaign Act (FECA) of 1971, as amended in 1974 and 1976, thanks to the corruption exposed in the Watergate Scandal.[137]

McCutcheon, founder and CEO of Coalmont Electrical Development Corporation, brought suit against the Federal Election Commission

---

[134] Kenneth P. Vogel, "Christie apologizes for 'occupied territories,' " *Politico*, March 29, 2014. https://www.politico.com/story/2014/03/chris-christie-occupied-territories-apology-105169.

[135] Ibid.

[136] Jesse Burns, "Trump: Rubio a perfect little puppet," *The Hill*, Oct. 13, 2015. https://thehill.com/blogs/ballot-box/presidential-races/256737-trump-rubio-a-perfect-little-puppet.

[137] "The Federal Election Campaign Laws: A Short History," transition.fec.gov/info/appfour.htm.

arguing that the spending limits imposed under FECA unconstitutionally infringed on his First Amendment rights of political expression. He wished to make contributions to more candidates than then law allowed. With a 5–4 plurality decision in McCutcheon's favor, the Supreme Court of the United States further jettisoned Congressional efforts to control excessive spending on political campaigns. The fifth vote upholding pruning of the FECA came from Justice Clarence Thomas, who opposed all restrictions on campaign spending.

As *Nation* magazine pointed out, the *McCutcheon* decision thus became part of a trilogy of Court campaign finance decisions liberals love to hate. A *Nation* editorial declared, "[T]hat started in 1976 with *Buckley v. Valeo,*[138] which reversed the Midas touch by turning money into speech."[139] The second part of the trilogy, *Citizens United v. Federal Election Commission,*[140] enormously weakened restrictions of the McCain-Feingold Act, formally known as the Bipartisan Campaign Reform Act of 2002.

Delivering the judgment of the Court, a four-justice plurality in *McCutcheon*, Chief Justice John Roberts wrote, "There is no right in our democracy more basic than the right to participate in electing our political leaders." Citizens, he wrote, can participate in a number of ways, including voting, urging others to support a particular candidate, doing volunteer campaign work, running for office and contributing money. "The right to participate in elections," Roberts wrote, "is protected by the First Amendment, but that right is not absolute. Our cases have held that Congress may regulate campaign contributions to protect against corruption or the appearance of corruption. See *Buckley v. Valeo*, 424 U.S. 1–27."[141] Justice Roberts added, "At the same time, we have made clear that Congress may not regulate contributions simply to reduce the amount of money in politics, or to restrict the political participation of some in order to enhance the influence of others."[142]

McCutcheon v. F.E.C. dealt with two kinds of campaign contribution limits: "base limits" (the amount that may be given to any one candidate by any individual donor) and "aggregate limits," the overall amount that any single donor can contribute to a number of candidates. A big spender,

---

[138] *Buckley v. Valeo*, 424 U.S. 1, 96 S.Ct. 612 (1977).

[139] "Assault on Democracy," editorial in *The Nation*, April 20, 2014, p. 3. *Buckley v. Valeo*, 424 U.S. 1, 96 S.Ct. 612 (1976) held that the Federal Election Campaign Act (FECA) of 1971, as amended in 1974 after the Watergate Scandal, violated the First Amendment by limiting contributions by candidates to their own campaigns. The 7–1 decision by the Court declared that in theory, control of campaign spending was constitutionally permissible, but that basically, political contributions were a form of speech protected by the First Amendment. After the decisions in *Citizens United v. Federal Election Commission*, 558 U.S. 310, 130 S.Ct. 876 (2010) as expanded by the *McCutcheon* decision of 2014, the Federal Election Commission would seem to have little left to do.

[140] *Citizens United v. Federal Elections Commission*, 558 U.S. 310, 130 S.Ct. 876 (2010).

[141] Chief Justice Roberts' opinion announcing the judgment of the Court, *McCutcheon et. al. v. Federal Election Commission*, 572 U.S. 185, 191, 134 S.Ct. 1434, 1441 (2014).

[142] Ibid.

McCutcheon felt unconstitutionally constrained because during the 2011–2012 election cycle—in compliance with contribution limits then in force-he contributed $33,088 to 16 different federal candidates. McCutcheon argued in his lawsuit against the Federal Election Commission that he wished to contribute $1,776 each to 12 additional candidates, but could not do so because of the aggregate limit on contributions to candidates.

For the 2013–2014 election, individuals could give a total of $123,200 to candidates,[143] national and state political committees, and PACS (political action committees). There is a limit of $48,600 on what individuals can contribute to candidates. McCutcheon's announced support exceeded $50,000.

McCutcheon v. Federal Election Committee struck down aggregate contribution limits. People favoring those limits, as *The Washington Post*'s Robert Barnes and Matea Gold analyzed the issues, "could dramatically increase the power and size of joint fundraising committees." They gave the example of the Obama Victory Fund merging the efforts of the Obama campaign with the Democratic National Committee.[144]

Justice Roberts wrote that the aggregate limits on campaign spending did not meet the express objectives of preventing corruption. In fact, "Because we find a substantial mismatch between the Government's stated objective [in preventing "quid pro quo" corruption] and the means selected to achieve it, the aggregate limits fail even under the 'closely drawn' test." The " 'closely drawn' " test, akin to "strict scrutiny" of measures impacting the First Amendment, was drawn from *Buckley v. Valeo*.[145]

Roberts' plurality opinion, however, went beyond *Buckley v. Valeo*, a decision concentrating on and upholding "base limits" on campaign spending. "Although *Buckley* provides some guidance, we think that its ultimate conclusion about the constitutionality of the aggregate limit under the FECA does not control here." *Buckley* spent only three sentences analyzing the aggregate limit, noting that the aggregate limit had not been separately addressed at length in the case.[146]

---

143 Id., p. 5. McCutcheon was joined in his lawsuit by the Republican National Committee.

144 Robert Barnes and Matea Gold, "Supreme Court case could give wealthy donors more latitude in elections," *The Washington Post*, Oct. 10, 2013. https://www.washingtonpost.com/politics/supreme-court-case-could-give-wealthy-donors-more-latitude-in-elections/2013/10/03/26a66d82-2ad4-11e3-b139-029811dbb57f_story.html.

145 *McCutcheon v. Federal Election Committee*, 572 U.S. 185, 196, 134 S.Ct. 1434, 1446, (2014).

146 Ibid. at 1462.

The *Buckley* decision had characterized aggregate limits on campaign spending as " 'a quite modest restraint upon protected political activity,' "[147] Chief Justice Roberts disagreed.[148]

> We cannot agree with that characterization. An aggregate limit on how many candidates an individual may support through contributions is not a "modest restraint" at all. The Government may no more restrict how many candidates or causes a donor may support than it may tell a newspaper how many candidates it may endorse.

Quoting the 2008 decision in *Davis v. Federal Election Commission,*[149] Roberts declared, "No matter how desirable it may seem, it is not an acceptable governmental objective to 'level the playing field'."

Chief Justice Roberts then took up Justice Stephen Breyer's dissenting argument that this Court failed to take adequate account of "any 'collective' interest that may justify restrictions on individual speech. Roberts responded,[150] "[W]e do not doubt the compelling nature of the 'collective' interest in preventing corruption of the electoral process."

But as Roberts read *Buckley v. Valeo,*[151]

> [W]hile preventing corruption or its appearance is a legitimate objective, Congress may target only a specific type of corruption-quid pro quo corruption. As Buckley explained, Congress may permissibly seek to rein in "large contributions [that] are given to secure a political quid pro quo from current and potential office holders.

"The Chief Justice's opinion conceded that although the line between quid pro quo corruption and general influence may seem vague," the distinction must be respected in order to safeguard basic First Amendment rights.[152]

> "[I]n drawing that line, the First Amendment requires us to err on the side of protecting political speech rather than suppressing it." *Federal Election Comm'n. v. Wisconsin Right to Life*, 551 U.S. 449, 457 (2007) (opinion of Roberts, C.J.)

Roberts asserted further that "[s]pending large sums of money in connection with elections, but not in connection with an effort to control the exercise of an officeholder's official duties, does not give rise to such quid pro quo corruption."

---

[147] Ibid. at 1465, quoting *Buckley v. Valeo*, 424 U.S. at 28 (1976).

[148] Ibid. at 1448.

[149] Ibid. at 1450, 207, quoting *Davis v. Federal Election Commission*, 554 U.S. 724, 741, 128 S.Ct. 2759, 2773 (2008).

[150] Ibid. at 1450.

[151] Ibid.

[152] Ibid. at 1451.

The Chief Justice placed reliance on disclosure requirements about political contributions as a "particularly effective means of arming the voting public with information." Large political contributions (within legal limits, of course) may cause party leaders to feel a particular gratitude. But such gratitude, in Roberts' view, was not corruption absent quid pro quo trading of votes for monetary support. The plurality decision was given force by a dissenting opinion by Justice Clarence Thomas. In Thomas' view, *Buckley v. Valeo*[153] "denigrates core First Amendment speech and should be overruled."

Quoting himself, Thomas contended,[154] " 'I am convinced that under traditional strict scrutiny, broad prophylactic caps on both spending and giving in the political process . . . are unconstitutional.' "

Justice Stephen Breyer wrote a combative dissent, in which he was joined by Justices Ginsburg, Sotomayor and Kagan.[155] Breyer declared that the plurality's conclusion that aggregate spending limits to control total amounts expended in political campaigns does not give rise to corruption was misguided. Breyer contended that the plurality defined corruption too narrowly, to quid pro quo corruption akin to bribery. Breyer contended:[156]

> In reality, as the history of campaign finance reform shows and as our earlier cases on the subject have recognized, the anticorruption interest that drives Congress to regulate campaign contributions is a far broader, more important interest than the plurality acknowledges. It is an understanding in maintaining the integrity of our public governmental institutions. And it is an interest rooted in the Constitution and in the First Amendment itself.
>
> * * *
>
> The upshot is that the interests the Court has long described as preventing 'corruption' or the 'appearance of corruption' are more than ordinary factors to be weighed against the constitutional right to political speech. Rather, they are interests rooted in the First Amendment itself. They are rooted in the constitutional effort to create a democracy responsive to the people-a government where laws reflect the very thoughts, views, ideas and sentiments, the expression of which the First Amendment protects.

Justice Breyer then provided lengthy appendices quoting lobbyists and elected politicians on the effects of huge soft money contributions to

---

153 Ibid. at 1462, quoting his opinion in *Colorado Federal Campaign Comm v. Federal Election Comm'n.*, 518 U.S. 604, 631–648, 116 S.Ct. 2309, 2323–2331.

154 Ibid.

155 Ibid. at 1464. Dissenting opinion of Justice Stephen Breyer.

156 Ibid. at 1466–1467.

political parties.[157] For example, Fred Rozen—a partner in a lobbying firm—said " ' "money is given so that the contributors can be close to, and recognized by, Members, Presidents, and Administration officials who have power." ' "

Justice Breyer quoted Fred Thompson, a former U.S. Senator from Tennessee, in a 2001 statement saying[158] " ' "We have gone from basically a small donor system . . . where the average person believed they had a stake, believed they had a voice, to one of extremely large amounts of money, where you are not a player unless you are in the $100,000 to $200,000 range [or more]. . . ." ' "

And outspoken former Senator Alan Simpson (D-Wyo) said,[159] " ' "Too often, Members' first thought is not what is right or wrong or what they believe, but how will it affect fundraising. Who, after all, can seriously contend that a $100,000 donation does not alter the way one thinks about—and quite possibly votes—on an issue?" ' "

157 Ibid. At Appendix A to Breyer opinion, p.1482.

158 Ibid.

159 Ibid. At. 1483.

CHAPTER 2

THE FIRST AMENDMENT: HISTORICAL BACKGROUND AND TODAY'S LAW

It has been said that the present is only the cutting edge of the past. This is especially true in law, with courts for the most part looking to earlier decisions, "following precedent." In studying struggles for freedom of expression, it is easy to wonder if there is much that is new. Old patterns of control—ancient enemies of freedom—may be traced to authoritarian philosophies hundreds and hundreds of years old. Major controls over the press well known in Seventeenth and Eighteenth Century England and America set the pattern for battles for freedom of expression which will continue in the Twenty-First Century.[1] Patterns of control continue, and so do the fights against them.

4. SEDITIOUS LIBEL: ANCIENT ENEMY OF FREEDOM

Sedition—defined roughly as expression attacking government's form, laws, institutions, or officers (including, in Seventeenth Century England, members of the Royal family)—is a criminal charge many centuries old. In the United States of the Twenty-First Century the crime has been restricted by court rulings.

The crime of seditious libel or "sedition" has a long and bloody history. Consider the case of William Prynne who advocated strict Puritanism. In his book, "*Histrio-Mastix*," he denounced such popular pastimes as dancing, hunting, Christmas-keeping, and play-going (although Prynne thought that reading plays was a perfectly fine diversion). How did this attack government? The attack was inferred from Prynne's assertion that lewd women and whores acted in plays: It

[1] Fredrick S. Siebert, *Freedom of the Press in England*, 1476–1776 (Urbana: Univ. of Illinois Press, 1952). This is the classic treatment of the instruments of control. See also Norman L. Rosenberg, *Protecting the Best Men: An Interpretive History of the Law of Libel* (Chapel Hill: Univ. of North Carolina Press, 1986), and Leonard W. Levy, *Emergence of a Free Press* (New York: Oxford, 1985).

seems Henrietta Maria, the Queen of England had taken part in private productions at Somerset House. Although the historical record suggests that Prynne did not refer to the Queen, Archbishop William Laud sought to have Prynne prosecuted on the grounds that the book[2] "*could* have been referring to the Queen." Prynne was fined £10,000 and given life imprisonment. In addition, he was pilloried (made to "stand in the stocks," held in a frame in a public square where passers-by could taunt him) and had his ears cropped off (A year later, in 1637, Dr. John Bastwick[3] and Henry Burton[4] were treated similarly by the infamous Court of the Star Chamber for their attacks on the Pope.).[5] Mob demonstrations against authority followed Prynne's sentencing. He was released from prison by the Long Parliament in 1641 after Puritan forces gained control of England and after the abolition of the Court of the Star Chamber.[6]

Treason is a crime punishable by death. It had been defined very broadly in England since 1352, in the time of Edward III. Treason then meant not only making war against the King or giving aid and comfort to enemies, it also included "compassing the death of the king," or imagining his death (A federal statute makes it a crime to threaten the life of the president or president-elect of the United States.[7] The statute distinguishes between actual threats and things spoken in jest or spoken with hyperbole. On the other hand, the utterance of the threat is sufficient to prosecute. The Supreme Court has held that the statute is constitutional.).

It wasn't only the people who originated dangerous ideas who were at risk. Printer John Twyn, suffered the harshest penalty possible when he printed a book called *"A Treatise on the Execution of Justice."* The book contended that a ruler is accountable to the people, and that the people may take up arms against and even kill a king who refuses accountability. Writing was included in "compassing the death of the king," and at a 1663 session of the Old Bailey court in London Twyn was indicted for treason. Although Twyn had not written the book, he refused to say who did. And as the printer, he then received the full weight of the

---

2 Dorothy Auchter, *Dictionary of Literary and Dramatic Censorship in Tudor and Stuart England* (Greenwood Publishing Group, Westport, Conn., 2001).

3 Dr. Bastwick wrote *Elenchus Religionis Papisticae* and *Flagellum Pontificis et Episcoporum Latialium*. The books objected to Archbishop William Laud's changes in the Church of England that Bastwick believed moved the church back to Roman Catholicism. Star Chamber judges refused to allow Dr. Bastwick to represent himself and reached a verdict of guilty even though some of the judges had not read his books. Leonard A. Parry, *Some Famous Medical Trials* (Beard Books, Washington, D.C., 1928).

4 Burton also wrote a book critical of changes in the Church of England by Archbishop William Laud.

5 3 Howell's State Trials 561 (1632–3).

6 Siebert, pp. 123–125.

7 18 U.S.C.A. § 871.

law's brutality. The judge pronounced the sentence—guilty and then the punishment:[8]

> * * * "that you be * * * drawn upon a hurdle [sledge] to the place of execution; and there you shall be hanged by the neck, and being alive, shall be cut down, and your privy-members shall be cut off, your entrails shall be taken out of your body, and you living, the same to be burnt before your eyes; your head to be cut off, your body to be divided into four quarters * * * And the Lord have mercy upon your soul."

Martyrs to the principle of free expression had their impact as spokesmen for a new philosophy such as John Milton and John Locke had theirs. But the legal principle of seditious libel remained in force. If people criticized government, they did so at their peril. Seditious libel soon was transported to the English colonies in America, although punishments for the crime never descended to the level of cruelty inflicted on the drawn-and-quartered John Twyn.

SEDITION IN COLONIAL AMERICA: THE ZENGER TRIAL

At least four colonial Americans faced sedition prosecutions for printed words before the most celebrated criminal trial of the colonial period took place in 1735. The outcome of that famous trial—involving *New York Weekly Journal* printer John Peter Zenger—still has meaning in the Twenty-First Century symbolizing press struggles for freedom to criticize government.

Zenger became a hero of press freedom by getting into the middle of a bitter factional dispute in politics of the New York colony. New York Gov. William Cosby, a greedy and autocratic man, was opposed by lawyer James Alexander.

A group, known as the Popular Party, spoke out against Cosby's administration. They started the *New York Weekly Journal* and Alexander wrote anonymous attacks labeling Governor Cosby a tyrant and oppressor of the colony.[9]

The colony's attorney general tried, unsuccessfully, to get a grand jury to indict the printer. Thwarted in that direction the attorney general brought charges of sedition on his own, filing an "information" with the New York court. Zenger was jailed, and remained there for eight months awaiting trial for seditious libel. Alexander prepared to defend Zenger. He was unable to do so, however, because Chief Justice James De Lancey, who had been appointed by Cosby, disbarred Alexander from practicing law. Alexander then turned to Andrew Hamilton of Philadelphia to plead Zenger's case.

---

[8] Howell's State Trials 513 (1663).

[9] Stanley Nider Katz, *A Brief Narrative of the Case and Trial of John Peter Zenger* (Cambridge: Harvard, 1963); Harold L. Nelson, "Seditious Libel in Colonial America," 3 *Am.Jour.Legal History* 160 (1959).

The original "Philadelphia lawyer," Hamilton had built a reputation as the ablest attorney in the colonies. His bold advocacy that the court discard old patterns of thinking about sedition came to bear in an irresistible way with jurors already sympathetic to Zenger's cause. The law of sedition then held that the defendant was not to be permitted to plead that his offending words against government were true. The truth, it was held, only aggravated the offense, for it was more likely than falsehood to cause the target to seek violent revenge and breach the community's peace. Furthermore, a jury then had only a minor role in a sedition trial: its job was to decide whether the accused had, indeed, published the words. It was up to the court to decide whether they were illegal words.

Jockeying with Chief Justice De Lancey, Hamilton urged the jury to recognize truth as a defense for Zenger, and argued that the jury should decide "the law"—whether the words were libelous—as well as the fact of printing. Blocked by the judge from expanding on these points, he shifted argument to the importance of permitting men to criticize their governments, saying:[10]

> Men who injure and oppress the people under their administration provoke them to cry out and complain, and then make that very complaint the foundation for new oppressions and prosecutions. * * * [T]he question before the Court and you, gentlemen of the jury, is not of small or private concern; it is not the cause of a poor printer, nor of New York alone, which you are trying. No! it may, in its consequences, affect every freeman that lives under a British government, on the main of America. It is the best cause; it is the cause of liberty; and I make no doubt but your upright conduct, this day, will not only entitle you to the love and esteem of your fellow citizens, but every man who prefers freedom to a life of slavery, will bless and honor you as men who have baffled the attempts of tyranny; and by an impartial and uncorrupt verdict, have laid a noble foundation for securing to ourselves, our posterity, and our neighbors, that to which nature and the laws of our country have given us a right—the liberty—both of exposing and opposing arbitrary power in these parts of the world at least, by speaking and writing truth.

Hamilton ended his plea before an emotion-charged courtroom; De Lancey delivered a confusing charge to the jury, which retired to deliberate. In a short time the jury emerged with a "not guilty" verdict. There were celebrations in the streets that night; there were printings and re-printings of the Hamilton plea for years to come, more even in England than in the colonies. The court trial for seditious libel was finished for the colonial period in America as an instrument for control

[10] Ibid. at 2–9.

of the press. Not for 40 years or more would seditious libel be used again in America by a court.[11] Not so for the colonial legislatures where sedition cases continued to be brought.

It was the elected Assembly, or lower house of the colonial legislature, that was the most successful and most active force in official control of Eighteenth-Century colonial printers. Jealous of its powers under the view that it was Parliament in miniature, and unwilling to have its acts criticized, this agency of government disciplined printer after printer. Even as it emerged as the main check on the powers of the Crown's governors, even as it showed itself as the seat of government support for the movement for independence, the Assembly demonstrated its aversion to popular criticism. Its instrument for control was the citation for contempt ("breach of privilege"), and it haled a long line of printers before it for their "seditious" attacks on its performance. The legislative contempt citation was a legislative sedition action.

Historian Leonard Levy has demonstrated the relative power and activity of the Assemblies in respect to the press. Up and down the seaboard, printers were brought to the legislative bar and there were forced to kneel and beg the pardon of the stern lawmakers, swear that they meant no harm by their writings, and accept rebuke or imprisonment. The brother of Benjamin Franklin, Printer James Franklin's irony put him in jail in 1722; he had speculated that the Massachusetts government might get around to outfitting a ship to pursue a pirate "sometime this month, wind and weather permitting." New Yorkers James Parker and William Weyman were jailed for publishing an article on the poverty of Orange and Ulster counties; the Assembly construed it as a reflection upon its stewardship. These were only two actions among many, repressive actions by legislatures that continued to the eve of the Revolutionary War in some colonies.[12]

The great article of faith that heads America's commitment to free expression was adopted in 1791 by men who had not yet thought through all that "free speech and press" implies. The First Amendment to the Constitution states that "Congress shall make no law * * * abridging freedom of speech, or of the press * * * ." Although some then argued over precisely what they meant by the words, none spoke doubts about the importance of the principle. They were deeply aware of the lasting symbolic power of the courageous Zenger in accepting jail in the cause of free press. They knew well the spirited, soaring arguments for free press by England's famed "Cato," whose essays were printed and re-printed in

[11] Harold L. Nelson, "Seditious Libel in Colonial America," 3 *Am.Journ.Legal History* 160 (1959).

[12] Levy, *Emergence of a Free Press*, pp. 71–84. No other historian has stimulated others to study Eighteenth-Century American press freedom as has Levy, whose thesis that the First Amendment was not intended by the Framers to end the British common law of seditious libel in America has aroused many to dissent. Revising his earlier, provocative Legacy of Suppression (1960) in Emergence of a Free Press (1985), and conceding some errors and misinterpretations in Legacy, he responds directly to many of the protestors but concedes nothing central to his main thesis. See *Emergence of a Free Press*, passim, for many of the confrontations.

the little colonial newspapers. Behind them lay the great pamphleteering and newspapering that had raised sedition to an art in bringing the colonies to revolt against the Mother country, printed words indispensable in bringing down the most powerful nation on earth.

Yet in the searing newspaper debates of the nation's first years, with Federalists and anti-Federalists indulging in heated political speech seen by many as seditious and thus criminal, the axioms of centuries were with them. It still seemed to many that no government could stand if it could not at some point punish its critics, if the new government was meant to last. Some words surely were illegal. Not, perhaps, in the realm of religion, where James Madison, among others, argued an unlimited freedom to speak and write; but could sedition be given such scope? It was the party of Thomas Jefferson that gave an answer, in the debates over the Alien and Sedition Acts of 1798–1800.

THE ALIEN AND SEDITION ACTS, 1798–1800

In the complex story about the reluctant retreat of the crime of sedition through more than 150 years of American history, no episode stands out more than the controversy of 1798–1800 over the Alien and Sedition Acts. It was only seven years after the adoption of the Bill of Rights and its First Amendment that the Acts were written, at a time of high public and official alarm. With France and England in conflict through the 1790s, America had been pulled by both toward war. The Republicans—Jefferson's party—had favored France, while the Federalists sided with England. Angered at Jay's Treaty of 1794 with England, which France believed placed America on the side of her enemy, France had undertaken the raiding of American shipping. America's envoys, sent to France to negotiate a settlement, were faced with a demand for an American war loan to France, and a bribe of a quarter-million dollars. This unofficial demand as a price for negotiations was revealed to Americans as the notorious "X, Y, Z Affair." Now most of America was incensed; President John Adams called for war preparation, which his Federalist Congress set about in 1797.[13]

The Republicans suffered heavy political losses because of the nation's war fever. But they did not abandon their support of France. Stigmatized in the refusal to do so, associated by the Federalists with the recent French Revolution and its Terror, and beleaguered on all sides for their continued opposition to Britain, the Republicans were in deep trouble.

Fear of an invasion by France, supported by French and Irish immigrants living in the United States who might attack American forces, added to the list of Federalist worries. They also were concerned about the possibility of another American revolution that would divide

[13] James M. Smith, *Freedom's Fetters* (Ithaca: Cornell Univ.Press, 1956), Chap. 2. This is the leading work on the Alien and Sedition Acts.

the country. The Whiskey Rebellion, Shays's Rebellion and insurrections in the Colonial period lent credence to Federalist concerns. President Adams, years before he was elected, had warned of the dangers inherent in having two opposing political parties working against each other and the battle between Republicans and Federalists appeared to be the embodiment of that prediction.

Contributing to the rancor between the two parties were the publications of the partisan newspapers of the time. Each side portrayed the other as the chief villain of the time. Criticisms, justified and otherwise, and name-calling filled their pages. Jefferson was called the Anti-Christ while Adams was portrayed as a man intent on creating a monarchy with himself as king. In this context, the Federalist Congress passed the Alien and Sedition Acts as measures to control opposition to America's war policy, to the Federalist majority party, and to ensure that the nation would remain united in a time of national crisis.

It was the Sedition Act that struck most lethally at opposition and at the Republicans. The Act made it a crime to publish or utter false, scandalous, and malicious criticism of the President, Congress, or the government with the intent to defame them or bring them into disrepute.[14] The one person not protected was Thomas Jefferson, the vice president. At the time, the candidate with the most votes was president and the runner-up was vice president. This predates the "ticket" of presidential and vice presidential running mates.

Fourteen indictments were brought under the Act—all 14 resulted in convictions.[15] The first prosecution put Rep. Matthew "Ragged Matt, the Democrat," Lyon in jail for four months and cost him a fine of $1,000. In a letter published by a newspaper he helped found, Lyon claimed that, under President Adams, the Executive Branch showed "an unbounded thirst for ridiculous pomp, foolish adulation, and selfish avarice," and that the public welfare was "swallowed up in a continual grasp for power."[16]

Lyon was tried in a case presided over by Supreme Court Justice William Paterson, who was sitting as a federal circuit judge.[17] Lyon pleaded not guilty and also filed a pleading that the Sedition Act was not constitutional. Justice and Judge Paterson rejected Lyon's contention that the Act was unconstitutional.

Anthony Haswell, Republican editor of the (Bennington) *Vermont Gazette*, came to Lyon's defense while the latter was in prison. He wrote that Lyon was held by "the oppressive hand of usurped power," and said that the federal marshal who held him had subjected him to indignities

14 Ibid. at Chap. 6.

15 Ibid. at 185.

16 Lyon was re-elected from jail by his district. Sedition Act Trials-Historical Background and Documents. http://www.fjc.gov/history/home.nsf/page/tu_sedbio_lyon.html.

17 In addition to sitting on the Supreme Court, justices would travel the circuit of judicial districts presiding over grand juries and trials.

that might be expected of a "hard-hearted savage." Prosecuted and convicted, Haswell's fine was $200 and his term in federal prison two months.[18]

Its back to the wall under the attempt of the Federalists to outlaw it as a party of disloyalty and subversion, the Republican Party found spokesmen who declared that the idea of sedition betrayed a self-governing society, and denied that the federal government had any kind of power over the press. The Acts, the Jeffersonian Republicans said, were unconstitutional in making it a crime to criticize the President and government. No matter that the Acts permitted the defenses for which Andrew Hamilton had argued in defending Zenger: truth was of little use in defending opinions (how to prove the truth of an opinion?). Also, jury power to find the law could be circumvented by judges in various ways. A people, they argued, cannot call itself free unless it is superior to its government, unless it can have unrestricted right of discussion. No natural right of the individual, they contended in philosopher John Locke's framework, can be more important than free expression. The Jeffersonians rested their case on their belief in reason as the central characteristic of men, and on the people's position of ascendancy over government.[19]

Lawyer Tunis Wortman in 1800 worked out philosophical ground for freedom in the fullest statement of his era. Others—including James Madison and St. George Tucker drove home the arguments for free expression, but the Jeffersonian Republican Wortman led the way in "*A Treatise Concerning Political Enquiry and the Liberty of the Press.*" Wortman argued that the Alien and Sedition Acts, which criminalized criticism of government, should be forbidden under the First Amendment to the Constitution. Without criticism of government, Wortman believed that tyranny would result. He also argued that truth must be a defense to libel.[20]

The radical Thomas Cooper demolished one-by-one the arguments for permitting a sedition power in government.[21] He attacked the Sedition Act on the basis of its incompatibility with democracy, asking, "have we advanced so far on the road to despotism in this republican country, that we dare not say that our President may be mistaken?"[22] Nonetheless, Cooper was tried and convicted for violating the Sedition Act. He was sentenced to six months in jail and fined $400.[23]

---

[18] Each trial is treated in Smith, Chaps. 11–17.

[19] Levy, Chap. 10. And see Chap. 9 for evidence that several Jeffersonians had no objection to a sedition power in *state* governments.

[20] See Dwight L. Teeter, Jr., "Tunis Wortman" in Roger K. Newman, ed., *The Yale Biographical Dictionary of American Law* (New Haven: Yale University Press, 2009), pp. 601–602.

[21] *Political Essays* (Phila.: Printed for R. Campbell, 1800), pp. 71–88.

[22] Thomas Cooper, *Account of the Trial of Thomas Cooper*, (J. Biren, Philadelphia, 1800), p. 20.

[23] Ibid. at 52.

Even so, the Sedition Act was not universally unpopular, at least at first. While Kentucky and Virginia passed resolutions opposing the Sedition Act, Delaware and Massachusetts took the opposite position.[24] Rhode Island, Massachusetts, New York, Connecticut, New Hampshire and Vermont refused to endorse the Kentucky or Virginia resolutions. Federalists pointed to the "Necessary and Proper" clause of the Constitution.[25] Congress had the power to create a law to protect the nation, the Congress and the presidency, they argued.

But perhaps most importantly at the time, none of the sitting justices of the Supreme Court found the Act to be unconstitutional. Chief Justice Oliver Ellsworth wrote, in a private letter, that rights to slander and incite sedition were not conceived of by the First Amendment.[26] James Morton Smith's study of the Sedition Act of 1798 noted the positions of Justices James Iredell, William Cushing and Bushrod Washington,[27] "all of whom presided in New Jersey in 1798–1799, pointedly instructed grand juries on the constitutionality of that statute."

Justice Iredell laid out his position on the Alien and Sedition Act in three editions of *The Independent Chronicle* and the *Universal Advertiser* in late May 1799. He, too, pointed to the "Necessary and Proper" clause to find the Act constitutional.[28]

> * * * What is necessary and proper in time of confusion and disorder would not, perhaps be necessary and proper in a time of tranquility and order. These are questions of policy not questions of law and upon which the legislature is bound to decide according to its real opinion of the necessity and propriety of any act in contemplation.

Justice Iredell both praised and condemned the power of the printing press, concluding that the risk from allowing libels against the president, the Congress and the United States justified the "necessary and proper" Alien and Sedition Act.[29]

> The liberty of the press is, indeed, valuable-long may it preserve its lustre. It has converted barbarous nations into civilized ones—taught science to rear its head—enlarged the capacity encreased the comforts of private life—and leading the banners of freedom, has extended her sway where he very name was unknown.
>
> * * * A pen in the hands of an amiable and virtuous man may enlighten a whole nation, and by observation of read wisdom

[24] Ethelbert Warfield, *The Kentucky Resolutions of 1798*, (1894), p. 102.

[25] Article I, Sec. 8, Clause 18: "To make all Laws which shall be necessary and proper for carrying into Execution the foregoing Powers, and all other Powers vested by the Constitution in the Government of the United States * * * ".

[26] William Garrott Brown, *The Life of Oliver Ellsworth* (MacMillan & Co. London 1905).

[27] James Morton Smith, *Freedom's Fetters* (Cornell University Press, Ithaca, 1956).

[28] Ibid.

[29] Ibid.

> grounded on pure morality, may lead it to the path of honor and happiness. The same pen in the hands of a man equally able, but with vices as great as the other's virtues, may be arts of sophistry easily attainable and inflaming the passions or weak minds, delude many into opinions the most dangerous and conduct them to actions the most criminal.
>
> * * * Such be unquestionably the case, can it be tolerated in any civilized society that any should be permitted with impunity to tell falsehoods to the people with an express intention to deceive them and lead them into discontent if not insurrection, which is so apt to follow? It is believed no government in the world was ever without such a power.

But the public soured on the Act. It had been used to punish political theorists and a popular member of Congress. It targeted the father of the New York public education system. Included among its victims were two men who, drinking in a tavern, had spoken disrespectfully about President Adams. The Federalists and Adams lost the elections of 1800. President Jefferson was committed to letting the Acts lapse, and they died in early 1801. The nation would see no federal peacetime sedition act again for 140 years. Furthermore, the alternative route of using the common law as a basis for federal sedition actions was closed to the government only a few years later. The Supreme Court ruled in cases of 1812 and 1816 that federal courts had been given no authority over common-law crimes by the Constitution, and that whatever question there had been about the matter had been settled by public opposition to such jurisdiction.[30]

Different fears, different hatreds led to suppressive laws as times changed. In the South about a generation later, states began passing laws to silence Abolitionists. The anti-slavery drive, coupled with incidents such as Nat Turner's slave rebellion, caused convulsions of fear among Southerners that their "peculiar institution" and the shape of society and government would be subverted and destroyed. Laws were passed—sedition laws, though not labeled as such in statute books—making it a crime to advocate the abolition of slavery or to argue that owners "have no property" in slaves, and denying abolitionist literature access to the mails.[31] The suppression of anti-slavery argument became almost total in most of the South by 1850.[32]

---

[30] *United States v. Hudson and Goodwin*, 11 U.S. (7 Cranch.) 32 (1812); *United States v. Coolidge*, 14 U.S. (1 Wheat.) 415 (1816).

[31] Three Virginia laws passed between 1832 and 1848 are in Harold L. Nelson, *Freedom of the Press from Hamilton to the Warren Court*, pp. 173–178.

[32] Readers should remember that it was politically correct at different periods of American history to say that women should not have the vote, that Catholics should not hold office, that a work week of only 40 hours would only coddle the working classes. Political correctness applies to those who complain about political correctness in that they object to the objections of others. Comments critical of "political correctness" were a large part of Donald Trump's presidential bid in 2016.

SEDITION IN WORLD WAR I

Sedition actions surfaced again in the early Twentieth Century when both state and federal lawmakers acted to halt criticism of government during the rise of socio-political protest. Prosecutions to punish verbal attacks on the form of government, on laws, and on government's conduct, found new life at the federal level some 100 years after they had been discredited by the Alien and Sedition Act prosecutions of 1798–1800. The actions focused on a new radicalism, flourishing in the poverty and sweat-shop conditions of industrial cities and in the lumber and mining camps of the West. Whether seeking an improved life for the deprived, driving for power, or fostering revolution, socialists, anarchists, and syndicalists (revolutionary workers who seek to seize government, as through general strikes) advocated drastic change in the economic and political system. Laws and criminal prosecutions rose to check their words.[33]

World War I brought a wave of legislation across the states to make criminal the advocacy of violent overthrow of government. Yet it was the federal government's Espionage Act of 1917 and its amendment of 1918 to include sedition that put most muscle into prosecution for criminal words. Foremost among forbidden and prosecuted statements were those that were construed to cause insubordination or disloyalty in the armed forces, or to obstruct enlistment or recruiting.[34] Some 1,900 persons were prosecuted for speech, and as many as 100 newspapers and periodicals barred from the mails.[35] Polemics in pamphlet form, as well as books, also were the cause of prosecutions.

The best-known of the Socialist newspapers prosecuted under the Espionage Act were the *New York Call*, the *Masses*, also of New York, and the *Milwaukee Leader*. In the last of these, editor Victor Berger had denounced the war, the United States government, and munitions makers. Postmaster General Albert Burleson considered this the kind of opposition to the war forbidden by the Espionage Act, and excluded it from the mails as the Act provided. Further, he said, the repeated attacks on the war effort in the *Leader* were evidence that it would continue doing the same in the future, and on these grounds, the *Leader*'s second-class mail permit should be revoked. He was upheld in his revocation of the permit by the United States Supreme Court, and the *Leader* was thus denied the low-rate mailing privilege from 1917 until after the war.[36]

Burleson's actions were not universally applauded. In February of 1919, Sen. William Borah of Idaho tried, unsuccessfully, to repeal

[33] William Preston, Jr., *Aliens and Dissenters, Federal Suppression of Radicals*, 1903–1933 (Cambridge: Harvard Univ.Press, 1963).

[34] 40 U.S. Statutes 217. For state laws, see Zechariah Chafee, Jr., *Free Speech in the United States* (Boston, 1941), pp. 575–597.

[35] Chafee, p. 52.

[36] *United States ex rel. Milwaukee Social Democratic Pub. Co. v. Burleson*, 255 U.S. 407, 41 S.Ct. 352 (1921).

sections of the Espionage Act that Burleson was using to censor the mail.[37]

> These provisions of the Espionage Act have resulted in a complete censorship of the American Press. In my opinion, if Congress should ever assume to usurp the power to establish a censorship, there could be no more effective and successful method adopted than that of giving the Postmaster General certain powers with reference to the exclusion of printed matter from the mails.

The majority of Congress disagreed, however. Minnesota Sen. Knute Nelson warned about the dangers of Bolshevism.[38] "Unless steps are taken to check this tide, grave danger threatens our republic. Some radical speakers now going about the country would bring America to the level of Russia."

Pamphleteers of the left were convicted under the Espionage Act as well as under state anarchy and sedition acts. The famous case of *Schenck v. United States* led to the articulation of the famous "clear and present danger" test discussed in Chap. 1.[39]

RATTLING THE SABERS OF THE 1917 ESPIONAGE ACT IN THE TWENTY-FIRST CENTURY

The Espionage Act of 1917 is no longer just a memory of wholesale prosecutions during World War I for words that did little if any damage to the United States' war effort. Two months after declaring war on Germany in 1917, President Woodrow Wilson signed the Espionage Act. The Act listed activities to be considered as spying and to be punished with jail terms. President Wilson also had asked for sweeping power to punish persons his administration believed published information harmful to the national defense. Constitutional scholar Geoffrey R. Stone quoted President Wilson's view that disloyal persons " 'had sacrificed their rights to civil liberties.' " That would have meant that a mere *accusation* of disloyalty could strip a person of civil liberties before or without a trial. Congress, however, declined to provide such power to the president seeing the proposed measures as an unconstitutional threat to the First Amendment.[40]

Reporters' use of information classified under the label of national security in 2005 and 2006 led to feverish pronouncements by members of Congress, by Bush administration Attorney General Alberto Gonzales, and by conservative pundits calling for use of the Espionage Act to punish

---

[37] "Mail Censorship Repeal Beaten: Senate 39 to 25 Rejects Amendment by Borah to Curtail Burleson's Power," *New York Times*, Feb. 8, 1919.

[38] Ibid.

[39] *Schenck v. U.S.*, 249 U.S. 47, 39 S.Ct. 247 (1919).

[40] Geoffrey R. Stone, *Perilous Times: Free Speech in Wartime from the Sedition Act of 1798 to the War on Terrorism*, New York, W.W. Norton & Co., 2004, pp. 137–138; Rani Gupta, "Reporters or Spies?," *The News Media and the Law*, Fall, 2006, p. 4.

"disloyalty" by the news media. Both Rep. Peter King, R-NY, and Sen. Jim Bunning, R-KY, angrily denounced *New York Times* journalists James Risen and Eric Lichtblau as "traitors." Rep. King urged using the Espionage Act of 1917 to prosecute journalists Risen and Lichtblau because they had written the investigative account revealing vast amounts of warrantless wiretapping by the National Security Administration (NSA).[41] In fact, the *Times* sat on this story for a year at the request of President George W. Bush. But once the story was published, Vice President Dick Cheney called it disloyal, harmful to national security and not deserving of the Pulitzer Prize it was awarded.[42]

THE "AIPAC" CASE: A MODEL FOR PROSECUTING REPORTERS?

A case involving the American Israel Public Affairs Committee (AIPAC) has been termed a model for potential prosecutions of reporters. In the case, two lobbyists were charged with violations of the Espionage Act of 1917. Even though lobbyists are not journalists, this case nevertheless has been suggested as a template to use against the news media.[43]

Steven J. Rosen and Keith Weissmann were indicted in 2006 on charges of violating the Espionage Act. They were accused of passing national defense information to reporters and foreign officials. Federal Judge T.S. Ellis III, presiding over a hearing in the case, said, "Persons who have unauthorized possession, who come into unauthorized possession of classified information, must abide by the law. That applies to academics, lawyers, journalists, professors, whatever."[44]

Lawyers for Rosen and Weissmann argued that their conduct was protected by the First Amendment and that because they were not government employees, they could not be prosecuted for leaks. The attorneys argued that the two men were doing exactly what reporters do. In response, the Justice Department said that the lobbyists were different from journalists. At the same time, the government lawyers refused to rule out the possibility of prosecuting reporters under the Espionage Act.[45] The case came to a quiet end when the Obama Administration had the charges dismissed in the spring of 2009.

---

[41] Eric Lichtblau and James Risen, "Spy Agency Mined Vast Data Trove, Officials Report," *New York Times*, Dec. 24, 2005, Sec. 1, P.1.

[42] David Remnick, "Nattering Nabobs," editorial, *New Yorker*, July 10, 2006; http://www.newyorker.com/magazine/2006/07/10/nattering-nabobs.

[43] Adam Liptak, "In Leak Cases, New Pressures on Journalists," *New York Times*, April 30, 2006.

[44] Scott Shane and David Johnston, "Pro-Israeli Lobbying Group Roiled by Prosecution of Two Ex-Officials," *New York Times*, March 5, 2006.

[45] Ibid.

Gonzales said in 2006 that the federal government had the power to prosecute journalists for disclosing classified information. "There are some statutes on the book, which if you read the language carefully, would seem to indicate that it is a possibility."[46]

One approach to shutting off leaks to reporters, as the Bush administration searched for unauthorized communications that didn't follow the White House's agenda, was to get rid of government officials who were seen as sources of unfavorable news items. In April, 2006, the CIA fired a 22-year-veteran intelligence officer over "unauthorized contacts with reporters."[47]

Another Pulitzer Prize-winning report was denounced by the Bush White House. Vice President Cheney and other Republican official attacked *Washington Post* reporter Dana Priest's article about the "rendition" (some called it kidnaping) of terrorism suspects to jails in Eastern Europe.[48]

The Bush administration vented its outrage after an article in the *New York Times* in June, 2006 (also by Lichtblau and Risen) about the U.S. Treasury Department and the CIA mining an international banking database in Brussels in search of movement of funds to or by Al Qaeda. Similar accounts soon appeared in the *Wall Street Journal* and the *Los Angeles Times. The New Yorker's* editor, David Remnick, said that Bush and Cheney were angered because they had asked for the story to be spiked. Remnick wrote, however, that this information "has been an open secret ever since it was trumpeted by—well, by George W. Bush, in mid-September, 2001."[49]

WIKILEAKS, NEWS MEDIA AND GOVERNMENT SECRETS

The English playwright-satirist Oscar Wilde famously declared a century ago, "Spies are of no use nowadays. Their profession is over. The newspapers do their work instead."[50] In 2010, WikiLeaks took Wilde's declaration a step further when it began to leak documents, including video, from American units fighting in Iraq and Afghanistan. A few months later, in November, WikiLeaks began to share the contents of more than 250,000 American diplomatic cables with four news organizations, *Le Monde, El Pais, Der Spiegel* and the *Guardian* (the *Guardian* then shared its documents with the *New York Times.*

---

[46] Adam Liptak, "Gonzales Says Prosecutions of Journalists are Possible," *New York Times*, May 22, 2006; see also Liptak, "In Leak Cases, New Pressure on Journalists," *New York Times*, April 30, 2006.

[47] Dafna Linzer, "CIA Officer is Fired for Media Leaks," *Washington Post*, April 22, 2006.

[48] Eve Berliner, "The Pulitzer Prize 'Traitors:' Assault on a Vigilant Press in a Time of Secrecy and War," http://www.evesmag.com/pulitizertraitors.htm.

[49] David Remnick, "Nattering Nabobs," editorial, *New Yorker*, July 10, 2006; http://www.newyorker.com/magazine/2006/07/10/nattering-nabobs.

[50] Oscar Wilde, "An Ideal Husband," Act III.

In the beginning, WikiLeaks existed simply as a site where people could make secret documents public. Those documents mostly came from the world of business as employees and former employees laid out for the world to see the wrongdoing of corporations. WikiLeaks drew the ire of those corporations with its postings of internal memos about questionable and illegal practices. It was the subject of an attempt to shut it down through prior restraint [covered later in this chapter]. WikiLeaks was founded and led by Julian Assange, an Australian.[51]

> Wikileaks is a self-described "not-for-profit media organization," launched in 2006 for the purposes of disseminating original documents from anonymous sources and leakers. Its website says: "Wikileaks will accept restricted or censored material of political, ethical, diplomatic or historical significance. We do not accept rumor, opinion, other kinds of first hand accounts or material that is publicly available elsewhere."
>
> The *New York Times* described WikiLeaks as an organization having a core of 40 volunteers, plus 800 "mostly unpaid" followers maintaining computer servers for WikiLeaks and protecting it from the sort of hacking that allowed the organization access to secret government documents. Among the revelations coming from WikiLeaks included documents on the detentions at Guantamo Bay, killings without legal authority in East Timor and Kenya, and then-vice presidential candidate Sarah Palin's e-mails.

Assange clearly delighted in flouting United States security classifications. The *New York Times* reported that one leak involved a video showing American Apache helicopters in Baghdad in 2007, killing at least a dozen persons, including two Reuters journalists.[52] Reuters had asked the military to investigate the killings. The news organization also filed FOIA requests for the gun camera footage from the Apache attack helicopter that killed the two staffers, photographer Namir Noor-Eldeen, 22, and driver Saeed Chmagh, 40.[53]

> The U.S. military in a statement issued just after midnight on Thursday described the incident as a firefight with insurgents. It has said the killings were being investigated.
>
> "Our preliminary investigation raises real questions about whether there was fighting at the time the two men were killed," said David Schlesinger, editor-in-chief of Reuters.
>
> * * *

[51] Jonathan Zittrain and Molly Sauter, "Everything You Need to Know About Wikileaks," *MIT Technology Review*. Dec. 9, 2010. https://www.technologyreview.com/s/421949/everything-you-need-to-know-about-wikileaks/.

[52] http://www.nytimes.com/video/multimedia/1248069533084/collateral-murder.html.

[53] David Viggers, "Reuters seeks U.S. probe into killing of Iraqi staff," July 17, 2007. http://blogs.reuters.com/photographers-blog/2007/07/17/reuters-seeks-us-probe-into-killing-of-iraqi-staff/.

> Residents and witnesses interviewed by Reuters said they saw no gunmen in the immediate area where Noor-Eldeen and Chmagh were killed in Baghdad's al-Amin al-Thaniyah neighborhood.

The military's investigation concluded that the helicopter pilots were justified in their use of force because they had spotted a rocket-propelled grenade (RPG) and that the long lens on the cameras the Reuters employees were carrying could be confused for weapons.

Assange's anti-war, anti-U.S. zeal also resulted in what the *Times* termed collateral damage. A release of documents about the war in Afghanistan was released without expunging names of Afghans providing intelligence information to NATO troops, clearly endangering their lives. And U.S. Army PFC Bradley Manning, now known as Chelsea Manning, formerly working in U.S. Army intelligence, was facing charges under the 1917 Espionage Act.

But the revelations kept on coming. At the end of 2010, The *New York Times* reported that cables released by WikiLeaks showed that the federal Drug Enforcement Administration (DEA) had been expanded into a global intelligence operation. The *Times* reported that the DEA's reach "... that expands far beyond narcotics, and an eavesdropping operation so expansive that it has to fend off foreign politicians who want to use it against their political enemies, according to secret diplomatic cables." Leaked cables included DEA spying activities from countries including Panama, Mexico, Venezuela, Paraguay, Afghanistan, Mali, Nigeria, Sierra Leone and Guinea.[54]

Scott Horton of Harper's Magazine blogged in early August of 2010 that the American intelligence community was looking to discredit or destroy Assange and WikiLeaks. A purportedly leaked memo revealed plans to achieve that, Horton wrote.[55]

> [T]he Army Counterintelligence Center had prepared a 32-page secret plan to destroy WikiLeaks. The memo notes that the American intelligence community has valuable allies in the struggle against WikiLeaks—China, North Korea, Russia, Vietnam, and Zimbabwe. It recommended emulating the tactics used by these tyrannical states:
>
> The identification, exposure, termination of employment, criminal prosecution, legal action against current or former insiders, leakers, or whistleblowers could potentially damage or destroy this center of gravity and deter others considering similar actions from using the Wikileaks.org website.

---

[54] Ginger Thompson and Scott Shane, "Cables Portray Expanded Reach of Drug Agency: Beyond Narcotics War," *New York Times*, December 26, 2010, p. 1.

[55] Scott Horton, "WikiLeaks: The National-Security State Strikes Back," *Harper's Magazine*, Aug. 3, 2010. http://harpers.org/blog/2010/08/wikileaks-the-national-security-state-strikes-back/.

* * *

Finally, it argued that WikiLeaks itself must be criminalized and put out of business.

In August, 2010, Swedish authorities began an investigation of Assange on rape and molestation charges raised by two Swedish women. A day later the rape charge was dismissed but lesser charges of molestation and harassment remained. The charges did not directly translate from Swedish to English, the *New York Times* reported.[56]

> Now that the more serious charge of rape has been dropped, Mr. Assange is being investigated to see if he might have committed the crime known in Swedish as "ofredande," which can be translated as "molestation" or harassment." In English, the terms 'sexual molestation' and 'sexual harassment' have very different meaning and connotations.
>
> As Gustav Sandstrom explains in the *Wall Street Journal*, under Swedish law, ofredande "is defined broadly and can refer to anything from groping someone to inappropriate, nonsexual behavior, such as disrupting public order."

Eventually, the specifics of the criminal complaints of the two women were explained, the *New York Times* reported.[57]

> According to accounts the women gave to the police and friends, Swedish officials said, they had consensual sexual encounters with Mr. Assange that became nonconsensual. One woman said that Mr. Assange had ignored her appeals to stop after a condom broke. The other woman said that she and Mr. Assange had begun a sexual encounter using a condom, but that Mr. Assange did not comply with her appeals for him to stop when it was no longer in use.

At the beginning of the investigation into the assault case, Assange protested that the charges were a pretext to get him to Sweden where the United States could take him into custody to face espionage and other charges related to the disclosure of hundreds of thousands of secret documents leaked by PFC Manning.[58] He fled to the Ecuadorean embassy in London after British courts declined to stop extradition proceedings to return him to Sweden.

During the first year of his stay in the embassy, WikiLeaks released 2.4 million emails from the Syrian regime of President Bashar al-Assad.[59]

---

[56] Robert Mackey, "Swedish Prosecutor Hopes to Conclude Investigation of WikiLeaks Founder Soon," *New York Times*, Aug, 24, 2010. http://thelede.blogs.nytimes.com/2010/08/23/swedish-prosecutor-hopes-to-conclude-investigation-of-wikileaks-founder-soon/.

[57] David Jolly, "Sweden Reopens Rape Investigation of WikiLeaks Founder," Sept. 1, 2010, *New York Times*. http://www.nytimes.com/2010/09/02/world/europe/02wikileaks.html?_r=0.

[58] Associated Press, "Briefing Set on Assange Asylum Request," June 23, 2012.

[59] Ravi Somaiya, "WikiLeaks Releasing Trove of Syria Documents," *New York Times*, July 5, 2012.

WikiLeaks reportedly said that the emails would disclose detailed information about Syria's government and economy and would prove embarrassing to both Assad and his opponents. Included in a sample of the emails, which had not been confirmed, was an exchange between Syrian officials and an Italian and Greek communication companies about providing secure communications used by military forces and police.

In August of 2015, Swedish prosecutors dropped their investigations of the lesser charges of misconduct against Assange. But, the prosecutors said they still wanted to question Assange on accusations of rape made against him.[60]

Assange spent seven years hiding out in an Ecuadorean Embassy in London. In 2019, his asylum was revoked and London police dragged Assange out of the embassy and charged him with skipping bail for failure to appear when he faced extradition to Sweden on the sexual assault and rape charges. Assange was sentenced to 50 weeks in prison on that charge.[61]

Assange now faces extradition to the United States where he was initially charged with one count of conspiring with Manning to break into a government computer. In 2019, U.S. prosecutors announced 17 new charges, under the Espionage Act, for his role in the publication of hundreds of thousands of classified military and diplomatic documents.[62]

EDWARD SNOWDEN, GLENN GREENWALD AND NSA SECRETS (AND CIA, AND FBI)

On June 14, 2013, the *Guardian* newspaper in Britain reported on a secret American court order enabling the NSA to require a Verizon subsidiary to provide all of its customers' records for a three-month time span. The National Security Agency (NSA), the mammoth, super-secretive electronic spying arm of the United States government, wanted to do data mining. This was a program classified Top Secret, one already underway for at least seven years. As in the case of PFC Chelsea (born Bradley Manning in 1987) Manning to WikiLeaks in 2010, there had been a massive, embarrassing leak of classified information. The Manning leaks of State Department cables, however, generally were at a lower security classification, "Secret" rather than the "Top Secret" revelations in the *Guardian*.

---

[60] Associated Press, "Sweden Drops Some Sex Cases Against Assange," Aug. 13, 2015.

[61] Alexander Smith, "WikiLeaks Founder Julian Assange Sentenced to 50 Weeks in Prison for Skipping Bail in England," NBC News (2019), *available at* https://www.nbcnews.com/news/world/wikileaks-founder-julian-assange-sentenced-50-weeks-prison-skipping-bail-n1000506.

[62] William Booth & Karla Adam, "Julian Assange to Face Full Extradition Hearing in 2020," *Washington Post* (2019), *available at* https://www.washingtonpost.com/world/europe/julian-assange-to-face-a-full-extradition-hearing-in-2020/2019/06/14/a91e7ed0-8e97-11e9-adf3-f70f78c156e8_story.html.

Edward Snowden, then 29, was a civilian contractor employed by Booz Allen Hamilton, a defense contractor headquartered in McLean, Virginia. The computer-adept Snowden, lived with his girlfriend at his home in Hawaii. He had a high-paying job and a Top Secret clearance for handling some of the most sensitive defense materials for the U.S. government. Then, Snowden became a fugitive by stealing NSA secrets and by working with Glenn Greenwald of the *Guardian*, an accomplished and aggressive reporter who works on U.S. and British defense stories.[63]

After lifting a huge but undetermined number of Top Secret electronic files, Snowden disappeared. He wound up keeping an extremely low profile in a Hong Kong hotel, and contacted the award-winning investigative reporter Greenwald through a series of cloak-and-dagger maneuvers including encryption of email messages. Greenwald's book about his work with Snowden—aptly titled *"No Place to Hide"*—is a cautionary tale about the perils of trying to break a major story that the government wants to keep under wraps. For example, the NSA has the capability to track people who are carrying cellphones. As a result, Greenwald was told by Snowden to be sure to remove the battery from his phone to try to thwart NSA tracking of him as an individual.[64] And both Snowden and the documentary filmmaker Laura Poitras, who encouraged Greenwald to follow this important story about NSA's unfettered spying, had to resort to elaborately encrypted emails in order to communicate. Also, Greenwald purchased a laptop to use but not to be connected with the Internet. He called it his "air gapped machine." He explained, "It is much more difficult to subject an Internet-free computer to surveillance."[65] Ultimately, Greenwald, who resides in Rio de Janiero, Brazil, went to Hong Kong to meet with Snowden and Poitras.[66] Although the NSA and other government security agencies fell back on their "we're protecting you from terrorists" gambit, it required a leak by a young NSA contract employer to reveal the enormity of NSA intrusions into individual's privacy, both domestic and international. The traditional press evidently was clueless about the vast extent of NSA snooping.

Greenwald wrote that as Snowden was instructing him to go to Hong Kong, he said:[67]

> "I want to spark a worldwide debate about privacy, Internet freedom, and the dangers of state surveillance. I'm not afraid of what will happen to me," he said. "I've accepted that my life will

---

[63] Siobhan Goran, Evan Perez, and Janet Hook, "U.S. Collects Vast Data Trove," *Wall Street Journal*, June 7, 2013.

[64] Glenn Greenwald, *"No Place to Hide: Edward Snowden, the NSA, and the U.S. Surveillance State"* (New York: Metropolitan Books, 2014), pp. 8–9.

[65] Ibid. at 22.

[66] Peter Maass, "How Laura Poitras Helped Snowden Spill His Secrets," *New York Times Magazine*, Aug. 13, 2013.

[67] Greenwald, *No Place to Hide*, p. 18.

likely be over from my doing this. I am at peace with that. I know it's the right thing to do."

Greenwald wrote that his agreement with the *Guardian* gave him full editorial independence, but still had to clear initial scrutiny from editors and from *Guardian* lawyers as he struggled to break the now-legendary exposé of NSA activities. Early in the process, Greenwald read thousands of documents taken by Snowden. Among them, the reporter found a Foreign Intelligence Surveillance Act (FISA) court order. The FISA court's orders are secret warrants to authorize government eavesdropping through electronic surveillance. Despite the command of the Sixth Amendment that courts shall be open to the public, "All of its rulings are automatically designated Top Secret, and only a handful of people are authorized to access its documents," Greenwald wrote. He noted that he had never seen a FISA court order before, but then,[68] "Almost nobody had." The order in question held that wholesale and indiscriminate collection of American telephone records was justified by Sec. 215 of the USA PATRIOT Act.

Other documents acquired by Edward Snowden showed the NSA program ominously called BOUNDLESS INFORMANT to have collected more than three billion pieces of data from U.S. communication systems alone in a 30-day period early in 2013. Greenwald compared that with an answer by U.S. Director of National Intelligence James Clapper to a question asked by Sen. Ron Wyden of Oregon. Sen. Wyden asked whether NSA collected any data whatsoever on millions or hundreds of millions of Americans. (Snowden wanted it made public that Clapper lied to Congress.) Clapper's answer:[69] "No, sir." Clapper's definition of PRISM? He termed it[70] " 'an internal government classification system used to facilitate the government's statutorily authorized collection of foreign intelligence information from electronic communication service providers under court supervision.' "[71]

One of Snowden's leaks involved the sealed Foreign Intelligence Surveillance Agency (FISA) court's standing order directing Verizon to hand over records to the NSA. Verizon was not alone in receiving many NSA requests. AT&T and Nextel, in spring, 2013, were subject to standing court orders too. Evidently just skimming the surface, Sen. Edward Markey, D-MA, said that four major carriers complied with tens of thousands of court orders each year. The *Wall Street Journal* reported Verizon alone "received 260,000 requests for customer data in 2011.[72] These records, known as metadata, involve telephone numbers, call duration, and at times, call locations. These FISA Court authorizations,

---

[68] Ibid. at 27.

[69] Ibid. at 30.

[70] Ibid. at 54–55.

[71] Authors' Note: Pay attention to the words "foreign intelligence."

[72] Danny Yadron, Spencer E. Ante, and Anton Troianovski, "When NSA Calls, Companies Answer," *Wall Street Journal*, June 7, 2013, p. A4.

renewable every three months, do not allow eavesdropping on the content of calls.

Greenwald was critical of a practice of leading American newspapers—the *New York Times* and the *Washington Post*-in delaying reporting of important stories if asked by government to do so. Greenwald declared that on occasion newsworthy information gets suppressed. That, Greenwald wrote, is what happened to a *Washington Post* story on illegal overseas CIA torture sites by concealing the names of those countries where the torture-enabling prisons were based.

During a 10-day period in Hong Kong with Snowden, Greenwald and Poitras chose which stories to report, and in what order. First up in the Greenwald reports based on documents supplied by Snowden: the Top Secret program known as PRISM. NSA collected data from nine of the largest internet companies, including Google, Facebook, Verizon, Skype, and Yahoo!.[73]

Law Professor Jonathan Turley of Georgetown University commented in 2013 that President Barack Obama was asking for supporters to back him in spying on every American, "fundamentally altering our society. Indeed, he and congressional allies are trying to convince Americans that they can free themselves from fear only by redefining privacy in a way that allows ubiquitous surveillance.[74] Supporters of the program argue that collecting metadata does not really invade personal privacy and does not reveal the contents, for example, of telephone conversations.[75]

Turley and others have warned, however, that if an individual's phone calls and email records are available, much can be learned about a person. Emails to a medical marijuana resource line? Repeated calls to an abortion clinic? To an Alcoholics Anonymous hotline? When government promises to protect Americans if they will "temporarily" give up some liberties, a benign government can protect them. Turley declared that Obama was repeating "the siren call of all authoritarian figures throughout history. . . ." Turley reiterated Benjamin Franklin's warning,[76] "[T]hose who would give up essential liberty to purchase a little temporary safety deserve neither liberty nor safety."

Because of Edward Snowden's disclosures, published initially through the *Guardian* newspaper, both conservatives and liberals in the United States now knew, and were alarmed by, NSA's overreaching spying activities. Snowden left Hong Kong and wound up in Russia. Snowden remains there. From time to time, stories arise about the

---

[73] Greenwald, pp. 20–21, 63–64, 75–76.

[74] Jonathan Turley, "Creeping surveillance state, creepy conclusions: Who, when and where reveal too much," *USA Today*, June 10, 2013, p. 6A.

[75] Kathleen Hennessey, "Obama defends data collection," *Los Angeles Times*, June 9, 2013, p. A1.

[76] Turley, op. cit.

possibility for Snowden to return to the United States, with or without the prospect of prosecution.

Snowden has said that he was willing to serve time in prison over the leaks. But, Snowden said, American officials have not responded to his offer.[77]

Snowden could face trial under the Espionage Act and without a plea agreement, could spend the rest of his life in prison. Snowden told the BBC that while he is willing to go to prison, he does not want to become an object lesson,[78] "I've volunteered to go to prison with the government many times. What I won't do is I won't serve as a deterrent to people trying to do the right thing in difficult situations."

In 2019, Snowden published "*Permanent Record*," a book explaining how he came to the decision to leak top secret documents revealing the government's plans for mass surveillance. Shortly afterwards, the U.S. government filed a civil lawsuit claiming that publication was in violation of the non-disclosure agreements he signed with both the CIA and the NSA. District Court Judge Liam O'Grady ruled that the U.S. government was entitled to the proceed of Snowden's book.[79]

THE SMITH ACT OF 1940

Immediately after World War I, the thrust of revolutionary communism spurred the Attorney General of the United States to urge the passage of a federal peacetime sedition act. His call for such a peacetime measure (the Espionage Act of 1917 had applied only to war) was defeated although widespread deportation of Russians and other aliens for their ideas and words was accomplished. But 20 years later, similar fears accompanied the coming of World War II and the activity of domestic communists brought passage of a similar bill. This was the Alien Registration Act of 1940, known as the Smith Act for Rep. Howard W. Smith of Virginia who introduced it.[80] For the first time since the Alien and Sedition Acts of 1798, America had a federal peacetime sedition law. The heart of its provisions, under Sec. 2, made it a crime to advocate forcible or violent overthrow of government, or to publish or distribute material advocating violence with the intent to overthrow government.

The Act was to have little or no impact upon the mass media of general circulation. Media generally advocated the *status quo*, not radical

---

[77] Ewen MacAskill, "Edward Snowden: US has not offered me plea deal; Whistleblower says he has offered to do time in prison as part of a deal to return to US, but 'we are still waiting for them to call us back'," *Guardian*, Oct. 5, 2015. http://www.theguardian.com/us-news/2015/oct/05/edward-snowden-us-has-not-offered-me-plea-deal.

[78] Ibid.

[79] Alison Flood, "Edward Snowden's Profits From Memoir Must Go to US Government, Judge Rules," *Guardian* (2019), *available at* https://www.theguardian.com/books/2019/dec/20/edward-snowden-profits-memoir-us-government-judge-rules-permanent-record.

[80] 54 U.S. Statutes 670.

change or revolution. But for speakers, teachers and pamphleteers of the Communist Party, the Smith Act came to mean a great deal. Fewer than 20 persons had been punished under the Alien and Sedition Acts of 1798–1801; it is estimated that approximately 100 persons were fined or imprisoned under the Smith Act between 1940 and 1960.[81] In one sense, however, the Smith Act was less suppressive than its ancestor: the Alien and Sedition Acts had punished criticism of government officials, Congress, and the laws. The Smith Act limited the ban to advocating violent overthrow of government.

The government made its first move in 1943. Leaders of a revolutionary splinter group, the Socialist Workers Party which followed Russia's banished Leon Trotsky, were the target. They were brought to trial in Minneapolis and convicted for the advocacy of violent overthrow in their printed polemics. The Court of Appeals sustained the conviction, and the United States Supreme Court refused to review the case.[82]

But the Communist Party was much more the target of government prosecution than the little group of Trotskyites. In the context of the Cold War between the United States and the Union of Soviet Socialist Republics following World War II, almost 10 years of prosecution took place. The first case, *Dennis v. United States*, brought major figures in the Communist Party to trial and convicted 11 of them.[83] The charges in *Dennis* were that the defendants had reconstituted the American Communist Party in 1945, and conspired to advocate violent overthrow of the government.

For almost nine months the trial went on in federal district court under Judge Harold Medina. The nation was fascinated and bored in turn as the defense introduced complex legal challenges to the trial and the prosecution introduced exhibit after exhibit. Newspapers, pamphlets, and books were employed as evidence of the defendants' intent, from the *Daily Worker* to *"The Communist Manifesto."*

Judge Medina followed the doctrine of the *Gitlow* case. He instructed the jury that advocacy or teaching of violent overthrow of the government was not illegal if it were only "abstract doctrine." What the law forbade was teaching or advocating "action" to overthrow the government.[84] The jury found that the 11 did, indeed, conspire to advocate forcibly overthrowing the government. The 2nd Circuit Court of Appeals upheld the conviction and the case was accepted for review by the Supreme Court of the United States.

---

81 Don R. Pember, "The Smith Act as a Restraint of the Press," Journalism Monographs #10, May 1969; Zechariah Chafee, Jr., *The Blessings of Liberty* (Phila., N.Y.: J.B. Lippincott Co., 1954), p. 22.

82 *Dunne v. United States,* 138 F.2d 137 (8th Cir.1943).

83 *Dennis v. United States,* 341 U.S. 494, 71 S.Ct. 857 (1951).

84 *United States v. Foster,* 80 F.Supp. 479 (S.D.N.Y.1948). Upon appeal, this case became *United States v. Dennis* et al., 183 F.2d 201 (2d Cir.1950).

The Supreme Court upheld the convictions in a plurality, that is a majority agreeing that the convictions should stand but no single opinion enjoying majority support. The justices wrote five opinions, three opinions concurring in conviction and two dissenting. Three justices joined Chief Justice Fred M. Vinson's opinion that concluded that the convictions were constitutional. He said that free expression is not an unlimited or unqualified right, and that "the societal value of speech must, on occasion, be subordinated to other values and considerations."[85] But a conviction for violation of a statute limiting speech, he said, must rest on the showing that the words created a "clear and present danger" that a crime would be attempted or accomplished. Thus he went to the famous Holmes rule first expressed in the *Schenck* case in 1919, and interpreted it as follows:[86]

> In this case we are squarely presented with the application of the "clear and present danger" test * * * Overthrow of the Government by force and violence is certainly a substantial enough interest for the Government to limit speech. Indeed, this is the ultimate value of any society, for if a society cannot protect its very structure from armed internal attack, it must follow that no subordinate value can be protected. * * * Certainly an attempt to overthrow the Government by force, even though doomed from the outset because of inadequate numbers or power of the revolutionists, is a sufficient evil for Congress to prevent.

Chief Justice Vinson thus rejected the position that likelihood of success in committing a criminal act is required under the Clear and Present Danger test. Chief Justice Vinson adopted the statement of the Court of Appeals in this case in interpreting the Clear and Present Danger test. Chief Judge Learned Hand of the 2nd Circuit had written: "In each case [courts] must ask whether the gravity of the 'evil,' discounted by its improbability justifies such invasion of free speech as is necessary to avoid the danger."[87] Vinson was arguing that the danger need not be immediate when the interest (here, self-preservation of government) is important enough. Vinson based the Clear and Present Danger test only on the Clear part, the harm that would result. The fact that the chances of the Communists succeeding in overthrowing the government was not part of the equation under Chief Justice Vinson's reasoning.

Deep disagreements split the Court over such limiting of free expression, as seen in the dissents of Justices Black and Douglas.

---

85 *Dennis v. United States*, 341 U.S. 494, 71 S.Ct. 857 (1951).

86 Ibid. at 508–509, 867.

87 Ibid. at 510, 868 quoting183 F.2d at 212.

Douglas could see no clear and present danger to the government and state in the words and papers of the 11 Communists, writing:[88]

> Communists in this country have never made a respectable or serious showing in any election * * *. Communism has been so thoroughly exposed in this country that it has been crippled as a political force. Free speech has destroyed it as an effective political party. It is inconceivable that those who went up and down this country preaching the doctrine of revolution which petitioners espouse would have any success.
>
> * * *
>
> Free speech—the glory of our system of government—should not be sacrificed on anything less than plain and objective proof of danger that the evil advocated is imminent.

Through most of the 1950's, cases under the Smith Act continued to move through the courts. But *Yates v. United States* in 1957, was the last significant prosecution. In *Yates*, the Supreme Court reversed the conviction of 14 Communist Party leaders under the Smith Act. Its decision turned in large part on the difference between teaching the need for violent overthrow as an abstract theory or doctrine, and teaching it as a spur to action.[89] Since the trial court had not required the jury which found the defendant guilty to make the distinction, the conviction was reversed. There was no reference to the famous Clear and Present Danger test.

The Warren Court—so called for Chief Justice Earl Warren who had been appointed in 1953—had grown less and less willing to uphold convictions under the Smith Act, and with the *Yates* decision, charges against many other defendants in pending cases were dismissed in lower courts. The Smith Act soon lapsed into disuse, and in 1977 disappeared from bills reforming the federal Criminal Code.[90]

ADVOCACY OF AN IDEA OR THE USE OF FORCE? BRANDENBURG V. OHIO (1969)

In 1969, the Supreme Court was presented with the appeal of a Ku Klux Klan leader who had been convicted under the Ohio Criminal Syndicalism statute for advocating the duty or necessity of crime, violence or unlawful methods of terrorism to accomplish political reform. The leader, Clarence Brandenburg, had been televised as he made a speech in which he said the Klan was "not a revengent [sic] organization, but if our President, our Congress, our Supreme Court, continues to suppress the white, Caucasian race, it's possible that there might have

[88] *Dennis v. United States*, 341 U.S. 494, 588, 71 S.Ct. 857, 906–907 (1951).

[89] *Yates v. United States*, 354 U.S. 298, 77 S.Ct. 1064 (1957).

[90] For other controls on news media embraced by the Act (S.1437), see Reporters Committee for Freedom of the Press, News Media Alert, Aug. 1977, pp. 4–5.

to be some revengeance [sic] taken." He added that "We are marching on Congress * * * four hundred thousand strong."

The Supreme Court reversed the conviction. Citing precedent since *Dennis,* it said in a per curiam holding that:[91]

> [T]he constitutional guarantees of free speech and free press do not permit a State to forbid * * * advocacy of the use of force or of law violation except where such advocacy is directed to inciting or producing imminent lawless action and is likely to incite or produce such action. * * * A statute which fails to draw this distinction impermissibly intrudes upon the freedoms guaranteed by the First and Fourteenth Amendments.

The Court here provided protection for expression that stops short of "inciting" or producing imminent lawless action. Less than an absolute barrier to government's control of expression, the *Brandenburg* test nevertheless was a strong element in crippling sedition prosecutions.[92] It requires lawmakers to craft statutes that include the protections afforded in *Dennis*, that unless the state can prove actual incitement, the speech can not be punished.

In December of 2010, an Internet blogger and radio host was sentenced to 33 months in prison for threatening the lives of three federal judges on the 7th Circuit Court of Appeals.[93] Harold "Hal" Turner was convicted of violating a federal statute that makes it illegal to make threats to assault or kill a federal judge with the intent of impeding, intimidating or interfering with their work.[94]

In June, 2009, after the three judges on a 7th Circuit panel upheld two Chicago laws banning guns, Turner posted a blog entry, quoting in part, Thomas Jefferson:

> " 'The tree of liberty must be replenished from time to time with the blood of tyrants and patriots' "
>
> * * *
>
> "It is time to replenish the tree! Let me be the first to say this plainly: These judges deserve to be killed. Their blood will replenish the tree of liberty. A small price to pay to assure freedom for millions."

It was Turner's third trial on the charge. Two prior prosecutions ended with hung juries.

---

91 *Brandenburg v. Ohio,* 395 U.S. 444, 89 S.Ct. 1827 (1969).

92 See Harry Kalven, "The New York Times Case: a Note on The Central Meaning of the First Amendment," 1964 *Sup.Ct.Rev.* 191.

93 Mark Fass, "Blogger Who Threatened Judges Is Sentenced to 33 Months in Prison," *New York Law Journal*, Dec. 22, 2010.

94 18 U.S.C. 115(a)(1)(B).

Sedition treats speaking against government as a criminal act but what about actions that convey messages? When are actions as loud as words?

SYMBOLIC SPEECH: U.S. V. O'BRIEN (1968) AS A "GIFT" TO COMMUNICATIONS LAW

"Mass communications law" is not an island unto itself. It often is affected—and buffeted—by winds of change touching other parts of American law and society. Take the example of a 1968 conviction of a young man who violated federal law by burning his draft card. Daniel James O'Brien claimed that his act was "symbolic speech" to protest the Vietnam War and thus was protected by the First Amendment. Congress, attempting to protect the draft process in support of the divisive war, had passed a law protecting draft documents, including the draft cards that all eligible men were required to carry. The law was written in response to anti-war protesters' attacks on Selective Service offices and records that were intended to impede the process of drafting young men to serve in Vietnam.

United States v. O'Brien[95] helped to establish a balance between the First Amendment rights of individuals and the interest of government in achieving its important goals. O'Brien sought to express his disagreement with U.S. policies on Vietnam. The government's goal was to provide for national defense. The Supreme Court found that Congress was well within its constitutional authority to "raise and support armies." While O'Brien's action was expressive, it conflicted with that Congressional power. Added to the mix was the question of whether burning a draft card was actual speech that deserved First Amendment protection or merely a criminal act.

Had O'Brien merely said he dissented, he would have been protected. But O'Brien "spoke" through his action in burning his draft card. The crucial analysis and conclusion regarding the appropriate treatment of this mixture of speech and action can be found in Chief Justice Earl Warren's opinion for the Court:[96]

> This court has held that when "speech" and "nonspeech" elements are combined in the same course of conduct, a sufficiently important governmental interest in regulating the non-speech elements can justify incidental limitations on First Amendment freedoms.
>
> * * *
>
> [W]e think it clear that a government regulation is sufficiently justified if it is within the constitutional power of the government; if it furthers an important or substantial

[95] *United States v. O'Brien*, 391 U.S. 367, 88 S.Ct. 1673 (1968).

[96] *United States v. O'Brien*, 391 U.S. 367, 376, 88 S.Ct. 1673, 1678–1679 (1968).

governmental interest; if the governmental interest is unrelated to the suppression of free expression; and if the restriction on alleged First Amendment freedom is no greater than is essential to the furtherance of that interest.

The case settled the question about relative weights given to the First Amendment and those laws of general applicability created for the purpose of the running of society. Where those laws only incidentally affect speech, that is to say they were not created to stifle expression, they will prevail. A law against robbery is a law of general applicability. A robbery defendant might argue that he was exercising his First Amendment rights when he said, "Stick 'em up! Give me all your money," but that claim would fail.

The *O'Brien* decision has been used by courts in cases upholding regulation of advertising[97] (see Chap. 12) and of cable television (see Chap. 11).[98]

A LESSON FROM O'BRIEN ABOUT LAWS OF GENERAL APPLICABILITY

The media must keep in mind the risks they face under laws applying to everyone, "laws of general applicability" as lawyers call them. The Supreme Court has ruled in a number of cases that it is constitutional to use such laws against media defendants.

In *Cohen v. Cowles Media*,[99] for example, the Supreme Court upheld an award of damages against two Minnesota newspapers for breaking a promise not to reveal the identity of a source for a story. (This case is treated in greater depth in Chap. 10: Shielding Information from Disclosure.)

The First Amendment did not bar the recovery of money where the newspapers breached their promise under a feature of contract law that allows plaintiffs recover damages where they suffered harm by relying on the broken promises of the defendant. In the case, Cohen lost his job after he was revealed as the source. His reliance on contract law could not be overcome by the newspapers' reliance on the First Amendment.

In *Food Lion v. Capital Cities/ABC, Inc.*,[100] a federal district court ruled and the Fourth Circuit affirmed that ABC violated trespass laws

---

[97] See, e.g., Chap. 12's treatment of the four-part test in *Central Hudson Gas & Electric Corp. v. Public Service Comm'n.*, 447 U.S. 557, 100 S.Ct. 2343 (1980); *Posadas de Puerto Rico v. Tourism Co.*, 478 U.S. 328, 340, 106 S.Ct. 2968, 2976 (1986), and *Board of Trustees of the State University of New York v. Fox*, 492 U.S. 469, 109 S.Ct. 3028 (1989).

[98] See, e.g., Chap. 11's discussion of key cable TV regulation decisions, including *Home Box Office v. FCC*, 567 F.2d 9 (D.C.Cir.1977); *Quincy Cable TV, Inc. v. FCC*, 768 F.2d 1434 (D.C.Cir.1985); *Century Communications Corp. v. FCC*, 835 F.2d 292 (D.C.Cir.1987); *Turner Broadcasting v. FCC*, 810 F.Supp. 1308 (D.D.C.1992); *Turner Broadcasting v. FCC*, 512 U.S. 622, 114 S.Ct. 2445 (1994), 22 Med.L.Rptr. 1865.

[99] *Cohen v. Cowles Media*, 501 U.S. 663, 111 S.Ct. 2513 (1991).

[100] *Food Lion v. Capital Cities/ABC, Inc.*, 194 F.3d 505 (4th Cir.1999).

when producers for ABC's Prime Time used fraud to gain access to stores. Although the initially staggering punitive damage award of $5.45 million was reduced, first at the trial court level and then by the Fourth Circuit,[101] the lesson continues to be that media are subject to the same laws as everybody else. This has been of particular concern in the area of newsgathering. In a series of recent cases, media defendants have faced liability for the use of surreptitiously recorded phone calls where someone else made the recordings and then turned them over to the press. (These cases are dealt with in more detail in Chap. 7: Newsgathering Torts and Related Areas of Law). Federal and state laws prohibiting such recordings have been brought to bear against the media in these cases. Because the wiretap laws are general in nature and do not single out the press, some courts have been willing to allow penalties against the media.

Lawrence Matthews, a veteran reporter, found out about the risks of laws of general applicability when he was arrested on child pornography charges. Matthews, a 25-year veteran reporter with broadcasting and print experience, broadcast a three-part series on child pornography on the Internet in 1995. Part of his story dealt with the efforts of law enforcement agencies to stop the traffic in child pornography. Matthews became a freelance reporter and continued to look into the topic.

In his reporting, Matthews used the Internet to contact persons involved in the trafficking of child pornography. Using aliases, he chatted with minors and also received and sent images of child pornography. Some of the "minors" he chatted with were, in fact, FBI agents posing as underage females for the purpose of identifying and arresting persons who were trafficking in child pornography and persons attempting to commit statutory rape by having sex with minors. Matthews said that he knew from his prior stories and research that some of the "minors" he talked with would be federal agents.

In 1997, Matthews was indicted on 15 counts each of receiving and transmitting child pornography over the Internet. He pleaded not guilty and argued that the First Amendment protected his activities as a reporter. Matthews contended that his use of child pornography was necessary to infiltrate rings of child pornographers and that he had not acted with illegal intent in doing so. The trial court rejected Matthews' newsgathering and First Amendment arguments, with the judge refusing to let Matthews plead or argue the defense of newsgathering and the First Amendment.

Matthews pleaded guilty to one count of receiving and one count of transmitting child pornography while reserving the right to appeal the trial court's ruling. His case was heard by a panel of judges on the Fourth Circuit Court of Appeals.[102] Judge Diana Motz, writing the opinion for

[101] The appellate panel reduced the damages to $2 for breach of the duty of loyalty and trespass. *Food Lion v. Capital Cities/ABC, Inc.*, 194 F.3d 505, 522 (4th Cir.1999).

[102] *U.S. v. Matthews*, 209 F.3d 338 (4th Cir.2000).

the panel, rejected Matthews' First Amendment argument. Judge Motz acknowledged the importance of First Amendment rights.

But then, she recognized limitations to those freedoms, citing cases where the government has the right and power to limit speech that harms the public or which does not contribute to the advancement of ideas. Included in the areas not protected by the First Amendment are laws required to address "extraordinary problems," Judge Motz wrote.[103]

> Of particular importance here, the Supreme Court has consistently upheld restrictions on First Amendment freedoms to combat the "extraordinary problem" of child pornography.

And, Judge Motz wrote, Matthews' conviction did not violate the First Amendment because of the gravity of the harm from child pornography, especially as it both constituted a record of children's participation in sexual activities as well as continuing to encourage persons to abuse children. The First Amendment did not give journalists the right to violate that law intended to protect children.

> The Supreme Court has expressly instructed that "generally applicable laws do not offend the First Amendment simply because of their enforcement against the press has incidental effects on its ability to gather and report the news."[104]

The lesson then is that professional communicators need to realize the limits of the protections of the First Amendment. In chapters on access rights, shielding information from disclosure, libel and commercial speech, we will see yet other examples of the boundaries of speech and press protection.

5. PRIOR RESTRAINT

Despite authoritative statements that the chief purpose of the First Amendment guarantee is to prevent previous restraints upon publication, prior restraints continued to be exerted into the Twenty-First Century.

In *Near v. Minnesota* (1931), perhaps the most influential First Amendment decision by the Supreme Court of the United States, Chief Justice Charles Evans Hughes wrote that it is generally considered " * * * that it is the chief purpose of the [First Amendment] guarantee to prevent previous restraint on publication."[105] Journalists and civil libertarians have long counted pre-publication censorship as the most despised of all controls. Prior restraint's origins may be traced back virtually as long as there has been printing. It was tied in Sixteenth and Seventeenth Century England to requiring printers to get permission or license from government to publish. Then, censors often pored over every

---

[103] Ibid.

[104] Ibid.

[105] *Near v. Minnesota ex rel. Olson*, 283 U.S. 697, 713, 51 S.Ct. 625, 630 (1931).

word, to make sure that nothing harmful to those in authority would be printed.

Obviously, if government can stop publication before it occurs, that is the ultimate in repressiveness. Although it is true that a person may be deterred from publishing by the threat of post-publication punishment (as in the case of libel, invasion of privacy, or obscenity), that is not the issue here. As the U.S. Supreme Court has said: "If it can be said that a threat of criminal or civil sanctions after publication 'chills' speech, prior restraint 'freezes' it * * * "[106]

Government attempts to use prior restraint have taken place, with almost predictable regularity, when some form of crisis occurs. During pre-Civil War days when Abolitionists' agitating threatened "the peculiar institution" of slavery, the South often used prior restraint as a weapon. Postmasters regularly refused to deliver mailings from Northern anti-slavery societies. And, during the Civil War, Northern generals would occasionally shut down pro-South ("Copperhead") publishers. President Abraham Lincoln himself ordered the closing of newspapers on one occasion.[107] Later in the Nineteenth Century, heavy restrictions on publishing and distributing of materials discussing sex were extensively used, and prior restraint was part of the control. Postal and customs officials' use of prior restraint, in peacetime to control materials labeled "obscene" and, in wartime, to stop "sedition," was vigorous and frequent through the first third of the Twentieth Century.[108]

The area of prior restraint expanded in the Twentieth Century in matters not related to governmental acts of self-protection. As discussed in Chap. 11, there still is the governmental licensing of all broadcasters to regulate who has access to the airwaves. There are also many areas in which courts can issue injunctions against speaking, publishing, or distributing words or symbols—and those are prior restraints. For example, the Federal Trade Commission can issue "cease and desist" orders against anti-competitive or deceptive ads, and can order advertisers to publish corrective statements.[109] Copyright law provides for court-issued injunctions to restrain illegal use of copyrighted materials.[110]

In 1984, the U.S. Supreme Court allowed a trial court to forbid newspaper publication of material from pre-trial "discovery" proceedings.[111] This echoed the 1970s, when a striking extension of prior restraint burst out as courts across the nation forbade publishing of

---

[106] *Nebraska Press Ass'n v. Stuart*, 427 U.S. 539, 559, 96 S.Ct. 2791, 2803 (1976).

[107] Russel Blaine Nye, *Fettered Freedom* (East Lansing: Michigan State, 1951).

[108] Vincent Blasi, "Toward a Theory of Prior Restraint," 66 *Minn.L.Rev.* 11, 14–15 (Nov. 1981).

[109] "Anon., The FTC's Injunctive Authority Against False Advertising of Food and Drugs," 75 *Mich.L.Rev.* 745 (March 1977).

[110] 17 U.S.C.A. §§ 502, 503.

[111] E.g. *Seattle Times Co. v. Rhinehart*, 467 U.S. 20, 104 S.Ct. 2199 (1984).

accounts of part or all of the records in pre-trial hearings and even in trials. (See Chap. 9).

Later chapters will detail additional aspects of prior restraint. In this chapter, the special concern goes to government's claims to suppress, on its own behalf, attacks on its personnel and structure, or words constituting danger to national security.

NEAR V. MINNESOTA

Chief Justice Hughes' majority opinion in *Near v. Minnesota,* a case from 1931, established groundwork that may be seen as a watershed which turned United States Supreme Court majorities in the direction of expanded press freedom.[112]

That decision grew out of scruffy origins. Howard Guilford and J.M. Near were publishing partners in producing *The Saturday Press,* a Minneapolis "smear sheet" which charged that gangsters were in control of Minneapolis' gambling, bootlegging and racketeering, and that the city law enforcement and government agencies and officers were derelict in their duties. It vilified Jews and Catholics. The newspaper case led the Supreme Court of the United States to make one of its most notable descriptions of the extent of freedom of the press in America.

Publication of *The Saturday Press* was halted when a Minnesota statute authorizing prior restraint of "nuisance" or "undesirable" publications was invoked.[113] That statute declared that any person publishing a "malicious, scandalous and defamatory newspaper, magazine or other periodical" could be found guilty of creating a nuisance and could be enjoined from future wrongdoing.[114] Near and Guilford were brought into court after a temporary injunction ordered cessation of all activity by their paper. After the hearing, the injunction was made permanent by a judge, but with the provision that *The Saturday Press* could resume publication if the publishers could persuade the court that they would run a newspaper without objectionable content described in the Minnesota "gag law" statute.[115]

Near and Guilford appealed to the Minnesota Supreme Court, but that court upheld the restraint declaring that the protections of free expression did not exist to protect publications that were "devoted to scandal and defamation."[116] Near and Guilford then turned to the U.S. Supreme Court, which found in their favor by the margin of five votes to

---

[112] *Near v. Minnesota ex rel. Olson,* 283 U.S. 697, 51 S.Ct. 625 (1931); Paul L. Murphy, "Near v. Minnesota in the Context of Historical Developments," 66 *Minn.L.Rev.* 95 (Nov. 1981); Fred W. Friendly, *"Minnesota Rag"* (N.Y. 1981).

[113] The statute had been passed by the Minnesota Legislature in response to a different, but similar nuisance newspaper.

[114] Chap. 285, Minn.Sess.Laws 1925, in Mason's Minn.Stats., 1927, Secs. 10123–1 to 10123–3.

[115] *Near v. Minnesota ex rel. Olson,* 283 U.S. 697, 702–707, 51 S.Ct. 625, 628 (1931).

[116] *State v. Guilford,* 174 Minn. 457, 219 N.W. 770 (1928).

four. Speaking for the Court, Chief Justice Charles Evans Hughes noted the importance of this case: "This statute, for the suppression as a public nuisance of a newspaper or periodical, is unusual, if not unique, and raises questions of grave importance transcending the local interest involved in the particular action." Hughes declared of this prior restraint, "This is the essence of censorship."[117]

Hughes then turned to history-as-precedent to answer the question of whether a statute authorizing such proceedings in restraint of publication was consistent with the concept of liberty of the press, declaring here that the chief purpose of the constitutional guaranty is to prevent previous restraints.

He embarked upon a two-fold modification of the old English authority, Sir William Blackstone. Blackstone would have had *no prior restraint,* period. The Chief Justice, however, conceded that such a prohibition against all prior restraint might be "stated too broadly," and said that " * * * the protection even as to previous restraint is not absolutely unlimited." In a few exceptional cases, limitation of the principle of "no prior restraint" could be recognized:[118]

> No one would question but that a government might prevent actual obstruction to its recruiting service or the publication of sailing dates of transports or the number and location of troops. On similar grounds, the primary requirements of decency may be enforced against obscene publications. The security of the community life may be protected against incitements to acts of violence and the overthrow by force of orderly government. The constitutional guaranty of free speech does not "protect a man from an injunction against uttering words that may have all the effect of force."

Although Blackstone's "no prior restraint" was thus modified, another aspect of Blackstone was liberalized. Blackstone had approved punishing the publication of criticisms of government or government officials. But Hughes said that the press had a right—and perhaps even a duty—to discuss and debate the character and conduct of public officers.[119]

> [T]he administration of government has become more complex, the opportunities for malfeasance and corruption have multiplied, crime has grown to most serious proportions, and the danger of its protection by unfaithful officials and of the impairment of the fundamental security of life and property by criminal alliances and official neglect, emphasizes the primary need of a vigilant and courageous press, especially in great cities.

[117] *Near v. Minnesota,* 283 U.S. at 707, 713, 51 S.Ct. at 627, 630.

[118] Ibid. at 716, 631.

[119] Ibid. at 719–720, 632–633.

> The fact that the liberty of the press may be abused by miscreant purveyors of scandal does not make any the less necessary the immunity of the press from previous restraint in dealing with official misconduct. Subsequent punishment for such abuses as may exist is the appropriate remedy, consistent with constitutional privilege.

Despite the four dissenting votes, *Near v. Minnesota* has stood since 1931 as one of the most important decisions of the Supreme Court. *Near* was the first case involving newspapers in which the Court applied the provisions of the First Amendment against states through the language of the Fourteenth Amendment.[120] And it was to serve as important precedent for protecting the press against government's demands for suppression.

THE "PENTAGON PAPERS" CASE: NEW YORK TIMES CO. V. U.S. (1971)

It was 40 years before the press again collided with government bent on protecting its own interest and functions through prior restraint. On June 30, 1971, the United States Supreme court cleared the confrontation with a decision hailed by many news media with such headlines as "VICTORY FOR THE PRESS" and "The Press Wins and the Presses Roll."[121] These triumphant headlines were tied to the "Pentagon Papers" case. Early in 1971, *New York Times* reporter Neil Sheehan was given photocopies of a 47-volume study of the United States involvement in Vietnam titled *History of the United States Decision-making Process on Vietnam Policy*. On Sunday, June 13, 1971, the *New York Times*—after a team of reporters had worked with the documents for three months—published a story headlined: "Vietnam Archive: Pentagon Study Traces 3 Decades of Growing U.S. Involvement." Within 48 hours after publication, Attorney General John Mitchell sent a telegram to the *Times*, urging that no more articles based on the documents be published, charging that the series would bring about "irreparable injury to the defense interests of the United States."[122] The *Times* chose to ignore Attorney General Mitchell's plea, and columnist James Reston angrily wrote: "For the first time in the history of the Republic, the Attorney General of the United States has tried to suppress documents he hasn't read about a war that hasn't been declared."[123]

After the *Times*' refusal to stop the series of articles, the Department of Justice asked U.S. District Court Judge Murray I. Gurfein to halt publication of the stories. Judge Gurfein, who was serving his first day

---

[120] William A. Hachten, *The Supreme Court on Freedom of the Press: Decisions and Dissents* (Ames, Iowa: Iowa State Univ. Press, 1968), p. 43.

[121] *Newsweek, Time,* July 12, 1971.

[122] Don R. Pember, "The Pentagon Papers Decision: More Questions Than Answers," Journalism Quarterly 48:3 (Autumn, 1971) p. 404; *New York Times,* June 15, 1971, p. 1.

[123] *New York Times,* June 16, 1971, p. 1.

as a federal judge, issued a temporary restraining order on June 15, putting a stop to the *Times'* publication of the articles. But after a hearing where both the *Times* and government put forth evidence and were able to make their own arguments, Judge Gurfein refused to issue an injunction. He continued the temporary restraining order until the case could be resolved by the appellate courts.[124] But silencing the *Times* did not halt all publication of the "Pentagon Papers." The *Washington Post*—and a number of other major journals—also weighed in with excerpts from the secret report. The Justice Department likewise applied for—and was granted—a temporary restraining order against the *Washington Post*.[125]

After two weeks of uncertainty, the decision by the Supreme Court of the United States cleared the papers for publication. *New York Times* Managing Editor A.M. Rosenthal was jubilant: "This is a joyous day for the press—and for American society." *Time* magazine added, "Certainly the Justice Department was slapped down in its efforts to ask the courts to enjoin newspapers, and will not likely take that route again."[126] Despite such optimism, some observers within the press were disturbed by the outcome of the "*Pentagon Papers*" case. Not only were there three dissents against lifting the injunction among the nine justices, there was also deep reluctance to do so on the part of two of the majority justices. Furthermore, federal court injunctions had now, for the first time in American history, been employed to impose prior restraint upon newspapers, and the courts had preserved those injunctions intact for two weeks.

The Court's decision was short. It refused to leave in effect the injunctions which the Justice Department had secured against the *Times* and the *Post*, and quoted *Bantam Books v. Sullivan*:[127]

> "Any system of prior restraints of expression comes to this Court bearing a heavy presumption against its constitutional validity." *Bantam Books, Inc. v. Sullivan*, 372 U.S. 58, 83 S.Ct. 631 * * * (1963); see also *Near v. Minnesota ex rel. Olson*, 283 U.S. 697, 51 S.Ct. 625 * * * (1931). The Government "thus carries a heavy burden of showing justification for the imposition of such a restraint." *Organization for a Better Austin v. Keefe*, 402 U.S. 415, 91 S.Ct. 1575, 1578 (1971).

With those words, a six-member majority of the Court ruled that the government had not shown sufficient reason to impose prior restraint. Of the six, four found nothing in the facts of the case to qualify their positions. Justices Hugo L. Black and William O. Douglas expressed abhorrence for prior restraint, Douglas saying "uninhibited, robust and

---

124 *U.S. v. New York Times*, 328 F.Supp. 324 (S.D.N.Y. 1971).

125 For a clear account of the cases' journeys through the courts, see Pember, pp. 404–405.

126 *Time*, July 12, 1971, p. 10.

127 *New York Times Co. v. United States*, 403 U.S. 713, 714, 91 S.Ct. 2140, 2141 (1971).

wide-open debate" on public questions was essential. "The stays in these cases that have been in effect for more than a week constitute a flouting of the principles of the First Amendment as interpreted in *Near v. Minnesota* * * * ."[128]

Justice William J. Brennan, Jr., although not subscribing to an absolutist position about prior restraint, nevertheless declared that it was permissible in only a "single, extremely narrow" class of cases, as when the nation was at war or when troop movements might be endangered. For all the government's alarms as to possible dangers of nuclear holocaust if secrecy were breached, it had not presented a case that publication of the Pentagon Papers would cause such an event. Therefore:[129]

> * * * every restraint issued in this case, whatever its form, has violated the First Amendment—and none the less so because the restraint was justified as necessary to examine the claim more thoroughly.

With reluctance, Justices Byron White and Potter Stewart joined the majority. Stewart approved secrecy in some contexts, and said he was convinced that the Executive branch of government was correct in attempting to suppress publication of some of the documents here. But he voted with the majority, he said, because he could not say that disclosure of any of the Pentagon Papers "will surely result in direct, immediate, or irreparable damage to our Nation * * * ."[130] Stewart said that the courts could be called upon to act should Congress pass new laws to punish the disclosure of governmental secrets.[131]

Justice White noted in his concurrence that Congress had considered and rejected giving the president powers to impose prior restraints on publication of defense secrets.[132]

> However, these same members of Congress appeared to have little doubt that newspapers would be subject to criminal prosecution if they insisted on publishing information of the type Congress had itself determined should not be revealed. Senator [Henry Fountain] Ashurst, for example, was quite sure that the editor of such a newspaper 'should be punished if he did publish information as to the movements of the fleet, the troops, the aircraft, the location of powder factories, and all that sort of thing.' [Cong.Rec. 2008] Id., at 2009, 55.

White said that if any of the published material proved, after publication, to be punishable under the Espionage Act of 1917, the newspapers now stood warned: "I would have no difficulty in sustaining

---

[128] Ibid. at 724, 2146.

[129] Ibid. at 727, 2148.

[130] Ibid. at 730, 2149.

[131] *New York Times v. United States*, 403 U.S. 713, 91 S.Ct. 2140, 2149 (1971).

[132] Ibid. at 734, 2151–52.

convictions under [the Espionage Act] on facts that would not justify * * * the imposition of a prior restraint."[133]

Justice Thurgood Marshall declared that Congress had twice rejected proposed legislation that would have given the President war-time powers to prohibit some kinds of publication. And, he said, it would be inconsistent within the concept of separation of powers for the Court to use its contempt power to prevent behavior that Congress had specifically declined to prohibit.[134]

Dissenting, Justice Harlan wrote that disputes about matters so grave as the alleged contempt and publication of the Pentagon Papers needed more time to resolve, and he voted to support the injunctions.[135] He found that the Court had been almost "irresponsibly feverish in dealing with these cases" of such high national importance in only a few days of time. Justice Blackmun agreed with Harlan, and added a shrill indictment of the press:[136]

> If, however, damage has been done, and if, with the Court's action today, these newspapers proceed to publish the critical documents and there results therefrom "the death of soldiers, the destruction of alliances, the greatly increased difficulty of negotiation with our enemies, the inability of our diplomats to negotiate," to which list I might add the factors of prolongation of the war and of further delay in the freeing of United States prisoners, then the Nation's people will know where the responsibility for these sad consequences rests.

It should be recognized that no new legal course was charted by the *Pentagon Papers* case. After a delay of two weeks—a prior restraint imposed by lower federal courts at the insistence of the Department of Justice—the Supreme Court allowed the press to resume publication of the documents. By a 6-to-3 margin, the Supreme Court adhered to *Near v. Minnesota*, that classic case which, by a 5-to-4 margin, forbade prior restraint except in time of war, or when the materials involved were obscene, or when there was incitement to violence or to the overthrow of the Government.

The *Pentagon Papers* case underlines the important truth that no freedom is ever won, once and for all.

UNITED STATES V. PROGRESSIVE, INC. (1979)

Historical fact was not the issue, however, when at the end of the decade the federal government learned that *The Progressive*, a magazine

---

[133] Ibid. at 735–738, 2152–2154.

[134] Ibid. at 746, 2157.

[135] Ibid. at 753, 2161.

[136] Ibid. at 763, 2165. Blackmun was quoting the dissent of Judge Wilkey in the Pentagon Papers case involving the *Washington Post* in the Court of Appeals for the Second Circuit, *United States v. Washington Post Co.*, 446 F.2d 1327 (D.C.Cir.1971).

founded and published in Madison, Wis., was about to print an article titled "The H-Bomb Secret: How We Got It, Why We're Telling It." The manuscript, the U.S. Attorney charged, carried the deepest of technical secrets relating to the security of our weapons. Publication would endanger national security and that of the world, and in the process would violate the U.S. Atomic Energy Act of 1954 by making public "restricted data" about thermonuclear weapons. The government sought and got a temporary injunction against publication of the article by journalist Howard Morland.[137]

Morland swore that everything in the article was in the public domain, that he had not been forced to use secret sources for the information; the government denied that this was the case. While the trial was in mid-course, it also came to light that similar information had been available to the public by accident, for a time, in a government science laboratory library.[138] Federal District Judge Robert Warren was fully aware of the Supreme Court's rule that "any prior restraint on publication comes into court under a heavy presumption against its constitutional validity." Warren found the revelation of secret technical details about the H-bomb quite different, however, from revealing a secret history of war-policy making. He found that publication offered the possibility of "grave, direct, immediate and irreparable harm to the United States," and said:[139]

> * * * because the government has met its heavy burden of showing justification for the imposition of a prior restraint on publication of the objected-to technical portions of the Morland article * * * the Court finds that the objected-to portions of the article fall within the narrow area recognized by the Court in *Near v. Minnesota* in which a prior restraint on publication is appropriate.

Yet Warren's deep concern at the possible outcome of publication ("I'd want to think a long, hard time before I'd give a hydrogen bomb to [dictator] Idi Amin.") was questioned in the national debate and discussion which surged over the case. The government, it was asserted, had not shown that publication would result in "direct, immediate, or irreparable damage to the Nation" that the *Pentagon Papers* decision had insisted was necessary to justify prior restraint. The field of journalism was divided in its support.[140]

The Progressive and Morland, seizing on implications of the Atomic Energy Act that conceivably rendered even innocent conversations about

---

[137] *United States v. Progressive, Inc.*, 467 F.Supp. 990 (W.D.Wis.1979). Major prior restraint cases are discussed by U.S. Circuit Judge J.L. Oakes in "The Doctrine of Prior Restraint Since the Pentagon Papers," 15 *U.Mich.Journ.L. Reform* 497 (Spring, 1982).

[138] *United States v. Progressive, Inc.*, 486 F.Supp. 5 (W.D.Wis.1979).

[139] *United States v. Progressive, Inc.*, 467 F.Supp. 990 (W.D.Wis.1979).

[140] Civil Liberties, No. 328, June 1979, p. 1; Ben Bagdikian, "A Most Insidious Case," *Quill*, 67:6, June 1979, pp. 21, 22; "Editors and Lawyers Share Mixed Views on Story Ban," *Editor & Publisher*, March 17, 1979, p. 13.

nuclear weapons subject to classification ("classified at birth") insisted that no real secrets had been told. They appealed, and prior restraint held through six months of court process. Suddenly intruding into the matter was the publication on Sept. 16, 1979, of a long letter in the (Madison, Wis.) *Press Connection,* a daily of 11,000 circulation, from an amateur student of the nuclear bomb. A copy of a letter from computer programmer Charles Hansen to Sen. Charles Percy of Illinois, it included a diagram and list of key components of an H-bomb. Other newspapers which had received copies had not yet published it when, on the following day, the government moved to drop its court action to bar publication of the Morland article. A U.S. Justice Department spokesman said that the Hansen letter had exposed three "crucial concepts" that the government was trying to protect from publication.

Morland's article was published. *The Progressive* set about trying to raise $200,000 from the public, which was the cost, it said, of defending. No prosecution of the *Press Connection* or other newspapers that published the Hansen letter materialized. Judge Warren dismissed the case against *The Progressive* on Sept. 4, 1980.[141]

Judge Warren's decision reflected the constitutional rule regarding prior restraint. In order for a prior restraint to be constitutional, it must meet a three-part test.

1. The government must show that it has a compelling interest that is strong enough to override First Amendment rights.
2. The prior restraint must be narrowly tailored, that is to say that it restrains only those things covered by the compelling government interest.
3. The prior restraint must be effective.

Once the information covered by Judge Warren's order was made public, by persons other than The *Progressive* magazine staff, the prior restraint no longer was effective and so Judge Warren dissolved the order. It was no longer constitutional.[142]

TECHNOLOGY AND PRIOR RESTRAINT: THE OKLAHOMA CITY BOMBING TRIAL (1997)

The requirement that prior restraints be effective and the ability to publish at the speed of the electron on the Internet came together to alter the practical law of prior restraint on Feb. 28, 1997, and again on March 11, 1997. On February 28, the *Dallas Morning News* published an exclusive story on its website detailing Timothy McVeigh's purported

[141] *Milwaukee Journal,* Sept. 4, 1980, Part 2, pp. 1, 10.

[142] As Judge Richard Owen, of the United States District Court for the Southern District of New York, once aptly reminded the author of [the *Progressive* case] while he was acting as counsel for a party at trial: "Once the cat is out of the bag, the ball game is over." *Gambale v. Deutsche Bank AG,* 377 F.3d 133 (2d Cir. 2004).

admission to the 1995 Oklahoma City bombing that killed 168 persons and injured hundreds more. On March 11, Playboy magazine published an on-line story by freelance reporter Ben Fenwick providing actual details from McVeigh defense team documents.

McVeigh defense attorney Stephen Jones blasted both stories and both periodicals, at first claiming that the documents underlying the stories were stolen, and later, fraudulent. Even so, federal investigators used some of the details from the Playboy website story to look for significant new evidence in the bombing case.[143]

Although the *Dallas Morning News* broke a version of the story first, *Playboy's* Fenwick had been working on the story for many months. He had contacted Professor Bill Loving at the University of Oklahoma where Fenwick had once been Loving's graduate assistant. Fenwick showed up at Loving's office early one evening and showed him the documents, asking for advice on what to do with them. The documents Fenwick possessed purported to be a chronology of the bombing and a detailing of the development of McVeigh's ideology, written down by members of McVeigh's defense team when its members interviewed McVeigh. Even as Fenwick worked to confirm details in the documents and to flesh out the story, he faced what seemed to be an insurmountable problem: how to publish his story.

Loving discussed with Fenwick the case of *United States v. Cable News Network*, 865 F.Supp. 1549 (S.D.Fla.1994), in which CNN was found guilty of criminal contempt of court for broadcasting secretly recorded tapes of telephone calls between deposed Panamanian dictator Manuel Noriega and his attorney. As discussed in Sec. 58, Chap. 9, after CNN announced that it had the tapes, presiding judge William Hoeveler concluded that the broadcast would harm Noriega's Sixth Amendment rights, violating his attorney-client privilege and also by revealing information that could harm his defense. After the 11th Circuit Court of Appeals upheld the injunction, but before the U.S. Supreme Court ruled on the case, CNN broadcast one of the taped conversations. Eventually, CNN was charged with and convicted of contempt by Judge Hoeveler.[144]

In McVeigh's case, the documents clearly fell within the attorney-client privilege and were damning to the defense. In chilling detail, they laid out the plans for bombing the Murrah Federal Building, the arrangement for the getaway car and McVeigh's touching off the fuse. One of the McVeigh defense documents read:[145]

---

143 Pete Slover, "McVeigh admitted bombing, memo says," *Dallas Morning News* website, March 1, 1997. See also Martha T. Moore and Tony Mauro, "Can both sides be right and wrong simultaneously?," *USA Today*, March 5, 1997; Jo Thomas, "Bomb Suspect's 'Confession' Is Called Ploy by the Defense," *New York Times*, March 6, 1997, and Gordon Witkin, "A Disputed Story Threatens a Trial," *U.S. News & World Report*, March 17, 1997, p. 36.

144 *U.S. v. CNN*, 865 F.Supp. 1549 (S.D.Fla.1994).

145 Documents provided to the author by Ben Fenwick.

> He pulled [the Ryder rental truck] carrying the explosives back into the street and at the light at Harvey and NW 5th Street he lit the fuse. When the light turned, he pulled into the parking spot in front of the Murrah Building. Possibly two vehicles passed the Ryder truck as he was parking it. One woman looked at Tim as she was headed down the steps to walk into the Murrah Building. She was a white woman, dirty blonde hair, probably mid thirties. He still had on his hat.

Fenwick and *Playboy* kept the CNN case in mind as they worked on the story. One idea they considered was holding the story until the jury was picked. They anticipated that presiding judge Richard Matsch would sequester the jury and that publication at that point would cause little or no harm to McVeigh's defense. But Judge Matsch decided that he would not sequester the jury.

That left Fenwick and *Playboy* with no safe time to publish. Any announcement of the story, any leak likely would draw an immediate injunction against *Playboy*, keeping the magazine from being distributed and keeping the story away from the public.

The *Dallas Morning News*, however, provided a key hint pointing to a way for *Playboy* to beat prior restraint. A *Morning News* reporter got similar information, though in no way as detailed as that which Fenwick had obtained, and wrote a story for its Feb. 28, 1997, edition. The *Morning News* was working to establish its Web presence and so the newspaper routinely put versions of its day's stories on its website before the printed version came out on the street. The newspaper promoted the news that it had appeared online before it appeared in print. The appearance of the Web version gave Loving the key to overcoming the prior restraint threat. The theory was based on the facts of the *Progressive* case and the constitutional requirement that prior restraints be effective.

With the *Morning News'* Web publication in mind, Loving contacted Fenwick and *Playboy*. If the magazine published its story on the Internet, the judge would have no legal grounds to support a prior restraint. *Playboy* had been prepared to release a one-thousand-word excerpt of the story on the Internet. Editors delayed the release in favor of publication of the complete full-length story on the McVeigh documents and Fenwick's reporting on the defense papers and on the bombing itself.

With the story in the hands of the public and no effective means of preventing further distribution, neither the prosecution nor the defense sought to prevent further publication of the articles. The article contained information that was helpful to the prosecution, particularly about how and where McVeigh obtained the nitro-methane fuel used in the bomb. Following the publication, federal investigators found the person who sold McVeigh the fuel and that person became a witness in the trial. McVeigh subsequently was convicted and sentenced to death.

McVeigh later asked to have his execution televised. That will be dealt with in Chap. 8, Reporting the Legislative and Executive Branches.

Use of the Internet to publish at a moment's notice has made the imposition of prior restraint less effective and more unlikely. Unless a party seeking to restrain a story can learn of a story before it reaches the Internet, there is no real means of preventing its publication. Judges still will have contempt power to persons or entities interfering with the orderly administration of justice, but that will come only after the news has been delivered.[146]

The WikiLeaks publications of secret documents shows just how difficult using prior restraint against Web publication is. The inability of a federal judge to shut down the Web leaker was illustrated by the case of *Bank Julius Baer v. WikiLeaks*.[147] The bank, which operates in the Cayman Islands, brought suit after confidential bank documents were posted on WikiLeaks.org.

In the *Baer* case, the bank sought an injunction against WikiLeaks over its posting of documents that the bank said were stolen by an angry former employee or forged by the former employee. WikiLeaks did not participate in the proceedings and U.S. District Judge Jeffrey White issued a temporary restraining order and, later, a permanent injunction.[148] As part of the order, Dynadot.com, the domain name registrar for WikiLeaks, disabled WikiLeaks.org. That closed the regular entry to the site. But, as news organizations and bloggers reported, Internet users continued to have access through mirror sites, located in other countries, and directly through its IP address.[149]

Less than two weeks later, Judge White dissolved the injunction saying that the order might conflict with constitutional principles.[150] Judge White also said that as the site was still available on the Internet, the injunction had not achieved its purposes. The requirement that prior restraints have to be effective to be constitutional remains.

When WikiLeaks released thousands of State Department cables in 2010, the government did not even try to get a prior restraint. Even so, when several websites blocked WikiLeaks, hundreds of mirror sites sprang up.[151] Hackers then attacked sites that stopped doing business with WikiLeaks and going after credit card companies that refused to

---

[146] Evan Ramstad, "Putting News on Internet First Seen Protective," *Wall Street Journal*, March 15, 1997, p. B6.

[147] *Bank Julius Baer & Co. Ltd v. Wikileaks*, 535 F.Supp.2d 980 (N.D.Cal. 2008).

[148] Ibid.

[149] Adam Liptak and Brad Stone, "Judge Shuts Down Web Site Specializing in Leaks," *New York Times*, Feb. 20, 2008.

[150] Cynthia Brumfield, "Judge Reverses Wikileaks Injunction; URL is Back Up," *USLaw.com*, March 1, 2008.

[151] Ravi Somaiya, "Hundreds of WikiLeaks Mirror Sites Appear," *New York Times*, Dec. 5, 2010.

process payments to the site, Amazon that had provided servers and PayPal which stopped accepting donations and payments to WikiLeaks.

Still, judges are asked to grant prior restraints in the context of trials and to protect privacy rights, reputations and business interests. In most cases, the courts defer to the longstanding principles from *Near*. Sometimes, though, judges will grant restraints leading to new case law.

In *Doe v. Holder*,[152] a library challenged a provision of the Patriot Act, requiring that FBI inquiries into the users of libraries and Internet Service Providers be kept secret. In *Doe*, an Internet Service Provider argued that the sorts of information that the FBI was seeking ought to be exempt from the secrecy provisions of the Act. Federal Judge Victor Marrero ruled that information about what the FBI was requesting including name, address, telephone number, account number, email address, and billing information should not be kept secret. On the other hand, Judge Marrero ruled that additional information sought by the FBI should be kept secret to protect anti-terrorism investigations.

CONTRACT AND ADMINISTRATIVE LAW RESTRICTIONS ON PUBLICATIONS

It is not only the security of the United States' war effort and the provisions of the Atomic Energy Act that have been argued in support of the government's demand for prior restraint. Rules of administrative agencies can furnish the same.[153] The CIA is experienced in the matter. Its employee Victor L. Marchetti resigned from the agency and, with John Marks, wrote "*The CIA and the Cult of Intelligence.*" This, the CIA charged upon learning of its existence in manuscript form, violated the secrecy contract Marchetti had signed when first employed, promising not to divulge any classified information without specific permission from the CIA.[154] It obtained an injunction in federal district court, the judge ordering Marchetti to submit all writings about the CIA or intelligence work to the Agency for review as to whether it contained classified information that had not been released to the public. As the case proceeded (the Supreme Court of the United States denied certiorari),[155] the CIA's scrutiny of the manuscript resulted in its demand that 339 deletions be performed. "It was the Devil's work we did that day," said Marchetti's attorney, Melvin L. Wulf, after he and the authors spent hours literally cutting out passages of the manuscript—perhaps as much as 20 percent.[156] Resisting all the way, Marchetti finally won agreement

[152] *Doe v. Holder*, 703 F.Supp.2d 313 (S.D.N.Y. 2010).

[153] Ithiel de Sola Pool, "Prior Restraint," *New York Times*, Dec. 16, 1979, p. E19, portrays unintended prior restraint on research publication through elaborate funding rules of the U.S. Dept. of Health, Education, and Welfare—"a nightmare of bureaucracy run wild, producing results that no one intended."

[154] *United States v. Marchetti*, 466 F.2d 1309 (4th Cir.1972).

[155] *Marchetti v. United States*, 409 U.S. 1063, 93 S.Ct. 553 (1972).

[156] Melvin D. Wulf, Introduction to Victor Marchetti and John D. Marks, *The CIA and the Cult of Intelligence* (New York: Alfred A. Knopf, 1974), p. xxv.

from the court that all but 27 of the 339 deletions would be restored.[157] The book was finally published with blank spaces and the prominent, repeated boldface notation: **"DELETED"**.

SNEPP V. UNITED STATES (1980)

Frank Snepp, strategy analyst for the CIA in Vietnam, succeeded in getting his case against the CIA to the Supreme Court. He, too, had resigned from the agency and written a book—*"Decent Interval"*—about his experiences. He, too, had signed an agreement not to publish without first submitting the manuscript to the CIA, and the agency brought legal action. The Supreme Court, by a 6–3 vote, ruled that Snepp had broken his contract, approved an injunction requiring Snepp to submit future writings for publication review, and ruled that he must give all profits from the sale of the book to the CIA through a "constructive trust" imposed on him by the court.[158] He had a fiduciary obligation to the CIA and had breached his trust by publishing.

The government had not alleged that classified or confidential information was revealed by the Snepp book. Rather, it alleged "irreparable harm" in his failure to clear the material with the CIA, and the Supreme Court approved the lower courts' finding that publication of unreviewed material "can be detrimental to vital national interests even if the published information is unclassified."[159]

If the agent published unreviewed material in violation of his fiduciary and contractual obligation, said the court, the constructive trust remedy simply "required him to disgorge the benefits of his faithlessness * * * ." Snepp "disgorged" about $138,000, the proceeds from *"Decent Interval."*[160]

Non-disclosure agreements similar to those Snepp and Marchetti had signed so appealed to President Ronald Reagan that in 1983, he issued a directive requiring them of all persons who had access to classified government information, numbering—declared protesting media—more than 100,000 employees. President Reagan withdrew the directive in the face of congressional and media protests.[161]

If the emergence of non-disclosure agreements in the decade beginning with Marchetti appeared as one more example of government creativity in devising prior restraints in the name of national security, predictably enough that newly minted instrument was not the end of invention in prior restraint.

---

157 Ibid. at xxiv.

158 *Snepp v. United States*, 444 U.S. 507, 100 S.Ct. 763 (1980).

159 Ibid. at 2411.

160 Herbert Mitgang, "Royalties to the Treasury," *New York Times Book Review*, Aug. 31, 1980.

161 "Directive on Safeguarding National Security Information," 9 Med.L.Rptr. 1759 (1983).

NONDISCLOSURE AGREEMENTS OR FEDERAL LAW FOR WHISTLEBLOWERS?

A quarter of a century after Reagan's excursion into the use of non-disclosure agreements to protect government secrets, federal contractors were using non-disclosure agreements in a bid to keep employees from revealing wrongdoing.[162] Some agreements included prohibitions on employees profiting from any disclosure. That violates federal whistleblower laws, attorneys representing whistleblowers said.

The non-disclosure agreements came to light after two contractor employees at the Hanford plutonium processing plant in Washington state reported wrongdoing "at the nation's most contaminated nuclear facility without getting approval from an agency supervisor," the *Washington Post* reported.

Donna Busche was among employees asked by the Department of Energy to sign the agreement. She was reluctant to do so, the *Post* reported.[163]

> "It was a gag order," said Busche, 51, who served as the manager of environmental and nuclear safety at the Hanford waste treatment facility for a federal contractor until she was fired in February after raising safety concerns. "The message was pretty clear: 'Don't say anything to anyone, or else.' "

More workers within and outside of the federal government report that they worry about retaliation if they reveal wrongdoing, the *Washington Post* reported. Congress, the Securities and Exchange Commission, the Special Inspector General for Afghanistan Reconstruction and the Office of Special Counsel are looking into the use of the non-disclosure agreements.

The Hanford nuclear plant's agreement preventing employees from getting a financial benefit from disclosures runs counter to U.S. whistleblower laws dating back to the 1860s.[164]

> The federal government has been encouraging whistleblowers to come forward and trying to protect them since the Civil War, when Congress passed the False Claims Act to punish war profiteers. Under the act, whistleblowers are entitled to collect a percentage of the fraud they uncover. In one of the largest such cases, American banker Bradley Birkenfeld reported secret deposits by U.S. citizens in the Swiss bank UBS. In 2012, he collected a $104 million bounty.

---

[162] Scott Higham and Kaley Belval, "Workplace secrecy agreements appear to violate federal whistleblower laws," *Washington Post*, June 29, 2014.

[163] Ibid.

[164] Ibid.

BUY THE BOOK; DON'T READ IT

The Pentagon hit on the novel approach of trying to buy all of the first edition of a book written by an Army officer who served in Afghanistan.[165] Army Reserve Lt. Col. Anthony Shaffer wrote a memoir, "*Operation Dark Heart*," about his experiences in the Special Operations Command. The Army Reserve Command approved the book but intelligence agencies objected when they got copies. The Defense Intelligence Agency complained that the book would compromise national security. Shaffer and his publisher, St. Martin's Press, made changes for the second edition, but the first edition had already been printed. So, the Department of Defense bought and destroyed the first printing. A seller on eBay later offered to sell a copy of the first edition for $2,000.

VALERIE PLAME: THE LEAST SECRET AGENT

Former CIA agent Valerie Plame lost her challenge to the CIA's nondisclosure policy in late 2009 when the Second Circuit Court of Appeals ruled that she could not publish any materials in her memoir, "*Fair Game: My Life as a Spy, My Betrayal by the White House*," about any possible employment by the CIA before 2002. In fact, the opinion makes the point in its first footnote that,[166] "All references in this opinion to Ms. Wilson's possible pre-2002 Agency affiliation are hypothetical and should not be understood to confirm or deny any information on that subject."

Ms. Plame, wife of former Ambassador Joseph Wilson, was "outed" by the Bush Administration ostensibly in retaliation for Wilson's op-ed piece that President George W. Bush's claim that Iraq had sought yellowcake uranium from the African nation of Niger was false. The specter of a nuclear-armed Iraq was one of the strongest arguments that the Bush Administration used in building support for the invasion of Iraq. I "Scooter" Libby, Vice President Dick Cheney's chief of staff, was convicted of lying to the FBI in connection with the investigation into the leak. Newspapers reported that two top administration officials had contacted a half dozen Washington reporters to disclose Plame's identity and CIA position.[167]

Her identity compromised, Plame resigned from the CIA. She began working on her memoir and submitted it to the CIA Publication Review Board. The CIA objected to information about Plame's service before 2002 and attempts to negotiate a mutually acceptable resolution failed. Plame then filed suit to prevent the CIA from barring publication of her memoir.

---

165 Chris Lawrence and Padma Rama, "Pentagon destroys thousands of copies of Army officer's memoir," *CNN*, Sept. 25, 2010.

166 *Wilson v. C.I.A.*, 586 F.3d 171, 174 (2d Cir. 2009).

167 Ibid. at 176.

The trial court ruled for the CIA holding that Plame's confidentially agreement gave the agency the right to control publication.[168]

Plame appealed to the Second Circuit which affirmed the trial court. The Second Circuit panel holding that her secrecy agreement was still in effect and that the CIA had shown that keeping the information about her pre-2002 activities needed to be kept secret to protect agency operations. Notwithstanding the publicity about her CIA employment, Plame could not overcome her secrecy agreement.[169]

> Ms. Wilson-like every other current and former Agency employee who has signed a Secrecy Agreement-"simply has no first amendment right to publish" the information here at issue, regardless of how "public" her past activities appear to have become.

On Oct. 22, 2007, Plame's book, complete with the redactions required by the Publication Review Board, was published. The material about her pre 2002 employment was removed. However, her publisher Simon & Schuster added an afterword written by Laura Rozem, a reporter. As the appellate panel noted, the material covers the parts of Plame's life that the CIA wanted kept secret.[170]

> Drawn from interviews and public sources, it provides historical background and recounts portions of Ms. Wilson's life and career that she was unable to include herself. When the afterword is read together with "*Fair Game*," a full and vivid picture of Valerie Plame Wilson emerges. Ms. Wilson has had no input or involvement in the creation of the afterword, which she has not seen before publication of this book.

PLAME'S SUIT AGAINST VICE PRESIDENT CHENEY, KARL ROVE AND I. "SCOOTER" LEWIS LIBBY

In 2006, Plame and her husband filed suit over the public disclosure of her position as a classified CIA employee. The suit alleged that the leak of her identity was an act of retaliation against Wilson for his op-ed piece that President Bush's assertion that Iraq had sought yellowcake uranium from the African nation of Niger was untrue.

The couple's suit alleged that the leak constituted a civil conspiracy to violate the couple's First and Fifth Amendment as well as their privacy rights. This was not a case brought directly under the Intelligence Identities Protection Act of 1982 but rested on other rights guaranteed under the Constitution. Specifically, the couple said that disclosure was an act or retaliation against Joseph Wilson for speaking out on the uranium claims that made up part of the Bush Administration justification for the invasion of Iraq. The couple also said that they were

---

[168] *Wilson v. McConnell*, 501 F.Supp.2d 545, 35 Media L. Rep. 2362 (S.D.N.Y. 2007).

[169] *Wilson v. C.I.A.*, 586 F.3d 171, 196 (2d Cir. 2009).

[170] Ibid. at 183.

denied equal treatment, that they were singled out by the Bush Administration.

A federal judge dismissed the case in 2007 on the grounds that they had not exhausted other means to seek redress and that the court did not have subject matter jurisdiction over the complaint.[171] Judge John D. Bates also concluded that the defendants were acting within their duties as members of the executive branch.[172]

> The alleged means by which defendants chose to rebut Mr. Wilson's comments and attack his credibility may have been highly unsavory. But there can be no serious dispute that the act of rebutting public criticism, such as that levied by Mr. Wilson against the Bush Administration's handling of prewar foreign intelligence, by speaking with members of the press is within the scope of defendants' duties as high-level Executive Branch officials.

CIA STRENGTHENS PUBLICATIONS REVIEW RULES (2006)

A year before Plame filed suit to be able to publish her book, the CIA reportedly strengthened its rules affecting existing and former employees' ability to write about agency activities. These new rules for its Publications Review Board were criticized as targeting those critical of Bush administration policies.[173]

> The CIA acknowledged for the first time last week that the Publications Review Board subjects former officials under contract to a two-part test. "First, material submitted for publication cannot contain classified information," CIA spokesman Paul Gimigliano wrote in an e-mail. "Second, it cannot impair the individual's ability to do his or her job or the CIA's ability to conduct its mission as a nonpartisan, nonpolicy agency of the executive branch."

A copy of the CIA's publication regulation from July 2005 limited the review of submitted material to determining whether it contained classified material, the *National Journal* reported. The 2005 regulation specifically rejected a test based on political considerations. "Permission to publish will not be denied solely because the material may be embarrassing to or critical of the agency."[174]

Mark Zaid, an attorney representing former CIA employees, also said the publication review had been toughened, and that the agency had

---

[171] *Wilson v. Libby*, 498 F.Supp.2d 74 (D.D.C. 2007).

[172] Ibid. at 21.

[173] Shane Harris, "CIA tightens limits on former employees' ability to speak out," *National Journal*, April 30, 2006.

[174] Ibid.

returned to attitudes of the past.[175] "There's been a fundamental shift in practice at the Publications Review Board. There's literally been a reinstitution of the 1950s attitude that what happens at the C.I.A. stays at the C.I.A."

Authors said that the agency has been sending warnings and reprimands for violations of the rules that include letters warning of possible Justice Department investigations.

The *New York Times* reported in the fall of 2003 that gubernatorial candidate Arnold Schwarzenegger had required his campaign staff to sign confidentiality agreements that they would not disclose any information about Schwarzenegger, his family, friends, associates or employees.[176] Disclosure would draw a $50,000 penalty.

PROCTER & GAMBLE V. BANKERS TRUST CO. (6TH CIR.1996)

When Business Week magazine was hit with a prior restraint order in 1995, it seemed as if U.S. District Judge John Feikens was oblivious to the precedent set in *Near v. Minnesota* (1931). Business Week, trying to report on manufacturing giant Procter & Gamble's (P&G's) take-no-prisoners lawsuit against Banker's Trust, a huge financial institution P&G was suing for millions of dollars in losses supposedly caused by bad investments. Presiding Judge Feikens put a restraining order on *Business Week*, ordering it not to reveal the contents of court-sealed documents sent to the magazine by a lawyer from the firm involved in the P&G-Bankers Trust litigation.[177]

As part of its reporting process, once it had the leaked documents, *Business Week* had told both sides of the litigation that it had a copy of Procter & Gamble's amended complaint against Bankers Trust, a judge-sealed document. *Business Week's* efforts to publish a story on this huge legal brawl between two giant companies were cut short by the arrival of Judge Feikens' faxed temporary restraining order, issued after complaints from both P&G and the bank. After three weeks passed—and after several hearings—Judge Feikens reluctantly ended his restraining order. The judge maintained, however, that his prior restraint order against the magazine was constitutionally defensible. The judge's anger at the magazine was evident: "I cannot permit *Business Week* to snub its nose at court orders."[178]

---

[175] Scott Shane and Mark Mazzetti, "CIA Crackdown Seeks to Tighten Agency's Secrecy," *New York Times*, April 24, 2006.

[176] Richard Blow, "Full disclosure on full disclosure," *New York Times*, Sept. 27, 2003.

[177] *Procter & Gamble v. Bankers Trust Co. and The McGraw-Hill Companies*, 78 F.3d 219 (6th Cir. 1996), 24 Med.L.Rptr. 1385, overturning U.S. district court ruling reported at 900 F.Supp. 186 (S.D.Ohio 1995). Note that Judge Feikens took over this complex litigation from a terminally ill judge who had allowed the parties virtually complete freedom in sealing documents, allowing the parties to keep many of their allegations and much of their evidence away from public view.

[178] 900 F.Supp. 186, 193 (S.D.Ohio 1995); for unsuccessful early efforts to appeal against the restraining order, see Keith H. Hammonds and Catherine Yang, "Business Week vs. the

On appeal, the Sixth Circuit declared the restraining order unconstitutional. Chief Judge Gilbert S. Merritt quoted *Bantam Books v. Sullivan*'s stirring language that " * * * prior restraint comes to a court 'with a heavy presumption against its constitutional validity.' "[179]

> * * * *Business Week* obtained information from a confidential source and prepared a story on a matter of public concern. Following standard journalistic protocol, Business Week sought comment from the parties and proceeded to take its story to print. Instead, the magazine received a facsimile transmission from a Federal District Court prohibiting publication * * * and citing "irreparable harm" as the reason.
>
> * * *
>
> * * * [P]rohibiting the publication of a news story is the essence of censorship and is allowed only under exceptional circumstances.

Chief Judge Merritt's understanding of—and denunciation of—prior restraint was applauded by civil libertarians. That he had to craft such a decision is a reminder that hard-won freedoms cannot be taken for granted.

PRIOR RESTRAINT AND CRIMINAL SPEECH

While the Supreme Court has declared that prior restraints are fundamentally antithetical to the First Amendment, it also has declared certain kinds of speech outside First Amendment protection. Criminal speech is one of those categories.[180]

In *U.S. v. Schiff*[181] a district court in Nevada granted an injunction against Irwin Schiff and two other defendants who were operating Freedom Book as well as three websites dedicated to a system to avoid federal income taxes. The defendants published *The Federal Mafia: How the Government Illegally Imposes and Unlawfully Collects Income Taxes* which told readers how to file tax returns and W-4 forms that would allow them to avoid income taxes. Judge Lloyd George granted the government's motion to enjoin the defendants from engaging in their business, including disseminating their message that taxes can legally be avoided.

Judge," *Business Week* cover story for Oct. 16, 1995; see also *McGraw-Hill Cos. v. Procter & Gamble*, 515 U.S. 1309, 116 S.Ct. 6 (1995) for Justice Stevens' order saying that only *permanent* restraining orders are appealable to the Supreme Court of the United States.

179 *Procter & Gamble v. Bankers Trust*, 78 F.3d 219, 224, 225 (6th Cir. 1996), citing *Bantam Books v. Sullivan*, 372 U.S. 58, 70, 83 S.Ct. 631 (1963).

180 See *U.S. v. Barnett*, 667 F.2d 835 (9th Cir. 1982). In this case, a defendant sought to suppress the results of a search in a drug case. Part of the argument was that pamphlets and other materials that gave instructions on the manufacture of phencyclidine (PCP). In rejecting the defendant's claim, the 9th Circuit panel noted that, "the First Amendment does not provide a defense to a criminal charge simply because the actor uses words to carry out his illegal purpose." At 842.

181 *U.S. v. Schiff*, 269 F.Supp.2d 1262 (D. Nev. 2003).

Judge George acknowledged the constitutional prohibition on prior restraint, citing *Near*. But Judge George noted that Schiff's speech was in a category that fell outside First Amendment protection.[182]

> [D]efendants knowingly promote and participate in an abusive tax scheme that teaches taxpayers that they may lawfully file zero-income tax returns and exempt withholding statements to avoid paying taxes and assists them in doing so. This message is subject to injunction as false, misleading and deceptive commercial speech, incitement, and aiding and abetting illegal conduct * * * .

Judge George cited *Brandenburg v. Ohio*[183] and its language that the government may forbid speech or advocacy that is aimed to incite or produce imminent lawless action. The *Federal Mafia* book did just that with its encouragement of tax law violation, the judge concluded.

PRIOR RESTRAINT AND THE HIGH SCHOOL PRESS

As was evident from the discussion of *Near v. Minnesota* (1931), the key case on prior restraint, not all pre-publication censorship is unconstitutional. Early in 1988, in *Hazelwood School District v. Kuhlmeier*,[184] the U.S. Supreme Court held that public school officials have the power to impose pre-publication censorship on student newspapers that are learning labs. The newspaper involved in this case, *Spectrum*, was published at Hazelwood High School near St. Louis, Missouri.

The newspaper was to be six pages long in its 1983 school-year-end edition as produced by the school's Journalism II class. On May 10, 1983, Principal Robert Reynolds was shown proofs for the edition due to appear on May 13. The proofs were taken to the principal by an interim newspaper adviser; the regular Journalism II instructor had left Hazelwood East for another job just 12 days earlier.

After Principal Reynolds was shown page proofs, he objected to publication of two stories. One described three Hazelwood East students' experiences with pregnancies; the other discussed the effect of divorce on students at the school. Although the pregnancy story used fictitious names to mask identities, the principal decided that the masking was insufficient. Evidently he also thought that the article's references to sex and birth control were not appropriate for some of the younger students in the school. Finally, he was concerned that a student was identified by name in the divorce story, and that the student's parents had not been given the opportunity to respond.

Apparently believing that there was no time for redoing the stories—and that the paper could not appear at all at school year's end if delays

[182] Ibid. at 1272.

[183] 395 U.S. 444, 89 S.Ct. 1827 (1969).

[184] 484 U.S. 260, 108 S.Ct. 562 (1988).

occurred—Principal Reynolds deleted two entire pages containing the stories he found offensive. The deleted pages contained other articles—on teen marriages, runaways, juvenile delinquency, and a general article on teenage pregnancy. Principal Reynolds later testified that he had no objection to those articles; they were deleted only because they were on the same pages with the articles that troubled him.[185]

Cathy Kuhlmeier and two other former Hazelwood East students who had been newspaper staffers claimed Reynolds' action violated their First Amendment rights, and sought injunctive relief and monetary damages in a federal district court.

The trial court upheld the principal's actions. Deletion of the divorce article on invasion-of-privacy grounds was held reasonable, as was the principal's desire to avoid younger students' exposure to "unsuitable material."[186]

The Eighth Circuit Court of Appeals, however, reversed the district court, holding that the newspaper was both a part of the school's curriculum *and* a public forum, " 'intended to be operated as a conduit for student viewpoints.' " Since the newspaper was a public forum, the appeals court held, school officials could not censor its contents except when necessary " ' * * * to avoid material and substantial interference with school work or discipline * * * or with the rights of others.' "[187]

The U.S. Supreme Court granted certiorari and reversed the Court of Appeals, thus upholding the principal's prior restraint of the newspaper. Justice White wrote for the majority in this 5–3 decision. He outlined circumscribed freedoms available to students in public high schools. Although quoting from the famous language of the Vietnam war armband protest case—*Tinker v. Des Moines Independent Community School District*[188]—public school students do not " 'shed their constitutional rights at the schoolhouse gate' "—Justice White then took a restrictive tack. He declared that "the First Amendment rights of students in the public schools 'are not automatically co-extensive with the rights of adults in other settings.' "[189]

Student rights must be applied " 'in the light of special characteristics of the school environment.' " Quoting *Bethel School District No. 403 v. Fraser* (1986), he wrote that a school need not tolerate speech that is inconsistent with its educational mission, even though government could not censor such speech outside the school. (The Bethel case involved disciplining a student who had made a campaign speech in

---

185 Ibid. at 264, 566 n.

186 *Hazelwood School Dist. v. Kuhlmeier*, 484 U.S. 260, 265, 108 S.Ct. 562, 566 (1988).

187 Ibid. at 265, 567.

188 See *Tinker*, 393 U.S. 503, 511, 89 S.Ct. 733, 739.

189 Ibid.

behalf of a student politician; the speech was full of sexual double entendres.)[190]

Justice White's majority opinion declared that the *Spectrum* was not a forum for public expression: It was a part of the school's curriculum, a regular educational activity. He also interpreted the school board's policy statement supporting free expression for school-sponsored publications as suggesting "at most that the administration will not interfere with the students' exercise of those First Amendment rights that attend the publication of a school-sponsored newspaper. It does not reflect an intent to extend those rights by converting a curricular newspaper into a public forum."[191]

The majority opinion also said that a school in its capacity of publisher may " 'disassociate itself' " from speech which is disruptive, or which sets a bad example in terms of speech that is "ungrammatical, poorly written, inadequately researched, biased or prejudiced, vulgar or profane, or unsuitable for immature audiences."

This meant, the Court said, that educators

> * * * do not offend the First Amendment by exercising editorial control over the style and content of student speech in school-sponsored expressive activities so long as their actions are reasonably related to legitimate pedagogical concerns.

In dissent, Justice William J. Brennan, Jr., joined by Justices Marshall and Blackmun, said that when the students enrolled in that Journalism II course, they expected a civics lesson. They argued that only substantially disruptive speech should be censored, conceding that poor grammar, writing or research would disrupt or subvert the school's curricular purpose.[192]

> The same cannot be said of official censorship designed to shield the *audience* or dissociate the *sponsor* from the expression. Censorship so motivated * * * in no way furthers the curricular purpose of a student *newspaper,* unless one believes that the purpose of the school newspaper is to teach students that the press ought never to report bad news, express unpopular views, or print a thought that might upset its sponsors.
>
> * * *
>
> The young men and women of Hazelwood East expected a civics lesson, but not the one the Court teaches them today.

---

[190] *Bethel School District No. 403 v. Fraser,* 478 U.S. 675, 106 S.Ct. 3159 (1986).

[191] *Hazelwood School Dist. v. Kuhlmeier,* 484 U.S. at 270, 108 S.Ct. at 569.

[192] Ibid. at 290, 580.

PRIOR CENSORSHIP IN HIGH SCHOOLS AFTER HAZELWOOD: THE "FORUM" QUESTION

As attorney Mark Goodman of the Student Press Law Center (SPLC) pointed out, not all censorship of official school newspapers is automatically constitutional. If censorship is not " 'reasonably related to pedagogical concerns,' " it may be overturned. Goodman also noted that if a newspaper had been "opened as a forum for student expression where student editors had been given control over content," a court could rule against school officials' censorship.[193]

In 2004 Judge Arthur J. Tarnow held that a public high school's newspaper was a limited public forum.[194] He held that the restrictive language of the U.S. Supreme Court's decision in *Hazelwood v. Kuhlmeier* (1988)[195] did not apply and that Utica High School's *Arrow* had the protection of the First Amendment.

Judge Tarnow ruled that *The Arrow* was a limited public forum, where students controlled the content and production of the paper and made all of the paper's major editorial decisions without significant administrative intervention. Staffers of that student newspaper were free to cover controversial topics, including teenage sex, drug and alcohol abuse, suicide and sexual orientation. Adviser Gloria Olman had never been ordered to change or to remove such stories from the newspaper.[196]

Judge Tarnow cited a college case *Kincaid v. Gibson*:[197] "The *Hazelwood* standard is inapplicable where a school-sponsored publication is a limited public forum." Unlike the *Hazelwood* decision, he found that *The Arrow* was a limited public forum "because it has been opened for use by the public for speech and discussion concerning matters that are relevant to the Utica High School community and its readership." Judge Tarnow's decision is in line with positions advocated by the Student Press Law Center that despite the *Hazelwood* decision, not all censorship of official school newspapers is automatically constitutional.[198]

---

[193] Goodman, p. 38, citing *Hazelwood School District v. Kuhlmeier*, pp. 273, 267. As Mr. Goodman noted, before *Hazelwood*, the rule on student freedom of expression came from *Tinker v. Des Moines Independent Community School Dist.*, 393 U.S. 503, 511, 89 S.Ct. 733, 739 (1969), where the U.S. Supreme Court declared that if school officials can "reasonably" predict that student expression would cause "material disruption" or interference with the rights of other students, then censorship could be justified.

[194] *Katherine Dean, a minor, through her mother and next friend, Coleen Elsarelli v. Utica Community Schools, and Joan C. Sergent,* U.S. District Court, Eastern District, Southern Division, 345 F.Supp.2d 799, accessed through the Student Press Law Center website, http://www.splc.org/.

[195] 484 U.S. 260, 108 S.Ct. 562 (1988).

[196] Ibid. at 3.

[197] *Kincaid v. Gibson*, 236 F.3d 342, 346, n. 5 (6th Cir.2001) (en banc). *Kincaid* is discussed in the textbook at pp. 72–74.

[198] See Mark Goodman, *Law of the Student Press* (Washington, D.C.: SPLC, 1995), 38, as referred to in the textbook's discussion of forum questions at p. 69.

PUNISHMENT FOR "BONG HITS 4 JESUS" BANNER UPHELD (2007)

The Supreme Court of the United States continued to support the right of public school administrators to limit speech that they consider to be at odds with school policies and goals in a case over a high school prank. Juneau (Alaska) High School senior Joe Frederick was part of a group of students who were allowed to leave class and watch the passage of the Olympic torch in 2002. Knowing that the event would draw TV coverage, Frederick and some friends made a 14-foot-long banner, lettered with duct tape, spelling out the nonsense phrase, "BONG HiTS4 Jesus." As the torch passed, they unfurled the banner.[199]

School Principal Deborah Morse walked across the street and told the students to put the banner away. Frederick did not comply and Morse took and crumpled up the banner. Frederick was suspended from school for eight days. Frederick said he saw the slogan on a snowboard sticker and that it was meant only to get attention. Principal Morse said the banner promoted drug use, specifically smoking marijuana. Displaying that message at the school-sanctioned event directly contradicted the school's policy of educating students about the dangers of drug use and discouraging their use.

The controversy was fanned by conservative pundits including former U.S. drug czar (and recovering gambling addict) William J. Bennett. The National School Boards Association backed punishment of the student. Former U.S. special prosecutor Kenneth Starr, best known for his dogged investigation leading to impeachment of President Bill Clinton, represented the Juneau School Board for no charge. It is possible that this high-powered concern over a student prank stemmed from anger over an Alaska Supreme Court decision allowing private possession of marijuana.[200]

Frederick sued for violation of his First Amendment rights. The U.S. District Court for Alaska ruled in favor of Principal Morse and the Juneau School Board in 2003, but the Ninth Circuit U.S. Court of Appeals reversed, holding in favor of Frederick. Circuit Judge Andrew Kleinfeld wrote that even though the banner was displayed at a high school event and might be a pro-marijuana message, schools should not be able to censor speech because it is contrary to a social message favored by the school.[201]

Writing for the 5–4 Court, Chief Justice John Roberts held that " 'the constitutional rights of students in public schools are not automatically coextensive with the rights of adults in other settings.' " Roberts agreed

---

[199] *Morse v. Frederick*, 551 U.S. 393, 127 S.Ct. 2618 (2007).

[200] Tom Kizzia, " 'Bong Hits 4 JESUS' goes to the Supreme Court," *Anchorage Daily News*, March 4, 2007, last modified March 21, 2007.

[201] *Frederick v. Morse*, 439 F.3d 1114 (9th Cir.2006). Late in 2006, the Supreme Court granted certiorari, 549 U.S. 1075, 127 S.Ct. 722 (2006).

with Principal Morse that the cryptic language of the sign promoted illegal drug use.[202]

> The message on Frederick's banner is cryptic. It is no doubt offensive to some, perhaps amusing to others. To still others, it probably means nothing at all. Frederick himself claimed "that the words were just nonsense meant to attract television cameras." 439 F.3d, at 1117–1118. But Principal Morse thought the banner would be interpreted by those viewing it as promoting illegal drug use, and that interpretation is plainly a reasonable one.

Concurring, Justice Clarence Thomas expressed regret that the Court did not dispense altogether with a key case supporting freedom of expression for students, *Tinker v. Des Moines Independent School District*.[203] Thomas, referring to the days when teachers could use corporal punishment to ensure that students were properly respectful and obedient, argued that elementary and secondary school students had no right of expression under the First Amendment.

In dissent, Justice John Paul Stevens objected to disciplining student Joe Frederick for making an ambiguous statement with an oblique reference to drug use. Stevens wrote: "The First Amendment demands more, indeed, much more."[204]

> In my judgment, the First Amendment protects student speech if the message itself neither violates a permissible rule nor expressly advocates conduct that is illegal and harmful to students. This nonsense banner does neither, and the Court does serious violence to the First Amendment in upholding—indeed, lauding—a school's decision to punish Frederick for expressing a view with which it disagreed.

KINCAID V. GIBSON (2001): SIXTH CIRCUIT REJECTS PRIOR RESTRAINT AT KENTUCKY STATE UNIVERSITY

Hazelwood has been applied at least once to the university level by a federal district court. In *Kincaid v. Gibson*,[205] the forum question was applied to the yearbook at Kentucky State University.

---

[202] *Morse v. Frederick*, 551 U.S. 393, 401, 127 S.Ct. 2618, 2622–2624 (2007). Roberts quoted *Bethel School Dist. No. 403 v. Fraser* (1986), 478 U.S. 675, 682, 106 S.Ct. 3159 (1986), and *Hazelwood School Dist. v. Kuhlmeier*, 484 U.S. 260, 266, 108 S.Ct. 562 (1988).

[203] Ibid. at 2630. Concurring opinion of Justice Thomas citing *Tinker v. Des Moines Independent School District*, 393 U.S. 503, 506, 89 S.Ct. 733 (1969).

[204] Ibid. at 2643–2644. Dissenting opinion of Justice Stevens.

[205] *Kincaid v. Gibson*, 236 F.3d 342 (6th Cir.2001). For earlier efforts at censorship at the public university level, see *Papish v. Board of Curators of the University of Missouri*, 410 U.S. 667, 93 S.Ct. 1197 (1973). (Graduate student expelled for on-campus distribution of an underground newspaper—with a cartoon of the statue of liberty being raped by a policeman—was ordered to be reinstated at the University of Missouri.), and *Dickey v. Alabama State Board of Education*, 273 F.Supp. 613, 618 (M.D.Ala.1967), vacated in *Troy State University v. Dickey*, 402 F.2d 515 (5th Cir.1968). (Student editor Gary Dickey, ordered by Troy State officials not to

Kincaid was Charles Kincaid, a student at KSU. His co-plaintiff was Capri Coffer, another KSU student and the editor of the "*Thorobred*" yearbook in the 1993–94 school year. Betty Gibson was the university's vice president for Student Affairs. Coffer put together the yearbook, in large measure by herself after her staff fell out of the project. The yearbook included material from the 1992–93 school year because the staff for that yearbook was behind schedule. It also featured photos from the university and surrounding community as well as national and international events. When the yearbook came back from the printer, Gibson objected to it. Among her objections was the fact that the yearbook cover was purple, not one of the university's colors, a lack of captions for many of the photographs and the inclusion of national and world events not directly related to the university.

Following consultation with the administration, Gibson confiscated the yearbooks. Kincaid, who had paid a mandatory student fee of $80 for his yearbook, and Coffer sued on several grounds, focusing on the violation of their First and Fourteenth Amendment rights.

U.S. District Judge Joseph Hood granted summary judgment to the university, saying that the Kentucky State yearbook was no different from yearbooks produced at high schools. Judge Hood wrote:[206]

> High school yearbooks are not usually vehicles for the expression of views, or for robust debate about societal issues, and they never have been. There can be no serious argument that this yearbook is a public forum.

A three-judge panel of the Sixth Circuit Court of Appeals affirmed Judge Hood's ruling. But in an unusual move, the entire Sixth Circuit decided to rehear the appeal. On January 5, 2001, the Sixth Circuit reversed Judge Hood, finding for the students. Judge R. Guy Cole, Jr., wrote the opinion for the circuit. In it, Judge Cole focused on the question of the forum status of the "*Thorobred*." In doing so, Judge Cole and the Sixth Circuit concluded that the "*Thorobred*" was a limited public forum. The university's policies left control of the yearbook in the hands of its student editor.

Governments are permitted limited controls on expression in limited public forums, Judge Cole wrote. Those controls are limited to regulation needed to meet a compelling state interest. Confiscation of the yearbooks was not a narrowly crafted regulation designed to preserve a compelling state interest, Judge Cole wrote.[207]

---

publish a "controversial" editorial, was expelled for publishing blank space with label "**censored**." The appeals court ordered Dickey reinstated.).

[206] *Kincaid v. Gibson*, CA 95–98 (E.D.Kentucky).

[207] *Kincaid v. Gibson*, 236 F.3d 342, 354 (6th Cir.2001). "KSU agrees to release yearbooks confiscated by school officials in 1994 in settlement with students," Student Press Law Center News Flash, at. http://www.splc.org/article/2001/03/ksu-agrees-to-release-yearbooks-confiscated-by-school-officialsin-1994-in-settlement-with-students.

> There is little if any difference between hiding from public view the words and pictures students use to portray their college experience, and forcing students to publish a state sponsored script. In either case, the government alters student expression by obliterating it. We will not sanction a reading of the First Amendment that permits government officials to censor expression in a limited public forum in order to coerce speech that pleases the government.

A Student Press Law Center news release reported that Charles Kincaid and Capri Coffer—the two students who sued Kentucky State University back in 1994 over the confiscation of 2,000 student yearbooks—settled their case. They agreed to settle for $5,000 each and for $60,000 in attorneys fees and costs. Most important, the yearbooks were at long last freed for distribution. The news release added that the university had spent more than $100,000 in its efforts to suppress the yearbooks.

HOSTY V. CARTER (7TH CIR. 2005)

The *Kincaid* victory over prior restraint (on public college campuses) in the Sixth Federal Circuit was only one battle. The prior censorship war continues elsewhere. By mid-2005, the full panel of the Seventh Circuit ruled that prior restraint of a state university's newspaper is permissible.[208]

At Governors [sic] State University in Illinois, Dean Patricia Carter ordered the off-campus printer of the school newspaper, the *Innovator*, to halt future issues until she could approve their content before publication. The *Innovator*, supported by student activity funds, had published articles under Margaret Hosty's byline accusing Arts and Sciences Dean Roger K. Oden of lacking integrity. Accused of irresponsible and defamatory journalism by Dean Oden and by university President Stuart Fagan, the newspaper nevertheless refused to retract statements characterized as false by the administration, nor would it print administration responses.

The newspaper staff would not submit to pre-publication review and the printer was unwilling to print it if he might not be paid. The newspaper ceased publication in November, 2000, although it later resumed publication under new management. Student journalists Margaret Hosty, Jeni Porche and Steven Barba sued, asserting that Dean Carter and other Governors State officials' threats to withdraw the *Innovator's* financial support violated their First Amendment rights. The students sought damages under 42 U.S.C. § 1983.

---

[208] *Hosty v. Carter*, 412 F.3d 731 (7th Cir.2005); Student Press Law Center, "Hosty v. Carter Information Page," https://splc.org/2006/01/hosty-v-carter-information-page/. Cases on collegiate press freedom include *Schiff v. Williams*, 519 F.2d 257 (5th Cir.1975); *Joyner v. Whiting*, 477 F.2d 456 (4th Cir.1973), and *Antonelli v. Hammond*, 308 F.Supp. 1329 (D.Mass.1970).

Although a U.S. district court granted summary judgments to other Governors State defendants, it held that the distinctions between the *Hazelwood* case and a case involving students at a state university were "* * * so clearly established that no reasonable person in Carter's position would have thought herself qualified to pull the plug on the *Innovator*." Dean Carter appealed, claiming qualified immunity.[209]

Illinois Attorney General James Ryan asked the U.S. Court of Appeals, 7th Cir., to extend the *Hazelwood* decision allowing prior restraint to apply to college publications as it did to high schools. A three-judge panel of the Seventh Circuit held that Hazelwood did not apply, but that decision was vacated, making possible an appeal to a full panel of the Seventh Circuit.

Two years later, writing for the seven-judge majority in the Seventh Circuit's en banc decision in *Hosty v. Carter*, Circuit Judge Frank Easterbrook referred to a footnote in *Hazelwood School District v. Kuhlmeier* (1988), concluding that college newspapers could be subjected to prior restraint. Footnote 7 said, " 'We need not now decide whether the same degree of deference is appropriate with respect to state-sponsored expressive activities at the college and university level.' "[210]

The Court of Appeals majority in Hosty found that " * * * there is no sharp difference between high school and collegiate papers." "We hold, therefore, that *Hazelwood's* framework applies to subsidized student newspapers at colleges as well as at elementary and secondary schools. * * * *Hazelwood* supplies the framework for evaluating collegiate speech and allows regulation when readers might infer the school's approval."[211]

Judge Easterbrook wrote that the *Innovator*, even though it was a student activity and not part of the Governors State Curriculum, could still be regulated if adjudged not to be a public forum. Easterbrook in effect concluded that academic freedom for administrators trumped student rights. "Let us not forget," he wrote, "that academic freedom includes the authority of the university to manage its academic community and evaluate teaching and scholarship free from interference by other units of government, including the courts."[212]

The majority opinion concluded that Dean Carter had qualified immunity from damages for her actions. "Public officials," Judge Easterbrook wrote, "need not predict, at their peril, how constitutional uncertainties will be resolved."[213]

---

[209] Ibid. at 733.

[210] Ibid. at 734, quoting *Hazelwood v. Kuhlmeier*, 484 U.S. at 273–274, 108 S.Ct. 562 (1988).

[211] Ibid. at 735.

[212] Ibid. at 736, citing *University of Pennsylvania v. EEOC*, 493 U.S. 182, 110 S.Ct. 577 (1990); *University of Michigan v. Ewing*, 474 U.S. 214, 106 S.Ct. 507 (1985), and *University of Wisconsin v. Southworth*, 529 U.S. at 237–239 (Souter, J., concurring).

[213] Ibid. at 739.

Dissenting, Circuit Judge Terence T. Evans wrote that college students are young adults who are more mature and thus more able to make their own decisions than high school students. A university has a different purpose from a high school—"to expose students to a 'marketplace of ideas.' " Judge Evans argued that *Hazelwood* did not apply because "no pedagogical concerns can justify suppressing the student speech here. Dean Carter violated clearly established First Amendment law in censoring the student newspaper. I would affirm the judgment of the district court [in favor of student Margaret Hosty and others]."[214]

By denying that the *Innovator* was a public forum, however, the majority opened the door to prior restraint. Although a U.S. Court of Appeals decision applies as precedent only in its particular circuit, such decisions can be persuasive in other circuits or jurisdictions. Professor Emeritus Wayne Overbeck of California State University, Fullerton, quoted from a revealing memorandum after the 2005 *Hosty* decision by Christine Helwick, J.D., lawyer for the 400,000-student California State University (CSU) system.

Helwick wrote that the *Hosty* decision means " ' * * * that CSU campuses may have more latitude than previously believed to censor the content of subsidized student newspapers, provided that there is an established practice of regularized content review and approval for pedagogical purposes.' " The CSU system attorney suggested, however, that prepublication review " ' * * * may very well expose the University to liability for that content against claims of defamation.' "

Legislation has since created protections for both collegiate and high school press in California.

DISTRIBUTION ON HIGH SCHOOL GROUNDS

Related to the forum question are issues involved in on-campus distribution. People with causes—including young people—want to publicize their views. Consider *Hemry by Hemry v. School Board* (1991), involving a group of Christian students who believed it their religious duty to distribute a religious newspaper to other students. This collided with school district policy forbidding distribution of any material that would interfere with normal educational activities at a school. The court held that hallways of a school are not a public forum, and that the distribution regulations—because they were not content-based and did not take away other avenues for distributing the religious newspaper—were appropriate under the First Amendment.[215]

On the other hand, if school's policy restricting distribution can be characterized as content-based, that may overturn the regulation. In *Johnston-Loehner v. O'Brien* (1994), a federal district court knocked

---

214 Ibid. at 744.

215 *Hemry by Hemry v. School Board*, 760 F.Supp. 856 (D.Colo.1991).

down a school's policy requiring students to get permission from the school superintendent before distributing materials. The court declared this to be a "content-based prior restraint" and therefore invalid. Furthermore, the school had not made a determination that distribution of particular religious materials would "materially and substantially interfere" with the rights of students or with normal school activities.[216]

Meanwhile, Justice Brennan's warning about the dangerous "civics lesson" offered by *Hazelwood* in permitting school authorities to habituate students to accepting governmental prior restraint is worrisome to civil libertarians.[217] If, indeed, secondary schools are primary training grounds for citizens who will be expected to take their place in a democracy, freedom from stultifying censorship is not too much to ask. Unfortunately, high schools and school boards, in their quest to be presented in a good light, too often have shown themselves willing to censor student expression, even expression that had no chance of causing a disruption or causing harm.

FORUMS, PUBLIC AND OTHERWISE

The public forum/nonpublic forum question has not traditionally been a concern of the mass media, except in terms of distribution. Mass media, after all, are private concerns and do not raise state action issues. Public forum questions have arisen in the area of purchase of advertising space in areas controlled by the government, such as airport terminals and on publicly controlled bus systems. The public forum question was determinative in the *Hazelwood* case as well as other controversies involving publications in schools.

Generally speaking, the forum issue rests on conduct by the governmental body and comes down to the question of whether the government has dedicated a place or other forum, such as a newspaper, yearbook, radio or television station to the expression of ideas.

The public forum doctrine got off to a rocky start in 1897 in the case of *Davis v. Commonwealth of Massachusetts*.[218] In that case, William Davis was convicted of making a public address, in his case a sermon, on the Boston Common in violation of a municipal ordinance that prohibited people from making public addresses, selling property, putting on shows or other public amusements without a permit from the mayor.

Davis appealed to the Supreme Court. There the Court concluded that the city of Boston, which held title to the park, had the right to control what occurred in the park, including expressive activity. Justice White, delivering the opinion of the Court, wrote:[219]

---

216 *Johnston-Loehner v. O'Brien*, 859 F.Supp. 575 (M.D.Fla.1994).

217 See the quotation from Justice Brennan's dissent in *Hazelwood*, discussed earlier in this chapter.

218 *Davis v. Commonwealth of Massachusetts*, 167 U.S. 43, 17 S.Ct. 731 (1897).

219 Ibid. at 733.

> For the legislature absolutely or conditionally to forbid public speaking in a highway or public park is no more an infringement of the rights of a member of the public than for the owner of a private house to forbid it in its house.

However, the opposite conclusion was reached in *Hague v. CIO*[220] when the Supreme Court held that the Committee for Industrial Organization had the right, as did all citizens, to discuss labor relations on the streets of Jersey City, New Jersey. Jersey City had an ordinance similar to the Boston ordinance challenged in *Davis*. Jersey City was using the ordinance to prevent the CIO from handing out leaflets and discussing the rights of working men and women under the National Labor Relations Act. That treatment violated the speech and assembly rights of the CIO protected by the 14th Amendment.

While the Court acknowledged the 1897 *Davis* decision, it chose to reverse in *Hague*.[221]

> Wherever the title of streets and parks may rest, they have immemorially been held in trust for the use of the public and, time out of mind, have been used for such purposes of assembly, communicating thoughts between citizens, and discussing public questions. Such use of the streets and public places has, from ancient times, been a part of the privileges, immunities, rights, and liberties of citizens. The privilege of a citizen of the United States to use the streets and parks for the communication of views on national questions may be regulated in the interest of all; it is not absolute, but relative, and must be exercised in subordination to the general comfort and convenience, and in consonance with peace and good order, but it must not, in the guise of regulation be abridged or denied.

This concept of the public park and street as a forum for communication has been applied to other places under the control of the government. The test for whether the venue is a public forum rests primarily on the analysis of the government's intent to create a public forum based on how the government has treated the venue. Therefore, when the public was allowed a road to travel through an Army base without restriction, the post commander lost the ability to prevent a peace activist from protesting on the road.[222] The action of the government in permitting the unrestricted traffic made that street that ran through the military reservation a public forum.

Among the factors used in determining whether the government has created a public forum are the expressed intentions of the government, government actions indicating the use of the venue, and degree of government support for and the degree of government involvement in the

---

220 *Hague v. CIO*, 307 U.S. 496, 59 S.Ct. 954 (1939).

221 Ibid. at 515–516.

222 *Flower v. U.S.*, 407 U.S. 197, 92 S.Ct. 1842 (1972).

use of the venue. In *Hazelwood*, the newspaper was supported financially by the district, the adviser was paid to advise, the students created the paper as a class assignment and were graded on their product. All of these pointed to an instructional venue and not a public forum.

In the search for the proper forum designation, the courts have found that there are public forums, nonpublic forums and limited purpose public forums. Each of these classifications helps determine the degree to which people can engage in expressive conduct without government control.[223] The forum question is of great importance in determining whether or not an official school publication has full First Amendment protection. For example, in *Planned Parenthood of Nevada v. Clark County School District*, the Ninth Circuit United States Court of Appeals upheld a school's decision to exclude advertising relating to birth control and pregnancy from a school publication. Crucial to the decision, the court said, was " * * * whether the school newspapers, yearbooks, and athletic programs are forums for public expression." The court held that under school policy, officials had substantial discretion to reject advertising, and that the school publications involved never had been opened to public forum status. The school's restrictions on advertising, based on the school's desire to appear neutral on controversial issues, was upheld as conforming to the reasoning of the *Hazelwood* decision discussed above.[224]

The three categories are, broadly stated:

1. **Public Forum**—The government has, either by direct action in dedicating a space to receive all ideas and speakers or failure to act as in the case of *Flower v. U.S.* where the government allowed unlimited traffic on a street running through an Air Force base. Permitting the traffic and the carriage of all message by any and all speakers meant that the government could not, later, prevent a peace activist from taking his message to that street.[225]

> Under such circumstances the military has abandoned any claim that it has special interests in who walks, talks, or distributes leaflets on the avenue. The base commandant can no more order petitioner off this public street because he was

[223] Several recent cases point to the continued vitality of the public forum concept. In *American Civil Liberties Union of Nevada v. City of Las Vegas*, 333 F.3d 1092 (9th Cir.2003), a 9th Circuit Court of Appeals panel ruled that the Fremont Street Experience, a pedestrian mall, was a public forum where government could not prevent people from handing out leaflets, setting up tables to sell goods or putting up information booths. In *First Unitarian Church of Salt Lake City v. Salt Lake City Corp.*, 308 F.3d 1114 (10th Cir. 2002), a panel of the 10th Circuit ruled that the Church of Jesus Christ of Latter-day Saints could not restrict expressive activities on a portion of a city street that the church had bought. A public easement, retained by Salt Lake City, that allowed continued pedestrian use of the street made it a public forum and prevented the church from banning "offensive speech, dress or conduct."

[224] *Planned Parenthood of Southern Nevada v. Clark County School District*, 887 F.2d 935 (9th Cir.1989), affirmed en banc 941 F.2d 817 (9th Cir.1991).

[225] *Flower v. U.S.*, 407 U.S. 197, 92 S.Ct. 1842 (1972).

distributing leaflets than could the city police order any leafleteer off any public street.

2. **Limited Public Forum**—The government has allowed particular categories of speech or speakers in a location. As long as the restriction on the content is reasonably related to the purpose or use of the forum, it is constitutional. On the other hand, restricting speakers or speech on the basis of a disagreement by the government is not permitted.

3. **Nonpublic Forum**—The government has not opened the space to speakers or ideas. Government's decision not to allow expression is judged on its reasonableness. Reasonableness is judged, in part, on the purpose of the forum. As Justice Sandra Day O'Connor wrote in *Cornelius v. NAACP Legal Defense and Educational Fund, Inc.*, the government has rights similar to that of any other property owner.[226]

> Nothing in the Constitution requires the Government freely to grant access to all who wish to exercise their right to free speech on every type of Government property*800 without regard to the nature of the property or to the disruption that might be caused by the speaker's activities.

Forum status then is key to the establishment of expressive rights.

OTHER FORMS OF PRIOR RESTRAINT

Government pre-publication censorship continues to be discouraged by courts, but—as discussed earlier—it can occur. In addition, prior restraint may occur in other contexts, cropping up in connection with topics covered in following chapters of this book. Courts are petitioned for prior restraint orders—injunctions against publication—in areas of law including defamation, privacy,[227] copyright,[228] obscenity,[229] access to government information,[230] and advertising/commercial speech.[231] Although courts, in general, grant prior restraint orders reluctantly, the issue lives on. In libel, for example, courts usually will not halt defamatory publications via injunction. In copyright law and other areas

[226] *Cornelius v. NAACP Legal Defense and Educational Fund, Inc.*, 473 U.S. 788, 105 S.Ct. 3439 (1985).

[227] Similarly to defamation, courts have been reluctant to issue injunctions to plaintiffs in privacy cases. See Abrams, op. cit., p. 506. See *Organization for a Better Austin v. Keefe*, 402 U.S. 415, 91 S.Ct. 1575 (1971).

[228] See Chap. 13, above, and Abrams, op. cit., pp. 515–531. Injunctions occur more frequently in trademark disputes, although they are occasionally granted—temporarily—in copyright cases. See, e.g., *Rosemont Enterprises, Inc. v. Random House, Inc.*, 256 F.Supp. 55 (S.D.N.Y.1966), reversed at 366 F.2d 303 (2d Cir.1966).

[229] The seminal prior restraint case, *Near v. Minnesota*, specifically listed obscenity—along with information of aid to an enemy in wartime and expression inciting to violence/governmental overthrow—as kinds of expression subject to prior restraint. 283 U.S. 697, 51 S.Ct. 625 (1931).

[230] See Chap. 8.

[231] See Chap. 13, esp. *Posadas de Puerto Rico Associates v. Tourism Co.*, 478 U.S. 328, 106 S.Ct. 2968 (1986).

dealing with business relationships, pre-publication injunctions may be found frequently enough that they are not aberrations. Prior restraint assumes so many guises that it cannot safely be said that battles against pre-publication controls are ever won, once and for all time.

6. PRIOR RESTRAINT: LICENSING

When licensing power over expression amounts to prior censorship, it is constitutionally forbidden. Broadcasting, however, has long been a special case, outside some protections of the print media.

Licensing is one aspect of prior restraint. And, where broadcast regulation is concerned, licensing is still alive and well in the United States: a government license is required to operate a broadcast station.

Past forms of licensing, as in England in the sixteenth and seventeenth centuries, meant that only licensed printers who had government's approval were allowed to print. At the beginning of the Twenty-First Century, licensed broadcast stations have the freedom to criticize government, knowing full well that broadcast re-licensing by the Federal Communications Commission has become largely a routine matter.

If licensing broadcasting stations seems a benign form of that ancient control, other kinds of official prior permission raise sharper-edged issues. Consider the American Nazis decision to march, displaying swastikas, through a mostly Jewish neighborhood in Skokie, Illinois, in 1977. Nazi leader Frank Collin asked a number of Chicago suburbs for permits (licenses) for demonstrations in their parks or on their streets.

Skokie officials reacted strongly to the request. More than half of the village residents were Jewish and more than 5,000 were survivors of Nazi concentration camps. Village officials obtained an injunction against the march. That injunction was stayed by the U.S. Supreme Court and reversed by Illinois courts. Following the defeat, Skokie adopted three ordinances to prohibit the kind of demonstration that the Nazis sought. The first ordinance required that applicants for assemblies or parades by more than 50 persons obtain $300,000 in public liability insurance and $50,000 in property damage insurance.[232]

The Nazis announced plans to protest the ordinances, in particular, that they obtain $350,000 in insurance coverage. Skokie sought and obtained an injunction from an Illinois court preventing the Nazis from conducting the demonstration. The Nazis then appealed and the case reached the Illinois Supreme Court.

---

[232] The other two ordinances prohibited the distribution of materials promoting or inciting hatred and denied people the right to engage in political demonstrations while wearing "military-style" uniforms.

The American Civil Liberties Union, which lost much of its membership over this issue, was cast in the ironic role of defending Nazis' right to demonstrate. The Illinois Supreme Court supported the ACLU's position, striking down the Village of Skokie's licensing attempt. The court invalidated the insurance requirement. Forcing groups to obtain $350,000 in insurance was unreasonable and unconstitutional, the court said.

Many times, unpopular ideas or groups help to establish rights simply because they are unpopular and are subject to restrictions by government. Major weapons against licensing in the Twentieth Century were hammered out by repeated battles by Jehovah's Witnesses. Repeatedly, they fought their cases all the way to the U.S. Supreme Court and ultimately won. This religious group endured great suffering. As Professor William A. Hachten noted, "The ACLU reported * * * that in one six-month period of 1940, 1,488 men, women and children in the sect were victims of mob violence in 355 communities in 14 states."[233] The Witnesses made themselves unpopular with their refusal to salute the American flag and by their disdain for other religions, particularly the Roman Catholic Church. And, their persistent street sales of literature and doorbell-ringing for their beliefs often irritated non-believers.[234]

The Jehovah's Witness cases are useful reminders that freedom of expression belongs to the people, not merely to media corporations. Furthermore, a landmark case won by the Witnesses—*Lovell v. City of Griffin, Georgia*—is crucially important because it explicitly sets out constitutional protection for *distribution* of information as well as to publication.

Alma Lovell, a Jehovah's Witness, was convicted in municipal court in Griffin, Georgia, and sentenced to 50 days in jail when she refused to pay a $50 fine. Her crime? She had not received advance permission from the City Manager of Griffin to hand out literature, as required by a municipal ordinance.

Alma Lovell simply could not be bothered with such technicalities. She saw herself as a messenger sent by Jehovah and believed that applying to the City Manager for permission would have been " 'an act of disobedience to His commandments.' " The Supreme Court, however, regarded the ordinance as far more than a technicality. Speaking for a unanimous Court, Chief Justice Charles Evans Hughes denounced the ordinance:[235]

> We think that the ordinance is invalid on its face. Whatever the motive which induced its adoption, its character is such that it

---

[233] William A. Hachten, *The Supreme Court on Freedom of the Press* (Ames, Iowa: Iowa State University Press, 1968), p. 73.

[234] Ibid. at 74; *Lovell v. City of Griffin, Georgia*, 303 U.S. 444, 58 S.Ct. 666 (1938).

[235] *Lovell v. City of Griffin*, 303 U.S. 444, 451–452, 58 S.Ct. 666, 669 (1938).

strikes at the very foundation of the freedom of the press by subjecting it to license and censorship.

The liberty of the press is not confined to newspapers and periodicals. It necessarily embraces pamphlets and leaflets. These indeed have been historic weapons in the defense of liberty, as the pamphlets of Thomas Paine and others in our own history abundantly attest. * * *

The ordinance cannot be saved because it relates to distribution and not to publication. "Liberty of circulation is as essential to that freedom as liberty of publishing; indeed, without circulation, the publication would be of little value." *Ex parte Jackson*, 96 U.S. 727, 733, 24 L.Ed. 877.

Because the ordinance of the City of Griffin was not limited to " 'literature' that is obscene or offensive to public morals or that advocates unlawful conduct," the ordinance could not be upheld. In *Schneider v. Town of Irvington, New Jersey*, the Supreme Court reviewed four cities' anti-littering ordinances. Three of these ordinances in effect punished distributors if the recipient of a leaflet threw it to the ground. The Supreme Court held such ordinances unconstitutional.[236]

The issues presented in *Lovell v. Georgia* arose again some 64 years later in another case involving Jehovah's Witnesses and a city ordinance banning canvassing without a permit. In *Watchtower Bible and Tract Society of New York, Inc. v. Village of Stratton*,[237] Jehovah's Witnesses sued to overturn the village ordinance that required that persons first obtain a permit from the mayor's office, complete and sign it before going door-to-door.

The Court, in an 8–1 opinion with Chief Justice Rehnquist as the lone dissenter, held that the ordinance violated the First Amendment when it was applied to persons engaged in "religious proselytizing, anonymous political speech and the distribution of handbills." Justice Stevens' opinion, concluded that the *Village* interest in preventing fraud and protecting the privacy rights of its residents was not sufficient to overcome First Amendment rights.

As in the *Lovell* case, the Court said that had the ordinance been confined to commercial canvassers and people soliciting funds, it would likely have withstood constitutional inquiry. But the ordinance was broadly construed to cover many different speakers and subjects. A special "no exemptions" list allowed residents to specifically exclude Jehovah's Witnesses along with

---

[236] *Schneider v. Town of Irvington, New Jersey*, 308 U.S. 147, 60 S.Ct. 146 (1939).

[237] *Watchtower Bible and Tract Society of New York, Inc. v. Village of Stratton*, 536 U.S. 150, 122 S.Ct. 2080 (2002).

> political candidates, trick or treaters, campaigners, Camp Fire Girls and Scouts.[238]

The Court explained that the ordinance violated three tenets of free expression, specifically, the right to engage in speech anonymously, the right to expression without having to meet the burden of obtaining permission and the ability to engage in spontaneous speech.[239]

> First, as our cases involving distribution of unsigned handbills demonstrate, there are a significant number of persons who support causes anonymously. "The decision in favor of anonymity may be motivated by fear of economic or official retaliation, by concern about social ostracism, or merely by a desire to preserve as much of one's privacy as possible." *McIntyre v. Ohio Elections Comm'n,* 514 U.S., at 341–342, 115 S.Ct. 1511. The requirement that a canvasser must be identified in a permit application filed in the mayor's office and available for public inspection necessarily results in a surrender of that anonymity.
>
> * * *
>
> Second, requiring a permit as a prior condition on the exercise of the right to speak imposes an objective burden on some speech of citizens holding religious or patriotic views. As our World War II-era cases dramatically demonstrate, there are a significant number of persons whose religious scruples will prevent them from applying for such a license. There are no doubt other patriotic citizens, who have such firm convictions about their constitutional right to engage in uninhibited debate in the context of door-to-door advocacy, that they would prefer silence to speech licensed by a petty official.
>
> * * *
>
> Third, there is a significant amount of spontaneous speech that is effectively banned by the ordinance. A person who made a decision on a holiday or a weekend to take an active part in a political campaign could not begin to pass out handbills until after he or she obtained the required permit. Even a spontaneous decision to go across the street and urge a neighbor to vote against the mayor could not lawfully be implemented without first obtaining the mayor's permission.

In his dissent, Chief Justice Rehnquist argued that the village had a strong interest in protecting its residents from the dangers associated with door-to-door canvassers. To bolster his point, he pointed to a double murder that took place in Hanover, New Hampshire. In that case, two

[238] Ibid. Footnote 6 at 155, 2084.

[239] Ibid. at 166–167, 2089–2090.

teenagers murdered a couple. In a confession, one of the teens said the duo planned to steal debit card numbers from homeowners and then kill them. The teens said they posed as canvassers telling homeowners they were conducting an environmental survey for their school and that was how they gained entrance to the murdered couple's home. A Stratton-style ordinance might have saved the couple's lives, Rehnquist reasoned, and that would be enough to make it constitutional.[240]

> The ordinance prevents and detects serious crime by making it a crime not to register. Take the Hanover double murder discussed earlier. The murderers did not achieve their objective until they visited their fifth home over a period of seven months. If Hanover had a permit requirement, the teens may have been stopped before they achieved their objective. One of the residents they visited may have informed the police that there were two canvassers who lacked a permit. * * * Or the police on their own may have discovered that two canvassers were violating the ordinance. Apprehension for violating the permit requirement may well have frustrated the teenagers' objectives; it certainly would have assisted in solving the murders had the teenagers gone ahead with their plan.

In addition, Chief Justice Rehnquist also dissented on the basis that the ordinance was content neutral, did not allow discretion to reject an application and was a negligible burden on persons wishing to go door-to-door.

"TIME, PLACE AND MANNER"

Cases like that of Alma Lovell or the Watchtower Society, of course, do not mean that advocates can distribute anything they want at any time or place. What the courts call "time, place and manner" restrictions may be upheld as lawful if they are administratively even-handed and do not favor some kinds of content over others. A city, in other words, may set reasonable hours when canvassing may be done.[241]

Similarly, local governments may restrict the use of sound amplification systems around medical facilities and otherwise regulate how expression may be undertaken. When governments do this, they are using their inherent police powers. These powers are considered to be part and parcel of a government's ability and obligation to maintain order.

> The police power of a state extends beyond health, morals and safety, and comprehends the duty, within constitutional limitations, to protect the well-being and tranquility of a

[240] Ibid. at 179, 2096.

[241] *Schneider v. Town of Irvington,* 308 U.S. 147, 60 S.Ct. 146 (1939).

> community. A state or city may prohibit acts or things reasonably thought to bring evil or harm to its people.[242]

In *Kovacs v. Cooper*, the case from which the quote above is taken, Charles Kovacs was convicted by Judge Albert Cooper of operating a sound truck within the Trenton, New Jersey, city limits in violation of an ordinance prohibiting "use on the city streets of sound amplifying devices making loud and raucous noises."[243]

The Supreme Court upheld the conviction, saying that the ordinance was not a complete bar to the use of sound amplification, but rather was related to the legitimate interests of the city in preventing distractions to traffic and denying residents the quiet and tranquility they desire.[244]

> City streets are recognized as a normal place for the exchange of ideas by speech or paper, but this does not mean the freedom is beyond all control. We think it is a permissible exercise of legislative discretion to bar sound trucks with broadcasts of public interest, amplified to a loud and raucous volume, from the public ways of municipalities.

Similarly, courts have required that people protesting the business practices of retailers to leave space for people to pass on the sidewalks and enter and leave the business. In cases where the interests of homeowners, businesses, commuters and other government constituents come into conflict with the rights of persons engaged in expressive activities, the courts examine the relationship between the goals of that expression and the rights of others to try to reach a balance.

SUPREME COURT TAKES AWAY ANTI-ABORTION COUNSELORS' BUFFER ZONE

The Supreme Court unanimously agreed to do away with a 35-foot buffer zone that the state of Massachusetts had established outside facilities that provided abortion services.[245] The buffer zone was created by the Massachusetts legislature more than a decade after two women, receptionists at two different clinics, were shot and killed by the same gunman.

In the opinion, written by Chief Justice John Roberts, the Court held that the buffer law violated the First Amendment rights of "counselors" who sought to speak to women entering the clinic. The Court did not apply Strict Scrutiny (found in Appendix B) but rather decided the case on First Amendment grounds. The Massachusetts law, the Reproductive Health Care Facilities Act, required protestors to remain outside the 35-

---

[242] *Kovacs v. Cooper*, 336 U.S. 77, 83, 69 S.Ct. 448, 451 (1949).

[243] Ibid.

[244] Ibid. at 86, 452–453.

[245] *McCullen v. Coakley*, 573 U.S. 464, 134 S.Ct. 2518 (2014).

foot buffer. But the counselors challenging the law were not protesting, Chief Justice Roberts wrote.[246]

> While the Act may allow petitioners to "protest" outside the buffer zones, petitioners are not protestors; they seek not merely to express their opposition to abortion, but to engage in personal, caring, consensual conversations with women about various alternatives. It is thus no answer to say that petitioners can still be seen and heard by women within the buffer zones. If all that the women can see and hear are vociferous opponents of abortion, then the buffer zones have effectively stifled petitioners' message.

In addition to differentiating between counselors and protestors, Chief Justice Roberts pointed to a solution to the conduct that Massachusetts wanted to prevent. The state had alternative means to protect access to its clinics, he wrote. It was contained, partly, in the challenged law.[247]

> Subsection (e) of the Act already prohibits deliberate obstruction of clinic entrances. Massachusetts could also enact legislation similar to the federal Freedom of Access to Clinic Entrances Act of 1994, 18 U.S.C. § 248(a)(1), which imposes criminal and civil sanctions for obstructing, intimidating, or interfering with persons obtaining or providing reproductive health services. Obstruction of clinic driveways can readily be addressed through existing local traffic ordinances. While the Commonwealth contends that individuals can inadvertently obstruct access to clinics simply by gathering in large numbers, that problem could be addressed through a law requiring crowds blocking a clinic entrance to disperse for a limited period when ordered to do so by the police.

Some commentators have noted that the plaza in front of the Supreme Court building is closed off to demonstrations and individual protestors have been arrested.[248] The rule was relaxed somewhat in 2013 when the Court issued a rule that required pedestrians to "maintain suitable order and decorum within the Supreme Court building and grounds." A few have suggested that people concerned about the Court's decisions regarding campaign finance reform and other issues of the day simply approach justices as counselors, offering guidance and handing them pamphlets explaining how their choices need not be final and irrevocable.

---

246 Ibid. at 2523.

247 Ibid. at 2524.

248 Brett Logiurato, "Here's The Ultimate Irony Of The Supreme Court Banning 'Buffer Zones' At Abortion Clinics." *Business Insider*, June 27, 2014.

CINCINNATI V. DISCOVERY NETWORK, INC. (1993)

A city has an interest in keeping litter off its streets, but can it limit distribution of free-circulation publications that get taken from newsracks and thrown about?

Discovery Network, Inc., had permission from Cincinnati to place its newsracks on public property to distribute free-circulation magazines consisting mostly of advertising. In 1990, because of littering around the newsracks, the city revoked permission, declaring that the magazines were "commercial handbills." A pre-existing Cincinnati ordinance forbade distribution of commercial handbills.[249]

A U.S. District Court held that although the city may regulate newsracks for safety and esthetics, its regulations must be "narrowly tailored to achieve the desired objective."[250] A government entity regulating commercial speech bears the burden of establishing a "reasonable fit" between the ends and the means chosen to achieve those ends.[251]

When this case reached the U.S. Supreme Court, Justice Stevens declared for a 6–3 majority that although the city's interest in protecting against litter had some validity, it was not a sufficient reason to discriminate against the free circulation of magazines that were predominantly advertising. Justice Stevens wrote:[252]

> In our view, the city's argument attaches more importance to the distinction between commercial and non-commercial speech than our cases warrant and seriously underestimates the value of commercial speech.

Dissenting, Chief Justice Rehnquist—joined by Justices Byron White and Clarence Thomas—complained that the Cincinnati newsracks decision will "unduly hamper our cities' efforts to come to grips with the unique problems posed by the dissemination of commercial speech."[253]

7. FORCING COMMUNICATION TO OCCUR

The other side of prior restraint (preventing communication in the first place) is forcing communication to occur. Except for the broadcast media, forcing communication to occur generally is forbidden.

Forcing communication to take place is closely connected with—is often the "flip side" of—a system of prior restraint. As Fredrick Siebert showed in his pathbreaking study of the development of freedom of

[249] *Cincinnati v. Discovery Network, Inc.*, 507 U.S. 410, 113 S.Ct. 1505 (1993).

[250] The District Court cited *Board of Trustees of State University of New York v. Fox*, 492 U.S. 469, 109 S.Ct. 3028 (1989).

[251] *Cincinnati v. Discovery Network, Inc.*, 507 U.S. 410, 113 S.Ct. 1505 (1993).

[252] Ibid. at 1165.

[253] Ibid. at 1173.

expression in England from 1476 to 1776, printers who did not publish what they were told to print by government often put themselves in real peril.[254] Similarly, in the early years of Britain's American colonies, printers—who needed government subsidies to survive—had to display "Published by Authority" on their newspapers. Such printers often learned that they dared not deviate from printing only the official accounts—edited for public consumption—of the meetings (held in secret) of colonial legislatures or Governor's councils.[255]

After the War for Independence and the creation of the United States, the development of strongly competing political factions—and later, political parties—helped distribute "official printing" business while criticizing government raucously.[256] Later, in the first four decades of the Nineteenth Century, the rise of mass circulation newspapers supported primarily by advertising helped free the press from government.[257]

Over time, the libertarian ideas borrowed from England evolved, with arguments taken from John Milton from the Seventeenth Century and from "Country Whig" philosophers of the Eighteenth Century.[258] Those ideas developed in the crucible of American politics into the ideas that government should keep hands off the press, allowing criticism of government through a "free marketplace of ideas," assuming that truth would win over falsehood in the process of argumentation.

This "marketplace of ideas" philosophy became a kind of received truth, cited with the force of binding precedent by the Supreme Court of the United States in important Twentieth Century decisions.[259] But when major riots occurred after the assassination of Martin Luther King, law professor Jerome Barron articulated a troubling and persistent viewpoint. He argued that lack of access to media of communication by disadvantaged minorities showed that government should intervene to give the voiceless a voice. Otherwise, people left voiceless were going to "take it to the streets," violently.[260]

In an age of mass communication, Barron asserted, the members of the public must have access to the columns and airwaves of the mass

---

[254] Siebert, *Freedom of the Press in England,* 1476–1776; Clyde A. Duniway, *The Development of Freedom of the Press in Massachusetts* (Cambridge: Harvard Univ. Press, 1906), pp. 104–05.

[255] Jean Folkerts, Dwight L. Teeter, Jr., and Edward Caudill, *Voices of a Nation,* 5th ed. (Boston: Pearson Allyn & Bacon, 2009), pp. 19–23.

[256] See, e.g., Jackson Turner Main, *The Antifederalists: Critics of the Constitution* (Chapel Hill: Univ. of North Carolina Press, 1961); Teeter, "Press Freedom and the Public Printing: Pennsylvania, 1775–1783," *Journalism Quarterly* XLV (Autumn, 1968), p. 445.

[257] Jean Folkerts, et. al., op. cit., pp. 108, 121–124.

[258] See Chap. 1, Sec. 1; see also Norman L. Rosenberg, *Protecting the Best Men* (Chapel Hill: Univ. of North Carolina Press, 1985).

[259] See, e.g., the classic newspaper antitrust case of *Associated Press v. United States,* 326 U.S. 1, 28, 65 S.Ct. 1416, 1418 (1945).

[260] Jerome A. Barron, "Access to the Press—a New First Amendment Right," 80 *Harv.L.Rev.* 1641 (1967).

media. Barron elaborated the position that for many decades the high cost of ownership had barred countless voices from a part in the "marketplace of ideas." The media—giant in size and cost, relatively few in number, and owned by largely like-minded entrepreneurs devoted to the economic and political *status quo*—have the power to deny citizens the right to have their message communicated widely.

The media themselves, in Professor Barron's view, are crucial barriers to a diversity of opinion and fact in the marketplace. "At the very minimum," Barron wrote, "the creation of two remedies is essential—(1) a nondiscriminatory right to purchase editorial advertisements in daily newspapers, and (2) a right of reply for public figures and public officials defamed in newspapers."[261]

Professor Barron's "right of access to the press" ideas were tested—and found wanting—in a famed 1974 decision by the U.S. Supreme Court. In *Miami Herald v. Tornillo,* the Supreme Court took on a case that had arisen in Florida under that state's "right of reply" statute. The *Miami Herald* had refused to print a reply by a political candidate, Pat L. Tornillo, Jr., to a *Herald* editorial criticizing his candidacy for the Florida legislature. When Tornillo asked for his right of reply in the columns of the newspaper, he was refused access, so he sued.

The Florida Supreme Court upheld Tornillo's arguments, and said he should have a right of reply to the print media similar to the right granted under the equal opportunities and fairness doctrines to persons attacked by broadcast media and cable. (See Chap. 11.) At this writing the "equal opportunities" ["equal time"] law for political candidates is still in force. However, the FCC's "fairness doctrine" requiring broadcasters to air controversial issues and responses to personal attacks was repealed. The First Amendment, said the Florida Court, "is not for the benefit of the press so much as for the benefit of us all," and added:[262]

> The right of the public to know all sides of a controversy and from such information to be able to make an enlightened choice is being jeopardized by the growing concentration of the ownership of the mass media into fewer and fewer hands, resulting ultimately in a form of private censorship.

The Supreme Court of the United States, however, reversed the Florida court.[263]

In so doing, the nation's highest court conceded the dangers of concentration of media ownership, cross-channel ownership and chains and syndicates all of which focused great power to inform and to influence public opinion in the hands of a few. However valid those arguments, the Court said, government coercion by a remedy such as a right of reply

[261] Barron, *Freedom of the Press for Whom?* (Bloomington: Indiana Univ. Press, 1973), p. 6.

[262] *Tornillo v. Miami Herald Pub. Co.*, 287 So.2d 78 (Fla.1973).

[263] *Miami Herald Pub. Co. v. Tornillo,* 418 U.S. 241, 94 S.Ct. 2831 (1974).

"brings about a confrontation with the express provisions of the First Amendment."

Chief Justice Warren Burger wrote for a unanimous court in rejecting the arguments advanced by Pat Tornillo and Jerome Barron. Reviewing past decisions of the Court, the Chief Justice declared:[264]

> The clear implication has been that any such compulsion to publish that which " 'reason' tells them [editors] should not be published" is unconstitutional. A responsible press is an undoubtedly desirable goal, but press responsibility is not mandated by the Constitution and like many other virtues it cannot be legislated.

The Florida statute, the Court said, penalized on the basis of the content of a newspaper. The penalty is increased cost of production, and taking up space that could go to other material the paper may have preferred to print. Infinite expansion of its size to accommodate replies that a statute might require is not to be expected of a newspaper.

But cost aside, the Florida statute failed "to clear the barriers of the First Amendment because of its intrusion into the function of editors." The functions of choosing content, determining size of the paper and treatment of public issues, may be fair or unfair, said the Chief Justice. He added that "[i]t has yet to be demonstrated how governmental regulation of this crucial process can be exercised consistent with First Amendment guarantees of a free press * * * "

The *Tornillo* decision developed no reasoning as to why newspapers were exempt, but broadcasting need not be, from the requirements of furnishing opportunities to reply. Once again, as in other circumstances, the First Amendment's shield proved stronger for print journalism than for broadcasting.[265]

"AG GAG BILLS: FORCED COMMUNICATION PLUS PRIOR RESTRAINT"

Heavily criticized by animal rights organizations such as People for the Ethical Treatment of Animals (PETA), ASPCA and the Humane Society of the United States, friendly legislators are trying to help livestock raisers and owners avoid scrutiny. Investigative videos and articles indeed are upsetting to those in various phases of livestock industries. For an example, see Ted Conover, "The Way of All Flesh: Undercover in an industrial slaughterhouse," Harper's Magazine, May, 2013, pp. 31ff.

---

264 Ibid. Quotes and paraphrases following are from Chief Justice Burger's majority opinion at 2838–2840.

265 See Chap. 12, Sec. 79.

In 2014, half of all states had tried or were trying to pass "Ag Gag" laws, but only seven became statutes.[266] The laws uniformly target secret filming of activities at farms, ranches feedlots and slaughterhouses. Some of the proposed statutes make it a crime to lie on an employment application in order to gain access. Others, like Montana, criminalizes the act of filming a crime.[267]

> 81–30–103. Unlawful acts: (2) A person who does not have the effective consent of the owner and who intends to damage the enterprise conducted at an animal facility may not:
>
> * * *
>
> (b) enter an animal facility that is at the time closed to the public with the intent to commit an act prohibited by this chapter;
>
> (c) remain concealed in an animal facility with the intent to commit an act prohibited by this chapter;
>
> (d) enter an animal facility and commit or attempt to commit an act prohibited by this chapter;
>
> (e) enter an animal facility to take pictures by photograph, video camera, or other means with the intent to commit criminal defamation * * *

Ag Gag laws in Utah and Idaho were challenged in federal courts in 2014.[268] Both suits contested the law on similar grounds. The Idaho law makes unauthorized recording is punishable by up to a year in jail and a $5,000 fine. Utah makes it a crime to provide false information to gain access to a farm. Both suits argued that the investigations by groups and individuals are protected by whistle blower laws and guarantees of freedom of speech. They also point to harms and risks that the undercover work helps to expose.[269]

> One such investigation was conducted by the Humane Society of the United States in Chino, California, in 2007, and led to the largest meat recall in U.S. history. Undercover video at a slaughterhouse showed cows too weak or sick to walk dragged by chains, rammed by forklifts and sprayed with high-pressure hoses. It was released after three attempts to get the facility's USDA inspectors to do something, and the government ended up recalling 143 million pounds of meat, including 37 million pounds intended for the school lunch program.

Legislation called the "Ag Gag" bill was passed by the Tennessee General Assembly in Spring, 2013, but Gov. Bill Haslam vetoed the bill after constitutional objections were raised. Gov. Haslam, a

[266] Idaho, Iowa, Kansas, Missouri, North Dakota and Utah.

[267] MCA 81–30–103(2).

[268] Associated Press, "2 ag-gag laws facing federal court challenges," July 19, 2014.

[269] Ibid.

nonconfrontational Republican, provided reasons for his veto, adding that he "respectfully encouraged the General Assembly to reconsider this issue." Gov. Haslam had received thousands of messages after the Humane Society mounted a campaign calling for the veto. The Tennessee Press Association (TPA) and the Tennessee Committee on Open Government (TCOG) called for the veto on open government grounds. Frank Gibson, TPA public policy director and a former chairman of TCOG, expressed approval of the veto and termed the bill a "backdoor attempt to repeal the Tennessee Shield Law."[270]

Tennessee Attorney General Bob Cooper called the bill "constitutionally suspect" on three grounds. Beyond that, he said the bill would repeal portions of the Tennessee Shield Law without explicitly saying so. Reporting for the Knoxville *News Sentinel*, Tom Humphrey noted objections from a number of district attorneys that the bill has the unintended consequence of making animal cruelty cases harder to prosecute.[271]

The original bill called for anyone making videos or photographs of livestock abuse to hand unedited materials over to law enforcement authorities within 48 hours. The Holt Dresden bill apparently was in response to a surreptitious Humane Society video, shot over a number of months, about abusive training methods used with Tennessee Walking Horses. The video led to a prosecution and conviction for animal cruelty.

8. CRIMINAL LIBEL

Control of words critical of officials and other citizens was provided by criminal libel law in the states the nation's early years, almost disappearing after World War II.

Like the vampire legend, criminal libel never quite seems to die out. Even though it was conventional wisdom late in the Twentieth Century to assert that criminal libel is dead in the United States, it showed up in Arkansas as recently as the end of 2003.[272]

In origins, criminal libel overlaps the old crime of sedition: laws making verbal attacks on government applied also to words that assailed government officials. That may be seen earlier in this chapter in Sec. 4's discussion of the Alien and Sedition Acts of 1798. After the death of the Alien and Sedition Acts in 1801, statutes making libel a crime began to proliferate in the states.

Keep the phrase *criminal libel* in mind, distinguishing it from *civil libel.* A *criminal* charge or case is brought by an official or agency of

---

270 Tom Humphrey, "Haslam vetoes 'Ag Gag' bill," *News Sentinel* (Knoxville), May 14, 2103, p. A1.

271 Ibid; see also editorial, "Haslam deserves praise for veto of 'Ag Gag' proposal," *News Sentinel*, March 15, 2013, p.B2.

272 "Trooper pursues criminal slander charges against chief, officer," *AP Newswire*, Nov. 17, 2003.

government; if a defendant is convicted at trial he or she is subject to imprisonment, payment of a fine, or possibly both. *Civil* libel—dealing with publications (including broadcasts) which are false and which harm a person's *reputation*—do not involve criminal penalties. The person winning a civil libel case can receive monetary "damages" for reputational damage caused by the defendant.

The Jeffersonians who successfully ended the Federalists' Alien and Sedition Acts had a limited sense of freedom themselves. The Jeffersonians, hating the *national* sedition law when brought to bear on their newspapers and editors, nevertheless accepted the power to punish political speech when it was held by the states.[273] Supposedly, citizens could control their local/state affairs and check tendencies toward oppression close to home more easily than they could check a remote, centralized national government.

Laws of the new states provided that libel could be a crime whether it was aimed at plain citizens or government men. That the laws went under the name "criminal libel" laws instead of under the hated term "seditious libel" made them no less effective as tools for prosecution of those who attacked officials.

Under the British common law tradition for criminal libel, truth was not a defense. The old reasoning was that the truer the disparaging words, the more likely the insulted person to seek violent revenge, breaching the peace. Thus the legal aphorism of the Eighteenth Century: "the greater the truth, the greater the libel."

The states drew up safeguards against some of the harshest features of the old English law of libel. The principles that Andrew Hamilton pleaded for in defending Zenger in colonial New York before there was a U.S.A. emerged as important ones early in the Nineteenth Century as states embarked upon prosecutions. Truth slowly was established as a defense in criminal libel actions, and juries were permitted to "find the law" (rule whether the words were defamatory) under growing numbers of state constitutions and statutes as the century progressed.

A celebrated early case in New York State encouraged the spread of new defenses. It stemmed from a paragraph reprinted by Federalist editor Harry Croswell from the *New York Evening Post* attacking President Thomas Jefferson:[274]

> Jefferson paid Callender [a Republican editor] for calling Washington a traitor, a robber, and a perjurer; for calling Adams a hoary-headed old incendiary, and for most grossly slandering the private characters of men who he well knew to be virtuous.

---

[273] Levy, *Emergence of a Free Press*, Chaps. 9 and 10; Berns, pp. 89–119.

[274] *People v. Croswell*, 3 Johns.Cas. 337 (N.Y.1804).

The great Federalist leader, Alexander Hamilton, in 1804 took the case after Croswell had been convicted of criminal libel in a jury trial in which he had not been permitted to show the truth of his charge. Hamilton argued that "the liberty of the press consists of the right to publish with impunity truth with good motives for justifiable ends though reflecting on government, magistracy, or individuals." This, of course, made the intent of the publisher crucial. He also urged that the jury be allowed to find both the law and the facts of the case. He lost, the appeals court being evenly divided. The result, however, was so repugnant to people and lawmakers that the New York Legislature in 1805 passed a law embracing the principles that Hamilton urged.[275]

Other states adopted Hamilton's formula, and a few, indeed, made truth a defense no matter what the intent of the writer. But the death of the vicious "the greater the truth the greater the libel" doctrine was slow and reluctant.

Nineteenth Century American courts were reluctant to give truth a protected position in the law, even though statutes seemed to endorse the position that the public needs to know the truth. As legislatures adopted truth as a defense in libel statutes during the Nineteenth Century, courts nevertheless clung tenaciously to the old idea that if the truth produced a breach of the peace, it could be punished.[276] Although few statutes or constitutions retained words' "tendency to breach the peace" as a basis for criminality in libel in the Twentieth Century, judges who wanted to employ it found it readily accessible in common law principles.

Criminal libel actions were few through most of the Nineteenth Century. They surged in number in the 1880s and held at some 100 reported cases per decade for 30 years or more. Not all, by any means, were brought for criminal defamation of public officials in the pattern of seditious libel actions.[277] But criticism of police, governors, mayors, judges, prosecutors, sheriffs, and other government officials was the offense in scores of criminal libel cases.

For whatever reasons, criminal libel actions dropped after World War I from about 100 per decade to much smaller numbers.[278] Courts increasingly held that civil libel suits to recover damages were much to be preferred to criminal libel prosecutions, which more and more seemed inappropriate to personal squabbles between citizens. Dueling, that extreme breach of the peace, was out of favor as a means of settling personal differences or avenging verbal insults, as in centuries past. Also,

---

[275] An Act Concerning Libels, Laws of the State of New York, Albany, 1805.

[276] Elizabeth Goepel, *"The Breach of the Peace Provision in Nineteenth Century Criminal Libel Law,"* (Univ. of Wis.1981), unpublished Master's thesis.

[277] John D. Stevens, et al., "Criminal Libel as Seditious Libel," 43 *Journalism Quar.* 110 (1966); Robert A. Leflar, "The Social Utility of the Criminal Law of Defamation," 34 *Texas L.Rev.* 984 (1956). Stevens et al. found that about one-fifth (31) of the 148 criminal libel cases reported in the half-century after World War I grew out of charges made against officials.

[278] Stevens, op. cit.

the defamed person ordinarily had more to gain through a civil judgment for money damages than through a criminal conviction.

CRIMINAL LIBEL OF OFFICIALS

In 1966, the U.S. Supreme Court focused on the concept of breach of the peace from common law criminal libel, finding that it did not square with the First Amendment. Merely to say that words which tend to cause breach of the peace are criminal is too indefinite to be understandable, the Court said. The case, *Ashton v. Kentucky*, involved a pamphlet in which Ashton charged, among other things, that a police chief had acted lawlessly during a strike of miners. Ashton was convicted under a judge's definition of criminal libel as "any writing calculated to create disturbances of the peace." The Supreme Court said that without more specificity, that was too vague an offense to be constitutionally permissible.[279]

GARRISON V. LOUISIANA (1966)

In a second 1966 criminal libel decision, *Garrison v. Louisiana*, the Supreme Court reached back to its 1964 ruling in the civil libel case, *New York Times v. Sullivan*. Applying the logic of *Sullivan* to a criminal libel case involving criticism of public officials had a heavy impact on the law. The *Sullivan* decision said that critical words must be used with actual malice if they were to be the object of a civil libel action against officials. In *Garrison v. Louisiana* (1966), the Court transferred the same rule into the field of criminal libel. There "Big Jim" Garrison, a flamboyant prosecuting attorney in the Louisiana, gave out a statement at a press conference saying several judges of his parish (county) were lazy and inattentive to their official duties. Garrison was convicted of criminal libel, and his case ultimately reached the Supreme Court.

The Court cited the *Sullivan* rule defining actual malice: a public official might recover damages for civil libel—or now, sustain a prosecution for criminal libel—only if it could be shown that there was knowing falsity or reckless disregard for the truth. The Court said:[280]

> The reasons which led us so to hold [in *Sullivan*] * * * apply with no less force merely because the remedy is criminal. * * * Truth may not be the subject of either civil or criminal sanctions where discussion of public affairs is concerned. And since " * * * erroneous statement is inevitable in free debate * * * " only those false statements made with a high degree of their probable falsity demanded by *New York Times* may be the subject of either civil or criminal sanctions. For speech concerning public

[279] *Ashton v. Kentucky*, 384 U.S. 195, 198, 86 S.Ct. 1407, 1409–1411.

[280] *Garrison v. Louisiana*, 379 U.S. 64, 85 S.Ct. 209 (1964); Harry Kalven, "The New York Times Case: A Note on the Central Meaning of the First Amendment," 1965 *Supreme Court Review* 191.

affairs is more than self-expression; it is the essence of self-government.

In the late 1990s, criminal libel seemed to have little in the way of constitutional support, but there are occasional signs that criminal libel is not yet buried. As Robert Sack has noted, a 1991 Colorado Supreme Court decision held that state's criminal libel statute invalid "only insofar as it reaches constitutionally protected statements about public officials or public figures on matters of public concern." The Colorado Supreme Court found that "where one private individual has disparaged the reputation of another private individual," the Colorado statute remains valid.[281]

So the good news is that criminal libel cases are rare. The bad news is that criminal libel won't quite go away. The Arkansas case in November 2003[282] is a reminder that criminal libel law slumbers in many states and may wake up and cause trouble. In this unusual case, the Tenth Circuit interpreted a 1988 Kansas statute in order to make it constitutional. That is, the court ruled that because the statute was enacted after *Garrison v. Louisiana* (1964), the Kansas legislature must have meant to include *Garrison's* twin pronouncements, (1) that truth must be allowed as a defense to criminal libel, and (2) that proof of actual malice is required to make a criminal libel conviction stick.[283]

In 2005, Paul McMasters, First Amendment ombudsman at the First Amendment Center, reported that criminal libel statutes were on the books in 20 states.[284] Utah had its criminal libel law invalidated by the Utah Supreme Court. The Utah court said in *I.M.L. v. State*[285] that the Utah statute was unconstitutional, in part, because it relied on the common law definition of malice and also because it allowed punishment for some truthful statements. In addition, a federal court of appeals ruled in 2003 that Puerto Rico's criminal libel law was unconstitutional.[286]

---

[281] *People v. Ryan*, 806 P.2d 935 (1991), cited in Sack, op. cit., at p. 174n. This case involved a fake "wanted poster" distributed to several bars and businesses in Fort Collins, Colo., by a disgruntled former date, falsely accusing a woman of being wanted for a number of crimes and falsely warning that she had sexually transmitted diseases.

[282] "Trooper pursues criminal slander charges against, chief, officer," AP Newswire, Nov. 17, 2003. An Arkansas state trooper alleged that the chief of police of Edmondson, Arkansas, and a police officer from the town made statements that damaged the trooper's standing within the state police. The case stemmed from statements made about a traffic stop involving the trooper and police chief.

[283] *Phelps v. Hamilton*, 59 F.3d 1058 (10th Cir.1995).

[284] Paul K. McMasters, "Inside the First Amendment: The crime of speaking ill of your betters," Gannett News Service, Nov. 7, 2005.

[285] *I.M.L. v. State*, 61 P.3d 1038 (Utah 2002).

[286] "Federal Appeals Court Rules Puerto Rico's Criminal Libel Law Unconstitutional," AP Newswire, Jan. 23, 2003. The case involved the newspaper El Vocero which had published a story linking a member of a police drug task force with a drug dealer. The officer in question filed a criminal complaint against the reporter. The Puerto Rican statute provided criminal penalties of six months in jail and fines for people making false statements about a public official's performance of his duties. The First Circuit Court of Appeals court ruled in *Mangual v. Rotger-Sabat*, 317 F.3d 45 (1st Cir. Puerto Rico 2003), that the statute did not require that

A number of states—including Alaska, Arizona, California, Hawaii, Indiana, Nebraska, Oregon, Vermont, and Wyoming—had repealed their criminal libel statutes. Most of these repeals came in the 1970s and 1980s, and Pennsylvania's criminal libel statute was declared unconstitutional in 1972.[287]

Still, criminal libel cases continue to pose threats to free and open discussion in Florida, Idaho, Kansas, Louisiana, Michigan, Montana, New Hampshire and North Carolina.[288]

In the first successful criminal libel prosecution of a newspaper in almost 30 years, the publisher and editor of a free, tabloid newspaper distributed in the Kansas City, Kansas, area were found guilty of seven counts of criminal defamation. David Carson, publisher, and Edward H. Powers Jr., editor, of the *New Observer* had frequently criticized Kansas City Mayor Carol Marinovich. During her third re-election bid, the newspaper reported a number of times that Marinovich did not live in the county that contained Kansas City. The statement was not correct. Following Marinovich's victory, the county's district attorney, another frequent target of the newspaper, filed 10 counts of criminal defamation against the two and they were convicted on seven of the charges.[289]

The case and convictions drew considerable media criticism and a failed attempt to repeal the Kansas law. The *New Observer* case was followed by another criminal defamation case filed by a Kansas official against a newspaper.[290] *Baxter Springs News* publisher Larry Hiatt and newspaper columnist Ron Thomas were charged with criminal defamation for a column and an advertisement carried in the newspaper. Both column and ad were critical of City Clerk Donna Wixom. Baxter Springs City Attorney Robert Myers filed criminal complaints against the two men and a candidate who paid for the political ad. The charges were dismissed on a technicality because the city did not obtain a special prosecutor in the case.[291]

CRIMINAL LIBEL OF GROUPS

Perhaps adding tenacity to the shrinking offense of criminal libel was a highly unusual case of 1952 that claimed the attention of much of the world of civil liberties. It involved a special and rarely employed version of the ancient criminal libel law—that under some circumstances, *groups* could be libeled and the state could bring criminal

---

prosecutors prove actual malice. This and the Utah case shows that even with the Garrison case as precedent, many criminal libel statutes do not conform to constitutional requirements.

[287] Criminal Defamation in the United States: A 2015 Update, https://kellywarnerlaw.com/criminal-defamation-in-the-united-states-a-2015-update/.

[288] Ibid.

[289] John Dvorak, "Publisher, editor of tabloid get fine, probation in Kansas libel case," *Kansas City Star*, Nov. 28, 2002.

[290] "Publisher, columnist, candidate charged with defamation," AP Newswire, March 16, 2003.

[291] "Baxter Springs newspaper staff, fights legal battles," AP Newswires, June 11, 2003.

action against the libeler. *Beauharnais v. Illinois* was decided in 1952 with a finding of "guilty."[292] It involved a leaflet attack on the African-Americans in Chicago, at a time when the memory of Hitler Germany's mass killing of Jews was fresh in the minds of the nation. Migration of blacks from the south into northern cities was swelling. Beauharnais, president of the White Circle League, had organized his group to distribute the leaflets, and they did so in downtown Chicago. Among other things the leaflet called for city officials to stop "the further encroachment, harassment, and invasion of the white people * * * by the Negro * * * ", and predicted that "rapes, robberies, knives, guns, and marijuana of the negro" surely would unite Chicago whites against blacks.

Beauharnais was prosecuted and convicted under an Illinois law making it unlawful to exhibit a publication which "portrays depravity, criminality, unchastity, or lack of virtue of a class of citizens, of any race, color, creed or religion which said publication * * * exposes the citizens of any race, color, creed or religion to contempt, derision, or obloquy or which is productive of breach of the peace or riots."[293]

The charges against "Negroes," said the Court, were unquestionably libelous; and the central question became whether the "liberty" of the Fourteenth Amendment prevents a state from punishing such libels when they are directed not at an individual, but at "designated collectivities." The Court said that only if the law were a "willful and purposeless restriction unrelated to the peace and well-being of the State," could the Court deny a state power to punish utterances directed at a defined group.

Justice Frankfurter found that for more than a century, Illinois had been "the scene of exacerbated tension between races, often flaring into violence and destruction." He cited the murder of abolitionist Elijah Lovejoy in 1837, the "first northern race riot"—in Chicago in 1908—in which six persons were killed, and subsequent violence in the state of Illinois down to the Cicero, Illinois, race riot of 1951. He concluded that "In the face of this history and its frequent obligato of extreme racial and religious propaganda, we would deny experience to say that the Illinois legislature was without reason in seeking ways to curb false or malicious defamation of racial and religious groups."[294]

Four members of the court delivered strong dissents to the majority opinion that sustained Beauharnais' conviction. Justice Hugo Black stated much of the case against the concept of group libel as an offense

---

[292] 343 U.S. 250, 72 S.Ct. 725 (1952). See also *People v. Spielman*, 318 Ill. 482, 149 N.E. 466 (1925). Also "Knights of Columbus" cases: *People v. Turner*, 28 Cal.App. 766, 154 P. 34 (1915); *People v. Gordan*, 63 Cal.App. 627, 219 P. 486 (1923); *Crane v. State*, 14 Okl.Crim. 30, 166 P. 1110 (1917); *Alumbaugh v. State*, 39 Ga.App. 559, 147 S.E. 714 (1929). And see Joseph Tannehaus, "Group Libel," 35 *Cornell L.Q.* 261 (1950).

[293] *Beauharnais v. Illinois*, 343 U.S. 250, 251, 72 S.Ct. 725, 728 (1952).

[294] Ibid. at 258–261, 731–733. Illinois dropped the statute, but later enacted a hate-crime law.

acceptable to American freedom. Calling the law a "state censorship" instrument, Black said that permitting states to experiment in curbing freedom of expression "is a startling and frightening doctrine in a country dedicated to self-government by its people."[295]

Attempts to create a color-blind society that accepted diversity in religion, philosophy, sexual orientation, national or ethnic origin took the form of law punishing persons for attacks on discrete and identifiable groups.

All but four states—South Carolina, Arkansas, Georgia, Michigan and Wyoming—had hate crime statutes in 2015.[296] Thirty-one states' laws closely followed a model of the Anti-Defamation League of B'nai B'rith calling for both criminal sanctions and civil penalties. In 1992, the U.S. Supreme Court decided *R.A.V. v. St. Paul*, a test of a city ordinance's application to a 17-year-old accused of cross-burning in a black family's fenced yard.[297]

The 17-year-old—identified as R.A.V. because he was a minor—was accused of violating a St. Paul, Minnesota "Bias-Motivated Crime Ordinance." That ordinance made it a misdemeanor disorderly conduct for anyone to place, on public or private property, any symbol, object or graffiti "including, but not limited to, burning a cross or placing a Nazi swastika, which one knows * * * arouses anger, alarm, or resentment in others on the basis of race, color, creed, religion or gender * * * "[298] The Minnesota Supreme Court upheld the ordinance, saying it merely made illegal speech of the "fighting words" variety, words long held to be beyond constitutional protection.[299]

Writing for five members of the Court, Justice Antonin Scalia declared the ordinance unconstitutional because "it prohibits otherwise permitted speech solely on the basis of the subject it addresses." He wrote,[300] burning a cross in someone's yard is reprehensible. But St. Paul has sufficient means at its disposal to control such behavior without adding the First Amendment to the fire."

Four justices who concurred in the holding concluded that the ordinance was underinclusive, in that it did not prohibit all words of its type. The concurring justices also wrote that the ordinance was overbroad in that it criminalized expression protected by the First Amendment.

---

[295] Ibid. at 270–273, 737–739.

[296] Polly Mosendzon, "Charleston Shooting May Be Hate Crime, But State Has No Such Law," *Newsweek*, June 19, 2015. http://www.newsweek.com/charleston-shooting-may-be-hate-crime-state-has-no-such-law-345304.

[297] Mary Deibel, "Hate Crimes," Scripps-Howard News Service, *Knoxville News-Sentinel*, Dec. 1, 1991, p. F–1, and see Hadley Arkes, "Civility and Restriction of Speech: Rediscovering the Defamation of Groups," 1974 *Sup.Ct.Rev.* 281–335; *City of Chicago v. Lambert*, 47 Ill.App.2d 151, 197 N.E.2d 448 (1964).

[298] *R.A.V. v. St. Paul*, 505 U.S. 377, 112 S.Ct. 2538, 2541 (1992).

[299] Ibid., citing *Chaplinsky v. New Hampshire*, 315 U.S. 568, 62 S.Ct. 766 (1942).

[300] *R.A.V. v. St. Paul*, 505 U.S. 377, 112 S.Ct. 2538, 2550 (1992).

Although the other four members of the Court concurred, they took aim on the majority's reasoning. For example, Justice White argued that by equating fighting words with political expression, the Court's majority showed disrespect for the latter:[301]

> Fighting words are not a means of exchanging views, rallying supporters, or registering a protest: they are directed against individuals to provoke violence or to inflict injury. Therefore, a ban on all fighting words or on a subset of the fighting words category would restrict only the social evil of hate speech, without creating the danger of driving viewpoints from the marketplace.
>
> * * *
>
> Indeed, by characterizing fighting words as a form of "debate," the majority legitimizes hate speech as a form of public discussion.

Justice White's dissent pointed to the potentially dual nature of using symbols that both express an idea and also create harm.

EFFECTS ON CAMPUS HATE SPEECH CODES?

Trying to curtail racist or ethnic hate speech, a number of colleges and universities have ladled good intentions into their student conduct codes. However, as Tim England wrote in 1992, speech codes of universities have been found unconstitutional when subject to court challenges.[302]

William Celis 3d reported in the *New York Times* that the *R.A.V.* case appeared to weaken if not invalidate some speech codes. He pointed out in 1992 that this was no small matter because perhaps as many as 100 universities had instituted codes to punish discriminatory or intimidating name-calling or symbolic acts based on racism or other prejudices: ethnic, religious, sex, sexual orientation, national origin, or handicap.[303]

Such codes collide with traditional ideas of free expression on campus. For example, if a sociology class discussed racial slurs, might that not violate a hate speech regulation? Because of such "overbreadth," codes at the University of Michigan and the University of Wisconsin-Milwaukee were found unconstitutional.[304]

---

[301] Ibid. at 2554.

[302] Tim England, "Racist Speech: A First Amendment Issue on College Campuses," Southwest Colloquium of the Association for Education in Journalism and Mass Communication, 1992.

[303] William Celis 3d, "Universities Reconsidering Bans on Hate Speech," *New York Times*, June 24, 1992, p. A11.

[304] England, op. cit. Cases discussed by him included *Doe v. University of Michigan*, 721 F.Supp. 852 (E.D.Mich.1989) and *The UWM Post v. Board of Regents, University of Wisconsin System*, 774 F.Supp. 1163 (E.D.Wis.1991).

More recently, universities have taken a look at practices that would avoid subjecting students to unexpected shocks from potentially upsetting content. These trigger warnings first arose on the Internet to warn visitors to sites that clicking on a link or scrolling would lead them to material that might affect them adversely. Some faculty use the warnings so that students can prepare themselves for the material so that they can more fully participate in classroom discussion. Some critics complain that students are being shielded from reality.

COMMUNITY EFFORTS TO PREVENT OFFENSIVE SPEECH AND CONDUCT

Two New York City firefighters and a police officer lost their challenge to being fired over a Labor Day parade appearance in which they evoked racial stereotypes.[305] The three float participants covered their faces in black lipstick and wore Afro wigs.[306] "The float itself featured two buckets of Kentucky Fried Chicken on the hood of a flatbed truck." One of the three clung to the back of the truck in a parody of the dragging death of James Byrd, Jr., an African-American man killed by three white men who dragged him behind a pickup truck.

The three lost their jobs following administrative hearings conducted by the police and fire departments. All three sued in federal court and the district court judge ruled for them. A panel of the Second Circuit Court of Appeals reversed. The Second Circuit found that the city's decision to terminate the three was constitutional. The three were fired because of the disruptive effects of their expressive activity on the ability of the police and fire departments to do their jobs.[307]

> Where a Government employee's job quintessentially involves public contact, the Government may take into account the public's perception of that employee's expressive acts in determining whether those acts are disruptive to the Government's operations.

Students may see a parallel to the right of the high school principal in Hazelwood who did not have to tolerate student expression that posed a risk of disruption of the educational mission of the high school.

The Second Circuit panel explained that terminations of public employees because of the disruption caused by their expressive activities would be legitimate as long as:[308]

> "(1) the employer's prediction of disruption is reasonable; (2) the potential disruptiveness is enough to outweigh the value of the

[305] *Locurto v. Giuliani*, 447 F.3d 159 (2d Cir. 2006).

[306] Ibid.

[307] Ibid. at 179.

[308] Ibid. at 173.

> speech; and (3) the employer took action against the employee based on this disruption and not in retaliation for the speech."

Those safeguards must be applied where government employees engage in expressive activities related to matters of public concern. Where employees are engaged in expression about private matters, the government has greater leeway as will be shown in the Tindle case below.

In a case with similar facts but a different outcome, the IOTA XI Chapter of Sigma Chi Fraternity at George Mason University won protection from university sanctions for its "ugly woman contest," charity fund-raiser, in which fraternity members dressed as caricatures of women.[309] One fraternity member was painted black and wore a dress, stuffed with pillows. His portrayal was described as an offensive caricature of a black woman.

Following the event, a number of students protested to the university administration that the skit had been sexist and racist. Shortly after that, the dean of students and the leaders of student government met and concluded that the fraternity, had created a "hostile learning environment" for women and blacks. The fraternity was suspended from a number of campus activities and ordered to set up an education program to deal with cultural differences.

The fraternity sued in federal court to overturn the sanctions and won its case at summary judgment on First Amendment grounds. The university appealed the judgment and the case made its way to the Fourth Circuit Court of Appeals where a three-judge panel affirmed the lower court.

While the Fourth Circuit Panel opinion gave no great credit to the fraternity's skit, describing it as "an exercise of teenage campus excess" and referring to its "sophomoric nature." Still, the panel concluded, that the performance constituted expressive entertainment that also conveyed a message to its audience.[310]

> What is evident is that the Fraternity's purposefully nonsensical treatment of sexual and racial themes was intended to impart a message that the University's concerns, in the Fraternity's view, should be treated humorously. From the Fraternity's conduct and the circumstances surrounding it, we have no difficulty in concluding that it intended to convey a message.

The panel declared that the university could not punish the fraternity's expressive conduct just because it disagreed with the message it conveyed.

---

309 *IOTA XI Chapter of Sigma Chi Fraternity v. George Mason University*, 993 F.2d 386 (4th Cir. 1993).

310 Ibid. at 392.

That is not to say that the racially insensitive practice of wearing blackface is protected in all cases. In *Tindle v. Caudell*, a white police officer lost a case in which he challenged a punishment for wearing blackface to a Halloween party at the Fraternal Order of Police Lodge.[311]

Officer Kevin Tindle was given a 30-day suspension by the Little Rock Police Department for his actions. Department policies prohibited officers from engaging in conduct that would result in justified criticism of the officer or department and also from ridiculing, mocking, taunting or deriding persons. Tindle sued, claiming the punishment violated his First Amendment rights.

Officer Tindle lost his challenge to the sanctions in federal district court and the case made its way to a three-judge panel of the Eighth Circuit Court of Appeals. That panel rejected Tindle's argument that the punishment violated his First Amendment right to wear the costume as a form of entertainment.

But the panel rejected the notion that mere entertainment was protected under the First Amendment. Tindle's actions contained no expressive intent, the panel concluded.[312]

> Tindle does not claim he intended to comment on any issue of interest to the public. He instead intended simply to entertain the other officers and their guests at the party by wearing an amusing costume. Amusing other guests at a private party with no showing of any intended message is not speech on a matter of public concern.

The panel then affirmed the lower court's ruling in favor of the police department and Tindle's punishment. So, where arguably offensive speech is considered an attempt to convey ideas, it receives protection under the First Amendment. At the same time, though, conduct that is illegal still can be punished by the state.

9. TAXATION

The mass media are constitutionally protected from discriminatory or punitive taxation.

Taxation has long been a fighting word to the press. Taxes on the press instituted in England were called "taxes on knowledge" because they raised the purchase price of pamphlets and other printed materials beyond the means of most persons. Taxation also came to be a hated symbol of control and oppression in American history. The British Stamp Act of 1765 imposed great hardships on printers in colonial America, taxing newspapers, advertisements, pamphlets and many legal documents and became a great rallying cry for colonists who resisted

[311] *Tindle v. Caudell*, 56 F.3d 966 (8th Cir. 1995).

[312] Ibid. at 970.

British authority.[313] A huge storm of protest arose in the colonies, reflected in angry writings in newspapers and pamphlets and, ultimately, in mobs which forced British stamp agents to resign. Faced with such furious opposition, Parliament repealed the Stamp Taxes as they affected printer-editors.

If American colonists hated the Stamp Act taxes and argued against them in terms of "freedom of the press," American memories also were very short. In 1785, only two years after the War of Independence officially ended, the state of Massachusetts passed a newspaper stamp tax.

Protests echoing the Stamp Act disturbances soon resounded from the Massachusetts newspapers.[314] Such protests quickly led to the repeal of the Massachusetts stamp tax on newspapers later in 1785, although the state's legislature soon enacted a tax on newspaper ads.[315] The advertising tax was repealed in 1788.[316]

Newspapers and other units of the mass media of communications are businesses. As such, the media are not immune from taxation just like other business enterprises, as long as the taxes fall with a more or less even hand upon the press as well as other businesses. *Discriminatory* or *punitive* taxation, however, raises quite different issues. The classic case in United States constitutional law occurred during the 1930s and involved the flamboyant Huey "Kingfish" Long, the political boss and governor of Louisiana who entertained dreams of someday becoming president. The Supreme Court decision in *Grosjean, Supervisor of Accounts of Louisiana v. American Press Co., Inc.*[317] effectively halted a Huey Long-instigated attempt to use a punitive tax to injure newspapers which opposed Long's political regime.

During the 1930s, Louisiana's larger daily newspapers were increasingly expressing opposition to Long's political machine. Louisiana's larger newspapers' sniping at Governor Long's dictatorial posturings soon brought about retaliation. The Louisiana legislature passed a special 2 percent license tax on the gross receipts of all newspapers, magazines, or periodicals having a circulation of more than 20,000 copies per week.[318] Of Louisiana's 163 newspapers, only 13 had circulations of more than 20,000 per week. Of these 13 newspapers to which the tax applied, 12 were opponents of Long's political machine.[319]

---

[313] Arthur M. Schlesinger, *Prelude to Independence: The Newspaper War on Britain, 1763–1776* (New York: Knopf, 1958), p. 68.

[314] *Massachusetts Centinel*, May 28, 1785.

[315] Ibid., July 6, July 30, 1785.

[316] Clyde Augustus Duniway, *Freedom of the Press in Massachusetts* (New York, 1906), p. 137.

[317] *Grosjean, Supervisor of Accounts of Louisiana v. American Press Co., Inc.*, 297 U.S. 233, 56 S.Ct. 444 (1936).

[318] Ibid. at 240, 445.

[319] J. Edward Gerald, *The Press and the Constitution* 1931–1947 (Minneapolis, University of Minnesota Press, 1948) p. 100; William A. Hachten, *The Supreme Court on Freedom of the*

This transparent attempt to silence newspaper critics was challenged in the courts by nine Louisiana newspaper publishers who produced the 13 newspapers which had circulations of more than 20,000 copies a week.

In declaring the Louisiana tax unconstitutional, a noted conservative—Justice George Sutherland—spoke for a unanimous Supreme Court. Justice Sutherland, a man not revered for his felicity of expression, may indeed have had some able assistance in writing what has come to be known as "Sutherland's great opinion in *Grosjean.*" It has been asserted that Sutherland's opinion included a proposed concurring opinion which had been drafted by the famed liberal Justice Benjamin Nathan Cardozo, and which the Court wished to add into Justice Sutherland's opinion.[320]

Whether assisted by Cardozo or not, the Sutherland opinion in Grosjean remains noteworthy. Justice Sutherland began with a historical overview of government-imposed dangers to freedom of expression, including reference to John Milton's 1644 "Appeal for the Liberty of Unlicensed Printing" and to the end of the licensing of the press in England in 1695. As Sutherland noted, "mere exemption from previous censorship was soon recognized as too narrow a view of the liberty of the press."[321]

Justice Sutherland asserted that if taxes had been the only issue, many of England's best men would not have risked their careers and their lives to fight against them. The issue in England for many years, however, involved discriminatory taxation designed to control the press and silence criticism of government. The *Grosjean* opinion added:[322]

> The framers of the First Amendment were familiar with the English struggle, which had then continued for nearly eighty years and was destined to go on for another sixty-five years, at the end of which time it culminated in a lasting abandonment of the obnoxious taxes. The framers were likewise familiar with the then recent [1785–1788] Massachusetts [stamp tax] episode * * *

Justice Sutherland rejected the State of Louisiana's argument that the English common law in force when the Constitution was adopted forbade only prior restraints on the press and said nothing about forbidding taxation.[323] In reply, Sutherland's opinion quoted from a great Nineteenth Century American constitutional scholar, Judge Thomas Cooley, and declared that Cooley had laid down the test to be applied.[324]

Press: Decisions and Dissents (Ames, Iowa: Iowa State University Press 1968) p. 77; *Grosjean v. American Press Co.*, 297 U.S. 233, 56 S.Ct. 444, 445 (1936).

320 Irving Brant, *The Bill of Rights: Its Origin and Meaning* (New York: Bobbs-Merrill, 1965), pp. 403–404.

321 *Grosjean v. American Press Co.*, 297 U.S. 233, 249, 56 S.Ct. 444, 449 (1936).

322 Ibid.

323 Ibid.

324 Ibid. at 249, 449, quoting 2 Cooley's *Constitutional Limitations* (8th ed.) p. 886.

> The evils to be prevented were not the censorship of the press merely, but any action of the government by means of which it might prevent such free and general discussion of public matters as seems absolutely essential to prepare the people for an intelligent exercise of their rights as citizens.

Application of this test led Justice Sutherland to rule that the Louisiana gross receipts tax on its larger newspapers was an unconstitutional abridgement of the First and Fourth Amendments. Sutherland declared:[325]

> It is not intended by anything we have said to suggest that the owners of newspapers are immune from any of the ordinary forms of taxation for support of the government. But this is not an ordinary form of tax, but one single in kind, with a long history of hostile misuse against the freedom of the press.
>
> * * *
>
> The tax here involved is bad not because it takes money from the pockets of the appellees. If that were all, a wholly different question would be presented. It is bad because, in the light of its history and of its present setting, it is seen to be a deliberate and calculated device in the guise of a tax to limit the circulation of information to which the public is entitled in virtue of the constitutional guaranties. A free press stands as one of the great interpreters between the government and the people. To allow it to be fettered is to fetter ourselves.

Despite these ringing words, it should be noted again that the communications media are not exempt from paying non-discriminatory general business taxes. A case in point involved the *Corona Daily Independent,* a California newspaper which challenged a $32-a-year business license tax imposed by the City of Corona. The newspaper, which had paid the tax in a number of previous years, in 1951 refused to pay the tax. The newspaper went to court, arguing that the tax violated freedom of the press as guaranteed by the First and Fourteenth Amendments. However, a California Appellate Court held:[326]

> There is ample authority to the effect that newspapers and the business of newspaper publication are not made exempt from the ordinary forms of taxes for the support of local government by the provisions of the First and Fourteenth Amendments.

---

[325] Ibid. at 25–251, 449. Accord: See *City of Baltimore v. A.S. Abell Co.*, 218 Md. 273, 145 A.2d 111, 119 (1958). It was held that Baltimore city ordinances imposing taxes on advertising media were unconstitutional in that they discriminatorily taxed newspapers and radio and television stations. About 90 percent of the impact of the taxes was on those businesses.

[326] *City of Corona v. Corona Daily Independent*, 115 Cal.App.2d 382, 252 P.2d 56 (1953), certiorari denied 346 U.S. 833, 74 S.Ct. 2 (1953). See also *Giragi v. Moore*, 49 Ariz. 74, 64 P.2d 819 (1937) (general sales tax law placing a one per cent tax upon businesses' sales or gross income not unconstitutional as applied to newspapers); *Arizona Publishing Co. v. O'Neil*, 22 F.Supp. 117 (D.Ariz.1938), affirmed 304 U.S. 543, 58 S.Ct. 950 (1938).

Grosjean v. American Press Co. remains the leading case for the proposition that the mass media are constitutionally protected from discriminatory or punitive taxation. The *Grosjean* case, seen earlier, dealt with a garish fact situation, a transparent attempt by Louisiana Governor Huey "Kingfish" Long and his allies to silence newspaper critics.

Unlike the *Grosjean* situation, the State of Minnesota was operating out of more defensible motives during the 1970s when it enacted a "use tax" on paper and ink consumed applicable to newspapers. This apparently was only a revenue measure, not an attempt to control or to punish the press. Even so, the Supreme Court of the United States voided the tax by an 8–1 margin. The tax was held unconstitutional because it singled out the press for special treatment.

"Use taxes" are imposed by states to discourage their citizens from purchasing items in other states which have lower sales taxes. Minnesota's newspapers were exempted from use taxes until 1971, when the state began taxing the cost of paper and ink used in producing a publication.[327] In 1974, another change in the tax law exempted a publication's first $100,000 of ink and paper consumed from the 4 percent use tax.[328]

The $100,000 exemption meant that only the largest of Minnesota's publishers were liable to pay the tax. Only 11 publishers, producing 14 of the state's 388 paid-circulation newspapers, had to pay the tax in 1974. The Minneapolis Star and Tribune Company was the major revenue source from the tax. Of $893,355 collected in 1974, $608,634 was paid by the *Star* and *Tribune*.[329]

The Star and Tribune Company sued, asking a refund of the use taxes paid from January 1, 1974, to May 31, 1975. The company contended that the use tax violated freedom of the press and equal protection of the laws as guaranteed by the First and Fourteenth Amendments.[330] The Minnesota Supreme Court ruled the use tax constitutional,[331] and the Supreme Court of the United States then noted probable jurisdiction.[332]

Justice Sandra Day O'Connor wrote for an 8–1 Supreme Court in declaring the Minnesota tax unconstitutional on its face because it singled out publications for unique treatment under the state's law. She declared that there is evidence that differential taxation of the press

[327] Minn.Stat.Ann. §§ 297A.14, 287A.25i.

[328] Minn.Stat.Ann. § 297A.14.

[329] *Minneapolis Star and Tribune Co. v. Minnesota Commissioner of Revenue*, 460 U.S. 575, 103 S.Ct. 1365, 1368 (1983).

[330] Ibid.

[331] *Minneapolis Star and Tribune Co. v. Commissioner of Revenue*, 314 N.W.2d 201 (Minn.1981).

[332] *Minneapolis Star and Tribune Co. v. Minnesota Commissioner of Revenue*, 457 U.S. 1130, 102 S.Ct. 2955 (1982).

would have troubled the Framers of the First Amendment. "A power to tax differentially, as opposed to a power to tax generally, gives government a powerful weapon against the taxpayer selected."[333] Her opinion also suggested the threat of burdensome taxes might operate as a form of censorship, making the press wary of publishing the critical comments which often allow it to serve as an important restraint on government.

In *Leathers v. Medlock*, the Supreme Court took up the kind of issue that could make it the High Court of Taxation for some years. In *Leathers,* the Court framed the issue as "whether the First Amendment prevents a state from imposing its sales tax on only selected segments of the media." This case involved a complaint by Arkansas cable TV operators that a state sales tax applied to cable TV but excluded or exempted the media categories of newspapers, magazines and satellite broadcast services.

The U.S. Supreme Court held that cable operators' rights were not violated because the Arkansas tax did not apply just to the media but was a tax generally applicable to businesses. Furthermore, unlike the Minnesota use tax on print and ink, applying to only 14 of 388 newspapers in that state, the Arkansas tax applied to all 100 cable TV operations in the state.[334]

In California, Sacramento Cable Television (SCT) and a cable subscriber challenged a city ordinance including cable TV under a city utility user's tax along with gas, electric, and telephone services. The California Court of Appeals, Third Circuit, agreed with the prevailing view that cable TV is speech protected by the First Amendment. Even so, that appellate court held it constitutional for Sacramento to tax cable TV because cable logically could be categorized along with other utilities.[335]

What of a tax applied to some publications but not others on the basis of their content? In *Florida Department of Revenue v. Magazine Publishers of America* (1992), the Florida Supreme Court ruled that a state sales tax imposed upon publications based on their content did not pass muster under the First Amendment.

The Florida Supreme Court found that the state's sales tax was not "content neutral" in exempting some publications while allowing others to be taxed. Although some of the requirements publications had to meet to be termed "newspapers" were content-neutral (usually published weekly or daily, intended for general circulation to the public), one requirement was a problem. One provision called for the Department of

---

[333] Ibid. at 586, 1372. Justice—later Chief Justice William H. Rehnquist was the sole dissenter.

[334] *Leathers v. Medlock*, 499 U.S. 439, 111 S.Ct. 1438, 1443 (1991).

[335] *Sacramento Cable Television v. Sacramento*, 234 Cal.App.3d 232, 286 Cal.Rptr. 470 (1991). See also *Cox Cable Hampton Roads, Inc. v. Norfolk*, 242 Va. 394, 410 S.E.2d 652 (1991), holding that although cable TV may be taxed as a utility, the case should be returned to the trial court to consider Cox Cable's equal protection claim.

Revenue to determine whether publications—to be "newspapers" and thus exempt from the sales tax—contain " 'reports of current events and matters of general interest which appeal to a wide spectrum of the general public.' "[336] That criterion added up to an impermissible content-based judgment which invalidated the Florida tax exemption of newspapers under the First Amendment.

The magazine publishers—who hoped to join newspaper publishers in Florida in a tax exemption—were disappointed. Ironically, instead of invalidating the tax on magazines, the Florida Supreme Court invalidated the newspapers' exemption.

The basic rule remains: the press may not be singled out for "differential treatment" when being taxed. That differential treatment can be targeting some members of a particular category of media, as in the newspaper cases where larger papers were subject to the tax while smaller newspapers were not; targeting publications in order to punish them or to deter them from publishing stories critical of the government; or applying a tax (or exemption) on the basis of content. This, of course, does not mean the press will pay less in taxes than other kinds of businesses.

TAXING THE INTERNET: STATE V. FEDERAL INTERESTS

In the late 1990s, Congress passed the Internet Tax Freedom Act. The law barred state taxes on virtually all of the Internet and was passed in order to help nurture the growing communication medium. The ban on taxes is focused on taxes on internet connections so that companies and consumers are not discouraged from going online.

On the other hand, e-commerce continues to rise and the business being conducted online is attractive to states looking to maintain their revenues. In November 2010, the Census Bureau reported that e-commerce continued to rise. For the third quarter of 2010, the Census Department estimated that e-commerce totaled $41.5 billion or roughly 4 percent of total U.S. retail sales.[337] The Internet Tax Freedom Act expired in 2014.

States are free to impose use tax on their residents' Internet purchases. Online retailers are obligated to collect and remit the taxes to the states that have instituted the tax. More than half the states now do so.

---

[336] *Department of Revenue v. Magazine Publishers of America*, 604 So.2d 459 (Fla.1992).

[337] "Quarterly retail e-commerce sales 3rd quarter 2010," *U.S. Census Bureau News*, Nov. 17, 2010.

CHAPTER 3

TESTING THE BOUNDARIES OF CONSTITUTIONAL PROTECTION: FIGHTING WORDS, INCITEMENT/OUTRAGE AND OBSCENITY

They're not people from polite society, and you probably wouldn't invite them to have lunch with you. That said, let's consider some of the men and women who have made law with words that courts in the United States have ruled may be forbidden or punished. Examples considered in this chapter include two troublesome (and often hard to define) categories of words:

(1) Fighting Words and Incitement

(2) Obscenity

10. FIGHTING WORDS AND INCITEMENT

In *Chaplinsky v. New Hampshire*,[1] the Supreme Court of the United States held that words likely to injure by being communicated or that result in violence are harmful and so bereft of value that saying or publishing them may, constitutionally, lead to punishment. And, although the *Chaplinsky* case has much less impact today, it is instructive when looking speech that lies on or outside the boundaries of First Amendment protections. The case starts with Walter Chaplinsky a Jehovah's Witness who was distributing

[1] *Chaplinsky v. New Hampshire*, 315 U.S. 568, 62 S.Ct. 766 (1942).

literature on the streets of Rochester, N.H., one Saturday afternoon.[2]

An aside: The Jehovah's Witnesses have been involved in a number of Supreme Court cases centering on First Amendment rights. From *Lovell v. City of Griffith,*[3] through *Watchtower Society*[4], Witnesses have ignored statutes and ordinances as they honored their religious principles. Justice Robert H. Jackson described them when he wrote[5], "The Witnesses are an unincorporated body teaching that the obligation imposed by law of God is superior to that of laws enacted by temporal government."

The Witnesses denounced other religion, calling them "rackets." They were disliked and public anger translated into acts of violence after they refused to pledge allegiance.[6]

> In 1935, the movement's leadership had declared saluting the flag a form of idolatry, an edict that transformed an obscure sect into a widely known pariah. The public's contempt took on a sharper, more paranoid edge during the Second World War. Amid the patriotic fervor, Jehovah's Witnesses were denounced as cowards or traitors. Physical attacks upon believers were not uncommon.

In this environment Walter Chaplinsky went to Rochester, N.H. to spread the word of Jehovah. City Marshal James Bowering encountered Chaplinsky one day and warned him that his activities would cause problems. A month later, Chaplinsky stood on a street corner offering pamphlets to passers by and playing records of Witness speeches. The passers by were not amused and a crowd gathered.[7]

> Some time later, a disturbance occurred and the traffic officer on duty at the busy intersection started with Chaplinsky for the police station, but did not inform him that he was under arrest or that he was going to be arrested. On the way they encountered Marshal Bowering who had been advised that a riot was under way and was therefore hurrying to the scene. Bowering repeated his earlier warning to Chaplinsky who then addressed to Bowering the words set forth in the complaint.

---

[2] Ibid. at 569.

[3] *Lovell v. City of Griffin*, 303 U.S. 444, 58 S.Ct. 666, 82 L.Ed. 949 (1938).

[4] *Watchtower Bible and Tract Society of New York, Inc. v. Village of Stratton* 536 U.S. 150, 122 S.Ct. 2080, 153 L.Ed.2d 205 (2002).

[5] *West Virginia State Board of Education v. Barnette*, 319 U.S. 624, 629, 63 S.Ct. 1178, 1181 (1943).

[6] Jelani Cobb, "Innocence of Americans," *New Yorker*, Sept. 17, 2012. http://www.newyorker.com/news/news-desk/innocence-of-americans.

[7] *Chaplinsky v. New Hampshire*, 315 U.S. 568, 570, 62 S.Ct. 766, 768 (1942).

Bowering reported that Chaplinsky called him, a "God-damned racketeer and a damned fascist." Chaplinsky testified at trial that Bowering had begun the name calling.[8]

> He testified that when he met Bowering, he asked him to arrest the ones responsible for the disturbance. In reply Bowering cursed him and told him to come along. Appellant admitted that he said the words charged in the complaint with the exception of the name of the Deity.

Those words, with or without the reference to the Deity, were enough to send Chaplinsky to municipal court and eventually to the United States Supreme Court. Chaplinsky was convicted of violating a state law, which essentially criminalized speaking harsh words to another.[9]

The Court found that Chaplinsky's utterance constituted "fighting words." Justice Frank Murphy's opinion said that "fighting words" were those that could be expected to cause injury to the recipient and also cause violence. In a famous statement the Justice Murphy outlined the kinds of words which are not protected by the First Amendment:[10]

> There are certain well-defined and narrowly limited classes of speech, the prevention and punishment of which have never been thought to raise any Constitutional problems. These include the lewd and obscene, the profane, the libelous and insulting or "fighting" words—those which by their very utterance inflict injury or tend to incite an immediate breach of the peace. * * * [Such words] are of such slight social value that any benefit that may be derived from them is clearly outweighed by the social interest in order and morality.

In 1971, the Supreme Court revisited the concept at the heart of *Chaplinsky* in *Cohen v. California*.[11] In *Cohen*, Paul Robert Cohen was convicted of disturbing the peace when he wore a jacket expressing his opposition to the Vietnam War and the draft. The jacket had the sentiment, "Fuck the Draft" emblazoned on it. Cohen was arrested and charged with disturbing the peace when he wore the jacket to the Los Angeles County Courthouse. California had a statute similar to the one in New Hampshire.[12]

> Appellant was convicted of violating that part of Cal. Penal Code S 415 which prohibits 'maliciously and willfully disturb(ing) the peace or quiet of any neighborhood or person * * * by * * *

---

[8] Ibid.

[9] *Chaplinsky v. New Hampshire*, 315 U.S. 568, 569, 62 S.Ct. 766 (1942). New Hampshire law made it a crime to, " * * * address any offensive, derisive or annoying word to any other person who is lawfully in any street or other public place, nor call him by any offensive or derisive name, nor make any noise or exclamation in his presence and hearing with intent to deride, offend or annoy him, or to prevent him from pursuing his lawful business or occupation."

[10] Ibid. at 568, 766.

[11] *Cohen v. California*, 403 U.S. 15, 91 S.Ct. 1780 (1971).

[12] Ibid. at 15, 1783.

> offensive conduct,' for wearing a jacket bearing the words 'Fuck the Draft' in a corridor of the Los Angeles Courthouse. The Court of Appeal held that 'offensive conduct' means 'behavior which has a tendency to provoke others to acts of violence or to in turn disturb the peace,' and affirmed the conviction.

Cohen appealed his conviction and it was sustained by the California Court of Appeals. In language similar to that in *Chaplinsky*, the California court reasoned that,[13]

> It was certainly reasonably foreseeable that such conduct might cause others to rise up to commit a violent act against the person of the defendant or attempt to forceably remove his jacket. The fact that the police intervened and that the defendant was arrested before violence occurred does not make his conduct any the less provocative. We think it also a reasonable inference from the time and place of defendant's act that he intended to provoke disorder.
>
> It is our conclusion that the defendant's acts constituted the type of offensive conduct prohibited by sec. 415 in that it had a tendency to incite others to violent behavior or to disturb the peace.

But the Supreme Court disagreed. Justice John Marshal Harlan, writing for the 5–4 majority noted that no one had, in fact, tried to remove Cohen's jacket. Justice Harlan said that while the word that Cohen used was generally used in a provocative manner,[14]

> [I]n this instance it was clearly not 'directed to the person of the hearer.' *Cantwell v. Connecticut*, 310 U.S. 296, 309, 60 S.Ct. 900, 906, 84 L.Ed. 1213 (1940). No individual actually or likely to be present could reasonably have regarded the words on appellant's jacket as a direct personal insult. Nor do we have here an instance of the exercise of the State's police power to prevent a speaker from intentionally provoking a given group to hostile reaction.

Justice Harlan summarized California's position as a claim that the state had the power to punish speech on the grounds that it might provoke disturbance. That, Justice Harlan wrote, was not sufficient to overcome the First Amendment especially on the record of the case.[15]

> We have been shown no evidence that substantial numbers of citizens are standing ready to strike out physically at whoever may assault their sensibilities with execrations like that uttered by Cohen. There may be some persons about with such lawless and violent proclivities, but that is an insufficient base upon

---

[13] *People v. Cohen*, 1 Cal.App.3d 94, 99–100, 81 Cal.Rptr. 503, 506 (Cal.App. 2 Dist. Oct 22, 1969).

[14] *Cohen v. California*, 403 U.S. 15, 20, 91 S.Ct. 1780, 1785–1786 (1971).

[15] Ibid. at 23, 1787.

> which to erect, consistently with constitutional values, a governmental power to force persons who wish to ventilate their dissident views into avoiding particular forms of expression.

In *Texas v, Johnson*[16], the Court reinforced the point made in Cohen: no one had reacted violently. The *Johnson* case arose from the conviction of Gregor Lee Johnson for burning an American flag during demonstrations against President Ronald Reagan at the Republican National Convention in 1984. Johnson was convicted of,[17] "desecration of a venerated object in violation of Tex.Penal Code Ann. § 42.09(a)(3) (1989)."

A Texas appellate court had reversed the conviction and Texas appealed the reversal to the Supreme Court. Justice William Brennan wrote the majority opinion that said that the government could not simply punish expression (here expressive conduct) by declaring a flag or any other thing and making it a crime to desecrate it. Texas' lawyers also said the statute was intended to prevent breaches of the peace.

But, there had been no immediate breaches of the peace, Justice Brennan wrote.[18]

> Texas claims that its interest in preventing breaches of the peace justifies Johnson's conviction for flag desecration. However, no disturbance of the peace actually occurred or threatened to occur because of Johnson's burning of the flag. Although the State stresses the disruptive behavior of the protestors during their march toward City Hall, Brief for Petitioner 34–36, it admits that "no actual breach of the peace occurred at the time of the flagburning or in response to the flagburning." Id., at 34. The State's emphasis on the protestors' disorderly actions prior to arriving at City Hall is not only somewhat surprising given that no charges were brought on the basis of this conduct, but it also fails to show that a disturbance of the peace was a likely reaction to Johnson's conduct.

Johnson repeated his flag burning protest outside the 2016 Republican Convention in Cleveland, Ohio. Police officers used fire extinguishers to put out the burning flag and Johnson claimed they pushed him to the ground during the protest. Johnson was charged with misdemeanor assault after two people claimed they had been burned in the incident. The charges were later dropped, and the judge dismissed charges against 15 other people arrested at the protest. "[T]hree decades after the court invalidated prohibitions on flag desecration in 48 states, the city of Cleveland agreed to pay Mr. Johnson $225,000 to settle his

---

16 *Texas v. Johnson*, 491 U.S. 397, 109 S.Ct. 2533 (1989).

17 Ibid. at 400, 2537.

18 Ibid. at 408, 2541–2542.

claim that officers retaliated against him for an exercise of free expression."[19]

In both the *Cohen* and *Johnson* cases, the courts looked only at the reaction to the expression. Where there were no fights or other breaches of the peace, there were no "fighting words." The Courts essentially ignored Justice Murphy's second reason for finding that "fighting words" had no First Amendment value. Murphy had written that those words inflicted injury on the person to whom the words were directed.

Considering the Courts' analysis, observers of contemporary society may wonder what words would constitute "fighting words." Popular culture has employed every vulgarity, epithet and expletive without violence. It must be remembered that the breach of the peace must be considered from the point of view of the reasonable person hearing the words. It is true that the words "please excuse me" said to a drunk patron of a bar can lead to a punch in the nose, but the especially sensitive or the very drunk are not the true test of the likely breach of the peace test of words. As Justice Harlan wrote, the existence of some people who exhibit "lawless and violent proclivities"[20] are not sufficient to prove that some words cause a breach of the peace.

"INCITEMENT" AND SOLDIER OF FORTUNE MAGAZINE

A different kind of media liability results from "incitement." Where the media are concerned, that means bringing a lawsuit against the publishers of a story, movie, song or any other medium of popular expression, and blaming that media content for some harmful outcome.

Incitement at its most basic is communication intended to encourage other to take lawless action, and calculated or likely to bring about imminent harm the State has the substantive power to prevent. It has the mens rea or mental element in the intent to encourage others and the actus reus, the action of communicating the encouragement. In the media context, incitement is raised where something is published that a plaintiff argues has resulted in a real harm because of the publication.

An early example of an incitement suit directed against a publisher *Eimann v. Soldier of Fortune Magazine, Inc.*, where a 1988 jury award of $9.4 million ($7.2 million in punitive damages) was made against the magazine. A jury ordered the civil damage award, concluding that *Soldier of Fortune's* publication of a classified advertisement resulted in a murder for hire. The classified ad by John Wayne Hearn offered his services as a Vietnam veteran, a weapons specialist who knew jungle warfare, to perform "high risk assignments." Robert Black saw the ad and contacted Hearn, ultimately paying him $10,000 to kill Sandra Black, Robert's wife. Hearn committed the murder, was caught and is

[19] Nicholas Bogel-Burroughts, "Cleveland Settles 2016 Suit With Flag Burner Who Set Free-Speech Precedent in 1989", *New York Times*, June, 15, 2019.

[20] *Cohen v. California*, 403 U.S. 15, 23, 91 S.Ct. 1780, 1787 (1971).

serving several life terms for shooting Sandra Black to death in her home in Bryan, Texas. Robert Black was sentenced to death.

This case's outcome led *Editor & Publisher*, a trade journal for the newspaper industry, to call for a reversal of the huge civil damage verdict. "The Texas decision," *Editor & Publisher* said, "would mean that a reader with a grudge against a publication could bring suit claiming damages for ads believed to be untruthful or misleading unless the publisher investigated every advertising claim."[21]

Soldier of Fortune avoided liability in the case, because the Fifth Circuit Court of Appeals concluded that Hearn's advertisement was innocuously worded and that the magazine, therefore, had no duty to refuse to publish it.[22] Although the ad allowed Robert Black to connect with Hearn, *Soldier of Fortune* was not responsible. The ad it carried did not on its face suggest that a contract killing would take place.

BRAUN V. SOLDIER OF FORTUNE MAGAZINE (1992)

In a 1991 decision, however, an Alabama federal court found *Soldier of Fortune* liable for damages totaling $4,375,000 in another incitement case. In *Braun v. Soldier of Fortune*, brothers Michael and Ian Braun sued the magazine for its involvement in the contract murder of their father and wounding of Michael.

Richard Braun was in business with Bruce Gastwirth. Gastwirth decided to terminate the partnership and he began to look for someone who would kill for money. He found a classified ad in *Soldier of Fortune*. It read: "GUN FOR HIRE: 37-year-old professional mercenary desires jobs. Vietnam Veteran. Discreet and very private. Body guard, courier, and other special skills. All jobs considered."

Richard Savage placed the classified advertisement in *Soldier of Fortune* in 1985. Initially, the ad drew interest from men who wanted to become contract killers.[23]

> In addition to calls from young would-be soldiers of fortune, Savage got countless calls from people wanting everything from surveillance work to murder. They seemed to come from all walks of life. The common denominator was that they wanted someone followed, beaten up or killed a husband, a lover, a business competitor.

Sean Trevor Doutre, calling himself Peter Tosh Marley, saw Savage's ad and contacted him seeking work as a contract killer. He went

---

[21] "Responsibility for ad content," *Editor & Publisher*, March 12, 1988.

[22] *Eimann v. Soldier of Fortune Magazine, Inc.*, 880 F.2d 830 (5th Cir.1989), 16 Med.L.Rptr. 2148, 2152.

[23] Rowland Stitler, " 'til Death Do Us Part A Rude Awakening Anita Spearman Thought They Had Their Whole Lives Ahead Of Them. Her Husband Had Other Plans. . . . ." *Orlando Sentinel*, April 12, 1987. http://articles.orlandosentinel.com/1987-04-12/news/0120220111_1_spearman-doutre-palm-beach.

to work for Savage at his strip club near Knoxville, Tenn., as a bouncer after Savage interviewed him. Doutre eventually would commit two contract killings that Savage arranged after being contacted through the ad.

Gastwirth contacted Savage and hired him to kill Braun. Doutre got the assignment and on Aug. 26, 1985 carried it out. As Richard Braun and his 16-year-old son Michael drove from their suburban Atlanta home, Doutre stepped in front of the car and fired several shots with a MAC-11 automatic pistol. Braun and his son rolled out of the car on opposite sides. Doutre stepped up and fired two shots into Richard Braun's head. Doutre then pointed the gun at Michael, but did not fire. Instead, Doutre put his finger to his lips, signaling Michael to be quiet, and ran into the woods. Savage, Doutre and Gastwirth were caught and convicted of conspiracy in the murder and shooting.

The *Braun* court distinguished Savage's *Soldier of Fortune* ad from the classified ad involved in the *Eimann* case discussed above, refusing to grant the magazine a summary judgment, holding that the advertisement carrying phrases such as "Gun for Hire" and "All jobs considered" was far more explicit than the "innocuous" language of the ad in the *Eimann* case. The court held that the *Soldier of Fortune* ad had harmed the Braun family.[24]

The U.S. Court of Appeals, 11th Circuit, allowed the jury verdict to stand, voting 2–1 that a standard of legal duty may be set for publishers. Advertisements should not be published that expose the public to a substantial danger of harm.[25]

> We agree with the district court that "the language of this advertisement is such that, even though couched in terms not explicitly offering criminal services, the publisher could recognize the offer of criminal activity as readily as its readers obviously did." * * *

For the most part, however, outcomes of incitement cases against the media favor defendants. There are some exceptions.

HIT MAN MANUAL CROSSES THE LINE BETWEEN MERE ADVOCACY AND INCITEMENT

James Perry did some research. He purchased two books published by Paladin Enterprises ("*Hit Man: A Technical Manual for Independent Contractors*" and "*How to Make a Disposable Silencer*") as he prepared to go into the killing-for-hire business.

In 1992, Perry was contacted by Lawrence Horn. Horn wanted to get his hands on a $2 million settlement that his 8-year-old son, Trevor, had

[24] Ibid. at 1729.

[25] *Braun v. Soldier of Fortune Magazine*, 968 F.2d 1110, 1121 (11th Cir.1992), 20 Med.L.Rptr. 1777, 1786. The Supreme Court denied certiorari. "See High Court Shuns Two Free Speech Cases," *New York Times*, Jan. 12, 1993, p. A9.

been awarded for injuries that left him a quadriplegic. Horn's ex-wife Mildred had custody of their son. Perry killed Mildred and Trevor Horn and Trevor's nurse Janice Saunders using an AR-7. He had modified the rifle using instructions from the two books.[26] Perry followed a number of the instructions from the two books but despite his best efforts, police arrested him. Both Perry and Horn were convicted of murder and sentenced to life in prison without parole.

Mildred Horn's family and the survivors of Janice Saunders sued Paladin arguing that the publisher aided and abetted Perry and Horn in the commission of the murders. District Court Judge Williams expressed loathing toward the books involved, finding that Paladin engaged in a marketing strategy to assist criminals. Even so, he found that First Amendment principles commanded granting a summary judgment to Paladin Enterprises.

The judge noted that several classes of speech receive limited or no protection under the First Amendment. He listed obscenity, fighting words, libel, commercial speech, and "words likely to incite imminent lawless action." The court ruled that the books published by Paladin Enterprises did not fit these categories and, further, that they were not actionable incitement to unlawful activity.[27]

The Fourth Circuit reversed the grant of summary judgment in Paladin's favor and sent the case back for trial. The Circuit Court panel said that the jury could judge whether Paladin had the required intent for a finding of liability.[28]

> Paladin has stipulated that it provided its assistance to Perry with both the knowledge and the intent that the book would immediately be used by criminals and would-be criminals in the solicitation, planning, and commission of murder and murder for hire, and even absent the stipulations, a jury could reasonably find such specific intent.

The 4th Circuit dealt with the distinction drawn by the district court that *Hit Man* did not amount to a call to action and was, instead, within the category of speech that was a mere teaching of the abstract idea of murder for hire. The distinction between advocacy of action and abstract philosophy came into play in the *Yates* and *Brandenburg* cases from Chap. 2.[29] The 4th Circuit said:

> Paladin assisted Perry through the quintessential speech act of providing Perry with detailed factual instructions on how to prepare for, commit, and cover up his murders, instructions

---

[26] *Rice v. Paladin Enterprises, Inc.*, 940 F.Supp. 836 (D.Md.1996).

[27] Ibid. at 844–848, 2187–2189, citing key cases discussed elsewhere in this chapter of Law of Mass Communications, 9th ed.: *Miller v. California* (obscenity), 413 U.S. 15, 93 S.Ct. 2607 (1973) and *Brandenburg v. Ohio*, 395 U.S. 444, 89 S.Ct. 1827 (1969) (incitement to imminent lawbreaking).

[28] *Rice v. Paladin*, 128 F.3d 233, 248 (4th Cir.1997).

[29] Ibid. at 266.

> which themselves embody not so much as a hint of the theoretical advocacy of principles divorced from action that is the hallmark of protected speech.

Paladin sought review by the Supreme Court but was rejected in 1998.[30] Faced with the prospect of another trial, Paladin settled with the families of Janice Saunders and Mildred Horn for an amount believed to be in the multi-million dollar range.

The 4th Circuit distinguished *Hit Man* from so-called copycat cases where criminal conduct in fictional movies, television shows, books and magazines are mimicked in real life (Discussed later in this section). The producers of such entertainment would avoid liability because there would be no evidence that they intended to promote criminal conduct.

MICHELLE CARTER CONVICTED OF INVOLUNTARY MANSLAUGHTER FOR TEXTS URGING BOYFRIEND TO COMMIT SUICIDE (2018)

A Massachusetts' court found that cyber bullying is not protected by the First Amendment. "In 2014, when Michelle Carter was 17 years old, she encouraged her 18-year-old boyfriend Conrad Roy III to kill himself both in days leading up to his death and as he was attempting suicide."[31]

Carter was convicted of involuntary manslaughter in a Massachusetts juvenile court.[32] Appealing her conviction all the way to the Supreme Judicial Court of Massachusetts, Carter argued that her conviction of involuntary manslaughter violated her right of free speech under the First Amendment and article 16 of the Massachusetts Declaration of Rights.[33] The court disagreed stating:

> As the Supreme Court has explained, "From 1791 to the present . . . the First Amendment has permitted restrictions upon the content of speech in a few limited areas . . . which have never been thought to raise any constitutional problems," including "speech integral to criminal conduct" (quotations and citations omitted). We do not apply the narrow tailoring required by strict scrutiny in these contexts but rather determine whether the speech at issue falls within these "well-defined and narrowly limited classes of speech" (quotation and citation omitted). Thus, there is nothing in the prosecution or conviction of the

---

[30] *Paladin v. Rice*, 523 U.S. 1074, 118 S.Ct. 1515 (1998).

[31] Ephrat Livni, *The Teen Convicted in a Controversial Suicide Texting Case has Appealed to the US Supreme Court*, QZ.com (2019), *available at* https://qz.com/1665616/teen-whose-texts-urged-boyfriend-to-suicide-appeals-to-supreme-court/.

[32] Lawrence Hurley, "U.S. Supreme Court Rejects Woman's Appeal in Teen Texting Suicide Case," *Reuters*, Jan. 13, 2020.

[33] *Commonwealth v. Carter*, 481 Mass. 352, 365–66, 115 N.E.3d 559, 2019 Mass. LEXIS 83, 2019 WL 453373 (Supreme Judicial Court of Massachusetts February 6, 2019, Decided), *available at* https://advance-lexis-com.proxy.lib.utk.edu/api/document?collection=cases&id=urn:contentItem:5VBY-YF11-DY89-M35D-00000-00&context=1516831.

> defendant * * * to suggest that the First Amendment has been violated in any way. The only verbal conduct punished as involuntary manslaughter has been the wanton or reckless pressuring of a vulnerable person to commit suicide, overpowering that person's will to live and resulting in that person's death. We are therefore not punishing words alone, as the defendant claims, but reckless or wanton words causing death. The speech at issue is thus integral to a course of criminal conduct and thus does not raise any constitutional problem[34]

The U.S. Supreme Court refused to hear her appeal and left in place the involuntary manslaughter conviction that drew attention to cyber bullying.[35]

3D-PRINTED GUNS: FIRST AMENDMENT RIGHTS VERSUS FIREARM REGULATIONS

In 2013, Cody Wilson, founder of the Texas-based company Defense Distributed, manufactured the first 3D-printed hand gun and posted blueprints for it on the Internet.[36] Shortly thereafter the State Department demanded that he remove the designs from his website because it could put unregulated and difficult to detect guns in the wrong hands.

The State Department, under the Obama administration, argued that the company violated an arms export law.[37] Wilson sue the State department over its demands that he remove the blueprints from the web. The State Department, under the Trump administration, reversed course in June 2018 and entered into an agreement permitting Wilson to publish his firearms blueprints online.[38] Attorneys General for 19 states and the District of Columbia filed a lawsuit seeking to invalidate a "settlement that had been negotiated quietly between the federal government and Defense Distributed" because the "State Department failed to consider the national security implications of deregulation in light of the unique properties of untraceable, undetectable, 3D-printable plastic firearms."[39] The suit claimed the agreement violated the 10th Amendment by eroding the states' police powers. Defense Distributed argued that the state violated the First Amendment by restricting what it can publish.

Judge Robert S. Lasnik, of the U.S. District Court for the Western District of Washington, found that even though Defense Distributed

---

[34] Ibid at 367–68.

[35] Hurley, op. cit.

[36] Deanna Paul, "Federal Judge Blocks Publication of 3-D Printed Gun Blueprints," *Washington Post*, August 27, 2018.

[37] Erik Larson & Bloomberg, "Are Blueprints for 3D-Printed Guns Protected by the Constitution? A U.S. Judge Is Considering the Question," *Fortune*, August 27, 2019.

[38] Paul, op. cit.

[39] Larson, op. cit.

argued that the prohibition from posting the files constituted a prior restraint that is presumed to be unconstitutional, and that any regulation should be subject to strict scrutiny, found that the First Amendment issue was not relevant because the State Department acted in an arbitrary and capricious manner when it issued a temporary modification to the arms act and entered into an agreement with Defense Distributed.[40] Lasnik found that the procedure the State Department followed in modifying the arms export law was unlawful and vacated the agreement with Defense Distributed.[41]

LIABILITY IN POPULAR CULTURE

Even so, film maker Oliver Stone and Time Warner faced a civil suit for Stone's film "*Natural Born Killers*." The family of Patsy Ann Byers sued Time Warner, Stone and others for making and distributing the movie arguing that the film led a young man and woman to go on a shooting spree and shoot Byers, leaving her a paraplegic.

The case arose following the robbery of a convenience store in Ponchatoula, Louisiana, on March 8, 1995, in which Sarah Edmondson and Benjamin Darrus shot Byers. Edmondson and Darrus, were so obsessed with the movie that they started their own crime spree, emulating the two young killers in the film. Byers was their first victim. Byers and her family filed the suit claiming that Time Warner and the other defendants were responsible for Byers wounds. Byers, who died of cancer during the case, alleged that "the Warner defendants intended to incite viewers of the film to begin, shortly after viewing the film, crime sprees such as the one that led to the shooting of Patsy Byers." There have been more than a dozen murder cases in which "*Natural Born Killers*" has been cited as a factor. In the Byers case, the media have reported that Edmondson and Darrus watched the movie a half dozen times a day during their crime spree.[42]

But on March 12, 2001, a Louisiana judge dismissed the lawsuit saying that Byers' family had not established that there was enough evidence to show that Stone or Time Warner had intended to incite violence through the film.

Another "incitement" case which received substantial publicity was *Herceg v. Hustler*, in which a teenage boy died experimenting with "autoerotic asphyxiation" after he read about it in *Hustler* magazine. The

---

40 *State of Washington, et. al. v. Department of State, et.al.*, No. C18-1115RSL, at *23–24 2019 (W.D. Wash. Nov. 12, 2019).

41 Ibid at *25.

42 Frank Murray, "FTC adds ammo to lawsuits for deaths Lawyers say study hurts Hollywood," *Washington Times*, Sept. 13, 2000, A-section.

U.S. Court of Appeals, 5th Circuit, in 1987 reversed a damage award of nearly $200,000 against *Hustler*. There, the court said:[43]

> The constitutional protection accorded to the freedom of speech and of the press is not based on the naive belief that speech can do no harm but on the confidence that the benefits society reaps from the free flow and exchange of ideas outweighs the costs society endures by receiving reprehensible and dangerous ideas.

INCITEMENT AND ROCKERS OZZY OSBOURNE AND SLAYER

Rock star Ozzy Osbourne was sued by surviving family members of an adolescent who committed suicide after listening repeatedly to the song. The grieving relatives, however, were unable to collect damages from Osbourne because his lyrics in his song "Suicide Solution" were held to be entertainment. In any event, the survivors could not prove that Osbourne's music had been intended to cause suicide.

The band Slayer, described as a musical group performing in the death metal genre, was sued by David and Lisanne Pahler, the parents of a 15-year-old who was kidnaped, tortured, raped and murdered by three adolescent males.[44] The Pahlers also sued their daughter's killers. In their suit, the Pahlers contended that the three boys who victimized their daughter had been inspired by Slayer. The three said that they intended to form their own death metal band. "They believed that killing Elyse Pahler would advance their careers in death metal music and said their decision to murder her was influenced by Slayer music and lyrics."[45]

The Pahlers argued in their third amended complaint that the band and its promoters and distributor should be liable under California law that prohibits businesses from creating, producing and marketing indecent musical products to minors. They also had a claim for wrongful death against the recording industry.

The district court ruled that nothing in the California statute barred the marketing strategies used by Slayer and the recording industry. Further, the court said, "the content of Slayer compositions is protected by the First Amendment. Marketing unregulated, protected speech can never constitute an unlawful business practice."[46]

Citing *Brandenburg*, Judge E. Jeffrey Burke wrote "it must appear that the Slayer lyrics (1) were directed and intended to cause listeners to commit specific criminal acts; and (2) that they were likely to produce the

---

[43] *Herceg v. Hustler Magazine*, 814 F.2d 1017, 1019 (5th Cir.1987), 13 Med.L.Rptr. 2345. The quoted passage was used by the court in deciding the case discussed above, *Rice v. Paladin Enterprises*, 940 F.Supp. 836 (D.Md.1996).

[44] *Pahler v. Slayer*, 29 Med.L.Rptr 2627. This case, decided in the California Superior Court for San Luis Obispo County, was not reported in the California Reporter.

[45] Ibid. at 2627.

[46] Ibid.

violent acts urged by the speaker."[47] Judge Burke noted that the California Supreme Court had concluded that lyrics and poetry,[48]

> cannot be construed to contain the requisite "call to action" for the elementary reason that they simply are not intended to be and should not be read literally on their face, nor judged by a standard of prose oratory.

Judge Burke found the Slayer lyrics repulsive and profane but not incitement. He granted the defendants' motion to dismiss the Pahlers' claim because "Slayer lyrics cannot be found to have incited Elyse Pahler's murder, the music industry did not unlawfully aid and abet her killers."[49]

Even so, some media companies have taken steps to avoid inciting violence. YouTube banned video content that it believed incited violence.[50]

> "We realise it's not always obvious where we draw the line on content that's acceptable to upload," said YouTube in a blog post.
>
> "We've updated the community guidelines . . . included in the update are a few new things to steer clear of, like not directly inciting violence."

BEYOND INCITEMENT—DUTY OF CARE

In addition to finding liability where media defendants have been found to have "incited" others to commit violence, courts have had to deal with civil suits filed by survivors of violence "inspired" by media content. The theory advanced by plaintiffs is that a media defendant is at fault because its release of the content to the public created a risk of harm that was foreseeable and led to the harm. It is a long-accepted theory of negligent liability for the producers of dangerous products and for those who allow dangerous conditions to exist and create a risk for others. The theory is that the defendant had a duty not to create that risk and so must bear liability for the result if something bad happens.

An early media case involving such a claim arose over the killing of a Texas Highway Patrol officer in 1992. In *Davidson v. Time Warner,*[51] the family of Bill Davidson, a Texas Highway Patrol Officer, sued Time Warner and Tupac Amaru Shakur claiming that Shakur's *2Pacalypse Now* led to Davidson's death.

---

[47] Ibid. Citing *Hess v. Indiana*, 414 U.S. 105, 108–109, 94 S.Ct. 326 (1973); *McCollum v. CBS, Inc.*, 202 Cal.App.3d 989, 1000, 249 Cal.Rptr. 187 (1988).

[48] Ibid. *Citing McCollum v. CBS, Inc.*, 202 Cal.App.3d 989, 1002, 1000, 249 Cal.Rptr. 187 (1988).

[49] Ibid. at 2627.

[50] Mark Sweeney, "YouTube bans violent videos," *Guardian*, Sept. 12, 2008.

[51] *Davidson v. Time Warner*, 1997 WL 405907 (S.D.Tex.), 25 Media L. Rep. 1705. The case was not reported in F. Supp.

Trooper Davidson stopped Ronald Howard, driving a stolen car, on a traffic violation. Howard, who was listening to the Shakur's music, shot Davidson with a 9 millimeter Glock pistol. Howard claimed in his murder trial that listening to the music caused him to shoot Trooper Davidson.[52]

The Davidsons' suit claimed, among other things, that the defendants were liable because they had a duty not to release music that would cause injury or death. Such a duty would be predicated by an awareness of the risk of harm resulting from the public release of the album. The court explained that a finding of liability would rest on the outcome of a balancing test.[53]

> In determining whether to impose a duty we are to consider the risk, foreseeability, and likelihood of injury weighed against the social utility of the actor's conduct, the magnitude of the burden of guarding against the injury and the consequences of placing that burden on the actor.

The court did not agree that either Time Warner or Shakur owed a duty of care. For one thing, the Davidson shooting was an isolated case. The court cited the *Eimann* case in concluding that the killing was not foreseeable by the defendants.[54]

> In *Eimann*, the plaintiff presented evidence that at least seven of the magazine's classified ads were tied to criminal activity. By contrast, the Davidsons present no evidence that *2Pacalypse Now* has been the source of "music-inspired crime"; after more than 400,000 sales of *2Pacalypse Now*, the case at bar is the only one alleging violence after listening to Shakur's virulent music. Thus, the probability of harm is very low.

The Davidsons also included an incitement claim arguing that Shakur's music caused Howard to kill. The court rejected that claim as well. It noted that *2Pacalypse Now* had been in general release for three years before the shooting and that 400,000 copies had been sold. The fact that Howard was listening to the music at the time of the killing did not sway the court.[55]

The court's analysis of evidence and expert testimony in the case led it to conclude that the music did not incite imminent violence. It certainly did not overcome Shakur's First Amendment right to express his opinion even if it was revolutionary in nature.[56]

> At best, the recording reveals that weak-willed individuals may be influenced by Shakur's work. As the Supreme Court

---

52 Howard was convicted and sentenced to death. Ibid. at 1.

53 Ibid. at 10.

54 Ibid. at 12.

55 Ibid. at 20.

56 Ibid. at 21.

explained, swaying the weak-willed does not remove constitutional protection from speech.

In a number of cases, plaintiffs have combined both incitement and duty of care claims in seeking to hold media defendants liable for violence. The killings at Columbine High School in 1999 led to a federal court suit, *Sanders v. Acclaim Entertainment*, against several video game and movie companies.[57] The widow and stepchildren of William Sanders, a teacher killed by Dylan Klebold and Eric Harris, filed suit claiming that the violent content of games, including Mortal Kombat, Doom, Redneck Rampage, Final Fantasy, Nightmare Creatures and Resident Evil had contributed to the attack on students and teachers at the high school.[58]

> Plaintiffs allege that the Video Game Defendants manufactured and/or supplied to Harris and Klebold these video games which made violence pleasurable and attractive and disconnected the violence from the natural consequences thereof, thereby causing Harris and Klebold to act out the violence * * * [and] trained [them] how to point and shoot a gun effectively without teaching either of them any of the constraints, responsibilities, or consequences necessary to inhibit such an extremely dangerous killing capacity.

In addition, Sanders' survivors argued that movie makers had contributed to the killings by releasing violent films. In particular, the family pointed to the movie "*Basketball Diaries*" in which the protagonist shoots and kills his teacher and his classmates. Sanders' family argued that the film influenced Harris and Klebold. The family also sued the producers and providers of adult content on the Internet.

The judge hearing the case dismissed the claims against the video game and movie companies. His decision was based on applicable Colorado state law and the First Amendment. Under Colorado law, the game and movie defendants had to have owed the victims a duty of care not to take actions that would have endangered them. In addition, the defendants must have been able to foresee that the two teens would have gone on their killing spree as a result of playing the games and seeing the movie. Finally, Colorado law did not allow the makers of movies and video games to be held to account under a theory of strict liability.

The federal judge also concluded that the games and movie were protected by the First Amendment. After noting that the creation and distribution of "works of imagination" are part of the core of expression, the judge disposed of the plaintiffs' argument that the violent content of the games and movie deprived them of protection against civil suits. "[I]t is manifest that there is social utility in expressive and imaginative forms of entertainment even if they contain violence."[59] Allowing liability

---

[57] *Sanders v. Acclaim Entertainment, Inc.*, 188 F.Supp.2d 1264 (D.Colo. 2002).

[58] Ibid. at 1269.

[59] Ibid. at 1274. The judge quoted heavily from a Seventh Circuit decision overturning a municipal ordinance that would have limited minors' access to violent video games. "[T]he

for expression would conflict with First Amendment values, the judge reasoned. Similarly, he wrote, Colorado case law did not allow for the imposition of a duty to identify dangers from expression where that duty would interfere with important societal values.[60]

> Given the First Amendment values at stake, the magnitude of the burden that Plaintiffs seek to impose on the Video Game and Movie Defendants is daunting. Furthermore, the practical consequences of such liability are unworkable. Plaintiffs would essentially obligate these Defendants, indeed all speakers, to anticipate and prevent the idiosyncratic, violent reactions of unidentified, vulnerable individuals to their creative works.

A *USA Today* story on the 10th anniversary of the Columbine killings reported that much of what the public had been told about Dylan Klebold and Eric Harris was not correct.[61]

The article targets many claims made about the pair, including the assertions that they were in the "Trenchcoat Mafia," were disaffected videogamers, were on anti-depressants, were the victims of bullies and targeted jocks, blacks or Christians. "That story about a student being shot in the head after she said she believed in God? Never happened, the FBI says now."[62]

Instead of being prompted to commit the attack by violent videogames, movies and adult Web sites, authors of new books on the pair and the attacks, say that both Klebold and Harris were seriously disturbed.[63]

> "These are not ordinary kids who were bullied into retaliation," psychologist Peter Langman writes in his new book, "*Why Kids Kill: Inside the Minds of School Shooters*." "These are not ordinary kids who played too many video games. These are not ordinary kids who just wanted to be famous. These are simply *not ordinary kids*. These are kids with serious psychological problems."

Seventh Circuit observed, '[v]iolence has always been and remains a central interest of humankind and a recurrent, even obsessive theme of culture both high and low.' "*American Amusement Mach. Ass'n v. Kendrick*, 244 F.3d 572, 577 (7th Cir.2001), cert. denied, 534 U.S. 994, 122 S.Ct. 462, 151 L.Ed.2d 379 (2001). Indeed, "[c]lassic literature and art, and not merely today's popular culture, are saturated with graphic scenes of violence, whether narrated or pictorial." Id. at 575. Moreover, the *Kendrick* Court acknowledged that video games that include pictorial representations of violence are "stories" and contain "age-old themes of literature." Id. at 577–78. The Court flatly rejected the notion that society is better served by insulating the vulnerable from exposure to such images: To shield children * * * from exposure to violent descriptions and images would not only be quixotic, but deforming; it would leave them unequipped to cope with the world as we know it. Id. at 577.

[60] Ibid. at 1275.

[61] Gregg Toppo, "10 years later, the real story behind Columbine," *USA Today*, April 14, 2009.

[62] Ibid.

[63] Ibid.

Several other federal courts have rejected liability for video game and movie content. In *James v. Meow Media*, a federal court rejected similar claims over violent video games and the movie "*The Basketball Diaries*."[64]

One of the poster children for the category of violent video games, "*Grand Theft Auto*," was the subject of a $246 million suit filed in the fall of 2003.[65] William and Joshua Buckner, teen stepbrothers, said they were inspired by the game to shoot at vehicles on Interstate 40. They killed one motorist and wounded a passenger in another car. The families alleged that Sony Computer Entertainment and Rockstar Games failed to warn consumers about the harm the game could cause by inspiring copycat behavior. Sony and Rock Star Games were sued in state court. The case was removed to federal court where the defendants moved to dismiss the case on First Amendment grounds. The plaintiffs' moved to have the case returned to state court where they could pursue a product liability claim. After their motion was rejected, they filed to dismiss.

CALIFORNIA TAKES ON VIOLENT VIDEO GAMES—AND LOSES

First a federal district court, then a three-judge panel of the 9th U.S. Circuit Court of Appeals struck down a California law that would prevent the sale or rental of violent video games to anyone younger than 18. The panel said the law violated minors' rights under the First and Fourteenth Amendments.[66]

> Judge Consuelo Callahan said there were less restrictive ways to protect children from "unquestionably violent" video games. For example, the justices said the industry has a voluntary rating system and that parents can block certain games on video consoles.

In creating the law, California lawmakers relied on studies that suggested that violent games could be linked to aggression, anti-social behavior and desensitization to violence. Judge Callahan's opinion rejected that justification for the law.[67]

"None of the research establishes or suggests a causal link between minors playing violent video games and actual psychological or

---

[64] *James v. Meow Media, Inc.*, 90 F.Supp.2d 798 (W.D.Ky.2000). This case arose following the murders of three students at Heath High School in Paducah, Ky., in 1997. Michael Carneal, 14, took a .22-caliber pistol and five shotguns to the school and fired on other students there. The families of the three students killed brought the suit against the makers and distributors of violent video games, movies and adult Web sites. The families alleged that the games and movies desensitized Carneal and that without those influences he would not have committed the killings. The trial court dismissed the suit on the grounds that the defendants had no duty of care with respect to Carneal's victims and that they did not cause the deaths.

[65] J.J. Stambaugh, "Maker of violent video game sued; Fatal Cocke County spree draws suit asking millions from firms, teens' parents," *Knoxville News-Sentinel*, Oct. 21, 2003.

[66] "Court strikes down California video game law," Associated Press, Feb. 20, 2009.

[67] Ibid.

neurological harm, and inferences to that effect would not be reasonable," Callahan said in her ruling.

SUPREME COURT STRIKES CALIFORNIA RESTRICTIONS ON VIOLENT VIDEO GAMES

In 2011, the Supreme Court affirmed the 9th Circuit ruling that the California restrictions on the sale and rental of violent video games.[68] Justice Antonin Scalia wrote the Court's opinion in *Brown v. Entertainment Merchants Ass'n*, that was joined by Justices Kennedy, Sotomayor, Ginsburg and Kagan. Justice Samuel Alito wrote a concurring opinion joined by Chief Justice John Roberts. Justices Clarence Thomas and Stephen Breyer dissented.

Violent video games were defined as games,[69] "in which the range of options available to a player includes killing, maiming, dismembering, or sexually assaulting an image of a human being."

The law focused on those games that,[70] "Enables the player to virtually inflict serious injury upon images of human beings or characters with substantially human characteristics in a manner which is especially heinous, cruel, or depraved in that it involves torture or serious physical abuse to the victim."

Torture of the virtual victims included mental as well as physical abuse. The statute required that the virtual victim of torture be aware of the torture and that the human player intend to torture the virtual victim, going beyond the killing of the computer character.

In order to place the violent video games outside the protection of the First Amendment, the California Legislature included a three-part test, drawn from the landmark obscenity case of *Miller v. California* (discussed later in this chapter).[71] The three-part test applied the law to those games that had elements that would meet all three parts,[72]

(A) Comes within all of the following descriptions:

(i) A reasonable person, considering the game as a whole, would find appeals to a deviant or morbid interest of minors.

(ii) It is patently offensive to prevailing standards in the community as to what is suitable for minors.

(iii) It causes the game, as a whole, to lack serious literary, artistic, political, or scientific value for minors.

The California law made it a crime, punishable by fine of up to $1,000, to sell or rent a violent video game to a minor. It also required

[68] *Brown v. Entertainment Merchants Ass'n*, 564 U.S. 786, 131 S.Ct. 2729 (2011).

[69] West's Ann.Cal.Civ.Code § 1746 (d)(1).

[70] West's Ann.Cal.Civ.Code § 1746 (d)(1)(B).

[71] *Miller v. California*, 413 U.S. 15, 93 S.Ct. 2607 (1973).

[72] West's Ann.Cal.Civ.Code § 1746 (d)(1)(A)(1).

that violent video games have a 2-inch-square label with the number "18" on a white field notifying purchasers that the game had violent content. The law allowed the parents and legal guardians of minors to purchase the games and, presumably, let them play.

In ruling that the California law was not constitutional, Justice Scalia focused his opinion on the First Amendment protections that video games were entitled to. California had agreed that games were entitled to those protections but had argued that the violent nature of the games and the vulnerabilities of persons under 18 meant that the state should be able to keep them out of the hands of minors, at least those whose parents or guardians wouldn't buy the games for them.[73]

> California correctly acknowledges that video games qualify for First Amendment protection. The Free Speech Clause exists principally to protect discourse on public matters, but we have long recognized that it is difficult to distinguish politics from entertainment, and dangerous to try.

Justice Scalia also addressed the concerns raised in a concurrence by Justice Samuel Alito. Although Justice Alito concurred in the result, he wrote an opinion in which he concluded that the California law was unconstitutional because of the way it defined the games it would apply to. Justice Alito instead argued that California should have the power to limit the exposure of minors to the games. He wrote about the potential effects of the violent content on children.[74]

> In some of these games, the violence is astounding. Victims by the dozens are killed with every imaginable implement, including machine guns, shotguns, clubs, hammers, axes, swords, and chainsaws. Victims are dismembered, decapitated, disemboweled, set on fire, and chopped into little pieces. They cry out in agony and beg for mercy. Blood gushes, splatters, and pools. Severed body parts and gobs of human remains are graphically shown. In some games, points are awarded based, not only on the number of victims killed, but on the killing technique employed.

But, as Justice Scalia wrote,[75] "Justice Alito recounts all these disgusting video games in order to disgust us—but disgust is not a valid basis for restricting expression."

---

[73] *Brown v. Entertainment Merchants Ass'n*, 564 U.S. 786, 790, 131 S.Ct. 2729, 2733 (2011). Justice Scalia then turned to the law's *Miller*-like, three-part test. Trying to shoehorn violent content into the obscenity category of speech that falls outside the protection of the First Amendment does not work, Justice Scalia wrote.[71] California has tried to make violent-speech regulation look like obscenity regulation by appending a saving clause required for the latter. That does not suffice. Our cases have been clear that the obscenity exception to the First Amendment does not cover whatever a legislature finds shocking, but only depictions of "sexual conduct," *Miller*, supra, at 24, 93 S.Ct. 2607. See also *Cohen v. California*, 403 U.S. 15, 20, 91 S.Ct. 1780, 29 L.Ed.2d 284 (1971); *Roth*, supra, at 487, and n. 20, 77 S.Ct. 1304.

[74] Ibid. at 2749.

[75] Ibid. at 2738.

Because California's law targeted the video games because of their violent content, the Court had to apply a Strict Scrutiny test to determine its constitutionality (Strict Scrutiny is defined in Appendix).

The first part of the test requires that the government show that it had a compelling interest that was important enough to overcome First Amendment concerns. The law did not, Scalia wrote.[76]

> California cannot meet that standard. At the outset, it acknowledges that it cannot show a direct causal link between violent video games and harm to minors.
>
> * * *
>
> The State's evidence is not compelling. California relies primarily on the research of Dr. Craig Anderson and a few other research psychologists whose studies purport to show a connection between exposure to violent video games and harmful effects on children. These studies have been rejected by every court to consider them, and with good reason: They do not prove that violent video games cause minors to act aggressively (which would at least be a beginning). Instead, "[n]early all of the research is based on correlation, not evidence of causation, and most of the studies suffer from significant, admitted flaws in methodology." *Video Software Dealers Assn.* 556 F.3d, at 964. They show at best some correlation between exposure to violent entertainment and minuscule real-world effects, such as children's feeling more aggressive or making louder noises in the few minutes after playing a violent game than after playing a nonviolent game.

Justice Stephen Breyer's dissent concluded that California had proven its compelling government interest. He cited both the record from the lower courts as well as independent research[77] that he conducted on his own.[78]

> There are many scientific studies that support California's views. Social scientists, for example, have found causal evidence that playing these games results in harm. Longitudinal studies, which measure changes over time, have found that increased exposure to violent video games causes an increase in aggression over the same period.

---

[76] Ibid. at 2738–39.

[77] The issue of Justice Breyer's insertion of research that lay outside the record and pleadings raised concerns in some quarters. The inclusion of such material, however well researched by a justice and his clerks, still leaves the parties without the opportunity to do their own vetting and, more importantly, prepare their own responses to the new material. Critics likened Justice Breyer's conduct to allowing a referee to punch a fighter after a fight has ended to try to influence the judges who will decide who the winner should be.

[78] Ibid. at 2768.

Justice Breyer appended a list of more than 150 peer-reviewed articles on the subject.[79]

> Experts debate the conclusions of all these studies. Like many, perhaps most, studies of human behavior, each study has its critics, and some of those critics have produced studies of their own in which they reach different conclusions. (I list both sets of research in the appendixes.) I, like most judges, lack the social science expertise to say definitively who is right. But associations of public health professionals who do possess that expertise have reviewed many of these studies and found a significant risk that violent video games, when compared with more passive media, are particularly likely to cause children harm.

But the majority's opinion went beyond the existence of the compelling government interest. Justice Scalia concluded that the law failed the constitutional test because it was underinclusive. Even if California had correctly concluded that violence in popular media, including video games and Saturday morning cartoons, was harmful, it chose only to regulate the games. Constitutional principles require that government regulation of speech be evenhanded.[80] "Here, California has singled out the purveyors of video games for disfavored treatment—at least when compared to booksellers, cartoonists, and movie producers—and has given no persuasive reason why."

Justice Scalia pointed to another problem with underinclusiveness in the law. It did not protect all minors.[81]

> The Act is also seriously underinclusive in another respect—and a respect that renders irrelevant the contentions of the concurrence and the dissents that video games are qualitatively different from other portrayals of violence. The California Legislature is perfectly willing to leave this dangerous, mind-altering material in the hands of children so long as one parent (or even an aunt or uncle) says it's OK. And there are not even any requirements as to how this parental or avuncular relationship is to be verified; apparently the child's or putative parent's, aunt's, or uncle's say-so suffices. That is not how one addresses a serious social problem.

Justice Clarence Thomas dissented, arguing that the First Amendment did not extend to the sale or rental of video games to minors. Justice Thomas, as he has in other cases, argued that minors have no First Amendment rights and that parents have sole authority in determining what information is passed to their children. Starting with references to the Puritans in the 1600s through the mid 1800s, Justice

[79] Ibid. at 2769.

[80] Ibid. at 2740.

[81] Ibid. at 2740.

Thomas cited letters, books and other sources that showed parental power over children. As such, the historical precedent showed that the authors of the First Amendment would not see the rights under that amendment as applying to the California statute and the First Amendment could not be used to strike it down.[82]

> The question is not whether certain laws might make sense to judges or legislators today, but rather what the public likely understood "the freedom of speech" to mean when the First Amendment was adopted. See *District of Columbia v. Heller*, 554 U.S. 570, 634–635, 128 S.Ct. 2783, 171 L.Ed.2d 637 (2008). I believe it is clear that the founding public would not have understood "the freedom of speech" to include speech to minor children bypassing their parents. It follows that the First Amendment imposes no restriction on state regulation of such speech. Because the First Amendment could not be applied to a state law affecting the right of parents, solely, to choose what video games they would buy for their minor children and minor children do not have the right to acquire the ideas contained within such games without their parents' consent. . . .

Justice Thomas would have held the California law constitutional.

THE NUREMBERG SITE: WANTED POSTERS AND FREE EXPRESSION

In the spring of 2001, a panel of the 9th Circuit Court of Appeals reversed a judgment of $107 million and lifted an injunction against the operators of a controversial anti-abortion Internet site called the Nuremberg Site.[83] In doing so, the panel continued its protection of speech and limiting the use of incitement.

The case had its beginnings in 1995 at a meeting of the American Coalition of Life Activists (ACLA). At the meeting, which took place on the anniversary of *Roe v. Wade*, the anti-abortion group unveiled a poster with the name and addresses of doctors who performed abortions. The poster declared the "Dirty Dozen" guilty of crimes against humanity and offered a reward of $5,000 for information leading to their arrests, convictions and revocations of their licenses to practice medicine. The poster was reproduced in an ACLA affiliate magazine.

The ACLA later targeted individual doctors and eventually produced a dossier which it called the "Nuremberg Files," which contained information about abortion providers. The stated purpose for the files was for use in Nuremberg-style trials for abortion providers once the United States decided to end abortion and prosecute the killers of "God's

---

[82] Ibid. at 2759.

[83] *Planned Parenthood of Columbia/Willamette, Inc. v. American Coalition of Life Activists*, 244 F.3d 1007 (9th Cir.2001).

children."[84] In 1996, the ACLA sent the materials to a fellow activist who put them on the Web site. The site identified abortion providers and asked those visiting the site to provide more information. It paid attention to violence against abortion providers.[85]

> The website marked the names of those already victimized by anti-abortion terrorists, striking through the names of those who had been murdered and graying out the names of the wounded. * * *
>
> Neither the posters nor the website contained any explicit threats against the doctors. But the doctors knew that similar posters prepared by others had preceded clinic violence in the past. By publishing the names and addresses, ACLA robbed the doctors of their anonymity and gave violent anti-abortion activists the information to find them.

Some of the doctors and two health centers fired back with a lawsuit alleging that the Web wanted poster violated state and federal law, including the Freedom of Access to Clinic Entrances Act of 1994 (FACE), 18 U.S.C. § 248.[86] U.S. District Judge Robert E. Jones concluded in granting the permanent injunction against the ACLA that the "Deadly Dozen" poster was a threat to "bodily harm, assault, or kill one or more of the plaintiffs."[87] Judge Jones noted that the ACLA had published wanted posters of several abortion providers before they were murdered.[88] The judge also focused on published statements by ACLA members lauding the murderers of abortion providers, including the sniper killing of Canadian abortion doctor Garson Romalis.[89]

> Defendant Treshman praised the shooting of Dr. Romalis on national television, stating "I would say that was certainly the superb tactic. It was certainly far better than anything seen in the States because the shooting was done in such a way that the perpetrator got away. I would think more abortionists would quit as a result of it."

---

[84] The Nuremberg Files website listed a number of public figures as abortion supporters (and future war crimes defendants), including six current members of the Supreme Court, Bill Clinton, Al Gore, Janet Reno, Jack Kevorkian, C. Everett Koop, Mary Tyler Moore, Whoopi Goldberg and Retired Justice Byron White. Justice White's inclusion is puzzling as he dissented in *Roe v. Wade.*

[85] Ibid. at 2.

[86] The Act provides for appropriate relief in the form of injunctions and compensatory and punitive damages for persons who are "aggrieved" by threats of violence as they seek access to medical clinics or provide medical services.

[87] *Planned Parenthood of Columbia/Willamette, Inc. v. American Coalition of Life Activists,* 41 F.Supp.2d 1130, 1131 (D.Ore.1999).

[88] "On March 10, 1993, Dr. David Gunn was shot and killed outside of the Pensacola, Florida, clinic where he performed abortions. * * * Prior to his murder Dr. Gunn's name, photograph and other identifying information appeared on WANTED posters. * * * On August 21, 1993, Dr. George Patterson, an abortion provider, was shot and killed in Mobile, Alabama. Prior to Dr. Patterson's murder, his name, physical description and address were published on a WANTED poster." Ibid. at 1135.

[89] Ibid. at 1135.

Based on his findings of fact, Judge Jones concluded that the defendants engaged in illegal communication of true threats against the plaintiffs in an attempt to interfere or intimidate them from continuing their abortion activities. Judge Jones also presided over the jury trial which resulted in the $107 million judgment against the defendants under the Freedom of Access to Clinic Entrances Act.

A three-judge panel reversed, finding that ACLA's speech was protected by the First Amendment. But the full 9th Circuit reheard the appeal and reversed the three-judge panel. In a decision written by Circuit Judge Pamela Ann Rymer, the majority of the circuit ruled that the content of the Web site constituted a "true threat" under the Freedom of Access to Clinic Entrances (FACE) Act, 18 U.S.C. § 248.[90] The Act gives a right of action when a person or persons uses a threat of force or intentionally intimidate persons because they provide reproductive health services.

The circuit majority looked to the findings of the district court jury which found in favor of the health care providers. The circuit majority rejected the three-judge panel's finding that the First Amendment protected the anti-abortion group's speech. Under that interpretation, the ACLA Web site would have to be shown to have threatened the health care providers in order to find the ACLA liable.

The full panel of the 9th Circuit concluded that the ACLA speech should be judged in light of the FACE Act. In that context, the ACLA speech would be judged on the basis of its "intent to intimidate."[91]

> Thus, the jury must have found that ACLA made statements to intimidate the physicians, reasonably foreseeing that physicians would interpret the statements as a serious expression of ACLA's intent to harm them because they provided reproductive health services. Construing the facts in the light most favorable to the physicians, the verdict is supported by substantial evidence. ACLA was aware that a "wanted"—type poster would likely be interpreted as a serious threat of death or bodily harm by a doctor in the reproductive health services community who was identified given the previous pattern of "WANTED" posters identifying a specific physician followed by that physician's murder.

The 9th Circuit's full panel said that the threat existed in the part of the ACLA Web site that featured crossed-out photographs of doctors who had been murdered or wounded. Because the speech constituted true threats, they were not protected speech, Judge Rymer wrote. The case was sent back down for consideration of the punitive damages awarded.

---

[90] *Planned Parenthood of Columbia/Willamette, Inc. v. American Coalition of Life Activists,* 290 F.3d 1058 (9th Cir. en banc 2002).

[91] Ibid. at 1063.

11. OBSCENITY AND AMERICAN LAW

Obscene expression has never been considered worthy of constitutional protection, but the growth of the hard-core pornography industry during the 1950s prompted the Supreme Court to create standards to establish what could legally be classified as obscene.

Obscenity was not considered a significant legal issue during the first 170 years of this nation's history. In fact, the Supreme Court did not decide to review the constitutionality of existing obscenity laws until 115 years after the first federal anti-obscenity law had been enacted.[92]

The main reason for this long era of judicial neglect was the limited scope of pornographic business in the United States prior to the 1950s. Before this time those who engaged in the sale of sexually explicit materials tended to be small-time operators, specializing in procuring a few erotic books or batches of grainy French postcards for a very select and secretive clientele.[93]

During the 1950s, however, as organized crime began to move into the field, its operation became much more efficient and profitable, employing mass mailings for the first time to promote the sale of slickly produced erotic magazines to a much broader segment of the population.[94] By 1960, annual revenues from the sale of sexually explicit materials were estimated to be in excess of $500 million, earnings that at the time rivaled those of both the American television and motion picture industries.[95] Estimates of the earnings from Internet sex sites

---

[92] The first federal anti-obscenity law was contained in the Tariff Act of 1842, U.S. Public Statutes at Large, Vol. 5, Chap. 270, forbidding the, "importation of all indecent and obscene paintings, lithographs, engravings and transparencies." In 1957, the United States Supreme Court ruled on the constitutionality of such anti-obscenity laws for the first time in *Roth v. United States*, 354 U.S. 476, 77 S.Ct. 1304 (1957). In this regard it is informative to note that the word "pornography" itself did not exist in the English language until sometime during the early 1850s, and that it originally referred only to the scientific (or pseudo-scientific) study of prostitutes. See Walter Kendrick, *The Secret Museum*, New York, Viking Press, 1987.

[93] See the Gathings Committee: U.S. Congress, House, Select Committee on Current Pornographic Materials, Hearings Before Select Committee, and Report of Select Committee to the House, 83rd Cong. 2d Sess. 1952.H. Rept. 2510 and the Kefauver Committee: U.S. Congress, Senate, Committee on the Judiciary, Obscene and Pornographic Materials, 84th Cong., 2d Sess. 1956, H. Rept. 2381.

[94] Federal Bureau of Investigation: Report Regarding the Extent of Organized Crimes Involvement in Pornography (1978). Also see, Attorney General's Commission on Pornography: Final Report (1986), pp. 291–301. Although an earlier government study, the Report of the President's Commission on Obscenity and Pornography (1970), found insufficient evidence to document the extent of mob involvement in this field, (pp. 142–143), its efforts to establish such a connection were admittedly quite limited.

[95] The Granahan Committee: U.S. Congress, House, Committee on the Post Office and Civil Service, Subcommittee on Post Operations, Hearings before Subcommittee and Report of Subcommittee to Committee, 86th Congress, 2d sess. 1960. Although both the Kefauver and the Granahan Committee reports acknowledged the difficulty of accurately estimating the revenues generated by an illegal industry whose major operators were not likely to disclose this information on their tax forms, the figures were considered to be rather conservative projections of actual earnings. For comparative purposes, the total revenues earned by all TV stations in the United States in 1960 was $962 million, while the total domestic box office receipts for all films shown in the U.S. that year was $710 million. Christopher H. Sterling and Timothy R.

ranges from $200 million to $1.8 billion. In 2015, the range for the American porn industry was between $10 and $12 billion.[96] The wide range is attributed to the fact that the people who own these businesses do not publish their books.

Prior to this time, obscenity always had been assumed to be an illegal form of expression, denied any First Amendment protection. As Justice Holmes had declared in *Frohwerk v. United States*[97]

> The First Amendment * * * cannot have been, and obviously was not, intended to give immunity for every possible use of language.

But in 1957, just as hard-core pornography was emerging as a major industry throughout the nation, the Supreme Court decided to intervene in this field of law for the first time. Concerned that overly broad anti-obscenity statutes might be improperly infringing on protected free speech, the Court acted to impose its own federal guidelines on these laws, requiring them to conform to one uniform standard in determining what could legally be classified as "obscene."[98] Unfortunately, this decision of the Court to assume ultimate authority over obscenity law in the United States was made on the eve of the "sexual revolution," a frenzied era that would soon cast the nine Justices adrift in a flood of obscenity appeals, floundering aimlessly for a time upon its surging waves of controversy.

12. THE COMMON LAW ORIGINS

British common law principles drawn from an era of soapbox orators and humble printers could offer only limited guidance to American courts facing the need to develop a legal definition of obscenity for a modern society.

Although Nineteenth Century America was never a hot-bed of erotic literature, the moral and religious fervor that swept the nation during the 1870s launched crusades to seek out every kind of depravity or vice, wherever it might be found. In 1873, Anthony Comstock, a sexually fixated religious crusader whose slogan was "Morals! Not Art or Literature," was able to convince Congress to adopt federal legislation making it a crime to use the mail to distribute obscene materials. During the next few years several state legislatures also responded to the demands of Comstock and his followers by passing their own anti-obscenity laws.

Haight, The Mass Media: Aspen Institute Guide to Communication Industry Trends. New York, Praeger Publishers, 1976. Table 380–A, p. 207 and Table 340–B, p. 182.

[96] Chris Morris, "Things Are Looking Up in America's Porn Business," *NBC News*, Jan. 20, 2015.

[97] *Frohwerk v. United States*, 49 U.S. 204, 206, 39 S.Ct. 249, 250 (1919).

[98] *Roth v. United States*, 354 U.S. 476, 77 S.Ct. 1304 (1957).

After these laws had been enacted, it was then up to each state court to decide how the term "obscene" should be defined. In the absence of any precedents from earlier American case law, these courts were forced to seek guidance from English common law where a number of judges eventually discovered and applied the standard an English court had established in 1868 in the case of *Regina v. Hicklin.*

THE HICKLIN RULE

The *Hicklin* rule was created in the enforcement of Lord Campbell's Act, a Parliamentary measure aimed at stamping out the trade in obscenity in England. The act was intended to protect works of art while it targeted truly offensive works that posed a threat to the youth and which were calculated to shock the common feelings of decency in the minds of ordinary people. In *Hicklin,* the distributor of an anti-Catholic pamphlet, *"The Confessional Unmasked,"* was brought up under provisions of Lord Campbell's Act. Part of the pamphlet targeted the Catholic Church while the other part told the story of "depravities" that took place in the confessional and other structures in the Catholic Church. Although he granted that Mr. Hicklin's intent was to defend Protestant England from Catholicism, Lord Chief Justice Cockburn ruled that *"The Confessional Unmasked"* was obscene. Lord Cockburn set down this test for obscenity:[99]

> Whether the tendency of the matter charged as obscene is to deprave and corrupt those whose minds are open to such immoral influences and into whose hands a publication of this sort might fall.

In states that followed the *"Hicklin* rule" it was not necessary to prove that any publication under review was likely to harm or offend a normal adult.[100] The rule needed only assertions that the work in question could have a damaging effect on children or abnormal adults—"those whose minds are open to such immoral influences"—in order to satisfy its standard. In time, some state courts added the so-called "partly obscene" test to the *Hicklin* rule. If a publication contained one or more obscene passages, the entire work could be classified as obscene.[101]

Perhaps the most troublesome portion of the *Hicklin* rule, though, was the concept that a book could be classified as obscene if it suggested "thoughts of a most impure and libidinous character."[102] In the law of obscenity, no harm or even likelihood of harm to readers need be shown in order to suppress a book.[103] In 1913, Judge Learned Hand wrote an

[99] *Regina v. Hicklin,* L.R.3 Q.B. 360, 370 (1868).

[100] See *United States v. Bennett,* 24 Fed.Cas. 1093, 1103–1104, No. 14,571 (C.C.S.D.N.Y.1879); *Commonwealth v. Friede,* 271 Mass. 318, 320, 171 N.E. 472, 473 (1930).

[101] Lockhart & McClure, op. cit., p. 343.

[102] Ibid.

[103] See *Roth v. United States,* 354 U.S. 476, 490, 77 S.Ct. 1304, 1312 (1957); see also dictum by Justice Frankfurter, *Beauharnais v. Illinois,* 343 U.S. 250, 266, 72 S.Ct. 725, 735 (1952).

often quoted protest against the *Hicklin* rule, which he termed "mid-Victorian precedent." Although Judge Hand felt compelled to uphold the condemnation as obscene of Daniel Goodman's novel *"Hagar Revelley,"* the judge wrote:[104]

> I question whether in the end men will regard that as obscene which is honestly relevant to the adequate expression of innocent ideas, and whether they will not believe that truth and beauty are too precious to be mutilated in the interests of those most likely to pervert them to base uses. * * *

Despite his protest, the *Hicklin* rule remained the leading test of obscenity in America until the 1930s.[105]

THE ULYSSES DECISION

About this time, however, other American courts began to relax enforcement of the *Hicklin* rule to some extent. A mother who wrote a book to help her children learn about sex—and who later published the book at the suggestion of friends—successfully defended herself against charges that the book (*"Sex Side of Life"*) was obscene.[106] And in 1933, James Joyce's famed stream-of-consciousness novel *"Ulysses,"* now an acknowledged classic, was the target of an obscenity prosecution under the Tariff Act of 1930.[107]

Customs officers had prevented an actress from bringing *"Ulysses"* into the United States.[108] When *"Ulysses"* reached trial, Judge John Woolsey decided that a literary work deserved be judged in its entirety, rather than by the contents of a few selected passages. On this basis he attacked the *Hicklin* test head-on and ruled that *"Ulysses"* was art, not obscenity.

His decision has become one of the most noted in the law of criminal words, even though it by no means brought the end of the *Hicklin* rule, which continued to applied in the decisions of other courts.[109] Overrated or not, the *"Ulysses"* decision represents an often-cited step toward nullifying some of the most restrictive aspects of the old *Hicklin* standard. Judge Woolsey's ruling was upheld by a panel of the Second Circuit Court of Appeals.[110]

---

[104] *United States v. Kennerley*, 209 Fed. 119 (S.D.N.Y.1913).

[105] See, e.g., *Commonwealth v. Friede*, 271 Mass. 318, 320, 171 N.E. 472, 473 (1930).

[106] *United States v. Dennett*, 39 F.2d 564, 76 A.L.R. 1092 (2d Cir.1930).

[107] *United States v. One Book Called "Ulysses,"* 5 F.Supp. 182 (S.D.N.Y.1933); Paul and Schwartz, op. cit., p. 66.

[108] Seized as contraband, the United States initiated a forfeiture proceeding naming the book at the defendant. It is common practice but most defendants, facing their own trials, do not try to defend the contraband. In the case of seized drugs, no defense would work. But in this case, Random House, a publisher, hired a lawyer for her book.

[109] See e.g., *United States v. Two Obscene Books*, 99 F.Supp. 760 (N.D.Cal.1951), affirmed as *Besig v. United States*, 208 F.2d 142 (9th Cir.1953).

[110] *U.S. vs. One Book Entitled, Ulysses by James Joyce* (Random House Claimant), 72 F.2d 705 (2d Cir. 1934).

The *"Ulysses"* decision provided a new definition of obscenity for other courts to consider: That a book is obscene if it[111]

> tends to stir the sex impulses or to lead to sexually impure and lustful thoughts. Whether a particular book would tend to excite such impulses must be the test by the court's opinion as to its effect (when judged as a whole) on a person with average sex instincts.

Only one portion of the old *Hicklin* rule appeared in Judge Woolsey's *Ulysses* opinion: the emphasis on thoughts produced by a book as an indicator of a book's obscene effect on a reader. This judicial preoccupation with thoughts—and the tests outlined by Judge Woolsey in 1933—are markedly similar to rules for judging obscenity laid down in the Supreme Court's landmark decision in the 1957 case of *Roth v. United States*.[112]

13. THE ROTH LANDMARK

In *Roth v. United States* (1957), the Supreme Court held that obscenity is not constitutionally protected expression.

The Supreme Court tried to establish one uniform national standard to define the obscene in 1957. In *Roth*, the Court declared that obscene speech was outside protections of the First Amendment, the decision also tried to create safeguards to limit the sweep of anti-obscenity laws to deal only with expression that was correctly classified as obscene.[113] Because this decision also dealt with *People v. Alberts*, a case arising under a state statute, the Roth ruling settled the general question of the constitutionality of both federal and state anti-obscenity laws.

In the federal case, Roth was convicted of violating the statute by mailing a book, *"American Aphrodite,"* plus various pamphlets. Roth received the maximum sentence: a $5,000 fine plus a five-year penitentiary term. His conviction was affirmed by the U.S. Court of Appeals, Second Circuit, even though a powerful concurring opinion by Judge Jerome N. Frank termed obscenity laws unconstitutionally vague. Judge Frank objected that there was no proof that obscene publications tended to have an effect on normal, average adults. He added, [U]nder the [federal] statute * * * punishment is apparently inflicted for provoking, in such adults, undesirable sexual thoughts, feelings or

[111] *United States v. One Book Called "Ulysses,"* 5 F.Supp. 182, 184 (S.D.N.Y.1933).

[112] *Roth v. United States*, 354 U.S. 476, 77 S.Ct. 1304 (1957).

[113] Ibid. Although this decision is usually referred to simply as the *Roth* case, the Supreme Court decision actually involved two different appeals. The Court simultaneously decided a case under the federal obscenity statute, *United States v. Roth*, 237 F.2d 796 (2d Cir.1956), and a case arising under a state statute. West's Ann.Cal.Pen. Code, Art. 311; *People v. Alberts*, 138 Cal.App.2d Supp. 909, 292 P.2d 90 (1955).

desire—not overt dangerous or anti-social conduct, either actual or probable.[114]

Justice Brennan wrote the majority opinion, influencing the direction of obscenity law developments in two ways. First, he affirmed the prevailing common law view that obscenity laws could be used to punish *thoughts.* Overt sexual actions were not needed to support a conviction. Second, and more significantly, he affirmed the common law holding that obscenity is not legally protected expression.[115]

Those are the two main strands in the law of obscenity. Other strands found in by concurring and dissenting Justices in *Roth v. United States* foreshadowed major and minor themes for the next 40 years in the complex fabric of obscenity law.[116]

THE ROTH TEST

Writing for the Court, Justice Brennan offered this definition of obscenity: "Obscene material is material which deals with sex in a manner appealing to prurient interest."[117] "Prurient interest," refers to sexually oriented thoughts that are shameful or morbid. Brennan then articulated "the Roth test" for judging whether or not material is obscene:[118]

> * * * whether to the average person, applying contemporary community standards, the dominant theme of the material taken as a whole appeals to prurient interest.

Subsequent decisions have returned for guidance to these words again and again. This "*Roth* test" repudiated the adoption by some American courts of the *Hicklin* rule.[119] The practice of judging books by the presumed effect of isolated passages upon the most susceptible persons was rejected because it "might well encompass material legitimately dealing with sex."[120]

However, Justice Brennan's words were obviously not wholly libertarian. Under *Roth,* a book could be declared obscene if it could be

---

114 237 F.2d, 796, 802 (2d Cir.1956). See Stanley Fleishmann, "Witchcraft and Obscenity: Twin Superstitions," Wilson Library Bulletin, April, 1965, p. 4.

115 354 U.S. 476, 482, 77 S.Ct. 1304, 1307 (1957).

116 For example, Chief Justice Earl Warren's concurrence in *Roth* argued that the conduct of a defendant was the key point in an obscenity prosecution. For a case which turned on the defendant's conduct, see *Ginzburg v. United States,* 383 U.S. 463, 86 S.Ct. 942 (1966).

117 *Roth v. United States,* 354 U.S. 476, 486–487, 77 S.Ct. 1304, 1310 (1957). The terms used in the three "tests" approved in *Roth*—"lustful desire," "lustful thoughts," and "appeal to prurient interest"—all imply that if a book can be assumed to cause or induce "improper" sexual thoughts, that book can be "banned." The "appeal to prurient interest" test was drawn from the American Law Institute's Model Penal Code, Tentative Draft No. 6 (Philadelphia, American Law Institute, May 6, 1957).

118 Ibid. at 489, 1311.

119 Ibid. at 489: "The *Hicklin* test, judging obscenity by the effect of isolated passages upon the most susceptible persons, might well encompass material legitimately treating with sex, and so it must be rejected as unconstitutionally restrictive of the freedoms of speech and press."

120 Ibid. at 489, 1311.

assumed that it might induce obscene thoughts in a hypothetical average person.[121] There was no need for the prosecution to prove that there is a "clear and present danger"[122] or even a "clear and possible danger"[123] that the reading of the book in question would lead to antisocial conduct.

ROTH: CONCURRENCES AND DISSENTS

Chief Justice Earl Warren was evidently puzzled by the idea that *books* rather than persons were defendants in obscenity prosecutions. His brief concurring opinion in *Roth* proved to be remarkably predictive of future issues in the law. Chief Justice Warren stated that in an obscenity trial, the conduct of the defendant rather than the obscenity of a book should be the central issue.[124] He concluded that both Roth and Alberts had engaged in "the commercial exploitation of the morbid and shameful craving for materials with prurient effect" and said that the state and federal governments could constitutionally punish such conduct.[125]

Justice Brennan's majority opinion in *Roth* has influenced the course of the law of obscenity. So has Chief Justice Warren's concurring opinion, which insisted that the behavior of the defendant, rather than the nature of the book itself, was the "central issue" in an obscenity case.[126]

Justice William O. Douglas was joined by Justice Hugo L. Black in a scathing attack on obscenity laws and obscenity prosecutions. This dissent foreshadowed arguments these Justices would advance in obscenity cases which subsequently followed *Roth* to the Supreme Court. Douglas wrote that Roth and Alberts were punished "for thoughts provoked, not for overt acts nor antisocial conduct." He was unimpressed by the possibility that the books involved might produce sexual thoughts: "The arousing of sexual thoughts and desires happens every day in normal life in dozens of ways."[127]

Problems involving freedom of speech and press, it was argued, must not be solved by "weighing against the values of free expression, the judgment of a court that a particular form of expression has 'no redeeming social importance.' " Justice Douglas declared:[128]

> [T]he test that suppresses a cheap tract today can suppress a literary gem tomorrow. All it need do is incite a lascivious thought or arouse a lustful desire. The list of books that judges or juries can place in that category is endless.

---

[121] Ibid. at 486, 1310.

[122] Ibid.

[123] Ibid. at 481, 1310, citing *Dennis v. United States*, 341 U.S. 494, 71 S.Ct. 857 (1951).

[124] Ibid. at 495, 1314.

[125] Ibid. at 496, 1315.

[126] Ibid. at 495, 1314–1315.

[127] Ibid. at 509, 1321.

[128] Ibid. at 514, 1324.

14. MONITORING COMPLIANCE: THE FEDERAL REVIEW ERA

Once the federal court system had asserted its right to review the constitutionality of all State obscenity laws, it found itself overwhelmed not only by the case-load it assumed, but also by the difficulty of defining obscenity in any uniform or clearly consistent way.

Although *Roth* remained the leading decision on obscenity and said much, later court decisions showed that it actually settled very little. Five years after *Roth* the Supreme Court attempted to refine its definition of obscenity in *Manual Enterprises, Inc. v. Day*, Postmaster General of the United States. In writing for the Court, Justice Harlan termed "*MANual*" [sic], "*Trim,*" and "Grecian Pictorial" to be "dismally unpleasant, uncouth and tawdry" magazines which were published "primarily, if not exclusively, for homosexuals."[129]

Despite this, a majority of the Supreme Court held that these magazines which presented pictures of nude males were not obscene and unmailable because they were not "patently offensive." Harlan wrote:[130]

> Obscenity under the federal statute * * * requires proof of two distinct elements: (1) patent offensiveness; and (2) "prurient interest" appeal.

In 1966, the Supreme Court again tackled the tough problem of defining obscenity as decisions were announced in the "*Fanny Hill*" case,[131] and *Ginzburg v. United States.*[132]

First announced was the decision in the *Fanny Hill* case. *"Fanny Hill,"* or more accurately, *"Memoirs of a Woman of Pleasure,"* was written in England about 1749 by John Cleland. The book was well known in the American colonies and was first published in the United States around 1800. *"Fanny Hill,"* was also one of the first books in America to be the subject of an obscenity trial; in Massachusetts in the year 1821.[133] More than 140 years later, *"Fanny Hill"* was back in the courts of Massachusetts, as well as in New York, New Jersey and Illinois.

In *"Fanny Hill,"* there is not one of the "four letter words" which have so often brought modern literature before the courts. But although the language was quite sanitary, author Cleland's descriptions of Fanny's sexual gyrations left little to the imagination. Even so, some experts—including poet and critic Louis Untermeyer—testified that *"Fanny Hill"*

---

[129] *Manual Enterprises, Inc. v. Day*, 370 U.S. 478, 481, 82 S.Ct. 1432, 1434 (1962).

[130] Ibid. at 487, 1437. Prurient interest is defined as a shameful or morbid interest in sex, nudity or excretion while patently offensive refers to materials that, generally speaking, shocks community standards regarding how sexual matters are presented or represented.

[131] *A Book Named John Cleland's Memoirs of a Woman of Pleasure v. Attorney General*, 383 U.S. 413, 86 S.Ct. 975 (1966).

[132] *Ginzburg v. United States*, 383 U.S. 463, 86 S.Ct. 942 (1966).

[133] *Commonwealth v. Peter Holmes*, 17 Mass. 336 (1821).

was a work of art. The experts, however, were asked by a cross-examining prosecuting attorney if they realized that the book contained "20 sex acts, four of them in the presence of others; four acts of lesbianism, two acts of male homosexuality, two acts of flagellation and one of female masturbation."[134]

"Fanny Hill," then, is a frankly erotic novel. Justice Brennan summed up the tests for obscenity which the highest court had approved:[135]

> We defined obscenity in *Roth* in the following terms: "[W]hether to the average person, applying contemporary community standards, the dominant theme of the material taken as a whole appeals to prurient interest." 354 U.S. at 489, 77 S.Ct. at 1311. Under this definition, as elaborated in subsequent cases, three elements must coalesce: it must be established that (a) the dominant theme of the materials taken as a whole appeals to a prurient interest in sex; (b) the material is patently offensive because it affronts contemporary community standards relating to the description or representation of sexual matters; and (c) the material is utterly without redeeming social value.

The Supreme Court ruled that the Massachusetts courts had erred in believing that a book could be deemed obscene even though not "unqualifiedly worthless." Justice Brennan, writing for himself and two other justices, stated that a book "can not be proscribed unless it is found to be *utterly* without redeeming social value."[136] Two other justices concurred in the result but not Brennan's reasoning in a plurality victory for the book and its distributors.

The *Ginzburg* case involved three publications: "*EROS*, a hardcover magazine of expensive format; *Liaison*, a bi-weekly newsletter; and *"The Housewife's Handbook on Selective Promiscuity,"* * * * a short book." Justice Brennan took notice of abundant evidence from Ralph Ginzburg's federal district court trial "that each of the accused publications was originated or sold as stock in trade of the sordid business of pandering— the business of purveying textual or graphic matter openly advertised to appeal to the erotic interest of their customers."[137]

Included as evidence of this "pandering"[138] were *EROS* magazine's attempts to get mailing privileges from the whimsically named hamlets of Intercourse and Blue Ball, Pennsylvania. Mailing privileges were

---

[134] Cf. the outraged dissent by Justice Tom C. Clark, 383 U.S. 413, 441–445, 86 S.Ct. 975, 989–996 (1966).

[135] *A Book Named John Cleland's Memoirs of a Woman of Pleasure v. Attorney General*, 383 U.S. 413, 418, 86 S.Ct. 975, 977 (1966).

[136] Ibid. at 419, 978.

[137] *Ginzburg v. United States*, 383 U.S. 463, 467, 86 S.Ct. 942, 945 (1966).

[138] Pandering is defined as "catering to the gratification of the lust of another" *Black's Law Dictionary* (5th ed. 1989).

finally obtained in Middlesex, New Jersey.[139] Also, Justice Brennan found "the leer of the sensualist" permeating the advertising for the three publications. *Liaison,* for example, was extolled as "*Cupid's Chronicle,*" and the advertising circulars asked, "Are you a member of the sexual elite?"[140]

> The Court split severely over the *Ginzburg* case, however, with Justices Black, Douglas, Harlan and Stewart all registering bitter dissents. Justice Black set the tone for his dissenting brethren, declaring:[141]
>
> * * * Ginzburg * * * is now finally and authoritatively condemned to serve five years in prison for distributing printed matter about sex which neither Ginzburg nor anyone else could possibly have known to be criminal.

Justice Harlan accused the court's majority of rewriting the federal obscenity statute in order to convict Ginzburg, and called the new "pandering" test unconstitutionally vague.[142] And Justice Stewart asserted in his dissent that Ginzburg was not charged with "commercial exploitation," with "pandering," or with "titillation," and to allow him to be convicted on such grounds was to deny him due process of law.[143]

Justice Douglas added his denunciation of the condemnation of materials as obscene not because of their content, but because of the way they were advertised.[144]

PROTECTING THE YOUNG: THE GINSBERG CASE AND THE "VARIABLE OBSCENITY" CONCEPT

As if to confound careless spellers, it happens that one of the most important cases after the Ralph *Ginzburg* case involved a man named Ginsberg: Sam Ginsberg. In the 1968 *Ginsberg* case, the Supreme Court held by a 6–3 vote that a New York statute which defined obscenity on the basis of its appeal to minors under 17 was not unconstitutionally vague.

Sam Ginsberg and his wife operated Sam's Stationery and Luncheonette in Bellmore, Long Island. In 1965, a mother discovered that her son, and other teenage boys, were able to buy "girlie" magazines at Sam's Stationery. She called police and sent her 16-year-old son to the Ginsbergs' store to buy some of the magazines. The boy purchased two magazines—apparently *Sir* and *Gent* or similar publications—walked out of the luncheonette and handed them to a waiting police officer.

---

[139] *Ginzburg v. United States,* 383 U.S. 463, 467, 86 S.Ct. 942, 945 (1966).

[140] Ibid. at 469n, 946.

[141] Ibid. at 476, 950.

[142] Ibid. at 495, 955.

[143] Ibid. at 497, 956.

[144] Ibid.

On the basis of this sale, Sam Ginsberg was convicted of violation of a New York law making it a misdemeanor "knowingly to sell * * * to a minor under 17 any picture * * * which depicts nudity * * * and which is harmful to minors" and "any * * * magazine * * * which contains * * * [such pictures] and which, taken as a whole, is harmful to minors."[145]

It should be noted that magazines such as the 16-year-old boy purchased from Sam Ginsberg's luncheonette in 1965 would be found two years later *not* to be obscene for adults by the Supreme Court.[146] However the judge at Sam Ginsberg's obscenity trial found pictures in the two magazines which depicted nudity in a manner that was in violation of the New York statute. The trial judge found that the pictures were harmful to minors under the terms of the New York statute.

In affirming Ginsberg's conviction, Justice Brennan approved the concept of "variable obscenity."[147] Brennan acknowledged that the magazines involved in the *Ginsberg* case were not obscene for sale to adults. However, he upheld the right of a state to accord to minors under the age of 17 a more restricted right of access than assured to adults to judge and determine for themselves what sex material they may read or see.[148]

In the case that resulted in the fining and jailing of *Eros* publisher Ralph Ginzburg, the Supreme Court served notice that not only *what* was sold but *how* it was sold would be taken into account.[149] The *how* of selling or distributing literature can include a legitimate public concern over the materials which minor children see. In essence, *Ginsberg* established the concept of "variable obscenity", holding that materials not obscene for adults can be found to be obscene if children are allowed access to them.[150]

INDECISIVENESS: REDRUP AND STANLEY

In 1967, the Supreme Court of the United States openly admitted its confusion over obscenity law in a case known as *Redrup v. New York*.[151] This decision did not *look* important: it took up only six pages in United States Reports and only about four pages were devoted to its unsigned *per curiam* ["by the court"] majority opinion. The other two pages were

[145] *Ginsberg v. New York*, 390 U.S. 629, 633, 88 S.Ct. 1274, 1276 (1968). The statute is Article 484–H of the New York Penal Law, McKinney's Consol. Laws c. 40.

[146] *Redrup v. New York*, 386 U.S. 767, 87 S.Ct. 1414 (1967). Justice Brennan noted that *Redrup* had been decided before Ginsberg's case made it to the Supreme Court, but declared that *Redrup* would not invalidate Ginsberg's conviction.

[147] *Ginsberg v. New York*, 390 U.S. 629, 635 n., 88 S.Ct. 1274, 1278 n. (1968), quoting Lockhart and McClure, "Censorship of Obscenity: The Developing Constitutional Standards," 45 *Minnesota Law Review* 5, 85 (1960).

[148] Ibid. at 635, 1277–1278; see *Butler v. Michigan*, 352 U.S. 380, 77 S.Ct. 524 (1957); *Roth v. United States*, 354 U.S. 476, 77 S.Ct. 1304, 1309 (1957).

[149] *Ginzburg v. United States*, 383 U.S. 463, 86 S.Ct. 942 (1966).

[150] *Ginsberg v. New York*, 390 U.S. 629, 88 S.Ct. 1274 (1968).

[151] *Redrup v. New York*, 386 U.S. 767, 87 S.Ct. 1414 (1967).

given over to a dissent by Justice John Marshall Harlan, with whom Justice Tom C. Clark joined.

Redrup was a significant case simply because the Court said that a majority of its members could not agree on a standard which could declare so-called "girlie magazines" and similar publications to be obscene. *Redrup* seemed for a time to be the most important obscenity case since *Roth v. United States* because it was used by both state and federal courts for several years to avoid many of the complexities of judging whether works of art or literature are obscene.

On June 12, 1967, the date the Court's term ended that year and less than two months after *Redrup* was decided, the Court reversed 11 obscenity convictions by merely referring to *Redrup v. New York.*[152] Another dozen state or federal obscenity convictions were reversed during the next year, with *Redrup* being listed as an important factor in each reversal.

STANLEY V. GEORGIA (1969)

In 1969, there was hope that the Supreme Court—clearly frustrated by its growing caseload of obscenity appeals—would find some way to bring order to this complex and troublesome area of law. The Court's resolution of *Stanley v. Georgia* added to this hope.[153]

The *Stanley* case arose when a Georgia state investigator and three federal agents, operating under a federal search warrant, searched the home of Robert E. Stanley, looking for bookmaking records. Evidence of bookmaking was not found, but the searchers found three reels of 8 millimeter film and a projector. They treated themselves to a showing and decided—as did the court—that the films were obscene. When Stanley's appeal reached the Supreme Court, Justice Thurgood Marshall—writing for a unanimous Court—overturned the conviction, naming two constitutional rights.[154]

(1) A right growing out of the First Amendment, a "right to receive information and ideas, regardless of their social worth."[155]

(2) A constitutional right to privacy against government intrusions interfering with receiving information and ideas in the privacy of one's home:[156]

[152] Dwight L. Teeter, Jr., and Don R. Pember, "The Retreat from Obscenity: Redrup v. New York," *Hastings Law Journal* Vol. 21 (Nov., 1969), pp. 175–189.

[153] *Stanley v. Georgia,* 394 U.S. 557, 89 S.Ct. 1243 (1969).

[154] Black, J., concurred in the decision.

[155] Ibid. at 564, 1247, citing *Winters v. New York,* 333 U.S. 507, 510, 68 S.Ct. 665 (1948).

[156] Ibid. at 564–565, 1247–1248.

Additionally, Justice Marshall wrote that "States retain broad power to regulate obscenity; that power simply does not extend to mere possession by the individual in the privacy of his own home."[157]

OVERREADING STANLEY

Taken together, *Redrup* and *Stanley* indicated to some judges that prohibitions on obscenity had been loosened by the Supreme Court. *Redrup* suggested that the Court wouldn't define anything but hard-core pornography as obscene. Further, the right to possess obscene materials would make little sense if persons could not acquire it. And so, a U.S. District Court judge in *Reidel v. United States* reasoned that " 'if a person has the right to receive and possess this material, then someone must have the right to deliver it to him.' " He concluded that § 1461 of the United States Code could not be validly applied unless obscene material is directed at children or unwilling adults.[158]

In doing so, the judge ignored both the precedent of *Roth* and the Supreme Court's own express limitation on the reach of Stanley. The Supreme Court quickly made clear that the judge had misread *Stanley*.[159]

> The District Court gave *Stanley* too wide a sweep. * * * Whatever the scope of the "right to receive" referred to in *Stanley,* it is not so broad as to immunize the dealing in obscenity in which Reidel engaged here—dealings that Roth held unprotected by the First Amendment.

Also, in *Byrne v. Karalexis* (1971),[160] the U.S. Supreme Court upheld the prosecution of a theater owner for showing the Swedish film, *"I Am Curious (Yellow)."* This mentioned a U.S. district court reading of *Stanley* saying that people ought to be able to watch sexy movies in the relative privacy of a theater's darkness. The Supreme Court, however, voted to allow states to prosecute theater owners exhibiting this film.[161]

OVERREACHING BY A DISTRICT COURT

In 2005, a federal judge declared federal obscenity laws unconstitutional applying privacy rights that echoed the Supreme Court's decision in *Stanley*. Judge Gary Lancaster dismissed a 10-count indictment against the operators of an adult video company that operated a Web site featuring graphic sexual content.[162] Extreme Associates, the defendants, had been charged with nine counts of violating federal

---

157 Ibid. at 564, 1247–1248.

158 Quoted in *United States v. Reidel,* 402 U.S. 351, 355, 91 S.Ct. 1410, 1412–1413 (1971).

159 *United States v. Reidel,* 402 U.S. 351, 355–356, 91 S.Ct. 1410, 1412–1413 (1971).

160 *Byrne v. Karalexis,* 401 U.S. 216, 91 S.Ct. 777 (1971).

161 Ibid., overturning 306 F.Supp. 1363 (D.Mass.1969).

162 *U.S. v. Extreme Associates, Inc.,* 352 F.Supp.2d 578 (W.D.Pa. 2005).

obscenity statutes and a single count of conspiracy in connection with the distribution of obscene materials through the mail and over the Internet.

The defendants did not dispute the government's contention that the videos were obscene. They opposed the indictments on the grounds that they violated constitutional rights to privacy and liberty.[163] Their arguments were similar to those advanced, and rejected, in *Reidel* but had an additional proposition. They argued that as the federal statute affected constitutional rights, the statutes had to be examined under a Strict Scrutiny standard.

Judge Lancaster ruled that speech, privacy and liberty rights were affected by the obscenity statute and the Strict Scrutiny standard should be applied.

Judge Lancaster found that there was no compelling interest that allowed the government to prosecute persons who sought the materials available through Extreme Associates.[164]

> We find that the federal obscenity statutes do not survive the strict scrutiny test as applied to the circumstances of this case. First, we find that after *Lawrence* the government can no longer rely on the advancement of a moral code i.e., preventing consenting adults from entertaining lewd or lascivious thoughts, as a legitimate, let alone a compelling, state interest.

Lawrence was the Supreme Court case that held that Texas' homosexual sodomy law was unconstitutional. In Lawrence, a majority of the Supreme Court concluded that the government had no interest, including promoting a moral code, that was strong enough to justify invading the privacy rights of consenting adults.[165]

In December, 2005, a three-judge panel of the Third Circuit reversed the dismissal. The panel reversed Judge Lancaster largely on the grounds that his court lacked authority to rule the obscenity statutes unconstitutional. The appellate panel's reasoning rested on the fact that federal obscenity laws have withstood constitutional challenges for more than 30 years and also on explicit direction from the Supreme Court itself on the discretion of lower courts.[166]

> In *Rodriguez de Quijas v. Shearson/American Express Inc.*, 490 U.S. 477, 484, 109 S.Ct. 1917, 104 L.Ed.2d 526 (1989), the Supreme Court explicitly admonished lower courts that "[i]f a precedent of this Court has direct application in a case, yet appears to rest on reasons rejected in some other line of decisions, the Court of Appeals should follow the case which

[163] Ibid. at 585.

[164] Ibid. at 3586–587.

[165] Ibid. at 591.

[166] Ibid. at 155.

directly controls, leaving to this Court the prerogative of overruling its own decisions."

In short, the appellate panel said that Judge Lancaster could not overrule well-established Supreme Court precedent. That is not to say that Supreme Court decisions are inviolate in perpetuity. Lower courts are free to consider positions that run counter to Supreme Court precedent. But those courts must defer in their judgments until the Supreme Court chooses to change its interpretation of the law and the constitution.

The Supreme Court chose not to re-examine the issue and denied certiorari in the case in May 2006.[167]

15. CREATING A NEW CONSENSUS: THE MILLER STANDARD

In 1973, Chief Justice Burger succeeded in developing a new set of obscenity standards that a majority of the Court could accept.

MILLER V. CALIFORNIA

Most important of the five obscenity cases decided by the Supreme Court on June 21, 1973—and indeed the most important such case since *Roth v. United States* (1957)—was *Miller v. California.* In that case, as in the four others decided that same day, the Court split 5–4, revealing a new coalition among the Justices where obscenity and pornography were concerned.[168]

Miller v. California began when Marvin Miller mailed five unsolicited—and graphic—brochures to a restaurant in Newport Beach. The envelope was opened by the restaurant's manager, with his mother looking on, and they complained to police. The brochures advertised four books, *"Intercourse, Man-Woman," "Sex Orgies Illustrated,"* and *"An Illustrated History of Pornography,"* plus a film titled *"Marital Intercourse."* After a jury trial, Miller was convicted of a misdemeanor under the California Penal Code.[169]

---

[167] *Extreme Associates, Inc. v. U.S.,* 547 U.S. 1143, 126 S.Ct. 2048 (2006).

[168] *Paris Adult Theatre I v. Slaton,* 413 U.S. 49, 93 S.Ct. 2628 (1973); *United States v. Orito,* 413 U.S. 139, 93 S.Ct. 2674 (1973); *Kaplan v. California,* 413 U.S. 115, 93 S.Ct. 2680 (1973), and *U.S. v. Twelve 200-ft. Reels of Super 8mm. Film,* 413 U.S. 123, 93 S.Ct. 2665 (1973). That coalition included Justice Byron R. White (appointed by President Kennedy) plus four justices appointed by President Nixon: Chief Justice Warren Burger, plus Justices Harry Blackman, William H. Rehnquist, and Lewis Powell. Dissenting in *Miller* plus the four cases listed were Justices Thurgood Marshall, Potter Stewart, William O. Douglas, and the author of the *Roth* test of 1957 and of many obscenity decisions thereafter, Justice William J. Brennan, Jr.

[169] *Miller v. California,* 413 U.S. 15, 93 S.Ct. 2607 (1973). West's Ann. California Pen. Code § 312.2(a) makes it a misdemeanor to knowingly distribute obscene matter. After the jury trial, the Appellate Department, Superior Court of California, Orange County, summarily affirmed the conviction without offering an opinion.

Writing for the majority in *Miller,* Chief Justice Burger ruled that California could punish such conduct. He noted that the case involved "a situation in which sexually explicit materials have been thrust by aggressive sales action upon unwilling recipients or juveniles."

Endeavoring to formulate a new standard, Chief Justice Burger first returned to *Roth's* declaration that obscene materials were not protected by the First Amendment.[170] Then, he denounced the test of obscenity outlined in the *"Fanny Hill (Memoirs of a Woman of Pleasure)"* case in 1960, nine years after *Roth.* In that case, three justices, in a plurality opinion, held that material could not be judged obscene unless it were proven to be "utterly without redeeming social importance." Burger wrote that such a standard forced prosecutors to "prove a negative," which he termed a "burden virtually impossible to discharge under our criminal standards of proof."[171]

The Chief Justice wrote that since the 1957 decision in *Roth,* the Court had not been able to muster a majority to agree to a standard of what constitutes "obscene, pornographic material subject to regulation under the states' police power."[172] In 1973, however, Burger found himself in substantial agreement with four other Justices. He made the most of it, setting out general rules on what states could regulate ("hard-core pornography") and re-wording the *Roth* and *Memoirs* tests into a standard reducing the states' burden of proof necessary to convict persons for distribution or possession of sexually explicit materials.[173]

> * * * [W]e now confine the permissible scope of such regulation to works which depict or describe sexual conduct. That conduct must be specifically defined by the applicable state law, as written or authoritatively construed. A state offense must also be limited to works which, taken as whole, appeal to the prurient interest in sex, which portray sexual conduct in a patently offensive way, and which, taken as a whole, do not have serious literary, artistic, political, or scientific value.

---

[170] *Miller v. California,* 413 U.S. 15, 20, 93 S.Ct. 2607, 2613 (1973), citing *Roth v. United States,* 354 U.S. 476, 77 S.Ct. 1304 (1957).

[171] Ibid. at 22, 2613–2614, citing *Memoirs of a Woman of Pleasure v. Massachusetts,* 383 U.S. 413, 86 S.Ct. 975 (1966). Emphasis the Court's.

[172] Ibid.

[173] Ibid. at 23–24, 93 S.Ct. 2607, 2614, 2615 (1973). Emphasis the Court's. Chief Justice Burger wrote that a state could, through statute, forbid:

> "(a) Patently offensive representations or descriptions of ultimate sexual acts, normal or perverted, actual or simulated.
>
> (b) Patently offensive representations or descriptions of masturbation, excretory functions, and lewd exhibition of the genitals."

Burger also stated: "Sex and nudity may not be exploited without limit by films or pictures exhibited or sold in places of public accommodation any more than live sex and nudity can be exhibited or sold without limit in such public places. At a minimum, prurient, patently offensive depiction or description of sexual conduct must have serious literary, artistic, political or scientific value to merit First Amendment protection."

> The basic guidelines for the trier of fact must be: (a) whether "the average person, applying contemporary community standards" would find that the work, taken as a whole, appeals to the prurient interest * * * (b) whether the work depicts or describes, in a patently offensive way, sexual conduct specifically defined by the applicable state law, and (c) whether the work, taken as a whole, lacks serious literary, artistic, political or scientific value. We do not adopt as a constitutional standard the "*utterly* without redeeming social value" test of *Memoirs v. Massachusetts* * * *: that concept has never commanded the adherence of more than three Justices at one time.

The majority opinion also declared that it would be unwise to attempt to formulate a uniform national standard to determine what appeals to "prurient interest" or what is "patently offensive." "[O]ur nation is simply too big and diverse for this Court to reasonably expect that such standards could be articulated for all 50 states in a single formulation * * * "[174] The First Amendment, Burger said, did not force citizens in Maine or Mississippi to accept all depictions of sexual conduct that might be tolerated in Las Vegas or New York City.

This new recognition of "community standards" in the area of obscenity law also appeared to furnish the Court the justification it had been seeking to reduce its obscenity appeal workload: let obscenity be defined on a state-by-state basis. That way, the Court might not have to review the contents of each allegedly obscene book or film that had been banned in order to decide whether it actually was obscene under federal law.[175] Because *Miller* permitted "community standards" to be a factor evaluated in determining what was obscene, the Supreme Court could now defer in those matters to the lower courts, pointing out that local judges and juries were much better situated than Supreme Court Justices to interpret and apply local sexual standards. Unfortunately, once again, those who hoped for this result had underestimated the inherent capacity of obscenity law to confound the judicial system.

Justice Brennan's opposition to these decisions founded in on his growing belief that no matter what set of standards were used, obscenity statutes would always be unconstitutionally vague. That is, there are *"scienter"* problems: obscenity laws are by their nature so formless that defendants can not have fair notice as to whether publications or films they distribute or exhibit are obscene. Without fair notice, there will be a "chilling effect" upon protected speech.

---

[174] Ibid. at 302618.

[175] Although the *Roth* decision did not specifically require that a single uniform federal standard be applied in all obscenity cases, Justice Brennan interpreted it that way in *Jacobellis v. Ohio*, 378 U.S. 184, 84 S.Ct. 1676 (1964).

Brennan wrote:[176]

> I am convinced that the approach initiated 15 years ago in *Roth v. United States* * * * culminating in the Court's decision today, cannot bring stability to this area of the law without jeopardizing First Amendment values, and I have concluded that the time has come to make a significant departure from that approach.
>
> * * *
>
> Our experience with the *Roth* approach has certainly taught us that the outright suppression of obscenity cannot be reconciled with the fundamental principles of the First and Fourteenth Amendments. * * * [W]e have failed to formulate a standard that sharply distinguishes protected from unprotected speech
>
> * * *
>
> I would hold, therefore, that at least in the absence of distribution to juveniles or obtrusive exposure to unconsenting adults, the First and Fourteenth Amendments prohibit the state and federal governments from attempting wholly to suppress sexually oriented materials on the basis of their allegedly "obscene" contents. Nothing in this approach precludes those governments from taking action to serve what may be strong and legitimate interests through regulation of the manner of distribution of sexually oriented material.

From the *Miller* decision of 1973 well into the 1980s, the Court split 5–4 in many of the obscenity cases it has decided. The majority followed *Miller,* and favored stringent regulation of sexually explicit material. Time and time again, including many *per curiam* decisions in which the Court upheld obscenity prosecutions without an explanatory opinion, Justice Brennan dissented, constantly contending that obscenity can not be described with sufficient clarity to give defendants fair notice.[177]

THE MEANINGS OF MILLER: DEFINING "COMMUNITY STANDARDS"

If the Supreme Court Justices had expected that the new "contemporary community standards" test introduced by the *Miller* case would significantly reduce their obscenity caseload, they were soon to be disappointed.

---

[176] Brennan dissent in *Paris Adult Theatre I v. Slaton,* 413 U.S. 49, 73–74, 83, 93 S.Ct. 2628, 2642, 2647, 2662 (1973), which concentrated, however, on the reasoning in *Miller.* This dissent relied on the Court's conclusion in *Redrup v. New York,* 386 U.S. 767, 87 S.Ct. 1414 (1967).

[177] See, e.g., *Trinkler v. Alabama,* 414 U.S. 955, 94 S.Ct. 265 (1973); *Raymond Roth v. New Jersey,* 414 U.S. 962, 94 S.Ct. 271 (1973); *Sharp v. Texas,* 414 U.S. 1118, 94 S.Ct. 854 (1974); *J-R Distributors, Inc. v. Washington,* 418 U.S. 949, 94 S.Ct. 3217 (1974). See also *Hamling v. United States,* 418 U.S. 87, 140–152, 94 S.Ct. 2887, 2919–2924 (1974).

JENKINS V. GEORGIA

Take a Georgia case involving Mike Nichols' serious and much-praised film, "*Carnal Knowledge*," a film containing no frontal nudity or explicit depictions of sex acts. Nevertheless, in *Jenkins v. Georgia*, theater manager Billy Jenkins was convicted under a Georgia statute forbidding distribution of obscene material. This state action was so ludicrous that the Supreme Court of the United States was compelled to intervene, granting certiorari. Writing for the Court, Justice William H. Rehnquist declared that the film was not patently offensive and therefore not obscene because it contained none of the actions listed in *Miller v. California*:[178]

> "representations or descriptions of ultimate sexual acts, normal or perverted, actual or simulated," and "representations or descriptions of masturbation, excretory functions, and lewd exhibition of the genitals."

In essence, the Court was saying that although it was now willing to accept the fact that "contemporary community standards" regarding sexual matters might vary to some extent from region to region, there could be no finding of obscenity anywhere in the United States unless the material in question could reasonably be considered to be obscene.

HAMLING V. UNITED STATES: LOCAL STANDARDS NEED NOT APPLY

In one of the first obscenity cases to reach the Supreme Court after it enunciated the *Miller* test, a majority of the Court determined that the exclusion of a local survey on obscenity standards was permissible. William Hamling and several co-defendants were convicted on 12 counts of using the mails to deliver obscene advertisements in 1971, two years *before* the *Miller* decision recognized the relevance of local community standards in determining whether the average person could reasonably find that a work appealed to prurient interest. Although Hamling was convicted before *Miller* came down, his case followed *Miller* to the Supreme Court.

Hamling and friends were attempting to sell an illustrated version of the government's own *Presidential Report of the Commission on Obscenity and Pornography*, offering in their promotional mailer a wide assortment of graphic photographs illustrating those lurid and obscene sexual activities the government report had simply described.

During the trial, conducted in San Diego, California, the judge had refused to allow the defense to introduce the results of a survey of 718 San Diego residents. The survey results suggested that a majority of those surveyed felt the brochure should be made available to the public. The judge ruled that the jury was to use a national standard and the

[178] *Jenkins v. Georgia*, 418 U.S. 153, 160, 94 S.Ct. 2750, 2755 (1974).

introduction of a local survey would be inappropriate because local views would only constitute a part of the national standard he would require the jury to follow in determining whether the brochure was obscene.[179]

When the Supreme Court reviewed the case in 1974, Justice Rehnquist, writing for the majority, concluded that the refusal of the trial judge to admit evidence of community standards did not prejudice the rights of the defendants because the brochure itself was clearly obscene.[180] Further, the majority concluded that the trial court's decision to keep the local survey out of evidence did not constitute error. The majority also concluded that when the trial judge instructed the jury to gauge the obscenity of the brochures based on national standards of obscenity, the instruction did not rise to the level of reversible error because the jury would have reached the same conclusion even if they considered local standards.

Dissenting, Justice Brennan wrote forcefully that the local survey should not have been withheld from jurors' deliberations because it could have changed their verdict. He also criticized the Supreme Court's majority for allowing the trial court to use a national rather than a local test for obscenity.[181]

> The emphasis on 'national' standards is the very core of the instructions, because the trial judge made 'national' standards the central criterion of the determination of the obscenity of the brochure. He referred to 'national' standards in his instructions no less than 18 times, 14 of them within the space of four transcript pages.
>
> * * *
>
> But in addition to the palpable absurdity of the court's surmises that introduction of the San Diego study could not have affected the jurors' deliberations, and that petitioners would not have introduced additional evidence or done anything materially different had they known the jurors would be instructed on local standards, the Court's assertion that the jurors could not have ruled differently if instructed to apply local, not national, standards evinces a claim of omniscience hardly mortal. It is the more remarkable in light of the contrary supposition of *Miller v. California*, 413 U.S. 15, 93 S.Ct. 2607, 37 L.Ed.2d 419 (1973), that a jury instructed to apply national standards could indeed reach a different conclusion from what it might if instructed to apply local standards * * *

---

179 The judge's instructions read, in part, "You must measure the material by contemporary or current national community standards and determine whether the material so exceeds the customary limits of candor in the descriptions and representations of sex and nudity which are reasonably acceptable in the national community, that they are patently offensive."

180 *Hamling v. United States*, 418 U.S. 87, 94 S.Ct. 2887 (1974).

181 Ibid. at 145–151.

In addition, Justice Brennan, joined by Justices Stewart and Marshall, asserted that material should not be suppressed unless there is distribution to juveniles or obtrusive exposure to non-consenting adults.[182] He also criticized the concept of "community standards" itself, pointing out that national distributors, facing "variegated standards * * * impossible to discern," will be forced to abide by the most repressive standard when distributing sexually oriented materials.[183]

POPE V. ILLINOIS

One example of the difficulties lower courts have had in knowing exactly how the "community standards" test should be applied is illustrated by *Pope v. Illinois.*[184] Here the question was whether the artistic value of a work was to be determined by the typical citizen in the community where the case was being tried. As in *Hamling*, the Supreme Court gave substantially less weight to the community standard than was suggested in *Miller*.

It should be recalled that *Miller v. California* set out a what amounts to a "saving grace" rule in the three-part test for determining whether material is obscene and therefore outside the protections of the First Amendment.[185]

> (3) Then, even though the material does appeal to prurient interest in a patently offensive manner, does it deserve free speech protection despite such qualities because of having serious literary, artistic, political or scientific value?

In this case—involving sales of magazines to undercover agents in a Rockford, Illinois adult bookstore—the constitutionality of judge's instructions to the jury were challenged. At their trials, the defendants argued that the literary or artistic value of a work should be based on a uniform national standard.[186] The judge rejected this argument, instructing the jury instead to consider its value in terms of, "how it would be viewed by ordinary adults in the whole state of Illinois." Writing for the majority, Justice White stated:

> There is no suggestion in our cases that the opinion of the value of an allegedly obscene work is to be determined by reference to community standards. Indeed, *Smith v. United States,* 431 U.S. 291, 97 S.Ct. 1756 (1977) held that, in a federal prosecution for

---

[182] Ibid. at 141–142, 2919.

[183] Ibid. at 144, 2921.

[184] *Pope v. Illinois*, 481 U.S. 497, 107 S.Ct. 1918 (1987). For other examples of the type of problems lower courts have encountered in attempting to apply this standard see *Pinkus v. United States*, 436 U.S. 293, 98 S.Ct. 1808 (1978)—children not to be included in considering community standards-and *Smith v. United States*, 431 U.S. 291, 97 S.Ct. 1756 (1977)—jury can find material obscene under federal law even if state in which offense occurs has no anti-obscenity law.

[185] *Miller v. California*, 413 U.S. 15, 23–24, 93 S.Ct. 2607, 2614–2615 (1973).

[186] This has come to be known as the "SLAPS" test; does the material have *S*erious *L*iterary, *A*rtistic, *P*olitical or *S*cientific value that protects it from being classified as obscene.

> mailing obscene materials, the first and second prongs of the *Miller* test—appeal to prurient interest and patent offensiveness—are issues of fact for the jury to determine applying contemporary community standards. The Court then observed that unlike prurient appeal or patent offensiveness, "[L]iterary, artistic, political, or scientific value * * * is not discussed in *Miller* in terms of contemporary community standards."

White maintained that "artistic value" was not a relative term that each community could be permitted to establish for itself.

> Just as the ideas a work represents need not obtain majority approval to merit protection, neither, insofar as the First Amendment is concerned, does the value of a work vary from community to community based on the degree of local acceptance it has won. The proper inquiry is * * * whether a reasonable person would find such value in the material, taken as a whole.

However, instead of reversing Pope's conviction outright, the Supreme Court sent the case back to a lower court to determine whether the use of the national standard constituted reversible error or mere harmless error that would allow the conviction to stand. On remand, the Illinois appellate court determined that the use of the national standard to ultimately decide whether the magazines were obscene was mere harmless error and affirmed the conviction. The appellate court ruled that the magazines were clearly obscene on their face.[187]

DETERMINING WHICH COMMUNITY STANDARDS APPLY ON THE INTERNET

One of the most interesting aspects of the evolution of obscenity today is which community standard should apply when determining whether material is obscene or not. Should the determinative community be the place where users download or view allegedly obscene material or should the courts use a different community, one defined by the Web?

In an early case predating the widespread use of the Internet, the 6th Circuit had to deal with the question of venue and community standards arising from the use of a computer bulletin board. Before the advent of widespread access to Web sites with adult content, computer users would dial on telephone lines to bulletin boards maintained on remote computers. Once connected, users could examine the contents of the bulletin board and then download files in a point-to-point transmission. The Internet has largely supplanted bulletin boards with Web sites.

---

[187] *Pope v. Illinois*, 162 Ill.App.3d 299, 113 Ill.Dec. 547, 515 N.E.2d 356 (2d Dist.App.Ct.1987).

In *U.S. v. Thomas*,[188] a 6th Circuit panel considered the argument advanced by Robert and Carleen Thomas that the material they were convicted of transmitting from their computer bulletin board should not have been judged by a jury applying the community standards of Memphis, Tenn.

The Thomases operated a bulletin board from their hometown of Milpitas, California. Customers could obtain a password and then log into the bulletin board where they could view images and download them into their own computers. A postal inspector learned of the bulletin board service, purchased a password and downloaded images. Subsequently, federal agents raided the Thomas' home and seized their computer system. The couple was indicted by a federal grand jury in Memphis and eventually convicted of conspiracy, transportation of obscene materials in interstate commerce and sending images of minors engaged in sex.

The Thomases appealed arguing, among other things, that because the postal inspector downloaded the images, they were not guilty of transporting the images to Tennessee. Along with that argument came their contention that the Internet required a different community standard because bulletin board operators had no way of knowing who would download their images and where. As a result, if traditional venue and community standards rules were applied, Internet content providers would have to censor themselves for fear that they would be prosecuted in some restrictive community.

But the appeals court rejected that argument saying that the Thomases knew who had purchased passwords to their bulletin board. If they wanted to avoid prosecution in Tennessee, they should have refused to sell passwords to anyone from there. But bulletin board operations are different from Web sites. For one thing, Web site operators, as a general principle, do not have control over who accesses their sites. There are systems that are intended to restrict access to adults that use credit card information or subscription to services like Adult Check but even those do not restrict where the content is viewed. And, just as with the Thomases, federal investigators can choose to access Internet content in the most restrictive communities.

The question of the community standard was at least raised tangentially in Justice Stevens opinion in *Reno v. ACLU*,[189] the case that found the indecency provisions of the Communications Decency Act to be unconstitutional (The case is taken up later in this chapter.). In looking at the effect of the CDA on Internet content, Justice Stevens said that the act created a national standard for acceptable content that ran counter to the notion of individual community controls created in *Miller*. Community standards provide protection for speech, Stevens noted.[190]

---

[188] *U.S. v. Thomas*, 74 F.3d 701, 24 Media L. Rep. 1321 (6th Cir.1996).

[189] *Reno v. ACLU*, 521 U.S. 844, 117 S.Ct. 2329, 25 Media L. Rep. 1833 (1997).

[190] Ibid. at 873.

> This "societal value" requirement, absent in the CDA, allows appellate courts to impose some limitations and regularity on the definition by setting, as a matter of law, a national floor for socially redeeming value. The Government's contention that courts will be able to give such legal limitations to the CDA's standards is belied by Miller's own rationale for having juries determine whether material is "patently offensive" according to community standards: that such questions are essentially ones of fact.

Without the protections afforded by having individual communities establish what they found acceptable, the CDA impermissibly limited Internet speakers who would censor themselves rather than risk prosecution.[191]

> Moreover, the "community standards" criterion as applied to the Internet means that any communication available to a nation wide audience will be judged by the standards of the community most likely to be offended by the message.

With that, Stevens pointed out the problem of using community standards in a *Miller* determination of whether materials are patently offensive or appeal to prurient interest. The Internet is unlike other means of mass communication. While magazine and video distributors can choose to avoid sending their arguably obscene content to particular locales, the Internet content provider has no such control. That is illustrated with a comparison between the cases of *ACLU v. Reno,*[192] the challenge to the Child Online Protection Act, and *Sable Communications v. FCC.*[193]

In *Sable*, the operators of a dial-a-porn business, sued to prevent enforcement of changes in the federal communications act as well as prohibitions on the trafficking in interstate commercial obscene phone messages. The *Sable* plaintiffs argued that a prohibition on obscene messages violated their rights as it would subject them to prosecution even though the messages might not be obscene in some communities because of their standards. The Supreme Court concluded that the federal ban did not create a national obscenity standard but instead allowed communities to set their own levels of what was acceptable and what was obscene. And, in a key part of the decision, at least for purposes of this discussion, the court said that Sable could avoid prosecution by exercising discretion.[194]

> There is no constitutional barrier under *Miller* to prohibiting communications that are obscene in some communities under local standards even though they are not obscene in others.

---

[191] Ibid. at 877–878.

[192] *ACLU v. Reno*, 217 F.3d 162 (3d Cir.2000).

[193] *Sable v. FCC*, 492 U.S. 115, 109 S.Ct. 2829 (1989).

[194] Ibid.

> Sable, which has the burden of complying with the prohibition, is free to tailor its messages, on a selective basis, to the communities it chooses to serve.

But compare that with the Child Online Protection Act case. COPA, referred to in the industry as "Son of CDA," was a Congressional attempt to create a statute that would restrict adult content on the Internet by using a "harmful to minors" rationale. It made it a crime to operate a commercial Web site what allowed minors to see material that is harmful to them. A federal court enjoined the enforcement of the Act and that injunction was upheld by a panel of the 3rd Circuit Court of Appeals. The 3rd Circuit panel focused on the constitutional problems of imposing a national community standard on Internet content providers.[195]

> Because material posted on the Web is accessible by all Internet users worldwide, and because current technology does not permit a Web publisher to restrict access to its site based on the geographic locale of each particular Internet user, COPA essentially requires that every Web publisher subject to the statute abide by the most restrictive and conservative state's community standards in order to avoid criminal liability. Thus, because the standard by which COPA gauges whether material is "harmful to minors" is based on identifying "contemporary community standards" the inability of Web publishers to restrict access to their Web sites based on the geographic locale of the site visitor, in and of itself, imposes an impermissible burden on constitutionally protected First Amendment speech.

The Supreme Court, in a plurality opinion, rejected the 3rd Circuit panel's conclusion.[196] While eight members agreed to vacate the appellate court's findings and send it back for reconsideration, there was considerable disagreement as to the ultimate constitutionality of "contemporary community standards" in the statute. Justice Stevens wrote the sole dissent.

Justices Thomas wrote the plurality opinion. Only justices Rehnquist and Scalia joined in the key section on the application of "community standards" to the Internet. Justice Thomas' key argument relied on decisions by the Court involving mailings and distribution in traditional media. Justice Thomas quoted from *Hamling* and *Sable* in arguing that distributors bear the responsibility for the reactions of communities that they send their materials to.[197]

> The fact that distributors of allegedly obscene materials may be subjected to varying community standards in the various federal judicial districts into which they transmit the materials does not render a federal statute unconstitutional.

---

195 *ACLU v. Reno*, 217 F.3d 162, 166 (3d Cir.2000).

196 *Ashcroft v. ACLU*, 535 U.S. 564, 122 S.Ct. 1700 (2002).

197 Ibid. at 580–581. Quoting from *Hamling v. U.S.*, 418 U.S. 87, 106, 94 S.Ct. 2887 (1974).

Quoting from *Sable*, Justice Thomas noted that under *Miller*, some communications will be obscene in some communities and not others.[198] "*If Sable's audience is composed of different communities with different local standards, Sable ultimately bears the burden of complying with the prohibition on obscene messages.*" (Emphasis added by Justice Thomas.)

Justice Thomas concluded that the burden of self-protection falls on publishers and distributors. Notwithstanding the government's stipulation that Internet publishers have no control on where consumers access the Web, Justice Thomas said it is still the publishers' responsibility.[199]

> If a publisher wishes for its materials to be judged only by the standards of particular communities, then it need only take the simple steps of utilizing a medium that enables it to target the release of those materials into those communities.

So, Justice Thomas, joined by Justices Rehnquist and Scalia resolved the issue of the application of community standards to the Internet by suggesting that publishers stay off the Internet if they wish to avoid prosecution in the most restrictive communities that exist.

Justice Stevens' dissent responded directly to Justice Thomas' advice by suggesting that a more constitutionally correct approach would be for those people who would be adversely affected to avoid the medium themselves.[200]

> It is hardly a solution to say, as Justice Thomas suggests that a speaker need only choose a different medium in order to avoid having its speech judged by the least tolerant community. Our overbreadth doctrine would quickly become a toothless protection if we were to hold that substituting a more limited forum for expression is an acceptable price to pay. Since a content-based restriction is presumptively invalid, I would place the burden on parents to [quoting Justice Thomas] "take the simple step of utilizing a medium that enables" them to avoid this material before requiring the speaker to find another forum.

Justice Stevens argued that the nature of the Internet would mean that application of COPA would result in some members of the Internet audience being denied access to materials simply because some other parts of the audience found it offensive.

Justice O'Connor rejected the argument that COPA could be found unconstitutional solely on the basis of the application of community standards to the Internet. Justice O'Connor rejected the application of

---

[198] *Sable Communications v. FCC*, 492 U.S. 115, 124, 109 S.Ct. 2829.

[199] *Ashcroft v. ACLU*, 535 U.S. 564, 583, 122 S.Ct. 1700, 1712 (2002).

[200] Ibid. at 605, 1724.

Hamling and *Sable* to the Internet, at least where speech aimed at adults is concerned.[201]

> [G]iven Internet speakers' inability to control the geographic location of their audience, expecting them to bear the burden of controlling the recipients of their speech, as we did in *Hamling* and Sable, may be entirely too much to ask, and would potentially suppress and inordinate amount of expression.

Justice Breyer's concurrence focused on the use of the word "community" in the statute. Justice Breyer concluded that "community" should refer to the community of all adults in the United States. He cited the House Report on the statute.[202]

> The Committee recognizes that the applicability of community standards in the context of the Web is controversial, but understands it as an "adult standard" rather than a "geographic" standard, and one that is reasonably constant among adults in America with respect to what is suitable for minors.

But Justice Breyer then reasoned that the application of variations of this national standard by local juries in different communities would not violate the First Amendment.

COPA BACK IN THE 3RD CIRCUIT

The case was reconsidered by the 3rd Circuit[203] and it found COPA to be unconstitutional, avoiding the issue of "community standards" that the Supreme Court found so troubling. The 3rd Circuit concluded that COPA failed to pass muster under Strict Scrutiny. Applied in many First Amendment cases, the doctrine requires that statutes (1) serve a compelling government interest, (2) be narrowly tailored and (3) be the least restrictive way of achieving that government interest.

While the 3rd Circuit acknowledged that the government had a compelling interest in protecting minors from harmful material, the statute was not narrowly tailored. For one thing, the 3rd Circuit noted, only commercial operators were at risk. A person who placed "harmful materials" on the Web without commercial purpose would be exempt from the penalties.

More troubling to the 3rd Circuit was the definition and probable application of the "material harmful to minors" section. The appellate panel began with a recitation of its concerns about allowing discrete geographic communities to apply their restrictive approaches to the Web. "This limitation by definition burdens speech otherwise protected under

---

201 Ibid. at 587, 1714.

202 H.R. Report No. 105–775, p. 28 (1998).

203 *American Civil Liberties Union v. Ashcroft*, 322 F.3d 240 (3d Cir. 2003).

the First Amendment for adults as well as minors living in more tolerant setting."[204]

The 3rd Circuit also found the question of context to raise serious constitutional questions. Since the *Roth* case, courts have been required to judge works as a whole rather than on isolated passages or sections. COPA defined "harmful material" as, among other things, "any communication, picture, image file." As such, the 3rd Circuit found the selective judgment of individual pictures or images to violate the First Amendment.[205]

> For example, one sexual image, which COPA may proscribe as harmful material, might not be deemed to appeal to the prurient interest of minors if it were to be viewed in the context of an entire collection of Renaissance artwork.
>
> * * *
>
> Because we view such a statute, construed as its own text unquestionably requires, as pertaining only to single individual exhibits, COPA endangers a wide range of communications, exhibits, and speakers whose messages do not comport with the type of harmful materials legitimately targeted under COPA

Because minors have the same access to materials as adults, publishers of nonobscene Web content aimed at adults would find themselves the target of COPA. That overly broad application also violates the strict scrutiny requirement of narrow tailoring of the statute.

Finally, the 3rd Circuit concluded, the statute failed to take into consideration the differences in the wide range of ages and maturity encompassed by the term "minor." The differences between toddlers and teens would mean different results in deciding whether the Web content appealed to prurient interest or had serious literary, artistic, political or scientific value, the appellate panel reasoned.[206]

> [E]ven the Government does not argue, as it could not, that materials that have "serious literary, artistic, political or scientific value" for a sixteen-year-old would have the same value for a minor who is three years old. Nor does any party argue, despite Congress's having targeted and included all minors seventeen or under, that pre-adolescent minors (i.e., ages two, three, four, etc.) could be patently offended by a "normal or perverted sexual act" or have their "prurient interest" aroused by a "post-pubescent female breast," or by being exposed to whatever other material may be designed to appeal to prurient interests.

---

[204] *American Civil Liberties Union v. Ashcroft*, 322 F.3d 240, 252 (3d Cir. 2003).

[205] Ibid.

[206] Ibid. at 253–254.

The case was appealed again to the Supreme Court which affirmed the court of appeals and remanded the case for trial.[207]

The multi-year saga of the Child Online Protection Act came to an end in March of 2007 when U.S. District Judge Lowell A. Reed, Jr. held that the statute was unconstitutionally overbroad and vague. Judge Reed also ruled that the Act was not the least restrictive means to accomplish the job of protecting minors from sexually explicit materials.[208] Judge Reed issued a permanent injunction against enforcement of the Act.

At the outset, Judge Reed concluded that, as the regulation targeted the content of speech, the standard of review for the Act should be strict scrutiny (defined in the Glossary).[209]

Because COPA suppresses a large amount of speech that adults have a constitutional right to receive, under the strict scrutiny standard, COPA may only be upheld as constitutional if defendant meets his burden of proving that COPA is narrowly tailored to the compelling interest that COPA was enacted to serve and there are no less restrictive alternatives that would be at least as effective in achieving that interest.

But Judge Reed found that filtering software was less restrictive than COPA. Filtering software would allow the parents of minor children to block out objectionable material while leaving adults the freedom to access adult materials, Judge Reed wrote. The effectiveness of filtering software had been demonstrated in the expert testimony provided to the court. "Even defendant's own study shows that all but the worst performing filters are far more than COPA would be at protecting children from sexually explicit material on the Web," Reed wrote.[210] With that less burdensome alternative to the criminal sanctions, COPA was not as narrowly tailored as it needed to be to withstand strict scrutiny review.

The worldwide nature of the Internet formed the basis of Judge Reed's conclusion that COPA was underinclusive. Expert witnesses said that about half of the adult content on the Web came from foreign sources.[211] As the Act did not address foreign Web site operators posting adult content, it did not apply uniformly to all Web content. Because only the American Web site operators would be at risk, the Act was unconstitutional.

The Act also was overbroad in that it posed a risk to operators of Web sites whose content was constitutionally protected for use by adults or even by older minors. COPA left the publishers of content that would be shielded under the SLAPS test for adults at risk when viewed by younger minors. "[W]hat would be 'patently offensive' to an eight-year-

---

207 *Ashcroft v. American Civil Liberties Union*, 542 U.S. 656, 124 S.Ct. 2783 (2004).

208 *American Civil Liberties Union v. Gonzales*, 478 F.Supp.2d 775 (E.D.Pa. 2007).

209 Ibid. at 810.

210 Ibid. at 815.

211 Ibid. at 816.

old would logically encompass a broader spectrum of what is available on the Web than what would be considered 'patently offensive' for a sixteen-year-old," Judge Reed wrote.[212]

That lack of notice as to what could be prosecuted under COPA also impelled Judge Reed to conclude that COPA was unconstitutional. Questions about which minor age group would serve as the test of patent offensiveness of Web content as well as the Act's failure to set up a clear definition of which context would be used to judge content led to Judge Reed's holding that the Act was unconstitutionally vague. Old media tests of obscenity enunciated by courts require that the finder of fact judge the objectionable content in the context of the whole work. For books, magazines or movies, the context is clear: it is the whole book, magazine or movie. On the Internet, context is less well defined. Is the context the single Web page or the entire Web site? Is it the entirety of a search result for a particular term or is it all pages linked to the site being judged? This lack of clarity meant that Web publishers would not be able to anticipate what the government might prosecute. It would result in self-censorship and that sort of chill on speech is not constitutional.

SUPREME COURT FINDS FILTERING REQUIREMENT CONSTITUTIONAL FOR LIBRARIES

By a 6–3 vote, the U.S. Supreme Court upheld a Congressional effort to protect children from Internet pornography. On June 23, 2003, the Court held that the Children's Internet Protection Act (CIPA) is constitutional.[213]

The statute, which had been challenged by the *American Library Association in U.S. v. American Library Ass'n*, required that filters be placed on computers in public libraries to prevent children from seeing harmful materials. The statute was upheld in a plurality opinion in which Chief Justice William H. Rehnquist was joined by only three others, Justices O'Connor, Scalia, and Thomas. In separate opinions, Justices Stephen Breyer and Anthony Kennedy concurred in the judgment but filed separate opinions. Justices Stevens and Souter filed dissents and Justice Ginsburg joined Justice Souter's dissent.

CIPA was based on the federal government's ability to place conditions on its aid. The federal government helps public libraries pay for Internet access through the E-rate program and the Library Services and Technology Act. Congress passed CIPA after numerous stories and complaints about people accessing pornography in public libraries. The statute gave libraries the choice between not accepting federal Internet assistance or installing the blocking software.

---

212 Ibid. at 817.

213 *U.S. v. American Library Ass'n*, 539 U.S. 194, 123 S.Ct. 2297 (2003).

The plurality concluded that CIPA did not implicate First Amendment issues, but rather was a test of the government's spending powers.[214]

> CIPA does not "penalize" libraries that choose not to install such software, or deny them the right to provide their patrons with unfiltered Internet access. Rather CIPA simply reflects Congress' decision not to subsidize their doing so.

The plurality rejected the contention that the statute infringed on the "public forum" status of libraries and that the filters would reduce adult patrons to the level of children. The government declared in oral argument that patrons could simply ask library staffs to turn off the filters. Justice Kennedy noted, though, that if the filtering software could not be turned off, it could form the basis for an "as-applied" challenge to the policy.

Justice Souter compared the upholding of CIPA to a library buying a book and then withholding it from adults who did not seem to have a proper "purpose," or cutting any pages from an encyclopedia that might somehow offend.[215]

RENO V. ACLU, THE FIRST BATTLE OVER INTERNET CONTENT

In 1997, the Supreme Court of the United States pondered the nature of the Internet and World Wide Web following a challenge to the Communications Decency Act (CDA) by a group of business, library, and non-commercial organizations led by the American Civil Liberties Union. The CDA, part of the Telecommunications Act of 1996, made it a crime to send "indecent" or "patently offensive" communications to persons under 18 years of age.[216]

The CDA also made it a crime to transmit information about abortions. The Act § 223(a)(1)(B) provided for fines and imprisonment for any person convicted of making or soliciting and transmitting "any comment, request, suggestion, proposal, image or other communication which is obscene or indecent knowing that the recipient is under 18 years of age."

In a trial before a three-judge panel in Philadelphia, the plaintiffs argued that the CDA violated the First Amendment, and that terms "indecent" and "patently offensive" were so vague that they violated the free speech and due process clauses of the Constitution and the Bill of Rights.

---

214 Ibid. at 2308.

215 Ibid. at 2321–2322.

216 The Court noted: that the major part of The Telecommunications Act of 1996, Pub. L. 104–104, 110 Stat. 56, was an unusually important legislative enactment. Its first 103 pages deal with reducing regulation and hastening " 'the rapid deployment of new telecommunications technologies.' " Whereas the bulk of The Telecommunications Act of 1996 was the product of extensive committee hearings, the CDA and its challenged portions were added either after the hearings were ended or during floor debate on legislation. See 25 Med.L.Rptr. at 1839.

After studying computers, the Internet, and the uses people make of electronic communication, the three-judge panel concluded that freedom should win out in this new medium. In the end, the panel concluded that the CDA was unconstitutional. These judges declared that "With the possible exception of e-mail to a known recipient, most content providers cannot determine the identity and age of every user accessing their material."[217] At issue was a section of the CDA which declared the "knowing" transmission of obscene and indecent messages to any recipients under 18 years old to be a crime.[218]

RENO V. ACLU IN THE U.S. SUPREME COURT

Unusually lengthy oral arguments occurred before the Supreme Court of the United States, dealing with technology and the reach of the CDA. Justice John Paul Stevens, who later wrote the Court's decision, asked about the liability of a library which might put sexually explicit materials on-line where children as well as adults might view them. Deputy Solicitor General Seth P. Waxman answered for the government that in such a situation, sexual materials could not be sent. And what, then, of an adult who indicated that he would let his 16-year-old son see such materials. Again, that would violate the CDA. Justice Scalia broke in at that point: "You're saying that any adult has a heckler's veto on the whole operation by simply saying, 'I'm going to let my son watch it.' "[219]

Justice John Paul Stevens wrote for the seven-Justice majority:[220]

> Notwithstanding the legitimacy and importance of the congressional goal of protecting children from harmful material, we agree with the three-judge federal court that the statute abridges "the freedom of speech" protected by the First Amendment.

True, communication over the Internet via the World Wide Web makes enormous amounts of information available to an explosively growing list of users.[221] " 'Once a provider posts its content on the Internet, it cannot prevent that content' "—including sexually explicit language or images—" 'from entering any community.' "

Justice Stevens then distinguished the Internet, which requires that persons seek content, from radio and television in which the audience passively receive broadcast content:[222]

---

[217] *ACLU v. Reno*, 929 F.Supp. 824, 853 (E.D.Pa.1996).

[218] Title U.S.C.A. § 223(a)(1)(B)(ii) (Supp. 1997). Sec. 223(d) approached defining obscenity and indecency with this language about sending persons under 18 years old any message "that, in context, depicts or describes, in terms patently offensive as measured by contemporary community standards, sexual or excretory activities or organs."

[219] 1997 WL 136253 (U.S.Oral.Arg.).

[220] *Reno v. American Civil Liberties Union*, 521 U.S. 844, 849, 117 S.Ct. 2329, 2334 (1997), 25 Med.L.Rptr. 1833, 1835.

[221] 521 U.S. at 853, 117 S.Ct. at 2336, Ibid. at 1837.

[222] *Reno v. American Civil Liberties Union*, 521 U.S. at 854, 117 S.Ct. at 2336, Ibid. at 1837–1838, citing Findings 88 and 89, from 929 F.Supp. at 844–845.

> Though [sexually explicit] material is widely available, users seldom encounter such content accidentally. * * * Almost all sexually explicit images are preceded by warnings as to the content. For that reason, " 'odds are slim' that a user would enter a sexually explicit site by accident." Unlike communications received by radio and television, "the receipt of information on the Internet requires a series of affirmative steps more deliberate and directed than merely turning a dial. A child requires some sophistication and some ability to retrieve material and thereby to use the Internet unattended."
>
> * * *
>
> The Internet is not as "invasive" as radio or television. The District Court specifically found that "[c]ommunications over the Internet do not 'invade' an individual's home or appear on one's computer screen unbidden. Users seldom encounter content 'by accident.' " 929 F.Supp., at 844 (finding 88). It also found that " '[a]lmost all sexually explicit images are preceded by warnings as to the content,' " and cited testimony that "odds are slim" that a user would come across a sexually explicit sight by accident. *Ibid.*

Justice Stevens' opinion declared that ambiguities in the language of the CDA " * * * rendered it problematic for purposes of the First Amendment."[223]

> We are persuaded that the CDA lacks the precision that the First Amendment requires when a statute regulates the content of speech. In order to deny minors access to potentially harmful speech, the CDA effectively suppresses a large amount of speech that adults have a right to receive and to address to one another. That burden on adult speech is unacceptable if less restrictive alternatives would be at least as effective in achieving the legitimate purpose that the statute was enacted to serve.
>
> In evaluating the free speech rights of adults, we have made it perfectly clear that "[s]exual expression which is indecent but not obscene is protected by the First Amendment." *Sable*, 492 U.S., at 126. See also *Carey v. Population Services Int'l*, 431 U.S. 678, 701, 97 S.Ct. 2010 (1977).

The Court stated that "parental control software" could help to restrict access to sexually explicit materials.[224] Parental control is one thing; blanket control by the Government is another. Justice Stevens wrote that "the CDA is a content-based blanket restriction on speech,

---

[223] Ibid. at 870–871, 874, 2344, 2346.

[224] Ibid. at 854–855, 2335, 2336.

and, as such, cannot be 'properly analyzed as a form of time, place and manner regulation.' "[225]

In any event, the Supreme Court of the United States did not demolish all government weapons against transmitting obscenity and child pornography. However transmitted, whether via the Internet or by other means, obscenity and child pornography already were illegal under federal law.[226]

OTHER OBSCENITY ISSUES

To what extent can federal enforcement officials involve themselves in the process of distributing obscene materials without being found to have improperly enticed a defendant into committing a crime?

In *United States v. Kuennen,*[227] the Supreme Court refused to review the conviction of an individual whose shipment of obscene materials from Denmark was first intercepted by U.S. Customs officials and then re-mailed to him by that agency. Kuennen claimed that he had not violated federal postal laws because the law simply prohibited "causing" obscene materials to be sent through the mail and in this case it was the federal agency that "caused" these materials to be mailed to him. The federal court was unmoved by his argument, finding that although a Customs official may have mailed the package to Kuennen, it was the defendant himself who "caused" the mailing of these materials when he ordered them from his foreign supplier.

However, in *Jacobson v. United States*[228], in a 5–4 decision, the Supreme Court held that a government enforcement agency could not actively solicit customers for obscene materials and then charge them criminally for having responded to the solicitation. In this case an organization secretly sponsored by the government was sending promotional materials offering a wide assortment of explicit child pornography books and magazines to individuals it suspected were already purchasing these materials from other sources.

Keith Jacobson, an elderly Nebraska farmer, received such advertisements for more than two years before he finally ordered a pornographic magazine, *"Boys Who Love Boys"*, from the organization. On the basis of his order, Jacobson was convicted of violating a federal mail statute by knowingly receiving materials showing minors engaged in sexually explicit activities.

Justice White, writing for the majority, held that while government agents might be permitted to offer citizens an opportunity to commit

---

[225] Ibid. at 868, 2342.

[226] 25 Med.L.Rptr. at 1848, n. 44 (1997), citing 18 U.S.C. §§ 1464–1465 (criminalizing obscenity), and § 2251 (criminalizing child pornography).

[227] *United States v. Kuennen*, 901 F.2d 103 (8th Cir.1990), cert. denied 498 U.S. 958, 111 S.Ct. 385 (1990).

[228] *Jacobson v. United States*, 503 U.S. 540, 112 S.Ct. 1535 (1992).

crimes they are already predisposed to commit, it was illegal entrapment for them to engage in such an elaborate subterfuge to induce an innocent person to commit a crime.

THE MAPPLETHORPE EXHIBIT CASE

Concern that mid-American juries lacked the sophistication to distinguish between "art" and "smut" lessened to some extent in October 1990 after a Cincinnati, Ohio, jury acquitted a local museum director charged with displaying obscene works.[229] Dennis Barrie, director of Cincinnati's Contemporary Arts Center, had scheduled an exhibition of pictures by Robert Mapplethorpe, a nationally recognized photographer who died of AIDS in 1989.

The exhibition included five photos of nude men in sadomasochistic poses and two of children with their genitals exposed. The exhibit had attracted little attention in its previous showings in Philadelphia and Chicago, but at its opening in Cincinnati, Barrie and the Museum were charged with pandering obscenity, and unlawfully displaying pictures of nude children, both misdemeanor offenses carrying maximum sentences of one year in jail, and a fine of $5,000. To simplify the issue, the state called just one witness to testify as to the artistic merit of the exhibit, a self-styled communications "specialist" whose only claimed expertise as an art critic involved writing songs for the "*Captain Kangaroo*"[230] television show. In contrast, the defense called more than a dozen expert witnesses, including directors from some of the nation's leading art museums who were unanimous in their assessment of Mapplethorpe as a serious and important artist.

If the prosecution believed the photos themselves would be enough to shock the mostly working class, church-going jury of four men and four women into returning a guilty verdict, they clearly underestimated the jury. After the trial had ended, several jurors admitted being personally offended by these pictures they felt were "lewd", "grotesque" and "disgusting."[231] But even though they felt that these photos did appeal to prurient interests and were patently offensive, they accepted the judgment of art experts who believed these works also had artistic merit, and therefore could not be classified as being obscene.

Reacting in part to public criticism of the federal funding Mapplethorpe had received, Congress amended the statute governing awards made by National Endowment for the Arts, requiring the NEA to consider "general standards of decency" in deciding who might qualify for

---

[229] *Contemporary Arts Center v. Ney*, 735 F.Supp. 743 (S.D.Ohio 1990). Also see "Jury Finds Merit in Mapplethorpe Exhibit with Verdict of Not Guilty," *Milwaukee Journal*, October 7, 1990, p. A1.

[230] A children's television show that ran from 1955 to 1981. http://www.imdb.com/title/tt0047718/.

[231] Isabel Wilkerson, "Obscenity Jurors Were Pulled 2 Ways But Deferred to Art," *New York Times* October 10, 1990, p. B1. Five of the eight jurors had never visited an art museum.

funding from the organization. Applying this new standard, NEA denied requests for government funds from several artists who applied for grants, including one who planned theatrical performances of simulated masturbation and another who intended to smear her body with excrement to portray the debasement of women. When these individuals were unable to obtain taxpayer funding they sought, they challenged the new "decency" standard in court.

A California federal district court upheld their challenge, finding the term "decency" to be unconstitutionally vague and overbroad because it prevented applicants from fully understanding what was required of them in order to qualify for federal financial support.[232]

2 LIVE CREW CASE

In March 1990, a Florida judge in Fort Lauderdale, Florida entered a decree forbidding the sale or distribution of a music video "*Nasty As They Wanna Be*" by rap group 2 Live Crew anywhere within the jurisdiction of the Court. District Judge Jose A. Gonzales conducted extensive hearings before deciding that the music video was in fact obscene, and therefore could be prevented from being sold.[233]

A local music store owner, Charles Freeman, sold a copy of the music video to an undercover police officer a few days after the decree had been entered and was convicted of violating this ban. Shortly after Freeman's arrest, 2 Live Crew performed selections from the music video during an all-adult concert in Fort Lauderdale. The three members of the group were each charged with one misdemeanor count of disseminating obscene material, and were tried in October 1991, soon after Freeman's conviction.

The defense maintained that white jurors on the six-member jury panel would be incapable of understanding this unique form of black artistic expression, but the jury voted unanimously for acquittal, finding that the performance was not obscene.[234] Once again, the verdict turned on the "artistic merit" issue, for the jury accepted the judgment of a black English professor that "rapping" represented a serious black cultural art

---

[232] *Finley v. National Endowment for the Arts*, 795 F.Supp. 1457 (C.D.Cal.1992).

[233] *Skyywalker Records, Inc. v. Navarro*, 739 F.Supp. 578 (S.D.Fla.1990), 17 Med.L.Rptr. 2073. According to testimony presented at the hearings, this single music video contained more than a dozen references urging violent sex, some 200 descriptions of women as either "bitches" or "ho" (whores), 115 explicit terms for male or female genitalia, 87 descriptions of oral sex, 9 descriptions of male ejaculation, 4 extensive descriptions of group sex, all within a general theme glorifying the debasement and humiliation of women. The declaratory judgment of obscenity entered by the District Judge was later vacated on appeal. The reviewing court pointed out that the judge who had tried the case had not demonstrated that he possessed either the artistic or literary background necessary to find that the work lacked "serious artistic, scientific, literary or political value." *Luke Records v. Navarro*, 960 F.2d 134 (11th Cir.1992).

[234] "Rap Members Found Not Guilty in Obscenity Trial," *New York Times*, October 21, 1990, p. 1.

form, whose words were not to be taken at their face value but to be understood in the historical context of black culture.[235]

In both of these censorship cases, those who had been predicting that a new wave of artistic censorship would sweep across the nation could take some comfort in the verdicts of two predominately white, working-class juries who respected their obligations as jurors to decide these emotion-packed obscenity issues impartially and objectively. Perhaps, then, there is reason to believe that the time-honored American trial by jury system deserves more respect than its erudite critics have sometimes been willing to accord it.

CHILD PORNOGRAPHY

Although American law has been unsympathetic to the pleas of women to stop the flood of pornographic materials in the United States, child pornography has been treated in an entirely different fashion. Child pornography is something of a misnomer. It isn't pornography. Pornography is sexual material that is not obscene. Pornography is protected by the First Amendment. What is referred to as Child Pornography is the crime of using children in sexual performances. That is not protected by the First Amendment. Legislation has been created to outlaw using minors to perform or act in the creation of films, books, or magazine articles or other items depicting the sexual exploitation of children.[236]

The measure was designed to put a stop to magazines which could be purchased in 1977 such as *Chicken Delight*, *Lust for Children*, *Lollitots*, and *Child Discipline* that were then being sold. Dr. Judianne Densen-Gerber, president of the Odyssey Institute, made this outraged statement to the Subcommittee on Crime of Congress' Committee on the Judiciary:[237]

> There comes a point where we can no longer defend by intellectualization or forensic debate. We must simply say "I know the difference between right and wrong and I am not afraid to say 'no' or demand that limits be imposed."
>
> Common sense and maternal instinct tell me that this [child pornography that she found in New York, Philadelphia, Boston, Washington, New Orleans, Chicago, San Francisco, and Los Angeles] goes way beyond free speech. Such conduct mutilates

---

[235] Another factor that may have aided the defense is that the vocals the prosecution recorded at the concert were virtually unintelligible to the jury, providing very little basis for the jury to find the lyrics to be obscene.

[236] Senate Bill 1585, 95th Congress, 1st Session, No. 95–438, "Protection of Children Against Sexual Exploitation Act of 1977;" Report of the Committee on the Judiciary, United States Senate, on S. 1585.

[237] Prepared Statement of Judianne Densen-Gerber, J.D., M.D., F.C.L.M., President, Odyssey Institute, for submission to The U.S. House of Representatives, Committee on the Judiciary, Subcommittee on Crime, May 23, 1977.

children's spirits; they aren't consenting adults, they're victims. The First Amendment isn't absolute.

The legislation, signed into law in 1978 by President Carter, was formally called the "Protection of Children Against Sexual Exploitation Act of 1977." The law, in the words of U.S. Senators John C. Culver of Iowa and Charles Mathias of Maryland, was intended to do the following:[238]

- Make it a Federal crime to use children in the production of pornographic materials.
- Prohibit the interstate transportation of children for the purpose of engaging in prostitution, and
- Increase the penalty provisions of the current Federal obscenity laws if the materials adjudged obscene involve the use of children engaging in sexually explicit conduct.

This measure tried to correct loopholes in federal obscenity statutes. Before this law was passed, there was no federal statute prohibiting use of children in production of materials that depicted explicit sexual conduct. This statute defined "minor" as any person under the age of 16 years. Penalties for violation of this statutory provision are two-ten years imprisonment and/or a fine of up to $10,000 on first offense, or five-fifteen years imprisonment and/or a fine of up to $15,000 for subsequent offenses.[239]

Committees of the U.S. Senate and House of Representatives found a close connection between child pornography and the use of young children as prostitutes. For example, a 17-year-old Chicago youth who had sold himself on the streets for two years, could often earn close to $500 a week in 1977—the equivalent of perhaps $2,000 a week in 1997—by selling himself two or three times a night to perform various sex acts with "chicken hawks" or pose for pornographic pictures or both.[240]

KIDPORN AND NEW YORK V. FERBER (1982)

In 1982, the Supreme Court of the United States made one thing clear about the murky law of obscenity: it will uphold state efforts to punish individuals for the production or sale of "kidporn."

In *New York v. Ferber*, the Court declared valid a New York criminal statute prohibiting persons from knowingly authorizing or inducing a

[238] Form letter sent to the author by Senators Culver and Mathias, circa September 1977; letter to the author of October 19, 1977, by Rep. John Conyers, Jr. of Michigan's First District. See Public Law 95–225.

[239] 18 U.S.C.A. § 2251, Chap. 110—Sexual Exploitation of Children. The Mann Act, 18 U.S.C.A. § 2423, prohibits the interstate transportation of minor females for purposes of prostitution and did not include young males until amended in 1977.

[240] Report of the Committee on the Judiciary, United States Senate on S.1585, Protection of Children Against Sexual Exploitation Act of 1977 (Washington, D.C., 1977), p. 7. See also Robin Lloyd, *For Money or Love: Boy Prostitution in America* (New York: Vanguard Press, 1976).

child less than 16 years old to engage in a sexual performance.[241] "Sexual performance" was defined by the New York statute as, "any performance or part thereof which includes sexual performance or part thereof which includes sexual conduct by a child less than sixteen years of age."

The case began when Paul Ira Ferber, proprietor of a Manhattan bookstore specializing in sexually oriented materials, sold two films to undercover police officers. The two films dealt almost exclusively with depictions of boys masturbating. A jury trial convicted Ferber of two counts of promoting a sexual performance and Ferber was sentenced to 45 days in prison.

Ferber's convictions were upheld on first appeal, but the New York Court of Appeals said that the statute section under which Ferber was convicted was too sweeping, that it might be used to punish sale or promotion of material protected by the First Amendment, including "medical books and educational sources, which deal with adolescent sex in a realistic but not obscene manner."[242]

The Supreme Court of the United States granted certiorari and overturned the New York Court of Appeals. Writing for the Court, Justice Byron White said:

> Like obscenity statutes, laws directed at the dissemination of child pornography run the risk of suppressing protected expression by allowing the hand of the censor to become unduly heavy. For the following reasons, however, we are persuaded that the States are entitled to greater leeway in the regulation of pornographic depictions of children.
>
> *First.* It is evident beyond the need for elaboration that a state's interest in "safeguarding the physical and psychological well being of a minor" is "compelling." *Globe Newspaper Co. v. Superior Court,* 457 U.S. 596, 607, 102 S.Ct. 2613, 2620 (1982), 8 Med.L.Rptr. 1689.
>
> * * *
>
> *Second.* The distribution of photographs and films depicting sexual activity by juveniles is intrinsically related to the sexual abuse of children in at least two ways. First, the materials produced are a permanent record of the children's participation and the harm to the child is exacerbated by their circulation. Second, the distribution network for child pornography must be closed if the production of material which requires the sexual exploitation of children is to be effectively controlled.

Justice White noted the economic motive involved in the production of such materials. "It rarely has been suggested that the constitutional freedom for speech and press extends immunity to speech or writing used

---

241 *New York v. Ferber,* 458 U.S. 747, 752–753, 102 S.Ct. 3348 (1982), 8 Med.L.Rptr. 1809.

242 Ibid.

as an integral part of conduct in violation of a valid criminal statute."[243] Further, classifying child pornography as a category outside protection of the First Amendment is compatible with the Supreme Court's earlier rulings.

COURTS EXTEND PROTECTION AGAINST "KIDPORN"

Two 1994 federal court decisions illustrate how far courts will extend the "Protection of Children Against Sexual Exploitation Act of 1977." Government efforts continue to discourage traffic in forms of sexually suggestive depiction of minors.

In *United States v. Knox* (1994), a U.S. Court of Appeals affirmed the conviction of a man who obtained films through the mails of minors engaging in "lascivious exhibition of the genitals or pubic area." These convictions were affirmed even though all of the under-age females in the films wore some form of clothing covering their private parts. The court held that these films, featuring young girls dancing provocatively or spreading their legs as cameras focused on their pubic areas, were clearly intended to produce images "sexually arousing to pedophiles."[244]

Then, in *United States v. X-Citement Video, Inc.*, the U.S. Supreme Court affirmed the conviction of an X-rated film distributor for selling one of the first films featuring porn star Traci Lords, produced when she was 15 years old. The Court held that even though Ms. Lords might have sought such roles eagerly, she could not consent retrospectively to having appeared in films made when she was still a minor. Because the distributor knew that Ms. Lords was under-age when this film was made, the Court upheld the defendant's conviction for knowingly distributing pornography involving minors.[245]

VIRTUAL CHILD PORNOGRAPHY

As computer technology, computer imaging capabilities in particular, continued its development, it became possible to digitally create images and animations that replicated actual child pornography. Congress addressed the issue with the Child Pornography Prevention Act of 1996. That act expanded the ban on child pornography to include any "computer or computer-generated image or picture" The CPPA[246] expanded the federal prohibition on child pornography to include not only pornographic images made using actual children, but also "any visual depiction, including any photograph, film, video, picture, or computer or computer-generated image or picture," that "is, or appears to be, of a minor engaging in sexually explicit conduct."

[243] Quoting *Giboney v. Empire Storage & Ice Co.*, 336 U.S. 490, 69 S.Ct. 684 (1949).

[244] *United States v. Knox*, 32 F.3d 733 (3d Cir.1994).

[245] *United States v. X-Citement Video, Inc.*, 513 U.S. 64, 115 S.Ct. 464 (1994).

[246] 18 U.S.C. § 2256.

The Supreme Court found the statute unconstitutional in 2002.[247] The Court, in an opinion by Justice Kennedy, rejected the government's contention that the statute did little more than extend the prohibitions found in Ferber. The Court distinguished between the crime of child sexual abuse recorded in child pornography and the ideas expressed in materials that do not involve the participation of actual children. If children are not involved, then the otherwise legal speech cannot be prohibited, Justice Kennedy reasoned.

The government argued that the existence of virtual child pornography might well whet the appetites of pedophiles and could serve to encourage producers of such materials to continue and expand to the use of actual children. But Justice Kennedy rejected that contention.[248]

> [T]he mere tendency of speech to encourage unlawful acts is not a sufficient reason for banning it, *Stanley v. Georgia,* 394 U.S. 557, 557, 89 S.Ct. 1243, absent some showing of a direct connection between the speech and imminent illegal conduct, see, e.g. *Brandenburg v. Ohio,* 395 U.S. 444, 447, 89 S.Ct. 1827.

Some astute observers might well predict that child pornography defendants would try to avoid conviction by claiming that the subjects of the materials were virtual rather than real and placing the burden on the prosecution to prove that the "children" actually were children. In a number of cases, regrettably many not formally "published" by the courts, appeals courts have concluded, among other things, that (1) juries are competent to examine materials and judge whether the participants are actual children, (2) the issue of real as opposed to virtual children is not raised by the state statute and, (3) the prosecution does not bear the burden of proof regarding the existence of the participants.

Congress passed the Prosecutorial Remedies and Other Tools to End the Exploitation of Children Today Act in 2003. The Act makes it a crime to pass off computer-generated materials as actual child pornography and provides penalties for people who market materials "in a manner that reflects the belief, or that is intended to cause another to believe, that the material or purported material," is child pornography.[249]

GETTING CAUGHT WITH CHILD PORN BECAUSE OF A VIRUS

In 2009, the Associated Press reported on a new danger from computer viruses, having child pornography downloaded on a user's computer.[250] The story reported that pedophiles have used computer viruses to store illegal materials on other people's computers, that pranksters have used viruses to create the appearance that someone has

---

[247] *Ashcroft v. Free Speech Coalition,* 535 U.S. 234, 122 S.Ct. 1389 (2002).

[248] Ibid. at 236, 1394.

[249] Pub.L.No.108–21, 117 Stat. 650.

[250] Jordan Robertson, "AP Impact: Framed for child porn-by a PV virus," Associated Press, Nov. 9, 2009.

downloaded child pornography and that some malware targets computer users with child porn.

An investigation by the news service found a number of instances where people were accused of and charged with crimes because of child pornography found on their computers. Clearing their names and fighting the criminal charges is difficult. Many prosecutors are skeptical of claims that someone whose computer is found with child pornography is innocent.[251]

> "It's an example of the old 'dog ate my homework' excuse," says Phil Malone, director of the Cyberlaw Clinic at Harvard's Berkman Center for Internet & Society. "The problem is, sometimes the dog does eat your homework."

In one case, a Massachusetts state workers compensation investigator was charged with possession of child pornography, fired from his job and was the target of death threats. Michael Fiola faced years in prison until defense experts examined his state-issued laptop.

> An inspection for his defense revealed the laptop was severely infected. It was programmed to visit as many as 40 child porn sites per minute—an inhuman feat. While Fiola and his wife were out to dinner one night, someone logged on to the computer and porn flowed in for an hour and a half.

Prosecutors performed another test and confirmed the defense findings. The charge was dropped—11 months after it was filed.

The AP reported that some persons found with child porn on their computers were using file sharing programs, had visited sites to obtain pirated software or had visited sites to be able to play computer games without paying for them.

MOTION PICTURE INDUSTRY STANDARDS

Until the late 1940s, five major film companies dominated the motion picture business in the United States. Paramount, MGM, Warner Brothers, Twentieth Century Fox and RKO owned more than 3,000 of the nation's first-run motion picture theaters and controlled film industry production, distribution and exhibition by following a policy of trade-offs and cross-preferences with other studio-owned theaters to deny some 15,000 independently owned theaters access to these feature films until their box office appeal had diminished.

This concentration of control within the film industry also allowed the major studios to cooperate in adopting and enforcing a code of industry standards to ensure that no feature film would contain themes or scenes that might be offensive to certain segments of the film

---

[251] Ibid.

audience.[252] Independent film producers had no choice but to conform to these standards of decency, because without the industry's "Production Code Seal of Authority" they would be denied access to those essential first-run theaters owned by the major studios.[253]

Then, in 1948, the Justice Department was able to force the major film studios to enter into a Consent Decree in which they agreed to rid themselves of their motion picture theaters.[254]

Losing control of these major first-run theaters also meant that these studios lost the capacity to impose industry standards on feature film content. As television viewing increased during the 1950s, film attendance plunged downward from 90 million a week in 1948 to less than 40 million a week only a decade later.[255] To lure audiences back to the film theaters, their new owners needed motion pictures promising special attractions television couldn't provide. One technique was to use technology to expand the screen, surround the viewer with sound, and portray action on a massive scale.

Another was to show sexier or more provocative dramas than television offered the public. Freed of the constraints of the Hollywood Production Code, theater chains began turning to European producers for daring, far more explicit motion pictures than American audiences had ever seen in the past.

At this point a number of local film boards originally formed in the early 1900s, but then dormant for decades as Hollywood closely supervised motion picture content, suddenly came to life as these new independent films began appearing in their communities. Now as such boards, operating under state authority, began trying to fill that void left by the collapse of industry controls, the issue soon arose about their legal right as government agencies to impose conditions on the local exhibition of feature films.

---

[252] The Motion Picture Producers and Distributors of American (MPPDFA) established a film review office in 1922, largely as a public relations gesture to reduce the bad image resulting from a rash of personal scandals in Hollywood. Known as the "Hays' Office", because of its first director, Will Hays, its role in reviewing film content did not become significant until the major studios adopted a much more stringent set of standards, known as the Production Code, in the mid 1930s.

[253] In many ways this private content supervisory system closely resembled that employed by National Association of Broadcasters. In both cases, a small group of studios or networks were able to avoid offending audiences by exerting their control over the main channels of distribution, and this power that gave them to deny distribution to material they believed was in bad taste. In television as in film, the later fragmentation of that power diminished their ability to continue to perform that function.

[254] *United States v. Paramount Pictures*, 334 U.S. 131, 68 S.Ct. 915 (1948). The studios were actually given the option of divesting themselves of either their role as film distributors or film exhibitors, but sensing the threat that television would soon pose for film theaters, they chose to retain their more profitable distribution role.

[255] Christopher Sterling and Timothy Haight, eds. *The Mass Media: Aspen Institute Guide to Communication Industry Trends* (New York: Praeger, 1978), pp. 34–35.

The first of these cases to challenge the authority of a state to control film content was *Burstyn v. Wilson*, a 1952 Supreme Court decision involving Roberto Rossellini's film, "*The Miracle*."[256]

This was a story about a simple-minded goatherd who had been raped by a bearded stranger whom she believed to be St. Joseph. The film was accused not of obscenity but of "sacrilege." The New York Education Department had issued a license to allow showing of "*The Miracle*," but the Education Department's governing body, the New York Regents, ordered the license withdrawn after the regents had received protests that the film was "sacrilegious." Burstyn appealed the license's withdrawal to the New York Courts, claiming that the state's licensing statute was unconstitutional. New York's courts, however, rejected that argument.

The Supreme Court of the United States ultimately ruled unanimously that the New York statute and the term "sacrilegious" were both so vague that they abridged freedom of expression. Although the Court said in *dicta* that a clearly drawn obscenity statute to regulate motion pictures might be upheld, the main thrust of the *Burstyn* decision was toward greater freedom. Not only were films given protection under the First and Fourteenth Amendments, movies which offended a particular religious group need not, for that reason alone, be banned. Thus "sacrilege" can no longer be a ground for censoring movies.

Seven years after the *Burstyn* decision, the Supreme Court—in *Kingsley International Pictures Corp. v. New York*—again upheld the concept that films are within the protection of the First Amendment. In *Kingsley*, however, the Court specifically refused to decide whether "the controls which a state may impose upon this medium of expression are precisely co-extensive with those allowable for newspapers, books, or individual speech."[257]

In 1961 Times Film Corporation paid the City of Chicago the customary license fee to exhibit the film "*Don Juan*" but then refused to submit the film as required by local ordinance to Chicago's Film Review Board for pre-screening and a license. Instead, in *Times Film Corp. v. City of Chicago*, it challenged the city's authority to impose these conditions on the exhibition of a motion picture, contending that the ordinance constituted an unconstitutional prior restraint on free speech.

---

[256] *Joseph Burstyn, Inc. v. Wilson*, 343 U.S. 495, 72 S.Ct. 777 (1952). Some film historians claim that *Mutual Film Corp. v. Industrial Commission of Ohio*, 236 U.S. 230, 35 S.Ct. 387 (1915) was the first test of film's free speech rights, a test in which a federal court held that a state law could restrict film distribution because film was not a form of protected expression, but rather only a business. What these historians overlook is that it was not until 1925 in Gitlow v. New York that the Supreme Court finally recognized the power of federal courts to overturn state laws restricting free speech, so that in this case, determining whether or not film was a protected form of free speech was really irrelevant to the actual decision, and therefore not a precedent controlling future federal court decisions in this field.

[257] Ibid. at 689, 1362.

The Supreme Court upheld the city's right to impose the conditions on its local film exhibitors by a 5–4 vote. The majority denied that there was complete freedom to exhibit any motion picture and added, "Nor has it been suggested that all previous restraints are invalid."[258]

Four years later, *in Freedman v. Maryland* (1965), the Supreme Court invalidated a state prior restraint system. This time, unlike the *Times Film* case, *all* prior restraint was not challenged as unconstitutional. Instead, the Maryland Film Review Board was challenged because it could arbitrarily halt the showing of a film until the exhibitor was able to complete a time-consuming appeal procedure through the state court system. The Maryland review process was held invalid because of insufficient procedural safeguards for the protection of the film exhibitor. But even Justice Brennan—the legendary First Amendment supporter—suggested that an orderly, speedy procedure for prescreening films could be constitutional.[259]

In fact, a later Maryland-based film review system was upheld by an affirming vote of the Supreme Court—in *Al Star v. Preller* (1974)—demonstrating that a reasonably structured process was constitutional. The provisions of the new statute, cited with approval by the Court[260]

- Granted the Review Board only five days in which to review and license a film.
- Required, if a license is denied, that the Review Board begin review proceedings within 3 days before the Baltimore City Circuit Court.
- Required that a court make a prompt determination of obscenity (or lack of it) in an adversary hearing before the Review Board can make final denial of the license.
- Required the Board to bear the burden of proof at all stages of the proceeding.

At this time, then, prior restraint of film is still constitutional, but only when strict procedural safeguards are followed. These film industry decisions reflect the difficult role the Supreme Court has had to play when attempting to balance the free speech rights of a film distributor against the inherent right of each state to protect the welfare of its citizens.

In 1968 the major film studios began a new effort to enhance the image of the industry. Unable any longer to enforce standards of good taste, the studios instead established a rating system designed to inform audiences in advance what type of content each film contained. In the

---

[258] *Times Film Corp. v. Chicago*, 365 U.S. 43, 47, 81 S.Ct. 391, 393 (1961), citing *Near v. State of Minnesota ex rel. Olson*, 283 U.S. 697, 51 S.Ct. 625 (1931).

[259] *Freedman v. Maryland*, 380 U.S. 51, 85 S.Ct. 734 (1965). For a similar result, see *Interstate Circuit, Inc. v. Dallas*, 390 U.S. 676, 88 S.Ct. 1298 (1968).

[260] *Al Star v. Preller*, 419 U.S. 956, 95 S.Ct. 217 (1974), affirming 375 F.Supp. 1093 (D.Md.1974).

original rating system, a "G" designated films suitable for all audiences; "PG" meant parents were cautioned that some material might not be suitable for children; "R" indicated that children under 17 would not be admitted unless accompanied by a parent or guardian; and "X" meant no one under 17 would be admitted.

The rating system had at least two unintended effects. One was to destroy the appeal of the "G" rated film, as children began refusing to attend those films that adults thought were good for them. In 1968, 32 percent of the films released by major studios had a "G" rating, but by 1990, only 4 percent were rated "G."[261]

In contrast, "R" rated films rose from 22 percent of all major releases in 1968 to 48 percent in 1990, as average age of the film audience dropped from 22 to 16, and "R" became virtually synonymous with this age group's favorite film genre; violent, action packed adventures laced with suitable amounts of mayhem, some nudity and gore.

The other was to make it virtually impossible to successfully market an "X" rated film. Soon after the code was adopted, a number of major newspaper chains established the policy of refusing to accept display ads for "X" rated films, and several television groups began following the same policy a few years later. In addition, most major video rental organizations refused to handle "X" rated films. In view of these severe constraints an "X" rating imposed on the earnings potential of a picture, Hollywood producers generally insisted on contractual agreements that allowed them to re-edit any feature film rated as "X" to delete any scenes that prevented it from receiving a "R" rating.[262]

Because of the bitter controversies these agreements created between producers-investors and directors attempting to make serious but extremely graphic films such as "*Henry and June*" or "*Tie Me Up! Tie Me Down,*" the film code was revised in 1990. Then, NC-17 (No One Under 17 Admitted) replaced the X rating. Jack Valenti of the MPAA said that over time, the "X" had "taken on a surly meaning."

Unfortunately for the film industry, several states, as well as most newspapers, television stations and video rental organizations, were unimpressed by this distinction drawn by the rating group, continuing to treat the "NC-17" rating as nothing more than an artsy "X."[263]

Although the film industry's rating system is far from perfect, it has at least been designed to perform a public service by notifying audiences

---

[261] "MPAA Film Ratings 1968–90" *Variety* November 8, 1991, p. 26. One example of this film industry fear of the dreaded "G" rating was the John Wayne, Katharine Hepburn film, "*Rooster Cogburn*" where the producers insisted that one violent scene be inserted to guarantee a "PG" rather than "G" rating.

[262] "Taking the Hex Out of X" *Time,* October 8, 1990, p. 79. Jack Valenti, The Voluntary Movie Rating System, http://www.mpaa.org/the-voluntary-rating-system-promotes-free-speech/.

[263] "NC-17 X'd Out at Blockbuster; Wildmon, AFA Boycott," *Variety* January 21, 1991, p. 27.

in advance what type of content they can expect from each film the industry releases.

Efforts to persuade the music industry to adopt a similar code system have been far less successful to date. After agreeing in principle in 1985 to label all violently pornographic or sexually explicit record and music video releases, several years passed before six major music distributors finally declared their willingness in 1990 to begin on a voluntary basis to establish standards for applying notification stickers on all musical cassettes and albums containing obscene or otherwise patently offensive material.

As soon as this agreement was reached, however, several states began consideration of legislation that would prevent anyone under the age of 18 from purchasing any record or cassette bearing such a label. The music industry immediately went on the offensive, declaring that they would abandon this labeling effort if any state passed such a law abridging their right of free speech.[264]

While this concern for freedom of expression is certainly praiseworthy, another factor that might have some effect on the attitude of these music distributors is that purchasers under the age of 18 not only accounted for 32 percent of all revenues earned by the music industry in 1988, but also represented the largest age segment of buyers for "heavy metal" and "black/urban" music, the two types of music most likely to be affected by any labeling law.[265]

ELECTRONIC MEDIA STANDARDS

For broadcasters, transmission of obscene programming is a federal criminal offense, and also grounds for FCC revocation of a broadcast license.[266] In addition, however, the Commission has been attempting to establish more rigorous standards for sexually oriented broadcast programs, prohibiting "indecent" content, which the agency has defined in general terms as being patently offensive descriptions of sexual or excretory activities.[267]

The public appears to expect a far higher standard of good taste from broadcasters, and particularly from television networks, than from other media simply because even in an era when these networks attract a smaller percentage of the nation's primetime viewers, they still remain the most powerful and pervasive force in American mass culture. On a typical evening, any modestly popular situation comedy scheduled by one

---

[264] Kevin Zimmerman, "Music Biz Rising to Free-Speech Challenge," *Variety,* July 25, 1990, p. 53.

[265] Charles Fleming, "Stickers for Minors a Major Headache," *Variety,* July 25, 1990, p. 1.

[266] For radio and television, this prohibition against the transmission of obscene content is contained in the criminal provisions of 18 U.S.C.A. § 1464. A similar prohibition against the carriage of obscene cable TV programming is contained in the Cable Policy Act, 47 U.S.C.A. § 559.

[267] The FCC's indecency activities are discussed in Chap. 12.

of the major television networks will be viewed by more Americans than will read any best-selling novel or attend any single feature film that entire year. In other words, virtually every network television series producer has a greater opportunity to influence public sentiments, beliefs and values than even the most popular of novelists or film makers.

Until the early 1980s, all broadcast programming was regulated by the federal government. Although the amount of supervisory control the FCC actually exerted over television network program policies was minimal, the fact that a federal agency was authorized by law to make television responsive to the concerns of the public was in itself sufficient to satisfy most citizens.

The deregulation of broadcasting closed this one channel of legal influence that had been open to the average citizen, at a time when the industry was dismantling its own private system of program content standards and looking for ways to attract a younger, more affluent and less traditional group of listeners and viewers.

Competition from the Fox Network and a wide array of cable services forced the three major television networks to become slightly more venturesome during the 1980s, as both series and made-for-TV movies began treating topics that would have been summarily rejected only a decade before. Although very little that was broadcast during this era could have been classified as "indecent," much less obscene, American audiences were not accustomed to even mildly risqué programs from a medium readily accessible to children in the home.

Even so, because of widespread concern caused by broadcasting being released from virtually all of its "public interest" obligations, one of the major results of broadcast deregulation has been to popularize the forming of countless local and national private pressure groups, ranging from religious right to radical left, from Gay and Lesbian League to the AFL-CIO, to fight for each group's own perceived interests in broadcast programming. Using a broad range of economic, legal and political threats, these groups have already forced a number of stations to modify their programming policies in response to their demands.

PART 2

DEFAMATION, PRIVACY AND NEWSGATHERING TORTS

CHAPTER 4

DEFAMATION: LIBEL AND SLANDER

16. DEFAMATION DEFINED

Defamation is false communication which exposes persons to hatred, ridicule, or contempt, lowers them in the esteem of others, causes them to be shunned, or injures them in their business or calling. Its categories are libel—broadly, printed, written or broadcast material—and slander—broadly, spoken words of limited reach.

We have long been concerned with our reputations in the communities in which we live. The words of the children's rhyme, "sticks and stones may break my bones, but words will never hurt me" do not apply in the field of mass communications. Words can injure and under the civil law, the victims of hurtful words have a right to sue for the damage they cause.

Juries have no problem delivering damage awards in the millions of dollars for the sting of words. In the spring of 1997, a jury in Houston, Texas, came back with a $222.7 million award against the publisher of the *Wall Street Journal* over an article which defamed a Texas securities company.[1] That award, subsequently eliminated by the presiding judge because of misconduct on the part of the plaintiff, MMAR, in the discovery process, topped the previous record libel award of $58 million awarded to a Texas district attorney over statements made about him in a television station's investigative reports about ticket fixing.[2]

Although more attention to fair play and ethical considerations might well stave off many of the libel suits now brought against the

1 *MMAR Group, Inc. v. Dow Jones & Co., Inc.*, 187 F.R.D. 282 (S.D.Tex.1999).

2 McLennan County District Attorney Vic Feazell sued KDFW-TV in Dallas over an 11-part series that claimed that he had taken kickbacks in drunk driving cases. During the appeal by the station, Feazell settled the case for $16 million.

media, a free society by its nature is going to allow communication which results in harm to some reputations. Freedom, after all, is a risk. On the other hand, though, while society has a strong interest in the free flow of information, there is also a social stake in allowing protection of one's good name. The competition between the two has resulted in a balancing of interests. And, as with attempts to balance matters of great weight, there are oscillations from one side to the other and back, again. This is one of the reasons that libel law is so confusing for both media and legal professionals.

Protection of reputations is not a new concept, and neither is punishment for people who defame. The Law of the 12 Tables, compiled about 300 years after the founding of Rome, declared that anyone who slandered another and injured his reputation would be beaten with a club. We can recall the Biblical injunction against bearing "false witness against thy neighbor." In ancient Britain at the time of Alfred in the Ninth Century, slander was either painful or expensive, depending on the slanderer's standing in society. "The penalty for slander was the tearing out of tongue."[3] The only way to avoid mutilation was to pay the *wergild*, the price set for each social class. According to a set and firmly fixed system of social worth, a prince was worth 500 shillings, a nobleman 300, a farmer 100 and an agricultural serf between 40 and 80. That reflected a social view of the worth of the person and his words. A prince's words were dear while a serf's were insignificant (unless you were a serf trying to raise up to 80 shillings to keep a civil tongue in your head).[4] The system took into account the greater weight and broader distribution of the words of a prince compared with the impact and import of the words of a serf. Similarly, traditional libel, printed defamation, has been considered more damaging than slander, spoken defamation.

Early on, the English church court had jurisdiction over slander cases in connection with its jurisdiction over the conduct and morality of its members (church courts could prosecute sins). Harmful statements about a person were enough to subject him to the jurisdiction of the church courts. Such a defendant was referred to as a *diffamatus*, one whose reputation was bad enough to justify bringing him to trial putting him at risk of excommunication.[5] In those cases where bad reputation was determined to be unfounded, the church court then had to deal with the people who spread the now-proven-false statements about the defendant. The slanderers had therefore committed a crime in the eyes of the church and faced punishment as provided for in the Langston Constitution of 1222,[6] "furthermore, we excommunicate all those who for lucre, hate, favour, or any other cause maliciously impute a crime

[3] Winston S. Churchill, *A History of the English Speaking Peoples, The Birth of Britain* (New York: Barnes & Noble, 1993), p. 67.

[4] The shilling of the time was the price of a cow or sheep.

[5] Theodore F.T. Plucknett, *A Concise History of the Common Law* (London: Butterworth, 1948), p. 455 (Chap. 5).

[6] Ibid.

whereby anyone is defamed among good and grave persons in such wise that he has been put to his purgation at least, or otherwise aggrieved." More modernly, Supreme Court Justice Potter Stewart addressed the issue of reputation in the 1966 Supreme Court case of *Rosenblatt v. Baer* which we will discuss later in this chapter:[7]

> The right of a man to the protection of his own reputation from unjustified invasion and wrongful hurt reflects no more than our basic concept of the essential dignity and worth of every human being—a concept at the root of any decent system of ordered liberty.

But the protection of reputation as a legal concept within the structure of secular government arose more than 700 years ago with the creation of *De Scandalis Magnatum*, an act of the English crown in 1275 which made it a crime to slander the leading men of England—the king and his magnates. Its re-enactment in 1378 made clear the purpose of the protection of those men declaring that false statements regarding the character, conduct and reputations of the leaders of the nation, now extended to peers, prelates, justices and specifically named officials, threatened peril and mischief "to all the realm, and quick subversion and destruction of the said realm."[8] The penalties for such statements were severe, the loss of the ears for spoken words and the loss of the right hand where the statements were in writing. These acts and their punishments were intended to preserve the political power of the government, an aim that has lain at the heart of much of defamation law and which became of paramount importance in preserving the freedom of the press and public in the United States.

The Court of the Star Chamber became the forum for many of these cases where defamatory statements carried criminal penalties as breaches of the peace, seditious libel or criminal libel. In large measure, the Star Chamber took jurisdiction because it was considered more reliable (more likely to render the "right" decision in the eyes of the monarchy) than local courts when dealing with political criminals. While there were legislative acts that could provide justification for the defamation prosecutions, the Star Chamber relied on the "absolute power" of the realm as well as the "law of God."[9] That was invoked in the case *De Libellis Famosis*.[10]

---

[7] *Rosenblatt v. Baer*, 383 U.S. 75, 92, 86 S.Ct. 669, 679 (1966).

[8] Norman L. Rosenberg, *Protecting the Best Men: An Interpretive History of the Law of Libel*, (Chapel Hill: University of North Carolina Press, 1986), p. 4 (Introduction).

[9] Theodore F.T. Plucknett, *A Concise History of the Common Law*, (London: Butterworth, 1948), p. 458 (Chap. 5).

[10] *De Libellous Famosis*, (1606) 77 Eng. Rep. 250. "That every Libel [* * *] is made either against a private man, or against a Magistrate or publick person. If it be against a private man it deserveth a severe punishment, for although the Libel be made against one, yet it inciteth all those of the same family, kindred, or society to revenge, and so may be the cause of per consequens to quarrels and breach of the peace, and may be the cause of shedding of blood, and of great inconvenience: if it be against a Magistrate, or other publick person, it is a greater offence; for it concerneth not onely the breach of the peace, but also the scandal of government;

But in the Sixteenth Century, local and church courts in England began to hear cases regarding spoken attacks on personal and business reputations. The rise of the merchant class made reputation a valuable property and the courts began awarding monetary damages for injuries to both personal reputation and reputations affecting business relationships with others. From a legal point, the evolution of monetary damages came about under a doctrine that held that where a statute created a punishment for conduct that harmed others, then the person harmed could sue for damages even where the statute did not mention the possibility of a civil suit. Plaintiffs then applied the *scandalum magnatum* in the civil courts, supplementing the body of common law regarding defamation.

English colonists brought many legal traditions to America and with them, attitudes about defamation. But these colonial suits were unlike the multimillion dollar cases we see played out in the courts these days. For one thing, the purpose of the defamation suit was to repair the damage to the plaintiff's reputation. Damage awards were often small and often the losing defendant was forced to acknowledge the falsity of his statement either in court or at some public place where the retraction would quickly be spread, and the reputation of the plaintiff rehabilitated. To help restore the status quo, the courts would sometimes offer the losing defendant the choice of paying a large damage award or making his public apology and retraction.

There also was concern about the effect of slanderous words on the community and government and several colonies passed laws against making false or vilifying statements against others. A Pennsylvania statute called for punishment of "Spreaders of False News." A Connecticut law made it a crime to knowingly tell lies about people and made the penalties more severe for each subsequent offense. All told, defamation cases made up about 17 percent of the criminal cases of colonial courts. The *Zenger* case had a symbolic impact on the treatment of seditious libel in the courts, but the prosecution of speech attacking the established power structure continued in the colonial assemblies.

Following the excesses of the Sedition Act of 1798, defamation law evolved with public officials turning more often to purely civil libel suits rather than criminal libel actions to deter criticism against them. It was not just public officials, either. The novelist and political essayist James Fenimore Cooper[11] carried on a series of libel suits against newspapers. Cooper was initially angered by the treatment of his literary works in the

for what greater scandal of government can there be than to have corrupt or wicked Magistrates to be appointed and constituted by the King to govern his Subjects under him? And greater imputation to the State cannot be, than to suffer such corrupt men to sit in the sacred seat of Justice, or to have any medling in or concerning the administration of Justice." A rule from the case was that truth could not be used a defense. The reasoning: a false statement could be denied but a truthful libel would be even more likely to harm the Magistrate and government.

[11] Cooper wrote *The Last of the Mohicans, The Deerslayer* and *The Leatherstocking Tales* among other titles in a long literary career.

popular press and more outraged by the press coverage of a dispute surrounding a controversy over property owned by the Cooper family. In many ways similar to current criticisms of the media, Cooper was concerned that the popular press was inflaming the masses and threatening to replace reasoned government with the tyranny of public opinion. As Norman Rosenberg wrote in his "*Protecting the Best Men*":[12]

> Cooper could still hope that the republic's descent into tyranny might be halted if, among other things, the landed gentry—Cooper's version of the best men—regained political power; this could only happen, he believed, if strict defamation laws prevented the press from destroying the characters and reputations of these worthy citizens.

Opinion leaders and the political and social elite still sue to advance or protect their own agendas, but while many defamation suits arise from stories about the powerful and famous, many others come about from the "routine" and "everyday" stories and communications generated in the modern media.

Even "routine" libels can be expensive. The average cost of defending a libel suit easily may run into the hundreds of thousands of dollars, and that refers only to legal costs and not to money paid out as part of a judgment. And those costs could include the expenses run up by the winning plaintiff. Actor and director Clint Eastwood won $150,000 in damages against the *National Enquirer* in 1996. The court ordered the *Enquirer* to pay an additional $653,000 to Eastwood to cover the costs of his lawsuit. Litigation that might sting a large newspaper or broadcast chain station or its insurance company could ruin a small media outfit.

In one extraordinary case in 1985, costs to *Time* magazine were estimated as $3 million for its successful defense of a suit by Ariel Sharon; and in *Westmoreland v. CBS*—arguably one of the most-publicized libel cases in the nation's history—one estimate was $8 million in legal costs for both sides, although Gen. William Westmoreland dropped his suit before it reached the jury. Such prospects may lead media to avoid the huge costs of defending a drawn-out trial by settling out of court—for $800,000 in the case of a 1984 agreement by the *Wall Street Journal*. Insurance, which is not required and not always available, does not eliminate the expenses of defamation litigation. As with car or homeowner insurance, libel insurance comes with a deductible, the amount the policy holder must pay to cover the first part of the costs and award. In one libel case in which one of the authors was involved in a consulting capacity, the deductible was $100,000 and that is what the defendant television station had to pay before its insurance carrier opened its checkbook. Regular business or homeowner's

---

[12] Norman L. Rosenberg, *Protecting the Best Men: An Interpretive History of the Law of Libel*, (Chapel Hill: University of North Carolina Press, 1986), p. 138 (Chap. 6).

insurance does not cover libel, special coverage called Errors and Omissions is needed to provide such protection.

It is not just the newspaper, television or radio station that need to be wary of defamation suits. Press releases and advertising copy can give rise to a costly defamation suit. Statements made in a press conference by the Anti-Defamation League cost the organization more than $10 million in 2004.[13] Novels and short stories have resulted in courtroom cases and multimedia presentations and social media are new and fertile fields for litigation. This chapter will then discuss the elements of defamation with an eye toward incorporating the liabilities involved in every form of mass communication.

Although the case comes from England, printed in *The Mirror* newspaper on Aug. 1, 1997, the story offers food for thought for all professional communicators: "One little word was all that was needed to save four and a half years of courtroom agony for Poinsias de Rossa. The word was 'sorry' but it was not a part of the vocabulary of writer Eamon Dunphy and his bosses at the *Sunday Independent.* A simple apology could have saved the newspaper group an estimated £1 million in damages and costs. The former minister said last night he'd never have sued if the paper had printed the apology he sought. 'They failed to do the decent thing,' he said." (The pound was worth about $1.68 at the time of the story.)

It will be a sometimes-confusing excursion. The late William L. Prosser, long considered America's leading torts scholar, assessed this area of the law in this way:[14]

> It must be confessed * * * that there is a great deal of the law of defamation which makes no sense. It contains anomalies and absurdities for which no legal writer ever has had a kind word, and it is a curious compound of a strict liability imposed upon innocent defendants * * * with a blind and almost perverse refusal to compensate the plaintiff for real and very serious harm.

As a distinguished study asserted decades ago, the law of libel aims at one thing and hits another. The study, entitled "*Libel Law and the Press: Myth and Reality*", noted that the law assumes that by suing, plaintiffs whose reputations have been injured can somehow be made whole by receiving money. That study found, however, that plaintiffs tend to be more interested in correction of falsity and in "setting the record straight."[15]

---

[13] *Quigley v. Rosenthal, Anti-Defamation League,* 327 F.3d 1044 (10th Cir. 2003), cert. denied 540 U.S. 1229, 124 S.Ct. 1507 (2004).

[14] Prosser, *Law of Torts,* 4th ed. (1971), p. 737.

[15] Randall P. Bezanson, Gilbert Cranberg, and John Soloski, *Libel Law and the Press: Myth and Reality* (New York: The Free Press, 1987).

Moreover, many defamation cases are filed because of the treatment that the subjects of these publications receive once they bring the matter to the attention of the publisher. In many of the suits, the plaintiffs reported that they would have been willing to listen to an explanation for the harmful words from the defendant.[16] But, more often than not, the reaction they got was a harsh and abrupt, "we stand by our story." Adding insult to injury was the critical factor in bringing about the lawsuit. All publishers, managers and administrators will develop their own policies to deal with complaints about stories, but a key factor in avoiding costly and risky litigation is a willingness to hear the aggrieved person out. It is unnecessary and improvident to apologize or accept responsibility for what one person claims are errors or misstatements about him, but it is possible and very helpful to take a complaint seriously and relay the matter to the appropriate supervisor.

The Web's ability to make anyone with access to a computer a publisher has expanded the possibilities for suit. People make use of websites and social media to express themselves on issues and people in their communities, failing to realize that what could be said late at night in someone's kitchen at the end of a party is something else when it is posted where anyone can see.[17] A number of libel suits have arisen in recent years over intemperate remarks posted on websites, social media sites and bulletin boards operated by universities, cities and businesses. All the rules pertaining to traditional libel apply to the Web as we will see in the following pages.

INFOWARS AND PARKLAND HIGH SCHOOL SHOOTING

The *Infowars* website is no stranger to controversy. From the Sandy Hook shooting to the murder of DNC employee Seth Rich and a shout out from President Trump, the site has generated considerable attention, though more for the outrage generated by the conspiracy theories trumpeted by guests and founder Alex Jones. Jones is facing lawsuits over comments about the Sandy Hook shootings based on stories carried on the *Infowars* radio show. The site itself is the target of a libel suit filed in Texas state court by Marcel Fontaine, wrongly identified by photograph and caption as the Marjory Stoneman Douglas High School shooter in Parkland, Florida.

Infowars and *Infowars* reporter Kit Daniels moved to dismiss the suit on the grounds that there was no evidence to support Fontaine's suit. The Texas trial court ruled against *Infowars* and Daniels allowing the suit to proceed. The defendants appealed to the Texas Court of Appeals. The appellate court affirmed the trial court's decision with regard to Infowars and Daniels.[18] The appellate court began its holding recounting

---

16 Ibid.

17 Jenn Abelson, "Uncivil discourse blights online debates," *Boston Globe*, Jan. 5, 2004.

18 *Infowars, LLC v. Fontaine*, WL 5444400, Oct. 24, 2019.

what happened on February 14, 2018, the day Nikolas Cruz killed seventeen people at Marjory Stoneman Douglas High School in Parkland, Florida.[19]

> That same day, the Infowars.com website published an article authored by Daniels entitled "MSM already covering it up." The article provided information and commentary relating to the Parkland shooter, Nikolas Cruz, and included a clear photo of Marcel Fontaine below the text "another alleged photo of the suspect shows communist garb" and with the caption "Shooter is a commie." In the photo, Fontaine is wearing a red shirt that features several famous communist leaders engaging in merriment.

Infowars and Daniels conceded that Fontaine was not the shooter who had already been identified. But, the defendants argued, they merely reported on what appeared on social media. Daniels downloaded the photograph from 4chan.org and also from a Twitter account Laguna Beach Antifa. The court noted that,[20] "the day before the Parkland shooting, the top Google search result for Laguna Beach Antifa's Twitter account described it as a parody account." The 4chan text that ran with the photo of Fontaine read,[21]

> "Florida Shooter Was Commie!" and the text "FLORIDA SHOOTER WAS A CONFIRMED LIBERAL COMMIE!!! What r we going to do to help the country defend itself against the red scare/pol? A million bucks says he supports ANTIFA too!"

Reliance on 4chan did not help *Infowars* or Daniels as the appellate court noted that 4chan had been described in another legal proceeding as unreliable as a news-gathering agency in the opinion affirming the trial court.

SOCIAL MEDIA SPEED LIBELS AND LIBEL SUITS

Years ago, people could react to events in their communities and news stories by writing letters to the editor in their local newspapers. It took time to write, either by hand or on a typewriter. It took more time for a letter to reach the paper and editors there would reject those letters that amounted to libel. Now, things that happen in communities or around the world generate reactions instantly through social media but without the benefit of time to reconsider an intemperate thought or having an editor to block libel. Mind you, the thousands of libel cases from the pre-digital age prove that even giving people time doesn't eliminate the risk of libel. Since 2013, more than 200 cases involving social media were or are moving through state and federal courts.

---

19 Ibid. at 2, 3.

20 Ibid. at 4.

21 Ibid.

FACEBOOK

With its reach and popularity, Facebook has been at the heart of a number of libel suits. A case involving a mother in Colorado and a martial arts instructor in Texas illustrates the power and danger of using social media.[22] Michelle Hall of Aurora, Colo., created a Facebook group page in 2011 called, "Please help me stop a child molester!"[23] Hall accused Paul Hawbecker of sexually molesting and taking pictures of her daughter.[24] Hall wrote on the page that law enforcement investigations were active against Hawbecker in Colorado and Texas. The claims were not true. U.S. District Court Judge Royce C. Lamberth concluded that Hall either knew or should have known the statement was false.[25]

> Hall posted a comment in November 2011 that Hawbecker taught karate to kids. In another post in April 2014, she stated that Hawbecker lived and worked in San Antonio, worked with and around children, and asked group members to spread his name to anyone they knew in San Antonio. She also "liked" Hawbecker's employer, enabling him to see many of her posts. It was only in April 2014, nearly three years after the group was created, that Hawbecker found out about the existence of the group.

After Hall's page went up, a parent of a child who attended the school where Hawbecker taught martial arts raised concerns about the connection between Hawbecker and the school. Hawbecker was put on a reduced teaching schedule and prevented from teaching classes with children or female students. In 2017, Hawbecker fired and any mention of him was scrubbed from the school's website. Hawbecker tried to find additional employment after his hours were cut at the school. No one would hire him. Prospective employers would either not respond to his applications or simply say that something had come up in his background checks.[26]

> At least one employer sat down with Hawbecker and showed him that a search for the name "Paul Eric Hawbecker" yielded results showing Hall's accusations and documents from this very lawsuit. That employer bluntly informed Hawbecker that companies, particularly ones who conduct business online, are

---

[22] *Hawbecker v. Hall*, 276 F.Supp.3d 681 (W.D.Texas 2017).

[23] Ibid. at 685.

[24] Hall testified that at some unspecified date in 2005, Hawbecker, a friend of a mutual friend, was traveling through Colorado and needed a place to stay for the night. Hawbecker stayed at the Hall residence. Hall believes that Hawbecker took pictures of her daughter that night and in some unspecified manner engaged in sexual misconduct with her. She has no personal knowledge that any improper act occurred, has not been able to identify any pictures that allegedly exist of her daughter, and is not aware of any evidence that indicates that Hawbecker engaged in any sexual misconduct. *Hawbecker v. Hall*, WL 7187642 (W.D.Texas 2016).

[25] *Hawbecker v. Hall*, 276 F.Supp.3d 681, 685 (W.D.Texas 2017).

[26] Ibid. at 686.

> protective of their images and "could not take a chance" in hiring someone with his background.

Evidence showed that Hawbecker suffered emotional and mental harm. His romantic relationship failed, he lost friends and sought therapy to help manage his anxiety regarding Hall's allegations. Hawbecker testified about his fear of being in public or even leaving the house. Hawbecker won his case on a motion for summary judgment in a different federal district court. His case made it to Judge Lamberth's court for determination of damages. Hall did not appear in the courtroom in Texas saying that she did not have the money to be present or to hire an attorney to represent her. Despite a request from Hawbecker to take down the page, Hall continued to maintain it. Hall tried to minimize the nature of her Facebook efforts.[27]

> In response to a summary judgment motion, Hall claimed she had limited knowledge of how Facebook worked, that she thought the group was "private and closed" and that she never intended any of the statements to get out. However, the evidence shows that Hall repeatedly expressed her intent to contact Hawbecker's friends and employers about the allegations contained in the Facebook group, and during this lawsuit, she relinquished admin privileges over the page to another Facebook user to allow the page to continue. It remains unclear, however, to what extent the group page is still active or whether the defamatory statements have been removed.

Judge Lamberth awarded Hawbecker $343,000 for lost wages, loss of future income, damage to his reputation noting that he did not know how Hall would pay the judgment (Hall could not afford to travel to Texas to appear in court). He awarded Hawbecker an additional $100,000 in exemplary, or punitive, damages.

THE MILLION-DOLLAR BLOG

A Texas jury found a Dallas "lifestyle and beauty blogger" and her husband liable for defaming a wedding photographer through her blogs and other social media and awarded the photographer $1 million.[28] But before the jury reached its decision, photographer Andrea Polito reportedly had lost hundreds of thousands of dollars, shut down her studio and drained her life and retirement savings. All of that was driven by Andrew and Neely Moldovan's blog post attacks that were picked up by local, national and international media. "I called it an online public smear campaign by a blogger," Polito's attorney Dave Wishnew, partner in the firm of Gruber Elrod Johansen Hail Shank LLP, said.[29]

---

[27] Ibid. at 685.

[28] Avi Selk, "They trashed their wedding photographer over a $125 fee, so a jury told them to pay her $1 million," *The Washington Post*, Aug. 1, 2017.

[29] Telephone conversation with Dave Wishnew.

The case had its beginnings in 2014 when the couple hired Polito to photograph the wedding and preparations. Polito's company shot the ceremony in October of that year. In January Neely Moldovan told Twitter followers that she was starting to pick out the photographs for the couple's wedding album. The same day Andrew Moldovan was tweeting,[30] "We want our f---ing wedding album, which we already paid for." The Moldovans did not want to pay the contracted price of $150 for the album cover. After trying to work out the problems with the Moldovans, Polito said she planned to absorb the cost to satisfy her customers, *Dallas News* reported.[31]

But, the Moldovans had already started using social media to trash Polito and to push the story to local media.[32]

> The couple expressed in conversations obtained in discovery that they did not want Polito to find out about their contacting news outlets. They asked people they contacted about Polito to keep the issue quite because, as one conversation showed they "prefer the surprise."

Dallas NBC affiliate KXAS-TV picked up on the story as did the British newspaper, *The Daily Mail*, which ran a headline reading, "Wedding photographer holds couple's pictures hostage." Wishnew criticized that characterization.[33] "No one was holding their pictures hostage; it was just false." He said the Moldovans hoped their story would go viral. Neely Moldovan used her blog, *A Complete Waste of Makeup*, and then a later blog, *It Starts With Coffee*, to claim that Polito had done the same thing to almost two dozen other couples. Neely Moldovan's blogs appeared to benefit from the attention, Wishnew said.[34] "Her sponsored blog posts tripled in 2015."

Blogging has led to more than 120 suits in state and federal courts by 2019.

TWITTER LIBEL SUITS

As Internet communication evolves, Twitter—the micro-messaging service—was bound to cause libel litigation. True, no "tweet"—a Twitter message—can be more than 280 characters, but even a short message can draw litigation. Eriq Gardner reported for Reuters that Courtney Love, that cynosure of stoners, was the first celebrity to be sued for tweeting.

---

[30] Avi Selk, "They trashed their wedding photographer over a $125 fee, so a jury told them to pay her $1 million," *The Washington Post*, Aug. 1, 2017.

[31] Claire Z Cardona, "Bride, groom who slammed Dallas wedding photographer online, in media must pay $1.08M," *Dallas News*, July 31, 2017.

[32] Telephone conversation with Dave Wishnew.

[33] Ibid.

[34] Ibid.

Courtney Love, widow of Nirvana frontman Kurt Cobain, is above all a celebrity, but has been variously a singer, a lyricist, and an actress and a producer. Most recently, she appeared in an obviously pixilated condition at such venues as televised celebrity roasts. Love's credits include a substantial role in "The People versus Larry Flynt" (1996), leading a mostly female band ("Hole") for several years. Her life, often fodder for tabloids, included loss of the custody of her 11-year-old daughter after arrests for cocaine possession and for prescription drug abuse.

The suit was filed in Los Angeles, the BBC reported March 28, 2009 (citing Reuters). Love was being sued for messages on her Twitter and Myspace pages by Dawn Simorangkir, an Austin, Texas, designer with a clothing line called Boudoir Queen. Simorangkir says the messages were libelous, invaded her privacy, interfered with her business, breach of contract, and causing her emotional distress.[35] Simorangkir reportedly cited remarks from Love's Internet postings, claiming that Love called her, among other things, " 'nasty lying hosebag thief.' "[36] *The Hollywood Reporter* carried a story that quoted Love's Twitter as saying, "oi vey don't f---with my wardrobe or you will end up in a circle of corched [sic] eaeth [sic] hunted til your dead."[37] A Los Angeles jury found that Love had not libeled Simorangkir. Actor James Woods filed a $10 million suit over a Tweet that called him a cocaine addict.[38] If a Tweeter can identify a person and say something false and damaging, a libel suit can follow. Retweeting is another matter Sec. 230(c)(1) provides immunity for netizens. "No provider or user of an interactive computer service shall be treated as the publisher or speaker of any information provided by another information content provider."

Questions have come up about Donald and President Trumps' active Twitter account. In 2017 he tweeted,[39] "Arnold Schwarzenegger isn't voluntarily leaving the Apprentice, he was fired by his bad (pathetic) ratings, not by me. Sad end to great show." In 2012,[40] "While @BetteMidler is an extremely unattractive woman, I refuse to say that because I always insist on being politically correct." In 2018, he tweeted about Omarosa Manigault Newman, one of his senior adviser and former

---

[35] BBC News, "Rocker Love sued over net 'libel,' " http://news.bbc.co.uk/2/hi/entertainment/7969987.stm; "Courtney Love sued for Twitter defamation," http://www.reuters.com/article/us-love-idUSTRE52R00020090331.

[36] "Courtney Love: Apparent online rants now in court," http://www.accesshollywood.com/articles/courtney-loves-apparent-online-rants-now-in-court-69278/.

[37] Eriq Gardner, "Courtney Love sued for Twitter Defamation," *Hollywood Reporter*, Mar. 30, 2009.

[38] Josh Feldman, "James Woods files $10 million defamation suit against twitter troll," *Mediate,* July 30, 2015. http://www.mediaite.com/online/james-woods-files-10-million-defamation-lawsuit-against-twitter-troll/. The defendant died during the proceedings ending the suit.

[39] Donald J. Trump @realDonaldTrump, March 4, 2017.

[40] Donald J. Trump @realDonaldTrump, Oct. 28, 2012.

Apprentice cast member,[41] "When you give a crazed, crying lowlife a break, and give her a job at the White House, I guess it just didn't work out. Good work by General Kelly for quickly firing that dog!"

Although the tweets are offensive and arguably untrue, President Trump is protected because of a number of elements of libel law: 1) his targets are public figures and so would have a harder time of proving fault (discussed in Chap. 5); 2) most of his tweets are words of opinion and so are not actionable (discussed in Chap. 5); and, 3) filing a libel suit would mean that the plaintiff would have to go through what would likely be a very public and ugly discovery process in which the most personal questions could be asked.

As such, simple retweets should be immunized by the CDA. But, if a re-tweeter adds comments, those comments would be treated as an original publication creating exposure for a libel suit. A total of 23 Twitter libel cases had been or were making their way through the courts by 2019. That does not include any suits that ended through settlement before a final judgment.

READER COMMENTS

Anyone who has read stories posted on news sites is aware of the reader comments that appear after. While many comments are non-actionable opinion (See, Opinion and Rhetorical Hyperbole in Chap. 5), some comments are flat-out statements of arguable fact. When supposedly factual statements harm someone's reputation, libel lawyers come into play.

In *McGlothlin v. Hennelly*,[42] comments in social media and in reader comments for an online news site, withstood a challenge in pretrial proceedings to allow a libel suit to go forward. James McGlothlin is a founding member of The United Company, which is the parent company of Scratch Golf, LLC, which owns Hilton Head National Golf Course. Kevin Hennelly made three separate posts on Facebook and on the website of the *Island Packet*, a local newspaper, in which he criticized McGlothlin and asserted that he was corrupt and engaged in criminal activity. In a reader comment section in response to an *Island Packet* newspaper story: Hilton Head National developers: Why golf lost its swing there and what the future holds ("*Island Packet* Comment")[43]

> Statement: It looks like they left out a few pertinent facts. The most glaring is the corrupt people involved. [* * *] James Woodrow McGlothlin gave the corrupt Governor McDonald of Virginia wife a "no show" job. The McDonalds never reported income, $36,000. These guys are crony capitalists and will break

[41] Donald J. Trump @realDonaldTrump, Aug. 14, 2018.

[42] *McGlothlin v. Hennelly*, 370 F.Supp.3d 603 (D.S.C.2019).

[43] Ibid. at 609–610.

every rule in the book to get a government favor or handout. [* * *]

In ruling on Hennelly's motion to dismiss the libel suit, U.S. District Judge David C. Norton held that the reader comment and one Facebook post stated a libel claim sufficient to overcome the motion to dismiss (Judge Norton *did not say* that Hennelly had libeled McGothlin. His holding just allowed the suit to go forward allowing a jury to decide whether McGlothlin had been libeled.).

FINDING THE ONLINE DEFENDANT

Sometimes, it's easy to identify the defendant, the person who published the libel. In an age of anonymous bloggers and postings, it can be difficult to find the person responsible. In *Cohen v. Google*, a model sought the identity of an anonymous blogger on the, now removed, Google site *Skanks in NYC*.[44]

In August 2008, model Liskula Cohen learned about the existence of several Weblogs under the heading *Skanks of NYC*. The five blogs referred to Cohen using the terms "skank," "skanky," "ho" and "whoring."[45]

The question of identifying anonymous speakers is a significant one in First Amendment law. Anonymity is a protection against government or private party retaliation. *New York Times* Ethicist Randy Cohen wrote about the competing interests involved in the case.[46]

There are times when anonymity is legitimately practiced—by political dissidents in repressive regimes, for example. Donna Lieberman, the executive director of the New York Civil Liberties Union, told me: "We've defended the right to anonymous speech successfully on some occasions," including "Iranian students in masked protest at the time of the shah." Journalists reasonably use anonymous sources when doing so is the only way to obtain significant information. Rate My Professors and the like, though not without their faults, are useful enterprises that rely on the shield of anonymity. Without it, what student, mindful of the wrath of a teacher scorned, would post the scathing, though well-thought-out, denunciation of a prof?

And so, mindful of the use of discovery to locate and punish dissent, the courts have adopted standards requiring that plaintiffs show that they have legitimate claims before the cloak of anonymity is stripped from a publisher. In the *Cohen* case, trial court Judge Joan Madden ruled that Cohen had satisfied the requirement that she present a valid claim.[47]

---

[44] *Cohen v. Google, Inc.*, 25 Misc.3d 945, 887 N.Y.S.2d 424 (N.Y.Sup., 2009).

[45] *Cohen v. Google, Inc.*, 25 Misc.3d 945, 887 N.Y.S.2d 424 (N.Y.Sup., 2009).

[46] Randy Cohen, "Is It O.K. to Blog About This Woman Anonymously?" *Ethicist.Blogs. NyTimes.com*, Aug. 24, 2009.

[47] *Cohen v. Google, Inc.*, 25 Misc.3d 945,949, 887 N.Y.S.2d 424, 427 (N.Y.Sup., 2009).

> Here, petitioner is entitled to pre-action disclosure of information as to the identity of the Anonymous Blogger, as she has sufficiently established the merits of her proposed cause of action for defamation against that person or persons, and that the information sought is material and necessary to identify the potential defendant or defendants.

So, while the bar is set higher in determining the identity of an anonymous blogger or poster, it can be met and defendants identified. In the *Cohen* case, the blogger's identity was revealed, and Cohen named Rosemary Port, an acquaintance who was the blogger, in a $3 million libel suit.[48]

In a suit brought by a city council member in Scranton, Penn., a state district court rejected an attempt to uncover the identities of six persons who posted comments on an online discussion board. Judy Gatelli, president of the Scranton City Council and a council member, sued Joseph Pichelsky, the operator of the dohertydeceit.com bulletin board, a site critical of the city government of Scranton and its mayor, Christopher A. Doherty.

In 2008, Gatelli sought the identities of persons who posted messages to the *Scranton Political Times Message Board* claiming that they and Pichelsky had libeled her. The trial court refused to allow the subpoenas and that decision was appealed. Early in 2011 a Pennsylvania appellate court affirmed the ruling.[49] In doing so, the three-judge panel cited *Melvin v. Doe*, a 2003 Pennsylvania Supreme Court decision holding that the identification of an anonymous poster on an Internet site required a balancing of the interests of plaintiffs with the First Amendment rights of the anonymous speakers.[50] "[A]ny ruling that does not fully protect the anonymity of the anonymous Internet speaker may deter anonymous Internet speech." And so, anonymous publishers on the Internet need to be aware that their identities may be discovered in the course of a defamation suit and they could find themselves in court.

The ability to create a name for a person's wifi network gives people the ability to identify themselves to device users who are looking for wifi access.[51] In an Idaho Supreme Court case, whether the name of a wifi network was libelous was a fact question for a jury to decide. In *Irish v. Hall*,[52] the former mayor of Harrison, Idaho, and her husband sued a

---

[48] Randy Cohen, "Is It O.K. to Blog About This Woman Anonymously?" *Ethicist.Blogs.NyTimes.com*, Aug. 24, 2009.

[49] *Pichelsky v. Gatelli*, 12 A.3d 430 (Pa.Super. 2011).

[50] Ibid.

[51] This can be problematic, though. Many wifi routers come with a regular password that is not usually guessable, but still should be changed regularly. More importantly, many routers have a second administrative password. For one brand, the password is "administrative" giving persons with bad intent the ability to log into the wifi network where they will have access to all the devices linked to it. Personalizing the name of the wifi network simply makes it easier for hackers to pick likely targets.

[52] *Irish v. Hall*, 163 Idaho 603, 416 P.3d 975 (Idaho 2018).

sitting city council member and his wife over the change of the name of their home wifi network. Problems between Mayor Wanda Irish and Jeffrey and Dona Hall had been ongoing for some time over the city's easement near the marina that the Halls owned in Harrison.[53]

> The dispute underlying the present case began in May 2012, after the Halls' boat and trailer were towed off of the public easement. Upon discovering his boat had been towed, Jeffrey Hall called Wanda Irish eight times within one hour calling her vulgar names and accusing her of having his boat towed, which Wanda Irish denied doing. Following this incident, Jeffrey Hall placed posters in his vehicle that read, "MAYOR IRISH LIED!!!" and "MAYOR IRISH LIES!!!"

Later in 2012, the Halls found several cameras around Harrison and in a campground near the Halls' marina. The cameras belonged to Dennis Irish and the Irishes said that the cameras had been put up to enhance security because of taggers (graffiti artists). The next year, the Halls complained to the Kootenai County Sheriff's Office that Dennis Irish was stalking Dona Hall. The conflict continued with confrontations between Jeffrey Hall and Wanda Irish. In the summer of 2015, Jeffrey Hall changed the name of his marina's wifi network to "Mayor Wanda Irish Terrorist."[54]

> Wanda Irish saw the wireless name on her cell phone, and the Irishes' attorney subsequently sent a cease-and-desist letter to the Halls. The Halls responded by changing the Gateway Marina's wireless designation to, "she really is a [t]errorist." The Halls then changed their home wireless internet designation to read, "[D]ennis and [W]anda Irish stocking u2." In August 2015, the Halls again changed their home wireless designation to "Move Irish."

The Irishes filed a libel suit over the wifi names. The case went to trial but after the first day of the Irishes' case, the trial judge granted a directed verdict to the Halls. Judge Cynthia K.C. Meyer held that the wifi name was, first, ambiguous and, second, an opinion that the Halls were expressing.[55]

> "Dennis and Wanda stocking U2," again, who are they talking about? And then with the misspelling of "stalking," again, we know that what was intended is s-t-a-l-k, stalking, harassing, spying on, or at least I think that's the intent. I think that's a reasonable inference based on the evidence that that was the intent of that name, but it's misspelled s-t-o-c-k-i-n-g, and then there's U2, you, the letter, and 2, the numeral.

[53] Ibid. at 605, 977.

[54] Ibid. at 606, 978.

[55] Ibid.

> For someone who is seeing that for the first time, what does that mean? Does it mean that they're actually stocking U2 albums for sale? Sounds kind of preposterous, but I don't know that it's any more preposterous than another interpretation. And, again, I believe it's an opinion. I don't believe it's subject to something that can be proven or disproven.

The opinion by Idaho Supreme Court Chief Justice Roger S. Burdick focused on the trial court judge's explanation of "stocking U2,' noting that the judge had correctly determined that the words could refer to stalking, a crime. The ambiguity as to the meaning was a fact question and therefore a matter for a jury to decide. The standard for a directed verdict under Idaho state law is that a finder of fact could only reach one conclusion based on the facts. The question about the ultimate meaning of the words was not one that had only one conclusion and should not have been resolved by a directed verdict. The case was sent back to the trial court for further proceedings.

17. THE FIVE ELEMENTS OF LIBEL

The plaintiff in a libel suit must plead that there was Publication, Identification, Defamation, Injury and Fault.

Potential libel suit defendants—and that includes all of us—need to know (as do lawyers filing libel suits) that five conditions must be present before a suit can hope to succeed. The five necessary conditions for suit are:

1. Publication
2. Identification
3. Defamation
4. Injury
5. Fault

18. PUBLICATION

There is an old saying: "They can't lock you up for what you think." The same holds true for defamation suits. You can think all the nasty things you want to about people, organizations and corporations. It is not until you publish the statement that we start down the painful path of litigation. Publication means that someone other than the publisher and the subject of the statement receives the communication. You may speak harshly to someone or write about them or paint pictures, but until some other person perceives the message you have little to fear from defamation. But as soon as someone else sees or hears, you are in for a bumpy ride. Even when we broadcast or put our

defamatory statement on the Internet, we still call it publication, a term of art in defamation.

The reason for the publication requirement is easy to understand when we keep in mind that defamation arises over damage to reputations, the esteem in which we are held by others. In professional communication we think of defamatory stories appearing in newspapers with hundreds of thousands of readers, seen or heard by millions in broadcast audiences or accessible by the millions hooked into the Web. But in defamation law, it takes only one person to make up an audience for purposes of publication. In one case, a man dictated a letter to his secretary accusing the addressee of grand larceny. The secretary typed the letter and it was sent through the mail. The letter's recipient brought a successful libel suit: the court held that publication took place at the time the stenographic notes were read and transcribed.[56] Some states hold that when one employee or member of a group communicates with another, there has been no publication. The reasoning is that the company, corporation, church or other group constitutes an entity made up of its employees or members. Communication among employees essentially is like a person talking to himself. Even so, intra-corporate communication can lead to suit if the communication goes beyond the boundaries of the entity.

Litigation Note: *Even if you are in a jurisdiction where intra-company communication is not considered publication, those memos can create significant legal problems. In a defamation suit, a good plaintiff's attorney will seek to develop evidence to show the defendant's bad motives and create a bad image of the defendant before the jury. To that end, the plaintiff's attorney will demand that the defendant produce all notes, memos and even emails that have relevance to the suit. Rule 34 of the Federal Rules of Civil Procedure has been interpreted to require the disclosure of email, voice-mail telephone records and back-up tapes. And discovery, discussed in detail in Sec. 26, is intended to bring out any materials arguably related to the case, so it can be far reaching. The National Law Journal has reported on the growing use of discovery for email and its potential for damage to clients. "Think of email as a corporate CB radio," one litigation support firm said of electronic discovery. "It is full of corporate gossip, and derogatory or indiscreet remarks. It paints a very down-to-earth picture of corporate knowledge and behavior. And it is meticulously transcribed and stored."*[57] *An mail message in which a reporter or editor crows that, "we are going to get that #%* & @$" or which speaks unflatteringly about the subject of a story can*

[56] *Ostrowe v. Lee,* 256 N.Y. 36, 175 N.E. 505 (1931). See also *Arvey Corp. v. Peterson,* 178 F.Supp. 132 (E.D.Pa.1959). This is the majority position although there is a significant minority of jurisdictions which hold that communication between employees of a company does not create publication because it is akin to talking to one's self. Remember though, that the odds are that you will be in a jurisdiction where you incur liability.

[57] Martha Middleton, "A Discovery: There May Be Gold in E-Mail," *The National Law Journal,* Sept. 20, 1993.

significantly increase the risk of losing a defamation suit and adding to the size of a damage award. Such statements help to turn juries against media defendants and provide fuel for the plaintiff's attorney who will seek to inflame the passions and prejudices of the jurors against the "mean spirited, arrogant and willful" media defendants.

One significant question that arises in defamation is the extent of liability from a published defamatory statement. If your newspaper or magazine has a circulation of 250,000, how many libel suits can be brought? Similarly, what is the extent of liability for a broadcast that has 500,000 viewers, a home page on the Internet that can be accessed by millions of persons or the 20,000 copies of a novel? The answer comes in two parts. The first is liability for all of the copies of the single edition of the newspaper, book, generation of the home page or broadcast seen or heard in each of the homes. Those are considered to be a single publication and would create liability for only one defamation suit. The second question arises when that edition, home page or broadcast crosses state lines. Can a plaintiff sue in each and every state in which the defamatory statement was published? In most states, the single publication rule applies, especially with respect to Internet libels. The rule allows only one lawsuit per single publication.

The single-publication rule also applies to the statute of limitations. The statute of limitations, already mentioned above, is the time in which a plaintiff has to commence the suit. This limitation on the time in which a plaintiff can start a suit is based on the idea that potential defendants should not have to look over their shoulders for potential plaintiffs for their whole lives. It also means that plaintiffs will bring their suits in a timely fashion when evidence and witnesses are more likely to be reliable.

In 25 states and the District of Columbia, the statute of limitations for libel is one year after publication. Among the rest, 19 states set their statute of limitations at two years and six give the plaintiff three years to file suit. As you can see from the range of statutes of limitations, the 50 states and the District of Columbia have developed the law of defamation in their own ways. There are general principles, but each state is free to follow its own judicial philosophies, subject to the requirements of the First Amendment and the Constitution. With the existence of mail subscriptions and Internet sites that carry content for newspapers, radio, TV, advertisers, PR firms and general publishers, a defendant who has its place of business in a one-year statute of limitations state might well find itself sued in a two-or three-year statute of limitations state.

States with two-year statutes are Alabama, Alaska, Connecticut, Delaware, Florida, Hawaii, Idaho, Indiana, Iowa, Maine, Minnesota, Missouri, Montana, Nevada, North Dakota, South Carolina, South Dakota, Washington, and Wisconsin. Arkansas, Massachusetts, New

Hampshire, New Mexico, Rhode Island and Vermont's limitations are three years. The rest of the states have one-year statutes of limitation.

Because deadlines are so important,[58] one consideration in defamation is when the statute begins to run. For newspapers or other daily publications, it is simple enough—the day the publication comes out. For magazines, the question becomes more complicated. In *Tocco v. Time, Inc.*[59], it was held that the publication takes place at the time a magazine is mailed to subscribers or put in the hands of those who will ship the edition to wholesale distributors. That approach, however, is not universally accepted. To the contrary, *Osmers v. Parade Publications,* Inc.,[60] held that a publication date is when the libel was "substantially and effectively communicated to a meaningful mass of readers—the public for which the publication was intended, not some small segment of it." For Internet publishers, the more reasonable rule would appear to be when the statement became available.

But even when the beginning of the statute of limitations can be identified, the question remains which statute to apply. If the statute of limitations has expired in one jurisdiction, can a plaintiff still sue in another state where the statute of limitations is longer? In *Keeton v. Hustler,*[61] the United States Supreme Court allowed the plaintiff to sue *Hustler* magazine in New Hampshire, the only state where the statute of limitations had not expired.[62] The key to the case was the fact that *Hustler* magazine had circulation in New Hampshire. Having taken advantage of doing business in the state, the magazine had to accept the jurisdiction of the state. The magazine pointed out that it sold only between 10,000 and 15,000 copies in New Hampshire out of its entire circulation, but the Supreme Court found that to be sufficient to confer jurisdiction. New Hampshire's libel statute of limitations is now 3 years.

While courts limit liability by applying a specific statute of limitations, publishers (including station management and those on the Internet) need to understand the limitations on the single-publication rule. It does not apply when a defamatory statement is republished. This can be a tricky issue. If a defamatory statement is published on May 1, the publisher has a year to worry about. On May 2 of the next year, the statute of limitation will have tolled (in the majority of jurisdictions) and the plaintiff will be barred from bringing suit. It does not matter if the newspaper or magazine sells a back issue on the following May 3. The initial publication is the controlling date for purposes of the statute of limitation.

---

[58] Civil procedure textbooks provide many examples of cases where plaintiffs (through their attorneys) failed to comply with the rules and so lost their cases or the right to bring their cases.

[59] *Tocco v. Time, Inc.*, 195 F.Supp. 410 (E.D.Mich 1961).

[60] *Osmers v. Parade Publications, Inc.*, 234 F.Supp. 924, 927 (S.D.N.Y.1964).

[61] *Keeton v. Hustler*, 465 U.S. 770, 104 S.Ct. 1473 (1984).

[62] At the time, New Hampshire's statute of limitation was six years.

The problem arises when the publisher publishes the defamatory statement again. If a newspaper publishes, in a later edition, a story it published earlier, the newspaper faces the possibility of a new defamation suit with a newly begun statute of limitations. This can be a significant problem for those media entities that create "remember when" or "10 years ago today" features. The reprinting of those articles from 10, 20 or 50 years earlier creates a new publication and lawsuit. The same applies to book publishers who may issue a subsequent edition of a book. In *Rinaldi v. Viking Penguin,*[63] a New York court of appeals ruled that although the allegedly defamatory statements in a hard-cover book were protected from suit by the statute of limitations, a paperback edition of the same book started a new statute of limitations. For newspapers, subsequent editions of the same day's newspaper can be considered new publication of defamatory materials. The same holds true for re-broadcasts. The key in these cases is the choice the publishers made to publish again and the opportunity, whether they took advantage of it, to correct the statement.

Updating a website does not create a new statute of limitations, a panel of the 7th Circuit Court of Appeals[64] held in 2019.[65] In that case, a luxury car share service owner, George Kiebala, was the subject of multiple website postings made by Derek Boris. Boris had joined the program and allowed Kiebala to rent his Lamborghini Gallardo. He withdrew from the program but Kiebala's final check to him did not clear. Boris posted what the court called "angry and derogatory" statements about Kiebala and the car share service on customer review websites including *Scamexposure.com*, *Privatecomplaints.com*, and *Ripoffreport.com*. In 2010 and 2011. Boris offered Kiebala a final chance to resolve the dispute in 2014. When that failed, Boris took to the Web again, the court said.[66]

> On July 21, 2015, on a new website called scamorg.com, Boris posted a statement almost identical to his Ripoff Report post of July 20, 2011. And on July 22, 2015, Boris returned to Ripoffreport.com and "updated" his original July 20, 2011 post.
>
> Kiebala filed a libel suit. [* * *] we assume for purposes of the appeal, that by indicating that his 2011 negative review was "updated," Boris caused the post to reflect a date of 2015, making it more likely to be prioritized in new online search results.

Kiebala filed a libel suit. It was dismissed by a federal district court and the 7th Circuit panel took up the appeal. One of the issues was whether

---

63 *Rinaldi v. Viking Penguin*, 52 N.Y.2d 422, 438 N.Y.S.2d 496, 420 N.E.2d 377 (1981).

64 In this case, the federal appellate court applied Illinois law. Federal courts are required to must apply state law on issues of substantive law where federal statutes or federal procedure are not involved. In this case, Illinois law was applied.

65 *Kiebala v. Boris*, 928 F.3d 680 (7thCir. 2019).

66 Ibid. at 682.

Boris' "updating" his review or putting the content of a previous review constituted a republication starting a new statute of limitations clock. The 7th Circuit panel held that the update, which did not have any new information, was not a new publication.[67] With respect to the re-posting of the 2011 negative review to a new site in 2015, the panel concluded that as the post was unchanged, it was nothing more than a copy of the original review and not a new publication.

Republication can be a particular problem when periodicals repackage their investigative series in book or other form. In *Warford v. Lexington Herald-Leader Co.,*[68] the 1986 reprint of a 1985 series charging an assistant basketball coach with recruiting violations brought a lawsuit. The Kentucky Supreme Court noted that a basketball player who was a source for damaging information originally published by the newspaper about assistant coach Reggie Warford had promptly denied and retracted his statements, and his denial was published by the *Herald-Leader*.

The series, which won a Pulitzer Prize, was then republished in 1986, retitled "1985: A Year of Crisis in College Athletics." The 1986 publication, which omitted the athlete's denial, was sent to "the president, athletic director, faculty representative, and head football and basketball coaches at each [NCAA] member university, as well as 100 major newspapers * * *" Assistant Coach Warford, who asserted that the series had damaged his employment chances, won his lawsuit against the newspaper.

INTERNET LINKS AND REPUBLICATION

It isn't exactly republishing someone else's story but linking is a way to send people to stories. A 2009 case out of Kentucky helped resolve the question about whether a link is a republication.[69] Attorney Robert Salyer sued the Southern Poverty Law Center over its *Intelligence Report,* an examination of extremism in the military. A section of the report, "A Few Bad Men," said that Salyer was part of an extremist group in the military, had been dishonorably discharged and barred from practicing law in military courts. The report was published on the Southern Poverty Law Center's website on July 7, 2006.

On July 28, 2008, Salyer asked the Law Center to take his name from the article. The Law Center took out the references. Salyer sued over the article. His suit was dismissed on the grounds that he filed after the one-year statute of limitations had expired. He then advanced an argument that a hypertext link to the original article constituted a new publication. The trial court looked at the nature of links and concluded

---

[67] Ibid. at 687.

[68] *Warford v. Lexington Herald-Leader Co.*, 789 S.W.2d 758, 759–760 (Ky.1990).

[69] *Salyer v. Southern Poverty Law Center, Inc.*, 701 F.Supp.2d 912 (W.D.Ky. 2009).

that while links would send new readers to the article, it was little more than a reference.[70]

> Traditional republication occurs when the substance of the previously published defamatory statements are altered or the defamatory statements themselves are put forth in a new form. Neither of those methods of republication occurred in this case. The hyperlinks, while adding a new method of access to "A Few Bad Men," did not restate the allegedly defamatory statements and did not alter the substance of that article in any manner.

A link, accompanied by an excerpt from a defamatory publication, might well constitute a new publication, though. It is, after all, action that allows the defendant to have made changes to remove the defamatory material.

THE DOCTRINE OF REPUBLICATION: WHEN NOT TO REPEAT

Republication is a major concern publishers[71] because in most cases, the defamation suit is brought because the media defendant has quoted or paraphrased someone else's statement about the plaintiff. Both students and professionals (who ought to know better) have claimed the "defense" of merely quoting another person's defamation. "It was the person I interviewed who said the defamatory thing. I merely reported it" is not a defense. This holds true even when the person quoted is saying the defamatory statement in her own voice in a recording, video or audio.

"The common law of libel has long held that one who republishes a defamatory statement 'adopts' it as his own and is liable [for false, defamatory statements] in equal measure to the original defamer."[72] Modern defamation law holds that the original speaker also can be held liable if he knew it would be republished or reasonably could foresee the statement being repeated. In practical terms, the original speaker is less likely to be the primary target for the defamation suit because it will be the media entity that has the deeper pockets.

A 1988 case from Illinois makes clear that repetition of a libelous statement carries great risk for a media defendant. In *Owens v. CBS*,[73] a network-owned station in St. Louis, Mo., carried a story about a Secret Service investigation into a threatening letter sent to President Ronald Reagan. The letter carried a return address from a residence in Centreville, Ill., and was signed with the name Michael Brown.

The Secret Service interviewed Brown and his sister, Delores, who both denied writing the letter. The sister suggested the handwriting was

---

[70] Ibid. at 916.

[71] Here, publisher means the person who published, broadcast, posted to social media or wrote anywhere the statement could be perceived.

[72] *Liberty Lobby, Inc. v. Dow Jones & Co.*, 838 F.2d 1287, 1298 (D.C.Cir.1988), 14 Med.L.Rptr. 2249.

[73] *Owens v. CBS*, 173 Ill.App.3d 977, 123 Ill.Dec. 521, 527 N.E.2d 1296 (5 Dist.1988).

that of a neighbor, Carolyn Owens. Owens was interviewed by the Secret Service and denied writing the letter. Robin Smith, a reporter for the station, and cameraman from KMOX-TV, the CBS-owned station, learned of the letter and investigation and traveled to Centreville where Smith interviewed the Browns and Owens. The Secret Service agents declined to speak with her. In the course of her reporting, Smith was told that there were "problems" between the Browns and Owens. Smith said that, "it did not occur to her that Michael might have some reason not to be accurate or truthful."[74] It also turned out that Owens held the job that Delores Brown had once held herself. That night, KMOX-TV ran stories on its 5, 6 and 10 p.m. newscasts. The 10 p.m. story was seen by more than half a million viewers.[75]

> ROBIN SMITH: Nineteen-year-old Michael Brown, his 29-year-old sister, Delores Brown, and their 31-year-old neighbor, Carolyn Owens, say they were all taken to the Centreville Police Department, and they identified these two men as the Secret Service agents who asked them if they wrote a letter which included threats to kill President Reagan. Secret Service agents confirmed the existence of a letter but would not give us a copy. Michael Brown says he did not write it, but he saw the letter. It was signed in his name with his home address, and he and his sister explained other details included in the letter.
>
> * * *
>
> ROBIN SMITH: Michael and Delores Brown and Carolyn Owens told me they were shown a copy of the threatening letter and then Secret Service agents asked them to rewrite that letter in its entirety for purposes of handwriting analysis. Both of the Browns accused their neighbor, Carolyn Owens, of writing that letter (emphasis added), but she also denied it, and she refused to make any other comments.
>
> CAROLYN OWENS: I just am not at liberty to say anything about the letter.
>
> ROBIN SMITH: All three say federal agents told them they may be contacted again-soon-after handwriting analysis is completed. Robin Smith, Newsroom report tonight.

No one was charged in connection with the letter and Owens and the Browns were told by the Secret Service that they had been cleared. Owens asked the station to run a story about her exoneration, but the station refused to do so after the Secret Service would not comment on the investigation. Owens and her family were harassed at work, school and when they were out in the community. She sued CBS for libel and was awarded $280,000. CBS appealed and one of the points of its appeal was that it was merely "setting forth the particulars of the secret service

[74] Ibid. at 1301.

[75] Ibid. at 1303.

investigation and explaining why the Browns and plaintiff were involved in it."[76] The network argued that when it said that the Browns were accused Owens of writing the letter it was just presenting allegations. The appellate court rejected that argument.[77]

> [T]he law in Illinois remains that the republisher of a defamatory statement made by another is himself liable for defamation even though he gives the originator's name. In light of this rule, we fail to see how a person who republishes a defamatory statement can evade liability merely by showing that he has repeated it with precision. Indeed, a faithful retelling of a defamatory statement may be the most damning kind.

Republication does not necessarily apply to the independent parties who distribute defamatory publications. The courts have said that it would be unreasonable to hold a newsstand operator liable for the contents of all the publications sold at the newsstand. Before a court will hold a distributor liable, it must first determine that the distributor knew of the defamatory content. The Minnesota Supreme Court applied this to a libel suit brought by the Church of Scientology against the Minnesota State Medical Association Foundation:[78] "Those who merely deliver or transmit defamatory material previously published by another will be considered to have published the material only if they knew, or had reason to know, that the material was false and defamatory." This also can protect broadcasters who carry network programs containing defamatory statements as well as newspapers republishing defamatory wire service reports.

INTERNET SERVICE PROVIDERS AND REPUBLICATION

There are two considerations when looking at the impact of the doctrine of republication as applied to the Internet. The first is the application of the doctrine to content providers, the people who put up websites, blog, tweet, create postings for newsgroups and email. The second applies to the Internet Service Providers, the people who carry the content created by others.

Generally speaking, the content providers bear the same responsibilities as any other publisher. There is not a difference between uploading a defamatory statement onto a website and putting words on paper. Just as a letter to the editor page must not contain defamatory messages, a Web page must avoid carriage of defamation. If a website allows visitors to post messages or other content on the site, the operator

---

[76] Ibid. at 1305.

[77] Ibid. at 1308.

[78] *Church of Scientology v. Minnesota State Medical Ass'n. Found.*, 264 N.W.2d 152, 156 (Minn.1978).

must be wary of defamation. When an ISP bears responsibility for what it carries, it can have liability.

In a pre-Internet case, *Hellar v. Bianco*,[79] the owners of a bar were found liable for republication over a defamatory statement written on a bathroom wall. It was a familiar sort of statement, "for a good time, call * * *" that gave the name and telephone number of a woman living in Placer County, California. A bar patron who had visited the bathroom called the number. In the course of a conversation with the woman and her husband, the patron explained how he got the number. The woman's husband called the bar and notified the bartender and sought to have the offending message removed. In a subsequent visit to the bar, the woman's husband found that the statement had not been removed from the bathroom wall. The woman, who was the subject of the defamatory statement, sued. The California appellate court found for the woman saying that while the bar owners might not have written the message, they had republished it by failing to remove it.[80]

> Republication occurs when the proprietor has knowledge of the defamatory matter and allows it to remain after a reasonable opportunity to remove it.
>
> * * *
>
> Persons who invite the public to their premises owe a duty to others not to knowingly permit their walls to be occupied with defamatory matter. See *Burns v. Dean*, 1 King's Bench 818, wherein it was held that the proprietors of a club were liable for allowing a defamatory statement to be put upon their walls in a position in which it could be read by any one who came into the club. The theory is that by knowingly permitting such matter to remain after reasonable opportunity to remove the same the owner of the wall or his lessee is guilty of republication of the libel.

And so the site or bulletin board operator must be careful not to permit others to create liability by allowing defamatory statements to remain. While liability is based on knowledge of the defamation and allowing it to remain, operators should not merely try to avoid knowing what has been added to the site. An official with Virtual Town Hall LLC, a company that helps create and operate official websites for more cities and towns, said his company advises clients not to host official message boards because of the nature of some of the messages posted.[81] Randy Perry said that the company shut down two city message boards in Connecticut and New York because of personal attacks.

It is a different picture for Internet Service Providers, like Comcast Xfinity, Time Warner, AT&T or Verizon, selling Internet access to

---

[79] *Hellar v. Bianco*, 111 Cal.App.2d 424, 244 P.2d 757 (Cal.Dist.Ct.App.3d 1952).

[80] Ibid. at 759.

[81] Jenn Abelson, "Uncivil discourse blights online debates," *Boston Globe*, Jan. 5, 2004.

subscribers. The ISP serves as a conduit and so does not create or, generally speaking, control content. Congress provided specific protection for ISPs following a split in cases as to whether ISPs were liable for defamatory statements carried in their systems. In the first case to be decided on the issue, *Cubby, Inc. v. CompuServe, Inc.,*[82] a federal judge held that Compuserve was a distributor and not a publisher. But in another case brought in 1995, *Stratton Oakmont, Inc. v. Prodigy,*[83] a court in New York said that Prodigy's conduct and declaration that it was "an online service that exercised editorial control over the content of messages posted on its computer bulletin boards,"[84] made it a publisher. Although the parties resolved their differences, the presiding court rejected an attempt to drop its conclusions and avoid a troubling precedent.

Congress specifically overruled *Stratton Oakmont* in Sec. 230 of the Communications Decency Act.[85] "No provider or user of interactive computer services shall be treated as the publisher or speaker of information provided by another information content provider." ISPs are likened to mere conduits, rather than content providers. As such, they have no real control and, thus, no liability.

Two cases involving online publication of defamation firmly established the scope of Sec. 230 protection. In *Zeran v. America Online*[86] and *Blumenthal v. Drudge,*[87] the Internet Service Provider America Online avoided liability through application of Sec. 230.

In *Zeran,* Kenneth Zeran, a Seattle, Washington, artist, photographer and film maker, was the subject of an anonymous posting on an American Online bulletin board on April 25, 1995. The posting described the sale of T-shirts and posters featuring tasteless and insensitive slogans relating to the bombing of the Alfred P. Murrah Federal Building in Oklahoma City.[88] In addition to the descriptions of the "sale" items, Zeran's phone number was included. Zeran began receiving a large volume of angry calls. He was unable to simply change his telephone number because he worked from his home and he conducted his business by phone. Zeran contacted AOL and was told that the posting would be removed. AOL declined to publish a retraction. An AOL official reportedly offered Zeran an account[89] through which he could respond to the postings with his own. In the next five days, other

---

82 *Cubby, Inc. v. CompuServe, Inc.,* 776 F.Supp. 135 (S.D.N.Y.1991).

83 *Stratton Oakmont, Inc. v. Prodigy,* Not reported (N.Y.Sup.1995), 23 Med.L.Rptr. 1794.

84 Ibid.

85 47 U.S.C.A.§ 509 230(c)(1).

86 *Zeran v. America Online,* 129 F.3d 327 (4th Cir.1997), 25 Med.L.Rptr. 2526.

87 *Blumenthal v. Drudge,* 992 F.Supp. 44 (D.D.C.1998), 26 Med.L.Rptr. 1717.

88 Some of the materials made insensitive references to children who were in the daycare center in the building who were killed in the terrorist bombing.

89 An early AOL business model had the company giving computer users free hours of service before charging them an hourly rate for access. The number of free hours of access topped out at 1,000. After the 1,000 hours, the bills came.

postings repeating the original message and instructing readers to "ask for Ken" appeared. By April 30, Zeran was receiving an abusive call, on average, every two minutes. To add to Zeran's troubles, announcers at an Oklahoma City radio station learned of the AOL postings. They broadcast the content of the postings and encouraged their listeners to call Zeran and let him know what Oklahomans thought of his business.

Zeran sued AOL on the grounds that the ISP took an unreasonable amount of time to remove the initial defamatory message, refused to publish a retraction and failed to screen the later postings. The district court dismissed the case against AOL on the grounds that Sec. 230 provided immunity for ISPs. Zeran appealed to the 4th Circuit on the grounds that giving notice to AOL of the defamatory posting made AOL something more than a mere distributor of Internet content.

But the 4th Circuit disagreed, saying that Congress had clearly chosen to make ISPs immune. The fact that Zeran notified AOL of the defamation did not create a duty on the part of AOL. In other words, AOL was not like the bar owners in *Hellar*, at footnote 79 above (You may recall that in *Hellar* the defamatory graffiti was written in a bar bathroom where the owners could control what was written.). The 4th Circuit held:[90]

> * * * liability upon notice reinforces service providers' incentives to restrict speech and engage in self-regulation. If computer service providers were subject to distributor liability, they would face potential liability each time they receive notice of a potentially defamatory statement from any party concerning any message. Each notification would require a careful yet rapid investigation of the circumstances surrounding the posted information, a legal judgment concerning the information's defamatory character, and an on the spot editorial decision whether to risk liability by allowing the continued publication of that information. Although this might be feasible for the traditional print publisher, the sheer number of postings on interactive computer services would create an impossible burden in the Internet context.

Zeran sought a review by the Supreme Court but was turned down.[91]

Internet journalist/purveyor of gossip Matt Drudge helped refine the understanding of Sec. 230 when, on Aug. 10, 1997, he published a story about Clinton advisor Sidney Blumenthal in his column, *The Drudge* Report, carried by America Online and by direct email to subscribers.[92]

> The DRUDGE REPORT has learned that top GOP operatives who feel there is a double standard of only reporting Republican shame believe they are holding an ace card: New White House

[90] *Zeran v. America Online*, 129 F.3d 327, 332 (4th Cir.1997).

[91] *Zeran v. American Online*, 524 U.S. 937, 118 S.Ct. 2341 (1998).

[92] *Blumenthal v. Drudge*, 992 F.Supp. 44, 46 (D.D.C.1998).

> recruit Sidney Blumenthal has a spousal abuse past that has been effectively covered up.
>
> The accusations are explosive.
>
> There are court records of Blumenthal's violence against his wife, one influential Republican, who demanded anonymity, tells the DRUDGE REPORT.

On Aug. 11, 1997, Drudge retracted the story through his email mailing list and on Aug. 12, he retracted the story on AOL. The Blumenthals sued for defamation, naming Drudge and AOL as defendants. AOL moved for summary judgment and U.S. District Judge Friedman granted the motion citing Sec. 230 of the CDA.[93] "Whether wisely or not, it has been made the legislative judgment to effectively immunize providers of interactive computer services from civil liability in tort with respect to material disseminated by them but created by others."

The Blumenthals argued that the relationship between Drudge and AOL was more than that of content provider and conduit. They pointed to the fact that AOL sought a business arrangement with Drudge, that it paid him $3,000 a month for his column, that AOL reserved the right to remove content from Drudge's column if the content violated the terms of AOL's service. Finally, the Blumenthals argued, AOL promoted the *Drudge Report*. In doing so, the Blumenthals contended, AOL assumed liability for Drudge's content. But Judge Friedman disagreed, reluctantly so.[94]

> If it were writing on a clean slate, this Court would agree with plaintiffs. AOL has certain editorial rights with respect to the content provided by Drudge and disseminated by AOL, including the right to require changes in content and remove it; and has affirmatively promoted Drudge * * *

But, Judge Friedman added, Congress gave ISPs immunity even where they took an active or aggressive role in providing content. The Blumenthals' case ended with the grant of summary judgment. Not so the case against Matt Drudge. That continued despite a challenge to the Washington, D.C., lawsuit by Drudge, a California resident. Drudge argued that the D.C. courts did not have jurisdiction over him because he wrote his column in California.

Judge Friedman rejected Drudge's motion to dismiss the case, recognizing that the Internet is a system without geographic boundaries. In Drudge's case, he pursued and published gossip about political figures living and working in the District of Columbia. That was enough to place him under the jurisdiction of the federal court there.

---

93 Ibid. at 49.

94 Ibid. at 51.

Sec. 230 continues to provide protection for Internet Service Providers. In *Johnson v. Arden,*[95] Sec. 230 resulted in dismissal of claims against persons who hosted an Internet discussion board. Susan and Robert Johnson, operators of the Cozy Kitten Cattery in Unionville, Missouri, sued Elizabeth Arden and Michelle Reitenger, doing business as http://www.complaintsboard.com/, three persons who posted damaging statements about the Johnsons and their business and a California company that hosted http://www.complaintsboard.com/. The Third Circuit ruled that Sec. 230 immunized the Web companies from the defamation claims.[96]

> The CDA states that "[n]o provider or user of an interactive computer service shall be treated as the publisher or speaker of any information provided by another information content provider," 47 U.S.C. § 230(c)(1), and expressly preempts any state law to the contrary, id. § 230(e)(3). The CDA defines an "information content provider" as "any person or entity that is responsible, in whole or in part, for the creation or development of information provided through the internet or any other interactive computer service." Id. at § 230(f)(3).

The court explained that where ISPs merely allow the posting of information, Sec. 230 applies. However, the court noted that where Internet sites require persons to post information, the Sec. 230 protections no longer work.[97]

> See *Fair Housing Council of San Fernando Valley v. Roommates.com*, LLC, 521 F.3d 1157, 1162–64 (9th Cir.2008) (holding that CDA immunity did not apply to website that was designed to force subscribers to divulge protected characteristics, but that CDA immunity did apply to the "Additional Comments" section of the website where the information was created by third parties and not required by the website ISP).

Additionally, Sec. 230(c)(1) provides immunity for Internet users who simply repeat content. "No provider or user of an interactive computer service shall be treated as the publisher or speaker of any information provided by another information content provider." Adding material or posting a defamatory comment still creates a risk of suit.

PUBLICATION AND JURISDICTION: WHERE CAN THE PLAINTIFF SUE?

The *Drudge* case raises the question about proper jurisdiction. We have already seen the benefits of being able to choose the place where

---

95 *Johnson v. Arden*, 614 F.3d 785 (8th Cir. 2010).

96 Ibid. at 790–791.

97 Ibid. at 791.

you sue. In *Keeton v. Hustler*[98] being able to sue in New Hampshire gave life to Keeton's suit, which was time barred everywhere else. It is, of course, the plaintiff who starts the forum selection dance because the plaintiff begins the suit.

Traditional analysis for jurisdiction has turned on notions of fairness and predictability. Did the defendant intentionally enter the state where the suit is being brought? Could the defendant have anticipated being sued in that state? How fair is it to make the defendant defend the lawsuit in the state? All these questions bear on whether a plaintiff can force a defendant to go to a particular state to defend itself.

It is easy enough to see that a periodical's circulation area or the limits of a broadcaster's signal carve out an area where plaintiffs can show publication took place. How much circulation is enough? A newspaper case decided in 1996 provides a good deal of guidance. Berry Gordy, famous as the founder of Motown Records, sued *The New York Daily News* over an article it published about him.[99] Gordy was a resident of California and the paper was published on the opposite side of the country. More than 99 percent of the copies of the newspaper published by the *Daily News* were circulated within 300 miles of the New York area. Only 13 copies of the *Daily News* and 18 copies of the *Sunday Daily News* were circulated in California but that was enough to create jurisdiction in California. The Ninth Circuit said that the actions of the defendants were aimed at Gordy, a California resident, that the *Daily News* had distributed the 13 to 18 copies of its paper in California, and that Gordy had suffered the damage to his reputation in California. All of these together created jurisdiction.

For publishers on the Web, the question of jurisdiction is more of a problem. Anyone, anywhere in the world with a computer and modem can open up a page. Is the Internet publisher actually sending the content to that person in that state? If not, is the Internet publisher doing something else that would subject it to jurisdiction in a state other than its home state? Courts have wrestled with the question for some time and it appears that each case must be decided on its own particular facts.

To begin with, an Internet publisher, say a television station with its own website, operates in its home state. It is likely incorporated there. It is physically located there. Jurisdiction in that state is a given. A television station that operates near the border between two states and which serves both states will have to face lawsuits in each state. The business presence of the station in each state makes it amenable to suit in each state.

But if a station is located in New York, what are the chances it will be doing business in California? Without "sufficient minimum contacts" in California, the New York station cannot be sued in California. But it

---

98 *Keeton v. Hustler*, 465 U.S. 770, 104 S.Ct. 1473 (1984).

99 *Gordy v. Daily News*, 95 F.3d 829 (9th Cir.1996), 24 Med.L.Rptr. 2301.

is possible for a New York station to have those "sufficient minimum contacts." If the New York station created and sold a syndicated television program to California stations, it would be said to have a presence in California. Similarly, if the New York station committed some intentional act that had a result in California, it might be subject to jurisdiction. For example, the top-rated evening anchor in New York leaves the station for California. The New York station issues a statement in New York falsely accusing the anchor of sexual harassment. If that statement has the effect of damaging the anchor's reputation in California, the New York station might well be subject to California jurisdiction. This notion of jurisdiction based on the effects of the Internet use was applied in the *Drudge* case where the federal court found that his activities subjected him to the jurisdiction of the District of Columbia courts. Here, in defamation, that effect would be a likely reason to allow a plaintiff to sue in what would be considered a foreign forum. The effect reason is similar to the reason that Keeton was allowed to sue *Hustler Magazine* in New Hampshire.

Several cases have turned on the question of a defendant's contacts with the plaintiff's state of residence. In *Young v. New Haven Advocate,*[100] the warden of a prison in Virginia sued the *Hartford Courant* and the *New Haven Advocate*, alleging that the newspapers had libeled him in their print and Web editions. Following several articles,[101] Young sued the two newspapers alleging that they had implied that he was "a racist who advocates racism" and that he encouraged "abuse of inmates by guards."[102] The *Advocate* did not circulate to Virginia and the *Courant* had only eight subscribers in the state. No reporter from either newspaper had visited Virginia in preparation for the story. Young's attorneys argued that the two newspapers' Web publication amounted to worldwide publication, including Virginia. Not surprisingly, both newspapers objected to being hauled into Virginia courts. They filed motions to dismiss. The federal district court denied the motions saying that the Internet publications were acts that had caused injury in Virginia and that publishing on the Internet was enough to let Virginia courts have jurisdiction over the newspapers.[103] The newspapers appealed to the 4th Circuit Court of Appeals. The 4th Circuit panel reversed the district court saying that the mere posting of a story on the Internet did not, in and of itself, create jurisdiction.[104]

---

[100] *Young v. New Haven Advocate,* 315 F.3d 256 (4th Cir. 2002), cert. denied *Young v. New Haven Advocate,* 538 U.S. 1035, 123 S.Ct. 2092 (2003).

[101] Connecticut, facing overcrowding in its own prison system, had sent hundreds of inmates to Virginia. The two newspapers had written about a prison run by Warden Stanley Young and reported critically on conditions, inmate complaints and the presence of Confederate memorabilia in Young's office.

[102] *Young v. New Haven Advocate,* 315 F.3d 256, 259 (4th Cir. 2002).

[103] *Young v. New Haven Advocate,* 184 F.Supp.2d 498 (W.D.Va. 2001).

[104] *Young v. New Haven Advocate,* 315 F.3d 256, 263 (4th Cir. 2002).

> [T]he fact that the newspapers' websites could be accessed anywhere, including Virginia, does not by itself demonstrate that the newspapers were intentionally directing their website content to a Virginia audience. Something more than posting and accessibility is needed to "indicate that the [newspapers] purposefully (albeit electronically) directed activity in a substantial way to the forum state" * * * The newspapers must, through Internet postings, manifest an intent to target and focus on Virginia readers.

Having set the requirements for a finding of jurisdiction, the 4th Circuit panel then looked at the websites. Neither paper's websites contained any advertisements aimed at Virginia readers and both websites focused on local news.[105] "In sum, it appears that these newspapers maintain their websites to serve local readers in Connecticut, to expand the reach of their papers within their local markets," the panel concluded. The articles in question focused on Connecticut inmates and were geared toward public debate of the issue in Connecticut. As such, the Web stories did not create jurisdiction for courts in Virginia.

In *Hy Cite Corp. v. Badbusinessbureau.com,*[106] a federal court in Wisconsin dismissed a defamation and trademark complaint brought by a Wisconsin company against the operator of a website in St.Kitts/Nevis, West Indies. Badbusinessbureau.com operates the *Rip-Off Report* where consumers can complain about businesses. At the time of the suit, the *Rip-Off Report* had received some 61,000 complaints. Between 30 to 40 complaints targeted Hy Cite Corp. Badbusinessbureau.com allows companies that have been criticized to post rebuttals, for a fee. Hy Cite learned that it was the subject of complaints on the Badbusinessbureau.com website. Badbusinessbureau.com informed the company that it would cost $50,000 to enroll in the site and post rebuttals to the complaints.[107] Hy Cite responded to the offer by filing a defamation suit in federal court in Wisconsin. Badbusinessbureau.com moved to dismiss on the grounds that the court in Wisconsin did not have jurisdiction. The judge agreed noting that when a defendant is not a resident of the state where the case is filed, there must be some reason to give that state jurisdiction.[108]

> Due process requires that a nonresident defendant have "certain minimum contacts with [the forum state] such that the maintenance of the suit does not offend 'traditional notions of fair play and substantial justice,'" *International Shoe v. Washington*, 326 U.S. 310, 316, 66 S.Ct. 154 (1945).

---

[105] Ibid.

[106] *Hy Cite Corp. v. Badbusinessbureau.com*, 297 F.Supp.2d 1154 (W.D.Wis. 2004).

[107] Ibid. at 1156.

[108] Ibid. at 1157.

The judge, looking at the contacts that Badbusinessbureau.com had with residents of Wisconsin, noted that the Internet firm had not solicited business in Wisconsin and had entered into no business arrangements with anyone in Wisconsin. There were insufficient contacts to give a Wisconsin court jurisdiction over Badbusinessbureau.com. the judge ruled.

One case that has been cited by a number of courts in deciding Internet jurisdiction makes the test one of the "nature and quality of commercial activity that an entity conducts over the Internet." *Zippo Manufacturing v. Zippo Dot Com*[109] over use of the trademark name "Zippo" used for a brand of lighters. While this is not an Internet defamation case, its jurisdiction analysis applies.

Zippo Manufacturing sued the Internet company, which operated a Web news service, alleging dilution of its trademark name and noting that some of the newsgroups that *Zippo Dot Com* provided access to featured sexually explicit matter. The lighter company operated in Pennsylvania while *Zippo Dot Com* was based in California. The case was brought in a Pennsylvania federal court and the California company moved to dismiss the case on the grounds that the Pennsylvania court did not have jurisdiction. In this case, unlike the Wisconsin matter above, the court concluded that *Zippo Dot Com* had purposefully availed itself of doing business in Pennsylvania and was subject to the jurisdiction of the court there. In his analysis, Judge McLaughlin employed a sliding scale to determine whether jurisdiction was proper.[110]

> At one end of the spectrum are situations where a defendant clearly does business over the Internet. * * * At the opposite end are situations where a defendant has simply posted information on an Internet website which is accessible to users in foreign jurisdictions.

The first example creates jurisdiction in the state where the business takes place. The second does not create jurisdiction. But, Judge McLaughlin noted, the middle of the spectrum could be problematic. He gave an example of an "interactive website where a user can exchange information with the host computer." He concluded that the test for jurisdiction would be the level of interactivity and commercial nature of the information exchange. In the case of *Zippo Dot Com*, Judge McLaughlin reasoned that because the Internet company had entered into contracts with 3,000 users and seven ISPs in Pennsylvania, it had established the minimum contacts necessary to give Pennsylvania court's jurisdiction.

Not all courts or federal circuits have adopted the *Zippo* test. The 4th Circuit in the *Young v. New Haven Advocate* rejected Judge McLaughlin's approach. Until a uniform rule is applied to all U.S. courts,

---

[109] *Zippo Mfg. v. Zippo Dot Com*, 952 F.Supp. 1119 (W.D.Pa. 1997).

[110] Ibid. at 1124.

media professionals would be well advised to act as if they could be brought into any court in any state.

A question for both paper and Internet publishers is how their activities will be analyzed in a foreign country. No other nation has the First Amendment. Foreign governments and individuals have their own court and justice systems for dealing with embarrassing or defamatory publications. What happens if a person in another country sues over a story that is carried in international editions or on the Internet? The person may well win, based on the legal system in place. What then is the consequence for the losing U.S. defendant?

A federal judge ruled in 1995 in favor of U.S. defendants when plaintiffs sought to enforce a libel judgment they won in England,[111] where the laws favor plaintiffs. Judge Ricardo Urbina said that a "repugnant" foreign judgment could not be enforced in the U.S. Judge Urbina's decision made the denial of enforcement mandatory. The holding by Judge Urbina would not affect the enforcement of a libel judgment in the nation where the case was tried. That means that people and businesses with assets in those foreign countries could still lose their property.

Litigation Note: *The issue of jurisdiction plays into what is known as "forum shopping," looking for a jurisdiction where a party will have an undue advantage. In some instances, it will be a tendency for juries to find for plaintiffs or a jurisdiction with higher-than-average awards. In the Keeton v. Hustler case, it was a matter of finding the one jurisdiction where the statute of limitations had not expired. While this should not drive circulation and distribution decisions, it should be kept in mind as a litigation issue. There are special rules that can come into play with forum choice but those are best left to the attorneys who have already endured Civil Procedure class.*

DEFAMATION "LIVE!"

The issue of responsibility for republishing the statements of another is of particular importance to broadcasters, especially with the increasing ability to go "live" to the scene of news stories and also for radio stations that feature the call-in talk show. We begin our analysis by looking at one of the first cases of "live" defamation encountered by the courts and the resolution applied there.

In *Summit Hotel Co. v. National Broadcasting Co.*,[112] the Pennsylvania Supreme Court was faced with a new legal issue, how to assign liability in a case of an extemporaneous remark made in the course of a live radio broadcast. NBC had sold airtime to an advertising company which put together a radio series featuring Al Jolson, the singer/actor. The advertising company hired all the performers and

[111] *Matusevitch v. Telnikof*, 877 F.Supp. 1 (D.D.C. 1995).

[112] *Summit Hotel Co. v. National Broadcasting Co.*, 336 Pa. 182, 8 A.2d 302 (1939).

provided the scripts which were reviewed and approved by NBC in advance. In the June 15, 1935 show, Jolson was to interview the winner of a golf tournament. During that interview, Jolson made his extemporaneous remark:

> Jolson: But tell me, Sam, what did you do after you got out of college?
>
> Sam: I turned golf professional and in 1932 I got a job at the Summit Golf Club in Uniontown, Pennsylvania.
>
> Jolson: That's a rotten hotel.

The Summit Hotel was not amused and sued NBC, winning $15,000 (In 2019 dollars the judgment would be about $281,000). NBC appealed and the Pennsylvania Supreme Court had to figure out what to do with this new medium which had little legal history surrounding it. The justices rejected the approach of treating broadcasts just like newspapers. Unlike newspapers which are written ahead of time and subjected to the scrutiny of the copy desk, broadcasts were live and changes made in previously reviewed scripts or ad libs might not be foreseen. The justices noted that Jolson had been employed by the advertising company and that the script, previously reviewed and approved, had nothing offensive in it. Further, there was no means by which NBC could have prevented the spontaneous remark. The Pennsylvania court reversed the judgment.

But the court did not grant NBC, or any other broadcasters for that matter, absolute immunity from liability in live broadcasts, either its own or those who bought airtime. It placed strict limits on the protections it gave to NBC in the *Summit Hotel* case.[113]

> We therefore conclude that a broadcasting company that leases its time and facilities to another, whose agents carry on the program, is not liable for an interjected defamatory remark where it appears that it exercised due care in the selection of the lessee, and, having inspected and edited the script, had no reason to believe an extemporaneous defamatory remark would be made. Where the broadcasting station's employee or agent makes the defamatory remark, it is liable, unless the remarks are privileged83 [e.g. as part of a public record]* * *

And so, broadcasters may have a means of avoiding liability, if they exercise proper care in the manner of their live broadcasts. It is not automatic. The broadcaster must have taken adequate steps to try to prevent any spontaneous defamation. A good example of what happens when a broadcast simply throws open the microphone to anyone comes from the Louisiana case of *Snowden v. Pearl River Broadcasting Corp.*[114]

---

113 Ibid. at 204, 312.

114 *Snowden v. Pearl River Broadcasting Corp.*, 251 So.2d 405 (La.App.1971), appeal denied, 259 La. 887, 253 So.2d 217 (La.1971).

In *Snowden*, radio station WBOX in Bogalusa, La., had created a radio call-in program in early 1968 to increase its audience ratings. It was called *Call and Comment* and ran from January or February of 1968 until April 3, 1968, when the station broadcast the program that cost it a libel judgment of $11,500 (of course that was in addition to the costs of the suit). On April 3, 1968, the station opened up its microphones to any topic, except segregation, integration and religion. Drug use was in the news. The previous day, the moderator had read a wire service story about drug addiction and suggested drugs as a topic for the April 3 program.

The station had chosen not to purchase equipment that would have allowed it to delay callers' comments and allow the moderator to block statements. The station manager said that he did not think the station could afford the device. The only controls the station placed on callers was the request that, "in fairness to all people and jobs unless you are willing to identify yourself and to tell us who is calling, we would rather you would not use specific names or places."[115] In the course of the program, callers talked about drug use and drug sales in Bogalusa. The names of three residents and one business were linked to drug sales:[116]

> Unidentified Caller: I've been listening to your program every day for two or three weeks here.
>
> Announcer: Yes, sir.
>
> Unidentified Caller: And I've been noticing that its very evidence that there is proof being narcotics been going around here in town at these certain places. The police know about it but the facts that I've heard over at the station and you all know about it. It looks like they could to down there and they could do something to the Pizza Shanty and stop this stuff.
>
> Announcer: Sir.
>
> Unidentified Caller: It's obvious that Doctor Newman is writing those prescriptions and Guerry Snowden is filling them and they are selling them down there.
>
> Announcer: Who's calling please?
>
> * * *
>
> Unidentified Caller: Well I didn't hear anybody else say who they were.
>
> Announcer: Okay.

Snowden, Newman and the owners of the Pizza Shanty sued and were awarded, respectively, $4,000, $5,000 and $2,500. The station appealed,

---

[115] Ibid. at 407.

[116] Ibid.

and in upholding the judgments, the Louisiana Appeals Court explained in detail why the station's behavior was indefensible:[117]

> The question here presented is whether a radio station, having invited the public to speak freely through its facilities on a matter of public interest, is impressed with the duty of preventing such persons from making defamatory statements over the air. We would have no difficulty in finding a station liable, if it received defamatory material from an anonymous source, and broadcast the report without attempting verification. The direct broadcast of such anonymous defamatory material, without the use of any monitoring or delay device, is no less reprehensible in our judgment.

We can apply *Summit* and *Snowden* to live news. If a station goes live to a scene and broadcasts defamatory statements from field, it may have liability as in *Snowden.* There will, of course be significant differences. The field crew will have the opportunity to see the person or persons they are going to put on the air. They will have the ability to judge for themselves whether or not the subjects are credible. They will, more likely than not, have had the chance to at least introduce themselves and get an idea of what the source is going to say. If that source appears to be unreliable, the remote crew would be better served by avoiding the live interview. To put someone on the air live or to stream live just because the technology makes it possible, puts the station at risk because it will have adopted the statement. The analysis will then turn on what the field crew observed about the source, how they assessed the source's credibility and whether it was reasonable for the station to rely on the source's being able to provide information without defaming. Of course, the judgment of the station employees on the scene will be assessed by a jury or judge who will have the benefit of 20/20 hindsight in evaluating the correctness of the broadcaster facing suit for getting something wrong.

Because broadcasting no longer operates as it did at the time of *Summit Hotel*, students should be cautioned against concluding that there will be no liability for defamatory statements made on air. Stations now produce and are responsible for the content they air. In radio broadcasting at the time of *Summit*, the networks would sell blocks of time on their networks. They did not control content. Today, broadcasters sell advertisements during programs that they either produce themselves or buy. Where they are the creators of the shows, they will not evade liability by claiming they did not know the defamatory statement would be made.

The equivalent of "live" broadcasting may be found on the Internet with Tweets, blogs and websites providing content as quickly as broadcasters. While Sec. 230 will provide protections where the Internet

---

[117] Ibid. at 410.

site merely allows content to be posted, liability will exist where the Internet site is creating the content itself.

19. IDENTIFICATION

To bring a successful libel action—once publication has been established—a plaintiff must also demonstrate that he or she was *identified* in the alleged libel. Plaintiffs must show that the statement complained about refers to them. In legal terms this is known as the requirement that the publication be "of and concerning" the plaintiff.

Most of the time, the identification is obvious. A plaintiff's name or picture is used, right along with the statements claimed to be defamatory. But sometimes identification may occur in a less direct way: in one case, a camera shop answered a competitor's ads with these words:[118]

> USE COMMON SENSE * * * You Get NOTHING for NOTHING! WE WILL NOT
>
> 1. Inflate the prices of your developing to give you a new roll free!
>
> 2. Print the blurred negatives to inflate the price of your snapshots!

The Cosgrove Studio sued for libel, claiming that ad implied Cosgrove used dishonest business practices. In upholding a damage award for Cosgrove, a Pennsylvania appeals court made an important point: Identification of the defamed need not be by name. "A party need not be specifically named, if pointed to by description or circumstances tending to identify him," the court held.

In the majority of the states, the rule generally is that the recipient of the communication understands it to refer to the plaintiff. This rule means that statements that refer to subjects generally may pose as much or more of a problem than a specific reference to a particular person. For example, in *Eyal v. Helen Broadcasting,*[119] a radio station broadcast the following: "The owner of a Brookline [d]elicatessen and seven other people are arrested in connection with an international cocaine ring." Haim Eyal, the owner of Haim's Delicatessen in Brookline, Mass., brought suit claiming that the broadcast defamed him and his business. The Massachusetts Supreme Court said that the broadcast could support a claim of defamation and could have identified Eyal and his business. The court said:[120] "If the defendant intends to refer to a particular person,

---

[118] *Cosgrove Studio & Camera Shop, Inc. v. Pane*, 408 Pa. 314, 182 A.2d 751 (1962). See also *Grove v. Dun & Bradstreet, Inc.*, 438 F.2d 433 (3d Cir.1971), and *Dictaphone Corp. v. Sloves* (N.Y.Sup.1980), 6 Med.L.Rptr. 1114.

[119] *Eyal v. Helen Broadcasting*, 411 Mass. 426, 583 N.E.2d 228 (1991).

[120] Ibid. citing *New England Tractor-Trailer Training of Conn., Inc. v. Globe Newspaper Co.*, 395 Mass. 471, 483, 480 N.E.2d 1005, 1012 (1985).

the communication will be deemed 'of and concerning' that person, if it is so understood by the recipient of the communication, no matter how bizarre or extraordinary it is that the communication was in fact so understood."

Photographs create ready identification. The composition of a photograph, caption or context within an article or advertisement can create liability. Although defamatory content comes later in this chapter, the case of *Holmes v. Curtis Publishing*[121] provides a warning. James Holmes was depicted in one of two photographs that appeared in the *Saturday Evening Post* to illustrate the story, "The Mafia: Shadow of Evil on an Island in the Sun." The photograph in question showed a group of four tourists, including Holmes, playing blackjack. The photo caption referred to "High-Rollers at the Monte Carlo club," and said that the club's casino grossed $20 million a year with a third "skimmed off for American Mafia 'families'." Holmes, the focal point of the picture and a man in no way connected with Mafia, said that he was identified as a participant in organized crime activities.

Surprising as it may seem, the intent of the defendant does not determine the final outcome. But, if one considers the heart of defamation is the standing in which the plaintiff is held by the community, then the intent of the defendant cannot decide the case. Courts have found identification even when defendants have truthfully claimed that they were referring to someone other than the plaintiff. In *Washington Post Co. v. Kennedy,*[122] *The Washington Post* reported on the arrest of Harry P.L. Kennedy, an attorney, in Michigan. Kennedy was brought back to Washington, D.C. to face charges. The *Post* reported on the arrest and ran the following headline and story:

> Attorney Held as Forger
>
> Harry Kennedy Brought Back from Detroit to Face Charge.
>
> Harry Kennedy, an attorney, 40 years old, was brought back to Washington from Detroit yesterday to face a charge of forgery.
>
> According to Headquarters Detective Vermillion, who trailed Kennedy to Detroit, the man forged the name of a client for $900.

Harry Kennedy, 37, and the only Harry Kennedy known as an attorney in the District of Columbia, brought suit. The D.C. Circuit found that Harry Kennedy had been identified, saying:[123]

> Unless the true intent of the publisher of libelous matter is to be gathered from the contents of the article, rather than from what the writer subsequently says was in his mind, innocent parties may suffer without redress.

---

[121] *Holmes v. Curtis Pub. Co.*, 303 F.Supp. 522 (D.S.C.1969).

[122] *Washington Post Co. v. Kennedy*, 3 F.2d 207 (D.C.Cir.1925).

[123] Ibid.

And, in an old case from English courts that has been quoted and followed by U.S. courts, including the D.C. Circuit in the *Kennedy* case, a completely fictional character cost a newspaper substantial damages. The *Manchester (England) Sunday Chronicle* published a humorous article about the adventures of one Artemus Jones. Jones was a churchwarden (a lay officer of the Anglican Church) who led a quiet and respectable life at home, but who engaged in wild orgies across the English Channel in France. It so happened that there was a lawyer by the name of Artemus Jones and he complained that other members of the bar were giving him a hard time about "his" exploits. Even though the *Chronicle* said it was a completely fictitious Artemus Jones and even published a story to that effect, a jury took only 15 minutes to award the real-life Jones £1,750.[124] The lesson to be drawn from this is to be aware of the risks of using fictitious names, or, more likely to occur, granting anonymity to subjects of stories in return for their cooperation or to protect them. The false identity or name given to a subject or source may open the door to a successful claim by someone who bears the name in reality.

The Web has resulted in an astronomical increase in the number of potential plaintiffs who can claim identification. Those entities that have begun to put their pages and broadcasts on the Internet need to be aware of the increased danger. Those who communicate directly through email or on their home pages should take notice of one recent case of mistaken identity involving an Alabama Supreme Court justice who more recently was a United States Senate candidate and a New Mexico State University engineer. The Alabama justice and candidate, Roy S. Moore, gained notoriety for fighting to keep the Ten Commandments on state property. The New Mexico engineer has received email in support of the judge's position and has not been pleased. "I had gotten very tired of writing telling people that I had no clue what they were talking about, especially since I do not agree with them," Moore told the Associated Press. Moore's home page features a Viking proverb, "Praise not beer, till it is drunk." Judge Moore did not have email or a home page at the time.[125] The former justice's position on beer is not known.

The identification issue becomes more difficult for the plaintiff when dealing with works of pure fiction. But even then, plaintiffs have won cases, though far less often than with nonfiction. The disclaimer that, "the work is purely fictional and does not depict any persons living or dead," can help to build a defense that the allegedly defamatory statement is not "of and concerning" the plaintiff but it is not the end to the case. Fiction based on real-life occurrences carry greater risk as in *Bindrim v. Mitchell*.[126] A best-selling author, Gwen Davis Mitchell, was

---

[124] Robert H. Phelps and E. Douglas Hamilton, *Libel: Rights, Risks, Responsibilities*, New York: Macmillan Co., (1966), p. 31, quoting from *E. Hulton & Co. v. Jones*, 2 K.B. 444 (1910).

[125] In Flux, "Moore of the Same is Keeping a New Mexico Man in E-Mail," *The National Law Journal*, May 5, 1997.

[126] *Bindrim v. Mitchell*, 92 Cal.App.3d 61, 155 Cal.Rptr. 29 (1979).

working on a project about women of the leisure class. She tried to join Bindrim's therapy group that incorporated nudity in group therapy. Bindrim refused to allow Mitchell to join the group if she were to write about it. Mitchell denied any intention to write about the experience and even signed an agreement not to disclose what occurred in the sessions.

Two months after joining the therapy group, Mitchell signed a book deal with Doubleday for a novel and got an advance royalty payment of $150,000. After the book came out, Bindrim sued Mitchell and Doubleday. The defendants said that Bindrim had not been identified in the book, which dealt with a nude therapy session and its leader. The California appellate court analyzed the issue in this way,[127] "In the case at bar, the only differences between plaintiff and the Herford character in 'Touching' were physical appearance and that Herford was a psychiatrist rather than psychologist. Otherwise, the character Simon Herford was very similar to the actual plaintiff. We cannot say that no one who knew plaintiff Bindrim could reasonably identify him with the fictional character."

The risks of "fiction" rose again late in 2009 when a Georgia jury found that best-selling author Haywood Smith defamed a childhood friend in her novel, "*The Red Hat Club*."[128] The book is the story of a group of women who are "of a certain age" who meet regularly and wear red hats.[129] Vickie Stewart sued over the depiction of her as the character SuSu, who was written as an atheist, right-wing reactionary,[130] "an alcoholic who drank while working as a flight attendant and frequently engaged in casual sex with airplane passengers and others."

Smith moved for summary judgment on the libel claim and was denied by the trial court. She appealed and the Georgia Court of Appeals held that the label of fiction did not protect it in a libel suit.[131]

> Simply because a book is labeled "fiction" does not mean that it may not be defamatory. See *Muzikowski v. Paramount Pictures Corp.*, 322 F.3d 918, 925(III)(A) (7th Cir.2003). In other words, the test for libel "is not whether the story is or is not characterized as 'fiction,' or 'humor,' but whether the charged portions, in context, could be reasonably understood as describing actual facts about the plaintiff or actual events in which she participated."

---

[127] Ibid. at 37, 76.

[128] Andy Peters, "Best-Selling Novel Defamed Woman, Jury Finds," *Fulton County Daily Record*, Dec. 1, 2009.

[129] In the interest of full disclosure, Bill Loving, one of the authors, served as a consultant for the plaintiff in the *Red Hat* case.

[130] Ibid.

[131] *Smith v. Stewart*, 660 S.E.2d 822, 830–831 (Ga.Ct.App 2008).

Stewart's attorney Jeffrey D. Horst brought witnesses who testified that they saw elements of Stewart's life incorporated into the SuSu character through 39 different traits that the character and Stewart shared.[132]

> "We put on the stand people who knew Vickie pretty well who immediately recognized SuSu as depicting Vickie Stewart's life," Horst said. "But they said they didn't know if these other things were true, like whether she drank on the job or had sex with stud puppies."

Using a forensic computer expert, Horst uncovered damaging emails that Haywood had written.[133] "In the email, Smith told the colleague that she had received an email from the woman who was the basis for her fictional 'slut' and that the woman was threatening to sue her."

The defense team, representing Haywood and her publisher St. Martin's Press, argued that using real-life persons as inspiration for fictional characters was a common practice. The defense team brought two experts on that point, defense lawyer Peter C. Canfield said. The experts testified that[134] "well-known authors such as Ernest Hemingway, F. Scott Fitzgerald and John Irving 'all modeled characters in their books after people they knew,' Canfield said." Canfield explained that the jurors had been instructed that[135] "in Georgia, modeling a fictional character after a real person is a strict liability offense."

Litigation Note: *Discovery also can help play a part in determining who the fictional character really was. In Bindrim, the plaintiff introduced tape recordings that the defendant made at the therapy sessions to show that the novel was based on the actual sessions and that Bindrim was the lead character. Notes, character profiles bibles and correspondence can help establish that the plaintiff was the one written about. Today, discovery of emails can be particularly useful. Where an author is successful, stories, transcripts or recordings of speeches, presentations and Q & As can be a gold mine of damaging evidence. Such evidence also can be helpful in establishing that the defendant did not intend to write or actually did not write about the plaintiff but, as explained above, that may not resolve the case.*[136]

---

[132] Andy Peters, "Best-Selling Novel Defamed Woman, Jury Finds," *Fulton County Daily Record*, Dec. 1, 2009.

[133] Ibid.

[134] Ibid.

[135] Ibid.

[136] In his reference work *Law of Defamation*, Prof. Rodney Smolla offers 11 factors to establish identity in works of fiction:

1. Whether the plaintiff's name, or a very similar name, is used;
2. whether there are physical similarities between the plaintiff and the character;
3. whether the ages of the plaintiff and the character are close;
4. whether there are similarities in geographic location and setting;
5. whether there are similarities in occupation or career progress;
6. whether there are similarities in relationships and personality characteristics;
7. whether the work as a whole is clearly presented as fiction;

Students should keep in mind that disclaimers, such as that in 8 of Professor Smolla's list, does not create immunity from suit. Indeed, any number of cases have been won by plaintiffs despite such disclaimers as seen in the *Stewart* case above.

Identification cannot be established by a person who says that an attack on a large heterogeneous group libels her because she happens to belong to it. To suggest some examples, derogatory statements about a political party, an international labor union, the Presbyterian Church, or the Rotary Club do not identify individuals with sufficient particularity so as to allow them to bring a libel action. The only exception comes in the case law of the individual states. In Arkansas, for example, a plaintiff who is part of a large group must prove that the statement applied to him personally.

More generally speaking, such defamation cases arise when the defamatory statement is made about a small sub-group of an organization, that's quite different. Suppose a defamatory attack is made on the directors of the Smithjones County Democratic Party, on the officers of a labor union (whether it be a national or local unit), or the presiding elders of a church, or on the civic club's officers. Then, each individual member of the attacked sub-group may be able to establish identification—even though his or her name was not used—and bring suit.

A sleazy book—"*U.S.A. Confidential*"—resulted in the often cited—and often misinterpreted—case known as *Neiman-Marcus Co. v. Lait.*[137] That case set down these guidelines:

> (1) Where the group or class libeled is large, none can sue even though the language used is inclusive.
>
> (2) When the group or class libeled is small, and each and every member of the group or class is referred to, then any individual member can sue.
>
> (3) That while there is a conflict in authorities where the publication complained of libeled some or less than all of a designated small group, the federal court ruling in the *Neiman-Marcus* case said it would allow such an action.

Those guidelines were drawn from a sleazy fact situation. Authors Jack Lait and Lee Mortimer claimed in "*U.S.A. Confidential*" that swingers

---

8. whether a disclaimer labeling the work as fiction and similarities as "coincidental" is employed;

9. whether there are similarities between the plot of the fictional work and real events in the plaintiff's life;

10. whether the use of the plaintiff's name or the fictional character allegedly representing the plaintiff play prominent roles in the fictional work or have only "fleeting and incidental" significance; and,

11. whether the events that take place in the fictional work are so fantastical or bizarre that no reasonable reader would treat them as realistic depictions.

[137] *Neiman-Marcus v. Lait*, 107 F.Supp. 96 (S.D.N.Y.1952); 13 F.R.D. 311 (1952).

looking for a "good time" need look no further in Dallas than that city's famed department store, Neiman-Marcus. The book's chapter on Dallas asserted[138] that all of the store's models (there were nine) were prostitutes, the highest-paid in town. The book also said that the "nucleus of the Dallas fairy colony" was in the Neiman-Marcus men's store (which had 25 salesmen). Finally, these fearless authors declared that the store's "salesgirls" (there were 382) were prostitutes too, cheaper and more fun than the models. Using the guidelines, the court dismissed the lawsuits of the saleswomen (382 was simply too large a group to have identification take place), but allowed the suits of the models and the salesmen.

But please note what the *Neiman-Marcus* case did NOT say. It did not say that if a group is larger than 25, you can publish anything you want about that group. In point of cold legal fact, identification has been held to take place when an unnamed person was a member of a large group. In *Fawcett Publishing v. Morris,*[139] the Oklahoma Supreme Court held that a member of the University of Oklahoma football team made up of 60 to 70 players had been identified in an article that referred to the OU football team and was defamatory.

Fawcett was the publisher of *True Magazine* which had printed a story in 1958 about, amphetamine use by athletes under the headline, "The Pill That Can Kill Sports." The story contained the following passages:[140]

> The amphetamines are administered to athletes by hypodermic injection, nasal spray, or in tablets or capsules, but pills are the most common form, at least according to those athletic figures who are willing to talk.
>
> There is, however, one statistic which is available, and which strongly indicates that consumption is rapidly increasing. Recently I was able to buy 30 cc.'s of dextroamphetamine sulphate for 95 cents. This amount—enough to hop up an entire football team—cost three times this much a few years ago. Also, I was able to buy a thousand amphetamine pills for $1.40 less than a third of the 1954 price. When sales go up, prices go down.
>
> Speaking of football teams, during the 1956 season, while Oklahoma was increasing its sensational victory streak, several physicians observed Oklahoma players being sprayed in the nostrils with an atomizer. And during a televised game, a close-up showed Oklahoma spray jobs to the nation. "Ten years ago," Dr. Howe observed acidly, "when that was done to a horse, the case went to court. Medically, there is no reason for such

[138] Ibid. at 97. Footnote quoting pages 39–40.

[139] *Fawcett Publications, Inc. v. Morris*, 377 P.2d 42 (Okl.1962), cert. denied, 376 U.S. 513, 84 S.Ct. 964 (1964).

[140] Ibid. at 47.

> treatment. If players need therapy, they shouldn't be on the field."

Dennit Morris, the plaintiff, was a fullback on the alternate squad of the 1956 football team that went to and won in the Orange Bowl. He also played in 1957 and 1958. Morris brought evidence at the trial conducted in Oklahoma that it was spirits of peppermint that was administered to the football team. Spirits of peppermint was used for the relief of "cotton mouth," or dryness of mouth, resulting from prolonged or extreme physical exertion. Morris also presented evidence that he did not use amphetamines or any other drugs. Morris won his case and $75,000.

Fawcett appealed and one of the bases for that appeal was it contention that because Morris had not been individually named, that it was just the team, consisting of 60 to 70 players, that he was not identified sufficiently to have been libeled. But the Oklahoma Supreme Court was not persuaded. It agreed that there was a substantial precedent for the proposition that a member of a large group could not recover unless he was referred to personally. But in this case, the court said, Morris was not just some anonymous member of a large group. He was a readily identifiable member of a group that had been defamed by the article and that:[141]

> the article libels every member of the team, including the plaintiff, although he was not specifically named therein; that the average lay reader who was familiar with the team, and its members would necessarily believe that the regular players, including the plaintiff, were using an amphetamine spray as set forth in the article; that the article strongly suggests that the use of amphetamine was criminal; and that plaintiff has sufficiently established his identity as one of those libeled by the publication.
>
> In reaching the conclusion that plaintiff has established his identity in the mind of the average lay reader as one of those libeled, we are mindful that a full-back on the alternate squad of a university team who has played in nine out of eleven all victorious games in one season will not be overlooked by those who were familiar with the team, and the contribution made by its regular players.

Apart from *Fawcett*, other courts have held that groups made up of as many as 53 still permit individual members to bring their suits.[142] The

[141] Ibid. at 52.

[142] See *Brady v. Ottaway Newspapers, Inc.*, 84 A.D.2d 226, 445 N.Y.S.2d 786 (1981), 8 Med.L.Rptr. 1671, where a plaintiff policeman who was a member of a group of 53 unnamed policemen was not barred from bring a libel suit. Courts also have held that members of a jury can be defamed [*Byers v. Martin*, 2 Colo. 605 (1875)]; all four officers of a labor union [*De Witte v. Kearney & Trecker Corp.*, 265 Wis. 132, 60 N.W.2d 748 (1953)]. Another court, however, has held that a libel action would not work against a magazine which attacked all distributors of the controversial anti-cancer drug laetrile [*Schuster v. U.S. News & World Report, Inc.*, 602 F.2d 850 (8th Cir.1979), 5 Med.L.Rptr. 1773.] Also, a newspaper was ruled not to have identified

number will depend on both precedent within the jurisdiction and the facts of the case. There is no magic number, above which publishers are safe, though when the possible plaintiffs are in the hundreds or thousands, the risk is virtually nonexistent.

A final note on identification deals with who can be the plaintiff in a defamation suit. Defamation is a tort that is personal to the person harmed. That means that only the person identified can bring the suit. Husbands cannot file defamation suits for statements made about their wives. Wives cannot sue when their husbands were the subjects of the defamatory statements. Friends, acquaintances and business associates have no standing to sue.

The question of defamation of the dead has generally been settled in that dead people have no reputations to be harmed. Although Louisiana had a criminal defamation statute that made defaming the memory of the dead a crime, that state's supreme court rejected any civil actions for defamation of the dead saying dead people have no reputations.[143] A Rhode Island statute provides for a slander or libel suit based on a person's obituary.

The other issue dealing with death and the defamation suit is the question of the effect of the plaintiff's death[144] on the suit. More than half of the states and the District of Columbia say that the defamation suit dies with the plaintiff (some with the death of the defendant).

20. DEFAMATION

Is the publication or broadcast defamatory? The third necessary part of the defamation suit is that the published statement that identified the plaintiff did indeed defame. That says that the words injured reputation, or, in some circumstances, caused emotional distress. Plaintiffs must assert that defamation occurred and prove the same at trial. What can constitute defamation? Noted libel experts Robert Sack and Sandra Baron summed it up in their reference work on libel when they said:[145] "* * * what is defamatory shares with hard-core pornography the characteristic that, whatever its precise definition, judges and jurors think they 'know it when [they] see it.' "

individuals when 21 individuals of a town police department sued following publication of a printed rumor about one unidentified officer. *Arcand v. Evening Call Pub. Co.*, 567 F.2d 1163 (1st Cir.1977).

[143] *Gugliuzza v. K.C.M.C., Inc.*, 606 So.2d 790 (La.1992), 20 Med.L.Rptr. 1866.

[144] Rhode Island General Laws § 10–7.1–1.

[145] Quoting Justice Potter Stewart's concurrence in *Jacobellis v. Ohio*, 378 U.S. 184, 197, 84 S.Ct. 1676 (1964). Robert Sack and Sandra Baron, *Libel Slander, and Related Problems*, (Michie and Practising Law Institute, New York, 1996).

The first rule is that the statement must be false. In the case of *Philadelphia Newspapers, Inc. v. Hepps,*[146] a 5–4 decision in the U.S. Supreme Court overturned a decision by the Pennsylvania Supreme Court which held that the defendant would have to bear the burden of proving the truthfulness of an allegedly defamatory statement. That was based on an old common law presumption that defamatory statements were untrue. Justice O'Connor wrote for the majority that protections for free expression required that the plaintiff shoulder the burden of proving that the allegedly defamatory statement was false.[147]

> In a case such as this one, where a newspaper publishes speech of public concern about a private figure, the private-figure plaintiff cannot recover damages without also showing that the statements at issue are false. Because in such a case the scales are in an uncertain balance as to whether the statements are true or false, the Constitution requires that the scales be tipped in favor of protecting true speech. To ensure that true speech on matters of public concern is not deterred, the common-law presumption that defamatory speech is false cannot stand.
>
> And so, as a practical matter, it is the plaintiff who will have to show that the statement was false. This comports with our understanding that truth is the strongest privilege (otherwise stated as truth is the strongest defense in defamation) to publish.

Apart from being false, what are the hallmarks of defamatory statements? Generally, what judges and juries will not find to be defamatory are words that merely annoy, embarrass or hurt the feelings of the plaintiff. The words or other communication must affect the plaintiff's reputation in the community or some portion of the community. The plaintiff does not need to prove that the entire community would change its opinion of him or that "all the right-thinking people" now think less of him.

This approach differs from the English approach, which American courts followed until the early part of the Twentieth Century. Under the English approach, defamation would be determined by seeing how the "right-thinking Englishman" would view the statement. The difficulties in using this approach are illustrated in the case of *Mawe v. Piggott*[148] in which an Irish priest was accused of informing on Catholic insurgents. Even though such an accusation would strongly damage anyone's reputation in Ireland, the courts ruled that the statement was not defamatory. The reason given by the court was that no reasonable person would think less of a person for telling the authorities about law

---

[146] *Philadelphia Newspapers, Inc. v. Hepps,* 475 U.S. 767, 106 S.Ct. 1558 (1986), 12 Med.L.Rptr 1977.

[147] Ibid. at 767.

[148] *Mawe v. Piggott,* 4 Ir. R.–C.L. 54 (1869).

breakers.[149] "The very circumstances which will make a person be regarded with disfavour by the criminal classes will raise his character in the estimation of right-thinking men," the court said. Under this English approach, defamation would depend on orthodoxy rather than the effect of words on reputations.

The case that turned American defamation law away from the English approach was *Peck v. Tribune*.[150] Elizabeth Peck, a resident of Chicago, discovered an advertisement in the *Chicago Sunday Tribune* which featured her picture and a testimonial for a brand of whisky. The name attached to the ad was that of a Mrs. A. Schuman who was identified as a nurse who both consumed Duffy's Pure Malt Whisky and gave it to her patients as part of her treatment of them. Peck was not a nurse and she was a teetotaler (she did not drink any alcohol). Peck sued, but her case was tossed out by the trial court because, the trial court concluded, there was no general disapproval of drinking whisky and therefore the statement could not harm Peck's reputation.

The Seventh Circuit Court of Appeals had ruled that the publication was not libelous. "It was pointed out that there was no general consensus of opinion that to drink whisky is wrong," Justice Oliver Wendell Holmes said of the circuit decision. But Justice Holmes disagreed with that approach.[151] "If the advertisement obviously would hurt the plaintiff in the estimation of an important and respectable part of the community, liability is not a question of a majority vote." Justice Holmes' reference to a "respectable part of the community" places some limitations on how defamation is determined.

Courts will not support a conclusion that a statement is defamatory if the finding would go against public policy or be so far out of step with the community as to constitute a greater harm. Before the 1954 decision in *Brown v. Board of Education*,[152] some courts ruled that making the statement that a white person was black was defamatory. The Supreme Court and society's demand that people be treated equally regardless of race meant that after *Brown* it would be difficult for any court to support a finding that a white person's being described as black was defamatory.[153] Similarly, a statement that a person was a law-abiding member of the community would not be considered defamatory even if a group of anarchists or criminals found the statement to be repugnant.

---

149 Ibid. at 62.

150 *Peck v. Tribune*, 214 U.S. 185, 29 S.Ct. 554 (1909).

151 Ibid. at 190, 556.

152 *Brown v. Board of Education*, 347 U.S. 483, 74 S.Ct. 686 (1954).

153 One of the few cases following *Brown* where a court held a newspaper's publication that a white woman was black amounted to defamation, *Bowen v. Independent Pub. Co.*, 230 S.C. 509 96 S.E.2d 564 (S.Carolina) 1957. The South Carolina Supreme Court held that "in view of the social habits and customs deep-rooted in this State, such publication is calculated to affect her standing in society and to injure her in the estimation of her friends and acquaintances." At 566, 513. In *Northern Indiana Public Service Co. v. Dabagia*, 721 N.E.2d 294 (Ct.App.Indiana 1999), an Indiana appellate court held that calling someone a "camel jockey" or "arab" was not defamatory, although they are epithets. At 303.

The problem for the media professional is knowing how to "know it when they see it," or, more importantly when they write, broadcast or post it. Words will have different meanings in different contexts including the social, temporal and regional settings where the statements appear. Perhaps the best way to avoid defaming is to look at the legal analysis that statements are subjected to.

In addition to being false and damaging to reputations, the defamatory statement must be believable, that is to say that the audience could believe the damaging statement actually described the plaintiff. Such was the jury's conclusion in the celebrated case of *Falwell v. Flynt.*[154] In that case, the Rev. Jerry Falwell sued *Hustler* publisher Larry Flynt over an advertising parody that asserted that Falwell's first sexual experience was with his mother in an outhouse while both were drunk. It was a part of the continuing feud between Falwell and Flynt. Falwell sued Flynt for libel, invasion of privacy and intentional infliction of emotional distress. While Flynt won on his claim of infliction of emotional distress, he lost his defamation claim as,[155] "[t]he jury returned a verdict for the defendants on the libel claim, finding that no reasonable man would believe that the parody was describing actual facts about Falwell." The tabloid *Sun*, published by Globe International, ran a story about Nellie Mitchell, a resident of Mountain Home, Ark. Mitchell had run a newsstand and delivered newspapers for 50 years. She gained notoriety for her long service and was featured in a number of stories in 1980. On Oct. 2, 1990, the *Sun* ran Mitchell's photograph in connection with a story that appeared under the headline, "Pregnancy Forces Granny to Quit Work at Age 101." A second photograph of Mitchell appeared with a story about an Australian woman named Audrey Wiles. According to the *Sun*, Wiles, who was 101, had to quit her paper route after a millionaire customer made her pregnant. Mitchell sued. Globe International built part of its defense on the claim that no one believed what it ran in the pages of the *Sun*. Although Mitchell did not recover on her libel claim, she did receive an award of $650,000 in compensatory damages and $850,000 in punitive damages on a related claim.[156]

DEFAMATION PER SE AND PER QUOD

Defamatory statements fall into two analytical categories: defamation *per se* and defamation *per quod*. Defamation *per se* is libel on its face and the courts will presume that such defamatory statements automatically damage reputations. The list below provides the categories of words that are defamatory *per se*. Defamation *per quod* is libel arising from the context of the words. Here, the courts (and juries) must determine whether the statement did, in fact, damage the plaintiff's

[154] *Falwell v. Flynt*, 797 F.2d 1270 (4th Cir.1986), 13 Med.L.Rptr. 2281.

[155] Ibid. at 1274.

[156] The Eighth Circuit Court of Appeals reduced the damage award saying it was excessive under the facts of the case.

reputation. Unlike defamation *per se*, under defamation *per quod* plaintiffs must plead and prove special damages.[157] The *per se* and *per quod* distinction is a part of the legacy of slander, spoken defamation.

Understanding the nature of people and the process of communication, the English courts divided slanderous statements into two categories—slander *per se* and *per quod*. Slander *per se* consisted of those categories of spoken statements that would, by their very speaking, cause harm to the plaintiff. The four categories are:

1. Words that impute to the plaintiff a crime for which he can be made to suffer corporally by way of punishment;
2. Words that impute to the plaintiff a contagious or infectious disease;
3. Words that impute adultery or unchastity to a plaintiff who is a woman or a girl (based on the Slander of Women Act of 1891[158]); and,
4. Words that, when spoken of the plaintiff in relation to his office, profession, or trade, would tend to injure his reputation therein.

These slanders/libels were considered to be serious enough to merit treatment based on their presumed damage to the plaintiff's reputation. But if a plaintiff complained of slander/libel that fell outside these categories, he would have to prove that the words, in fact, damaged his reputation. This meant that words that were simply annoying or personally troublesome would not justify the awarding of damages. This approach was carried by English colonists to America and applied to American cases. The distinction still applies as illustrated by the case of *Wardlaw v. Peck*.[159]

Robert Newton Peck, an author of children's books, was to speak at the convocation at Erskine College in South Carolina. Mary Jo Wardlaw, an Erskine student, was to meet Peck at an airport, about an hour away, and drive him to the college. Wardlaw did not show up and Peck, angry and complaining about the treatment, took a cab to the college which paid the fare. Despite receiving additional apologies for Wardlaw's mistake, Peck remained angry and said he would[160] "deal with Mary Jo the next day in convocation."

During his speech, Peck began referring to Wardlaw as "Mary Jo Warthog" and "Warthog." Peck said that he hated her because she was late in picking him up at the airport. Peck likened Wardlaw to "Janice,"

---

[157] Special damages are treated under the harm section, but generally, special damages means that the plaintiff suffered an actual pecuniary (measurable in actual dollars) loss as the result of the defamatory statement.

[158] Generally, Clement Gatley, *Law and Practice of Libel and Slander*, (London: Sweet & Maxwell Ltd., 1929), at 45.

[159] *Wardlaw v. Peck*, 282 S.C. 199, 318 S.E.2d 270 (S.C.App.1984).

[160] Ibid. at 200, 272.

a character in one of his books, a person "built like a garbage truck" who was the "bully of his childhood." At some point in the speech, Peck said that he had a recurring nightmare that Wardlaw and another Erskine student "were breeding under his sink."

Wardlaw sued, alleging that Peck had slandered her, causing her great emotional distress and forcing her to remain secluded in her room the day after the convocation and making it impossible for her to face people in public. Her suit included Peck's statement regarding her "breeding under his sink." Peck's statements about Wardlaw, calling her "Warthog" and comparing her to the character in one of his books, did not fall into any of the four categories of speech that are slander *per se*. They were slander *per quod* and in order to prove that the words were defamatory, Wardlaw had to show that she suffered damages, for if she was not damaged, then the statement was not damaging or defamatory.

The trial court dismissed the first part of her suit. The South Carolina Court of Appeals affirmed and explained its ruling on the *per quod* claim saying:[161]

> We do not view Wardlaw's hurt feelings, however genuine, as special damage making Peck's words actionable *per quod*. The gist of defamation lies not in the hurt to the defamed person's feelings, but in the injury caused his reputation * * * Where special damage is necessary to maintain an action, that special damage must consist of some provable material loss to the plaintiff as a result of the injury to his reputation.

The trial court allowed the portion of Wardlaw's suit over the charge of unchastity, a slander *per se* statement, to go forward under a South Carolina statute that allowed women to win damages for such allegations without having to put forth proof of special damages. Wardlaw won her case on that claim and was awarded $4,000 in actual damages and $20,000 in punitive damages.

This slander analysis is important in those jurisdictions that treat broadcast defamation as slander, rather than libel. The requirement that the plaintiff plead and prove special damages makes lawsuits more difficult and give broadcasters an edge in defamation cases. California and South Carolina treat broadcast defamation as slander as a matter of law. Case law suggests that broadcasts would be treated as slander in Colorado, Nevada and Arizona. Depending on circumstances, in Texas and Tennessee, the distinction between slander and libel is based on how the defamatory statement is created. Scripted broadcast defamation is libel while extemporaneous broadcasts are slander.

As literacy grew and the greater impact of the printed word was recognized, the courts created the category of libel. The distinctions between *per se* and *per quod* accompanied the growth of libel law. Today, libel *per se* is classified as a statement whose defamatory meaning is

[161] Ibid. at 205, 274–275.

apparent on its face. Libel *per quod* is a statement whose defamatory meaning is based on the extrinsic knowledge of the recipient. This distinction applies to an essential element of the defamation case—damages. In the majority of jurisdictions, libel *per se* carries a presumption of damage. That is because of the apparent damage to reputation from the statement on its face. For cases of libel *per quod*, where the reputational damage must rely on outside fact, the plaintiff must plead and prove actual damage. The significance of this becomes apparent in the damage section below.

Per se should be fairly easy to see in many cases. The categories follow those laid out in slander *per se*. In short, any published statement that on its face would injure a person's reputation in the community or hinder him or her in a chosen occupation or trade falls under libel *per se*.

IMPUTING CRIME

Publishing falsely that a person is held in jail on a forgery charge,[162] or to say incorrectly that one has illicitly sold or distributed narcotics,[163] is libelous on its face. To say without legal excuse that one made "shakedown attempts"[164] on elected officers, or committed bigamy,[165] perjury,[166] or murder[167] is libelous. Some "crimes" are so minor that courts will not find them libelous *per se*. But some allegations, while not charging that the plaintiff committed a specific crime may still be considered libelous *per se*. In *Clemente v. Espinosa,*[168] a claim that an attorney had an association with the Mafia was sufficient as an accusation of criminality.[169]

But some *per se* statements may not seem so obvious. Robert Sack and Sandra Baron gave this example to show how libel *per se* may crop up, even in a case that appears to be one of libel *per quod*.

If, for example, a Mr. Johnson were falsely reported by a newspaper to have withdrawn funds kept in the bank account of the firm of Johnson, Smith, and Jones, but in fact, as members of the community knew, Johnson had been thrown out of the firm a month before, in a *per se/per*

---

[162] *Oklahoma Pub. Co. v. Givens*, 67 F.2d 62 (10th Cir.1933); *Barnett v. Schumacher*, 453 S.W.2d 934 (Mo.1970).

[163] *Snowden v. Pearl River Broadcasting Corp.*, 251 So.2d 405 (La.App.1971).

[164] *Bianco v. Palm Beach Newspapers, Inc.*, 381 So.2d 371 (Fla.App.1980), 6 Med.L.Rptr. 1484.

[165] *Taylor v. Tribune Pub. Co.*, 67 Fla. 361, 65 So. 3 (1914); *Pitts v. Spokane Chronicle Co.*, 63 Wash.2d 763, 388 P.2d 976 (1964).

[166] *Milan v. Long*, 78 W.Va. 102, 88 S.E. 618 (1916); *Riss v. Anderson*, 304 F.2d 188 (8th Cir.1962).

[167] *Shiell v. Metropolis Co.*, 102 Fla. 794, 136 So. 537 (1931); *Frechette v. Special Magazines*, 285 App.Div. 174, 136 N.Y.S.2d 448 (1954).

[168] *Clemente v. Espinosa*, 749 F.Supp. 672, 679 (E.D.Pa.1990).

[169] Ibid. at 679.

quod jurisdiction, Johnson might or might not have a cause of action without proving "special damages." The analysis is as follows:[170]

> The statement's defamatory meaning can be understood only by reference to an extrinsic fact, that Johnson is no longer with the firm. It is thus libel *per quod*. Special damages must therefore be proven. In some *per se/per quod* jurisdictions, however, the further question must be asked: Does the statement fall within one of the slander *per se* categories? It does, because the charge is the crime of theft. In those jurisdictions, the necessity to plead and prove special damages would first arise because the statement is libelous *per quod* and then would be removed because it falls within one of the slander *per se* categories.

IMPUTING UNCHASTITY

Beyond *Wardlaw v. Peck*,[171] it should be obvious that one should beware of publishing words imputing sexual acts either outside the bounds of a marital relationship or outside prevailing moral codes. Courts have found that charging without foundation that a woman is immoral as actionable libel. The charge of indiscretion need not be pronounced; any statement fairly imputing immoral conduct is actionable.[172]

Pat Montandon, author of "*How To Be a Party Girl*", was to discuss her book on the Pat Michaels "Discussion" show. *TV Guide* received the show producer's advance release, which said that Montandon and a masked, anonymous prostitute would discuss "From Party-Girl to Call-Girl?" and "How far can the 'party-girl' go until she becomes a 'call-girl'." *TV Guide* ineptly edited the release, deleting reference to the prostitute and publishing this: "10:30 Pat Michaels—Discussion 'From Party Girl to Call Girl.' Scheduled guest: TV Personality Pat Montandon and author of '*How to Be a Party Girl*'." Montandon sued for libel and won $150,000 in damages.[173]

On the other hand, a woman who posed in the nude for a film maker but later got his agreement not to show the film, was unsuccessful in a libel action following his breaking of the agreement. She charged that his showing of the film to people who knew her caused her shame, disgrace and embarrassment. But the court said that "a film strip which includes

[170] Robert Sack and Sandra Baron, *Libel Slander, and Related Problems*, (Michie and Practising Law Institute, New York, 1996).

[171] *Wardlaw v. Peck*, 282 S.C. 199, 318 S.E.2d 270 (S.C.App.1984).

[172] *Baird v. Dun and Bradstreet*, 446 Pa. 266, 285 A.2d 166 (1971); *Wildstein v. New York Post Corp.*, 40 Misc.2d 586, 243 N.Y.S.2d 386 (1963); *Youssoupoff v. Metro-Goldwyn-Mayer*, 50 Times L.R. 581, 99 A.L.R. 864 (1934).

[173] *Montandon v. Triangle Publications, Inc.*, 45 Cal.App.3d 938, 120 Cal.Rptr. 186 (1975).

a scene of plaintiff posing in the nude does not necessarily impute unchastity," and that it was not libel *per se*.[174]

Under the strict interpretation of the unchastity category, the sexual conduct need not violate law regulating sexual conduct but rather requires only a statement that the plaintiff had engaged in intimate relations. There has been a movement to loosen the tight constraints of the category, especially in light of changing mores. However, the rule still remains and poses risks for the publisher. Of special concern is the publication of defamatory statements on the Internet. Statements regarding sexual activity which might not raise a single eyebrow in some places might constitute the gravest defamation in a foreign jurisdiction.

The apparent protection solely for women against a false statement alleging unchastity was included in Robert Newton Peck's appeal in *Wardlaw v. Peck*.[175] Peck argued that a South Carolina statute allowing women to be awarded damages for claims of unchastity without proof of special damages was unconstitutional because it did not provide the same protections for men. The South Carolina Court of Appeals rejected that argument saying that nothing in the statute would prevent a man from seeking damages for allegations of unchastity.[176] "There is no reason to distinguish between men and women in the application of this rule. Surely, a man's reputation for decency and honor is no less dear to him than is a woman's to her." The court also mentioned in a footnote that a number of jurisdictions had allowed suits by men over such allegations.

IMPUTING LOATHSOME DISEASE

The law has long held that diseases which may be termed "loathsome, infectious, or contagious" may be libelous when falsely attributed to an individual. This category of *per se* defamation is a holdover from English law and prejudices that date back centuries. It comes from misunderstandings and ignorance of the disease process that meant that the sick were shunned. Professor Rodney Smolla reports that there have been relatively few American cases regarding this category.[177] Those diseases that have been found to be loathsome generally have been venereal diseases such as gonorrhea and syphilis. Leprosy also is counted among the loathsome diseases, probably because of the ancient fear of the disease.

Perhaps because of its linkage with sex, AIDS has been treated as a loathsome disease in a number of cases. The authors have not found any cases where the inclusion of AIDS as a loathsome disease was disputed.

---

[174] *McGraw v. Watkins*, 49 A.D.2d 958, 373 N.Y.S.2d 663 (1975). But contra, see *Clifford v. Hollander* (N.Y.Civ.1980), 6 Med.L.Rptr. 2201, where a photo of a nude woman, identified falsely as that of a woman journalist, was held libelous.

[175] *Wardlaw v. Peck*, 282 S.C. 199, 318 S.E.2d 270 (S.C.App.1984).

[176] Ibid. at 211, 278.

[177] Rodney A. Smolla, *Law of Defamation*, (Clark, Boardman Callaghan, New York, 1995).

In a case which represents a more enlightened approach to the disease category, *Chuy v. Philadelphia Eagles Football Club,*[178] the Third Circuit held that the false statement that the plaintiff had cancer was not defamatory, because cancer is not a "loathsome disease" and the public reaction to it "is usually one of sympathy rather than scorn, support and not rejection."[179] Publication of a statement that a person is an alcoholic falls into the *per se* category.[180]

An incorrect assignment of mental impairment or of mental illness to a person is libel on its face.[181] The magazine *Fact* published in its September-October issue of 1964; an article billed as "The Unconscious of a Conservative: A Special Issue on the Mind of Barry Goldwater." Goldwater was the Republican Party's candidate for president and a senator from Arizona at the time. He was portrayed in one of two articles as "paranoid," his attacks on other politicians stemming from a conviction that "everybody hates him, and it is better to attack them first." A *Fact* poll of psychiatrists, asked to judge whether Goldwater was psychologically fit to serve as president, also was reported on. A jury found libel and awarded Goldwater $1.00 in compensatory damages and $75,000 in punitive damages

IMPUTING INCOMPETENCE IN TRADE, OCCUPATION OR PROFESSION

So long as one follows a calling that is lawful, he has a claim not to be defamed unfairly in the performance of it. The possibilities are rich for damaging one through words that impugn honesty, skill, fitness, ethical standards, or financial capacity in his chosen work, whether it be banking or basket-weaving. Observe some of the possibilities: that a university was a "degree mill;"[182] that a contractor engaged in unethical trade;[183] that a clergyman was "an interloper, a meddler, a spreader of distrust;"[184] that a schoolmaster kept girls after school so that he could court them;[185] that a jockey rode horses unfairly and dishonestly;[186] that

---

[178] *Chuy v. Philadelphia Eagles Football Club*, 595 F.2d 1265, 1281–82 (3d Cir.1979), 4 Med.L.Rptr. 2537 (en banc).

[179] Ibid. at 1281–82. Readers should note that in this case the plaintiff was able to recover damages on a theory of intentional infliction of emotional harm so the defendant did not avoid responsibility.

[180] *Hedrick v. Center for Comprehensive Alcoholism Treatment*, 7 Ohio App.3d 211, 454 N.E.2d 1343 (1982).

[181] *Cowper v. Vannier*, 20 Ill.App.2d 499, 156 N.E.2d 761 (1959); *Kenney v. Hatfield*, 351 Mich. 498, 88 N.W.2d 535 (1958). But not in *Virginia: Mills v. Kingsport Times-News*, 475 F.Supp. 1005 (W.D.Va.1979), 5 Med.L.Rptr. 2288.

[182] *Laurence University v. State*, 68 Misc.2d 408, 326 N.Y.S.2d 617 (1971). Reversed on grounds that State official's words were absolutely privileged, 41 A.D.2d 463, 344 N.Y.S.2d 183 (1973).

[183] *Greenbelt Co-op. Pub. Ass'n v. Bresler*, 253 Md. 324, 252 A.2d 755 (1969), reversed on other grounds 398 U.S. 6, 90 S.Ct. 1537 (1970).

[184] *Van Lonkhuyzen v. Daily News Co.*, 195 Mich. 283, 161 N.W. 979 (1917).

[185] *Spears v. McCoy*, 155 Ky. 1, 159 S.W. 610 (1913).

[186] *Wood v. Earl of Durham*, 21 Q.B.D. 501 (1888).

an attorney was incompetent,[187] and that a corporation director embezzled.[188]

By no means is every statement to which a businessman, tradesman or professional takes exception, however, libelous. Thus Frederick D. Washington, a church bishop, sued *The New York Daily News* and columnist Robert Sylvester for his column that said Washington had attended a nightclub performance at which a choir member of his church sang. The bishop argued that his church did not approve of its spiritual leaders' attending nightclubs, and that he had been damaged. The court said the account was not, on its face, an attack on the plaintiff's integrity, and called the item a "warm human interest story" in which there was general interest. This was not libel on its face and the court upheld dismissal of Bishop Washington's complaint.[189]

Nor did David Brown convince the court that there was libel in a pamphlet that opposed his attempt to get a zoning change from the City Council of Knoxville, Tenn. The pamphlet attacked a change that would have permitted Brown to build apartments in a residential district, and asked the question: "Have the 'Skids Been Greased' at City Council?" Brown sued for libel, arguing that the question suggested he had bribed the City Council and that it had accepted the bribe. But the court held that the question did not suggest bribery in its reasonable and obvious meaning; but rather, that pressure in the form of political influence had been brought to bear on certain Council members to expedite matters. This was not libel. Had the pamphlet said that,[190] "palms are greased at the City Council," that would have been libel on its face and actionable.

A margin of protection also exists in the occasional finding by a court that mistakenly attributing a single instance of clumsiness or error to a professional man is not enough to damage him. Rather, such cases have held, there must be a suggestion of more general incompetency or lack of quality before a libel charge will hold. One court said:[191]

> To charge a professional man with negligence or unskillfulness in the management or treatment of an individual case, is no more than to impute to him the mistakes and errors incident to fallible human nature. The most eminent and skillful physician or surgeon may mistake the symptoms of a particular case without detracting from his general professional skill or

---

187 *Hahn v. Andrello,* 44 A.D.2d 501, 355 N.Y.S.2d 850 (1974).

188 *Weenig v. Wood,* 169 Ind.App. 413, 349 N.E.2d 235 (1976).

189 *Washington v. New York News Inc.,* 37 A.D.2d 557, 322 N.Y.S.2d 896 (1971).

190 *Brown v. Newman,* 224 Tenn. 297, 454 S.W.2d 120 (1970). An official who resigned from a "financially troubled bank" was not libeled: *Bordoni v. New York Times Co., Inc.,* 400 F.Supp. 1223 (S.D.N.Y.1975).

191 *Blende v. Hearst Publications,* 200 Wash. 426, 93 P.2d 733 (1939); *November v. Time Inc.,* 13 N.Y.2d 175, 244 N.Y.S.2d 309, 194 N.E.2d 126 (1963); *Holder Const. Co. v. Ed Smith & Sons, Inc.,* 124 Ga.App. 89, 182 S.E.2d 919 (1971). But see *Cohn v. Am-Law, Inc.* (N.Y.Sup.Ct.1980), 5 Med.L.Rptr. 2367, where defamation was found in a magazine story saying an attorney went "unprepared" to a single hearing.

> learning. To say of him, therefore, that he was mistaken in that case would not be calculated to impair the confidence of the community in his general professional competency.

This also applies to the reputations of corporations, the artificial legal entities created to carry on business. It is possible to damage the reputation of a corporation or partnership by defamation that reflects on the conduct, management, or financial condition of the corporation.[192] To say falsely that a company is in shaky financial condition, or that it cannot pay its debts, would be libelous, as would the imputation that it has engaged in dishonest practices. While a corporation is an entity quite different from the individuals that head it or staff it, there is no doubt that it has a reputation, an "image" to protect.

Publishing or broadcasting casual statements that a business or corporation is "broke" or "going bankrupt" or "has a rotten credit rating" can be risky business indeed unless you are prepared to prove the truth of such statements in court. When Dun & Bradstreet—which is in the business of giving credit ratings—published erroneous information indicating falsely that a Greenmoss Builders had filed for bankruptcy, that was held to be defamatory. Both the Vermont courts and the United States Supreme Court agreed that a $350,000 award should be paid to the firm.[193]

Charging dishonest or unethical behavior by a firm can also result in a successful defamation suit. In a case that may be difficult to understand in light of the damaging revelations and admissions by tobacco companies in 1996 and 1997, the Chicago TV station WBBM—owned by the CBS Network—found in 1988 that such a firm could still be libeled. The Supreme Court denied *certiorari*, leaving intact a $3 million damage award in the case of *Brown & Williamson Tobacco Corp. v. Jacobson and CBS, Inc.*[194] Back in 1981, Walter Jacobson had delivered a "Perspective" report denouncing the makers of Viceroy cigarettes for hiring advertising "slicksters" to create an advertising strategy to "hook" the young. The strategy used by Brown & Williamson, Jacobson said, was taken from a report recommending that smoking be portrayed to youth as a kind of rite of passage involving wearing a bra or shaving or drinking wine or beer. The broadcast added up to an accusation of unethical youth-oriented advertising by Brown & Williamson for its Viceroy cigarettes, thus endangering the health of the impressionable young.[195] But in the case, the cigarette maker was able to show that it had not put the plan into effect. It even presented evidence

---

[192] *Dupont Engineering Co. v. Nashville Banner Pub. Co.*, 13 F.2d 186 (M.D.Tenn.1925); *Electric Furnace Corp. v. Deering Milliken Research Corp.*, 325 F.2d 761 (6th Cir.1963); *Golden Palace, Inc. v. National Broadcasting Co., Inc.*, 386 F.Supp. 107 (D.D.C.1974).

[193] *Dun & Bradstreet, Inc. v. Greenmoss Builders, Inc.*, 472 U.S. 749, 105 S.Ct. 2939 (1985).

[194] *Brown & Williamson Tobacco Corp. v. Jacobson*, 827 F.2d 1119 (7th Cir.1987).

[195] Certiorari denied 485 U.S. 993, 108 S.Ct. 1302 (1988), upholding the judgment of the United States Court of Appeals, Seventh Circuit. See 827 F.2d 1119 (7th Cir.1987) 14 Med.L.Rptr. 1497.

that it had fired the advertising agency that developed the advertising strategy.[196] (We will have more on the case, including the cautionary tale about destroying evidence, later.)

OTHER STATEMENTS DAMAGING REPUTATION

Esteem and social standing can be lowered in the eyes of others by statements concerning political belief and conduct other than that grouped under crime and under sexual immorality in the preceding pages. To take political belief first, many important cases since the late 1940's have largely involved false charges of "Communist" or "Red" or some variant of these words indicating that one subscribes to a generally hated political doctrine. But before these, a line of cases since the 1890's produced libel convictions against those who had labeled others as anarchists, socialists, or fascists. Gay once was used to describe someone who was happy. It also meant bright colors. Over time, it became a term to call someone homosexual. It was actionable defamation to publish that a person was gay. Today, with the legalization of same-gender marriage and a maturing of society, the term, on its own, no longer has the power to harm a reputation. In the days of Emma Goldman and Big Bill Haywood, it was laid down by the courts that to call one an "anarchist" falsely was libelous;[197] when socialism protested capitalism and America's involvement in World War I, "red-tinted agitator" and "Socialist" were words for which a wronged citizen could recover;[198] In the revulsion against Nazi Germany and Japan during World War II, false accusations of someone being "Fascist" or "pro-Jap" brought libel judgments.[199]

Magazines, columnists, newspapers, and corporations have paid for carelessness indulged in by charging others as "Communist" or "representative for the Communist Party."[200] The "basis for reproach is a belief that such political affiliations constitute a threat to our institutions * * *." In the famous case of *Gertz v. Robert Welch, Inc.*,[201] the trial court

---

[196] Years too late for Walter Jacobson, Liggett Group acknowledged that tobacco companies aimed sales pitches at 14-to-18-year-olds. That admission came in March of 1997, more than a decade after the libel verdict against him and his Chicago television station. "I smiled inwardly, yes," Jacobson was quoted in *Electronic Media*. "I dug out a wonderful picture taken a few years ago when the tobacco executives testified before Congress and said, 'Look what they're saying now.' " Jeff Borden, "Jacobson buoyed by new tobacco headlines," *Electronic Media*, April 28, 1997, p. 9.

[197] *Cerveny v. Chicago Daily News Co.*, 139 Ill. 345, 28 N.E. 692 (1891); *Wilkes v. Shields*, 62 Minn. 426, 64 N.W. 921 (1895).

[198] *Wells v. Times Printing Co.*, 77 Wash. 171, 137 P. 457 (1913); *Ogren v. Rockford Star Printing Co.*, 288 Ill. 405, 123 N.E. 587 (1919).

[199] *Hartley v. Newark Morning Ledger Co.*, 134 N.J.L. 217, 46 A.2d 777 (1946); *Hryhorijiv v. Winchell*, 180 Misc. 574, 45 N.Y.S.2d 31 (1943).

[200] Anon., "Supplement," 171 A.L.R. 709, 712 (1947). *Grant v. Reader's Digest Ass'n, Inc.*, 151 F.2d 733 (2d Cir.1945). And see *Wright v. Farm Journal*, 158 F.2d 976 (2d Cir.1947); *Spanel v. Pegler*, 160 F.2d 619 (7th Cir.1947); *MacLeod v. Tribune Pub. Co.*, 52 Cal.2d 536, 343 P.2d 36 (1959).

[201] *Gertz v. Robert Welch, Inc.*, 306 F.Supp. 310 (N.D.Ill.1969); 418 U.S. 323, 94 S.Ct. 2997 (1974).

found that the publication of the John Birch Society had libeled Chicago Attorney Elmer Gertz in charging falsely that he was a "Leninist," a "Communist-fronter," and a member of the "Marxist League for Industrial Democracy." Gertz was awarded $400,000. In another case, where one organization called another "communist dominated" and failed to prove the charge in court, $25,000 was awarded to the plaintiff organization.[202]

Not every insinuation that a person is less than American, however, is libelous. Abraham Goodman, a selectman of Ware, Mass., phoned a call-in radio talk-show of the Central Broadcasting Corp. station, WARE, to explain his opposition to a proposed contract for the local police union, at issue in the town prior to a citizen vote on the matter. During his extended and agitated discussion, he said that "* * * if we do not get together and stop the inroad of communism, something will happen." A libel suit was brought by the police local's parent union against Central Broadcasting, and the Massachusetts Supreme Judicial Court held that this fragment of Goodman's statement was "mere pejorative rhetoric," and an "unamiable but nonlibelous utterance."[203]

Finally, there are many words among those lowering esteem or social standing that defy classifying. Appellations that may be common enough in the excited conversation of neighborhood gossips can turn to actionable libel when reduced to print or writing. It has been held actionable on its face to print and publish that one is "a liar,"[204] "a skunk,"[205] or "a scandalmonger";[206] "a drunkard,"[207] "a hypocrite,"[208] or "a hog";[209] or to call one heartless and neglectful of his family.[210] Other actionable epithets include linking a person to a swastika symbol,[211] or calling one a "despicable human being,"[212] or a "bitch" (implying a woman is a prostitute in a dated way).[213] Name-calling where private citizens are concerned is occasionally the kind of news that makes a lively paragraph,

---

[202] *Utah State Farm Bureau Federation v. National Farmers Union Service Corp.*, 198 F.2d 20 (10th Cir.1952). See also *Cahill v. Hawaiian Paradise Park Corp.*, 56 Haw. 522, 543 P.2d 1356 (1975).

[203] *National Ass'n of Government Employees, Inc. v. Central Broadcasting Corp.*, 379 Mass. 220, 396 N.E.2d 996 (1979). Also *McAuliffe v. Local Union No. 3*, 29 N.Y.S.2d 963 (Sup.1941); *McGaw v. Webster*, 79 N.M. 104, 440 P.2d 296 (1968); "pro-Castro," *Menendez v. Key West Newspaper Corp.*, 293 So.2d 751 (Fla.App.1974).

[204] *Melton v. Bow*, 241 Ga. 629, 247 S.E.2d 100 (1978); *Paxton v. Woodward*, 31 Mont. 195, 78 P. 215 (1904); *Smith v. Lyons*, 142 La. 975, 77 So. 896 (1917); contra, *Bennett v. Transamerican Press*, 298 F.Supp. 1013 (S.D.Iowa 1969); *Calloway v. Central Charge Service*, 142 U.S.App.D.C. 259, 440 F.2d 287 (1971).

[205] *Massuere v. Dickens*, 70 Wis. 83, 35 N.W. 349 (1887).

[206] *Patton v. Cruce*, 72 Ark. 421, 81 S.W. 380 (1904).

[207] *Giles v. State*, 6 Ga. 276 (1849); cf. *Smith v. Fielden*, 205 Tenn. 313, 326 S.W.2d 476 (1959).

[208] *Overstreet v. New Nonpareil Co.*, 184 Iowa 485, 167 N.W. 669 (1918).

[209] *Solverson v. Peterson*, 64 Wis. 198, 25 N.W. 14 (1885).

[210] *Brown v. Du Frey*, 1 N.Y.2d 190, 151 N.Y.S.2d 649, 134 N.E.2d 469 (1956).

[211] *Mullenmeister v. Snap-On Tools*, 587 F.Supp. 868 (S.D.N.Y.1984).

[212] *Smith v. McMullen*, 589 F.Supp. 642 (S.D.Tex.1984).

[213] *Stone v. Brooks*, 253 Ga. 565, 322 S.E.2d 728 (1984).

but the alert and responsible reporter recognizes it for what it is and decides whether to use it on better grounds than its titillation value.

Ridicule also falls into this general category. It is pointless to try to draw a narrow line to separate words that ridicule from those that lower esteem and social standing. That which ridicules may at times have the effect of damaging social standing. Yet that which attempts to satirize, or which makes an individual appear uncommonly foolish, or makes fun of misfortune has a quality distinct enough to serve as its own warning signal.

Ridicule must be more than a simple joke at another's expense, for life cannot be so grim that the thin-skinned, the solemn, and the self-important may demand to go entirely unharried. A number of courts have specifically included ridicule in the laundry list of definitions of defamation. In New York, defamation is defined picturesquely as,[214] "words which tend to expose one to public hatred, shame, obloquy, contumely, odium, contempt, ridicule, aversion, ostracism, degradation or disgrace * * *" When the jocular barb penetrates too deeply or carries too sharp a sting, or when a picture can be interpreted in a deeply derogatory manner, ridicule amounting to actionable libel may have occurred.

To sensationalize the poverty of a woman so as to bring her into ridicule and contempt, and to make a joke out of the desertion of a bride on her wedding day[215] have been held libelous. A famed case arose from a photo in an advertisement that accidentally gave the illusion of a "fantastic and lewd deformity" of a steeplechaser holding a riding crop and his saddle.[216]

Yet there is room for satire and exaggeration. *Boston Magazine* published a page titled "Best and Worst Sports," including the categories "sports announcer," "local ski slopes," and "sexy athlete," some categories plainly waggish, some straightforward and complimentary. Under "sports announcer," the best was named and given kudos; and then appeared: "*Worst:* Jimmy Myers, Channel 4. The only newscaster in town who is enrolled in a course for remedial speaking." Myers sued, lost at trial for failure to establish defamation, and appealed.[217]

The Massachusetts Supreme Judicial Court described the appearance of the magazine's page, with its title, lampooning cartoons, and a mood of rough humor in the words, including "one-liners" and preposterous propositions under such titles as "Sports Groupie." It ruled

---

[214] *Kimmerle v. New York Evening Journal,* 262 N.Y. 99, 102, 186 N.E. 217 (1933).

[215] *Moffatt v. Cauldwell,* 3 Hun. 26, 5 Thomp. & C. 256 (N.Y.1874), but "poverty" and "unemployment" have been held not actionable words: *Sousa v. Davenport,* 3 Mass.App.Ct. 715, 323 N.E.2d 910 (1975); *Kirman v. Sun Printing & Pub. Co.,* 99 App.Div. 367, 91 N.Y.S. 193 (1904).

[216] *Burton v. Crowell Pub. Co.,* 82 F.2d 154 (2d Cir.1936).

[217] *Myers v. Boston Magazine Co., Inc.,* 380 Mass. 336, 403 N.E.2d 376 (Mass.Sup.Jud.Ct.1980), 6 Med.L.Rptr. 1241.

that the statement about Myers made on such a page would not reasonably be understood by a reader to be an assertion of fact. "Taken in context, it can reasonably be considered to suggest that Myers should have been so enrolled," even though the words read "is enrolled." The words stated "a critical judgment, an opinion." And since Myers was himself available to the critic's audience, being often on view, his performances were in line with the rule that facts underlying opinions could be assumed—the performances "furnished the assumed facts from which the critic fashioned his barb." The court said that words such as these are meant to "sting and be quickly forgotten". Although for the plaintiff who "is the victim of ridicule, the forgetting may not be easy," the law refuses to find a statement of fact where none has been uttered.[218] This was opinion, and if such "is based on assumed, nondefamatory facts, the First Amendment forbids the law of libel from redressing the injury."

Perhaps the case that best illustrates the fine line that the courts draw between actionable statements and the price one pays for public recognition came in the case of the *Rev. Jerry Falwell v. Larry Flynt*, mentioned above. Flynt's ad parody asserting that Falwell had lost his virginity to his mother in a drunken state in an outhouse led to suits for libel, invasion of privacy and intentional infliction of emotional distress. While the libel and privacy claims were eliminated at the trial level the jury found for Falwell on the emotional distress claim. The Fourth Circuit affirmed, and the case went to the Supreme Court where the justices by an 8–0 vote reversed the lower court. Chief Justice Rehnquist, writing the decision, concluded that the nature of the publication, a commentary on a public figure, deserved the utmost protection of the First Amendment.[219] Falwell had not made his case sufficiently to overcome that protection.

A more recent case shows that the existence of humor, or more precisely parody, rests in the eyes of the courts. In *New Times v. Isaacks*,[220] a Texas court of appeals concluded that a parody in a weekly alternative newspaper could be interpreted to be libelous. The case began after Judge Darlene Whitten sent a 13-year-old boy to jail for five days for his Halloween essay about the shooting of a teacher.[221] The student and his classmates had been assigned to write a "scary story."

The *Dallas Observer* ran a parody piece in which Judge Whitten jailed a 6-year-old girl for a book report on the Maurice Sendak book "*Where the Wild Things Are.*" The parody, which portrayed the 6-year-old in handcuffs and ankle shackles, explained that the judge had ordered the jail time because the book report contained "cannibalism, fanaticism

---

[218] Ibid. at 1243, 1245.

[219] The nature of the First Amendment defense is taken up in the next chapter on defenses to libel claims.

[220] *New Times, Inc. v. Isaacks*, 91 S.W.3d 844 (Tex.App. 2002).

[221] John C. Ryan, "Texas court to rule: Can fiction be libel?" *Christian Science Monitor*, Dec. 1, 2003.

and disorderly conduct."[222] The piece contained a quote attributed to Judge Whitten.[223]

> "Any implication of violence in a school situation, even if it was just contained in a first-grader's book report, is reason enough for panic and overreaction," Whitten said from the bench. "It's time for you to grow up, young lady, and it's time for us to stop treating kids like children."

Judge Whitten was not amused, and neither was Bruce Isaacks, Criminal District Attorney for Denton County, who was "quoted" in the story. They both sued for libel. The *Observer* moved for summary judgment arguing that its publication was parody and thus protected because it was not a statement of fact. The newspaper lost the case and appealed. The court of appeals affirmed the trial court's denial of summary judgment for the newspaper. The appellate court held that there was a "genuine issue of material fact" regarding the possibility that a reasonable person could take the parody as a statement of fact.

After spending a good deal of time defining satire and parody as literary method of criticism using "shocking and cruel language," "often employed" "to humble political leaders and public figures" and "often calculated to injure the feelings of the subject of the portrayal," the appeals court focused on the article's reference to Judge Whitten.[224] The test is whether persons of ordinary intelligence would take the statements to be assertions of fact, the court said.

The *Observer*'s use of a photograph of a small child and inclusion of quotes attributed to Judge Whitten, the district attorney and then-Gov. George W. Bush all lent credence to the article, the court said. In addition, the court said, the fact that Judge Whitten had sent a teenager to jail recently suggested that readers might well believe that she would hold a 6-year-old to jail in shackles in her courtroom.[225]

TEXAS SUPREME COURT FINDS IN FAVOR OF SATIRE

The Texas Supreme Court finally put an end to the not-so-funny libel case when it ruled that political satire really was protected speech.[226] The 2004 ruling came just a month shy of the anniversary of the original publication of the *Observer* story. In its analysis, the Texas court looked to the entirety of the article and found a number of clues to the satirical nature of the story. They included an unorthodox headline and photo, outrageous quotes and reference to a special interest group called God-

[222] Ibid.

[223] *New Times, Inc. v. Isaacks*, 91 S.W.3d 844, 850 (Tex.App. 2002).

[224] Ibid. at 854.

[225] The article reported that courthouse security officers had ordered the 6-year-old placed in shackles after reviewing her school record which included "reprimands for spraying a boy with pineapple juice and sitting on her feet." Ibid. At 850.

[226] John Council, "Satire's Not Free Speech-Wait, Just Kidding," *Texas Lawyer*, Sept. 13, 2004.

Fearing Opponents of Freedom, otherwise known as GOOF. The plaintiffs had argued that only readers who made it through the entire story would get the joke and that others would form opinions based on partial reading of the article. The Texas court disposed of that argument while acknowledging that some readers would come to conclusions without reading the whole story.[227]

> [W]e cannot impose civil liability based on the subjective interpretation of a reader who has formed an opinion about the article's veracity after reading a sentence or two out of context; that person is not an objectively reasonable reader.

Because the article was largely fictional, the plaintiffs argued that the defendant newspaper must have published with actual malice, that is to say they knew that the article was false when they published it. The Texas court disagreed saying that the First Amendment protects speech that ridicules public officials.

While a living man whose obituary has mistakenly been printed may feel annoyed and injured and may attract unusual attention and perhaps a rough joke or two as he walks into his office the next morning, he has not been libeled. As one court said, death "is looked for in the history of every man," and where there is notice of a death that has not occurred, "Prematurity is the sole peculiarity."[228] Yet an erroneous report of death has been held to be the cause of an action for "negligent infliction of emotional distress"—an injury closely related to defamation.[229] The court decides whether a publication is libelous *per se* (by itself). But when the words complained of can have two meanings—one innocent and the other damaging—it is for the jury to decide in what sense the words were understood by the audience. Both judge and jury, in their interpretation of the statement claimed to be defamatory, should give language its common and ordinary meaning.[230]

DEFAMATION IN DIFFERENT FORM

Defamation comes in as many forms as there are means of communication. Defamation can be expressed by the broadcast or printed word. It can come in the form of gesture. For example, publishing a picture or video of someone being stopped by a security guard and frisked could amount to defamation. Pictures in and of themselves can be defamatory if they convey false impressions about the conduct and character of those depicted. That is a particular concern with the current ability to digitally manipulate pictures. Photographs may be scanned

---

227 Ibid.

228 *Cohen v. New York Times Co.*, 153 App.Div. 242, 138 N.Y.S. 206 (1912); *Cardiff v. Brooklyn Eagle, Inc.*, 190 Misc. 730, 75 N.Y.S.2d 222 (1947).

229 *Rubinstein v. New York Post Corp.* (N.Y.Sup.Ct.1983), 9 Med.L.Rptr. 1581. Emotional distress is treated later in this book.

230 *Peck v. Coos Bay Times Pub. Co.*, 122 Or. 408, 259 P. 307, 311 (1927); Prosser, 4th ed., p. 746.

into a computer or taken with a digital camera. The elements can be rearranged, or new elements introduced with the click of a mouse button. Plaintiffs can find themselves with a cause of action after being digitally imposed into a defamatory picture.

In *Kiesau v. Bantz*, the Iowa Supreme Court upheld a jury verdict for defamation over an altered photograph that falsely showed a deputy sheriff standing in front of her squad car with her breasts exposed.[231] Deputy Crystal Kiesau was the first female deputy in the Buchanan County Sheriff's Department. She worked with Deputy Tracey Bantz, the son-in-law of the sheriff, who was the subject of numerous complaints within the department. Bantz got a picture of Deputy Kiesau and altered it on his home computer to make it appear that Deputy Kiesau was posed with her breasts exposed. Deputy Kiesau sued for defamation as well as negligent hiring on the part of the sheriff for making his son-in-law a deputy. Kiesau won and the verdict was upheld by the Iowa Supreme Court.

Researchers are examining new methods for finding alterations in digital photographs.[232] The cutting and pasting process used to remove or replace elements leave traces, duplicated details that do not occur in nature or digital stamps that show that an image has been doctored. The pixel patterns in digital photographs also can be examined for sequences that are not naturally occurring and clone stamping provides evidence of alteration of individual photographs (Deep Fakes are treated in Chap. 6).

But almost invariably in the mass media, illustration is accompanied by words, and it is almost always the combination that carries the damaging impact. In an issue of *Tan*, a story titled "Man Hungry" was accompanied by a picture taken several years earlier in connection with a woman's work as a professional model for a dress designer. With it were the words "She had a good man—but he wasn't enough. So she picked a bad one!" On the cover of the magazine was the title, "Shameless Love." The woman sued for libel, and the court granted her claim for $3,000. "There is no doubt in this court's mind that the publication libeled plaintiff," the judge wrote. "A publication must be considered in its entirety, both the picture and the story which it illustrates."[233]

During a program broadcast in Albuquerque, N.M. over station KGGM-TV, the secretary of a Better Business Bureau was speaking about dishonest television repairmen. He held up to the camera a newspaper advertisement of the Day and Night Television Service Company. The BBB official said that some television servicemen were cheating the public:

---

[231] *Kiesau v. Bantz*, 686 N.W.2d 164 (Iowa 2004).

[232] Anick Jesdanun, "Researchers look to spot photo hoaxes," *Associated Press*, Feb. 24, 2010.

[233] *Martin v. Johnson Pub. Co.*, 157 N.Y.S.2d 409, 411 (1956). See also *Farrington v. Star Co.*, 244 N.Y. 585, 155 N.E. 906 (1927) (wrong picture); *Wasserman v. Time, Inc.*, 138 U.S.App.D.C. 7, 424 F.2d 920 (1970), certiorari denied 398 U.S. 940, 90 S.Ct. 1844 (1970).

> This is what has been referred to in the trade as the ransom. Ransom, the ransom racket. The technique of taking up the stuff after first assuring the set owner that the charges would only be nominal, and then holding the set for ransom * * *

The New Mexico Supreme Court pointed up the effect of combining the picture and the words:[234] "Standing alone, neither the advertisement nor the words used * * * could be construed as libel. But the two combined impute fraud and dishonesty to the company and its operators."

In a few states, headlines may be libelous even though modified or negated by the story that follows. A 1956 decision explains how headlines and closing "tag-lines" of a news story can be libelous (even though in this case the newspaper defended itself successfully). One story in a series published by the *Las Vegas Sun* brought a libel suit because of its headline and closing tagline advertising the next article in the series. The headline read "Babies for Sale. Franklin Black Market Trade of Child Told." The tagline promoting the story to appear the next day read "Tomorrow-Blackmail by Franklin." The body of the story told factually the way in which attorney Franklin had obtained a mother's release of her child for adoption. Franklin sued for libel and won. But the *Sun* appealed, claiming among other things that the trial judge had erred in instructing the jury that the words were libelous. The *Sun* said that the language was ambiguous, and susceptible of more than one interpretation.

But the Nevada Supreme Court[235] said that the headline and tagline were indeed libelous. Under any reasonable definition, it said, "black market sale" and "blackmail" "would tend to lower the subject in the estimation of the community and to excite derogatory opinions against him and hold him up to contempt."

But in the majority of jurisdictions, headlines and cutlines must be read in the context of the entire article and a headline that defames may be rehabilitated by explanatory or correcting copy. Does this mean that a publisher can defame with impunity in a headline as long as she explains away the defamatory statement somewhere in the body of the story? The West Virginia Supreme Court, faced a case involving outsize headlines that were clearly defamatory but not necessarily supported by the text of the stories they ran with. In *Sprouse v. Clay Communication, Inc.*,[236] an unsuccessful candidate for governor of West Virginia sued over a series that suggested that he had used a dummy corporation to make substantial profits in real estate. Included in the headlines were: "Pendleton Realty Bonanza By Jim Sprouse Disclosed," "More Asks Federal Probe in Sprouse's Land Grab," and "Dummy Firm Seen Proving

[234] *Young v. New Mexico Broadcasting Co.*, 60 N.M. 475, 292 P.2d 776 (1956); *Central Arizona Light & Power Co. v. Akers*, 45 Ariz. 526, 46 P.2d 126 (1935).

[235] *Las Vegas Sun, Inc. v. Franklin*, 74 Nev. 282, 329 P.2d 867 (1958). The *Sun* won the appeal on other grounds.

[236] *Sprouse v. Clay Communication, Inc.*, 158 W.Va. 427, 211 S.E.2d 674 (1975).

Corruption." The court noted the extraordinary size of the headlines in deciding the issue of whether the headlines should be judged by themselves or should be taken as a whole with the texts of the stories:[237]

> Generally, where the headline is of normal size and does not lead to conclusion totally unsupported by the body of the story, both headlines and story should be considered together for their total impression. However where outsized headlines are published which reasonably lead the average reader to an entirely different conclusion than the facts recited in the story, and where the plaintiff can demonstrate that it was the intent of the publisher to use such misleading headlines to create a false impression on the normal reader, the headlines may be considered separately with regard to whether a known falsehood was published.

In terms of Internet publishing, the lessons to be learned from this section are especially important. Because the Internet appears anywhere a user accesses a page, newsgroup or email, it can be easy for a plaintiff to find that she has been defamed in a jurisdiction that allows consideration only of headlines. Further, the type of "headline" used in the Internet communication may have the same effect as the oversize and clearly defamatory headlines found in *Sprouse*.

Broadcasters also must take care in preparing teases and promos. Promos, in and of themselves, may be considered to constitute a separate publication from the actual newscast or story. Therefore, a sexy promo which hypes a story that later proves to be more conservative may have the effect of landing the broadcaster in court. Teases, which precede the story and are separated by introductions of other stories and commercial breaks, can be problematic as well. Prof. Rodney Smolla notes in his work, *The Law of Defamation*, that the tease in a *60 Minutes* report on U.S. involvement in Vietnam was one of the strongest negative statements at issue. In the tease, reporter Mike Wallace told the viewing audience that CBS would present evidence of what it had come to believe was a "conspiracy" of U.S. military intelligence to conceal the strength of enemy troops in Vietnam.

21. ACTUAL INJURY

The fourth element that needs to be pleaded by a plaintiff in a libel suit: "actual injury." The private-person plaintiff must demonstrate loss or reputational injury of some kind. Actual injury may include a showing in court of out-of-pocket money loss, of impairment of reputation and standing in the community, of personal humiliation, and of mental anguish

---

[237] Ibid. at 441, 686.

and suffering, as the Supreme Court of the United States said in *Gertz v. Robert Welch, Inc.*[238]

Before publishing, broadcasting, making movies, writing novels or going online, students need to realize how many zeroes juries can put in a damage award. The *Wall Street Journal* was hit with a libel award of $222.7 million, the largest libel award on record. Dow Jones, the publisher of the *Journal,* appealed the award and the court reduced it by $200 million, roughly the amount of the punitive damages. That still left $22.7 million in actual damages and a personal punitive damage award of $20,000 against a *Wall Street Journal* reporter. That remaining judgment was later overturned in its entirety because of misconduct on the part of the plaintiffs during discovery. Barricade Books, a New York publisher, faced closure after losing a defamation suit that carried a $3 million award. Barricade published a biography of casino owner Steve Wynn, *"Running Scared: The Life and Treacherous Times of Las Vegas Casino King Steve Wynn."* Barricade had published a catalog and the description of the book included a reference to "why a confidential Scotland Yard report calls Wynn a front man for the Genovese crime family." Barricade could not post an appeal bond in order to challenge the decision. The publisher chose not to obtain libel insurance because of the cost, estimated by Barricade owner Lyle Stuart to range from $25,000 to $100,000.[239]

Courts and statutes are not entirely consistent in their labeling of the kinds of damages that may be awarded to a person who is libeled. Generally, however, three bases exist for compensating the injured person.

The first is that injuring reputation or causing humiliation ought to be recognized as real injury, even though it is impossible to make a scale of values and fix exact amounts due the injured for various kinds of slurs. If such injury is proved, "general" or "compensatory" damages are awarded.

There is also harm of a more definable kind—actual pecuniary loss that a person may suffer as a result of a libel. It may be the loss of a contract or of a job, and if it can be shown that the loss is associated with the libel, the defamed may recover "special" damages—the cost to him. It is plain, however, that some states use the term "actual damages" to cover both pecuniary loss and damaged reputations. Thus it was held in *Miami Herald Pub. Co. v. Brown*:[240]

In addition to Massachusetts, the Oregon Supreme Court has held that punitive damages are not permitted. Damages are limited to

---

[238] *Gertz v. Robert Welch, Inc.*, 418 U.S. 323, 348–350, 94 S.Ct. 2997, 3011–3012 (1974).

[239] Doreen Carvajal, "Defamation Suit Leaves Small Publisher Near Extinction," *New York Times*, Oct. 8, 1997.

[240] *Miami Herald Pub. Co. v. Brown*, 66 So.2d 679, 680 (Fla.1953). See, also, *Ellis v. Brockton Pub. Co.*, 198 Mass. 538, 84 N.E. 1018 (1908); *Osborn v. Leach*, 135 N.C. 628, 47 S.E. 811 (1904).

compensation for damage to reputation. Michigan has reached a similar conclusion.

Actual damages are compensatory damages and include (1) pecuniary loss, direct or indirect, or special damages; (2) damages for physical pain and inconvenience; (3) damages for proven mental suffering; and (4) damages for injury to reputation.

The third basis for awarding damages is public policy—that persons who maliciously libel others ought to be punished for the harm they cause. Damages above and beyond general and actual damages may be awarded in this case and are called punitive or exemplary damages. Some states deny punitive damages, having decided long ago that they are not justified. For more than a century, Massachusetts, for example, has rejected punitive damages, under a statement by the famed Oliver Wendell Holmes, Jr., then judge of the Massachusetts high court:[241]

> "The damages are measured in all cases by the injury caused. Vindictive or punitive damages are never allowed in this State. Therefore, any amount of malevolence on the defendant's part in and of itself would not enhance the amount the plaintiff recovered by a penny * * *."

The Supreme Court has laid down some rules regarding punitive damages. In *Gertz v. Robert Welch, Inc.*,[242] the Court acknowledged that the states have a "strong and legitimate * * * interest in compensating private individuals for injury to reputation," but compensation may not be limitless. A private plaintiff proving negligence can collect only "compensation for actual injury," otherwise known as "compensatory" or "general" damages.[243] To collect punitive damages, private persons (like public officials or public figures) have to prove "actual malice" rather than mere negligence. It found that awarding presumed damages ("compensatory" or "general" damages) or punitive damages where there is no demonstrated loss, "unnecessarily compounds the potential of any system of liability for defamatory falsehood to inhibit the vigorous exercise of First Amendment freedoms."[244]

Precisely what the Court meant by the permitted "compensation for actual injury" was not spelled out, but Justice Powell made it plain that he was not speaking strictly of compensation for proved dollar losses flowing from defamation:[245]

> We need not define "actual injury," as trial courts have wide experience in framing appropriate jury instructions in tort action. Suffice it to say that actual injury is not limited to out-of-pocket loss. Indeed, the more customary types of actual harm

241 *Burt v. Advertiser Newspaper Co.*, 154 Mass. 238, 245, 28 N.E. 1, 5 (1891).

242 *Gertz v. Robert Welch, Inc.*, 418 U.S. 323, 348, 94 S.Ct. 2997, 3011 (1974).

243 Ibid.

244 Ibid. at 348–351, 3011–3012.

245 Ibid. at 349–350, 94 S.Ct. At 3011, 3012.

> inflicted by defamatory falsehood include impairment of reputation and standing in the community, personal humiliation, and mental anguish and suffering. * * * all awards must be supported by competent evidence concerning the injury, although there need be no evidence which assigns an actual dollar value to the injury.

Huge amounts in damages are often claimed, and sometimes awarded although juries' judgments in the multimillion-dollar range are most often reduced by trial judges or by appeals courts. A jury awarded an Oberlin, Ohio, grocery more than $44 million in a libel case against Oberlin College.[246] The case in 2016 began after an Oberlin College student was caught trying to steal a bottle of wine from Gibson's Bakery, a small grocery. A grocery employee chased the student, who is black, outside and got into an altercation with two other Oberlin students, who are black. The three students were arrested and pled guilty to criminal charges in 2017.[247]

> Despite the students' admissions of guilt, campus racial grievance groups were not satisfied. Student groups accused Gibson's of having racially profiled the three students and pushed Oberlin to sever all ties with the bakery, which had supplied its cafeterias with food.
>
> Soon, the Oberlin Student Senate passed a resolution stating Gibson's "had a history of racial profiling and discriminatory treatment." Dean of Students Meredith Raimondo joined the demonstrations, using a bullhorn to shout that the Gibsons were "racist."

The college stopped doing business with Gibson's Bakery. The Gibson family sued alleging libel and intentional infliction of emotional distress. The jury verdict, which has since been reduced by the judge in the case, was $11.2 million in compensatory damages and $33 million in punitive damages. Ohio has a cap on punitive damages of $22 million.

A California court jury in 1981 awarded $1.6 million to comedienne Carol Burnett, who was falsely portrayed by the *National Enquirer*, said the judge in the case, as "drunk, rude, uncaring and abusive" in the Rive Gauche restaurant, Los Angeles.[248] The judge disagreed with the jury only in the amount of damages, which he cut in half to $50,000 compensatory plus $750,000 punitive, and the punitive total was cut to $150,000 by the California Court of Appeal more than two years after the jury trial.[249]

---

[246] Christian Schneider, "Family-owned grocery store smeared by Oberlin College just got $33 million in punitive damages," *The College Fix*, June 13, 2019.

[247] Ibid.

[248] *Burnett v. National Enquirer* (Cal.Super.Ct.1981), 7 Med.L.Rptr. 1321, 1323.

[249] *Burnett v. National Enquirer, Inc.*, 144 Cal.App.3d 991, 193 Cal.Rptr. 206 (1983), 9 Med.L.Rptr. 1921, appeal dismissed 465 U.S. 1014, 104 S.Ct. 1260 (1984).

"Miss Wyoming" of 1978, Kimerli Jayne Pring, won a jury award of $25 million in punitive damages plus $1.5 million in compensatory damages from *Penthouse* magazine in 1981. She alleged that a *Penthouse* humorous piece of fiction falsely implied that she was sexually promiscuous and immoral. The staggering punitive award was quickly halved by Federal District Court Judge Clarence C. Brimmer, *Penthouse* appealed the enormous remainder, and after another year reversed the judgment clearing it of liability: the article could be reasonably understood by readers as only a "pure fantasy," not as defamation of Pring.[250] That meant the magazine would only have to deal with the costs of defending itself and appealing the case.

But even when reduced, an award of a million dollars is still a million dollars that a company or its insurance carrier must pay. In at least one case, a libel judgment drove one family from the newspaper business. The *Alton Telegraph* lost a $9.2 million judgment in 1980 in an Illinois court over a memo sent by two reporters to a Justice Department task force on crime.[251] The memo dealt with a realtor who learned of the memo some time later. The paper filed for bankruptcy protection (the judgment exceeded the net worth of the paper) pending the conclusion of the appeals process. During the appeal, the paper and the plaintiff settled the case for a reported $1.4 million. After that the family that had owned the paper sold it to a media chain.

It should be noted, though, that the numbers of victories and losses do not include many cases that are settled rather than tried. In the three most recent cases in which one of this textbook's authors participated, the media defendant settled for amounts in the six-figure range. Additionally, many cases do not make it to trial because the media defendant has won by summary judgment.

What are some of the things that give rise to these less frequent but still staggering libel awards? Studies point to three significant factors: (1) a sympathetic plaintiff; (2) an unsympathetic defendant; and, (3) jurors' perceptions about the nature of big media entities. Abrasive lawyers add to the mix.

A study of libel cases written by Thomas B. Kelley for the Practising Law Institute considered these and other factors in which juries awarded large amounts to plaintiffs, amounts that appeared to be disproportionate to the evidence regarding the plaintiff's actual injuries. The plaintiff was a significant factor. In the cases studied, the plaintiffs were people who had enjoyed the respect of the community and whose career was based on public trust. Juries could categorize the plaintiff as

---

[250] *Pring v. Penthouse Intern., Ltd.*, 695 F.2d 438 (10th Cir.1982), 8 Med.L.Rptr. 2409.

[251] The memo alleged that the building contractor was involved in organized criminal activity. It was originally given to the Justice Department. The memo found its way into the hands of banking regulators and a local bank which then began its own investigation of the contractor who found it difficult to get financing. The contractor found out that the memo had caused his problems and sued the newspaper.

a person of integrity who stood for the truth and justice. Because the nature of news means that so many stories involve persons in public office or who occupy positions of public trust, professional communicators need to exercise due care.

While juries were finding the plaintiff to be deserving of their sympathy, the media defendants were found to be the opposite. Juries saw media defendants as smug, arrogant and incompetent. In his analysis of about First Amendment cases for the Practising Law Institute, James J. Brosnahan wrote "Many jurors probably have a healthy skepticism about the accuracy of what is published and may have a fixed opinion about the defendant newspaper." Other commentators have pointed to behaviors that jurors find disturbing and that help them reach overly large damage awards. Included in the laundry list are the use of leading questions during interviews, an apparent attempt to get a source to make damaging statements, a failure to contact obvious and available sources, the emotional involvement of the reporter in the story or regarding the plaintiff, and reliance on sources who are clearly not credible or bear a grudge against the plaintiff.

The *Houston Chronicle* interviewed jurors in the original $222.7 million libel award against the *Wall Street Journal* over its reporting on the activities of MMAR, a Houston securities firm. The newspaper talked with three of the seven members of the jury. They told the newspaper that the damage figure was based on the worth of the *Journal's* parent company, Dow Jones. Evidence at the trial set Dow Jones' worth at between $2 billion to $3 billion. The jurors said that a damage award that amounted to 10 percent of the company's worth would be a warning but not cripple the company.

The *Journal* reported that Money Management Analytical Research Group was reckless with clients' money, had acted in a fraudulent manner on some occasions and was living high on the hog. MMAR was a firm that had grown by dealing in securities that traditional Wall Street bond firms avoided. Jurors said that they started the case with substantial confidence in the *Journal*. They also said that they valued the role that the media play. "We depend on the media as our protectors of the First Amendment," juror Mike Johnson was quoted by the *Chronicle*. But the jury found that the *Journal*'s reporting included eight false and defamatory statements. Sources for the story testified that the *Journal* reporter misquoted them. A juror recalled that one source for the *Journal* article denied ever talking to the reporter. The evidence showed that the reporter also failed to read some key documents that would have shown that one of the most damaging statements in the story was not true.[252] "We wanted to punish them for betraying a trust," Johnson was quoted as saying.

[252] Deborah Tedford, "Jurors Hope Libel Award Will Scream a Message," *The Houston Chronicle*, March 27, 1997.

It turns out that the *Journal* had not betrayed that trust. Subsequent revelations showed that MMAR had concealed evidence that it had, in fact, engaged in the sorts of behavior that the *Journal* reported on. Still, it is instructive to see how the general public sees the media and the standards it would hold professional communicators to.

Getting to the particulars of damage awards, Judge Posner of the 7th Circuit said in *Douglass v. Hustler Magazine*,[253] "[w]e have repeatedly emphasized—and take this opportunity to emphasize again—that we will not allow plaintiffs to throw themselves on the generosity of the jury; if they want damages they must prove them."

But not in all cases. In a number of jurisdictions, the courts will permit presumed damages. Presumed damages are compensatory damages for which the plaintiff need not give evidence. It is part of a doctrine of compensation that assumes that in many cases it is not possible to show the extent of the harm from a defamatory publication. The Supreme Court said in *Dun & Bradstreet v. Greenmoss Builders* that[254] " 'proof of actual damage will be impossible in a great many cases where, from the character of the defamatory words and the circumstances of the publication, it is all but certain that serious harm has resulted in fact.' " In those jurisdictions where the presumed harm doctrine is applied, the jury is told that it may presume that the plaintiff was injured as a result of the publication of the defamation. That does not mean that the plaintiff will not offer evidence of damage, only that the plaintiff can rely on the jury to assess the impact of the defamatory statement if she so chooses.

In other jurisdictions, the plaintiff must plead and prove special damages, actual pecuniary losses. This is a significant burden and many cases are disposed of early on when the plaintiff has not met his burden. Special damages apply in defamation per quod cases, those cases where the defamation is not apparent on its face, cases which rely on extrinsic facts to make the defamatory meaning apparent. Special damages are actual economic losses. These may include the loss of employment, contracts, customers, credit, and being denied accommodation at restaurants and other public houses. Social losses, including the loss of friends, is not considered a pecuniary loss unless those social losses can be tied to some monetary loss. Mental distress in and of itself is not considered sufficient as proof of pecuniary loss.

When a plaintiff comes to court, she may introduce any number of elements to show the jury the extent of the damage her reputation has suffered and which the jury will use to compute its damage award. The jury will consider a number of things, including the nature of the publication, the extent to which the defamation was believed, and her

---

[253] *Douglass v. Hustler Magazine, Inc.*, 769 F.2d 1128, 1144 (7th Cir.1985), 11 Med.L.Rptr. 2264 (Posner, J.), cert. denied, 475 U.S. 1094, 106 S.Ct. 1489 (1986).

[254] *Dun & Bradstreet, Inc. v. Greenmoss Builders, Inc.*, 472 U.S. 749, 760, 105 S.Ct. 2939, 2946 (1985).

prior good reputation. Here, less credible media outlets have an advantage. That advantage may turn into a liability later, but in this area less credibility can help.

The defendant, on the other hand, may introduce evidence to show the jury that the damages suffered by the plaintiff were not so serious. That will include evidence that the plaintiff had a bad reputation to begin with, the defendant's reason for publishing the defamatory statement and the plaintiff's ability to respond to the statement. The defendant also may introduce evidence of retraction or correction. A number of states have passed retraction statutes that require that a plaintiff first notify the media defendant of the defamation and allow the defendant to retract the statement. If the defendant does publish a retraction, the statutes will limit the damages the plaintiff can recover.

22. FAULT

The final element of libel that the aggrieved person must allege and persuasively demonstrate is "fault" on the part of the publisher or broadcaster.

Before recovery, the plaintiff must prove that the defendant was at fault in publishing the defamatory statement. There are two general levels of fault in defamation cases: negligence and actual malice. Actual malice is a term of art and means that the publisher published the defamatory statement either with knowledge that it was false or with reckless disregard of its probably falsity. Actual malice does not mean, as most people commonly understand it, that the publisher published with ill will or bad motives. It should be evident that the actual malice standard gives the media a very large benefit of the doubt; it is difficult for a public person to prove that the news organization knew something was false, for example.

Private persons—that is, people who are not classed as public officials or public figures by a court—often have to meet a lesser, easier standard of proof. They have to prove only that the defamation complained of was negligently published, or published without the "due care" that would be used by an "average person of ordinary sensibilities."[255] Some states have decided to apply a negligence standard based on the conduct of the reasonable professional in the same industry. This means that the defendant will bring evidence that his conduct conformed to the general standards of others in the profession. It can work to the advantage of the defendant who will not have his conduct gauged by the common sense of the juror, but rather by standards set in the industry and which fellow professionals and academics will testify to. One can argue that the reasonable professional standard in fact allows

[255] See *Gertz v. Robert Welch, Inc.*, 418 U.S. 323, 94 S.Ct. 2997 (1974); see also *Black's Law Dictionary*.

sloppy practices in an industry to protect the poor reporting of individual defendants.

This split approach has resulted from the Supreme Court case of *Gertz v. Robert Welch, Inc.* The Court told private people they would not have to meet the constitutional demand of proving actual malice against publishers in bringing libel suits. What, then, would be required of them? Justice Powell wrote for the majority that the states might set their own standards of liability for private people to prove, except that the Constitution would not permit states to impose "liability without fault." Powell was saying that state standards could not include an ancient rule in libel *per se*—that for those words which are damaging on their face, the law presumes injury to reputation and liability for libel by the publisher; the only question is the amount of damages that may be recovered.[256] This was the long-standing rule of "strict liability" in libel, and the Court was saying that the media must be shielded from strict liability. The standard of fault for private people to prove, Powell said, need be no more than "negligence," instead of the "actual malice" of *Sullivan*. The Powell opinion significantly returned to the states much of the jurisdiction in libel cases that had been lost to them through the sweep of *Sullivan*, even as it made it plain that there must not be a return to "automatic" liability for defamation.

And so, *Gertz*, put the burden of defining the standard of fault to be used onto the state courts:[257] "We hold that, so long as they do not impose liability without fault, the States may define for themselves the appropriate standard of liability for a publisher or broadcaster of defamatory falsehood injurious to a private individual." The result, unsurprisingly, has been to encourage lack of uniformity in libel law among the states. Note, also, that the majority in *Gertz v. Welch*—by not spelling out a lesser standard of fault—by indirection invited the states to fall back to the familiar (if squishy) concept of negligence. The dissent by Justice William O. Douglas made that point:[258]

> The standard announced today leaves the States free to "define for themselves the appropriate standard of liability for a publisher or broadcaster" in the circumstances of this case. This of course leaves the simple negligence standard as an option with the jury free to impose damages upon a finding that the publisher failed to act as "a reasonable man." With such continued erosion of First Amendment protection, I fear that it may well be the reasonable man who refrains from speaking.

---

[256] Ibid. at 346, 3010 (1974); Prosser, pp. 780–781.

[257] Ibid.

[258] Douglas dissent, 418 U.S. 323, 360, 94 S.Ct. 2997, 3017 (1974).

WHICH GUIDELINE? "REASONABLE JOURNALIST" OR "REASONABLE PERSON"?

As John B. McCrory, Robert D. Sack, and others have noted, the question arises whether the standard of conduct is going to be the traditional "reasonable man" or "reasonable person" standard of general negligence law, or whether a standard of conduct set by the media industry will be the guidepost.[259]

Both kinds of standards pose problems for media defendants. With the reasonable person standard, the non-journalists sitting on juries seem to have an inborn belief that by definition, journalists are not reasonable persons: journalists are intrusive and tell things that shouldn't be told. And if an industry standard is used—such as Justice Harlan's formulation,[260] "standards of investigation and reporting ordinarily adhered to by responsible publishers," then expert witnesses for a lawsuits two sides will no doubt disagree over what those standards properly should be. And once again, non-journalists—jurors and judges—will sit in a position to second-guess reporters, editors, and broadcasters.

COURTS AND THE SETTING OF JOURNALISTIC STANDARDS

In no part of journalism law have the courts more clearly and consistently entered the realm of setting journalistic standards than where they judge the level of "fault"—whether the fault of actual malice or the fault of negligence or gross irresponsibility. Courts examine carefully the reporting and writing process at least as much when a plaintiff is private as when he is public.

In Tennessee, the state Supreme Court decided that it was up to the jury to say whether there had been negligence in a reporter's reliance on a single police record to suggest mistakenly that a woman was an adulterer. Using the "arrest report" of the Memphis police, a *Press-Scimitar* reporter wrote a story saying that a Mrs. Nichols had been shot. The suspect was a woman who went to the Nichols home and found her own husband there with Mrs. Nichols. The story used "police said" and "police reported" in attribution, the reporter testifying that these were common terms used to indicate that a source was either a written police record or a policeman's spoken words.

Had the reporter gone to see the police record called the "offense report," he would have learned that not only was Mrs. Nichols with the suspect's husband (named Newton), but also Mr. Nichols and two neighbors. There would thus have been no suggestion that Mrs. Nichols was having an adulterous affair and had been "caught" by Mrs. Newton. Almost a month later, the newspaper printed a story correcting the

---

[259] John B. McCrory, Robert C. Bernius, Robert D. Sack, et al., "Constitutional Privilege in Libel Law" in James C. Goodale, chairman, *Communications Law 1993,* Vol. 2, pp. 322–327; Sack and Baron, op. cit., p. 344.

[260] *Curtis Pub. Co. v. Butts,* 388 U.S. 130, 87 S.Ct. 1975 (1967).

implication of the first story. But Mrs. Nichols sued for libel, and testified at trial that the article had torn up her home, children, and reputation, that the family had to move, that she had telephone calls asking how much it cost to get the newspaper to run the correcting account. A friend testified that after the initial story, people gossiped about Mrs. Nichols and "said that she was a whore."

Before the case went to the jury for decision, the trial court granted the newspaper a directed verdict: While "no fault had been shown" on the part of the reporter, the trial court said, it did note its uncertainty as to what standard of fault was required on the basis of *Gertz*. The Tennessee Court of Appeals, which reversed the trial court decision on several grounds, said that the standard of liability was "ordinary care." The case then went to the Tennessee Supreme Court, which in upholding the Court of Appeals and sending the case back for trial, laid down Tennessee's requirement upon private libel plaintiffs: negligence.[261]

In determining the issue of liability, the conduct of defendant is to be measured against what a reasonably prudent person would, or would not, have done under the same or similar circumstances. This is the ordinary negligence test that we adopt, not a "journalistic malpractice" test whereby liability is based upon a departure from supposed standards of care set by publishers themselves * * *.

In *General Products v. Meredith*, an article on wood stoves in *Better Homes and Gardens Home Plan Ideas Magazine* warned against fire danger with the use of triple-walled chimneys in certain stoves. The manufacturer (found to be "private") of one type, not subject to the hazards of creosote buildup, brought suit. The federal District Court denied part of the magazine's motion for summary judgment, saying that there was evidence of possible negligence by the reporter in his fact gathering:[262]

> * * * he relied on an earlier book and article and did not examine them directly, but drew on his general recall of their content. He did not contact the author of either source for an update, was not aware that the information in the magazine article had been repudiated by a subsequent article in another publication, and did not contact anyone in the industry on testing relevant to his subject.

A KARK-TV reporter who happened to be near the scene of police activity in a shopping center store was alerted to the fact, and a camera crew from the station was sent. The crew filmed the scene of police handcuffing two men and placing them in a squad car. The reporter questioned the police but got no comment and interviewed a store clerk from whom she received vague responses. Her story accompanying the broadcast video

[261] *Memphis Pub. Co. v. Nichols*, 569 S.W.2d 412, 418 (Tenn.1978), 4 Med.L.Rptr. 1573.

[262] *General Products Co., Inc. v. Meredith Corp.*, 526 F.Supp. 546 (E.D.Va.1981), 7 Med.L.Rptr. 2257, 2261.

called the event a "robbery attempt," and said that the two men "allegedly held a store clerk hostage." But the handcuffed men were never arrested, merely detained until police determined that the "tip" on which they acted was false and there had been no robbery attempt. In a libel trial, each plaintiff was awarded $12,500.[263]

The Arkansas Supreme Court said there was enough evidence of reporting negligence for the trial court to send that issue to the jury: a news report relying completely on information from a police scanner, without any checking, an on an eye-witness account from a reporter who didn't know the context for what she observed, was not,[264] "found to be due care as a matter of law."

An Ohio court found no negligence in another case, was there negligence in a reporter's failure to interview all eight persons arrested on drug charges, before publishing a story in which a father and son of the same name were confused. The court said that the reporter "undoubtedly could have taken additional steps to ensure the accuracy of his facts." But he had talked with several officials, with an attorney, and with neighbors of the raided house, and had listened to a tape of a news conference about the event. His[265] "procedures were well within the bounds of professionalism in the news gathering business."

Illinois' Supreme Court adopted negligence as its standard, saying recovery might be had on proof that the defendant knew the statement to be false, or "believing it to be true, lacked reasonable grounds for that belief." It added that a journalist's[266] "failure to make a reasonable investigation into the truth of the statement is obviously a relevant factor." And it quoted the Kansas Supreme Court with approval as further elaboration of what "negligence" means:[267] "* * * the lack of ordinary care either in the doing of an act or in the failure to do something. * * * The norm usually is the conduct of the reasonably careful person under the circumstances." If it is any help to the reporter, it may be noted that the word "care" is used in various courts' discussions of negligence. It is simply the "care" of the reasonably prudent person in the Arizona and Tennessee cases discussed above. And in the Illinois and Kansas cases just mentioned, the guideline is "ordinary care," while it is "reasonable care" (Washington),[268] and "due care" (Ohio).[269]

One analyst found that the use of the negligence standard demonstrated high uncertainty and severe contradictions in results, plus

[263] *KARK-TV v. Simon*, 280 Ark. 228, 656 S.W.2d 702 (1983), 10 Med.L.Rptr. 1049. The Arkansas Supreme Court reversed and remanded the case because of the trial court's error in permitting the jury to consider punitive damages, even though it granted none.

[264] Ibid. at 704, 10 Med.L.Rptr. at 1051.

[265] *Horvath v. Telegraph* (Ohio App.1982), 8 Med.L.Rptr. 1657, 1662.

[266] *Troman v. Wood*, 62 Ill.2d 184, 340 N.E.2d 292, 298–299 (1975).

[267] Ibid. at 299; *Gobin v. Globe Pub. Co.*, 216 Kan. 223, 531 P.2d 76 (1975).

[268] *Taskett v. KING Broadcasting Co.*, 86 Wash.2d 439, 445, 546 P.2d 81, 85 (1976).

[269] *Thomas H. Maloney and Sons, Inc. v. E.W. Scripps Co.*, 43 Ohio App.2d 105, 334 N.E.2d 494 (1974).

a likelihood that it produces self-censorship by media. He wrote in 1984 that the *Gertz* approach has failed.[270]

"GROSS IRRESPONSIBILITY"

In New York, the fault of negligence is not serious enough for a private individual to maintain a libel suit. The New York Court of Appeals has specified that, where the subject matter is of public concern, recovery for the private individual depends on his establishing[271] "that the publisher acted in a grossly irresponsible manner without due consideration for the standards of information gathering and dissemination ordinarily followed by responsible parties." The *Utica Observer-Dispatch* had reported two different episodes involving drug-charge arrests in a single story. At one point, it incorrectly brought together school teacher Chapadeau and two other men at a drug-and-beer party, referring to "the trio." Chapadeau was not there, and he brought a libel action. The Court of Appeals noted the error but also pointed out that the story was written only after two authoritative agencies had been consulted, and that the story was checked by two desk hands at the newspaper. "This is hardly indicative of gross irresponsibility," said the court.[272] "Rather it appears that the publisher exercised reasonable methods to ensure accuracy." Summary judgment for the newspaper was upheld. It was denied, however, where a television reporter who had broadcast an account of fraudulent practices concerning burial expenses could recall little or nothing about his sources and how he obtained the information, and made little or no effort to authenticate his report.[273] The appeals court said that a jury would have to decide whether that was gross irresponsibility.

Litigation Note: *If a case goes to trial, the plaintiff's attorney will focus on the conduct of the media defendant in allowing the defamatory statement to be published. The attorney will ask the reporter the steps he took in gathering the information. No matter how careful the reporter, the plaintiff's attorney will point to "that one last call that would have let the reporter know that the story was wrong." The plaintiff's attorney will present witnesses who will testify that they would have told the reporter that vital piece of information, "if he had only asked." A good plaintiff's attorney will create a time line to show the jury that the reporter spent days or weeks working on his investigation, but called the defendant for a*

---

[270] Marc Franklin, "What Does Negligence Mean in Defamation Cases?", 6 *Hastings Comm/Ent* 259 (Winter, 1984), and see pp. 266–271 of the article for an excellent analysis of journalistic practices as examined by courts under the negligence standard.

[271] *Chapadeau v. Utica Observer-Dispatch, Inc.*, 38 N.Y.2d 196, 379 N.Y.S.2d 61, 64, 341 N.E.2d 569, 571 (1975). The similarity to U.S. Supreme Court Justice Harlan's recommended standard for public figures to meet, in *Curtis Pub. Co. v. Butts*, 388 U.S. 130, 87 S.Ct. 1975 (1967), above, p. 117, is too striking to avoid a connection.

[272] Ibid. at 65, 341 N.E.2d at 572. See also *Goldman v. New York Post Corp.*, 58 A.D.2d 769, 396 N.Y.S.2d 399 (1977).

[273] *Meadows v. Taft Broadcasting Co., Inc.*, 98 A.D.2d 959, 470 N.Y.S.2d 205 (1983), 10 Med.L.Rptr. 1363.

response only a day before publication. At each stage of the way, the plaintiff's attorney will be sending a message to the jury, asking in effect: "would you have done such a poor job and ruined my client's reputation?" The answer will be a "no." And since jurors will think of themselves as reasonably prudent people, the plaintiff's attorney will be building his case that the defendant failed to live up to that reasonable standard of conduct. In those jurisdictions that use the reasonable professional standard, the plaintiff's attorney will look for experts to lay out standards of conduct that the defendant did not meet in preparing the story. Under these circumstances, the defendant may wind up putting on a case to show the miserable state of the profession.

23. DISCOVERY

In the course of litigation, both sides have the opportunity to learn about the other side. This process, called discovery, is intended to avoid trial by ambush. More practically, it means that the parties will be able to get an idea of the strengths and weaknesses of the other side. The defendant can delve into the plaintiff's past in order to show that the plaintiff's reputation was far from pristine.

The plaintiff can go into the defendant's conduct in the course of preparing the story. That discovery can go into great detail. Every interview, every telephone call can and will be intensely scrutinized. The plaintiff's lawyer will even look to the editorial process and what the publisher was thinking while preparing to publish.

In one of the most celebrated media cases of the 1970s, Barry Lando and Mike Wallace of CBS' *60 Minutes* refused to answer questions in discovery proceedings that sought to probe their "state of mind" in preparing a segment on one Col. Anthony Herbert. Herbert, a public figure (the public figure issue is discussed in Chap. 5), was suing for words in the broadcast which, he said, portrayed him as a liar in his accusations that his superiors covered up reports of Vietnam War crimes. He was seeking evidence of actual malice on the part of Lando and Wallace. Confronted in discovery proceedings that lasted a year and produced almost 3,000 pages of Lando's testimony alone, Lando refused to respond when it came to inquiries into his state of mind in editing and producing the program, and into the editorial process in general. He said this was a realm of journalistic work that must not be intruded upon for fear of its chilling effect on expression protected by the First Amendment.

While the Court of Appeals, Second Circuit, held on a 2–1 vote that First Amendment interests warranted an absolute evidentiary privilege for Lando, the U.S. Supreme Court reversed, saying that the First Amendment does not prohibit plaintiffs from directly inquiring into the editorial processes of those whom they accuse of defamation.[274]

[274] *Herbert v. Lando*, 441 U.S. 153, 99 S.Ct. 1635 (1979), 4 Med.L.Rptr. 2575.

Journalists in libel cases had been testifying as to their motives, discussions, and thoughts relating to their copy, for a century and more before *Times v. Sullivan* without objecting to the process, said Justice White in writing the majority opinion; and *Times v. Sullivan* "made it essential to proving liability that plaintiffs focus on the conduct and state of mind of the defendant." He elaborated:[275]

> To be liable, the alleged defamer of public officials or of public figures must know or have reason to suspect that his publication is false. In other cases proof of some kind of fault, negligence perhaps, is essential to recovery. Inevitably, unless liability is to be completely foreclosed, the thoughts and editorial processes of the alleged defamer would be open to examination.

A few newspaper editorials and media voices recognized that the *Herbert* decision had broken no new ground and presented no fresh menace to the First Amendment, but attacks on the Supreme Court were far more common as media took the view that the justices had violated the integrity of the "editorial process" and the First Amendment.[276] Alarmed reactions of shock over presumed new damage by the Court to the First Amendment were often without understanding that what the Court was finding was in line with what lower courts had found for decades or for a century. In general, press reactions spoke eloquently to journalists' superficial education in the history of press freedom, and to their necessary occupational fix upon the world's current "hot scoop," unalloyed by knowledge of the history in which their own First Amendment roots were embedded.

Discovery in libel had arrived to stay, the *Herbert* case confirming its applicability. Said one media attorney at the time:[277] "While there was an outcry from some representatives of the press at the time, it now seems unlikely that the opinion will have any dramatic effect. Before *Herbert* journalists had routinely testified about the editorial process in establishing their freedom from 'actual malice' or 'fault.' As a result of *Herbert*, they will continue to do so."

A federal judge opened up the discovery process even further in a 1997 libel case against *Time Magazine* that predated the "fake news" meme of recent years.[278] Richard Ellis, a former Moscow photographer for Reuters sued *Time*, claiming that the magazine had gotten him fired for exposing faked photographs in the magazine. Ellis said that *Time* had a policy and practice of using false or doctored pictures and that *Time* had libeled him in a letter and story to keep him from exposing the practice.

---

[275] Ibid. at 160, 1641, 2578.

[276] *Editorials on File*, April 16–30, 1979, pp. 437–446.

[277] Robert D. Sack, "Special Discovery Problems in Media Cases," *Communications Law 1980*, I, 235, 242 (Practising Law Institute 1980).

[278] Iver Peterson, "Court Broadens Scrutiny in Time Libel Case," *New York Times*, April 28, 1997.

The controversy arose over the publication of a number of pictures purporting to show prostitution in Moscow. Ellis suggested that the photos were faked because they showed crimes being committed in the light of day with the people pictured unconcerned about being photographed. Ellis contacted one of the people pictured, a Russian pimp, and talked about the photos. The pimp contacted *Time* and offered them a recording which allegedly contained a promise from Ellis to the pimp of money from *Time* if he were to say the photos were faked. Ellis finally posted a statement on Compuserve calling the photos fakes. *Time* published a letter to its readers accusing Ellis of trying to bribe the Russian pimp. It was on the basis of that letter that Ellis filed his suit. U.S. Magistrate Patrick Attridge ordered *Time* to comply with discovery and disclose the editors' states of mind in the publication of the Moscow prostitution pictures.

The inquiry did not end there. Judge Attridge's order also required that *Time*'s editors also reveal the decisions that led to the publication of a computer-altered photograph of O.J. Simpson and a photograph of a frowning Bill Clinton where the photo used was not related to the headline on the cover. The order went so far as to include "instances of other deceptive photographs at *Time* involving one or all of the persons" in the Moscow pictures. The sweep of the discovery order went far beyond the traditional libel inquiry, which would normally go only to the editorial process involved in the allegedly libelous publication. In addition, the discovery covered publication decisions made at dates later than the first allegedly faked photos.

Because the discovery process can be so intrusive, sensible journalists (or public relations or advertising people who get involved in litigation) should always conduct themselves carefully. Self-protective reporters have long understood that their story notes (or tape recordings, or video out-takes) may be subpoenaed as part of the discovery process in litigation. If you and your newspaper are being sued for libel by a mayor, do you want to explain to a jury the doodles you've sketched on your note pad? What if you've drawn a passable likeness of the mayor but added fangs? But even if you have embarrassing materials in your notes or in video out takes, do *not* destroy any materials relating to litigation once "the papers have been filed" to start a legal action. Don't destroy such materials while there is still any possibility of an appeal or further proceedings. If you do, the court may assume that destruction of materials subject to discovery is evidence of actual malice or may be punishable as contempt of court.

Remember the case of *Brown & Williamson Tobacco Corp. v. Jacobson*?[279] In 1981, Jacobson had delivered a "Perspective" report denouncing the makers of Viceroy cigarettes for hiring advertising "slicksters" to create an advertising strategy to "hook" the young. The

[279] *Brown & Williamson Tobacco Corp. v. Jacobson*, 827 F.2d 1119, 1123 (7th Cir.1987).

strategy used by Brown & Williamson, Jacobson said, was taken from a report recommending that smoking be portrayed to youth as a kind of rite of passage involving wearing a bra or shaving or drinking wine or beer. The broadcast added up to an accusation of unethical youth-oriented advertising by Brown & Williamson for its Viceroy cigarettes, thus endangering the health of the impressionable young.[280]

The report was said to be based on a "confidential report in the files of the federal government." Such a report did exist in the files of the Federal Trade Commission (FTC); it had been prepared by a research firm working for Ted Bates & Co., an ad agency once employed by Viceroy Cigarettes' parent company, Brown & Williamson. At one point, a *confidential* FTC report had assumed, apparently erroneously, that Viceroy had adopted a "hook the young" ad strategy. A researcher for the CBS station—Michael Radutzky—had learned of the FTC report from a newspaper article, and even received copies of some pages of that report. However, Radutzky couldn't persuade FTC staffers to send him copies of the confidential report; the staffers would only "confirm that the report and its findings were accurate."

The FTC's ambiguous response to Radutzky, however, was contradicted directly by a Thomas Humber, a spokesman for Brown & Williamson. Humber told Radutzky that Brown & Williamson had rejected the strategy suggested in documents submitted by the Ted Bates ad agency. Humber stated [to Radutzky, according to Humber's notes] that the proposals referred to in the FTC report were similar to a proposed libelous story that a young inexperienced reporter might submit to his editors but that it was corrected by a news organization's editors and attorneys. Humber stated that in such a case no legitimate criticism could be leveled at the news organization.

In response to a request from Jacobson, researcher Radutzky had searched unsuccessfully for "pot, wine, beer and sex" ads for Viceroy cigarettes. Radutzky had made lengthy notes as he conducted interviews and read those pages of the FTC report provided to him by a newspaper reporter. Radutzky also made handwritten entries on the margins of the FTC report pages he had, and also developed an 18-page sample script.

The jury, however, never saw this work by Radutzky. Before the trial, Radutzky[281] "destroyed all of his contemporaneous interview notes, five of the ten pages of the FTC report * * * and fifteen of the original eighteen pages of the sample script."

Radutzky testified that he had destroyed those materials while "housecleaning" after a district court had dismissed an original *Brown & Williamson* libel complaint. The lawsuit, however, was later reinstated and, as the Court of Appeals noted, the destruction of materials violated

[280] Cert. den, 485 U.S. 993, 108 S.Ct. 1302 (1988), upholding the judgment of the United States Court of Appeals, Seventh Circuit. See 827 F.2d 1119 (7th Cir.1987) 14 Med.L.Rptr. 1497.

[281] Ibid.; see Stuart Taylor, Jr., "Justices Uphold $3 million Libel Award on CBS," *New York Times*, April 4, 1988.

CBS policy. The Court of Appeals concluded that Brown & Williamson had proved[282]

> "by clear and convincing evidence that the defendants either knew the Perspective [Jacobson's commentary] was false or in fact entertained serious doubts as to its truth," thus allowing the district court jury's verdict against the TV station to stand. Furthermore, "[t]he most compelling evidence of actual malice submitted to the jury was the intentional destruction of critical documents by Jacobson's researcher* * *"

An important lesson to be learned from this case is that publishers and broadcasters need to develop clear policies about preparation of news or commentary reports. In any event, once a legal proceeding has started—and until it has concluded, beyond possibility of re-filing or appeal—notes, memos, tapes, or videotapes may not be destroyed safely.

It does not require the actual filing of a lawsuit to require a media entity to preserve records. A threat of suit or a reasonable expectation of suit should make destruction of materials inadvisable.

Although the primary focus in this section has been on discovery of defendants, there are important considerations for the plaintiff as well. Consider the *MMAR* case in which the Houston bond firm that sued the *Wall Street Journal* over an article that MMAR claimed forced it out of business.

The article focused on the high-risk aspects of MMAR's business and its business practices. One passage from the article said that,[283] "Among traders, MMAR'S style and lineage earned it the nickname 'Make Money and Run.' " One of MMAR's largest clients was the Louisiana Employees Retirement System, known as LASER. LASER later sued MMAR over its conduct and settled the case for $2.7 million.

MMAR sued over eight statements in the *Wall Street Journal* article. The jury found that five of the statements were false and defamatory. One dealt with the firm's spending habits.[284] "In one year, the firm ran up $2 million in limousine bills, according to Raphael Grinburg, a former employee who used to monitor travel expenses for the firm."

But perhaps the most damning statement dealt with MMAR's conduct in the sale of IOs, securities that represented the interest-only portion of mortgage payments. Buyers of these securities would make money as mortgages were paid. But, in 1992, homeowners started prepaying their mortgages and that meant a decline in mortgage interest.[285] "For a time, MMAR hid the portfolio's losses by mismarking

[282] Ibid.

[283] Laura Jereski, "Regulators Study Texas Securities Firm and Its Louisiana Pension Fund Trades," *The Wall Street Journal*, Oct. 21, 1993.

[284] Ibid.

[285] Ibid.

the IOs by three points or more, equal to as much as 10% of the bonds' market value, according to one former salesman."

MMAR went out of business shortly after the article came out and the court noted the probable impact of the statement about the misrepresentation. "Not every statement found by the jury to have been false and defamatory, however, could plausibly explain the sudden demise and failure of MMAR as a business entity within one month after the Article was published. For example, another of the five statements[286] found by the jury to be libelous—that in one year MMAR 'ran up $2 million in limousine bills'—may have led the reader to view the company as one that was foolishly self-indulgent and profligate with its own property. But this is quite different than the mismarking statement, which assails the basic integrity and fidelity of MMAR in handling its customer's property."

But, it turns out that MMAR had an extensive taping system and had recorded numerous conversations, including conversations that bore directly on the allegedly libelous statements published by the *Wall Street Journal*. In fact, the tape recordings supported the truth of the *Wall Street Journal* story.

In one tape recording, two company officials discussed a request by the National Association of Securities Dealers to interview the head of MMAR's trading desk.[287]

> "Forrester asked what did MMAR do, 'except for mispricing?' Dobson responded that that was 'pretty major.' Equally damning inferences regarding MMAR's mispricing of IOs may be drawn from another tape recorded conversation between MMAR principal Paul Brown and MMAR's salesman Richard Evans. In this July, 1992, conversation, in which the price of IOs owned by LASERS was discussed, Mr. Brown asked if Mr. Evans was 'on market.' Mr. Evans replied that he was not yet on market, but would be in 'like three months.' Further dialogue between these two revealed that the securities were priced 'down to around 31 right now,' but that they 'did go 26-and-a-half.' A reasonable inference is that the securities were at that time mispriced or mismarked by four and one-half points, or about 17 percent above what Mr. Evans knew the market to be. Such evidence would have been highly relevant to Dow Jones's defense that the mismarking statement was truthful."

The existence of the tapes came to light when William Fincher, a former MMAR employee, contacted Dow Jones in 1988. He revealed that MMAR had a taping system and that he had been ordered to review the tapes while still an employee. Fincher said he had been pressured to erase certain tapes. He said he made copies of dozens of tapes.

---

[286] *MMAR Group, Inc. v. Dow Jones & Co., Inc.*, 187 F.R.D. 282, 386 (S.D.Tex.1999).

[287] Ibid. at 286–287.

None of the tapes Fincher had reviewed had been made available during discovery. Dow Jones filed a motion for new trial and for modification of the judgment based on the information that Fincher provided. On April 8, 1999, the district court granted Dow Jones' motion saying,[288] "From clear and convincing evidence the Court finds that MMAR obtained its favorable verdict through its own misconduct and misrepresentations; that MMAR's misrepresentations and other misconduct did prevent Defendants from fully and fairly presenting their defense; and that MMAR's verdict was unfairly obtained."

Fincher did not see the outcome of the motion. After contacting Dow Jones, but before his deposition could be taken in the case, he was killed in a private plane crash in Belize.[289] The lesson here is that plaintiffs, as well as media defendants must comply with the rules and intent of discovery, written to ensure that cases are decided on the whole story.

NBC'S "DATELINE" AND THE PICKUP TRUCK FIRE RISK DEBACLE

NBC discovered the hazards of diligent discovery and the effective use of public relations in litigation. It also provided a lesson in what happens when a media defendant does not stand by its reporters or aggressively pursue discovery itself.

A November 17, 1992 *Dateline NBC* television program ran a story about a design problem with GM pickup trucks. GM full-size pickup trucks made with side-mounted gasoline tanks from 1973 to 1987 were blamed for a number of truck fires. To illustrate the problem, NBC showed a staged accident in which a GM truck burst into flames after a side-impact crash.

After the NBC broadcast showing the staged crashes, General Motors officials told NBC News the *Dateline NBC* segment was unfair and asked to inspect the vehicles used in the crashes. The network responded that,[290] "the vehicles had been junked and were not available."

In January 1993, after discovering the identity of the company that staged the crash, GM got an injunction against the Indianapolis-based Institute for Safety Analysis, which had conducted the crash tests for NBC. The judge ordered the Institute not to destroy the vehicles used in the crash tests. The vehicles later were retrieved from a junkyard by GM.[291]

In February, 1993, after asking NBC for a retraction, GM filed a libel suit against the network, claiming the rigged tests were blatantly deceptive and caused irreparable harm, GM charged that the "crash test"

[288] Ibid. at 291.

[289] Ibid. at 286.

[290] Doron P. Levin, "In Suit, GM Accuses NBC of Rigging Crash Tests," *New York Times*, Feb. 2, 1993.

[291] Ibid.

fires had been touched off by radio transmitters which caused model rocket engines affixed to gasoline tanks to ignite.

Michael Gartner, then NBC News president, at first defended the *Dateline NBC* segment, comparing the sparking devices used in the crash tests to a heated headlight lamp filament, and declared the broadcast to be "fair and accurate."[292] But a short time later, at Gartner's direction, NBC anchors Stone Phillips and Jane Pauley apologized on *Dateline* for the rigged pickup crash tests. General Motors quickly dropped its lawsuit against NBC, and, on March 2, Gartner resigned from the presidency of NBC News, although no one had accused him of having personal knowledge of the deception.[293] Slipshod journalism has its price. As pointed out by Paul McMasters, executive director of the Freedom Forum First Amendment Center at Vanderbilt University, the crash test flap enabled GM to divert attention from the real issue: Were those pickup trucks as safe as they should be?[294]

An article in *The American Lawyer*[295] revealed some of the secrets that GM managed to keep from *Dateline*. The article dealt with the Shannon Moseley lawsuit against GM. Moseley was a 17-year-old in Georgia who died in a fiery GM pickup crash.

Moseley's parents believed GM was responsible and their attorney set out to find out what the company knew about its trucks. The lawyers, James Butler and Bob Cheeley, found a key witness who had worked for GM as a safety expert before becoming embittered about his work experiences and leaving. Ronald Elwell, a former top GM expert witness on vehicle safety, told Cheeley about some secret crash tests it had conducted on its trucks.[296]

> Perhaps most important, Elwell told Cheeley about a highly sensitive series of 22 truck crash tests that GM had staged in the early eighties but had failed to disclose to any of the more than 100 plaintiffs who had sued the company over post-collision fuel-fed truck fires. Elwell said he himself had been in the dark about the tests until September 1983. In a story Elwell would tell with great emotion on the witness stand in the Moseley trial, Alex McKeen, then the head of GM's engineering analysis division, allegedly took him aside and told him to check out the safety research and development lab at the company's 1,000-acre proving grounds in Milford, Michigan.
>
> * * *

---

[292] Adler, op.cit.

[293] Ken Auletta, "Changing Channels," *The New Yorker*, March 15, 1993, p. 38.

[294] Remarks at Region 3 Society of Professional Journalists conference, Knoxville, TN, March 6, 1993.

[295] Terence Moran, "GM Burns Itself," *The American Lawyer*, April, 1993.

[296] Ibid.

> The next time Elwell made one of his frequent visits to the proving grounds, he later testified, he took McKeen up on his suggestion. There he saw a row of pickup trucks that had been crash-tested, obviously for the purpose of exploring the performance of the outside-the-frame-rail fuel tanks. Virtually all the fuel systems had failed. ("They were very badly smashed," Elwell told the jury in Atlanta. "There were holes in them as big as melons. They were split open.")
>
> Even more damaging were Elwell's revelations about GM's conduct when plaintiffs' attorneys would seek GM records pertaining to its crash tests.[297] He brought out, for instance, that GM allegedly used a sliding scale in complying with discovery requests: For vehicles that performed well in the field, a "poundage rule" was applied, he claimed, meaning an abundance of documentation would be produced. For more vulnerable vehicles, a narrowing rule applied: Give nothing not specified in a request, down to the jot and tittle. "It was very, very constricted," Elwell said. "So that if you had to give anything, you gave only one test, or maybe you would say none [existed] because none [of the vehicles in the test] were painted red with white sidewalls [like the vehicle described in the request]."

If NBC had had more faith in its own reporters' investigation, it would have benefitted from seeing the story in *The American Lawyer*. The story came out within a month of GM's libel complaint and the revelations there would have shown that the GM threat of the libel suit was not so significant. After all, a GM expert had revealed that the company itself had demonstrated the failure of the fuel tanks.

---

[297] Ibid.

CHAPTER 5

THE CONSTITUTIONAL DEFENSE AGAINST LIBEL SUITS

24. THE PUBLIC PRINCIPLE

Media defend against libel suits on grounds of their service to the public interest.

Libel may be an old area of law, but its dangers are exceedingly real today. This chapter deals with defenses to libel both new and old. Sweeping changes in libel law since 1964 have changed not only the law of defamation but also have altered key interpretations of the Constitution of the United States.

The American Constitution was nearly two hundred years old before courts, attorneys, and journalists concluded that it ought to protect speech and press against libel actions. It was in 1964 that the Supreme Court of the United States ruled in *New York Times Co. v. Sullivan*[1] that public officials who sued for libel would have to clear a First Amendment barrier rather than the long-used lesser barriers of state laws and precedents. The emergence of multiple suits claiming formerly unheard-of amounts of damages threatened losses so high as to turn "watchdog" media into sheep. The public interest in vigorous, unintimidated reporting of the news was endangered. Society could not accept self-censorship on the part of media "chilled" by fear of libel awards. The United States Constitution itself, through the First Amendment, would provide the shield for discussion of public matters that the narrow vagaries of many state libel laws denied and that the public welfare demanded.

1 *New York Times Co. v. Sullivan*, 376 U.S. 254, 84 S.Ct. 710 (1964).

Striking as the new application of the Constitution was, it really amounted to an expansion of the "public principle" inherent in centuries-old defenses against libel suits. Defenses had grown in the context of the need of an open society for information. Society needs full discussion in media if its citizens are to participate in decisions that affect their lives, are to have the opportunity to choose, and to maintain ultimate control over government. Those who claimed harm to their reputations might find their suits unavailing if certain public concerns and values were furthered by the publication. Where the hard words were the truth, or were privileged as in news of court proceedings, or were fair criticism of performances by artists and others, the public had a real stake in receiving those words.

The First Amendment protection raised by the Supreme Court in the 1964 *Sullivan* case told public officials they would have to accept more fully the verbal rough-and-tumble of political life. Most notably, they would have to show that the news medium published the offending words with *actual malice*—knowledge of falsity, or reckless disregard for falsity.

Though there are relatively few libel suits in the area of media law, they remain at the forefront of media legal concerns. Although he has not followed through on the 15-plus suits he threatened to file during the 2016 campaign and through the first three years of his presidency, Donald Trump did sue an author over statements in a book about his net worth, a woman who filed a class action suit over practices of the now-defunct Trump University and TV host and political commentator Bill Maher over a joke he made about Trump's birth certificate. Trump lost the first two suits and settled the Maher suit. The self-censorship and "chill" that the *Sullivan* decision was intended to avert nevertheless has penetrated some newsrooms, diluting investigative reporting. Journalists, legal scholars, the American Civil Liberties Union, and others have urged strengthening of the *Sullivan* doctrine.[2] They are of course opposed by some, including Associate Justice Clarence Thomas and Donald Trump, who feel that *Sullivan* has been too protective of media.[3]

---

2 Anthony Lewis, "The Sullivan Case," *The New Yorker*, Nov. 5, 1984, 52; Marc Franklin, "Good Names and Bad Law: a Critique of Libel Law and a Proposal," 18 *Univ.S.F.L.Rev.* 1, Fall 1983; "Symposium, Defamation and the First Amendment: New Perspectives," 25 *William & Mary L.Rev.* 1983–1984, Special Issue; Michael Massing, "The Libel Chill: How Cold Is It Out There?," *Columbia Journ. Rev.*, May/June, 1985, 31; Gilbert Cranberg, "ACLU Moves to Protect All Speech on Public Issues from Libel Suits," *Civil Liberties*, Feb. 1983, 2.

3 Jan Greene, Libel Plaintiffs Organize Against Media, *1985 Report of Society of Professional Journalists*, Sigma Delta Chi, Freedom of Information '84–'85, 4; Bruce E. Fein, "New York Times v. Sullivan: an Obstacle to Enlightened Public Discourse * * *," quoted in 11 *Med.L.Rptr.* #3, 12/18/84, News Notes.

25. DEFENSE AGAINST PUBLIC OFFICIALS' SUITS

Under the doctrine of *New York Times Co. v. Sullivan*, the First Amendment broadly protects the news media from judgments for defamation of public officials.

When the Supreme Court of the United States handed down its decision in 1964, it added a great new dimension of protection to news media in the field of libel. It said that news media are not liable for defamatory words about the public acts of public officials unless the words are published with "actual malice." This defined the word "malice"[4] with a rigor and preciseness that had been lacking for centuries and in a way that gave broad protection to publication. Public officials, it said, must live with the risks of a political system in which there is "a profound national commitment to the principle that debate on public issues should be uninhibited, robust, and wide-open * * *." Even a factual error, it said, will not make one liable for libel in words about the public acts of public officials unless actual malice is present. The case was a watershed decision in that it gave publishers and speakers just enough protection from libel suits to let them question or even challenge the political power structure. As Justice Brennan wrote in his opinion for the Court:[5]

> We are required in this case to determine for the first time the extent to which the constitutional protections for speech and press limit a State's power to award damages in a libel action brought by a public official against critics of his official conduct.

New York Times Co. v. Sullivan[6] wasn't based on a news story or editorial. It stemmed from an "editorial advertisement"[7] in the *Times*, written and paid for by a group intensely involved in the struggle for equality and civil liberties for African Americans. The suit was brought by L. B. Sullivan, Commissioner of Public Affairs for the city of Montgomery, Ala. He sued the *Times* and four black clergymen who were among the 64 persons whose names were attached to the advertisement.[8] The inclusion of the four ministers guaranteed that the trial would be held in Alabama. That was because the ministers were from Alabama. If

[4] Malice, which will be defined later, is not meant in this context to mean hatred or ill will. It is a term of art in the law of mass communications.

[5] *New York Times Co. v. Sullivan*, 376 U.S. 254, 256, 84 S.Ct. 710, 713 (1964).

[6] *New York Times Co. v. Sullivan*, 376 U.S. 254, 84 S.Ct. 710 (1964).

[7] It should be noted that no matter what form of communication, all speakers, writers, filmmakers and multimedia creators share in the risks of defamation and all rely on the First Amendment for protection of their rights of expression.

[8] Realizing that parties might be at a disadvantage when facing a plaintiff in her home state, federal civil practice allows for removal to federal court, a court perceived as less vulnerable to state partisanship. If a case is removed to federal court, the federal judge applies the appropriate state's laws and precedent. But in order to go to federal court, the parties must be "diverse," that is to say that there can be no overlap of state citizenship. Each side must be from a different state than the opposing side. By including the four ministers, the plaintiffs destroyed diversity and kept the trial in state court where the state district judge would make rulings, oversee the jury selection and set the tone of the trial. Only seven states do not have judicial elections. Delaware, Hawaii, Massachusetts, New Hampshire, New Jersey, Rhode Island and Virginia.

the suit had been limited to the *Times*, a New York corporation, on one side and Sullivan, an Alabama plaintiff on the other, the case might have been removed to federal court under rules created to ensure that out-of-state parties get a fair shake. The case would still have applied Alabama libel law, but it would be a federal judge who would not have to bear public pressure that could turn lead a local judge to make rulings in a case based on popular opinion rather than the law.

The now-famous advertisement, titled "Heed Their Rising Voices," recounted the efforts of Black students to affirm their rights at Alabama State College in Montgomery and told of a "wave of terror" that met them. It invoked the name of the Reverend Martin Luther King, Jr. and his leadership in the civil rights movement:[9]

HEED THEIR RISING VOICES

> As the whole world knows by now, thousands of Southern Negro students are engaged in wide-spread, nonviolent demonstrations in positive affirmation of the right to live in human dignity as guaranteed by the U.S. Constitution and the Bill of Rights. In their effort to uphold these guarantees, they are being met by an unprecedented wave of terror by those who would deny and negate that document which the whole world looks upon as setting the pattern for modern freedom * * *.
>
> * * *
>
> In Montgomery, Alabama, after students sang "My Country, 'Tis of Thee" on the State Capitol steps, their leaders were expelled from school, and truck-loads of police armed with shotguns and tear-gas ringed the Alabama State College Campus. When the entire student body protested to state authorities by refusing to re-register, their dining hall was padlocked in an attempt to starve them into submission.
>
> * * *
>
> Again and again the Southern violators have answered Dr. King's protests with intimidation and violence. They have bombed his home almost killing his wife and child. They have assaulted his person. They have arrested him seven times—for "speeding," "loitering" and similar "offenses." And now they have charged him with "perjury"—a *felony* under which they could imprison him for *ten years*. Obviously, their real purpose is to remove him physically as the leader to whom the students and millions of others—look for guidance and support, and thereby to intimidate *all* leaders who may rise in the South * * *. The defense of Martin Luther King, spiritual leader of the

[9] *New York Times Co. v. Sullivan*, 376 U.S. 254, 84 S.Ct. 710, facing 292; see also Anthony Lewis, *Make No Law* (New York: Random House, 1991).

student sit-in movement, clearly, therefore, is an integral part of the total struggle for freedom in the South.

Sullivan, one of three elected Commissioners of the City of Montgomery, was commissioner of Public Affairs. His duties included supervision of the police department, fire department, department of cemetery and department of scales. Sullivan had not seen the advertisement when it came out. He was shown the ad in the mayor's office.[10] Sullivan was not named in the advertisement but claimed that because he supervised the Montgomery Police Department, people would identify him as the person responsible for police action at the State College campus. He said also that actions against the Rev. King would be attributed to him by association.

It was asserted by Sullivan, and not disputed, that there were errors in the advertisement. The errors were key in the outcome of the suit in Alabama state court and supreme court. Police had not "ringed" the campus although they had been there in large numbers. Students sang the National Anthem, not "My Country, 'Tis of Thee." The expulsion had not been protested by the entire student body, but by a large part of it. They had not refused to register but had boycotted classes for a day. The campus dining hall was not padlocked, and the Rev. King had only been arrested by Montgomery police two times, once for speeding and the other for "loitering" when he waited outside a courtroom to observe a case.[11]

The manager of the *Times* Advertising Acceptability Department said that he had not checked the copy for accuracy because he had no cause to believe it false, and some of the signers were well-known persons whose reputation he had no reason to question.

Because Alabama libel law required plaintiffs to seek retraction of the offending article before a libel suit could be started, Sullivan wrote to the *Times* and complained about the advertisement which, he said, imputed to him all of the actions taken by police including the "ringing of the campus," "padlocking of the dining hall," and "arresting the Rev. King seven times." In fact, three of the Rev. King's arrests took place before Sullivan became commissioner. Sullivan also wrote similar letters to the four black ministers whose names were appended to the advertisement. None of the ministers responded because they had not consented to having their names attached and so did not consider that they had published anything. The *Times'* response was to ask Sullivan what his complaint was. The letter said, "we * * * are somewhat puzzled as to how you think the statements in any way reflect on you," and "you might, if you desire, let us know in what respect you claim that the statements in the advertisement reflect on you." Sullivan then filed his suit without explaining his retraction demand. The *Times* ran a retraction of the advertisement for Alabama Gov. John Patterson who also complained,

---

10 *New York Times Co. v. Sullivan*, 273 Ala. 656, 144 So.2d 25 (Ala. 1962).

11 Ibid.

saying that the advertisement charged him with "grave misconduct and * * * improper actions and omissions as Governor of Alabama and Ex-Officio Chairman of the State Board of Education of Alabama." The *Times* later explained that it had published the retraction for Gov. Patterson because,[12] "we didn't want anything that was published by The *Times* to be a reflection on the State of Alabama and the Governor was, as far as we could see, the embodiment of the State of Alabama and the proper representative of the State and, furthermore, we had by that time learned more of the actual facts which the ad purported to recite * * *"

Even so, Gov. Patterson sued. So did three other current and former Montgomery officials. Each suit sought $500,000 in damages. Each suit named the four ministers as co-defendants. The case was straightforward under Alabama law. The jury's role, according to the judge's instructions, was only to decide if the *Times* had published the advertisement and whether the advertisement was "of and concerning" L.B. Sullivan. Judge Walter B. Jones had already ruled that the advertisement constituted libel per se (see Chap. 4).[13] "After a three-day trial, an all-white jury deliberated for two hours and 20 minutes and ruled in favor of Mr. Sullivan, awarding him $500,000 (the equivalent of nearly $4 million today).[14] In August 1962, the Alabama Supreme Court upheld the finding saying that the First Amendment did not protect libel."

The impact was profound, as Anthony Lewis noted in his book "*Make No Law*." Lewis wrote:

> Sullivan and Governor Patterson and the others were out to transform the traditional libel action, designed to repair the reputation of a private party, into a state political weapon to intimidate the press. The aim was to discourage not false but true accounts of life under a system of white supremacy:
>
> Stories about men being lynched for trying to vote, about cynical judges using the law to suppress constitutional rights, about police chiefs turning attack dogs on men and women who wanted to drink a Coke at a department-store lunch counter. It was to scare the national press—newspapers, magazines, the television networks—off the civil rights story.
>
> The *Times* appealed to the Supreme Court of the United States. In addition to procedural issues, the *Times* argued that the First Amendment should not permit a public official like Sullivan to collect damages for presumed damages for statements critical of his performance in office. Such an approach would leave open

[12] Anthony Lewis, *Make No Law*, New York: Random House, 1991, p.35.

[13] Bruce Weber, "M. Roland Nachman, Lawyer in Times v. Sullivan Libel Case, Dies at 91," *New York Times*, Dec. 4, 2015.

[14] The *Times* was in shaky financial shape at the time and the effect of the damage awards from the cases brought by Sullivan, Gov. Patterson and others which amounted to more than $3 million (more than $24 million in today's dollars) could have jeopardized its continued existence.

> the door for public officials and governments to silence their opponents by using the courts and the tool of the libel case.
>
> In the oral argument before the Supreme Court, M. Roland Nachman, Jr., the attorney for Commissioner Sullivan, and Justice White took up the matter of how careful publishers would have to be in printing stories about public officials.[15]
>
> White: But if were held here that a newspaper could publish a falsehood which it thought to be true, that would still not save the *Times* here?
>
> Nachman: You mean a reasonable belief in truth?
>
> White: Yes.
>
> Nachman: No, sir, not under Alabama law.

Alabama law, like that in most states, held publishers liable for defamatory statements. Truth could serve as a defense. But if it was wrong, if it held inaccuracies even when published in good faith, truth could not be used as a defense and that would leave publishers open to damage awards. That meant that, without a First Amendment defense, the *Times* would have to pay all the libel judgments. The effect would be to stop the *Times* and every other news organization covering the civil rights movement. Beyond that, every publisher would have to stop coverage of public officials for fear that some story would contain an error and result in a costly defamation suit.

The Supreme Court saw such libel actions as threatening freedom of expression, especially as it related to comments about government and reversed the decision. It held that the Alabama rule of law was "constitutionally deficient for failure to provide the safeguards for freedom of speech and of the press that are required by the First and Fourteenth Amendments * * *."

One issue raised by Sullivan's lawyers and the Alabama Supreme Court was the fact the statements were published came in an advertisement. Sullivan had argued, and the Alabama Supreme Court agreed, that advertisements did not deserve the First Amendment protection sought by the *Times*. Justice Brennan disagreed, saying that the advertisement:[16]

> * * * communicated information, expressed opinion, recited grievances, protested claimed abuses, and sought financial support on behalf of a movement whose existence and objectives are matters of the highest public concern * * * That the *Times* was paid for publishing the advertisement is as immaterial in this connection as is the fact that newspapers and books are sold * * * Any other conclusion would discourage newspapers from

---

[15] Peter Irons, editor, *May It Please The Court The First Amendment,* (New York, The New Press, 1997), at 176.

[16] *New York Times Co. v. Sullivan,* 376 U.S. 254, 266, 84 S.Ct. 718 (1964).

> carrying "editorial advertisements" of this type, and so might shut off an important outlet for the promulgation of information and ideas by persons who do not themselves have access to publishing facilities—who wish to exercise their freedom of speech even though they are not members of the press. The effect would be to shackle the First Amendment * * *

Justice Brennan's opinion recognized the unsettled times and divisive issues, including civil rights, facing the nation in the period. But, he wrote, the *Times* case was a part of the country's commitment to free expression.[17] "The constitutional safeguard, we have said, 'was fashioned to assure unfettered interchange of ideas for the bringing about of political and social changes desired by the people.' *Roth v. United States*, 354 U.S. 476, 484, 77 S.Ct. 1304, 1308."

Change does not come easily. Consider the fractured nature of politics in the first part of the Twenty-First Century. But what standard should govern the manner in which ideas are expressed and arguments made? Justice Brennan framed the fundamental issue in *New York Times v. Sullivan* case this way:[18]

> Thus we consider this case against the background of a profound national commitment to the principle that debate on public issues should be uninhibited, robust, and wide-open, and that it may well include vehement, caustic, and sometimes unpleasantly sharp attacks on government and public officials. See *Terminiello v. Chicago*, 337 U.S. 1, 4, 69 S.Ct. 894, 93 L.Ed. 1131; *DeJonge v. Oregon*, 299 U.S. 353, 365, 57 S.Ct. 255, 81 L.Ed. 278. The present advertisement, as an expression of grievance and protest on one of the major public issues of our time, would seem clearly to qualify for the constitutional protection. The question is whether it forfeits that protection by the falsity of some of its factual statements and by its alleged defamation of respondent.

The answer? No, Brennan wrote. He rejected the position that the falsity of some of the factual statements in the advertisement destroyed the First Amendment protection for the *Times* and the clergymen.[19] "[E]rroneous statement is inevitable in free debate, and * * * it must be protected if the freedoms of expression are to have the 'breathing space' that they need to survive, * * *" it ruled. Quoting the holding in *Sweeney v. Patterson*,[20] he added that, " 'Cases which impose liability for erroneous reports of the political conduct of officials reflect the obsolete doctrine that the governed must not criticize their governors * * *

---

17 Ibid. at 270, 721.

18 Ibid. at 270–271, 721.

19 Ibid.

20 *Sweeney v. Patterson*, 76 U.S.App.D.C. 23, 128 F.2d 457, 458 (1942).

Whatever is added to the field of libel is taken from the field of free debate.' "

Elaborating on the matter of truth and error, it said that it is not enough for a state to provide in its law that the defendant may plead the truth of his words, although that has long been considered a bulwark for protection of expression, Brennan wrote:[21]

> A rule compelling the critic of official conduct to guarantee the truth of all his factual assertions—and to do so on pain of libel judgments virtually unlimited in amount—leads to * * * "self-censorship." Allowance of the defense of truth, with the burden of proving it on the defendant, does not mean that only false speech will be deterred. Even courts accepting this defense as an adequate safeguard have recognized the difficulties of adducing legal proofs that the alleged libel was true in all its factual particulars. [* * *] Under such a rule, would-be critics of official conduct may be deterred from voicing their criticism, even though it is believed to be true and even though it is in fact true, because of doubt whether it can be proved in court or fear of the expense of having to do so. They tend to make only statements which 'steer far wider of the unlawful zone.' *Speiser v. Randall* 357 U.S. 513, 78 S.Ct. 1332, 2 L.Ed.2d 1460. The rule thus dampens the vigor and limits the variety of public debate. It is inconsistent with the First and Fourteenth Amendments.

This was the end for Alabama's rule that, "the defendant has no defense as to stated facts unless he can persuade the jury that they were true in all their particulars." But the decision reached much farther than to Alabama: Most states had similar rules under which public officials had successfully brought libel suits for decades. In holding that the Constitution protects even erroneous statements about public officials in their public acts, the Court was providing protection that only a minority of states had provided previously.

Having decided that the constitutional protection was not destroyed by the falsity of statements in the advertisement, Justice Brennan added that the protection also was not lost because the statement was made about an official. "Criticism of their official conduct," Brennan's opinion held, "does not lose its constitutional protection merely because it is effective criticism and hence diminishes their official reputations."[22]

That did not mean that public officials were left without recourse when they were libeled. Justice Brennan set forth the circumstances under which a public official could recover damages for defamation: Only if the official could prove that the statement was false and defamatory,

---

[21] *New York Times Co. v. Sullivan*, 376 U.S. 254, 270, 84 S.Ct. 710, 725–726 (1964).

[22] Ibid. at 273, 84 S.Ct. at 722.

and the publisher knew it was false or published knowing that it was probably false. This is the actual malice rule.

Malice in the new context was no longer the vague, shifting concept of ancient convenience for judges who had been shocked or angered by words harshly critical of public officials. It was not the oft-used "evidence of ill-will" on the part of the publisher; it was *not* "hatred" of the publisher for the defamed; it was *not* "intent to harm" the defamed. Rather, the actual malice which the plaintiff would have to plead and prove lay in the publisher's knowledge that what he printed was false, or else disregard on the part of the publisher as to its probable falsity.

The old, tort-based libel requirement that the publisher would have to prove the truth of his words disappeared in Brennan's formulation:[23] No longer would the publisher carry the burden; instead, the plaintiff official would have to prove falsity. Further, it would not be enough for the plaintiff to prove knowing or reckless falsity by "the preponderance of evidence." Instead, he would have to prove it "with convincing clarity." Also, to learn whether the trial court had properly applied the law in this important case over how expression might be regulated, the appellate courts were to independently review the trial record itself to make sure that there had been no forbidden intrusion on free expression.[24]

As court interpretation and litigation carried on after these drastic revisions of the libel law of centuries, *New York Times Co. v. Sullivan* came to be recognized as the most important First Amendment case for decades. Famed attorney Floyd Abrams termed the decision[25] "majestic," and[26] "one of the most far reaching, extraordinary, and beautiful decisions in American history."

CRITICISM OF THE "ACTUAL MALICE" STANDARD?

The constitutional defense ("actual malice") from *New York Times v. Sullivan* continues to face challenges to its philosophy. Justice Clarence Thomas wrote in a 2019 decision by the court to turn down an appeal in a recent libel case, that *Sullivan* should be reconsidered.[27] Thomas argued that the Constitution, as it was written in 1787,[28] made no

[23] This was made explicit in *Philadelphia Newspapers, Inc. v. Hepps*, 475 U.S. 767, 106 S.Ct. 1558 (1986), 12 Med.L.Rptr 1977 where the Court held that the burden was on the plaintiff to prove the "defamatory" statement was false.

[24] Ibid. at 285, 84 S.Ct. at 728. Reaffirmed 20 years later by the Supreme Court in *Bose Corp. v. Consumers Union*, 466 U.S. 485, 104 S.Ct. 1949 (1984), 10 Med.L.Rptr. 1625, 1636–1639, this rule was held to govern all appellate courts in the determination of actual malice under *Sullivan*, rather than a lesser legal standard which provides that trial-court findings of fact are not to be set aside by appellate courts unless they are "clearly erroneous." Appeals courts have usually practiced independent review: *LDRC Bulletin #13*, Spring 1985, 2.

[25] 10 *Med.L.Rptr.* #17, 4/24/84, News Notes.

[26] 10 *Med.L.Rptr.* #17, 4/24/84, News Notes.

[27] Adam Liptak, "Justice Clarence Thomas Calls for Reconsideration of Landmark Libel Ruling," *New York Times*, Feb. 19, 2019.

[28] Readers may remember Justice Thomas' dissent in *Brown v. Entertainment Merchants Ass'n*, 564 U.S. 786, 131 S.Ct. 2729, 180 L.Ed.2d 708 (2011). Brown was the case in which video game companies successfully opposed a California law forbidding the sale or rental of violent

provision for protecting speech from libel suit or libel prosecution.[29] The First Amendment did nothing to limit the authority of states to protect the reputations of their citizens and leaders as they saw fit, Thomas wrote. When the First Amendment was ratified, he wrote, many states made it quite easy to sue for libel in civil actions and to prosecute libel as a crime. That was, he wrote, as it should be.[30]

> "We did not begin meddling in this area until 1964, nearly 175 years after the First Amendment was ratified," Justice Thomas wrote of the Sullivan decision. "The states are perfectly capable of striking an acceptable balance between encouraging robust public discourse and providing a meaningful remedy for reputational harm."

Justice Thomas might want to consider his position in light of a headline that ran in the *Montgomery Advertiser* after the libel suits were filed against the *Times*:[31] "State Finds Formidable Legal Club to Swing at Out-of-State Press." The *Alabama Journal*, suggested that the suits[32] "could have the effect of causing reckless publishers of the North" to make a re-survey of their habit of permitting anything detrimental to the South and its people to appear in their columns"

The multiple suits by Sullivan, Gov. Patterson and the other Alabama officials made clear that the state had no interest in "striking an acceptable balance." The Northern newspapers and network news shows that covered the civil rights movement were considered agents of disruption that encouraged the demonstrations in favor of equal rights.

---

video games to minors. A majority of the court found the law impermissibly regulated speech that was directed at children. Thomas argued that the majority wrongly decided the case by failing to apply the First Amendment as it was understood in the late Eighteenth Century. "[* * *] the freedom of speech," as originally understood, does not include a right to speak to minors (or a right of minors to access speech) without going through the minors' parents or guardians." As such, any law regulating the ability of the video game companies to market to children was constitutional as it was consistent with practices more than 200 years ago. "The historical evidence shows that the founding generation believed parents had absolute authority over their minor children and expected parents to use that authority to direct the proper development of their children. It would be absurd to suggest that such a society understood "the freedom of speech" to include a right to speak to minors (or a corresponding right of minors to access speech) without going through the minors' parents. [* * *] In the Puritan tradition common in the New England Colonies, fathers ruled families with absolute authority. "The patriarchal family was the basic building block of Puritan society." S. Mintz, *Huck's Raft* 13 (2004) (hereinafter Mintz); see also R. MacDonald, *Literature for Children in England and America From 1646 to 1774*, p. 7 (1982) (hereinafter MacDonald). The Puritans rejected many customs, such as godparenthood, that they considered inconsistent with the patriarchal structure. Mintz 13.

Part of the father's absolute power was the right and duty "to fill his children's minds with knowledge and . . . make them apply their knowledge in right action." E. Morgan, *The Puritan Family* 97 (rev. ed.1966) (herein-after Morgan). Puritans thought children were "innately sinful and that parents' primary task was to suppress their children's natural depravity." S. Mintz & S. Kellogg, *Domestic Revolutions* 2 (1988).

[29] Adam Liptak, "Justice Clarence Thomas Calls for Reconsideration of Landmark Libel Ruling," *New York Times*, Feb. 19, 2019.

[30] Ibid.

[31] Anthony Lewis, *Make No Law*, New York: Random House, 1991, p. 35.

[32] Ibid. at 34.

The-late Justice Antonin Scalia also criticized *Sullivan* for the same reason.[33]

> "For the Supreme Court to say that the Constitution requires [that ruling], that's not what the people understood when they ratified the First Amendment," Scalia said.
>
> At the time it was adopted, nobody thought that the First Amendment would encompass the ability to libel somebody, according to Scalia. "Who told Earl Warren and the Supreme Court that what had been accepted libel law for a couple hundred years was no longer?" he asked.

In a 2012 interview by Charlie Rose, Scalia summed up actual malice in this way:[34]

> You can libel public figures at will so long as somebody told you something, some reliable person told you the lie that you then publicized to the whole world—that's what *New York Times v. Sullivan* says.

That is not entirely true and the ways that the courts have found to establish publication with actual malice is found on the pages below.

Justice Scalia's death in 2016 leaves Justice Thomas the lone member of the Supreme Court arguing to overturn *Sullivan*.

Donald Trump has criticized the news media and said he would work to change libel law.[35]

> On the campaign trail, then-candidate Donald Trump pledged to somehow "open up" American libel laws. "One of the things I'm going to do if I win . . . is I'm going to open up our libel laws so when they write purposely negative and horrible and false articles, we can sue them and win lots of money," said Trump at a February 2016 campaign event in Fort Worth, Texas.

Then, in a Cabinet meeting in January of 2019, he repeated his promise to alter the libel landscape.[36]

> On a separate front, we are going to take a strong look at our country's libel laws so that when somebody says something that is false and defamatory about someone, that person will have meaningful recourse in our courts. If somebody says something that's totally false, and knowingly false, that the person that has been abused, defamed, libeled will have meaningful recourse. Our current libel laws are a sham and a disgrace and do not represent American values or American fairness. So we're going

---

[33] Abby Rogers, "Justice Scalia 'Abhors' The Supreme Court's 1964 Ruling On Libel," *Business Insider*, Dec. 4, 2012.

[34] Erik Wemple, "Antonin Scalia hates 'NYT v. Sullivan' " *The Washington Post*, Dec. 4, 2012.

[35] Erik Wemple, "President Trump calls libel laws 'a sham and a disgrace,' pledges review," *The Washington Post*, Jan. 10, 2019.

[36] Ibid.

to take a strong look at that. We want fairness, can't say things that are false, knowingly false, and be able to smile as money pours into your bank account. We're going to take a very, very strong look at that and I think what the American people want to see is fairness.

What Donald Trump apparently did not realize is that the change in libel law that he wants, took place in 1964 in *New York Times v. Sullivan*. Under the *Sullivan* rule, a person who publishes a defamatory statement with knowledge of its falsity, has liability making it appear that Donald Trump apparently is championing a decades-old rule of law as something completely new.

26. ACTUAL MALICE

Courts examine reporting procedures in testing for actual malice and find reckless disregard for falsity much more often than knowledge of falsity.

If a libel plaintiff is found by the judge to be a public official or public figure[37], the plaintiff's next move is to try to show that the offending words were published with actual malice. This term, as we have seen, is defined by the Supreme Court as reckless disregard for falsity in the words, or, as knowledge that the publication is false. The burden is on the plaintiff to prove falsity, although the defendant may well undertake to demonstrate truth—a complete privilege.

It is worth remembering that, as was said earlier, the actual malice of *Sullivan* is quite different from the concept "malice" as it is usually understood. The word ordinarily has to do with hostility, ill will, spite, intent to harm—as, indeed, it was defined in libel law for generations before *Sullivan*, and as it continues to be defined in its tort-related sense in state libel law where the constitutional standard does not apply. But old-style malice can play a part in determining the existence of constitutional malice. Evidence that the publisher harbored ill feelings toward the plaintiff may help the jury conclude that such hatred took the form of publishing knowing falsehoods or a willingness to publish with reckless disregard of the falsity.

The Supreme Court has said that "actual malice" is a[38] "term of art, created to provide a convenient shorthand expression for the standard of liability that must be established" where public persons bring libel suits. The court that is trying the libel issue must direct itself to the factual issue as to the defendant's subjective knowledge of actual falsity or his high degree of awareness of probable falsity before publishing.[39]

---

[37] The determination of whether a plaintiff is a public official or public figure is dealt with later in this chapter.

[38] *Cantrell v. Forest City Pub. Co.*, 419 U.S. 245, 95 S.Ct. 465 (1974).

[39] *Orr v. Argus-Press Co.*, 586 F.2d 1108 (6th Cir.1978).

Very soon after *Sullivan* had established the new definition of actual malice, the Supreme Court began the process of defining "reckless disregard." In *Garrison v. Louisiana*,[40] a criminal libel action, it said that reckless disregard means a "high degree of awareness of probable falsity" of the publication. In a non-media civil libel case where one candidate for public office sued his opponent (*St. Amant v. Thompson*), the Supreme Court said that for reckless disregard to be found,[41] "There must be sufficient evidence to permit the conclusion that the defendant in fact entertained serious doubts as to the truth of his publication."

Garrison v. Louisiana, 379 U.S. 64, 85 S.Ct. 209 (1964) arose in a dispute between D.A. Earling Carothers "Jim" Garrison, who achieved national notoriety for his investigation of the John F. Kennedy assassination, and eight judges of the Criminal District Court. It began with a judge denying Garrison money from a fines and fees fund for office furnishings. Garrison obtained the money by going to a different judge and misrepresenting that the first judge had withdrawn his objection. The eight judges responded by requiring that at least five approve further disbursements to Garrison's office. Garrison then asked for money for undercover agents investigating vice in the Bourbon and Canal Street districts. The judges refused citing Louisiana constitutional concerns. The judge from the original controversy then criticized Garrison's conduct in office. Garrison replied with a press conference of his own in which he suggested that the judges had been influenced by racketeers and were lazy.

Garrison was convicted of criminal libel, and the Supreme Court of the United States reversed the conviction. It said that the fact that the case was a criminal case made no difference to the principles of the *Times v. Sullivan* rule, and that malice would have to be shown. And the "reckless disregard" of truth or falsity in malice, it said, lies in a "high degree of awareness of probable falsity" on the part of the publisher. Nothing indicated that Garrison had this awareness of falsity when he castigated the Louisiana judges.[42]

Since *New York Times v. Sullivan*, the courts have been at pains to distinguish between "reckless disregard of truth" and "negligence."[43] Negligence is not enough to sustain a finding of actual malice. In the leading case, the Court went to this point. Errors in the famous advertisement, "Heed Their Rising Voices," could have been discovered by the *New York Times* advertising staff had it taken an elevator up a floor to the morgue and checked earlier stories on file. Failure to make this check, the Supreme Court said, did not constitute "reckless

[40] *Garrison v. Louisiana*, 379 U.S. 64, 74, 85 S.Ct. 209, 216 (1964).

[41] *St. Amant v. Thompson*, 390 U.S. 727, 731, 88 S.Ct. 1323, 1325 (1968).

[42] *Garrison v. Louisiana*, 379 U.S. 64, 85 S.Ct. 209 (1964).

[43] *Priestley v. Hastings & Sons Pub. Co. of Lynn*, 360 Mass. 118, 271 N.E.2d 628 (1971); *A.S. Abell Co. v. Barnes*, 258 Md. 56, 265 A.2d 207 (1970).

disregard;" at the worst it was negligence, and negligence is not enough to indicate actual malice.[44]

In *Washington Post v. Keogh*,[45] Congressman Eugene Keogh sued the newspaper for columns written by Drew Pearson that claimed that Keogh engaged in bribe splitting. The *Post* carried and syndicated Pearson's column. The *Post* brought a motion for summary judgment. A U.S. district court in the nation's capitol denied the motion and the *Post* appealed to the D.C. Circuit Court of Appeals.

Keogh opposed the motion for summary judgment. He argued that the case should go to trial and be judged by a jury. In his appeal, Keogh offered excerpts from magazine and newspaper stories about Pearson and his reputation for accuracy and truthfulness. Pearson's reputation was such, he argued, that the *Post* should not have simply published what he wrote. The *Post* should have checked and verified Pearson's allegations. That failure to check, Keogh's attorneys argued, showed the *Post* published with actual malice.

The appellate judges, in an opinion written by Judge J. Skelly Wright, held that the *Post* showed no reckless disregard and granted the *Post*'s motion for summary judgment. Judge Wright looked at Pearson's credentials in light of the standards articulated in *Sullivan* and *Garrison*.[46]

> Proof of isolated instances of inaccuracy, therefore, in a 35-year career during which Pearson has published well over 10,000 columns, cannot be accorded significance, since the relevant rule of law contemplates that 'erroneous statement is inevitable in free debate, and * * * it must be protected if the freedoms of expression are to have the breathing space they need to survive.' *Garrison v. State of Louisiana*, supra, 379 U.S. at 74, 85 S.Ct. at 216.

In addition, the *Post* offered depositions from the editor, an assistant managing editor and three employees that they read the columns and had not seen any evidence that would cause them to suspect the information was false.

The issue of the accuracy of the columns had not been judged. But the *Post* did not need to prove the columns were correct at that stage of the litigation. Remember, Keogh would have to prove actual malice. In *Sullivan*, the Supreme Court held that the *Times'* failure to ensure the accuracy of the advertisement was not sufficient to show actual malice. No actual malice, no libel. Imposing a requirement for the Post or any other newspaper would retain the burdens of the pre-*Sullivan* era. Judge Wright wrote:[47]

---

[44] *New York Times Co. v. Sullivan*, 376 U.S. 254, 288, 84 S.Ct. 710, 730 (1964).

[45] *Washington Post Co. v. Keogh*, 125 U.S.App.D.C. 32, 365 F.2d 965, 972–973 (1966).

[46] Ibid. at 971–972, 38–39.

[47] *Washington Post Co. v. Keogh*, 125 U.S.App.D.C. 32, 365 F.2d 965, 972–973 (1966).

> Verification is * * * a costly process, and the newspaper business is one in which survival has become a major problem. * * * We should be hesitant to impose responsibilities upon newspapers which can be met only through costly procedures or through self-censorship designed to avoid risks of publishing controversial material.

In *Garrison* and *Keogh*, courts defined reckless disregard by saying what it is not. Defining reckless disregard can be difficult for lawyers and judges and so it is a troubling issue for professional communicators. A more easily understandable, common sense analysis was offered in *Dombey v. Phoenix Newspapers, Inc.*,[48] where the Arizona Supreme Court said:[49]

> The disregard must be more than "reckless"—conscious disregard would be a better description of the test.
>
> [R]eckless conduct is not measured by whether a reasonably prudent man would have published, or would have investigated before publishing. There must be sufficient evidence to permit the conclusion that the defendant in fact entertained serious doubts as to the truth of his publication. Publishing with such doubts shows reckless disregard for truth or falsity and demonstrates actual malice.

The Arizona court acknowledged that its preference in analyzing reckless disregard would protect some less-than-admirable publishers, but that it was a cost of doing business under the First Amendment.[50]

> It may be said that such a test puts a premium on ignorance, encourages the irresponsible publisher not to inquire, and permits the issue to be determined by the defendant's testimony that he published the statement in good faith and unaware of its probable falsity. Concededly the reckless disregard standard may permit recovery in fewer situations * * * But to insure the ascertainment and publication of the truth about public affairs, it is essential that the First Amendment protect some erroneous publications as well as true ones.

In the actual malice analysis we spend less time on knowledge of falsity than on reckless disregard. That is a matter of practicality. It is rare that a publisher will have admitted to publishing, knowing that the defamatory statement is false. Where such evidence exists, the fault issue will be a moot point. But there are some knowing falsity cases that come up from time to time.

---

[48] *Dombey v. Phoenix Newspapers, Inc.*, 150 Ariz. 476, 724 P.2d 562, 573 (1986), 13 Med.L.Rptr. 1282.

[49] Ibid. at 487.

[50] Ibid. Quoting *St. Amant v. Thompson*, 390 U.S. 727, 88 S.Ct. 1323 (1968).

KNOWING FALSITY

Publishing with knowledge of falsity is rare in reported libel law cases. A publisher of a libel who publicly admits to knowing the statement was false to begin with is not likely to reach trial. Instead, knowledge of falsity comes when objective evidence proves that the publisher knew it was false. An illustrative case involved a suit by State Sen. Richard Schermerhorn of New York.[51] He was interviewed by reporter Ron Rosenberg of the Middletown *Times Herald Record* about a bill that Schermerhorn proposed to create a development corporation that would issue $50 million in bonds to redevelop portions of the city of Newburgh. The Newburgh Development District Corporation, known as the NDDC in Newburgh, aroused public concerns.[52]

> [T]he proposal was causing serious concern in Newburgh's black and Hispanic communities which had suffered inordinate disruption and dislocation during earlier attempts at urban renewal in the city. It was apparently feared that the new bill would not provide adequately for relocation of displaced families and would also result in the dilution of minority voting strength. In an attempt to prevent those consequences, efforts were begun to assure community representation on the board of directors of the proposed NDDC, and those efforts became a subject of inquiry by the defendant *Times Herald Record.*

Rosenberg interviewed Shermerhorn by phone. He asked about black leaders' insistence that the senator's bill be amended to guarantee black and Hispanic representation on the board of directors. Schermerhorn replied that guaranteeing minority representation might be unconstitutional but that he wanted board members to best qualified, regardless of color, and willing to serve without expecting to benefit. Schermerhorn stressed the need for board members with training and experience in financing. When Rosenberg pressed Schermerhorn about the minority demands, he responded,[53] "I can't help what the Black community wants. I want to be able to have qualified Blacks that can serve. I want to be able to have people who are representative of the community who are, above all, qualified to serve on this Board."

Rosenberg later wrote a story which was published under the headline, "SCHERMERHORN SAYS NDDC CAN DO WITHOUT BLACKS." There was no reference to the words of the headline in the story. A storm of protest against the senator arose, and fellow Senators Vander L. Beatty and Sidney von Luther proposed a resolution of censure in the Senate against Schermerhorn. In a later story, Beatty was quoted as saying that he had access to tapes in which Schermerhorn made subtle

[51] *Schermerhorn v. Rosenberg*, 73 A.D.2d 276, 426 N.Y.S.2d 274 (1980), 6 Med.L.Rptr. 1376.

[52] Ibid. at 278–279.

[53] Ibid. at 279. Schermerhorn testified that he recommended a black faculty member at West Point be appointed to the board.

anti-black and anti-Semitic statements. Sen. von Luther, who introduced the censure resolution against Schermerhorn, said that Rosenberg had told him he had recorded his interview and that he had the tape in which Schermerhorn made racial and ethnic slurs. Rosenberg offered the tape to von Luther and Beatty for their attempt to oust Schermerhorn from the senate. Despite requests from Senators von Luther and Beatty, no tape of the telephone interview was produced.

Schermerhorn denied making the headline statement and told his Senate colleagues that if there were tapes showing he had made such statements; he would be unfit to serve in the Senate and would resign. He brought a libel suit and alleged that the newspaper and reporter published with knowledge of falsehood.[54] At trial, Rosenberg testified that Schermerhorn had not said the words that the headline reported. von Luther and Beatty testified for Shermerhorn and said that they believed that,[55] "No tape recording had been made of Rosenberg's interview with Schermerhorn; there was never any recording of Schermerhorn making racial or ethnic slurs; and Schermerhorn had never made the statement attributed to him in the *Times Herald* headline."

Rosenberg testified that he had not written the headline. He said a copy editor, Ira Rifkin, wrote the words. The court hearing the appeal, was not convinced.[56] "On the evidence before us, however, we are of the view that the jury was justified in rejecting that testimony. Rifkin had unaccountably become unavailable and was never produced at trial." The jury found for Schermerhorn and awarded him $36,000. The newspaper appealed citing, among other reasons, that the case should be overturned because it was entitled to protection from the First Amendment. The appellate court held that the newspaper and reporter could not rely on the First Amendment for protection where the jury found that Rosenberg himself wrote the headline knowing it was false.[57]

> A newspaper simply may not shield itself from a libel action by reporting the utterance of a false and defamatory accusation of which it was the source. To hold otherwise would be to denigrate rather than to advance the values encompassed within and protected by the First Amendment.
>
> The public looks to the press not only as a forum for divergent ideas and opinions but, equally important, as a source of accurate accounts of newsworthy events. Permitting the press intentionally to disseminate false and defamatory reports with

---

[54] *Schermerhorn v. Rosenberg*, 73 A.D.2d 276, 426 N.Y.S.2d 274 (1980), 6 Med.L.Rptr. 1376.

[55] Ibid. at 282.

[56] Ibid. at 285.

[57] Ibid. at 288.

impunity would be to damage its credibility and ultimately to injure the press as an institution.

RECKLESS DISREGARD

The more frequently encountered situation is one involving reckless disregard. It is a term of art meaning that the publisher published the defamatory statement even though he entertained serious doubts about its truth or published with reckless disregard of the probable falsity of the statement. The following cases illustrate ways in which the courts have found defendants acted with the required level of fault. These cases fall into several general categories, including:

(1) a reliance on a source or sources who are not believable or who are relied on despite their known biases,

(2) publishing an inherently improbable story,

(3) failing to contact a necessary and proper source, and,

(4) recognizing that the publisher has doubts about the truthfulness of the story and still publishing.

CURTIS PUBLISHING CO. V. BUTTS & ASSOCIATED PRESS V. WALKER

Curtis Publishing Co. v. Butts,[58] a case decided along with the case of *Walker v. Associated Press*, helped to establish what would and would not constitute actual malice in publication by a libel defendant. The two cases were not related on the facts, but they were related by subject matter as each plaintiff was not a public official but rather a public figure (public figure status is covered later in this chapter) and the Court had to decide whether the actual malice standard applied. It was a circumstance of two cases following the *Sullivan* case and dealing with issues of fault in libel. The Supreme Court took both cases and decided them together with two opposite results based on the application of the reckless disregard test.

Wally Butts was the athletic director at the University of Georgia. He was the subject of an "investigative" story in the *Saturday Evening Post* that ran under the headline, "The Story of a College Football Fix."

The story ran with the following editor's note,[59]

> Not since the Chicago White Sox threw the 1919 World Series has there been a sports story as shocking as this one * * * Before the University of Georgia played the University of Alabama * * * Wally Butts * * * gave [to its coach] * * * Georgia's plays,

---

[58] *Curtis Publishing Co. v. Butts, Associated Press v. Walker*, 388 U.S. 130, 87 S.Ct. 1975 (1967).

[59] Ibid. at 136.

> defensive patterns, all the significant secrets Georgia's football team possessed.

The story began when Atlanta insurance salesman George Burnett and another man stopped at a restaurant to make a telephone call. Through some crossed wires, Burnett overheard a conversation between Butts and Alabama football coach Paul "Bear" Bryant about a week before Georgia played Alabama.

Burnett took what he said he heard to the *Saturday Evening Post.* Burnett told the *Post* that he heard Butts giving Bryant Georgia's game plan and plays. The *Post* reported that,[60] "the Georgia players, their moves analyzed and forecast like those of rats in a maze, took a frightful physical beating." The *Post* reported on Alabama's victory and said that players and those on the sidelines knew of the betrayal. The magazine reported that Burnett turned his notes of the telephone conversation over to Georgia's head coach, that Butts resigned his position for health and business reasons and what it expected the article would do to the former athletic director,[61]

> "The chances are that Wally Butts will never help any football team again. * * * The investigation by university and Southeastern Conference officials is continuing; motion pictures of other games are being scrutinized; where it will end no one so far can say. But careers will be ruined, that is sure."

Butts sued, claiming that while Burnett had overheard the conversation between him and Bryant, he gave no secrets away. He was awarded $60,000 in actual damages and $3 million in punitives. The trial court reduced the total to $460,000.[62] He appealed. Justice Harlan wrote the plurality opinion for the court in *Butts.* His opinion was joined by three other justices and Chief Justice Warren concurred in the result to affirm the judgment.

Justice Harlan's analysis emphasized the failures of reporting in that the *Post* published its story based on Burnett's affidavit about what he said he heard without checking to see if they were true.[63]

> Burnett's notes were not even viewed by any of the magazine's personnel prior to publication. John Carmichael, who was supposed to have been with Burnett when the phone call was overheard, was not interviewed. No attempt was made to screen the films of the game to see if Burnett's information was accurate, and no attempt was made to find out whether Alabama had adjusted its plans after the alleged divulgence of information.

---

[60] Ibid.

[61] Ibid.

[62] Bryant filed his own suit but settled with Curtis Publishing.

[63] *Curtis Publishing Co. v. Butts*, 388 U.S. 130, 157–158, 87 S.Ct. 1975, 1993 (1967).

> The *Post* writer assigned to the story was not a football expert and no attempt was made to check the story with someone knowledgeable in the sport. At trial such experts indicated that the information in the Burnett notes was either such that it would be evident to any opposing coach from game films regularly exchanged or valueless.

The *Post* was not under deadline pressure, Justice Harlan wrote. The story was not,[64] " 'hot news' and the editors recognized the need for a thorough investigation." In some ways, the *Butts* case focused on failures to check readily available sources in ways that are similar to the Court's holding in in *Harte-Hanks Communications, Inc. v. Connaughton*, 491 U.S. 657, 109 S.Ct. 2678 (1989) discussed later in this chapter. And so, Harlan's opinion affirmed the lower courts' judgments.

Things were markedly different in the case of Edwin Walker, a former Army general who sued the Associated Press over a story of his involvement in a riot on the campus of the University of Mississippi. Retired Maj. Gen. Walker, had resigned from the Army in 1961 after a storm of controversy over his troop-indoctrination program. Opposed to the integration of the University of Mississippi, he had in 1962 appeared on the scene there when James H. Meredith became the school's first black student. Dan Rather, covering the story for CBS, wrote in his autobiography, "*The Camera Never Blinks*," about Walker's appearance on the campus where he addressed, "the students and rednecks who poured in." Rather described the scene, writing,[65]

> It struck me as rather comic, a former Army general standing under those hundred-year-old trees, rallying southern manhood against the threat of one lonely black freshman. But I quickly changed my mind. I could see what was coming like a storm at sea.

Thousands rioted. Two people were killed, including a foreign reporter and a man who had gotten lost while driving with his family who stopped to find directions. Hundreds were injured and it took federal marshals and troops to restore order.

The Associated Press reporter Van Savell wrote a story that said that Walker,[66] "had taken command of the violent crowd and had personally led a charge against federal marshals sent there to effectuate the court's decree and to assist in preserving order. It also described Walker as encouraging rioters to use violence and giving them technical advice on combating the effects of tear gas."

Walker sued the Associated Press and eight other news organizations that carried the AP story. In his suit, Walker admitted he

---

[64] Ibid. at 157, 1992.

[65] Dan Rather and Mickey Herskowitz, *The Camera Never Blinks*, (William Morrow, New York, 1977), at 74.

[66] *Associated Press v. Walker*, 388 U.S. 130, 140, 87 S.Ct. 1975, 1983–1984 (1967).

went to the campus and said that he had spoken to a group of students. But, he claimed, he had counseled restraint and peaceful protest. He said the protesters rejected his counsel and that he did not have any control over them. He denied any involvement in any charge against federal marshals. Walker won his suit against the AP over the publication of the story in the *Fort Worth Star-Telegram* and was awarded $500,000. The AP appealed and wound up before the Supreme Court.

Justice Harlan found the reporting and circumstances completely different from the *Post*'s in *Butts*.

> The Associated Press received the information from a correspondent who was present at the scene of the events and gave every indication of being trustworthy and competent. His dispatches in this instance with one minor exception, were internally consistent and would not have seemed unreasonable to one familiar with General Walker's prior publicized statements on the underlying controversy. Considering the necessity for rapid dissemination, nothing in this series of events gives the slightest hint of a severe departure from accepted publishing standards.

Walker's own actions and words suggested that he could well have been an instigator, Justice Harlan pointed out in a footnote.[67]

> On September 26, 1962, Walker had made a statement on radio station KWKH at Shreveport, Louisiana, urging people to '(r)ise to a stand beside Governor Ross Barnett at Jackson, Mississippi.' He contended that the people had 'talked, listened and been pushed around far too much * * *.' He promised that he would 'be there,' on 'the right side.' The next morning in a television appearance in Dallas he repeated the same sentiments, and he set out his views once again from New Orleans on the evening of September 28, 1962. On September 29, 1962, Walker arrived in Jackson, Mississippi, and held another press and television conference in which he called for 'violent vocal protest.' On the afternoon of September 30, 1962, Walker held a final press conference at which he again urged defiance of court orders and federal power.

Justice Harlan's plurality opinion used the term "a severe departure from accepted publishing standards." The Associated Press reporting did not constitute such a "severe departure" and so Justice Harlan concluded that Walker should not be entitled to damages from the Associated Press. Chief Justice Warren's concurrence in the result framed the question in terms of the New York Times standard.[68]

> I have no difficulty in concluding that No. 150, *Associated Press v. Walker*, must be reversed since it is in clear conflict with *New*

---

[67] Ibid.

[68] Ibid. at 165, 1997–1998.

> *York Times*. The constitutional defenses were properly raised and preserved by the petitioner. The trial judge expressly ruled that no showing of malice in any sense had been * *1997 made, and he reversed an award of punitive damages for that reason. The seven members of this Court who reach the question agree with that conclusion, and all agree that the courts below erred in holding the First Amendment inapplicable.

ST. AMANT V. THOMPSON

A year later, the Court took up the issue of reckless disregard and laid out a whole laundry list of things that could lead to a finding of reckless disregard. *St. Amant v. Thompson*[69] arose over a radio broadcast by a political candidate. St. Amant, the candidate, made a televised speech in Baton Rouge, Louisiana. In the course of his speech, St. Amant read a series of questions which he had put to J. D. Albin, a member of a Teamsters Union local, and Albin's answers to those questions. The exchange concerned the allegedly nefarious activities of E. G. Partin, the president of the local, and the alleged relationship between Partin and St. Amant's political opponent. Albin said that Partin had stolen union funds and had decided to get rid of a safe containing union records. Albin also referred to Herman A. Thompson, an East Baton Rouge Parish deputy sheriff and the person who sued St. Amant:[70]

> "Now, we knew that this safe was gonna be moved that night, but imagine our predicament, knowing of Ed's connections with the Sheriff's office through Herman Thompson, who made recent visits to the Hall to see Ed. We also knew of money that had passed hands between Ed and Herman Thompson * * * from Ed to Herman. We also knew of his connections with State Trooper Lieutenant Joe Green. We knew we couldn't get any help from there and we didn't know how far that he was involved in the Sheriff's office or the State Police office through that, and it was out of the jurisdiction of the City Police."

Thompson sued over the statement. A Louisiana trial court found that the statement was defamatory and that St. Amant had broadcast with actual malice. The Louisiana Supreme Court agreed and affirmed the trial court. The U.S. Supreme Court disagreed, Justice White's opinion holding, that the test required proof of knowing falsity or serious doubts as to truth.[71] In St. Amant's case, he had known Albin for eight months. St. Amant had verified other parts of Albin's claims and collected affidavits from others. Albin also gave an affidavit to reporters and St. Amant believed that Albin was placing himself at personal risk by revealing details about the union's activities.

---

69 *St. Amant v. Thompson*, 390 U.S. 727, 88 S.Ct. 1323 (1968).

70 Ibid. at 728–729, 1324.

71 Ibid. at 731, 1324.

It is the subjective belief of the defendant that is the test for finding reckless disregard, the Court said. But that does not mean that defendants can slide off the hook simply by swearing that they published with belief in the truth of what they said.[72]

> "Professions of good faith will be unlikely to prove persuasive, for example, where a story is fabricated by the defendant, is the product of his imagination, or is based wholly on an unverified anonymous telephone call. Nor will they be likely to prevail when the publisher's allegations are so inherently improbable that only a reckless man would have put them in circulation. Likewise, recklessness may be found where there are obvious reasons to doubt the veracity of the informant or the accuracy of his reports."

Justice White's opinion lays out the key to actual malice cases. Although it is a subjective test, based on the belief of the defendant publisher, *those subject claims can be overcome by objective evidence.*

FINDING RECKLESS DISREGARD

Court-determined indicators of "reckless disregard" include: where a reporter did not make personal contact with anyone involved in the event before writing;[73] where a publication relied on an obviously biased source, was advised of the falsity of information, and published with no further investigation of the story;[74] where the publication printed although the story was inherently improbable.[75] Ill will of the reporter toward the subject of the story may in some cases contribute to a finding of reckless disregard.[76]

LOBBYIST VICKI ISEMAN SETTLES LIBEL SUIT AGAINST THE NEW YORK TIMES, DESPITE OMBUDSMAN'S COLUMN CRITICAL OF OWN PAPER

On December 30, 2008, lobbyist Vicki Iseman filed a $27 million libel suit against *The New York Times* in a federal court in Richmond, Va. She contended that her reputation was injured by the newspaper's falsely implying that she had "an illicit 'romantic' relationship with Sen. John McCain.[77] On February 19, 2009, Ms. Iseman settled the lawsuit, evidently with no monetary payment involved.

---

[72] Ibid. at 732, 1326.

[73] *Akins v. Altus Newspapers, Inc.*, 609 P.2d 1263 (Okl.1977).

[74] *Stevens v. Sun Pub. Co.*, 270 S.C. 65, 240 S.E.2d 812 (1978).

[75] *Hunt v. Liberty Lobby*, 720 F.2d 631 (11th Cir.1983), 10 Med.L.Rptr. 1097, 1107.

[76] *Cochran v. Indianapolis Newspapers, Inc.*, 175 Ind.App. 548, 372 N.E.2d 1211 (1978), 3 Med.L.Rptr. 2131.

[77] Neil H. Simon, "Libel Suit Against New York Times Filed in Richmond," *Media General News Service*, Dec. 30, 2008.

The lawsuit seemed worrisome to the news media, as indicated by substantial coverage of its filing by *The News Media & the Law*, the useful quarterly publication of the *Reporters Committee on Freedom of the Press*. That coverage was headlined:[78] "An unlikely weapon in the libel arsenal: Could an ombudsman's column be used as ammunition against his own paper?"

The New York Times had published an article on February 21, 2008 headlined "For McCain, Self-Confidence on Ethics Poses Its Own Risk." The article[79] quoted un-named McCain aides who believed that Senator McCain, during his 2000 run for the presidency, had an affair with lobbyist Iseman. Further, the article suggested Iseman used her access to McCain to seek concessions from the Federal Communications Commission for owners of broadcast. After the *Times*' story, McCain called a news conference, denying an improper relationship with Iseman or that he had behaved unethically.

Iseman filed her lawsuit[80] against the *Times* in Richmond, Virginia., late in December 2008, roughly seven weeks after Senator McCain lost the presidential election to Barack Obama. Public Editor Clark Hoyt, the ombudsman for *The New York Times*, had published an article just three days after the initial *Times* coverage of Iseman and McCain. In a comment titled "What That McCain Article Didn't Say," Hoyt wrote:[81] "The article was notable for what it did not say: It did not say what convinced the advisers [of McCain] that there was a romance. It did not make clear what McCain was admitting when he acknowledged behaving inappropriately—an affair or just an association with a lobbyist that could make him look bad." [The Iseman lawsuit complained[82] that the February 21, 2008, *Times* article had wrongly "created the impression that Senator McCain had *confessed* unethical and inappropriate behavior with Ms. Iseman, including a suggestion that McCain had confessed to having a romantic relationship with Ms. Iseman."]

Iseman's lawsuit seized on Hoyt's column, declaring: "Most significantly, of all, *The New York Times'* own public editor, Clark Hoyt, interpreted the column as communicating that Ms. Iseman and Senator McCain engaged in an inappropriate romantic relationship." The Complaint said:[83] "As Mr. Hoyt wrote about his own paper, *The New York Times*, 'if a paper is going to suggest an improper sexual affair, whether editors think that is the central point or not, it owes readers more proof

---

[78] Kathleen Cullinan, with reporting by Dana Liebelson and Ahnalese Rushman, *The News Media & The Law* (Winter, 2009), p. 29.

[79] Jim Rutenberg, Marilyn W. Thompson, David Kirkpatrick and Stephen Labaton, "For McCain, Self-Confidence on Ethics Poses Its Own Risk," *New York Times*, February 16, 2008.

[80] *Vicki L. Iseman v. The New York Times Company, William Keller, James Rutenberg, Marilyn Thompson, Stephen Labaton, Dean Kirkpatrick, and Dean Baquet*, Case No. 3:08CV848, United States District Court for the Eastern District of Virginia, pp. 1, 36.

[81] Clark Hoyt, "What That McCain Article Didn't Say," *New York Times*, Feb. 24, 2008.

[82] Complaint, *Iseman v. New York Times* et al., p.15. Emphasis in Complaint.

[83] Complaint, *Iseman v. New York Times*, et. al., pp. 34–35. Emphasis in Complaint.

than the *Times* was able to provide'" It showed that this was "reckless disregard for truth or falsity in the classic sense—it was a publication that deliberately created the impression that *The New York Times* defendants had *no doubt* that Ms. Iseman and Senator McCain had an improper relationship, when in fact they had failed to ever 'nail down' the story.' *The New York Times* Defendants *knew they did not know*—and brazenly published anyway."

Although the Iseman lawsuit against *The New York Times* was short-lived—it was settled less than two months after it was filed—it is likely to cast a chill on ombudsmen's columns (where such columns still exist). The settlement was characterized differently by the parties on each side.

ADDING TO THE RECKLESS DISREGARD DEFINITION: HARTE-HANKS V. CONNAUGHTON (1989)

The *Connaughton* decision[84] of 1989 marked the first time in two decades that the U.S. Supreme Court held against the media in a public figure libel case. (Keep in mind, however, that the media have lost some public figure libel cases over the years in lower courts. See, for example, the $3.05 million libel loss incurred in *Brown & Williamson v. Jacobson*[85] in 1987.

Harte-Hanks Communications, Inc. v. Connaughton says that the media may be held responsible for defamation in reporting on a candidate for public office if a jury could reasonably find "actual malice" misconduct by news organizations. The key here turned on how "reckless disregard for the truth" was defined.

The case began 1983 during a judicial election that was reported on by the Hamilton, Ohio, *Journal News* (owned by Harte-Hanks until 1986). The story is both complicated and simple. The complicated part deals with the events surrounding the election. The simple part about the conduct of the newspaper in researching and presenting its story.[86]

> A little over a month before the election, the incumbent's Director of Court Services resigned and was arrested on bribery charges. A grand jury investigation of those charges was in progress on November 1, 1983. On that date, the *Journal News* ran a front-page story quoting Alice Thompson, a grand jury witness, as stating that Connaughton had used "dirty tricks" and offered her and her sister jobs and a trip to Florida "in appreciation" for their help in the investigation.

[84] *Harte-Hanks Communications, Inc. v. Connaughton*, 491 U.S. 657, 660, 109 S.Ct. 2678, 2682 (1989), 16 Med.L.Rptr. at 1883.

[85] *Brown & Williamson Tobacco Corp. v. Jacobson*, 827 F.2d 1119 (7th Cir.1987), 14 Med.L.Rptr. 1497, cert. denied 485 U.S. 993, 108 S.Ct. 1302 (1988).

[86] Ibid. at 660.

Connaughton was involved in the controversy. He had Patsy Stephens, the most important witness to the bribery charges to his home where he conducted a tape-recorded interview with her with eight other persons present. In the interview, Stephens explained,[87] "how, on 40 or 50 occasions, she had visited with the Court Administrator, Billy Joe New, in his office and made cash payments to dispose of "DUI" and other minor criminal charges against her former husband and various other relatives and acquaintances."

Less than a week later, Stephens took a lie detector test. Connaughton arranged the test at the suggestion of the county prosecutor. After Stephens passed the test, Connaughton filed a written complaint against New who was arrested, indicted and convicted.

Alice Thompson, Stephens' sister, was present at the recorded interview. Stephens said one of the payments was made over a shoplifting charge against her sister, Alice. The two sisters spent hours with Connaughton, his wife and two of Connaughton's supporters.[88]

> They discussed a number of subjects, including the fact that Billy Joe New had just resigned, the question whether there was reason to be concerned about the safety of the two sisters, the fact that Martha Connaughton might open an ice cream parlor sometime in the future, the possibility that the two sisters might be employed there as waitresses, and a vacation in Florida planned by the Connaughtons for after the election.

In the next month, Thompson contacted the *Journal News* through her lawyer. She wanted to tell the newspaper about the "dirty tricks" Connaughton used in the grand jury investigation. The newspaper's editor and a reporter met with Thompson and recorded an interview with her.[89]

> [* * *]Thompson made these specific charges:
>
> —that Connaughton had stated that his purpose in taping the interview with Patsy Stephens was to get evidence with which he could confront New and Judge Dolan and "scare them into resigning" without making any public use of the tapes;
>
> —that he would pay the expenses for a 3-week vacation in Florida for the two sisters;
>
> —that he would buy a restaurant for the two sisters' parents to operate;
>
> —that he would provide jobs for both Patsy Stephens and Alice Thompson;

[87] Ibid.

[88] Ibid. at 669.

[89] Ibid. at 670–672, 2687–2689.

—that he would take them out to a victory dinner at an expensive French restaurant after the election; and

—that Connaughton would not allow knowledge of the sisters' involvement to become public.

Thompson said Connaughton had asked leading questions and turned the recorder off and on so his voice would not be heard on the tape. The editor and reporter asked Thompson if her sister would confirm what she told them. Thompson replied, saying,[90] "I think she's scared right now to talk to anyone, because the *Cincinnati Enquirer* has been trying to get her to talk to them. She's getting scared now since this is all reality. * * *"

After the interview, the *Journal News* put together a team of reporters and told them interview all of the witnesses to the conversation between Connaughton and Thompson with one exception—Patsy Stephens. No reporter was asked to interview her and no one at the *Journal-News* made any attempt to do so.

The newspaper interviewed Connaughton and asked him about Thompson's charges. Connaughton denied them. He said that many of the topics Thomson spoke of had come up in the conversation, but he said he had not offered Stephens a job for her testimony nor did he promise a vacation for the sisters. He gave a copy of the recording to the reporters.

The next day the *Journal News* published its story, "Bribery case witness claims jobs, trip offered." The story laid out Thompson's claims and Connaughton's denials. Connaughton lost the election and sued. At trial, *Journal News* reporters testified that they had interviewed everyone, apart from Stephens, present when Connaughton interviewed Stephens. All of the six witnesses said that Connaughton had not made promises, offers or any other inducements for Stephen's information. The newspaper asked Connaughton to be able to listen to the tape and he provided a copy.[91]

> Much of what Thompson had said about the interview could easily have been verified or disproved by listening to the tapes. Listening to the tapes, for example, would have revealed whether Thompson accurately reported that the tape recorders were selectively turned on and off and that Connaughton was careful not to speak while the recorders were running. Similarly, the tapes presented a simple means of determining whether Stephens and Thompson had been asked leading questions, as Thompson claimed.

But the newspaper did not listen to the tape. The editor of the *Journal News* testified that the paper did not interview Stephens because

---

[90] Ibid. Footnotes.

[91] Ibid. at 682, 2693.

Connaughton did not put her in touch with the reporter. Justice Stevens' opinion for the Court focused on those failures.[92]

> It is [* * *] undisputed that Connaughton made the tapes of the Stephens interview available to the *Journal News* and that no one at the newspaper took the time to listen to them. Similarly, there is no question that the *Journal News* was aware that Patsy Stephens was a key witness and that they failed to make any effort to interview her. Accepting the jury's determination that petitioner's explanations for these omissions were not credible, it is likely that the newspaper's inaction was a product of a deliberate decision not to acquire knowledge of facts that might confirm the probable falsity of Thompson's charges. Although failure to investigate will not alone support a finding of actual malice, see *St. Amant*, 390 U.S., at 731, 733, 88 S.Ct., at 1325, 1326, the purposeful avoidance of the truth is in a different category.

Justice Stevens used the phrase, "purposeful avoidance of the truth" twice in his opinion. It is key to helping reporters understand the difference between the statement in *Keogh* that *The Washington Post* had no obligation to verify its columnist's facts and the *Journal News'* failing to check a key and necessary source. Failing to interview every single possible source does not automatically lead to a finding of actual malice. Failing to interview the source who could determine the truth or falsity of a story is likely to lead to a finding of actual malice.[93]

> * * * [I]t is clear that the conclusion concerning the newspaper's departure from accepted standards and the evidence of motive were merely supportive of the court's ultimate conclusion that the record "demonstrated a reckless disregard as to the truth or falsity * * * [of the largely unsupported allegations against Connaughton] * * * and thus provided clear and convincing proof of 'actual malice' as found by the jury." 842 F.2d at 847. Although courts must be careful not to place too much reliance on such factors, a plaintiff is entitled to prove the defendant's state of mind through circumstantial evidence, see *Herbert v. Lando*, 441 U.S. 153, 99 S.Ct. 1635 (1979).

A failure to check carefully the facts regarding Daniel Connaughton has sometimes been called a "failure to contact a necessary and obvious source." But students should be wary of turning the failure on the part of the *Journal News* into a requirement for interviewing every possible source for every bit of information that could be used in a story. The *Journal News'* failure can be likened to "willful blindness" in which a party deliberately turns a blind eye to important information. As life has proven, sometimes not all sources are available before publication,

---

92 Ibid. at 691, 2697.

93 Ibid. at 667–668.

posting or broadcast. If other sources can provide the information from the missing source, the search for the truth will be satisfied and it will not be a "deliberate effort" to avoid the truth.

PROZERALIK V. CAPITAL CITIES, INC.

The case of *Prozeralik v. Capital Cities Communications, Inc.* provides a warning about the need to double check facts and what happens if a jury believes that a reporter did not have a source for a key element of a story. Prozeralik began with a report of an abduction and beating in the Niagara Falls area of New York. The identity of the victim was not released, but the case was linked to organized crime and it was suggested that the victim was a local restaurateur. During a news meeting at a Capital Cities television and radio station, the news staff speculated about the identity of the beating victim. John Prozeralik's name came up. It was pure speculation, based only on the fact that Prozeralik was a restaurateur in the area, the owner of John's Flaming Hearth Restaurant.

The station's noon news anchor Cindy DiBiasi took that name and contacted the FBI. What happened during that telephone call was hotly disputed. The anchor testified that she brought up Prozeralik's name and the FBI's media coordinator, an Agent Thurston, told her,[94] "You can go with that unless I call you back." Thurston hotly denied saying that. He told the trial court that he did not provide Prozeralik's name or confirm that he was the victim (The victim was David Pasquantino and not Prozeralik). Thurston denied telling the anchor she could go with the name unless he called back. The evidence showed that such procedure was not Thurston's normal method of operation.[95]

The station ran stories on its noon TV newscast and its 12:45, 1:45 and 2:45 p.m. news segments on its radio station identifying Prozeralik as the victim.[96]

> "The FBI is investigating a beating and abduction in Cheektowaga last night. Today, investigators are questioning John Prozeralik, the owner of John's Flaming Hearth Restaurant, in Niagara Falls, New York. Prozeralik was either tricked or forced to the Howard Johnson's in Cheektowaga according to police, where he was beaten with a baseball bat or pipe, and tied up. Today, the FBI is investigating the possibility that Prozeralik owed money to organized crime figures."

Prozeralik and his attorney called and denied any involvement. The station news director then called Thurston back and Thurston said he

---

[94] *Prozeralik v. Capital Cities Communications, Inc.*, 82 N.Y.2d 466, 605 N.Y.S.2d 218, 626 N.E.2d 34 (1993), 21 Med.L.Rptr. 2257, 2258.

[95] Reporters who have dealt with the FBI know that the agency has a hard, fast rule that it does not comment on active investigations.

[96] *Prozeralik v. Capital Cities Communications, Inc.*, 82 N.Y.2d 466, 471, 605 N.Y.S.2d 218, 220–221, 626 N.E.2d 34, 36–37 (1993), 21 Med.L.Rptr. 2257, 2258.

did not know the victim's identity when the anchor called, nor did he confirm it was Prozeralik. The station then ran retractions on its television newscasts at 6 and 11 p.m. that included the following:[97]

> "Tonight, we have developments on two fronts in the abduction that ended yesterday in a Cheektowaga motel. First, the victim is not, and I repeat, is not, John Prozeralik, the operator of John's Flaming Hearth Restaurant. The FBI earlier today said and confirmed the victim was Prozeralik, but our independent investigation is revealing he was not involved * * *"

As a practical matter, it probably did not advance the station's cause to publicly blame the FBI for the mistaken identity and further take credit for eliminating Prozeralik as the victim when Prozeralik himself called the station to deny being the beating victim. Additional problems arising in the case included the fact that a rival television station had correctly identified the victim the day before the defendant station broadcast its first story and the fact that the plaintiff's attorney could point to the pressures of the sweeps competition at the time.

The jury found for Prozeralik and awarded him $18 million. The judgment was reduced to $15.45 million by the judge. Capital Cities appealed and the New York appellate court found reversible error in the trial judge's jury instructions. Judge Irving Fudeman concluded that the broadcast news stories and the station's retractions were false and that meant that the plaintiff did not have to prove falsity in his case.[98]

> Defendant demonstrates that the jury instructions impermissibly impinged on the jury's resolution of credibility and actual malice by, in effect, directing the jury to accept FBI Agent Thurston's version of the telephone conversation between him and DiBiasi.

The question of falsity was a fact question and therefore a matter for the jury, not the judge. The case was retried and the jury in the second trial found the broadcasts false and awarded Prozeralik $9.5 million.

ALTERED QUOTES: MASSON V. THE NEW YORKER, ALFRED A. KNOPF AND JANET MALCOLM (1991)

If a writer alters an interview subject's quotations materially, is that "knowing falsity"? That was a key issue in a decade-long defamation suit which resulted in a Supreme Court decision[99] and which finally seemed to have been resolved by a November, 1994, jury verdict. The case, described as a soap-opera for the highly literate, involved a defamation suit by a flamboyant psychiatrist against a gifted writer of biographical profiles. In 1983, psychiatrist Jeffrey M. Masson sued for defamation

---

[97] 221, 37, 47.

[98] Ibid.

[99] *Masson v. New Yorker Magazine, Inc.*, 501 U.S. 496, 111 S.Ct. 2419 (1991), 18 Med.L.Rptr. 2241.

based on a two-part article by Janet Malcolm, first appearing in *The New Yorker*, and later published in book form by Knopf. The article/book were drawn from Ms. Malcolm's extensive tape-recorded interviews with Dr. Masson and covered his dismissal from his post as projects director of the Sigmund Freud Archives.

In his lawsuit, Dr. Masson argued that Ms. Malcolm had " * * * fabricated words attributed to him with quotation marks, and misleadingly edited his statements to make him appear 'unscholarly, irresponsible, vain and lacking in personal honesty or moral integrity.' "[100] Masson contended that the magazine and Knopf knew of author Malcolm's misconduct before the book and the article were published. The trial court had granted summary judgment in favor of Ms. Malcolm, the *New Yorker* and Knopf. The 9th Circuit had affirmed, and Dr. Masson appealed to the Supreme Court.

One of the disputed passages as published in Ms. Malcolm's writings involved her use of quotation marks around Dr. Masson's description of his plans to occupy Maresfield Gardens (home of the Freud Archives) after the elderly Anna Freud's death. Consider Justice Kennedy's repetition of that passage, and his remark upon it:[101]

> " 'It was a beautiful house, but it was dark and somber and dead. * * * I would have renovated it, opened it up, brought it to life. Maresfield Gardens would have been a place of scholarship but also of sex, women, fun. It would have been like the change in The Wizard of Oz, from black-and-white into color.' " In the Freud Archives 33.
>
> [Justice Kennedy then commented:] The tape recordings contain a similar statement, but in place of the reference to "sex, women and fun," and the Wizard of Oz, petitioner [Masson] commented [in the tape recorded interview]:
>
> "[I]t is an incredible storehouse. I mean, the library, Freud's library alone is priceless in terms of what it contains; all his books with his annotations in them; the Schreber case annotated, that kind of thing. It's fascinating."
>
> The passage was similar but not verbatim. That was key in the opinion. Justice Kennedy wrote that deliberate misquotation of a public figure *cannot be libelous* unless the wording changes the meaning of what really was said.[102]
>
> In general, quotation marks around a passage indicate to the reader that the passage reproduces the speaker's words verbatim. They inform the reader that he or she is reading the

[100] *Masson v. New Yorker Magazine, Inc.*, 881 F.2d at 1453, 16 Med.L.Rptr. at 2089–2090.

[101] *Masson v. New Yorker Magazine, Inc.*, 501 U.S. at 503, 111 S.Ct. at 2426 (1991), 18 Med.L.Rptr. at 2245.

[102] *Masson v. New Yorker Magazine, Inc.*, 501 U.S. at 516, 111 S.Ct. at 2432 (1991), 18 Med.L.Rptr. at 2250–2251.

> statement of the speaker, not a paraphrase or other indirect interpretation by an author. By providing this information, quotations add authority to the statement and credibility to the author's work.
>
> * * *
>
> Second, regardless of the truth or falsity of the factual matters asserted within the quoted statement, the attribution may result in injury to reputation because the manner of expression or even the fact that the statement was made indicates a negative personal trait or an attitude the speaker does not hold.
>
> * * *

Justice Kennedy noted that in some circumstances, as in a printed hypothetical conversation or in a work of fiction, a writer's use of quotation marks taken by readers to mean the reproduction of actual conversations.[103] "* * * In some sense, any alteration of a verbatim quotation is false. But writers and reporters by necessity alter what people say, at the very least to eliminate grammatical and syntactical infelicities."

Justice Kennedy's decision spoke cautiously to the issue of liability for altered quotes:[104]

> If every alteration constituted the falsity required to prove actual malice, the practice of journalism, which the First Amendment standard is designed to protect, would require a radical change, one inconsistent with our precedents and First Amendment principles.
>
> * * *
>
> We conclude that a deliberate alteration of the words uttered by a plaintiff does not equate with knowledge of falsity for purposes of *New York Times v. Sullivan* * * * and *Gertz v. Robert Welch* * * * unless the alteration results in a material change in the meaning conveyed by the statement. The use of quotations to attribute words not in fact spoken bears in a most important way on that inquiry, but it is not dispositive in every case.
>
> Deliberate or reckless falsification that comprises actual malice turns upon words and punctuation only because words and punctuation express meaning. Meaning is the life of language. And for the reasons we have given, quotations may be a devastating instrument for conveying false meaning. * * * [R]eaders of In the Freud Archives may have found Malcolm's portrait of petitioner especially damning because so much of it

[103] *Masson v. New Yorker Magazine, Inc.*, 501 U.S. at 514, 111 S.Ct. at 2431 (1991), 18 Med.L.Rptr. at 2248.

[104] *Masson v. New Yorker Magazine, Inc.*, 501 U.S. at 514, 517–518, 111 S.Ct. at 2431, 2433 (1991), 18 Med.L.Rptr. at 2241, 2249, 2251.

> appeared to be a self-portrait, told by petitioner in his own words. And if the alterations of petitioner's words gave a different meaning to the statements * * * then the device of quotations might well be critical in finding the words actionable.

Justice White dissented with respect to part of Justice Kennedy's opinion that said that publishing an altered quote did not, on its face, amount to actual malice.[105] "Malcolm, wrote that Masson said certain things that she knew Masson did not say. By any definition of the term, this was 'knowing falsehood': Malcolm asserts that Masson said these very words, knowing that he did not."

Justice Scalia joined Justice White in his dissent to that part of Justice Kennedy's opinion.

The Supreme Court's majority returned the case to the trial court to proceed with the lawsuit. Journalists and legal commentators differed on the potential impact of *Masson v. New Yorker*. Jane Kirtley, then-director of the Reporters Committee for Freedom of the Press, said,[106] " '[a] lot more reporters are going to start using tape recorders in addition to notebooks—a kind of belt and suspenders protection.' " The *New York Times*, however, said editorially that the Supreme Court had produced a measured decision meaning that,[107]

> * * * fallible journalists won't be held to stenographic exactitude for everything they put between quotation marks. Yet if a deliberately altered quote makes the speaker look like a self-confessed fool or rascal, the journalists had better be prepared to defend themselves in court.

MASSON V. MALCOM AND NEW YORKER MAGAZINE, INC.: THE JURY RETURNS AND RETURNS (1994)

In 1993, Dr. Masson won, sort of, in the trial court.[108] "The jury found that The *New Yorker* was not liable. The jury also found that Malcolm had libeled Masson, but was unable to reach a verdict regarding the damages that should be awarded." Because the jury could not reach a unanimous decision on damages, the judge granted Ms. Malcolm's motion for a new trial.

In 1994, a different jury came back with a different verdict.[109]

> The jury found that Masson had not carried his burden of persuasion that the "Intellectual Gigolo," "Greatest Analyst Who Ever Lived," and "Sex, Women, Fun" quotations were false. It found that the "I Don't Know Why I Put It In" quotation was

---

[105] Ibid. at 526, 2348.

[106] Tony Mauro, "Journalists may need taped evidence of quotes," *USA Today*, June 21, 1991.

[107] "Misquotations, Measured," *New York Times*, June 21, 1991.

[108] *Masson v. New Yorker Magazine, Inc.*, 85 F.3d 1394 (9thCir. 1996).

[109] Ibid. at 1397.

> not defamatory. Additionally, the jury found that Malcolm either did not "know that the ['He Had The Wrong Man'] quotation was false, or she [did not] act with a reckless disregard as to the truth or falsity of [the quotation]."
>
> Dr. Masson appealed and the 9th Circuit affirmed the trial court.

WRONG BUT NOT RECKLESS DISREGARD

Juries don't often find that journalists acted with reckless disregard. In those cases where they have, appellate courts have, more often than not, found negligence on the part of the journalist but that the journalist has acted with actual malice.

Some decisions have held that "internal inconsistencies" in a reporter's story do not make reckless disregard;[110] nor does the possibility that the reporter harbored "animosity", or a "grudge" or "ill will" toward the plaintiff;[111] nor does a combination of a reporter's failure to investigate, his possession (but omission from the story) of material contradictory to the hard words, plus the fact that the material was not "hot news" and so could have been further checked.[112] And to repeat, reckless disregard is not carelessness or negligence, which are flaws found often enough in news stories but which must be accepted in news about public issues and public persons if freedom is to have the "breathing space" it requires to survive.

A jury found flaws in the famous case of *Ariel Sharon v. Time, Inc.* Former Israeli Defense Minister Ariel Sharon had sued *Time* magazine over its story about the Israeli investigation into the massacre of hundreds of Palestinian civilians in two refugee camps near Beirut. Israel had invaded Lebanon in 1982 in order to destroy PLO (Palestinian Liberation Organization). The Sabra and Shatila refugee camps were surrounded by the Israeli army.[113]

> During Israel's occupation of West Beirut, and by prior arrangement with the Israel Defense Forces ("IDF"), members of the Christian Phalangist militia entered two Palestinian refugee camps, Sabra and Shatila. From September 16 to September 18, 1982, the Phalangists killed hundreds of Palestinian civilians, many of them women and children.

Time published an article on the findings of the Israeli investigation of the massacre, "The Verdict Is Guilty: An Israeli commission apportions

---

[110] *Foster v. Upchurch*, 624 S.W.2d 564 (Tex.1981), 7 Med.L.Rptr. 2533.

[111] *Lancaster v. Daily Banner-News Pub. Co., Inc.*, 274 Ark. 145, 622 S.W.2d 671 (1981), 8 Med.L.Rptr. 1093; *Curtis v. Southwestern Newspapers*, 677 F.2d 115 (5th Cir.1982), 8 Med.L.Rptr. 1651.

[112] *McNabb v. Oregonian Pub. Co.*, 69 Or.App. 136, 685 P.2d 458 (1984), 10 Med.L.Rptr. 2181.

[113] *Sharon v. Time, Inc.*, 599 F.Supp. 538, 542 (S.D.New York 1984).

the blame for the Beirut massacre."[114] The article reported on the Kahan Commission's findings and recommendations. It was, the article said, a "stinging indictment" of Sharon. The commission found that Sharon failed to consider the possibility of innocent Palestinians and that he had indirect responsibility for the massacre.[115]

> One section of the report, known as Appendix B, was not published at all, mainly for security reasons. That section contains the names of several intelligence agents referred to elsewhere in the report. *Time* has learned that it also contains further details about Sharon's visit to the Gemayel family on the day after Bashir Gemayel's assassination. Sharon reportedly told the Gemayels that the Israeli army would be moving into West Beirut and that he expected the Christian forces to go into the Palestinian refugee camps. Sharon also reportedly discussed with the Gemayels the need for the Phalangists to take revenge for the assassination of Bashir, but the details of the conversation are not known.

Sharon filed a $50 million suit for libel claiming the *Time* story said that he,[116] "instigated, encouraged, or condoned the massacres at Sabra and Shatilla, and because it suggests that the Commission had secret evidence or found secretly that he had lied when he testified that he had not known in advance that a massacre would occur."

There was no such statement in Appendix B. The reporter who wrote the finished story had taken David Halevy's[117] notes about Sharon's meeting with the Phalangists and revised them in one key way.[118]

> Where Mr. Halevy wrote that Mr. Sharon, "gave them the feeling" that "he understood their need to take revenge," Mr. Smith wrote that Mr. Sharon "discussed" their need for revenge.

The jury found that the statement about the meeting between Sharon and the Phalangists was false and damaging to his reputation. Jury foreman Richard Peter Zug read a statement conveying the jury's criticism of *Time*.[119]

> "We find," he said, "that certain *Time* employees, particularly correspondent David Halevy, acted negligently and carelessly in reporting and verifying the information which ultimately found its way into the published paragraph of interest in this case."

---

114 William E. Smith, " "The Verdict Is Guilty: An Israeli commission apportions the blame for the Beirut massacre," *Time*, Feb. 21, 1983.

115 Ibid.

116 *Sharon v. Time, Inc.*, 599 F.Supp. 538, 543 (S.D.New York 1984).

117 *Time* had sought documents from the U.S. Department of State and testimony from Sharon about the commission report and documents in the report from the Israeli government. All were denied.

118 Arnold H. Lubasch, "Time Cleared of Libeling Sharon But Jurors Criticize Its Reporting," *New York Times*, Jan. 25, 1985.

119 Ibid.

That wasn't enough for Sharon to win. As a public figure and former public official, he had to prove that *Time* published with actual malice. The jury did not find that. Both sides claimed victory. Sharon had proven the falsity of the *Time* report. *Time* continued to defend its reporting and pointed out that Israel had not provided adequate access to documents and witnesses needed to support the truth of the article. Time also was not permitted to call confidential sources to testify.

The cases of public-person plaintiffs who must accept without compensation the negligent, the careless—indeed the "irresponsible" and the "unreasonable"[120]—sometimes warrant the journalist's reflection: Floyd Rood, a tireless worker and publicist in youth assistance efforts including drug rehabilitation, was said in a news story to have begun a money-raising project "to help solve his drug addiction problem." The word "his" was wrong[121]; it had accidentally been changed from "the" in wire transmission. He lost his suit.

St. Louis Alderwoman Delores Glover, said erroneously by a newspaper to have had abortions, could not recover for libel, for the newspaper had been no more than negligent in its mistake.[122] Mrs. Glover attended a meeting on equipment required at clinics performing abortions. Mrs. Glover, an opponent of abortion, did not speak. In the discussion, fellow Alderwoman Lerel Stewart objected to requiring certain equipment. She said that, as she had gone through two abortions, she did not believe the equipment was necessary. Mrs. Stewart's remarks caused something of a furor.

After the meeting, Mrs. Stewart clarified what she said, explaining she had two involuntary miscarriages. A *Globe-Democrat* reporter covering the meeting phoned her story in[123]. A rewrite man took the call and confused the names writing that Mrs. Glover told the meeting she had two abortions. Ms. Glover had to be sedated when the newspaper with the story was published the next day. She sued for libel and won. The *Globe-Democrat* appealed to the Missouri Supreme Court which overturned the judgment.[124]

> We hold that notwithstanding the obvious and regrettable upset suffered by Mrs. Glover, as a public official she has failed as a matter of law to demonstrate that the *Globe-Democrat* published its story with the actual malice required to overcome the qualified constitutional privilege recognized in *New York*

[120] *Lawrence v. Bauer Pub. & Printing Ltd.*, 89 N.J. 451, 446 A.2d 469 (1982), 8 Med.L.Rptr. 1536, 1543.

[121] *Rood v. Finney*, 418 So.2d 1 (La.App.1982), 8 Med.L.Rptr. 2047.

[122] *Glover v. Herald Co.*, 549 S.W.2d 858 (Mo.1977), 2 Med.L.Rptr. 1846.

[123] In the days before smart phones and tablets, reporters covering news would telephone their newspapers and dictate their stories. A rewrite man, so called because the person would rewrite the notes into a story, would put everything together for a story. *Some may notice the gender-specific reference. Newspapers carried over the terminology of times when newspaper staffs were mainly men.

[124] *Glover v. Herald Co.*, 549 S.W.2d 858, 860 (Mo.1977), 2 Med.L.Rptr. 1846.

Times Co. v. Sullivan, 376 U.S. 254, 84 S.Ct. 710, 11 L.Ed.2d 686 (1964), and therefore, the judgment and verdict in the circuit court are reversed.

MURPHY V. BOSTON HERALD, INC. ET AL.

The "actual malice" shield for news media is not bulletproof. That was demonstrated by Massachusetts Superior Court Judge Ernest B. Murphy's $2.01 million libel verdict against the *Boston Herald* and reporter David Wedge. On May 7, 2007, the $2.09 million verdict—reduced by the trial judge to $2.01 million—was upheld by Massachusetts' highest tribunal, the Supreme Judicial Court. The verdict also echoed the United States Supreme Court's finding in *Harte-Hanks v. Connaughton* (1989) that slipshod reporting could result in liability for a publication characterized by knowing falsity or reckless disregard for the truth.[125]

By itself, the *Boston Herald* libel case represents a cautionary tale for news media, emphasizing lessons that should already have been learned about: (1) not relying on second-hand versions of statements supposedly made in closed meetings which the reporter could not attend; (2) not using shaky information to build a crusade to try to get rid of a public official; (3) not republishing damaging information without checking the facts (or lack of facts) underlying the original story; (4) not multiplying the reach of a shaky news report by appearing on a national television program, and (5) not losing or destroying a reporter's notes.

Early in 2002, the *Boston Herald* published a front-page story written by David Wedge and another reporter, Jules Crittenden, headlined "Murphy's Law: Lenient judge frees dangerous criminals." One of the news stories critical of Judge Murphy, published Feb. 13, 2002, said that judge " 'heartlessly demeaned victims.' "

The article was accompanied by a photograph of Judge Murphy, captioned "Under Fire." The article's lead began, "A wrist-slapping New Bedford Superior Court judge under fire for letting four accused rapists return to the streets has a pro-defendant stance and has heartlessly demeaned victims, according to records and sources." The February 13, 2002, article continued,[126]

> According to several courthouse sources, Judge Ernest B. Murphy said of a teenage rape victim, "She can't go through life as a victim. She's [fourteen].
>
> She got raped. Tell her to get over it."
>
> The exchange occurred in Murphy's New Bedford Superior Court chambers last week, when prosecutors confronted

---

[125] *Murphy v. Boston Herald, Inc.*, 449 Mass. 42, 865 N.E.2d 746, 35 Media L. Rep. 1865 (Massachusetts 2007). Citing *Harte-Hanks v. Connaughton*, 491 U.S. 657, 691–692, 109 S.Ct. 2678 (1989).

[126] Ibid. at 44, 750.

> Murphy over his lenient sentencing practices. He also belittled a [seventy-nine] year old robbery victim when prosecutors pushed for a tough jail term for her attackers, reportedly saying, "I don't care if she's [one hundred and nine]," sources said.

A subsequent story in the *Boston Herald*, on February 14, 2002, under David Wedge's byline, was headlined "Rape victim's mom pleads . . . dump the judge." The article's lead said,[127] "A criminal-coddling judge who has let four accused rapists walk out of court in the past week should be removed by acting Gov. Jane Swift, the enraged mother of one of the rape victims said yesterday." This story then repeated the first story's words about what the judge reportedly said to a 14-year-old rape victim: " 'She's [fourteen]. She got raped. Tell her to get over it.' " Nine other *Boston Herald* article used those word, even though eight of the nine articles were written by reporters other than Wedge.[128]

At trial, Wedge testified that he had heard of a controversy about sentencing practices and was assigned to investigate growing public criticism of the judge. Wedge testified that an assistant district attorney and the district attorney told him about Judge Murphy's comments but said they had not heard the judge themselves. Wedge met with the prosecutor who was in the courtroom when Judge Murphy made his comments. He testified that prosecutor David Crowley confirmed to Wedge that the district attorney had correctly characterized the statements. Wedge read from his notebook the quotations that would appear in the Herald, and Crowley did not indicate that any of the information was inaccurate. The interview took place before the story was published, he testified.

But, as Justice John Greaney wrote in his opinion for the court, Wedge's testimony in court did not match up with his testimony in depositions. At deposition, Wedge said he did not talk to Crowley until after his story ran.[129]

> Wedge conceded that his sources for the statement (FitzGerald, Walsh, and Crowley) related the statement using slightly different words, and that, instead of "tell her to get over it," the words told him may have been, "she's got to get over it." At one point in his deposition, Wedge testified that all three of his sources had told him that the plaintiff had said, "She's a [fourteen year old] girl, she got raped, she's got to get on with her life and get over it."

Wedge testified that he tried to talk to Judge Murphy before the article ran. He said he went to the New Bedford courthouse to interview

[127] Ibid. at 45, 750.

[128] Ibid. at footnotes.

[129] Ibid. at 53, 755–756.

Judge Murphy but was turned away by a clerk. He asked a court officer to pass on a note, but the officer said no, Wedge testified.[130]

> When asked to describe the court officer at the courthouse who had (as Wedge testified) barred his access to the plaintiff on February 12, Wedge was unable to provide any details. Wedge admitted, in deposition testimony, that he did not know the location, in the courthouse, of the court room in which the plaintiff was sitting that day, and admitted, essentially, that there had been no note.
>
> [* * *]
>
> In the end, Wedge also was unable to identify any source for his reported statements that the plaintiff "heartlessly demeaned victims." Finally, Wedge conceded that the statement in the February 14 article reporting that the rape victim "took the stand and tearfully told the [plaintiff] how the rape had affected her" was false.

Wedge appeared on March 7, 2002, on *Fox*'s "The O'Reilly Factor." Host Bill O'Reilly asked Wedge whether he was sure that Judge Murphy had said that the rape victim should get over it, and Wedge replied,[131] "Yes, he said this. He made this comment to three lawyers. He knows he said it, and everybody else that knows this judge knows that he said it."

Judge Greaney, however, pointed out that at the time Wedge made the comment on the O'Reilly Factor, he "knew that three lawyers did not tell him that they heard the statement."

Judge Greaney's opinion included a devastating indictment of slipshod journalism at the newspaper:[132] "Neither Wedge, nor any other person at the trial, could name one person at the *Herald* who either edited, or checked for accuracy of, the content of Wedge's articles. It is fair to say that, by the end of Wedge's testimony, his credibility on any material factual point at issue was in tatters."

> Judge Murphy testified that the statements in the newspaper had damaged his reputation, caused him other injuries, and had been published with actual malice. Judge Murphy had received boxes of irate letters from persons he did not know, many of them referring to the "tell her to get over it" phrase. Death threats arrived in some of those letters.[133] The first death threat was slipped under the door of Judge Murphy's chambers. It consisted a picture of Judge Murphy taken from the Herald's coverage, with a target superimposed on the judge's face. A bullet hole was drawn on Judge Murphy's forehead in that

---

[130] Ibid. at 53–54, 756.

[131] Ibid. at 45, 750.

[132] Ibid. at 53, 756.

[133] Ibid. at 66, 764.

picture, and the photo carried the handwritten message, " 'YOU'RE DEAD! "GET OVER IT" YOU BASTARD!' "

Justice Greaney and the rest of the Massachusetts Supreme Court upheld the libel award.

27. PUBLIC OFFICIALS AND FIGURES

WHO BEARS THE ACTUAL MALICE BURDEN IN DEFAMATION?

Did "public official" in *New York Times v. Sullivan* mean every person who is employed by government at any level? Justice Brennan foresaw that this question would arise, but said simply in a footnote in the *Sullivan* case:[134] "It is enough for the present case that respondent's position as an elected city commissioner clearly made him a public official * * *"

Discussions of "who is a public official" (or "public figure") all too often come up in newsrooms after a publication or broadcast has been made that looks as if it may result in a defamation lawsuit. Some of the time, it will be apparent that the individual involved is a public official: the President of the United States, a governor, a state legislator. It would be simple if holding a government position automatically gave one the status of public official. But in the famous 1979 decision in *Hutchinson v. Proxmire*, the U.S. Supreme Court said in a footnote that "public official" is not synonymous with "public employee."

Over the years, the courts evolved the definition as it applied or declined to apply the Sullivan standard to plaintiffs.

In 1966, *Rosenblatt v. Baer* helped the definition. Newspaper columnist Alfred D. Rosenblatt wrote in the *Laconia Evening Citizen* that a public ski area, which in previous years had been a financially shaky operation, now was doing "hundreds of percent" better. He asked, "What happened to all the money last year? And every other year?" Baer, who had been dismissed from his county post as ski area supervisor the year before, brought a suit charging that the column libeled him. A New Hampshire court upheld his complaint and awarded him $31,500. But when the case reached the United States Supreme Court, it reversed and remanded the case. It said that Baer did indeed come within the "public official" category:[135]

> Criticism of government is at the very center of the constitutionally protected area of free discussion. Criticism of those responsible for government operations must be free, lest criticism of government be penalized. It is clear, therefore, that the "public official" designation applies at the very least to those

---

134 *New York Times Co. v. Sullivan*, 376 U.S. 254, 282 n. 23, 84 S.Ct. 710, 727 n. 23 (1964).

135 *Rosenblatt v. Baer*, 383 U.S. 75, 86 S.Ct. 669 (1966).

among the hierarchy of government employees who have, or appear to the public to have, substantial responsibility for or control over the conduct of governmental affairs.

The Court applied the *Sullivan* rule to Baer, who had left public service before publication. Continuing public interest in the issue regarding Baer while he was a public official was a substantial factor.

Discussions of "who is a public official" (or "public figure") all too often come up in newsrooms after a publication or broadcast has been made that looks as if it may result in a defamation lawsuit. Some of the time, it will be apparent that the individual involved is a public official: the president of the United States, a governor, a state legislator. It would be simple if holding a government position automatically gave one the status of public official. But in the famous 1979 decision in *Hutchinson v. Proxmire*,[136] the U.S. Supreme Court said in a footnote that "public official" is not synonymous with "public employee."

Such uncertainty comes from the legal fact of life that every libel suit is tried on a case-by-case basis. Because, as has been said, courts move with adequate precedent if not with adequate grace, it is not surprising that courts sometimes reach inconsistent and even contradictory conclusions about who is and who is not designated a "public official."

Consider these examples:

A coach and athletic director at a 130-student Texas high school is a public official,[137] yet a wrestling coach known state-wide in Ohio was held to be a private figure.[138]

As Robert D. Sack and Sandra S. Baron have noted,[139] "authorities are sharply divided over whether a public school teacher * * * is a public official."

Cases that did not reach the United States Supreme Court have provided some guidance, starting soon after *Times v. Sullivan* was decided. During 1964, the Pennsylvania Supreme Court applied public figure status to a senator who was candidate for re-election.[140] Shortly,

---

[136] *Hutchinson v. Proxmire*, 443 U.S. 111, 99 S.Ct. 267, 561 L.Ed.2d 411, 5 Media L. Rep. 1279 (1979). See David A. Elder, "The Supreme Court and Defamation: a Relaxation of Constitutional Standards," *Kentucky Bench and Bar*, Jan. 1980, pp. 38–39.

[137] *Johnson v. Southwestern Newspapers Corp.*, 855 S.W.2d 182 (Tex.App.1993), 21 Med.L.Rptr. 1746.

[138] *Milkovich v. News-Herald*, 15 Ohio St.3d 292, 473 N.E.2d 1191 (1984), 11 Med.L.Rptr. 1598.

[139] Robert D. Sack and Sandra S. Baron, *Libel, Slander and Related Problems* (New York: Practising Law Institute, 1994) p. 255, citing *Basarich v. Rodeghero*, 24 Ill.App.3d 889, 321 N.E.2d 739 (1974) (teacher is public figure) and *Richmond Newspapers, Inc. v. Lipscomb*, 234 Va. 277, 362 S.E.2d 32 (1987), 14 Med.L.Rptr. 1953, and others (teacher not public figure.)

[140] *Clark v. Allen*, 415 Pa. 484, 204 A.2d 42 (1964).

state legislators were included,[141] a former mayor,[142] a deputy sheriff,[143] a school board member,[144] an appointed city tax assessor,[145] and a police sergeant.[146] A state legislative clerk was ruled a public official, in his suit against a former state senator who accused the clerk of wiretapping when he was actually doing his clerk's duty in trying to identify a telephone caller who used obscenities.[147]

In some cases, it has been held that one retains public-official status despite lapse of time: A former federal narcotics agent was designated a "public official" in his libel suit for a story about his official misconduct, despite the fact that he had left the agency six years earlier.[148] And since 1971, the Supreme Court's rule has been that a charge of criminal conduct against a present official, no matter how remote in time or place the conduct was, is always "relevant to his fitness for office," and that he must prove actual malice in a libel suit.[149]

Although "public official" would seem to be readily identifiable, many questions remain. Courts and commentators have long taken the view that holding a government position almost automatically gives one the status of public official. There are others who are paid by government, but who are not government employees. Consultants and contractors who earn their entire livelihoods from government may escape the "public official" label.[150] In a Texas case, a county surveyor who brought a libel suit against a newspaper for its criticism of his work as an engineering consultant to a municipality was ruled not to be a public official but a private person in his consultant's work.[151] And the Court of Appeals for the Fourth Circuit ruled that the Iroquois Research Institute, employed by the Fairfax County (Va.) Water Authority as a research consultant in a county project, did not have public official status. Relying on the *Rosenblatt v. Baer* decision, the court said that Iroquois was in the sole role of a scientific fact finder, merely reporting the facts it found to the Water Authority. It had no control over the conduct of government

---

141 *Washington Post Co. v. Keogh,* 125 U.S.App.D.C. 32, 365 F.2d 965 (1966); *Rose v. Koch and Christian Research, Inc.,* 278 Minn. 235, 154 N.W.2d 409 (1967).

142 *Washington Post Co. v. Keogh,* 125 U.S.App.D.C. 32, 365 F.2d 965 (1966); *Rose v. Koch and Christian Research, Inc.,* 278 Minn. 235, 154 N.W.2d 409 (1967).

143 *St. Amant v. Thompson,* 390 U.S. 727, 88 S.Ct. 1323 (1968).

144 *Cabin v. Community Newspapers, Inc.,* 50 Misc.2d 574, 270 N.Y.S.2d 913 (1966).

145 *Eadie v. Pole,* 91 N.J.Super. 504, 221 A.2d 547 (1966).

146 *Suchomel v. Suburban Life Newspapers, Inc.,* 84 Ill.App.2d 239, 228 N.E.2d 172 (1967).

147 *Martonik v. Durkan,* 23 Wash.App. 47, 596 P.2d 1054 (1979), 5 Med.L.Rptr. 1266.

148 *Hart v. Playboy Enterprises* (D.C.Kan.1979), 5 Med.L.Rptr. 1811.

149 *Monitor Patriot Co. v. Roy,* 401 U.S. 265, 91 S.Ct. 621 (1971).

150 *Hutchinson v. Proxmire,* 443 U.S. 111, 119 n. 8, 99 S.Ct. 2675, 2680 n. 8 (1979). See David A. Elder, "The Supreme Court and Defamation: a Relaxation of Constitutional Standards," *Kentucky Bench and Bar,* Jan. 1980, pp. 38–39.

151 *Foster v. Laredo Newspapers, Inc.,* 541 S.W.2d 809 (Tex.1976), certiorari denied 429 U.S. 1123, 97 S.Ct. 1160 (1977).

affairs, made no recommendations, was little known to the public, and exercised no discretion.[152] It was private.

Nine major media organizations unsuccessfully urged the United States Supreme Court to review the appeals court decision for *Iroquois*, asserting that the case,[153] "presents perhaps the most significant unresolved issue in the constitutional law of defamation * * *." The Supreme Court denied review and the case went back to trial court with Iroquois confirmed for trial as a private figure.

John B. McCrory and Robert C. Bernius described a good analytical frame for determining when a person could be classed as a public official. If a person is in a position to make policy and has access to the press (presumably for self-defense), that can add up to classification as a public official.[154] That analysis—doubtless making too much sense to apply uniformly to defamation cases—cuts across whether an official is elected or appointed. Such an approach even meant that a receptionist in a public clinic was a public official, because she had sole responsibility for making appointments, making her job performance a matter of undeniable public interest.[155]

EXTENDING THE PUBLIC OFFICIAL STATUS TO PUBLIC FIGURES

The doctrine of *New York Times Co. v. Sullivan* extends the requirement of proving actual malice to public figures, such as non-official persons who involve themselves in the resolution of public questions. After all, persons who throw themselves into public controversies in an attempt to influence their outcomes are more than just anonymous residents of a community caught up in a newspaper story.

In the *Rosenblatt*, Justice Douglas wrote a separate concurring opinion. In it he raised the question of what persons and what issues might call for an extension of the *Sullivan* doctrine beyond "public officials." He said:[156]

> * * * I see no way to draw lines that exclude the night watchman, the file clerk, the typist, or, for that matter, anyone on the public payroll. And how about those who contract to carry out governmental missions? Some of them are as much in the

---

[152] *Arctic Co., Ltd. v. Loudoun Times Mirror et al.*, 624 F.2d 518 (4th Cir.1980), 6 Med.L.Rptr. 1433, 1435.

[153] 6 Med.L.Rptr. #31 (Dec. 9, 1980), News Notes; John Consoli, "Consultants to Gov't. Aren't Public Figures," *Editor & Publisher*, Jan. 17, 1981, 9.

[154] 1993 edition of "Constitutional Privilege in Libel Law," by John B. McCrory and Robert C. Bernius, updated by Robert D. Sack et. al., in James C. Goodale, chairman, *Communications Law* 1993, Vol. II, p. 259.

[155] Ibid. at 261, citing *Auvil v. Times Journal Co.* (E.D.Va.1984), 10 Med.L. Rptr. 2302.

[156] *Rosenblatt v. Baer*, 383 U.S. 75, 89, 86 S.Ct. 669, 678 (1966).

> public domain as any so-called officeholder * * * [T]he question is whether a public issue not a public official, is involved.

Back in 1966, the decision in a suit brought by the noted scientist and Nobel Prize winner, Dr. Linus Pauling, indeed said that it wasn't just "public officials" who would have to prove actual malice if they were to succeed with libel suits. Pauling sued the *St. Louis Globe-Democrat* claiming libel in an editorial entitled "Glorification of Deceit." It referred to a non-appearance by Pauling before a subcommittee of the United States Senate, in connection with Pauling's attempts to promote a nuclear test ban treaty. It read in part: "Pauling contemptuously refused to testify and was cited for contempt of Congress. He appealed to the United States District Court to rid him of the contempt citation, which that Court refused to do." Pauling said that he had not been cited for contempt, that he had not appealed to any court to rid himself of any contempt citation, and that no appeal was expected.

The federal court conceded that Pauling was not a "public official" such as the plaintiff in *New York Times Co. v. Sullivan*. But it added:[157]

> We feel, however, that the implications of the Supreme Court's majority opinions are clear. Professor Pauling, by his public statements and actions, was projecting himself into the arena of public controversy and into the very "vortex of the discussion of a question of pressing public concern". He was attempting to influence the resolution of an issue which was important, which was of profound effect, which was public and which was internationally controversial * * *.

Pauling took his case to the United States Supreme Court, but the justices denied certiorari,[158] and the lower court's decision stood.

WALKER V. A.P. (1967)

While public figure Linus Pauling was thus being embraced within the *Sullivan* rules, a retired general in the United States Army was undertaking a set of "chain" libel suits. Maj. Gen. Edwin A. Walker (whose case was discussed above) had been involved in a controversy when he was forced to leave the service after it was disclosed that he was conducting political indoctrination of U.S. troops stationed in Germany.

Walker had opposed integration in the military and he continued to voice his opposition after he entered civilian life. Segregationists looked to him for leadership and Walker consented to the creation of a "Walker for president" political exploration committee. A little-known fact is that Lee Harvey Oswald said that he had tried to assassinate Walker in Dallas, but failed when the pistol shot he took at the former general missed. Walker was a "public figure," said Justice Harlan in writing for

---

[157] *Pauling v. Globe-Democrat Pub. Co.*, 362 F.2d 188, 195–196 (8th Cir.1966).

[158] *Pauling v. National Review, Inc.*, 49 Misc.2d 975, 269 N.Y.S.2d 11 (1966).

four members of the Court,[159] "by his purposeful activity amounting to a thrusting of his personality into the 'vortex' of an important public controversy."

Under any reasoning, General Walker was a public man in whose public conduct society and the press had a legitimate and substantial interest.

Harlan argued that the public figure should not have to meet as difficult a standard of proof as the public official. He articulated a lower barrier for public figures:[160]

> We consider and would hold that a "public figure" who is not a public official may * * * recover damages for a defamatory falsehood whose substance makes substantial danger to reputation apparent, on a showing of highly unreasonable conduct constituting an extreme departure from the standards of investigation and reporting ordinarily adhered to by responsible publishers.

Justice Warren disagreed, writing in his concurrence: "Under any reasoning, General Walker was a public man" in whose conduct society had a substantial interest. Warren said that giving a public figure, such as Walker, an easier burden to meet than a public official in recovering damages for libel,[161] "* * * has no basis in law, logic or First Amendment policy. Increasingly in this country, the distinction between governmental and private sectors are blurred * * *"

ROSENBLOOM V. METROMEDIA

In 1971, the Supreme Court took up the case of *Rosenbloom v. Metromedia*, Inc.[162] George Rosenbloom, a distributor of nudist magazines in Philadelphia, was a private citizen arrested in a crackdown on obscenity. Metromedia radio station WIP had said Rosenbloom had been arrested on charges of possessing obscene literature and linked him to the "smut literature rackets." Later acquitted of obscenity charges, Rosenbloom sued for libel in the WIP broadcasts, and won $275,000 in trial.

But the station took the case up to the Supreme Court. There was no majority opinion, but five justices agreed that Rosenbloom should not recover. The largest block, a plurality of three justices, approved extending the actual malice requirement in libel whenever the news was a "matter of public interest." It was a substantial extension of the protections for the media. The three justices endorsed the "matter of public interest" rationale, laid out by Justice William J. Brennan:[163]

---

[159] *Associated Press v. Walker*, 388 U.S. 130, 155, 87 S.Ct. 1975, 1991 (1967).

[160] Ibid. at 155, 1991.

[161] Ibid. at 163–165, 1995–1997.

[162] *Rosenbloom v. Metromedia*, 403 U.S. 29, 91 S.Ct. 1811 (1971).

[163] Ibid. at 43, 91 S.Ct. at 1819.

> If a matter is a subject of public or general interest, it cannot suddenly become less so merely because a private individual is involved, or because in some sense the individual did not "voluntarily" choose to become involved. The public's primary interest is in the event * * *. We honor the commitment to robust debate on public issues, which is embodied in the First Amendment, by extending constitutional protection to all discussion and communication involving matters of public or general concern, without regard to whether the persons involved are famous or anonymous.

Lower courts accepted the plurality opinion as gospel. The sweep of "matter of public or general interest" was so powerful that few libel suits, whether by public or private persons were won. Commentators on press law predicted the disappearance of libel suits. But in mid-1974, hardly three years after *Rosenbloom*, the three-justice plurality for the "matter of public interest" interpretation revealed itself as a shaky foundation. A five-justice majority of the U.S. Supreme Court rejected it as a rule in *Gertz v. Robert Welch, Inc.*[164] *Gertz* would restore certainty to the process of deciding when professional communicators would have the protections of actual malice and when private persons would be able to recover after proving negligence.

Rosenbloom is alive, sort of. The Indiana Supreme Court breathed new vitality into the doctrine in 1999 in the case of *Journal-Gazette Co., Inc. v. Bandido's*.[165] The case had its beginnings in an unappetizing headline about a restaurant in Fort Wayne. Bandido's had three restaurants in Fort Wayne and another in Lima, Ohio. In 1988, the Allen County Board of Health inspected the north-side Bandido's in Fort Wayne. The inspector's report included these remarks:[166] "Evidence of flies, roaches and rodents noted. Advise exterminator to do a full clean-out of premises. Rodent droppings noted only in restroom."

A second inspection conducted three weeks later found no evidence of rodents. But the day after that second inspection, the Board of Health revoked the restaurant's permit and closed the north-side Bandido's. When the *Journal-Gazette* published a story about the closure, the article had the following headline:[167] "Health Board shuts doors of Bandido's Inspectors find rats, roaches at local eatery."

The problem with the headline lay in the fact that rodent droppings do not rats make. The health inspector never found rats in the restaurant and there was no statement that rats were found in the restaurant in the story but rather evidence of rodents. The restaurant owner asked for a

164 *Gertz v. Robert Welch, Inc.*, 418 U.S. 323, 94 S.Ct. 2997 (1974). For the position that the "public interest" criterion should be the rule, see Anthony Lewis, "New York Times v. Sullivan Reconsidered * * *," 83 *Columbia L.Rev.* 603 (1983).

165 *Journal-Gazette Co., Inc. v. Bandido's*, 712 N.E.2d 446 (Ind.1999), 27 Med.L.Rptr. 2089.

166 Ibid. at 449.

167 Ibid. at 450.

retraction and the newspaper published a story under the headline, "Owner says Bandido's likely to open today."

Initially, the owner was satisfied with the retraction and sent a letter to that effect. But ten days after sending the letter, the owner hired a new attorney who wrote a new letter saying that the follow-up story was not adequate. The headline did not indicate that the newspaper was retracting its story, the letter explained. The attorney asked the newspaper to print an equal-size retraction headline in the same location in the newspaper as the original story.

The *Journal-Gazette* refused to do that and Bandido's sued. The trial judge ruled that Bandido's was a limited-purpose public figure (more on public figure categories later in this chapter) which would have to prove that the newspaper published with actual malice. The jury found for Bandido's and awarded the plaintiff $985,000.

The Indiana Court of Appeals reversed the trial court, concluding that the record failed to show that there was sufficient evidence of actual malice. Both Bandido's and the *Journal-Gazette* appealed to the Indiana Supreme Court which also overturned the trial court verdict. In doing so, the Indiana court declared that libel plaintiffs in Indiana would have to prove actual malice whether they were public figures or private persons. The mechanism by which the Indiana high court made that choice was the affirmation of a prior holding in a case from the Indiana Court of Appeals. In *Aafco Heating and Air Conditioning Co. v. Northwest Publications, Inc.*,[168] the court of appeals applied the *Rosenbloom* plurality holding that when published statements dealt with matters of public interest there should be no difference in the treatment between private persons and public figures.[169]

The Indiana Court of Appeals properly noted that applying a negligence standard to private individuals and an actual malice standard to public figures "assumes that society has a greater interest in protecting 'private' reputation than safeguarding the community standing and repute of 'public officials' and 'public figures.'" Such an assumption does not exist in Indiana in matters of public or general concern where "[t]he reputations of public figures and public officials merit the same quantum of protection as those of private citizens."

The Indiana Supreme Court also concluded that there was little difference between the abilities of public figures and private figures to gain access to "channels of effective communication" so that they could respond to defamatory statements. The Indiana court's reasoning was that relatively few public officials or public figures actually have the means by which to command the attention of the media. Most public

---

[168] *Aafco Heating and Air Conditioning Co. v. Northwest Publications, Inc.*, 162 Ind.App. 671, 321 N.E.2d 580 (Ind.Ct.App.1974), 1 Med.L.Rptr. 1683.

[169] *Journal-Gazette Co., Inc. v. Bandido's*, 712 N.E.2d 446 (Ind.1999), 27 Med.L.Rptr. 2089.

figures and officials are more like private persons with respect to access to the media.

Finally, the Indiana Supreme Court rejected the notion that public figures accepted the risks and differential standard of proof by being in the public. Quoting from the *Rosenbloom* plurality, the Indiana Court advanced the argument that:[170]

> the idea that certain "public" figures have voluntarily exposed their entire lives to public inspection, while private individuals have kept theirs carefully shrouded from public view is, at best, a legal fiction.

The Indiana Supreme Court, recognizing that it could not impose a negligence standard for public figures and public officials because of the *Sullivan* rule, instead chose to apply the actual malice standard to private persons where stories were of public or general interest.

28. DEFINING "PUBLIC FIGURE"

Distinguishing a public from a private person under *Gertz* rests on either of two bases: 1.) fame, notoriety, power or influence that render one a public figure for all purposes, or 2.) the status that makes one a public figure only for a limited range of issues. In either case, the person assumes special prominence in the resolution of public controversy.

The *Gertz* case came a scant three years after *Rosenbloom*. In *Gertz*, the Supreme Court found a balanced approach to deciding which plaintiffs would have to prove actual malice and which would be able to win their cases with a lesser burden, in most cases proving that the defendant published the story negligently.

Elmer Gertz, a Chicago lawyer, was retained by a family to bring a civil action against Policeman Richard Nuccio who had shot and killed their son and had been convicted of second-degree murder. *American Opinion*, a monthly publication given to the views of the John Birch Society, carried an article saying that Gertz was an architect of a "frame-up" of Nuccio, that he was part of a communist conspiracy to discredit local police, and that he was a Leninist and a "Communist-fronter." Gertz, who was none of these things, brought a libel suit and for six years battled the shifting uncertainties of the courts' attitudes toward "public official," "public figure," and "matter of public interest" for the purposes of libel. A jury found libel per se and awarded Gertz $50,000 in damages. The award was disallowed by the trial judge and also by the Seventh Circuit Court of Appeals:[171] Because the *American Opinion* story

[170] Ibid. at 453.

[171] *Gertz v. Robert Welch, Inc.*, 471 F.2d 801 (7th Cir.1972). A dozen years after Gertz brought his first action, a federal jury awarded him $400,000 upon re-trial, and the Seventh Circuit Court of Appeals upheld the award: *Gertz v. Robert Welch, Inc.*, 680 F.2d 527 (7th Cir.1982), 8 Med.L.Rptr. 1769.

concerned a matter of public interest, Gertz would have to show actual malice on its part, even though he might be a private citizen. Objecting, Gertz appealed to the U.S. Supreme Court.

PRIVATE INDIVIDUALS EXEMPTED FROM ACTUAL MALICE RULE

With four other justices agreeing, Justice Powell wrote for the majority.[172] The plurality opinion in *Rosenbloom v. Metromedia*, relied on by the Circuit Court, should not stand. Justice Powell had no quarrel with requiring public officials and public figures to prove actual malice in their libel suits. But he reasoned that the legitimate state interest in compensating injury to the reputation of private individuals—of whom, it was found, Gertz was one—requires that such persons be held to less demanding proof of fault by the offending news medium—only "negligence," rather than the stern actual malice standard. They are at a disadvantage, compared with public officials and public figures, where they are defamed:[173]

> Public officials and public figures usually enjoy significantly greater access to the channels of effective communication and hence have a more realistic opportunity to counteract false statements than private individuals normally enjoy. Private individuals are therefore more vulnerable to injury, and the state interest in protecting them is correspondingly greater. * * *
>
> An individual who decides to seek governmental office must accept certain necessary consequences of that involvement in public affairs. He runs the risk of closer public scrutiny than might otherwise be the case. * * *

Those classed as public figures stand in a similar position. Hypothetically, it may be possible for someone to become a public figure through no purposeful action of his own, but the instances of truly involuntary public figures must be exceedingly rare. For the most part those who attain this status have assumed roles of special prominence in the affairs of society.

> * * * the communications media are entitled to act on the assumption that public officials and public figures have voluntarily exposed themselves to increased risk of injury from defamatory falsehoods concerning them. No such assumption is justified with respect to a private individual. He has not accepted public office nor assumed an "influential role in ordering society." * * *

---

[172] *Gertz v. Robert Welch, Inc.*, 418 U.S. 323, 94 S.Ct. 2997 (1974).

[173] Ibid. at 344–346, 3009–3010.

Dissenting Justices Douglas and Brennan wanted to affirm the Court of Appeals finding that anyone—including Gertz—would have to prove actual malice in offending words from a story of general or public interest. Brennan argued that the *Gertz* decision damaged the protection which mass media ought to have under the First Amendment. Douglas repeated his view that the First Amendment would bar Congress from passing any libel law; and like Congress,[174] "States are without power 'to use a civil libel law or any other law to impose damages for merely discussing public affairs.' "

Brennan, who had written the plurality opinion in *Rosenbloom*, reiterated his point there: "Matters of public or general interest do not,[175] 'suddenly become less so merely because a private individual is involved, or because in some sense the individual did not "voluntarily" choose to become involved.' " He said it is unproved and highly improbable that the public figure will have better access to the media. The ability of all to get access will depend on the "same complex factor * * *: the unpredictable event of the media's continuing interest in the story." As to the assumption that private people deserve special treatment because they do not assume the risk of defamation by freely entering the public arena, Brennan stated that,[176] "* * * voluntarily or not, we are all 'public' men to some degree."

GERTZ IS NOT A "PUBLIC" PERSON

In *Gertz v. Welch,* the Supreme Court first brushed off the notion that he might be a public official. Gertz had never had a paid government position and his only "office" had been as a member of mayors' housing committee years before. As for the suggestion that he was a "de facto public official" because he had appeared at the coroner's inquest into the murder (incidental to his representing the family in civil litigation), if that made him a "public official," the court said, all lawyers would become public officials in their status as "officers of the court," which would make little sense.

But the troublesome possibility that Gertz was a *public figure* remained. Because lower courts have so frequently relied on the Supreme Court's treatment of the matter in *Gertz,* detail is called for here.

To begin, the court said, persons in either of two cases,[177] "assume special prominence in the resolution of public questions." Also, "they invite attention and comment."

> [A public figure] designation may rest on either of two alternative bases. In some instances, an individual may achieve

[174] Ibid. at 356, 3015.

[175] Ibid. at 362, 3018.

[176] Ibid. at 364, 3019.

[177] Ibid. at 352, 3013. Succeeding definitions and procedures in determining "public figure" are taken from *Gertz,* pp. 343 and 351, 94 S.Ct. at 3009 and 3013.

such pervasive fame or notoriety that he becomes a public figure for all purposes and contexts. More commonly, an individual voluntarily injects himself or is drawn into a particular public controversy and thereby becomes a public figure for a limited range of issues. In either case such persons assume special prominence in the resolution of public questions.

1. The first of the two—deemed a public figure for all purposes and in all contexts: One should not be deemed a public personality for all aspects of his life, "absent clear evidence of general fame or notoriety in the community and pervasive involvement in the affairs of society."

Gertz was not a public figure under this first category. He had, indeed, been active in community and professional affairs, serving as an officer of local civil groups and various legal agencies. He had published several works on law. Thus, he was well-known in some circles. But he had "achieved no general fame or notoriety in the community." No member of the jury panel, for example, had ever heard of him.

2. The second of the two—where "an individual voluntarily injects himself * * * into a particular public controversy and thereby becomes a public figure for a limited range of issues." Alternative wording used by the court was that "commonly, those classed as public figures have thrust themselves[178] 'into the vortex' of particular public controversies in order to influence the resolution of the issues involved."

In determining the status of this person who has no general fame or notoriety in the community, the court said the procedure should be one of "looking to the nature and extent of an individual's participation in the particular controversy giving rise to the defamation." In this statement, the Court was rejecting the trend under *Rosenbloom* to examine the *topic* of the news to determine whether the public principle held, and instead to examine the *individual* and his role in public life. Doing this for attorney Gertz, the court found again that he was not a public figure: He had played only a minimal role at the coroner's inquest, and only as the representative of a private client; he had no part in the criminal prosecution of Officer Nuccio; he had never discussed the case with the press; and he "did not thrust himself into the vortex of this public issue * * *" nor "engage the public's attention in an attempt to influence its outcome." Gertz was not, by this second basis, a public figure, and he would not, consequently, have to prove that *American Opinion* libeled him with actual malice. The Supreme Court ordered a new trial.

The modification of *Sullivan* and *Rosenbloom* by *Gertz* was a damaging retreat in protection in the eyes of media commentators. Some, journalists suspected that although there were gains for the media under *Gertz*—in requiring plaintiffs to show fault and in limiting the reach of

---

[178] As a variant of the "limited range of issues" public figure, the Court identified the person who has not voluntarily entered a public controversy, but is drawn into it. Subsequent decisions have heavily vitiated this concept. See M.L. Rosen, "Media Lament: the Rise and Fall of Involuntary Public Figures," 54 *St. John's L.Rev.* 487, Spring 1980.

punitive damages—it was on the whole a great door-opener for libel suits by private plaintiffs who no longer had to prove actual malice.

David A. Anderson, legal scholar and former journalist, argued that even under the protection of the *Rosenbloom* interpretation, the self-censorship by the press which *Sullivan* had sought to minimize in establishing the malice rule and other safeguards, was real.[179] He wrote that the unconventional, non-established media, sometimes known as the "alternative" press, and the world of magazines, are forced to self-censorship under *Gertz*. The people about whom the alternative press writes are frequently from spheres of life not much handled by the established newspaper media, and thus not established as "public figures." Often financially marginal, the unconventional media face a further problem in the high cost of legal defense. Anderson's worry over self-censorship, whether under *Gertz* or under draconian jury awards even where the greater protection of *Sullivan* applies, runs strongly through the world of the media.[180]

COURTS DETERMINE "PUBLIC" AND "PRIVATE" UNDER GERTZ

Whatever the level of press self-censorship under *Gertz* may be, subsequent cases show that media need to be discriminating. Sometimes, distinguishing the "public" from the "private" is not easy, even for the judge, who makes the decision before the case goes to the jury. One judge has said[181] that the two concepts are "nebulous:" "Defining public figures is much like trying to nail a jellyfish to the wall."

Recall that the *Gertz* decision set up two categories of public figures:

(1) Persons (including organizations) who are "all purpose" or "pervasive" public figures because they have pervasive fame or influence, in their own communities if not regionally or nationally.

(2) "Limited purpose" (sometimes called "vortex") public figures (including organizations), who voluntarily have injected themselves into a matter of public controversy, to help resolve that controversy.

"ALL-PURPOSE" PUBLIC FIGURES

Sometimes it is easy to see that a person is an "all purpose" or "pervasive" public figure: entertainers Carol Burnett[182] and Johnny Carson,[183] famed evangelist Jerry Falwell,[184] who commented constantly

179 David A. Anderson, "Libel and Press Self-Censorship," 53 *Tex.L.Rev.* 422 (1975); for an historic pattern supporting Anderson, see Norman L. Rosenberg, *Protecting the Best Men* (Chapel Hill: University of North Carolina Press, 1986).

180 10 Med.L.Rptr. #13, 3/27/84, *News Notes*; 10 Med.L.Rptr. #34, 8/21/84, *News Notes*.

181 *Rosanova v. Playboy Enterprises, Inc.*, 411 F.Supp. 440, 443 (S.D.Ga.1976).

182 *Burnett v. National Enquirer* (Cal.Super.1981), 7 Med.L.Rptr. 1321.

183 *Carson v. Allied News Co.*, 529 F.2d 206 (7th Cir.1976).

184 *Hustler v. Falwell*, 485 U.S. 46, 108 S.Ct. 876 (1988).

on politics and who talked of running for President. Courts found that they were public figures in libel suits that they filed. Today, Whoopi Goldberg, Stephen Colbert and Stefani Joanne Angelina Germanotta[185] are all purpose public figures.

But what about candidates, persons who want to be public officials. Should they enjoy the protections of private persons, subject only to their ability to win a majority of an ever-shrinking electorate? *Monitor Patriot Co. v. Roy*[186] established that candidates are subject to the same requirements as office holders. The controversy began on September 10, 1960. It was three days before the New Hampshire Democratic Party's primary election of candidates for the United States Senate and the *Concord Monitor*, published a syndicated column discussing the forthcoming election. In the course of the column there appeared references to the criminal records of several of the candidates. The column said Alphonse Roy, one of the candidates, was a "former small-time bootlegger." Roy lost and he sued both the paper and the column's distributor.

The trial court concluded that Roy would have to meet the actual malice standard required of public officials. But the judge added that the actual malice standard would apply to official acts only and statements pertaining to private conduct, which might include bootlegging, would be tested by a different fault standard. The jury found for Roy and the case made its way eventually to the U.S. Supreme Court. There, the justices overturned the libel award saying that the *New York Times* rule would apply to candidates.[187]

> "[I]t might be preferable to categorize a candidate as a 'public figure,' if for no other reason than to avoid straining the common meaning of words. But the question is of no importance so far as the standard of liability in this case is concerned, for it is abundantly clear that, whichever term is applied, publications concerning candidates must be accorded at least as much protection under the First and Fourteenth Amendments as those concerning occupants of public office."

And the Court rejected the trial court's approach that made statements about public office activities different from private activities. In doing so, the Court drew from the case of *Garrison v. Louisiana:*[188]

> "Of course, any criticism of the manner in which a public official performs his duties will tend to affect his private, as well as his public, reputation. The *New York Times* rule is not rendered inapplicable merely because an official's private reputation, as well as his public reputation, is harmed. The public-official rule

185 Known professionally as Lady Gaga.

186 *Monitor Patriot v. Roy*, 401 U.S. 265, 91 S.Ct. 621 (1971).

187 *Monitor Patriot v. Roy*, 401 U.S. 265, 91 S.Ct. 621 (1971).

188 Ibid. at 274, 626.

protects the paramount public interest in a free flow of information to the people concerning public officials, their servants. To this end, anything which might touch on an official's fitness for office is relevant. Few personal attributes are more germane to fitness for office than dishonesty, malfeasance, or improper motivation, even though these characteristics may also affect the official's private character. 379 U.S., at 76–77."

In seeming contradiction, however, a famous jetsetter with the household-word name of Firestone was held to be a private person.[189] This famous case is discussed later in this chapter.

For an example of a case with local or community involvement, consider the libel suit of attorney Myron Steere, who was labeled an all-purpose public figure. Steere had represented a woman charged with shooting to death her husband; Nellie Schoonover was convicted of first-degree murder.[190] Later, an Associated Press story said the Kansas State Board of Law Examiners had recommended that the Kansas Supreme Court publicly censure Steere for his conduct of her defense. The examiners found that Steere had entered into a "contingency agreement" with Mrs. Schoonover to get all but $10,000 of her late husband's estate if she were acquitted. She would be left with the $10,000.

Steere sued broadcasters and newspapers that had carried the AP account for defamation, claiming inaccuracies. The trial court held that he would have to prove actual malice because—the Kansas Supreme Court said—"appellant was a public figure for all purposes by virtue of his general fame and notoriety in the community." Then it described the reach and breadth of Steere's involvement in the life of the community: He had practiced law in the county for 32 years and had been the county attorney for 8 of those years.[191]

> * * * He has achieved a position of some influence in local affairs capped by his representation of Nellie Schoonover in her well-publicized, famous murder trial. We find the totality of his experience in Franklin County gave Myron Steere the requisite fame and notoriety in his community to be declared a public figure for all purposes.

Not only a person may be a "public figure." In *Ithaca College v. Yale Daily News Pub. Co., Inc.*, the facts started with the publication of "The Insider's Guide to the Colleges 1978–79," 404 pages of material compiled and edited by the *Yale Daily News*. Through stringers, the editors obtained information on many colleges, and published of Ithaca College

---

[189] *Time, Inc. v. Firestone,* 424 U.S. 448, 96 S.Ct. 958 (1976).

[190] Some years later, Mrs. Schoonover filed a $5.5 million legal malpractice suit against Steere, "$5.5 Million Lawsuit Filed," *The Hays Daily News*, Nov. 16, 1976.

[191] *Steere v. Cupp,* 226 Kan. 566, 602 P.2d 1267 (1979), 5 Med.L.Rptr. 2046. And see *Sprouse v. Clay Communication,* 158 W.Va. 427, 211 S.E.2d 674 (1975), 1 Med.L.Rptr. 1695, 1704.

such statements as: "Sex, drugs, and booze are the staples of life." Ithaca College sued for libel, charging falsity and damage to its business and academic reputation. While Ithaca terms itself a "private" college, the New York Supreme Court said it could not be such in a libel suit.[192]183 The college assumes a role as a qualified educator of many students, serves the public good, is responsible for fair dealing with its students, the court ruled. It is recognized to be of "general fame or notoriety in the community [with] pervasive involvement in the affairs of society." The court decided that the college was a "public figure for all purposes." Similarly, corporations also may be classified as "public figures."[193]

Efforts to define public figures become especially troublesome where corporations are concerned.[194] For example, an insurance company, because of its power and influence, was held to be a public figure inviting attention and comment from the media.[195] On the other hand, the Supreme Court of the United States refused to hear an Oregon case holding that corporations—specifically banks—are not automatically public figures.[196] Note that this case was decided in 1985, several years before the savings and loan/banking crisis became big news, complete with U.S. senators' involvement in keeping regulators at bay in apparent exchange for campaign donations. The Great Recession of 2008, driven by the lending practices of major financial institutions and bank likely has made banks more "public figure" than not.

"LIMITED PURPOSE" PUBLIC FIGURES

Far more common than the person of general fame or notoriety who is a public figure for all purposes is the individual who is such for a "limited range of issues." Thus Dr. Frederick Exner for two decades and more had been "injecting" and "thrusting" himself into the fluoridation-of-water controversy through speeches, litigation, books, and articles. When he brought a libel suit for a magazine's criticism of his position,[197] he was adjudged a public figure for "the limited issue of fluoridation" by having assumed leadership and by having attempted to influence the outcome of the issue. He had taken the role of "attempting to order society" in its concern with fluoridation.

Harry Buchanan and his firm were retained to perform accounting services for the Finance Committee to Re-elect the President (CREEP) in

---

[192] *Ithaca College v. Yale Daily News Pub. Co., Inc.*, 105 Misc.2d 793, 433 N.Y.S.2d 530 (1980), 6 Med.L.Rptr. 2180.

[193] See *WTSP-TV, Inc. v. Vick* (Fla.Cir.Ct.1985), 11 Med.L.Rptr. 1543. But see *Blue Ridge Bank v. Veribanc, Inc.*, 866 F.2d 681 (4th Cir.1989).

[194] Robert Drechsel and Deborah Moon, "Corporate Libel Plaintiffs and the News Media," 21 *Am. Bus. L. Journ.* 127 (Summer, 1983).

[195] *American Benefit Life Ins. Co. v. McIntyre*, 375 So.2d 239 (Ala.1979), 5 Med.L.Rptr. 1124.

[196] *Bank of Oregon v. Independent News, Inc.*, 298 Or. 434, 693 P.2d 35 (1985), cert. denied 474 U.S. 826, 106 S.Ct. 84 (1985).

[197] *Exner v. American Medical Ass'n*, 12 Wash.App. 215, 529 P.2d 863 (1974).

1971. Common Cause brought suit in 1972 to force the Committee to report transactions, and Buchanan's deposition was taken in the matter. In reporting the suit, Associated Press compared matters involving Buchanan with the handling of money by convicted Watergate conspirator Bernard L. Barker. Buchanan sued AP for libel. Was he a public figure? The court said "yes."[198] There was intense interest in campaign finances at the time Buchanan was working for CREEP. The system he helped set up for the committee and the cash transactions in which he took part were legitimate matters of public scrutiny and concern. Buchanan was a key person for attempts to investigate. He was an agent of the committee who voluntarily accepted his role, and as such a public figure.

Some examples of Limited Purpose Public Figures: The businessman-president of a state bail-bond underwriters' association attacked a Pennsylvania state commission's report on bail-bond abuses and attempted to have the commission dissolved. He had injected himself into controversy and was a public figure.[199] Also, the United States Labor Party is a public political organization actively engaged in publishing articles, magazines, and books, and is a public figure[200] "at least in regard to those areas of public controversy * * * in which [it has] participated." The Church of Scientology seeks to play an influential role in ordering society, has thrust itself onto the public scene, and is a public figure.[201] So is a Roman Catholic priest who has actively involved himself in the debate over the independence of Northern Ireland, through radio, television, and speeches.[202]

If the list of persons and organizations strike you as plainly appropriate public figures in the contexts described, where does the problem arise? The fact is that there are hard cases disturbing to media people who are dismayed by courts' finding certain individuals to be private even though in the public eye. Consider that to be a problem caused by *Gertz v. Robert Welch, Inc.* (1974). Before that decision of the U.S. Supreme Court, the presumption was that government proceedings are public and almost inevitably made public figures out of participants. Thanks to the *Gertz* decision, such public figure presumptions need to be used with great caution. Take a notorious case attempting to draw a line between public figures and private persons, *Time, Inc. v. Firestone.*

---

[198] *Buchanan v. Associated Press,* 398 F.Supp. 1196 (D.D.C.1975).

[199] *Childs v. Sharon Herald* (Pa.Ct.Com.Pl.1979), 5 Med.L.Rptr. 1679.

[200] *United States Labor Party v. Anti-Defamation League* (N.Y.Sup.Ct.1980), 6 Med.L.Rptr. 2209.

[201] *Church of Scientology of California v. Siegelman,* 475 F.Supp. 950 (S.D.N.Y.1979), 5 Med.L.Rptr. 2021.

[202] *McManus v. Doubleday & Co., Inc.,* 513 F.Supp. 1383 (S.D.N.Y.1981), 7 Med.L.Rptr. 1475.

TIME, INC. V. FIRESTONE (1976)

Mary Alice Firestone—wife of a prominent member of the wealthy industrial family and member of the "society" elite of Palm Beach, Fla. (the "sporting set," as U.S. Supreme Court Justice Marshall called it)—went to court to seek separate maintenance (in common terms, a separation) from her husband, Russell. He counterclaimed for divorce on grounds of adultery and extreme cruelty. The trial covered 17 months, both parties charging extramarital escapades ("that would curl Dr. Freud's hair," the trial judge said). Several times during the 17 months, Mrs. Firestone held press conferences. She subscribed to a clipping service. *Time* magazine reported the trial's outcome: Russell Firestone was granted a divorce on grounds of extreme cruelty and adultery, *Time* said. But the trial judge had not, technically, found adultery, and Mrs. Firestone sued *Time* for libel.[203] The judge had granted the divorce on the grounds that " 'neither party is domesticated, within the meaning of that term as used by the Supreme Court of Florida,' " and that " 'the marriage should be dissolved.' " A jury awarded her $100,000 and *Time* appealed, arguing that Mrs. Firestone was a public figure and as such would have to prove actual malice in *Time*'s story.

Justice Rehnquist, writing for the majority of five of the U.S. Supreme Court, said "no" to *Time*'s appeal. He quoted various passages from the *Gertz* definition of "public figure" which he said did not fit Mrs. Firestone:[204] "special prominence in the resolution of public questions," "pervasive power and influence," "thrust themselves to the forefront of particular public controversies in order to influence the resolution of the issues involved." The crux of the matter was that, for all the publicity involved:

> Dissolution of marriage through judicial proceedings is not the sort of "public controversy" referred to in *Gertz*, even though the marital difficulties of extremely wealthy individuals may be of interest to some portion of the reading public.

In spite of her position in the "Palm Beach 400," her press conferences, and her clipping service, Mrs. Firestone was a "private" individual, and her "private" marital affairs did not "become public for the purposes of libel law solely because they are aired in a public forum."

Predictably, news media were outraged at the designation of Mrs. Firestone as "private." Accustomed to thinking of official proceedings including divorce trials as public matters which could be reported without fear of injuring the privacy of the participants, journalists had to make a conscious effort to think of Mrs. Firestone as in some sense private. Their effort was made more difficult in that her position in society had for years before the divorce placed her among the "newsworthy" and in the public eye. And with her use of clipping services

---

[203] *Time, Inc. v. Firestone,* 424 U.S. 448, 96 S.Ct. 958 (1976).

[204] Ibid. at 454, 965.

and press conferences during the drawn-out divorce trial, her "public" character had seemed confirmed. What might the decision mean for future cases?

WOLSTON V. READER'S DIGEST (1979)

Three years after *Firestone*, the Supreme Court took up another case whose background was also a public court proceeding. And again, the fact that a libel plaintiff's suit arose from his involvement in an official public matter did not destroy private status for his libel suit. Ilya Wolston had been summoned in 1958 to appear before a grand jury that was investigating espionage but failed to appear. Later, he pleaded guilty to a charge of criminal contempt for failing to respond to the summons and accepted conviction. Sixteen years later, *Reader's Digest* published a book by John Barron on Soviet espionage in the U.S. The book said erroneously that the FBI had identified Wolston as a Soviet intelligence agent. Wolston sued for libel. He asserted that he had been out of the limelight for many years, and that if he had been a public figure during the investigations, he now deserved to be considered private. The lower courts disagreed, saying the long lapse of time was immaterial, that Soviet espionage of 1958 continued to be a subject of importance, and that Wolston thus remained a public figure.

He appealed to the Supreme Court, which by a vote of 8–1 reversed the lower courts and determined that Wolston was a private person who would not have to prove actual malice in his libel suit against the *Reader's Digest*. Justice Rehnquist wrote:[205]

> We do not agree with respondents and the lower courts that petitioner can be classed as such a limited-purpose public figure. First, the undisputed facts do not justify the conclusion of the District Court and the Court of Appeals that petitioner "voluntarily thrust" or "injected" himself into the forefront of the public controversy surrounding the investigation of Soviet espionage. * * * It would be more accurate to say that petitioner was dragged unwillingly into the controversy. The government pursued him in its investigation.

HUTCHINSON V. PROXMIRE (1979)

On the date of the *Wolston* decision, another Supreme Court ruling on the definition of public figure was handed down, and again the decision cast the public figure into a narrower light than many journalists felt warranted. This time, the Court said that researcher Ronald Hutchinson, who had received some $500,000 in federal government grants for his experiments, including some on primates'

[205] *Wolston v. Reader's Digest Ass'n, Inc.*, 443 U.S. 157, 99 S.Ct. 2701 (1979).

response to aggravating stimuli,[206] was not a private figure.[207] He would not have to prove actual malice in his libel suit against Sen. William Proxmire of Wisconsin, who had labeled Hutchinson's work "monkey business" and had given a "Golden Fleece of the Month Award" to government funding agencies which he ridiculed for wasting public money on grants to Hutchinson. A Proxmire press release, a newsletter, and a television appearance were involved, all following Proxmire's announcement of the Award on the Senate floor.

Concerned about the narrowing of the definition of "public figure," media attorney James C. Goodale had reasoned in advance of the decision that the lower courts' holding that Hutchinson was, indeed, a public figure deserved to be upheld in the Supreme Court.[208] "Clearly information about how our government grants money and who gets it," he said, "should be the subject of unlimited comment by anyone—especially by a U.S. Senator."

The Supreme Court, however, did not see it that way. It reversed the lower courts, saying that their conclusion that Hutchinson was a public figure was erroneously based upon two factors: one, his success in getting federal grants and newspaper reports about the grants, and two, his access to media as represented by news stories that reported his response to the Golden Fleece Award. But:[209]

> Hutchinson did not thrust himself or his views into public controversy to influence others. Respondents have not identified such a particular controversy; at most, they point to concern about general public expenditures. But that concern is shared by most and relates to most public expenditures; it is not sufficient to make Hutchinson a public figure. If it were, everyone who received or benefitted from the myriad public grants for research could be classified as a public figure.

"Subject-matter classifications"—such as general public expenditures—had been rejected in *Gertz* as the touchstone for deciding who would have to prove actual malice, the Court said: instead, the person and his activities must be the basis. And, finally, the Court said it could not agree that Hutchinson had such access to the media that he

[206] The bulk of Hutchinson's research was devoted to the study of emotional behavior. In particular, he sought an objective measure of aggression, concentrating upon the behavior patterns of certain animals, such as the clenching of jaws when they were exposed to various aggravating stressful stimuli. The National Aeronautics and Space Agency and the Navy were interested in the potential of this research for resolving problems associated with confining humans in close quarters for extended periods of time in space and undersea exploration. *Hutchinson v. Proxmire*, 443 U.S. 111,115, 99 S.Ct. 2675, 2678 (1979).

[207] *Hutchinson v. Proxmire*, 443 U.S. 111, 99 S.Ct. 2675 (1979).

[208] *Hutchinson v. Proxmire*, 443 U.S. 111, 99 S.Ct. 2675 (1979).

[209] *Hutchinson v. Proxmire*, 443 U.S. 111, 134–135, 99 S.Ct. 2675, 2688 (1979). Proxmire was reported to have settled the suit out of court for $10,000, and the Senate was reported to have assumed his trial costs of more than $100,000. D.S. Greenberg, "Press Was a Co-Villain in Proxmire's Golden Gimmick," *Chicago Tribune*, April 17, 1980.

should be classified as a public figure; his access was limited to responding to the announcement of the Golden Fleece Award.

"VORTEX" PUBLIC FIGURES NOT CLEARLY DEFINED

Other circumstances complicate the defining of public figures. Justice Powell's definition in *Gertz* and various courts' since (as in *Firestone, Wolston,* and *Hutchinson*), make it crucial to decide whether the person has voluntarily injected himself into a matter of public controversy to help resolve that controversy. American courts, unfortunately, have not drawn clear or predictable lines to separate "public figures" from "private persons." Even so, it may be said that there are many public figures besides those who voluntarily "get involved" and try to influence the outcome of public issues. (Please note, as discussed later, that older tort law, dating back long before *New York Times v. Sullivan,* has traditionally provided the defense of "fair comment" for media that are sued for their critiques of authors' works, restaurants, plays, celebrities and public entertainers.)[210]

If persons truly were not public figures before getting media coverage, the mere fact of that coverage will not make them public figures. At times however—although rarely—unwilling persons, through no fault of their own, can become "involuntary public figures."[211] For the most part, however, there are mainly two kinds of "public figures:" The person who, nationally or locally, has pervasive or all-purpose fame, and the "vortex" public figures who thrust themselves into public issues, particularly in an effort to influence the course of events in some significant way.

The safest generalization for journalists is not to generalize: Get legal advice on close calls whether a person is a "public figure" or a "private figure." At times, courts have ruled that some persons holding elective office—such as an elected but unsalaried county surveyor[212] or a justice of the peace[213]—are private persons.

BOOTSTRAPPING

Bootstrapping refers to a physical and legal impossibility. It comes from a humorous story from the pulp fiction days (not the movie, the actual 1930s publications) featuring a surprise ending in which the

---

210 Prosser, *Law of Torts,* (1971 St. Paul, Minn., West Pub.) 813.

211 See, e.g., *Wolston v. Reader's Digest Ass'n, Inc.,* 443 U.S. 157, 167, 99 S.Ct. 2701, 2707 (1979), and *Waldbaum v. Fairchild Publications, Inc.,* 627 F.2d 1287, 1295 (D.C.Cir.1980), citing *Gertz v. Robert Welch, Inc.,* 418 U.S. 323, 94 S.Ct. 2997 (1974), recognizing that—at least in theory—an involuntary public figure could exist.

212 *Foster v. Laredo Newspapers, Inc.,* 541 S.W.2d 809 (Tex.1976), cert. denied 429 U.S. 1123, 97 S.Ct. 1160 (1977).

213 *Guinn v. Texas Newspapers, Inc.,* 738 S.W.2d 303 (Tex.App.1987), 16 Med.L.Rptr. 1024, cert. denied 488 U.S. 1041, 109 S.Ct. 864 (1989). An error-filled article referred to "Guinn," not to Judge Guinn, asserting that Guinn had been convicted of a felony. (In point of fact, Guinn had been the attorney for the convicted thief.)

protagonist grasps his own bootstraps (pieces of leather on the sides of boots that boot wearers use to help slip on their footwear) and lifts himself out of danger. It is used in defamation to refer to a process in which a defendant will try to take a private person plaintiff and turn him into a public figure in order to require the plaintiff to pass the actual malice hurdle. Some defense attorneys will try to apply *Rosenbloom*, suggesting to the trial court that the allegedly defamatory story is proof that the plaintiff is widely known in the community. The determination of public figure or private person status is a matter of law, that is to say, it is a decision by the court rather than any jury.

Sometimes, this attempt to bootstrap the plaintiff will take the form of offering up copies of the defendant's own stories that led to the libel suit and its aftermath, stories of other media outlets reporting on the defendant's stories and other stories laying out the progress of the defamation suit. Stories published subsequent to the initial, defamatory story will not make a private person a public figure. *The public/private figure determination is made at that point in time when the initial and allegedly defamatory statement is published.* The courts must look to the conduct of the plaintiff to see if she is an all-purpose public figure or a limited purpose public figure. Merely being caught up in an event that draws the attention of the media or a single media outlet does not necessarily make an otherwise private person a public figure. As the Supreme Court said in *Wolston*, to make people public figures just because they are caught up in a newsworthy event would reimpose the failed doctrine set forth in the plurality in *Rosenbloom*.[214] "We repudiated this position in *Gertz* and in *Firestone*, however, and we reject it again today."

29. SUMMARY JUDGMENT

WINNING THE LIBEL SUIT WITHOUT HAVING TO GO TO TRIAL

If a judge at the threshold of a libel trial finds that a plaintiff is a public figure or public official, the case moves at once to a second pretrial consideration, of great importance to the defending news medium and the plaintiff. The plaintiff alleges actual malice, and the defendant ordinarily denies it and moves that the judge dismiss the case in a "summary judgment" for the defendant. Winning such a motion avoids a trial.

Summary judgment is a way to maintain judicial efficiency. If a party cannot win a case, there is no need to go through the lengthy and costly process of trying a case. There can be two bases for coming to the conclusion that a party cannot win—either the facts won't support a case or the law will not let a party win. For example: John Doe makes a $1,000

[214] *Wolston v. Reader's Digest Association*, 443 U.S. 157, 99 S.Ct. 2701 (1979).

bet with Jane Roe on the outcome of an election. Doe loses. Roe wants to collect but Doe refuses to pay. Roe sues in state court. Doe may be able to dispose of the case through summary judgment. Some states will not allow their courts to be used to enforce a gambling debt. There, the law will make it impossible for Roe to win and the case may be disposed of through summary judgment. On the other hand, if Doe is able to produce evidence that he has paid, such as a signed receipt from Roe, he can win on summary judgment based on the facts.

Avoiding trial is desirable for a number of reasons. First, to defend the average libel suit through a trial can costs tens of thousands of dollars. Second, the extended distraction and emotional drain of a libel suit add up to a real threat to vigorous reporting. The importance of summary judgment to the media's defense and to the public need for robust, uninhibited, wide-open reporting was laid out in the decision in *Washington Post Co. v. Keogh*, an early case that interpreted *Times v. Sullivan*:[215]

> In the First Amendment area, summary procedures are * * * essential. For the stake here, if harassment succeeds, is free debate. One of the purposes of the Times principle, in addition to protecting persons from being cast in damages in libel suits filed by public officials, is to prevent persons from being discouraged in the full and free exercise of their First Amendment rights with respect to the conduct of their government.

In ruling on the motion for summary judgment by the defendant, the judge must make a decision: Is there a "genuine issue of material fact"—a substantial claim by the plaintiff supported by evidence—that there was knowing or reckless falsity in the publication?[216]

Chief Justice Warren Burger of the United States Supreme Court in 1979 wrote a famous footnote—number 9 in *Hutchinson v. Proxmire*—casting doubt on the appropriateness of summary judgment in libel cases. Lower courts take his admonition into account and sometimes have found it a basis for denial of summary judgment, but summary judgments seem to be granted defendants far more often in libel suits brought by public people than they are denied.[217] Despite the famed footnote, many defamation actions—perhaps as many as 75 per cent of those brought by public figures or officials in the last decade—have been ended by grants of summary judgments to media defendants.

---

[215] *Washington Post v. Keogh*, 125 U.S.App.D.C. 32, 365 F.2d 965, 968 (1966).

[216] Restatement, Second, Torts, Vol. 3, p. 220. *Cerrito v. Time, Inc.*, 449 F.2d 306 (9th Cir.1971); *Hayes v. Booth Newspapers, Inc.*, 97 Mich.App. 758, 295 N.W.2d 858 (1980), 6 Med.L.Rptr. 2319.

[217] *Hutchinson v. Proxmire*, 443 U.S. 111, 99 S.Ct. 2675 (1979). *Yiamouyiannis v. Consumers Union of U.S., Inc.*, 619 F.2d 932 (2d Cir.1980), 6 Med.L.Rptr. 1065. Defendants' motions for summary judgment in the 1980s have been successful about 75% of the time, and Burger's "footnote 9" has been used rarely: *Libel Defense Resource Center Bulletin* #13, Spring 1985, 10.

In a decision helpful to the media, the Supreme Court ruled in *Jack Anderson v. Liberty Lobby, Inc.* (1986)[218] that public official or public figure suits must be ended before trial by summary judgment unless libel can be shown with "convincing clarity." Anderson was sued after articles said to portray Willis Carto and Liberty Lobby as Neo-Nazi, racist, and fascist.

Plaintiffs Carto and Liberty Lobby argued against the summary judgment, saying that the researcher for the Jack Anderson column's articles had relied on several unreliable sources and because there were inaccuracies in the articles. Writing for the Supreme Court, Justice White wrote that trial judges must decide, based on pre-trial affidavits, whether a public plaintiff can meet the actual malice standard by "clear convincing evidence." If not, summary judgment should be granted.

Police Chief Robert Prease alleged in a suit that stories in the Akron, (Ohio) *Beacon Journal* libeled him. Assistant Managing Editor Timothy Smith said that all statements in the stories were made in good faith with no serious doubts about their accuracy, and the chief did not refute Smith. Thus, the judge found that there was no issue between them about actual malice—no "genuine issue of material fact" that would have to be argued before a jury for decision. He granted summary judgment for the newspaper.[219]

But the United States Court of Appeals, Fourth District, found such an issue in *Fitzgerald v. Penthouse Intern., Ltd.*,[220] and reversed a trial court's grant of summary judgment to *Penthouse*. Fitzgerald, a specialist in the use of dolphins as military weapons, sued *Penthouse* for an article about his work that might have been construed as an allegation of espionage—selling dolphins trained as "torpedoes" to other nations, for "fast bucks." The Court found that *Penthouse* relied almost exclusively for its story upon a questionable source, and detailed his "many bold assertions about the United States intelligence community" which in some cases "invite skepticism." It quoted *St. Amant v. Thompson*:[221] Recklessness may be found "where there are obvious reasons to doubt the veracity of the informant or the accuracy of his reports." Fitzgerald had presented a factual question about whether *Penthouse* had "obvious reasons to doubt" its source; *Penthouse* would have to go to trial on the matter of actual malice.

Litigation Note: *Experienced litigators will use summary judgment to throw a wrench into the plaintiff's case. Once the case is underway, the defendant's attorney will obtain affidavits from the publisher and other involved persons. Those affidavits will attest to the subjective belief of the affiants that they entertained no doubts as to the accuracy of the story and*

---

218 *Anderson v. Liberty Lobby, Inc.*, 477 U.S. 242, 106 S.Ct. 2505 (1986), 12 Med.L.Rptr. 2297.

219 *Prease v. Poorman* (Ohio Com.Pl.1981), 7 Med.L.Rptr. 2378.

220 *Fitzgerald v. Penthouse Intern., Ltd.*, 691 F.2d 666 (4th Cir.1982), 8 Med.L.Rptr. 2340.

221 *St. Amant v. Thompson*, 390 U.S. 727, 732, 88 S.Ct. 1323, 1326 (1968).

they surely did not publish with knowing falsity. The defense attorney will then move for summary judgment on the basis of those affidavits. The plaintiff will not have had time to complete discovery and so will have little evidence to present in opposing the motion. Some judges, willing to keep their dockets as clear as possible, will grant the motion. The plaintiff must then go through the appellate process to revive the case. The added time and expense will do much to discourage the plaintiff. The plaintiff's attorney, who most likely took the case on contingency, will have added expense. The attorney may wind up taking a bigger chunk of any ultimate recovery because of the extra steps in the lawsuit.

NEUTRAL REPORTAGE

A sometimes useful—but not-to-be-trusted—defense against libel lawsuits goes under the name of "neutral reportage." The neutral reportage argument is one which lawyers sometimes use on behalf of media clients, but that defense has not attained the status of a reliable constitutional defense.

Back in 1977, Judge Irving Kaufman of the U.S. Court of Appeals, Second Circuit, pioneered the neutral reportage concept in *Edwards v. National Audubon Society, Inc.*[222] Judge Kaufman wrote for the court that the Constitution protects accurate, unbiased news reporting of accusations made against public figures regardless of the reporter's view of their truth. This concept is related to the long-standing common-law and statutory doctrine of qualified privilege immunity from successful libel suit for fair and accurate reports of official proceedings.

The case arose when *The New York Times* carried a story reporting accurately a National Audubon Society's written statement that some scientists were paid to lie about the effects of the pesticide DDT upon birds. This outraged the scientists who were implicated, and they brought a libel suit against the Society and the *Times*. Overturning a jury verdict for the scientists, Judge Kaufman wrote for the Court of Appeals that "a libel judgment against the *Times*, in face of this finding of fact, is constitutionally impermissible." He reasoned:[223]

> At stake in this case is a fundamental principle. Succinctly stated, when a responsible, prominent organization like the National Audubon Society makes serious charges against a public figure, the First Amendment protects the accurate and disinterested reporting of those charges, regardless of the reporter's private views of their validity. * * * What is newsworthy about such accusations is that they were made. We do not believe that the press may be required under the First

[222] *Edwards v. National Audubon Society, Inc.*, 556 F.2d 113 (2d Cir.1977). See Kathryn D. Sowle, "Defamation and the First Amendment: The Case for a Constitutional Privilege of Fair Report," 54 *NYU Law Review* 469 (June, 1969).

[223] *Edwards v. National Audubon Society, Inc.*, 556 F.2d 113, 120 (2d Cir.1977).

> Amendment to suppress newsworthy statements merely because it has serious doubts regarding their truth.

Judge Kaufman applied this doctrine only to situations where the press was not taking sides or was deliberately distorting statements in order to launch a personal attack. But in this case, the judge said, reporter John Devlin of *The Times* wrote an accurate account, did not take the Audubon Society's side in his article. Further, Devlin's article included the scientists' indignant responses to the Audubon Society's charges. Judge Kaufman's opinion termed Devlin's work "an exemplar of fair and dispassionate reporting * * * Accordingly, we hold that it was privileged under the First Amendment."[224]

Welcome as the "neutral reportage" concept was to the news media; it quickly was met by an opposing view from another U.S. Court of Appeals. Writing in *Dickey v. CBS* (1978), Judge James Hunter held in the 3rd Circuit Court of Appeals decision that,[225] "no constitutional privilege of neutral reportage exists." That case involved a libel action resulting from a television broadcast of a pre taped talk show in which a Pennsylvania Congressman accused a public figure of accepting payoffs. Although CBS won the case, it was not on "neutral reportage" grounds, which Judge Hunter said flew in the face of the much-cited decision in *St. Amant v. Thompson* (1964)[226] (discussed earlier) Judge Hunter criticized the *Audubon* decision:[227]

> While the Second Circuit [in *Edwards v. Audubon Society*] found that there can be no liability despite the publisher's "serious doubts" as to truthfulness, *St. Amant* holds that for libel against a public figure to be proved, "[t]here must be sufficient evidence to permit the conclusion that the defendant in fact entertained *serious doubts* as to the truth of his publication. Publishing with such doubts shows reckless disregard for truth or falsity and demonstrates actual malice."
>
> * * *
>
> We therefore conclude that a constitutional privilege of neutral reportage is not created * * * merely because an individual newspaper or television or radio station decides that a particular statement is newsworthy.

Since the *Dickey* case of 1978, the concept of neutral reportage has had an uneven and generally unpredictable history of acceptance and rejection, but it may be said that at times it has proven to be a useful defense for the media. A number of states have accepted the neutral

---

224 Ibid.

225 *Dickey v. CBS Inc.*, 583 F.2d 1221 (3d Cir.1978).

226 *St. Amant v. Thompson*, 390 U.S. 727, 731, 88 S.Ct. 1323, 1325 (1968).

227 *Dickey v. CBS Inc.*, 583 F.2d 1221, 1225–1226 (3d Cir.1978).

reportage doctrine, including Florida and Ohio;[228] others have rejected it.[229] In Illinois in the 1980s, one appellate court adopted the neutral report privilege, another rejected it, and the state's supreme court refused to consider the issue.[230]

Efforts to use—and get wider recognition for—the defense of neutral reportage continued through the 1990s. When the defense has succeeded, it has been in situations where the plaintiff was a public figure and where the report involved was fair and accurate without the espousal of a point of view by the news medium.[231] For example, the defense failed in *Cianci v. New Times Publishing Co.* There, *New Times* was found by the Second Circuit (enunciator of the *Edwards* doctrine) to have violated many of the qualifications limiting the privilege.[232] The publication was flatly denied the neutral reportage privilege for its story suggesting falsely that the mayor had been accused of being a rapist.

In 1989, in a case setting (if only temporarily) a record for punitive damages against a newspaper in a case surviving the appeals process, the neutral reportage case was rejected as inapplicable. The *Pittsburgh Post-Gazette* paid (including $561,000 in interest) damages totaling $2.8 million. (Of that amount, a total of $2 million was in punitive damages.) In that case, *DiSalle v. P.G. Publishing Co.*, a Pennsylvania superior court held:[233]

> * * * [I]f neutral reportage is to be recognized as a constitutional privilege, it can offer protection irrespective of the publisher's belief in the truth or falsity of the charges only when a public official or public figure levels a false charge against a public official or figure.
>
> On the other hand, as attorney Robert McGough said after representing the *Pittsburgh-Post Gazette* in this case, newspapers commonly report on accusations by private parties against public officials,[234] " 'without knowing or caring whether

[228] *El Amin v. Miami Herald Pub. Co.* (Fla.Cir.Ct.1983), 9 Med.L.Rptr. 1079; *Horvath v. Telegraph* (Ohio App.1982), 8 Med.L.Rptr. 1657. See especially John B. McCrory et al., "Constitutional Privilege in Libel Law," 1993 Revision by Robert D. Sack et.al., in James C. Goodale, *Communications Law* 1993, Vol. II (New York: Practising Law Institute, 1993), pp. 355–363.

[229] 220 New York: *Hogan v. Herald Co.*, 84 A.D.2d 470, 446 N.Y.S.2d 836 (1982), 8 Med.L.Rptr. 1137, affirmed 58 N.Y.2d 630, 458 N.Y.S.2d 538, 444 N.E.2d 1002 (1982), 8 Med.L.Rptr. 2567; Kentucky: *McCall v. Courier-Journal and Louisville Times Co.*, 623 S.W.2d 882 (Ky.1981), 7 Med.L.Rptr. 2118; Michigan: *Postill v. Booth Newspapers, Inc.*, 118 Mich.App. 608, 325 N.W.2d 511 (1982), 8 Med.L.Rptr. 2222.

[230] *Fogus v. Capital Cities Media, Inc.*, 111 Ill.App.3d 1060, 67 Ill.Dec. 616, 444 N.E.2d 1100 (1982), 9 Med.L.Rptr. 1141, 1143.

[231] Goodale, loc. cit.

[232] *Cianci v. New Times Publishing Co.*, 639 F.2d 54 (2d Cir.1980), 6 Med.L.Rptr. 1625.

[233] Albert Scardino, "Pittsburgh Paper Pays $2.8 million Libel Award," *New York Times*, July 12, 1989, p. 9; *DiSalle v. P.G. Publishing Co.*, 375 Pa.Super. 510, 544 A.2d 1345, 1363 (1988), 15 Med.L.Rptr. 1873.

[234] Scardino, loc. cit.

the accusation is true * * * In Pennsylvania, it is now not enough to report the accusation accurately.' "

Neutral reportage, then, is an unreliable defense. The policy decision to publish or broadcast a story involving defamatory charges in an unprivileged situation—even against a person or entity appearing to be a "public official" or a "public figure"—should be checked out not only by journalists but by their legal advisers before publication.

CALIFORNIA REJECTS NEUTRAL REPORTAGE FOR PRIVATE PERSONS

In a 1996 case that showed the continuing controversy over the doctrine, *Khalid Khawar v. Globe International Inc.*,[235] the California Court of Appeals upheld a judgment against the *Globe* tabloid over a story that reported that a California farmer and former reporter was the "real assassin" of Sen. Robert F. Kennedy. The *Globe* ran a story about a book about the assassination. Author Robert Morrow published a book on the senator's murder, "*The Senator Must Die: The Murder of Robert F. Kennedy*," in which he claimed that Kennedy was killed by the Iranian secret police at the direction of the Mafia. Morrow, whose claims were not supported by any other investigators into the assassination, identified Khawar as the actual assassin and gave his name as Ali Ahmand, the name of Khawar's father.

Khawar sued and was awarded $1.1 million. The court found Khawar a private figure and said that neutral reportage would not apply. Further, the appellate court affirmed the jury's conclusion that the *Globe* published its article with actual malice. As with *Connaughton*, the jury concluded that the *Globe* had failed to contact sources who could have revealed the inaccuracy of the story. "The article is not merely false, but glaringly false—it makes assertions that on the surface seem extraordinarily improbable—a fact that certainly is circumstantial evidence that *Globe*'s representatives had a very high degree of skepticism concerning the truthfulness of the charges."[236] The California Supreme Court accepted the case for consideration in the fall of 1996.[237] It issued its opinion in 1998.[238]

Complicating the matter in the *Khawar* case was the fact that the trial court held that Khawar was a private person. In most neutral reportage privilege cases, the plaintiff has been a public figure. The

---

[235] *Khawar v. Globe International*, 51 Cal.App.4th 14, 54 Cal.Rptr.2d 92 (1996), 24 Med.L.Rptr. 2345.

[236] B.J. Palermo, "Who Killed RFK? Not This Guy," *The National Law Journal*, A–1, A–20, Aug. 25, 1997.

[237] *Khawar v. Globe International*, 57 Cal.Rptr.2d 277, 923 P.2d 766 (1996).

[238] *Khawar v. Globe Intern., Inc.*, 19 Cal.4th 254, 79 Cal.Rptr.2d 178 (1998).

California appeals court declined to apply neutral reportage to private persons and the California Supreme Court agreed.[239]

> In concluding that the neutral reportage privilege is unavailable here because Khawar is a private figure, we do not decide or imply either that the neutral reportage privilege exists as to republished defamations about public figures or that *Globe* established other possible requirements of the privilege here.
>
> * * *
>
> We hold only that the Court of Appeal did not err when it concluded that "in California there is no neutral reportage privilege extending to reports regarding private figures."

SUPREME COURT DECIDES NOT TO DECIDE NEUTRAL REPORTAGE

The United States Supreme Court decided not to take up the issue of neutral reportage in 2005 when it declined, without comment, to hear a case involving a newspaper's reporting of defamatory statements about two elected officials in a Pennsylvania town.[240] Instead, it let stand a Pennsylvania Supreme Court decision[241] that held that neither the Pennsylvania nor U.S. constitutions created a neutral reportage protection for media.

The case began with a story in the *Chester County Daily Local* that reported on a dispute that took place in and around a meeting of the Parkerburg Borough Council. The article "Slurs, insults drag town into controversy," detailed heated exchanges both in and outside council chambers. William Glenn, a member of the council, made allegations that Council President James Norton III and Borough Mayor Alan Wolfe were homosexuals, that the two men had access to children and that Norton had grabbed Glenn's penis.

The reporter covering the story, relayed Glenn's accusations to Norton who said in reply,[242] "If Mr. Glenn has made comments as bizarre as that, then I feel very sad for him, and I hope he can get the help he needs." Norton and Wolfe sued Glenn and the newspaper. The trial court granted summary judgment for the newspaper on the grounds that they were entitled to protection under the neutral reportage privilege.

In doing so, the trial judge concluded that neutral reportage was the same as the fair report privilege that protects media when they accurately report official government proceedings (see Qualified Privilege below in this chapter). Under that privilege, actual malice is

---

[239] Ibid. at 189–190.

[240] Hope Yen, "Supreme Court Declines to Hear Cases Involving Media Protections, Abortion," *Associated Press*, March 29, 2005.

[241] *Norton v. Glenn*, 580 Pa. 212, 860 A.2d 48, 49 (2004).

[242] Ibid. at 215, 50.

not at issue.[243] "The trial court opined that pursuant to this privilege, 'the subjective awareness of the publisher, of the truth or falsity of the statement, is irrelevant.' "

Wolfe and Norton won their case against Glenn and then appealed the trial court's decision regarding the newspaper. The appellate court reversed saying that there was no constitutional or statutory basis for the neutral reportage privilege. The newspaper defendants appealed to the Pennsylvania Supreme Court which confined its analysis to the question of whether the U.S. or Pennsylvania constitutions provided a basis for application of neutral reportage.

The Pennsylvania Supreme Court first disposed of the trial court's conclusion that neutral reportage was the same as the fair report privilege. Fair report and neutral reportage are two distinct and different entities, the state supreme court reasoned.[244]

> The fair report doctrine adopted in *Sciandra*[245] is a common-law privilege protecting media entities which publish fair and accurate reports of governmental proceedings. At issue here, however, is whether there is a constitutional privilege to publish accounts of statements that were not made in the course of official proceedings.

In states where the issue has been taken up by the courts, there is a split in acceptance and rejection of neutral reportage. The U.S. Supreme Court has not ruled directly on neutral reportage, the Pennsylvania court said. Looking at U.S. Supreme Court cases, especially those following *New York Times v. Sullivan*, the Pennsylvania court concluded that the use of the actual malice standard and it concomitant protection of reputational rights meant that the court had not granted wholesale immunity to media defendants.[246]

> [W]e conclude that the existing case law from the U.S. Supreme Court indicates that the high Court would not so sharply tilt the balance against the protection of reputation, and in favor of protecting the media, so as to jettison the actual malice standard in favor of the neutral reportage doctrine.

The newspaper defendants also argued that the Pennsylvania constitution could serve as the basis for a finding that the state adopted the neutral reportage privilege. The Pennsylvania court rejected that citing precedent holding that the state constitution would not afford

---

[243] Ibid. at 215, 50.

[244] Ibid. at 234, 62.

[245] *Sciandra v. Lynett*, 409 Pa. 595, 187 A.2d 586 (1963), which held that:

> [A] newspaper has the privilege to report the acts of the executive or administrative officials of government. . . . If the newspaper account is fair, accurate and complete, and not published solely for the purpose of causing harm to the person defamed, it is privileged and no responsibility attaches, even though information contained therein is false or inaccurate.

[246] *Norton v. Glenn*, 580 Pa. 212, 860 A.2d 48, 57 (2004).

greater free speech protections than the federal constitution.[247] The Pennsylvania Supreme Court then sent the case back for retrial on the claims made by Norton and Wolfe against the newspaper.

30. QUALIFIED PRIVILEGE AS A DEFENSE

News media may publish defamation from legislative, judicial or other public and official proceedings without fear of successful libel or slander action; fair and accurate reports of these statements are privileged.

In the law, privilege carries a pretty straightforward definition, one that everyone can relate to:[248] A benefit or advantage enjoyed by a person or category of persons that ordinary citizens don't have. Privilege exists for many social, civil and political institutions. Clubs admit their members and exclude others, member of Congress are the only persons allowed to vote on the bills that will become the law of the United States and the Democrats and Republicans keep their own counsel.

These privileges make it possible for members to carry out their jobs. The privilege to speak out plainly and without fear of retaliation is important to those who operate the government. Society benefits when a lawmaker can speak his or her mind in the furnace of political debate. Justice can be more easily reached when judges and the participants in legal proceedings are permitted to say what needs to be said without being held accountable.[249] And, members of the executive, the branch that carries out the laws of the nation, state and local community, need the privilege to express themselves freely.

The privilege, or immunity, carries into defamation law.[250] For members of the legislative, judicial and executive branches in federal, state and local setting, the privilege is absolute. There is no defamation liability for what these people say in the performance of their official duties. This is "absolute" privilege. No words relevant to the business of the proceeding will support a suit for defamation. If a person is defamed in these proceedings, he cannot recover damages.

The *absolute privilege* given to the three branches would be of little use if the media, which reports on the conduct and activities of government would wind up facing suit for printing the defamatory words of officials. So, since long before the landmark year 1964 and the constitutional defense developed in and after *New York Times Co. v. Sullivan*, libel suits have been defended under statutory and common law provisions termed *qualified privilege, fair comment and criticism*, and

---

[247] See *Sprague v. Walter*, 518 Pa. 425, 543 A.2d 1078 (1988).

[248] Drawn from *Black's Law Dictionary*, West Publishing.

[249] This is not to suggest that perjury is protected. False statements made under oath are criminal and carry penalties. It is the words that must be spoken to carry out the process of government that are protected.

[250] For other circumstances where it applies, see Prosser, pp. 804–805; see also Robert Sack and Sandra Baron, op. cit., .Chap. 6, pp. 361–408.

truth. As noted earlier, the theory that free expression contributes to the public good in a self-governing society underlies the older defenses as well as the constitutional defense.

Public policy also demands, in an open society, that people know to the fullest what goes on in the proceedings. For this reason, anyone who reports proceedings is given a limited or "qualified" immunity from successful suit for defamation. For the public at large, "anyone" ordinarily means the mass media. The protection is ordinarily more limited for the reporter of a proceeding than for the participant in the proceeding. It is thus called "qualified" (or "conditional") privilege.[251]

Students should know that they, and all other folks, have their own privilege. It has been held that any citizen has absolute immunity in any criticism he makes of government. The City of Chicago brought a libel suit against the *Chicago Tribune*, claiming damages of $10 million through the *Tribune*'s campaign coverage in 1920. The stories had said that the city was broke, that its credit "is shot to pieces," that it "is hurrying on to bankruptcy and is threatened with a receivership for its revenue."

The court denied the city's claim.[252] It said that in any libelous publication concerning a municipal corporation, the citizen and the newspaper possess absolute privilege.

> Every citizen has a right to criticize an inefficient government without fear of civil as well as criminal prosecution. This absolute privilege is founded on the principle that it is advantageous for the public interest that the citizen should not be in any way fettered in his statements * * *[253]

Qualified privilege in reporting official proceedings is the heart of the concern here. The privilege arose in the law of England, the basic rationale having been developed before the start of the Nineteenth Century in connection with newspaper reports of court proceedings.[254] While American courts relied on English decisions, America was ahead of England in expanding the protection for press reports. The immunity was broadened to cover the reporting of legislative and other public official proceedings by the New York legislature in 1854,[255] 14 years before privilege for reporting legislative bodies was recognized in England. Other states readily adopted the New York rule.

---

[251] A few states give absolute privilege to press reports of official proceedings, e.g. Thompson's Laws of New York, 1939, Civ.P. § 337, Wis.Stats.1931, § 331.05(1). Broadcasters are immune from defamation suits brought for the words of politicians in campaign ads under FCC rules: *Farmers Educational & Co-op. Union of America v. WDAY, Inc.*, 360 U.S. 525, 79 S.Ct. 1302 (1959).

[252] *City of Chicago v. Tribune Co.*, 307 Ill. 595, 139 N.E. 86, 90 (1923).

[253] See also *Grafton v. ABC*, 70 Ohio App.2d 205, 435 N.E.2d 1131 (1980), 7 Med.L.Rptr. 1134, 1136, quoting *Capital District Regional Off-Track Betting Corp. v. Northeastern Harness Horsemen's Ass'n*, 92 Misc.2d 232, 399 N.Y.S.2d 597, 598 (1977).

[254] *Curry v. Walter*, 170 Eng.Rep. 419 (1796); *King v. Wright*, 101 Eng.Rep. 1396 (1799).

[255] New York Laws, 1854, Chap. 130; *Wason v. Walter*, L.R. 4 Q.B. 73 (1868).

In America a famous figure in jurisprudence stated the heart of the rationale for qualified privilege in an early case that has been relied upon by American courts countless times since. Judge Oliver Wendell Holmes, Jr., then of the Massachusetts bench and later a Justice of the United States Supreme Court, wrote the words in *Cowley v. Pulsifer*.[256] Publisher Royal Pulsifer's *Boston Herald* had printed the content of a petition seeking Charles Cowley's removal from the bar, and Cowley sued. Judge Holmes wrote that the public must have knowledge of judicial proceedings, not because one citizen's quarrels with another are important to public concern,[257]

> * * * but because it is of the highest moment that those who administer justice should always act under the sense of public responsibility, and that every citizen should be able to satisfy himself with his own eyes as to the mode in which a public duty is performed.
>
> The advantage to the nation in granting privilege to press reports, he stressed, is "the security which publicity gives for the proper administration of justice."

The privilege is "qualified" in the sense that it must be fair and accurate. (For example, an accurate quote misleadingly published out of context may not be privileged if defamatory.) Also, in some jurisdictions, the privilege will not hold if the report of the proceeding is made with malice (in the sense of ill will). Fundamentally, however, if a news account is a fair and accurate summary of a public official proceeding or record, the citizen or reporter will be protected by the "reporter's privilege." Also, the story must be one of a "public and official proceeding," not a report of related material that emerges before, after, or in some way outside the proceeding.

FAIR AND ACCURATE REPORTS

Errors can destroy qualified privilege. Ponder the perils of careless notetaking, the constant danger of a misspelled name, the arcane and technical jargon and findings of law courts, and all the slip-ups of life that happen under tight deadlines. Further, if the report of an official proceeding is not fair to people involved in it, the reporter can be in trouble. We have seen in the previous chapter how Mrs. Firestone won a libel judgment for $100,000 from *Time, Inc.*, for its error in reporting that her husband's divorce was granted on grounds of adultery.

In the case of Anthony Liquori of Agawam, Mass., a newspaper reporter made an error in an address after extracting other materials from a court record about a "breaking" case in which a man of the same name from Springfield pleaded guilty and was convicted. The reporter took an address from a phone book; the innocent Liquori was wrongly

[256] *Cowley v. Pulsifer*, 137 Mass. 392, 394 (1884).

[257] Ibid. at 394.

identified and sued the Republican Company, publisher of the Springfield papers which carried separate stories, both erroneous. The Republican Company defended with a plea of qualified privilege, arguing that the defense should hold,[258] "because the newspaper articles were a substantially accurate report of a judicial proceeding." It asserted that since only the address of the accused was inaccurate, it had published an article which was "substantially true and accurate and entirely fair," and that no more was required. But citing several previous cases about fair and accurate press reports of official proceedings, the Massachusetts Appeals Court said:[259]

> " * * * an article which labels an innocent man as a criminal because it refers erroneously to his street address, which the reporter gained from a source outside the court records, is neither substantially accurate nor fair."

It denied qualified privilege for the Republican. A wrong name, taken accurately from official police records, on the other hand, is privileged.[260]

Not every inaccuracy in reporting proceedings is fatal, however. Privilege did not fail in *Mitchell v. Peoria Journal-Star, Inc.*,[261] merely because the news story of a court action for liquor ordinance violation got the violators' place of arrest wrong. In *Josephs v. News Syndicate Co., Inc.*,[262] the newspaper did not lose privilege because somehow the reporter incorrectly slipped into his story of a burglary arrest the statement that the accused had been found under a bed at the scene of the burglary. Where he was actually discovered is not mentioned.

OPINION AND EXTRANEOUS MATERIAL

One way to destroy immunity for a news story is to add opinion or material extraneous to the proceeding. It is necessary for reporters to stick to the facts of what comes to light under officials' surveillance. Radio station KYW in Philadelphia broadcast a "documentary" on car-towing rackets, and Austin Purcell sued for defamation. The broadcast had used a judicial proceeding as a basis: a magistrate's hearing at which Purcell was convicted of violating the car-tow ordinance. (Purcell later was exonerated, on appeal.) But the producer of the documentary wove into his script some material he had gathered from other sources—the voices of a man and a woman claiming that they had been cheated and a

---

[258] *Liquori v. Republican Co.*, 8 Mass.App.Ct. 671, 396 N.E.2d 726, 728 (1979), 5 Med.L.Rptr. 2180.

[259] Ibid. at 728–29.

[260] *Biermann v. Pulitzer Pub. Co.*, 627 S.W.2d 87 (Mo.App.1981), 7 Med.L.Rptr. 2601. See also *Murray v. Bailey*, 613 F.Supp. 1276 (N.D.Cal.1985), 11 Med.L.Rptr. 1369. Report saying plaintiff arrested for drunk driving and assault and battery privileged as fair report when in fact plaintiff had been arrested for public intoxication and resisting arrest. Book author's later erroneous statement "convicted of drunken driving" held not privileged.

[261] *Mitchell v. Peoria Journal-Star, Inc.*, 76 Ill.App.2d 154, 221 N.E.2d 516 (1966).

[262] *Josephs v. News Syndicate Co., Inc.*, 5 Misc.2d 184, 159 N.Y.S.2d 537 (1957).

conversation with detectives. Anonymous voices on the tape called Purcell a "thug" and a "racketeer." The producer added comment of his own to the effect that "the sentencing of a few racketeers is not enough." That was defamation, the court said, and it was not protected by qualified privilege. The documentary lost the protection of qualified privilege because it contained[263] "exaggerated additions."

"OLD-STYLE MALICE"

New York Times Co. v. Sullivan (1964) gave the term "actual malice" a restricted meaning where public officials and figures are concerned. Actual malice means that the publisher knew the words were false, or had reckless disregard for whether they were false or not. Malice before that decision was defined in many ways, including ill will toward another, hatred, intent to harm, bad motive, or lack of good faith. It used to be that people who claimed that news stories of government proceedings libeled them, often charged "malice" in the stories, in terms such as these. Such definitions of "old-style malice" are still alive for libel that does not proceed under the constitutional protection provided by *New York Times v. Sullivan*.

Consider a case in which the *St. Paul Dispatch* was accused of a malicious report based on a complaint filed in district court. The newspaper's story said that William and Frank Hurley had been accused of depleting almost all of the estate of an aged woman before her death. Some $200,000 was involved. The Hurleys sued for libel, saying that the report was malicious and therefore not privileged.

The court did not agree, and in effect said the paper had showed neither "old style malice" (an inaccurate report " 'made solely for the purpose of causing harm to the person defamed' ") nor the harder to prove "actual malice" under the *New York Times* rule.[264] The court ruled the Hurleys could not win their suit because they could produce no evidence of malice at the trial. Other courts have used old definitions of malice, where qualified privilege is pleaded, alongside knowing or reckless falsehood. Thus, one says there is no malice in that which "the publisher reasonably believed to be true;" another speaks of malice as "intent to injure," and another of malice as "ill will."[265]

---

[263] *Purcell v. Westinghouse Broadcasting Co.*, 411 Pa. 167, 191 A.2d 662, 666 (1963). Ibid., 668. See also *Jones v. Pulitzer Pub. Co.*, 240 Mo. 200, 144 S.W. 441 (1911); *Robinson v. Johnson*, 152 C.C.A. 505, 239 Fed. 671 (1917); *Embers Supper Club, Inc. v. Scripps-Howard Broadcasting Co.*, 9 Ohio St.3d 22, 457 N.E.2d 1164 (1984), 10 Med.L.Rptr. 1729.

[264] *Hurley v. Northwest Publications, Inc.*, 273 F.Supp. 967, 972, 974 (D.Minn.1967).

[265] *Bannach v. Field Enterprises, Inc.*, 5 Ill.App.3d 692, 284 N.E.2d 31, 32 (1972); and *Brunn v. Weiss*, 32 Mich.App. 428, 188 N.W.2d 904, 905 (1971). See, also, *Orrison v. Vance*, 262 Md. 285, 277 A.2d 573, 578 (1971).

OFFICIAL PROCEEDINGS

Reports of official activity outside the proceeding—the trial, the hearing, the legislative debate or committee—may not be protected. Some official activity has the color of official proceeding but not the reality. To start with the courts:[266] Any trial including that of a lesser court "not of record" such as a police magistrate's furnishes the basis for privilege. The *ex parte* proceeding in which only one party to a legal controversy is represented affords privilege to reporting.[267] So does the grand jury report published in open court.[268]

In many states, the attorneys' "pleadings" filed with the clerk of court as the basic documents starting a lawsuit are *not* proceedings that furnish protection. In those states the judge must be involved; an early decision stated the rule that for the immunity to attach, the pleadings must have been submitted[269] "to the judicial mind with a view to judicial action," even if only in pretrial hearings on motions.

A 1927 New York decision, as so often in defamation, led the way for several states' rejecting this position and granting protection to reports of pleadings. Newspapers had carried a story based on a complaint filed by Mrs. Elizabeth Nichols against Mrs. Anne Campbell, claiming the latter had defrauded her of $16,000. After the news stories had appeared, Mrs. Nichols withdrew her suit. Mrs. Campbell filed libel suit. Acknowledging that nearly all courts had refused qualified privilege to stories based on pleadings not seen by a judge, the New York Court of Appeals said it would no longer follow this rule.

The New York high court conceded that it is easy for malicious persons to file pleadings in order to vent hostility against others in news stories, and then withdraw the lawsuits. But it said that this can happen also after judges are in the proceeding; suits have been dropped before verdicts have been reached. It added that newspapers had so often printed stories about actions started before they reached a judge that[270] "the public has learned that accusation is not proof and that such actions are at times brought in malice to result in failure." The newspapers won.

That set up what is sometimes called the "Campbell Rule," which says that pleadings may be reported on, fairly and accurately, as soon as they are filed with a court and before a judge has acted upon them. Perhaps 20 states follow this rule today. That is, the filing of a pleading is a reportable public and official act appears to be a public and official act in the course of judicial proceedings.

---

[266] *McBee v. Fulton*, 47 Md. 403 (1878); *Flues v. New Nonpareil Co.*, 155 Iowa 290, 135 N.W. 1083 (1912); See also Sack, loc. cit.

[267] *Metcalf v. Times Pub. Co.*, 20 R.I. 674, 40 A. 864 (1898).

[268] *Sweet v. Post Pub. Co.*, 215 Mass. 450, 102 N.E. 660 (1913).

[269] *Barber v. St. Louis Dispatch Co.*, 3 Mo.App. 377 (1877); *Finnegan v. Eagle Printing Co.*, 173 Wis. 5, 179 N.W. 788 (1920).

[270] *Campbell v. New York Evening Post*, 245 N.Y. 320, 327, 157 N.E. 153, 155 (1927).

The Campbell Rule, increasingly, seems to be "the modern rule," with more and more courts' language tending toward making the contents of pleadings starting a lawsuit a public record to be reported upon.[271] That is fortunate for reporters, editors and broadcast news directors, many who long have assumed that once a pleading is filed with a court clerk, it is fair game.

But other states have not chosen to follow this rule. Massachusetts specifically rejected it in 1945. The *Boston Herald-Traveler* had published a story based on pleadings filed in an alienation of affections case, had been sued for libel, and had lost. The state Supreme Court said:[272]

> * * * the publication of accusations made by one party against another is neither a legal nor a moral duty of newspapers. Enterprise in that matter ought to be at the risk of paying damages if the accusations prove false. To be safe, a newspaper has only to send its reporters to listen to hearings rather than to search the files of cases not yet brought before the court.

Even in those jurisdictions where "pleadings" are privileged, careful adherence to basic rules of reporting is a must. That is, it should be made clear where the information is from: Attribution to the privileged document is good self-protection. The best rule, of course, is to play fair. Ethical reporters and editors will want to make sure that stories explicitly say that a pleading beginning a lawsuit tells only the plaintiff's side of the story. Reporters may wish to go further, phoning lawsuit defendants or the defendants' attorneys to give them an opportunity to comment. (It is likely that defendants may be unwilling to comment in the face of pending litigation, but it never hurts to ask, and it will indicate reportorial fairness.)

Stories based on the following situations were outside "official proceedings" of courts and did not furnish news media the protection of qualified privilege: A newsman's interview of ("conversation with") a United States commissioner, concerning an earlier arraignment before the commissioner;[273] the words of a judge[274] and of an attorney[275] in courtrooms, but just before trials were convened formally, and the taking by a judge of a deposition in his courtroom, where he was acting in a "ministerial capacity" only, not as a judge.[276] In *Bufalino v. Associated Press,*[277] the wire service did not actually demonstrate that it relied on FBI records, nor did it identify "officials" who were unnamed sources. So,

---

[271] Henry R. Kaufman, ed., *Libel Defense Resource Center (LDRC) 50-State Survey,* 1991 (New York: LDRC, 1991).

[272] *Sanford v. Boston Herald-Traveler Corp.,* 318 Mass. 156, 61 N.E.2d 5 (1945): But see *Sibley v. Holyoke Transcript-Telegram Pub. Co., Inc.,* 391 Mass. 468, 461 N.E.2d 823 (1984), 10 Med.L.Rptr. 1557.

[273] *Wood v. Constitution Pub. Co.,* 57 Ga.App. 123, 194 S.E. 760 (1937).

[274] *Douglas v. Collins,* 243 App.Div. 546, 276 N.Y.S. 87 (1934).

[275] *Rogers v. Courier Post Co.,* 2 N.J. 393, 66 A.2d 869 (1949).

[276] *Mannix v. Portland Telegram,* 144 Or. 172, 23 P.2d 138 (1933).

[277] *Bufalino v. Associated Press,* 692 F.2d 266 (2d Cir.1982), 8 Med.L.Rptr. 2384.

the AP could not show that it was within the scope of privilege.[278] In a Louisiana case,[279] a newspaper reporter was held to be outside the privilege because he relied on another newspaper's story, even though the latter was based on a sheriff's press release.

EXECUTIVE OFFICERS AND PRIVILEGE

Shift now to news stories about the executive and administrative branch of government. When government officials hold a hearing or issue a report or even a press release, absolute privilege usually protects them. And where absolute privilege leads, qualified privilege for press reports ordinarily follows. Yet while major and minor federal officials enjoy the privilege under federal decisions, state courts have not been unanimous in granting it.[280]

The formal hearings of many administrative bodies have a quasi-judicial character, in which testimony is taken, interrogation is performed, deliberation is engaged in, and findings are reported in writing. The reporter can have confidence that such proceedings are "safe" to report. The minutes of a meeting and audits of a city water commission were the basis for a successful plea of privilege by a newspaper whose story reflected badly on an engineer.[281] The Federal Trade Commission investigated a firm and an account based on the investigation said that the firm had engaged in false branding and labeling; the account was privileged.[282] A news story reporting that an attorney had charged another with perjury was taken from a governor's extradition hearing, a quasi-judicial proceeding, and was privileged.[283]

Also, informal hearings or investigations carried out by executive-administrative officers, even those outside of hearing-chambers and without the banging of a gavel, usually furnish privilege. For example, a state tax commissioner audited a city's books and reported irregularities in the city council's handling of funds. A story based on the report caused a suit for libel, and the court held that the story was protected by privilege.[284]

Yet not every investigation provides a basis for the defense of qualified privilege; reporters and city editors especially need to know what the judicial precedent of their state is. In a Texas case, a district attorney investigated a plot to rob a bank and obtained confessions. He made the confessions available to the press. A successful libel suit brought was brought on the basis of the resulting news story. The

---

[278] Ibid., 271–272, 2389.

[279] *Melon v. Capital City Press*, 407 So.2d 85 (La.App.1981), 8 Med.L.Rptr. at 1167.

[280] *Barr v. Matteo*, 360 U.S. 564, 79 S.Ct. 1335 (1959); Prosser, pp. 802–803; Kaufman, LDRC 50-State Survey.

[281] *Holway v. World Pub. Co.*, 171 Okl. 306, 44 P.2d 881 (1935).

[282] *Mack, Miller Candle Co. v. Macmillan Co.*, 239 App.Div. 738, 269 N.Y.S. 33 (1934).

[283] *Brown v. Globe Printing Co.*, 213 Mo. 611, 112 S.W. 462 (1908).

[284] *Swearingen v. Parkersburg Sentinel Co.*, 125 W.Va. 731, 26 S.E.2d 209 (1943).

confessions were held insufficient as executive proceedings to provide the protection.[285]

Police reporters need to be especially alert to libel dangers. "Blotters" listing the records of arrests and charges made are sources for many news stories. Their status as a basis for a plea of privilege varies from state to state.[286] Police stations generally have a written record—now often kept on computer—which keeps track of incidents and activities around the clock. These reports vary in form and completeness; blotters usually are starting points in the reporting process, with additional checking—including interviewing of officials—needed to get reasonably complete information. As suggested earlier, larger departments often establish some form of police "hot line," which—for safety's sake—probably ought to be regarded as unprivileged.[287]

Oral reports of preliminary investigations by policemen do not support a plea of privilege in some states. The *Rutland Herald* obtained information from police officers and published a story about two brothers arrested on charges of robbery, and included this paragraph:[288]

> Arthur was arrested on information given to police by the younger brother, it is said. "*According to authorities*," [emphasis added by authors] Floyd in his alleged confession stated that Arthur waited outside the window in the rear of the clothing store while Floyd climbed through a broken window the second time to destroy possible clues left behind.

A suit for libel was brought, and the court denied qualified privilege to the story. It reviewed other states' decisions on whether statements attributed to police were a basis for privilege.[289] "It has been held that reports made to police officers charging persons with crime are not judicial proceedings the publication of which are privileged."

The State of New Jersey has provided by statute that "official statements issued by police department heads" protect news stories, and Georgia has a similar law. In other states, courts have provided the protection through decisions in libel suits. In *Kilgore v. Koen*,[290] an Oregon case, privilege was granted to a story in which deputy sheriffs' statements about the evidence and arrest in a case involving a school principal were the newspaper's source.

---

[285] *Caller Times Pub.Co. v. Chandler*, 134 Tex. 1, 130 S.W.2d 853 (1939). But see *Woolbright v. Sun Communications, Inc.*, 480 S.W.2d 864 (Mo.1972).

[286] *Sherwood v. Evening News Ass'n*, 256 Mich. 318, 239 N.W. 305 (1931); M.J. Petrick, "The Press, the Police Blotter and Public Policy," 46 *Journalism Quarterly* 475, 1969.

[287] See *Phillips v. Evening Star Newspaper Co.*, 424 A.2d 78 (D.C.App.1980), 6 Med.L.Rptr. 2191.

[288] *Lancour v. Herald & Globe Ass'n*, 111 Vt. 371, 17 A.2d 253 132 A.L.R. 486 (Vermont 1941).

[289] Ibid. at 384, 259; *Burrows v. Pulitzer Pub. Co.*, 255 S.W. 925 (Mo.App.1923); *Pittsburgh Courier Pub. Co. v. Lubore*, 91 U.S.App.D.C. 311, 200 F.2d 355 (1952).

[290] *Kilgore v. Koen*, 133 Or. 1, 288 P. 192 (1930).

LEGISLATIVE BRANCH REPORTING

As for the legislative branch, the third general sphere of government, state statutes have long declared that the immunity holds in stories from legislative settings. The legislative privilege is of paramount importance if the media are to fulfill their watchdog function.[291] For debates on the floor of Congress or of a state legislature, there has been no question that protection would apply to news stories. A few early cases indicated that stories of petty legislative bodies such as a town council[292] would not be privileged; but today's reporter need have little fear on this count.

In news stories about a New Jersey municipal council meeting, the city manager was quoted as saying that he was planning to bypass two policemen for promotion because they were insubordinate and "I should have fired them." There was some question as to whether the meeting was the regular one, or a session held in a conference room later. The New Jersey Supreme Court said that that didn't matter. It was not only an official but also a public meeting, at which motions were made by councilmen, heated discussion ensued, and the city manager was questioned by councilmen. Privilege held for the newspaper.[293]

One question about reporting legislatures was settled in a series of "chain" libel suits in the 1920s against several major newspapers. The "qualified privilege" immunity holds for news reports of committees of legislative bodies.[294] (Chain libel suits exist where one plaintiff sues a publisher in several states or jurisdictions on the basis of one allegedly defamatory report. Only one recovery is allowed, however.)

Legislative committees have a long history of operating under loose procedural rules.[295] Irregular procedures raise the question whether committee activity always meets the requirements of a "legislative proceeding" which is the basis for immunity in news reports.[296] In reporting committee activity, the reporter may sense danger signals if the committee:

Holds hearings without a quorum;

Publishes material that its clerks have collected, without itself first investigating charges in the material;

---

291 New York Laws, 1854, Chap. 130; *Wason v. Walter*, L.R. 4 Q.B. 73 (1868).

292 *Buckstaff v. Hicks*, 94 Wis. 34, 68 N.W. 403 (1896).

293 *Swede v. Passaic Daily News*, 30 N.J. 320, 153 A.2d 36 (1959).

294 *Cresson v. Louisville Courier-Journal*, 299 Fed. 487 (6th Cir.1924).

295 Walter Gellhorn (ed.), *The States and Subversion* (Ithaca: Cornell Univ.Press, 1952); Ernst J. Eberling, *Congressional Investigations* (New York: Columbia Univ.Press, 1928); more recently, lax legislative evidence rules have resulted in dropping prosecutions against "Iran-contra" scandal defendants. (Because of such loose procedures, it was determined those defendants who testified before Congress on TV later could not get a fair trial.) See, e.g., David Johnston, "Judge in Iran-Contra Trial Drops Case Against North After Prosecutor Gives Up," *New York Times*, Sept. 17, 1991.

296 H.L. Nelson, *Libel in News of Congressional Investigating Committees* (Minneapolis: Univ. of Minn.Press, 1961), Chs. 1, 2.

> Has not authorized the work of its subcommittees;
>
> Has a chairman given to issuing "reports" or holding press conferences on matters that the committee itself has not investigated?

When state and congressional investigating committees relentlessly hunted "subversion" in the 1940s and 1950s, thousands of persons were tainted with the charge of "communist" during the committee proceedings. High procedural irregularity was common. Yet only one libel case growing out of these irregular proceedings reached the highest court of a state, and the newspaper successfully defended with a plea of privilege.[297]

Again, there is much variation concerning privilege from jurisdiction to jurisdiction. It may be generalized that accurate and fair accounts of meetings which are both open to the public and deal with matters of public concern are privileged.[298] Matters get trickier when there is a newsworthy story which becomes available through confidential or secret reports dealing with charges of official misconduct.

The American Broadcasting Co. was sued after it ran correspondent Bettina Gregory's five part series about scandals in the General Services Administration (GSA). From a confidential source, ABC received—and used as source material—some leaked GSA internal reports. Those reports led to broadcasting assertions that Excelon Security Co., which had been under GSA contract to provide security services, had provided guards who did not have security clearances.

The ABC broadcast added that unnamed top federal, county, and city officials said "the President of Excelon is alleged to have connection with organized crime."

Excelon president Salvatore J. Ingenere sued, arguing that the documents were erroneous and were not privileged because the GSA documents were internal memos not intended for publication. Ingenere lost his suit when the U.S. district court ruled that,[299] "* * * the Massachusetts common law fair use report privilege extends to the fair and accurate reporting of confidential government reports that reveal possible government misconduct."

PUBLIC PROCEEDINGS

The Restatement (Second) of Torts, that oft quoted and influential summary of how law *ought* to be, says:[300]

> The publication of defamatory matter * * * in a report of an official action or proceeding or of a meeting open to the public

---

297 *Coleman v. Newark Morning Ledger Co.*, 29 N.J. 357, 149 A.2d 193 (1959).

298 Sack, in Goodale, ed., *Communications Law 1991*, Vol. I, p. 62.

299 *Ingenere v. ABC* (D.Mass.1984), 11 Med.L.Rptr. 1227.

300 Restatement (Second) of Torts, S 611 (1977).

that deals with a matter of public concern is privileged if the report is accurate and complete and a fair abridgement of the occurrence is reported.

In 1854, the New York legislature enacted a statute saying something quite similar to the passage from the Restatement, dealing with a[301] "fair and true report * * * of any judicial, legislative or public official proceeding." Some 102 years later, in 1956, the New York legislature removed the word "public" from that statute. The change was made after editorial campaigning by New York City newspapers.[302] The deletion of the word "public" made it possible to have immunity in publishing news of an official proceeding even though the proceeding was not public.

In some cases, efforts to use the fair report privilege as a defense to libel suits growing out of coverage of secret government proceedings do not succeed. Despite the elimination of the word "public" from the New York statute, the state Court of Appeals ruled in 1970 that news stories of matrimonial proceedings—secret under New York law—are not protected by qualified privilege.

That New York situation carries a message to all mass communicators: *Know the law of the state in which you work.* Outside of New York, journalists sometimes have lost immunity when they reported libelous stories after gaining access to secret governmental or quasi-governmental proceedings. In a case from the 1930s, *McCurdy v. Hughes,*[303] a newspaper reported on a secret meeting of a disciplinary board of a state bar association in which a complaint against an attorney was considered. The attorney brought a libel suit for derogatory/defamatory statements in the story and won.

Reporting gets tricky for the news media in those times where a meeting or record is not both *public* and *official.* Obviously, some government records do not have public status. If news media publish such non-public or secret materials containing defamatory information, the public interest in those materials needs to be compelling to afford the media protection from liability.

Take, for example, *Time* magazine's 1978 publication of an article about suspected criminal activities of a Congressman from Pennsylvania named Daniel J. Flood. The *Medico v. Time, Inc.*[304] defamation suit resulted, beginning when the magazine—in an article tying the Congressman to the Mafia—published these words: "The suspected link,

---

[301] New York Laws, 1854, Chap. 130; *Danziger v. Hearst Corp.*, 304 N.Y. 244, 107 N.E.2d 62 (1952).

[302] *Editor & Publisher,* May 5, 1956, p. 52; See *New York State Legislative Annual,* 1956, pp. 494–495. *Shiles v. News Syndicate Co.*, 27 N.Y.2d 9, 313 N.Y.S.2d 104, 107, 261 N.E.2d 251 (1970).

[303] *McCurdy v. Hughes,* 63 N.D. 435, 248 N.W. 512 (1933).

[304] *Medico v. Time, Inc.*, 643 F.2d 134 (3d Cir.1981), 6 Med.L.Rptr. 2529, cert. denied 454 U.S. 836, 102 S.Ct. 139 (1981).

the Wilkes-Barre firm of Philip Medico and his brothers. The FBI discovered more than a decade ago that [Congressman Daniel] Flood steered Government business to the Medicos and often traveled in their company jet." *Time*'s article was based on secret FBI files.[305]

In addition, the magazine story called Medico a member of an organized crime "family" and referred to him as a Mafia "capo" or chief. *Time* magazine, however, argued that the gist of its article was that the Federal Bureau of Investigation had recorded "Pennsylvania Rackets Boss" Russell Bufalino's description of Philip Medico.

The trial court refused to find that *Time*'s article could be defended as true, but ultimately held that the article was protected under Pennsylvania's common law privilege to report official proceedings. The court recognized that *Time* had summarized secret FBI reports which had been given the magazine without authorization. But because *Time*'s article was a fair and accurate report of the FBI documents, the trial judge ruled that publication was privileged. Recognizing the great public concern over allegations of wrongdoing by a member of Congress, it was held that secret FBI documents concerning Philip Medico were,[306] " 'a report of an official proceeding or meeting.' "

Upholding the trial court, a U.S. Court of Appeals found that important "policies underlie the fair report privilege." First is an "agency theory," where one who reports on a public, official proceeding represents people who could not attend. But, said the appeals court, the agency rationale would not work for proceedings or reports not open to the public. A second policy—and the one the appeals court embraced—is a "theory of public supervision."[307]

As public inspection of courtroom proceedings may further the just administration of the laws, public scrutiny of the records of criminal investigatory agencies may often have the equally salutary effect of fostering among those who enforce the laws "the sense of public responsibility." For example, exposing the content of agency records may, in some cases, help ensure impartial enforcement of the laws.

A final note about the word "public" in connection with qualified privilege: The immunity to lawsuit for reporting is clearest when the meeting or record is both *public* and *official*. Perhaps there is an emerging standard suggesting that even if a meeting or record is not both public and official, it is important for the community to know what is happening where matters of public welfare and concern are involved.[308] As for private gatherings of stockholders, directors, or members of an

---

[305] Ibid. at 141, 2535.

[306] Ibid. at 137–139.

[307] Ibid. at 141, quoting Judge (later Mr. Justice) Holmes from *Cowley v. Pulsifer*, 137 Mass. 392, 394 (1884).

[308] See Robert D. Sack, op. cit., pp. 105–108, citing *Kilgore v. Younger*, 30 Cal.3d 770, 796, 180 Cal.Rptr. 657, 673, 640 P.2d 793, 797 (1982), and *Crane v. Arizona Republic*, 729 F.Supp. 698 (C.D.Cal.1989).

association or organization, they are no basis for privilege in news reports.

31. TRUTH AS A DEFENSE

Most state laws provide that truth is a complete defense in libel cases, but some require that the publisher show "good motives and justifiable ends." The United States Supreme Court has not ruled on whether truth may ever be subjected to civil or criminal liability.

The defense of truth (often called "justification") in civil libel has ancient roots developed in the common law of England. It was taken up by American courts as they employed the common law in the colonial and early national periods and was transferred from the common law to many state statutes. Its basis appeals to common sense and ordinary ideas of justice: Why, indeed, should an individual be awarded damages for harm to his reputation when the truth of the matter is that his record does not merit a good reputation? To print or broadcast the truth about persons is no more than they should expect. In addition, the social good may be served by bringing to light the truth about people whose work involves them in the public interest.

It is held by some courts that truth alone is a complete defense, regardless of the motives behind its publication, and this squares with the libel statutes in most states. Some state laws continue to qualify, and provide that truth is a defense if it is published,[309] "with good motives and justifiable ends." The qualifying term goes back to 1804, when Alexander Hamilton used it in his defense of newspaperman Harry Croswell in a celebrated New York criminal libel case.[310] So far as the comatose *criminal* libel offense is concerned, however, the United States Supreme Court has ruled that the Hamiltonian qualification is unconstitutional, and may not be required of a defendant.[311]

The Supreme Court has shied away from ruling that truth is always a defense. Justice White wrote in *Cox Broadcasting Co. v. Cohn*[312] that the Court had not decided the question "whether truthful publications may ever be subjected to civil or criminal liability." Earlier cases, he said, had "carefully left open the question" whether the First Amendment requires,[313] "that truth be recognized as a defense in a defamation action brought by a private person * * *."

---

[309] State statutes and constitutional provisions are collected in Angoff, op. cit. See also Note, 56 *N.W.Univ.L.Rev.* 547 (1961); *Garrison v. Louisiana,* 379 U.S. 64, 85 S.Ct. 209 (1964), footnote 7.

[310] *People v. Croswell,* 3 Johns.Cas. 337 (N.Y.1804).

[311] *Garrison v. Louisiana,* 379 U.S. 64, 85 S.Ct. 209 (1964).

[312] *Cox Broadcasting v. Cohn,* 420 U.S. 469, 95 S.Ct. 1029 (1975), a privacy decision. But see Restatement, Second, Torts, § 581A, p. 235, which says "There can be no recovery in defamation for a statement of fact that is true * * *."

[313] Ibid. at 490, 1043–1044.

THE BURDEN OF PROVING TRUTH

Since the Supreme Court rules of *Sullivan* and *Gertz* have made it plain that some level of fault on the part of the media must be shown—from knowing falsity to negligence—the burden of pleading and showing falsity has largely been on the plaintiff where he is a public person. Yet the *Restatement of Torts (Second)* takes the position that it cannot yet be said that the burden is inescapably on the plaintiff:[314]

Placing the burden on the party asserting the negative necessarily creates difficulties, and the problem is accentuated when the defamatory charge is not specific in its terms but quite general in nature. Suppose, for example, that a newspaper published a charge that a storekeeper short-changes his customers when he gets a chance. How is he expected to prove that he has not short-changed customers when no specific occasions are pointed to by the defendant?

Some courts have said that the burden of proof rests on the plaintiff to show defamation and to prove damages. It is clear that defendants in libel suits frequently have been at pains to prove that an alleged libel is true.[315] In 1986, however, in *Philadelphia Newspapers v. Hepps*,[316] the U.S. Supreme Court held 5–4 that it is unconstitutional to put the burden of proving truth on a media defendant where the story involved deals with a matter of public concern.

The *Hepps* case was a close call, a 5–4 decision, but it nevertheless tilted the scales in favor of the media for expression "of a public concern." Justice Sandra Day O'Connor wrote for the majority that the old,[317] " * * * common-law presumption that defamatory speech is false cannot stand when a plaintiff seeks damages against a media defendant for speech of public concern."

The news media, in other words, should not be punished for statements that may be true. This decision invalidated similar rules in eight other states, including New Jersey. Before the *Hepps* decision, a dozen or more other states—including New York and Connecticut—had already shifted the burden of proof concerning falsity to the plaintiffs.[318]

Not every detail of an allegedly libelous story must be proved accurate in order to rebut a charge of "falsity," but rather, that the story is "substantially" true.[319] But no formula can measure just what inaccuracy will be tolerated by a particular court.

---

[314] Ibid., § 613, p. 310.

[315] See *Memphis Pub. Co. v. Nichols*, 569 S.W.2d 412 (Tenn.1978), 4 Med.L.Rptr. 1573.

[316] *Philadelphia Newspapers, Inc. v. Hepps*, 475 U.S. 767, 777, 106 S.Ct. 1558, 1564 (1986), 12 Med.L.Rptr. 1977, 1981.

[317] Ibid. at 77, 1564.

[318] Stuart Taylor, Jr., "Supreme Court Adds Protection for News Media in Libel Actions," *New York Times*, April 22, 1986.

[319] *Hein v. Lacy*, 228 Kan. 249, 616 P.2d 277, 282 (1980), 6 Med.L.Rptr. 1662, 1666; Prosser, 825.

A U.S. district court held that a 2015 *Buzzfeed* article claiming that the CEN news agency in Britain was, "The King of Bullshit News" was substantially true.[320] CEN (the Central European News agency) was founded by Michael Leidig in 1995 to sell stories from non-English speaking countries to third-party media services in and outside of Britain. *Buzzfeed* reporters started working on the story following reports in other news media that pointed out inaccuracies in CEN stories. At the conclusion of the investigation, the BuzzFeed team members summarized that,[321] "the evidence assembled by BuzzFeed News suggests that an alarming proportion of CEN's 'weird news' stories are based on exaggeration, embellishment, and outright fabrication[.]" (Dkt. No. 1-1 at 4.)

Leidig and CEN sued *Buzzfeed* for libel seeking $5 million in damages. The case ended in summary judgment for *Buzzfeed*. U.S. District Judge Victor Marrero held that:[322]

1 statement implying that news agency and its founder manufactured false quotes was at least substantially true;

2 statement debunking tapeworm story published by news agency was at least substantially true;

3 statement disproving story that a kitten died was substantially true;

4 statement alleging news agency and its founder copied photos was substantially true;

5 statement implying quotes in two-headed goat story by news agency and its founder were fabricated was substantially true;

6 statement regarding origins of news agency was substantially true; and

7 statement article implying news agency falsified quotes was substantially true.

In one part of *Buzzfeed*'s story, its reporters looked at a CEN story about people in China who "walked cabbages" in order to escape feelings of loneliness.[323] "The story included quotes from 'Chinese psychiatrist Wen Chao', explaining how walking a cabbage on a lead can help reduce feelings of isolation." The story was accompanied by photos of Chinese teens walking cabbages. *Kotaku*, *The Wall Street Journal* and *Buzzfeed* ran stories at the time debunking the story. The photo of the teens was real but they were pulling the cabbages along as part of an art installation by Han Bing, the Chinese artist who has incorporated cabbage walking in his art for more than a decade.

---

[320] *Leidig v. BuzzFeed, Inc.*, 371 F.Supp.3d 134 (S.D.New York 2019).

[321] Ibid. at 138.

[322] Ibid. at 134.

[323] Ibid. at 138.

CEN sold a story about a Chinese man who purportedly contracted tapeworms from eating too much sashimi (a Japanese dish of sliced raw fish). The CEN article was accompanied by a photo of the man's X-ray "showing the spots of disseminated cysticercosis."[324] That photo was debunked by *Snopes.com*, the widely known fact-checking site. *Snopes* found the photos were much like photos of X-rays published by the *British Medical Journal* in an article about a man who contracted a rare case of disseminated cysticercosis through the consumption of uncooked pork. The *Daily Mail, Buzzfeed* and other sites carried the story in 2014.

> Buzzfeed noted that CEN managed to get interviews with persons in remote locations in other countries where English is not commonly spoken. The interviews of contain quotations,[325] "from someone that no one else could persuade to talk, including the local media. And many of those quotes, especially those from anonymous 'officials', include phrases that one would expect to hear from someone who grew up in the UK."

Judge Marrero's analysis of instances of manufactured news on the part of CEN resulted in a finding that they were "substantially true" and not actionable.

Late in 1995, the Ninth Circuit Court of Appeals upheld summary judgment for the popular CBS weekly news magazine, *60 Minutes*. In 1989, the show broadcast a segment titled "A is for Apple," which made disparaging reference to Alar, a chemical growth regulator sprayed on apples. The story was based primarily on a National Defense Resources Council (NDRC) report titled, "Intolerable Risk: Pesticides in Our Children's Food."

The NDRC report used by CBS discussed the Environmental Protection Agency's (EPA) knowledge of the carcinogenic properties of the chemical daminozide, trade name Alar. In the *60 Minutes* story Ed Bradley said that the most powerful cancer-causing "agent in our food supply is a substance sprayed on apples to keep them on the trees longer and make them look better. That's the conclusion from a number of scientific experts." Bradley cited a number of sources to bolster the conclusion that the EPA, which could remove Alar from the market, hesitated to do so for fear of being sued by its manufacturer, Uniroyal.[326]

Grady and Lillie Auvil sued on behalf of themselves and other Washington state apple growers, claiming that the broadcast caused apple sales to drop markedly. The Auvils countered claims made in the course of the broadcast with statements that no scientific studies had yet shown that Alar caused cancer in people. The studies were limited to lab animals. The U.S. district court nonetheless granted CBS summary

---

[324] Disseminated Cysticercosis is a parasitic tissue infection caused by larval cysts of the tapeworm. https://www.cdc.gov/parasites/cysticercosis/.

[325] *Leidig v. BuzzFeed, Inc.*, 371 F.Supp.3d 134, 140 (S.D.New York 2019).

[326] *Auvil v. CBS "60 Minutes,"* 67 F.3d 816, 819 (9th Cir.1995), 23 Med.L.Rptr. 2454, 2456.

judgment on the grounds that the plaintiffs had failed to advance evidence to sustain a workable issue of fact as to the falsity of the broadcast.[327]

The Ninth Circuit cited a number of precedents in concluding that,[328] "animal studies are routinely relied on by the scientific community in assessing the carcinogenic effects of chemicals on humans." That was enough for the Ninth Circuit to affirm the district court.

In an old but illustrative case, the *New York World-Telegram and Sun* tried to establish truth of the following statement from its pages, but failed:[329]

> John Crane, former president of the UFA now under indictment, isn't waiting for his own legal developments. Meanwhile, his lawyers are launching a $,$$$,$$$ defamation suit.

Focusing on the word "indictment," Crane brought a libel suit against the newspaper and the columnist who wrote the item. He said that the defendant knew or could have learned the falsity of the charge by using reasonable care.

The defendants tried to dodge the libel action, arguing that the facts about John Crane already had been widely published and commented up by the press of the city. The lame argument that the phrase "under indictment" was used in a figurative, non-legal sense failed, and Crane won his suit against the newspaper. The court held that "under indictment" means a legal action by a grand jury to begin criminal charges, and that the use of the term to mean accusation by private persons is rare.[330] In any case, you cannot prove the truth of one charge against a person by showing he or she was suspected or guilty of another.[331]

The same term—"indictment"—was used by another newspaper in an incorrect way, but was held *not* to be libelous. The word appeared in connection with conflict-of-interest findings discussed in an editorial. A councilman was never truly indicted, but rather was charged by delivery of a summons, and convicted. The court held that "indictment" was substantially accurate, and although technically incorrect, did not constitute defamation.[332]

Thus, loose usage of certain technical terms does not always destroy a plea of truth. This is what a court ruled when a Massachusetts newspaper said that a man named Joyce had been "committed" to a

---

[327] *Auvil v. CBS*, 836 F.Supp. 740 (E.D.Wash.1993), 21 Med. L.Rptr. 2059.

[328] *Auvil v. CBS*, 67 F.3d 816, 821 (9th Cir.1995), 23 Med. L.Rptr. 2454, 2457.

[329] *Crane v. New York World Telegram Corp.*, 308 N.Y. 470, 126 N.E.2d 753 (1955).

[330] Ibid. at 475, 756.

[331] *Sun Printing and Pub. Ass'n v. Schenck*, 40 C.C.A. 163, 98 Fed. 925 (1900); *Kilian v. Doubleday & Co.*, 367 Pa. 117, 79 A.2d 657 (1951); *Yarmove v. Retail Credit Co.*, 18 A.D.2d 790, 236 N.Y.S.2d 836 (1963).

[332] *Schaefer v. Hearst Corp.* (Md. Super.1979), 5 Med.L.Rptr. 1734.

mental hospital when actually he had been "admitted" to the hospital at the request of a physician as the state law provided. The newspaper's words that caused the man to bring a libel suit were that the man "charges * * * that his constitutional rights were violated when he was committed to the hospital last November." In ruling for the newspaper which pleaded truth, the court said:[333]

> Strictly * * * "commitment" means a placing in the hospital by judicial order * * * But the words [of the news story] are to be used in their "natural sense with the meaning which they could convey to mankind in general." This meaning of the word "commitment" was placing in the hospital pursuant to proceedings provided by law. In so stating as to the plaintiff * * * the defendant reported correctly.

Of course, writers or broadcasters who are highly attuned to nuances in word meanings may save their employers the expense and trouble of even successful libel defenses by avoiding gaffes such as confusing "commit" with "admit." While news media continue to be staffed in part by writers insensitive to shades of meaning, however, they may take some comfort in the law's willingness—however unpredictably—to bend on occasion.

Courts frequently hold that truth will not be destroyed by a story's minor inaccuracies. Thus truth succeeded although a newspaper had printed that the plaintiff was in police custody on August 16, whereas he had been released on August 15;[334] and it was not fatal to truth to report in a news story that an arrest, which in fact took place at the Shelly Tap tavern, occurred at the Men's Social Club.[335]

In accord with the maxim that "tale bearers are as bad as tale tellers," it is no defense for a news medium to argue that it reported accurately and truthfully someone else's false and defamatory statements. The broadcaster or newspaper reporter writes at the employer's peril and at his or her own peril, too. The words "it is reported by police" or "according to a reliable source" do not remove from the news medium faced with a libel suit the job of proving that the allegation or rumor itself is true. Liability under the "republication" rule persists.

Even though every fact in a story is truthful, an error of omission can result in libel. Recall now, in Chap. 4, the *Memphis Press-Scimitar's* accurate facts about the shooting of Mrs. Nichols. A woman had gone to the home of Mrs. Nichols, and there, the newspaper said, reporting on the basis of a police arrest report, found her own husband (Newton) with Mrs. Nichols. The implication of an adulterous affair between the two was plain in the story, which reported some facts accurately. Mrs. Nichols

---

[333] *Joyce v. George W. Prescott Pub. Co.*, 348 Mass. 790, 205 N.E.2d 207 (1965).

[334] *Piracci v. Hearst Corp.*, 263 F.Supp. 511 (D.Md.1966), affirmed 371 F.2d 1016 (4th Cir.1967).

[335] *Mitchell v. Peoria Journal-Star, Inc.*, 76 Ill.App.2d 154, 221 N.E.2d 516 (1966).

brought libel suits. The *Press-Scimitar* had omitted much from the story, as shown by a separate police document (the "offense report"): Not only were Mrs. Nichols and Mr. Newton at the home, but also Mr. Nichols and two other people. Had these facts been in the news story, there would have been no suggestion of an affair. The *Press-Scimitar* pleaded truth of its words, but the Tennessee Supreme Court said:[336]

> In our opinion, the defendant's reliance on the truth of the facts stated in the article in question is misplaced. The proper question is whether the meaning reasonably conveyed by the published words is defamatory * * * The publication of the complete facts could not conceivably have led the reader to conclude that Mrs. Nichols and Mr. Newton had an adulterous relationship. The published statement, therefore, so distorted the truth as to make the entire article false and defamatory. It is no defense whatever that individual statements within the article were literally true.

An article about a public official's criminal conviction failed to state that, upon retrial, the official was acquitted, and the defense of truth was denied the magazine. Also, courts have refused to accept the plea of truth where news media would not identify anonymous sources upon whom defamatory stories were based.[337]

SUBSTANTIAL ACCURACY

Mass communicators should keep in mind that "accuracy" and "truth" are not identical in law. Suppose that your source, a member of Congress, stops you on the street and says: "Your hometown banker, J.Q. Milquetoast, has embezzled thousands of dollars from three different banks." If you quote your source exactly, that will be accurate.

To prove truth, however you will have to prove that your source's statement about the banker is accurate too, and that Milquetoast indeed had embezzled thousands of dollars from banks.[338]

32. OPINION AND FAIR COMMENT AS DEFENSES

State statutes and the common law provide the doctrine of fair comment and criticism as a defense against libel suits brought by people and institutions who offer their work to the public for its approval or disapproval, or where matters of public interest are concerned. Despite assertions that the old fair comment defense was superseded by constitutional

[336] *Memphis Pub. Co. v. Nichols*, 569 S.W.2d 412, 420 (Tenn.1978), 4 Med.L.Rptr. 1573, 1579. See also for true facts but false implication, *Dunlap v. Philadelphia Newspapers, Inc.*, 301 Pa.Super. 475, 448 A.2d 6 (1982), 8 Med.L.Rptr. 1974.

[337] *Dowd v. Calabrese*, 577 F.Supp. 238 (D.D.C.1983), 10 Med.L.Rptr. 1208, 1213.

[338] See, e.g., *Rouch v. Enquirer & News*, 440 Mich. 238, 487 N.W.2d 205 (1992), 20 Med.L.Rptr. 2265.

protections for opinion, its principles still are in use by media and courts. Furthermore, the effect of *Milkovich v. Lorain Journal* (1990) on the "opinion defense" stemming from expansive readings of *Gertz v. Robert Welch, Inc.* (1974) must be considered.

FAIR COMMENT UNDER COMMON LAW AND STATE STATUTES

Opinion embraces comment and criticism. The defense of fair comment was shaped to protect the public stake in the scrutinizing of important public matters. Comment and criticism have permeated news and editorial pages and broadcasts, explaining, drawing inferences, reacting, evaluating. The law protects even scathing criticism of the public work of persons and institutions who offer their work for public judgment: public officials and figures; those whose performance affects public taste in such realms as music, art, literature, theater, and sports; and institutions whose activities affect the public interest such as hospitals, schools, processors of food, public utilities, drug manufacturers. Under fair comment legal immunity against a defamation action is given for the honest expression of opinion on public persons and/or matters of public concern.[339]

Even the most public persons have some small sphere of private life. Although one's private character of course can deeply affect one's public acts, there are circumstances in which comment on private acts and personal character is not embraced by the protection of fair comment.[340] The wide sweep of *Sullivan*, it will be remembered, protects only statements about public persons' *public* acts; and courts continue to hold that public persons retain a private sphere.

TRUE AND FALSE STATEMENTS OF "FACT"

States have varied in their fair comment rules. Most have said that the protection for comment does not extend to that which is falsely given out as "fact." This presents at the outset the often-difficult problem of separating facts—which are susceptible of proof—from opinion—which cannot be proved true or false. As you will see, courts efforts to distinguish between statements of fact and of opinion have created one of the slipperiest slopes in all of American law. Beyond the problem of making that often cloudy distinction is the diversity of rules from state to state. The majority of states have insisted on the rule of "no protection

---

339 Prosser, 812–816; Harper and James, *Law of Torts* (Boston, 1956). See also *New York Times Co. v. Sullivan*, 376 U.S. 254, 271, 84 S.Ct. 710, 721 (1964) quoting *Cantwell v. Connecticut*, 310 U.S. 296, 310, 60 S.Ct. 900, 906 (1940).

340 *Post Pub. Co. v. Moloney*, 50 Ohio St. 71, 89, 33 N.E. 921, 926 (1893); Harper and James, 461.

for misstatement of fact." Oregon's Supreme Court, for example, held,[341] "it is one thing to comment upon or criticize * * * the acknowledged or proved act of a public man, and quite another to assert that he has been guilty of particular acts of misconduct." Under this interpretation,[342] "charges of specific criminal misconduct are not protected as 'opinions.' "

A question of "fact" faces the writer under some states' rules of fair comment: the comment must be based on facts—facts stated with the comment, or facts that are known or readily available to the reader. The Fisher Galleries asked art critic Leslie Ahlander of *The Washington Post* to review an exhibition of paintings by artist Irving Amen. Later, Mrs. Ahlander's column carried this comment:[343]

> [The Amen prints and paintings] are so badly hung among many commercial paintings that what quality they might have is completely destroyed. The Fisher Galleries should decide whether they are a fine arts gallery or a commercial outlet for genuine "hand-painted" pictures. The two do not mix.

Fisher sued for libel, and the *Post* defended on the grounds of fair comment and criticism. Fisher argued that in order for opinion to be protected by the fair comment doctrine, the facts upon which it is based must be stated or referred to so that the reader may draw his own conclusions. The court acknowledged that this is the rule in some jurisdictions. But it instead took that view that the facts do not necessarily have to be stated in the article, but may be facts,[344] "known or readily available to the persons to whom the comment or criticism is addressed * * *."

Besides the problem of "fact," the ancient question of what constituted "malice" entered the picture and had much to do with what was "fair." Malice would destroy the protection of fair comment; and malice for centuries before *New York Times Co. v. Sullivan* had been defined in various ways. Furthermore, various characteristics of "unfair" expression were sometimes treated as suggesting malice. Thus from state to state and jurisdiction to jurisdiction, malice could be pretty much what the court felt it ought to be: ill-will, enmity, spite, hatred, intent to harm; "excessive publication,"[345] vehemence,[346] words that were not the honest opinion of the writer,[347] words which there was no "probable cause to believe true,"[348] words showing reckless disregard for the rights of others,

---

[341] *Marr v. Putnam*, 196 Or. 1, 32, 246 P.2d 509, 523 (1952); *Otero v. Ewing*, 162 La. 453, 110 So. 648 (1926).

[342] *Cianci v. New Times Pub. Co.*, 639 F.2d 54, 66 (2d Cir.1980), 6 Med.L.Rptr. 1625, 1635; Restatement (Second) of Torts, #571.

[343] *Fisher v. Washington Post Co.*, 212 A.2d 335, 336 (D.C.App.1965).

[344] Ibid. at 338.

[345] *Fisher v. Washington Post Co.*, 212 A.2d 335, 338 (D.C.App.1965).

[346] *England v. Daily Gazette Co.*, 143 W.Va. 700, 104 S.E.2d 306 (1958).

[347] *Russell v. Geis*, 251 Cal.App.2d 560, 59 Cal.Rptr. 569 (1967).

[348] *Taylor v. Lewis*, 132 Cal.App. 381, 22 P.2d 569 (1933).

words which a reasonable man would not consider fair.[349] Malice still can be "adduced"[350] from such qualities of expression in some jurisdictions where qualified privilege or fair comment is at issue.

Thus the West Virginia Supreme Court held in denying fair comment's protection against the *Charleston Gazette* which had tongue-lashed several legislators who sued it for saying, among other things, that they had sold their votes. The court said that,[351] "* * * if such comment is unfair or unreasonably violent or vehement, immunity from liability is denied."

OPINION UNDER THE CONSTITUTION

Opinion defenses against defamation, although remarkably useful, sometimes promise more than they deliver. True, as in the *Old Dominion* union dispute, the First Amendment was held to protect exaggerated, extravagant give-and-take in labor and political disputes. In such settings, deep feelings give rise to name-calling, to "rhetorical hyperbole" that is not to be construed literally.

Examples of epithets protected in labor or political disputes include:

- "Scabs" and "traitors" as used in a union publication against non-union workers.[352]
- "Blackmail" and "unethical trade" in a land-use dispute.[353]
- "Fellow traveler of the fascists" in a denunciation of a leader of a political fringe group.[354]

Such opinion was protected by courts, defined as immunized by *the context in which it occurred*, in labor or political disputes.[355]

With less than perfect consistency, courts distinguish hyperbole from specific charges of crime and wrongdoing. For example, charging one with a "SS [Nazi] background" and being associated with the Gestapo are not opinion or hyperbole, nor is "outright extortion" spoken of a councilman.[356]

In addition to such protection for rhetorical hyperbole, additional constitutional immunity was deduced by many courts from a dictum—a

---

349 *James v. Haymes*, 160 Va. 253, 168 S.E. 333 (1933).

350 *Goldwater v. Ginzburg*, 414 F.2d 324, 342 (2d Cir.1969).

351 *England v. Daily Gazette Co.*, 143 W.Va. 700, 718, 104 S.E.2d 306, 316 (1958).

352 *Old Dominion Branch No. 496, Nat. Ass'n of Letter Carriers, AFL-CIO v. Austin*, 418 U.S. 264, 94 S.Ct. 2770 (1974).

353 *Greenbelt Cooperative Pub. Ass'n v. Bresler*, 398 U.S. 6, 90 S.Ct. 1537 (1970).

354 *Cianci v. New Times Pub. Co.*, 639 F.2d 54, 62 (2d Cir.1980), 6 Med.L.Rptr. 1625, 1631, quoting *Buckley v. Littell*, 539 F.2d 882 (2d Cir.1976).

355 Sack, 157–58, 160–61.

356 *Good Government Group of Seal Beach, Inc. v. Superior Court*, 22 Cal.3d 672, 150 Cal.Rptr. 258, 586 P.2d 572 (1978).

kind of judicial aside—written by U.S. Supreme Court Justice Lewis Powell in the majority opinion in *Gertz v. Robert Welch, Inc.*[357]

> Under the First Amendment there is no such thing as a false idea. However pernicious an idea may seem; we depend for its correction not on the conscience of judges and juries but on the competition of other ideas. But there is no constitutional value in false statements of fact.

Under this statement apparently giving an absolute protection for opinion, the Second Restatement of Torts (1977) said—prematurely, it has turned out—that common-law fair comment had been obliterated. It declared that only where a statement in the form of opinion implies the allegation of undisclosed defamatory facts as the basis is the statement actionable.[358]

Such a statement is "mixed" opinion, and not protected as "pure" opinion is. ("Mixed" opinion refers to an opinion expressed in such a way to appear to be based on facts, and where the opinion is expressed so as to imply there are undisclosed facts justifying the defamatory statement. "Pure" opinion, on the other hand, is based on provable facts which are explicitly stated as support for the opinion. [Restatement (Second) of Torts (1977), § 566, Comment b.])

After *Gertz*, many courts enthusiastically supported—and added to—the Supreme Court's statement that "there is no thing as a false idea." Under that slogan, constitutional support flourished, protecting expressions of opinion against defamation lawsuits. For example, the Massachusetts Supreme Judicial Court, using approaches from *Gertz*, from the Restatement of Torts, and from elements of rhetorical hyperbole. In doing so, it illustrated the horrendous difficulty in distinguishing between fact and opinion.

In that case, reporter Cole was fired from WBZBTV for "reasons of misconduct and insubordination," an official statement from the general manager said. Newspapers reported the firing and the reasons and added that station spokesman Konowitz elaborated by telephone to them that "unofficially" the firing also was based on "sloppy and irresponsible techniques." Cole sued for libel, seeking damages for those "unofficial words." In upholding the station's position, the court ruled that Konowitz's words could be viewed only as expressions of opinion regarding Cole's reporting abilities. It said:[359]

---

357 *Gertz v. Robert Welch, Inc.*, 418 U.S. 323, 339–340, 94 S.Ct. 2997, 3007 (1974). For a case boldly using Gertz to create an "opinion defense," see *Miskovsky v. Oklahoma Publishing Co.*, 654 P.2d 587 (Okl.1982), cert. denied 459 U.S. 923, 103 S.Ct. 235 (1982), 8 Med.L.Rptr. 2302; see also discussion in Goodale, ch., *Communications Law 1993*, Vol. II, at p.153, including *In re Yagman*, 796 F.2d 1165, 1186 (9th Cir.1986): " 'an opinion is simply not actionable defamation.' "

358 Restatement (Second) Torts (1977), S566, Comment b.

359 *Cole v. Westinghouse Broadcasting Co., Inc.*, 386 Mass. 303, 435 N.E.2d 1021 (1982), 8 Med.L.Rptr. 1828, 1832–1833. See also Marc A. Franklin, "The Plaintiff's Burden in Defamation * * *," 25 *William and Mary L.Rev.* 825, 868 (1983–1984), arguing that "goodness" and "badness"

> Whether a reporter is sloppy and irresponsible with bad techniques is a matter of opinion. The meaning of these statements is imprecise and open to speculation. They cannot be characterized as assertions of fact. They cannot be proved false. "An assertion that cannot be proved false cannot be held libelous." *Hotchner v. Castillo-Puche*, 551 F.2d 910, 913 * * *

It may puzzle journalists that one cannot prove such charges false. After all, the United States Supreme Court and other courts often have canvassed reporters' techniques, finding them acceptable at times despite angry charges by plaintiffs, flawed and faulty at other times, and on the basis of the latter sometimes have granted libel judgments.[360]

But the Massachusetts Court found precedent for its judgment: One writer, for example, had called a judge one of the ten worst judges in New York, said he had made a sufficient pattern of incompetent decisions and should be removed from office. The New York court denied recovery for these "opinions," saying that the defendants had simply expressed "their opinion of his judicial performance," and the judge could not recover[361] "no matter how unreasonable, extreme or erroneous these opinions might be." (The statement that the judge was "probably corrupt," on the other hand, was an accusation of crime that could be proved true or false.) In another case, "liar" merely expressed an opinion and could not be libelous however mistaken the opinion might be.[362] In another, "fascist" and fellow traveler of fascism were matters of opinion and protected ideas—but in this case,[363] the claim that the plaintiff had lied about people in his work as a journalist was ruled to be an assertion of fact.

The unsettled nature of the law as to opinion and comment under the Constitution was strikingly illustrated in *Evans v. Ollman*,[364] a 1984 decision of the Court of Appeals, District of Columbia Circuit. Eleven judges sitting *en banc* delivered seven opinions. The majority found for two defendant newspaper columnists, and the U.S. Supreme Court refused to accept the plaintiff's appeal, in effect upholding the decision.

---

are evaluative statements, "simply not concepts that can be judicially characterized as being either true or false."

[360] *Curtis Pub. Co. v. Butts*, 388 U.S. 130, 87 S.Ct. 1975 (1967), finding the Associated Press reporter's techniques blameless and the *Saturday Evening Post's* constituting "reckless disregard." Where reckless disregard is found, it is commonly for bad reporting techniques.

[361] Citing *Rinaldi v. Holt, Rinehart & Winston, Inc.*, 42 N.Y.2d 369, 376, 380–382, 397 N.Y.S.2d 943, 950–951, 366 N.E.2d 1299, 1306 (1977).

[362] Citing *Edwards v. National Audubon Soc., Inc.*, 556 F.2d 113, 121 (2d Cir.1977).

[363] *Buckley v. Littell*, 539 F.2d 882, 890–891 (2d Cir.1976). Decisions that have found indications of "undisclosed defamatory facts" and denied protection include: *Braig v. Field Communications*, 310 Pa.Super. 569, 456 A.2d 1366 (1983), 9 Med.L.Rptr. 1057, allegation that "Judge Braig is no friend of the Police Brutality Unit"; *Nevada Independent Broadcasting Corp. v. Allen*, 99 Nev. 404, 664 P.2d 337 (1983), 9 Med.L.Rptr. 1769, in a statement questioning whether a political candidate was "honorable"; *Grass v. News Group Publications, Inc.*, 570 F.Supp. 178 (S.D.N.Y.1983), 9 Med.L.Rptr. 2129, saying that Lew made the business a great success, while "Alex minded the store back home" and "was always in the shade when Lew was around."

[364] *Ollman v. Evans*, 750 F.2d 970 (D.C.Cir.1984), 11 Med.L.Rptr. 1433; appeal refused by Supreme Court, L. Greenhouse, "Supreme Court Roundup," *New York Times*, 5/29/85, 8.

Bertell Ollman, a Marxist professor of political science at New York University who was going through the process of being appointed to head the department of government at the University of Maryland, sued syndicated newspaper columnists Evans and Novak. Their column stated that Ollman "is widely viewed in his profession as a political activist," whose "candid writings avow his desire to use the classroom as an instrument for preparing what he calls 'the revolution'." It also reported that an unnamed political scientist said that Ollman "has no status within the profession but is a pure and simple activist."

Writing for himself and three others, Judge Kenneth W. Starr found this to be opinion protected under the First Amendment and the *Gertz* dictum. Judge Robert Bork, joined by three others, considered the statements in the column to be rhetorical hyperbole, and as such a category of words different from either "fact" or "opinion," but protected by the First Amendment. Judge (later Justice) Antonin Scalia, writing as one of five who dissented in part from the judgment, called the statement as to Ollman's status in the profession "a classic and cooly crafted libel," and treated it as an unprotected statement of fact.[365]

Judge Starr noted the difficulty and the "dilemma" that courts often face in distinguishing between fact and opinion. For doing so, he shaped a four-part test which periodically is used in decisions grappling with this perplexing realm of libel law:[366]

> 1. The inquiry must analyze the common usage or meaning of the words. Do they have a precise meaning such as a direct charge of crime, or are they only loosely definable?
>
> 2. Is the statement verifiable—"objectively capable of proof or disproof?"
>
> 3. What is the "linguistic" context in which the statement occurs? Here the article or column needs to be taken "as a whole": "The language of the entire column may signal that a specific statement which, standing alone, would appear to be factual, is in actuality a statement of opinion."
>
> 4. What is the "broader social context into which the statement fits?" Here there are signals to readers or listeners that what is being read or heard is likely to be opinion, not fact. An example would be the labor dispute of *Old Dominion*, with its exaggerated rhetoric common in such circumstances. Another signal would be whether the article appeared on an editorial page—where opinion is expected—or in a front-page news story.

Despite the assertion in the Restatement (Second) of Torts in 1977, *Gertz v. Robert Welch, Inc.*, did not obliterate the old libel defense of fair

[365] Ibid. at 1038.

[366] Ibid. at 979–983.

comment. Years later, some courts were still using common-law fair comment.[367]

For example, the Illinois Appellate Court, Fifth District, in 1982 held that repeated charges of "liar" against a county official in a newspaper editorial, and warning of two more years of his "lying leadership," were not protected opinion. For while a single charge of "liar" about a single event had been held not actionable in Illinois, the cumulative force of several such charges was[368] "an actionable assault on the plaintiff's character in general, not mere criticism of his conduct in a particular instance." The Court found that these were factual assertions, not expressions of opinion and not rhetorical hyperbole as argued by the defendant. Once more, the charge of "liar" had been found to be unprotected. It is unsafe, like accusations of criminal activity even in the form of[369] "In my *opinion*, he is a rapist" * * * a dangerous form of comment taken up in the 1990 U.S. Supreme Court decision discussed below.

MILKOVICH V. LORAIN JOURNAL CO. (1990)

As is evident from the preceding pages, *Gertz v. Welch, Inc.* (1974) generated numerous court decisions referred to under the general label of a "constitutional opinion defense." This defense was warmly welcomed by many commentators, adopted by many appellate courts, and rejected by some others.[370] When this defense was accepted, it meant that statements of opinion—variously defined—were held not to be actionable defamation. That opinion defense has been diluted, in substantial measure, by the U.S. Supreme Court decision in 1990 in a 15-year-old (the case had begun 15 years earlier) libel case, *Milkovich v. Lorain Journal Co.*[371]

Michael Milkovich, Jr., a retired high school wrestling coach whose teams won numerous state championships, taught the news media a practical lesson. It may sound like opinion, but it needs to be checked for objectively provable statements. In 1974, Milkovich was coaching the Maple Heights (Ohio) High School wrestling team against Mentor High School when a fight broke out. Several persons were hurt. Later, Coach

---

367 Sack, 178–82; Note, Fact and Opinion after *Gertz v. Robert Welch, Inc.*, 34 *Rutgers L.Rev.* 81, 126 (Fall 1981); Jerry Chaney, "Opinion Dicta New Law of Libel?" 10 *Med.Law Notes* #2, 5 (Feb., 1983); 10 Med.L.Rptr. #15, 4/10/84, News Notes; Prosser & Keeton, *Law of Torts*, 5th ed. (1984), 831; *Cianci v. New Times*, 639 F.2d 54 (2d Cir.1980), 6 Med.L.Rptr. 1625, 1634. *Goodrich v. Waterbury Republican-American, Inc.*, 188 Conn. 107, 448 A.2d 1317 (1982), 8 Med.L.Rptr. 2329; *Orr v. Argus-Press Co.*, 586 F.2d 1108 (6th Cir.1978); *Tawfik v. Loyd* (N.D.Tex.1979), 5 Med.L.Rptr. 2067.

368 *Costello v. Capital Cities Media, Inc.*, 111 Ill.App.3d 1009, 67 Ill.Dec. 721, 445 N.E.2d 13 (1982), 9 Med.L.Rptr. 1434.

369 *Cianci v. New Times Pub. Co.*, 639 F.2d 54, 63 (2d Cir.1980), 6 Med.L.Rptr. 1625, 1631; *Ollman v. Evans*, 750 F.2d 970 (D.C.Cir.1984), 11 Med.L.Rptr. 1433, 1443.

370 See discussion in David A. Anderson, "Is Libel Law Worth Reforming?", 140 *Pa.L.Rev.* (Dec.1991), pp. 505–510.

371 *Milkovich v. Lorain Journal Co.*, 497 U.S. 1, 110 S.Ct. 2695 (1990), 17 Med.L.Rptr. 2009.

Milkovich was among those testifying in an investigation by the Ohio State High School Athletic Association (OSHAA). His Maple Heights team was put on probation and ruled ineligible for the 1975 state tournament, and Coach Milkovich was censured for his role in the fight. After OSHAA was sued by some Maple Heights parents and wrestlers, an Ohio Court of Common Pleas overturned the probation and ineligibility orders.[372]

The following day, a column by sportswriter J. Theodore Diadiun appeared in the *News-Herald,* a newspaper published by the Lorain Journal Co. The column's headline said: "Maple beat the law with the 'big lie.' " A headline on the jump page read, "* * * Diadiun says Maple told a lie." The column said, in part:[373]

> " '* * * a lesson was learned (or relearned) yesterday by the student body of Maple Heights High School, and by anyone who attended the Maple-Mentor wrestling meet of last Feb. 8.
>
> * * *
>
> " 'It is simply this: If you get in a jam, lie your way out.
>
> * * *
>
> " 'The teachers responsible were mainly Maple wrestling coach, Mike Milkovich, and former superintendent of schools, H. Donald Scott.
>
> * * *
>
> " 'Anyone who attended the meet, whether he be from Maple Heights or Mentor, or impartial observer, knows in his heart that Milkovich and Scott lied at the hearing after each having given his solemn oath to tell the truth.
>
> " 'But they got away with it.
>
> " 'Is this the kind of lesson we want our young people learning from their high school administrators and coaches?
>
> " 'I think not.' "

Milkovich sued for defamation, and 15 years later—in 1990—the U.S. Supreme Court granted certiorari,[374] "to consider the important questions raised by the Ohio courts' recognition of a constitutionally required 'opinion' exception to the application of its defamation laws."

Writing for the Court, Chief Justice William H. Rehnquist summarized cases constitutionally limiting the application of state defamation laws, from *New York Times v. Sullivan* (1964) through *Gertz* and *Philadelphia Newspapers v. Hepps.* (See discussions of these cases at text, Secs. 28 and 34.) In addition, the Chief Justice cited *Harte-Hanks*

---

[372] Ibid. at 4, 2698, 2010.

[373] Ibid. at 6, 2698, 2011.

[374] Ibid. at 10, 2701, 2013.

v. Connaughton (1989):[375] " 'The question whether the evidence in the record in a defamation case is sufficient to support a finding of actual malice is a question of law.' " That meant that the judge would make the determination. The jury exists to resolve fact questions.

The Chief Justice wrote:[376]

> Respondents would have us recognize * * * still another First Amendment-based protection for defamatory statements which are categorized as "opinion" as opposed to "fact." For this proposition they rely on the following dictum from our opinion in *Gertz*:
>
> "Under the First Amendment there is no such thing as a false idea. However pernicious an opinion may seem; we depend for its correction not on the conscience of judges and juries but on the competition of ideas. But there is no constitutional value in false statements of fact."
>
> Judge Friendly appropriately observed that this passage "has become the opening salvo in all arguments for protection from defamation actions on ground of opinion, even though the case did not remotely concern the question." *Cianci v. New Times Publishing Co.*, 639 F.2d 54, 62 (C.A.2 1980). Read in context, though, the fair meaning of the passage was merely a reiteration of Justice Holmes' classic "marketplace of ideas" concept * * * [See Chap. 1, Sec. 1.]
>
> Thus, we do not think this passage from *Gertz* was intended to create a wholesale defamation exemption for anything that might be labeled "opinion." * * * Not only would such an interpretation be contrary to the tenor and context of the passage, but it would also ignore the fact that expressions of "opinion" may often imply an assertion of objective fact.
>
> If a speaker says, "In my opinion John Jones is a liar," he implies a knowledge of facts which led to the conclusion that Jones told an untruth. Even if the speaker states the facts upon which he bases his opinion, if those facts are either incorrect or incomplete, or if his assessment of them is erroneous, the statement may still imply a false assertion of fact. Simply couching such statements in terms of opinion does not dispel these implications; and the statement, "In my opinion Jones is a liar," can cause as much damage to reputation as the statement "Jones is a liar."

Chief Justice Rehnquist wrote:[377] "It is worthy of note that at common law, even the privilege of fair comment did not extend to 'a false

---

[375] Ibid. at 17, 2705, 2016.

[376] Ibid. at 17, 2705–2706, 2017.

[377] Ibid. at 19, 2706, 2017.

statement of fact, whether it was expressly stated or implied from an expression of opinion.' Restatement (Second) of Torts * * * Sec. 566 Comment a."

The Chief Justice expressed a desire to avoid drawing lines between opinion and fact.[378] "* * * [W]e think the 'breathing space' which 'freedoms of expression require' to survive (*Hepps*, 475 U.S. at 772, 106 S.Ct. at 1561, quoting *New York Times*, 376 U.S. at 272, 84 S.Ct. at 721), is adequately secured by existing constitutional doctrine without the creation of an artificial dichotomy between 'opinion' and 'fact.' "[379]

> Thus, unlike the statement, "In my opinion Mayor Jones is a liar," the statement "In my opinion, Mayor Jones shows his abysmal ignorance by accepting the teachings of Marx and Lenin" would not be actionable. *Hepps* ensures that a statement of opinion relating to matters of public concern which does not contain a provably false factual connotation will receive full constitutional protection.

It is to be doubted that the preceding paragraphs are going to settle legal squabbles over what is "fact," "opinion," or, as the Chief Justice stated earlier, an expression of opinion implying an "objective fact."[380]

Chief Justice Rehnquist listed several decisions limiting the severity of libel laws against defendants:[381]

- The *Bresler-Letter Carriers-Falwell* line of cases, protecting name-calling statements that cannot reasonably be interpreted as representing "actual facts" about a person.
- "The *New York Times, Butts*, and *Gertz* culpability requirements further ensure that debate over public issues remains 'uninhibited, robust and wide-open.' *New York Times*, 376 U.S., at 270 [1964]."
- Finally, the enhanced independent appellate review required by *Bose Corp.* provides assurance that determinations about libel will be made so as not to "constitute a forbidden intrusion into the field of free expression. *Bose*, 466 U.S. at 490 * * *"

Chief Justice Rehnquist concluded that the language the newspaper columnist used against Coach Milkovich was "loose, figurative or hyperbolic," and that the column's connotation that the coach had committed perjury was susceptible of being proved true or false.[382]

Dissenting, Justice Brennan—joined by Justice Marshall—seemingly agreed with the majority's rendition of the facts in the

---

[378] Ibid. at 20, 2706, 2017.

[379] Ibid.

[380] 497 U.S. at 19, 110 S.Ct. at 2706 (1990), 17 Med.L.Rptr. at 2018.

[381] Ibid. at 20–22, 2706–2707, 2018.

[382] Ibid.

Milkovich case. Unlike the majority, however, Brennan characterized the columnist's words about the coach as "patently conjecture." Therefore, he disagreed with the finding that columnist Diadiun's statements were actionable because they implied an assertion of fact that the coach had perjured himself. Brennan countered:[383]

Diadiun not only reveals the facts upon which he is relying but makes it clear at which point he runs out of facts and is simply guessing. Read in context, such statements simply cannot reasonably be interpreted as implying such an assertion of fact.

The *Milkovich* decision means that news organizations are well advised to look to their ethics. Reporters and their bosses had best repress the desire to clobber reputations—especially *private* reputations—with opinion statements if the underlying facts are squishy. The noted media attorney Bruce Sanford put it another way: He predicted that[384] " 'our public debate will be more flannel-mouthed and more cautious' " because of self-censorship to avoid possible libel suits. Caution may be indicated. The Lorain Journal Co. reportedly spent more than $500,000 in defending and losing the *Milkovich* libel suit.[385] And, the *Milkovich* decision does have its strange aspects. As Sanford noted, it is ironic that the more far-fetched "* * * or obviously absurd the commentary, the more constitutional protection it will have." Unsurprisingly, Sanford—along with a number of other lawyers who defend media clients—initially looked at this decision and predicted tough times ahead for the news media where defamation is concerned.[386]

ARE STATEMENTS "OPINION" OR PROVABLE FACT?

Milkovich v. Lorain Journal proved perplexing for commentators, some who believed that the opinion defense based on a selective reading of *Gertz v. Welch* was all but defunct. Perhaps not. For, as Robert Sack and Sandra Baron have suggested, "* * *most courts considering opinion since Milkovich have reached the results they likely would have reached before."[387]

Opinions, by their nature, are not objectively provable. Consider *Unelko Corp. v. Rooney*, a useful case making an effort find a fact/opinion distinction involving CBS curmudgeon Andy Rooney. Rooney had a weekly commentary at the end of "Go Minutes." In one commentary, he talked about all the things that people sent to him, perhaps to get him to mention the product. Unelko sent a bottle of its Rain-X a windshield rain-

---

383 Ibid. at 28, 2711, 2019.

384 Bruce Sanford, "Libel Defeat Is Troublesome For Broadcast News," *RadioWeek* July 16, 1990, p. 4.

385 David Margolick, "How a '74 Fracas Led to a High Court Libel Case," *New York Times*, April 20, 1990.

386 Sanford, loc. cit.

387 Robert D. Sack and Sandra S. Baron, *Libel, Slander and Related Problems*, 2nd ed. (New York: Practising Law Institute, 1994), p. 214.

repellent. In the briefest of sentences, almost a throw-away line, Rooney said, "It didn't work." The Ninth Circuit Court of Appeals held this was an objectively supportable comment, a statement of fact not protected under *Milkovich*. The court expressed three tests for trying to draw a line between fact and opinion:[388]

> 1) Is figurative or hyperbolic language used of the kind not to be understood literally?
>
> 2) Was the general tenor of Rooney's broadcast commentary perceived as satirical or humorous?
>
> 3) Could the statement "It didn't work" be proved true or false?

Rooney and CBS actually defended successfully against this suit brought under California defamation law. Even though their case was undermined by the court's reading of *Milkovich v. Lorain Journal*, the defendants won because Unelko did not show that Rooney's statement was false and because of public interest in whether products actually work as represented.

MOLDEA V. NEW YORK TIMES CO. (1994)

Litigation brought by an author[389] against *The New York Times Book Review* may provide additional clues for what the *Milkovich* decision of 1990 (see above) means to protection of statements of opinion from libel suits. Dan Moldea wrote a book titled *Interference: How Organized Crime Influences Professional Football*. He asserted that an unfavorable review by *Times* sportswriter Gerald Eskenazi damaged the book's reception and injured Moldea's reputation and earning ability. The review said of Moldea's book,[390]

> [* * *] there is some really hot stuff in here, albeit warmed over. [Moldea's] examination of the 1980 Super Bowl ticket selling scandal involving Georgia Frontiere, the multimillionaire owner of the Los Angeles Rams, and her husband, Dominic, who went to prison for tax evasion, shows that greed has no bottom line. And [Moldea] raises truly disturbing questions about connections between some owners and friends who may be mob-connected, as well as about newspapers and television shows that regularly pander to people who bet on sports events. But there is too much sloppy journalism to trust the bulk of this book's 512 pages—including its whopping 64 pages of notes.

Moldea's defamation and false light invasion of privacy suit against *The Times* was at first unsuccessful, with a U.S. district court granting the newspaper summary judgment. That court ruled that the reviewer's

---

[388] *Unelko Corp. v. Rooney*, 912 F.2d 1049, 1051 (9th Cir.1990), 17 Med.L.Rptr. 2317, 2320–2321.

[389] *Moldea v. New York Times Co.*, 793 F.Supp. 335 19 Media L. Rep. 1931 (D.D.C. 1992).

[390] Ibid. at 335.

statements could not be legally actionable as defamation because they were merely statements of opinion and thus unverifiable; no reasonable juror, this court said could find them to be true or false.[391]

In a 2–1 decision, however, a panel of the Court of Appeals, D.C. Circuit, at first found in favor of Moldea, holding that some of the characterizations in Moldea's book were potentially actionable because they were verifiable, and could not be held to be true as a matter of law.

But on rehearing, the Court of Appeals held that Gerald Eskenazi's review of Moldea's book was not defamatory. First, the genre of the writing and the context in which it appears must be taken into effect:[392]

> In contrast to the situation in *Milkovich*, the instant case involves a context, a book review, in which the allegedly libelous statements were evaluations quintessentially of a type readers expect to find in that genre. The challenged statements in the *Times* review consist solely of the reviewer's comments on a literary work and therefore must be judged with an eye toward readers' expectations and understandings of book reviews. * * *
>
> There is a long and rich history in our cultural and legal traditions of affording reviewers latitude to comment on literary and other works. The statements at issue in the instant case are assessments of a book, rather than direct assaults on Moldea's character, reputation, or competence as a journalist. * * * [W]hile a critic's latitude is not unlimited, he or she must be given the constitutional "breathing space" appropriate to the genre. *New York Times v. Sullivan*, 376 U.S. 254, 272 (1964).

The *Times*' reasoning in its petition for rehearing had real impact, for the court said in "*Moldea* (II)":[393] "We believe that the *Times* has suggested the appropriate standard for evaluating critical reviews: 'The proper analysis would make commentary actionable only when the interpretations are unsupportable by reference to the written work.' " The court declared that this,[394] "supportable interpretation" standard provides that a critic's interpretation must be rationally supportable by reference to the actual text he or she is evaluating,[395] and thus 396 would not immunize situations analogous to *Milkovich* in which a writer launches a personal attack, rather than interpreting a book.

---

[391] *Moldea v. New York Times Co.*, 793 F.Supp. 335 (D.D.C.1992).

[392] *Moldea v. New York Times Co.*, 22 F.3d 310 (D.C.Cir. 1993).

[393] Ibid. at 315.

[394] Ibid.

[395] The Court of Appeals found similar approaches to the "supportable interpretation" standard in *Bose Corp. v. Consumers Union*, 466 U.S. 485, 104 S.Ct. 1949 (1984), and in *Masson v. New Yorker Magazine, Inc.*, 501 U.S. 496, 518, 111 S.Ct. 2419, 2434, quoting *Bose*, 466 U.S. at 512, 513, concerning statements not so obviously false as to sustain a finding of "actual malice.

The Court of Appeals decision in "*Moldea* (II)" meant that the district court's original grant of summary judgment to the *Times* was upheld, and thus halted Moldea's claims for both defamation and false light privacy.

The Supreme Court's decision in *Milkovich* appears to have encouraged many persons, upset with negative opinions, to try to sue for defamation. But the *Moldea* opinion, which protects opinion based on generally accurate statements of fact, has given guidance to courts leading to grants of summary judgment for media defendants.

And so, despite some early concerns about the effects of *Milkovich*, subsequent decisions show that the opinion defense remains quite vigorous. In *Brewer v. Capital Cities/ABC,* Inc.,[396] for example, a Texas appellate court found protection for opinion expressed in an investigative report on nursing homes.

On Oct. 25, 1991, *20/20* broadcast a story on the quality of care in Texas nursing homes titled "Victims of Greed." The story looked at two facilities owned and operated by Don Leonard Brewer focusing on patient abuse and wretched conditions inside. Tom Jarriel, reported on the homes, Brewer's salary and the profitability of nursing homes. At one point of the story, Jarriel said,[397] "If Medicaid can provide enough money for good patient care, as the experts claim, the most likely emphasis for patient neglect is profiteering on the part of the owners."

Brewer and his partner sued for defamation. The trial court granted summary judgment for the defendants and the plaintiffs appealed. The Texas appellate court concluded that the term profiteering was, in fact, a term of opinion. Judge David Richards, writing for the court, said:[398]

> The report makes it clear that ABC presented the notion of "profiteering" to the viewing audience as its opinion, not a statement of fact. The complained-of-language does not say profiteering is an absolute fact, proven to be the only conceivable reason for patient neglect, where Medicaid funds are provided; it merely asserts that "profiteering is the most likely reason."

[396] *Brewer v. Capital Cities/ABC, Inc.*, 986 S.W.2d 636 (Tex.App.2d Dist.1998), 27 Med.L.Rptr. 1235.

[397] Ibid. at 642.

[398] Ibid. at 643.

CHAPTER 6

THE LAW OF PRIVACY AND THE MEDIA

Sec.

33. DEVELOPMENT OF PRIVACY LAW

Privacy—"the right to be let alone"—is protected by evolving areas of tort law and is recognized as a constitutional right by the Supreme Court of the United States.

Privacy—roughly defined as "the right to be let alone"[1]—is one of the nation's hottest and most multifaceted issues in the Twenty-First Century.

PRIVACY AS A CONSTITUTIONAL RIGHT

Keep in mind that the Constitution guards the public against governmental excesses, not against misdeeds by fellow citizens. The Bill of Rights was agreed to in order to provide protections for the people from excesses of the new federal government. The people of the United State were shielded from unreasonable government searches and seizures by the Fourth Amendment. They didn't have to let the government house soldiers in their homes. Their private thoughts were protected by the right to remain silent when questioned by the government. When those protections are taken together with the Declaration of Independence's demands for "life, liberty, and the pursuit of happiness," it can be seen that concerns were expressed early in this nation's life for something close to a "right to be let alone."

Since 1961 the Supreme Court of the United States has recognized privacy as a constitutional right. This recognition is rather narrow, but to some extent it protects individuals from unwarranted intrusions by government or by police agencies.[2]

---

1 Thomas M. Cooley, *A Treatise on the Law of Torts*, 2nd ed. (Chicago: Callaghan and Co., 1888), p. 29.

2 See *Mapp v. Ohio*, 367 U.S. 643, 81 S.Ct. 1684 (1961) (a search and seizure case), and *Griswold v. Connecticut*, 381 U.S. 479, 85 S.Ct. 1678 (1965) (overturned state law regulating birth control practices of married couples).

When it came to protecting people from other people, it was entirely different. There is no direct Constitutional prohibition on people, businesses and institutions intruding on the privacy of other people.

DISTINGUISHING BETWEEN THE RIGHT OF PRIVACY AND PRIVACY TORTS

Here, a useful distinction may be made between the *right* of privacy and the tort *law* of privacy. As James Willard Hurst of the University of Wisconsin Law School wrote, American legal history is full of concern for a broad *right* to privacy, represented by interests protected in the Constitution's Bill of Rights. (The Constitution, again, protects individuals only against *government* actions.) The narrower tort *law* of privacy as enunciated by judges and by legislatures deals with invasions of personal privacy by individuals or businesses, making possible civil lawsuits for monetary damages.[3]

The tort law of privacy, although older than the right first discovered by the Supreme Court in 1961, was also a latecomer to American law. It has been traced to an 1890 *Harvard Law Review* article written by two young Boston law partners, Samuel D. Warren and Louis D. Brandeis. This article, often named as the best example of the influence of law journals on development of law, was titled (or perhaps mis-titled) "The Right to Privacy." The article, in fact, did not argue for a new constitutional right, but did contend that a privacy tort was an existing principle based on common law and could be constructed by taking pieces of existing law from a variety of areas, including copyright, defamation and trespass to property. This new concept of a personal right to be let alone was part of the evolving nature of the rights of individuals. The right to be protected in person and property was as old at common law (See Chap. 1) itself. And now, Warren and Brandeis wrote:[4]

> [I]t has been found necessary from time to time to define anew the exact nature and extent of such protection. Political, social, and economic changes entail the recognition of new rights, and the common law, in its eternal youth, grows to meet the demands of society.

Early on the law protected people from physical assaults on life and property, Warren and Brandeis wrote. People were protected from battery[5] and trespass. But the law was confined to protection from physical acts that affected life and property. Later, the laws that

[3] James Willard Hurst, *Law and Conditions of Freedom* (Madison: University of Wisconsin Press, 1956), p. 8.

[4] Samuel Warren and Louis D. Brandeis, "The Right to Privacy," 4 *Harvard Law Review* (1890), pp. 193–220. See also *Munden v. Harris*, 153 Mo.App. 652, 659–660, 134 S.W. 1076, 1078 (1911), where a state judge declared that the concept of privacy was not new: "Life, liberty, and the pursuit of happiness are rights of all men."

[5] Battery is a physical act that is harmful or offensive contact without consent. Students should keep in mind that battery is the contact as distinct from assault, an intentional act that creates a fear of an imminent harmful or offensive contact.

regulated interactions among people began to realize that life in communities also had a spiritual component and included feelings and intellect.[6]

> Thus, with the recognition of the legal value of sensations, the protection against actual bodily injury was extended to prohibit mere attempts to do such injury; that is, the putting another in fear of such injury. From the action of battery grew that of assault. Much later there came a qualified protection of the individual against offensive noises and odors, against dust and smoke, and excessive vibration. The law of nuisance was developed. So regard for human emotions soon extended the scope of personal immunity beyond the body of the individual. His reputation, the standing among his fellow-men, was considered, and the law of slander and libel arose.

This was a function of what Warren and Brandeis called,[7] "the beautiful capacity for growth which characterizes the common law." Warren and Brandeis did not see the issue as one to be dealt with by new statutes, but it needed attention.

> Recent inventions and business methods call attention to the next step which must be taken for the protection of the person [* * *] Instantaneous photographs and newspaper enterprise have invaded the sacred precincts of private and domestic life; and numerous mechanical devices threaten to make good the prediction that "what is whispered in the closet shall be proclaimed from the house-tops."

And, Warren and Brandeis were critical of the mass media of the day and its audience.

> The press is overstepping in every direction the obvious bounds of propriety and of decency. Gossip is no longer the resource of the idle and of the vicious but has become a trade which is pursued with industry as well as effrontery. To satisfy a prurient taste the details of sexual relations are spread broadcast in the columns of the daily papers. To occupy the indolent, column upon column is filled with idle gossip, which can only be procured by intrusion upon the domestic circle.

Warren and Brandeis suggested that common rights to intellectual and artistic property provided an example of a system for dealing with privacy. Common law copyrights existed before and side-by-side with copyright statutes. The common law copyright gave the creators of works a right of first publication. No one could publish the work and the work enjoyed a perpetual copyright.[8] When an author published for the first time, his perpetual copyright was ended. "In every such case the

6 *Harvard Law Review*, Vol. 4, No. 5. (Dec. 15, 1890), p. 193–194.

7 Ibid.

8 Ibid. at 199.

individual is entitled to decide whether that which is his shall be given to the public. No other has the right to publish his productions in any form, without his consent."

Warren and Brandeis proposed guidelines for applying this new right of privacy.[9]

> 1. The right to privacy does not prohibit any publication of matter which is of public or general interest. [* * *]
>
> 2. The right to privacy does not prohibit the communication of any matter, though in its nature private, when the publication is made under circumstances which would render it a privileged communication according to the law of slander and libel. Under this rule, the right to privacy is not invaded by any publication made in a court of justice, in legislative bodies, or the committees of those bodies [* * *]
>
> 3. The law would probably not grant any redress for the invasion of privacy by oral publication in the absence of special damage. [* * *]
>
> 4. The right to privacy ceases upon the publication of the facts by the individual, or with his consent. [* * *]
>
> 5. The truth of the matter published does not afford a defence. Obviously, this branch of the law should have no concern with the truth or falsehood of the matters published. It is not for injury to the individual's character that redress, or prevention is sought, but for injury to the right of privacy. [* * *]
>
> 6. The absence of "malice" in the publisher does not afford a defence. [* * *]

A violation of this privacy right could result in an award of damages or, in a limited set of circumstances, an injunction against publication and possibly imposition of criminal penalties.

Legal protections would vary depending on whether the person was "truly private" and those who "renounced the right to live their lives screened from public observation." They offered the following example:[10]

> To publish of a modest and retiring individual that he suffers from an impediment in his speech or that he cannot spell correctly, is an unwarranted, if not an unexampled, infringement of his rights, while to state and comment on the same characteristics found in a would-be congressman could not be regarded as beyond the pale of propriety.

---

[9] Ibid. at 216–218.

[10] Ibid. at 215.

THE "RIGHT" TO PRIVACY GETS A CHANCE IN COURT

In what appears to be the first reported case to invoke the idea of privacy as a right involved a New York family and an association that wanted to create a statue to honor their deceased mother. Phillip Schuyler, representing his sisters and other relatives of Mrs. Mary Hamilton Schuyler, sued to prevent the creation of a statue of her.[11] The Woman's Memorial Fund Association of New York wanted to put up two statues at the Columbian Exposition of 1893. One was to represent "Woman as the Reformer" and the other "Woman as the Philanthropist." The association chose Susan B. Anthony as the "reformer" and Mary Hamilton Schuyler as the "philanthropist." Phillip Schuyler read about the plan in a newspaper story. He and the rest of Mrs. Schuyuler's family got in touch with the association to tell them that the project was not authorized by the family and to stop. The association refused to abandon the project. It denied that Mrs. Schuyler's relatives needed to be consulted and said it would continue raising money for the statue.

The family sought an injunction against the association. Judge Morgan O'Brien ruled in favor of the family. But the grounds? She was dead. It wasn't a reputational issue. The family members were not a part of the statue. It was a matter of a privacy interest.

Judge O'Brien applied the new concept of privacy that Warren and Brandeis wrote about in their law review article, acknowledging that there were no case precedents.[12]

> It is true that there is no reported decision which goes to this extent in maintaining the right of privacy; and in that respect, this is a novel case. But the gradual extension of the law in the direction of affording the most complete redress for injury to individual rights, makes this an easy step from reported decisions much similar in principle. In a recent article of the Harvard Law Review (Dec., 1890, vol. 4, No. 5), entitled "The Right to Privacy," we find an able summary of the extension and development of the law of individual rights, which well deserves and will repay the perusal of every lawyer.

Mrs. Schuyler appeared to be the type of person the privacy right ought to apply to, Judge O'Brien wrote.[13]

> It has not been shown that Mrs. Schuyler ever came within the category of what might be denominated public characters. She was undoubtedly a woman of rare gifts and of a broad and philanthropic nature; but these she exercised as a private

[11] *Schuyler v. Curtis*, 27 Abb.N.Cas 38741, 40 N.Y.St.Rep. 289,15 N.Y.S. 787 (1891) The relationship was not that complicated. Phillip Schuyler's father George Schuyler married Elizabeth Hamilton. She died in 1863. George Schuyler married Mary Morris Hamilton in 1869. She gave birth to Phillip, Louisa Lee and Georgina Schuyler. Mary Moris Hamilton Schuyler died in 1877.

[12] Ibid. at 400.

[13] Ibid. at 400–401.

> citizen, in an unobtrusive way. There is no refutation of the status given her by the complaint, which alleges that, "she was in no sense either a public character or even a person generally known either in the community in which she lived or throughout the United States, but that her life was pre-eminently the life of a private citizen.

The association argued that giving family members the right to veto the project would mean that distant relatives of George Washington or Abraham Lincoln or any other famous person would then be able to prevent everyone from putting up a statue to honor, "any other great or distinguished man or woman." Judge O'Brien said that the famous and prominent had made conscious choices that distinguished them from private persons such as Mrs. Schuyler.[14]

> The moment one voluntarily places himself before the public, either in accepting public office or in becoming a candidate for office, or as an artist or literary man—he surrenders his right to privacy pro tanto, and obviously cannot complain of any fair or reasonable description or portraiture of himself.

The *Harvard Law Review* was quick to note the adoption of Warren and Brandeis' reasoning and the prescience of a line in the article.[15]

> "The right of one who has remained a private individual to prevent his public portraiture presents the simplest case for such extension."
>
> In Judge O'Brien's decision given last month in the case of *Schuyler v. Curtis, Donlevy and Others*, this hinted prophecy has its fulfillment.
>
> [* * *]
>
> That no reported decision has hitherto gone so far in protecting the right to privacy, Judge O'Brien freely recognizes; but he feels the tendency to extend the law in the direction of affording the most complete redress for injury to individual rights makes the new step an easy one.

Warren and Brandeis' article was cited two years later in a case that pitted two actors against the editor of a New York City newspaper, *Der Wachter*. The editor planned a contest in which he would publish a photograph of each man and then invite readers to vote for the man they thought was more popular. Neither man agreed to the contest and they sought an injunction to prevent the publication of their photos.[16]

Judge David McAdam granted the injunction and referred to the *Schuyler* case and Warren and Brandeis' article.[17]

---

[14] Ibid. at 399.

[15] *Harvard Law Review*, Vol. 5, No. 3. (Oct. 15, 1891), p. 148.

[16] *Marks v. Jaffa*, 6 Misc. 290, 26 N.Y.S. 908 (1893).

[17] Ibid. at 292, 909.

> An individual is entitled to protection in person as well as property, and now the right to life has come to mean the privilege to enjoy life without the publicity or annoyance of a lottery contest waged without authority, on the result of which is made to depend, in public estimation at least, the worth of private character or value of ability. See 4 *Harv. Law Rev.* 193; *Scrib. Mag.* July, 1890, pp. 65, 67.

RESISTANCE TO A RIGHT TO PRIVACY

Michigan's Supreme Court was not impressed in 1899 with Warren and Brandeis' law review article. A well-known lawyer and politician, Col. John Atkinson, died. A cigar maker brought out a new cigar named the John Atkinson cigar. It was marketed with a label bearing the likeness of Col. Atkinson. His widow sued to prevent the cigar maker from using her late husband's name and image. She lost at the trial court. A Michigan appellate court upheld the trial court's decision and the case was appealed to the Michigan Supreme Court. There Justice James A. Hooker upheld the lower courts. Justice Hooker began by noting that there are no controls on names.[18]

> As a rule, names are received at the hands of parents,—surnames by inheritance, and Christian names at their will. But this is not an invariable rule, for many names are adopted or assumed by those who bear them. But in neither case is the right to the use of a name exclusive. A disreputable person or criminal may select the name of the most exemplary for his child, or for his horse or dog or monkey. We have never heard this questioned. No reason occurs to us for limiting the right to apply a name, though borne by another person, to animate objects.

Justice Hooker took more time to dispose of the widow's assertion of a privacy right to protect her late husband's name and likeness. He noted the *Harvard Law Review* article and its claim of a new right to privacy based on the right of an individual to be an inviolate personality.[19]

> The right to privacy in a broader sense than before known to the common law is asserted. The article cites a number of cases, some of them relating to pictures, and criticises the courts for basing their decisions upon property or contract rights. These cases relate to letters, diaries, and other private writings, paintings, sculptures, music, etc.
>
> [* * *]
>
> Notwithstanding the unanimity of the courts in resting the decisions adverted to upon property rights, the authors assert that 'it is in reality not the principle of private property, but that

[18] *Atkinson v. John E. Doherty & Co.*, 121 Mich. 372, 373, 80 N.W. 285, 286, 46 L.R.A. 219, 80 Am.St.Rep. 507 (Michigan 1899).

[19] Ibid. at 375, 286.

> of an inviolate personality.' An examination of the article will show that authoritative decisions which support the theory advocated are wanting.

Col. Atkinson's widow could not prevent the cigar maker from marketing and selling the cigar bearing her late husband's name. Justice Hooker held up the *Schuyler* case and pointed to its reversal by the New York Court of Appeals (the highest appellate court in New York) in 1901 to show how untenable the proposed right of privacy is. But Justice Hooker is a bit disingenuous in this reference because the New York Court of Appeals reversed the *Schuyler* case on the grounds that any privacy right Mrs. Schuyler had died with her.[20]

In his opinion for the court in *Schuyler*, New York's Justice Rufus Peckham left the door open to a living person asserting a right of privacy.[21]

> Death deprives us all of rights, in the legal sense of that term; and, when Mrs. Schuyler died, her own individual right of privacy, whatever it may have been, expired at the same time. The right which survived (however extensive or limited) was a right pertaining to the living only.

If she were not dead, Mrs. Schuyler might have been able to assert the privacy right that her family sued to maintain.

> If the defendants had projected such a work in the lifetime of Mrs. Schuyler, it would, perhaps, have been a violation of her individual right of privacy, because it might be contended that she had never occupied such a position towards the public as would have authorized such action by any one so long as it was in opposition to her wishes.

Perhaps the most famous case on privacy rights also came from the New York Court of Appeals. *Roberson v. Rochester Folding Box Co.*[22] It's the one that makes it into the law and history books. The Rochester Folding Box Company obtained an image of Abigail Roberson who was 17 when the case began. It printed about 25,000 copies. "[U]pon the paper upon which the likenesses were printed and above the portrait there were printed, in large, plain letters, the words, 'Flour of the Family,' and below the portrait, in large capital letters, 'Franklin Mills Flour,' and in the lower right-hand corner, in smaller capital letters, 'Rochester Folding Box Co." The advertisements were posted in public places including stores, warehouses and saloons. The likeness was so good that friends and strangers recognized when she was out. Ms. Roberson was jeered at and scoffed; her complaint alleged. She sued asking the courts to order the Rochester Folding Box Company to stop using her image and also to

---

20 *Schuyler v. Curtis*, 147 N.Y. 434, 42 N.E. 22 (1895).

21 Ibid. at 447.

22 *Roberson v. Rochester Folding Box Co.*, 171 N.Y. 538, 64 N.E. 442, 447 (1902).

pay $15,000 for the shock, treatment by a physician and confinement to bed.

The trial court found for her and the appellate division of the New York courts submitted it to the state's highest court, the Court of Appeals. Chief Justice Alton Parker, like Justice Hooker in Michigan, found no precedent for, "The so called 'right of privacy.' " Justice Parker similarly found that the cases cited by Warren and Brandeis in support of the new right provided no support.[23] All of the cases were based on a property right or a breach of trust.

Justice Parker described the privacy right as one that would give persons vast powers.[24]

> The so-called "right of privacy" is, as the phrase suggests, founded upon the claim that a man has the right to pass through this world, if he wills, without having his picture published, his business enterprises discussed, his successful experiments written up for the benefit of others, or his eccentricities commented upon either in handbills, circulars, catalogues, periodicals, or newspapers; and, necessarily, that the things which may not be written and published of him must not be spoken of him by his neighbors, whether the comment be favorable or otherwise.

Justice Parker framed Ms. Roberson's complaint in terms that show his disapproval of her claim.[25] The use of her image, "is to plaintiff very distasteful, and thus, because of defendants' impertinence in using her picture, without her consent, for their own business purposes, she has been caused to suffer mental distress where others would have appreciated the compliment to their beauty implied in the selection of the picture for such purposes."

As Justice Hooker suggested in *Atkinson*, Justice Parker said that a right to privacy would have to come from the legislature as the courts had no power to create the new right.

Justices John Gray, William Bartlett, and Albert Haight dissented. Justice Gray wrote the dissent in which he framed the advertisers in far less flattering light than Justice Parker.[26]

> These defendants stand before the court, admitting that they have made, published, and circulated, without the knowledge or the authority of the plaintiff, 25,000 lithographic portraits of her, for the purpose of profit and gain to themselves; [* * *]that the effect has been to humiliate her, and to render her ill; and yet claiming that she makes out no cause of action. They say that no law on the statute books gives her a right to action, and

[23] Ibid. at 550, 445.

[24] Ibid. at 544, 443.

[25] Ibid. at 543, 443.

[26] Ibid. at 558–559, 448.

> that her right to privacy is not an actionable right at law or in equity.

Justice Parker's argument that equity law provided no recourse because no prior case established such a rule ignored the principles and practices of equity, the law of fairness (see Chap. 1).[27]

> It would be a reproach to equitable jurisprudence if equity were powerless to extend the application of the principles of common law or of natural justice in remedying a wrong, which, in the progress of civilization, has been made possible as the result of new social or commercial conditions.

The 4–3 majority decision was greeted with outrage and newspaper editorials railed against the refusal of the court to protect Ms. Roberson. The following year the New York legislature passed a statute making it both a misdemeanor and a tort to use the name, portrait, or picture of any person for advertising or "trade purposes" without that person's consent. Note that this was narrowly drawn legislation, limited to the kind of fact situation found in the *Roberson* case.[28] The statute has been applied liberally, though and covers most of the recognized privacy torts.

In 1905, the Georgia Supreme Court found a right of privacy in the common law on its own. It didn't wait for a legislative enactment.[29] The statute, however, was construed to allow for suits beyond the use of a person's likeness in trade to include false light claims discussed later in this chapter.

Like Ms. Roberson, Paolo Pavesich discovered a picture of him had been published for purposes of trade. New England Life had placed an advertisement in the *Atlanta Constitution*. The ad showed a photo of Pavesich next to a photo of another man who looked sickly and was ill-dressed.[30]

> Under the plaintiff's picture the following appeared: "In my healthy and productive period of life I bought insurance in the New England Mutual Life Insurance Co., of Boston, Mass., and to-day my family is protected and I am drawing an annual dividend on my paid-up policies." Under the other person's picture was a statement to the effect that he had not taken insurance, and now realized his mistake.

Pavesich never had a policy with New England Life. He sued asking for $25,000 (the equivalent of $747,341 today) in damages. Andrew Jackson Cobb wrote the opinion for the unanimous court which found for Pavesich. Justice Cobb did not find the same bar to expanding common

---

27 Ibid. at 561, 449.

28 New York Session Laws 1903, Ch. 132, §§ 1–2, now known as §§ 50–51, New York Civil Rights Law.

29 *Pavesich v. New England Life Insurance Co.*, 122 Ga. 190, 50 S.E. 68, 79 (1905).

30 Ibid. at 69.

law rights to include privacy.[31] "The novelty of the complaint is no objection, when an injury cognizable by law is shown to have been inflicted on the plaintiff. In such a case, 'although there be no precedent, the common law will judge according to the law of nature and the public good.' " Justice Cobb was not put off by the novelty of expanding common law. Just as the law recognized rights against public rights, the court had the ability to recognize private rights. Despite the resistance and even outright dismissal by jurists like Hooker and Parker, Justice Cobb was confident this new protection for privacy would become the accepted rule of law.[32]

> So thoroughly satisfied are we that the law recognizes, within proper limits, as a legal right, the right of privacy, and that the publication of one's picture without his consent by another as an advertisement, for the mere purpose of increasing the profits and gains of the advertiser, is an invasion of this right, that we venture to predict that the day will come that the American bar will marvel that a contrary view was ever entertained by judges of eminence and ability,

Justice Cob proved to be correct. Since the 1905 *Pavesich* decision, the tort law of privacy has grown mightily. The late William L. Prosser, for many years America's foremost torts scholar, outlined four kinds of torts under the broad label of "invasion of privacy."[33]

1. **Intrusion** on plaintiffs physical solitude (This area will be discussed at length in the following chapter; it is now often referred to where the media are concerned as a "NEWSGATHERING Tort.").

2. **False light.** Dean Prosser wrote of putting plaintiff in a false position in the public eye, as by signing that person's name to a letter or petition, attributing views not held by that person. This is the area of privacy law most resembling defamation.

3. **Appropriation** of some element of plaintiffs personality—his or her name or likeness—for commercial use.

4. **Publication of Private Matters** violating the ordinary decencies.

---

[31] Ibid.

[32] Ibid. at 80–81.

[33] See *Barbieri v. News-Journal Co.*, 56 Del. 67, 69–70, 189 A.2d 773, 774 (1963). The Delaware Supreme Court summarized Dean Prosser's analysis of the kinds of actions to be included by the law of privacy. For organizational purposes in this chapter and the next, the elements of privacy are presented in a different order. Dean Prosser had listed them in this sequence: (1) Intrusion; (2) Publication of Private Matters; (3) False Light, and (4) Appropriation. For an historically important treatment, see Prosser's much-quoted "Privacy," 48 *California Law Review* (1960), pp. 383–423. See also his *Handbook of the Law of Torts*, 4th ed. (St. Paul, Minn.: West Publishing Co., 1971), pp. 802–818.

It is emphasized that these categories are **not** mutually exclusive. More than one of these four kinds of privacy actions may be present in the same lawsuit.

THE SPREAD AND NATURE OF PRIVACY TORTS

The law of privacy—or at least one of its four main sub-tort areas as listed above—now has been recognized by federal courts, in the District of Columbia, and—in one form or another—in all 50 states.[34] Not every state has recognized all four torts. False light has encountered resistance because of various courts' assumption that it is the same thing as libel. Court (common law) recognition arrived first in the majority of states, with statutes recognizing at least some aspects of the law of privacy passed in others. Even in those states which were slow to recognize the law of privacy, privacy interests were apt to be protected under other legal actions such as libel or trespass.

Professor Prosser noted that an action for invasion of privacy is similar to the old concept *libel per se*: a plaintiff does not have to plead or prove actual monetary loss ("special damages") in order to have a cause of action. In addition, a court may award punitive damages. But while actions for defamation and for invasion of privacy have similarities, there also are differences. In a 1990 decision, the Arizona Supreme Court said that the fundamental difference between the two tort areas is that privacy law deals with freedom from emotional distress, while defamation's primary concern is reputation.[35]

That may be a distinction without a difference. It is difficult to imagine one having peace of mind if one's reputation has been unjustly harmed. In real life, the distinction between defamation and invasion of privacy is blurred. Privacy, it would seem, may often be regarded as a close cousin of defamation. Some publications, indeed, may be both defamatory and an invasion of privacy. Shrewd attorneys often sue for both libel and invasion of privacy on the basis of a single publication.

---

[34] Robert D. Sack and Sandra S. Baron, *Libel, Slander and Related Problems*, 2nd ed. (New York: Practising Law Institute, 1994), pp. 557–560; Libel Defense Resource Center, *LDRC 50-State Survey 1996–1997: Media Privacy and Related Law* (New York: LDRC, 1996). *Lake v. Wal-Mart Stores*, 582 N.W.2d 231 (Minn. 1998).

[35] *Godbehere v. Phoenix Newspapers*, 162 Ariz. 335, 783 P.2d 781 (1989); see also *Themo v. New England Newspaper Pub. Co.*, 306 Mass. 54, 27 N.E.2d 753, 755 (1940). Note that when Dean Prosser first categorized privacy torts in 1960, he could not have foreseen the U.S. Supreme Court decision in the libel case of *Gertz v. Robert Welch*, 418 U.S. 323, 94 S.Ct. 2997 (1974), which demolished the old *libel per se* that if words were held defamatory, a plaintiff did not have to prove harm in order to collect damages.

Usually, however, courts do not allow a plaintiff to collect for both actions in one lawsuit.[36] Florida's single publication/single action rule says that a single publication gives rise to one cause of action.[37]

> "The rule is designed to prevent plaintiffs from circumventing a valid defense to defamation by recasting essentially the same facts into several causes of action all meant to compensate for the same harm." *Gannett Co., Inc. v. Anderson*, 947 So.2d 1, 13 (Fla. 1st DCA 2006)

Privacy lawsuits also resemble defamation in that the right to sue, in general, belongs only to the injured person. As a rule, relatives or friends cannot sue because the privacy of someone else close to them is invaded, unless their own privacy also is invaded. In general, as with defamation, the right to sue for invasion of privacy dies with the individual.[38]

Keep two things in mind when considering privacy law:

First, the law of privacy is not uniform. One judge once compared the state of the privacy law to a haystack in a hurricane, so there is great conflict of laws from state to state and jurisdiction to jurisdiction.

Second, when courts or legislatures become involved with privacy, they are attempting to balance interests. On one side of the scale are public interests in an open society, and in freedom of expression and the right to publish. On the other, you have the individual's desire to be protected by zones of privacy. Both sides of the scale contain worthy interests, but clumsy balancing can produce horrid results. Congress passed the Privacy Protection Act in 1994 restricting access to DMV records. It did so, in part, to shield people from stalkers following the murder of actress Rebecca Schaeffer. But the law also prevents reporters from finding school bus drivers who have been convicted of drug offenses or of driving while intoxicated and learning how drivers continue to drive despite more than a dozen DUI convictions. What price "privacy"?

34. "FALSE LIGHT": COMMUNICATIONS INVADING PRIVACY

ELEMENTS OF FALSE LIGHT PRIVACY

The area of privacy known as "putting plaintiff in a false light in the public eye" holds great dangers of lawsuits for communications media. It is privacy law's area of greatest similarity to defamation. Some courts

[36] "Duplication of Damages: Invasion of Privacy and Defamation," 41 *Washington Law Review* (1966), pp. 360–377. See also Donald Elliott Brown, "The Invasion of Defamation by Privacy," 23 *Stanford Law Review* (Feb. 1971), pp. 547–568, and Sack and Baron, op. cit., pp. 562, 570–571.

[37] *Klayman v. Judicial Watch, Inc.*, 22 F.Supp.3d 1240, 1256 (S.D.Fla. 2014).

[38] *Bremmer v. Journal-Tribune Pub. Co.*, 247 Iowa 817, 76 N.W.2d 762 (1956). In at least one state, heirs can sue for false light invasion of privacy. See the Utah intrusion statute, U.C.A. §§ 76–9–401–403, 406.

have concluded that the false light tort is so similar to libel that they have declined to recognize it as a legitimate cause of action. Also, the first invasion of privacy case dealing with the mass media to be decided by the Supreme Court of the United States involved "false light."[39] Required elements of a false light lawsuit include:

(1) Publication and Identification. Like libel, false light requires distribution of an offending communication and identification of the plaintiff.

(2) The falsity must be substantial, and it must be proven by the plaintiff.[40]

(3) The false light—as stated in the Restatement (Second) of Torts—must be "highly offensive to a reasonable person."

(4) The defendant must have "had knowledge of or acted in reckless disregard as to the truth or falsity of the publicized matter and the false light in which the other would be placed."[41]

LORD BYRON AND OTHER "FALSE LIGHT" PLAINTIFFS

False light privacy has roots going back to an outraged English poet, the flamboyant Lord Byron. Back in 1816, His Lordship sued successfully to prevent the publication of a book of inferior poems offered as works written by to Lord Byron.[42] In more recent years, the media—or people who use the media—have misrepresented the views of other people at their peril.

A little more modernly, the case of *Dempsey v. National Enquirer*[43] provides a clear statement of the nature of the false light tort. In that case, the *Enquirer* and the *Star*, a News America Publishing, Inc.,

---

[39] *Time, Inc. v. Hill*, 385 U.S. 374, 87 S.Ct. 534 (1967). Note that the "false light" area overlaps another area discussed elsewhere in this chapter, "appropriation of some element of plaintiff's personality for commercial use." This overlap is apparent in cases involving spurious testimonials in advertisements. See, e.g., *Flake v. Greensboro News Co.*, 212 N.C. 780, 195 S.E. 55 (1938), where a woman's picture was placed, by mistake, in an advertisement, and *Fairfield v. American Photocopy Equipment Co.*, 138 Cal.App.2d 82, 291 P.2d 194 (1955).

[40] Sack and Baron, op. cit., pp. 563–564.

[41] Restatement (Second) of Torts, § 652E.

[42] *Lord Byron v. Johnson*, 2 Mer. 29, 3 Eng.Rep. 851 (Chancery, 1816). The Defendant, a publisher advertised for sale certain poems, which he represented by the advertisement to be the work of Lord Byron on whose behalf a Bill was filed (His Lordship being himself abroad,) for an Injunction to restrain the publication under the title described in the advertisement; and, on affidavits made by his Lordship's agents, both as to their belief and as to circumstances rendering it highly probable that the work was not His Lordship's, an application was made to the Vice-Chancellor accordingly; when His Honor, upon the ground that the affidavits were not sufficiently positive, and might be contradicted, ordered that notice of the motion should be given to Defendant. Notice having been given pursuant to this order, the application was now rendered before the Lord Chancellor, who approved of the course which had been taken by the Vice-Chancellor; and upon the Defendant declining to swear as to his belief that the poem in questions was actually the work of Lord Byron, granted the motion. An Injunction was issued accordingly, to restrain the Defendant from publishing, in the Plaintiff's name, or as his work, the several poems mentioned in the advertisement. Or any parts thereof, til answer or further order.

[43] *Dempsey v. National Enquirer*, 702 F.Supp. 934 (D.Me. 1989).

publication reported the story of a pilot who survived falling out of his plane. He clung to the boarding ladder (his co-pilot landed the plane after the pilot fell out). The *Enquirer/Star* claimed that the article was written by the pilot and included "quotes" and a first-person recollection that the *Star* attributed with a byline solely to the pilot, Henry Dempsey:[44]

> "This is it, pal. You're a goner." We were flying at about 2,500 ft. above the ocean, and I was hanging face-down out of the rear passenger door, just kind of twitching in the slipstream like a bit of old rag.
>
> It was crazy. One minute I'd been checking the door for a rattle. The next thing I knew the door had burst open and I was being sucked out of the plane.
>
> Only an instinctive grab for a rail on the passenger stairway stopped me from being sucked all the way out.
>
> Below me, I could see the Atlantic Ocean.
>
> "You're fish bait, pal," I said to myself. That's all I could think about at first as the plane lurched and bounced in the wind—not a big wind by ordinary standards, but when you're hanging out of an aircraft clipping along at 180 mph, any wind is big."

The *Enquirer* and *Star* moved for dismissal. U.S. District Judge Gene Carter[45] dismissed the claim against the *Enquirer*. The *Enquirer* "quoted" Dempsey but only the *Star* claimed that Dempsey had given the interview with the faked quotes and what it claimed were his recollections of what he felt and thought during the ordeal. Judge Carter held that the *Enquirer* "quotes" did not rise to the level of being "highly offensive to a reasonable person." He allowed the false light claim to go forward against the *Star*. The claim that Dempsey had written his own fake story was a matter for a jury to decide how offensive it would be to a reasonable person. He explained the interests protected by the false light tort embodied in the Restatement (Second) of Torts § 652E.:[46]

> "The interest protected * * * is the interest of the individual in not being made to appear before the public * * * otherwise than as he is * * * It is not, however, necessary to the action * * * that the plaintiff be defamed. It is enough that he is given unreasonable and highly objectionable publicity that attributes to him characteristics, conduct or beliefs that are false, and so is placed before the public in a false position."

Judge Carter invoked the *Lord Byron* case saying the facts in Dempsey were akin to those in that case.[47]

---

[44] Ibid. at 939.

[45] The case was heard in U.S. District Court because it was a diversity action (See, *New York Times v. Sulllivan* in Chap. 5 for an explanation of diversity.)

[46] Ibid. at 936.

[47] Ibid. at 937.

DUNCAN V. WJLA-TV

The case of *Duncan v. WJLA-TV* (1984) warns that mixing words with images, here in a "voice-over," can cause legal trouble. A young woman named Linda K. Duncan was on a street corner in Washington, D.C. Close by, WJLA-TV was shooting a story using a field report by reporter Betsy Ashton. The WJLA cameraman shot video showing K Street. He caught Ms. Duncan facing the camera and then shifted to reporter Ashton who reported a story (ostensibly related to a National Institutes of Health building nearby). The story was about a new treatment for genital herpes. That was the 6 p.m. story.

WJLA ran the story in the 11 p.m. newscast. For that newscast the editors cut the portion of the video that showed Ms. Ashton. The station broadcast the video of K Street as news anchor David Schoumacher started his voice-over. Ms. Duncan was seen turning toward the camera, and then pausing. As she did so, Schoumacher intoned, "For the twenty million Americans who have herpes, it's not a cure." Then, the news video showed Mrs. Duncan turning away and walking off down the street.

A United States district court judge ruled that the 6 p.m. broadcast was neither defamatory nor a false light invasion of privacy. The early broadcast provided sufficient context for viewers not to associate the subject matter of the news story with Ms. Duncan. The court said, however, that the 11 p.m. newscast presented different questions and should be submitted to a jury for consideration.[48] Jurors awarded Ms. Duncan a small damage award from WJLA-TV.

FALSE LIGHT DOES NOT NEED TO BE BAD, JUST FALSE

Unlike defamation, which requires that a person's reputation be damaged, the False Light tort requires only that the published statement be false, substantial and objectionable. Being falsely praised is as actionable as being falsely damned. A fictionalized biography of Warren Spahn[49] raised the issue of false statements about Spahn's military service and other parts of his life. Spahn had moved up to the major leagues and played the 1942 season. He entered the Army and through World War II, returning to the major leagues in 1946 and was a 13-time All-Star player.

In 1958 at the height of Spahn's career and popularity, Julian Messner, Inc., published a biography written by Milton J. Shapiro.[50] Spahn objected to the book and sued claiming false light and appropriation (covered later in this chapter). Spahn said the book was filled with inaccuracies and in the period covering his service in World War II made false claims about his heroism, including the false statement that he was awarded a Bronze Star for valor (a check of

---

48 *Duncan v. WJLA-TV, Inc.*, 106 F.R.D. 4 (D.D.C.1984), 10 Med.L.Rptr. 1395, 1398.

49 Spahn holds the record for most wins by a left-handed pitcher with 363.

50 *The Warren Spahn Story*, Julian Messner, Inc. 1958.

Internet sources will find multiple sites that tell readers that Spahn won the Bronze Star proving the old saying, "A lie can travel halfway around the world before the truth can get its boots on," which, incidentally, has been falsely attributed to Mark Twain.).

The book made Spahn out to be a fearless soldier working on the only bridge crossing the Rhine into Nazi Germany. But it was not true:[51]

> Sergeant Spahn was not in charge of "supervision of the repairs" of the Bridge at Remagen; Spahn did not go "from man to man, urging them on"; Sergeant Spahn did not go "into the town of Remagen to check with his company commander on his orders for the day" and, consequently, the whole description thereof is imaginary; Spahn had not "raced out into the teeth of the enemy barrage"

The book was filled with other made-up episodes of Spahn's life including scenes of his learning to pitch from his father and even what the book presented as Spahn's own inner thoughts.[52]

> "His confidence began to slip. He wasn't sure he could put the ball where he wanted to anymore. He was afraid to try for the corners, afraid to throw the fast balls, afraid he was through" [* * *]"Then the feeling had turned to fear. Then desperation. Finally, he even began to feel a little sorry for himself'

The author testified that his sources were newspaper stories, other articles and some background books. He never interviewed Spahn, his family, friends, fellow players or even Spahn's team, the Milwaukee Braves. Even with the many instances of false assertions about Spahn, the book did not cross the line into defamation. Here is the distinction between the rights protected by false light and libel. Libel protects a person's reputation, how the person is perceived by others. False light preserves a person's right to be left alone and not have lies told about him/herself.

Spahn was awarded $10,000. But a series of appeals meant that it was not until 1969 that the case was over with Spahn finally prevailing.

CAN PHOTOGRAPHS LIE?

The cliché "photos don't lie" shouldn't be trusted. An example from the presidential race in 2004 gives ample proof of that. Computer allows photographs to be manipulated or created and in February 2004, one such "photograph" appeared in the media. "The composite, which carried a false Associated Press credit, purported to show John Kerry and Jane Fonda, known for her stance against the Vietnam War, sharing a speaker's platform at a 1971 antiwar rally."[53] Conservative groups

---

[51] *Spahn v. Messner, Inc.*, 43 Misc.2d 219, 228, 250 N.Y.S.2d 259 (1964).

[52] Ibid. at 231.

[53] Katie Hafner, "The camera never lies but the software can," *New York Times*, March 11, 2004.

circulated the manipulated photo for several days, and it appeared in several publications before it was revealed to be a fake, apparently stitched together by someone opposed to Mr. Kerry's presidential run.

THE DEEPFAKE: SEEING (AND LISTENING) IS BELIEVING

In the days of analog, faked photos were fairly easy to detect. Overlaying negatives or cutting pictures to make a mosaic image were, for the most part, obvious. Then Adobe Photoshop came along and created the ability to digitally alter or combine images. The Photoshopped images were much better than cut-and-paste photos but even then it was possible to detect fakes. Shadows that were out of place or the direction of the sun in two or more places in one image would give the game away. But AI and deep learning has changed things, making it easier to create faked images and video. The implications for the democratic process are disturbing. Simple manipulations already have been seen by millions.[54]

> On May 22, a Donald Trump superfan and occasional sports blogger from the Bronx named Shawn Brooks posted a video clip of Nancy Pelosi on his personal Facebook page. The clip showed Pelosi at her most excitable, stammering during a press conference as she voiced frustration over an abortive infrastructure meeting with the president. Brooks' commentary on the video was succinct: "Is Pelosi drunk?"
>
> Thirteen minutes later, a Facebook official told *The Daily Beast*, Brooks posted a very different Pelosi video to a Facebook page called Politics WatchDog—one of a series of hyperpartisan news operations Brooks runs (with help, he claims). This clip had been altered to slow Pelosi down without lowering the pitch of her voice. The effect was to make it sound as though the Speaker of the House was slurring her words drunkenly while criticizing Donald Trump.

The video was seen 4 million times and it was shared 60,000 times on Facebook. The actor James Woods tweeted, "Drunk as a skunk." It got 55,000 likes and was retweeted17,000 time.[55] "What is wrong with Nancy Pelosi?", wrote Rudy Giuliani, the president's personal lawyer, in a tweet linking to the AllNews 24/7 post. "Her speech pattern is bizarre."

Brooks earned $1,000 in shared ad revenue before Facebook stopped giving him his share a day and a half after it went up. Facebook's fact checkers took that long to determine the video was a fake.

---

[54] Kevin Poulsen, "We Found the Guy Behind the Viral 'Drunk Pelosi' Video," *The Daily Beast.com*, June 2, 2019.

[55] Ibid.

An altered video that didn't rely on AI was offered by White House Press Secretary Sarah Sanders to justify revoking CNN reporter Jim Acosta's press pass.[56]

> The edited video looks authentic: Acosta appeared to swiftly chop down on the arm of an aide as he held onto a microphone while questioning President Trump. But in the original video, Acosta's arm appears to move only as a response to a tussle for the microphone. His statement, "Pardon me, ma'am," is not included in the video Sanders shared.

U.S. District Judge Timothy J. Kelly noted the alteration during the hearing at which he ordered Acosta's White House press pass restored.[57] "[* * *] the record strongly suggests that one of the initial specific reasons for the revocation cited by the government—that Mr. Acosta laid his hands on the White House intern—was likely untrue and was at least partly based on evidence that was of questionable accuracy."

With the splintering of the American audience, it is likely that deep fakes will be seen and, perhaps more importantly, believed by millions. The implications for the democratic process are profound and frightening.[58]

> The Rachel Thomas, the co-founder of Fast.ai, a machine-learning lab in San Francisco, says a disinformation campaign using deepfake videos probably would catch fire because of the reward structure of the modern Web, in which shocking material drives bigger audiences—and can spread further and faster than the truth.

Deepfakes create new liabilities for content producers and providers under the false light privacy tort. As with the Nancy Pelosi video, a deepfake that shows or seems to show a widely known political figure making a speech while drunk, creates a false impression. The creator and publisher of the deepfake would have liability but finding and suing a single person would be like trying to destroy an anthill by hitting each ant with a hammer. The key would be the social media sites that carried the video and allowed it to be copied and retransmitted by their millions of users.

But Internet Service Providers are protected from false light and libel lawsuits from those harmed by deep fakes. That is because of Sec. 230 of the Communications Decency Act. Internet Service Providers are immunized from liability for the content they carry.[59] Remember that

---

[56] Drew Harwell, "White House shares doctored video to support punishment of journalist Jim Acosta," *The Washington Post*, Nov. 8, 2018.

[57] *CNN v. Donald J. Trump*, No.-18-cv-2610 (D.C.) Nov. 16, 2018.

[58] Drew Harwell, "White House shares doctored video to support punishment of journalist Jim Acosta," *The Washington Post*, Nov. 8, 2018.

[59] "[n]o provider or user of an interactive computer service shall be treated as the publisher or speaker of any information provided by another information content provider," 47 U.S.C. § 230(c)(1).

AOL was protected from a libel suit in *Zeran v. America Online*[60] (discussed in Chap. 4). Congress has begun to look at the issue of immunity under Sec. 230 in light of the development of deep fakes.[61]

> At the hearing, members of Congress, including committee chairman Adam Schiff (D-Calif.), argued that deepfakes could be justification for altering laws that exempt technology companies from legal liability for harmful content on their platforms.
>
> "If the social media companies can't exercise the proper standard of care when it comes to a variety of fraudulent or illicit content, then we have to think about whether that immunity still makes sense," Schiff said.

Congressional action is not guaranteed. Both the major tech and social media companies and members of Congress oppose any changes to Sec. 230.

That is not to say that there could be no recourse. The use of the images of famous political figures or any celebrity for that matter could lead to a suit for violating the privacy right of appropriation and right of publicity (These are dealt with later in this chapter.).

CONTEXT FOR PHOTOS

Photos—and especially their captions—must be watched carefully by editors. Pictures or videos which give or are used so that they give a misleading impression about a person's character, are especially dangerous. Two old—and interrelated—cases make the point that if a picture—or photo caption—puts someone in a false light, don't use it. Two invasion of privacy lawsuits filed by Mr. and Mrs. John W. Gill, one successful and one not, are instructive.[62]

Mr. and Mrs. Gill were seated on stools at a confectionery shop they operated at the Farmer's Market in Los Angeles, visible from a public walkway. Famed photographer Henri Cartier-Bresson took a photo of the Gills, with Mr. Gill's arm around his wife. The photograph was used in *Harper's Bazaar* magazine to illustrate a brief article on the theme that love makes the world go "round." The Gills sued over publication of the photo. The publisher objected to the claim and the trial court sustained the objection. The case made it to the California Supreme Court which reversed the trial court allowing the Gills to proceed with their suit. Even so, the opinion by Justice Homer Spence concluded that the photo would not seriously offend the feelings of an ordinary man. There are no more

In a different false light lawsuit against a different magazine, however, Mr. and Mrs. Gill fared better. *Ladies Home Journal* magazine

---

[60] *Zeran v. America Online*, 129 F.3d 327 (4th Cir.1997), 25 Med.L.Rptr. 2526.

[61] Ali Breland, "Deepfakes Could Finally Bring Accountability to Big Tech Companies," *Mother Jones*, June 13, 2019.

[62] *Gill v. Hearst Pub. Co.*, 40 Cal.2d 224, 253 P.2d 441 (1953).

had published the same photo taken at the Farmers Market but had made the photo an invasion of privacy by using a misleading caption. The *Journal* used the Gills' picture to illustrate an article titled "Love." Underneath the picture was this caption: "Publicized as glamorous, desirable, 'love at first sight' is a bad risk." The story termed such love "100% sex attraction" and the "wrong" kind. Justice Jesse Carter's opinion lays out the key to the Gil's claim.[63] "It is not unreasonable to believe such would be seriously humiliating and disturbing to plaintiffs' sensibilities, and it is so alleged, especially when we consider it deals with the intimate and private relationship between the opposite sexes and marriage." The trial court judge had entered a judgment for the magazine ending the Gill's suit. But the California Supreme Court reversed the trial court saying that it was not the judge's role to make the decision about the meaning of the article. That was a matter for a jury, which decides questions of fact.[64] "It is said the allegation that the publication depicts plaintiffs as dissolute persons and holds them up to public scorn and ridicule are conclusions of law. We do not think so. The published article and likeness are attached to the complaint, and as seen from the foregoing discussion, they are susceptible of the construction placed thereon by plaintiffs."

There are no further proceedings reported suggesting strongly that the magazine settled with the Gills.

A 1984 Texas case suggests that the context of a whole magazine in which something is published can cause lawsuits for defamation or for invasion of privacy. Jeannie Braun, trainer of "Ralph the Diving Pig" at Aquarena Springs Resort, San Marcos, Texas, took exception to publication of her photograph published in *Chic*, a Larry Flynt-published magazine specializing in female nudity and photos and cartoons of an overtly sexual nature.

Part of Mrs. Braun's job at Aquarena Springs was to tread water while holding out a baby bottle. Ralph the pig would then jump into the pool and feed from the bottle. The resort made pictures and postcards from a photo of an airborne Ralph jumping toward Mrs. Braun. She had signed a release saying the picture could be used for advertising and publicity so long as it was used in good taste, without embarrassment to her family.

Once the photo appeared in *Chic*—surrounded by pictures and cartoons with sexual content (captions on other items included "Lust Rock Rules" and "Chinese Organ Grinder")—Mrs. Braun sued for a total of $1.1 million for defamation and invasion of privacy. After ruling that Mrs. Braun was a private individual, the Fifth Circuit Court of Appeals held that Mrs. Braun could not receive damages for both defamation and

---

[63] *Gill v. Curtis Pub. Co.*, 38 Cal.2d 273, 280, 239 P.2d 630, 635 (1953).

[64] Ibid. at 281–282, 635–636.

privacy. Assessing damages only for false light privacy invasion, the court awarded Mrs. Braun $65,000.[65]

CHER V. FORUM INTERNATIONAL

Actress and entertainer Cher brought a false light suit against the tabloid, *Star*, and the adult magazine, *Forum*, over their use of an interview that she gave. Cher said she consented to a taped interview with writer-talk show host Fred Robbins with the understanding that it would appear in *US* magazine, an innocuous people-celebrities feature publication. *US* did not publish the interview, but instead returned it to Robbins with a "kill" fee. Robbins then sold the interview to the *Star* and to *Forum*.

Cher's lawsuit did not claim that the interview was defamatory, nor that private facts had been published without her consent, instead claiming that publication in *Star* and *Forum* International put her in a false light, and further alleged breach of contract, unfair competition, and misappropriation of her name and likeness and of her right to publicity.[66]

The trial court found for Cher on her claim that the *Star* falsely represented that she had given that publication an "Exclusive Interview," degrading her as a celebrity given the nature of that publication. A panel of the Ninth Circuit Court of Appeals held, however, that The *Star* had a right to promote the publication of the interview and further that the promotional materials did not amount to an endorsement. Therefore, the judgment against *Star* magazine was reversed.

Forum magazine, had a different result. *Forum* used Cher's name and likeness in promotional subscription "tear-out" ads saying: "There are certain things that Cher won't tell *People* and would never tell *US*. She tells *Forum*."[67]

It is true, the Ninth Circuit Court of Appeals panel ruled that publishers can use promotional ads or literature so long as there is no false claim that a celebrity endorsed a publication. But Judge Goodwin wrote: "[T]he advertising staff [of *Forum*] engaged in the kind of knowing falsity that strips away the protection of the First Amendment." The Court of Appeals then cut the original damage award to Cher from the trial court amount of $600,000 to about $200,000.[68]

FICTIONALIZATION

Out-and-out *fictionalization*, as the term is used by the courts in certain false light cases. It involves more than mere incidental falsity.

---

[65] *Braun v. Flynt*, 726 F.2d 245, 258 (5th Cir.1984), 10 Med.L.Rptr. 1497, 1498, 1499, 1507–1508.

[66] *Cher v. Forum International, Ltd.*, et. al., 692 F.2d 634, 638 (9th Cir.1982).

[67] *Cher v. Forum International, Ltd.*, et al, 692 F.2d 634, 640 (9th Cir.1982).

[68] Ibid.

Fictionalization appears to mean the deliberate or reckless addition of untrue material, perhaps for entertainment purposes or to exaggerate to "make a good story better." Although courts' rules for determining fictionalization are by no means crystal clear, communicators should be warned to look to their ethics and their accuracy. "Hyping" or "sensationalizing" a story by adding untrue material so that a false impression is created about an individual may well be actionable. For a plaintiff to collect damages, the fictionalization must be found to be *highly offensive*.

CANTRELL V. FOREST CITY PUBLISHING CO.

Major fact errors—or large swatches of fictionalizing in something purporting to be a news story—can mean serious difficulty for the media. Mrs. Margaret Mae Cantrell and her son sued the *Cleveland Plain Dealer* newspaper ("Forest City Publishing") for an article published in 1968. The underlying facts: Mrs. Cantrell's husband was killed, along with 43 others, when the Silver Bridge across the Ohio River at Point Pleasant, W.Va., collapsed. *Cleveland Plain Dealer* reporter Joseph Eszterhas (who later became wealthy as a Hollywood screen writer) covered the disaster and wrote a much-praised news feature on Mr. Cantrell's funeral. Five months later, Eszterhas and a photographer returned to Point Pleasant and visited the Cantrell residence. Mrs. Cantrell was not there, so the reporter talked to the Cantrell children and the photographer took 50 pictures. Eszterhas' story appeared as the lead article in the August 4, 1968, edition of the *Plain Dealer*'s Sunday magazine.

The article emphasized the children's old clothes and the poor condition of the Cantrell home. Even though Mrs. Cantrell had not been home, Eszterhas wrote:[69]

> "Margaret Cantrell will talk neither about what happened nor about how they are doing. She wears the same mask of non-expression she wore at the funeral. She is a proud woman. She says that after it happened, the people in town offered to help them out with money and they refused to take it."

Ruling that Mrs. Cantrell should be allowed to collect the $60,000 awarded by a U.S. District Court jury, Justice Stewart, writing the opinion for the Supreme Court said:[70]

> The District Judge was clearly correct in believing that the evidence introduced at trial was sufficient to support a jury finding that * * * [Eszterhas and the publishing company] had published knowing and reckless falsehoods about the Cantrells. * * * In particular, his article plainly implied that Mrs. Cantrell had been present during his visit to her home and that

[69] *Cantrell v. Forest City Pub. Co.*, 419 U.S. 245, 248, 95 S.Ct. 465, 468 (1974), quoting Eszterhas, "Legacy of the Silver Bridge," The *Plain Dealer Sunday Magazine*, Aug. 4, 1968.

[70] Ibid. at 253,470–471.

Eszterhas had observed her "wearing the same mask of non-expression she wore at her husband's funeral."

Editors, news directors and publishers should keep in mind that the newspaper was found liable for Eszterhas' fictionalization under the doctrine of respondeat superior.[71]

DEFENSES TO FALSE LIGHT PRIVACY LAWSUITS

(1) While it may seem a semantic distinction, unlike defamation, truth is not a defense in false light cases. Instead, falsity is a required element of the tort and if the falsity of the statement is not proved, the plaintiff cannot win. Note that false light is the only of the four privacy torts in which falsity is required (Also, of course, if the matter is covered by qualified privilege, the privilege will defeat false light litigation. Qualified privilege is covered in Chap. 5.).

(2) In false light cases where public interest is involved, the plaintiff must meet a standard of fault borrowed from the constitutional defense to libel:[72] *actual malice* (proof of publication with knowledge that it was false or with reckless disregard for the truth.)

(3) *Consent*—as in all privacy tort areas—can serve as a defense if two conditions are present. First, the consent must be provable. Second, the consent must be broad enough to cover the situation complained of; consent to one thing is not consent to another and traditional contract law principles apply.

THE "ACTUAL MALICE" CONSTITUTIONAL REQUIREMENT FROM TIME, INC. V. HILL

When the Supreme Court weighed the law of privacy against the First Amendment freedom to publish, the freedom to publish was given precedence. The key case, *Time v. Hill* (1967) was noteworthy because it was the first time that the Supreme Court decided a privacy case involving the mass media.[73]

In 1952, the James J. Hill family was living quietly in the upscale suburban Philadelphia town of Whitemarsh. The Hills' anonymity was shattered, however, when three escaped prisoners entered their lives, holding the Hills hostage in their own home for 19 hours. The family was not harmed, but the Hills—completely against their wishes—were thrust into the news. The story became even more sensational when two of the

---

[71] Respondeat superior: "let the master answer." Any act of an employee or agent, to become the act of the corporation, must be performed by the employee while acting within the scope of his employment.

[72] *Time, Inc. v. Hill*, 385 U.S. 374, 87 S.Ct. 534 (1967), which imported the "actual malice" standard of libel law into false light privacy. As discussed in Chap. 5, the landmark case on actual malice in defamation is *New York Times v. Sullivan*, 376 U.S. 254, 84 S.Ct. 710 (1964).

[73] This decision also was noteworthy because the Hill family's attorney was Richard M. Nixon, who later became president of the United States.

three convicts who had held them hostage were killed in a shoot-out with police.[74]

In 1953, Random House published Joseph Hayes' novel, "*The Desperate Hours*", a tale of a family taken hostage by escaped convicts. The novel later became a successful play and motion picture.

The publicity that prompted Hills to sue for invasion of privacy was an article published in *Life* magazine in 1955 and titled,[75] "True Crime Inspires Tense Play," describing the Hills' ordeal. The Hills won in trial court, but *Life* appealed to the New York Court of Appeals and eventually wound up before the U.S. Supreme Court. The Hills won their appeal in the New York appellate court. Judge Harold Stephens made note of the fact that when *Life* magazine decided to publish and article on the play, it used the Hill's actual home[76] for a photo shoot with actors from the play. In the article, *Life* wrote about the play and forthcoming movie as giving people the chance to see what happened to the Hills.[77]

> 'Three years ago, Americans all over the country read about the desperate ordeal of the James Hill family, who were held prisoners in their home outside Philadelphia by three escaped convicts. Later they read about it in Joseph Hayes's novel, *The Desperate Hours*, inspired by the family's experience. Now they can see the story re-enacted in Hayes's Broadway play based on the book, and next year will see it in his movie, which has been filmed but is being held up until the play has a chance to pay off.'

Life's photographs showed a depiction of the son being "roughed up" by one of the escaped convicts. This picture was captioned "brutish convict." Also, a picture titled "daring daughter" showed the daughter biting the hand of a convict, trying to make him drop a gun.

It was not what happened to the Hills. The Hills had not been harmed by the escapees, while in the Hayes novel the father and son were beaten and the daughter "subjected to a verbal sexual insult."

The Hills sued[78] and sought damages for invasion of privacy claiming that the article falsely gave the impression that the play mirrored the family's experience, and that the magazine knew this was untrue. The magazine defended itself arguing that article was of legitimate news interest, " 'published in good faith without any malice whatsoever * * *' "

---

[74] *Time, Inc. v. Hill*, 385 U.S. 374, 377, 87 S.Ct. 534, 536 (1967); Pember, *Privacy and the Press*, p. 210.

[75] *Life*, Feb. 28, 1955; 385 U.S. 374, 377, 87 S.Ct. 534, 536–537 (1967).

[76] The Hills had moved to Connecticut because of a job promotion.

[77] *Hill v. Hayes*, 18 A.D.2d 485, 488, 240 N.Y.S.2d 286 (1963).

[78] The Hills sued under §§ 50–51, New York Civil Rights Law, McKinney's Consol. Laws, Ch. 6; see 385 U.S. 374, 378, 87 S.Ct. 534, 537 (1967).

The Hills were awarded damages,[79] but those damages were overturned by the Supreme Court of the United States.[80] Writing for the court, Justice Brennan focused on the fact that the New York law protecting people from unauthorized use of their likeness for advertising did not include language protecting people in the Hills's situation. Court cases had liberally interpreted the statute and allowed suits by people like Warren Spahn, who sued over grossly untrue statements about him in a biography. But, the First Amendment required a test for the fault requirement. Because the statute did not provide one, the Supreme Court would have to create one. First, Brennan asserted that it was[81] "crystal clear * * * that truth is a complete defense in actions under the [New York] statute based upon reports of newsworthy people or events." Thus, "[c]onstitutional questions which might arise if truth were not a defense are * * * of no concern."

Justice Brennan analyzed the issue of fictionalization. He noted that James Hill was a newsworthy person essentially without privacy with regard to his involvement in the hostage experience. He was entitled to sue to the extent that *Life* magazine "fictionalized" and exploited Hill for the magazine's benefit. But, as a person who occupied a public space, he could not use negligence as the standard for judging *Life*. That would chill the press, he wrote.[82]

> In this context, sanctions against either innocent or negligent misstatement would present a grave hazard of discouraging the press from exercising the constitutional guarantees. Those guarantees are not for the benefit of the press so much as for the benefit of all of us. A broadly defined freedom of the press assures the maintenance of our political system and an open society. Fear of large verdicts in damage suits for innocent or merely negligent misstatement, even fear of the expense involved in their defense, must inevitably cause publishers to 'steer * * * wider of the unlawful zone,'

Brennan used his opinion in *New York Times v. Sullivan* to set a rule that would balance the interest of society in having access to information

---

[79] A jury awarded $50,000 compensatory and $25,000 punitive damages. When a new trial was granted on the issue of damages, a jury was waived, and the court awarded $30,000 in compensatory damages with no punitive damages. See *Hill v. Hayes*, 18 A.D.2d 485, 489, 240 N.Y.S.2d 286 (1963).

[80] *Time, Inc. v. Hill*, 385 U.S. 374, 87 S.Ct. 534 (1967).

[81] At the outset of his opinion, Justice Brennan relied heavily on *Spahn v. Julian Messner, Inc.*, 18 N.Y.2d 324, 274 N.Y.S.2d 877, 221 N.E.2d 543 (1966). *Spahn*, which is addressed earlier in this chapter, dealt with a biography of the pitcher which falsely related experiences in his life. The New York courts held that he could recover under the statute created following the *Roberson v. Rochester Folding Box Co.* case which created a statutory right to sue for the consensual use of a person's likeness in trade. That statute subsequently was held to allow for suits like Spahn's which was not based on the selling of an item in commerce but rather on the false manner in which he was portrayed.

[82] *Time, Inc. v. Hill*, 385 U.S. 374, 389, 87 S.Ct. 534, 545 (1967).

against the rights of people like the Hills who had become subjects of public interest:[83]

> Material and substantial falsification is the test. However, it is not clear whether proof of knowledge of falsity or that the article was prepared with reckless disregard for the truth is also required.
>
> * * *
>
> We hold that the Constitutional protections for speech and press precluded the application of the New York statute to redress false reports of matters of public interest in the absence of proof that the defendant published the report with knowledge of its falsity or in reckless disregard of the truth.

Note that Justice Brennan's adaptation of the malice rule from the libel case of *Times v. Sullivan* to privacy applies only to instances involving falsity. Furthermore, the Court was badly split in *Time v. Hill.* A five-justice majority did vote in favor of the magazine, but only two justices—Potter Stewart and Byron White—agreed with Brennan's use of the "*Sullivan* rule."

To Justice Brennan, if innocent, non-malicious error crept into a story, that was part of the risk of freedom, for which a publication should not be liable. Justice Brennan wrote:[84]

> Erroneous statement is no less inevitable in * * * [a situation such as discussion of a new play] than in the case of comment upon public affairs, and in both, if innocent or merely negligent, * * * it must be protected if the freedoms of expression are to have the "breathing space" that they "need * * * to survive."

"Breathing space"—a phrase borrowed from *New York Times v. Sullivan*—indicated that the Court was giving the press a healthy benefit of the doubt. Press freedom, Brennan declared, is essential "to the maintenance of our political system and an open society." Yet this freedom could be dangerously invaded by lawsuits for libel or invasion of privacy. "We have no doubt," Brennan wrote,[85] "that the subject of the *Life* article, the opening of a new play linked to an actual incident, is a matter of public interest. 'The line between informing and entertaining is too elusive for the protection of * * * [freedom of expression].' "

Time, Inc. v. Hill erected an important constitutional shield in false-light privacy cases. If persons caught up in the news are to recover damages for falsity, they must prove "actual malice." Making an important point, Robert Sack and Sandra Baron wrote that,[86] "[u]nder

---

83 *New York Times Co. v. Sullivan*, 376 U.S. 254, 84 S.Ct. 710 (1964), used in *Time, Inc. v. Hill*, 385 U.S. 374, 386–388, 87 S.Ct. 534, 541–542 (1967).

84 Ibid. at 388–389, 542–543.

85 Ibid. at 388, 542, quoting *Winters v. New York*, 333 U.S. 507, 510, 68 S.Ct. 665, 667 (1948).

86 Sack and Baron, op. cit., p. 575.

Time, Inc. v. Hill, whether [a privacy] plaintiff is a public official or public figure is immaterial. The pivotal question is whether the offending publication is about a matter of legitimate public interest." As they pointed out, such a position distinguishes false-light privacy from the law of libel. In the 1974 defamation landmark, *Gertz v. Welch*, the Supreme Court rejected the rule that a private figure libel plaintiff caught up in a newsworthy event must prove actual malice.

CONSENT AS A DEFENSE TO FALSE-LIGHT PRIVACY LAWSUITS

In addition to truth (not so much as a defense as a legal privilege) and the constitutional actual malice defense, consider *consent*. Logically, if persons have consented to have their privacy invaded, they should not be able to sue. As Warren and Brandeis wrote in their 1890 *Harvard Law Review* article,[87] "The right to privacy ceases upon the publication by the individual or with his consent."

The defense of consent, however, poses some difficulties. To make this defense stand up, it must be *pleaded* and *proved* by the defendant. An important rule here is that the consent must be as broad as the invasion. Consider the well-known New York case of *Metzger v. Dell Publishing* (1955).[88] Three young men were standing in front of a print shop where one worked and near the home of another. They were discussing the World Series. A reporter for *Front Page Detective* took their picture and used it, with several others, to illustrate a story called "Gang Boy." The story. The story, which had its beginnings in the case of a young man who had been arrested in connection with the beatings of two men. The story showed,[89]

> [* * *]Brooklyn youths who have little to do in their spare time have a habit of standing around on the streets, looking longingly through tavern windows at the light, warmth, entertainment, and companionship to be seen therein, and of playing cards or throwing dice in hallways, and have organized themselves into lawless gangs [* * *]

The three young men had no connection with gangs, not looked through tavern windows nor been arrested, the judge wrote.[90] "They were simply dragged into the article by the purely fortuitous circumstance that at the particular moment when this reporter (author of the article) appeared in their neighborhood in search of 'local color' * * *"

The three had given oral consent to have their pictures taken. But,[91] "[* * *] there is nothing to support the idea that they consented to a use of their picture in connection with this article or to any publication

---

[87] Warren and Brandeis, op. cit., p. 218.

[88] *Metzger v. Dell Pub. Co.*, 207 Misc. 182, 136 N.Y.S.2d 888 (1955).

[89] Ibid. at 184.

[90] Ibid. at 185.

[91] Ibid. at 185–186.

whatever of the picture so taken. Furthermore, under the statute an oral consent is not enough—a written consent is thereby expressly required." The jury awarded them $9,000 which the judge reduced to $5,100.

CONSENT AS AN ISSUE: RUSSELL V. MARBORO BOOKS

A professional model was held to have a suit for invasion of privacy despite having signed a release. In states having privacy statutes, including California, New York, Oklahoma, Utah, Virginia and Wisconsin, prior consent in writing is required to use a person's name or likeness in advertising or "for purposes of trade." Ms. Russell, a successful and highly paid professional model, had worked at a photo shoot by the famed photographer Richard Avedon. She signed a printed release form:[92]

MODEL RELEASE

> The undersigned hereby irrevocably consents to the unrestricted use by * * * [photographer's name], advertisers, customers, successors and assigns of my name, portrait, or picture, for advertising purposes or purposes of trade, and I waive the right to inspect approve such completed portraits, pictures or advertising matter used in connection therewith * * *.

Ms. Russell maintained that her job as a model involved portraying "an intelligent, well-bred, pulchritudinous, ideal young wife and mother in * * * socially approved situations." The shoot was for Marboro Books, a publisher and operator of bookstores. The photograph that Avedon would create was to be used for a *New York Times* advertisement and for posters promoting Marboro's educational books. The photo showed Ms. Russell and a male model sitting in two adjacent beds reading Marboro books. The caption read, "For People Who Take Their Reading Seriously." The ad ran in the *Times* and the posters were displayed in the bookstores.

Marboro Books, however, sold the photograph to Springs Mills, Inc., a manufacturer of bedsheets with a reputation for publishing[93] "national advertising which was offensive and in bad taste to such an extent that they have been unable to obtain for their bedsheet advertising photographic illustrations created and participated in by persons of the professional stature and talents of the plaintiff and of Avedon."

The photo of Ms. Russell and the male model was retouched so that, instead of "her husband," she was with an elderly male and instead of an educational work, she appeared to be reading a book by Springs entitled "Clothes Make the Man."[94] "This book had for some years been nationally advertised to contain reading matter and illustrations so vulgar in

[92] *Russell v. Marboro Books*, 18 Misc.2d 166, 183 N.Y.S.2d 8 (1959).

[93] Ibid. at 171.

[94] Ibid.

content that publication thereof had been refused by editors." Springs used the altered photograph in magazines with millions of readers and turned it into a contest.[95] "We bought this picture to advertise SPRINGMAID Sheets, but we can't write the caption. Elliott Springs tried, but all he came up with was Lost Weekend, Knight Errant, Lost Between the Covers and You Can't Go Wrong With On a SpringMaid Sheet."

Ms. Russell sued Marboro Books, Springs Mills and magazines that published the ad. She alleged in her suit that the publication of the altered photo created the impression that she was "portraying a willing call girl waiting to be used by a stranger whetting his sexual appetite" by reading the dirty book.

The defendants argued that Ms. Russell's consent and waiver made her case unwinnable. Judge Matthew M. Levy acknowledged that,[96]

> [* * *]the consent would clearly entitle an assignee to use the same picture that was used by the original advertiser. The waiver of the right to inspect or to approve means, at the least, that the plaintiff could not object to publication by the assignee of an unflattering portrait of the plaintiff, *if that were the one taken by Avedon* (emphasis added by author)."
>
> But if the picture were altered sufficiently in situation, emphasis, background or context, I should think that it would no longer be the same portrait, but a different one. And as to that changed picture, I would hold that the original written consent would not apply, and that liability would accrue where the content of the picture has been so changed that it is substantially unlike the original.

If the photo had not been altered but simply used in an advertisement for sheets instead of books, the release would still be effective, Judge Levy wrote.

A BOGUS CONSENT: WOOD V. HUSTLER MAGAZINE

The topic of consent ought to make publishers wary. *Hustler* magazine was hoaxed by a snapshot and an un-neighborly neighbor, losing a $150,000 privacy judgment as a result.[97] Billy and LaJuan Wood, husband and wife, had gone skinny-dipping in a river in a secluded area of a Texas state park. After swimming, they playfully took several photos of each other in the nude. Billy had the film developed by a business using a mechanical developing process, and they treated the snapshots as private, not showing them to others and keeping them out of sight in a drawer in their bedroom.

---

[95] Ibid. at 183.

[96] Ibid.

[97] *Wood v. Hustler Magazine, Inc.*, 736 F.2d 1084, 1085–1086 (5th Cir.1984), 10 Med.L.Rptr. 2113, 2114.

Steve Simpson, a neighbor living on the other side of the Woods' duplex, broke into the Woods' home and stole some of the photos.[98] Simpson and Kelley Rhoades, who was then his wife, submitted a nude photo of LaJuan to *Hustler* magazine for publication in its "Beaver Hunt" section.[99]

Simpson and Rhoades filled out a consent form requesting personal information. They gave some true information about LaJuan Wood (her identity, and her hobby of collecting arrowheads) but also gave some false information such as her age and a lurid sex fantasy attributed to her. Ms. Rhoades forged LaJuan Wood's signature and the photography and consent form were mailed to *Hustler* in California. The faked consent form did not list a telephone number but gave Ms. Rhoades' address as the place where *Hustler* was to send the $50 it was to pay for each photo used in its "Beaver Hunt" section. *Hustler*'s policy was to call the "model" to ensure she was the person in the photo and also to allow her to change her mind. Where no telephone number was listed, *Hustler* would send a mailgram (a telegram sent to a post office which would deliver it).

After *Hustler* selected LaJuan's photo, Kelley Rhoades received and answered a mailgram addressed to LaJuan Wood. She phoned *Hustler* as the magazine requested. A *Hustler* staff member then had about a two-minute conversation with Ms. Rhoades matching her answers with the information on the form. That was the extent of the magazine's checking for consent.[100]

The Woods found out about the photo from friends. Not believing the, the Woods bought a copy of the magazine and found LaJuan's picture. LaJuan was humiliated. She received obscene phone calls and needed counseling. They filed a libel and invasion of privacy suit against *Hustler*. The libel suit was dismissed because the Woods did not file before the end of the one-year statute of limitations on libel suits in Texas. Texas has a two-year statute of limitations on privacy torts. LaJuan Wood won her false light suit[101] and *Hustler* appealed.[102] The magazine argued that it should not be held liable for placing LaJuan Wood in a false light because it did not publish in reckless disregard of the truth, having no serious doubts about the consent form. The trial court found that Hustler published with reckless disregard. However, a panel of the Fifth Circuit Court of Appeals held that since LaJuan Wood was a private figure she needed to prove only negligent behavior by *Hustler* in order to collect

---

[98] It was not clear how Simpson learned of the photos.

[99] The magazine ran a contest in which it sought nude photos of women from its readers. If picked for publication, the women photographed would receive $50 and the "fame" of having appeared in the pages of the magazine.

[100] *Wood v. Hustler Magazine, Inc.*, 736 F.2d 1084, 1092 (5th Cir.1984).

[101] The false light was that LaJuan had consented to submit a nude photo of herself and have *Hustler*, "a coarse and sex-centered magazine" publish a photograph of her in the nude.

[102] Ibid. at 1089.

damages. Upholding the trial court damage award of $150,000, Judge Thomas Morrow Reavley wrote:[103]

> *Hustler* carelessly administered a slipshod procedure that allowed LaJuan to be placed in a false light in the pages of *Hustler* Magazine. The nature of material published in the Beaver Hunt section would obviously warn a reasonably prudent editor or publisher of the potential for defamation or privacy invasion if a consent form were forged.

Judge Reavley noted that *Time v. Hill* had required proof of actual malice for false light. But that case involved a matter of public interest.

SPECIFICITY OF CONSENT: RAIBLE V. NEWSWEEK

Good intentions are not much of a defense without consent. It may be pleaded that defendants believed they had consent, but this can do little more than mitigate punitive damages. Some consequences of a publication's not getting a specific consent for photographs may be seen in the case of *Raible v. Newsweek*.[104] A *Newsweek* photographer visited Eugene Raible's home in 1969, asking to take a picture of Mr. Raible and his children in their yard for use in "a patriotic article." The October 6, 1969, issue of *Newsweek* featured an article which was headlined on the cover, "The Troubled American—A Special Report on the White Majority." *Newsweek* used Mr. Raible's photograph (with his children cropped out); he was shown wearing an open sport shirt and standing next to a large American flag mounted on a pole on his lawn. The article ran for many pages, with such captions as "You'd better watch out, the common man is standing up," and "Many think the blacks live by their own set of rules." Mr. Raible sued for libel and for invasion of privacy.

Although Raible's name was not used in the story, the court said it was understandable that his neighbors in Wilkinsburg, Pa., might consider him to be typical of the "square Americans" discussed in the article. Raible argued that his association with the article meant that he was portrayed as a[105] " 'Troubled American,' a person considered 'angry, uncultured, crude, violence prone, hostile to both rich and poor, and racially prejudiced.' "

Raible's libel claims were dismissed via summary judgment with Judge William W. Knox saying that if Raible was libeled, so was the white majority in the United States. Judge Knox, however, ruled that the privacy lawsuit should go to trial, saying that if Raible had consented to use of his photograph in connection with that particular article, he would have given up his right to sue for invasion of privacy. "However," the judge added, "it would appear * * * that the burden of proof is upon the defendant [*Newsweek*] to show just what plaintiff consented to * * *" and

---

[103] Ibid. at 1092.

[104] *Raible v. Newsweek, Inc.*, 341 F.Supp. 804, 805, 806, 809 (W.D.Pa.1972).

[105] Ibid. at 809.

that such a factual issue would have to be resolved in a trial. Raible said he had not consented to a photo with his children cut out and he did not consent to the photo in connection with the article.

Newsweek's attorneys argued that the case should be dismissed because there was no suggestion that the magazine had published with reckless disregard. But Judge Knox distinguished Raible's case from that of the Hills in *Time v. Hill* which dealt with events that captured the attention of the nation.

> It would seem apparent from the depositions in this case that while the subject of the article, to wit: the public concern of troubled Americans is obviously a matter of public interest, nevertheless there is nothing to show that plaintiff was ever involved either willfully or unintentionally in these matters. Plaintiff contends that a photographer for the defendant merely asked to take the picture of himself and his children in his yard for use in "a patriotic article".

CONSENT AND TIME-LAPSE

Even if a signed release is in one's possession, it would be well to make sure that the release is still valid. In a Louisiana case, *McAndrews v. Roy*,[106] a man had taken a body-building course in a health studio. He agreed to have "before" and "after" photos taken of his physique, showing the plaintiff wearing swim trunks. Ten years later, the health studio again used the pictures in an ad. The court held that privacy had been invaded. In *McAndrews*, the plaintiff had agreed to have the "before-and-after" pictures taken and used some 10 years before the photos actually were used. Cole McAndrews had his photos taken when he started to work out at the health club owned by Alvin Roy. Roy testified that while his business was starting out, he would use the photos of students to get new customers. McAndrew was not paid for the use of the pictures and, in any event, they were not used for a period of 10 years. The court held that the passage of time rendered the expectation that the pictures would be not be used to be a reasonable one.[107] It said that the owner of the health studio should have gotten a renewal of McAndrews' permission.

RESISTANCE TO FALSE-LIGHT PRIVACY LAW: CAIN V. HEARST

False-light privacy has been accepted by courts of most states, although growing resistance to this rather shapeless, defamation-like tort has been growing since 1980. In *Cain v. Hearst*,[108] the Texas Supreme Court renounced its earlier, if guarded, acceptance of the false

[106] *McAndrews v. Roy*, 131 So.2d 256 (La.App.1961).

[107] Ibid. at 259.

[108] *Cain v. Hearst Corp.*, 37 Tex.S.Ct.Jrnl. 1151, 878 S.W.2d 577 (Tex.1994), citing Diane Leenheer Zimmerman, "False Light Invasion of Privacy: The Light that Failed," 64 *N.Y.U. Law Rev.* 364, 452 (1989).

light tort. Clyde Cain, a Texas prison inmate serving a life sentence, had sued the *Houston Chronicle*, claiming the newspaper put him in a false light by calling him a burglar, thief, pimp, and killer. Cain's lawsuit objected to the newspaper's statement that he was part of the "Dixie Mafia," a criminal association and that he had killed as many as eight people.

The *Chronicle*, owned by the Hearst Corporation, moved the case to federal court because the parties were from diverse states. Its lawyers filed a motion to dismiss arguing that Cain's false light suit was more properly a libel suit. Texas' one-year statute of limitations on libel meant the case would be time-barred. The two-year statute of limitations on false light would let him move forward. The federal courts, unsure as to the state of the law in Texas referred the question of the state's recognition of false light to the Texas Supreme Court.[109]

A closely divided court rejected false light. The majority said that false light,[110] "duplicates the tort of defamation while lacking many of its procedural limitations." Justice Raul A. Gonzalez, writing the opinion for the majority, noted that most jurisdictions required that false light claims show proof of the falsity of the published statement complained of. Furthermore, the elements of damages that have been recognized in false light actions are similar to those awarded for defamation.[111] "The principal element of actual damages for false light claims is typically mental anguish [* * *] physical illness and harm to the plaintiff's commercial interests have also been recognized. [* * *] Thus many, if not all, of the injuries redressed by the false light tort are also redressed by defamation."

Justice Gonzalez invoked protections for the media in libel suits that do not exist in false light cases. They include absolute and qualified privilege, though privilege has been recognized in false light suits to protect publishers and a 1991 decision by a Texas intermediate appellate court held that publications being sued for false light[112] "are subject to the same protections as are publications alleged to be defamatory." The Texas Supreme Court would not allow the false light cause of action because of the impact on news organizations and free speech.[113]

> On balance, the marginal benefit to be achieved by permitting recovery against non-defamatory speech not addressed by any existing tort is outweighed by the probable chilling effect on speech and, in some cases, on freedom of the press, that would

---

109 *Cain v. Hearst Corp.*, 878 S.W.2d 577, 22 Media L. Rep. 2161, 878 S.W.2d 577 (Texas 1994).

110 Ibid. at 580–581.

111 Ibid. Citing William L. Prosser, "Privacy", 48 *Cal.L.Rev.* 383, 409 (1960).

112 *Wavell v. Caller-Times Publishing Co.*, 809 S.W.2d 633 (Tex.App.—Corpus Christi 1991, writ denied).

113 *Cain v. Hearst Corp.*, 878 S.W.2d 577, 584, 22 Media L. Rep. 2161, 878 S.W.2d 577 (Texas 1994).

> result from recognition of the false light tort. For the reasons expressed in this opinion, we expressly decline to recognize the tort of false light.

Justice Jack Hightower wrote a dissent for himself and three other justices. He noted that inferior Texas courts had recognized false light suits for a decade. False light and libel claims may share some elements, but the two exist for different purposes.[114]

> Defamation preserves individuals' reputation interests, but false light invasion of privacy, as the other branches of the right of privacy, safeguards individuals' sensitivities about what people know and believe about them. E.g. *Godbehere v. Phoenix Newspapers, Inc.*, 162 Ariz. 335, 783 P.2d 781, 787 (1989).

MINNESOTA ADOPTS PRIVACY TORTS, EXCEPT FOR "FALSE LIGHT"

Minnesota, the last state to adopt privacy torts, finally adopted three out of four in 1998: intrusion upon seclusion, appropriation, and publication of private facts. The vehicle for this adoption was the Minnesota Supreme Court decision in *Lake v. Wal-Mart Stores, Inc.*[115] That court, however, specifically rejected the false light privacy tort.

Lake v. Wal-Mart Stores was not a media case. It started in 1995 when the Dilworth, Minn., Wal-Mart refused to print a nude photo of 19-year-old Elli Lake and Melissa Weber, 20, from a roll of film taken during a vacation in Mexico. They received their developed photographs and negatives, minus a print of the nude shot. Included was a written notice saying that one or more of the negatives had not been returned because of their "nature."

Ms. Lake learned in 1996 that one copy—or possibly more—of the nude photograph was circulating in Dilworth, and that aspersions were being cast on her presumed sexual orientation. She filed suit against Wal-Mart and the unidentified Wal-Mart employee who circulated the photo alleging all four privacy torts. The trial court dismissed her suit because Minnesota did not recognize invasion of privacy as an actionable tort. The intermediate court of appeals, while sympathetic, affirmed the dismissal. The case then went to the Minnesota Supreme Court. The Court found for Ms. Lake and recognized most of the privacy torts, belatedly joining the majority of states. Chief Justice Katherine Blatz wrote for the court:[116]

> Today we join the majority of jurisdictions and recognize the tort of invasion of privacy. The right to privacy is an integral part of our humanity; one has a public persona, exposed and active, and a private persona, guarded and preserved. The heart of our

[114] *Cain v. Hearst Corp.*, 878 S.W.2d 577, 586, 22 Media L. Rep. 2161, 878 S.W.2d 577 (Texas 1994).

[115] *Lake v. Wal-Mart Stores, Inc.*, 582 N.W.2d 231 (1998).

[116] Ibid. at 235.

liberty is choosing which parts of our lives shall become public and which parts we shall hold close.[117]

Chief Justice Blatz wrote that Ms. Lake and Ms. Weber had stated a triable cause of action, reversing the lower courts and allowing her to proceed with most of her lawsuit. But Minnesota would not recognize false light, Chief Justice Blatz wrote.[118] "We are concerned that claims under false light are similar to the claims of defamation, and to the extent that false light is more expansive than defamation, tension between this tort and the First Amendment is increased."

FLORIDA REJECTS FALSE LIGHT

Florida joined Texas and Minnesota in not recognizing false light.[119] Florida paving contractor Joe Anderson Jr. sued the *Pensacola News-Journal* story which he said implied that a hunting accident that killed his wife (after he had sued for divorce) was really murder. His libel suit was dismissed under Florida's two-year statute of limitations. He refiled his suit as a false light claim, taking advantage of Florida's four-year statute of limitations in privacy actions.

Even though the newspaper article had truthfully reported that Anderson had shot and killed his wife in 1998 while deer hunting and that this had been ruled an accident, Anderson sued claimed the implication was that he had murdered his wife. A jury agreed with Anderson, awarding him $18.28 million in damages. In 2006, the Florida Court of Appeal, 1st Dist., overturned the damage award,[120] reasoning that if libel and false light privacy were similar, both should have two-year statutes of limitations. In October 23, 2008, the Florida Supreme Court upheld the Court of Appeal and declared that Florida does not recognize false light. Any benefit from the false light remedy, Justice Barbara Pariente wrote,[121] "is outweighed by the danger in unreasonably impeding constitutionally protected free speech."

35. APPROPRIATION OF PLAINTIFF'S NAME OR LIKENESS

The appropriation or "taking" of some element of a person's personality for commercial or other economic advantage is at the heart of the beginning of the recognition of the privacy torts.

It is understandable. A person has one face. If someone uses that face without permission to advertise a prophylactic, the owner of that face is permanently changed, and not necessarily for the better. The

[117] Ibid, citing *Cain v. Hearst Corp.*, 37 Tex. S.Ct. Jrnl. 1151, 878 S.W.2d 577 (Tex.1994).

[118] Ibid.

[119] *Gannett Co. v. Anderson*, 947 So.2d 1 (Fla.App. 1 Dist. 2006).

[120] Ibid.

[121] *Anderson v. Gannett Co., Inc.*, 994 So.2d 1048, 1050, 33 Fla. L. Weekly S856, 36 Media L. Rep. 2553 (Florida) 2008.

owner of the face will be associated with that product and the association might not be welcome. If the person whose face was used is a member of a community that does not hold with either premarital sex or birth control, it is likely to result in criticism or ostracism. The person whose face was used may get a "reputation" (an archaic term for promiscuity) and have to deal with unwelcome advances. Most importantly, the person has been robbed of the right to be left alone.

The first widely known privacy cases—*Roberson v. Rochester Folding Box Co.*[122] and *Pavesich v. New England Life Insurance Co.*,[123] both discussed earlier in this chapter, turned on using a person's picture or name *without permission* for advertising purposes. In Ms. Roberson's case, she complained that her picture had,[124] "been recognized by friends of the plaintiff and other people, with the result that plaintiff has been greatly humiliated by the scoffs and jeers of persons who have recognized her face and picture on this advertisement, and her good name has been attacked, causing her great distress and suffering, both in body and mind * * *" The Georgia Supreme Court recounting of the facts in the *Pavesich* case said that, "The publication is malicious, and tends to bring plaintiff into ridicule before the world, and especially with his friends and acquaintances, who know that he has no policy in the defendant company."

Justice Cobb, writing the opinion for the Court in recognizing this new right of privacy, said that privacy and liberty were intertwined.[125]

> [T]he body of a person cannot be put on exhibition at any time or at any place without his consent. The right of one to exhibit himself to the public at all proper times, in all proper places, and in a proper manner is embraced within the right of personal liberty. The right to withdraw from the public gaze at such times as a person may see fit, when his presence in public is not demanded by any rule of law, is also embraced within the right of personal liberty. Publicity in one instance, and privacy in the other, are each guarantied. If personal liberty embraces the right of publicity, it no less embraces the correlative right of privacy * * *

ELEMENTS OF THE APPROPRIATION TORT

As with false light and publication of private facts, appropriation begins with publication, that someone else saw or heard or read it. The second element is that the publication constitutes a commercial use, that the publication was used to sell something. The third requirement is identification, that the publication was of and concerning the plaintiff.

---

122 *Roberson v. Rochester Folding Box Co.*, 171 N.Y. 538, 64 N.E. 442, 447 (1902).

123 *Pavesich v. New England Life Insurance Co.*, 122 Ga. 190, 50 S.E. 68, 79 (1905).

124 *Roberson v. Rochester Folding Box Co.*, 171 N.Y. 538, 542–543, 64 N.E. 442, 447 (1902).

125 *Pavesich v. New England Life Insurance Co.*, 122 Ga. 190, 50, 70, S.E. 68, 79 (1905).

IDENTIFICATION

Generally speaking, the use of a private person's (someone not famous) name, by itself, is not enough to bring about a successful appropriation lawsuit. A company could publish an advertisement for its breakfast cereal, saying that the cereal "gives Fred Brown his high hurdling energy" without much fear of a successful appropriation suit. There are, of course, many Fred Browns in the nation. However, should the cereal company—without explicit permission, identify a *particular* individual—that's trouble. For example, if a real-life person—we'll make up the name of "Olympic High Hurdle Champion Fred Brown"—has his name used without permission in the cereal ad, he would have an action for invasion of privacy. So, a name can be used as long as a person's *identity* is not somehow appropriated.

Brooklyn resident Joseph Angelo Maggio sued over the use of the name Angelo Maggio in James Jones' best-selling novel, "*From Here to Eternity*". A New York court held that though the names were almost the same, Maggio's identity had not been taken. The fictional Angelo Maggio was not the same as the real-life Joseph Angelo Maggio.[126]

However, there are circumstances where using a name can lead to a successful appropriation suit. If the facts show that the publication 1) uses a name and 2) only one person has the name and 3) the public understands that the name is referring to the person, then an appropriation suit is possible. Take, for example, the old case of *Kerby v. Hal Roach Studios.*[127] The case began when the studio promoted "Topper",[128] the first Hal Roach screwball comedy. Before television and social media, studios had to figure out a way to generate buzz, to get people to talk about a movie. The studio hit on a publicity gimmick to boost interest. It sent out 1,000 perfumed letters to men in the Los Angeles area. The letters read:[129]

> Dearest:
>
> "Don't breathe it to a soul, but I'm back in Los Angeles and more curious than ever to see you. Remember how I cut up about a year ago? Well, I'm raring to go again, and believe me I'm in the mood for fun.
>
> "Let's renew our acquaintanceship and I promise you an evening you won't forget. Meet me in front of Warners Downtown

---

[126] *People on Complaint of Maggio v. Charles Scribner's Sons,* 205 Misc. 818, 130 N.Y.S.2d 514 (1954).

[127] *Kerby v. Hal Roach Studios,* 53 Cal.App.2d 207, 127 P.2d 577 (1942).

[128] "Topper" was a 1930s screwball comedy in which characters George and Marion Kerby die in an automobile accident. At first, they don't realize that they have died. They come to know the truth, but they have not gone to heaven. George and Marion conclude that they are short on good deeds. The two ghosts decide to help their old boss, Cosmo Topper, learn to live a little. The movie was a success and was followed by two more *Topper* comedies. https://www.rottentomatoes.com/m/topper

[129] *Kerby v. Hal Roach Studios,* 53 Cal.App.2d 207, 208–209, 127 P.2d 577, 579 (1942).

Theatre at 7th and Hill on Thursday. Just look for a girl with a gleam in her eye, a smile on her lips and mischief on her mind!

"Fondly,

"Your ectoplasmic playmate,

"Marion Kerby."

Marion Kerby was the name of one of the characters—a female ghost—portrayed in that series of movies. Unfortunately for Hal Roach Studios, there was a real-life Marion Kerby. She was the only Marion Kerby in the telephone directory. After being annoyed by numerous phone calls and one in-person visit, she sued for invasion of privacy. As in *Roberson* and *Pavesich*, the impact of the campaign to increase ticket sales, had an effect on Ms. Kerby. She,[130] "became terribly excited, nervous, unhappy; she had a feeling of disgrace and anguish; she was heartsick and didn't care what happened, whether she had the rest of a career or not; in the case of a lady caller plaintiff was afraid of being shot." Ms. Kerby won her suit.

DEFINING COMMERCIAL USES FOR APPROPRIATION CASES

The survivors of the swordfish fishing captain depicted in the Warner Brothers movie "The Perfect Storm" lost their appropriation case in Florida when that state's supreme court held that using an element of a person's personality in a movie was not a commercial purpose as long as the movie did not directly promote a product or service.

Jodi Tyne, the widow of fishing captain Billy Tyne, and the couple's two daughters sued Warner Brothers alleging that the movie company's use of Billy Tyne in the movie, "The Perfect Storm" constituted an appropriation of his name and likeness. The Tynes sued in federal court because the parties were diverse. A U.S. District Court granted summary judgment holding that the Florida appropriation statute did not apply to using a person's name or likeness in a movie and that the advertising for the movie itself did not constitute a commercial use of the men's names. The case eventually made it to the Florida Supreme Court to rule on how the Florida appropriation statute would apply to the facts.[131]

The Florida Supreme Court looked to the state statute and to a prior Florida case in which a family sued over a book that told the story of an airline crew that died in a crash in 1972 and appeared as apparitions on subsequent flights. Author John Fuller saw news reports of the appearances of Captain Robert Loft and some of the crew members who all died in the crash. He wrote a book, "*The Ghost of Flight 401*", which was made into a movie. Captain Loft's family sued for appropriation. The trial court dismissed their claims saying neither the book nor movie gave rise to an appropriation claim under Florida law. A Florida intermediate

[130] Ibid. at 209, 579.

[131] *Tyne v. Time Warner Entertainment*, 901 So.2d 802 (Fla.2005).

appellate court upheld the decision.[132] Appellate court held that appropriation required more than just making money to put a publication under the appropriation statute.[133]

> While we agree that at least one of the purposes of the author and publisher in releasing the publication in question was to make money through sales of copies of the book and that such a publication is commercial in that sense, this in no way distinguishes this book from almost all other books, magazines or newspapers and simply does not amount to the kind of commercial exploitation prohibited by the statute.

In *Lane v. MHRA,*[134] another Florida intermediate appellate case, the terms "trade," "commercial," or "advertising purpose" were defined to mean using a person's name or likeness to directly promote a product or service. Citing *Loft, Lane* and several other appropriation cases from Florida's appellate courts, Justice Charles Wells held that the Florida appropriations statute did not apply to *The Perfect Storm*.[135]

> Not only do these decisions demonstrate that the common usage of the term "commercial" in the commercial misappropriation and right of publicity context is indeed limited to the promotion of a product or service as the courts construing section 540.08 have concluded, but they also indicate that such works should be protected by the First Amendment

Some students question the reasoning. After all, "The Perfect Storm" made $328.7 million. But the fact that it made money did not mean that Captain Billy Tyne was used for commercial purposes. He simply "appeared" in the movie. Now, if Time Warner had George Clooney, playing Billy Tyne, look into the camera halfway through the movie and urge audience members to sign up for basic cable with Time Warner, it would have been a commercial use.

GOING FROM NON-COMMERCIAL TO COMMERCIAL USE

We can see where the line between commercial and noncommercial use in *Bosley v. Wildwett.com*.[136] Catherine Bosley, whose legal name is Catherine Balsley, worked as a reporter and new anchor for the CBS affiliate in Youngstown, Ohio, for more than 10 years. On a vacation to Florida, she participated in a wet T-shirt contest. Her participation, which included removing some of her clothes, was videotaped by a Florida company called Dream Girls, Inc., in the nightclub where the contest was held. The video of Bosley was shown on websites, ads and videos of the "naked anchor woman." DreamGirlsVideos.com, released a

---

[132] *Loft v. Fuller,* 1408 So.2d 619 (Fla. 4th DCA 1981).

[133] Ibid. at 622–623.

[134] *Lane v. MRA Holdings, LLC,* 242 F.Supp.2d 1205 (M.D.Fla.2002).

[135] *Tyne v. Time Warner Entertainment,* 901 So.2d 802, 810 (Fla.2005).

[136] *Bosley v. Wildwett.com,* 310 F.Supp.2d 914 (N.D.Ohio 2004).

video of the wet t-shirt contest, called "Dream Girls' Spring Break 2003, volume one." WildWetT.com, another Dream Girls company, released a second version of the video. The video was promoted as featuring Bosley, the "naked anchor woman."

After that, a different company operating as SexBrat.com, obtained a license to use the video. SexBrat is a subscription adult website. For a $37 monthly fee, members got access to the "members only" portion of the website where they could see the Bosley video and others. Bosley was asked to resign from the station. Bosley sued alleging appropriation and other torts. As part of her suit, she sought a temporary restraining order against the media defendants displaying or selling her video. In particular, she objected to the use of her image and name in the packaging and promotion of the defendants' videos and services. In granting her the restraining order, U.S. District Judge James Gwin agreed.

> The prominent display of Plaintiff Bosley's name, image, and likeness on the cover of the WildeT video—as well as promotional images of Plaintiff Bosley posted on WildWetT.com—clearly constitute an advertisement for the video. Meanwhile, the use of images of Catherine Bosley in the "Spring Break 2003" video and in the "members only" portion of SexBrat.com constitute direct promotion of Defendants' products or services.

ARRINGTON V. NEW YORK TIMES

A well-dressed young African-American man's photograph was used on the cover of *The New York Times* Sunday magazine. His face was recognizable, although his name was not used. The newspaper had taken his picture walking in a public area along Wall Street to illustrate an article titled "The Black Middle Class: Making It." The newspaper argued that it had used his picture to illustrate upward mobility of blacks. The use of Clarence Arrington's photograph in those circumstances was held not to violate New York Civil Rights Act, §§ 50–51, dealing with appropriation of a person's name or likeness for commercial purposes, meaning advertising. New York's highest court—the Court of Appeals—emphasized in its *Arrington* decision that the state's statute will be narrowly construed, limiting it to advertising and *not* interfering with publication of news stories.[137]

[137] *Arrington v. New York Times Co.*, 55 N.Y.2d 433, 440, 449 N.Y.S.2d 941, 944, 434 N.E.2d 1319, 1322 (1982), 8 Med.L.Rptr. 1351. See also *Estate of Hemingway v. Random House, Inc.*, where Mary Hemingway—widow of the Nobel laureate novelist Ernest Hemingway—sued to prevent publication of a biographical study by A.E. Hotchner. Mrs. Hemingway complained about references to her in Hotchner's book as an invasion of privacy, but the court held that with a biography of such a renowned figure, the public's interest in information outweighed privacy interests.

36. APPROPRIATION'S WEALTHIER, MORE FAMOUS COUSIN: "THE RIGHT OF PUBLICITY"

Courts have found property rights in athletes and performers' likenesses or personalities on the grounds that they have a right to control how their fame is used.

Athletes led the way in trying to control the use of their images in commercial settings. A 1953 baseball trading card lawsuit provided one of the first cases where popular figures' rights to profit from their fame and to prevent others from using that fame was employed.[138] Baseball cards were a popular premium included in packages of gum in post-World War II America.[139] Topps, the leading gum maker in the United States signed baseball players to agreements for the use of their pictures. Haelan Laboratories had also signed agreements with many of the same athletes and sued Topps. Haelan framed the case as one of tortious interference (discussed in Chap. 7) in which Topps tried to get the baseball players to break their contracts with Haelan. Topps, on the other hand, said that the contract between Haelan and the players was nothing more than a release of liability for use the players' pictures for trade. The New York statute, passed in the public outcry over the *Roberson* case, created a privacy right against the use of a person's likeness in trade.[140] A signed release, normally in consideration of some payment,[141] was required to avoid a lawsuit under the statute. As such, Haelan's agreement was just a way to avoid being sued and did not create any real property interest that deserved protection, Topps' lawyers argued,[142] "because a man has no legal interest in the publication of his picture other than his right of privacy, i.e., a personal and non-assignable right not to have his feelings hurt by such a publication."

When the case reached the 2nd Circuit Court of Appeals, Judge Jerome D. Frank declared that the New York law was more than that. It created a right to give permission to use a likeness and to be compensated for the value of the association between himself and the product or service.[143]

---

[138] *Haelan Laboratories, Inc. v. Topps Chewing Gum, Inc.*, 202 F.2d 866 (2d Cir. 1953).

[139] Trading cards have been used as premiums for candy, ice cream, crackers, gasoline and tobacco. It isn't just baseball players. Over the history of trading cards, athletes of all kinds, celebrities, historical figures and more have been depicted.

[140] New York Session Laws 1903, Ch. 132, §§ 1–2, now known as §§ 50–51, New York Civil Rights Law. "Any person whose name, portrait or picture is used within this state for advertising purposes or purposes of trade without the written consent first obtained . . . may maintain an equitable action . . . against the person . . . so using . . . to prevent and restrain the use thereof; and may also sue and recover damages for any injuries sustained by reasons of such use . . . ."

[141] The ball players received a small payment of $100 or less, provided they made the roster and stayed on it.

[142] *Haelan Laboratories, Inc. v. Topps Chewing Gum, Inc.*, 202 F.2d 866, 868 (2d Cir.1953).

[143] Ibid.

> This right might be called a 'right of publicity.' For it is common knowledge that many prominent persons (especially actors and ball-players), far from having their feelings bruised through public exposure of their likenesses, would feel sorely deprived if they no longer received money for authorizing advertisements, popularizing their countenances, displayed in newspapers, magazines, busses, trains and subways. This right of publicity would usually yield them no money unless it could be made the subject of an exclusive grant which barred any other advertiser from using their pictures.

The recognition of the right of publicity made it possible for athletes and other celebrities to prevent, punish or monetize the use of their identities by those who seek to gain commercial advantage or corporate goodwill by association.[144] Basketball great Kareem Abdul-Jabbar (who changed his name from Lew Alcindor in 1970) had an actionable lawsuit against General Motors Corporation.[145] In an advertisement for Oldsmobile, a GM ad broadcast during the 1993 NCAA basketball tournament asked who had the record for being named Most Valuable Player most often in that tournament. The answer given in the advertisement: Lew Alcindor, with the voice-over asserting that Oldsmobile also was a definite first-round pick.

The right of publicity moved well into the digital age with suits by a former collegiate players against Electronic Arts, the company that makes the NCAA Football series. Samuel Keller, former Nebraska and Arizona State quarterback, basketball player Edward C. O'Bannon, Jr.; Byron Bishop; Michael Anderson; Danny Wimprine; Ishmael Thrower; Craig Newsome; Damien Rhodes; Samuel Jacobson filed a class action suit over EA's use of their likenesses.[146] The game used avatars that represent actual collegiate players. It copied the teams of each school with avatars matching team members. Keller began the suit and Circuit Judge Jay S. Bybee, writing the opinion for the Ninth Circuit Court of Appeals, noted his depiction in the games.[147]

> In the 2005 edition of the game, the virtual starting quarterback for Arizona State wears number 9, as did Keller, and has the same height, weight, skin tone, hair color, hair style, handedness, home state, play style (pocket passer), visor preference, facial features, and school year as Keller. In the 2008 edition, the virtual quarterback for Nebraska has these

[144] California, Florida, Indiana, Illinois, Kentucky, Massachusetts, New York, Nebraska, Nevada, Ohio, Oklahoma, Pennsylvania, Rhode Island, Tennessee, Texas, Utah, Virginia, Washington and Wisconsin have statutes protecting the right of publicity. These and other states also have common law which provided the basis for the original movement to establish privacy rights.

[145] *Abdul-Jabbar v. General Motors*, 85 F.3d 407 (9th Cir.1996).

[146] *In re NCAA Student-Athlete Name & Likeness Licensing Litigation*, 724 F.3d 1268, 107 U.S.P.Q.2d 1629 (9th Cir. 2017).

[147] Ibid. at 1272.

same characteristics, though the jersey number does not match, presumably because Keller changed his number right before the season started.

The close replication of Keller and the other collegiate players in "realistic virtual versions of actual stadiums" was enough to defeat EA's First Amendment defense based on transformative use (discussed in Chap. 13). Ultimately, the NCAA and EA reached a $60 million settlement to end the case. Some 25,000 collegiate athletes who were depicted in EA's sports video games, received checks.[148] Changes in NCAA rules and changes in state law, particularly a California law that allows collegiate athletes to be compensated for the use of their names, images and likenesses, means that EA could revive its NCAA Football series.[149] EA discontinued the game after the 2014 version.

A group of former NFL players sued the league[150] over its use of their images in a combined 155 NFL Films productions.[151] John Frederick Dryer, Elvin Lamont Bethea, and Edward Alvin White, along with 20 other former NFL players,[152] claimed, among other things,[153] that their rights of publicity were violated. U.S. District Judge Paul A. Magnuson held that the case turned on a determination of whether the players' right of publicity outweighed First Amendment protections for NFL Films. Precedent held that when the publication was not commercial speech, rights of publicity would not succeed. In *Bolger v. Youngs Drug Products Corp.*, Justice Marshall addressed the difference in treatment.[154]

> With respect to noncommercial speech, this Court has sustained content-based restrictions only in the most extraordinary circumstances. [* * *] By contrast, regulation of commercial speech based on content is less problematic.

Dryer and his fellow plaintiffs acknowledged that a finding that the films were expressive, noncommercial works would mean they would lose their suit. At its most basic, commercial speech is speech that proposes a

---

[148] O'Bannon filed an additional class action suit alleging that the NCAA had engaged in anti-trust conduct with respect to players' names, images, and likenesses. A federal district court ruled in his favor and a panel of the Ninth Circuit Court of Appeals affirmed the portion of the judgment that related to NCAA rules prohibiting student-athletes from being paid. *Edward C. O'Banon, Jr., On Behalf of Himself and All Others Similarly Situated v. National Collegiate Athletic Association*, 802 F.3d 1049 (9thCir. 2015).

[149] Bryan Wiedey, "The door is finally open for 'NCAA Football' franchise to return," *Sporting News*, Oct. 10, 2019.

[150] *Dryer v. National Football League*, 55 F.Supp.3d 1181 (D.Minn. 2014).

[151] NFL Films presented "Game of the Week," "Season Highlights" and specialty films on standout players and themed films including, "Cliffhangers, Comebacks & Character: The 1981 San Diego Chargers."

[152] The 20 other players settled their cases with the NFL. The NFL created a fund that would benefit all former professional players and also established a licensing agency to help players make use of their publicity rights. Dryer, Bethea and White opted out of the settlement and continued to pursue their suit.

[153] The three also claimed violations of the Lanham Act (discussed in Chap. 12).

[154] *Bolger v. Youngs Drug Products Corp.*, 463 U.S. 60, 103 S.Ct. 2875, 77 L.Ed.2d 469 (1983).

transaction. Commercial speech sometimes serves to advance an advertiser's position by creating goodwill or engendering loyalty to a brand. Judge Magnuson looked to indicators that would show the films were a form of commercial speech. He didn't find any.[155]

> The productions cannot be distinguished from the other content; the productions are the content. This contrast matters. The NFL does not pay television networks to broadcast NFL Films productions. Rather, those networks pay the NFL for the right to air those productions. In addition, other advertisers pay to have their advertisements inserted into the production's broadcast. The productions themselves are not advertising.
>
> Nor do the productions exploit players' images for the singular purpose of brand enhancement or other commercial gain. Instead, the productions tell the story of a football game, or a football team, or even of a particularly great football player. They are, in that sense, a history lesson of NFL football. The only way for NFL Films to tell such stories is by showing footage of the game—the plays, the players, the coaches, the referees, and even the fans. The NFL is capitalizing not on the likenesses of individual players but on the drama of the game itself, something that the NFL is certainly entitled to do.

In addressing the players' state-law right of publicity claims, Judge Magnuson noted that each of the states, New Jersey, California, New York, Minnesota and Texas had exceptions to the right of publicity based on whether the use was newsworthy or in the public interest. There was substantial interest in the performance of NFL players, the circumstances of their games and the plays themselves. In addition to the First Amendment protections and the exceptions to the state right of publicity claims, the films were also protected by the Copyright Act.[156] That meant they were covered by the federal copyright statute. Sec. 301 of the Copyright Act preempts state-law claims including right of publicity actions.

Dryer, Bethea and White appealed to the Eighth Circuit Court of Appeals and lost there as well.[157] The appellate panel concluded that the Copyright statute's protection of copyright holders' rights to exploit their works trumped the players' publicity rights. The players' other state claims were not addressed because of the resolution of the copyright claim.

---

[155] *Dryer v. National Football League*, 55 F.Supp.3d 1181, 1192 (D.Minn. 2014).

[156] 17 U.S.C. §§ 101–810.

[157] *Dryer v. National Football League*, 814 F.3d 938, 117 U.S.P.Q.2d 1812 (8th Cir. 2016).

THE RIGHT OF PUBLICITY IN NEWS: ZACCHINI V. SCRIPPS-HOWARD BROADCASTING (1977)

Although the cases on right of publicity dealt with advertising, games and films, news is not exempt. Hugo "The Human Cannonball" Zacchini catapulted into privacy law when he won a decision before the United States Supreme Court in 1977 over a newscast. The case arose when Zacchini was shot out of a cannon into a net 200 feet away at the Geauga County Fair in Burton, Ohio. Zacchini took exception to being filmed by a free-lancer working for Scripps-Howard Broadcasting, and more importantly, having the station broadcast his 15-second flight. Zacchini had spotted the free-lancer before he performed and asked him not to film his performance.[158] Zacchini performed in a fenced area surrounded by grandstands. The only people who could see the act were fairgoers. Despite Zacchini's request, the station broadcast the video with the anchor calling the act a "thriller" and urging viewers to go to the fair: "[Y]ou really need to see it *in person* to appreciate it."

Zacchini sued for infringement of his "right of publicity," claiming that the television station's showing of his act amounted to an appropriation of his professional property. The trial court granted summary judgment to the television station. The intermediate appellate court reversed the trial court in Zacchini's favor. The Ohio Supreme Court reversed the appellate court allowing summary judgment for the station. After the Ohio court rejected Zacchini's claims, the Supreme Court of the United States did not. Justice White, writing the opinion for the 5–4 majority, held:[159]

> Wherever the line * * * is to be drawn between media reports that are protected and those that are not, we are quite sure that the First and Fourteenth Amendments do not immunize the media when they broadcast a performer's entire act without his consent.

The Supreme Court declared that broadcasting a film of Zacchini's "entire act poses a substantial threat to the economic value of that performance." A five-member majority of the Court sent the *Zacchini* case back to the Ohio courts for a decision on whether the Human Cannonball could recover damages.

Apart from the peculiar facts of *Zacchini*, news is not considered a commercial use.

---

[158] The freelancer, on direction by the producer of the newscast, went back the next day and filmed the act.

[159] *Zacchini v. Scripps-Howard Broadcasting Co.*, 433 U.S. 562, 574, 97 S.Ct. 2849, 2857 (1977).

DEEP FAKES, PHOTOSHOP AND THE RIGHT OF PUBLICITY

Some commentators have suggested that the right of publicity might allow persons harmed by deep fakes to pursue actions against the social media networks that make it possible for people to construct fake and damaging videos and images. So far, celebrities mostly have been the targets of deep fakes. A Redditor by the name "deepfakes" has posted hardcore porn videos featuring the faces of Scarlett Johansson, Maisie Williams, Taylor Swift, Aubrey Plaza, and Gal Gadot on Reddit.[160] The videos use existing porn videos and images found through Google search and video from YouTube. One of deepfakes' videos placed images of Gal Gadot's face into a porn video about incest.[161] "[H]e trained the algorithm on porn videos and Gal Gadot's face. After enough of this 'training,' the nodes arrange themselves to complete a particular task, like convincingly manipulating video on the fly."

Gadot did not participate in the original porn video and the quality of the deepfake was such that the falsity was relatively easy to detect. But, as the technology continues to develop, the substitution of real celebrities for porn actors will become more believable. And, researchers are developing algorithms that will allow a user to take an image of a person and turn it into a figure making it walk, dance or *do other things*. Those will be posted to social media and reach an audience of most of the adults in the United States. The Pew Research Center reported in 2019 that,[162]

- 73 percent of adults use YouTube,
- 69 percent Facebook,
- 37 percent Instagram,
- 28 percent Pinterest,
- 27 percent LinkedIn,
- 24 percent Snapchat,
- 22 percent Twitter,
- 20 percent WhatsApp, and,
- 11 percent Reddit.

For the small-time troll who fakes a photo and posts it online, the ability to sue does little to fix the false impressions created by posts. A jury may award the celebrity victim a substantial amount. If the troll has no assets, his target will win only the satisfaction of having a jury declare the publication to be false and little else. As such lawsuits will have little deterrent effect, leaving the door open for noxious and damaging deep

[160] Samantha Cole, "AI-Assisted Fake Porn Is Here and We're All Fucked," *Vice*, Dec. 11, 2017.

[161] Ibid.

[162] Andres Perrin and Monica Anderson, "Share of U.S. adults using social media, including Facebook, is mostly unchanged since 2018," The Pew Research Center, April 10, 2019.

fakes. The entities that have both the ability to regulate content and billions of dollars that a plaintiff could go after are the social media companies that reach most Americans.

Sec. 230 protects social media companies from libel and false light suits. But, Sec. 230 contains an exemption for claims relating to intellectual property.[163] Some states have held that the right of publicity is similar to intellectual property in that it is the product of a person's efforts in the public sphere. Both the U.S. Supreme Court[164] and the Ohio Supreme Court[165] held in *Zacchini* that his suit was for the protection of his right of publicity. The Ohio Supreme Court[166] held that the right was "a right of exclusive control over the publicity given to his performances, which the plaintiff seeks to protect. For a performer, this right is a valuable part of the benefit which may be attained by his talents and efforts, and we think that this right is entitled to legal protection [* * *]. But the Ohio Supreme Court held that the language of *Time v. Hill* required that a right of publicity plaintiff would have to prove actual malice where the TV station broadcast a matter of public interest.[167] "Here, the TV station was privileged to report the facts of Mr. Zacchini's performance in a newscast, because the performance was a matter of legitimate public interest. No abuse appears which would defeat that privilege."

The U.S. Supreme Court reversed and remanded. Justice White held that *Hill* was not applicable to the *Zacchini* case. Hill was a false light suit. Zacchini was asserting his right of publicity. The two torts serve different purposes and have different elements, Justice White wrote.[168] "The interest protected' in permitting recovery for placing the plaintiff in a false light 'is clearly that of reputation, with the same overtones of mental distress as in defamation.' " In right of publicity cases,[169] "the State's interest is closely analogous to the goals of patent and copyright law, focusing on the right of the individual to reap the reward of his endeavors and having little to do with protecting feelings or reputation."

---

[163] 47 U.S.C.A. § 230(e) Effect on other laws

(2) No effect on intellectual property law

Nothing in this section shall be construed to limit or expand any law pertaining to intellectual property.

(3) State law

Nothing in this section shall be construed to prevent any State from enforcing any State law that is consistent with this section. No cause of action may be brought, and no liability may be imposed under any State or local law that is inconsistent with this section.

[164] *Zacchini v. Scripps-Howard Broadcasting Co.*, 433 U.S. 562, 574, 97 S.Ct. 2849, 2857 (1977).

[165] *Zacchini v. Scripps-Howard Broadcasting Co.*, 47 Ohio St.2d 224, 351 N.E.2d 454 (Ohio 1976).

[166] Ibid. at 232, 460.

[167] Ibid. at 235–236, 462.

[168] *Zacchini v. Scripps-Howard Broadcasting Co.*, 433 U.S. 562, 573, 97 S.Ct. 2849, 2856 (1977).

[169] Ibid.

Nonconsensual use of a person's fame in commerce is the most common basis for right of publicity cases. Trolls, political operatives and others who use photo manipulation or AI-based deep fakes are not engaging directly in sales. But right of publicity cases also can be brought where the user has gained a benefit apart from sales. Social media monetization is based on volume, how many people visit, so a person creating deep fakes can meet the self-benefit category of right of publicity. In addition, courts have recognized that damage to future rights of publicity is enough to bring suit. Boxing great Muhammad Ali sued *Playgirl Magazine* over a cartoon that used an image that was recognizable as him.[170] The image depicted a nude black man sitting in the corner of a boxing ring. Identification of Ali was easy, District Court Judge Lee Gagliardi wrote,[171] "Even a cursory inspection of the picture which is the subject of this action strongly suggests that the facial characteristics of the black male portrayed are those of Muhammad Ali. The cheekbones, broad nose and wideset brown eyes, together with the distinctive smile and close-cropped black hair are recognizable as the features of the plaintiff, one of the most widely known athletes of our time." Ali sought an injunction to stop the distribution of the edition with the image, surrender of all unsold copies and items used to print the edition of the magazine. While *Playgirl* had used the image in trade, Ali had another basis for his right of publicity claim, Judge Gagliardi wrote,[172]

> As has been noted, in the course of his public career plaintiff has established a commercially valuable proprietary interest in his likeness and reputation, analogous to the good will accumulated in the name of a successful business entity.
>
> [* * *]defendants appear not only to be usurping plaintiff's valuable right of publicity for themselves but may well be inflicting damage upon this marketable reputation. As described previously, the "likeness" of Ali which has been published is a full-frontal nude drawing, not merely a sketch or photograph of him as he appears in public.

Judge Gagliardi issued the injunction.

It is not difficult to see a celebrity, politician or other public figure bringing a right of publicity suit against a social media company. If courts agree that the right of publicity is an intellectual property, Sec. 230 immunity will not apply. As in *Ali*, the plaintiff could seek an injunction to force the social media company to take down the offending image or video. One of the complaints about an Elizabeth Warren altered sign photo is that Twitter declined to take down the image even after the campaign contacted the company and notified them of the image. The

[170] *Ali v. Playgirl, Inc.*, 447 F.Supp. 723, 206 U.S.P.Q. 102, 13 Media L. Rep. 2540 (S.D. N.Y.1978).

[171] Ibid. at 726.

[172] Ibid. at 729.

Digital Millennium Copyright Act (DMCA)[173] provides that ISPs get protection from suit, in part, by complying with § 512(c).[174]

> As a preliminary matter, a service provider can only receive safe harbor protection if it:
>
> (A) has adopted and reasonably implemented, and informs subscribers and account holders of the service provider's system or network of a policy that provides for the termination in appropriate circumstances of subscribers and account holders of the service provider's system or network who are repeat infringers; and [* * *]

Failure to remove content expeditiously can leave an ISP exposed to claims of contributory infringement. If, or when, the right of publicity comes under the terms of the DMCA either by court decision or statute, both the failure to remove and a finding of contributory infringement would be a powerful inducement to stop deep fakes and image alteration. Although most cases involve companies being notified of an infringing work, case law provides for responsibility where the facts show a company allows infringing works to remain online despite being aware of the infringement.[175]

> Actual knowledge is not necessary to deprive an infringer of safe harbor. Motherless would also lose its safe harbor if it was "aware of facts or circumstances from which infringing activity is apparent" and did not "act [ ] expeditiously to remove, or disable access to, the material." This is different from actual knowledge because instead of looking at subjective thoughts, we look at objective facts and circumstances from which the specific infringement would be obvious to a reasonable person.

But it is not all jelly and ice cream. A 2003 case involving secretly videotaped athletes demonstrates that even if Sec. 230 does not immunize an ISP, the ISP may not have any liability. In *Doe v. GTE,*[176] collegiate athletes at Northwestern University, Illinois State University and several other schools were videotaped in locker rooms. The footage was sold on the Internet under the titles, "Voyeur Time" and "Between the Lockers," by Franco Productions, Rodco and Hidvidco—Atlas Video Release. The athletes[177] sued Franco and the other companies. They also sued officials at their colleges claiming that the officials had not adequately protected them and three Internet service providers. Qualified immunity protected the college officials. Franco and the other

---

[173] 17 U.S.C. § 512 (1999).

[174] *BMG Rights Management and Round Hill Music v. Cox Communications*, 2015 WL 7756130 (E.D. Va. 2015).

[175] *Ventura Content, Ltd. v. Motherless, Inc.*, 885 F.3d 597, 609, 2018 Copr.L.Dec. P 31, 242, 125 U.S.P.Q.2d 1924 (9thCir. 2018).

[176] *Doe v. GTE Corp.*, 347 F.3d 655 (7th Cir. 2003).

[177] The athletes sued as John Doe and others to avoid their real names from being associated with the videos.

sellers never showed up and defaulted or were dismissed because they could not be found or served. The only defendants left were the Internet service providers, GTE, Genuity and PSInet. PSInet declared bankruptcy. GTE and Genuity moved to dismiss the athletes' case. The trial court granted the motion and the case was dismissed. The athletes appealed to the Seventh Circuit Court of Appeals. A three-judge panel upheld the lower court with Circuit Judge Frank Easterbrook explaining how the Internet service providers were not liable for simply providing Internet access to Franco and the others.[178]

> A web host, like a delivery service or phone company, is an intermediary and normally is indifferent to the content of what it transmits. Even entities that know the information's content do not become liable for the sponsor's deeds. Does a newspaper that carries an advertisement for "escort services" or "massage parlors" aid and abet the crime of prostitution, if it turns out that some (or many) of the advertisers make money from that activity? How about Verizon, which furnishes pagers and cell phones to drug dealers and thus facilitates their business? [* * *] That web hosting services likewise may be used to carry out illegal activities does not justify condemning their provision whenever a given customer turns out to be crooked.

If an ISP has not created the content that violate a person's right of publicity, the only recourse is to sue the creator of the deep fake or other manipulation of their images. Establishing an intellectual property right would allow the target of the altered or created image to appeal to ISPs on the ground that DMCA protections ought to be extended to protect the right of publicity. The DMCA only covers copyrighted work. Patents and trademarks are not protected. Whether ISPs will choose to protect intellectual property remains to be seen. ISPs generally have declined requests for take downs of altered images like the one used against the Warren campaign explaining that the content does not violate the ISP's terms of use or a reliance on the marketplace of ideas to provide remedies as people can find the truth themselves.

PARODIES IN NAME OR LIKENESS

Efforts at social commentary through parody collided with celebrities' efforts to control their images in *Cardtoons v. Major League Baseball Players Association* (1996).[179] The association sued Cardtoons, producer of satiric baseball playing cards, featuring pictures on one side and making fun of players on the other. San Francisco Giants' outfielder Barry Bonds—one of the game's highest-salaried players—was termed "Treasury Bonds" and, in reference to the nation's gold depository, was said to use a "Fort Knoxville Slugger" for his baseball bat. The U.S. Court

[178] *Doe v. GTE Corp.*, 347 F.3d 655, 659 (7th Cir. 2003).

[179] *Cardtoons v. Major League Baseball Players Association*, 95 F.3d 959 (10th Cir.1996).

of Appeals (10th Cir.) held that although the players' publicity rights were infringed, there was sufficient social commentary on the cards to entitle them to First Amendment protection.[180]

On the other hand, TV celebrity Vanna White, famous for her role on the "Wheel of Fortune," was awarded $403,000 by a jury for a Samsung Electronics advertisement used a quiz show with a robot resembling Ms. White.[181] The game show setting and the manner of the robot's dress were found to make use of her celebrity. White's legal victory was upheld by a U.S. Court of Appeals, despite fiery dissents claiming that such parodies should be protected under the First Amendment.

A distinctive singing voice and style also are elements of identity. Ford Motor Company's use of a singer who sounded much like Bette Midler resulted in a $400,000 court victory for "the Divine Miss M."[182] Ford tried to hire Ms. Midler to sing a signature song in an advertisement for the Ford Taurus. She refused. Ford's ad agency, Young & Rubicam, hired a singer to perform the song and documents produced in the trial showed that the agency was directed to find a voice that was like hers.

DESCENDABILITY OF THE RIGHT OF PUBLICITY

If the right of publicity is a form of intellectual property, what happens when the famous person dies? Technology has been used to recreate actors and singers in commercials, videos and concerts. In an early right of publicity case, the legal ghost of the late horror-film star Bela Lugosi came back to haunt Universal Pictures Company in a courtroom battle over the exploitation of his fame after his death in 1956.[183] Universal capitalized on Lugosi's fame, especially his role as Dracula. The movie company entered into licensing agreements to allow manufacturing of items including shirts, cards, games, kites, bar accessories, and masks, all with the likeness of Lugosi's Count Dracula. His widow and son sued but the California Supreme Court, however, held 4–3 that the exclusive right to profit from the actor's name and likeness did not survive him. The Court held that the right could not be created after his death. If Lugosi had entered into agreements to exploit his celebrity before he died, his survivors could have sued the makers of products using his likeness under state laws regarding unfair competition. But, as the Court noted in its *per curiam* opinion, the right of publicity, like other rights, died with him.[184] Such, "* * * a right of value to create a business product or service of value is embraced in the law of privacy and is protectable during one's lifetime [* * *]."

---

[180] Ibid. at 962.

[181] *White v. Samsung Electronics*, 971 F.2d 1395 (9th Cir.1992), rehearing denied, 989 F.2d 1512 (9th Cir.1993), cert. den., 508 U.S. 951, 113 S.Ct. 2443 (1993).

[182] *Midler v. Ford Motor Company*, 849 F.2d 460 (9th Cir.1988).

[183] *Lugosi v. Universal Pictures*, 25 Cal.3d 813, 819, 160 Cal.Rptr. 323, 326, 603 P.2d 425, 428 (1979).

[184] Ibid. at 819, 326, 428.

Later cases upheld discernibility of aspects of famous deceased persons include the famed mystery novelist Agatha Christie,[185] Martin Luther King, Jr.,[186] and the legendary rock star Janis Joplin.[187]

California and 27 other states passed statutes since giving protection to the names, likenesses, voices and images.[188] California's law provides protection to celebrities, who were California residents at the time of their deaths. Initially, the California statute gave rights of publicity, which could be bequeathed along with the rest of their estates, to those who died as long ago as 1935. Two court cases over the rights of publicity belonging to the estate of Marilyn Monroe led the California Legislature to amend the law to give protection to dead celebrities regardless of when they died.[189]

DEFENSES TO APPROPRIATION AND RIGHT OF PUBLICITY SUITS

Defendants in appropriation and publicity suits can always defend on the grounds that the use was consensual. Some states require such consent to be in writing and signed by the parties. Otherwise, defenses focus mainly on the nature of the publication. If there is no commercial use as in a news story, the defendant has a good chance of winning. But, remember that in *Ali*, Muhammad Ali won his case largely based on the harm to his image and subsequent right of publicity and Zacchini sued over TV news story.

37. PRIVATE FACTS

With the law of privacy, "truth can hurt." Unlike the law of defamation, truth is not necessarily a defense to an invasion of privacy lawsuit.

All people have things that they would prefer no one find out about. When those private matters wind up in the pages of a newspaper, magazine, in a broadcast or on the Internet, they can lead to a lawsuit under the third privacy tort, private facts.

ELEMENTS OF PRIVATE FACTS

The private fact tort starts with publication. It doesn't matter if the publication is news or commercial in nature. Identification is necessary

[185] *Hicks v. Casablanca Records*, 464 F.Supp. 426 (S.D.N.Y.1978).

[186] *Martin Luther King, Jr. Center for Social Change v. American Heritage Products*, 508 F.Supp. 854 (N.D.Ga.1981), reinterpreted in the Georgia Supreme Court, 8 Med.L.Rptr. 2377 (Ga. 1982).

[187] *Joplin Enterprises v. Allen*, 19 Med.L.Rptr. 2093 (W.D.Wash.1991), reinterpreted in 795 F.Supp. 349 (W.D.Wash.1992).

[188] Matthew Belloni, "Monroe, money fueling right of publicity battle," The *Hollywood Reporter*, Sept. 14, 2007.

[189] Jordana Lewis, "Long-Dead Celebrities Can Now Breathe Easier," *New York Times*, Oct. 23, 2007.

to show that the plaintiff's privacy was invaded. It must reveal a fact, a truth that is private, though the tort does not require that no one but the plaintiff know it. The publication also will "violate the ordinary decencies," in other words, the publication would be highly offensive to a reasonable person.

REPORTING A MEDICAL CONDITION

Dorothy Barber was stuck in a hospital room with a condition that caused her to lose weight while eating constantly. She clearly believed her medical problem was her private business. A sneaky photographer's picture taken in her hospital room wound up being published in *Time* magazine under the remarkably insensitive caption, "Starving Glutton."[190] The article recounted how her doctor admitted her to the hospital because, "although she had eaten enough in the past year to feed a family of ten, she had lost 25 pounds." Mrs. Barber's lawsuit illustrates overlapping of privacy torts, for she clearly had legal actions because the magazine revealed private facts about her—publication of private matters violating the ordinary decencies. Also, as will be discussed in the next chapter—Mrs. Barber had an action for intrusion for the unwanted entry into her hospital room by the photographer and for him photographing her despite her protests. Although Mrs. Barber's family and others close to her knew about her condition, it was still private with respect to the readership of a national magazine.

SIPPLE V. CHRONICLE PUBLISHING CO.

Much in the law of privacy is unpredictable, and the private facts area is no exception. Consider the lawsuit brought by ex-Marine Oliver Sipple, who saved President Gerald Ford's life in 1975 by disrupting the aim of would-be assassin Sarah Jane Moore. On Sept. 22, 1975, Moore was in a crowd outside San Francisco's St. Francis Hotel, about 40 feet away from President Ford, who was riding in a convertible in a motorcade. When Moore aimed pistol at the president, Sipple noticed and hit her arm just as she fired, sending the shot high above President Ford's head. (The bullet's ricochet slightly injured a bystander in the crowd.).[191] Two days after the incident, *San Francisco Chronicle* columnist Herb Caen wrote that the city's gay community was proud of Sipple and that his heroism might dispel stereotypes about homosexuals. The *Los Angeles Times* and other newspapers picked up the story from the *Chronicle* and noted,[192] "that he was a prominent member of the San Francisco gay community. Some of the articles speculated that President

---

[190] *Barber v. Time, Inc.*, 348 Mo. 1199, 159 S.W.2d 291 (1942). Mrs. Barber won $3,000 from the magazine.

[191] Randal C. Archibald, "One of Ford's Would-Be Assassins is Paroled," *New York Times*, Jan. 1, 2008. Archibald reported that Sarah Jane Moore's attempt on Ford's life came just 17 days after Lynnette (Squeaky) Fromme, a follower of Charles Manson, tried to kill Ford in Sacramento.

[192] *Sipple v. Chronicle Publishing Co.*, 154 Cal.App.3d 1040, 1044 (1984).

Ford's failure to promptly thank Sipple for his heroic act was a result of Sipple's sexual orientation."

Sipple objected that his sexual orientation had nothing to do with saving the President, and filed suit against *The Chronicle*, against columnist Caen, and against the *Los Angeles Times* and several other newspapers, seeking $15 million in damages.[193] Sipple said that the publications,[194]

> [* * *]were highly offensive to plaintiff inasmuch as his parents, brothers and sisters learned for the first time of his homosexual orientation; and that as a consequence of disclosure of private facts about his life plaintiff was abandoned by his family, exposed to contempt and ridicule causing him great mental anguish, embarrassment and humiliation."[195]

The Los Angeles Times countered that Sipple was a person "thrust into the vortex of publicity" of an event of worldwide importance, claiming that "* * * many aspects of his life became matters of legitimate public interest." The trial court granted summary judgment to the newspapers and dismissed his suit. Sipple appealed. The appellate court held Sipple was so newsworthy after saving President Ford's life that he could not collect damages for an invasion of his privacy. Sipple was involved in an event of international importance. The court also found that Sipple was not secretive about his orientation. He had been involved in gay parades and was known by hundreds of people in Dallas, New York, Houston, San Diego, Los Angeles and San Francisco. His friendship with Harvey Milk[196] had been reported in several gay magazines.[197]

> In fact, appellant quite candidly conceded that he did not make a secret of his being a homosexual and that if anyone would ask, he would frankly admit that he was gay. In short, since appellant's sexual orientation was already in public domain and since the articles in question did no more than to give further publicity to matters which appellant left open to the eye of the public, a vital element of the tort was missing [* * *]

But when the newsworthiness is less, the privacy protection for an individual can be correspondingly greater. Toni Ann Diaz, for example, had achieved a far more limited newsworthiness as the first woman student body president at a Northern California junior college, the College of Alameda.

---

[193] Ibid. at 1051 (1984).

[194] Ibid. at 1044–1045.

[195] In this and earlier periods of time, sexual orientation was a taboo subject and being gay or seen as being gay led to multiple attacks, some deadly, by homophobes.

[196] Milk was the first self-acknowledged gay man to be elected in California when he won a seat on the San Francisco Board of Supervisors.

[197] *Sipple v. Chronicle Publishing Co.*, 154 Cal.App.3d 1040, 1048 (1984).

DIAZ V. OAKLAND TRIBUNE

In 1978, *Oakland Tribune* columnist Sidney Jones published truthful—yet highly private—information about dealing with a sex change operation undergone by Ms. Diaz:[198]

> More Education Stuff: The Students at the College of Alameda will be surprised to learn their student body president Toni Diaz is no lady, but is in fact a man whose real name is Antonio.
>
> Now I realize, that in these times, such a matter is no big deal, but I suspect that his female classmates in P.E. 97 may wish to make other showering arrangements.

Diaz sued. Justice Betty Barry-Deal noted that Ms. Diaz was a transexual.[199] "Suffice it to say that for most of her life Diaz suffered from a gender identification problem and the anxiety and depression that accompanied it. She testified that since she was young, she had had the feeling of being a woman." Antonio Diaz underwent gender corrective surgery in 1975. Her therapist testified that her physical and psychological identities were in harmony after the operation. Ms. Diaz kept her gender reassignment private.[200]

> Diaz scrupulously kept the surgery a secret from all but her immediate family and closest friends. She never sought to publicize the surgery. She changed her name to Toni Ann Diaz and made the necessary changes in her high school records, her social security records, and on her driver's license. She tried unsuccessfully to change her Puerto Rican birth certificate.

She enrolled in Alameda College and was elected student body president in 1977. While president Ms. Diaz charged that college administrators were misusing money from the student association account, money that students paid. Within days of Ms. Diaz' charges, Jones received calls from confidential sources telling him that Ms. Diaz was a man. On March 26, 11 days after the student newspaper broke the story about the allegations of misuse of student money, Jones' column was published. Ms. Diaz sued for invasion of privacy. The trial court jury awarded Ms. Diaz a total of $775,000, finding that the information about the sex change surgery was not newsworthy and would be offensive to ordinary readers. Jones and the newspaper appealed. The appeals court found that the trial judge had made two mistakes that required a retrial: 1) the instruction about the right to privacy, the judge gave the jury a definition that was overly broad, and, 2) the judge required that the defendants prove the newsworthiness defense. The appellate court held there would have to be a new trial. But the opinion by Judge Betty Narry-

---

198 *Diaz v. Oakland Tribune, Inc.*, 139 Cal.App.3d 118, 188 Cal.Rptr. 762, 766 (1983).

199 Ibid. at 123.

200 Ibid.

Deal made clear that even though Ms. Diaz would have to prove the column was not newsworthy, it would not be difficult.[201]

> [W]e cannot state that the fact of her gender was newsworthy per se.
>
> Contrary to defendants' claim, we find little if any connection between the information disclosed and Diaz's fitness for office. The fact that she is a transsexual does not adversely reflect on her honesty or judgment.
>
> [* * *]
>
> Nor does the fact that she was the first woman student body president, in itself, warrant that her entire private life be open to public inspection. The public arena entered by Diaz is concededly small. Public figures more celebrated than she are entitled to keep some information of their domestic activities and sexual relations private.

Judge Barry-Deal delivered her most pointed comments about the defendants' claim that the column was newsworthy because it dealt with the changing roles of women in society.[202]

> This assertion rings hollow. The tenor of the article was by no means an attempt to enlighten the public on a contemporary social issue. Rather, as Jones himself admitted, the article was directed to the students at the College about their newly elected president. Moreover, Jones' attempt at humor at Diaz's expense removes all pretense that the article was meant to educate the reading public.

The appellate court then sent the case back to the trial level, but a second jury never heard this case. After the decision by the California Court of Appeal, First District, the case settled out of court reportedly for between $200,000 and $300,000.

HOWARD V. DES MOINES REGISTER

Like so many other cases in privacy law, *Howard v. Des Moines Register and Tribune Co.*[203] raised both ethical and legal concerns. Reporter Margaret Engel did an investigative story on a county home[204] where patients died from scalding baths, women were sterilized though they were not retarded[205] and illegal shipments of drugs reportedly took

---

201 Ibid. at 134.

202 Ibid.

203 *Howard v. Des Moines Register and Tribune Co.*, 283 N.W.2d 289 (Iowa 1979).

204 Such government-run facilities were used to house people who could not take care of themselves. In some cases, these homes were used to hold young women and girls who were deemed to be at risk of an unplanned pregnancy.

205 For decades, 32 state and uncounted numbers of local governments sterilized immigrants, people of color, poor people, unmarried mothers, the disabled, the mentally ill as a way of preventing harmful traits like criminality, mental impairment or promiscuity from being

place. The home eventually was closed by the state. Before the closure, Myrle J. Corso, a former staff member, contacted Opal M. Snyder, a columnist for a local newspaper and publisher of a newsletter. Snyder suggested that Corso write a column for her newsletter about her concerns. Corso wrote about patient abuse and neglect, mishandling of drugs and two instances of involuntary sterilization. Corso sent copies of her column to the Iowa Gov. Robert Ray, State Department of Health and the *Des Moines Register*. Snyder started her own investigation of the home and sent a letter to Gov. Ray including a statement that Collene Blakely, a former nurse's aide, had made. Blakely recounted how a young woman, Robbin Woody (who would marry and become Robbin Howard) was sterilized.[206]

> One day, when I came to work, I found Robin on her bed, crying. When I inquired as to the problem, she told me that she had been called to Riva Ripper's office and was told by Mrs. Ripper that she, Robin, would be released if she agreed to be sterilized. Mrs. Ripper is the stewardess at the County Home. If she didn't agree she would have to remain at the Jasper County Home indefinitely.
>
> [* * *]
>
> About a year later I saw her at a park in Newton. She told me at that time that she had been released because she "gave up her rights to be a person".

Ms. Engel covered the controversy about the home, reporting on multiple meetings of the county board of supervisors who were discussing the 120 reported deficiencies at the home. She reported on the resignations of the administrator and head nurse. Engel spent weeks investigating the home and spoke to Snyder who gave her copies of the documents sent to the governor. She interviewed the home's psychiatrist about the sterilization of Robbin Woody. The psychiatrist said,[207]

> "That child she was a young girl was a very explosive, impulsive young girl largely without controls over her aggressive and, at times, irrational behavior."
>
> He said she was sterilized because "she would be a very questionable risk as far as having and rearing a baby. The people who hold on that way are those who move on to child abuse."
>
> Robin's mother, Mrs. Gladys Woody of Newton, said she agreed with the decision then and now. She would not discuss the matter further.

---

passed down through children. The theory, not proven, was that preventing the reproduction of these persons would improve the quality of the whole population.

[206] *Howard v. Des Moines Register and Tribune Co.*, 283 N.W.2d 289, 296 (Iowa 1979).

[207] Ibid. at 293.

Engel testified that she could not find Robbin Woody. And so, Robbin (Woody) Howard learned about the story when she read it in the *Register* story. She filed a private facts lawsuit. The trial court dismissed her suit and she appealed to the Iowa Supreme Court. The Court affirmed the trial court on the basis of 1) the newsworthiness of the story, and, 2) the story was based on public records obtained under the Iowa public records statute. As in Diaz, the burden was on the plaintiff to prove the story was not newsworthy. Howard acknowledged that the story was newsworthy but argued that including her name was still an invasion of privacy.[208]

> Here the disclosure of plaintiff's involuntary sterilization was closely related to the subject matter of the news story. It documented the article's theme of maladministration and patient abuses at the Jasper County Home. [* * *]Plaintiff's experience in 1971 was plainly relevant with other past events in evaluating the home's administration.
>
> In the sense of serving an appropriate news function, the disclosure contributed constructively to the impact of the article. It offered a personalized frame of reference to which the reader could relate, fostering perception and understanding. Moreover, it lent specificity and credibility to the report.

Beyond that, the Iowa court held that because the story and the information about Howard had been obtained under the state's public records act, the documents were public records and so could not constitute an invasion of privacy.[209] "Liability for disclosing public information is foreclosed on this basis because matters of public record are, as a matter of law, of legitimate concern to the public."

In most cases, the existence of a public record usually has precluded recovery for invasion of privacy. Even if persons are embarrassed by publication of dates of a marriage or birth,[210] or other information from a public record,[211] publication accurately based on such records has been protected by qualified privilege and escaped successful lawsuits. This can be true even in some extreme fact situations, as when the *Albuquerque Journal* published a story—based on records of a court proceeding—that a 16-year-old boy had sexually assaulted his younger sister. The sister sued claiming private facts but lost based on the public record.[212]

---

[208] Ibid. at 303.

[209] Ibid. at 298.

[210] *Meetze v. Associated Press*, 230 S.C. 330, 95 S.E.2d 606 (1956).

[211] *Stryker v. Republic Pictures Corp.*, 108 Cal.App.2d 191, 238 P.2d 670 (1951).

[212] *Hubbard v. Journal Pub. Co.*, 69 N.M. 473, 474, 368 P.2d 147, 148 (1962). {5} Sec. 13–8–66, 1953 Supp., being § 48, Ch. 205, L.1955, provides: 'The court's official records, excluding all written reports of the probation officer and records kept in the probation office or in the juvenile attorney's office, shall be public records and open to inspection.'

STATUTORY PROHIBITIONS ON PUBLICATION

Attitudes about rape led to the passage of state laws to prevent the publication of the names of victims. Beliefs that rape was shameful coupled with ideas of victim responsibility meant that, unlike other crimes of violence, rape should not be a matter of public discussion. Cases where news organizations were either sued or prosecuted led to the revision of those laws. Today, it is largely an editorial decision whether to disclose names with most news organizations choosing not to make victims' names public.

COX BROADCASTING CORP. V. COHN

In 1971, 17-year-old Cynthia Cohn was gang-raped and murdered. Six youths were indicted for the crimes. There was heavy coverage of the event, but the identity of the rape victim was not disclosed until one defendant's trial began. Five of the six youths entered pleas of guilty to rape or attempted rape after murder charges were dropped. Those guilty pleas were accepted, and the trial of the defendant who pleaded not guilty was set for a later date. A Georgia statute forbade publication of the identity of a rape victim. Despite this, a reporter employed by WSB-TV learned Cynthia Cohn's identity from indictments open to public inspection and broadcast her identity as part of his story. The report was repeated the next day.

Martin Cohn sued the TV station, claiming that the broadcasts identifying his daughter invaded his own privacy.[213] After hearing the *Cohn* case twice, the Georgia Supreme Court ruled that the statute forbidding publication of the name of a rape victim was constitutional,[214] " 'a legitimate limitation on the right of freedom of expression contained in the First Amendment.' "

The Supreme Court of the United States overturned the Georgia court by a vote of 8–1. Writing for the Court, Justice White said:[215]

> The version of the privacy tort now before us—termed in Georgia the "tort of public disclosure" * * * is that in which the plaintiff claims the right to be free from unwanted publicity about his private affairs, which, although wholly true, would be offensive to a person of ordinary sensibilities. * * * [I]t is here that claims of privacy most directly confront the constitutional freedoms of speech and press.

Justice White wrote that truth may not always be a defense in either defamation or privacy actions. First, concerning defamation,[216] "The Court has * * * carefully left open the question whether the First and

---

[213] *Cox Broadcasting v. Cohn*, 420 U.S. 469, 470–474, 95 S.Ct. 1029, 1034–1035 (1975).

[214] Ibid. at 475, 1036.

[215] Ibid. at 489, 1043.

[216] Ibid. at 491–492, 1044.

Fourteenth Amendments require that truth be recognized as a defense in a defamation action brought by a private person as distinguished from a public official or a public figure." Writing about privacy, he continued:[217] "In similar fashion, *Time v. Hill*, supra, [385 U.S. 374, 383 n. 7, 87 S.Ct. 534, 539 (1967)] expressly saved [reserved] the question whether truthful publication of very private matters unrelated to public affairs could be constitutionally proscribed." Thus, the Supreme Court recognized—but backed away from—a troubling constitutional question: May a state ever define and protect an area of privacy free from unwanted *truthful* publicity in the press?

Having recognized this problem, Justice White then turned his majority opinion to narrower and safer ground. In *Cox*, the key question was whether Georgia might impose punishment for the accurate publication of the name of a rape victim, when that name was obtained from an official record open to public inspection. Justice White concluded that the news media could not be published from quoting accurately from such a record.[218] He wrote that the news media have a great responsibility to report fully and accurately the proceedings of government,[219] "and official records and documents open to the public are the basic data of governmental operations."

THE FLORIDA STAR V. B.J.F.

In 1989, the U.S. Supreme Court cautiously upheld the generalization that if material is part of a public record, it can be reported truthfully and accurately without legal penalty. A woman sued a Jacksonville weekly newspaper after it published an item identifying her and saying that she had been robbed and sexually assaulted.[220] This information was made available in the sheriff's department, which had prepared a report using her full name and put it in the department's press room. Access to reports in this room was unrestricted.

A reporter-trainee for *The Florida Star* copied the report verbatim, and a reporter then wrote an accurate one-paragraph "Police Reports" item, which was published. This violated the newspaper's own policy against identifying rape victims; the newspaper had not done so previously. This mistake by the newspaper led to B.J.F.'s lawsuit under a Florida statute[221] making it unlawful to publish or broadcast the name of a victim of a sexual offense.

The U.S. Supreme Court overturned the directed verdict that awarded B.J.F. $100,000 in damages. By a 6–3 vote, the Court carefully confined itself to the specific fact situation. The Court again avoided

[217] Ibid.

[218] Ibid. at 490–491, 1044.

[219] Ibid. at 492, 1044–1045 (1975), citing *Sheppard v. Maxwell*, 384 U.S. 333, 350, 86 S.Ct. 1507, 1515 (1966).

[220] *Florida Star v. B.J.F.*, 491 U.S. 524, 538, 109 S.Ct. 2603, 2611 (1989).

[221] Florida Stat. § 794.03.

deciding the tough constitutional issue of whether the press can ever have criminal responsibility or civil liability for publishing a privacy-invading news story. Note also that this decision did not declare unconstitutional the Florida statute making it a crime to publish a rape victim's name.

Writing for the Court, Justice Thurgood Marshall turned to *Smith v. Daily Mail* (1979)[222] for his rationale in *The Florida Star* case, carefully limiting this decision to the context of this case. The *Smith v. Daily Mail* principle, Justice Marshall wrote, protects only publication of information which a news medium has "lawfully obtained."[223] "It is undisputed that the article describing the assault on B.J.F. was accurate * * * [and] lawfully obtained * * *" Some of Justice Marshall's words, however, suggested that the Court *might* look favorably upon punishment for publishing truthful information if the statute authorizing such punishment was precise and narrowly drawn. But where government did not "police itself in disseminating information," imposition of damages against the media cannot stand.[224]

DEFENSES TO PRIVATE FACTS SUITS

There are three defenses in private fact suits. The publisher-defendant can argue that it cannot be held liable because the publication was: 1) newsworthy, 2) based on public or official records, 3) did not violate the ordinary decencies, or, 4) consented to by the plaintiff.

VIRGIL V. TIME, INC.: QUESTIONING "CONSENT"

What happens if a source calls back and says, "I withdraw my consent to be in your story!" It has happened. *Virgil v. Time, Inc.*[225] began with a feature story that a writer for *Sports Illustrated* wanted to do on body surfing at a beach acknowledged to be the most dangerous in the world. He learned about Mike Virgil, a daredevil body surfer. He met Virgil and began working on the story. Once the story reached the editing process, a fact-checker called the Virgil home and spoke with his wife to double check on some information in the story. At this point—evidently because Mrs. Virgil disapproved of the interview—Virgil "revoked all consent" for use of his name in the article and for use of the photographs.

---

[222] *Smith v. Daily Mail Pub. Co.*, 443 U.S. 97, 105, 99 S.Ct. 2667, 2672 (1979). A 14-year-old high school student shot and killed a 15-year-old. The *Charleston Daily Gazette* learned the name from police radio traffic and published it. A West Virginia statute forbade the publication of the names of juveniles accused of crimes without a court order and the newspaper was prosecuted. The Supreme Court held 8–0 that criminal sanctions could not be imposed on a newspaper that lawfully obtained it.

[223] Ibid. at 536, 2611.

[224] Ibid. at 492, 1044–1045 (1975), citing *Sheppard v. Maxwell*, 384 U.S. 333, 350, 86 S.Ct. 1507, 1515 (1966).

[225] *Virgil v. Time*, 527 F.2d 1122, 1125 n. (9th Cir.1975).

One of the sections of the story laid a foundation for Virgil's approach to surfing[226]

> 'Virgil's carefree style at the Wedge appears to have emanated from some escapades in his younger days, such as the time at a party when a young lady approached him and asked where she might find an ashtray. 'Why, my dear, right here,' said Virgil, taking her lighted cigarette and extinguishing it in his mouth. He also won a small bet one time by burning a hole in a dollar bill that was resting on the back of his hand. In the process he also burned two holes in his wrist.'

The article revealed that Virgil once dove headfirst down a flight of stairs at a ski resort.[227] "Because why? Well, there were these chicks all around. I thought it would be groovy. Was I drunk? I think I might have been." Virgil told the reporter that he would get jobs in construction and then deliberately injure himself so he could collect unemployment and support his surfing.

Sports Illustrated ran the story anyway. Virgil filed a privacy suit. Time, Inc., publisher of the magazine moved for summary judgment arguing that because Virgil had not claimed that anything in the story was not true and so he should not be able to sue. But, remember that private facts cases are based on the disclosure of facts. The trial judge denied the motion and Time appealed. Circuit Court Judge Charles Merrill, writing for the three-judge panel, was not sympathetic. He wrote that Virgil had understood that the article was going to be limited to his prowess as a surfer at The Wedge, and that he did not know it would contain references to some "bizarre incidents" in his life not "directly related to surfing." He disposed of the consent issue fairly quickly.[228]

> Talking freely to a member of the press, knowing the listener to be a member of the press, is not then in itself making public. Such communication can be said to anticipate that what is said will be made public since making public is the function of the press, and accordingly such communication can be construed as a consent to publicize. Thus if publicity results it can be said to have been consented to. However, if consent is withdrawn prior to the act of publicizing, the consequent publicity is without consent.

Merrill noted that some situations that would make revocation impossible. "There may be cases where requiring that an eleventh-hour change of mind be honored would unfairly burden the publisher and where it could not, for that reason, be regarded as a timely revocation of consent. This is not such a case."

---

226 Ibid. at 1132.

227 Ibid.

228 Ibid. at 1127.

He turned to the newsworthiness defense that Time, Inc., might raise. Quoting again from the Restatement, he pointed to the distinction between what were and were not matters of legitimate public interest and therefore newsworthy or not.[229]

> The line is to be drawn when the publicity ceases to be the giving of information to which the public is entitled, and becomes a morbid and sensational prying into private lives for its own sake, with which a reasonable member of the public, with decent standards, would say that he had no concern. * *

Merrill acknowledged a public interest could exist in an activity like body surfing. But, he added, a public interest did not mean the right of the public to know private facts about the persons who engage in that activity.[230] "The fact that they engage in an activity in which the public can be said to have a general interest does not render every aspect of their lives subject to public disclosure." The case was remanded to the trial court.

U.S. District Judge Gordon Thompson, Jr., applied the new test for newsworthiness that Judge Merrill had drawn and concluded that Virgil would not be able to meet his burden with respect to the newsworthiness of the article.[231]

> The facts themselves putting out cigarettes in his mouth and diving off stairs to impress women, hurting himself in order to collect unemployment so as to have time for bodysurfing at the Wedge during summer, fighting in gang fights as a youngster, and eating insects are not sufficiently offensive to reach the very high level of offensiveness necessary under Virgil to lose newsworthiness protection.

And so, reporters and editors can rely on the newsworthiness of their stories if a source should withdraw consent. That is, as long as any private facts are, in the words of Judges Merrill and Thompson, "not offensive to the degree of morbidity or sensationalism."

38. INTRUSION: AN INTRODUCTION

Invading a person's solitude, either in person or through the use of devices, can lead to an intrusion claim.

Personal privacy can seem a quaint and old-fashioned idea. Today, people willingly surrender their privacy in order to make use of the Internet, wireless phone services and IOT (Internet of Things) devices. TVs listen to people and cameras record who comes and goes. Alexa, Cortana and Google Assistant listen for their activation words, or something like their activation words. Visiting a website means picking

---

[229] Ibid. Quoting Restatement (Second) of Torts s 652D (Tentative Draft No. 21, 1975).

[230] Ibid. at 1131.

[231] Ibid. at 1289.

up tracking tools that tell marketers where you've been, how long you spent looking at the site and what you bought. It seems that the only time people are concerned about their privacy is when their activities are viewed by people who are not supposed to see or hear or read what they've been doing. And that's where journalism walks, drives, flies, or boats in.

The tort of intrusion is taken up in the next chapter along with other matters related to the behavior of media professionals in the course of gathering news.

CHAPTER 7

NEWSGATHERING TORTS AND RELATED AREAS OF LAW

39. NEWSGATHERING TORTS: AN OVERVIEW

Newsgathering torts—which often are privacy torts in new clothes—continue to be significant areas of concern in the Twenty-First Century

Much of the development of newsgathering torts comes from intrusion, a very old concept in English law. In 1765, Sir William Blackstone's "*Commentaries*"[1] described eavesdroppers as "people who listen under windows, or the eaves of a house, to conversation, from which they frame slanderous and mischievous tales." While we still deal with eavesdroppers (consider how many people listen in to cellphone conversations while pretending to read a tablet or smartphone). But, technology has added a whole raft of ways to intrude.

This chapter takes up a variety of legal areas lumped together under the label "newsgathering torts." The follow a much-followed pattern in a 1960 law review article by Dean William L. Prosser. He included the following under the broad label of "invasion of privacy:"[2]

(1) Intrusion on the plaintiff's physical solitude.

(2) Publication of private matters violating the ordinary decencies.

(3) Putting plaintiff in a false position in the public eye, as by signing that person's name to a letter or petition, attributing to that individual views not held by that person.

---

1 *Sir William Blackstone's Commentaries on the Law*, ed. by Bernard C. Gavit (Washington, D.C.: Washington Book Co., 1892).

2 *Barbieri v. News-Journal Co.*, 56 Del. 67, 189 A.2d 773, 774 (1963). The Delaware Supreme Court summarized Dean Prosser's analysis of the kinds of actions to be included in the law of privacy. See Prosser's "Privacy," 49 *California Law Review* (1960), pp. 383–423, and his *Handbook of the Law of Torts*, 4th ed. (St. Paul, Minn.: West Publishing Co., 1971), pp. 802–818.

(4) Appropriation of some element of plaintiff's personality—his or her name or likeness—for commercial use.

40. ELEMENTS OF INTRUSION

Invading a person's solitude by trespassing, intercepting communications, using hidden microphones or cameras can lead to successful intrusion claims.

Understanding intrusion is easy: What are the places in your life that you consider off-limits? Think of your day. You get up. You go into the bathroom, sit down and meditate on life. How comfortable would you be if strangers walked in to watch or listen. The same for the shower in your private home. When you go to the bedroom preparing to sleep, how receptive would you be to having strangers show up as you stripped. Now, there may be places and circumstances, such as the communal showers at the gym or beds in a bunkhouse at summer camp, that wouldn't make you as uncomfortable. The toilet, likely will always be a place where you expect privacy (that is unless you are in boot camp where the toilets simply back up to a wall).

And so, the elements of intrusion are:

1) A reasonable expectation of privacy. You cannot reasonably expect people to avert their eyes as you walk down the street. And, despite what a public irate against "the media" may think, it is not an invasion of privacy to take someone's photograph in a public place.

2) Intrusion. Having someone (personally or by instrumentality, such as telephoto lenses, hidden camera) go into that place where you have a reasonable expectation of privacy.

That's it. Someone, and in this context, it is a reporter, went someplace and someone objected and sued. Now, the reason we have most of a chapter devoted to this, is the fact that intrusions can take many forms and the expectations of privacy are variably reasonable. Unlike the other privacy torts, there is no publication requirement. Nothing needs to be printed, broadcast or posted. The mere intrusive presence is what triggers the tort.

A KEY PRECEDENT: DIETEMANN V. TIME, INC.

Arguably the most important precedent involving intrusion torts is *Dietemann v. Time, Inc.*,[3] a ruling that says loud and clear that the First Amendment gives the media no right to violate the privacy interests of people, even when legitimate news is being pursued.

The case began in 1963 when *Life* magazine, published by Time, Inc., and the Los Angeles District Attorney agreed to work together on a story

[3] *Dietemann v. Time, Inc.*, 449 F.2d 245 (9th Cir.1971).

and investigation of medical quackery.[4] A.A. Dieteman had been identified as a person who was practicing medicine without a license and *Life* sent a reporter, Mrs. Jackie Metcalf, and a photographer, William Ray, to his home, where he practiced. Dieteman was a disabled veteran who had little formal education. Dieteman worked as a plumber but made claims to be a scientist as well as a healer.[5] "He made no charges when he attempted to diagnose or to prescribe herbs and minerals. He did accept contributions."

On Sept. 20, 1963, the reporter and photographer went to his home and claimed they had been sent by a friend. They entered and went to Dieteman's den where he "diagnosed" and "treated" people using clay, minerals and herbs. As he asked Mrs. Metcalf about her condition and complaint of a lump in her breast, Ray took pictures using a hidden camera.[6]

> One of the pictures taken by him appeared in *Life* Magazine showing plaintiff with his hand on the upper portion of Mrs. Metcalf's breast while he was looking at some gadgets and holding what appeared to be a wand in his right hand. Mrs. Metcalf had told plaintiff that she had a lump in her breast. Plaintiff concluded that she had eaten some rancid butter 11 years, 9 months, and 7 days prior to that time. Other persons were seated in the room during this time.

Dieteman's diagnosis and conversation with Mrs. Metcalf was broadcast to a car parked near his home where it was recorded. A few weeks later, Dieteman was arrested there on a charge of practicing medicine without a license, a felony. *Life* was there to cover it and its photographer took a number of photos inside Dieteman's house. The magazine carried the story and photographs in November under the headline, "Crackdown on Quackery." Dieteman pleaded nolo contendere[7] to a misdemeanor in a plea agreement. Dieteman then sued Time, Inc., for $300,000 on an invasion of privacy claim based on the use of the hidden camera and transmitter. A federal district court (the parties were diverse, so the case was removed to federal court) jury found for Dieteman and he was awarded $1,000 for injuries to his feelings and peace of mind. Time appealed on grounds that California had not recognized a right of privacy against using subterfuge to gain entrance and then photographing and transmitting what happened inside a home. Time also argued that its use of the camera and transmitter were

---

4 Quackery is a term that has fallen out of use, that refers to engaging in dishonest practices often associated with spurious claims about medical knowledge and the ability to heal. It is condemned because it gives false hope to patients and turns them away from actual medicine that could have cured them.

5 *Dietemann v. Time, Inc.*, 449 F.2d 245, 245 and 256 (9th Cir.1971).

6 *Dietemann v. Time, Inc.*, 449 F.2d 245, 245 and 256 (9th Cir.1971).

7 Nolo contendere Latin for "I will not contend," and is a plea in which a defendant accepts his conviction but does not admit guilt.

protected by the First Amendment. A three-judge panel of the Ninth Circuit Court of Appeals rejected Time's defense.

Circuit Judge Shirley Hufstedler, writing a scathing opinion for the panel, disposed of Time's arguments that Dieteman couldn't sue for intrusion because that cause of action didn't exist in California. Four other states and the District of Columbia had previously found that such a tort existed under common law, she wrote. Although the issue had not been settled in California,[8] "we have little difficulty in concluding that clandestine photography of the plaintiff in his den and the recordation and transmission of his conversation without his consent resulting in his emotional distress warrants recovery for invasion of privacy * * *" Judge Hufstedler was even more pointed about the use of new technology and its impact on the right to be let alone.[9]

> Plaintiff's den was a sphere from which he could reasonably expect to exclude eavesdropping newsmen. He invited two of defendant's employees to the den. One who invites another to his home or office takes a risk that the visitor may not be what he seems, and that the visitor may repeat all he hears and observes when he leaves. But he does not and should not be required to take the risk that what is heard and seen will be transmitted by photograph or recording, or in our modern world, in full living color and hi-fi to the public at large or to any segment of it that the visitor may select.

Time's lawyers argued that the First Amendment would protect the use of the devices claiming that they were "indispensable tools of investigative reporting" and that cases like *New York Times* meant that using the devices was immunized from torts like the one Dieteman sued over. Judge Hufstedler was not impressed, noting that "the ancient art of investigative reporting" was practiced long before those electronic devices came into being.

Judge Hufstedler was quick to distinguish between the publication in *New York Times* and the conduct of its employees with respect to the immunity claim Time was trying to make. Time argued that, because the story would be protected by the First Amendment, the conduct should also be shielded. Judge Hufstedler replied, in effect, that the First Amendment protections in *New York Times* were based on what appeared in its pages, not the process by which the advertisement came to be.[10]

> The First Amendment has never been construed to accord newsmen immunity from torts or crimes committed during the course of newsgathering. The First Amendment is not a license to trespass, to steal, or to intrude by electronic means into the

[8] *Dietemann v. Time, Inc.*, 449 F.2d 245, 248 (9th Cir.1971).

[9] Ibid. at 249.

[10] Ibid.

precincts of another's home or office. It does not become such a license simply because the person subjected to the intrusion is reasonably suspected of committing a crime.

Later intrusion cases would recite many of the points that Judge Hufstedler made in *Dietemann*.

JOHN DOES 1 THROUGH 30 AND UNKNOWN ILLINOIS STATE UNIVERSITY ATHLETES VS. FRANCO PRODUCTIONS, ET AL.

A federal district court awarded 46 male college athletes damages totaling $506 million in their intrusion suits against several Internet companies over the sale of videos[11] secretly taken in campus locker rooms, showers, and restrooms. The giant award made headlines,[12] even though no money was ever paid. That was because none of the defendants could be found to serve a complaint and summons.[13] The athletes' attorney Cindy Fluxgold said there was no expectation of collecting the full damages awarded, but that money was not the athletes' main priority.[14] "It was to try to close these people down and try to put Pandora back in its box. The only way the court can send a strong message to the bad guys is to say, 'We're going to hit you where it hurts; the pocketbook.' " If found, any of the defendants will be subject to the judgment and accompanying orders to surrender the footage from the hidden cameras, stop advertising and selling the videos.

The 46 athletes were a handful of the estimated 1,000 athletes who were secretly videotaped in the 1990s. Cameras were hidden in gym bags and pointed toward areas where the athletes would be nude or in a state of undress. Video footage identified Northwestern, Illinois, Eastern Illinois, Illinois State, Iowa State, Michigan State, Indiana, and Penn among the campuses targeted. The plaintiffs were identified in court records as John Doe Number 1, Number 2 and so on, so that they would not be further identified in a case over "gay porn" videos.

Elements of intrusion explains that people will have a lowered expectation of privacy in campus locker rooms or communal showers. That was the case with the athletes in this case. Whoever was in the

---

[11] The videos were marketed as gay porn tapes and had titles like, "Straight off the Mat" and "Voyeur Time."

[12] Associated Press, "Pay up: Judge orders $506 million payment to videotaped athletes," *USA Today*, Dec. 122, 2004. Jere Longman, "Videotaped Athletes Win Federal Lawsuit," *New York Times*, Dec. 5, 2002.

[13] Finding defendants or suspects in criminal or civil cases on the Internet can be difficult. It is estimated that more than 60 percent of porn available in the United States comes from offshore operations. U.S. jurisdiction ends at the national border. Careful Internet criminals also use multiple websites as cutouts to avoid having content traced to their own IP addresses. Defendants in the case included Franco Productions; Dan Franco; George Jachem and R.D. Couture, individually and d/b/a Rodco; Hidvidco; Logan Gaines Entertainment and Campfire Video.

[14] Jere Longman, "Videotaped Athletes Win Federal Lawsuit," *New York Times*, Dec. 5, 2002.

shower or dressing room could see them without violating their privacy rights. But even with that lowered expectation of privacy, the athletes still had a reasonable expectation of privacy that they would not be videotaped and have the imagery sold as porn tapes.

A 2016 juvenile proceeding points out the harms of invading the privacy of a person in a bathroom.[15] M.H., a 16-year-old and identified only by initials, used his smartphone to surreptitiously record another high school student in a school bathroom stall while the other student was either masturbating or pretending to do so. The video didn't show the student's face but did reveal his distinctive socks and shoes, which were visible in the gap between the stall wall and the floor.[16]

> M.H. uploaded the 10-second video to his Snapchat application with the caption, "I think this dude is jacking off" or some similar title.
>
> M.H. intended the video to be funny and to get a laugh. But tragically, about two weeks later, [the student in the video] took his own life, stating in a suicide note, "I can't handle school anymore and I have no friends."[17]

M.H. appealed the finding that he was a delinquent and his probation. The California appellate panel hearing his case affirmed, denying multiple points challenging the district court's finding, including M.H.'s First Amendment claim that his conduct was protected as his recording in the bathroom stall was "a matter of concern to his school community," "a matter of "public interest," and constituted "news gathering." He contends (the student) was engaged in an unlawful act.[18]

> Not surprisingly, the Attorney General contends exactly the opposite, stating the evidence does not show [the student] committed any unlawful act, and M.H.'s conduct was designed and intended not to report a crime or other newsworthy event, but rather to invade [the student's] privacy to ridicule, embarrass, and deprive him of dignity in front of his peers.

Because M.H. failed to raise his newsgathering defense in the district court and the appellate panel declined to explore it.

BARBER V. TIME, INC.

Barber v. Time[19] provides a classic example from a pre-digital age of place and circumstance that determine intrusion. In 1939, Mrs. Dorothy Barber was a patient in a Kansas City hospital, under treatment for a

---

15 *In Re M.H.* 1 Cal.App.5th 699 (2016).

16 Ibid. at 702.

17 Ibid. at footnotes. Matthew's suicide note also states, "P.S. I've been planning this for months now." The causal relationship, if any, between M.H.'s video and Matthew's suicide is not before us and we express no opinion on that issue.

18 Ibid. at 714.

19 *Barber v. Time, Inc.*, 348 Mo. 1199, 159 S.W.2d 291 (1942).

condition or disease which caused her to eat constantly but still lose weight.[20] Information about her condition reached reporters in the Kansas City area and reporters showed up. Mrs. Barber refused to be interviewed. Justice Laurance Mastick Hyde's opinion described the wire service reporters,[21]

> coming back with a photographer after being refused her consent to publish an article about her ailment and taking her picture surreptitiously while she was voicing her protests against any publicity in a conversation with one of them, by means of which he attracted her attention away from the photographer.

The photos and stories appeared in Kansas City newspapers. *Time Magazine* then purchased the picture from the wire service that reported the story originally.[22] *Time*'s headline read: "Starving Glutton;" a cutline under the picture said "Insatiable-Eater Barber; She Eats for Ten." Mrs. Barber sued, alleging a violation of her right to privacy. She won $3,000 in damages from Time, Inc.,[23] $1,500 in actual damages and $1,500 in punitive damages. After the judgment, *Time* appealed to the Missouri Supreme Court. Justice Hyde noted that Missouri had only in court cases adopted a privacy right and that right only in connection with the use of a likeness in advertising. But he added that 12 states and the District of Columbia recognized privacy and the right had been recognized in the Restatement of Torts and American Law Institute, which he quoted,[24] "The interest which one has to maintain his privacy and to live an individual life, which is the basis of the rule, is similar to the much more strongly protected interest to have one's person free from unwanted intentional physical contacts by others."

Justice Hyde then laid out the conduct to intrusion liability, writing that when defendants should have realized that their intrusion,[25] "would be offensive to persons of ordinary sensibilities." Mrs. Barber's hospital room and her treatment fell squarely under that standard.[26]

> Certainly, if there is any right of privacy at all, it should include the right to obtain medical treatment at home or in a hospital for an individual personal condition (at least if it is not contagious or dangerous to others) without personal publicity.

The Missouri Supreme Court affirmed damages in the amount of $1,500 for the invasion of privacy but reversed and remanded on the award of $1,500 for punitive damages. Because *Time* had bought the

---

[20] The private facts aspect of the case is discussed in Chap. 6.

[21] *Barber v. Time, Inc.*, 348 Mo. 1199, 1209 S.W.2d 291, 296 (1942).

[22] When *Time* purchased the rights to the photos and story, it also bought any liability that attached to them. That's why *Time* was the defendant.

[23] Ibid. at 1203, 293.

[24] Ibid. at 1204, 293.

[25] Ibid.

[26] Ibid. at 1208, 295.

story, it did not know that Mrs. Barber objected to a picture and the reporter, it hadn't published with express malice.

SHULMAN V. GROUP W: EMERGENCY MEDICAL TREATMENT

A case almost 50 years after *Barber* made clear that the privacy of medical treatment could include treatment outside a hospital, in this case—inside a rescue helicopter.[27] In 1990, Ruth Shulman and her son Wayne were in an automobile that ran off Interstate 10 in California's Riverside County, tumbling down an embankment and coming to rest on its top. Mrs. Shulman was pinned under the car; both she and her son had to be pried out of the wreckage by rescue workers using a "jaws of life" device.

A Mercy Air rescue helicopter was sent to the accident scene carrying a nurse, the helicopter pilot, and Joel Cooke, a video camera operator employed by Group W Productions. As California Supreme Court Justice Kathleen Mickle Werdegar described the accident scene and how it later was made into a part of a television program:[28]

> Cooke roamed the accident scene, videotaping the rescue. Nurse Carnahan wore a wireless microphone that picked up her conversation with both Ruth [Shulman] and the other rescue personnel. Cooke's tape was edited into a piece approximately nine minutes long, which, with the addition, of narrative voice-over, was broadcast on September 29, 1990, as a segment of "On Scene: Emergency Response."
>
> [* * *]
>
> During her extrication from the car, Ruth asks at least twice if she is dreaming. At one point, she asks [Nurse] Carnahan, who has told her she will be taken to a hospital in a helicopter, "are you teasing?" At another point, she says: "This is terrible. Am I dreaming?" * * * While being loaded into the helicopter on a stretcher, Ruth says: "I just want to die."

Ruth Shulman was left a paraplegic by the accident. When the program was broadcast, her son called her in the hospital, telling her that "Channel 4 is televising our accident now." Several hospital workers told her the same thing. Later, Mrs. Shulman understandably objected that she had been exploited, that the videotaped segment of her accident had been gathered and shown without her consent. She sued for invasion of privacy: private facts and intrusion.[29]

The trial court granted Group W summary judgment[30] "on the ground that the events depicted in the broadcast were newsworthy and

---

[27] *Shulman v. Group W Productions*, 18 Cal.4th 200, 74 Cal.Rptr.2d 843, 955 P.2d 469 (1998).

[28] Ibid. at 475–476.

[29] Ibid. at 477.

[30] Ibid. at 475.

the producers' activities were therefore protected under the First Amendment to the United States Constitution." A California Court of Appeals panel reversed, narrowing the issues and eliminating part of Mrs. Shulman's claim that dealt with the taping at the accident scene.[31]

> Appellants' accident occurred on a heavily traveled public highway. . . . The videotape itself shows a crowd of onlookers peering down at the rescue scene below. Appellants could be seen and heard by anyone at the accident site itself and could not have had a reasonable expectation of privacy at the scene in regard to what they did or said. Their statements or exclamations could be freely heard by all who passed by and were thus public, not private.

In so doing, the appellate court held that Ruth Shulman had no reasonable expectation of privacy at the accident scene, a heavily traveled Interstate highway where a crowd of onlookers stood on the embankments, watching the rescue efforts. However, once inside the rescue helicopter, the California Court of Appeal found, Mrs. Shulman had a reasonable expectation of privacy.

The California Supreme Court reversed the Court of Appeal on the matter of intrusion inside the rescue helicopter.[32] Justice Werdegar agreed that the rescue helicopter was a private place, but held that triable issues[33] existed over whether defendants[34]

> [* * *] tortiously intruded by listening to Ruth's confidential conversation with Nurse Carnahan at the rescue scene without Ruth's consent. Moreover, we hold that defendant had no constitutional privilege to intrude on plaintiff seclusion and private communications.

All told, the California Supreme Court was protective of television news coverage of accidents and disasters at an accident scene or on adjoining public property. Group W's video account of the rescue was newsworthy. *Shulman* also is notable for the declaration that, citing *Dieteman*,[35] "the First Amendment does not immunize the press from liability for torts or crimes committed in an effort to gather news." Justice Werdegar distinguishing the First Amendment protections for publication or news versus decisions that made clear that the process of newsgathering was not as protected. The cameraman's presence and videotaping of the accident scene and Ruth Shulman as she was pulled from the wreckage did not fit the evolving definition of intrusion because that part of her rescue was "in public" and of legitimate public interest.

---

[31] *Shulman v. Group W Productions, Inc.*, 59 Cal.Rptr.2d 434, 449 (2d Dist. 1996).

[32] *Shulman v. Group W Productions, Inc.*, 18 Cal.4th 200, 955 P.2d 469, 74 Cal.Rptr.2d 843 (1998).

[33] Triable issues mean that the question needed to be judged by a jury or judge in a trial.

[34] Ibid. at 210, 475, 848.

[35] *Shulman v. Group W Productions*, 18 Cal.4th 200, 236, 74 Cal.Rptr.2d 843, 867, 955 P.2d 469, 493 (1998).

But placing a microphone on the nurse to hear everything the accident victim said—and pursuing the victim all the way into the rescue helicopter—was seen as a fact question to be decided by a jury, whether it was highly offensive to a reasonable person and so amount to actionable intrusion. After the case was remanded but before that jury question could be considered, the *Shulman* case was settled out of court.

LE MISTRAL V. CBS

In the late 1970s, a television crew's intrusion, with lights on and camera rolling, onto private property caused huge legal costs for a CBS-owned station. The actual damages were $1,200, but the costs of trial and appeal added up. In addition, a jury award of $250,000 punitive damage award that was sent back to the trial court for retrial meant additional costs. *Le Mistral v. Columbia Broadcasting System*[36] underlines the lesson that, while it may make good video, to surprise people with cameras in their private businesses, it may not be worth it. In *Le Mistral*, reporter Lucille Rich and a camera crew were sent to restaurants that had been cited for violations of New York's health code. The reporting team was told to go in with cameras rolling (at this stage of news video, cameras needed bright lights to capture a good image). And so, the CBS crew caused quite a scene when they walked into the famous and fashionable Le Mistral restaurant in New York City. The reporter-camera team was doing a series on restaurants cited for health-code violations and the fact that well-known restaurants that catered to the city's elite were failing health inspections would draw viewers. The president of the Le Mistral corporation and the manager refused to be interviewed about the poor inspection and ordered the CBS crew to leave. The record is not clear whether the crew took one minute or 10. However long, the cameras kept rolling capturing the scene inside.[37] The restaurant corporation sued CBS invasion of privacy and trespass. The jury found that the restaurant suffered $1,200 in actual damages. They returned a $250,000 punitive award. CBS appealed.

As Time, Inc., had done in *Dieteman*, CBS argued that it was immunized from the privacy tort by the First Amendment. The appellate panel also invoked *Dieteman*.[38]

> In *Dietemann v. Time, Inc.*, [* * *], it was observed that "(t)he First Amendment has never been construed to accord newsmen

---

[36] *Le Mistral, Inc. v. Columbia Broadcasting System*, 61 A.D.2d 491, 402 N.Y.S.2d 815 (1st Dept.1978).

[37] Patrons waiting to be seated left the restaurant. Others who had finished eating, left without waiting for their checks. Still others hid their faces behind napkins or tablecloths or hid themselves beneath tables. (The reluctance of the plaintiff's clientele to be videotaped was never explained and need not be. Patronizing a restaurant does not carry with it an obligation to appear on television) Ibid. In footnotes. It was suggested that while some diners simply did not want to be videotaped in the restaurant, others did not want to be videotaped in the restaurant dining with people not their spouses.

[38] *Le Mistral, Inc. v. Columbia Broadcasting System*, 61 A.D.2d 491, 494, 402 N.Y.S.2d 815, 817 (1st Dept.1978).

> immunity from torts or crimes committed during the course of news-gathering. The First Amendment is not a license to trespass . . . ."

While it allowed the actual damages, the appellate judges returned the question of punitives. At trial, the judge did not allow CBS to put on a witness to testify why the crew entered the restaurant with the cameras rolling. That testimony would have been important to the jury considering punitive damages, the appellate panel held. Presiding Justice Francis Murphy dissented with regard to retrial on punitive damages.[39]

> It is clear from the record that, in dispatching reporters to plaintiff restaurant, defendant was not motivated by actual malice or such an intentional disregard of plaintiff's rights as would justify the imposition of punitive damages (87 C.J.S. Trespass s 112, p. 1068). The defendant was merely pursuing a newsworthy item in the overly aggressive but good faith manner that characterizes the operation of the news media today.

But, Justice Murphy warned, news organizations should consider that, now that the *Le Mistral* case was precedent future trespasses could well support punitive damages. The media had been warned.

In comparison, a Louisiana newspaper's defense, that its taking pictures on a public street did not invade privacy, led to a victory.[40] Mr. and Mrs. James Jaubert were away from home when a photographer for the *Crowley Post-Signal* took a picture of their home.[41] The caption read: "One of Crowley's stately homes, a bit weatherworn and unkempt, stands in the shadow of a spreading oak." Mrs. Jaubert's mother saw the photo and called the couple. The Jauberts cut short their trip and returned home. The caption did not identify the Jauberts as the owners or show the house number. Still, the Jauberts recognized their home as did friends and neighbors. The Jauberts filed an invasion of privacy suit alleging the publication of the photo caused them,[42] "mental suffering, embarrassment, and humiliation." The trial court jury found in their favor awarding the couple $500 each. The newspaper appealed. A three-judge intermediate appellate panel, with one dissent, held that the photograph was not newsworthy because of the uncomplimentary caption.[43] "The argument of the *Crowley Post* may have had some merit if only the photograph had been published without the remarks contained in the caption." Identification was proved because people approached the Jauberts after the publication to talk about the picture

---

39 Ibid. at 496, 818.

40 *Jaubert v. Crowley Post-Signal, Inc.*, 375 So.2d 1386 (La.1979).

41 Newspapers used to run "wild art," photos that were not coupled with stories. In the days before newspapers shrank because of declining readership and advertising income, newspapers would use wild art to fill up pages.

42 *Jaubert v. Crowley Post-Signal, Inc.*, 375 So.2d 1386, 1387 (La.1979).

43 *Jaubert v. Crowley Post Signal, Inc.*, 368 So.2d 475 (La. App. 3d Cir. 1979).

meaning that they knew both the house and the couple. Finally, the appellate court held,[44]

> The fact that the photograph as (sic) taken from a public street and could be viewed by any passersby is of no legal consequence. Plaintiffs enjoy the right to be free from unreasonable intrusion. Discovering during one's absence that his home has been given front page attention, without his permission, accompanied by a less than flattering caption, is an invasion of the right of privacy."

The Jaubert's had a right to be let alone without being subjected to the unwarranted and undesired publicity from the publication of the photo, the appellate court held.

But when the Louisiana Supreme Court took the case,[45] it reversed the lower courts saying,[46]

> It is clear from the record that the Jauberts' home was plainly visible from the public street, and that passersby were presented with a view of the property which was identical to that published by the defendant. Therefore, plaintiffs had no right to privacy, regarding the house and its condition [* * *]

Jaubert made clear an uncomfortable fact that what can be seen by the public, as on a street, is public and not private. A Florida appellate court held a similar view in a case that raised ethical questions as well as legal one.

In *Cape Publications v. Bridges*,[47] Hilda Bridges Pate sued for invasion of privacy for a photograph published by a Florida newspaper, *Cocoa Today*. She had been abducted by her estranged husband, who forced her at gunpoint to go with him to their former apartment. The husband forced her to undress in an effort to prevent her from trying to escape. Police surrounded the apartment building. During the standoff, the husband shot and killed himself. When police heard the gunshot, they stormed the apartment, and rushed a partially clad Ms. Pate to safety across a parking lot as she clutched a dish towel to cover her body. A photographer for *Cocoa Today* took pictures and the newspaper published them. Ms. Pate sued and won an intrusion suit, the jury awarding her $1 million in compensatory damages and $9 million in punitive damages.

A Florida appellate court overturned all damage awards, saying: "The published photograph is more a depiction of grief, fright, emotional tension and flight than it is an appeal to sensual appetites." In short, it

---

44 Ibid. at 478, 479.

45 *Jaubert v. Crowley Post-Signal, Inc.*, 375 So.2d 1386 (La. 1979).

46 Ibid. at 1391.

47 *Cape Publications, Inc. v. Bridges*, 423 So.2d 426 (Fla.App. 5th Dist.1982).

was a newsworthy story. Judge James Dauksch wrote,[48] "The photograph revealed little more than could be seen had * * * [Ms. Pate] been wearing a bikini, and somewhat less than some bathing suits seen on the beaches." The judge added that courts should be slow to interfere with publication of news in the public interest.

Journalists still should be sensitive to concerns of persons in public events, in a time of mass shootings. It is a balancing of the obligation to report the news and consideration for people on the worst day of their life. You can, legally, take the video or photograph. But being able to do something doesn't mean you should do it. Journalists should employ their ethics and find the "third door"[49] to do their jobs while not adding to the trauma.

People who are not journalists continue to have an impact on newsgathering and the news. Every person with a smartphone is a potential news photographer or videographer who can provide the truth of what happens in newsworthy events. The use of videotapes to show police activity and, sometimes, misconduct became nationally prominent in 1991 with the video of the Rodney King beating by Los Angeles police officers.[50] A Los Angeles plumber, George Holliday, grabbed his camcorder and stepped onto the balcony of his apartment and recorded four Los Angeles police officers beating King. The footage was shown on national news programs and the officers charged. A jury acquitted the officers,[51] sparking the LA riots

One early cellphone-documented shootings by a police officer led to a criminal conviction of the officer.[52] At 2 in the morning New Year's Day 2009, 22-year-old Oscar Grant III was on a BART train when a scuffle occurred. Police were called and BART officers[53] pulled Grant and several of his friends from the train at Fruitvale Station. Passengers and bystanders took video on cell phones and digital camera because of the aggressive way the officers behaved. BART police officer Johannes Mehserle arrived and was told to arrest Grant. After he forced Grant

---

[48] Ibid. In footnote 2, the judge quoted the Restatement (Second) of Torts, § 652D, Comment G, on the definition of news: Authorized publicity, customarily referred to as "news," includes publications concerning crimes, arrests, police raids, suicides, marriages, divorces, accidents, fires, catastrophes of nature, narcotics-related deaths, rare diseases, etc., and many other matters of genuine popular appeal.

[49] The "third door" is a teaching tool developed by author Bill Loving in his ethics classes. It addresses the tendency of journalists, both collegiate and professional, to employ binary thinking: I do it this way or it doesn't get done." The third door approach asks the media practitioner to consider an alternative way to accomplish a journalistic goal in an ethical manner. Is the only way to get an interview subject to reveal racist or sexist beliefs, to pretend to hold the same? Are some choices in newsgathering a matter of efficiency or ethics?

[50] Erik Ortiz, "George Holliday, Who Taped Rodney King Beating, Urges Others to Share Videos," *NBC News*, June 9, 2015.

[51] Two of the officers were convicted in federal court of violating King's constitutional rights.

[52] Demian Bulwa and Rachel Swan, "10 years since Oscar Grant's death: What happened at Fruitvale Station?" *San Francisco Chronicle*, Dec. 31, 2018.

[53] BART (Bay Area Rapid Transit) had its own police force because its trains passed through multiple cities, meaning none of the cities had jurisdiction on the whole rail line.

chest down and tried to handcuff his hands behind his back, Mehserle pulled his pistol, stood and shot Grant in the back. His defense was that he thought he had drawn his taser. BART surveillance and passenger cameras recorded the shooting. It made national news and the footage was played in Mehserle's trial. A Los Angeles jury found Mehserle guilty of involuntary manslaughter.

The killing of Walter Scott by police officer Michael Slager likely would have been treated as a justified police shooting based on "the officer's fear of imminent death or serious injury" if cellphone video had not been taken. Moments after the struggle, Officer Slager reported on his radio: "Shots fired and the subject is down. He took my Taser," according to police reports. A man walking to work noticed Officer Slager and Scott and began to record what happened.[54]

> The video begins in the vacant lot, apparently moments after Officer Slager fired his Taser. Wires, which carry the electrical current from the stun gun, appear to be extending from Mr. Scott's body as the two men tussle and Mr. Scott turns to run.
>
> Something—it is not clear whether it is the stun gun—is either tossed or knocked to the ground behind the two men, and Officer Slager draws his gun, the video shows. When the officer fires, Mr. Scott appears to be 15 to 20 feet away and fleeing. He falls after the last of eight shots.

Slager was fired, arrested and prosecuted for Scott's killing. A jury deadlocked in state court on a murder charge and Slager entered into a plea bargain under which he pled guilty to violating Scott's civil rights. He was sentenced to 20 years. Cellphone video of Eric Garner saying, "I can't breathe," as he was placed in a chokehold by a New York City police officer led to nationwide protests following his death.[55]

VIDEO RIGHTS IN THE PRESENCE OF POLICE

Some police have responded to the use of cellphone cameras with threats and arrests, in some cases relying on statutes forbidding the recording of conversations.[56] While it is legal to photograph while on public property and the use of smartphone camcorders is similarly protected, the manner of the recording can result in prosecution.

Boston police arrested several people after they used their cell camcorder feature to record police activity. Boston police cited a Massachusetts law banning audio recordings unless all of the people being recorded have agreed. The law was intended to protect people from surreptitious recordings of telephone conversations, but Boston police

---

[54] Michael S. Schmidt and Matt Apuzzo, "South Carolina Officer Is Charged With Murder of Walter Scott," *New York Times*, April 7, 2015.

[55] Niraj Chokshi, "New video purports to show aftermath of the chokehold that led to Eric Garner's death," *The Washington Post*, July 19, 2014.

[56] Daniel Rowinski, "Police fight cellphone recordings," *Boston.com*, Jan. 12, 2010.

began to use it to deter people from videotaping them in action.[57] "The police apparently do not want witnesses to see what they do in public," said Sarah Wunsch, a staff attorney with the American Civil Liberties Union of Massachusetts.

A Boston police representative said that police were enforcing the state's wiretapping law. Elaine Driscoll, the department representative then invoked the shopworn claim of interference with the police.[58] "If an individual is inappropriately interfering with an arrest that could cause harm to an officer or another individual, an officer's primary responsibility is to ensure the safety of the situation," she said.[59]

The cases in Massachusetts turned on whether the recording was done openly or surreptitiously. When the videotaping or other recordings have been obvious, defendants have had charges dismissed. But when the recording was hidden, the courts found defendants guilty of violating the state's wiretapping law.

It happens to journalists, too. Police arrested a *Washington Post* reporter covering the protests over the death of Michael Brown in Ferguson, Mo.[60] Wesley Lowery and other reporters were at work in a McDonald's that was near a protest staging area. Police ordered the reporters to leave. Lowery started taking video on his phone. One officer objected. On his way out, Lowery was "slammed into a soda dispenser."[61] He was restrained and taken to jail. Martin D. Baron, executive editor of *The Washington Post,* said the police illegally ordered him to stop filming.[62] "That behavior was wholly unwarranted and an assault on the freedom of the press to cover the news," Baron said. "The physical risk to Wesley himself is obvious and outrageous." The rights of ordinary people to take videos of law enforcement officers in the performance of their duties has created tension and a number of arrests and civil rights lawsuits. To be clear, as in the *Jaubert* and *Cape Publications,* people have a right to take pictures and video when they are in public spaces. But some police officers have taken exception to the practice and a number of people recording arrests, stops and patrol have been arrested with some charged with crimes.

The right to record is based on two considerations, usually found in state law: 1) Whether the video or audio recording is open, and, 2) whether the state has a law against secret audio recording as in the

57 Ibid.

58 Ibid.

59 Police have arrested bystanders, camera in hand or not, for interfering with police in the performance of their duties. In court, it is the word of the officer versus the claim of the bystander with most juries accepting the word of the officer. The use of cellphone and smartphone cameras has resulted in a decline in the number of these arrests. Video and audio footage can show who was telling the truth.

60 Mark Berman, "Washington Post reporter arrested in Ferguson," *Washington Post,* Aug. 13, 2014.

61 Ibid.

62 Ibid.

Boston cases. But a trend that has begun to emerge appears to favor the public's right to take video and audio of police as they perform their duties. In 2011, the First Circuit Court of Appeals held in *Glik v. Cunniffe*[63] that there was a First Amendment right to film police. Simon Glik sued Boston police officers after they arrested him while he filmed an arrest taking place on the Boston Common.

Simon Glik caught sight of three police officers arresting a young man. Glik heard another bystander say something to the effect of, "You are hurting him, stop." Concerned that the officers were employing excessive force to effect the arrest, Glik stopped roughly ten feet away and began recording video footage of the arrest on his cell phone.

After placing the suspect in handcuffs, one of the officers turned to Glik and said, "I think you have taken enough pictures." Glik replied, "I am recording this. I saw you punch him."

Another officer asked if Glik's phone recorded audio. Glik replied that it did, and the officer arrested him for violating the state wiretapping law and for disturbing the peace. A Boston Municipal Court quickly dismissed the charges.[64]

The municipal court judge noted that the fact that the "officers were unhappy they were being recorded during an arrest . . . does not make a lawful exercise of a First Amendment right a crime." Glik then sued in U.S. District Court for violation of his First Amendment rights. He won and a panel of the First Circuit affirmed saying that the right to gather information about the conduct of public officials was an important First Amendment issue. The First Circuit denied the officers' claims of qualified immunity.

The First Circuit was the first of the federal circuit courts of appeal to find a First Amendment right to film police. The rest of the federal circuits have either directly acknowledged such a right or noted longstanding protections of First Amendment right in the context of a police stop. In all circuits, First Amendment rights are tempered where filming or speaking interferes with the performance of police duties. It should be noted that standing some distance away and filming has not been found to interfere.

The New York City Police Department issued a memo to its officers in August 2014[65] reminding them that the public has a right to take video of them. The memo makes clear that officers can take action when the persons using cameras interfere with their operations. But, absent that interference, the public has a constitutional right to video. "Members of the public are legally allowed to record police interactions," the memo states. "Intentional interference such as blocking or obstructing cameras

[63] *Gericke v. Begin*, 753 F.3d 1 (1st Cir. 2014).

[64] Ibid. at 80.

[65] Caitlin Nolan and Thomas Tracy, "Cops have been put on notice: Let the cameras roll," *New York Daily News*, Aug. 10, 2014.

or ordering the person to cease constitutes censorship and also violates the First Amendment."

WHEN INTRUSION BECOMES STALKING

Photographers known as "*paparazzi*"—Italian slang for a small, annoying insects, were a topic of debate in journalism ethics classes. These photographers earned a living by taking photographs of celebrities to sell to photo agencies that would, in turn, sell to magazines and tabloids like the *National Enquirer* and *Star* that catered to gossip about the famous, mostly actors, singers and sports stars. Photographs of celebrities doing mundane, everyday things "just like me" would bring in good money in the heyday of the paparazzo (single for paparazzi). Photos of celebrities doing things they ought not to, like an actor kissing someone who was not her partner, would command more money. Paparazzi would gather outside restaurants, hotels and any other place that a celebrity had gone to. They would start photographing as soon as the person stepped out and continued until their target drove away or, in some cases, managed to evade pursuit by paparazzi in cars.[66] Often times, the paparazzi would shout provocative things at the celebrities in the hopes of getting a reaction that could be photographed and sold for more money.

There are, in fact, ample laws and court precedents against stalking and against the forms of invasion of privacy listed above. Before the death of Princess Diana, the American poster boy for paparazzi behaving badly was Ron Galella. He proudly called himself a paparazzo, and made a career taking photos of America's own version of royalty, Jacqueline Kennedy Onassis, and her children. Mrs. Onassis, widow of President John F. Kennedy and also of Greek shipping magnate Aristotle (Ari) Onassis, was hounded so enthusiastically by Galella that U.S. Circuit Judge Irving Ben Cooper used him as a defining example of paparazzi. The judge declared that paparazzi[67] "make themselves as visible to the public and obnoxious to their photographic subjects as possible to aid in the advertisement and wide sale of their works."

Galella's fixation on photographing Mrs. Onassis and her children ultimately led to issuance of an injunction against the photographer. A 1975 injunction forbade Galella from approaching within 25 feet of Mrs. Onassis or within 30 feet of her children. A major fear was that Galella's intrusiveness might endanger the Kennedy children, John and Caroline, whom he stalked photographically at their private schools in addition to

---

[66] When Princess Diana and her lover, Dodi Fayed, died in a 1997 high-speed auto crash in Paris, paparazzi were widely blamed for her death: James Fallows, "Are Journalists People?" *U.S. News & World Report*, Sept. 15, 1997; Marianne MacDonald, "Hunted down by paparazzi, Diana lived a nightmare," *London Observer Service for Scripps Howard News Service*, published in *The Knoxville News-Sentinel*, Sept. 8, 1997, p. A1 (Never mind that the death car's driver was intoxicated and also had the anti-depressant Prozac in his system when he drove at high speeds to get away from pursuing paparazzi.)

[67] *Galella v. Onassis*, 533 F.Supp. 1076, 1106 (S.D.N.Y.1982).

lurking outside the New York high-rise where Mrs. Onassis and her children lived, following them to the theater, and so forth.

Temptation, however, proved too great for Ron Galella. He disobeyed the injunction on four different occasions in 1981, again getting too close and becoming too obnoxious in his photographic shadowing of Mrs. Onassis and her children. Judge Cooper found Galella to be in contempt of the court's 1975 order, subjecting the persistent paparazzo to liability for a heavy fine and/or imprisonment.[68]

"STALKING" BY MEDIA: WOLFSON V. LEWIS

What seemed to be egregious misconduct—trespass plus stalking of a family—led to issuance of a temporary injunction against broadcast journalists in *Wolfson v. Lewis*.[69] Paul Lewis and Steve Wilson, award-winning journalists for the syndicated television news show *Inside Edition* were investigating Leonard Abramson, chairman and owner of the U.S. Healthcare HMO. The story's focus was on the high salaries being paid to the executives of U.S. Healthcare including some who happened to be members of Abramson's family. This occurred in the mid 1990s, when complaints about HMO profits and denial of claims were being debated.[70] The *Wall Street Journal* reported in 1994 that the president of U.S. Healthcare, Abramson, made $21.2 million ($36.5 million today) in one a year as patient satisfaction scores in for-profit HMOs was falling.

Their investigation led them to seek an interview with U.S. Healthcare Board Chairman and principal executive Leonard Abramson. Abramson's son-in-law Richard Wolfson directed pharmacy and dental operations for U.S. Healthcare. His wife, Nancy Abramson Wolfson, directed the firm's health education department. Marcy Shoemaker, Nancy Wolfson's sister, was president of a video post-production company in which U.S. Healthcare owned the majority of stock.

Wilson traveled to Pennsylvania where the Abramson/Wolfson families lived. Before he went, he sent a faxed letter requesting an on-camera interview to Abramson. Wilson sent two more faxed letters to Abramson. Abramson did not reply to any of the letters. Once in Pennsylvania, Wilson called to request an interview. He was referred to U.S. Healthcare's PR firm.[71]

---

[68] *Galella v. Onassis*, 533 F.Supp. 1076, 1108 (S.D.N.Y.1982).

[69] *Wolfson v. Lewis*, 924 F.Supp. 1413 (E.D.Pa.1996).

[70] Philip M. Nudelman & Linda M. Andrews, "The "Value Added" of Not-for Profit Health Plans," 334 *New Eng. J. Med.* 1057, 1058 (1996) (criticizing for-profit HMOs for spending 20–30% on administration, marketing and dividends, leaving much less to be spent on health care needs of community); Ron Winslow, *HMO Juggernaut: U.S. Health-care Cuts Costs, Grows Rapidly and Irks Some Doctors*, *WALL ST. J.*, Sept. 6, 1994, at Al (noting that president of U.S. Healthcare made $21.2 million while doctors were being squeezed).

[71] *Wolfson v. Lewis*, 924 F.Supp. 1413, 1423 (E.D.Pa.1996).

> Public relations strongly indicated on February 12, 1996 and informed Mr. Wilson definitively on February 13, 1996 that neither Mr. Abramson nor any other executive at U.S. Healthcare would be interested in providing an on-camera interview to *Inside Edition.*

Abramson and his wife went to their Florida home about this time and Lewis and Wilson focused on Richard Wolfson and his wife. They did not request on-camera interviews with either. After concluding that Abramson nor any other U.S. Healthcare officials would take part in an on-camera interview, Lewis and Wilson began preparations for an ambush interview.[72] They identified Richard Wolfson's car in the U.S. Healthcare parking lot. They obtained the Wolfsons' home address. Wilson parked a rented Jeep in front of a neighboring house and Lewis waited in a van with a camera team in the company's parking lot. When Wilson saw Wolfson leave for work, he notified Lewis. Wilson waited and followed the next car to leave the Wolfson home. The car, driven by one of the family's security guards, happened to be carrying Nancy Wolfson and the Wolfson's 3-year-old daughter to school. Wilson followed and passed the car, looking over to see who the passenger was. That frightened the guard and Mrs. Wolfson. The Jeep reappeared when Mrs. Wolfson drove herself to work. A security guard who followed Mrs. Wolfson to work testified that he believed Mrs. Wolfson's life was in danger. Both the Wolfsons testified about their fears for their daughter. Using the license plate from the Jeep, the Wolfsons learned that it had been rented by Lewis. They had their PR firm contact *Inside Edition* and relayed the Wolfsons' fears for their child insisting that the journalists stop. The *Inside Edition* producer contacted Lewis and Wilson. Wilson called Mrs. Wolfson, identified himself as an *Inside Edition* reporter and tried to assure her that he intended no harm to her children.[73] "Mrs. Wolfson testified that she thought it was a "threatening phone call" because he referred to her two children."

Later that day, Wolfson spotted the *Inside Edition* van parked across the street from his home. He testified he had his children kept inside for fear for their safety. A security guard confronted the *Inside Edition* team when they drove onto the entrance of their driveway. *Inside Edition* got another call from the PR firm asking for the reporters to stop. Mrs. Wolfson was pregnant, *Inside Edition* was told. In both calls, *Inside Edition* asked that Mr. Abramson either provide a statement or be interviewed.

The Wolfsons fled to Florida and the Abramson's home which backs up to the Intracoastal Waterway. The waterway, a public water highway,

---

[72] As described by Mr. Wilson, Mr. Lewis and by their expert witness Robert Greene, a two-time Pulitzer Prize-winning journalist, an "ambush interview" refers to a confrontational, surprise interview with an unwilling subject, generally a person who has previously refused to be interviewed. The TV journalist approaches the subject surreptitiously with cameras and sound rolling and asks a question calculated to embarrass the subject. Ibid. at 1424.

[73] Ibid. at 1426.

runs the length of the state of Florida. The *Inside Edition* crew rented a boat and anchored just outside a chain that separates the public waterway from the Abramson home. A security guard told the people in the house about the boat, microphones and camera equipment. Mrs. Wolfson testified about her reaction.[74]

> I basically was outraged; that we tried to get away, we tried to live a normal life, we tried to just maintain some kind of, again, normalcy for our kids and here we take them away and they are following us. We just couldn't hide, we couldn't get away from anything, and it was horrible because it was a beautiful day and kids want to go outside and play. We couldn't take them out to the swimming pool or let them play in the playground because that was all outside in the back of the house where these people were.

The security guards warned the family to stay away from windows in the event of "gunplay." During their time near the Abramson home, the *Inside Edition* crew had three encounters with police and several with private security personnel. The Wolfsons returned to Pennsylvania where they sought an injunction against the reporters to keep them from keeping them under surveillance and harassing them.

U.S. District Judge Raymond Broderick issued the injunction writing that he believed that:[75]

> A reasonable jury could well find that Mr. Wilson and Mr. Lewis intentionally intruded, in a manner that would be highly offensive to a reasonable person, upon the solitude and seclusion of the Wolfsons by engaging in a course of conduct apparently designed to hound, harass, intimidate and frighten them. The intrusions committed by Mr. Wilson and Mr. Lewis consisted of a pattern of conduct involving physical and sensory invasions into Mr. and Mrs. Wolfson's privacy. Mr. Wilson's and Mr. Lewis's actions deprived the Wolfsons of the right to live their life quietly and peacefully.

Judge Broderick noted that Abramson testified that before *Inside Edition* arrived in Pennsylvania, he had received threats. No evidence regarding the threats was introduced in the course of the proceedings. Judge Broderick granted the injunction prohibiting Wilson and Lewis from engaging in conduct:[76]

> [* * *] which invades the privacy of Richard Wolfson, Nancy Wolfson and their children, including but not limited to actions of: harassing, hounding, following, intruding, frightening,

[74] Ibid. at 1429.

[75] Ibid. at 1432.

[76] Ibid. at 1435.

terrorizing or ambushing Plaintiffs Richard and Nancy Wolfson or their children;

Judge Broderick noted that the reporters would not be harmed by the injunction and could still report on the high salaries that Abramson and the Wolfson's were paid. They just could not report it in a way that intruded on the Wolfson family. Remarkably, the *Wolfson* case was settled out of court just before appellate arguments began, reportedly with no payments involved.[77] The injunction against *Inside Edition* journalists was ended, the Wolfsons' lawsuit was withdrawn, and the journalists promised not to follow the Wolfsons or go to their homes.

Wolfson is significant in that the reporters were following norms in reporting, albeit with an excess of zeal. None of the reporting tactics were, in and of themselves, illegal.

41. INTRUSION: NONCONSENSUAL ENTRY, REFUSAL TO LEAVE AND EXPECTATIONS OF PRIVACY

Photographers and journalists enter private property at their legal peril if they do not have appropriate permission.

Intrusion is a tort, a civil wrong. It is based on a reasonable expectation of privacy. Trespass is a civil wrong. Trespass also is a criminal offense. It is based on rights of ownership and dates back to the earliest days of the common law. If a journalist enters the property of a corporation, there is no intrusion. A person has to sue for an invasion of her privacy. But the journalist who has entered a corporation's property could be both arrested and sued for trespass.

The elements can vary in detail, but the general definition of criminal trespass is:

1) Knowingly or intentionally entering or remaining on
2) someone else's property
3) without authorization.

During deer hunting season, hunters sometimes walk through a forest onto land belonging to someone who does not want deer hunted on his property. When charged or sued for trespass, the hunter will say, truthfully, "I didn't know I walked onto the other person's land. There was no sign. How was I to know?" And so, the hunter may think he has proven he did not commit knowing or intentional trespass. But then, the judge says, "For the definition of trespass, the "knowingly entering" requirement refers to the actor's knowledge of the literal act of entering property. It does not matter whether the actor actually knows the property belongs to someone else."

---

[77] "HEALTH: HMO Execs Drop Suit Against TV Show," *Los Angeles Times*, Jan. 29, 1997.

Civil trespass is defined as:

Intrusion upon the property of another without permission.

A property owner can file a civil lawsuit against someone who trespasses in order to recover actual damages or receive compensatory relief for injury suffered as a direct result of a trespass. Annoyance or discomfort are considered injury in trespass. It is no defense that the reporter is performing a "public service" by gathering news to be delivered to an audience about an important matter. As explained by a California appellate court more than 20 years ago, a trespass is a trespass.[78]

> The essence of the cause of action for trespass is an unauthorized entry onto the land of another. Such invasions are characterized as intentional torts, regardless of the actor's motivation. Further, defendant is liable for an intentional entry although he has acted in good faith, under the mistaken belief, however reasonable, that he is committing no wrong.

DEFENSES TO TRESPASS

Apart from proving that the property did not belong to the plaintiff, the defense to civil trespass is consent.

Consent can be:

1) Express, or,

2) Implied.

Express consent is easy. The person who owns the property says, "Come on in." Express consent also can be nonverbal as when the property owner beckons or waves you in.

Implied consent has multiple forms.

Implied consent arising from:

1) a relationship. When a student returns home from college, the family relationship means she does not have to ask permission to enter the family home. The same relationship rule applies to roommates.

2) a business relationship or invitation. When you go to a McDonald's, you don't have to ask permission to go in to buy a Happy Meal. You are a customer and so you have an implied consent to enter. Businesses open to the public create an implied consent.

Consent can be conditional. McDonald's has a sign in its stores, "No shoes, no shirt, no service." That means that customers must meet those conditions or there is no consent. Many businesses prompted by the *Food Lion* case (discussed later in this chapter) have signs that do not allow entry if a person has a camera. Cases like *Franco* (discussed earlier in

[78] *Miller v. NBC*, 187 Cal.App.3d 1463, 232 Cal.Rptr. 668 (1986).

this chapter) have prompted "no cell or smartphones allowed in locker room or showers" signs.

Both express and implied consent can be withdrawn. "Get out" destroys consent and the person who loses consent must leave the property in a reasonable amount of time. Reasonableness is governed by circumstances and judged by the rule of reason.

Consent can be denied through the use of "no trespassing" signs.

CONSENT IS CONSENT: BAUGH V. CBS

Another ethics and law issue comes from a 1993 case. *Baugh v. CBS*[79] hung up another caution flag for broadcasters. CBS's *Street Stories* public affairs magazine program broadcast an episode titled "Stand By Me." The broadcast covered the Alameda County [CA] Mobile Crisis Intervention Team. The story followed Elaine Lopes, a domestic violence survivor and supervising victim witness consultant in helping victims through crises. Reporter Bob McKeown and a CBS camera crew followed Ms. Lopes as she counseled victims of domestic violence. At one point in the story, a police dispatch call is heard,[80] "husband beat up wife. Broke windows in the house. And she's waiting there." McKeown does a voice over as video shows Ms. Lopes and others in Yolanda Baugh's house.[81]

> "Minutes after the police arrive, Elaine Lopes and her team are on the scene. They're professional victims' advocates, trained to pick up the pieces of lives touched—sometimes shattered—by crime.
>
> Unidentified Woman # 1:1
>
> He started beating on me and kicking on me and hitting me in the face. And then he kept bullying at me, talking about, 'You ain't going to do nothing.' You know, just bullying me like, you know, he knew I was scared of him.

Mrs. Baugh is seen in the video, at one point demonstrating how her husband attacked her. Mrs. Baugh testified that the first time she saw Ms. Lopes team and camera crew, she ordered them out of her house because she didn't know who they were. But, she said, she allowed them because a police officer told her that it was a team from the DA's office and that they were there to help. Ms. Lopes introduced herself and her team from the crisis intervention team. The camera crew was not introduced, she testified.[82]

> I asked the group what the camera was for. One of the crew members said they were doing a segment on Elaine for the District Attorney's office.

[79] *Baugh v. CBS, Inc.*, 828 F.Supp. 745 (N.D.Calif 1993).

[80] Ibid. at 750.

[81] Ibid. at 751.

[82] Ibid. at 751–752.

> The crew member did not say they were doing this for CBS, KPIX, or the *Street Stories* program. Nor did they mention that the film would be used commercially in any way.
>
> I said I had no objections to them doing some filming of Elaine for the DA's office, as long as I was not going to be on anyone's television. The crew member said, "Okay." If they had not agreed to my condition, I would not have permitted them to stay.

Months later, Mrs. Baugh heard from Ms. Lopes about the upcoming segment of the news show. She objected and said she had not agreed to let the crew in as long as she was not going to be on television. More than two weeks before CBS aired the episode of *Street Stories* containing footage of Mrs. Baugh, she talked to a producer at CBS who told her that he might be able to obscure her face on the screen. Mrs. Baugh told him that was not sufficient, but her plea got nowhere. Mrs. Baugh said:[83] "* * * about a week later, I was contacted on the phone by a man who identified himself as a CBS lawyer in New York. In a rude, uncaring and arrogant manner, he told me that I had no case against CBS and there is nothing I could do."

Mrs. Baugh sued, alleging appropriation of likeness, intrusion on seclusion, trespass, unfair competition, disclosure of private facts, fraud and both negligent and intentional infliction of emotional distress. U.S. District Judge Fern Smith dismissed all but the disclosure of private facts, fraud and intentional infliction of emotional distress.

She failed in her allegation of trespass or intrusion because she consented to the presence of the camera crew, Judge Smith wrote.[84]

> No California cases indicate that the consent must be knowing or meaningful and the Court does not find any reason to add that requirement to the tort. In a case where consent was fraudulently induced, but consent was nonetheless given, plaintiff has no claim for trespass. Of course, a plaintiff in this predicament may still have a remedy based on fraud or intentional misrepresentation.

A month after making her ruling, Judge Smith dismissed the remaining counts because CBS and Mr. and Mrs. Baugh had reached a settlement over her remaining three causes of action. Some readers may wonder why *Dieteman* was not applied. In both cases, the journalists did not identify themselves and were granted consent to enter. The key difference is that the equipment was hidden in *Dieteman* while in *Baugh*, it was clearly seen.

---

[83] Ibid. at 752.

[84] Ibid. at 757.

OFFICIALS CAN'T CONSENT FOR THE HOMEOWNER: AYENI V. CBS

The ability to give consent has its limits. The property owner or homeowner has the power to consent. Government agents do not. A 1994 U.S. district court decision in *Ayeni v. CBS*[85] held that federal agents' grant of permission for TV journalists to attend a search of a home was insufficient for the journalists to avoid liability. Tawa Ayeni, wife of a man suspected of involvement in a credit card fraud ring, was home with her son Kayode, a minor, when U.S. Treasury Department agents carried out a search warrant. Six federal agents—four from the Secret Service and two postal inspectors—went to the Ayeni's residence about 6 p.m. Mrs. Ayeni, clad in her dressing gown, opened her door only slightly, but the agents pushed their way into her home.

About 8:15 p.m., Treasury Agent James Mottola entered the Ayeni apartment with a CBS news crew from *Street Stories*. Mrs. Ayeni later complained in her intrusion suit that the crew members were not identified as CBS employees, saying that she thought the CBS camera crew and producer Meade Jorgensen were[86] " 'part of the team executing the warrant.' "

When Mrs. Ayeni filed her intrusion suit, CBS and *Street Stories* producer Jorgensen both claimed a qualified immunity because[87] "they were acting with the permission of government agents * * * [and] should be entitled to the qualified immunity enjoyed by government officials." This audacious claim was slapped down by U.S. District Judge Jack Bernard Weinstein. Judge Weinstein held that the CBS employees had been invited into the residence by a U.S. agent "so they could titillate and entertain others was beyond the scope of what was lawfully authorized by the warrant." Concluding that the Ayeni lawsuit against CBS should not be dismissed, Judge Weinstein declared:[88]

> CBS had no greater right than that of a thief to be in the home, to take pictures, and to remove the photographic record. * * * The images, though created by the camera, are a part of the household; they cannot be removed without permission or official right. The television tape was seizure of information for non-government purposes.

In addition, a panel of the 2nd Circuit Court of Appeals held that Treasury Agent Mottola violated the Fourth Amendment protections against unreasonable search and seizure by allowing the CBS crew into the Ayeni home.[89] Mottola was held personally liable for damages for

---

[85] *Ayeni v. CBS Inc.*, 848 F.Supp. 362 (E.D.N.Y.1994).

[86] Ibid. at 364.

[87] Ibid. at 367.

[88] Ibid. at 368.

[89] *Ayeni v. Mottola*, 35 F.3d 680 (2d Cir.1994).

permitting the videotaping intrusion. See *Ayeni v. Mottola*, 35 F.3d 680 (2d Cir.1994).

In a similar case with slightly different results, police officers who allowed a TV crew to accompany them as they searched a home were not held liable for invasion of privacy, being immune from suit under 42 USC § 1983. But, the TV crew members the police allowed to enter the home, however, could be held liable for intrusion because their action was not state action. *Parker v. Boyer*, 93 F.3d 445 (8th Cir.1996). See also *Anderson v. WROC-TV*, 109 Misc.2d 904, 441 N.Y.S.2d 220 (1981), where a humane society investigator invited TV station personnel into a private residence as he served a warrant. Employees of the TV station ignored a tenant's request to leave the residence, taking some footage and later broadcasting it. The station was held liable for intrusion.

WILSON V. LAYNE

In search of both bad guys and good publicity, the U.S. Marshals Service in 1992 began "Operation Gunsmoke," a nationwide program of working with state and local police to catch fugitives. "Gunsmoke" led to more than 3,000 arrests across 40 metropolitan areas.

Dominic Wilson was among those sought. He had violated probation "on previous felony charges of robbery, theft, and assault with intent to rob." Marshals said he was likely to be armed and to resist arrest violently. Federal records listed Wilson's street address in Rockville, Maryland, but this was actually the home of his parents.

On the morning of April 16, 1992, a Gunsmoke team of deputy U.S. marshals and Montgomery County police officers set out to serve three arrest warrants on Wilson. The warrants did not mention reporters or photographers. The U.S. Marshals, however, had their own ride-along policy of taking journalists with them to inform the public and to gain good press. A reporter and a photographer from the *Washington Post* accompanied the team at the invitation of U.S. Marshals.

About 6:45 a.m., accompanied by the journalists, the Gunsmoke team entered the residence of Dominic Wilson's parents, Charles and Geraldine Wilson. Hearing the commotion, Charles Wilson ran into the living room clad only in his underwear, angrily and profanely asking the intruders to explain what they were doing. Evidently thinking they had apprehended an angry and dangerous fugitive, the officers threw Charles Wilson to the floor. His wife also ran into the living room, dressed only in her nightgown, in time to see her husband being restrained by armed officers.

While the officers swept through the house, however, the *Washington Post* photographer took many pictures, and the reporter evidently was in the house during the raid. Once the Gunsmoke officers found that Dominic Wilson was not there, they left the Wilson house. The newspaper never published the photographs. The Wilsons sued the marshals but not the *Washington Post*.[90] They alleged that bringing the media to their home violated their Fourth Amendment rights against unreasonable search and seizure. Chief Justice Rehnquist's opinion differentiated between the press and law enforcement personnel executing a search warrant.[91]

> Certainly, the presence of reporters inside the home was not related to the objectives of the authorized intrusion. Respondents concede that the reporters did not engage in the execution of the warrant, and did not assist the police in their task. The reporters therefore were not present for any reason related to the justification for police entry into the home—the apprehension of Dominic Wilson.

Allowing police to bring reporters in violated basic principles regarding the sanctity of the home going back hundreds of years, Chief Justice Rehnquist wrote. "In 1604, an English court made the now-famous observation that 'the house of everyone is to him as his castle and fortress, as well for his defence against injury and violence, as for his repose.' *Semayne's Case*, 5 Co. Rep. 91a, 91b, 77 *610 Eng. Rep. 194, 195 (K.B.)." The marshals argued that the presence of reporters helped raise public understanding of the efforts that government was making to fight crime. Having the press on the scene would also help ensure the accuracy of the reporting. The presence of reporters would also minimize police abuses, protect suspects and even help protect police. Chief Justice Rehnquist was not moved.[92]

> It may well be that media ride-alongs further the law enforcement objectives of the police in a general sense, but that is not the same as furthering the purposes of the search. Were such generalized "law enforcement objectives" themselves sufficient to trump the Fourth Amendment, the protections guaranteed by that Amendment's text would be significantly watered down.

Chief Justice Rehnquist held that it violates Fourth Amendment rights when police bring members of the media or others when they execute a warrant. The marshals were protected, though, by the fact that the law was not settled before *Wilson*. But the Supreme Court, having spoken, law enforcement was now and thereafter on notice that they could face suits. Chief Justice Rehnquist also warned journalists.[93]

> This, however, should make it clear to journalists that if they don't have legal permission to accompany officers on raids such as "Operation Gunsmoke," they could face liability if they enter

[90] *Wilson v. Layne*, 526 U.S. 603, 119 S.Ct. 1692 (1999).

[91] Ibid. at 611, 1699.

[92] Ibid. at 611, 1698.

[93] Ibid. at 1701, citing 141 F.3d at 118–119; *Ayeni v. Mottola*, 35 F.3d 680 (2d Cir. 1994), cert. denied 514 U.S. 1062, 115 S.Ct. 1689; *Parker v. Boyer*, 93 F.3d 445 (8th Cir. 1996), cert. denied 519 U.S. 1148, 117 S.Ct. 1081 * * *; *Berger v. Hanlon*, 129 F.3d 505 (9th Cir.1997).

> private property during a police action without permission from the tenants or landowners.

In combined oral arguments in *Wilson v. Layne* and *Hanlon v. Berger*, Supreme Court Justices were scathingly critical of law enforcement officials who allow reporters and photographers to accompany them on searches of residences. Justice David H. Souter, for example, asked:[94] " 'Why do you have to take photographers into someone's house? You can have a news conference when it is over.' " Further, Justice Souter disdainfully characterized an argument that news media presence at police searches serves the public interest by recording police activities as " 'fluff.' "

HANLON V. BERGER: MEDIA AS STATE ACTORS

The same day that the Supreme Court announced its decision in *Wilson*, the justices issued a *per curiam* (unsigned) opinion in *Hanlon v. Berger*.[95] U.S. Fish and Wildlife Service agents conducted a daylong search of Paul and Erma Berger's Montana ranch looking for evidence of "taking of wildlife in violation of Federal laws" (killing eagles). The agents allowed CNN reporters and camera operators to accompany them. The Bergers sued both the federal agents and CNN, alleging a Fourth Amendment violation. Because the law was not settled at the time of the search, the Court held that the federal agents were entitled to qualified immunity.

The case began in U.S. District Court as the Bergers sued the federal agents and CNN. The U.S. District Court dismissed his claims against both writing that the law was not settled at the time of the search and because CNN was not a government actor.

A Ninth Circuit panel hearing the appeal, reversed the trial court. The ultimate decision was rendered regarding the Fish and Wildlife agents in the Supreme Court. The question of CNN's liability was not. Circuit Court Judge Mary Schroeder's opinion for the Ninth Circuit three-judge panel reversed the lower court on CNN's liability. CNN was deeply involved in the search, Judge Schroeder wrote. CNN had heard about the Fish and Wildlife Service receiving a tip about the Bergers. The network contacted the federal agents to try to work out a television deal. About two weeks before the search was carried out, CNN and the federal agents had entered into a written agreement.[96]

> This confirms our agreement that the United States Attorney's Office for the District of Montana agrees to allow CNN to accompany USFWS Agents as they attempt to execute a criminal search warrant near Jordan, Montana, some time

[94] Linda Greenhouse, "Justices Question Presence of News Crews in Police Searches," *New York Times*, March 25, 1999.

[95] *Hanlon v. Berger*, 526 U.S. 808, 119 S.Ct. 1706 (1999).

[96] *Berger v. Hanlon*, 129 F.3d 505, 508 (9th Cir.1997).

> during the week of March 22, 1993. Except as provided below, CNN shall have complete editorial control over any footage it shoots; it shall not be obliged to use the footage; and does not waive any rights or privileges it may have with respect to the footage.
>
> In return, CNN agrees to embargo the telecast of any videotape of the attempt to execute the search warrant until either: (1) a jury has been empaneled and instructed by a judge not to view television reports about the case; or (2) the defendant waives his right to a jury trial and agrees to have his case tried before a judge; or (3) a judge accepts a plea bargain; or (4) the government decides not to bring charges relating to the attempt to execute the search warrant.

CNN was allowed to see the search warrant and supporting material in a briefing the day before the search. The warrant and materials were supposed to remain under seal and not available to the public until after the search. CNN's crew and Fish and Wildlife Service officers met outside the Bergers' ranch and discussed the search. Cameras were mounted on the outside or placed inside the Fish and Wildlife vehicles. A special agent wore a concealed microphone that transmitted live to the CNN techs. Judge Schroeder found that the joint actor test would determine whether CNN had gone from being a news organization to being a government actor.

The test says that "willful participation" in joint actions with the government or its agents makes an otherwise private person a government actor.

42. PROBLEMS WITH HIDDEN CAMERAS AND RECORDERS

The *Dietemann* case should encourage journalists to think carefully about their use of concealed cameras and other electronic gear and whether or not their subjects have a reasonable expectation of privacy.

DETERESA V. AMERICAN BROADCASTING COMPANIES, INC.

This lawsuit arose out of ABC-TV's coverage of the stabbing deaths of Nicole Brown Simpson and Ronald Goldman.[97] Just a few hours after the murders, suspect O.J. Simpson flew from Los Angeles to Chicago on an American Airlines flight. Beverly Deteresa was a flight attendant. In January 1994, ABC producer Anthony Radziwill went to the door of Deteresa's condominium in Irvine, California, and she answered the door. Radziwill identified himself, asking if she would appear on an ABC TV show to discuss the flight. Interest in O.J. Simpson's behavior on the flight was high, as Simpson had a cut on his hand that he said happened

[97] *Deteresa v. American Broadcasting Companies, Inc.*, 121 F.3d 460 (9thCir.1997).

in his hotel room in Chicago. Some suspected he was cut in the slaying of Brown Simpson and Goldman. Deteresa told Radziwill that she did not wish to appear on the TV show but did say that she was frustrated by inaccurate news reports about the flight. In the words of the 9th Circuit Court of Appeal Judge Diarmuid O'Scannlain,[98] "* * * contrary to the reports she had heard, Simpson had not kept his hand in a bag during the flight," and told Radziwill she would consider appearing on the TV show he was producing.

Radziwill called Deteresa the next morning. He asked her again whether she would go on camera. When Deteresa declined, Radziwill told her that he had audiotaped their entire conversation the previous day. He also had directed a cameraperson to videotape them from a public street adjacent to Deteresa's home. Deteresa hung up on Radziwill and told her husband Matthew what had happened. Matthew Deteresa called Radziwill and told him that his wife did not want ABC to broadcast the videotape. Radziwill replied that ABC did not need consent to broadcast the videotape. That night, ABC broadcast a five-second clip of the conversation on a program called *Day One*. Along with the clip, an ABC announcer stated that "the flight attendant who had served Simpson in the first-class section told '*Day One*' that she did not, as widely reported, see him wrap his hand in a bag of ice." ABC did not broadcast any portion of the videotape.

A federal district court granted ABC's summary judgment petition, and the Deteresas appealed. The Deteresas contended that Radziwill and ABC had violated state law, California Penal Code, § 632 (a):

> Every person who, intentionally and without the consent of all parties to a confidential communication, by means of any electronic amplifying or recording device, eavesdrops upon or records a confidential communication * * * shall be punished.

Another section of the California Penal Code, §§ 632(a), 637.2., allows a civil lawsuit against a person who violates the eavesdropping statute.

The meaning of the words "confidential communication" was at the heart of the case. Judge O'Scannlain's opinion examined Ms. Deteresa's "expectation of privacy."[99]

> * * * Radziwill immediately revealed that he worked for ABC and wanted Deteresa to appear on television to discuss the flight; Deteresa did not tell Radziwill that her statements were in confidence; Deteresa did not tell Radziwill that the conversation was just between them; and Deteresa did not request that Radziwill not share the information with anyone else. Radziwill, for his part, did not promise to keep what Deteresa had told him in confidence. We agree, from these

[98] Ibid. at 463.

[99] Ibid. at 465.

> undisputed facts, that no one in Deteresa's shoes could reasonably expect that a reporter would not divulge her account of where Simpson had sat on the flight and where he had not kept his hand.

The Ninth Circuit panel then upheld the district court's grant of summary judgment to ABC.

DESNICK V. AMERICAN BROADCASTING COMPANIES

Courts will look to the context of statements made in the course of reporting stories to determine the reasonableness of an expectation of privacy.[100] *PrimeTime Live*, an ABC network program, was sued by Dr. J.H. Desnick and associates of the Desnick Eye Center for trespass, defamation, and violation of federal and state. The *PrimeTime Live* broadcast was anchored by Sam Donaldson. A *PrimeTime Live* producer approached Desnick asking him to agree to be a part of a story on medical practices that did large numbers of cataract surgeries. He assured Desnick that it would be a fair, balanced report with no undercover surveillance or ambush interviews. Desnick Eye Center allowed videotaping of a cataract operation in the clinic's Chicago office. Desnick also consented to interviews with doctors and patients.

Unknown to Desnick, the ABC producer also sent persons with hidden cameras into Desnick Eye Center locations in Wisconsin and Indiana. These persons, posing as patients, asked for eye exams, and two doctors were secretly videotaped while examining these "test patients."

When the *PrimeTime Live* broadcast was made, Donaldson introduced the segment on Desnick Eye Centers with these words:[101]

> "We begin tonight with the story of a so-called 'big cutter,' Dr. James Desnick. . . . [I]n our undercover investigation of the big cutter you'll meet tonight, we turned up evidence that he may also be a big charger, doing unnecessary cataract surgery for the money."

And, despite the producer's promise, there was an ambush interview. Sam Donaldson accosted Dr. James H. Desnick at O'Hare Airport, asking:[102]

> "Is it true, Doctor, that you've changed medical records to show less vision than your patients actually have? We've been told, Doctor, that you've changed the glare machine so we have a different reading? Is that correct? Doctor, why won't you respond to the questions?"

This broadcast also asserted that of the seven "test patients," two were under 65 and thus ineligible for Medicare reimbursement. They

---

[100] *Desnick v. American Broadcasting Companies*, 44 F.3d 1345 (7th Cir.1995).

[101] Ibid. at 1348.

[102] Ibid. at 1349.

were told they did not need cataract surgery. Four of the other five patients who were on Medicare were told they did.[103]

Desnick Eye Services filed suit on multiple claims, including defamation, trespass, and fraud. The Court of Appeals declined to dismiss the defamation part of Desnick's lawsuit, saying that charges of tampering with equipment [to give false readings indicating need for cataract surgery] and Medicare fraud needed further investigation through a pre-trial discovery process.[104]

That left questions of *how PrimeTime Live* gathered information: Claims by Desnick of trespass, fraud, and violating federal and state statutes regulating electronic surveillance. The three-judge panel of the Seventh Circuit Court of Appeals held in its opinion by Judge Richard Posner that,[105]

> There was no invasion in the present case of any of the specific interests that the tort of trespass seeks to protect. The test patients entered offices that were open to anyone expressing a desire for ophthalmic services and videotaped physicians engaged in professional, not personal, communications with strangers (the testers themselves). The activities in the offices were not disrupted. * * * Nor was there any "invasion of a person's private space."
>
> * * *
>
> The federal and state wiretapping statutes that the plaintiffs invoke allow one party to a conversation to record the conversation unless his purpose in doing so is to commit a crime or a tort. * * * The defendants did not order the camera-armed testers into the Desnick Eye Center's premises in order to commit a crime or a tort.

Desnick's lawyers argued that ABC committed fraud to get his to cooperate with the story in the first place. Judge Posner's opinion concluded that the type of fraud alleged by Desnick Eye Centers could not go forward because Illinois did not provide a remedy for a fraudulent promise, unless it was part of a scheme to defraud.[106] Not all frauds are the same. Restaurant critics could not gain entry to do their reviews, Judge Posner wrote, if they had to disclose their identities to restaurants. ABC's promise was not in furtherance of a crime and so was not actionable. Judge Posner adopting a kind of "journalists will be journalists" stance comforting to media lawyers and troubling to

[103] Ibid. at 1348.

[104] Ibid.

[105] Ibid. at 1352.

[106] Ibid. at 1353.

ethicists. Judge Posner also noted that Desnick was approached by a news program that made extensive use of hidden cameras:[107]

> Investigative journalists well known for ruthlessness promise to wear kid gloves. They break their promise, as any person of normal sophistication would expect. If that is "fraud," it is the kind against which potential victims can arm themselves by maintaining a minimum of skepticism about journalistic goals and methods. Desnick, needless to say, was no tyro, or child, or otherwise a member of a vulnerable group. He is a successful professional and entrepreneur.

The appellate panel affirmed summary judgment for most of Desnick's claims.

SANDERS V. ABC

The test patients in *Desnick* had conversations that were not deemed private because they were between patients and staff members testing them for cataracts. They also were in offices that were open to the public. In *Sanders v. ABC*,[108] an employee of a tele-psychic company sued over recorded conversations made secretly by an ABC *PrimeTime* reporter. It was *Dieteman* in new clothes.

ABC reporter Stacy Lescht applied for a job at Psychic Marketing Group (PMG) as part of a story on the quality, reliability and whether callers were actually talking to psychics. Telepsychic call lines were a $100 million industry in the 1990s with psychics promising to help by predicting the future, solving financial and personal problems and finding love and happiness. Lescht told the company she had no experience or training as a psychic. Still, she was hired. PMG offered psychic readings and advice over the phone at a rate of $3.95 a minute through a 900 number. The employees were given scripts for phone calls. They were encouraged to keep callers on the line and so increase income for the company.

Lescht wore a hidden camera in a hat and recorded video and audio in the office when she was not on a telephone with customers. She recorded conversations with Sanders and another employee including one in which she was a participant. Sanders testified that he discussed very personal matters with her,[109]

> "including her self-esteem and her inner child, which he considered to be 'personal, private and confidential.' RT 726:18–727:3. He told her about his creating self-esteem products for

---

[107] Ibid. at 1354–1355, 1168. Desnick also lost a libel case growing out of the same fact situation. See *Desnick v. ABC*, 233 F.3d 514 (7th Cir.2000).

[108] *Sanders v. American Broadcasting Companies, Inc.*, 20 Cal.4th 907, 978 P.2d 67, 85 Cal.Rptr.2d 909 (1999).

[109] *Mark Sanders, Plaintiff, Respondent, and Cross-Appellant v. American Broadcasting Companies, Inc.*, Reply Brief, 12, 13, WL 33454358 1996.

> children, something he considered a very personal matter, and she told him she was scattered emotionally, which he considered a very personal matter, just between the two."

Another recorded conversation suggested that employees did not believe what they were telling callers. When the story, "Hello Telepsychic," was broadcast, it included six seconds of one of Sanders' conversations. Sanders filed suit alleging that the recording violated California law against using electronic devices to "record a confidential communication." He also sued for intrusion. A jury found in his favor on the intrusion claim awarding him $1.2 million. The jury verdict ruled against him on the violation of state law for recording the conversations. An intermediate court of appeals reversed the intrusion verdict.[110] The three-judge panel said that when the jury found against Sanders on the state law claim against recording confidential communication, it means that he had no expectation of privacy. The judges also concluded that because the employees worked in cubicles that offered no real privacy and allowed their conversations to be heard by other employees, Sanders had no expectation of privacy. The California Supreme Court took up the case.

Justice Kathleen Mickle Werdegar's opinion for the court acknowledged that Sanders would not have an expectation of privacy in his workplace conversations. After all, other people could hear him. But, she added, the question before the court was whether Sanders had a reasonable expectation of privacy under the circumstances of the hidden camera reporting.[111]

> In an office or other workplace to which the general public does not have unfettered access, employees may enjoy a limited, but legitimate, expectation that their conversations and other interactions will not be secretly videotaped by undercover television reporters, even though those conversations may not have been completely private from the participants' coworkers.

Even though, Justice Werdegar's opinion reversed the intermediate appellate court, she was not granting judgment to Sanders. She was, instead, laying out the factors that must be considered by any lower courts. That court would have to consider:

1) the conduct and the circumstances surrounding the recording,

2) whether the intrusion would be highly offensive to a reasonable person,

3) the motive for the recording

Justice Werdegar cited *Dieteman, Shulman, Desnick* along with another dozen or so cases in her analysis of the legal issues. She

---

[110] *Sanders v. ABC,* 52 Cal.App.4th 543, 60 Cal.Rptr.2d 595, 596 (2d Dist.1997).

[111] *Sanders v. American Broadcasting Companies, Inc.*, 20 Cal.4th 907, 911, 978 P.2d 67, 69, 85 Cal.Rptr.2d 909, 911 (1999).

concluded that the lower courts should have considered whether the use of the hidden camera and microphone would make a conversation with limited expectations of privacy, an intrusion. If a jury found intrusion, would it be highly offensive, Justice Werdegar wrote. ABC would still have the opportunity to rebut a finding of offensiveness.[112]

> Nothing we say here prevents a media defendant from attempting to show, in order to negate the offensiveness element of the intrusion tort, that the claimed intrusion, even if it infringed on a reasonable expectation of privacy, was "justified by the legitimate motive of gathering the news."
>
> ABC settled with Sanders for a reported $900,000.[113]

THE ACORN VIDEO

Conservative "muckraker" James O'Keefe III and his assistant found themselves on the defensive following his wildly successful, albeit fake, take down of community organizing group ACORN[114] in September 2009. O'Keefe got wall-to-wall coverage on conservative and soon after in mainstream news programs with a video that he claimed showed ACORN employees offering to aid prostitution and tax evasion. The video turned out to have been heavily edited to create a false impression of the employees and organization. ACORN challenged the videos and the editing came to light, but too late. Congress halted ACORN's funding, Census Bureau and IRS canceled contracts and the organization lost many of its private donors. ACORN shut its doors not long after. ACORN had long been a target of conservatives. Founded in the 1970s, the group advocated for affordable housing. It conducted multi-state voter registration drives, provided free tax return assistance with the IRS and advocated for a "living wage."

O'Keefe and Hannah Giles visited three ACORN offices and secretly videotaped conversations with employees. At the San Diego office, the two met with ACORN employee Juan Carlos Vera and discussed bringing in young girls for the purpose of prostitution.[115]

> While Mr. Vera had no idea he was being surreptitiously videotaped—which is not surprising given that California law expressly bars the secret recording of one's voice or image—there was also something Mr. O'Keefe did not know until after he released the damaging video of his conversation with Vera for broadcast.

---

[112] Ibid. at 919, 77, 927.

[113] "Network settles hidden camera claim for $900,000," *News Media & The Law*, Spring 2000.

[114] Association of Community Organizations for Reform Now.

[115] Rick Ungar, "James O'Keefe Pays $100,000 To ACORN Employee He Smeared-Conservative Media Yawns," *Forbes*, March 8, 2013.

> As soon as O'Keefe and his partner-in-crime left the ACORN location, Mr. Vera called the police to report the entire incident. It turns out that Vera had been playing along with O'Keefe in an effort to ensnare O'Keefe and Giles whom Vera believed were in the act of breaking the law by proposing to engage in the importing of young women to become prostitutes.

Then-California Attorney General Edmund "Jerry" Brown began an investigation. O'Keefe handed over all the video from his California ACORN visits in return for immunity for himself and Giles. Brown released his report the same day that ACORN closed its doors.[116] "The evidence illustrates," Brown said, "that things are not always as partisan zealots portray them through highly selective editing of reality. Sometimes a fuller truth is found on the cutting room floor."

Vera sued O'Keefe and Giles[117] alleging that they had violated the state's Invasion of Privacy Act.[118] In addition to criminal penalties, the law provides for civil suit where a person has been injured by a violation of the privacy law.

O'Keefe and Giles moved for summary judgment arguing that their activities were protected by the First Amendment. U.S. District Court Judge M. James Lorenz denied the motion, allowing the case to move forward. In his order, Judge Lorenz cited *Shulman*.[119]

> [N]o constitutional precedent or principle of which we are aware gives a reporter general license to intrude in an objectively offensive manner into private places, conversations or matters merely because the reporter thinks he or she may thereby find something that will warrant publication or broadcast. . . . In short, the state may not intrude into the proper sphere of the news media to dictate what they should publish and broadcast, but neither may the media play tyrant to the people by unlawfully spying on them in the name of newsgathering.

Vera received a payment of $100,000 to settle the case against O'Keefe and Giles

JUROR DISLIKE FOR "HIDDEN CAMERA" REPORTING

Appellate courts sometimes seem quite protective of the news media—even when hidden cameras are involved. However, because of the great cost of defending against privacy lawsuits, the media really "lose"

---

[116] https://oag.ca.gov/news/press-releases/brown-releases-report-detailing-litany-problems-acorn-no-criminality.

[117] *Vera v. O'Keefe*, 791 F.Supp.2d 959 (S.D.Calif. 2011).

[118] California Invasion of Privacy Act, Penal Code § 632: Eavesdropping on or recording confidential communications:

"(a) Every person who, intentionally and without the consent of all parties to a confidential communication, by means of any electronic amplifying or recording device, eavesdrops upon or records the confidential communication, [* * *] shall be punished" by fine, imprisonment or both.

[119] *Vera v. O'Keefe*, 791 F.Supp.2d 959, 968 (S.D.Calif. 2011).

even though cases often have a favorable outcome. Case in point, *People for the Ethical Treatment of Animals [PETA] v. Berosini.*[120] In *PETA*, animal trainer Bobby Berosini won a $4.2 million jury verdict for defamation and invasion of privacy. Animal rights activists took backstage videotape before a Las Vegas show—without Berosini's knowledge or consent—of Berosini "shaking and punching his trained orangutans and hitting them with some kind of rod." The videotapes later were distributed and shown to the public, and the animal rights advocates also stated that "Berosini regularly abuses his orangutans."

Berosini also sued the individuals responsible for videotaping him—including a Stardust Hotel dancer, Ottavio Gesmundo, who actually carried out the videotaping—for intrusion and appropriation The Nevada Supreme Court, however, overturned the jury award. First, the Nevada Supreme Court held that the defense of truth covered the videotapes. Second, the court ruled that Gesmundo's taping was not conduct of the kind that would be highly offensive to a reasonable person. The court observed that Gesmundo and his camera did not violate Berosini's expectation of privacy, because stagehands and others—including Gesmundo—had permission to be backstage as part of their jobs. Further, Gesmundo[121] "* * * caused no * * * interference. Neither Berosini nor his animals were aware of the camera's presence. If Gesmundo had surprised Berosini and his animals with a film crew and caused a great commotion, we might view this factor differently."

The Nevada Supreme Court also found that what Gesmundo and the animal rights activists had done did not amount to actionable "appropriation," thus reversing all damages awarded by the trial court.

43. TELEPHONES AND PRIVACY

Reporters should know better than to tap someone's telephone. What happens if someone else does it for the journalist?

THE FEDERAL WIRETAP STATUTE

The Federal Wiretap Statute[122] makes it a crime to intercept "any wire or oral communication," and assigns penalties of fines up to $250,000 and up to five years imprisonment. "Wiretapping" statutes also can be used to impose penalties, either criminal or civil, on interception of wireless or smartphone communications.

The statute also makes the intentional disclosures or attempted disclosure of the contents of telephone conversations illegal if the person trying to make the disclosure knows or had reasons to know the

---

[120] *People for the Ethical Treatment of Animals v. Bobby Berosini, Ltd.*, 111 Nev. 615, 895 P.2d 1269 (1995).

[121] *PETA v. Berosini*, 111 Nev. 615, 634, 895 P.2d 1269, 1280 (1995).

[122] 18 U.S.C. § 2511.

information was obtained illegally.[123] The use or attempted use of the intercepted communication also is a violation of the wiretap statute.

There is a "participant monitoring" provision in this statute allowing a party to a telephone call or conversation to make a recording.[124] The "one-party consent" provision of the statute says:[125]

> It shall not be unlawful under this chapter for a person not acting under color of law [e.g., a private citizen without a court order] to intercept a wire or oral communication where such person is a party to the communication or where one of the parties to the communication has given prior consent to such interception. . . .

That provision, however, is quickly followed by a huge exception which says, in effect, that the message interception may not be for the purpose of committing a crime or a tort.[126]

BARTNICKI V. VOPPER

In *Bartnicki v. Vopper aka Williams*,[127] a key issue was whether a media defendant could be held liable for publication of illegally recorded cellular phone calls, if the media defendant did not make the illegal recording.

Gloria Bartnicki, a teacher's union negotiator, sued Frederick W. Vopper, a WILK radio talk show host known as Fred Williams. Williams had broadcast a tape of an illegally recorded phone call between Bartnicki and Anthony F. Kane, Jr., president of the West Wyoming Valley Teachers Union. The audiotape was provided by Jack Yocum, president of the local taxpayers' association, who found it in his mailbox. The recording included some remarks critical of school board members' reluctance to provide raises to teachers, and some threatening words about the board from Kane:[128] "If they're not going to move for 3 percent, we'll have to go to their, their homes * * * to blow off their front porches, we'll have to do some work on some of those guys."

The U.S. Court of Appeals, 3rd Circuit, held that the government interest in protecting privacy would not justify penalties placed on free

---

[123] 18 U.S. Code Chap. 119—Wire and Electronic Communications Interception and Interception of Oral Communications § 2511. Interception and disclosure of wire, oral, or electronic communications prohibited.

[124] California, Connecticut, Delaware, Florida, Illinois, Maryland, Massachusetts, Michigan, Montana, Nevada, New Hampshire, Oregon, Pennsylvania, Vermont and Washington are "all party" states. All participants in a call must agree to the recording. If a call is made from a one party" state to an "all party" state, the "all party" rule applies.

[125] 18 U.S.C.A. § 2511(2)(d).

[126] Ibid.

[127] *Bartnicki v. Vopper aka Williams*, 200 F.3d 109 (3d Cir.1999). Relevant federal wiretap statute provisions are at 18 U.S.C.A. §§ 2511, 2520, 2520(c)(2). See also Pennsylvania statutes: 18 Pa. C.S.A. §§ 5703, 5725, 5725(a).

[128] Ibid. at 113 (3d Cir.1999).

speech under federal and state wiretapping statutes.[129] The U.S. Supreme Court agreed with the 3rd Circuit's conclusion, with Justice Stevens writing for the Court in an 8–1 decision.[130] Justice Stevens' opinion emphasized that the persons disclosing the tape, including the radio station, did not know the identity of the person who made the illegal recording of a cell phone message. "Second, their access to the information was obtained lawfully, even though the tapes were intercepted unlawfully by someone else. Third, the subject matter of the conversation was a matter of public concern."

Justice Stevens declared that in this case,[131] " * * * privacy concerns give way when balanced against the interest in publishing matters of public importance." He concluded that "* * * a stranger's illegal conduct does not suffice to remove the First Amendment shield from speech about a matter of public concern." Following the Supreme Court's reasoning in *Bartnicki*, when reporters actively participate in illegal interceptions of electronically conveyed conversations, news media are likely to be found liable.

PEAVY V. WFAA-TV

On May 29, 2001—just eight days after deciding *Bartnicki v. Vopper*, the U.S. Supreme Court refused to grant certiorari in *Peavy v. WFAA-TV*.[132] Like *Bartnicki*, the *Peavy* case involved secretly made recordings of phone calls. The case started out with a neighborhood dispute. Carver Dan and Sally Peavy had longstanding disagreements with neighbors Charles and Wilma Harman. Charles Harman heard Carver Peavy's cordless telephone calls on a police scanner. Peavy, a board member of the Dallas Independent School District, was in charge of purchasing insurance for the district which had about 20,000 employees. Harman said he heard Peavy talking about getting kickbacks on multi-million dollar insurance contracts for the district.[133] Harman started taping the calls. He contacted authorities about his concerns. When the police did not react quickly enough, Harman contacted WFAA-TV. Investigative reporter Robert Riggs began to work on the story. Riggs met with the Harmans and they played tapes of recorded conversations for him. Riggs knew that Peavy and the people in the phone calls did not know about and did not consent to the recording.[134] Harman gave Riggs a copy of the call. Riggs gave Harman instructions about taping, including not turning

---

[129] Ibid. at 129.

[130] *Bartnicki v. Vopper aka Williams* and *U.S. v. Vopper*, 532 U.S. 514, 121 S.Ct. 1753 (2001).

[131] Ibid. at 18–19, 20.

[132] *Peavy v. WFAA-TV, Inc.*, 221 F.3d 158 (5th Cir. 2000), cert. den. 532 U.S. 1051, 121 S.Ct. 2191 (2001).

[133] Jim Schutze, "Big Man Bites Back," *Dallas Observer*, Aug. 17, 2000.

[134] *Peavy v. WFAA-TV, Inc.*, 221 F.3d 158, 164 (5th Cir. 2000).

off the recorder during the calls and not editing the tape if anyone challenged their authenticity.

Riggs took the recording back to the station and the news director agreed that Peavy should be investigated. WFAA's outside counsel said he thought that it was legal to record cordless telephone conversations and advised Riggs that he could continue to accept tapes from Harman.[135] Several months later, WFAA staffers learned that the taping, contrary to earlier advice, was unlawful.[136] WFAA's outside counsel told the station to stop accepting tapes from the Harmans, but contended that the First Amendment protected broadcast of the tapes already received because Riggs had obtained them lawfully. The station told Harman that the recording was illegal. He recorded anyway giving Riggs information about at least one of the calls. Harman later pled guilty and was fined $5,000 for violating the federal wiretap statute. After Riggs learned the tapes were illegal, he contacted federal authorities and Dallas police. They got to hear the tapes. Peavy was indicted on federal charges that he took $459,000 to steer insurance contracts to a Dallas insurance agent.

WFAA and Riggs investigated Peavy using other resources. During the summer of 1995, WFAA broadcast three reports about Peavy's alleged wrongdoing in connection with school district insurance. Riggs won a Peabody Award broadcast journalism for his series. Prosecutors were not able to get any of the people involved to testify in the case against Peavy and he was acquitted.[137] He sued WFAA for $100 million claiming violations of the federal and state wiretapping laws. A U.S. District court granted summary judgment to the station and Riggs. A panel of the Fifth Circuit Court of Appeals took the case and reversed many of the district court's rulings. Keying in on the part of Peavy's claim over procurement or obtaining the phone calls. Circuit Judge Rhesa Hawkins Barksdale wrote:[138]

> Although intercepted conversations were *not* played on the broadcasts, the district court held that, in violation of the Federal and Texas wiretap acts, WFAA and Riggs "disclosed" portions of the tapes' contents during them.

The district court found that the Harmans made an independent decision to record the calls and that WFAA had not actively participated in the decision or recording. That was key to the station's defense.[139]

---

[135] Ibid. at 165.

[136] Cordless telephones are radio stations. The base connected to the telephone line and then transmitted to handheld receivers. The conversations over the telephone lines were protected by the wiretap statute. The radio portion, which the Harmans were intercepting, was not. Amendments to the wiretap statute provided protections for that. It is the basis for protecting the communications using smartphones.

[137] Jim Schutze, "Big Man Bites Back," *Dallas Observer*, Aug. 17, 2000.

[138] Ibid. at 166.

[139] *Peavy v. WFAA*, 37 F.Supp.2d 495, 512–513 (N.D.Texas 2000).

But Judge Barksdale found that Riggs had taken an active role in the wiretapping.[140]

> When the Harmans asked Riggs whether he wanted a copy of the tape listened to at their initial meeting, and any future tapes they might make, he replied that he did. Riggs instructed Harman not to turn the recorder on and off while listening to the intercepted conversations, and not to edit the tapes, to prevent authenticity challenges.

Judge Barksdale's opinion returned the case to district court for further proceedings saying that a jury could determine at trial whether Riggs had procured or obtained the recordings through the Harmans and whether Harmans were encouraged by WFAA's pursuit of the story to continuing to intercept Peavy's calls. Peavy reportedly settled his suit against WFAA for $5 million before the case was tried.[141] *Peavy* squared with *Bartnicki* in that it allowed liability where a journalist was more than a recipient of illegally recorded conversations.

WHEN MEDIA RECEIVE OTHER IMPROPERLY OBTAINED MATERIAL: PEARSON V. DODD

In a case that predates Bartnicki, Peavy and cellphones, a sitting senator tried and failed to collect from a reporter who made use of documents stolen from his office. Senator Thomas Dodd of Connecticut filed an intrusion lawsuit against sensational columnists Drew Pearson and Jack Anderson.[142] Pearson and Anderson had published papers taken from Dodd's office showing appropriation of campaign funds for personal use.[143]

Two employees and two former employees of Senator Dodd took documents from his files, photocopied them, and then replaced the originals in their filing cabinets. The copies were turned over to Anderson. Anderson had knowledge of how they had been obtained. The Pearson-Anderson "Washington Merry-Go-Round" column then ran six stories about Senator Dodd, dealing—in addition to his use of campaign funds—with his relationship with lobbyists for foreign interests.

Dodd sued, arguing that the way the information was obtained invaded his privacy, winning a judgment in a U.S. district court.[144] Pearson and Anderson appealed. D.C. Court of Appeals Judge J. Skelly

---

[140] *Peavy v. WFAA-TV, Inc.*, 221 F.3d 158, 171 (5th Cir. 2000).

[141] Eric Celeste, "Lawyered to death," *Dallas Observer*, Oct. 25, 2001.

[142] *Dodd v. Pearson*, 279 F.Supp. 101 (D.D.C.1968).

[143] The conversion of campaign money for personal use is a recurring theme with elected officials. In 2019, Rep. Duncan Hunter (Republican) pleaded guilty to conspiracy to misuse campaign funds. Prosecutors alleged that he took more than $250,000 in campaign funds to spend on himself and his wife. Hunter declared, as has become the pattern for political figures under investigation, that he was the target of a "witch hunt," in 2018 when he was indicted. Later he blamed his wife. When he pled guilty, his comment to reporters was that he had "made mistakes."

[144] *Dodd v. Pearson*, 279 F.Supp. 101 (D.D.C.1968).

Wright said that it was Dodd's employees and former employees who had committed improper intrusion, removing files and showing them to outsiders. Journalists Pearson and Anderson escaped liability, with Judge Wright declaring:[145]

> If we were to hold appellants [Pearson and Anderson] liable for invasion of privacy on these facts, we would establish the proposition that one who receives information from an intruder knowing it has been obtained by improper intrusion, is guilty of a tort. In an untried and developing area of tort law, we are not prepared to go so far.

44. FRAUD CLAIMS AND UNDERCOVER REPORTING

Many of the suits claiming damages from newsgathering practices of journalists include claims that the reporters engaged in fraud in getting access to places of business.

FOOD LION WINS $2

Food Lion, a grocery chain based in North Carolina, was making headlines in the 1990s. The chain was making an industry high 3.1 percent profit while the average for everyone else was 1 percent. It was moving into new territories, skipping over its neighbors to target states that offered opportunities for low-price grocery stores. And then ABC's *PrimeTime Live* broadcast a story about practices that helped the chain make its high profits. The "Food Lion" segment was devastating.[146]

> The broadcast included, for example, videotape that appeared to show Food Lion employees repackaging and re-dating fish that had passed the expiration date, grinding expired beef with fresh beef, and applying barbeque sauce to chicken past its expiration date in order to mask the smell and sell it as fresh in the gourmet food section.

The impact on the chain's financial fortune was immediate and disastrous.[147]

> Talk about the power of television: During the week of the broadcast the company's market value plummeted by $1.3 billion. And the show helped hammer Food Lion's profits, which

---

[145] *Pearson v. Dodd,* 133 U.S.App.D.C. 279, 410 F.2d 701, 704–705 (D.C. Cir. 1969). See also *Bilney v. Evening Star Newspaper Co.,* 43 Md.App. 560, 406 A.2d 652 (1979), 5 Med.L.Rptr. 1931, in which a newspaper was sued for intrusion because it had published confidential academic records of members of the University of Maryland basketball team. The records involved were held to be newsworthy, and the lawsuit against the paper was dismissed because it had not shown that reporters had solicited or encouraged reading of confidential records. The material involved came unasked for, from an unnamed source.

[146] *Food Lion, Inc. v. Capital Cities/ABC, Inc.,* 194 F.3d 505 (4th Cir.1999).

[147] Mark Gunther, "Yikes, Diane Sawyer's Downstairs! When ABC'S *PrimeTime* Live Burned Food Lion in a A TV Expose About Rotten Food, the Supermarket Chain Mishandled the Crisis and Made Matters Worse," *Fortune,* Dec. 23, 1996.

fell from $178 million in 1992 to a mere $3.9 million the following year, as the chain curbed its expansion plans and eventually closed 88 stores.

Food Lion sued but not for libel. If it had, it would have had to prove that the story was false. It would also have the burden of proving actual malice (discussed in Chap. 5). The chain instead sued for $2.47 billion over the methods that ABC reporters had used. The producers who got jobs at Food Lion Ms. Linne Litt (Dale) and Susan Barnett had made false statements on job applications in order to get hired by Food Lion. After they were hired, they were outfitted with tiny "jacketcam" or "lipstick" hidden cameras and recorders to gather information for ABC.

The investigation was inspired by tips from the United Food and Commercial Workers Union (UFCW). The union was waging an aggressive campaign against non-union Food Lion recruiting employees with claims of "off-the-clock"[148] practices of the chain. The UFCW had supplied the names of disgruntled workers to ABC producers. The union enlisted Food Lion workers to help the two producers write their resumes.[149]

Food Lion alleged in its suit that ABC had committed fraud, breach of duty of loyalty, trespass, and unfair trade practices in its undercover, hidden camera investigation. Although the suit got national headlines when a North Carolina jury[150] returned a verdict for the chain in the amount of $1,402 in actual damages and $5.545 million in punitive damages,[151] it turned out to be a tempest in a teapot.

The jury awarded Food Lion $1,400 in compensatory damages on its fraud claim, $1.00 each on its duty of loyalty and trespass claims. The $5.545 million in punitive damages was based on the fraud claim. The trial court found the punitive damages excessive and reduced them to $315,000.[152] ABC appealed. A three-judge panel of the Fourth Circuit Court of Appeals looked at Food Lion's fraud claims. Judge Martin Blane Michael wrote the opinion for the panel.[153]

> To prove fraud under North Carolina law, the plaintiff must establish that the defendant (1) made a false representation of material fact, (2) knew it was false (or made it with reckless disregard of its truth or falsity), and (3) intended that the

[148] Workers reported that in order to keep labor costs down, Food Lion made them clock out and stay to finish their work if they were not done by the end of their shifts.

[149] "Notably, the applications failed to mention the reporters' concurrent employment with ABC and otherwise misrepresented their educational and employment experiences." *Food Lion, Inc. v. Capital Cities/ABC, Inc.*, 194 F.3d 505, 511 (4th Cir.1999).

[150] In fact, the jury never got to watch the segment. It was told by U.S. District Judge Carlton S. Tilley to regard the TV report as accurate.

[151] Barry Meier, "Jury Says ABC Owes Damages of $5.5 Million," *New York Times*, Jan. 23, 1997.

[152] *Food Lion v. Capital Cities/ABC, Inc.*, 984 F.Supp. 923, 940 (M.D.N.C.1997).

[153] *Food Lion, Inc. v. Capital Cities/ABC, Inc.*, 194 F.3d 505. 512 (4th Cir. 1999).

> plaintiff rely upon it. In addition, (4) the plaintiff must be injured by reasonably relying on the false representation.

The first three elements were evident from the facts of the case. The fourth factor, damages turned out to be the key to the case. Food Lion claimed that it spent $1,944.62 in administrative costs for applicant screening, interviews, completing all forms and putting the two producers in the chain's payroll system. Food Lion also included costs for lower productivity by new employees and the money it paid the two producers, Dale and Barnett. Judge Michael found that those costs, necessary to prove injury for fraud, were not the result of fraud but rather the costs that Food Lion would incur when it hired any new employee. Food Lion sought to reclaim the wages it paid the producers. But, it was not fraud that Food Lion was paying for, Judge Michael wrote.[154]

> Dale and Barnett were paid because they showed up for work and performed their assigned tasks as Food Lion employees. Their performance was at a level suitable to their status as new, entry-level employees. Indeed, shortly before Dale quit, her supervisor said she would "make a good meat wrapper." And, when Barnett quit, her supervisor recommended that she be rehired if she sought reemployment with Food Lion in the future. In sum, Dale and Barnett were not paid their wages because of misrepresentations on their job applications. Food Lion therefore cannot assert wage payment to satisfy the injurious reliance element of fraud. The fraud verdict must be reversed.

Food Lion's administrative costs were the costs of any new hire. Although the two producers worked for three weeks, Food Lion could not claim that it suffered because it had expected the two to work longer. North Carolina is an at-will employment state meaning that either employer or employee could end the job relationship at any time.[155]

> As one of its payroll managers acknowledged on cross-examination, "when Food Lion hires a new deli clerk or a new meat clerk . . . it assume[s] the risk that that person might stay only a few days." Dale and Barnett were, in short, at-will employees.

Without any proof of injury, Food Lion's fraud claims disappeared. Because the punitive award was based on its fraud claim, that too disappeared. The trespass and breach of the duty of loyalty were upheld. The two producers were working for ABC and that breached their duty of loyalty.[156]

> They went into areas of the stores that were not open to the public and secretly videotaped, an act that was directly adverse

---

[154] Ibid. at 514.

[155] Ibid. at 513.

[156] Ibid. at 519.

> to the interests of their second employer, Food Lion. Thus, they breached the duty of loyalty, thereby committing a wrongful act in abuse of their authority to be on Food Lion's property.
>
> In sum, we are convinced that the highest courts of North and South Carolina would hold that Dale and Barnett committed trespass because Food Lion's consent for them to be on its property was nullified when they tortiously breached their duty of loyalty to Food Lion.
>
> Food Lion's $2 awards on those claims was affirmed.

Judge Paul Niemeyer dissented with respect to the fraud claim. He reasoned because that the two producers falsely represented themselves and that their intentions were to advance ABC's agenda and not Food Lion's, they should not be treated the same as any short-term employee.

CHIQUITA BRANDS INTERNATIONAL V. GALLAGHER

Powerful corporations make tempting targets for aggressive investigative reporters, but reporters must remember the lessons of that key precedent, *Dietemann v. Time, Inc.*, discussed near the start of this chapter. Recall that Court of Appeals Judge Shirley Hufstedler stated the law basic law of newsgathering: "The First Amendment has never been construed to accord newsmen immunity from torts or crimes committed during the course of newsgathering."

Michael Gallagher was an investigative reporter with the *Cincinnati Enquirer*, which published an 18-page special section about Chiquita Brands International on May 1998. Chiquita, formerly named United Fruit Company, a Cincinnati-based food giant. The splashy special section, bearing the headline "Chiquita Secrets Revealed," accused Chiquita Brands of improperly dodging foreign laws that would limit the size of its banana plantation holdings. Chiquita also was accused of endangering farm workers in Central America with dangerous pesticides.

It was said the articles were based on more than 2,000 employee voice mail messages. This was a major reporting effort, a point of pride for the *Cincinnati Enquirer*. Chiquita Brands, however, clearly saw trouble coming, complaining to the newspaper before the series was published. The company claimed biased reporting, possibly unlawful newsgathering, and expressed the expectation that libelous stories would result.[157] Despite these warnings, the newspaper published its special section on May 3. By June 28, 1998, journalistic pride had turned into journalistic embarrassment, with a six-column page one headline apologizing to Chiquita Brands.[158] The voice mail messages, which the newspaper had boldly cited as major sources for the Chiquita reportage,

---

157 Nicholas Stein, "Banana Peel," *Columbia Journalism Review*, September/October 1998.

158 Stein. Ibid.

were believed by the newspaper to have been leaked to reporter Gallagher by a Chiquita executive. Chiquita, however, persuaded the newspaper that Gallagher had illegally penetrated the corporation's voice mail system. The paper fired Gallagher and apologized:[159] " 'Despite [Gallagher's] assurances to his editors prior to publication that he obtained his information in an ethical and lawful manner, we can no longer trust his word.' "

The *Cincinnati Enquirer* also paid $14 million as part of the out-of-court settlement with Chiquita Brands, a settlement which included the newspapers renunciation of its articles and the front-page apology, published over three days. The parent company, Gannett, also pledged to investigate its employees and to inform Chiquita whether any had committed illegal acts in newsgathering. Ironically, Gannett also promised to give Chiquita unlimited access to recordings or transcripts of the voice-mail messages, and to seal documents and reporters' notes used in preparing the Chiquita articles.[160]

The settlement obviously damaged a major newspaper's reputation as well as its finances. Early in 2001, former *Cincinnati Enquirer* Editor Lawrence Beaupre was pursuing a lawsuit against Gannett, contending that Gannett made him a scapegoat and damaged his reputation. Gannett denied those claims, retorting that the Chiquita settlement was necessary because[161] " 'illegal newsgathering that occurred on Mr. Beaupre's watch.' "

As for reporter Gallagher, he pleaded guilty to criminal charges involving Ohio wiretapping and computer secrecy laws and was sentenced to five years of probation and 200 hours of community service.[162] Gallagher identified George G. Ventura, a former lawyer for Chiquita, as a crucial source for his articles about the huge banana company.[163], based here. and was sued by Chiquita Brands for a laundry list of civil wrongs, including defamation, trespass, conversion, and fraud by either hacking into the corporate voice mail or by using a code provided to him illegally by a Chiquita employee.

---

159 Ibid.

160 Dan Horn, "Lawsuit details revealed: Enquirer paid Chiquita $14 million in settlement, magazine reports," *Cincinnati Enquirer*, January 24, 2001, quoting *Editor & Publisher* magazine's site, from http://enquirer.com/editions/2001/01/24/loc_enquirer_paid.html.

161 Horn. Ibid.

162 "Reporter sentenced over Chiquita voice-mail theft," *Reporters Committee for Freedom of the Press*, July 26, 1999. https://www.rcfp.org/reporter-sentenced-over-chiquita-voice-mail-theft/.

163 Douglas Frantz, "Reporter in Chiquita Case Reveals Source in Court," *New York Times*, April 6, 1999.

CRIMINALIZING UNDERCOVER FILMING

If the Food Lion story was enough to put people off going to the grocery store, other hidden camera exposés had folks reconsidering vegetarianism.[164]

> A 2009 investigation at Hy-Line Hatchery in Iowa revealed hundreds of thousands of unwanted day-old male chicks being funneled by conveyor belt into a macerator to be ground up live.[165] That same year, undercover investigators at a Vermont slaughterhouse operated by Bushway Packing obtained similarly gruesome footage of days-old calves being kicked, dragged, and skinned alive.[166] A few years later, an undercover investigator at E6 Cattle Company in Texas filmed workers beating cows on the head with hammers and pickaxes and leaving them to die. And later that year, at Sparboe Farms in Iowa, undercover investigators documented hens with gaping, untreated wounds laying eggs in cramped conditions among decaying corpses.[167]

Undercover video recording the treatment of animals at farms and slaughterhouses continues to be documented with stories published in 2016, 2017, 2018 and 2019.[168] The publication of stories and broadcast of videos has had significant impact on agriculture. State and federal official have shut down operations and forced recalls of meats. Major buyers, like McDonald's have canceled contracts. And, abuses that have been documented by animal rights advocates who have either gotten jobs at the companies or snuck in with video cameras, have led to ballot initiatives as well as new laws to prevent abuses.

States with significant agriculture industries have responded by passing laws that make getting undercover videos a crime.[169]

> Ag-gag laws generally fall into one of three categories or a combination of two or all types. The first modern-day ag-gag laws are known as "agricultural interference" laws, and they ban recording images or sounds at industrialized farming operations without the owner's consent. "Agricultural fraud" laws were also introduced early on; this kind of ag-gag law bans

---

[164] *Animal Legal Defense Fund v. Herbert*, 263 F.Supp.3d 1193, 1197 (D. Utah 2017).

[165] Associated Press, "Agriculture Industry Defends Itself Over Grisly Iowa Chick Video," *Los Angeles Times*, Sept. 5, 2009.

[166] Associated Press, "Vermont Slaughterhouse Closed Amid Animal Cruelty Allegations," *Los Angeles Times*, Nov. 3, 2009.

[167] Tiffany Hsu, "McDonald's Cuts Egg Supplier After Undercover Animal Cruelty Video," *Los Angeles Times*, Nov. 18, 2011.

[168] https://www.miamiherald.com/news/nation-world/world/article155990889.html; https://www.nbcchicago.com/news/local/natural-prairie-fairlife-dairy-undercover-investigation-animal-recovery-mission/78242/; https://www.chicagotribune.com/business/ct-biz-undercover-video-pig-abuse-20180731-story.html.

[169] Alicia Prygoski, "Brief Summary of Ag-gag Laws," Animal Legal & Historical Center, Michigan State University College of Law, 2015.

> entering or applying for employment at industrialized farming operations under false pretenses. Many ag-gag bills introduced in 2011–2012 were "agricultural interference" and "agricultural fraud" hybrids. Because legislators ran into problems passing these kind of ag-gag laws, a new type of ag-gag emerged in late 2012. This kind is known as "rapid-reporting" legislation and it mandates that anyone who records an image or sound at an industrialized farming operation turn the recording over to authorities within a specified amount of time, usually twenty-four to forty-eight hours.

At least 25 state legislatures have considered passing such laws and six: Iowa Utah, Missouri, Idaho, Wyoming, and North Carolina passed laws criminalizing practices used by animal rights activists and journalists. These laws protect the rights of agricultural businesses making it illegal to gain access, either by sneaking in or by applying for a job under false pretenses. North Carolina included a right for farmers to file civil suits. As expected, animal rights groups have challenged the laws, winning cases in Idaho, Utah and Iowa. A U.S. District Court in Iowa struck down the state's Iowa Code § 717A.3A in 2019.[170] The Iowa Legislature passed the "agricultural production facility fraud" act in 2012. The act made it a crime to get access to an agricultural production facility by false pretenses or by making false statements on an employment application. U.S. District Judge James E. Gritzner noted in his ruling that the bill followed several industrial farm investigations "that brought critical national attention to the state's agricultural industry." Judge Gritzner listed several undercover investigations that found[171] "reports of workers hurling small piglets onto a concrete floor, mistreatment of hens and chicks and another where workers at a Hormel Foods supplier in Iowa beating pigs with metal rods and kicking "a young pig in the face, abdomen, and genitals to make her move while telling the investigator, 'You gotta beat on the bitch. Make her cry.' "

With irony or not, Judge Gritzner quoted members of the state legislature speaking about the need for the law.[172] "For example, as to security, then-Representative Annette Sweeney provided: "With this bill we want to make sure everybody involved in our livestock facilities and working within in those facilities is forthright, and want to make sure our livestock is being kept safe," Lawmakers also said the law would help ensure the biosecurity of the state's farms by preventing the spread of dangerous viruses and have the benefit of stopping groups that "work to give agriculture a bad name."

The plaintiffs, non-profit groups that advocate for animal rights, the well-being of agriculture workers and safety of the nation's food

---

170 *Animal Legal Defense Fund v. Reynolds*, 353 F.Supp.3d 812 (S.D. Iowa 2019).

171 Ibid. at 816–817.

172 Ibid. at 817.

supply,[173] argued that they wanted to but could not conduct undercover investigations of agriculture companies or make use of such investigations by others because of the law. It prevented their speech. As such, the challenge focused on the First Amendment aspects of the law. The state of Iowa replied that the First Amendment did not protect lying on employment applications or using false pretenses in order to get access to agriculture production facilities.

Judge Gritzner's analysis concluded that the law was aimed at particular speakers and points of view. As such, Strict Scrutiny (see Appendix B) would be applied. Under that test a content-based law is presumed to be unconstitutional. It can be justified only if the government serves a compelling state interest and is narrowly tailored. Iowa did not pass the test on narrow tailoring and compelling interest.[174]

> Defendants have produced no evidence that the prohibitions of § 717A.3A are actually necessary to protect perceived harms to property and biosecurity. [* * *]
>
> Defendants have made no record as to how biosecurity is threatened by a person making a false statement to get access to, or employment in, an agricultural production facility. Nor, in the absence of any record to the contrary, will the Court assume that biological harm turns on a human vector making a false statement unrelated to such harm in order to gain access to the facility. Protecting biosecurity is therefore purely speculative and cannot constitute a compelling state interest.

Judge Gritzner declared the law to be unconstitutional and issued a permanent injunction against its enforcement.[175] The case was appealed, and the Iowa Legislature was working on a new ag-gag law in 2019.

Utah's ag-gag law was found unconstitutional in 2017 on similar grounds.[176] In the Utah case, animal rights activist Amy Meyer and one of the plaintiffs was arrested while filming[177] "what appeared to be a bulldozer moving a sick cow at a slaughterhouse in Draper City, Utah. Meyer was on public property at the time—meaning her actions did not fall within the statute—but the State nonetheless brought charges. It later dismissed the case against Meyer without prejudice." Utah's ag-gag law criminalized[178] "obtain[ing] access to an agricultural operation under false pretenses," bugging an agricultural operation, filming an

[173] The *New York Times* reported in 2008 on the recall of 142 million pounds of meat, 37 million pounds of which went to school lunch programs because the slaughterhouse processed cows that were sick. Andrew Martin, "Largest Recall of Ground Beef Is Ordered," *New York Times*, Feb. 18, 2008.

[174] *Animal Legal Defense Fund v. Reynolds*, 353 F.Supp.3d 812, 825 (S.D. Iowa 2019). Quoting *United States v. Alvarez*, 567 U.S. 709, 132 S.Ct. 2537.

[175] *Animal Legal Defense Fund v. Reynolds*, 353 F.Supp.3d 812 (S.D.Iowa 2019).

[176] *Animal Legal Defense Fund v. Herbert*, 263 F.Supp.3d 1193 (D. Utah 2017).

[177] Ibid. at 1199.

[178] Utah Code § 76–6–112 (2012).

agricultural operation after applying for a position with the intent to film and filming an agricultural operation while trespassing."

U.S. District Judge Robert J. Shelby's analysis led to a finding that the law did not pass strict scrutiny because, among other things, it lacked a compelling state interest. The state argued that the act was intended to protect animals from diseases brought in by workers, to protect animals from unqualified and inattentive workers and to protect unqualified workers.[179]

> As an initial matter, it is not clear that these were the actual reasons motivating the Act. Indeed, the legislative history surrounding the Act appears entirely devoid of any reference to an intention by the State to protect the safety of animals or workers. Rather, as discussed, it is rife with discussion of the need to address harm caused by "national propaganda groups," and by "the vegetarian people" who are "trying to kill the animal industry," "a group of people that want to put [agricultural facilities] out of business."

Judge Shelby found the act violated the First Amendment rights of the plaintiffs.

EXTENDING MISREPRESENTATION AND PRIVACY CONCEPTS AGAINST THE NEWS MEDIA: VEILLEUX V. NBC

Five Maine teenagers were in the breakdown lane of a Maine Turnpike in 1993. The Ford Escort they were in had broken down. Then, their car was struck by a semi-tractor trailer driven by Robert Hornbarger.[180] "State police said it appeared that Hornbarger nodded off at the wheel when his southbound rig drifted into the breakdown lane and ran over a disabled Ford Escort, killing four of the five teen-agers inside." Hornbarger was not charged in the deaths of the teens. Instead, Hornbarger pled guilty to doctoring his log book to show that he had not driven more than the 10 hours allowed each day. He was sentenced to four months in jail. "Hornbarger said at his sentencing he was sorry the accident happened, but it wasn't his fault. He also said he could not remember what happened, but he denied having fallen asleep."

Alan Handel, a freelance producer, learned of that incident and called a *Dateline* producer about the accident and about long-distance trucker fatigue. The producer proposed a story to be called "Truckers—Asleep at the Wheel."[181] NBC agreed and assigned a *Dateline* associate producer and reporter to assist with the story. *Dateline* initially did interviews with the parents of one of the teens killed. The parents were founders of PATT (Parents Against Tired Truckers) and advocated

---

179 *Animal Legal Defense Fund v. Herbert*, 263 F.Supp.3d 1193, 1212 (D. Utah 2017).

180 Associated Press, "Truck driver in teens' deaths freed from jail," *Bangor Daily News*, Dec. 3, 1994.

181 *Veilleux v. National Broadcasting Co.*, 206 F.3d 92, 103 (1st Cir. 2000).

stronger regulation of trucking. The broadcasters had more trouble finding a trucking company and truck driver to feature in the story. Eventually, they contacted Peter Kennedy, a truck driver, and Kennedy's employers Ray and Kelly Veilleux who operated a trucking company in Maine. Much of the testimony about the discussions between *Dateline* and the plaintiffs was disputed.[182]

> Kennedy testified that Handel stated that he had "heard you guys had a lot of negative publicity up there in Maine" and that "he'd like to do a trip on a truck to see what it was really like, and do a little thing to put us in a positive light, instead of all the negative publicity we've had."
>
> * * *
>
> Ray testified at trial that when Handel contacted him and his wife, he asked Handel his "intentions" with regard to the program. Handel responded that *Dateline* was seeking a company that operated lawfully and safely to show "what it's really like to run a trip cross-country." Ray testified that Handel agreed that PATT had already gotten enough publicity, and that he "wanted to show the other side of the coin," the "positive side." Ray's wife, Kelly Veilleux, similarly testified that Handel had stated that he had no intention of including PATT in the program, and that she and Ray had made clear that they "did not want to be involved in the show if PATT had anything to do with it."

Handel denied making the statements. Whatever the conversations, *Dateline*, Kennedy and Ray and Kelly Veilleux agreed that reporters could accompany Kennedy on a run from California to Maine. On his outbound trip and before he connected with the *Dateline* crew, Kennedy was required to take a drug test. Kennedy met with the *Dateline* team in California and they rode with him back to Maine. During the trip, they filmed and interviewed him. Some of the video showed Kennedy falsifying his driver's log and telling the reporters that he was violating transportation regulations. Sometime later, Kennedy was notified that he had failed his drug test.[183] During a later interview, he disclosed the results of the test and told *Dateline* that he had been fired by Veilleux.

Some months later, NBC broadcast its *Dateline* report showing Kennedy violating trucking regulations and reporting on his failed drug test. *Dateline* also included interviews with PATT members whose children had died in trucking accidents and Department of Transportation officials. Kennedy and Ray and Kelly Veilleux sued[184] claiming defamation, fraudulent and negligent misrepresentation,

---

[182] Ibid. at 102–103.

[183] Kennedy testified that his conversation about the drug test was off the record. The *Dateline* defendants said it was not. Ibid. at 104.

[184] *Veilleux v. National Broadcasting Co.*, 8 F.Supp.2d 23 (D.Maine 1998).

intentional and negligent infliction of emotional distress, unreasonable publication of private facts, and false light invasion of privacy. A jury found for the plaintiffs and awarded them a total of $525,000.

A three-judge panel of the First Circuit Court of Appeals reversed the judgments on all but the fraudulent and negligent misrepresentation based on the plaintiff's assertion that the *Dateline* team had promised them that PATT would not be a part of the story. Circuit Court Judge Levin Campbell, writing the opinion, held that *Dateline* promise that PATT would not be involved was a specific misrepresentation. The *Dateline* team had already completed its interviews with PATT founders before it contacted was a specific misrepresentation.

> One who fraudulently makes a misrepresentation of fact, opinion, intention or law for the purpose of inducing another to act or to refrain from action in reliance upon it, is subject to liability to the other in deceit for pecuniary loss caused to him by his justifiable reliance upon the misrepresentation.
>
> * * *
>
> Looking first at defendants' alleged promise not to include PATT in the *Dateline* program, we believe this to be a misrepresentation made in circumstances that a Maine court today would find actionable. Defendants' statements concerning PATT can reasonably be considered "specific facts" about aspects of the program within defendants' exclusive control upon which Ray reasonably could have relied.

The court was less receptive to the claim that the "promise" to put trucking in a "positive light" created an obligation on the part of *Dateline* that the plaintiffs could recover on. In part, the court reasoned, those particular words might be considered "puffing" or "trade talk."[185] More importantly, the court reasoned that the promise might not be absolute.[186]

> An initial difficulty is whether the promise to provide "positive" coverage was unconditional or whether it should be interpreted as containing an implied condition that plaintiffs' own conduct, while driving cross-country under defendants' scrutiny, must at least be consistent with such favorable treatment. *Dateline* is, after all, a news program; reporters do not normally overlook newsworthy conduct, and it is hard to imagine that the parties expected positive coverage no matter how badly plaintiffs later behaved. Here, subsequent to the alleged promise, Kennedy admitted on camera to various regulatory violations and to taking illegal drugs. Should the alleged promise be construed to

---

[185] The terms come from contract law and refer to positive comments made about a product or service that, while intended to get a buyer to think more positively about the product or service, are not actual representations of fact.

[186] *Veilleux v. National Broadcasting Co.*, 206 F.3d 92, 103, 121 (1st Cir. 2000).

> require defendants to ignore this evidence of misconduct and to present plaintiffs in all respects favorably? If we read the promise to contain an implied condition that plaintiffs behave appropriately in order to receive positive coverage, then it is hard to see that defendants can be held liable for misrepresentation.

The appeals court sent the case back to the trial court so that it could reconsider the misrepresentation claims.

45. EMOTIONAL DISTRESS

Accompanying libel's damage to reputation and invasion of privacy's reputation to feelings is a newer tort: emotional distress. Sometimes referred to as "intentional," sometimes termed "negligent," causing emotional distress can refer to the power of words or pictures to carry psychological harm.

HUSTLER MAGAZINE V. FALWELL

In the mid-1980s, the emerging separate tort of infliction of mental injury was a major threat to the media. But in 1988, that threat was lessened somewhat by the U.S. Supreme Court's unanimous decision in *Hustler v. Falwell*.[187] The Court held that the First Amendment protects parodies—even *Hustler* magazine's mock ad which said Rev. Jerry Falwell's first sexual experience was in an outhouse, with his mother, while they were both drunk.

Following a scattergun tort approach, Rev. Falwell sued *Hustler* and its publisher, Larry Flynt, for libel *plus* invasion of privacy *plus* intentional infliction of emotional distress.

Not surprisingly, even though the fine print said "ad parody—not to be taken seriously"—a U.S. district court jury in Virginia, where Rev. Falwell preached and had his Liberty University, was sympathetic to Rev. Falwell. (After all, Flynt had declared, while giving a pre-trial deposition, that his intent in publishing the parody was to "assassinate" the minister's reputation.)[188] Sympathetic or not, the jury did not believe that Falwell had been libeled: "no reasonable person would believe that the parody was describing actual facts about Falwell." The jury also declined to find that his privacy had been invaded. Jurors, however, seized upon the idea of infliction of mental injury and awarded Falwell $200,000: $100,000 in compensatory damages, plus $50,000 in punitive damages against Flynt and $50,000 against his magazine.

The Court of Appeals, Fourth Circuit—like the trial court—concluded Falwell was a public figure.[189] That public figure status meant

---

[187] *Hustler Magazine v. Falwell*, 485 U.S. 46, 108 S.Ct. 876 (1988).

[188] David Margolick, "Some See Threat in Non-Libel Verdict of Falwell," *New York Times*, Dec. 10, 1986.

[189] *Falwell v. Flynt*, 797 F.2d 1270, 1274 (4th Cir.1986).

that defendants Flynt and *Hustler* magazine were entitled to "the same level of first amendment protection in an action for intentional infliction of mental distress that they would receive in an action for libel." Even so, the Court of Appeals found the ad parody so obnoxious that it affirmed the trial court's ruling.[190]

The Supreme Court disagreed. Chief Justice William H. Rehnquist defined the issue as whether the First Amendment limits a state's authority to protect its citizens from intentional infliction of mental distress. He wrote,[191] "We must decide whether a public figure may recover damages for emotional harm caused to him by an ad parody offensive to him and doubtless gross and repugnant in the eyes of most."

To the surprise of many, Chief Justice Rehnquist set out on a sweeping reaffirmation of First Amendment principles—principles which he had questioned in other cases.[192] He wrote approvingly of the free flow of ideas and opinions on matters of public interest as being at the heart of the First Amendment.[193] " '[T]he freedom to speak one's mind is not only an aspect of individual liberty—and thus a good unto itself—but also is essential to the common quest for truth and the vitality of society as a whole.' "

He declared that under the First Amendment robust political debate will result in speech critical of public officials or public figures who are[194] " 'intimately involved in the resolution of important questions, or by reason of their fame, shape events in areas of concern to society at large.' "

Rehnquist did not treat freedom of expression as an absolute: The First Amendment does not mean that ". . . any speech about public figures is immune from sanction in the form of damages. Although unknowingly false statements will be protected to ensure breathing space needed for open debate, knowingly or recklessly false statements have no value and are not protected."

The Chief Justice wrote that the law does not regard an intent to inflict emotional harm with much solicitude. He termed it understandable that most jurisdictions have created civil liability when such conduct is sufficiently outrageous. But Rev. Falwell, a powerful individual and sometime candidate for president, was a public figure involved,[195] ". . . in the world of debate about public affairs, [where] many

---

190 Ibid.

191 *Hustler Magazine, Inc. v. Falwell*, 485 U.S. 46, 108 S.Ct. 876 (1988).

192 See the Rehnquist opinion in *Wolston v. Reader's Digest Ass'n*, 443 U.S. 157, 99 S.Ct. 2701 (1979), rejecting the argument that a person who engages in criminal conduct automatically becomes a limited-purpose public figure. See also his opinion in *Time, Inc. v. Firestone*, 424 U.S. 448, 96 S.Ct. 958 (1976).

193 *Hustler Magazine, Inc. v. Falwell*, 485 U.S. 46, 50, 108 S.Ct.876, 879 (1988).

194 Ibid. at 53, 880. Quoting *Associated Press v. Walker*, 388 U.S. 130, 164, 87 S.Ct. 1975, 1996 (1967).

195 Ibid.

things done with motives that are less than admirable are protected by the First Amendment."

Rehnquist declared that any system of civil damages that might teach Flynt a lesson also would endanger a long and valued tradition of caustic American political caricatures—verbal and visual—and political cartoons. He pointed to the prominent role in political debate played by satire and political cartoons, and to the impact of images over the years: Lincoln's gangly frame, Teddy Roosevelt's glasses and teeth, Franklin D. Roosevelt's cigarette holder and jutting jaw.

Even though Falwell argued that the *Hustler* magazine parody was so outrageous that it lacked First Amendment protection, Rehnquist disagreed. True, he wrote,[196] "*Hustler* is at best a distant cousin of . . . political cartoons . . . and a rather poor relation at that." But the Chief Justice expressed doubts that a sufficiently precise standard could be found safely to distinguish Flynt's publication from political cartoons in general.

Two respected communications lawyers, Robert D. Sack[197] and Sandra S. Baron, asserted after *Hustler* that for there to be a successful emotional distress claim, the conduct must be[198] "extreme and outrageous, must cause severe emotional distress, and must be made with conscious disregard of a high degree of probability that severe emotional distress will result."

KOLEGAS V. HEFTEL BROADCASTING CORP.

Emotional distress cases often share characteristics of extreme and juror-offending conduct by media employees. When jurors perceive a powerful, arrogant mass medium "kicking around" individual citizens, is it any wonder that jury verdicts unfavorable to the media may result?

Consider the case of *Kolegas v. Heftel Broadcasting Corp.*,[199] a confrontation arising when two Chicago radio show hosts did a telephone interview with Anthony N. Kolegas. Mr. Kolegas had called station WLUP to promote a cartoon festival he had organized. Some of the proceeds were to support works of the Neurofibromatosis Foundation (NF). That foundation works to assist persons suffering from the condition commonly called Elephant Man's Disease. Kolegas had purchased airtime for a commercial on the station.

While talking to the hosts, Tim and Beth Disa, Kolegas mentioned that both his wife and his son suffered from NF. The radio show hosts

[196] *Hustler Magazine, Inc. v. Falwell*, 485 U.S. 46, 55, 108 S.Ct. 876, 881 (1988).

[197] Now Circuit Court of Appeals Judge Robert Sack.

[198] Robert D. Sack and Sandra S. Baron, *Libel, Slander, and Related Problems*, 2nd ed. (New York: Practicing Law Institute, 1994), pp. 676–677.

[199] *Kolegas v. Heftel Broadcasting Corp.*, 154 Ill.2d 1, 180 Ill.Dec. 307, 607 N.E.2d 201 (1992).

expressed disbelief that there was such a cartoon festival, and one said that Kolegas was "scamming" them. One host then said:

> "Why would someone marry a woman if she had Elephant Man disease? It's not like he couldn't tell—unless it was a shotgun wedding. * * * If he is producing it [the cartoon festival], he's only producing it part-time. The rest of the time he's too busy picking out their wardrobe * * * to make sure they have large hats to cover their big heads * * *"

Mr. and Mrs. Kolegas sued alleging that the radio hosts had defamed them, invaded their privacy and inflicted reckless infliction of emotional distress. A trial court dismissed their complaint and an intermediate appellate court affirmed in part and reversed in part. The case then went to the Illinois Supreme Court. Justice Michael Anthony Bilandic wrote the opinion for the Court which restored all the Kolegas' claims, sending the case back to trial. He recited the elements of the intentional infliction of emotional distress tort:[200] The conduct must be extreme and outrageous. The defendant must have known there was a high probability that his conduct would cause severe emotional distress. And, that the conduct, in fact, caused severe emotional distress.[201]

> The Disas responded to Kolegas' truthful statements by implying that Kolegas' wife was so hideous that no one would marry her except under duress. The Disas also broadcast statements implying that Kolegas' wife and five-year-old child had deformed heads. Had these comments been expressed privately, we might be more inclined to consider them "mere insults." Here, however, the Disas broadcast their derogatory remarks on the radio throughout the Chicago metropolitan area and outlying counties. We agree with the plaintiffs that conduct that is trivial between private parties may become extreme and outrageous by virtue of its publication to the community at large.

Justice Bilandic also held that the case should go back for trial because it was reasonable to infer that the Disas knew that the plaintiffs would be particularly susceptible to emotional distress especially when the Disas made which implied that they were hideous and deformed as a result of their disease.

There are no further proceedings suggesting that the defendants settled with the Kolegas' rather than run the risk of going to trial.

RICH V. FOX NEWS

The killing of a young Democratic National Committee staffer led to an emotional distress tort over Fox News' efforts to promote a conspiracy

---

[200] Ibid. at 20, 317, 211.

[201] Ibid. at 22, 212, 318.

theory about the leak of DNC emails.[202] Seth Rich was shot and killed near his home in Washington, D.C., months before the 2016 presidential election. The Metropolitan Police Department investigated and concluded that Rich was killed in a botched robbery attempt. But within days of his death, conspiracy websites began to claim that Rich was responsible for leaking the DNC emails to WikiLeaks and was murdered because of that.[203] Joel and Mary Rich, Seth's parents, opposed the conspiracy claims and asked that people, "refrain from pushing unproven and harmful theories about Seth's murder." But Fox News reporter Malia Zimmerman and Fox News commentator Ed Butowsky allegedly set out make the conspiracy national news even though the Department of Homeland Security and the office of the Director of National Intelligence on Election Security had debunked the conspiracy theory,[204]

Butowsky contacted Seth Rich's parents in Nebraska, through religious and social media connections. He had posted on Facebook that he was "looking to connect with anyone Jewish in Omaha." Once he had gotten to know Joel and Mary Rich and having won their confidence, Butowsky got them to hire a private investigator "to get closure as a family."[205] He contacted newly hired Fox News contributor Rod Wheeler, a former detective and private investigator, to help with the scheme. Butowsky brought Wheeler and the Riches together and persuaded them to allow him to pay for Wheeler's work. Even so, the Riches were Wheeler's clients and when they signed the contract with Wheeler, they "expressly prohibited 'media representation, unless otherwise permitted by the [Riches] in writing,' and stated that Wheeler 'shall not release any information regarding the investigation . . . without prior authorization.' "[206] Butowsky told the Riches he would respect the obligation that Wheeler not speak to him or anyone else.

On May 10, 2017, Butowsky and Zimmerman called Wheeler[207] "to falsely inform him that they had developed an FBI source supposedly confirming" that Seth had been in contact with WikiLeaks. Zimmerman and Butowsky both pressured Wheeler to go public with the false FBI source story which would run on Fox News. A few days later, he agreed.[208]

> [O]n May 16, Fox News published two pieces—both penned by Zimmerman.

---

[202] *Rich v. Fox News Network, LLC*, 939 F.3d 112 (2d Cir. 2018).

[203] U.S. intelligence agencies have concluded that Russian hackers got into the DNC server and gave the trove of emails to WikiLeaks.

[204] DHS Press Office, Joint Statement from the Department of Homeland Security and Office of the Director of National Intelligence on Election Security, Dep't Homeland Sec. (Oct. 7, 2016), https://www.dhs.gov/news/2016/10/07/joint-statement-department-homeland-security-and-office-director-national.

[205] *Rich v. Fox News Network, LLC*, 939 F.3d 112, 118 (2d Cir. 2018).

[206] Ibid.

[207] Ibid. at 118–119.

[208] Ibid. at 119.

> The first article was titled: "Slain DNC Staffer Had Contact with WikiLeaks Say Multiple Sources." [* * *] The article attributed a quote to an anonymous federal investigator: "I have seen and read the emails between Seth Rich and WikiLeaks." Id. The article continued: "The revelation is consistent with the findings of Rod Wheeler, former DC homicide detective and Fox News contributor and whose private investigation firm was hired by Rich's family to probe the case."
>
> The second article was titled: "Family of slain DNC staffer Seth Rich blasts detective over report of WikiLeaks link."[* * *]It read: "Rod Wheeler, a retired Washington homicide detective and Fox News contributor investigating the case on behalf of the Rich Family, made the WikiLeaks claim, which was corroborated by a federal investigator who spoke to Fox News." [* * *] It also added: "[A] spokesman for Rich's family on Tuesday said Wheeler was not authorized to speak for the family."

Emails, telephone calls and texts made clear that Fox News was aware of the scheme all along, Circuit Court of Appeals Judge Guido Calabresi, wrote in his opinion. Fox News reporters and talk show hosts continued to push the story, focusing on Wheeler's connection to the Rich family.[209]

> "HANNITY: [F]ormer D.C. homicide detective, Rod Wheeler, who was hired by a third party to investigate the murder on behalf of the family, says Mr. Rich was communicating with WikiLeaks before he was killed. Now, Seth's family has been pushing back today . . . . I have known you a long time, Rod, you are a man of honor and integrity, so tell us who hired you. WHEELER: Well, actually, I was hired by the family, Joel and Mary Rich. They signed the contract."

The Riches had asked Fox News to retract the story. Fox retracted, explaining that "[t]he article was not initially subjected to [a] high degree of editorial scrutiny." Even so, guests that Fox News invited to speak continued to repeat the story, and Fox kept two videos of the story on its website.

Butowsky continued to exploit the story and the Riches. He wrote to Joel Rich that Zimmerman had found the person and gun used to shoot your son.[210] "When you find out who did it you are going to be very very emotional." Butowsky told the *Washington Times* in 2018 that the Riches confirmed that Seth transmitted the DNC emails to WikiLeaks.

The Riches filed an intentional infliction of emotional distress claim against Fox News, Zimmerman and Butowsky. A U.S. District Court dismissed their claims with prejudice meaning that they could not amend

[209] Ibid. at 120.

[210] Ibid.

or re-file their suit. A three-judge panel of the Second Circuit Court of Appeals took up the case and reversed. Judge Calabresi, writing for the panel, held that on its face, the Riches' complaint met the requirements for an intentional infliction of emotional distress claim.[211]

> We have no trouble concluding that—taking their allegations as true—the Riches plausibly alleged what amounted to a campaign of emotional torture. In order to publish a knowingly false article accusing Seth of leaking the DNC emails, Butowsky and Zimmerman needed a reliable source. They settled on a purportedly independent investigator, hired by the Riches. But they had to fabricate that source. So Butowsky—through lies, religious appeals, and financial support—convinced the Riches to hire Wheeler, a Fox News contributor, as their private investigator.

Judge Calabresi remanded the case back to the district court to continue proceedings.

46. CONTRACT CLAIMS AND TORTIOUS INTERFERENCE

Private businesses affect the public, whether it is an airplane that has dangerous faults or an ingredient in a baby or personal hygiene product. The resourceful journalist will seek out corporate sources for details or confirmation. That can lead to the courtroom if attempts to get information runs afoul of a non-disclosure agreement.

In the first days of November 1996, CBS lawyers ordered *60 Minutes* not to broadcast an interview with Dr. Jeffrey Wigand, a former tobacco company scientist and executive. It turned out that the Wigand formerly worked for Brown & Williamson and the company was going to court to prevent him from violating a non-disclosure agreement. Bill Carter reported in The *New York Times* that CBS lawyers did not fear a libel suit from Brown & Williamson. The concern was that CBS could be sued for *tortious interference with contractual relations* because of tobacco company secrecy agreement with its former executive.[212]

Late in November 1995, Dr. Wigand was subpoenaed to testify in Mississippi in a Medicaid reimbursement lawsuit brought by that state's attorney general, Mike Moore. Documents Dr. Wigand brought with him—plus more Brown & Williamson inside reports on tobacco and health which were then put on the World Wide Web by a West Coast medical school—promised that the matter would not die quietly.[213]

---

211 Ibid. at 123.

212 Bill Carter, " '60 Minutes' Ordered to Pull Interview in Tobacco Report," *New York Times*, Nov. 9, 1995. See also Lawrence K. Grossman, "CBS, 60 Minutes, and the Unseen Interview," *Columbia Journalism Review*, Jan./Feb. 1996.

213 Barnaby J. Feder, "Former Tobacco Official Begins Giving Deposition," *New York Times*, November 30, 1995.

Finally, relieved that some of Dr. Wigand's testimony had been given in that deposition in Mississippi, CBS decided to broadcast the interview. Parts of Dr. Wigand's sworn testimony, although sealed, already had been published in The *Wall Street Journal* and closely matched what Dr. Wigand said in his broadcast interview, aired on CBS on January 28, 1996. Dr. Wigand's remarks included the charge that Dr. Thomas Sandefur, former Brown & Williamson chairman, committed perjury before a Congressional committee when he swore that he did not believe that nicotine is addictive.

A law review article by Maura Strassberga[214] suggests that there is a substantial risk of reporters being sued for intentional interference with a contract agreement. If a reporter tries to convince a corporate employee to divulge company secrets, he may be at risk of attempting to breach of a confidential or fiduciary relationship or disclosing trade secrets. Most states have established tort liability for disclosure of trade secrets.[215]

[214] Maura Irene Strassberga, "An Ethical Rabbit Hole: Model Rule 4.4 Intentional Interference With Former Employee Non-Disclosure Agreements and the Threat of Disqualification," 90 *Neb. L. Rev.* 141 (2011).

[215] Ibid. at 148.

PART 3

ACCESS TO GOVERNMENT INFORMATION

CHAPTER 8

REPORTING THE LEGISLATIVE AND EXECUTIVE BRANCHES

Sec.

47. THE PROBLEM OF SECRECY IN GOVERNMENT

Following World War II, obtaining access to information at various levels of government became an acute problem in American journalism.

A democracy is a political system in which the people dictate the course of their government by electing leaders whose policies and goals are in line with their own. But making choices in the voting booth requires information. Without reliable, contextual information, democracy becomes a joke. Getting that information, having openness even in democratic societies is not easily accomplished. The pressures to keep information from the people are many and compelling, especially when those pressures are the result of rationalizing, saying that the greater good requires secrecy. Or, it can simply be a way of avoiding accountability.

The Washington Post uncovered information in 2019 about a series of pessimistic assessments of the Afghan military campaign that had been kept secret by three different presidential administrations: Bush, Obama and Trump. The bottom line:[1] "John Sopko, the head of the federal agency that conducted the interviews, acknowledged to *The Post* that the documents show, "the American people have constantly been lied to."

Afghanistan, the longest military operation in U.S. history has sent almost three quarters of a million servicemen and servicewomen to the country. Many served multiple tours. Some 2,300 died in the campaign and 20,589 were wounded.[2] Apart from the human toll, Afghanistan cost $2 trillion (some estimates put the cost at $1.5 trillion). The cost of making war was $1.5 trillion. The interest paid on the money spent was $500 billion. The United States spent $115 billion on reconstruction. The

[1] Craig Whitlock, "At War With The Truth," *The Washington Post*, Dec. 9, 2019.

[2] Thomas Gibbons-Neff, "Documents Reveal U.S. Officials Misled Public on War in Afghanistan," *New York Times*, Dec. 9, 2019.

cost of training Afghan military and police was $87 billion. Economic development cost $24 billion and efforts to halt the drug trade cost $10 million.

Congress created the Office of the Special Inspector General for Afghanistan Reconstruction (SIGAR) to investigate waste and fraud in the Afghan war zone. In 2014, John Sopko, the head of SIGAR, ordered the agency begin a project known as "Lessons Learned." It was intended to help the United States avoid repeating the mistakes of Afghanistan. The Lessons Learned team interviewed more than 600 people who had firsthand experience in Afghanistan, the interviews taking place between 2014 and 2018. Most were Americans. SIGAR analysts also interviewed NATO allies and. About 20 Afghan officials were interviewed about reconstruction and development programs. Because the interviews were conducted by an inspector general's office and because they were promised anonymity if they wanted, the subjects were unusually open and direct.[3] Interviewees sometimes allowed their names to be used.

> Some described focused efforts to deliberately mislead the public. They said it was common at military headquarters in Kabul—and at the White House—to distort statistics to make it appear the United States was winning the war when that was not the case.
>
> "Every data point was altered to present the best picture possible," Bob Crowley, an Army colonel who served as a senior counterinsurgency adviser to U.S. military commanders in 2013 and 2014, told government interviewers. "Surveys, for instance, were totally unreliable but reinforced that everything we were doing was right and we became a self-licking ice cream cone."

Since 2016, SIGAR published seven reports on Lessons Learned. Those reports took the clear language from the interviews and condensed them into a bureaucratic prose that left out the harshest criticisms that were spoken, *The Post* reported.[4]

> "We found the stabilization strategy and the programs used to achieve it were not properly tailored to the Afghan context, and successes in stabilizing Afghan districts rarely lasted longer than the physical presence of coalition troops and civilians," read the introduction to one report released in May 2018.

The experience of Vietnam was brought up time and again in interviews. Early on, a reporter asked Bush whether he could avoid a Vietnam quagmire.

> "We learned some very important lessons in Vietnam," Bush replied confidently. "People often ask me, 'How long will this last?' This particular battlefront will last as long as it takes to

---

[3] Craig Whitlock, "At War With The Truth," *The Washington Post*, Dec. 9, 2019.

[4] Ibid.

> bring al-Qaeda to justice. It may happen tomorrow, it may happen a month from now, it may take a year or two. But we will prevail."
>
> In those early days, other U.S. leaders mocked the notion that the nightmare of Vietnam might repeat itself in Afghanistan.
>
> "All together now—quagmire!" Rumsfeld joked at a news conference on Nov. 27, 2001.

And, as in Vietnam every administration worked at manipulating public opinion, *The Post* reported. "In news conferences and other public appearances, those in charge of the war have followed the same talking points for 18 years. No matter how the war is going—and especially when it is going badly—they emphasize how they are making progress."

> Even when casualty counts and other figures looked bad, the senior NSC official said, the White House and Pentagon would spin them to the point of absurdity. Suicide bombings in Kabul were portrayed as a sign of the Taliban's desperation, that the insurgents were too weak to engage in direct combat. Meanwhile, a rise in U.S. troop deaths was cited as proof that American forces were taking the fight to the enemy.
>
> "It was their explanations," the senior NSC official said. "For example, attacks are getting worse. 'That's because there are more targets for them to fire at, so more attacks are a false indicator of instability.' Then, three months later, attacks are still getting worse. 'It's because the Taliban are getting desperate, so it's actually an indicator that we're winning.' "

Shortly after American and international forces entered Afghanistan, 9 percent of Americans said it was a mistake. That compared to 89 percent who said it was not.[5] Over the years the numbers have changed 43 percent saying it was a mistake to send troops and 52 percent saying it was not. But what would the numbers have been if three different presidencies disclosed what people on the ground were saying? That is a function of democracy, providing people with information to make informed choices with.

The Washington Post used the Freedom of Information Act to, first, request the reports and interview materials. It used elements of the Act to file a suit to force the release of the documents. FOIA is discussed later in this chapter. President Trump was critical of the practice of SIGAR to release its reports to the public.[6]

> "What kind of stuff is this?" the president asked about the reports, adding that "the public means the enemy" when it comes to who can read them. He did not specify the reports to

---

[5] R.J.Reinhart, "U.S. Views Mixed on War in Afghanistan," *Gallup*, Sept. 11, 2019. https://news.gallup.com/poll/266546/views-mixed-war-afghanistan.aspx.

[6] Dan Lamothe, "After Trump's broadside on inspectors general scrutinizing Afghanistan, silence from those under fire," *The Washington Post*, Jan. 4, 2019.

> which he was referring, but he told acting Defense Secretary Patrick M. Shanahan that he did not want watchdog reports from his department detailing the war to be released anymore.

President Trump said the enemy, without identifying who that was, reads "every line," although the reports do not include classified information. He said SIGAR should continue preparing the reports but that they should be private and "locked up." Members of Congress would be able to read the reports in secure locations. Mandy Smithberger, the director of the Straus Military Reform Project for the Project on Government Oversight, said that the American people deserve to know whether U.S. efforts in Afghanistan are achieving their goals or resulting in a fair return on investment.[7]

> "Classification decisions should be based on what information must be kept secret to keep our troops safe, but not as a way to obscure the public debate about our current wars," Smithberger said.

Ironically, while looking at how different presidencies treated information about Afghanistan it turns out that secrets are becoming more difficult to keep. The WikiLeaks revelations of hundreds of thousands of secret U.S. documents on war and diplomacy and treatment of prisoners of war showed that in the Internet Era, thousands of pages of secret material can be stolen and distributed in mere moments. The 2016 WikiLeaks leak of DNC emails demonstrated the power of such leaks to influence presidential elections. But no matter where the raw information comes from, it is up to journalists to evaluate, decide what is newsworthy and credible and what is too dangerous to individual lives or national security to be published. WikiLeaks, coming from secure servers beyond the reach of the laws of the United States, is just an early denizen of a Brave New World of document insecurity.

Information about government must be available to all concerned in order to allow for the existence of self-government. It may or may not be channeled through the mass media. Some critics have suggested that the media, owned by an increasingly smaller number of conglomerates, are spending a correspondingly smaller amount of their energies looking at societal problems. Norman L. Rosenberg and others have suggested that "the media's attention to social problems in the 1950s and 1960s [and arguably into the 2000s] primarily ebbed and flowed in relationship to nonlegal pressures within the communications industry itself * * * and to the complex links between the Fourth Estate and other powerful institutions * * *."

If such a state of affairs exists, what have journalists been doing about it? Not enough, if one believes Robert M. Entman's gloomy contentions:

---

7 Ibid.

> Restricted by the limited tastes of the audience and reliant upon political elites for most information, journalists participate in an interdependent news system, not a free market of ideas. In practice * * * the news media fall far short of the ideal version of a free press as civic educator and guardian of democracy.

Layoffs, firings and the deaths of newspapers and magazines have further diminished the ability of the news media to report, much less find information about what governments do, especially in the coronavirus pandemic when advertisers stopped buying ads. Decades ago, news organizations assigned reporters to each of the federal cabinet agencies. The reporters would know the people, the policies and the processes of the Department of Commerce or Interior. They were in a position to spot developing stories and provide more complete reports. Today, reporters find themselves parachuting into breaking stories like smokejumpers dropping in to fight a raging wildfire. Newspaper reporters find themselves covering their communities by telephone as they try to fill shrinking news holes as outlets with too few staffers.[8] Local TV news lacks resources to be able to provide viewers with the context, background and broader perspective of community, regional or state government. The result is a voting public with less and less information with which to make informed decisions at the ballot box.

And so, it is necessary to make the process of getting access to information about government more efficient and less difficult for both media and citizen. The media can provide a focus and the resources to fight for information. Informed citizens can make government accountable and also become speakers in their own right. The Internet has recreated that time when anyone could become a pamphleteer and freely publish her views. The growth of cable and satellite television delivery has increased channels by a hundredfold, and a flood of news, opinion and commentary fill the Internet. All of these have the potential of adding to public understanding and control of its institutions of government and society, as long as they have access to the facts.

The failure of mainstream media coverage in the run up to the invasion of Iraq in 2003 demonstrated the dangers of listening to the spin of public officials without having facts in hand. The Center for International and Security Studies at Maryland and the University of Maryland examined how 11 major media outlets reported on the issue.[9] The Center concluded that most reporters accepted the Bush administration's coupling of terrorism with Weapons of Mass Destruction.

> Many stories stenographically reported the incumbent administration's perspectives on WMD, giving too little critical

[8] The news hole is a newspaper term for the amount of space in a newspaper's edition for news.

[9] "Study faults media coverage of WMD," *Editor and Publisher*, Mar. 9, 2004.

examination of the way officials framed the events, issues, threats and policy options.

John Steinbrunner, director of the center, said that,[10] "the American media did not play the role of checking and balancing the exercise of power that the standard theory of democracy requires."

Underscoring the point, a Knight-Ridder investigative team reported in March 2004[11] on assertions made by the Bush administration that Saddam Hussein had ties to Al-Qaeda. The investigative team was one of the few to critically examine the pre-war statements of the administration before the invasion of Iraq.[12] The team concluded that the linkage, made on a number of occasions by President Bush and Vice President Dick Cheney, between Hussein and Bin Laden was overstated and that the administration had withheld other information.[13]

> Vice President Dick Cheney told *National Public Radio* in January that there was "overwhelming evidence" of a relationship between Saddam and Al-Qaida. Among the evidence was Iraq's harboring of Abdul Rahman Yasin, a suspect in the 1993 World Trade Center bombing. Cheney did not mention that Iraq had offered to turn over Yasin to the FBI in 1998. The Clinton administration refused the offer, because it was unwilling to reward Iraq for returning a fugitive.

Communicating effectively requires that the First Amendment now be given expanded meaning where access to government information is concerned. Growth of governmental power has coincided with expanding government secrecy at all levels and the digitization of records. The need for computer-literate reporters and citizens is increasingly important as records once freely available in file cabinets now require the involvement of a government gatekeeper. Computer searches for information—and finding patterns in that information—can be far more informative to society than yesterday's paper-chases, but only if citizen access is protected under the Constitution and under supporting statutes.[14] As is discussed in Sec. 48 of this chapter, the Supreme Court of the United States has viewed the Constitution and the First Amendment as something apart from the concept of "a public's right to know" or a "citizen's right to gather information."[15]

No defined segment of American society has been more concerned about tendencies to secrecy in government than journalists. Some believe

---

[10] Ibid.

[11] The story covered statements made before and after the invasion.

[12] "Knight Ridder team pursues 'most important story,' " *Editor and Publisher*, March 4, 2004.

[13] Ibid.

[14] For a philosopher's thoughtful appraisal of openness, see Sissela Bok, *Secrets: On the Ethics of Concealment and Revelation* (New York: Pantheon, 1983).

[15] See Dwight L. Teeter, Jr., "The First Amendment at Its Bicentennial: Necessary But Not Sufficient?" *Journalism and Mass Communication Quarterly*, Vol. 69, No 1. (Spring, 1992), pp. 18–27.

secrecy is the central threat to freedom of expression in Twenty-First Century America. During World War II, the need for extensive secrecy for an enormous war machine in a government bureaucracy grown gigantic was tolerated. But journalists after the war soon detected a broad pattern of continued secrecy in government operations. Access to meetings was denied; reports, papers, documents at all levels of government seemed less available. An intense, insistent campaign for access to government information was launched in the 1950's by editors, publishers, reporters, and news organizations. It went under a banner labeled "Freedom of Information," and under the claim that the press was fighting for the "people's right to know."[16]

To combat what they viewed as a severe increase in denial of access to the public's business, journalists took organized action. "Freedom of Information" committees were established by the American Society of Newspaper Editors[17] (ASNE) and by the Society of Professional Journalists—Sigma Delta Chi. The ASNE commissioned newspaper attorney Harold L. Cross to perform a major study on the law of access to government activity. His book, "*The People's Right to Know*", was published in 1953 and served as a central source of information and argument for openness. State and local chapters of professional groups worked for the adoption of state access laws. In 1958, a Freedom of Information Center was opened at the University of Missouri School of Journalism, as a clearinghouse and research facility for those concerned with the subject of access. Meanwhile, an early and vigorous ally was found in the House Subcommittee on Government Information under Rep. John E. Moss of California, created to investigate charges of excessive secrecy in the Executive branch of government.[18]

Journalism also had powerful allies in the scientific community. It found that the advance of knowledge in vast areas of government-sponsored science was being slowed, sometimes crippled for years, in the blockage of the flow of research information between and even within agencies of the federal government. Fear of "leakage" of secrets important to defense in the Cold War with the Soviet Union brought administrative orders that were contrary to the tenets of scientists and researchers. Stories about roadblocks in research and a too-real snarl of regulations, rules and red tape prevented scientists from sharing their findings with others. Their concern about the damage to the advance of knowledge in science paralleled journalists' alarm about damage to the

---

[16] See Annual Reports, Sigma Delta Chi Advancement of Freedom of Information Committee (Chicago, Sigma Delta Chi).

[17] Now the American Society of News Editors.

[18] Rep. John E. Moss, Preface to Replies from Federal Agencies to Questionnaire Submitted by the Special Subcommittee on Government Information of the Committee on Government Operations, 84 Cong. 1 Sess. (Nov. 1, 1955), p. iii.

democratic assumption that free institutions rest on an informed public.[19]

The Sept. 11 and anthrax attacks of 2001 brought a return to practices of the Cold War. *Science & Nature, Proceedings of the National Academy* and more than 17 other scientific journals agreed in 2003 to delete information from articles that might harm national security. The editors of the journals issued a statement at a meeting of the American Association for the Advancement of Science laying out their policy.[20]

> We recognize that on occasion an editor may conclude that the potential harm of publication outweighs the potential societal benefits. Under such circumstances, the paper should be modified or not be published.

The discussion was prompted by the presentation of a paper "that showed how to synthesize the polio virus from ordinary chemicals." It should be noted, though, that the editors who spoke in favor of the policy said that the polio paper would still have been published because its scientific and research value outweighed the risk of terrorism. Not all scientists agreed with the policy. Critics said that journal editors did not have the means to decide what research would pose more risk than benefit as scientists.[21]

Public understanding of the dangers of official secrecy broadened in the exposé of the Executive's abuse of power in the Watergate episode of the mid-1970's and in the debates over President Donald Trump's impeachment inquiry. During Watergate, Earl Warren, retired Chief Justice of the United States, credited the news media with a share in exposing the fraud and deceit, said if we are to learn from[22] "the debacle we are in, we should first strike at secrecy in government wherever it exists, because it is the incubator for corruption." New recruits entered the battle against official secrecy—Common Cause and the Center for National Security Studies among them. Groups of concerned citizens in states joined to promote openness in their state and local governments and coalitions formed to work to ensure the rights of the people to know what their governments were doing. The National Freedom of Information Coalition came into being to foster cooperation among state access groups and help bring into being organizations in states where none existed.

As different presidential administrations and changing leadership of federal agencies has meant sometimes more and sometimes less access being given, the key to reporting of the legislative and executive branches will always be persistence: stubbornness in asking questions and

---

[19] "Science, Education and Communications", 12 *Bulletin of Atomic Scientists*, 333 (Nov.1956); Walter Gellhorn, *Security, Loyalty, and Science* (Ithaca: Cornell Univ. Press, 1950).

[20] Amy Harmon, "Journals to consider U.S. security in publishing," *New York Times*, Feb. 16, 2003.

[21] Ibid.

[22] "Governmental Secrecy: Corruption's Ally", 60 *ABA Journal* 550 (May, 1974).

virtually endless patience that is often needed in filing and re-filing FOIA (Freedom of Information Act) requests.

LAQUAN MCDONALD SHOOTING AND THE FIGHT FOR POLICE DASHCAM VIDEOS

The story was one that seemed to appear with depressing regularity in American life. A young black man, armed, confronted police officers and attacked them forcing one officer to shoot and kill him.

And then came the open records requests.[23]

Chicago police were called to a trucking yard on the Southwest Side of Chicago on the night of Oct. 20, 2014. The two officers responding to the call said they found a man, later identified as 17-year-old Laquan McDonald. He was holding a folding knife, they said, and refused to drop it when ordered. Instead, McDonald walked and jogged away. Officers followed him, one on foot, the other in their police car. They called for backup. McDonald punctured a tire on the police car and pounded on the windshield, the officers said.

By the time, McDonald reached a section of Pulaski Road, six officers were at the scene. One, Officer Jason Van Dyke, shot McDonald hitting him 16 times. McDonald told his supervisors that McDonald was swinging his knife in an aggressive manner and moving toward police.[24] He had no choice, Van Dyke said. Five other officers corroborated Van Dyke's recitation of the events.[25]

The story might have ended there. Some of the people at the scene said McDonald had not tried to attack the officers but nothing outweighed the statements of the six police officers, including Van Dyke. Questions remained, though. Reporters knew the Chicago police cars had dashcams that could have recorded exactly what happened that night.

Even so, the video of the McDonald killing might not have seen the light of day without the efforts of several journalists in Chicago. Invisible Institute's[26] reporter Jamie Kalven wrote a story for *Slate* in which he went through the report of the shooting in which police claimed that McDonald lunged at them with a knife and was shot in the chest.[27]

---

[23] Monica Davey and Mitch Smith, "Video of Chicago Police Shooting a Teenager Is Ordered Released," *New York Times*, Nov. 19, 2015.

[24] Monica Davey, "Officers' Statements Differ From Video in Death of Laquan McDonald," *New York Times*, Dec. 5, 2015.

[25] Ibid.

[26] The Invisible Institute describes itself a journalism production company on the South Side of Chicago. "Our mission is to enhance the capacity of citizens to hold public institutions accountable. Among the tactics we employ are human rights documentation, investigative reporting, civil rights litigation, the curating of public information, conceptual art projects, and the orchestration of difficult public conversations."

[27] Jamie Kalven, "Sixteen Shots Chicago police have told their version of how 17-year-old black teen Laquan McDonald died. The autopsy tells a different story." *Slate*, Feb, 10, 2015.

> The Chicago press dutifully reported the police account of the incident. The reporter for the local NBC station called it "a clear-cut case of self-defense." It was also reported that the Independent Police Review Authority (IPRA), the city agency charged with investigating police shootings, would conduct an investigation, as it does in the case of every "police-involved shooting."
>
> In its broad outlines, this is a familiar Chicago story: A black American is shot by a Chicago police officer. A police source says the shooting was justified. IPRA announces it is investigating. Then silence. After a year or two, IPRA issues a report confirming that the shooting was indeed justified.

But, as Kalven reported, there were some things that didn't fit into the police narrative. Alma Benitez, a witness that night, said that there was no need to shoot McDonald. The officers had control of the situation, she said.[28]

And then there was the autopsy. Press reports said the coroner's office ruled McDonald's death was caused by multiple gunshot wounds, Kalven wrote. The Chicago Police Department had only said that McDonald had been shot in the chest. Kalven decided to use the Illinois equivalent of the Freedom of Information Act.[29]

> The question the press didn't ask—how many gunshot wounds are covered by the word "multiple"?—has now been definitively answered by the recently finalized autopsy report, which I have obtained via a Freedom of Information Act request: Laquan McDonald was shot 16 times.
>
> [* * *]

Kalven's story also revealed that a police dashboard camera had recorded the shooting. He and more than a dozen national and local journalists filed FOIA requests for the video. They were told that the video could not be released because it was part of an ongoing investigation.

Freelance journalist Brandon Smith filed one of the requests and was denied along with everyone else.[30] Smith, 29, was described by the *Columbia Journalism Review* as a former journalism student working part-time in marketing and restaurant jobs who also works as an Uber and Lyft driver. Smith then filed suit in state court asking the court to force the release of the video under the FOI Act. The Chicago Police Department replied that it was cooperating with state and federal

---

[28] Ibid.

[29] Ibid.

[30] Jeremy Borden, "How a little-known, Uber-driving freelancer brought the lawsuit that forced Chicago to release a police shooting video," *Columbia Journalism Review*, Nov. 25, 2015.

investigations and that the video was therefore exempt from disclosure.[31] The Department also argued that[32] "disclosure of the dashboard camera video could affect the recollections and testimony of witnesses to the incident."

Cook County Judge Franklin Valderrama noted that the body investigating the shooting was the Independent Police Review Authority was not a part of the Chicago Police Department, but rather was an office of the City of Chicago.[33] "Thus, the Department and IPRA are distinct and independent, if interrelated, Offices of the City of Chicago."

Because the Chicago Police Department was not conducting the federal, state and IPRA investigations, it could not rely on the sections of the Illinois FOIA to exempt the dashboard camera video, Judge Valderrama ruled.

Hours before the video was released, Officer Van Dyke was arrested on first-degree murder charges. Smith was not present to witness the release of the video.[34] He was denied entry because he did not have a press credential. Van Dyke was sentenced to 6 3/4 years in prison after his conviction on charges of second-degree murder and 16 counts of aggravated battery (one for each of the 16 shots Van Dyke fired into McDonald's body).[35] Three other Chicago police officers, including Van Dyke's partner Joseph Walsh, were acquitted of lying in police reports and covering up the killing. Four other officers were fired. Deputy Chief David McNaughton, who was the highest-ranking officer at the scene, and four other supervisor or investigative officers resigned or retired before disciplinary action could be taken against them.[36]

PRESIDENT NIXON AND THE 12-YEAR FIGHT FOR THE WATERGATE TAPES

It took a dozen years of struggle, including three lawsuits, to open the first 1.5 million pages of documents from the Administration of President Nixon, and those pages were mostly trivia and represented less than 4 per cent of the total body of papers. From beyond the grave, Nixon seemed determined to thwart public knowledge about the inner workings of his presidency. *The New York Times* reported in 1994 that the Nixon's heirs were continuing the late President's two-decade fight "to control

[31] Sec. 7(1)(D)(I) of Ill. FOIA exempts from disclosure records that would "interfere with pending or actually and reasonably contemplated law enforcement proceedings conducted by any law enforcement or correctional agency that is the recipient of the request."

[32] *Smith v CPD* MSJ Memorandum Opinion and Order, 15 CH 11780 at 12–13, Nov. 19, 2015.

[33] Ibid. at 14–15.

[34] Jeremy Borden, "How a little-known, Uber-driving freelancer brought the lawsuit that forced Chicago to release a police shooting video," *Columbia Journalism Review*, Nov. 25,2015.

[35] *Chicago Tribune* Staff, "Beyond Jason Van Dyke: Officers who faced criminal charges and/or discipline over Laquan McDonald shooting," *Chicago Tribune*, July 19, 2019.

[36] Ibid.

more than 3,000 hours of White House tapes and 150,000 pages of Presidential papers."

But Professor Stanley Kutler, a University of Wisconsin historian who sued to get access to the papers, won several significant victories to gain access, including the release of more than 200 hours of recordings. Kutler published a book on the Nixon tapes, "*Abuse of Power: The New Nixon Tapes*." *The New York Times* reported that "The tapes show one of the century's most skilled politicians in a prolonged act of self-destruction, lying to the public, to his political allies, to his closest aides and advisers, and finally to himself. They depict him as eloquent and profane, charming and chilling, brilliant and hapless, powerful and helpless."

It was *The New York Times'* report on the Pentagon Papers that led to Watergate.[37] Former National Security Council aide Daniel Ellsberg had given *The New York Times* a copy of a 47-volume study of U.S. involvement in Vietnam. Nixon and his staff created a special covert team called the Plumbers to stop leaks of classified information. As one tape excerpt made clear, Nixon intended to stop any and all leaks.[38]

" 'We're up against an enemy, a conspiracy,' Mr. Nixon told his chief of staff, H.R. Haldeman, on July 1, 1971. 'They're using any means. *We are going to use any means.* Is that clear?' " According to the tapes, the conspiracy included anti-war activists, former aides, the Kennedy family, "rich Jews" at the Internal Revenue Service, the Ford Foundation and others.

A head-on confrontation emerged in the Watergate investigations, as President Nixon refused to turn over to a grand jury, tape recordings of conversations with his White House aides. Federal Judge John J. Sirica ruled that the tapes must be submitted to him for *in camera* scrutiny [in private, before only the judge] and possible forwarding to the grand jury. President Nixon refused, asserting executive privilege, and said he was protecting "the right of himself and his successors to preserve the confidentiality of discussions in which they participate in the course of their constitutional duties." Special prosecutor Archibald Cox argued it was intolerable that "the President would invoke executive privilege to keep the tape recordings from the grand jury but permit his aides to testify fully as to their recollections of the same conversations." The President fired Cox, and the Attorney General resigned, and his deputy was fired before the President yielded the tapes (which of course were to prove central to the discrediting of him and his aides) amid a public cry for his impeachment.

---

[37] Tim Weiner, "Transcripts of Nixon Tapes Show the Path to Watergate," *New York Times*, Oct. 31, 1997.

[38] Ibid.

The Supreme Court ruled that executive privilege is not absolute, but qualified.[39] Chief Justice Warren Burger's opinion for the court held that the in-camera court inspection of the tapes that Sirica ordered would be a minimal intrusion on the President's confidential communications. The President's claim was not based on grounds of national security—that military or diplomatic secrets were threatened—but only on the ground of his "generalized interest in confidentiality." That could not prevail over "the fundamental demands of due process of law in the fair administration of justice." It would have to yield to the[40] "demonstrated, specific need for evidence in a pending criminal trial."

Subsequent assertions of executive privilege by Nixon involved his post-resignation claim to custody of presidential papers from his term in office—millions of pages of documents and almost 900 tapes—and also his denial of the rights of record companies and networks to copy, sell, and broadcast tapes that had been played at one of the trials arising from Watergate. The Supreme Court ruled in one case[41] that the government should have custody of all but Nixon's private and personal papers, and in the other,[42] it granted Nixon's plea to deny networks and record companies the right to copy, sell, or broadcast the tapes. Almost eight years after his resignation, a three-judge panel of the D.C. Circuit held[43] that government archivists had the authority to listen to the former president's Dictabelt recordings to determine which would be available at public listening centers. Nixon could not simply claim make a claim to that all the recordings were diaries and so get possession of them. Years later, taping systems in the Johnson and Kennedy administrations came to light. Public access to the Kennedy tapes provide insight into White House discussions surrounding the Cuban Missile Crisis. The Johnson tapes show that his fear that Republican presidential candidate Barry Goldwater would use a pullout from Vietnam to claim that Johnson was weak in the face of Communist aggression. The tapes and other documents from different presidential administrations show that domestic politics was the cause for many decisions that sent America's military into harm's way.

President Trump rarely invoked executive privilege in the first three years of his administration. It was in the background, though, as members of his administration said that executive privilege allowed them to ignore Congressional subpoenas. Trump mostly claimed that Congress did not have the authority to investigate conduct of the executive branch.[44]

---

[39] *United States v. Nixon*, 418 U.S. 683, 94 S.Ct. 3090 (1974).

[40] Ibid. at 684–685, 713; 3095–3096.

[41] *Nixon v. Administrator of General Services*, 433 U.S. 425, 97 S.Ct. 2777 (1977).

[42] *Nixon v. Warner Communications, Inc.*, 435 U.S. 589 98 S.Ct. 1306 (1978).

[43] *Nixon v. Freeman*, 670 F.2d 346 (D.C.Cir. 1982).

[44] Amelia Thomson-DeVeaux, "Could Executive Privilege Protect Trump In The Impeachment Inquiry?" *FiveThirtyEight.com*, Oct. 23, 2019. https://fivethirtyeight.com/features/could-executive-privilege-protect-trump-in-the-impeachment-inquiry/.

48. ACCESS AND THE CONSTITUTION

Courts have given little support to the position that the First Amendment includes a right of access to government information.

In many journalists' view, freedom of speech and press and the First Amendment encompass a right to gather government information as much as they embrace the right to publish and distribute it. Constitutional protection against denial of access seems to them only reasonable. The legal scholar Harold Cross argued that[45] "Freedom of information is the very foundation for all those freedoms that the First Amendment of our Constitution was intended to guarantee."

Famed First Amendment legal scholar Thomas I. Emerson held that[46] "we ought to consider the right to know as an integral part of the system of freedom of expression, embodied in the first amendment and entitled to support by legislation or other affirmative government action." He found the argument for "starting from this point * * * overwhelming," and further, that the Supreme Court has in some respects recognized a constitutional right to know. Decisions since have pointed the other way.

While an occasional lower court or dissenting judge has found reasons for the First Amendment to protect a right of access to government information, the Supreme Court of the United States has done so only in the setting of public, criminal trials. Justice Potter Stewart delivered a rationale for the denial of a constitutional right of access to government in a famous 1974 speech:[47]

> So far as the Constitution goes, the autonomous press may publish what it knows, and may seek to learn what it can.
>
> But this autonomy cuts both ways. The press is free to do battle against secrecy and deception in government. But the press cannot expect from the Constitution any guarantee that it will succeed. There is no constitutional right to have access to particular government information, or to require openness from the bureaucracy. The public's interest in knowing about its government is protected by the guarantee of a Free Press, but the protection is indirect. The Constitution itself is neither a Freedom of Information Act nor an Official Secrets Act.
>
> The Constitution, in other words, establishes the contest, not its resolution. Congress may provide a resolution, at least in some instances, through carefully drawn legislation. For the rest, we

---

[45] Harold L. Cross, *The People's Right to Know* (Morningside Heights: Columbia Univ. Press, 1953).

[46] Thomas I. Emerson, "Legal Foundations of the Right to Know," (1976) *Faculty Scholarship Series* 2800.

[47] Potter Stewart, "Or of the Press", 26 *Hastings L.J.* 631 (1975).

> must rely, as so often in our system we must, on the tug and pull of the political forces in American society.

Justice Stewart's words proved true. The courts have provided scant acknowledgment of a "right of access" under the First Amendment, except for access to public, criminal court trials. That declaration of a First Amendment right came *Richmond Newspapers v. Virginia*[48] (detailed in Chap. 9, below).

MCBURNEY V. YOUNG: NO FIRST AMENDMENT RIGHT TO INFORMATION

In a case that tested the right of states to grant records access to their own citizens but withhold them from citizens of other states, the Supreme Court again rejected a First Amendment right of access to government information.[49] Mark J. McBurney of Rhode Island and Roger W. Hurlbert of California each requested documents from Virginia under that state's Freedom of Information law. In both cases, the men's requests were denied because they were not Virginia citizens.[50] The two men, "filed suit under U.S.C. § 1983, seeking declaratory and injunctive relief for violations of the U.S. Constitution's Privileges and Immunities Clause[51] and, in Hurlbert's case, the dormant Commerce Clause."[52] A federal district court granted Virginia's motion for summary judgment, and the Fourth Circuit Court of Appeals affirmed.

But the U.S. Court of Appeals for the Third Circuit held that denying a New York journalist's records request under Delaware's FOIA statute that excluded non-citizens of Delaware Constitution's Privileges and Immunities Clause violated the Privileges and Immunity Clause.[53]

Justice Alito wrote the opinion for a unanimous (with a brief concurrence by Justice Thomas) Court. He rejected both arguments made by the men.[54]

> We hold [* * *] that petitioners' constitutional rights were not violated. By means other than the state FOIA, Virginia made available to petitioners most of the information that they sought, and the Commonwealth's refusal to furnish the

---

[48] *Richmond Newspapers v. Virginia*, 448 U.S. 555, 100 S.Ct. 2814 (1980).

[49] *McBurney, et al v. Young, Deputy Commissioner and Director, Virginia Division of Child Support Enforcement, et. al.*, 569 U.S. 221, 133 S.Ct. 1709 (2013).

[50] McBurney eventually got most of the information he sought under another Virginia statute.

[51] Art. IV, § 2, cl 1, "The Citizens of each State stall be entitled to all Privileges and Immunities of Citizens in the several States."

[52] The "Dormant" or "Negative" Commerce Clause is derived from Article I, Sec. 8 of the United States Constitution. It holds that state regulations that improperly burden interstate commerce are unconstitutional. Hurlbert argued that Virginia's restriction on information that he obtained and sold across state lines, was therefore not constitutional.

[53] *Lee v. Minner*, 458 F.3d 194 (3d Cir. 2006). *McBurney* abrogated the decision.

[54] *McBurney, et al v. Young, Deputy Commissioner and Director, Virginia Division of Child Support Enforcement, et. al.*, 569 U.S. 221,133 S.Ct. 1709, 1713 (2013).

> additional information did not abridge any constitutionally protected privilege or immunity. Nor did Virginia violate the dormant Commerce Clause. The state Freedom of Information Act does not regulate commerce in any meaningful sense, but instead provides a service that is related to state citizenship.

Justice Alito then expanded the scope of his opinion in dicta[55], going beyond the issues raised by McBurney and Hurlbert. Before the Freedom of Information Act, people did not have a right to get information that the government held, he wrote. English case law held that there was no general right to look at records or documents[56] unless the person who wanted to see them had an interest.[57] The same applied in early American law, Alito wrote.[58]

> Nineteenth Century American cases, while less uniform, certainly do not support the proposition that a broad-based right to access public information was widely recognized in the early Republic. See, e.g., *Cormack v. Wolcott*, 37 Kan. 391, 394, 15 P.245, 246 (1887) (denying mandamus to plaintiff seeking to compile abstracts of title records; "At common law, parties had no vested rights in the examination of a record of title, or other public records, save by some interest in the land or subject of record").

Perhaps Justice Alito should have read John Adams, "*A Dissertation on the Canon and Feudal Law*", written in 1765 and reflective of the thoughts of at least one of the founding fathers.[59]

> [The people] have a right, an indisputable, unalienable, indefeasible, divine right to that most dreaded and envied kind of knowledge, I mean, of the characters and conduct of their rulers. Rulers are no more than attorneys, agents, and trustees for the people; and if the cause, the interest and trust, is insidiously betrayed, or wantonly trifled away, the people have a right to revoke the authority that they themselves have

---

55 *Black's Law Dictionary* defines dictum as "[a] statement of opinion or belief considered authoritative because of the dignity of the person making it." In a judicial opinion, dicta are the statements made by the court about the law that were not necessary for the court to decide the case. *Black's Law Dictionary* (5th ed. 1989).

56 It can be easily understood when looking at the historical record. Many of the English districts were entirely owned outright by a major landowner. "In such cases, the entire electorate were the landowner's tenants, obliged to vote (in a public ballot) as directed or face eviction. In the 1760s, 205 of the 406 English constituencies were controlled by just 111 aristocratic owners." https://www.english-heritage.org.uk/learn/story-of-england/georgians/power-and-politics/ And so English courts would not envision the notions of public accountability or the right of the governed to know what their governors were doing in determining the direction of the country.

57 Interest is a right, claim or privilege in property.

58 *McBurney, et al v. Young, Deputy Commissioner and Director, Virginia Division of Child Support Enforcement, et. al.*, 569 U.S. 221, 233, 133 S.Ct. 1709, 1718–1719 (2013).

59 John Adams, *A Dissertation on the Canon and Feudal Law*, 1765.

> deputed, and to constitute abler and better agents, attorneys, and trustees.

A few years after *McBurney*, the Superior Court of New Jersey, Appellate Division[60] held that *McBurney* did not apply in that state. In *Scheeler v. Atlantic County Municipal Joint Insurance Fund*,[61] the appellate court held that New Jersey's Open Public Records Act use of the term "citizens" did not restrict access to records only for citizens of New Jersey. A former New Jersey citizen moved to North Carolina. Harry Scheeler then twice requested records under the OPRA. In a separate case, a national non-profit civil rights organization, sought records from the Atlantic City Board of Education. In all three requests, municipalities or agencies refused to provide records. They cited the New Jersey Open Records Act, "The Legislature finds and declares it to be the public policy of this State that: government records shall be readily accessible for inspection, copying, or examination *by the citizens* [emphasis added] of this State . . . ."[62] Justice Alito referred to New Jersey as one of several states that restricted public records request to citizens in *McBurney*. Not so, said the Superior Court.[63]

> Reading N.J.S.A. 47:1A–1 sensibly, 934 bearing in mind the context in which the phrase "citizens of this State" is used, the terms the Legislature used in the rest of OPRA, and considering the statute's history and purpose, we cannot conclude that the Legislature intended to preclude out-of-state residents from making OPRA requests.
>
> [* * *]
>
> "[A] public agency has a responsibility and an obligation to safeguard from public access a citizen's personal information with which it has been entrusted when disclosure thereof would violate the citizen's reasonable expectation of privacy . . . ."
>
> Clearly the term "citizen" in the last paragraph does not refer to New Jersey residents. It would produce an absurd result if the government were only required to protect personal information of New Jersey residents and could freely disseminate medical records, school transcripts, and other personal information of out-of-state residents. It is more logical to construe the term "citizen" as simply meaning "a person" or "an individual."

---

[60] The Superior Court of New Jersey, Appellate Division, is the second highest appeals court in the state and has jurisdiction over appeals from administrative decisions and court cases.

[61] *Scheeler v. Atlantic County Municipal Joint Insurance Fund*, 454 N.J.Super. 621 186 A.3d 930 (App. Div. 2018).

[62] Ibid. at 627, 933.

[63] Ibid. at 627, 933–934.

Justice Alito also referred to Professor Harold Cross in McBurney, using his research to buttress his argument that public access to government records was just a recent development.

> It certainly cannot be said that such a broad right has "at all times, been enjoyed by the citizens of the several states which compose this Union, from the time of their becoming free, independent, and sovereign." *Corfield*, 6 F.Cas., at 551. No such right was recognized at common law. See H. Cross, "The People's Right to Know" 25 (1953). ("[T]he courts declared the primary rule that there was no general common law right in all persons (as citizens, taxpayers, electors, or merely as persons) to inspect public records or documents").

As Dwight L Teeter, one of the authors of this textbook wrote in response to Justice Alito's citation, when Harold L. Cross published his path-breaking book, "*The People's Right to Know*,"[64] he wrote in an era of Cold War secrecy. He studied British precedents not to justify their narrowness but to demonstrate that in the American republic, the people needed more access to be and to remain a free people. Justice Alito's opinion carelessly (if not dishonestly) used Cross's research into autocratic British precedents out of context. Cross's book was a key part of the right to know movement that led Congress to enact the Freedom of Information Act signed into law in 1966 by President Lyndon B. Johnson. As Cross wrote in his classic study,[65] "Freedom of information is the very foundation for all those freedoms that the First Amendment of our Constitution was intended to guarantee." Justice Alito or his clerks either missed the point or distorted Cross' book to produce an argument in favor of closed government.

A RIGHT TO GO PLACES?

Unlike citizens of many other nations, Americans have long been blessed in their ability to take for granted a right to travel freely from state to state without having to show an "identity papers." And for the most part, Americans think they can travel anywhere they wish. But reporter William Worthy was thwarted in his attempt—in the 1950s period of the Cold War tensions with the Soviet Union and other Communist states—to travel to China to report. Worthy, of the *Baltimore Afro-American*, in 1956 ignored an order by Secretary of State John Foster Dulles barring American reporters from going to "Red China"[66] to report. When Worthy returned to the United States, the State Department revoked his passport and refused to give him another. Worthy went to court to attempt to regain it. The trial court held, without

[64] Harold L. Cross, *The People's Right to Know* (Morningside Heights, Columbia University Press, 1953).

[65] Ibid. at xiii–xiv.

[66] After the Communists won the civil war in China, the U.S. government refused to recognize it, continuing to deal with the nationalists in Taiwan as the legitimate China.

elaborating, that Dulles' refusal to issue the passport did not violate Worthy's rights to travel under the First Amendment. Worthy appealed, but his argument for First Amendment protection failed, the Court of Appeals holding:[67]

> The right to travel is a part of the right to liberty, and a newspaperman's right to travel is a part of freedom of the press. But these valid generalizations do not support unrestrained conclusions * * *
>
> Freedom of the press bears restrictions * * * Merely because a newsman has a right to travel does not mean he can go anywhere he wishes. He cannot attend conferences of the Supreme Court, or meetings of the President's Cabinet or executive sessions of the Committees of Congress.

In a 1965 case,[59] Louis Zemel, a private citizen, argued that a State Department ban on travel to Cuba was a direct interference with the First Amendment rights of citizens to inform themselves at first hand of events abroad. In making his request to the State Department for the needed validation of his passport to travel to Cuba, Zemel explained that the purpose of his trip was "to satisfy my curiosity about the state of affairs in Cuba and to make me a better informed citizen." The United States Supreme Court agreed that the Secretary of State's denial rendered "less than wholly free the flow of information concerning that country," but denied that a First Amendment right was involved.[68] "The right to speak and publish does not carry with it the unrestrained right to gather information," Chief Justice Warren said.[69]

On occasion, the U.S. State Department may deny a passport to a person whose foreign travel is thought to create "substantial likelihood of 'serious damage' to national security or foreign policy."[70] The Supreme Court upheld such a passport revocation involving Philip Agee, a dissident former Central Intelligence agent accused of working to expose the cover and sources of CIA employees.

PELL V. PROCUNIER

SAXBE V. WASHINGTON POST

From restrictions on foreign travel, turn to the question of whether there is a "right" to report on inmates in American prisons.[71] This is not

[67] *Worthy v. Herter*, 270 F.2d 905 (D.C.Cir.1959), certiorari denied 361 U.S. 918, 80 S.Ct. 255 (1959).

[59] *Zemel v. Rusk*, 381 U.S. 1, 85 S.Ct. 1271 (1965).

[68] Ibid. at 17–18, 1281 (1965). See also *Trimble v. Johnston*, 173 F.Supp. 651 (D.D.C.1959); *In re Mack*, 386 Pa. 251, 126 A.2d 679 (1956).

[69] Justices Black, Douglas and Goldberg dissented.

[70] *Haig v. Agee*, 453 U.S. 280, 287, 288, 101 S.Ct. 2766, 2771, 2772 (1981).

[71] Readers who believe that there is no need for journalists to keep an eye on prisons should read *The New York Times* story from April 2019 revealing horrific conditions in Alabama's prisons where inmates endured the highest rates of murder and rape in the nation.

a minor question; to protect freedom, journalists and other citizens need to be able to inquire into the health of the criminal justice system, from beginning[72] to end. That is, the system needs surveillance: from arrest to arraignment, to preliminary hearings, to plea bargains, or trials, to appeals, to sentencing of convicted criminals, to incarceration on through parole. Are all persons caught up in the criminal justice system treated alike, or are members of minority groups treated more harshly than other people? Once in prison, are inmates being rehabilitated and given useful skills to make a living or are they simply warehoused in overcrowded prisons? Finding out requires visits to prison and interviews with specific inmates.

Pell v. Procunier[73] arose when journalists Eve Pell, Betty Segal, and Paul Jacobs challenged a California prison regulation (#415.071) which barred media interviews with specific, individual inmates. Denied their requests to interview prison inmates Booker T. Hillery, Jr.; John Larry Spain; Bobby Bly and Michael Shane Guile, they asserted that the rule limited their news-gathering activity and thus infringed freedom of the press under the First and Fourteenth Amendments. The four inmates also sued alleging that the rule denied them their First Amendment rights. The inmates won in district court. The journalists lost and both they and the California prison officials appealed to the U.S. Supreme Court where both the inmates and journalists lost. Justice Stewart wrote for the majority that the inmates had alternative means of communicating with the press.[74] They could write letters. They could have visits by family, clergy, attorneys and any person of prior acquaintance.[75] The reporters had a right, the same as that of the general public, to take tours of prisons. But prison staff picked the tour routes.[76]

> In addition, newsmen are permitted to visit both the maximum security and minimum security sections of the institutions and to stop and speak about any subject to any inmates whom they might encounter. If security considerations permit, corrections personnel will step aside to permit such interviews to be confidential. Apart from general access to all parts of the institutions, newsmen are also permitted to enter the prisons to

Katie Benner and Shaila Dewan, "Alabama's Gruesome Prisons: Report Finds Rape and Murder at All Hours," *New York Times*, April 3, 2019.

With depressing regularity, news organizations find shocking conditions in America's prisons including forcing inmates to fight gladiator style, killings of inmates by prison staffs and sexual abuse by both inmates and staff. The United States has the highest rate of incarceration in the world. The Brennan Center for Justice reported that more than 2.2 million people are incarcerated in the United States. The United States accounts for a quarter of all prisoners in the world even though it has only 5 percent of the world's population. https://www.brennancenter.org/issues/end-mass-incarceration.

[72] From "stop and frisk," which targeted primarily young men of color; through coerced confessions, as happened with the Central Park 5, to the death penalty.

[73] *Pell v. Procunier*, 417 U.S. 817, 94 S.Ct. 2800 (1974).

[74] Ibid. at 824–825, 2805.

[75] That would include journalists if the journalist and inmate had been friends before.

[76] *Pell v. Procunier*, 417 U.S. 817, 830, 94 S.Ct. 2800, 2808 (1974).

> interview inmates selected at random by the corrections officials. By the same token, if a newsman wishes to write a story on a particular prison program, he is permitted to sit in on group meetings and to interview the inmate participants.

California created regulation #415.071 in 1971 after an escape attempt at San Quentin in which three staff members and two inmates were killed. California prison officials blamed the deaths on its former policy of allowing journalists to interview specific inmates. Under the policy, press attention was focused on a limited number of inmates. The inmates, as Justice Stewart wrote,[77] "became virtual 'public figures' within the prison society and gained a disproportionate degree of notoriety and influence among their fellow inmates. Because of this notoriety and influence, these inmates often became the source of severe disciplinary problems." California prison officials blamed the escape attempts and deaths on mounting disciplinary problems caused by press attention to a few inmates. Justice Powell spent less time in disposing of the journalists' assertion that the prison regulation was an "unconstitutional state interference with a free press." He framed the issue as one in which the journalists were asking for something that the public did not have.[78]

> The First and Fourteenth Amendments bar government from interfering in any way with a free press. The Constitution does not, however, require government to accord the press special access to information not shared by members of the public generally.

Saxbe v. Washington Post Co.,[79] dealt with a challenge to a federal prison policy that was similar to that of California.[80] Justice Stewart wrote the opinion for the Court and, as in *Pell*, held that reporters had no right to interview specific inmates. He wrote that federal prison officials said that the policy was motivated by the same disciplinary and administrative considerations that California relied on its press inmate policy. As in *Pell*, Justice Stewart focused on the opportunities and methods the press had.

> Except for the limitation [* * *] on face-to-face press-inmate interviews, members of the press are accorded substantial access to the federal prisons in order to observe and report the conditions they find there. Indeed, journalists are given access to the prisons and to prison inmates that in significant respects exceeds that afforded to members of the general public. For

[77] Ibid. at 831–832, 2808–2809.

[78] Ibid. at 834, 2810.

[79] *Saxbe v. Washington Post Co.*, 417 U.S. 843, 94 S.Ct. 2811 (1974).

[80] Policy Statement 1220.1A of the Federal Bureau of Prisons: 'Press representatives will not be permitted to interview individual inmates. This rule shall apply even where the inmate requests or seeks an interview. However, conversation may be permitted with inmates whose identity is not to be made public, if it is limited to the discussion of institutional facilities, programs and activities.'

example, Policy Statement 1220.1A permits press representatives to tour the prisons and to photograph any prison facilities. During such tours a newsman is permitted to conduct brief interviews with any inmates he might encounter. In addition, newsmen and inmates are permitted virtually unlimited written correspondence with each other.

Dissenting in both *Pell* and *Saxbe,* Justice Powell said that "sweeping prohibition of prisoner-press interviews substantially impairs a core value of the First Amendment." In these cases, he argued, society's interest "in preserving free public discussion of governmental affairs" was great and was the value at stake. Since the public is unable to know most news at first hand, "In seeking out the news the press * * * acts as an agent of the public at large. * * * By enabling the public to assert meaningful control over the political process, the press performs a critical function in effecting the societal purpose of the First Amendment."

Justice Powell was joined by Justices Douglas, Brennan and Marshal in dissent in *Saxbe.*

HOUCHINS V. KQED INC.

Much more restrictive access to a jail was at issue when Sheriff Thomas Houchins of Alameda Co., Calif., was ordered by a U.S. District Court to open up his facility to reporters and their cameras and recorders.[81] The controversy arose over conditions in Little Greystone, a part of the jail complex at Santa Rita. U.S. District Judge Alfonso Zirpoli found that the "shocking and debasing conditions which prevailed [at Santa Rita] constituted cruel and unusual punishment for man or beast as a matter of law."[82] After he visited the facility, Judge Zirpoli wrote that he had reached the[83] "inescapable conclusion . . . that Greystone should be razed to the ground."

One suicide had occurred there, and a psychiatrist said that inmates who were his patients were deteriorating in the facility.[84] Sheriff Houchins denied that conditions in the jail were responsible. Television station KQED and the NAACP sued to gain access to the jail saying that Houchins' policies provided no "means by which the public may be informed of conditions prevailing in Greystone or by which prisoners' grievances may reach the public." Shortly after the suit was filed, Sheriff Houchins announced the creation of a monthly tour. The tours were limited to 25 persons and did not visit Little Greystone. No cameras or recorders were allowed, nor was access to a part of the jail where violence had reportedly broken out earlier. Prisoners were shuffled to different parts of the jail before the tours started so they could not talk to the

[81] *Houchins v. KQED, Inc.,* 438 U.S. 1, 98 S.Ct. 2588 (1978).

[82] *Brenneman v. Madigan,* 343 F.Supp. 128 (N.D. Cal.1972).

[83] Ibid. at 132–133.

[84] The psychiatrist was fired.

visitors. KQED, which made a practice of covering prisons in the area and wanted access to shoot film of conditions and interview prisoners, pressed Houchins. The sheriff objected that the access sought would infringe the privacy of inmates, create jail "celebrities," cause attendant difficulties and disrupt jail operations. He said that the jail's mail, visitation and phone call regulations let inmates contact the public.[85] The district court agreed with KQED's contentions, and enjoined the sheriff from further blocking of media access "at reasonable times," cameras and recorders included. The California Court of Appeals upheld the injunction, saying that the U.S. Supreme Court's *Pell* and *Saxbe* decisions were not controlling.

But Houchins appealed to the U.S. Supreme Court, and it reversed the lower courts, Chief Justice Burger, writing the opinion, said that the Court had not held that there was a constitutional right to gather news, or a constitutional right of access to government. He agreed that news of prisons was important for the public to have, and that media serve as "eyes and ears" for the public. He said, however, that the Supreme Court had never held that the First Amendment compels anyone, private or public, to supply information. He said the legislative branch was free to pass laws opening penal institutions if it wished. Separately, Justice Stewart joined in the decision, differing only to the extent of saying that reporters on tour with the public should be allowed to carry and use their tools of the trade, including cameras and recorders. Justices Stevens wrote a dissent that Justices Brennan and Powell joined. Justice Stevens noted that KQED had done reporting on jail and prison issues. He referred to conditions in the Santa Rita jail complex and how the public was not able to learn about them. Excluding KQED and other reporters meant that the public's right to be informed of the way both convicted and prisoners awaiting trial were being housed and treated.[86]

> Petitioner's no-access policy, modified only in the wake of respondents' resort to the courts, could survive constitutional scrutiny only if the Constitution affords no protection to the public's right to be informed about conditions within those public institutions where some of its members are confined because they have been charged with or found guilty of criminal offenses.

Justice Stevens pointed to those prisoners who were confined awaiting trial. Those prisoners were subject to the same deplorable conditions as those convicted despite a presumption of their innocence.

---

[85] Inmates were allowed to send an unlimited number of letters to judges, attorneys, elected officials, the Attorney General, jail officials, or probation officers provided they had the postage. Those letters were not inspected. All others were opened and checked to make sure that they did not name any corrections officers or include anything about officers' actions. That rule prevented inmates from being able to communicate with the press about most topics of inmate complaints. Justice Stevens noted that inmate mail from the Santa Rita jail facility had been heavily censored,

[86] *Houchins v. KQED, Inc.*, 438 U.S. 1, 29, 98 S.Ct. 2588, 2604 (1978).

49. RECORDS AND MEETINGS OF THE FEDERAL GOVERNMENT

Access to records and meetings of federal executive and administrative agencies is provided under the "Freedom of Information" and the "Sunshine in Government" Acts; the Privacy Act provides for secrecy of records.

THE FREEDOM OF INFORMATION ACT

On July 4, 1966, President Lyndon B. Johnson signed the Federal Public Records Law, shortly to be known as the federal Freedom of Information Act (FOIA). President Johnson said the Act sprang,[87] "from one of our most essential principles: a democracy works best when the people have all the information that the security of the Nation permits." He expressed a "deep sense of pride that the United States is an open society in which the people's right to know is cherished and guarded."

FOIA replaced Sec. 3 of the Administrative Procedure Act of 1946, which had been described as a mechanism to prevent people from finding out what the government was doing,[88] permitted secrecy if it was required in the public interest or for "good cause."[89] The new law expressed neither this limitation nor another which had said disclosure was necessary only to "persons properly and directly concerned"[90] with

[87] John D. Pomfret, "Johnson Supports Greater Access to U.S. Data," *New York Times*, July 5, 1966.

[88] In a sense, "public information" is a misnomer for 5 U.S.C. § 1002, since the section permits withholding of Federal agency records if secrecy is required "in the public interest" or if the records relate "solely to the internal management of an agency." Government information also may be held confidential "for good cause found." Even if no good cause can be found for secrecy, the records will be made available only to "persons properly and directly concerned." Neither in the Administrative Procedure Act nor its legislative history are these broad phrases defined, nor is there a recognition of the basic right of any person—not just those special classes "properly and directly concerned"—to gain access to the records of official Government actions. Above all, there is no remedy available to a citizen who has been wrongfully denied access to the Government's public records. The present statute, therefore, is not in any realistic sense a public information statute. H.Rep.No.1497, 89th Cong., 2d Sess., p. 4 (1966).

[89] This vague language was susceptible of almost unlimited manipulation by an agency seeking justification for withholding information from the public. In 1961, for example, the Secretary of the Navy ruled that "telephone directories fall in the category of information relating to the internal management of the Navy," citing Sec. 3 as his authority. The following year, the National Science Foundation decided it would not be "in the public interest" to disclose cost estimates submitted by unsuccessful contractors in connection with a multimillion-dollar deep sea study. It appeared that the firm which had won the lucrative contract had not submitted the lowest bid; White House intervention was required to reverse the agency's decision that it had authority for this secrecy "in the public interest." "Administrative Agencies—In General—Any Person May Demand From Federal Agency Information Not Expressly Exempted as Privileged and May Bring Action for Improper Refusal to Disclose," 80 *Harv. L. Rev.* 909, (1967).

[90] Neither in the Administrative Procedure Act nor in its legislative history was there a recognition of the basic right of any person—not just those special classes "properly and directly concerned"—to gain access to the records of official government actions. 7 A.L.R. Fed. 876 (1971).

the subject at hand. In the words of Johnson's Attorney General Ramsey Clark, the FOI Act,[91]

> imposes on the executive branch[92] an affirmative obligation to adopt new standards and practices for publication and availability of information. It leaves no doubt that disclosure is a transcendent goal, yielding only to such compelling considerations as those provided for in the exemptions of the act.

The Department of Justice website has a useful section on FOIA, https://www.justice.gov/oip/doj-guide-freedom-information-act-0, which provides a guide to the act and its use. See also the 10th edition, Federal Open Government Guide of the Reporters Committee for Freedom of the Press, https://www.rcfp.org/open-government-guide. Every federal executive branch agency is required under the FOI Act to publish in the Federal Register its organization plan, and the agency personnel and methods through which the public can get information. Every agency's procedural rules and general policies are to be published. Every agency's manuals and instructions are to be made available for public inspection and copying, as are final opinions in adjudicated cases. The public has access to current indexes of these records. If records are improperly withheld, the U.S. district court can enjoin the agency from the withholding and order disclosure. And if agency officials fail to comply with the court order, they may be punished for contempt. The APA had no provisions to allow any remedies when a person was improperly denied records.

Exceptions to what must be made public are called "exemptions." Exemptions do not require that the federal agency withhold the records, they merely provide a justification for the non-release. In some instances, agencies may misinterpret the scope of an exemption or misapply one and refuse to release records. Federal courts can clarify things and have been called on to do so many times. There are nine exemptions:

1. Records "specifically authorized under criteria established by an Executive order to be kept secret in the interest of national defense or foreign policy" and which are properly classified.

2. Matters related only to "internal personnel rules and practices" of an agency.

3. Matters exempt from disclosure by statute.

4. Trade secrets and commercial or financial information obtained from a person and that are privileged or confidential.

---

[91] Foreword, *Attorney General's Memorandum on the Public Information Section of the Administrative Procedure Act* (1967).

[92] It is important to keep in mind that FOIA applies only to the federal executive branch and not to the legislative or judicial. It also is the federal openness law. Each state has its own version.

5. Inter-agency or intra-agency communications, such as memoranda showing how policymakers within an agency feel about various policy options.

6. Personnel, medical and similar files which could not be disclosed without a "clearly unwarranted invasion" of someone's privacy.

7. Investigatory files compiled for law enforcement purposes, if the production of such records would interfere with law enforcement, deprive one of a fair trial, constitute an unwarranted invasion of personal privacy, disclose the identity of a confidential source, disclose investigative techniques, or endanger the life or safety of law enforcement personnel.

8. Reports prepared by or for an agency responsible for the regulation or supervision of financial institutions.

9. Geological and geophysical information and data, including maps, concerning wells—particularly explorations by gas and oil companies.

OPENNESS: A NEVER-ENDING STORY

Every victory in open records or open meetings fights leaves the door open for the next battle. It is simply a fact of life that government officials, especially when under pressure or embarrassed because of mistakes within their agencies, tend to "stonewall" when citizens—including members of the news media—come around asking questions.

Although the Freedom of Information Act, as amended, has been useful in opening government files, federal courts for the most part have supported federal bureaucracies in keeping materials from the public in virtually every part of government.

Administrations have moved in the direction or more openness or less. President Jimmy Carter issued an executive order that only if a disclosure "reasonably could be expected to cause *identifiable* damage to national security," the information was confidential. However, any reasonable doubt should be resolved in favor of declassification, provided that the public interest in disclosure outweighed the damage to national security that "might be reasonably expected from disclosure."[93] President Ronald Reagan issued his own executive order telling federal agencies, to move from President Carter's presumption of openness to a presumption against disclosure. The George W. Bush Administration generally opposed access under the FOIA. Barack Obama's stated policies reversed those of the Bush Administration, but in practice his

[93] Alan S. Madens, "Developments Under the Freedom of Information Act—1979, 1980" *Duke L.J.* 139, 146–147.

administration set a record in 2014 for redacting files or outright denying access to them under FOIA, the Associated Press reported.[94]

President Obama's record was broken in the first eight months of the Trump Administration.[95] The statistics were driven by federal agencies responding to FOIA requests by saying more than ever it could not find a single page of requested files and asserting in other cases that it would be illegal under U.S. laws to release the information.

> People who asked for records under the Freedom of Information Act received censored files or nothing in 78 percent of 823,222 requests, a record over the past decade. When it provided no records, the government said it could find no information related to the request in a little over half those cases.

Federal agencies spent $40.6 million in that first eight months of the Trump Administration on the legal costs of defending denials and paying attorney's fees in cases where it lost lawsuits,[96] "for example, *The New York Times* was awarded $51,910 from the CIA in May in a fight over records about chemical weapons in Iraq." In more than one-in-three cases, the Trump Administration changed its position when challenged acknowledging that it had improperly tried to withhold documents.

Exemption 1—National Security Information. As outlined by the guidebook, "Litigation Under the Federal Open Government Laws", it may be seen that "national security" is an almost magical invocation. For example, the Central Intelligence Agency (CIA) is allowed, under a 1984 amendment to the National Security Act of 1947, to exempt "operational" files from the search and review requirements of the FOIA. The CIA's operations will become public at some point in time—when the operation is "over." When will the operation be declared "over?" That's up to the CIA to decide. The CIA hangs onto secrets: In some cases, the CIA may turn aside a request for information with the response that for national security reasons, it can neither confirm nor deny the existence of the requested records. For an example of the U.S. Supreme Court's deference to the CIA even in the face of massive wrongdoing by that agency, see the discussion of *CIA v. Sims* later in this chapter.

The CIA may have "good" reason to keep its secrets. The agency has blundered egregiously and tragically during its decades of existence for a good many years. In 1994, while the CIA guarded its warehouses full of secrets in the name of national security, it was revealed that Aldrich H. Ames, a CIA career operative, had sold out his country for money provided by Russian agents. Even though he lived well beyond his CIA paycheck for a decade, he was not apprehended until years after the Russians "turned" him and after he had compromised 20 CIA operations.

---

[94] Ted Bridis, "Obama administration sets new record for withholding FOIA requests," *Associated Press*, March 18, 2015.

[95] Ted Bridis, "First 8 months of Trump record year for censoring withholding FOIA," *Associated Press*, March 12, 2018.

[96] Ibid.

Because of Ames, 10 agents were executed, and presumably were tortured before they died.

Yet even after the end of the Cold War and the fall of the Soviet Union, U.S. intelligence operations are booming. The budget for U.S. spy agents had been an open secret—it was not published by Congress, but comments in *The New York Times* and elsewhere estimated the annual budget back in 1994 at about $28 billion. Facing a federal lawsuit filed by the Federation of American Scientists, the CIA revealed its budget was $26.6 billion. The CIA and other agencies in the "national intelligence community" really are not forthcoming about their budgets. In mid-2007, however, investigative blogger R J Williams published an article titled "Exclusive: Office of Nation's Top Spy Inadvertently Reveals Key to Classified Intel Budget." She wrote that the Defense Intelligence Agency (DIA) somehow allowed an unclassified Power Point presentation to be released on the DIA Website. She estimated the total budget of 16 U.S. intelligence agencies as topping $60 billion annually.

During the Reagan presidency, administration officials criticized FOIA saying that the Soviet KGB was a frequent FOI requester. But a skeptical lawyer challenged that claim with, what else, a FOIA request.[97] Paul Rosa sent FOIA requests to the secretary of defense, the branches of the military and American intelligence agencies for records of requests from Soviets or Soviet agencies.[98] "Most responses said, 'A review of our files indicates no requests or anyone acting on their behalf.' "

In another instance of deference to national security, a federal district court judge ruled in *Hayden v. National Security Agency/Central Security Service*[99] that disclosure of the existence of particular records, obtained through NSA monitoring of foreign electromagnetic signals, could be withheld, because providing proof of the existence of such records might be more sensitive than their substance.[100]

Challenges to refusals citing Exemption 1 are subject to judicial review as are all exemptions. The courts might not just accept the word of the federal government in every case. FOI case law holds that courts can examine documents *in camera* (in chambers) to determine the propriety of the exemption claim.

Exemption 2—Internal Agency Rules. The Internal Revenue Service (IRS) attempted to withhold its auditing manual,[101] on grounds

---

[97] George Lardner, Jr., "Lawyer Says FOIA is No pipeline to Soviets," *The Washington Post*, Sept. 13, 1983.

[98] Ibid.

[99] *Hayden v. National Security Agency/Central Sec. Service*, 608 F2d 1381 (D.C.Cir. 1979).

[100] Eleanor Randolph, "Is U.S. keeping too many secrets? Government's penchant for classifying information has helped conspiracy theories flourish. But Cold War's end, Internet access aid forces of openness," *Los Angeles Times*, May 17, 1997.

[101] The IRS audited a little more than 1 million federal income tax returns in 2016. In an audit, the agency examines a taxpayer's documentation for income, deductibles and other documents affecting the return. Persons being audited fall into three categories, generally, 1)

that the manual used by the agency was a document exempted as an internal document, that it was merely of internal concern. A federal circuit court, however, held—sensibly enough—that the auditing rules used by the IRS should be available to public inspection because Exemption No. 2 relates only to the internal personnel rules and practices of an agency. FOIA's legislative history showed that "Examples of these may be rules as to personnel's use of parking facilities or regulation of lunch hours, statements of policy as to sick leave and the like. Sen.Rep. at 8."

Exemption 3—Information Exempted by Other Statutes. Obviously, there are many such statutes which exclude information from disclosure. Tax returns, like Donald Trump's and completed census forms fall into this category. The label on this exemption may sound harmless, but this exemption has been used to defend failures to release information which the public clearly ought to know.

For an example of a Supreme Court decision based on other statutes, look to its holding upholding the Central Intelligence Agency's refusal to reveal names of universities and scientists who had dosed unsuspecting "subjects" with LSD (in the name of national security during the 1950s and 1960s), see *CIA v. Sims,* discussed in more detail later in this chapter. The CIA did not have to reveal identities of operatives or informants or employees under a section of the National Security Act, and thus found refuge in Exemption 3. The CIA has been protected by multiple statutes starting with the National Security Act of 1947.

Similarly, horror stories about experimenting on humans with nuclear radiation—information long held secret under Atomic Secrets legislation—finally surfaced late in 1993. Energy Secretary Hazel O'Leary, saying she was " 'appalled, shocked and deeply saddened,' " helped disclose experiments such as injecting plutonium into unsuspecting human "guinea pigs." Secretary O'Leary helped bring about the disclosure when she ordered declassification of millions of pages of documents at Department of Energy sites around the nation. More on this in the section on FOIA successes below.

Exemption 4—Trade Secrets, Commercial/Financial Information. David C. Vladeck, a professor of law at Georgetown University, has noted that this exemption is often criticized for its lack of clarity. Trade secrets or commercial and financial information about businesses in possession of the federal government are supposed to be privileged or confidential, and definitions of those terms vary somewhat among courts. This exemption came about because of concerns raised by the private sector. A company can spend millions of dollars to develop a new process for manufacturing its products. It also will have to file reports to government agencies on these processes for safety,

---

declaring too little income, 2) claiming improper deductions, and 3) mislabeling hobbies as businesses in order to deduct expenses.

environmental and other legitimate government concerns. Companies became concerned that competitors could avoid the expense of research and development by waiting for companies to file their government-mandated reports and then getting the information through FOIA. The result was a revolt in the private sector and threats to refuse to comply with government reporting requirements unless protections for trade secrets were put into place. Exemption 4 was created to address these industry concerns. The courts have developed the test for releasing or withholding "trade secrets" declaring that disclosure would be prevented when it could cause "substantial harm to the competitive position of the person from whom the information was obtained." The government does not need to show actual harm but only the existence of competition and a likelihood of injury.

The Supreme Court eliminated even the "harm" requirement in *Food Marketing Institute v. Argus Leader Media*. The *Argus Leader*,[102] a South Dakota newspaper, filed a FOIA request for Supplemental Nutrition Assistance Program (SNAP/food stamps) with the USDA for information, including names, addresses of all retail stores participating in SNAP from fiscal years 2005 to 2010. The newspaper also requested redemption data for each store. SNAP is an important resource in many states, especially farm states. Some 16 percent of SNAP recipients live in rural areas and another 15 percent live in small towns with populations less than 2,500. Only 23 percent of Americans live in these areas.

The USDA provided the names and addresses of the stores but denied the portion of the request for the redemption data. The agency cited Exemption 4 and the *Argus Leader* sued. A U.S. district court found that the redemption data could hurt stores; competitive positions by giving competitors an edge in deciding where to locate their own stores or trying to attract SNAP recipients. But, the district court, held, the competitive harm did not rise to the level of "substantial harm." The Supreme Court held, in an opinion by Justice Gorsuch, that nowhere in the statute did the requirement that denial would be based on "substantial harm," upholding the refusal to provide the records.

Exemption 5—Inter- and Intra-Agency Memoranda. Harry Hammitt wrote that this is the most unclear exemption in terms of its definition. It protects "pre-decisional documents" (presumably, "working papers") from "discovery processes."

Exemption 5 is also known as the "deliberative process" exemption meaning that it makes records used in the formulation of policy exempt.[103] "The deliberative process privilege under FOIA Exemption 5

---

[102] *Food Marketing Institute v. Argus Leader Media,* 139 S.Ct. 2356, 2363 (2019).

[103] *Knight First Amendment Institute at Columbia University v. U.S. Department of Homeland Security,* 407 F.Supp. 3d (S.D. NY 2019). The Knight Center sought "information relating to communications between government agencies and the White House concerning its authority to exclude or remove individuals from the United States based on certain beliefs and associations." The Knight Center wanted to know more about President Donald Trump's

protects 'documents reflecting advisory opinions, recommendations and deliberations comprising part of a process by which governmental decisions and policies are formulated.' *Dep't of Interior v. Klamath Water Users Protective Ass'n*, 532 U.S. 1, 8, 121 S. Ct. 1060, 149 L. Ed. 2d 87 (2001). To be protected by the deliberative process privilege, a document must be: 1) pre-decisional, that is, prepared to assist an agency decisionmaker in arriving at his decision; and 2) deliberative, that is, related to the process by which policies are formulated. See *Hopkins v. HUD*, 929 F.2d 81, 84 (2d Cir. 1991).

This exemption was expanded by the U.S. Supreme Court in *Federal Open Market Committee of the Federal Reserve Board v. Merrill*.[104] There, the Supreme Court upheld an agency's refusal to release monthly policy directives if they contained sensitive information not otherwise available, and if release of the directives would significantly harm the government's monetary functions or commercial interests.

Exemption 6—The "Privacy Exemption." (Personnel, medical, and similar records which could not be disclosed without a "clearly unwarranted invasion" of privacy.) Privacy is an important value in the United States, both sociologically and legally. As important as privacy is, there are countervailing—and sometimes more important—virtues in openness.

The phrase "similar records" in this exemption has taken material exempted from disclosure well beyond personnel or medical files. In *U.S. Department of State v. Washington Post*,[105] the newspaper sought to confirm information that officials of Iran's revolutionary government held U.S. passports/visas. The Department of State denied the request on grounds that its release might endanger the Iranians, and the Supreme Court upheld the refusal to release this information.

In *New York Times Co. v. NASA*, the newspaper asked for a duplicate of the tape recording of the voices of astronauts aboard the Challenger space shuttle at the time of its explosion on January 28, 1986.[106] The National Aeronautics and Space Administration declined to release a copy of the tape, which had been recovered from the ocean floor. NASA did provide a typed transcript of the recording. *The New York Times* sought the actual recording because the transcript was not the same as a recording and did not include the inflection and tone of the voices of the

---

executive order requiring "extreme vetting" of visa applicants and persons seeking admission to the United States as refugees.

[104] *Federal Open Market Committee of the Federal Reserve Board v. Merrill*, 443 U.S. 340, 99 S.Ct. 2800 (1979).

[105] *U.S. Department of State v. Washington Post*, 456 U.S. 595, 102 S.Ct. 1957 (1982).

[106] Members of the Challenger crew survived the explosion of the main fuel tank. Three manually operated air packs were turned on after the explosion occurred the wreckage revealed. "Dr. Joseph P. Kerwin, director of life sciences at NASA's Johnson Space Center in Houston, said the explosion that tore the crew compartment from the rest of the orbiter probably would not have killed or even seriously injured the crew members." Maura Dolan, "Challenger Crew Was Conscious After Blast: NASA Reports at Least 3 Emergency Air Packs Were Activated; 'Uh-Oh' Heard on Cabin Tape," *The Los Angeles Times*, July 29, 1986.

astronauts which would provide the listener with more information about what was happening and the astronauts' reaction. NASA said the tone and inflections on the recording was personal to the astronauts thus justifying the denial on privacy grounds. *The New York Times* then filed suit under the FOIA, but the Court of Appeals found that the tape might be a "similar record" to a medical or personnel file, and remanded the case to a district court. The district court then asserted that "[e]xposure to the voice of a beloved family member immediately prior to that family member's death is what would cause the Challenger families pain." The district court held that the families' privacy interest "* * *outweighs the public interest such that release of the tape would constitute a clearly unwarranted invasion of the families' personal privacy."

Terry Anderson, the Associated Press reporter, taken hostage in Lebanon in 1985 and held until 1991, sought information from the federal government on his abduction. Several agencies told him that they could not release information without getting signed releases from his captors first.

The privacy exemption has been stretched a good deal. In 2002, *The Washington Post* made a request for medical records of a giraffe that died in the National Zoo. The paper's request was rejected on the grounds that[107] "disclosure would violate the dead animal's privacy rights." But a 2019 case seems to have foreclosed animal privacy as a means of denying requests. The Animal Legal Defense Fund sought a USDA Animal Welfare Act inspection to determine the condition of a tiger being exhibited at a Louisiana truck stop. The group was involved in a state court case regarding the tiger's welfare. The ALDF made a request asking that it be expedited because of concerns about the tiger's life and safety. FOIA has a provision where requests can be expedited where "failure to obtain requested records on an expedited basis . . . could reasonably be expected to pose an imminent threat to the life or physical safety of an individual."[108]

The USDA refused the request saying that the tiger did not qualify as an "individual" for purposes of FOIA. The group sued. A three-judge panel in the Ninth Circuit held that the phrase "life or physical safety of an individual[109]" applied only to human beings.

In 2018, a GAO annual report on Freedom of Information showed that privacy statutes (for Exemption 6) were the most used in denying FOIA requests followed closely by national security for Exemption 1), then commercial (for Exemption 4) and law enforcement (for Exemption 7).

---

[107] Keith McKnight, "Media lose access to information; Government clamps down on what's allowed out," *Akron Beacon Journal*, Sept. 10, 2003.

[108] 5 U.S.C. § 552(a)(6)(E)(v)(I).

[109] *Animal Legal Defense Fund v. United States Department of Agriculture*, 933 F.3d 1088 (9th Cir 2019).

Reporters and editors suggest that the use of the privacy exemptions, Exemptions 6 and 7, is based on the public's desire to maintain their own privacy. The public is more likely to agree with or at least understand a federal agency's refusal to release information when it is put in terms of protecting people's privacy rights. The federal government cited the privacy rights of detainees when it refused to identify the people it held in Camp X-Ray at Guantanamo Bay.

Exemption 7—Investigatory files compiled for law enforcement purposes. This exemption is quoted at length, because it provides so many loopholes for federal investigatory agencies—most notably the Federal Bureau of Investigation—to withhold information. Exemption 7 says that the FOIA does not apply to information or records that are:

> * * * compiled for law enforcement purposes, but only to the extent that the production of such law enforcement records or information (A) could reasonably be expected to interfere with enforcement proceedings, (B) would deprive a person of a fair trial or a right to an impartial adjudication, (C) could reasonably be expected to constitute an unwarranted invasion of personal privacy, (D) could reasonably be expected to disclose the identity of a confidential source, including a state, local or foreign agency or authority or any private institution which furnished information on a confidential basis * * * or information compiled by a criminal law enforcement authority * * * or by an agency conducting a lawful national security intelligence investigation, information furnished by a confidential source, (E) would disclose techniques or procedures for law enforcement investigations or prosecutions * * *, or (F) could reasonably be expected to endanger the life or physical safety of any individual.

A key case showing the slipperiness of this exemption for those seeking records access is *Federal Bureau of Investigation v. Abramson.*[110] Journalist Howard Abramson was investigating President Richard Nixon's use of the FBI to collect information on persons he considered his political "enemies," the better to harass them. Abramson asked for the files on such enemies under the FOIA. The FBI rejected the request, calling release of the information an "unwarranted invasion of privacy" under Exemption 7(C) (quoted above), and also under Exemption 6, which also deals with privacy.

In *United States v. Landano*, however, the Supreme Court put at least a temporary crimp in the FBI's blanket use of Exemption 7(D), records or information compiled for law enforcement purposes that could reasonably be expected to disclose the identity of a confidential source.

---

[110] *Federal Bureau of Investigation v. Abramson*, 456 U.S. 615, 102 S.Ct. 2054 (1982).

Convicted cop-killer Vincent Landano argued that his claims of innocence were thwarted because the FBI refused to release sufficiently complete records that could cast doubt on his guilt. The FBI had interpreted Exemption 7(D) as giving it virtually unlimited authority to protect from disclosure confidential sources or the material they provide.[111]

Writing for a unanimous court, Justice Sandra Day O'Connor declared it is unreasonable to assume that all FBI investigative sources are confidential.

> We think this more particularized approach is consistent with Congress' intent to provide workable rules of FOIA disclosure. *Department of Justice v. Reporters Committee*, 489 U.S. at 779; 16 Med.L.Rptr. 1545, quoting *FTC v. Grolier*, 462 U.S. 19, 27, 103 S.Ct. 2209 (1983); see also *EPA v. Mink*, 410 U.S. 73, 80, 93 S.Ct. 827 (1973), 1 Med.L.Rptr. 2448. The government does not deny that, when a document is requested, it generally will be possible to establish factors such as the nature of the crime that was investigated and the source's relation to it. Armed with this information, the requester will have a more realistic opportunity to develop an argument that the circumstances do not support an inference of confidentiality.

Exemption 8—Reports prepared by or for an agency responsible for the regulation or supervision of financial institutions. The exemption exists to protect financial institutions from the harms of having financial records and reports made public. Consumer panic and depositors' demand to get their money back from their accounts in bank runs exacerbated the financial problems of the Great Depression.[112]

During a bank run, a large number of depositors lose confidence in the security of their bank, leading them all to withdraw their funds at once. Banks typically hold only a fraction of deposits in cash at any one time and lend out the rest to borrowers or purchase interest-bearing assets like government securities. During a bank run, a bank must quickly liquidate loans and sell its assets (often at rock-bottom prices) to come up with the necessary cash, and the losses they suffer can threaten the bank's solvency. The bank runs of 1930 were followed by similar banking panics in the spring and fall of 1931 and the fall of 1932. In some instances, bank runs were started simply by rumors of a bank's inability or unwillingness to pay out funds.

More modernly, concerns about the health of financial institutions that are publicly traded can cause declines in the value of their stock. In

---

[111] *U.S. Department of Justice v. Landano*, 508 U.S. 165, 171, 113 S.Ct. 2014, 2019, 2023 (1993); Linda Greenhouse, "Court Limits Shielding F.B.I. Sources," *New York Times*, May 25, 1994.

[112] Editors, "Bank Run," *History.com*, June 10, 2019. https://www.history.com/topics/great-depression/bank-run.

Consumers Union of U. S., Inc. v. Heimann,[113] the consumer advocate Consumers Union sought records showing whether banks in the New England region were complying with the Consumer Credit Protection Act, 15 U.S.C. § 1601–1691f (1976), otherwise known as the Truth in Lending Act. As the Office of the Comptroller of Currency explained, Truth in Lending "protects you against inaccurate and unfair credit billing and credit card practices. It requires lenders to provide you with loan cost information so that you can comparison shop for certain types of loans."

The banks had reported their compliance to the Comptroller of Currency which had analyzed and created a report. Consumers Union filed a FOIA request for the information. The Comptroller refused citing Exemption 8. Consumers Union sued and the case made it to the District of Columbia Circuit Court of Appeals where a three-judge panel held that Exemption 8 was properly applied to deny the request. A concurrence by Chief Judge J. Skelly Wright recited the legislative history of the exemption.[114]

> Both the House and Senate reports on the provision indicate that Congress was concerned that release of bank examination and operating reports could endanger the fiscal well-being of the subject banks. Thus, the Senate report states:
>
> Exemption No. 8 is directed specifically to insuring the security of our financial institutions by making available only to the Government agencies responsible for the regulation or supervision of such institutions the examination, operating, or condition reports prepared by(,) on behalf of, or for the use of such agencies.
>
> S.Rep.No.813, 89th Cong., 1st Sess. 10 (1965). And the House report observes:
>
> This exemption is designed to insure the security and integrity of financial institutions, for sensitive details collected by Government agencies which regulate these institutions could, if indiscriminately disclosed, cause great harm.

Exemption 9—Geological and geophysical information and data, including maps, concerning wells—particularly explorations by gas and oil companies. There are virtually no cases on Exemption 9. The legislative history points to concerns about how the information and data could be misused. Witnesses contended that the disclosure of the seismic reports and other exploratory findings of oil companies[115] "would give speculators an unfair advantage over the companies which spent millions of dollars in exploration."

---

[113] *Consumers Union of U. S., Inc. v. Heimann*, 589 F.2d 531 (D.C.Cir 1978).

[114] Ibid. at 536–537.

[115] H.R. Rep. No. 89-1497 (1966).

In one of the few Exemption 9 cases litigated, the environmental group AquAlliance requested records pertaining to water transfers in California.[116] Water is a major issue in that state which goes through periodic droughts lasting years. While the bureau complied, providing many of the requested documents, it withheld records of well construction, well completion and the physical location of wells. AquAlliance sued and lost. U.S. District Judge Ketanji Brown Jackson wrote,[117] "The dispute over Exemption 9 boils down to two questions: first, does the exemption cover water wells? And, second, does it cover the type of information that the Bureau has withheld here? This Court concludes that the answer to both questions is 'yes.'" Although water wells are not oil or gas wells, Judge Jackson reasoned that the plain language of the exemption. He recognized that at least one other court had declared that water[118] "is a precious, limited resource." And so, Judge Jackson concluded,[119] "the expressed purpose of including a FOIA exemption to prevent a windfall for speculators also applies in the context of water wells."

EVOLUTION OF FOIA

Long delays, high costs for searching and copying documents, and widespread agency reluctance to comply with the original act's provisions sum up the history of the FOIA.[120] Congress has acted on several occasions to improve access under FOIA. Not only were several exemptions tightened by the amendments; also, rules were passed requiring agencies to inform persons making requests for information within 10 days whether or not access would be granted, and to decide upon requests for appeals within 20 days. Uniform schedules of fees—limited to reasonable standard charges for document search and copying—were also mandated in the amendments.[121]

Even though the FOIA always listed deadlines, delays are the rule, not the exception. Requesters often referred to the Freedom of Information Act as the Freedom to Delay Information Act. Agencies could extend their processing time if they could show "unusual circumstances." Heavy workloads and short staffs combined to make the unusual the norm. Often, a department will turn down a request it deems too time-consuming.

---

[116] *AquAlliance v. United States Bureau of Reclamation*, 139 F.Supp.3d 203 (D.C.Cir. 2015).

[117] Ibid. at 209.

[118] *Starkey v. U.S. Dep't of Interior*, 238 F.Supp.2d 1188, 1195 (S.D.Cal.2002).

[119] *AquAlliance v. United States Bureau of Reclamation*, 139 F.Supp.3d 203, 210 (D.C.Cir. 2015).

[120] Wallis McClain, "Implementing the Amended FOI Act," *Freedom of Information Center Report No. 343*, Sept. 1975, p. 1; U.S. Congress, *Freedom of Information Act and Amendments of 1974 (P.L. 93–502) Source Book: Legislative History, Texts, and Other Documents. Joint Committee Print* (94th Cong., 1 Sess.), Washington: U.S. Government Printing Office, March 1975.

[121] Anon., "FOI Act Amendments Summarized," *FOI Digest*, 17:1, Jan.–Feb. 1975, p. 5.

The National Security Archive at George Washington University studied FOIA requests and found lengthy delays.[122] "[P]rocessing times for FOIA requests are as high as 905 business days at the Department of Agriculture and 1,113 business days (a little more than 3 years) at the Environmental Protection Agency." The Archive reported on its site www.nsarchive.gwu.edu/ that the oldest active request dated from 1987.[123] A FOIA Project report in 2016 showed that the Department of the Navy had the highest waiting period of agencies that responded to a request. The average wait for Navy FOIA requests was 354 days. The Air Force reported an average of 161 days. The CIA declined to take part in the survey.[124]

Time has not improved the track record for FOIA responses. *The Washington Post* reported in early 2019 on the longest-pending FOIA request in the 52 years of the law's history.

> The government's oldest pending FOIA request has been languishing for almost 25 years, and there are 111,334 FOIA requests waiting—a mountainous backlog. At many agencies, despite the law's requirement for a response within 20 business days, FOIA requests are rarely processed within a year.

And the worst year ever for FOIA was 2017, the Associated Press reported in 2018. Some 823,222 FOIA requests were made in 2017. In 78 percent of the requests, federal executive agencies provided nothing or censored files. Only 20 percent of the requesters received everything they asked for.

THE ELECTRONIC FREEDOM OF INFORMATION ACT

A significant change in the FOI Act came in September 1996 when Congress passed the Electronic Freedom of Information Act. The Act, sponsored in some form since 1991 by Sen. Patrick Leahy (D-Vt.), brought FOIA into the electronic age by widening the definition of records and requiring on-line access to them. The definition of a record now includes information stored electronically. That change addressed concerns about agencies storing vast quantities of information in databases and then refusing to create software to retrieve particular records.

The changes also required that records created on or after Nov. 1, 1996 be made available for inspection or copying on-line as well as in hard copy form. If an agency does not maintain on-line capabilities, the information must be made available through some other electronic means such as diskette or on CD-ROM. Agencies were to have complied with this in November 1997. As might be expected, the process took much

---

[122] Ibid.

[123] That request was one made by reporter Seth Rosenfeld. The case finally was resolved, and it is discussed later in this chapter.

[124] http://foiaproject.org/2016/01/26/good-news-and-bad-news-on-foia-responsiveness/ # more - 3572.

longer with the GAO reporting in 2002 that agencies were not putting materials online or making sure that the information was accurate or current.

Under EFOIA, Agencies also must make reasonable efforts to conduct database searches, except where such searches would significantly interfere with their operations. Requesters also may specify the format and form they want to receive the record it, provided the information can readily be produced in that format.

EFOIA also included clarifications about the way agencies could deny requests. Agencies had previously used a general rationale that releasing information would harm an interest protected by an exemption in saying no. After the passage of the amendments, agencies were required to withhold information "only if the agency reasonably foresees that disclosure would harm an interest protected by an exemption" or "disclosure is prohibited by law."

In addition, EFOIA made clear what agencies had to do in response to requests for certain records in electronic format. The four categories of information required to be made available for public inspection in an electronic format consist of:

- (A) "final opinions [and] . . . orders" rendered in the adjudication of administrative cases;
- (B) specific agency policy statements;
- (C) certain administrative staff manuals "that affect a member of the public;" and
- (D) records which have been released in response to a request and "that because of the nature of their subject matter, the agency determines have become, or are likely to become, the subject of subsequent requests for substantially the same records; or . . . that have been requested 3 or more times."

The requirement that agencies pro-actively post records that were requested three or more times benefits both requesters and agencies in that the posting eliminates new requests for records already provided and makes the records available online, speeding up the process.

But, even with the changes, records have not always been made available online.

The GAO's 2002 report said that agencies were making slow progress in complying with the EFOIA requirements. "Agencies are not devoting sufficient attention to the on-line availability of materials and ensuring that Web site content is adequately maintained, including accuracy and currency of the material and Web site links." The same study found that a number of agencies had removed or "scrubbed" information from their sites following the Sept. 11, 2001, attacks.

THE OPEN GOVERNMENT ACT OF 2007

On Dec. 31, 2007, President George W. Bush signed the Openness Promotes Effectiveness in our National Government Act, or "OPEN Government Act of 2007." The measure had passed the House by voice vote and by a unanimous Senate vote. At least 10 major journalism organizations, including the Society of Professional Journalists and the Reporters Committee for Freedom of the Press (RCFP) supported the Act. The RCFP termed it "arguably its most significant revision in 30 years." It went into effect on Dec. 31, 2008.

Among its provisions: creation of a Freedom of Information Officer position who has real power in a federal agency, plus appointment of an FOI liaison (an "ombudsman," some called this position) to help answer FOI requests. The RCFP quoted Thomas M. Susman, an experienced access litigator, as saying the ombudsman provision "has the potential to have the most universal effect on the FOIA process." Susman said such a system worked had worked well in some states and in other countries. Critics of the ombudsman approach, however, argue that it could serve to centralize FOI responses to provide pasteurized and homogenized news of federal agencies.

The Open Government Act of 2007 provides tracking numbers on document requests so requesters can check on progress, if any. This legislation retained the same 20-working-days disclosure requirement so often not complied with in the past. Timely compliance, given the flood of FOI requests and limited agency resources and personnel, still seems unlikely. As an RCFP *News Media Update* said on Dec. 19, 2007, however, new procedures will aid document-seekers ". . . by prohibiting FOIA agencies from charging search and duplication fees to non-commercial requesters when an agency has missed the 20-day deadline."

Rep. Henry Waxman (D-Calif.) said he regretted that a compromise in merging the House bill with the Senate bill had removed a provision to stop the "Ashcroft presumption of non-disclosure." In 2001, Attorney General John Ashcroft had reversed President Clinton's "presumption of disclosure."

THE FOIA IMPROVEMENT ACT OF 2016

President Obama signed into law the FOIA Improvement Act of 2016. The Act included changes to the Justice Department's Foreseeable Harm Standard. Previous administrations applied varying standard for non-disclosure which included withholding information based on "possible harm." Under the revision, agencies would withhold information "only if the agency reasonably foresees that disclosure would harm an interest protected by an exemption" or "disclosure is prohibited by law." The Act also requires agencies to make information that has been requested three times available in electronic format.

The Act puts a sunset provision on Exemption 5 denials. After 25 years, agencies cannot use Exemption 5's "deliberate process" to withhold them. Records in this category may be subject to other exemptions, but the overuse of Exemption 5 during the Obama administration made this change significant.

USING FOIA

The FOI Service Center, a project of the Reporters Committee on Freedom of the Press, periodically updates its Federal Open Government Guide. It summarizes the uses of the FOIA as a news-gathering tool, and also provides thumbnail sketches of the Act's disclosure exemptions. This is truly a "do-it-yourself" guide, and even includes sample FOI Act request letters—and, if needed—sample appeal letters. This material is available from The Reporters Committee, 1101 Wilson Blvd., Suite 1100, Arlington, VA 22209, (703) 807–2100, and from its invaluable Website, https://www.rcfp.org/wp-content/uploads/imported/FOGG.pdf and from the RCFP wiki, https://foia.wiki/wiki/Main_Page.

Essentially, a requester identifies a likely agency to have the records, files a request and then waits for the agency to make a decision about release.

Choosing the right agency is sometimes easy and sometimes difficult. If you lived near an Air Force base where nuclear-equipped bombers were stationed, where would you send your request for information on the bombs? It seems logical to say the Air Force or the Department of Defense. The proper agency, though, is the Department of Energy. Thermonuclear devices are nuclear materials that produce energy, though much faster and more energetically than any nuclear power plant (one hopes) and that falls under the Energy Department.

Once the agency has the request, it has 20 working days to make its decision. This probably will not be the case. Backlogs, time needed for research and labor shortages all add up to increased delays. If the agency decided to give you the information, everything ends. If the agency declines to give you the information, it must write to you explaining the exemption it claims. You have the option of appealing administratively to the agency or going to federal court. Administrative appeals take another "20 working days" [often, in fact, adding up to years] and the agency can either change its mind or stick with its denial.

If you decide to sue, you have a choice of filing in the federal court district where you live, the district where the records are kept or the District of Columbia (home to all executive agencies). The court will look at what you are requesting and the reasons the government offers for claiming its exemption. Whoever wins faces the possibility of an appeal to the next higher level by the losing side. The Supreme Court is the court of last resort for FOIA cases, but it accepts so few cases via its *certiorari* process that as a practical matter, a U.S. Court of Appeals may be the highest court available.

GETTING BACK YOUR LEGAL COSTS

Winning an FOI suit can mean reimbursement for the requester's legal fees. In *Davy v. CIA,*[125] author William A. Davy, Jr., requested records from the CIA about its involvement in the assassination of President Kennedy. Davy was the author of several articles and a book, "*Let Justice Be Done.*" The book looked at the investigation of the Kennedy assassination conducted by New Orleans District Attorney Jim Garrison. The CIA denied the request and Davy sued. At one point, the CIA produced some of the documents that Davy sought and then Davy won a summary judgment motion on the rest of his suit. Davy tried to get his legal costs reimbursed.

The trial court denied his request and the case made it to a three-judge panel of the D.C. Circuit Court of Appeals. There, Circuit Judge Judith Rogers reversed the denial of fees and sent the case back to the trial court to reconsider.

> This court, drawing on the Senate and House Committee reports for FOIA and its amendments, explained long ago that the provision for attorney's fees "was not enacted to provide a reward for any litigant who successfully forces the government to disclose information it wished to withhold," but instead "had a more limited purpose—to remove the incentive for administrative resistance to disclosure requests based not on the merits of exemption claims, but on the knowledge that many FOIA plaintiffs do not have the financial resources or economic incentives to pursue their requests through expensive litigation." *Nationwide Bldg. Maint., Inc. v. Sampson,* 559 F.2d 704, 711 (D.C.Cir.1977) (citing S.REP. NO. 93–854, at 17).

Judge Rogers pointed to the four criteria to be used in determining whether a FOIA plaintiff should be awarded fees. They are: "(1) the public benefit derived from the case; (2) the commercial benefit to the plaintiff; (3) the nature of the plaintiff's interest in the records; and (4) the reasonableness of the agency's withholding of the requested documents." The record showed that the factors weighed in Davy's favor and Judge Rogers remanded the case to the trial court with instructions to award his fees. "[H]e is entitled to an award of fees and costs, and upon remand the district court shall enter an appropriate order."

Before the FCC voted to repeal Net Neutrality (discussed in Chap. 11), it sought public comment. It got 22 million comments through the Internet. Compare that to the 3.9 million comments the FCC received before it adopted its Net Neutrality rules four years earlier.

During the run up to the FCC vote, some news reports pointed to comments that were not sent by the people whose names were attached to them. The Pew Research Center looked at comments as the FCC

---

[125] *William A. Davy, Jr. v. Central Intelligence Agency,* 550 F.3d 1155 (D.C. Cir. 2008).

prepared to vote. "Pew found that only 6 percent of submitted comments were unique while the rest had been submitted multiple times, in some cases, hundreds of thousands of times," Reuters reported. Of the seven most submitted comments, six favored repeal. "President Obama's order to take over Internet access is a exploitation of the open Internet" was a common, ungrammatical phrase.

In the wake of the vote and after hearing about people whose names were used without their knowledge, freelance writer Jason Prechtel filed a FOIA request asking for data that would point to who made bulk comments. The FCC denied the request. Prechtel sued. A year after that, a federal district court judge ordered the FCC to provide some, but not all, of the documents Prechtel asked for. The case settled. "A settlement agreement filed in court this week says the FCC agreed to pay Prechtel $43,000 to cover his attorneys' fees and court costs."

DEALING WITH A DELUGE OF DOCUMENTS

At some point, you get your FOIA documents, perhaps after going through the request and appeal process. You might get them after a lawsuit. When you take delivery, you have cartons filled with documents or gigantic files. How do you mine the mountain of words? It can be daunting. There is a cartoon that sums up the mixed blessing of fighting for winning records. It shows bloodied, beaten-up python that has just killed a hippopotamus, lying in the background. The caption reads" "Now I have to eat it, too?" Searching through thousands of pages of documents can take more time than a reporter has. If, as has happened, an agency has buried damaging portions in the middle of a document, the search can be all but impossible.

Technology provides a solution. Emily Bazelon, a staff writer for *The New York Times Magazine*, wrote a short piece on the tools she uses.[126] Once a request is filled, she has a tool to search for key information.[127]

> I've done investigative projects based on a relatively small number of documents, but if I ever have to sift through a huge data dump, looking for patterns and smoking guns, I'll use a software program called Everlaw. It lets you browse quickly without worrying about what format a document is in. (For example, you can switch back and forth between text messages and a PowerPoint.) I like the options it offers for organizing material. Full disclosure: My nephew Zach Sabin is a software engineer who helped develop this product.

SF Chronicle reporter Jason Fagone has used Everlaw to examine sometimes massive FOIA responses. "I think sometimes they do just dump a ton of records on you so you'll get bored or want to punch the

---

[126] Emily Bazelon, "An Arsenal of Skype, Voice Recorders and FOIAs," *New York Times*, Jan. 30, 2019.

[127] Ibid.

wall, he said. Fagone wrote a story on former Naval Station Treasure Island in San Francisco Bay. The station is a combination of a man-made island and a natural island. It was closed as a naval base and turned over to the city of San Francisco in 1997. Fagone used Everlaw to sift through documents on contamination at the base. It has become home to hundreds of families living in old Navy housing and is being developed into a "$6 billion development of condos and shops."

"It was a story on how, when Treasure Island was first analyzed by the EPA to see how contaminated it was and what might be done to clean it up," Fagone said. "They found Treasure Island was hazardous enough to be placed on the superfund list."

Treasure Island was not designated a superfund site, though the exact reason was not clear, Fagone and fellow *SF Chronicle* reporter Cynthia Dizikes reported in 2019. Using the Everlaw program, they found that,[128] "after the Navy closed the base and the city began reusing some buildings for housing, Navy contractors made a series of troubling discoveries, finding and removing more than 600 individual radioactive objects, some in housing areas." The base also was contaminated with industrial chemicals and toxic metals, they found.

Fagone also used Everlaw in FOIA requests about recent regulatory changes. "We were looking for information about changes to radiation regulation that had been proposed inside the Trump EPA and were trying to figure out who was sharing that information about the radiation rules. What was the background of people pushing those rules?"

Everlaw began as a tool for lawyers in complex litigation. Discovery, the sharing of evidence in lawsuits before the case goes to trial, is meant to help litigants understand the strengths and weaknesses of their and their opponent's cases. It often is abused, and legal publications write of burying opponents in an avalanche of paper or hiding "smoking gun" papers amid thousands of pages of documents. "The company started out with the premise that software automation could help with that, because humans can't consume the volume of documents in big cases," Chris Nguyen, head of corporate communication for Everlaw, said.

The company also undertook to provide a resource outside the legal system. "One of our core values as a company is helping organizations discover truth and get to the heart of justice" Nguyen said. "We value working with non-profits, journalists, educators and pro bono attorneys."

Those groups can access the system for free. The program gives reporters the ability to search through multiple formats, Nguyen said. It can review audio files, video files voice recordings, emails and other document types. "If you have a thousand videos and are looking for someone saying, 'red flag,' you're able to search for a video where somebody says the words, 'red flag,' " Nguyen said.

---

[128] Jason Fagone and Cynthia Dizikes, "SF's Treasure Island, poised for building boom, escaped listing as Superfund site," *S.F.Chronicle*, Sept. 19, 2019.

Fagone is using FOIA more now that he has access to the program. "You know that you're going to be able to feed it into the database," he said "no matter how many documents you are given by the agency no matter what shape or format they're in."

FOIA LOSSES

Court cases on FOIA are not always clear as courts have, variously clarified or muddied the water in access cases.

RECORDS, RECORDS, WHO'S GOT THE RECORDS

Federal executive agencies are supposed to provide records they possess in response to requests. But does it mean to possess. In *Forsham v. Harris*,[129] a 1980 Supreme Court decision, Justice Rehnquist held that written data held by a private research firm receiving federal grant money from HEW were not "agency records" if the agency providing the funds had not yet obtained the data. The FOI Act provided no direct access to such data in the hands of the research firm; therefore, HEW had not improperly "withheld the data. The Act applied not to records that could exist in agency files, but only to records that did exist. "We hold here that written data generated, owned, and possessed by a privately controlled organization receiving federal study grants are not "agency records" within the meaning of the Act when copies of those data have not been obtained by a federal agency subject to the FOIA.[130]

In *Kissinger v. Reporters Committee for Freedom of the Press*,[131] the Supreme Court held that the State Department had not "withheld" records of former Secretary of State Henry Kissinger's phone calls. Kissinger had donated, improperly by the way, the records to the Library of Congress where they would be unavailable to the public for 25 years. The Reporters Committee sued, arguing that the State Department needed to get the records back, even if it took a lawsuit. The Supreme Court held that agencies did not have to produce records they did not possess and that the district did not have the authority to order the transfer of Kissinger's notes from the Library of Congress to the State Department. Kissinger later agreed to a new review of documents to determine whether they were needed for departmental files.

PRIVACY CONCERNS OUTWEIGH PUBLIC INTEREST

Department of Justice v. Reporters Committee for Freedom of the Press

A CBS News correspondent and the Reporters Committee for Freedom of the Press sought rap sheets of four members of the Medico

[129] *Forsham v. Harris*, 445 U.S. 169, 100 S.Ct. 977 (1980).

[130] Ibid. at 171, 980.

[131] *Kissinger v. Reporters Committee for Freedom of the Press*, 445 U.S. 136, 100 S.Ct. 960 (1980).

crime family. The Medico family's ammunition companies were said by the Pennsylvania Crime Commission to be dominated by major figures in organized crime, And, the Medico family companies, thanks to a compliant and corrupt Congressman named Daniel J. Flood, were getting defense contracts.

The Reporters Committee asked for disclosure of any arrests, indictments, acquittals, convictions, and sentences of any of the four Medicos. Those materials were included in rap sheets[132] that the FBI had collected from across the country on a voluntary basis. It had 24 million of those records in the late 1980s. The FBI refused and an FOIA lawsuit was begun. The case eventually made it to the Supreme Court.[133]

Justice Stevens wrote the opinion for the Court with six other justices joining and two justices signing on to a concurring opinion. He laid out the reasons, in his view, of why the CBS correspondent and Reporters Committee wanted the rap sheets. More importantly, he provided his perspective on the value of the information demonstrating a fundamental misunderstanding of news.[134]

> [Medico] allegedly had improper dealings with a corrupt Congressman, and he is an officer of a corporation with defense contracts. But if Medico has, in fact, been arrested or convicted of certain crimes, that information would neither aggravate nor mitigate his allegedly improper relationship with the Congressman; more specifically, it would tell us nothing directly about the character of the Congressman's behavior. Nor would it tell us anything about the conduct of the Department of Defense (DOD) in awarding one or more contracts to the Medico Company.

The manner in which a company won a contract with the Department of Defense, the way in which a sitting congressman could steer a contract to that company and the background of the people involved would be a matter of public interest. Criminal records would raise questions about the manner in which bids and contracts were vetted. But Justice Stevens found the only value of the rap sheets, "would provide details to include in a news story."

That was not why FOIA was enacted, Justice Stevens said.[135]

> [* * *]this is not the kind of public interest for which Congress enacted the FOIA. In other words, although there is undoubtedly some public interest in anyone's criminal history, especially if the history is in some way related to the subject's

---

[132] Rap sheets contain descriptive information, such as date of birth and physical characteristics, as well as a history of arrests, charges, convictions, and incarcerations of the subject.

[133] *U.S. Dept. of Justice v. Reporters Committee For Freedom of Press*, 489 U.S. 749, 109 S.Ct. 1468 (1989).

[134] Ibid. at 772, 1482.

[135] Ibid. at 774, 1482.

> dealing with a public official or agency, the FOIA's central purpose is to ensure that the Government's activities be opened to the sharp eye of public scrutiny, not that information about private citizens that happens to be in the warehouse of the Government be so disclosed.

Rap sheets in the hands of local and state jurisdictions are not always public records, Justice Stevens noted. In 47 states, legislatures have placed substantial restrictions on the availability of criminal histories summaries even though arrests, indictments, convictions, and sentences in those summaries are matters of public record. Three Exemptions applied to the Medico rap sheet request, Justice Stevens said:[136]

> Exemption 3 applies to documents that are specifically exempted from disclosure by another statute. § 552(b)(3). Exemption 6 protects "personnel and medical files and similar files the disclosure of which would constitute a clearly unwarranted invasion of personal privacy." § 552(b)(6).7 Exemption 7(C) excludes records or information compiled for law enforcement purposes, "but only to the extent that the production of such [materials] . . . could reasonably be expected to constitute an unwarranted invasion of personal privacy." § 552(b)(7)(C).

It is clear that Exemption 7(C)'s protections for privacy, "could reasonably be expected to constitute," are easier to assert than that in 6, "would constitute." The Senate version of the 1974 FOIA amendments had the language, "clearly unwarranted invasion of personal privacy." That language conflicted with House language and in conference committee "clearly" was cut and the "could reasonably be expected to" was left in the resulting bill. Justice Stevens said the change was a response to concerns expressed by President Gerald Ford. Based on the legislative history, Justice Stevens held that the records sought by the reporters was exempt from disclosure.

CIA V. SIMS

CIA v. Sims[137] concerned a FOIA suit to get records on the CIA research project code-named "MKULTRA" The project, started in 1953, was intended to find ways to counter Chinese and Soviet advances in brainwashing and interrogation.[138] From 1953 to 1965, the CIA

---

[136] Ibid. at 755, 1473.

[137] *C.I.A. v. Sims*, 471 U.S. 159, 105 S.Ct. 1881 (1985).

[138] It was widely believed that a number of American servicemen, who were captured in the Korean War, had been subjected to chemical interrogation and brainwashing. The most significant instance occurred in early 1953 when Chinese state radio broadcast the statements of two captured Marine Corps aviators that the U.S. Joint Chiefs of Staff had ordered U.S. forces to carry out biological warfare. Thousands of American P.O.W.s were suspected of having collaborated with the communist forces. "A handful, on orders from their captors, had, in fact, falsely accused the United States of conducting germ warfare against North Korea. Congress

contracted with some 80 universities, research institutions, prisons and 185 researchers in the United States and Canada to test the efficacy of certain biological and chemical materials, including LSD, mescaline, nerve agents, PCP, electro shock and a drug identified as drug "Z" in altering human behavior.[139]

John C. Sims, an attorney, and Sidney M. Wolfe, M.D., the director of the Public Citizen Health Research Group, filed a request with the CIA for the names and institutions that worked on the project. The CIA refused and Sims and Wolfe sued. A U.S. District Court ordered the CIA to provide the names. After getting the case back from a three-judge panel of the D.C. Circuit, the court ordered the CIA to provide some of the names but found that others were exempt. The D.C. Circuit affirmed in part and reversed in part. The Supreme Court took up the case.

Chief Justice Burger wrote the opinion for the court with six other justices agreeing and Justice Marshall writing a concurring opinion that Justice Brennan joined. The case rested on the question of whether the National Security Act of 1947 exempted the disclosure of both institutions and researchers through Exemption 3, exempt by statute.[140]

> The plain statutory language is not to be ignored. [* * *] The legislative history of § 102(d)(3) also makes clear that Congress intended to give the Director of Central Intelligence broad power to protect the secrecy and integrity of the intelligence process. The reasons are too obvious to call for enlarged discussion; without such protections the Agency would be virtually impotent.

Some of the institutions had already been named. The CIA had contacted the universities, research foundations and institutions and gotten agreement from 59 to be identified. Sims and Wolfe argued that because most of the names had been identified, the names of the rest should be public. Chief Justice Burger noted that then-director Admiral Stansfield Turner had made the decision to make the names public where permission had been granted. William Casey, current director, also had the same power to disclose or keep the names secret under the National Security Act of 1947.

> And, Chief Justice Burger wrote, the release of seemingly trivial information could be damaging to the national security interests of the United States.[141]

> [T]he Director must, of course, do more than simply withhold the names of intelligence sources. Such withholding, standing

was transfixed by 'the fear that the soldiers could have been brainwashed by the Chinese and still be spying for them,' Col. Elspeth Cameron Ritchie wrote in the journal *Military Medicine*." Tim Weiner, "Remembering Brainwashing," *New York Times*, July 6, 2008.

139 Researchers, military officials and others envisioned being able to use psycho-chemical warfare to incapacitate enemy forces allowing war without killing.

140 *C.I.A. v. Sims*, 471 U.S. 159, 170, 105 S.Ct. 1881, 1888 (1985).

141 Ibid. at 178–179, 1892–1893.

> alone, does not carry out the mandate of Congress. Foreign intelligence services have an interest in knowing what is being studied and researched by our agencies dealing with national security and by whom it is being done. Foreign intelligence services have both the capacity to gather and analyze any information that is in the public domain and the substantial expertise in deducing the identities of intelligence sources from seemingly unimportant details.
>
> [* * *]
>
> In this context, the very nature of the intelligence apparatus of any country is to try to find out the concerns of others; bits and pieces of data "may aid in piecing together bits of other information even when the individual piece is not of obvious importance in itself." *Halperin v. CIA*, 203 U.S.App.D.C. 110, 116, 629 F.2d 144, 150 (1980). Thus, " '[w]hat may seem trivial to the uninformed, may appear of great moment to one who has a broad view of the scene and may put the questioned item of information in its proper context.' " *Halkin v. Helms*, 194 U.S.App.D.C. 82, 90, 598 F.2d 1, 9 (1978), quoting United States v. Marchetti, 466 F.2d 1309, 1318 (CA4), cert. denied, 409 U.S. 1063, 93 S.Ct. 553, 34 L.Ed.2d 516 (1972).

But it should be kept in mind that MKULTRA—hardly the CIA's finest hour—became known despite a determined effort to erase all evidence that it had ever existed. When Richard Helms—who had himself suggested the project as a CIA functionary in 1953—became President Nixon's CIA director in the 1970s, he ordered all evidence of the project wiped out. But some of the financial records of the project "inadvertently survived" and came to the attention of Admiral Stansfield Turner, CIA Director under President Carter. Turner turned the information over to the Senate Select Committee on Intelligence, resulting in a major Congressional investigation. But even there, the CIA request to treat the names of the MKULTRA researchers as confidential was honored.

At least two deaths were directly attributable to the MKULTRA though there were no records of what ultimately happened to many of the subjects.[142] Other test subjects went mad, and still others suffered psychological damage.[143] In at least 25 projects, subjects were given mid-

[142] One of the most notorious such cases involved Frank R. Olson, a CIA germ-warfare expert who died in a fall from a hotel window in 1953, nine days after a CIA doctor spiked Olson's after-dinner drink with LSD. In 1975, President Gerald R. Ford invited Olson's family to the White House to apologize; the government also paid the family $750,000. Thomas E. Ricks, "Experimenting with the Mind," *Washington Post*, June 27, 2007.

[143] One MKUltra subject was convicted of rape and murder of a girl in 1954. Jimmy Shaver, an airman, had no prior criminal history. The Army psychiatrist who was the expert witness on his state of mind was a senior MKULTRA researcher. Shaver's participation in MKULTRA was not disclosed in his trial. He was executed in 1958. Tom O'Neill, Dan Piepenbring, "Inside the Archive of an LDSD Researcher with Ties to the CIA's MKULTRA

altering substances without their knowledge of what they were getting and how it might affect them. The tests involved military personnel, college students, intelligence personnel and prison inmates. "Many of the human guinea pigs were mental patients, prisoners, drug addicts and prostitutes—"people who could not fight back," as one agency officer put it. In one case, a mental patient in Kentucky was dosed with LSD continuously for 174 days. The CIA ran "Operation Midnight Climax," an MKULTRA project in which government-employed prostitutes lured unsuspecting men to CIA "safe houses" where drug experiments took place.[144] "In 1954, a prison doctor in Kentucky isolated seven black inmates and fed them "double, triple and quadruple" doses of LSD for 77 days straight. No one knows what became of the victims."[145] The CIA also operated "black sites" in other countries at the time where an unknown number of foreign subjects were dosed with mind-altering substances.

The studies failed to include follow-ups on the subjects. The soldiers were simply returned to their units. Civilians were sent on their way, unaware of what had happened to them. Following Congressional hearings, such experiments were banned by executive order.

TESTING THE EFFECTS OF RADIATION

Access to information might have prevented other federal programs that experimented on American citizens and servicemen. Revelations by Secretary of Energy Hazel O'Leary led to the discovery of a number of government experiments in which people were exposed to harmful radiation. The radiation program was uncovered by a reporter from the *Albuquerque Tribune* in 1987. The tests were conducted during the Cold War when nuclear warfare was a very real possibility. *The New York Times* reported the chilling stories of five of victims of not only the radiation experiments, but also government secrecy.[146]

Anthony Guarisco was a sailor, assigned as a lifeguard on the officers' beach at Bikini Atoll. Following the detonation of two atomic bombs near some 90 unoccupied warships, Guarisco and other sailors were sent to the ships. Ostensibly, they were there to check radiation levels and try to decontaminate the ships by scrubbing them with brooms and mops. The real purpose of the experiment, in the words of one document was to see,[147] "how much radiation a man can take." In addition to a degenerative condition of his spine, Guarisco said his situation and that of others like him has been harmed by the government's secrecy. "A lot of us in this work have something like post-

---

Mind Control Project," *The Intercept*, Nov. 24, 2019. https://theintercept.com/2019/11/24/cia-mkultra-louis-jolyon-west/.

[144] History.com editors, "Operation Midnight Climax," *History.com*, June 16, 2017. https://www.history.com/topics/us-government/history-of-mk-ultra.

[145] Stephen Kinzer, "The Secret History of Fort Detrick, the CIA's Base for Mind Control Experiments," *Politico Magazine*, Sept. 15, 2019.

[146] Michael D'Antonio, "Atomic Guinea Pigs," *New York Times*, Aug. 31, 1997.

[147] Ibid.

traumatic stress disorder," the article quotes Guarisco. "But it is made a lot worse when no one believes you."

Guarisco uncovered a letter written by an Army scientist urging human experimentation in radiation research. The letter, which turned up in 1982, warned of the public relations risks, comparing them to reactions to Nazi experiments.[148] "Those concerned in the Atomic Energy Commission would be subject to considerable criticism, as admittedly this would have a little of the Buchenwald touch," the letter said.

In addition to sailors, government researcher's intent on discovering how the military would deal with an atomic battlefield, sent soldiers, Marines and air force personnel to open-air nuclear tests. All told, hundreds of thousands of military personnel were ordered to test sites and used as guinea pigs, without their knowledge.

Frederick Boyce, a child, was fed oatmeal with radioactive milk in a study of the body's absorption of different minerals. The researchers recruited Boyce and 23 other boys at the Water E. Fernald School for the Feebleminded in Boston by telling them they were joining a science club.[149]

> [I]n 1993, a librarian at Fernald discovered an old ledger book that described the way Boyce and other children in the 1950s had been seduced into taking part in medical experiments with promises of Red Sox tickets, Christmas parties, and other tokens.

Elmer Allen went to a San Francisco hospital with a knee injury. Doctors said he would have to have an amputation.[150] "Three days before the surgery, they secretly injected him with plutonium. Like 20 other patients in hospitals around the country, Allen had unknowingly been enrolled in an experiment financed by the A.E.C. to gather information to help protect workers at A-bomb plants." A 6-year-old leukemia patient was one of 89 persons subjected to high doses of radiation at the Institute of Nuclear Studies in Oak Ridge, Tenn., in the 1960s.[151]

In 1990, Congress passed the Radiation Exposure Compensation Act in 1990 to compensate the victims of radiation exposure, including persons exposed to radioactive fallout from nuclear weapons tests. In the 14 years since its passage, the fund paid $735 million on 11,174 claims from residents of Nevada, Utah, Colorado, Arizona, Texas, New Mexico, Wyoming, Idaho, South Dakota, North Dakota, Oregon and Washington.[152]

---

[148] Ibid.

[149] Scott Allenmay, "Even from deathbed, speaking up for justice," *New York Times*, May 3, 2006.

[150] Michael D'Antonio, "Atomic Guinea Pigs," *New York Times*, Aug. 31, 1997.

[151] Anna Snider, "A high level of criminal radioactivity." *Mother Jones*, March/April 1994.

[152] These were known as the "downwinders," because they lived downwind of nuclear tests and wound up in the plume of radioactive fallout.

In another instance of government abuse and secrecy, federal researchers studied 400 black men who had contracted syphilis. The researchers withheld treatment from the men even though effective treatments were then available. For four decades the researchers charted the progression of the disease. In 1972 after a former epidemiologist went public, the media reported on the Tuskegee Study of "Untreated Syphilis in the Negro Male." In the spring of 1997, President Clinton delivered a public apology for the experiments.

FOIA SUCCESSES

While federal government agencies have managed to thwart inquiries into their activities, FOIA and the genuine interest on the part of some public servants have allowed us to pierce the veil of secrecy of government. In many cases, the veil covered up horrendous conduct.

The U.S. Army conducted biological warfare tests around Washington, D.C., in the 1960s. Operatives sprayed travelers at a bus station with *bacillus subtilis*, a common bacterium, believed at the time to be harmless. Scientists later discovered that concentrated exposure could interfere with the immune systems of the elderly or those with debilitating diseases. In all, disclosures by the government showed that the Army conducted 239 secret tests of germ warfare in American cities. The Army also sprayed a chemical, later determined to be potentially cancer-causing, over Minneapolis in 1953.

While it was not the result of an FOIA request, additional information about military testing on American and foreign soil came to light in a congressional hearing in 2002. The Pentagon released summaries related to 28 chemical and biological warfare tests in Project 112, a program that operated in the 1960s and 1970s. The tests took place in Alaska, Hawaii, Canada and England and involved more than 7,000 service members. The military tested sarin and VX nerve gas and *Bacillus globigii*, a bacterium which was later found to be a hazard to people with weakened immune systems.

An FOI request revealed that a U.S. Air Force bomber accidentally dropped a hydrogen bomb near Albuquerque, New Mexico. The bomb, a 10-megaton bomb, fell from a B-36 bomber returning to base after practice maneuvers. Although the conventional explosives in the bomb detonated, the safety devices prevented a thermonuclear explosion.

Other disclosures showed that the FBI's COINTELPRO program had been used to spy on and harass Vietnam War protestors, that the FBI had the contents of a briefcase stolen from the 1968 Socialist Workers Party candidate for the presidency, that the CIA tried to get the gall bladder and other poisonous parts of a Tanganyikan crocodile and the services of a witch doctor to show them how to make poison from the parts.

FOIA disclosures led to the indictments and convictions of meat processors who had processed cows that died before making it to the slaughterhouse, revealed that plumbing valves purchased for $11 were being sold to the government for $140 apiece, uncovered evidence that defense contractors were charging the government to pay for their Washington lobbyists and that the Nixon administration tried to set up a drug bust on Beatle John Lennon in order to be able to deport him.

Seth Rosenfeld sued the Department of Justice and the Federal Bureau of Investigation under FOIA.[153] A journalist, Rosenfeld sought information about FBI investigations of a number of individuals and protests at the University of California, Berkeley, during the 1960s.

Rosenfeld filed open records requests with the FBI from late 1981 through early 1984, asking for FBI documents on investigations of people and organizations active in the Free Speech Movement (FSM) at Berkeley. The FBI found 8,432 documents, releasing 1,795 pages, plus another 4,985 in "redacted" form. The FBI withheld 1,652 pages in their entirety.

After lengthy litigation over documents in nine FBI files, the government appealed against release orders. But the appeal only dealt with three files. Those files contained information on the Free Speech Movement, US-Berkeley's then-president Clark Kerr, and journalist Marguerite Higgins. In 1991, the U.S. District Court for the Northern District of California ordered the release of all of the FSM documents generated after June 19, 1965, because none of the documents fell into the FOIA exemption for documents compiled for law enforcement purposes. The court also ordered the FBI files on Chancellor Kerr released as well.

The FBI appealed to the Ninth Circuit Court of Appeals. The Justice Department said the FBI should withhold the documents because they were related to national security, were compiled for law enforcement purposes and disclose investigatory techniques, disclose confidential information and invade the privacy of the persons the FBI investigated. The appellate court found that there was little to support a claim that the records would jeopardize national security. The court also found that some documents were not really law enforcement documents because the investigations of the subjects were not carried out for purposes of law enforcement.

Rosenfeld introduced evidence showing that the FBI waged a concerted effort in the late 1950s and 1960s to have Kerr fired from the presidency of UC-Berkeley. The documents Rosenfeld obtained all strongly support the suspicion that the FBI was investigating Kerr to have him removed from the UC administration, because FBI officials disagreed with his politics or his handling of administrative matters.

---

153 *Rosenfeld v. U.S. Dept. of Justice*, 57 F.3d 803 (9th Cir. 1999).

Conspicuously absent from these documents is any connection to any possible criminal liability by Kerr.

EXECUTIVE PRIVILEGE

A power to withhold records and information has always been asserted by the president and his executive department heads as "executive privilege." President George Washington was asked by Congress to make available documents relating to General St. Clair's defeat by Indians.[154] He responded that "the Executive ought to communicate such papers as the public good would permit, and ought to refuse those, the disclosure of which would injure the public * * *." In this case the records were made available to Congress, but many presidents since have refused to yield records, as have the heads of executive departments. Their power to do so was upheld early in the nation's history by the United States Supreme Court. The famous decision written by Chief Justice John Marshall was delivered in 1803 in *Marbury v. Madison*, where Marshall said that the Attorney General (a presidential appointee) did not have to reveal matters which had been communicated to him in confidence.

By the Constitution of the United States, the president is invested with certain important political powers, in the exercise of which he is to use his own discretion and is accountable only to the country in his political character and to his own conscience. Justice Marshall elaborated the principle in the trial of Aaron Burr, accused of treason, saying that "The propriety of withholding * * * must be decided by [the President] himself, not by another for him. Of the weight of the reasons for and against producing it he himself is the judge."

Executive privilege came to be asserted and used increasingly during the government's efforts to maintain security in the cold war with the U.S.S.R. following World War II. Presidents Truman and Eisenhower used the power to issue orders detailing what might and might not be released from the executive departments; both came under heavy attack from Congress and the news media. President Nixon's Executive Order No. 11–652 of March 8, 1972, replaced and modified rules set by President Eisenhower.

One of the most far-reaching directives of this period was issued by President Eisenhower in 1954. A senate subcommittee was investigating a controversy between the Army and Senator Joseph McCarthy of Wisconsin. President Eisenhower sent to Secretary of the Army Robert

---

[154] St. Clair was commander of American forces in the Northwest Territory (present-day Ohio, Indiana, Illinois, Michigan and Wisconsin. He led a force of 1,400 men against the tribes. He was defeated with casualties of nearly 900. It was the worst defeat of American forces by Native Americans.

Stevens a message telling him that his departmental employees were to say nothing about internal communications of the Department.[155]

> Because it is essential to efficient and effective administration that employees of the executive branch be in a position to be completely candid in advising with each other on official matters, and because it is not in the public interest that any of their conversations or communications, or any documents or reproductions, concerning such advice be disclosed, you will instruct employees of your Department that in all of their appearances before the subcommittee of the Senate Committee on Government Operations regarding the inquiry now before it they are not to testify to any such conversations or communications or to produce any such documents or reproductions.

While the directive was aimed at a single situation and a single Executive Department, it soon became used by many other executive and administrative agencies as justification for their own withholding of records concerning internal affairs. While journalists protested the spread of the practice and Congressional allies joined them, there was not much recourse apparent.

The president's powers to restrict access are substantial, used extensively by some and little by others. Journalists have widely asserted that President Ronald Reagan employed these powers more vigorously than his predecessors of many terms. In fact, one of President Reagan's directives placed a "lifelong" non-disclosure restriction on many government employees, although it was partially withdrawn. In his 1982 Executive Order 12,356, he tightened declassification rules set by President Jimmy Carter.

Access to federal officials' papers and claims of executive privilege were active issues during the latter half of the seventies. The Nixon papers cases and the Kissinger "phone calls" case both involved dispute about ownership of executive papers. President Carter signed the Presidential Records Act of 1978, effective January 1981, which clarified ownership of executive branch papers. The National Archives assumes control of presidential papers at the end of a president's last term. Records related to defense and foreign policy, plus presidential appointment records involving trade secrets, may be restricted for 12 years. Papers not restricted become available to the public under the FOI Act as soon as the Archives processes them.

On Nov. 2, 2001, President George W. Bush issued an executive order revising the Presidential Records Act.[156] The Act was created in the

---

[155] McCarthy became a household name for his hunt for reds (communists) in America. He variously claimed, in the space of about a month, to have a list of 205, 57 or 81 communists in the State Department. He never produced the list or proved any State Department employee was a communist. He later turned his attention to the Army.

[156] Deb Riechmann, "Bush Extends Rules on Docs Release," *AP Online*, Nov. 1, 2001.

wake of Watergate and former President Nixon's efforts to keep records from his White House from being made public. The Act required the disclosure of presidential and vice-presidential records 12 years after a chief executive leaves office and makes those records the property of the public rather than the president. Former President Reagan and his vice-president, George H.W. Bush, were to be the first presidential team to have its records released.

The change to the Act now gives former presidents power to decide whether the records will be made public. Before the Act was changed by Bush's executive order, the final decision was left up to the sitting president. Some observers expressed suspicions that Bush's order might have been issued to prevent disclosure of records of members of President Reagan's Administration who are now members of the Bush team, e.g. Vice President Dick Cheney and Secretary of Defense Donald Rumsfeld.

Other observers suggested that it was simply in keeping with George W. Bush's own philosophy. When Bush left the Texas governor's office, he sent his executive papers to his father's presidential library instead of taking them to the Texas State Library in Austin.

In October 2019, The Justice Department promised not to destroy records of President Trump's calls and meetings with foreign leaders as a federal district court considered a lawsuit in which three public interest groups allege that President Trump was violating his obligation to preserve records of his administration.

Citizens for Responsibility and Ethics in Washington (CREW), the National Security Archive and the Society for Historians of American Foreign Relations (SHAFR) filed their suit after details of a whistleblower complaint about the Sept. 25, 2019 phone call between President Trump and Ukraine's President Volodymyr Zelensky. The whistleblower wrote in his complaint that White House officials removed the electronic transcript of the call from the computer system used to store such calls and put it into a computer system used for highly classified information.

The plaintiffs asked U.S. District Judge Amy Berman Jackson to enforce the Act. "It has become increasingly evident that this president has no respect for legally required record-keeping if he thinks the record could make him look bad—or worse, reveal wrongdoing," CREW Executive Director Noah Bookbinder said.

The three groups said that the Trump Administration had mismanaged records of politically sensitive Trump conversations including meetings with Russian President Vladimir Putin where there were no note takers and a meeting with North Korean leader Kim Jong-Un in Vietnam with only two interpreters present and where no official record was created.

The Justice Department moved for dismissal of the suit saying that prior cases make clear that there can be no judicial review of presidential compliance with the act. "This long-standing bar on judicial review of the President's records creation, management, or disposal decisions, and of his day-to-day record keeping practices, requires dismissal" of the case, the government argued.

Judge Jackson agreed and wrote in her opinion that Congress had the power to amend the law to address the concerns being raised. And, she wrote,[157] "This opinion will not address, and should not be interpreted to endorse, the challenged practices; nor does it include any finding that the Executive Office is in compliance with its obligations."

WHITE HOUSE EMAIL

The Presidential Records Act came into play at the end of the Reagan presidency when administration officials sought to erase email communications in the White House computer system. Included in the email were references to a number of projects, including the Iran-Contra affair. Journalist Scott Armstrong filed suit to prevent Reagan administration officials from sweeping the system. The judge in the case ruled that the government could not simply erase the records. First, it would have to set up a system to determine how to decide which records to keep and which to destroy. The result was the creation of an email protocol. Under the rules, which went into effect in 1995, agencies will have to either automatically store business email electronically or make print outs for delivery to the National Archives.

Armstrong then sued President George H.W. Bush over his concerns that records from the Reagan Administration might be destroyed.[158] A U.S. District Court in Washington, D.C, dismissed and the D.C. Circuit Court of Appeals affirmed. The appellate panel held that given,[159]

> the intricate statutory scheme Congress carefully drafted to keep in equipoise important competing political and constitutional concerns, [* * *] the PRA precludes judicial review of the President's recordkeeping practices and decisions

The Clinton Administration came under fire in the 1990s for its failure to preserve White House emails. "Republicans * * * alleged that some of the missing correspondence may have related to the Monica S. Lewinsky investigation, a campaign finance probe of Gore and other controversies."

Journalist Scott Armstrong sued the Clinton Administration over records created and held by the National Security Council. Armstrong argued that the NSC should classify records held in its computers as either records subject to the Presidential Records Act or the Federal Records Act. Clinton declared the NSC was not an agency and therefore

[157] Spencer Hsu, "Judge dismisses lawsuit to compel White House to archive records of Trump calls, meeting with Putin, other foreign leaders," *The Washington Post*, Feb. 11, 2020.

[158] *Armstrong v. Bush*, 924 F.2d 282 (D.C. Cir. 1991).

[159] Ibid. at 290–291.

not subject to the FOIA. The District Court for the District of Columbia, noting the NSC's treatment as an agency in previous administrations, ruled that the NSC was, in fact, an agency. It would then have to comply with FOIA and the Federal Records Act for classifying and storing records. But Armstrong lost in the D.C. Circuit Court of Appeals, which ruled that the NSC was not an agency because it did not meet the test for agency classification. Instead, the majority concluded, the NSC was more like a presidential staff. Under that analysis, the NSC was not bound by the FOIA or Federal Records Act. The Supreme Court declined to take the case.

Early in 2008, the public learned that the George W. Bush administration had scrapped an email archiving system put into place by the Clinton Administration and that more than a year's worth of emails from different presidential offices had not been kept.[160] White House special counsel Emmet T. Flood told the House Oversight and Government Reform Committee that there were 473 days on which no electronic messages were stored.[161]

According to the study summary that the committee released, emails were not archived for Vice President Cheney's office on four days in early October 2003, coinciding with the start of a Justice Department probe into the leak of a CIA officer's identity, which later led to criminal charges against Cheney's chief of staff.

In addition, from 2001 to 2003, the George W. Bush White House recorded over computer backup tapes that were to have been a last line of defense in preserving emails. That period includes the run-up to the invasion of Iraq. The Clinton Administration had ended the practice or recording over backup tapes in 1999.

Not long after Donald Trump took office, reports of leaks from the White House led staff members to turn to a self-deleting app to prevent their messaging from being discovered by President Trump. Wary of having emails to journalists discovered, the staff members began using Confide, an app that deletes messages,[162] in fact, all traces of messages as soon as they are read.[163] In addition, *The Wall Street Journal* reported that White House staff members were using Signal, an encrypted peer-to-peer messaging app. Signal also has a timer feature that deletes messages. Those apps also were being used to communicate about presidential or federal business, Citizens for Responsibility and Ethics in Washington (CREW) and the National Security Archive said in a lawsuit to prohibit the White House from using any apps that deleted

[160] Elizabeth Williamson and Dan Eggen, "White House Has No Comprehensive E-Mail Archive," *The Washington Post*, Jan. 22, 2008.

[161] Ibid.

[162] Mara Gay, "Messaging App Has Bipartisan Support Amid Hacking Concerns," *The Wall Street Journal*, Jan. 24, 2017.

[163] Kaveh Waddell, "The Risks of Sending Secret Messages in the White House," *The Atlantic*, Feb. 17, 2017.

messages.[164] CREW and the National Security Archive said that use of such apps violates the Presidential Records Act (PRA)[165] requiring the preservation of official presidential records. The group sought a writ of mandamus prohibiting the use of such apps and requiring the White House to issue guidelines to ensure compliance with the PRA. The Act allows presidents to dispose of records that no longer have administrative, historical, informational, or evidentiary value. But the Act requires that presidents first[166] "obtain the views, in writing, of the Archivist."

A U.S. District Court dismissed the suit on the grounds that the Presidential Records Act does not get into the level of detail sought by CREW, that is, the Act does not require the president to go through all the steps that CREW was seeking.

When news of the use of the messaging apps came out, the House Oversight and Government Reform Committee sent a letter to the White House counsel expressing their concerns about the preservation of those communications.[167] "In response, a White House official assured the members that the President was 'committed to preserving records of activities' relating to his 'constitutional, statutory or other official or ceremonial duties.' " Additionally, the White House counsel sent out two memos to staff,[168]

> the Memo prohibits the use of "instant messaging systems . . . or other internet-based means of electronic communication to conduct official business," and directs White House personnel to "conduct all work-related communications on [their] official . . . email account[s]" and to "preserve electronic communications that are presidential records." [* * *] On the same day the Memo issued, White House Counsel sent a "Compliance Reminder Email" advising staff that the "[u]se of . . . messaging apps (such as Snapchat, Confide, Slack or others) . . . is not permitted" for any "work-related communications."

CREW appealed the dismissal and a three-judge panel of the D.C. Circuit Court of Appeals affirmed the trial court. Judge David Tatel wrote the opinion for the panel in which he laid out the two reasons the suit failed. First, in order to be able to issue a writ of mandamus, court must be satisfied that the government is, in fact, breaking the law in not doing what is required. The two memos instructed the White House staff to comply with the PRA, Judge Tatel wrote. The memos might not preserve the messages, but, the court did not have the authority to order

---

164 *Citizens for Responsibility and Ethics in Washington v. Trump*, 924 F.3d 602 (D.C. Cir. 2019).

165 44 U.S.C. § 2202.

166 § 2203(c).

167 *Citizens for Responsibility and Ethics in Washington v. Trump*, 924 F.3d 602, 605 (D.C. Cir. 2019).

168 Ibid. at 605.

the White House to correctly follow the PRA citing *Armstrong v. Bush*, 924 F.2d 282 (D.C. Cir. 1991).

PRIVACY ACT OF 1974

The Watergate scandal revealed the depths of the Nixon Administration's surveillance of American citizens as part of President Nixon's efforts to stop leaks from the government and to keep track of his "enemies." The increasing use of computerized records that used things like Social Security numbers to identify individuals led to concerns about how information might incorrectly be attributed to a person and how the collected information might be misused by government agencies.

"After long years of debate, a comprehensive federal privacy law passed the Congress * * * as a solid legislative decision in favor of individual privacy and the 'right to be let alone'," wrote attorney James T. O'Reilly.[169] It is a statute shaped to deal with the federal government's gargantuan systems of secret dossiers on citizens, to give citizens access to the content of files that may be kept on them, and to provide citizens with a means for correcting inaccurate content of these files. If agencies are not responsive in making changes, civil suits may be brought against them. A crucial element in the law is that no file may be transferred from one agency to another without the individual's consent, except where the purpose squares with the purpose for which the information was collected.

Under the law, a supposedly exhaustive index to all federal government data banks or personal information systems on individuals has been published. Also published in the Federal Register are the categories of individuals on whom records are maintained, and where one can learn whether a particular government agency has information about him.[170] No citizen who inquires about himself need give any reason for a request to examine the record, and may obtain a copy. Some exceptions to citizen access are provided, mostly dealing with law enforcement agencies' records, and including, notably, the CIA and the Secret Service.[171] However, foreign nationals working for the government have no access rights to personnel records about themselves under either the FOI Act or the Privacy Act, according to a U.S. Court of Appeals.[172]

---

[169] "The Privacy Act of 1974," *Freedom of Information Report No. 342*, Sept. 1975.

[170] Anon., "Citizens' Guide to Privacy Act Available," *FOI Digest*, 18:2 (March–April 1976), p. 2. For an editor's struggle of more than a year to get a file kept on him by the FBI, see John Seigenthaler, "Publisher Finally Gets His FBI Files, or Some of Them," (Memphis) *Tennessean*, July 10, 1977. False accusations, including one about his involvement in the Kennedy assassination, would be purged, the FBI said after finally releasing contents of the file.

[171] Anon., "Government Information and the Rights of Citizens," 73 *Mich.L.Rev.* 971, 1317. This study of more than 370 pages describes, analyzes, and criticizes the FOI Act, state open records and meetings laws, and the Privacy Act of 1974.

[172] *Raven v. Panama Canal Co.*, 583 F.2d 169 (5th Cir.1978), certiorari denied 440 U.S. 980, 99 S.Ct. 1787 (1979). See also, "Allows Personnel Files to be Kept From Alien," *News Media & The Law*, March–April 1980.

Privacy issues intensified during the 1970s and 1980s, as individuals made greater use of the Privacy Act to see records maintained about them and to amend those records or correct inaccuracies. States also were active in protecting privacy of financial, medical, and criminal records.

Recall that privacy issues also are part of the FOIA; as noted at earlier, Exemptions 6 (personnel or medical files) and 7 (law enforcement investigatory files) both list privacy. In *U.S. Department of Justice v. Reporters Committee for Freedom of the Press,*[173] the U.S. Supreme Court held—in part for privacy reasons—that FBI "rap sheets"—records of a person's arrests, charges, and jailings were exempt from release under FOIA. Release of such criminal identification records was held to be a "clearly unwarranted invasion of privacy" under the terms of the FOIA. Most states—all but Wisconsin, Florida, and Oklahoma—follow the federal lead in withholding rap sheets from public inspection.

The additional emphasis on secrecy brought about by the Privacy Act concerns some journalists about loss of inside sources of information in the federal government, and the possibility of tracing "leaks" through the agencies' records of who got access to various files.

The case of Wen Ho Lee raises another concern about the effectiveness of the Privacy Act in protecting people from the abuse of their government records. Lee was the a scientist at Los Alamos National Laboratory who was held in solitary confinement for nine months while the government investigated whether he gave nuclear secrets to China. During the investigation and his confinement, the media reported at length about the "evidence" that the federal investigation was following up on. They quoted unnamed sources within the federal government.

At the end of the investigation, the government's case collapsed. Lee was released after pleading guilty to a single felony charge of copying files to an unsecured cassette tape. Lee had originally faced 59 separate charges, many of which carried maximum life sentences. Presiding Judge James A. Parker apologized to Lee in the hearing, saying, "I sincerely apologize to you, Dr. Lee, for the unfair manner in which you were held in custody by the executive branch." Judge Parker noted that he ordered Lee held in solitary confinement because of representations by the Justice Department.[174]

> During December 1999, the then-United States attorney, who has since resigned, and his assistants presented me, during the three-day hearing between Christmas and New Year's Day, with information that was so extreme it convinced me that releasing you, even under the most stringent of conditions, would be a danger to the safety of this nation. The then-United

[173] *U.S. Department of Justice v. Reporters Committee on Freedom of the Press*, 489 U.S. 749, 109 S.Ct. 1468 (1989).

[174] "Statement by Judge in Los Alamos Case, With Apology for Abuse of Power," *New York Times*, Sept. 14, 2000.

> States attorney personally argued vehemently against your release and ultimately persuaded me not to release you.

Judge Parker said he was perplexed that the Justice Department suddenly agreed to Lee's release and did not set any conditions or restrictions.[175]

> What I believe remains unanswered is the question: What was the government's motive in insisting on your being jailed pretrial under extraordinarily onerous conditions of confinement until today, when the executive branch agrees that you may be set free essentially unrestricted? This makes no sense to me.

Lee sued alleging that government officials had violated the Privacy Act by leaking information about him to reporters. The case was complicated by the fact that the reporters who received the information refused to divulge their government sources. Lee's lawyers subpoenaed reporters at ABC, the Associated Press, *The Los Angeles Times*, *The New York Times* and *The Washington Post*. Lee's lawyers suspected that top officials of the Energy Department, including then-Secretary Bill Richardson and the department's director of counterintelligence, Notra Trulock had leaked the damaging information. Richardson, Trulock and other officials denied that they leaked the information about Lee to the media. Lee himself was critical of the actions by government officials.[176]

> "The rush to judgment that occurred in my case was prompted by a number of calculated, unlawful leaks by government officials," he said in a statement. The information leaked to the media "was in my case often misleading, harmful and disclosed with a political agenda," he added.

Lee's lawyers then subpoenaed the reporters who wrote about Lee's case and demanded they reveal the names of the unnamed sources cited in their stories. All of the reporters refused to reveal whom they had spoken to in confidence. The reporters' attempt to avoid testifying failed at the trial court and circuit court of appeals levels. The case was heading to the Supreme Court when the settlement was reached.[177]

> "This was never about whether the stories were right or wrong or about libel or about classified information," said Bob Drogin of *The Times*, who was one of the reporters subpoenaed. "We had fought this for four years and lost at every level. And we thought there was a great risk for the press if we took it before the Supreme Court and lost."

The settlement called for a $1.65 million payment. The U.S. government paid $895,000 and the five news organizations agreed to pay

---

[175] Ibid.

[176] David Savage, "Government, News Media Settle Suit by Wen Ho Lee," *Los Angeles Times*, June 3, 2006.

[177] Ibid.

$150,000 each. It was the first time that news organizations paid into a settlement where they were not being sued.

THE PRIVACY ACT AND DISABLED AMERICAN VETERANS

The law of unintended consequences applied to the Privacy Act. In 2004, The Disabled American Veterans appealed to Secretary of Defense Donald Rumsfeld to take action to allow the group to more freely visit with wounded service members.[178] The Department of Defense, citing the Privacy Act, limited information about the wounded and required the DAV to request permission to visit individual service members. DAV Executive Director David W. Gorman said that the restrictions were preventing the wounded from getting adequate information about their benefits and health care.

Gorman said that while Defense Department and Department of Veterans Affairs representatives provided some information about wounded veterans' rights, that information often was[179] "inadequate and fails to meet the needs of those injured. DAV national service officers offer the best knowledge, skill, experience, and representations available to disabled veterans today."

HIPAA: MAKING MEDICAL INFORMATION OFF-LIMITS

In the spring of 2003, police reporters all across the United States were suddenly having trouble getting hospital information, for example, on the condition of gunshot victims. And worried friends and relatives wanting to check up on a person injured in an auto crash were livid because they could get no information from the hospital.[180]

These are known as "HIPAA problems." HIPAA stands for Health Insurance Portability and Accountability Act of 1996. Under HIPAA, with rules that went into effect on April 17, 2003, limits are placed on how physicians, pharmacists, and health insurers can use and release medical information. Health care professionals are understandably nervous under HIPAA. Rachel Smolkin reported in the *American Journalism Review*[181] that health workers who release now-forbidden information could face fines up to $250,000 and 10 years in jail.

As originally conceived, the HIPAA rules would allow patients to decline listing in the hospital directory system if they so choose. Some hospitals, however, have assumed that patients wish to be left out of the directory unless they specifically say they want in. As Laurie Tarkan reported in *The New York Times*, "* * * if someone is unconscious, or

---

[178] "DAV urges defense secretary to get the facts to war wounded," *Newswire*, Jan. 7, 2004.

[179] Ibid.

[180] Laurie Tarkan, "Sorry, that information is off-limits: A privacy law's unintended results," *New York Times*, June 3, 2003.

[181] Rachel Smolkin, "A medical information crackdown," *American Journalism Review*, May 2003. P. 12.

otherwise unable to choose, the patient will not be in the directory, and relatives and friends may have trouble finding them."

HIPAA rules, written during the Clinton Administration, would have been even tougher had they not been watered down a bit by the Bush Administration. In any case, HIPAA privacy acknowledgment forms to be signed by patients are distributed in hospitals, doctors' offices, and pharmacies. The cost in information which the public needs seems substantial. Reporters are being given only one-word condition reports and then only if they have a person's first and last name. As Smolkin observed,[182]

> Hospital directory information, now largely off-limits, enabled journalists and the public to track victims felled during the September 11 terrorist attacks, the Oklahoma City bombing, the anthrax scares and school shootings.

GOVERNMENT IN THE SUNSHINE ACT

As the FOI Act is to federal government records, so the "Sunshine Act" is to federal government meetings.[183] The Act mandates open meetings for regular sessions and quorum gatherings of approximately 50 agencies—all those headed by boards of two or more persons named by the President and confirmed by the Senate. Included are the major regulatory agencies such as the Securities Exchange Commission and the Interstate Commerce Commission—whose meetings always had been secret—and such little-known entities as the National Council on Educational Research and the National Homeownership Foundation board of directors.[184]

All meetings of the named agencies are to be open—with at least one week's public notice—unless agendas take up matters in the 10 categories which permit closed sessions. Either a verbatim transcript or detailed minutes of all matters covered in closed sessions is to be kept. And as for the record of open meetings, it is to be kept as minutes and made available to the public at minimal copying cost.

Closed-to-the-public meetings will hardly be rare, whatever strength the Sunshine Act may prove to generate. The 10 categories of subject-matter whose discussion warrants closed doors for meetings of the boards and commissions are much like the exemptions to disclosure under the FOI Act. Abbreviated, they are:

1. National defense or foreign policy matters which are properly classified;

---

[182] Ibid. at 12–13.

[183] 5 U.S.C.A. § 552b. The FOI Act and the Privacy Act of 1974 are in the federal statutes under the same number, as 5 U.S.C.A. § 552a and 5 U.S.C.A. § 552c respectively.

[184] *Editor & Publisher*, Feb. 26, 1977, p. 32. This account's details of the Sunshine Act are taken largely from James T. O'Reilly, "Government in the Sunshine," *Freedom of Information Center Report 366*, Jan. 1977.

2. Internal agency personnel matters;

3. Matters expressly required by law to be held confidential;

4. Confidential commercial or financial information, and trade secrets;

5. Accusations of criminal activity, or of censure, against a person;

6. Matters which if disclosed would be clearly unwarranted invasions of a person's privacy;

7. Law enforcement and criminal investigatory records, subject to the same categories as FOI Act exemption (b)(7);

8. Bank examiners' records;

9. Matters which if disclosed would generate financial speculation (included to protect the Federal Reserve Board Open Market Committee) or which would frustrate agency action which has not been announced;

10. Matters which involve the agency's issuance of a subpoena or participation in hearings or other adjudication-related proceedings.

Violations of the Sunshine Act can result in suits for a transcript of the meeting. A federal court can also issue an injunction against illegal closures. If a secret meeting is discovered before it takes place, a court can enjoin the agency from meeting in secret. There are no financial penalties for illegal meetings, but courts may assign costs or fees against the United States—or against a plaintiff whose suit is found to be "dilatory or frivolous."

The 10 exemptions of the Sunshine Act apply to the roughly 1,300 Advisory Committees spread throughout the Executive Branch of government. These committees of private citizens contribute expertise, advice, and recommendations to government policy making. The members tend to be prominent persons from industries which deal with the agencies they advise. The Federal Advisory Committee Act[185] requires committees to comply with the Sunshine Act. But, a section of the FACA exempts[186] "any committee which is composed wholly of full-time officers or employees of the Federal Government."

CLINTON HEALTH CARE REFORM TASK FORCE

President Clinton proposed major changes in health care in his first term. He appointed Hillary Rodham Clinton, as the chairman of the Task Force, with the Secretaries of the Treasury, Defense, Veterans Affairs, Health and Human Services, Labor, and Commerce Departments, the Director of the Office of Management and Budget, the chairman of the

[185] Pub. L. 92–463, Sec. 1, Oct. 6, 1972, 86 Stat. 770.

[186] Sec. 3(2)(iii).

Council of Economic Advisers and three White House advisers. The task force was to "listen to all parties" and then "prepare health care reform legislation to be submitted to Congress.

The task force held one public hearing where interested parties could present comments on health care reform and 20 closed meetings to consider what advice to give to President Clinton. The Association of American Physicians and Surgeons, which represents physicians; the American Council for Health Care Reform, which represents health care consumers; and the National Legal & Policy Center, a government ethics group, sought access to the closed-door meetings. But the presidential counsel advised them that the task force was not an advisory committee and so did not have to meet in public. The groups filed suit alleged that Hillary Clinton's participation as chair of the task force meant that it did not meet the exemption from the Sunshine Act.[187] They argued that Hillary Clinton was First Lady and not a government employee. They sought a temporary restraining order and a preliminary injunction halting the operation of the Task Force until it complied with FACA and allowed the public to attend its meetings. A U.S. District Court found that Hillary Clinton was not a government employee and held that the task force did not qualify for an exemption under the FACA.

The case made it to a three-judge panel of the D.C. Circuit Court of Appeals. There, Judge Laurence Silberman's opinion concluded that Hillary Clinton was more than a First Lady. The Clinton Administration had made the argument that,[188]

> the traditional, if informal, status and 'duties' of the President's wife as 'First Lady' gives her de facto officer or employee status. The government invokes what it describes as 'a longstanding tradition of public service' by First Ladies—including, we are told, Sarah Polk, Edith Wilson, Eleanor Roosevelt, Rosalynn Carter, and Nancy Reagan—who have acted (albeit in the background) as advisers and personal representatives of their husbands.

Judge Silberman found the argument lacking and, also, out of step with the times.[189]

> We are not confident that this traditional perception of the President's wife, as a virtual extension of her husband, is widely held today. As this very case suggests, it may not even be a fair portrayal of Mrs. Clinton, who certainly is performing more openly than is typical of a First Lady. Indeed, in the future we may see a male presidential spouse, which could make the term "First Lady" anachronistic.

---

[187] *Association of American Physicians and Surgeons, Inc. v. Clinton*, 997 F.2d 898, 302 U.S.App.D.C. 208 (C.C. Cir. 1993).

[188] Ibid. at 904, 214.

[189] Ibid.

Instead, he wrote, Congress had recognized that First Ladies are more. Congress recognized that a president's spouse acts is the functional equivalent of an assistant. As such, Congress authorizes assistance and services authorized to be provided to the spouse of the president "in connection with assistance provided by such spouse to the president in the discharge of the president's duties and responsibilities." Judge Silberman said it was reasonable to see that a president using a spouse to carry out tasks that might be delegated to a White House aide.[190] "It is reasonable, therefore, to construe Sec. 105(e) as treating the presidential spouse as a de facto officer or employee."

IN RE CHENEY AND THE ENERGY TASK FORCE

Judicial Watch and the Sierra Club filed suits (later combined) to learn the identities of the participants in Vice President Dick Cheney's energy task force, the National Energy Policy Development Group.[191] Questions arose about the participation of energy company executives in the formation of the Bush energy policy which featured plans to increase energy production by removing protections of public lands from drilling and relaxation of environmental rules on the energy industry. It also called for a revival of the nation's nuclear energy program.

The complaint alleged that, because nonfederal employees and private lobbyists "regularly attended and fully participated in the Group's nonpublic meetings as de facto Group members," the Group could not benefit from the § 2(B) exemption and was therefore subject to FACA's requirements. The distinction was important because the FACA has requirements that each committee must[192] "be fairly balanced in terms of the points of view represented" and may "not be inappropriately influenced by the appointing authority or by any special interest." The Group "had one meeting with environmentalists on April 13th, 2001, which was about two months into the work of the task force. And by that time, the task force staff had at least 40-some-odd meetings with a whole range of industry groups, lawmakers, et cetera."[193]

Back in 2001, when first seeking the energy task force information, Judicial Watch Chairman and General Counsel Larry Klayman told *Natural Gas Week* magazine, "Judicial Watch is concerned that energy policy is being made in secret by individuals and interest with a financial and political stake in particular policies."

A complicating factor in the cases was the participation of the leading executives from now-defunct Enron in the creation of the Bush energy plan. Even before Enron's financial disintegration became a

---

190 Ibid. at 904–905, 214–215.

191 *Judicial Watch, Inc. v. National Energy Policy Development Group*, 219 F.Supp.2d 20 (D.D.C. 2002).

192 Pub. L. 92–463, Sec. 1, Oct. 6, 1972, 86 Stat. 770, §§ 5(b)(2), (3) & (c).

193 Robert Siegel, "Cheney's Energy Task Force Records Revealed," *National Public Radio*, July 18, 2007.

public scandal, Enron chairman Kenneth Lay had disclosed his role on the task force. *USA Today* reporter Jonathan Weissman, appearing on *The O'Reilly Factor* television commentary program, discussed the Bush administration's reluctance to reveal names of the participants along with Lay's disclosure.

> [O]fficials in the Bush administration say that there's a principle here, that they feel like they—they won't be able to get free and unfettered advice if whoever goes into the Oval Office is going to get grilled by the press afterwards.
>
> That doesn't make a lot of sense to me. I mean, a lot of people who go into the Oval Office go to the press and brag about it. In fact, I talked to the—the chairman of Enron, the big natural gas company, [and he] told me all about a meeting with the Cheney task force and the advice he had given him.

After a circuitous trip from the district court[194], through the D.C. Circuit Court of Appeals[195] and the Supreme Court[196], the case ended with a decision by the D.C. Circuit sitting *en banc*.[197] In an opinion by Judge A. Raymond Randolf, the court held that the participation by members of the fossil fuel and nuclear energy industry did not affect the status of the Group.[198] "We [* * *] hold that such a committee is composed wholly of federal officials if the President has given no one other than a federal official a vote in or, if the committee acts by consensus, a veto over the committee's decisions." The Circuit Court of Appeals ordered the district court to dismiss the case.

50. ACCESS TO BATTLEFIELDS AND NATIONAL SECURITY INFORMATION

As discussed elsewhere in this text, traditions of openness run afoul of restrictive executive orders, statutes and court decisions in areas where claims of "national security" are raised.

FIGHTING A NATIONAL SECURITY MENTALITY

It is likely that the crucial battle to preserve what journalists have come to see as the central meaning of the First Amendment will be fought in the arena of access to government information. What is talked about here goes beyond the traditional pushing and pulling between reporters and government. Resistance to access by government officials is to be expected: human nature, of course, dictates an unwillingness to look

194 *Judicial Watch, Inc. v. Nat. Energy Policy Development Group.*, 230 F.Supp.2d 12 (D.D.C. 2002).

195 *In re Cheney*, 334 F.3d 1096 (D.C.Cir. 2003).

196 *Cheney v. U.S. Dist. Court for Dist. of Columbia*, 542 U.S. 367, 124 S.Ct. 2576 (2004).

197 *In re Cheney*, 406 F.3d 723 (D.C.Cir. 2005).

198 Ibid. at 728.

foolish, and government officials—like all of us—dislike revealing mistakes.

During the late 1980s the phrase "national security" often was used as a reason why documents could not be released—or used in a federal court—to try Lt. Col. Oliver North on criminal conspiracy charges coming out of the Iran-Contra affair. (North, along with retired Admiral John M. Poindexter, the former National Security Adviser to President Reagan, was the subject of criminal charges relating to illegal sale of arms to Iran and diversion of the proceeds to fund the Nicaraguan Contras.) With those classified documents unavailable, the main charges against North were dropped early in 1989. The Central Intelligence Agency, itself so clandestine that its budget is secret, opposed release of security-classified documents needed to bring North to trial.

The task for reporters or other citizens who try to keep tabs on what government has done or is doing is monumental. With the terrorist attacks of Sept. 11, 2001, the federal government undertook domestic surveillance in an effort to uncover information about the attacks and to prevent new attacks. But questions immediately arose about the balance of government intrusion in the name of homeland security and the rights of personal privacy and association.

The federal government initiated sweeping changes to keep information from the public as it pursued its war on terrorism, domestic and international. Within days of the attacks the federal government detained an undisclosed number of persons in secret locations and began legal proceedings that were closed to public and press.[199]

A number of legal challenges to such secrecy were undertaken by media organizations and public interest groups, though public interest groups have led the fight and brought the majority of the challenges to secrecy. In most of the cases, courts have sided with the Administration, citing national security concerns for denying access to records and proceedings.

FINDING OUT WHO WAS DETAINED

On June 17, 2003, a three-judge panel of the D.C. Circuit ruled that the Freedom of Information Act would not allow the public to know who had been detained by the government.[200] That information had been sought by members of Congress, civil liberties and human rights groups and the media. They sought the names of the detainees, the number of detainees, the reasons for their detentions, the names of their lawyers and information relating to their locations. Many of the requests came following government claims that all of the detainees had always had the

---

[199] The government claimed that they were "material witnesses." As such, they were not eligible for bail and, because they were not charged with any crimes, they could be held indefinitely as the speedy trial act only applies to criminal defendants. Others were held on claims that they were in the country illegally, usually by overstaying a visa.

[200] *Center for Nat. Sec. Studies v. U.S. Dept. of Justice*, 331 F.3d 918 (D.C.Cir. 2003).

ability to contact their families and members of the public and to retain legal counsel.

A group of 22 public interest groups sued the Department of Justice for that information under the provisions of the FOIA.[201] U.S. District Judge Gladys Kessler denied part of the request and granted other parts giving access to the names of the detainees and their lawyers. Judge Kessler stayed her decision pending a decision by the court of appeals.

Because the case was brought under the FOIA, the government bore the burden of showing why the information fell within an exemption and could be, at the government's discretion, withheld from release.

The Justice Department invoked Exemption 7, investigatory files compiled for law enforcement purposes. Specifically the Justice Department relied on Exemptions 7(A), whenever disclosure could reasonably be expected to interfere with enforcement proceedings; 7(C) whenever disclosure could reasonably be expected to constitute an unwarranted invasion of personal privacy; or 7(F), whenever disclosure could reasonably be expected to endanger the life or physical safety of any individual. In addition, the Justice Department raised Exemption 3, matters exempt from disclosure by statute, for information related to material witnesses.

In support of its reliance on Exemption 7(A), the Justice Department argued that releasing the names could deter witnesses from cooperating, subject the witnesses to terrorist threats or exclusion from terrorist dealings and reveal "the direction and progress of the investigation by identifying where the DOJ is focusing its efforts." Armed with that information, terrorists could impede the investigations, the Justice Department argued.

Judge Kessler disposed of those arguments by pointing to the fact that the government already had identified persons it linked to al-Qaeda, had said publicly that detainees were entitled to inform anyone they want of their detention and already had publicly identified more than two dozen persons held as material witnesses. Judge Kessler also suggested that terrorist groups would probably know who in their terrorist cells had been detained.

Finally, the adverse effect on the government investigation from the non-disclosure of all the names would take place only if all the detainees were, in fact, linked to terrorists Judge Kessler wrote:

> The affidavits nowhere declare that some or all of the detainees have connections to terrorism. Nor do they provide facts that would permit the Court to infer links to terrorism. For example, the Government has provided no information on the standard used to arrest and detain individuals initially. Nor has it provided a general description of evidence that it obtained

[201] *Center for National Security Studies v. U.S. Department of Justice*, 215 F.Supp.2d 94 (D.D.C.2002).

> confirming any initial suspicions of links to terrorism. Indeed, when asked by the Court during the Motions Hearing to explain the standard used to arrest the detainees, or otherwise to substantiate the purported connection to terrorism, the Government was unable to answer.

To support her conclusion, Judge Kessler noted that some 677 original INS detainees had either been released or deported. None had been charged with terrorism. The government also failed to make a case through its affidavits that the detainees were material witnesses or informants. That lack was fatal to the arguments of the government. Judge Kessler declared:

> [T]he Court has uncovered no FOIA case that would permit the Government to do what it wants to do here: withhold information simply because of the possibility, however remote, that the detainees (even those who have been released) have information that might, at a later date, aid the Government's intelligence gathering and law enforcement efforts.

The government advanced what it called the "mosaic theory" to support its claim that revelations could interfere with its investigations. Under the theory, any information disclosure could be harmful. "[B]its and pieces of information that may appear innocuous in isolation, when assimilated with other information * * * will allow the organization to build a picture of the investigation and to thwart the government's attempts to investigate and prevent terrorism."

Judge Kessler's initial response was that there was no case law, no precedent, for applying the mosaic theory to the case. Secondly, the application of the "mosaic theory" would turn the FOIA into a blanket exception not authorized by the exemption itself.

> [A]pplication of the mosaic theory would essentially turn 7A into an exemption dragnet, as it would permit the government to lump together all information related to an ongoing government investigation and withhold it solely because innocuous parts of data might be pieced together by terrorist groups. This result is contrary to well-settled Exemption 7A case law.

A two-judge majority of the D.C. Court of Appeals reversed the part of Judge Kessler's decision giving the public access to the names of the detainees and their lawyers. The two judges concluded that the government properly invoked Exemption 7A which protects records compiled for law enforcement purposes whose release would interfere with enforcement. The majority concluded that because the Justice Department is a law enforcement agency, the courts should give deference to its claim that its documents have a law enforcement purpose.

> The terrorism investigation is one of DOJ's chief "law enforcement duties" at this time, see Reynolds Decl. Para. 2, and

> the investigation concerns a heinous violation of federal law as well as a breach of this nation's security. Moreover, the names of the detainees and their connections to the investigation came to the government's attention as a result of that law enforcement investigation.

The majority repeatedly made clear its tendency to accept the government's position with some 26 instances of "deference" or "defer" in the majority's opinion. In particular, the majority accepted the "mosaic" theory advanced by the government.

> [C]ourts have relied on similar mosaic arguments in the context of national security. In *Sims*, for example, the Supreme Court cautioned that "bits and pieces" of data " 'may aid in piecing together of other bits of information even when the individual piece is not of obvious importance in itself.' " 471 U.S. at 178, 105 S.Ct. at 1892, (quoting *Halperin*, 629 F.2d at 150). Thus, "[w]hat may seem trivial to the uninformed, may appear of great moment to one who has a broad view of the scene and may put the questioned item of information in its proper context." Id. (quotations omitted). Such a danger is present here. While the name of any individual detainee may appear innocuous or trivial, it could be of great use to al Qaeda in plotting future terrorist attacks or intimidating witnesses in the present investigation.

The majority similarly concluded that the release of the attorneys' names could allow the plaintiffs and others to construct a list of the detainees and thus risk having al-Qaeda obtain the list with "disastrous consequences."

In dissent, Circuit Judge David S. Tatel strongly criticized both the government's case and the reasoning of the two-judge majority.

> While the government's reasons for withholding some of the information may be legitimate, the court's uncritical deference to the government's vague, poorly explained arguments for withholding broad categories of information about the detainees, as well as its willingness to fill in the factual and logical gaps in the government's case, eviscerates both FOIA itself and the principles of openness in government that FOIA embodies.

Judge Tatel disagreed with the government's position that it be allowed to withhold the information requested on a blanket basis rather than the well-settled approach that information that information that can be disclosed be segregated from information that must be kept secret.

> Nothing in the statute requires requesters to seek only information not exempt from disclosure. To the contrary, the government bears the burden of reviewing the plaintiff's request, identifying functional categories of information that

are exempt from disclosure, and disclosing any reasonably segregable, non-exempt portion of the requested materials.

The Supreme Court declined to take up the case.

ACCESS TO MILITARY OPERATIONS

One of the true tests of how free a nation is comes when that nation's government is at war. Some of the givens of wartime include:

- There can be prior restraint when safety of military forces or civilians is at stake.
- Prior restraint can be imposed over dispatches sent or broadcast from a battle zone.
- Correspondents in a war zone may have both their mobility and their access to channels of communication curtailed.

Daniel C. Hallin's work "*The Uncensored War*" studied the media and the war in Vietnam. A myth has grown up, Hallin contends, that because the media were allowed, quite freely, to send home images of war in 'Nam, that the U.S. media somehow "lost the war."

President Nixon blamed television for demoralization at home during the latter stages of the Vietnam conflict. Such views of media—particularly, TV—coverage have affected policy. As Hallin noted,

> [I]t was the example of Vietnam, for instance, that motivated the British government to impose tight controls on news coverage of the Falklands crisis [of 1982]. Back at home, the Reagan administration, with Vietnam in mind, excluded the media from the opening phase of the invasion of Grenada.

COVERING THE FIRST PERSIAN GULF WAR

When President George H.W. Bush said that the Persian Gulf war was not to be "another Vietnam," he seemed to refer to his determination to bring enough military resources into play to assure a swift victory. The desire to avoid the "Vietnam syndrome" obviously had fallout for press coverage of the war in the Persian Gulf. Although camera operators on rooftops got spectacular footage of Nintendo-like displays of rockets and tracer bullets, the result of warfare—corpses—was little seen.

In the main, the American press acquiesced in the pooling arrangements. Daniel Hallin's comments on American news media in Vietnam are worth pondering in light of media's coverage of Persian Gulf warfare. Just how independent are the media? Hallin wrote:[202]

> Structurally the American news media are both highly autonomous from direct political control and, through the

[202] Daniel C. Hallin, *"The Uncensored War:" The Media and Vietnam* (Berkeley: University of California Press, 1986), p. 8.

> routines of the news-gathering process, deeply intertwined in the actual operation of government.

Hallin argued that news people combine suspicion of power with a respect for established order, institutions, and authority. Given this anomalous status, small wonder the press—watched most carefully by suspicious military officials—had severe problems in the Persian Gulf. The distinguished military correspondent Malcolm W. Browne, long known for his steadiness and balanced coverage, wrote in January 1991, that many[203]

> * * * news correspondents covering the war with Iraq are bridling under a system of conflicting rules and confusing censorship.
>
> For the first time since World War II, correspondents must submit to near-total military supervision of their work.

Military escorts tagged along with reporters, making it highly unlikely that servicemen and women who were interviewed would speak frankly. At times, escorts interrupted interviews, objecting to questions. When an enlisted man told a reporter how he continued to practice his Christian faith in a country where anything but Muslim rites are not legal, a military "information officer" cut off the interview. The reason?[204] "Military ground rules forbid questions about 'things that we don't know about necessarily."

Carol Rosenberg of the *Miami Herald* and Susan Sachs of *Newsday* were excluded from covering the First Marine Division in the Persian Gulf because they were thought to have asked "rude questions"[205] of Marine officers.

By 2003, the Pentagon began living up to a statement of principles on war coverage signed by military leaders and a number of American news bureau chiefs in 1992 to allow fuller coverage of military actions. This led to the "embedding" of some 600 journalists in military units after they had been sent to "boot camps" to toughen up and to learn how to stay, as much as possible, out of harm's way while reporting on firefights.

As pointed out by Lucy Dalglish in a *News Media and the Law* editorial, it is likely that control was the deciding factor in the military decision to allow greater freedom in reporting from combat zones. Evolving communication technology made it possible to provide live coverage from anywhere. "For the first time," Dalglish wrote,[206] "a television reporter would not have to rely on military communications

---

[203] Malcolm W. Browne, "Conflicting Censorship Upsets Many Journalists," *New York Times*, Jan. 21, 1991.

[204] Clarence Page, "Gulf between military, media is so wide that truth has been put in choke hold," *Milwaukee Sentinel*, Jan. 22, 1991, p. 8, Part 1.

[205] Ibid.

[206] Lucy Dalglish, "We all benefitted from the embeds: So what took so long?" *The News Media and the Law* (Spring, 2003).

equipment to send stories back to the newsroom. Censorship would be a practical impossibility."

Embedded reporters were able to report, as Defense Secretary Donald Rumsfeld suggested, only "slices of the war." Televised images of columns of Allied military equipment moving through a sandstorm were hardly edifying. Media coverage of battles was compared to[207] "seeing the battle through 'a soda straw.'" Despite lack of overview or context, the unaccustomed openness was welcomed by the American news media.

A Project for Excellence in Journalism study released on March 28, 2003, found that coverage by embedded reporters focused on combat and was predominantly live and unedited.[208] "Much of it lacks context but it is usually rich in detail. It has all the virtues and vices of reporting only what you can see."

In general, American reporters followed the Pentagon guidelines for embedded media.[209]

> These ground rules recognize the right of the Media to cover military to cover military operations and are in no way intended to prevent release of derogatory, embarrassing, negative or uncomplimentary information."
>
> * * *
>
> 4.a. All interviews with service members will be on the record. Security at the source is the policy. Interviews with pilots and aircrew members are authorized upon completion of missions; however, release of information must conform to these media ground rules.
>
> 4.b. Print or broadcast stories will be datelined according to local ground rules. Local ground rules will be coordinated through command channels with CENTCOM.
>
> 4.c. Media embedded with U.S. forces are not permitted to carry personal firearms.
>
> 4.d. Light discipline restrictions will be followed. [* * *]
>
> 4.e. Embargoes may be imposed to protect operational security. Embargoes will only be used for operational security and will be lifted as soon as the operational security issue has passed.

51. RECORDS AND MEETINGS IN THE STATES

The extent of access in the states varies under statutes providing what shall be open and what closed in the meetings and

---

[207] Project for Excellence in Journalism, Pew Charitable Trusts, Columbia University, "Embedded Reporters: What Are Americans Getting?," 7/2/03 http://www.journalism.org/2003/04/03/embedded-reporters.

[208] Ibid.

[209] *The News Media and the Law* (Spring, 2003), at pp. 6–7. The complete guidelines text is at www.defenselink.mil/news/Feb2003/d20030228pag.pdf.

records of executive, administrative, and legislative agencies.

All states have laws declaring that public policy demands substantial if not maximum disclosure of official business, both meetings and records. Rarely, however, is it conceded that every act or document of officialdom must be open to public scrutiny. Every branch of government in the United States conducts some of its work or maintains some of its records in secret. There are situations in the states as in the federal government's domain which favor secrecy as protection for the individual's private rights and for government's carrying out its work. But the principle of disclosure and openness is as important to the democratic spirit at the state and local levels as it is at the federal level. Thanks to open government efforts pushed by the press and by public spirited citizens in the 1960s and 1970s, all 50 states have open-meetings laws.

The range of and protections afforded state defies easy generalization or detailed discussion here. Citizens who need to know how to get information out of particular governmental units—including reporters—need to brief themselves on the special provisions of each state's access laws. The National Freedom of Information Coalition has a helpful guide to each state's statutes[210] as well as sample request letters and contact information for state hotlines. Failure to find and learn the statutes leaves the citizen or reporter at the mercy of officials who choose not to live up to open records or open meetings statutes.[211]

The Reporters Committee for Freedom of the Press also provides information on open records laws in the state through the "Tapping Officials Secrets" link on the Reporters Committee's Website: http://www.rcfp.org/open-government-guide. And the Reporters Committee even has freedom of information letters in draft form awaiting you at: https://www.ifoia.org/#!/.

Most state open records laws provide legal instruments for the record-seeker to use in trying to overcome denial of access. Usually, the record-seeker may apply to a court for an order to disclose (which may take several forms, such as an injunction against secrecy or a writ of mandamus ordering disclosure). In a number of states, denial of access to a record may be appealed to a state's attorney general, and, in Connecticut and New York, to a special, statutorily established, freedom of information review group. Penalties for illegal denial of access are provided in many statutes, ranging from the rare removal from office or impeachment to the more common fine and/or imprisonment. Many times, though, there is no penalty for denying records apart from the

---

[210] https://www.nfoic.org/coalitions/state-foi-resources/state-freedom-of-information-laws.

[211] On the other hand, it can be particularly satisfying to be able to quote chapter and verse when dealing with a less-than-helpful government employee. Oh, and as one of your authors has said, "Government is the people's business. We own it and have an interest in seeing that it is run properly."

agency paying the legal costs of the requestor leaving officials with no downside in keeping things secret.

Efforts are made periodically to generalize across state openness statutes, and even to "rank" state statutes in terms of "more open" or "less open." If one learns one is in a state with a highly rated statute, however, do not relax. Openness statutes—or court decisions, for that matter—tend to be rather like airline tickets—good for this time and purpose only. Keeping records and meetings open takes real diligence on the part of the news media and concerned citizens' groups.

To begin with, records kept by government offices are generically termed "public" but it does not necessarily mean "open to inspection by the public or press." The old common law (judge-made) definition of public record is something like this:[212] A written memorial by an authorized public officer in discharge of a legal duty to make a record of something written, said, or done.

Statutes further limit or expand the public's right to inspect "public records" exist:[213]

> Some documents which constitute public records under * * * an open records statute have been exempted from disclosure. There may be available to specified individuals [e.g. licensing examination data available only to the individual examined, or reports of mental examinations of school children available only to their parents.] * * * Not all state-affiliated organizations will meet the definition of "agency" within an open records act [e.g., consulting firms and quasi-public corporations are frequently outside the terms of an open records act.]

News media and private citizens regularly request and sue to get copies of records under state open records laws. Requests range from finding out what government agencies are spending on travel, who has been given a state credit card to how much state employees make. When requests are denied, some sue. In *Crocco v. Pennsylvania Department of Health*, a requester with the Pro-Life Action League sought records of professional license numbers and names of individuals on abortion facility applications. The department of health redacted the identifying information from the records. The Pennsylvania Office of Open Records affirmed the redaction of the information. The trial court affirmed, in part, citing the Personal Security Exemption to Pennsylvania's Right-to-Know Law.

> Section 708(b)(1)(ii) of the RTKL exempts records from public access that "would be reasonably likely to result in a substantial and demonstrable risk of physical harm to or the personal security of an individual." 65 P.S. § 67.708(b)(1)(ii). The

---

[212] *Amos v. Gunn*, 84 Fla. 285, 94 So. 615, 616 (1922).

[213] A qualified right of inspection does exist under common law. Harold L. Cross, *The Public's Right to Know* (New York: Columbia University Press, 1953), pp. xiii–xiv.

> personal security exception "embraces two notions: risk of physical harm and the risk to one's personal security."

The Department of Health cited studies of violence against abortion providers, statistics about violence along with declarations and affidavits from organizations and individuals about the risks to clinic personnel. Jean Crocco "emphasized" she lacked nefarious intent despite acting on behalf of the Pro-Life Action League. Crocco argued that disclosure of the names and license numbers was in the public interest. "She also submitted an affidavit attesting to her intention to use the information as she had when obtained in other states, purportedly to ensure proper patient care by licensed professionals."

There is also a common-law right of access to records that has been recognized by both state and federal courts.[214]

> Although the Right-to-Know Law makes a narrow class of documents unqualifiedly available, the common law makes a much broader class of documents available, but on a qualified basis.
>
> However, the common-law right of access to this broad category of records is contingent on two factors. First, the person seeking access must "establish an interest in the subject matter of the material." [* * *] Second, "the citizen's common-law right to gain access to [common-law] public records requires a balancing of interests." [* * *] Unlike a citizen's absolute statutory right of access, a plaintiff's common-law right of access must be balanced against the State's interest in preventing disclosure. [* * *] Finally, the common-law process, unlike the Right-to-Know process, "should be 'flexible and adaptable to different circumstances.' "

All the states have statutory provisions specifically providing for secrecy. One example is a provision in income tax laws mandating that individual income tax returns be protected from disclosure. Frequent exemptions appearing in state open records laws have much the same character as the exemptions in the Federal Freedom of Information Act (discussed earlier), including personnel or medical information, intra-or inter-agency memoranda, preliminary draft documents, and trade secrets. Most if not all states also exempt from disclosure a variety of health department records, juvenile and adoption records, licensing examination data, and public assistance or welfare records.

AGENCIES MAKE RECORDS PRICEY

The editorial board of the *Denver Post* wrote, "Public records in Colorado are no longer free—the default position of most state, local and judicial departments has become charge the maximum amount allowed,

---

214 *Higg-A-Rella, Inc. v. County of Essex*, 141 N.J. 35, 46–47, 660 A.2d 1163, 1168–1169 (1995).

estimate it'll take your employees days of work and then wait to see what happens." The editorial followed publication of an investigative report by *Denver Post* reporter David Migoya. Migoya exposed a scandal at the Colorado Judicial Department involving a $2.5 million contract that subsequently was canceled. Migoya followed that with a request for emails between Supreme Court Chief Justice Nathan Coats and the former court administrator, Christopher Ryan. The Colorado Judicial Department told the *Post* that fulfilling one request would cost $1,839.60 plus copying fees and the other $225 plus copying fees.

Agencies, both state and federal, are allowed to charge the cost of copying with the per page amounts varying from localities in states. A California appellate court held that charging $3.50 a page for direct and indirect costs was not arbitrary or capricious. An Oregon zoo said it would cost $18,000 for records on the zoo's elephant-breeding program. The *Denver Post* editorial questioned the costs to review emails and then collect them that the Judicial Department was going to charge.

> We understand that pulling emails from an archive does take time, but we cannot imagine why it'd take an employee 61.32 hours to run a query for those emails and print them out or create a digital copy. Even assuming that Coats required the attorney general himself to review the emails before their release, we are stumped at why it'd take someone an entire workweek plus 20 hours of overtime to complete such a task. Consider—those of you with office jobs—how many emails you read in a workweek and how many you respond to.

Some lawmakers have started imposing fees to provide records to the public. In Wisconsin, a retired educator, Sheila Plotkin, aske the members of Joint Finance Committee for correspondence they had received from Wisconsin residents about education funding.[215]

> All of the legislators Plotkin contacted provided responsive records for free. All, that is, except one: state Rep. John Nygren (R-Marinette), the panel's co-chair, wanted Plotkin to pay $100.41 for location costs.
>
> To Plotkin, this was a nonstarter.
>
> "I'm a citizen on a fixed income and cannot afford $100.41," said the 81-year-old retired educator from Madison. "I reject these charges. I think it is an attempt to price individual citizens out of" public records.
>
> Similarly, Wisconsin Freedom of Information Council President Bill Lueders asked Nygren in June for communications about the state budget. Nygren had claimed that the Republicans'

[215] Jonathon Anderson, "September: Lawmakers Use Costs To Rebuff Records Requests," *Wisconsin Freedom of Information Council*, Sept. 3, 2019.

> budget bill was crafted based on public input, so Lueders asked to see what members of the public said.
>
> Nygren agreed to produce the records—but only if Lueders paid an upfront search fee of $334.66. Lueders declined, noting that in numerous past requests no legislator had ever before charged him location fees.

The *Houston Chronicle* sought records from the Texas Department of Public Safety related to arrests of motorists. The *Chronicle* wanted to see if minorities were being singled out and ticketed when they drove through white neighborhoods. "The department initially asked for $75 million, and when the paper objected, offered the lower the price to $60 million." A friendly state lawmaker made it possible for the *Chronicle* to analyze the data for free. The paper then printed a story showing that minorities were twice as likely to be ticketed in certain white communities.

The Texas story is an example of state agencies trying to turn profits from the sale of public records. The idea has merit, as companies make money by mining records for saleable information. Commercial users can identify consumers and find out about their lifestyles by using the information in government databases. States, always strapped for cash, increasingly look at their records as a low-or no-cost resource that can be used to generate income. The problem is that news and public interest organizations are caught up in the money-making schemes.

The *Belleville News-Democrat* in Belleville, Ill., wanted to investigate voter fraud. One of the ways it could look at who was voting was to check state driver's license records. Illinois asked for $37.5 million for the records. The *Providence Journal-Bulletin* sought motor vehicle records to investigate ticket fixing. Rhode Island asked for $9.7 million. Some media organizations have asked for waivers of the fees, citing their public service use of the records. Others have simply refused to pay and forced agencies into public showdowns.

STATE ATTORNEYS GENERAL

Attorneys general have been called on to interpret meetings and records laws in many states. As for meetings, it is occasionally feasible for a reporter to seek "instant action" in the form of an attorney general's opinion, perhaps by placing a phone call even while an illegal secret meeting is in session. Through such maneuvers, enterprising reporters have, on occasion, forced meetings open.

More likely, however, before an opinion can be had, the meeting will have adjourned. Nevertheless, either a formal opinion delivered at the request of a state government agency, or an informal one delivered at the request of a non-official person or entity—such as a reporter or a newspaper—can have a future impact on the behavior of the secretive group or agency. Reporters, of course, should read up on the open-records, open-meetings opinions of attorneys general. The attorney general interprets the law of a state;[216] an AG's opinion does not have the force of a court opinion, but it is authoritative until a court has ruled on a particular question.

LOSING THE PUBLIC OPINION BATTLE

Conflicts between individual privacy rights and access, coupled with fears about what can or will be done with information, can impede the search for records. An example of that took place following the death of NASCAR driver Dale Earnhardt.

Earnhardt crashed into a wall during the 2001 Daytona 500 and was killed. A short time before that Daytona 500 race was run, a reporter for the *Orlando Sentinel* wrote a story that pointed to the risks to drivers because they didn't use a particular crash restraint system. The system, called the Head and Neck Support System, would prevent "head whipping" injuries that could result in the deaths of drivers.

NASCAR reported that Earnhardt had died because his seat belt was broken, but the newspaper wanted to determine for itself whether the lack of the restraint system might have contributed to his death. The paper asked for the autopsy report, including photos, so that its own expert could determine if head-whipping had been involved. But the request led to public outcry of fans and Earnhardt's family fought against the release of the autopsy information.[217]

> "The vast majority of NASCAR fans mistakenly believed that we wanted to publish the photos, Editor Tim Franklin says. 'Very few had any idea that we had just spent six months investigating NASCAR driver safety.'" After Earnhardt's widow, Teresa, appeared on television declaring that she didn't want photos of her husband's body displayed in public, angry racing fans bombarded the newspaper with more than 15,000 e-mails, letters, and phone calls. "Dozens of death threats poured in," Franklin says.

The newspaper reached an agreement with Earnhardt's widow and the newspaper's expert was able to see the autopsy photos. The expert said that Earnhardt had died of a head-whipping injury and not because of a broken seat belt. (NASCAR later required all of its drivers to use the Head and Neck Support system.)

But during the public outcry, the Florida Legislature changed the state's open records law to exempt autopsy photos from public view.[218]

---

[216] William Thompson, "FOI and State Attorneys General," *Freedom of Information Center Report No. 307*, July, 1973, University of Missouri.

[217] Charles Layton, "The Information Squeeze," *American Journalism Review*, Sept. 11, 2002.

[218] Ibid.

> "Florida's open government advocates were overwhelmed in their efforts to conduct a rational debate," Lucy Dalglish, executive director of the Reporters Committee for Freedom of the Press, later wrote. Gov. Jeb Bush signed the bill into law with Earnhardt's widow by his side.
>
> Observers said that the chance that Earnhardt's photos would wind up on Internet sites gave lawmakers enough reason to grant the exemption.

A big part of the problem was the Sentinel's failure to explain what it was looking for.[219]

> [* * *] the Sentinel never fully explained its reasons or internal thought processes in print because it was concerned about competitors who might seek the same information.
>
> "That's often the failure of news organizations—the will and inability to explain and justify what and how and why we do what we do," said Bob Steele, director of the ethics program at the Poynter Institute, which promotes excellence and integrity in journalism.
>
> "It's not a matter of defending what we do," Steele said, "but holding ourselves accountable by telling readers the purposes of our actions and justifying our processes based on our journalistic obligations and ethical standards. When we don't, that gets papers in trouble."

POLICE RECORDS

Police records are among the most important in all of government, yet rules of states and municipalities about disclosing such records vary tremendously. If citizens and reporters cannot get access to the "blotter" (the police calls log) and the arrest (booking) log and the jail log on a constant and continuous basis, the possibility of abuse of citizens' rights may tend to become a probability. According to yet another useful survey by the Reporters Committee on Freedom of the Press, most states have laws allowing sealing of investigatory files.

Just because a state does not spell out access to law enforcement records in statutory form, that does not mean that reporters or citizens are without remedy. Sometimes getting access to law enforcement records will take a willingness to sue under an open records statute—or, on a common law basis if no such statute applies—to try to get the records. Practical reporters will tell you, however, that developing a good working relationship with police probably is as valuable an avenue to access to their records as is reliance on statutes or courts to enforce access.

---

[219] Maya Bell, "Court Fight For Autopsy Photos Sparks Outrage," *Orlando Sentinel*, March 4, 2001.

Good working relationships with law enforcement officials obviously are not always available to reporters. When Sumter County, Georgia, Sheriff Randy Howard didn't appreciate news coverage in the *Sumter Free Press* about one of his sons in 1998, his office stopped its long-standing practice of faxing a copy of the daily arrest log and incident reports to local news media. Several months later, fax transmissions reappeared after some a favorable article about his son was published by the *Free Press*.[220]

In 1999, however, fax transmissions from the sheriff's office stopped after the *Free Press* published articles about possible discrepancies in the county's prisoner phone records. When the newspaper asked for relevant records, it was told the search and copying would cost $400. The newspaper filed suit under the Georgia Open Records Act.[221]

At trial, Sheriff Howard testified that although he knew the underlying records were public, the records he had faxed were merely press releases that he could send out as he pleased. Further, he argued that the newspaper had not made only oral requests for the records, not written. The newspaper replied that oral requests were sufficient, and the sheriff's office was not being asked to create any new records, only to release existing records. Also, it was argued that the sheriff's office should not discriminate among news organizations that were in favor and those that were not.

The Georgia Superior Court ordered the sheriff to treat news organizations equally. The sheriff's response was to stop all faxes to the media, and to say that records would be available only to individuals coming to the sheriff's office. When the *Sumter Free Press* returned to court, it won an order compelling Sheriff Howard to make them available to all local news organizations but also to distribute them, once again, by fax. That order, plus the Superior Court's assessment against the sheriff for $2,000 in attorney fees and court costs, was upheld by the Georgia Supreme Court.[222]

This, indeed, was an open records victory for the *Sumter Free Press*, but old-line reporters would hope that news media in that county actually show up at the sheriff's office to get additional information beyond bare-bones formats of incident reports and arrest log information.

ACCESS TO CAMPUS POLICE RECORDS

Many colleges and universities in the United States, said to be educating the young for democracy, have unfortunate histories where openness of campus police records is concerned. Part of the problem, in recent years, has been the United States Department of Education,

---

[220] *Howard v. Sumter Free Press*, 272 Ga. 521, 531 S.E.2d 698 (2000), 28 Med.L.Rptr. 1830.

[221] Ibid. at 183; see also "Sheriff ordered to give newspaper incident reports," *The News Media and the Law*, Summer, 2000.

[222] Ibid.

which was threatening universities with loss of federal funding if they violated student privacy by releasing "educational records." Strangely, the Department of Education functionaries argued that campus police incident reports were "educational records" under the Family Educational Rights and Privacy Act (FERPA).

The issue gained national notoriety in 1989 when Traci Bauer, a campus newspaper editor at Southwest Missouri State University (SMSU) claimed that she was entitled to SMSU Security Office incident reports.

Ultimately, Ms. Bauer sued Paul Kincaid, SMSU's director of university relations, seeking release of SMSU security office records. Triggering the controversy was Ms. Bauer's request to see an incident report about a rape involving a student athlete.[223]

In July, 1989, Kincaid had distributed a policy statement ordering the withholding of SMSU Security Office records, including the verbatim incident reports. The SMSU campus is located within the jurisdiction of the Springfield, Mo., police force.

Ms. Bauer's suit claimed that she was entitled to the SMSU incident reports, and that those reports—which were to be filed with the Springfield police by the campus Security Office—were sometimes delayed. She charged that this meant that the Springfield police thus were unable, at times, to investigate on-campus crime promptly. She sought access to the SMSU records under the Missouri Open Records or Sunshine Act.

SMSU Officials expressed fear of losing federal funding if the incident reports were released to the public and press contrary to the U.S. Department of Education's (DOE) understanding of FERPA. The DOE had urged campus officials to keep confidential police incident reports as "educational records," all in the name of privacy.[224]

U.S. District Judge Russell G. Clark, however, found that there was credible testimony that "* * * in the past SMSU has concealed or destroyed evidence of contraband and failed or refused to release selected criminal investigation and incident reports concerning sex offenses, student athletes, and university personnel." In addition, Judge Clark noted credible testimony from Mark Goodman, President of the Student Press Law Center, that no federal funds actually had been withheld as the result of disclosure of police information or incident reports.

The judge noted, however, that the U.S. Department of Education had issued warnings to some schools, and that all schools that had been issued warnings voluntarily fell into compliance with the DOE's interpretation of FERPA.

---

[223] *Bauer v. Kincaid*, 759 F.Supp. 575 (W.D.Mo.1991).

[224] Ibid. at 584; Sec. 610.25 of the Missouri Revised Statutes.

In sum, Judge Clark ruled that campus crime records were not "educational records," and thus could not be withheld under FERPA.[225]

> [T]his Court concludes that defendants' actions in withholding the criminal investigation and incident reports which contain names and other personally identifiable information, is unconstitutional under the equal protection. Judge Clark concluded that the criminal investigation and incident reports of SMSU are not exempt from disclosure under Missouri's Sunshine Law.

Evidently intent on making FERPA into a campus secrets act, the U.S. Department of Education was slow to comply with Judge Clark's ruling. As a result, the SPLC and student editors from the University of Tennessee and the University of Colorado sought—and were granted—an injunction to prevent the Department of Education from interfering with the release of campus crime reports.[226]

But obviously, it is the most troublesome or "sensitive" incidents (e.g. rape allegations against a star athlete, sexual harassment by professors, or some breach of law by an administrator) that tend to stir the human impulse to conceal damaging information. The trouble with "just a little secrecy"—whether on campus or elsewhere—is that what is hidden is likely to be precisely what society needs most to know.

In one telling example of that need and the risks that can result from secrecy, consider what happened at one Midwestern school. A master key disappeared from a dormitory office. It was promptly reported to university police, but the information was not made public.

Over the course of the next several weeks, students in the dormitory began to report thefts of personal belongings. Campus police officers came out and took reports but declined to list them as burglaries or thefts. The reason: there was no sign of forced entry to any of the dormitory rooms. Prompt reporting of the disappearance of the key in the first place might have let students take additional precautions to protect their belongings. Students may consider themselves lucky, though. Although their property was taken, no one was harmed in the series of incidents.

At another campus, two students reported being attacked while walking from a remote parking area to the main campus. The student newspaper learned of the attacks and sought campus police reports about them. During the battle over the university's refusal to release the reports, a third student was attacked while walking through the same area. This time, the student was raped. While universities may profit from the preservation of their images as safe places for parents to send

---

[225] Ibid. at 594.

[226] "Judge Orders Release of Campus Crime Reports," *New York Times,* March 15, 1991, on decision in *Student Press Law Center, Lyn D. Schrotgerber (CO), Sam G. Cristy and James C. Brewer, Jr. (TN) v. Lamar Alexander, U.S. Sec. of Education,* 778 F.Supp. 1227 (D.D.C. 1991).

their children, students run risks when they are not able to take measures to protect themselves.

ACCESS TO CAMPUS DISCIPLINARY RECORDS

Universities spend a good deal of time and effort promoting themselves as wholesome places where young people engage in the search for knowledge, guided by learned professors and aided by helpful staffs. Occasionally, students will depart from this quest and get into trouble. Just as universities have fought efforts to reveal risks of crime on their campuses, they likewise have tried to keep the lid on student disciplinary issues.

Student editors at the University of Georgia won a significant victory for access in the *Red & Black*[227] case in 1993 when the Georgia Supreme Court held that records of student disciplinary hearings fell outside the category of records made confidential by the Buckley Amendment. Further, the court said that the proceedings were subject to Georgia's open meetings law.

The controversy arose over hazing charges filed against two fraternities. The student editors of *The Red & Black* student newspaper sent reporters to both hearings, but the reporters were barred from both proceedings. The newspaper sued and won a partial victory at the trial court level.

Superior Court Judge Frank Hall rejected the position that the Buckley Amendment applied to the student disciplinary hearing records. But he also refused to grant the newspaper access to the records, saying that the school's judicial board did not fall under the state's open meetings law. It was not a covered body.

But the Georgia Supreme Court disagreed, siding with the newspaper's attorney who argued that openness was proper because it would allow the newspaper to monitor the hearing process. It declared that[228] "the policy of the state is that the public's business must be open, not only to protect against public abuse, but to maintain the public's confidence in its officials."

The Red & Black case has been disagreed with once in a university case, *U.S. v. Miami University*.[229] The Department of Education sued to prevent Ohio universities from releasing disciplinary records. A three-judge panel of the Sixth Circuit Court of Appeals held that FERPA did apply to student disciplinary records.[230]

---

[227] *Red & Black Publishing Co. v. Board of Regents of the University System of Georgia*, 262 Ga. 848, 427 S.E.2d 257 (1993).

[228] *Red & Black Publishing Co. v. Board of Regents of the University System of Georgia*, 262 Ga. 848, 845, 427 S.E.2d 257. 263 (1993); "Public Justice, Georgia Supreme Court opens campus proceedings: the ruling may be the start of a national trend," *Student Press Law Report*, Spring, 1993.

[229] *U.S. v. Miami University*, 294 F.3d 797 (6th Cir. 2002).

[230] Ibid. at 813.

> [A] detailed study of the statute and its evolution by amendment reveals that Congress intends to include student disciplinary records within the meaning of "education records" as defined by the FERPA. This intention is evinced by a review of the express statutory exemptions from privacy and exceptions to the definition of "education records."

The panel noted that there were two statutory exceptions that allowed the release of disciplinary records. The victim of a crime of violence can receive the final results of any disciplinary proceeding conducted by the institution against the alleged perpetrator. Also, institution can inform the public of the final results of any disciplinary proceeding if the institution determines that the student committed a violation of the institution's rules or policies[231]

> These two exemptions clearly evolve from a base Congressional assumption that student disciplinary records are "education records" and thereby protected from disclosure. Working from that base, Congress selected two particular situations in which otherwise protected student disciplinary records may be released. And even then, Congress significantly limits the amount of information that an institution may release and the people to whom the institution may release such information.

That ruling applies in the Sixth Circuit alone.

[231] Ibid.

CHAPTER 9

LEGAL PROBLEMS IN REPORTING COURTS

52. ACCESS TO JUDICIAL PROCEEDINGS

In a free society, judicial processes remain open to public view.

DISAPPEARING DOCKETS AND CLOSED COURTROOMS

Generations of journalism students have learned that justice needs the light of day. It is an article of professional faith that government should never be given the power of secret arrest, secret confinement or secret trial. But in the Twenty-First Century, that lesson and article of faith, based on the First Amendment, Sixth Amendment and common law principles, is in danger because of secret dockets and trials and imprisonments conducted in secret. Dockets are the courts' mechanism to announce their schedules; a case left off the public docket—or its disposition—may never be found or known. The constitutional and common law precedents are clear: Proceedings in criminal courts must be open based on First Amendment guarantees of the right of free expression, on the right to receive information, and on the Sixth Amendment promise of a public trial. These precedents and beliefs are undergirded by common law principles holding that the people are entitled to know by seeing how their justice system operates.

But in recent years, judges have favored the exigencies of a war on terror and a war on illegal drugs. Hundreds of cases in federal courts have been concealed from the public and press through the mechanism of secret dockets and closed courtroom proceedings.

The first widely publicized reports of the use of secret dockets and trials in American courts appeared in 2003. On May 12 of that year, the *Daily Business Review* of Miami reported that the U.S. District Court in

South Florida was concealing civil and criminal cases.[1] The secrecy scheme used a secret docketing system that operated side-by-side with the public docket.[2]

> With the start last week of the government's high-profile drug trafficking case against accused Colombian drug lord Fabio Ochoa, a fresh spotlight is shining on a little-known practice by the U.S. District Court in South Florida that's hiding civil and criminal cases from the public.
>
> Ochoa's defense team, including Miami super-lawyer Roy Black, says it has identified several drug cases in which the existence of events and pleadings were omitted from the public docket. The *Daily Business Review* learned that in one case drug defendant Nicholas Bergonzoli was convicted, sentenced and imprisoned last year in total secrecy.

Reporter Dan Christensen's story also raised the issue of secret proceedings in the federal government's case against Mohamed Kamel Bellahouel who would become known as M.K.B. in a habeas proceeding that took place in secrecy in both the 11th Circuit Court of Appeals and the United States Supreme Court.

Bellahouel, an Algerian married to an American woman, was detained for five months by federal authorities before being released on $10,000 bond, the *Daily Business Review* reported.[3]

> Bellahouel was a waiter at a Middle Eastern restaurant in Delray Beach, Fla., where he apparently served food to some of the Sept. 11 hijackers who dined at the restaurant. A Delray Beach movie theater employee told the FBI she thought she saw Bellahouel go into the theater with one of the hijackers. As a result, in October 2001, he was detained at the Krome Processing Facility in southwest Miami-Dade.

The newspaper reported that a reference to Bellahouel's case appeared for a short time on the 11th Circuit's computerized docketing system and a secret proceeding in Bellahouel's habeas corpus claim took place in Miami before a three-judge panel of the 11th Circuit.[4]

Bellahouel's case surfaced briefly because of a court clerk's mistake. Later, the *Daily Business Review* found, a court calendar and the 11th Circuit's computerized docketing system in Atlanta were altered to remove any trace of Bellahouel's case from the public record.

The newspaper asked the three judges on the panel to unseal the case, but received no reply, Christensen reported.

---

1 Dan Christensen, "Federal Court in Florida Hides Cases From Public," *Daily Business Review*, May 12, 2003.

2 Ibid.

3 Ibid.

4 Ibid.

Things have changed in the more than 10 years since the *Daily Business Review* story was published. Concealing cases and closing court proceedings have become more difficult, Black, of Black, Srebnick, Kornspan & Stumpf, P.A., said in 2015.[5] "When a judge seals a document, the judge must post a short note on the file explaining what the document is about."

But the history, even recent history, is not particularly hopeful. In 2006, The Reporters for News Media and the Law, a publication of the Reporters Committee for Freedom of the Press, wrote that there were more than 400 sealed cases in the U.S. District Court in Washington, D.C.[6]

> During the past five years, 469 cases in U.S. District Court in Washington, D.C., have been prosecuted and tried in complete secrecy, with no public knowledge even of the cases' existence and no way for the public to challenge the secrecy.

While the Bellahouel case was a terrorism-related proceeding, few of the secret cases in the D.C. court were linked to terrorism prosecutions, reporters Kirsten Mitchell and Susan Burgess found.[7]

> Cases missing from the criminal docket are typically gang-related prosecutions that tend to culminate in multi-defendant drug and murder conspiracy trials, say court officials and lawyers with access to the cases who were interviewed for this story.[8]

In most cases, the reporters found, cases were sealed at the request of federal prosecutors. The prosecutors are guided by the Justice Department's Policy With Regard to Open Judicial Proceedings.[9] That policy begins with a statement of the public interest in having public proceedings and refers to an overriding duty to oppose closing cases. And, the policy reads, there is "a strong presumption against closing proceedings or portions thereof, and the Department of Justice foresees very few cases in which closure would be warranted."[10]

---

[5] Telephone interview, October 2015.

[6] Kirsten B. Mitchell and Susan Burgess, "Disappearing Dockets," *News Media and the Law*, Winter 2006, Vol. 30, No. 1.

[7] Ibid.

[8] There were relatively few secret civil proceedings, the reporters found. They explained that most of the sealed civil cases were likely to be whistle blower cases. The enabling statute calls for sealing those cases for 60 days in order to give the government time to investigate the claims.

[9] 25 28 C.F.R. § 50.9.

[10] *Farr v. Superior Court of Los Angeles County*, 22 Cal.App.3d 60, 69, 99 Cal.Rptr. 342, 348 (1971).

In wording that tracks the 30-year-old language from the open courts cases of *Richmond Newspapers*,[11] *the Press-Enterprise* cases[12] and *Globe Newspapers*,[13] the guidelines prohibit federal prosecutors from seeking closure unless (1) there is no reasonable alternative, (2) the closure would prevent the harm feared and (3) the closure is as limited as is possible.

> Closure is restricted to those cases in which there is a substantial likelihood that (1) a defendant might be denied fair trial rights, (2) there is imminent danger to parties, witnesses or others and (3) that ongoing investigations would be seriously jeopardized. The guidelines do not apply when needed to protect national security information or classified documents.[14]

In any case, motions to close proceedings must be made publicly and advance notice provided. But the policy also allows the motion to be made secretly if announcing the move to close the proceeding or making the contents of the motion "would clearly defeat the reason for closure."[15]

Legal Times, the District of Columbia weekly covering government and legal issues, reported on government rationales for keeping proceedings secret in a March 6, 2006, story.[16] While information contained in the motions to seal cases was unavailable, reporter Sarah Kelley found lawyers and court officials who spoke about the practice. U.S. District Chief Judge Thomas Hogan said that protecting witnesses from harm was a valid reason to close cases. Stevan Bunnell, chief of the criminal division at the U.S. Attorney's Office in Washington, said the greater risk of retaliation against witnesses in the District of Columbia would account for the number of sealed cases in that court.

Washington defense attorney Joanne Slaight said:

> "The prosecutors want to protect their investigation, and it's in the defense lawyers' interest to seal the case for the protection of their client," Slaight said. "It serves both parties, but whether it serves the public is a different issue." [17]

The Justice Department's policy on open proceedings makes clear that the closing of trials is a serious matter. It requires a balancing of the public's interest in transparency in the administration of justice against clearly identified and real dangers to parties in criminal cases or the endangering of important criminal investigations which could be compromised unless kept secret. That is, at least, the theory of the

---

11 *Richmond Newspapers v. Virginia*, 448 U.S. 555, 100 S.Ct. 2814 (1980).

12 *Press-Enterprise Co. v. Superior Court of California*, 464 U.S. 501, 104 S.Ct. 819, 823 (1984) and *Press-Enterprise Company v. Superior Court*, 478 U.S. 1, 5, 106 S.Ct. 2735, 2739 (1986).

13 *Globe Newspaper Co. v. Superior Court for Norfolk County*, 457 U.S. 596, 603–607, 102 S.Ct. 2613, 2618–2620 (1982), 8 Med.L.Rptr. 1689, 1692–1694.

14 25 28 C.F.R. § 50.9 Policy With Regard to Open Judicial Proceedings.

15 Ibid.

16 Sarah Kelley, "D.C.'s Secret Docket," *Legal Times*, March 26, 2006.

17 Ibid.

Justice Department policy. The practice? Even with all the admonitions about the gravity of closure, a reading of the transcript in one secret case reveals the ease with which a case may be hidden from public view.

The 2005 11th Circuit decision in *U.S. v. Ochoa-Vasquez*[18] dealt with the appeal of convicted drug trafficker Fabio Ochoa-Vasquez. Part of Ochoa-Vasquez' appeal rested on his claim that the sealing orders in his and seven other drug defendants' cases violated his constitutional rights. Although it refused to overturn his conviction, a panel of the 11th Circuit nonetheless found that the closure violated requirements imposed by the First Amendment. The opinion contains a portion of the transcript showing the ad hoc nature of the secrecy arrangement.[19]

> THE COURT: * * * Anything else that I've left out?
>
> [Sanchez's counsel]: Judge, there's just—
>
> [Government]: There's the matter of docketing.
>
> MR. FOREMAN: There's just one other administrative matter.
>
> THE COURT: My feeling is that you just work that out however you can. I don't know what to do with it, if you want to—me to defer, I guess I could verbally order that—that the clerk retain custody of these documents and that they be filed either on Wednesday or however [Magistrate] Judge Vitunac orders it, and that they be held in the vault and not docketed.
>
> [Government]: That would work for us, Judge.
>
> [Sanchez's counsel]: That works, your Honor.
>
> * * *
>
> THE COURT: * * * So, I guess they can just put it in the vault—
>
> [Government]: That's fine, Judge.
>
> THE COURT:—without docketing.

The total number of cases kept secret is unknown, though in 2003 the Reporters Committee for Freedom of the Press reported that at least 46 U.S. district courts were using secret dockets.[20] It appears that closed courts may not be exceptions to longstanding assumptions that criminal courts, in particular, must be open to the public and thus to the press. Those assumptions rest on a fear of closed criminal proceedings, a central tenet of Anglo-American law, and with good reason.

A 2011 trade secrets case, that involved multiple and international defendants, revealed a secret parallel docketing system in Utah federal courts. In *Clearone Communications v. Bowers*,[21] one of the defendants

---

[18] *U.S. v. Ochoa-Vasquez*, 428 F.3d 1015 (11th Cir. 2005).

[19] *U.S. v. Ochoa-Vasquez*, 428 F.3d 1015, 1028 (11th Cir. 2005). The footnote also is found in the Winter 2006 edition of *News Media and the Law*, Vol. 30, No. 1.

[20] Sara Thacker, "Secret Justice: Secret Dockets," *Reporters Committee for Freedom of the Press*, Summer 2003.

[21] *Clearone Communications v. Bowers, et.al.*, 643 F.3d 735 (10th Cir. 2011).

filed an emergency motion to gain access to a "Court Only User Docket" claiming that the secret docket made it possible for the plaintiff to carry on communications with the trial court in secret.

> In that motion, the WideBand defendants alleged that "[o]n February 11, 2011, the Magistrate issued [an order] which acknowledged the existence of a dual docketing system called the 'Court User Only Docket,'" The WideBand defendants further alleged that they would be "severely prejudiced [in the appellate process] by not having access to ex parte communications between the court and ClearOne consisting of sealed Motions and any sealed Orders." * * * The WideBand defendants thus "request[ed] access to the 'Court Only User Docket' by giving the docket sheets and all filings to their attorney. . . ."

Tenth Circuit Court of Appeals Chief Judge Mary Beck Briscoe rejected the defendant's motion declaring that (1) the district court had not ruled on the emergency motion and (2) the issue was being raised in a reply brief in the appeal of the case.[22]

> Third, even ignoring these procedural deficiencies, there is clearly no merit to the WideBand defendants' arguments. Apparently, they are unaware that the district court, like this court, maintains both a publicly accessible docket and a docket intended for court personnel only. There is simply no basis for concluding that this system provided any litigation advantage to ClearOne.

Understand that the federal court system is big and that the appellate process takes place in locations distant from where trials occur. So, some two weeks before Judge Briscoe wrote her opinion laying out the reasons that the defendant did not understand how the system worked and concluded that the defendant had not been harmed by the separate docket used only by court personnel, U.S. Magistrate David Nuffer ruled on the defendant's motion to unseal the documents held in the "court use only" docket.[23]

Nuffer explained why many of the items were placed on that docket and adding other items had been filed secretly.[24]

> Many "court user only" entries have not appeared on the public docket because they are administrative in nature (such as information on service by mail or e-mail, transcript orders, or notes about docket corrections), make the public docket harder to read, and result in added PACER charges for persons downloading the public docket.

---

22 Ibid. at 782.

23 *Clearone Communications v. Chiang*, 2011 WL 2414396 (D.Utah 2011).

24 Ibid.

But, there were some additional items that did not fit into Nuffer's first categories.[25]

> On November 3, 2010, the magistrate judge issued an order explaining that some documents related to the Seizure Order were filed under seal because they contained information protected under the Confidentiality Order and that later, redacted versions of the sealed documents were filed. The order went on to unseal other sealed docket entries and documents related to the Seizure Order.

Without getting into the arcane and intricate mechanisms of federal civil procedure, the defendant seeking to have the docket unsealed argued that courts are required to show compelling reasons for sealing dockets.

But, citing a 2006 decision in the 9th Circuit, Nuffer noted that compelling reasons are only required for materials that would ultimately bear on a final decision. For everything else, a showing of "good cause" is sufficient justification for sealing.[26]

> The Kamakana court stated that it had previously reasoned "that when a district court grants a protective order to seal documents during discovery, 'it already has determined that "good cause" exists to protect this information from being disclosed to the public by balancing the needs for discovery against the need for confidentiality.' "

That would have seemed to have settled the matter. The documents and entries were sealed for "good cause" and would stay that way. Except.

> [A]fter a complete review of the docket in this case, the magistrate judge finds that making all the docket entries public would not reveal any protected information, except for one sealed minute entry, docket no. 277, which may contain proprietary information. Further, it appears there are means of ensuring trade secret and proprietary information is protected without sealing so many documents in their entirety.

Nuffer ordered that the documents, except for no. 277, be made public. The court-only docket had 2,500 entries.

In 2008, a federal judge in El Paso, Texas, denied a motion from a local activist to unseal documents and open up proceedings in a major corruption case in the U.S./Mexico border city.[27] Carl Starr sought to unseal plea agreements and all other documents in the case and have the court open all hearings to the public.

---

25 Ibid.

26 *Kamakana v. City & County of Honolulu*, 447 F.3d 1172, 1180 (9th Cir.2006).

27 *U.S. v. Ketner, et. al.*, 566 F.Supp.2d 568 (W.D.Texas 2008).

District Court Judge Frank Montalvo denied Starr's request. In his explanation for keeping documents and hearing secret, Montalvo cited journalism.[28]

> On every occasion in which a hearing and documents have been held confidentially, the Court has weighed the public's right of access against the Government's need to maintain the integrity of its lengthy, complex, and ongoing investigation into public corruption, which the media itself has conceded is critically important to the community's future prospects. As *Texas Monthly* columnist Paul Burka recently observed, "[t]he FBI's investigation of corruption in El Paso isn't just another crime story. It's the latest chapter in the frustrating saga of a city cheated of its destiny." Burka continues:
>
> Corruption is a betrayal of civic virtue, and this scandal could not have come at a worse moment for El Paso. * * * For the moment, however, El Paso's future rests with the FBI. Having started the crackdown on corruption, it must see things through to the end or there will be anarchy and the longed-for boom will not occur. No one is going to pour energy and effort and dollars into a city with a crooked government.
>
> It is for the benefit of the city and county that Montalvo will keep proceedings secret.
>
> At stake in this matter is not secrecy for its own sake. The rights of the defendants are not in peril, as they have each, through their respective counsel, asked for the plea proceedings to be held confidentially. Each of them pleaded guilty freely and voluntarily. Rather, the Court finds the need to respect prosecutorial discretion, preserve the integrity of the investigation, and protect the due process rights of unindicted co-conspirators overrides the public's right of access and the presumption of open proceedings.

It's not just criminal cases, where secrecy can prevail. In April, 2009, U.S. District Judge Marilyn Patel closed her courtroom in a civil suit over DVD encryption. The case pitted the Motion Picture Association of America against RealNetworks over DVD copying. The MPAA sued alleging the RealNetworks violated the Digital Millennium Copyright Act by selling DVD-backup software.

The court proceeding dealt with testimony about Content Scrambling System, an algorithm used to encrypt DVDs. Judge Patel closed the courtroom over the objections of reporters covering the case, including CNET which posted the story quoted from here. Attorney

---

[28] Ibid. at 583.

Reginald Steer said that testimony would cover licensing technology as well as the algorithm. Judge Patel agreed.[29]

"I find that this does meet the requirements for a trade secret," Patel said. "We're going to protect what needs to be protected. I'm ordering everyone not signed off on a confidentiality agreement to leave the courtroom."

SHARON STONE'S INVISIBLE SUIT

A case involving actress Sharon Stone appeared to disappear from the California courts in 2008, the *Los Angeles Times* reported. The suit, filed by Stone's former attorney, was the subject of a "supersealing" in which both the file was sealed in the case removed from the public docket.[30]

"It's not that we need to know what happens in every one of these cases. It's that we need to know in general how these cases are resolved," said Gregg Leslie, legal defense director for the Reporter's Committee for Freedom of the Press. "Especially with celebrity cases, the issue is do people who have certain power and money get different treatment? We need to know."

The plaintiff in the case, William P. Jacobson, had been identified in prior stories as Stone's entertainment lawyer. Stone and two motion picture companies were identified as defendants. The dispute was not revealed. The case was uncovered by accident when a reporter happened to be in a courtroom where the Stone case was called.

THE SIMPSON CIRCUS

Football hero, actor and television sports broadcaster O.J. Simpson's spectacular fall from grace and his subsequent criminal trial happened mostly on television. Accused in mid-1994 of the savage knife-slash murders of his ex-wife Nicole Brown Simpson and an acquaintance, Ron Goldman, Simpson was acquitted of murder charges on Oct. 3, 1995. But the resoundingly controversial jury verdict—coming after only three hours of deliberation following nine months of trial, by no means ended the legal gauntlet of O.J. Simpson. The criminal jury's finding of "not guilty" brought Simpson little peace. By late 1996, he was back in court, this time defending himself—unsuccessfully, as it turned out—against wrongful death suits brought by the families of Nicole Brown Simpson and Ron Goldman. Early in 1997, the civil jury found against Simpson and decided he should pay a multi-million-dollar judgment that exceeded his net worth and provided ammunition for those who believed that he escaped justice in his earlier trial.

---

[29] Greg Sandoval and Declan McCullagh, "Judge seals courtroom in MPAA DVD-copying case," *CNET News*, April 24, 2009.

[30] Harriet Ryan, "Secrecy of civil suit against Sharon Stone raises questions," *Los Angeles Times*, April 24, 2009.

These Simpson cases are significant because they focused public attention on both the criminal and civil justice systems in a way unprecedented in American media and legal history. All through the criminal trial, the public was subjected to saturation coverage of the case with updates, analysis and commentary from cable, national and local broadcast stations. Judge Lance Ito's decision to permit a camera in the courtroom provided an often-unflattering look at the process of trial. Alternately fascinated and appalled, TV viewers saw a trial in which a jury—sequestered for the longest period in American history—endured delays and rambling presentations of evidence that seemed to go on forever. This added up to a portrait of the criminal justice system as one in which lawyers spent their days in court grandstanding, making speeches and generally getting in the way of justice.

The criminal prosecution, which seemingly had a strong case bolstered by DNA evidence, appeared to be at cross purposes with itself without a unifying theme to support its theory of the case. The defense focused on the Los Angeles Police Department and played the race card, even though Simpson's lifestyle enjoyed more in common with the white establishment than the minority community. The jury, alternately lionized and vilified depending on who you talked to, came away with the conclusion that the prosecution had not met its burden of proving beyond a reasonable doubt that Simpson committed the murders. The media, which had the "story of the century," appeared to engage in a feeding frenzy over both the significant and the inconsequential.

When the verdict was in and the initial shock settled, the analysis began. The prosecution had put on a case that was mind-numbingly long and too complicated. The defense had latched onto the position that the investigating officers were racists and could not be trusted. The jury was blamed for voting for reasons of race rather than the evidence. The media were excoriated for having caused all of the participants to behave the ways they did.

The Simpson case came to stand as an example of the clash between the rights guaranteed under the First Amendment and those protected under the Sixth Amendment. That amendment says, in part:

> In all criminal prosecutions, the accused shall enjoy the right to a speedy and public trial, by an impartial jury of the State and district wherein the crime shall have been committed * * *

LEGAL LESSONS FROM THE SIMPSON TRIALS?

As Frank Rich of the *New York Times* suggested, there was "ancillary debate about the value of TV cameras in court—as if TV was the message rather than the messenger." It cannot be denied, though, that the criminal trial was a TV trial; Judge Lance Ito even delayed announcing the verdict, reached in mid-afternoon on Oct. 2, until the following day. That ensured that people in the earlier time zones would get the news in a timely fashion. Coverage of the verdict was massive and on the day the verdict was announced the volume of trading on the New York Stock Exchange was down by two-thirds during the time the verdict was being announced. Public relations practitioners were telling their clients to hold major announcements for several days, unless they wanted to "bury" a story.[31]

In the aftermath of the trial and verdict, *Time* magazine suggested that Judge Ito's inability to control the trial could mean that "TV may cease to be a fixture in American courtrooms." The judge in the re-trial of Erik and Lyle Menendez, who were accused of murdering their parents, excluded cameras from his courtroom. Even during the trial, other judges decided against allowing cameras in their courts. The cases of Susan Smith, found guilty of murdering her sons by drowning them, and the kidnaping murder case of Polly Klaas, were conducted without courtroom cameras.

Even so, Fred Goldman, the father of Ronald Goldman, later argued for cameras in the courtroom. Goldman was quoted in the *San Francisco Examiner* saying, "I'm glad cameras were there so that everyone could have a chance to see what can actually take place inside a courtroom." Many blamed Ito's failure to control his courtroom on the presence of the camera. But Goldman said that the camera showed what took place in the trial. "Here is the one place in our country where the principles of justice and fairness are supposed to be paramount and everyone could see for themselves how quickly that dishonesty and deceit can take the upper hand. I think it disturbed everyone in the country."[32]

A TRADITION OF PUBLIC PROCEEDINGS

Given the bloody English heritage of secret Star Chamber trials, secret court proceedings are very much against the American grain. The English tradition of public trials was transplanted to American shores during the colonial period. That English tradition arose as did the English Common Law, built upon the history and practices of the people and government which lives today.

> A man can only be accused of a civil or criminal offence which is clearly defined and known to the law. The judge is an umpire. He adjudicates on such evidence as the parties choose to produce. Witnesses must testify in public and on oath. They are examined and cross-examined, not by the judge, but by the litigants themselves or their legally qualified representatives. The truth of their testimony is weighed not by the judge but by twelve good men and true, and it is only when this jury has

[31] Wall Street Journal News Roundup, "Little Work Got Done Yesterday at 1 p.m.," *Wall Street Journal*, Oct. 4, 1995.

[32] Craig Marine, "Goldman Lashes Out at Ito Blasts Most of the Players of Criminal Trial in His Book," *San Francisco Examiner*, Feb. 26, 1997.

> determined the facts that the judge is empowered to impose sentence, punishment, or penalty according to law.[33]

But compare that to the Civil Code approach, employed by most European countries. Louisiana has the Civil Code as part of its legacy from French colonization. The Civil Code, otherwise known as Roman Law was derived from the Justinian Code. Winston Churchill described the differences between the two in the excerpt above and the unflattering description below.

> Under Roman law, and systems derived from it, a trial in those turbulent centuries, and in some countries even to-day, is often an inquisition. The judge makes his own investigation into the civil wrong or the public crime, and such investigation is largely uncontrolled. The suspect can be interrogated in private. He must answer all questions put to him. His right to be represented by a legal adviser is restricted. Witnesses against him can testify in secret and in his absence. And only when these processes have been accomplished is the accusation or charge against him formulated and published.[34]

Advocates of Civil Code point to the service of justice through a professional judiciary that makes the pursuit of truth more efficient and less prone to distortion from advocates who serve a particular party rather than the truth. Advocates of the Common law approach point to the protections of individual rights from abuses by government authority. The clash of advocates will more likely lead to the discovery of the truth rather than relying on a disinterested judiciary. And so, in the United States, we continue to rely on judges and juries to reach the truth. The issue for professional communicators is the extent to which we have access to those legal proceedings in order to report them to the public.

NATIONAL SECURITY AND SECRET JUSTICE

The Sept. 11, 2001, attacks changed many people's ideas about the need for public scrutiny of the legal process in the face of a determined and elusive enemy. Many prosecutors, judges and legal scholars concluded that news of detentions, arrests and prosecutions would give terrorist valuable information as to the status of their operations in the United States. As the government would have no way of knowing which detainees or defendants might be involved in terrorism and therefore of interest to terrorist groups, the government decided to try to keep all information about such cases secret. This secrecy applied to the proceedings themselves and even the public record of the existence of such proceedings.

---

[33] Winston S. Churchill, *The Birth of Britain, A History of the English Speaking Peoples*, (New York, Barnes & Noble, 1993) p. 222.

[34] Ibid.

Opponents of secrecy in justice argued that such practices were antithetical to the notion of public justice and public accountability. They argued that terrorists might be able to figure out from the disappearance of their confederates that something had gone wrong. In addition, they said, innocent persons would be caught up in the process and the lack of public scrutiny would permit violations of their rights and the basic tenets of American justice. America ought not to sacrifice its principles out of fear.

Two cases dealing with access to deportation hearings[35] resulted in diametrically opposed results. In the 6th Circuit, the *Detroit Free Press* brought one of the few media-led challenges to secrecy in deportation proceedings, winning the support of the three-judge panel in favor of access.

The 6th Circuit opinion began with a recognition of the power of Congress to set immigration policy, unfettered by judicial review and the responsibility of the executive branch to conduct immigration proceedings under immigration judges who work within that purview. And so, Congress has exercised its powers to exclude non-citizens because it concluded that their race or habits made them undesirable as citizens or their former associations branded them as undesirable.[36] Any review of the government's action or check on perceived abuses comes from the power of an informed citizenry, the panel wrote:[37]

> While the Bill of Rights jealously protects citizens from such laws, it has never protected citizens facing deportation in the same way. In our democracy, based on checks and balances, neither the Bill of Rights nor the judiciary can second-guess government's choices. The only safeguard on this extraordinary power is the public, deputizing the press as the guardians of their liberty.

Senior Judge Damon J. Keith employed strong language in his opinion for the panel, repeating words from First Amendment landmark decision *Grosjean v. American Press Co.* that "[a]n informed public is the most potent of all restraints upon misgovernment."[38]

Judge Keith wrote that the Executive Branch was seeking to eliminate that safeguard in conducting immigration proceedings away

[35] Days after the Sept. 11 attacks, Chief Immigration Judge Michael Creppy issued a directive to all immigration judges. The directive required that all "special interest" cases be closed to view. The closure is effective against the press, the public, family members and friends of deportees. The limitations include disclosure of whether a deportation case is scheduled for a hearing or on the docket. The only persons permitted knowledge of the proceeding are the deportee's attorney or representative. The Administration also has withheld the identities, numbers, and locations of persons it has detained.

[36] *Wong Wing v. U.S.*, 163 U.S. 228, 16 S.Ct. 977 (1896); *Chan Chae: Ping v. U.S.*, 130 U.S. 581, 9 S.Ct. 623 (1889), and *Harisiades v. Shaughnessy*, 342 U.S. 580, 72 S.Ct. 512 (1952).

[37] *Detroit Free Press v. Ashcroft*, 303 F.3d 681, 683, 30 Med.L.Rptr. 2313 (6th Cir.2002).

[38] Ibid. Quoting *Grosjean v. American Press Co.*, 297 U.S. 233, 250, 56 S.Ct. 444 (1936).

from public scrutiny against people in what it designated as "special interest" cases.[39] He wrote:

> The Executive Branch seeks to uproot people's lives, outside the public eye, and behind a closed door. Democracies die behind closed doors. The First Amendment, through a free press, protects the people's right to know that government acts fairly, lawfully and accurately in deportation proceedings. When government begins closing doors, it selectively controls information rightfully belonging to the people. Selective information is misinformation. The Framers of the First Amendment "did not trust any government to separate the true from the false for us."[40]

Relying on well-settled law on public access to trials,[41] the district court and the 6th Circuit panel ruled that the press had a First Amendment right of access to the hearings. While Judge Keith acknowledged the plenary power of the executive branch and of Congress in deciding who could immigrate and who could be excluded, that power was not unlimited. It did not, Judge Keith reasoned, allow the government to place restrictions on the First Amendment.

Judge Keith noted that the Supreme Court had placed limits on deportation proceedings where they had been found to violate fundamental due process. In *Kwock Jan Fat v. White*, a man of Chinese descent who claimed he was a U.S. citizen was subject to a deportation proceeding and prevented from entering the United States on the basis of anonymous information received by immigration officials. In reversing the exclusion order and remanding the case for reconsideration, Justice Clarke wrote for the Supreme Court in 1921:[42]

> The acts of Congress give great power to the Secretary of Labor over Chinese immigrants and persons of Chinese descent. It is a power to be administered, not arbitrarily and secretly, but fairly and openly, under the restraints of the tradition and principles of free government applicable where the fundamental rights of men are involved, regardless of their origin or race.

Judge Keith wrote that the Supreme Court had found that other Constitutional rights had been applied to deportation proceedings, notwithstanding the power of Congress and the executive branches to operate immigration courts. Judge Keith acknowledged the special circumstances of the war on terrorism. But he also pointed to the application to the numbers of cases involved, the fact that the directive closing the hearings without setting out standards for placing deportees

---

[39] Ibid.

[40] Quoting *Kleindienst v. Mandel*, 408 U.S. 753, 773, 92 S.Ct. 2576, 33 L.Ed.2d 683 (1972).

[41] Chiefly, *Richmond Newspapers, Inc. v. Virginia*, 448 U.S. 555, 100 S.Ct. 2814, 65 L.Ed.2d 973 (1980).

[42] *Kwock Jan Fat v. White*, 253 U.S. 454, at 464, 40 S.Ct. 566, 64 L.Ed. 1010 (1920).

in the category for closure and the government's tacit admission that persons with no links to terrorism would be included in closed hearings. The government has more targeted methods for keeping secret what needs to be kept secret, Judge Keith concluded. Closure would be warranted only on a showing of the need for secrecy. Constitutional rights, Judge Keith reasoned, cannot be swept away in the name of security.[43]

> The word "security" is a broad, vague generality whose contours should not be invoked to abrogate the fundamental law embodied in the First Amendment. The guarding of military and diplomatic secrets at the expense of informed representative government provides no real security for our Republic.

The 6th Circuit panel found for a right of access and affirmed the lower court's grant of an injunction against closure.

The 3rd Circuit reached the opposite conclusion in *North Jersey Media Group v. Ashcroft*.[44] In *North Jersey*, a group of media concerns sued to get access to "special interest" deportation proceedings based on the constitutional right of access to trials, specifically as articulated in the *Richmond Newspapers* case.[45]

In *North Jersey Media Group v. Ashcroft*, the district court found in favor of the media group and against government, concluding that openness should prevail. On appeal, however, a split panel of the 3rd Circuit held—despite the open trials precedent set by the U.S. Supreme Court in *Richmond Newspapers*—that courts should defer to the government's judgment about the need for secrecy in the war on terrorism. The 3rd Circuit focused on declaration filed by Dale Watson, Counterterrorism Chief of the Federal Bureau of Investigation, which laid out the government's concern.[46]

> In brief, the Watson Declaration represents that insight gleaned from open proceedings might alert vigilant terrorists to the United States' investigative tactics and could easily betray what knowledge the government does—or does not—possess. Watson submits that even details that seem innocuous in isolation, such as the names of those detained, might be pieced together by knowledgeable persons within the terrorist network, who could in turn shift activities to a yet-undiscovered terrorist cell. Because immigration judges cannot be expected accurately to assess the harm that might result from disclosing seemingly

---

[43] *Detroit Free Press v. Ashcroft*, 303 F.3d 681, 693, 30 Med.L.Rptr. 2313 (6th Cir. 2002), quoting the concurring opinion of Justice Black in the Pentagon Papers case, *New York Times Co. v. United States*, 403 U.S. 713, 717, 91 S.Ct. 2140, 29 L.Ed.2d 822.

[44] *North Jersey Media Group v. Ashcroft*, 308 F.3d 198, 200 (3d Cir. 2002).

[45] *Richmond Newspapers, Inc. v. Virginia*, 448 U.S. 555, 100 S.Ct. 2814, 65 L.Ed.2d 973 (1980).

[46] *North Jersey Media Group v. Ashcroft*, 308 F.3d 198, 200 (3d Cir. 2002).

trivial facts, Watson explains, seeking closure on a case-by-case basis would ineffectively protect the nation's interests.

The 3rd Circuit ruling held that a balancing between the good of allowing access to proceedings versus their potential harm was required and the panel majority concluded that the potential harm had the greater weight.

While the 3rd Circuit looked to the decision in the 6th Circuit holding in favor of access to the "special interest" deportation hearings, the 3rd Circuit court concluded from its own examination of immigration proceedings and case law that there was no First Amendment right of access.

The Supreme Court declined to hear the case[47] and left the split of authority between the two circuits. It allowed the federal government to continue to conduct secret proceedings in the Third Circuit while keeping such cases open in the Sixth Circuit. The federal government chooses where to try such cases.

53. Free Press Versus Fair Trial

Attorneys, judges and members of the press continue to try to settle long-standing issues in the "free press—fair trial" dispute.

Back in the 1960s, "trial by newspaper" or "trial by mass media" were phrases which were often heard as the bar-press controversy steamed up. Some attorneys blamed the mass media for many of the shortcomings of the American court system.[48] In reply, many journalists went to great lengths in trying to justify questionable actions of the news media in covering criminal trials.[49]

Many of the lawyers' arguments contained the assertion that the media were destroying the rights of defendants by publicizing cases before they got to court. Such publicity, it was said, prejudiced potential jurors to such an extent that a fair trial was not possible. Editors and publishers—and some attorneys, too—retorted that the media were not harmful, and contended with passion if not historical accuracy that the First Amendment's free press guarantees took precedence over other Constitutional provisions, including the Sixth Amendment.[50]

More than a century ago, Mark Twain asserted that when Alfred the Great invented trial by jury, news could not travel fast. Therefore, he could easily find a jury of honest, intelligent men who had not heard of

---

47 *North Jersey Media Group v. Ashcroft*, 538 U.S. 1056, 123 S.Ct. 2215 (2003).

48 See, e.g., Advisory Committee on Fair Trial and Free Press, Standards Relating to Fair Trial and Free Press (New York, 1966); see also draft approved Feb. 19, 1968, by delegates to the American Bar Association convention as published in March, 1968.

49 See, e.g., American Newspaper Publishers Association, Free Press and Fair Trial (New York): American Newspaper Publishers Association, 1967, p. 1 and passim.

50 American Newspaper Publishers Association, op. cit., p. 1.

the case they were to try. Mark Twain swore that with newspapers and the telegraph, the jury system "compels us to swear in juries composed of fools and rascals, because the system rigidly excludes honest men and men of brains."[51]

Actually, Mark Twain had the history of the jury system wrong. The jury began in Eleventh Century England, utilizing a defendant's neighbors who were called to serve both as witnesses and as arbiters of fact. It was not until several centuries later that juries stopped serving as witnesses and served only as triers of fact. In addition, Twain's Nineteenth Century exaggeration does not apply to jury selection procedures in the last quarter of the Twentieth Century. Jurors need not be absolutely ignorant of—or completely unbiased about—a case which is to go to trial. If jurors can set aside their prejudices and biases, and keep an open mind, that is sufficient.[52]

During the past five decades, the free press-fair trial controversy took place against a backdrop of several sensational, nationally publicized trials and the assassinations of President John F. Kennedy in 1963 and Senator Robert Kennedy and Martin Luther King in 1968. Resultant disputes arrayed the media's right to report against defendants' rights to a fair trial, generated new law in the form of several important Supreme Court decisions, and brought forth efforts to make rules to regularize dealings between the media and law enforcement officials.[53]

The assassination of President Kennedy brought problems of "trial by mass media" dramatically to public consciousness. That fact was underscored by the report of a Presidential Commission headed by Chief Justice Earl Warren. The Warren Commission was intensely critical of both the Dallas police and the news media for the reports of the news of that event. The accused assassin, Lee Harvey Oswald, never lived to stand trial, because he himself was assassinated by Jack Ruby in a hallway of Dallas police headquarters. The hallway was a scene of confusion, clogged with reporters, cameramen, and the curious.[54]

The month after Kennedy's slaying, the American Bar Association charged that "widespread publicizing of Lee Harvey Oswald's alleged guilt, involving statements by officials and public disclosures of the details of 'evidence' would have made it extremely difficult to impanel an

---

[51] Mark Twain, *Roughing It* (New York: New American Library, Signet Paperback, 1962), pp. 256–257.

[52] Rita J. Simon, *The Jury: Its Role in American Society* (Lexington, Mass. D.C. Health and Company, 1980), p. 5; *Murphy v. Florida*, 421 U.S. 794, 95 S.Ct. 2031 (1975).

[53] See Advisory Committee on Fair Trial and Free Press, op. cit., passim; see also *Irvin v. Dowd*, 366 U.S. 717, 81 S.Ct. 1639 (1961); *Rideau v. Louisiana*, 373 U.S. 723, 83 S.Ct. 1417 (1963); *Sheppard v. Maxwell*, 384 U.S. 333, 86 S.Ct. 1507 (1966).

[54] Report of the President's Commission on the Assassination of President John F. Kennedy (Washington: Government Printing Office, 1964), p. 241.

unprejudiced jury and afford the accused a fair trial."[55] Indeed, had Oswald survived to stand trial, he might not have been convicted. This was so even though the Warren Commission—after the fact—declared that Oswald was in all likelihood Kennedy's killer. Under American judicial procedures, it seems possible that Oswald could not have received a fair and unprejudiced trial, and that any conviction of him might have been upset on appeal.[56]

The Warren Commission placed first blame on police and prosecutors, but additionally criticized the media for their part in the events following the President's death. The Commission said that "part of the responsibility for the unfortunate circumstances following the President's death must be borne by the news media * * * ." Journalists were excoriated by Commission members for showing a lack of self-discipline, and a code of professional conduct was called for as evidence that the press was willing to support the Sixth Amendment right to a fair and impartial trial as well as the right of the public to be informed.[57]

The ABA's Code of Professional Responsibility says that lawyers who are involved in a criminal matter shall not make "extra-judicial statements" to the news media which go beyond unadorned factual statements.

Lawyers, again, are allowed to make general statements outside of court about "the general nature of the charges against the accused." This makes it possible for defense lawyers to try to counterbalance harmful pre-trial publicity against their clients. Lawyers, however, must refrain from making statements which are substantially likely to prejudice a criminal proceeding.

Reporters are not the only offenders in disrupting trials. A quick skimming of the General Index of a legal encyclopedia, *American Jurisprudence,* adds support for such a generalization. The General Index of "Amjur" contains nearly 1,000 categories under the topic, "New Trial." New trials may be granted because something went awry in the original trial, somehow depriving a defendant of the right to a fair trial under the Sixth Amendment. These categories include such things as persons fainting in the courtroom, hissing, technical mistakes by attorneys, prejudice of judges, and misconduct by jurors: Jurors who read newspapers, sleep or do other things that show that they will not fulfill their responsibilities.[58]

---

[55] William A. Hachten, *The Supreme Court on Freedom of the Press: Decisions and Dissents* (Ames, Iowa: Iowa State University Press, 1968), p. 106.

[56] Ibid.

[57] Report of the President's Commission on the Assassination of President John F. Kennedy, p. 241.

[58] 3 *American Jurisprudence,* Gen.Index, New Trial.

Findings of social scientists lend modest support to assumptions about jurors being prejudiced by the mass media.[59] Much more research, however, remains to be done before assertions can be made confidently that what a juror reads or learns from the mass media will affect the juror's subsequent behavior. On the other hand, it has been argued that lawyers, before casting aspersions at the press, might consider the question of whether their own legal house is in order.

Consider what psychologists can tell lawyers about a fair trial. Consider the rules of procedure in a criminal trial in many states as attorneys make their final arguments to a jury. First, the prosecution sums up its case. Then the defense attorney makes the final argument. And last, the prosecuting attorney makes the final statement to the jury. For years, psychologists have been arguing about order of presentation in persuasion. Some evidence has been found that having the first say is most persuasive; there is other evidence that having the last word might be best.[60] But in many jurisdictions, who gets neither the first say nor the last word during the final arguments before a jury? The defendant.[61]

Whatever the results, the impact of community sentiment on juries can best be explained by the *voir dire* examination of a prospective juror in the murder case that led to *Patton v. Yount*. The wife of a local minister, called as part of the pool of prospective jurors, known as the veniremen, was asked about talk in her community about the case.

> Q. Would your presence in serving as a juror create a difficulty in your parish?
>
> A. Why yes—when people heard my name on for this—countless people of the church have come to me and said they hoped I would take—the stand I would take in case I was called. I have had a prejudice built up from the people in the church.
>
> Q. Is this prejudice, has it been adverse to Mr. Yount?
>
> A. Yes it was. They all say he had a fair trial and he got a fair sentence. He's lucky he didn't get the chair.
>
> * * *

54. PRE-TRIAL PUBLICITY

Pre-trial publicity which makes it difficult—if not impossible—for a defendant to receive a fair trial was summed up in the

---

[59] See, e.g., Mary Dee Tans and Steven H. Chaffee, "Pretrial Publicity and Juror Prejudice," *Journalism Quarterly* Vol. 43:4 (Winter, 1966), pp. 647–654, and a list of juror prejudice studies on p. 647, notes 4, 5 and 6. But see Don R. Pember, "Does Pretrial Publicity Really Hurt?" *Columbia Journalism Review*, Sept./Oct. 1984, p. 16.

[60] See, e.g., Carl I. Hovland, et al., *The Order of Presentation in Persuasion*, (New Haven: Yale, 1957) passim.

[61] The authors are grateful to Professors Jack M. McLeod and the late Steven H. Chaffee, of the University of Wisconsin Mass Communications Research Center and Stanford University, respectively, for this insight.

Supreme Court cases of *Irvin v. Dowd* and *Rideau v. Louisiana.*

"Pre-trial publicity" is a phrase which is a kind of shorthand expression meaning strain between the press and the courts. The kind of publicity which "tries" a defendant in print or over the air before the real courthouse trial starts—that's the issue here. This section discusses two classic instances of pre-trial publicity, instances in which the news media did not cover themselves with glory: *Irvin v. Dowd* and *Rideau v. Louisiana*. It also takes up the Supreme Court's subsequent treatment of the issue in *Murphy v. Florida* and *Patton v. Yount.*

IRVIN V. DOWD

The *Irvin* case represents the first time that the Supreme Court overturned a state criminal conviction because publicity before the trial had prevented a fair trial before an impartial jury.[62]

The defendant in this murder case, Leslie Irvin, was subjected to a barrage of prejudicial news items in the hysterical wake of six murders which had been committed in the vicinity of Evansville, Indiana. Two of the murders were committed in December, 1954, and four in March, 1955. These crimes were covered extensively by news media in the locality, and created great agitation in Vanderburgh County, where Evansville is located, and in adjoining Gibson County.[63]

Leslie Irvin, a parolee, was arrested in April, 1955, on suspicion of burglary and writing bad checks. Within a few days, the Evansville police and the Vanderburgh County prosecutor issued press releases asserting that "Mad Dog Irvin" had confessed to all six murders, including three members of one family. The news media had what can conservatively be described as a field day with the *Irvin* case, and were aided in this by law enforcement officials. Many of the accounts published or broadcast before Irvin's trial referred to him as the "confessed slayer of six." Irvin's court-appointed attorney was quoted as saying he had received much criticism for representing Irvin. The media, by way of excusing the attorney, noted that he faced disbarment if he refused to represent the suspect.[64]

Irvin was soon indicted by the Vanderburgh County Grand Jury for one of the six murders. Irvin's court-appointed counsel sought—and was granted—a change of venue. However, the venue change, under Indiana law, was made only from Vanderburgh County to adjoining Gibson County, which had received similar prejudicial accounts about "Mad Dog Irvin" from the news media in the Evansville vicinity.[65]

The trial began in November of 1955. Of 430 prospective jurors examined by the prosecution and defense attorneys, 370—nearly 90 per

---

62 Gilmore, op. cit., pp. 116–117.

63 *Irvin v. Dowd,* 366 U.S. 717, 719, 81 S.Ct. 1639, 1641 (1961).

64 366 U.S. 717, 725–726, 81 S.Ct. 1639, 1641, 1645 (1961); Gilmore, op. cit., p. 11.

65 366 U.S. 717, 720, 81 S.Ct. 1639, 1641 (1961).

cent—had formed some opinion about Irvin's guilt. These opinions ranged from mere suspicion to absolute certainty.[66] Irvin's attorney had used up all of his 20 peremptory challenges. When 12 jurors were finally seated by the court, the attorney then unsuccessfully challenged all jurors on grounds that they were biased. He complained bitterly that four of the seated jurors had stated that Irvin was guilty.[67] Even so, the trial was held, Irvin was found guilty, and the jury sentenced him to death. Irvin's conviction was upheld by the Indiana Supreme Court, which denied his motions for a new trial.[68] Lengthy appeals brought Irvin's case to the Supreme Court of the United States twice,[69] but his case was not decided on its merits by the nation's highest court until 1961.

Then, in 1961, all nine members of the Supreme Court agreed that Irvin had not received a fair trial. The upshot of this was that Irvin received a new trial, although he was ultimately convicted. This time, however, his sentence was set at life imprisonment.[70]

In his majority opinion, Justice Tom C. Clark—a former attorney general of the United States—concentrated on the effect of prejudicial publicity on a defendant's rights. Clark noted that courts do not require that jurors be totally ignorant of the facts and issues involved in a criminal trial. It is sufficient if a juror can render a verdict based on the evidence presented in court.[71]

Justice Clark then considered the publicity Irvin had received, and concluded: "Here the build-up of prejudice is clear and convincing." He noted that arguments for Irvin presented evidence that "a barrage of newspaper headlines, articles, cartoons and pictures was unleashed against him during the six or seven months before his trial" in Gibson County, Indiana. Furthermore, "Evansville radio and TV stations, which likewise blanketed the county, also carried extensive newscasts covering the same incidents."[72]

TRIAL BY TELEVISION: RIDEAU V. LOUISIANA

If Leslie Irvin was mistreated primarily by newspapers during the period before his trial, Wilbert Rideau found that television was the major offender in interfering with his right to a fair trial. Early in 1961,

---

[66] 366 U.S. 717, 727, 81 S.Ct. 1639, 1645 (1961).

[67] 359 U.S. 394, 398, 79 S.Ct. 825, 828 (1959).

[68] *Irvin v. State*, 236 Ind. 384, 139 N.E.2d 898 (1957).

[69] Irvin's appeal for a writ of *habeas corpus* to a Federal District Court was denied on the basis that he had not exhausted his opportunities to appeal through the Indiana courts. 153 F.Supp. 531 (N.D.Ind.1957). A United States Court of Appeals affirmed the dismissal of the writ, 251 F.2d 548 (7th Cir.1958). In a 5–4 decision in 1959, the Supreme Court of the United States sent Irvin's case back to the Federal Court of Appeals for reconsideration. 359 U.S. 394, 79 S.Ct. 825 (1959). The Court of Appeals again refused to grant a writ of *habeas corpus* to Irvin, 271 F.2d 552 (7th Cir.1959). Irvin's case was then appealed to the Supreme Court for the second time.

[70] Gilmore, op. cit., pp. 11–12.

[71] *Irvin v. Dowd*, 366 U.S. 717, 723, 81 S.Ct. 1639, 1642–1643 (1961).

[72] Ibid. at 725, 1644.

a Lake Charles, Louisiana, bank was robbed. The robber kidnaped three of the bank's employees and killed one of them. Several hours later, Wilbert Rideau was arrested by police and held in the Calcasieu Parish jail in Lake Charles. The next morning, a moving picture—complete with a sound track—was made of a 20-minute "interview" between Rideau and the Sheriff of Calcasieu Parish. The Sheriff interrogated the prisoner and elicited admissions that Rideau had committed the bank robbery, the kidnaping, and the murder. Later in the day, this filmed interview was broadcast over television station KLPC in Lake Charles. Over three days' time, the film was televised on three occasions to an estimated total audience of 97,000 persons, as compared to the approximately 150,000 persons then living in Calcasieu Parish.[73]

Rideau's attorneys subsequently sought a change of venue away from Calcasieu Parish. It was argued that it would take away Rideau's right to a fair trial if he were tried there after the three television broadcasts of Rideau's "interview" with the sheriff. The motion for change of venue was denied, and Rideau was convicted and sentenced to death on the murder charge in the Calcasieu Parish trial court. The conviction was affirmed by the Louisiana Supreme Court,[74] but the Supreme Court of the United States granted *certiorari*.[75]

Justice Potter Stewart's majority opinion noted that three of the 12 jurors had stated during *voir dire* examination before the trial that they had seen and heard Rideau's "interview" with the Sheriff. Also, two members of the jury were Calcasieu Parish deputy sheriffs. Although Rideau's attorney challenged the deputies, asking that they be removed "for cause," the trial judge denied this request. Since Rideau's lawyers had exhausted his "peremptory challenges"—those for which no reason need be given—the deputies remained on the jury.[76]

Justice Stewart noted that the *Rideau* case did not involve physical brutality. However, he declared that the "kangaroo court proceedings in this case involved a more subtle but no less real deprivation of due process of law." Justice Stewart added:[77]

> * * * In this case the people of Calcasieu Parish saw and heard, not once but three times, a "trial" of Rideau in a jail, presided over by a sheriff, where there was no lawyer to advise Rideau of his right to stand mute.

Rideau's conviction was reversed, and a new trial was ordered by the Supreme Court. He was convicted again, sentenced to life imprisonment, and became well known again, this time as a journalist writing about prison conditions from inside the walls.

---

73 *Rideau v. Louisiana*, 373 U.S. 723, 724, 83 S.Ct. 1417, 1419 (1963).

74 *Rideau v. Louisiana*, 242 La. 431, 137 So.2d 283 (1962).

75 *Rideau v. Louisiana*, 371 U.S. 919, 83 S.Ct. 294 (1962).

76 *Rideau v. Louisiana*, 373 U.S. 723, 725, 83 S.Ct. 1417, 1418 (1963).

77 Ibid. at 727, 1419.

THE SUPREME COURT TAKES ANOTHER LOOK

There is no denying that prejudicial pre-trial publicity may deny a defendant a fair trial and provide a constitutional reason to reverse his conviction. But in 1975 and 1984, the Supreme Court took a step back in its consideration of pre-trial publicity. In *Murphy v. Florida,*[78] the Court was called on to consider the conviction of Jack Roland Murphy for robbery. Murphy argued that the jury that tried him had been prejudiced by news coverage that included references to his prior felony convictions and details of the crime he was being put on trial for.

Jack Murphy was already well known. Murphy, known as "Murph the Surf," had been involved in the 1964 theft of the Star of India sapphire from a New York Museum. His lifestyle, described by the Court as "flamboyant" had made him a popular media subject. Murphy had been charged with the robbery of a Miami Beach home. Before going on trial, he was indicted on two counts of murder. He also was indicted by a federal grand jury on a charge of conspiring to transport stolen securities in interstate commerce. Jury selection began with the summoning of 78 prospective jurors. Thirty were excused for various personal reasons, 20 were dismissed on peremptory challenges by prosecution and defense, and 20 more were excused by the court for have prejudged Murphy's guilt. The remaining eight served as the jury and two alternates.

Murphy tried to have the jury dismissed because it was aware of his connection with the Star of India theft and or the murder charges. When his motion was denied, Murphy refused to put on a defense. He did not testify and he did not cross examine any of the state's witnesses. He was convicted.

The Supreme Court, in an opinion by Thurgood Marshall, denied Murphy's contention that the jurors' knowledge of his prior crime and criminal charges denied him a fair trial. Acknowledging that the Constitution required a panel of "impartial" and "indifferent" jurors, Marshall wrote, "Qualified jurors need not, however, be totally ignorant of the facts and issues involved."[79] Marshall quoted from the opinion in *Dowd*:

> "To hold that the mere existence of any preconceived notion as to the guilt or innocence of an accused, without more, is sufficient to rebut the presumption of a prospective juror's impartiality would be to establish an impossible standard. It is sufficient if the juror can lay aside his impression or opinion and render a verdict based on the evidence presented in court."[80]

The Court looked at the *voir dire* process of questioning the prospective jurors and found no evidence that any member of the seated

[78] *Murphy v. Florida,* 421 U.S. 794, 95 S.Ct. 2031 (1975), 1 Med.L.Rptr. 1232.

[79] Ibid. at 799–800, 2036.

[80] *Irvin v. Dowd,* 366 U.S. 717, 723, 81 S.Ct. 1639, 1643–1644.

jury held a prejudiced view of Murphy's guilt. "Some of the jurors had a vague recollection of the robbery with which the petitioner was charged and each had some knowledge of petitioner's past crimes, but none betrayed any belief in the relevance of petitioner's past to the present crime."[81] This was radically different from *Dowd* in which 90 percent of the prospective jurors said they believed Dowd was guilty. Only 20 of the 78 called to the jury pool indicated enough prejudice to be excused, a little more than 25 percent. Chief Justice Burger noted the failure of the trial court to protect jurors from media coverage but still concurred in the result. Justice Brennan dissented.

In 1984, the Court was called on to consider once again the amount of information and bias that individual jurors could bear and still serve. In *Patton v. Yount,*[82] the Court was faced with a challenge to a conviction for rape and murder. Jon E. Yount was convicted of the rape and murder of 18-year-old Pamela Rimer. Yount, who had been Rimer's math teacher, turned himself in and gave police and oral and written confession. At his trial, Yount claimed temporary insanity but was convicted. Because Yount had not been advised of his Miranda rights, the Pennsylvania Supreme Court ordered a new trial. The trial judge ordered Yount's confession suppressed and the district attorney dismissed the rape charge.

The court then conducted extensive *voir dire*, interviewing 292 prospective jurors before seating a jury panel. Yount's attorneys sought a change of venue arguing that the widespread publicity the case and its predecessor would make it impossible for jurors to forget what they knew and decide the case on its own merits. The court denied the motion and said that the publicity surrounding the case was made up of stories that "merely reported events without editorial comment."[83] Yount was convicted again and appealed.

The Third Circuit Court of Appeals reversed his conviction saying that the pre-trial publicity had made it impossible for Yount to get a fair trial in Clearfield County. The Third Circuit noted that all but 163 of the prospective jurors questioned had heard of Yount's prior confession, plea of insanity and conviction (Most of the other jurors had been excused before individual questioning began. Four had been dismissed for cause before being questioned.). Of the 163 jurors questioned, 126, or 77 percent, "admitted they would carry an opinion into the jury box."[84] The court noted that one juror, a Mr. Hrin, and both alternates indicated in their responses to *voir dire* that they would have required evidence to overcome their beliefs about Yount's guilt. The Third Circuit opinion referred extensively to *Dowd.*

---

81 *Murphy v. Florida,* 421 U.S. 794, 800, 95 S.Ct. 2031, 2036 (1975).

82 467 U.S. 1025, 104 S.Ct. 2885 (1984).

83 Ibid. at 1027–1028, 2887.

84 Ibid.

The case then came before the Supreme Court which reversed the Third Circuit and upheld Yount's conviction.[85] First, the Court looked to the pre-trial publicity and found that there had been an average of less than one article a month in the two Clearview County newspapers in the 18 months between the reversal of Yount's first conviction and his second trial. The stories, the Court said, were not inflammatory and did not promote public passions against Yount. The passage of time had softened the prospective jurors' memories of the crime and previous case, the Court said.

Having disposed of the media's influence on the case, the Court in Justice Powell's opinion, turned to the Third Circuit's review of juror opinions.

> "The Court of Appeals * * * thought that the fact that the great majority of veniremen 'remembered the case' showed that time had not served to 'erase highly unfavorable publicity from the memory of [the] community.' 710 F.2d at 969. This conclusion, without more, is essentially irrelevant. The relevant question is not whether the community remembered the case, but whether the jurors at Yount's trial had such fixed opinions that they could not judge impartially the guilt of the defendant."[86]

Justice Powell pointed to the presumption of the impartiality of juries that attached to the *Yount* case. In part, that impartiality sprang from the *voir dire* process which has been used to determine the views of prospective jurors. Powell read the voir dire transcripts of the questioning of Hrin and the alternates and found no evidence of excludable bias.

Without a showing of "manifest error" in the selection of the jury, the appellate courts could not find that a defendant's fair trial rights were denied by pre-trial publicity.

The issue of pre-trial publicity played a significant part in the decision of *Playboy* magazine to publish it story about Timothy McVeigh's statement to his lawyers about his part in the bombing of the Murrah Federal Building in Oklahoma City. Reporter Ben Fenwick, who had covered the aftermath of the bombing for the Reuters News Service and others, gained access to a number of documents prepared by the defense, including a chronology of the events leading to the bombing itself. The documents included McVeigh's telling of his part in the attack that killed 168 men, women and children.

But Fenwick realized that because of the nature of the document he held, that the presiding judge could impose a prior restraint on the story. Fenwick developed his story and held onto it even though it meant a delay of months in publication.

---

85 Justice Marshall did not take part in the case.

86 Ibid. at 1035, 2890.

After confidential consultations, he decided that it would be best to wait until presiding Judge Richard Matsch sequestered the jury before publishing. Once the jury was locked away, they would be shielded from any prejudicial effects of the story. But Matsch chose not to sequester the jury and he announced that well before the trial began. Matsch did order the prospective jurors not to read or watch anything about the case and so provided at least some protection. Then, as discussed in Chap. 2, the use of the Internet to circumvent the threat of prior restraint led to the publication of the story. Matsch's warning appeared to work. Only one juror was luckless enough to admit to having read something about the case. The woman told Matsch that she did not think she would be called and that was why she read a brief story about problems with the FBI crime lab. Matsch responded sternly, asking, "How can we trust you to comply with the court's instructions when you have already violated them?" Matsch told the woman, "You'll be hearing from me."[87]

55. PUBLICITY DURING TRIAL: CAMERAS IN THE COURTROOM

The notorious *Lindbergh* kidnapping trial of the 1930s and the *Estes* case of 1965 severely limited still and television cameras in the courtroom. Cameras have returned in many states under the Supreme Court's 1981 decision in *Chandler v. Florida*.

"The Lindbergh Case" and "the trial of Bruno Hauptmann" are phrases heard whenever the free press—fair trial debate heats up. These phrases, of course, refer to the kidnaping in 1932 of the 19-month-old son of the aviator famed for the first solo crossing of the Atlantic. The child's kidnaping was front-page news for weeks, long after the child's body was found in a shallow grave not far from the Lindbergh home in New Jersey.

More than two years later, in September, 1934, Bruno Richard Hauptmann was arrested. His trial for the kidnap-murder of the Lindbergh child did not begin until January, 1935. The courtroom where Hauptmann was tried had a press section jammed with 150 reporters. During the Hauptmann trial, which lasted more than a month, there were sometimes more than 700 newsmen in Flemington, N.J., the site of the trial.[88]

Judge Thomas Trenchard issued orders that photographs could only be taken in the courtroom when he was not on the bench, and only four photographers would be allowed in the courtroom at one time.[89] A cooperative darkroom was set up in a bakery two blocks away to provide

---

[87] Jo Thomas, "Questioning of Jury Prospects in Oklahoma Bombing Trial Ends," *New York Times*, April, 22, 1997.

[88] John Lofton, *Justice and the Press* (Boston: Beacon Press, 1966), pp. 103–104.

[89] Alfred N. Delahaye, "The Case of Bruno Hauptmann (1935)", in *The Press on Trial: Crimes and Trials as Media Event*, (Lloyd Chiasson Jr. ed. 1997), p. 120.

copies of courtroom pictures.[90] Five newsreel companies agreed to operate sound motion-picture cameras in the courtroom.[91] Judge Trenchard allowed them to film provided they showed no footage until after the verdict.[92] Radio broadcasters had to rely on microphones outside the courtroom.[93]

The trial was criticized for its "carnival-like atmosphere."[94] One newspaper headline screamed "The Flemington Circus—This Way to the Big Tent."[95] Outside the courthouse vendors sold toy replicas of the ladder Hauptmann allegedly used to kidnap young Lindbergh, bookends the shape of the courthouse and photographs of Col. Lindbergh with a forged signature.[96]

The Union Hotel in Flemington, N.J., had received messages from 900 people from all over the world requesting rooms for the duration of the Hauptmann trial, but most spectators had to settle for accommodations in Trenton 20 miles away.[97] Six rooms on the top floor had been reserved for the jury; and newspaper and radio reporters had commandeered the other vacancies long before the messages started arriving.[98]

Reporters arrived in Flemington to cover what many were calling the "trial of the century."[99] Among the more famous were Walter Winchell, Edna Ferber, Arthur Brisbane, Fannie Hurst, Damon Runyon, Kathleen Norris, Alexander Woollcott and Adela St. Rogers.[100] Ginger Rodgers, Lynn Fontanne, Clifton Webb, Jack Benny and Jack Dempsey were among the movie and sports celebrities who joined the spectacle.[101]

The court normally accommodated no more than 500 spectators and folding chairs were borrowed to squeeze in wherever possible.[102] A gallery looked down at the rear of the court where 150 reporters were seated with 18-inch pine boards serving as writing tables.[103]

The attorneys ran a daily gauntlet of hundreds of reporters and photographers outside the courthouse.[104] David Wilentz, the prosecuting

---

90 Ibid.

91 Ibid.

92 Marjorie Cohn and David Dow, *Cameras in the Courtroom: Television and the Pursuit of Justice* (McFarland. 1998) p. 15.

93 Delahaye, op. cit., p. 120.

94 Cohn and Dow, op. cit., p. 15.

95 Ibid.

96 Ibid. at, 16.

97 George Waller, "Bruno Hauptmann," in *The Mammoth Book of Famous Trials* (Roger Wilkes ed. 2006), p. 185.

98 Ibid.

99 Ibid.

100 Ibid. at, 186.

101 Cohn and Dow, op. cit., p. 15.

102 Waller, op. cit., p. 188.

103 Ibid.

104 Cohn and Dow, op. cit., p. 16.

attorney, held nightly press conferences in Trenton, and Edward J. Reilly, the lead defense attorney, was generally available in Flemington to answer questions.[105]

Media coverage of the trial was excessive.[106] The *New York Herald Tribune's* Joseph Alsop was under orders to file 10,000 words a day.[107] The Hearst Corporation paid Reilly, Hauptmann's defense attorney, a $25,000 retainer and signed Anna Hauptmann to a contract promising that she would speak only to the *New York Evening Journal*.[108]

In the aftermath of the Hauptmann trial, the press was severely criticized for its actions. Reporters were accused of invading people's privacy and newspapers were faulted for printing rumors convicting Hauptmann in their columns.[109] Inside the courtroom, reporters were partly responsible for the disruption by frequently sending copy out by messengers.[110] An editorial in *Editor & Publisher* blamed newspapers, radio and newsreels for their part in "degrading the administration of Justice."[111]

Much of the publicity of the Hauptmann trial was prejudicial, and lawyers and newsmen authored statements which were clearly inflammatory. Hauptmann was described in the press, for example, as a "thing lacking in human characteristics."[112] After the trial—and after Hauptmann's execution—a Special Committee on Cooperation Between the Press, Radio, and Bar was established to search for "standards of publicity in judicial proceedings and methods of obtaining an observance of them." In a grim report issued in 1937, the 18-man committee—including lawyers, editors, and publishers—termed Hauptmann's trial "the most spectacular and depressing example of improper publicity and professional misconduct ever presented to the people of the United States in a criminal trial."[113]

One result of the committee's investigation of the Hauptmann trial was the American Bar Association's adoption in 1937 of Canon 35 of its Canons of Professional Ethics. Canon 35 forbade taking photographs in the courtroom, including both actual court sessions and recesses. As updated, Canon 35 declared that broadcasting or televising court proceedings "detract from the essential dignity of the proceedings,

---

[105] Delahaye, op. cit., p. 127.

[106] Cohn and Dow, op. cit., p. 16.

[107] Ibid.

[108] Ibid.

[109] Richard Kielbowicz, "The Story Behind the Adoption of the Ban on Courtroom Cameras," 63 *Judicature*, 19 (1979).

[110] Ibid.

[111] Delahaye, op. cit., p. 127.

[112] Lofton, op. cit., p. 124.

[113] American Bar Association, "Report of Special Committee on Cooperation between Press, Radio and Bar," Annual Report, Volume 62, pp. 851–866 (1937), at p. 861. See, also, *New Jersey v. Hauptmann*, 115 N.J.L. 412, 180 A. 809 (Err. & App.1935), certiorari denied 296 U.S. 649, 56 S.Ct. 310 (1935).

distract the participants and witnesses in giving testimony, and create misconceptions * * * and should not be permitted." This was replaced by ABA Canon of Judicial Conduct 3(7):[114]

> A judge should prohibit broadcasting, televising, recording, or taking photographs in the courtroom and areas immediately thereto during sessions of court or recesses between sessions * * * The only exceptions involved situations when the judge had given permission, or the filming was to be used only for ceremonial or instructional purposes.

ESTES V. TEXAS

Excesses in televising a trial in Texas during the 1960s meant the end of televising virtually all criminal trials for a period of more than a decade. As is discussed later in this section, however, developments in the late 1970s—capped by the January, 1981 decision of the Supreme Court of the United States *in Chandler v. Florida*[115]—have seen a substantial movement toward getting both television and still cameras back into state courtrooms.

The crucial case of the 1960s involved the swindling trial of flamboyant Texas financier Billie Sol Estes. Estes was ultimately convicted, but not until he had received a new trial as a result of the manner in which a judge allowed his original trial to be photographed and televised. Fallout from the U.S. Supreme Court decision which granted Estes a new trial seemed to rule out cameras in the courtroom.[116]

Estes came before a judicial hearing in Smith County, Texas, in 1962, after a change of venue from Reeves County, some 500 miles west. The courtroom was packed and about 30 persons stood in the aisles. A *New York Times* story described the setting for the pre-trial hearing in this way:[117]

> A television motor van, big as an intercontinental bus, was parked outside the courthouse and the second-floor courtroom was a forest of equipment. Two television cameras have been set up inside the bar and four more marked cameras were aligned just outside the gates.
>
> * * *
>
> Cables and wires snaked over the floor.

---

[114] American Bar Association, Code of Professional Responsibility and Code of Judicial Conduct, p. 59C. For Canon 35, see ABA, Annual Report, Vol. 62, at p. 1134; see it as updated by Justice John Marshall Harlan in his concurring opinion in *Estes v. Texas*, 381 U.S. 532, 601, n., 85 S.Ct. 1628, 1669 n. (1965).

[115] *Chandler v. Florida*, 449 U.S. 560, 101 S.Ct. 802 (1981).

[116] *Estes v. Texas*, 381 U.S. 532, 85 S.Ct. 1628 (1965).

[117] *Estes v. Texas*, 381 U.S. 532, 553, 85 S.Ct. 1628, 1638 (1965), from Chief Justice Warren's concurring opinion, with which Justices Douglas and Goldberg concurred.

With photographers roaming unchecked about the courtroom, Estes' attorney moved that all cameras be excluded from the courtroom. As the attorney spoke, a cameraman walked behind the judge's bench and took a picture.[118]

After the two-day hearing was completed on Sept. 25, 1962, the judge granted a continuance (delay) to the defense, with the trial to begin on October 22. Meanwhile, the judge established ground rules for television and still photographers. Televising of the trial was allowed, with the exception of live coverage of the interrogation of prospective jurors or the testimony of witnesses. The major television networks, CBS, NBC, and ABC, plus local television station KLTV were each allowed to install one television camera (without sound recording equipment) and film was made available to other television stations on a pooled basis. In addition, through another pool arrangement, only still photographers for the Associated Press, United Press, and from the local newspaper would be permitted in the courtroom.

At its own expense, and with the permission of the court, KLTV built a booth at the back of the courtroom, painted the same color as the courtroom. An opening in the booth permitted all four television cameras to view the proceedings. However, in this small courtroom, the cameras were visible to all.[119]

Despite these limitations the judge placed on television and still photographers, a majority of the Supreme Court held that Estes had been deprived of a fair trial in violation of the due process clause of the Fourteenth Amendment. Chief Justice Warren and Justices Douglas, Goldberg, and Clark asserted that a fair trial could not be had when television is allowed in any criminal trial. Justice Harlan, the fifth member of the majority in this 5–4 decision, voted to overturn Estes' conviction because the case was one of "great notoriety." Even so, it should be noted that Harlan reserved judgment on the televising of more routine cases.

In delivering the opinion of the Court, Mr. Justice Clark wrote:[120]

> We start with the proposition that it is a "public trial" that the Sixth Amendment guarantees to the "accused." The purpose of the requirement of a public trial was to guarantee that the accused would be fairly dealt with and not unjustly condemned. * * *

Justice Clark then took aim on an assertion that if courts exclude television cameras or microphones, they are discriminating in favor of the print media. Clark retorted, "[t]he news reporter is not permitted to

[118] *Estes v. Texas,* 381 U.S. 532, 553, 85 S.Ct. 1628, 1638 (1965). From concurring opinion by Chief Justice Warren.

[119] *Estes v. Texas,* 381 U.S. 532, 554–555, 85 S.Ct. 1628, 1638–1639 (1965), from Chief Justice Warren's concurring opinion.

[120] Ibid. at 538–539, 1631.

bring his typewriter or printing press." Clark did concede that technical advances might someday make television equipment and cameras quieter and less obtrusive.[121]

In a strongly worded dissent, Justices Stewart, Black, Brennan and White raised constitutional arguments in objecting to the ban on television from courtrooms, at least at that stage of television's development. Justice Stewart expressed doubt that Estes had been deprived of a fair trial by the limited televising of it.[122]

Brennan argued that the *Estes* decision was "*not* a blanket constitutional prohibition against the televising of state criminal trials."[123] Television, said Brennan, was barred by the majority side of *Estes* only from "notorious trials." Nevertheless, from 1965 to 1975, cameras—including television cameras—were kept out of virtually *all* courtrooms.

CAMERAS IN THE COURTROOM

After 1975, cautious efforts to get cameras back in the courtroom became evident in a number of states. In 1977, the Associated Press Managing Editors Association published a report titled "Cameras in the Courtroom: How to Get 'Em There." The report noted that if "you're going to get your Nikon into that courtroom you've got to have more tools than just a camera. For one thing, you've got to have the clout of your State Supreme Court."

The report described a process, beginning with work with a bench-bar-press committee, through demonstrations and carefully regulated experimental photo and TV coverage of either mock or actual trials. Then, a demonstration videotape should be made for use before a hearing to be conducted by the state's supreme court. The final step is writing guidelines for court coverage for adoption by the state supreme court.[124]

Tentatively, a number of states began to allow television, radio and photographic coverage of judicial proceedings. Modern cameras, available-light photography, smaller and quieter television and camera gear: technological advances have helped get cameras back into many courtrooms. More important, however, has been intelligent negotiation by thoughtful members of bench, bar and press who realize that photography in the courtroom, properly used, can be a valuable tool for educating and informing the public.

By 2003, all states allowed some form of television, radio or photographic coverage on a permanent basis. Coverage, in general, is

---

[121] Ibid. at 540, 1631.

[122] 381 U.S. 532, 601–602, 85 S.Ct. 1628, 1669 (1965).

[123] 381 U.S. 532, 617, 85 S.Ct. 1628, 1678 (1965).

[124] Freedom of Information Committee, APME, "Cameras in the Courtroom: How to Get 'Em There," 1977 *Freedom of Information Report*, p. 2.

subject to judicial discretion even in states with the most liberal rules. Camera coverage was not allowed in the District of Columbia.[125]

CHANDLER V. FLORIDA: THE LOWER COURTS

A key case testing admission of cameras to courtrooms is *Chandler v. Florida.*[126] It raised the issue of whether admitting television cameras to a courtroom, over the objection of a participant in a criminal case, made a fair trial impossible.[127]

The *Chandler* case stated the issue in rather extreme form, because in jurisdictions where coverage is permitted, consent of parties is required in most instances.[128] The Supreme Court of the United States held early in 1981 that television coverage had not denied Chandler a fair trial.[129]

Chandler v. Florida also is important because of its interrelationship with another Florida matter, *In re Petition of Post-Newsweek Stations, Florida, Inc.,* for Change in Code of Judicial Conduct.[130] In that proceeding, the Supreme Court of Florida ruled that electronic media coverage of courtroom proceedings is not in itself a denial of due process of law. However, the court also held that the First and Sixth Amendments do not mandate the electronic media be allowed to cover courtroom proceedings. The Florida Supreme Court then issued a rule to amend 3A(7) of Florida's Code of Judicial Conduct to allow still photography and electronic media coverage of public judicial proceedings in the appellate and trial courts, subject at all times to the authority of the presiding judge.[131]

The *Post-Newsweek Stations* ruling, with its lengthy appendices spelling out the deployment of equipment and personnel, the kind of equipment to be used, and pooling arrangements for coverage to cut down on in court distractions, has been used elsewhere as a primer for drafting petitions to seek changes in state judicial rules.

CHANDLER V. FLORIDA: THE TRIAL

Chandler v. Florida involved the burglary trial of two Miami Beach policemen, Noel Chandler and Robert Granger. During their trial, the defendants raised various objections to Florida's [then] Experimental Canon 3A(7). Under that canon, despite requests from the defendants

---

[125] Radio-Television Digital News Association, "Freedom of Information, Cameras in the Court: A State-by-State Guide." http://www.rtdna.org/content/cameras_in_court.

[126] *Chandler v. State,* 366 So.2d 64 (Fla.App.1978), certiorari denied 376 So.2d 1157 (1979), probable juris. noted 446 U.S. 907, 100 S.Ct. 1832 (1980).

[127] 366 So.2d 64, 69 (Fla.App.1978).

[128] See Appendix 2, "Television in the Courtroom—Recent Developments," National Center for State Courts, quoted in entirety in *Petition of Post-Newsweek Stations, Florida, Inc.,* 370 So.2d 764 (Fla.1979).

[129] *Chandler v. Florida,* 449 U.S. 560, 101 S.Ct. 802 (1981).

[130] *In re Petition of Post-Newsweek Stations, Florida, Inc.,* 370 So.2d 764 (Fla.1979).

[131] Ibid. at 781.

that live television coverage be excluded, cameras were allowed to televise parts of the trial.[132]

The Supreme Court of Florida denied a petition for a writ of certiorari, asserting a lack of jurisdiction. That court said, "No conflict has been demonstrated, and the question of great public interest has been rendered moot by the decisions in *Petition of Post-Newsweek Stations, Florida, Inc.*, 370 So.2d 764 (Fla.1979)."

The Supreme Court of the United States, however, noted probable jurisdiction in *Chandler v. Florida* in 1980.[133]

CHANDLER V. FLORIDA: THE SUPREME COURT

In 1981, the Supreme Court of the United States decided *Chandler* by an 8–0 upholding the convictions of the two Miami Beach police officers for burglarizing Piccolo's Restaurant. This case—regardless of its outcome—would have been memorable for its fact situation. Officers Chandler and Grander had been chatting with each other via walkie-talkies as they broke into the restaurant; they were overheard by an insomniac ham radio operator who recorded their conversations.[134]

Writing for that unanimous Court, Chief Justice Burger based his decision on the principle of federalism. States may work out their own approaches to allowing photographic and broadcast coverage of trials, as long as the Constitution of the United States is not violated.

Chandler and Granger had argued that the very presence of television cameras violated their rights to a fair trial because cameras were psychologically disruptive.[135] Chief Justice Burger wrote for the Court:[136]

> An absolute Constitutional ban on broadcast coverage of trials cannot be justified simply because there is a danger in some cases that prejudicial broadcast accounts of pretrial and trial proceedings may impair the ability of jurors to decide the issue of guilt or innocence. * * * [T]he risk of juror prejudice does not warrant an absolute Constitutional ban on all broadcast coverage. * * *

After the U.S. Supreme Court decision in *Chandler,* states increasingly experimented with cameras in courtrooms. The ABA model code's Sec. 3A(7) opposing cameras never was mandatory in any state unless adopted formally by a state's highest court. But in 1990, the ABA abandoned Canon 3A(7) completely, removing it from the ABA's model

---

132 *Chandler v. State,* 366 So.2d 64, 69 (Fla.App.1978).

133 *Chandler v. Florida,* 446 U.S. 907, 100 S.Ct. 1832 (1980).

134 *Chandler v. Florida,* 449 U.S. 560, 101 S.Ct. 802 (1981).

135 *The News Media & The Law,* 5:1 (Feb./Mar.1981) p. 5.

136 *Chandler v. Florida,* 449 U.S. 560, 575, 101 S.Ct. 802, 810 (1981).

code of judicial conduct.[137] The reason? The American Bar Association backed off on grounds that the canon did not deal with judicial ethics but was more properly an issue to be governed by separate court rules.[138] Note, that states do not have to admit cameras or broadcast equipment: they *may* do so according to their own rules. Further, any judge who finds cameras disruptive may exclude them.

As the Court said in *Chandler,*[139]

> Dangers lurk in this, as in most, experiments, but unless we are to conclude that television coverage under all conditions is prohibited by the Constitution, the states must be free to experiment. * * * The risk of prejudice to particular defendants is ever present and must be examined carefully as cases arise.

CAMERAS IN FEDERAL COURTROOMS

Even with the *Chandler* decision, the federal courts have not been receptive to cameras. Chief Justice Burger is famously quoted as saying that there would be cameras in the Supreme Court, "over my dead body." Burger's sentiment was repeated by Justice David Souter in 1996, in the wake of the O.J. Simpson case.[140] "I think the case is so strong," Justice Souter said, "that I can tell you the day you see a camera come into our courtroom, it's going to roll over my dead body."

With the growing number of state courts permitting cameras in the court, several media organizations petitioned the Judicial Conference to allow cameras in federal courts. This was an attempt at providing more judicial transparency in the federal court system. The 27-member Judicial Conference, which was headed by Chief Justice William H. Rehnquist, consisted of the chief judges of the 13 federal appellate circuits and judges from district courts in each circuit.

In 1983, a coalition of 28 broadcasters, publishers, news organizations and others led by CBS, petitioned the Judicial Conference to ask for changes in Canon 3A(7) and Rule 53. The group suggested the Florida guidelines as a model since the Supreme Court in *Chandler* had supported them.[141] The initial request was denied, but the issue was brought up again after several court cases were brought challenging the federal prohibition of electronic media coverage. In 1990, the Judicial Conference authorized an experimental program. The conference's hostility to cameras in the courtroom was long-standing and well known,

---

[137] Kate Aschenbrenner Pate, "Restricting Electronic Media Coverage of Child-Witnesses: A Proposed Rule," *University of Chicago Legal Forum* 1993, pp. 352–353.

[138] Ibid. at 353, citing Lisa L. Milord, *The Development of The ABA Judicial Code*, p. 22 (ABA, 1992).

[139] *Chandler v. Florida,* 449 U.S. 560, 581, 101 S.Ct. 802, 813 (1981).

[140] "On Cameras in Supreme Court, Souter Says, 'Over My Dead Body,' " Associated Press, March 30, 1996.

[141] Jane E. Kirtley, " 'A Leap Not Supported by History:' The Continuing Story of Cameras in the Federal Courts," 12 *Government Information Quarterly* 4 (1995), p. 372.

so it was a surprise when the group approved the pilot project. That action came after prodding by Robert W. Kastenmeier, a former member of the House of Representatives from Wisconsin, who at the time headed the House Judiciary subcommittee that oversees the administration of the federal courts.[142] Taking part were the Southern District of Indiana, District of Massachusetts, Eastern District of Michigan, Southern District of Pennsylvania and Western District of Washington.[143]

A set of guidelines was devised to govern the pilot program. One still photographer with one camera, one television operator with one camera and one stationary sound person were allowed in criminal courts. Two television cameras and two operators were allowed in appellate courts. The equipment should not produce distracting sound or light, and changing lenses, film or tape during the proceedings was prohibited. Journalists were required to wear appropriate business attire. Logos and markings of the news organization were forbidden. Pooling or sharing of the material with members of the media without access was required. Coverage of the jurors was prohibited.[144]

The first case covered actually took place three weeks before the official start date of the experiment. On June 10, 1991, New York District Court Judge William Connor allowed a Court TV crew in to cover a copyright dispute between the estate of actor James Dean and photographer Roy Schatt over fees for marketing Dean's image. Judge Connor said, "After a few hours you forget the camera is even there."[145]

The Federal Judicial Center, the research arm of the Judicial Conference, was charged with monitoring the experiment and providing a report at the end of the three-year experiment.[146] The report was favorable and stated that the attitudes of judges toward electronic media coverage of civil proceedings were initially neutral and became more favorable after experience under the pilot program and judges and attorneys generally reported observing small or no effects of camera presence on participants in the proceedings, courtroom decorum, or the administration of justice.[147] The report recommended that the Judicial Conference permanently extend coverage to civil trials in federal courts.[148] It appeared that the door to increased judicial transparency was going to open, with the exception of the United States Supreme Court, throughout the entire federal judicial system.

---

142 Linda Greenhouse, "U.S. Judges Vote Down TV in Courts," *New York Times*, Sept. 20, 1994.

143 Johnson, Molly Treadway, and Carol Krafka. "Electronic Media Coverage of Federal Civil Proceedings." Federal Judicial Center, 1994, p. iii.

144 Kirtley, op. cit., p. 377.

145 Ibid. at 378.

146 Ibid. at 377.

147 Johnson and Krafka, op. cit., p. 7.

148 Ibid. at 43.

In a secret vote, the Judicial Conference rejected the recommendation by the Federal Judicial Center and decided to continue the ban on cameras in federal courts. Spokesman David H. Sellars announced the decision at a press conference at the Supreme Court on Sept. 21, 1994. He said the Conference had convened on the prior day and voted roughly two-to-one in favor of upholding the absolute ban. The issue had taken 20 minutes of the six-hour meeting. The Conference offered no explanation for the decision, but Sellars said, "The tenor of concern was the potential impact on witnesses and jurors."[149] The decision came on the heels of media extravaganzas, mostly in the California state courts: O.J. Simpson, the Menendez brothers and Rodney King.[150]

Justice Souter remains alive and retired from the high court and cameras are still banned from the Supreme Court. The justices are still firm in their opposition to cameras in the nation's highest court, though Justice Stephen Breyer has spoken of a day when it might happen.[151] In a House subcommittee hearing on the court's budget, Breyer answered a question from Representative Adam B. Schiff, Democrat of California about cameras and the chance that the Supreme Court might try a pilot program for its oral arguments.[152]

> The justice told Mr. Schiff that he believed more serious studies needed to be conducted, and not by the news media, before cameras would be considered. He said he wouldn't favor a pilot program at the Supreme Court, but that at some point, through studies, justices would reach a comfort level with the notion.

But, Breyer, also said, the oral arguments represented just one percent of the process justices engage in when they decide cases. The public would not be helped much by showing arguments, he suggested.

Some might take comfort from the fact Breyer's suggestion about justices someday welcoming cameras. Then again, more than 20 years ago, Chief Justice Rehnquist said that he would welcome a report on the advisability of cameras in the Supreme and federal courts.[153]

Today, cameras are permitted in some nonjury civil cases in the Ninth Circuit as well as federal courts in the Southern and Eastern Districts of New York. Cameras also are permitted in the appellate courts of the Second and Ninth circuits. Cameras are still barred in federal courts for criminal and civil cases tried before juries.

---

149 Joan Biskupic, "Federal Ban Continued: Panel of Top Judges Breaks from Trend Taken by Majority of the States," *Washington Post*, Sept. 21, 1994.

150 Greg Kueterman, "Elimination of Cameras Surprises Federal Judge," *Indiana Lawyer*, Nov. 2, 1994.

151 Kate Phillips, "Justice Thomas Laughs at His Silent Streak," The Caucus Blog, *New York Times*, April 15, 2010.

152 Ibid.

153 David Margolick, "Federal Courts May Lift Ban on TV," *New York Times*, May, 23, 1990.

Even so, the most publicized case to come along in the Ninth Circuit after the camera ban was lifted was not televised. California's Proposition 8, a measure to overturn the right of gays and lesbians to legally marry in the state, passed with 52.3 percent of the vote after a bruising and expensive political campaign. Proposition 8 was challenged in federal court.

Judge Vaughn Walker issued an order shortly before the trial began permitting the Internet broadcast of the trial to five federal courthouses around the country.[154] The move was opposed by defenders of the same-sex marriage ban. They sought relief from the Supreme Court which responded with a stay and then an order forbidding the broadcast. Although the opinion was not signed, the dissent from Justice Breyer, joined by justices Ginsburg, Sotomayor and Stevens makes clear that it was Chief Justice Roberts and Justices Scalia, Alito, Thomas and Kennedy who stopped the broadcast.

In stopping the broadcast, the majority pointed to procedural errors made by Judge Walker. Judge Walker had made the decision to broadcast too quickly under the new rules being initiated by the Ninth Circuit, the justices said.[155]

> We are asked to stay the broadcast of a federal trial. We resolve that question without expressing any view on whether such trials should be broadcast. We instead determine that the broadcast in this case should be stayed because it appears the courts below did not follow the appropriate procedures set forth in federal law before changing their rules to allow such broadcasting.

Still, advocates of openness managed to show and tell what was happening in the courtroom.[156] Filmmaker John Ireland and actor John Ainsworth produced a reconstruction of the trial from daily transcripts of the proceedings on YouTube and the Web site marriagetrial.com,[157] "This court case is of great personal interest to us," Mr. Ainsworth said. "I wanted to see what was going on in that courtroom."

CAMERAS IN STATE COURTROOMS

Because of so much state-to-state variation, persons who would cover state courts with cameras will have to learn specific regulations applying to each court. The one constant is that the presiding judge is in control of his or her courtroom, and that judge's consent is required in virtually every state. The judge has discretionary control over camera coverage during proceedings. As might be expected, camera coverage of trials

---

[154] *Hollingsworth v. Perry*, 558 U.S. 183, 130 S.Ct. 705 (2010).

[155] Ibid. at 706.

[156] Malia Wollan, "No Live TV of a Trial on Marriage, but a Replay," *Los Angeles Times*, Feb. 2, 2010.

[157] Ibid.

involving juveniles generally is prohibited, and that also goes for victims of sex crimes, domestic relations cases, and trade secret litigation. Voir dire coverage is often forbidden, as is coverage of conferences in court. Each state will have specific rules, as suggested in the discussion of *Chandler v. Florida* (1981), discussed earlier at footnote 129 concerning the number of camera operators allowed, type of equipment allowed, and movement camera operators in the courtroom.[158]

The New Hampshire Supreme Court in 2002 limited the discretion of state court judges in banning cameras from courtrooms.[159] The case arose when WMUR, the *Boston Globe* and the New Hampshire Association of Broadcasters challenged a ruling by a New Hampshire trial court prohibiting them from photographing, recording or broadcasting a murder trial. The trial judge banned cameras and recorders as a matter of his court's standard policies.

While the court concluded that there was no constitutional right under state or federal constitutions to have cameras in New Hampshire courtroom, it also saw no constitutional prohibition against them. The court ruled for a presumption of access for cameras as "an extension of the reporting function of the more traditional arms of the press."[160] The New Hampshire court kept the door open to exclude cameras, but only if four requirements were met:[161]

> (1) closure advances an overriding interest that is likely to be prejudiced; (2) the closure ordered is no broader than necessary to protect that interest; (3) the judge considers reasonable alternatives to closing the proceeding; and (4) the judge makes particularized findings to support the closure on the record.

WEBCASTING NOT ALLOWED IN A U.S. DISTRICT COURT: IN RE SONY BMG MUSIC ENTERTAINMENT ET AL., PETITIONERS

Television and still photography are not allowed in federal courtrooms, but U.S. District Judge Nancy Gertner of the District of Massachusetts tried to use gavel-to-gavel Webcast coverage of a high-interest civil action in her court. Sony BMG Music Entertainment and other parties petitioned the Court of Appeals, First Circuit to avoid unwanted publicity in a music file-sharing/copyright case. The issue arose when Joel Tenenbaum, one of the individual defendants—many of them students—sued for copyright infringement for using file-sharing software to download and share copyrighted songs without paying royalties. Tenenbaum asked the district court to allow Courtroom View

[158] Ibid.

[159] *In re WMUR Channel 9*, 148 N.H. 644, 813 A.2d 455 (2002).

[160] Ibid. at 650.

[161] Ibid. at 650–651.

Network to Webcast a non-evidentiary motions hearing scheduled for January, 2009.[162]

As Senior U.S. Circuit Judge Bruce M. Selya framed the issue, "Does a federal district judge have the authority to permit gavel-to-gavel Webcasting of a hearing in a civil case?" Although sympathetic to the promise of new technologies in court coverage, he wrote for the Court of Appeals that local court rules and the policy of the Judicial Conference of the United States forbade Webcasting from a federal district court.[163]

Judge Selya's interpretation of Massachusetts District Court Rule 83.3's use of the term held that " . . . the phrase 'by order of the court' does not create a free-floating bubble of discretion but, rather, is confined to those situations . . . " including ceremonial functions such as naturalization proceedings.[164] The district court also has the authority under that rule to present evidence, perpetuate a record of proceedings, for security purposes, or "for the photographing, recording or broadcasting of appellate arguments."

Judge Selya concluded that Webcasting is a form of broadcasting, and that federal and local court rules forbid it. He wrote,

We also are mindful that emerging technologies eventually may change the way in which information—including information about court cases—historically has been imparted. Yet, this is not a case about free speech writ large, nor about the guaranty of a fair trial, nor about any cognizable constitutional right to public access to the courts. Our purview here is much more confined: this is a society dedicated to the rule of law; and if a controlling rule of law, properly interpreted, closes federal courtrooms in Massachusetts to webcasting and other forms of broadcasting (whether over the air or via the Internet), we are bound to enforce that rule.[165]

56. NOTORIOUS CASES: THE SHADOW OF SHEPPARD

The long ordeal of Dr. Samuel Sheppard ended with the reversal of his murder conviction on grounds that pre-trial and during-trial publicity had impaired his ability to get a fair trial.

---

[162] *In re Sony BMG Music Entertainment et. al,* Petitioners, Petition for a Writ of Mandamus or Prohibition to the United States District Court for the District of Massachusetts, Thanks to Professor Kyu Ho Youm, Jonathan Marshall First Amendment Chair, School of Journalism and Communication, University of Oregon, for bringing this decision to the attention of members of the Law & Policy Division, Association for Education & Mass Communication.

[163] Id. at 2–3, 6.

[164] Id. at 9.

[165] Ibid. at 17.

THE TRIAL OF DR. SAM SHEPPARD

When the free press—fair trial controversy is raised, the case most likely to be mentioned is that *cause celebre* of American jurisprudence, *Sheppard v. Maxwell.*[166] This case was one of the most notorious—and most sensationally reported—trials in American history. With perhaps the exception of the Lindbergh kidnaping case of the 1930s, the ordeal of Dr. Sam Sheppard may well have been the most notorious case of the Twentieth Century. His case continued to attract attention more than 40 years after the murder.

This case began in the early morning hours of July 4, 1954, when Dr. Sheppard's pregnant wife, Marilyn, was found dead in the upstairs bedroom of their home. She had been beaten to death. Dr. Sheppard, who told authorities he had found his wife dead, called a neighbor, Bay Village Mayor Spence Houk. Dr. Sheppard appeared to have been injured, suffering from severe neck pains, a swollen eye, and shock.

Dr. Sheppard, a Bay Village, Ohio, osteopath, told a rambling and unconvincing story to officials: that he had dozed off on a downstairs couch after his wife had gone upstairs to bed. He said that he heard his wife cry out and ran upstairs. In the dim light from the hall, he saw a "form" which he later described as a bushy haired man standing next to his wife's bed. Sheppard said he grappled with the man and was knocked unconscious by a blow to the back of his neck.

He said he then went to his young son's room, and found him unharmed. Hearing a noise, Sheppard then ran downstairs. He saw a "form" leaving the house and chased it to the lake shore. Dr. Sheppard declared that he had grappled with the intruder on the beach, and had been again knocked unconscious.[167]

From the outset, Dr. Sheppard was treated as the prime suspect in the case. The coroner was reported to have told his men, " 'Well, it is evident the doctor did this, so let's go get the confession out of him.' " Sheppard, meanwhile, had been removed to a nearby clinic operated by his family. While under sedation, Sheppard was interrogated in his hospital room by the coroner. Later, on the afternoon of July 4, he was also questioned by Bay Village police, with one policeman telling Sheppard that lie detector tests were "infallible." This same policeman told Dr. Sheppard, " 'I think you killed your wife.' " Later that same afternoon, a physician sent by the coroner was permitted to make a careful examination of Sheppard.[168]

As early as July 7—the date of Marilyn Sheppard's funeral—a newspaper story appeared quoting a prosecuting attorney's criticism of the Sheppard family for refusing to permit his immediate questioning.

---

[166] *Sheppard v. Maxwell,* 384 U.S. 333, 86 S.Ct. 1507 (1966).

[167] *Sheppard v. Maxwell,* 384 U.S. 333, 335–336, 86 S.Ct. 1507, 1508–1509 (1966).

[168] Ibid. at 337–338, 1509–1510.

On July 9, Sheppard re-enacted his recollection of the crime at his home at the request of the coroner. This re-enactment was covered by a group of newsmen which had apparently been invited by the coroner. Sheppard's performance was reported at length by the news media, including photographs. Front-page headlines also emphasized Sheppard's refusal to take a lie-detector test.[169]

On July 20, 1954, newspapers began a campaign of front-page editorials. One such editorial charged that someone was "getting away with murder." The next day, another front-page editorial asked, "Why No Inquest?" A coroner's inquest was indeed held on that day in a school gymnasium. The inquest was attended by many newsmen and photographers, and was broadcast with live microphones stationed at the coroner's chair and at the witness stand. Sheppard had attorneys present during the three-day inquest, but they were not permitted to participate.[170]

The news media also quoted authorities' versions of the evidence before trial. Some of this "evidence"—such as a detective's assertion that " 'the killer washed off a trail of blood from the murder bedroom to the downstairs section' "—was never produced at the trial. Such a story, of course, contradicted Sheppard's version of what had happened in the early morning hours of July 4, 1954.[171] A newspaper published a front-page picture of Marilyn Sheppard's blood-stained pillow. The picture had been altered to show the apparent imprint of a medical instrument.

The news media's activities also included playing up stories about Sheppard's extramarital love life, suggesting that these affairs were a motive for the murder of his wife. Although the news media repeatedly mentioned his relationship with a number of women, testimony taken at Sheppard's trial showed that Sheppard had only one affair with a woman named Susan Hayes.[172]

The Supreme Court of the United States, in Justice Tom C. Clark's majority opinion in the *Sheppard* case in 1966, summed up the news accounts in this way:[173]

> The publicity then grew in intensity until his indictment on August 17. Typical of the coverage during this period is a front-page interview entitled: "Dr. Sam: 'I Wish There Was Something I Could Get Off My Chest—but There Isn't.' " Unfavorable publicity included items such as a cartoon of the body of a sphinx with Sheppard's head and the legend below: " 'I Will Do Everything In My Power to Help Solve This Terrible Murder.'—Dr. Sam Sheppard." Headlines announced, *inter alia* [among

---

169 Ibid. at 338, 1510.

170 Ibid. at 339, 1510.

171 Ibid. at 340, 1511.

172 Ibid. at 340–341, 1511.

173 Ibid. at 341–342, 1511–1512.

other things], that: "Doctor Evidence is Ready for Jury," "Corrigan Tactics Stall Quizzing," "Sheppard 'Gay Set' Is Revealed by [Bay Village Mayor Spence] Houk," "Blood Is Found in Garage," "New Murder Evidence Is Found, Police Claim," "Dr. Sam Faces Quiz At Jail on Marilyn's Fear Of Him."

Although the record of Sheppard's trial included no excerpts from radio and television broadcasts, the Court assumed that coverage by the electronic media was equally extensive since space was reserved in the courtroom for representatives of those media.

Justice Clark also noted that the chief prosecutor of Sheppard was a candidate for common pleas judge and that the trial judge, Herbert Blythin, was a candidate for re-election. Furthermore, when 75 persons were called as prospective jurors, all three Cleveland newspapers published their names and addresses. All of the prospective jurors received anonymous letters and telephone calls, plus calls from friends, about the impending Sheppard trial.[174]

During the trial, pictures of the jury appeared more than 40 times in the Cleveland newspapers. And the day before the jury rendered its verdict of guilty against Dr. Sam Sheppard, while the jurors were at lunch in the company of two bailiffs, the jury was separated into two groups to pose for pictures which were published in the newspapers. The jurors, unlike those in the *Estes* case, were not sequestered ["locked up" under the close supervision of bailiffs]. Instead, the jurors were allowed to do what they pleased outside the courtroom while not taking part in the proceedings.[175]

The intense publicity given the *Sheppard* case in the news media continued unabated while the trial was actually in progress. Sheppard's attorneys took a "random poll" of persons of the streets asking their opinion about the osteopath's guilt or innocence in an effort to gain evidence for a change of venue. This poll was denounced in one newspaper editorial as smacking of "mass jury tampering" and stated that the bar association should do something about it.

A debate among newspaper reporters broadcast over radio station WHK in Cleveland contained assertions that Sheppard had admitted his guilt by hiring a prominent criminal lawyer. In another broadcast heard over WHK, columnist and radio-TV personality Robert Considine likened Sheppard to a perjurer. When Sheppard's attorneys asked Judge Blythin to question the jurors as to how many had heard the broadcast, Judge Blythin refused to do this. And when the trial was in its seventh week, a Walter Winchell broadcast available in Cleveland over both radio and television asserted that a woman under arrest in New York City for robbery had stated that she had been Sam Sheppard's mistress and had borne him a child. Two jurors admitted in open court that they had heard

---

[174] Ibid. at 342, 1512.

[175] Ibid. at 345, 1513.

the broadcast. However, Judge Blythin merely accepted the jurors' statements that the broadcast would have no effect on their judgment and the judge accepted the replies as sufficient.[176]

When the case was submitted to the jury, the jurors were sequestered for their deliberations, which took five days and four nights. But this "sequestration" was not complete. The jurors had been allowed to call their homes every day while they stayed at a hotel during their deliberations. Telephones had been removed from the jurors' hotel rooms, but they were allowed to use phones in the bailiffs' rooms. The calls were placed by the jurors themselves, and no record was kept of the jurors who made calls or of the telephone numbers or of the persons called. The bailiffs could hear only the jurors' end of the telephone conversations.[177]

When Sheppard's case was decided by the Supreme Court of the United States in 1966, Justice Tom C. Clark's majority opinion included this ringing statement of the importance of the news media to the administration of justice.[178]

> The principle that justice cannot survive behind walls of silence has long been reflected in the "Anglo-American distrust for secret trials." A responsible press has always been regarded as the handmaiden of effective judicial administration, especially in the criminal field. Its function in this regard is documented by an impressive record of service over several centuries. The press does not simply publish information about trials but guards against the miscarriage of justice by subjecting the police, prosecutors, and judicial processes to extensive public scrutiny and criticism.

Implicit in some of Justice Clark's other statements in his opinion was deep disapproval of the news media's conduct before and during the Sheppard trial. But the news media were by no means the only culprits who made it impossible for Sheppard to get a fair trial. There was more than enough blame to go around, and Justice Clark distributed that blame among the deserving: news media, police, the coroner, and the trial court. The trial judge, Herbert Blythin, had died in 1960, but Justice Clark nevertheless spelled out what Judge Blythin should have done to protect the defendant.

At the outset of Sheppard's trial, Judge Blythin stated that he did not have the power to control publicity about the trial. Justice Clark declared that Judge Blythin's arrangements with the news media "caused Sheppard to be deprived of that 'judicial serenity and calm to which [he] was entitled.'" Justice Clark added that "bedlam reigned at the courthouse during the trial and newsmen took over practically the

---

[176] Ibid. at 346, 1514–1515.

[177] Ibid. at 349, 1515.

[178] Ibid. at 349–350, 1515–1516.

entire courtroom hounding most of the participants in the trial, especially Sheppard."[179] Justice Clark asserted:

> The carnival atmosphere at trial could easily have been avoided since the courtroom and courthouse premises are subject to the control of the court. As we stressed in *Estes*, the presence of the press at judicial proceedings must be limited when it is apparent that the accused might otherwise be prejudiced or disadvantaged. Bearing in mind the massive pre-trial publicity, the judge should have adopted stricter rules governing the use of the courtroom by newsmen, as Sheppard's counsel requested. The number of reporters in the courtroom itself could have been limited at the first sign that their presence would disrupt the trial. They certainly should have not been placed inside the bar. Furthermore, the judge should have more closely regulated the conduct of newsmen in the courtroom. For instance, the judge belatedly asked them not to handle and photograph trial exhibits lying on the counsel table during recesses.

In addition, the trial judge should have insulated the jurors and witnesses from the news media, and "should have made some effort to control the release of leads, information, and gossip to the press by police officers, witnesses, and the counsel for both sides."[180] Justice Clark asserted that the trial's "carnival atmosphere" could have been avoided because the judge controls the courtroom and the courthouse. This control could have included "limiting the presence of the press" and more closely regulating reporters' conduct, such as keeping them outside the bar of the courtroom and preventing reporters from handling exhibits.[181]

The Sheppard case drew national attention again on Oct. 30, 1997, when an Indianapolis forensic scientist reported he could prove a second man was in the Sheppard home the night Marilyn Sheppard was murdered.[182] Mohammad A Tahir, a senior forensic scientist and DNA expert, said that samples taken from the Cuyahoga County coroner's office show that Marilyn Sheppard had sex with two men the night she died. During testing to isolate Marilyn Sheppard's own DNA, Tahir examined slides containing dried fluids gathered from her body in the autopsy. Tahir reported that he found traces of semen from two sources. The new evidence confirmed the presence of another man and was a significant development in Sam Reese Sheppard's attempts to clear his father's name.

Following the revelation about the DNA evidence, Sheppard said his next objective would be to identify that other man. Sheppard had previously identified a convicted killer, Richard Eberling, who operated

---

[179] Ibid. at 358, 1520.

[180] Ibid. at 359, 1521–1522.

[181] Ibid. at 358, 1520.

[182] R. Joseph Gelarden, "DNA Evidence Uncovered in Dr. Sheppard Murder Case," *Indianapolis Star*, Oct. 20, 1997.

a window washing service and had worked at the Sheppard home. A judge ordered Eberling to provide a blood sample for additional testing. Dr. Sheppard's body was exhumed to allow for DNA analysis of his blood. Investigators found a trail of blood running from the Sheppard's bedroom out of the house. Tahir has determined the blood did not come from Marilyn Sheppard. Investigators now believe Marilyn Sheppard bit her murderer. The DNA samples from the two men would help identify the source of the blood. Police examined Sheppard when he was arrested but found no fresh wounds.

Tahir announced his findings March 6, 1998, declaring that the blood found in the Sheppard bedroom did not come from Sam Sheppard and pointed to Eberling. The Cuyahoga County prosecutor's office announced in a news conference an hour later that it would not reopen the case.[183]

THE JUDGE'S ROLE

The decision in the *Sheppard* case left its mark in the recommendations of the American Bar Association's "Reardon Report" discussed later in this chapter. The cases discussed in this chapter—*Irvin, Rideau, Estes,* and *Sheppard*—generated new law and suggested strongly that American courts may insist more and more on tighter controls over the information released to the news media in criminal trials by police, prosecution and defense attorneys, and by other employees under the control of the courts. The primary responsibility, however, for seeing to it that a defendant receives a fair trial, rests with the courts. Judges are expected to remain in control of trials in their courts.

A judge with great respect for the press, Frank W. Wilson of a U.S. District Court in Nashville, Tennessee, wrote: "Certain it is that the press coverage of crimes and criminal proceedings make more difficult the job that a judge has of assuring a fair trial. But no one has yet shown that it renders the job impossible. In fact, no one has yet shown, to the satisfaction of any court, an identifiable instance of miscarriage of justice due to press coverage of a trial where the error was not remedied."[184] Note that Judge Wilson said that it is the *judge's* job to assure a fair trial. Judge Wilson declared, "show me an unfair trial that goes uncorrected and I will show you a judge who has failed in his duty."[185]

Judge Wilson thus placed great—some would argue *too* great—[186]reliance upon the remedies which a judge can use to attempt to set things right for the defendant once he has received what the judge

---

183 "Despite DNA Results, 'Fugitive' Case Closed," *Chicago Tribune*, March 6, 1998.

184 Frank A. Wilson, "A Fair Trial and a Free Press," presented at 33rd Annual convention of the Ohio Newspaper Association, Columbus, Ohio, Feb. 11, 1966.

185 Ibid.

186 Don R. Pember, Pretrial Newspaper Publicity in Criminal Proceedings: A Case Study (unpublished M.A. thesis, Michigan State University, East Lansing, Mich.) pp. 12–16.

considers to be an undue amount of prejudicial publicity. Some of the most important of these trial-level "remedies" are outlined below:

(1) *Change of venue*, moving the trial to another area in hopes that jurors not prejudiced by mass media publicity or outraged community sentiment can be found. This "remedy," however, requires that a defendant give up his Sixth Amendment right to a trial in the "State and *district* wherein the crime shall have been committed * * * ."[187]

(2) *Continuance or postponement*. This is simply a matter of postponing a trial until the publicity or public clamor abates. A problem with this "remedy" is that there is no guarantee that the publicity will not begin anew. It might be well to remember the axiom, "justice delayed is justice denied." A continuance in a case involving a major crime might mean that a defendant—even an innocent defendant—might thus be imprisoned for a lengthy time before his trial. A continuance means that a defendant gives up his Sixth amendment right to a *speedy* trial.

(3) *Voir dire*, examination of potential jurors. This refers to the procedure by which each potential juror is questioned by opposing attorneys and may be dismissed "for cause" if the juror is shown to be prejudiced. (In addition, attorneys have a limited number of "peremptory challenges" which they can use to remove jurors who may appear troublesome to one side or the other.) Professor Don R. Pember of the University of Washington says that the voir dire examination is an effective tool and one of the best available trial-level remedies.

(4) *Sequestration*, or "locking up" the jury. Judges have the power to isolate a jury, to make sure that community prejudices—either published or broadcast in the mass media or of the person-to-person variety—do not infect a jury with information during trial which might harm a defendant's chances for a fair trial by an impartial jury. As Professor Pember has said, judges are reluctant to do this today because of the complexities in the life of the average person.[188]

(5) *Contempt of Court*. This punitive "remedy" is discussed at length in Chap. 10. Courts have the power to cite for contempt those actions—either in court or out of court—which interfere with the orderly administration of justice. American courts—until the "gag order" controversies of recent years—have been reluctant to use the contempt remedy to punish pre-trial or during-trial publications. (See Sec. 61 of this chapter, on "restrictive" or "gag" orders.) Some critics of the American mass media would go even further: they would like to see the British system imported. That would mean using contempt of court

[187] Constitution, Sixth Amendment, emphasis added; Lawrence E. Edenhofer, "The Impartial Jury—Twentieth Century Dilemma: Some Solutions to the Conflict Between Free Press and Fair Trial," *Cornell Law Quarterly* Vol. 51 (Winter, 1966), pp. 306, 314.

[188] Another trial-level remedy which is more infrequently used is the blue-ribbon jury. When a case has received massive prejudicial publicity, a court may empower either the prosecution or the defense to impanel a special, so-called "blue ribbon" jury. Intelligent jurors are selected through the use of questionnaires and interviews, under the assumption that a more intelligent jury will be more likely to withstand pressures and remain impartial.

citations as a weapon to halt media coverage of ongoing or pending criminal cases.

THE INTERNET AND JURORS

If judges did not have enough trouble insulating jurors from news stories about high-profile trials, the use of the Internet, through both computers and mobile devices, has made the job more difficult. The *New York Times* reported in March of 2009 about a mistrial in a federal drug case in Florida. Nine of the 12 jurors had been doing research on the case on their own.[189]

> Jurors are not supposed to seek information outside of the courtroom. They are required to reach a verdict based on only the facts the judge has decided are admissible, and they are not supposed to see evidence that has been excluded as prejudicial. But now, using their cellphones, they can look up the name of a defendant on the Web or examine an intersection using Google Maps, violating the legal system's complex rules of evidence. They can also tell their friends what is happening in the jury room, though they are supposed to keep their opinions and deliberations secret.

In a number of cases, jurors have used Twitter to send updates about the progress of trials and their conclusions about cases. In others, jurors have used Google maps to look at intersections where accidents occurred or investigated how long, according the Google and other mapping and driving programs to check how long it would have taken for a defendant to have traveled from one location to another.

In the Florida case, the revelation about the jurors' misconduct came after eight weeks of trial. Jurors had looked up news stories about the case, looked up definitions for some terms used in the trial and had searched,[190] "for evidence that had been specifically excluded by the judge."

SECRET JURORS

One of the problems with the Sheppard case dealt with newspaper stories that gave the names and addresses of the veniremen from whom the trial jury would be picked. "As a consequence, anonymous letters and telephone calls, as well as calls from friends, regarding the impending prosecution were received by all of the prospective jurors."[191] That was a factor leading to the conclusion that Sheppard did not receive a fair trial.

---

[189] John Schwartz, "As Jurors Turn to Web, Mistrials Are Popping Up," *New York Times*, March 18, 2009.

[190] Ibid.

[191] *Sheppard v. Maxwell*, 384 U.S. 333, 342, 86 S.Ct. 1507, 1512 (1966).

In other cases, the fear that jurors might be subject to intimidation and harassment has led to the concealment of their identities.[192] Courts have barred access to jury lists and have prevented reporters from speaking to jurors even after trials have ended. One reason given is that jurors could be influenced during the trial if they knew that the defendant or those associated with the defendant could find them and retaliate long after the verdict was delivered.

Keeping juror information secret is analogous to the use of sequestration. In sequestration, jurors are shielded from improper outside influences. With secret juries, both jurors and their families are shielded from interference by their anonymity. In a case involving members of a criminal gang known as the Green Dragons, a trial court used an anonymous jury.[193]

> In support of its motion, the government argued that the evidence presented at trial would establish that the Green Dragons were a violent gang with a history of interfering with the judicial process, that gang members continued to seek to silence potential witnesses against them, and that press coverage of the case would be extensive.

As a result, trial courts have kept information about jurors secret. News organization have opposed such secrecy on the grounds that the information must be public as part of a public trial. Openness in the court system helps maintain public confidence in the justice process and public scrutiny helps keep the process of justice just.

The Pennsylvania Supreme Court took those factors into consideration in *Commonwealth v. Long*,[194] a highly publicized case in which the use of anonymous jurors were used. And while it did not rule for complete access, the Pennsylvania court did strike a balance to help preserve the integrity of the trial process and the integrity of the judicial process. The Pennsylvania Supreme Court held that while the addresses of jurors should remain secret, their names should be public.[195]

First, with respect to the value of openness in criminal trials, a trial by jury and public access to criminal trials serve the same function-ensuring the fairness of the judicial process. From the earliest days of this country, it was believed that the jury was the best way to assure a fair trial. * * * Likewise, public scrutiny of the criminal justice system enhances the quality and safeguards the integrity of the factfinding process, "with benefits to both the defendant and to society as a whole." *Globe*, 457 U.S. at 606, 102 S.Ct. 2613. * * *

While these considerations weigh in favor of disclosing jurors' names and addresses, we believe that revealing impaneled jurors' names is

---

[192] *U.S. v. Brown*, 250 F.3d 907, 911 (5th Cir. 2001).

[193] *U.S. v. Wong*, 40 F.3d 1347, 1376 (2d Cir. 1994).

[194] *Commonwealth v. Long*, 592 Pa. 42, 922 A.2d 892 (Pa. 2007).

[195] Ibid. at 60–61, 903–904.

sufficient. Openness is fostered by the public knowledge of who is on the impaneled jury. Armed with such knowledge, the public can confirm the impartiality of the jury, which acts as an additional check upon the prosecutorial and judicial process.

57. EXTERNAL GUIDELINES AND SELF-REGULATORY EFFORTS

An external regulatory threat—the fair trial reporting guidelines of the "Reardon Committee"—led to press-bar-bench efforts to agree to rules for covering the criminal justice process.

During the middle 1960s, the American Bar Association again got into the act in attempting to regulate prejudicial publicity.[196] As should be evident from preceding sections, there was plenty of pressure on the ABA to do something. First, as noted earlier, the Warren Commission investigating the assassination of President Kennedy had some harsh things to say about media coverage of the arrest of suspect Lee Harvey Oswald.[197] Then, there had been a chain of cases involving prejudicial publicity—*Irvin v. Dowd* (1961),[198] *Rideau v. Louisiana* (1963),[199] *Estes v. Texas* (1965)[200] and *Sheppard v. Maxwell* (1966).[201] Although the [Attorney General Nicholas deBelleville] Katzenbach Guidelines for federal courts and law enforcement officers had met with considerable approval, the ABA's concern continued. Early in 1968, the ABA Convention meeting in Chicago approved the "Standards Relating to Fair Trial and Free Press" recommended by the Advisory Committee headed by Massachusetts Supreme Court Justice Paul C. Reardon.[202] The "Reardon Report," as the document came to be known, was greeted with outraged concern by a large segment of the American media.[203] This report dealt primarily with things that attorneys and judges were *not* to say lest the rights of defendants be prejudiced. For example, if a defendant in a murder case had confessed before trial, that confession should not be revealed until duly submitted as evidence during an actual trial. Most frightening to the media, however, were suggestions that

---

[196] Advisory Committee on Fair Trial and Free Press, Standards Relating to Fair Trial and Free Press (New York, 1966); see also draft approved Feb. 19, 1968, by delegates to the ABA Convention as published in March, 1968. For earlier ABA involvement in trying to come to terms with prejudicial publicity see ABA, "Report of Special Committee on Cooperation Between [sic] Press, Radio and Bar," Annual Report, Volume 62, pp. 851–866 (1937).

[197] Report of the President's Commission on the Association of President John F. Kennedy (Washington: Government Printing Office, 1964) p. 241.

[198] *Irvin v. Dowd,* 366 U.S. 717, 81 S.Ct. 1639 (1961).

[199] *Rideau v. Louisiana,* 373 U.S. 723, 83 S.Ct. 1417 (1963).

[200] *Estes v. Texas,* 381 U.S. 532, 85 S.Ct. 1628 (1965).

[201] *Sheppard v. Maxwell,* 84 U.S. 333, 86 S.Ct. 1507 (1966).

[202] Advisory Committee on Fair Trial and Free Press (of the ABA), Approved Draft, op. cit.

[203] See, e.g., American Newspaper Publishers Association, Free Press and Fair Trial (New York: ANPA, 1967) p. 1 and passim.

contempt powers be used against the media if they were to publish statements which could affect the outcome of a trial.

The Reardon Report touched off many press-bar meetings, seeking to reach voluntary guidelines on coverage of the criminal arrest, arraignment, hearing and trial process.[204] More than two dozen states adopted voluntary agreements based on conferences among judges, lawyers, and members of the media. States with such guidelines include Colorado, Kentucky, Massachusetts, Minnesota, New York, Oregon, Texas, Washington, and Wisconsin.

In such a setting—in the aftermath of the Warren Commission Report on the Kennedy assassination (which called for curtailment of pretrial news)—the *Sheppard* case came along to illustrate once again just how wretchedly prejudicial news coverage of a criminal trial could become. In that setting, the ABA Advisory Committee on Fair Trial—Free Press (Reardon Committee) was formed.

In many places, a press-bar agreement occurred, leading to construction, by joint press-bar committees in roughly half of the states, of guidelines for the coverage of criminal trials.

WISCONSIN FAIR TRIAL AND FREE PRESS PRINCIPLES AND GUIDELINES

In Wisconsin, for example, informal rules titled "Wisconsin Fair Trial and Free Press Principles and Guidelines were drafted by a committee of lawyers and journalists in 1969. These guidelines were reworked and reissued in 1979 and in 1987 in response to changes brought about by cases such as *Nebraska Press Association v. Stuart* (1976) and pre-1987 free press-fair trial cases discussed earlier in this chapter."

These are *recommended* principles, for voluntary compliance, and the 2012 version emphasized that they are not binding on anyone. Further, and doubtless in some response to a Washington case which would have made voluntary guidelines mandatory as a condition for covering a trial, Wisconsin's 2012 guidelines specify that they are "not to be applied or used against anyone."[205]

The Wisconsin Guidelines, similarly to those of other states, ask for protection of criminal defendants' presumption of innocence as a shared responsibility among the judiciary, attorneys, news media, and law enforcement agencies. Both access to news of court proceedings and defendants' rights to a fair, unprejudiced trial are recognized as vital

[204] Advisory Committee on Fair Trial and Free Press, op. cit., 1966 and 1968; "Bar Votes to Strengthen Code on Crime Publicity," *Editor & Publisher*, Vol. 101 (Feb.24, 1968) p. 9.

[205] See Wisconsin News Reporter's Legal Handbook, 6th ed. (2012), prepared by the Media-Law Relations Committee, State Bar of Wisconsin, in cooperation with the Wisconsin Broadcasters Assn. and the Wisconsin Newspaper Assn. The Washington case is *Federated Publications v. Swedberg*. See below at footnote 206.

rights to be protected. The news media, which have a constitutional and statutory right to report on courts (subject to rare exceptions), and should strive for accuracy, balance, fairness and objectivity.

As to release of information in criminal trials, the guidelines say there should be no restraint on making available to the public, in criminal investigations, the following:

- Information in a public record;
- Information indicating that an investigation is in progress;
- Information on the general scope of an investigation, including a description of the offense and, if permitted by law, the identity of the victim;
- Requesting assistance in apprehending a suspect, or assistance in other matters, and the information necessary for those requests; and
- Warning the public of any dangers.

The guidelines also offer advice to lawyers including declining:

- Comments on the accused's character, reputation, or prior criminal record (including arrests, indictments, or other charges of crime);
- The possibility of a guilty plea to the offense charged or to a lesser offense;
- The existence or the contents of any confession, admission, or statement given by the accused, or a refusal or failure to make a statement;
- The performance or results of any examination or tests, or the refusal of the accused to submit to examinations or tests;
- The identity, testimony, or credibility of a prospective witness;
- Any opinion as to the guilt or innocence of the accused, the evidence, or the merits of the case.

FEDERATED PUBLICATIONS V. SWEDBERG

Voluntary guidelines may become a two-edged sword. In fact, some states reworked their guidelines after the harsh lesson of *Federated Publications v. Swedberg*[206] as decided by the Supreme Court of the State of Washington. Reworkings of the state guidelines were to re-emphasize their VOLUNTARY nature.

Judge Byron L. Swedberg presided over a trial involving charges of attempted murder. The case, in Whatcom County, north of Seattle, had great notoriety. It involved Veronica Lynn Compton, a woman reputedly

[206] *Federated Publications v. Swedberg*, 633 P.2d 74 (Washington 1981).

the girlfriend of Kenneth Bianchi. Bianchi was known regionally and even nationally as the "Hillside Strangler."

Judge Swedberg refused to grant a defense motion in the case of *State v. Compton* which would have closed a pretrial hearing to the public. However, the judge conditioned media attendance at the trial upon reporters' signing an agreement to abide by the Washington Bench-Bar-Press Guidelines. Federated Publications, publishers of the *Bellingham Herald*, challenged Judge Swedberg's order.

The Washington guidelines were created as a voluntary document and had no legal force until Judge Swedberg incorporated them in his order. In that situation, the guidelines—if enforced—would, for example, have stopped the media from reporting on the defendant's previous criminal record or on the existence of a pre-trial confession. In most cases, journalists will agree that pre-trial confessions should not be reported until officially accepted as evidence in court. However, situations could conceivably arise where the best judgment of journalists would be to include information about the existence of such a confession in pre-trial stories. As journalist Tony Mauro said in a Society of Professional Journalists Freedom of Information report in 1982,

> * * * [I]n a single stroke, Swedberg made suspect all the guidelines, developed in many instances only after years of delicate negotiations. Editors who were wary in the first place of sitting down with judges and lawyers were given new reasons to be suspicious—if we agree to talk about guidelines, the thinking went, someday they'll be used against us, as with Swedberg.

In upholding Judge Swedberg's ruling that members of the press must agree to abide by the Washington guidelines if so ordered by a judge, Justice Rosellini of the State of Washington's Supreme Court concluded that Swedberg's limitation was "reasonable." He compared the Swedberg situation to the Washington Supreme Court's holding in *Federated Publications v. Kurtz*.[207] In the *Kurtz* case, the court held that the public has a right under the state and federal constitutions to have access to judicial proceedings, including pretrial hearings.

Justice Rosellini listed alternatives to closing a courtroom (see discussion of a similar list elsewhere this chapter: Continuance (delay), change of venue, change of venire, voir dire, and so forth). Those alternatives, Justice Rosellini wrote, "all involved some compromise of a right or interest of the accused or the State. None of the suggested alternatives involved the exercise of some restraint on the part of the media." He concluded that since his court had the power to exclude all of

[207] *Federated Publications v. Kurtz*, 615 P.2d 440 (Washington 1980).

the public, including the media, he also had the power to impose reasonable conditions upon the media's attendance at a trial.[208]

58. RESTRICTIVE ORDERS AND REPORTING THE JUDICIAL PROCESS

After "gag orders" became a nationwide problem, *Nebraska Press Association v. Stuart* halted such prior restraints on the news media.

Bar-press guidelines such as those disclosed in the preceding sections tried to honor both the public's right to know about the judicial process and a defendant's right to a fair trial. Not all was well, however, despite the various meeting-of-minds between press and bar. Another disturbing counter-current was perceived during the late 1960s, starting mainly in California and involving judges issuing "restrictive" or "gag" orders in some cases.[209] In a Los Angeles County Superior Court in 1966, for example, a judge ordered the attorneys in a case, the defendants, the sheriff, chief of police, and members of the Board of Police Commissioners not to talk to the news media about the case in question. The order forbade "[r]eleasing or authorizing the release of any extrajudicial statements for dissemination by any means of public communication relating to the alleged charge or the Accused."

All that could be reported under such an order were the facts and circumstances of the arrest, the substance of the charge against the defendant, and the defendant's name, age, residence, occupation, and family status. If such an arrangement were to be worked out on a voluntary basis between press and bar, that might be one thing. However, the fact of a judge's *order*—a "gag rule"—worried some legal scholars, and with good reason.

In a New York case during 1971, Manhattan Supreme Court Justice George Postel, concerned about possibly prejudicial news accounts, called reporters into his chambers and laid down what he called "Postel's Law." The trial involved Carmine J. Persico, who had been charged with extortion, coercion, criminal usury ("loan sharking") and conspiracy. Justice Postel admonished the reporters not to use Persico's nickname ("The Snake") in their accounts and not to mention Persico's supposed connections with Joseph A. Columbo, Sr., a person said to be a leader of organized crime. The reporters, irked by Postel's declarations, reported

[208] *Federated Publications, Inc. v. Swedberg*, 96 Wash.2d 13, 633 P.2d 74, 75 (1981), 7 Med.L.Rptr. 1865, 1871, citing *Federated Publications, Inc. v. Kurtz*, 94 Wash.2d 51, 615 P.2d 440 (1980), 6 Med.L.Rptr. 1577. See also Tony Mauro, "Bench-media misunderstanding threatens press access to courts," FOI '82: A Report from the Society of Professional Journalists, p. 3.

[209] Robert S. Warren and Jeffrey M. Abell, "Free Press—Fair Trial: The 'Gag Order,' A California Aberration," *Southern California Law Review* 45:1 (Winter, 1972) pp. 51–99, at pp. 52–53.

what the judge had told them, including references to "The Snake" and to Columbo.

Persico's defense attorney then asked that the trial be closed to the press and to the public, and Judge Postel so ordered. However, the prosecutor—Assistant District Attorney Samuel Yasgur—complained that the order would set an unfortunate and dangerous precedent. For one thing, Yasgur declared, the absence of press coverage might mean that possible witnesses who could become aware of the trial through the media would remain ignorant of the trial and thus could not come forward to testify. Prosecutor Yasgur added:[210]

> But most importantly, Your Honor, as the Court has noted, the purpose of having press and the public allowed and present during the trial of a criminal case is to insure that defendants do receive an honest and a fair trial.

Newsmen appealed Judge Postel's order closing the trial to New York's highest court, the Court of Appeals. Chief Judge Stanley H. Fuld then ruled that the trial should not have been closed.[211]

> "Because of the vital function served by the news media in guarding against the miscarriage of justice by subjecting the police, prosecutors, and the judicial processes to extensive public scrutiny and criticism," the Supreme Court has emphasized that it has been "unwilling to place any direct limitations on the freedom traditionally exercised by the news media for '[w]hat transpires in the court room is public property.' "

Chief Judge Fuld added that courts should meet problems of prejudicial publicity not by declaring mistrials, but by taking careful preventive steps to protect their courts from outside interferences. In most cases, Judge Fuld suggested, a judge's cautioning jurors to avoid exposure to prejudicial publicity, or to disregard prejudicial material they had already seen or heard, would be effective. In extreme situations, he said, a court might find it necessary to sequester ("lock up") a jury for the duration of a trial.[212]

Although reporters were ultimately vindicated in the *Postel* case, a Louisiana case went against the press. This case, *United States v. Dickinson*, arose when reporters Larry Dickinson and Gibbs Adams of the Baton Rouge *Star Times* and the *Morning Advocate* tried to report on a U.S. District Court hearing involving a VISTA worker who had been indicted by a Louisiana state grand jury on suspicion of conspiring to murder a state official. The District Court hearing was to ascertain whether the state's prosecution was legitimate. In the course of this hearing, District Court Judge E. Gordon West issued this order:

---

[210] "Trial of Persico Closed to Public," *The New York Times*, Nov. 16, 1971, p. 1, 40.

[211] *Oliver v. Postel*, 30 N.Y.2d 171, 331 N.Y.S.2d 407, 414, 282 N.E.2d 306, 311 (1972).

[212] *U.S. v. Dickinson*, 465 F.2d 496 (5th Cir.1972). See, also, *People of the State of New York v. Holder*, 70 Misc.2d 31, 332 N.Y.S.2d 933 (1972).

> "And, at this time,—I do want to enter an order in the case, and that is in accordance with this Court's rule in connection with Fair Trial—Free Press provisions, the Rules of this Court.
>
> "It is ordered that no * * * report of the testimony taken in this case today shall be made in any newspaper or by radio or television, or by any other news media."

Reporters Dickinson and Adams ignored that order, and wrote articles for their newspapers summarizing the day's testimony in detail. After a hearing, Dickinson and Adams were found guilty of criminal contempt and were sentenced to pay fines of $300 each. Appealing to the Court of Appeals for the Fifth Circuit, the reporters were told that the District Court judge's gag order was unconstitutional.[213] They were not in the clear, however. The Court of Appeals sent their case back to the District Court so that the judge could reconsider the $300 fines. The judge again fined the reporters $300 apiece, and they again appealed to the Court of Appeals. This time, the contempt fines were upheld. The Fifth Circuit Court declared that the reporters could have asked for a rehearing or appealed against the judge's order not to publish. Once the appeal was decided in their favor, the court evidently reasoned, *then* they could publish.[214]

Attorney James C. Goodale—then vice president of *The New York Times*—was indignant.

> It doesn't take much analysis to see that what the Court has sanctioned is the right of prior restraint subject to later appeal. * * * What this case means, in effect, is that when a judge is disposed to order a newspaper not to report matters that are transpiring in public he may do so, and a newsman's only remedy is to appeal or decide to pay the contempt penalty, be it a fine or imprisonment.

In the fall of 1973, the Supreme Court—evidently not seeing a major issue requiring its attention—refused to grant certiorari, thereby allowing the lower court decision to stand.[215] By 1976, however, the gag issue was an obvious problem. Attorney Jack C. Landau, Supreme Court reporter for the Newhouse News Service and a trustee of the Reporters Committee for Freedom of the Press, came up with some agonizing statistics. From 1966 to 1976, hundreds of restrictive orders were issued by courts against the news media.

---

[213] *United States v. Dickinson*, 465 F.2d 496, 514 (5th Cir.1972).

[214] 476 F.2d 373, 374 (5th Cir.1973); 349 F.Supp. 227 (M.D.La.1972). See also James C. Goodale's "The Press 'Gag' Order Epidemic," *Columbia Journalism Review*, Sept./Oct. 1973, pp. 49–50.

[215] 414 U.S. 979, 94 S.Ct. 270 (1973), refusing certiorari in 465 F.2d 496 (5th Cir.1972).

NEBRASKA PRESS ASS'N V. STUART

Although the Supreme Court refused to hear the reporters' appeal in the *Dickinson* case[216]—thus allowing contempt fines against two reporters to stand—a virtual nationwide epidemic of restrictive orders quickly showed that the *Baton Rouge* case was no rarity.[217] A ghastly 1976 multiple-murder case in the hamlet of Sutherland, Nebraska (population 840) was reported avidly by the mass media. This provided the Supreme Court with the factual setting which led to the Court's clamping down on the indiscriminate issuance of gag orders. The issue was stated succinctly by E. Barrett Prettyman, the attorney who represented the news media in *Nebraska Press Association v. Stuart.*[218]

> The basic question before the Court is whether it is permissible under the First Amendment for a court to issue direct prior restraint against the press, prohibiting in advance of publication the reporting of information revealed in public court proceedings, in public court records, and from other sources about pending judicial proceedings.

The nightmarish Nebraska case involved the murder of six members of one family, including necrophilia. Police released the description of a suspect, 29-year-old Erwin Charles Simants, an unemployed handyman, to reporters who arrived at the scene of the crime. After a night of hiding, Simants walked into the house where he lived—next door to the residence where six had been slain—and was arrested.

Three days after the crime, the prosecuting attorney and Simants' attorney jointly asked the Lincoln County Court to enter a restrictive order. On Oct. 22, 1975, the County Court granted a sweeping order prohibiting the release or publication of any "testimony given or evidence adduced * * * ".[219] On October 23, Simants' preliminary hearing was open to the public, but the press was subject to the restrictive order. On that same day, the Nebraska Press Association intervened in the District Court of Lincoln County and asked Judge Hugh Stuart to set aside the County Court's restrictive order. Judge Stuart conducted a hearing and on October 27 issued his own restrictive order, prohibiting the Nebraska Press Association and other organizations and reporters from reporting on five subjects:[220]

> (1) the existence or contents of a confession Simants had made to law enforcement officers, which has been introduced in open court at arraignment; (2) the fact or nature of statements Simants had made to other persons; (3) the contents of a note he had written the night of the crime; (4) certain aspects of the

[216] *Dickinson v. U.S.,* 414 U.S. 979, 94 S.Ct. 270 (1973).

[217] Landau, p. 57.

[218] "Excerpts from the Gag Order Arguments," *Editor & Publisher,* May 1, 1976, p. 46A.

[219] *Nebraska Press Association v. Stuart,* 427 U.S. 539, 542, 96 S.Ct. 2791, 2795 (1976).

[220] Ibid. at 543–544, 2795.

> medical testimony at the preliminary hearing; (5) the identity of the victims of the alleged sexual assault and the nature of the assault.

This order also prohibited reporting the exact nature of the restrictive order itself, and—like the County Court's order—incorporated the Nebraska Bar-Press Guidelines.[221]

The Nebraska Press Association and its co-petitioners on October 31 asked the District Court to suspend its restrictive order and also asked that the Nebraska Supreme Court stop the gag order. Early in December, the state's Supreme Court issued a modification of the restrictive order "to accommodate the defendant's right to a fair trial and the petitioners' [i.e., the Nebraska Press Association, other press associations, and individual journalists'] interest in reporting pretrial events." This modified order prohibited reporting of three matters:[222]

> (a) the existence and nature of any confessions or admissions made by the defendant to law enforcement officers; (b) any confessions or admissions made to any third parties, except members of the press; and (c) other facts "strongly implicative" of the accused.

The Nebraska Supreme Court did not rely on the Nebraska Bar-Press Guidelines. After interpreting state law to permit closing of court proceedings to reporters in certain circumstances, the Nebraska Supreme Court sent the case back to District Judge Hugh Stuart for reconsideration of whether pretrial hearings in the Simants case should be closed to the press and public. The Supreme Court of the United States granted certiorari.[223]

Writing for a unanimous Supreme Court, Chief Justice Burger reviewed free press-fair trial cases and prior restraint cases. He wrote: "None of our decided cases on prior restraint involved restrictive orders entered to protect a defendant's right to a fair and impartial jury, but the opinions on prior restraint have a common thread relevant to this case." The Chief Justice then quoted from *Organization for a Better Austin v. Keefe:*[224]

> "Any prior restraint on expression comes to this Court with a 'heavy presumption' against its constitutional validity. * * * Respondent [Keefe] thus carries a heavy burden of showing justification for the imposition of such a restraint. He has not met that burden. * * * "

Chief Justice Burger noted that the restrictive order at issue in the Simants case did not prohibit publication but only postponed it. Some news, he said, can be delayed and often is when responsible editors call

---

221 Ibid. at 544, 2796.

222 Ibid. at 545, 2796.

223 *Nebraska Press Association v. Stuart,* 423 U.S. 1027, 96 S.Ct. 557 (1975).

224 *Organization for a Better Austin v. Keefe,* 402 U.S. 415, 91 S.Ct. 1575 (1971).

for more fact-checking. "But such delays," he added, "are normally slight and they are self-imposed. Delays imposed by governmental authority are a different matter."[225]

The Court then turned to an examination of whether the threat to a fair trial for Simants was so severe as to overcome the presumption of unconstitutionality which prior restraints carry with them. The Chief Justice borrowed Judge Learned Hand's language (oft criticized by libertarians) from a case involving the trial of Communists in 1950: whether the "gravity of the evil," discounted by its improbability, justifies such invasion of free speech as is necessary to avoid the danger.[226] The Court's review of the pretrial record in the Simants case indicated that Judge Stuart was justified in concluding that there would be intense and pervasive pretrial publicity. The judge could have concluded reasonably that the publicity might endanger Simants' right to a fair trial.

Even so, the restrictive order by the trial court judge was not justified in the view of the Supreme Court of the United States. Alternatives to prior restraint were not tried by the Nebraska trial court. Those alternatives included a change of venue; postponement of the trial to allow public furor to subside, and searching questioning of prospective jurors to screen out those who had already made up their minds about Simants' guilt or innocence. Sequestration ("locking up") of jurors would insulate jurors from prejudicial publicity only after they were sworn, but that measure "enhances the likelihood of dissipating the impact of pretrial publicity and emphasizes the elements of the jurors' oaths." The Chief Justice wrote:[227]

> * * * [P]retrial publicity, even if pervasive and concentrated, cannot be regarded as leading automatically and in every kind of criminal case to an unfair trial.
>
> * * *
>
> We reaffirm that the guarantees of freedom of expression are not an absolute prohibition under all circumstances, but the barriers to prior restraint remain high and the presumption against its use continues intact. We hold that, with respect to the order entered in this case prohibiting reporting or commentary on judicial proceedings held in public, the barriers have not been overcome; to the extent that this order restrained publication of such material, it is clearly invalid. To the extent that it prohibited publication based on information gained from other sources, we conclude that the heavy burden imposed as a condition to securing prior restraint was not met and the judgment of the Nebraska Supreme Court is therefore *reversed.*

---

[225] *Nebraska Press Association v. Stuart,* 427 U.S. 539, 560, 96 S.Ct. 2791, 2803 (1976).

[226] Ibid. at 562, 2804.

[227] Ibid. at 565, 2804.

Nebraska Press Association v. Stuart was hailed as a sizable victory for the news media. Nevertheless, some scholars were fretful about that decision's ultimate impact. Benno C. Schmidt, then a Columbia University law professor, found some "disturbing undertones." He expressed the fear that the[228]

> * * * Court may have invited severe controls on the press's access to information about criminal proceedings from principals, witnesses, lawyers, the police, and others; it is even possible that some legal proceedings may be closed completely to the press and public as an indirect result of *Nebraska*.

He also worried that the Supreme Court's decision might encourage trial judges to place increasing reliance on stipulations that parties in a trial—lawyers, witnesses, police, etc.—not provide information in the press.

Schmidt was correct in his gloomy assessment of the Simants case; the so-called victory of the press in *Nebraska Press Association* was hollow. As former *Washington Star* editor Newbold Noyes has observed:[229]

> It was Star Chamber, not publicity, that the founding fathers worried about. Defendants were guaranteed a public trial, not a cleared courtroom. The whole thrust of these amendments was—and must remain—that what happens in the courts happens out in the open, in full view of the citizenry, and that therein lies the individual's protection against the possible tyranny of government. There is no possible conflict between this idea and the idea of a free press.

RESTRICTIVE (GAG) ORDERS CONTINUE

Although judicial orders gagging the press were discouraged, by and large, by the Supreme Court decision in *Nebraska Press Association v. Stuart* (1976), discussed in the preceding paragraphs, struggles continue against restrictive orders silencing attorneys and trial participants. The news media won some and lost some where gag orders were concerned, but the basic fact is that gag orders will remain in force when they are issued unless challenged by journalists.

In Florida, for example, state court judge Robert Kaye ordered plaintiffs and their lawyers in a suit against tobacco companies not to talk to the media. The gag order was challenged successfully by a number of news heavyweights including Dow Jones & Co., the *New York Times*, the *Miami Herald*, and Gannett. Federal district court Judge Adelberto

---

[228] Schmidt, "The Nebraska Decision," *Columbia Journalism Review*, November/December, 1976, p. 51.

[229] Speech at the University of Oregon, Ruhl Symposium Lectures, November 21, 1975, reprinted in "The Responsibilities of Power," School of Journalism, University of Oregon, June, 1976, pp. 16–17.

Jordan held the gag order unconstitutional because no showing was made that it was necessary to bring about a fair trial.[230]

RESTRICTIONS IN THE JOHN WALKER LINDH CASE

In the first prosecution of an American citizen charged with providing assistance to al-Qaeda, protective orders kept confidential reports of interviews with detainees and others suspected of involvement with terrorist activities.[231]

The prosecution, obligated under the rules of criminal proceedings to provide certain of its investigative files to the John Walker Lindh defense team, sought to keep confidential the reports of its interviews. The protective order required the defense team to agree to keep information from the interviews confidential.

The defense team objected to the protective order, arguing that it made the defense more difficult because it would require that investigators be pre-screened before seeing or using the information, that it would limit the use of expert witnesses who would have to rely on the information and, finally, that the defense would not be able to battle for public opinion as effectively as the government, which had already released information about Lindh and his "crimes."

In granting the prosecution request, the judge noted that the issue of potential experts could be resolved by the court on a case-by-case basis. He also relied on the government's national security concerns involved in the dissemination of the information in granting the order.[232]

> Indeed, given the nature of al Qaeda and its activities, and the ongoing federal law enforcement investigation into al Qaeda, the identities of the detainees, as well as the questions asked and the techniques employed by law enforcement agents in the interviews are highly sensitive and confidential. Additionally, the intelligence information gathered in the course of the detainee interviews may be of critical importance to national security, as detainees may reveal information leading to the identification and apprehension of other terrorist suspects and the prevent of additional terrorist acts. Thus, a protective order prohibiting the public dissemination of the detainee interview reports will, in this case, serve to prevent members of international terrorist organizations, including al Qaeda, from learning, from publicly available sources, the status of, the methods used in, and the information obtained from the ongoing investigation of detainees.

---

[230] The *News Media & The Law*, Spring, 1999, pp. 8–9.

[231] *United States v. Lindh*, 198 F.Supp.2d 739 (E.D.Va.2002).

[232] Ibid. at 742.

With respect to the battle over public opinion and the defense ability to sway potential jurors, the judge noted the obligations of both sides to avoid the use of the media.[233]

> Finally, defendant argues that the proposed protective order would impair his ability to use the media, as he contends the government has done, to influence public opinion with respect to this case. Defendant has no constitutional right to use the media to influence public opinion concerning his case so as to gain an advantage at trial No such right inheres in either the Sixth Amendment right to a public trial, or the public's First Amendment right to a free press.

In October, 2002, Lindh pleaded guilty to a charge of illegally providing support for the Taliban regime and illegally carrying weapons while serving in the Taliban forces. He received a 20-year term in a plea bargain that avoided the possibility of a public trial where sensitive information could have come out and the possibility of multiple life terms.

THE TRIAL OF ZACARIAS MOUSSAOUI

The continuing legal saga of admitted al Qaeda member Zacarias Moussaoui took another turn in June of 2003 when the 4th Circuit Court of Appeals ruled against a government attempt to prevent Moussaoui from interviewing a captured al Qaeda leader and two other enemy combatants held by the United States.

Moussaoui, the only person charged and convicted in the Sept. 11 attacks, sought to interview Ramzi Binalshibh, reportedly a high-ranking al Qaeda member who was captured in Pakistan. Moussaoui, who represented himself, said that Binalshibh has information that would clear him of the charges. Moussaoui also sought to interview other terrorism suspects in U.S. custody.

The government moved to prevent Moussaoui from gaining access to the suspects on the grounds that any contacts between Moussaoui and the suspects would disrupt its ongoing interrogations and compromise national security. Presiding U.S. District Judge Leonie Brinkema granted Moussaoui's request but permitted only a closed-circuit interview with Binalshibh. The government appealed her ruling to the 4th Circuit. The appellate panel hearing the case rejected the government's appeal on procedural grounds.[234] Because Judge Brinkema's order was not a "final order" it could not be appealed.[235]

[233] Ibid. at 743.

[234] *U.S. v. Moussaoui*, 333 F.3d 509 (4th Cir.2003).

[235] This is similar to the position that the 6th Circuit found itself in in the Procter & Gamble case discussed in Chap. 2.

Judge Brinkema also ordered that Moussaoui's future pleadings be sealed because of their content or intent.[236] Brinkema ruled that Moussaoui, acting as his own attorney, was trying to use the court to communicate with the outside world. Any future pleadings containing threats, racial slurs, calls to action or other inappropriate language would be sealed, the judge said.

PRIOR RESTRAINT REVISITED: CNN AND THE NORIEGA TAPES

The prosecution of Panamanian dictator Manuel Antonio Noriega during 1991 showed that judicial prior restraint still could occur. Although *Nebraska Press Association v. Stuart* (see text, above) still is regarded as a major bulwark against prior censorship by judges, the bizarre *Noriega Tapes* case showed that courts, on occasion, still can crack the prior restraint whip.

General Noriega, of course, was a most unusual suspect. Taken into custody after a massive U.S. deployment of armed forces, Noriega took sanctuary in a Vatican consulate. After several days of listening to American rock music played by troops surrounding the Vatican property, General Noriega surrendered. He was then spirited away to a well-appointed jail cell in Florida (outfitted with TV, telephone, and even a paper shredder). (Concerns about a fair trial for a foreign head of state who surrendered after a potent military attack seemed strained: Could a U.S. court *really* find a jury of his peers?)

Suspicion grew that the last thing the U.S. government wanted after Noriega survived the attack on Panama was to get the ex-dictator on the stand where he could sing about his former chums at the Central Intelligence Agency (CIA). In any event, someone got hold of tape recordings of Noriega's Florida jail-cell calls to the office of his attorney, Frank Rubino. The tapes, which Rubino claimed were evidence of a government plot to spy on Noriega's legal defense plans, were given to the Cable News Network (CNN).[237]

After CNN announced that it had the tapes, U.S. District Judge William Hoeveler, on Nov. 8, 1990, granted defense attorneys' request for an injunction to prevent CNN's broadcast of the tapes. Although CNN broadcast no taped excerpts of conversations between the general and his attorneys, excerpts of Noriega's calls to others were broadcast.

Judge Hoeveler evidently saw CNN's eagerness to use the tapes as raising two Sixth Amendment questions: Violation of the attorney-client privilege and the possibility of revealing information harmful to Noriega's defense. Even though Judge Hoeveler noted that prior

---

[236] Tom Jackman, "Gag Rules Apply to Justice Officials, Judge Rules," *Washington Post*, Aug. 30, 2002.

[237] "Tales of the Tape," *Newsweek*, Dec. 17, 1990, p. 29; "Eavesdropping on Noriega," *Newsweek*, Nov. 19, 1990.

restraints are "presumptively unconstitutional," he held that the barrier laid down by a three-part test in *Nebraska Press Association v. Stuart* was not insurmountable. The *Nebraska Press* test for justifying prior restraint to prevent prejudicial publicity requires that:[238]

1. Publicity must impair the right to a fair trial.

2. No less restrictive alternative to prior restraint is available or practicable to mitigate effects of the publicity, and

3. A prior restraint would effectively prevent the harm to defendant's rights.

Judge Hoeveler found that in this instance, prior restraint was justifiable, and ordered a temporary injunction against CNN's broadcast of the tapes until the court could review the tapes in CNN's possession. The following day—Nov. 9, 1990—after an emergency appeal by CNN to the Eleventh Circuit Court of Appeals, Judge Hoeveler limited the temporary injunction to ten days. He complained about CNN's refusal to turn over the tapes to him, putting him in the position of having to make rulings without having heard them.

The next day—Nov. 10, 1990—the Court of Appeals ruled that the temporary restraining order should remain in effect. The appellate court upheld Judge Hoeveler's injunction against CNN and his demand for production of the tapes.[239] Meanwhile, CNN indeed had been defiant, for it repeatedly broadcast—on Nov. 9—a taped conversation said to be an interchange between Noriega and a legal secretary working for his attorneys. Noriega's attorneys asked for dismissal of the charges against their client and that CNN be fined $300,000 each time it played one of the tapes.[240]

CNN then withdrew a bit, agreeing on Nov. 12 to halt playing the tapes until the U.S. Supreme Court could rule. Noriega contended that he was being railroaded and was powerless before an unjust legal system.[241]

On Nov. 18, 1990, moving swiftly only eight days after the Court of Appeals ruling against CNN, the U.S. Supreme Court allowed the injunction to stand, denying CNN's petition for a writ of certiorari.[242]

After this defeat, CNN handed over the Noriega tapes to a federal magistrate who reported his evaluation of the tapes to U.S. District Judge Hoeveler. Anticlimactically, Judge Hoeveler ruled that CNN could broadcast the taped conversations. CNN, however, decided not to put the

---

[238] *United States v. Noriega*, 752 F.Supp. 1032, 1033 (S.D.Fla.1990), 18 Med.L.Rptr. 1348, 1349.

[239] *In re Cable News Network, Inc.*, 917 F.2d 1543, 1547 (11th Cir.1990), 18 Med.L.Rptr. 1352, 1358.

[240] "CNN to Delay Playing of Noriega Tapes," *New York Times*, Nov. 13, 1990.

[241] Ibid.; see also David Johnston, "Noriega Tells Judge He's at Mercy of an Unfair and Unjust System," *New York Times*, Nov. 17, 1990.

[242] *Cable News Network, Inc. v. Noriega*, 498 U.S. 976, 111 S.Ct. 451 (1990).

tapes on the air * * * at least, not immediately.[243] The *New York Times* confessed to being puzzled by CNN's behavior: Challenging a U.S. district judge, ultimately getting his permission to run the tapes, and then not doing so. A *Times* editorial said:[244]

> The network's actions and news judgments obscure the important feature of its own story. The existence, not the airing, of some tapes requires explanation from the [U.S.] Justice Department. What safeguards [for defendant Noriega] were in place at Miami's Metropolitan Correction Center and how were they violated?

On March 30, 1994, long after CNN's broadcast excerpts of the "Noriega tapes," CNN was charged with criminal contempt for " 'knowingly and wilfully' " disobeying Judge Hoeveler's November, 1990, injunction. Lawyers for CNN attended the arraignment proceeding, pleading not guilty before Judge Hoeveler in the cable network's behalf.[245]

In September, 1994, Judge Hoeveler began a non-jury trial, after offering to assign the case to another judge and to empanel and advisory jury to try questions of fact. Neither the Department of Justice, prosecuting, nor CNN, the defendant, accepted those offers.[246]

On November 1, 1994, Judge Hoeveler found CNN guilty as charged of criminal contempt of court, setting the hearing on sanctions to be levied against CNN for Dec. 9, 1994. Judge Hoeveler acknowledged the press's First Amendment responsibility to provide news of government misconduct, and then wrote:[247]

> * * * CNN, however, had already revealed the potential government misconduct. The intense pressure to play the tapes was actually coming from other news organizations, challenging CNN to show them the tapes or "where's the beef?" * * * [Such circumstances] do not justify the action taken by defendant. The 11th Circuit has held that even when a court's order is ultimately deemed to be invalid, the collateral bar rule requires parties to follow that order.
>
> * * *
>
> The thin bright line between anarchy and order—the delicate balance which ultimately is the vital protection of the individual and the public generally—is the rampart which litigants and the

[243] David Johnston, "Judge Lifts Ban on Noriega Tapes; No Broadcast is Planned," *New York Times*, Nov. 29, 1990.

[244] "Odd Behavior in the Noriega Case," *New York Times*, Dec. 1, 1990.

[245] Associated Press, "CNN charged in airing tape of Noriega's talks to lawyers," The Knoxville *News-Sentinel*, March 31, 1994, p. A12; Larry Rohter, "CNN Charged With Ignoring Court Order on Noriega Tapes," *New York Times*, March 31, 1994.

[246] District Judge William M. Hoeveler's decision in *United States v. Cable News Network, Inc.*, 865 F.Supp. 1549 (S.D.Fla.1994).

[247] Ibid. at 1564.

public have for the law and the orders issued by the courts. Defiance of court orders and, even more so, public display of such defiance cannot be justified or permitted.

Late in December, 1994, CNN complied with an order from Judge Hoeveler, ending the dispute by broadcasting an apology and paying $85,000 to reimburse the special prosecutor's costs.

59. ACCESS TO CRIMINAL TRIALS AND CIVIL MATTERS

Gannett v. DePasquale declared that pre-trial matters could be closed to press and public; _Richmond Newspapers v. Virginia_ held that there is a First Amendment right to attend trials.

The Supreme Court had some good news for the press in 1978, and it came in the decision in *Landmark Communications, Inc. v. Virginia*. *The Virginian Pilot*, a daily newspaper owned by Landmark, late in 1975 published an accurate article reporting on a pending investigation by the Virginia Judicial Inquiry and Review Commission. The article named a state judge whose conduct was being investigated. Because such proceedings were required to be confidential by the Constitution of Virginia and by related enabling statutes, a grand jury indicted Landmark for violating Virginia law.

The newspaper's managing editor, Joseph W. Dunn, Jr., testified that he had chosen to publish material about the Judicial Inquiry and Review Commission because he believed the subject was a matter of public importance. Dunn stated that although he knew it was a misdemeanor for participants in such an action to divulge information from that Commission's proceedings, he did not think that the statute applied to newspaper reports.[248]

Chief Justice Burger, writing for a unanimous Court, said the issue was whether the First Amendment allows criminal punishment of third persons—including news media representatives—who publish truthful information about proceedings of the Judicial Inquiry and Review Commission. The Court concluded that "the publication Virginia seeks to punish under its statute lies near the core of the First Amendment, and the Commonwealth's interests advanced by the imposition of criminal sanctions are insufficient to justify the actual and potential encroachments on freedom of speech and of the press."

Although the Commission was entitled to meet in secret, and could preserve confidentiality of its proceedings and working papers, the press could not be punished for publication of such information once it has obtained it.[249]

Obtaining information about judicial proceedings, of course, implies access by public and press to those proceedings. And then, after the "good

[248] *Landmark Communications, Inc. v. Virginia*, 435 U.S. 829, 98 S.Ct. 1535 (1978).

[249] Ibid. at 838, 1541.

news" of *Landmark Communications*, along came one of the Supreme Court's unpleasant surprises for the press: *Gannett v. DePasquale*.[250]

GANNETT V. DEPASQUALE

Journalists are taught that government should never be given the power of secret arrest, secret confinement, or secret trial. With its decision in *Gannett v. DePasquale*, the Supreme Court of the United States said, in effect, that two out of three aren't bad. In a badly fragmented 5–4 vote, with a total of five opinions written, the Court held that the public—including the press—has no right to attend pretrial hearings. The issue in *DePasquale* was narrow: the Gannett Company was seeking to overturn a ruling barring its reporter from a pretrial hearing and forbidding the immediate release of a transcript of a secret hearing.

The Court's majority, however, did not restrict itself to pretrial hearings. Justice Potter Stewart's majority opinion also declared that the rights guaranteed by the Sixth Amendment did not extend to the public or to the press. Instead, those rights "are personal to the accused. * * * We hold that members of the public [and thus the press] have no constitutional right to attend criminal trials." Joining Justice Stewart in that view were Justices William Rehnquist and John Paul Stevens.

Chief Justice Warren E. Burger joined the opinion of the Court, but argued that by definition, a " * * * ; hearing on a motion before trial is not a *trial:* it is a *pre*-trial hearing." Mr. Justice Lewis Powell, like the Chief Justice, concurred separately. Justice Powell expressed the belief that the reporter had an interest protected by the First Amendment to attend the pretrial hearing. However, he added that this right of access to courtroom proceedings is not absolute and must be balanced against a defendant's Sixth Amendment fair trial rights. In his concurring opinion, Justice William Rehnquist said that so far as the Constitution is concerned, it is up to the lower courts, "by accommodating competing interests in a judicious manner," to decide whether to open or close a court proceeding.

In a 44-page dissent joined by Justices William Brennan, Byron White, and Thurgood Marshall, Justice Harry Blackmun contended that the Sixth Amendment guarantees the public's right to attend hearings and trials. Justice Blackmun wrote that the Court's majority overreacted to "placid, routine, and innocuous" coverage of a criminal prosecution.

Gannett v. DePasquale arose when 42-year-old former policeman Wayne Clapp did not return from a July, 1976, fishing trip on upstate New York's Lake Seneca. He had been fishing with two men, aged 16 and 21, and those men returned in the boat without Clapp and drove away in Clapp's pickup truck. They were later arrested in Michigan after Clapp's

---

[250] *Gannett v. DePasquale,* 443 U.S. 368, 99 S.Ct. 2898 (1979).

disappearance had been reported and after bullet holes were found in Clapp's boat.

Gannett newspapers, the morning *Democrat & Chronicle* and the evening *Times-Union,* published stories about Clapp's disappearance and reported on police speculations that Clapp had been shot on his own boat and his body dumped overboard. In one story, the *Democrat & Chronicle* reported that the 16-year-old suspect, Kyle Greathouse, had led Michigan police to a place where he had buried Clapp's .357 magnum revolver. Defense attorneys then began taking steps to try to suppress statements made to police, claiming that those statements had been given involuntarily. The defense also tried to suppress evidence turned up in relation to the allegedly involuntary confessions, including the pistol.

During a pretrial hearing, when defense attorneys requested that press and public be excluded, Justice Daniel DePasquale granted the motion, evidently fearing that reporting on the hearing might prejudice defendants' rights in a later trial. Neither the prosecution nor reporter Carol Ritter of the *Democrat & Chronicle* objected to the clearing of the courtroom. On the next day, however, Ritter wrote Judge DePasquale, asserting a right to cover the hearing and asking to be given access to the transcript. The judge, refused to rescind his exclusion order or to grant the press or public immediate access to a transcript of the pre-trial hearing. Judge DePasquale's orders were overturned by an intermediate-level New York appeals court, but were upheld by the state's highest court, the Court of Appeals.[251] The Supreme Court of the United States subsequently granted certiorari.[252]

Although the issue of covering a pretrial hearing on suppression of evidence is technically narrow, it is important. As James C. Goodale, former vice president of the *New York Times,* has written:[253]

> Only a fraction of the criminal cases brought ever go to trial. The real courtroom for most criminal trials in the United States is the pre-trial hearing, where proceedings of a vital public concern often take place. * * * [A] successful suppression motion will probably mean that an account of the improper methods the police have used to extract a certain confession will be brought out only at the pretrial hearing, and nowhere else. * * * [T]his is information which the public needs to have if its public officers are to be held accountable. Without multiplying examples, we need only remember the shocking trials of Ginzburg and Scharansky behind closed doors in Russia in the summer of

[251] *Gannett Co., Inc. v. De Pasquale,* 43 N.Y.2d 370, 401 N.Y.S.2d 756, 372 N.E.2d 544 (1977), reversing the Supreme Court of the State of New York, Appellate Division, Fourth Department's decision in 55 A.D.2d 107, 389 N.Y.S.2d 719 (1976).

[252] *Gannett Co., Inc. v. De Pasquale,* 443 U.S. 368, 99 S.Ct. 2898 (1979).

[253] James C. Goodale, "Open Justice: The Threat of *Gannett,*" *Communications and the Law,* Vol. 1, No. 1 (Winter, 1979) pp. 12–13.

1978 to realize that criminal trials in this country must remain open.

Other constitutional scholars and a variety of publications expressed both shock and outrage at the Supreme Court's decision in *De Pasquale.* Fear of secret trials is in the American grain. Even though England's despised secret Court of the Star Chamber was abolished in 1641, it has been remembered as a symbol of persecution ever since. The assumption by both public and press has long been that open trials are needed to make sure that justice is done. Harvard Law Professor Lawrence Tribe, a leading scholar, said after *De Pasquale* was decided that there " ' * * * will be no need to gag the press if stories can be choked off at the source.' " Allen Neuharth, chairman of The Gannett Co., Inc., declared that " ' * * * those judges who share the philosophy of secret trials can now run Star Chamber justice.' "[254] In any event, the *De Pasquale* holding was far removed from Justice William O. Douglas's words in a 1947 contempt of court case, *Craig v. Harney*: "[w]hat transpires in the court room is public property."[255]

Justice Potter Stewart wrote for the Court:[256]

* * *

> Publicity concerning pretrial suppression hearings such as the one involved in the present case poses special risks of unfairness. The whole purpose of such hearings is to screen out unreliable or illegally obtained evidence and insure that this evidence does not become known to the jury. Cf. *Jackson v. Denno*, 378 U.S. 368, 84 S.Ct. 1774 (1964). Publicity concerning the proceedings at a pretrial hearing, however, could influence public opinion against a defendant and inform potential jurors of inculpatory information wholly inadmissible at the actual trial.

* * *

> The Sixth Amendment, applicable to the States through the Fourteenth, surrounds a criminal trial with guarantees such as the rights to notice, confrontation, and compulsory process that have as their overriding purpose the protection of the accused from prosecutorial and judicial abuses. Among the guarantees that the Amendment provides to a person charged with the commission of a criminal offense, and to him alone, is the "right to a speedy and public trial, by an impartial jury." The Constitution nowhere mentioned any right of access to a criminal trial on the part of the public; its guarantee, like the others enumerated, is personal to the accused. See *Faretta v.*

[254] "Slamming the Courtroom Doors," *Time Magazine*, July 16, 1979.

[255] *Craig v. Harney*, 331 U.S. 367, 374, 67 S.Ct. 1249, 1254 (1947).

[256] *Gannett Co., Inc. v. DePasquale*, 443 U.S. 368, 378–381, 99 S.Ct. 2898, 2905–2906 (1979).

> *California*, 422 U.S. 806, 846, 95 S.Ct. 2525, 2546 (1975) ("[T]he specific guarantees of the Sixth Amendment are personal to the accused.") (Blackmun, J., dissenting).
>
> Our cases have uniformly recognized the public trial guarantee as one created for the benefit of the defendant.

Chief Justice Burger's concurring opinion simply maintained that by definition, a hearing on a motion before trial to suppress evidence is not a *trial,* it is a *pre-trial* hearing. Trials should be open, but pre-trial proceedings are "private to the litigants" and could be closed.

Justice Powell's concurrence argued that the reporter had an interest protected by the First and Fourteenth Amendments in being present at the pretrial suppression hearing. He added:[257]

> As I have argued *in Saxbe v. Washington Post Co.*, 417 U.S. 843, 850, 94 S.Ct. 2811, 2815 (1974) (Powell, J., dissenting), this constitutional protection derives, not from any special status of members of the press as such, but rather because "[i]n seeking out the news the press * * * acts as an agent of the public at large," each individual member of which cannot obtain for himself "the information needed for the intelligent discharge of his political responsibilities." Id., at 863, 94 S.Ct., at 2821.

Justice Powell then swung into his balancing act, stating that the right of access to courtroom proceedings is not absolute. It is limited by both the right of defendants to a fair trial and by needs of governments to obtain convictions and to maintain the confidentiality of sensitive information and of the identity of informants. In his view, representatives of the public and the press must be given an opportunity to protest closure motions. Then it would be the defendant's burden to offer evidence that the fairness of his trial would be jeopardized by public and press access to the proceedings. On the other hand, the press and public should have to show that alternative procedures are available which would take away dangers to the defendant's chances of receiving a fair trial.[258]

Justice Rehnquist's concurring opinion scoffed that Justice Powell was advancing the idea " * * * that the First Amendment is some sort of constitutional 'sunshine law' that requires notice, an opportunity to be heard and substantial reasons before a governmental proceeding may be closed to public and press."[259]

Justice Blackmun's lengthy dissent was joined by Justices Brennan, White, and Marshall. Blackmun termed the news coverage of this case "placid, routine, and innocuous" and, indeed, relatively infrequent. After a long review of Anglo-American historical and constitutional

---

257 Ibid. at 397–398, 2914.

258 Ibid. at 398–399, 2915.

259 Ibid. at 405, 2918.

underpinnings for public trials, he pointed to dangers he saw in closing court proceedings.[260]

> I, for one, am unwilling to allow trials and suppression hearings to be closed with no way to ensure that the public interest is protected. Unlike the other provisions of the Sixth Amendment, the public trial interest cannot adequately be protected by the prosecutor and judge in conjunction, or connivance, with the defendant. The specter of a trial or suppression hearing where a defendant of the same political party as the prosecutor and the judge—both of whom are elected officials perhaps beholden to the very defendant they are to try—obtains closure of the proceeding without any consideration for the substantial public interest at stake is sufficiently real to cause me to reject the Court's suggestion that the parties be given complete discretion to dispose of the public's interest as they see fit. The decision of the parties to close a proceeding in such a circumstance, followed by suppression of vital evidence or acquittal by the bench, destroys the appearance of justice and undermines confidence in the judicial system in a way no subsequent provision of a transcript might remedy. * * *
>
> * * *
>
> It has been said that publicity "is the soul of justice." J. Bentham, *A Treatise on Judicial Evidence*, 67 (1825). And in many ways it is: open judicial processes, especially in the criminal field, protect against judicial, prosecutorial, and police abuse; provide a means for citizens to obtain information about the criminal justice system and the performance of public officials; and safeguard the integrity of the courts. Publicity is essential to the preservation of public confidence in the rule of law and in the operation of courts.

RICHMOND NEWSPAPERS V. VIRGINIA

On July 2, 1980—exactly one year after the Supreme Court of the United States ruled in *Gannett Co., Inc. v. DePasquale*[261] that pretrial hearings could be closed—the Court held 7–1 that the public and the press have a First Amendment right to attend criminal trials. The 1980 case, *Richmond Newspapers, Inc. v. Virginia*, brought joyous responses from the press.

Anthony Lewis of the *New York Times* wrote, "For once a Supreme Court decision deserves that overworked adjective, historic."[262] His newspaper editorialized: "Now the Supreme Court has reasserted the obvious, at least as it pertains to trials. 'A presumption of openness

---

[260] Ibid. at 438–439, 448, 2935–2936, 2940.

[261] *Richmond Newspapers v. Virginia*, 448 U.S. 555, 100 S.Ct. 2814 (1980).

[262] Anthony Lewis, "A Right To Be Informed," *New York Times*, July 3, 1980.

inheres in the very nature of a criminal trial under our system of justice.' "[263] Even though *Richmond Newspapers* did not overrule *Gannett* where pretrial matters are concerned, the Court's 1980 reliance on the First Amendment—and not on the Sixth Amendment as in *Gannett*—gave hope to journalists.

Justice John Paul Stevens' concurring opinion likewise saw *Richmond Newspapers* as remarkable: "This is a watershed case." He continued,[264]

> Until today the Court has accorded virtually absolute protection to the dissemination of information or ideas, but never before has it squarely held that the acquisition of newsworthy matter is entitled to any constitutional protection whatsoever.

Lewis said "the Court today established for the first time that the Constitution gives the public a right to learn how public institutions function: a crucial right in a democracy."[265] Attorney James Goodale said the *Richmond* case would help reporters to see " 'prisons, small-town meetings, the police blotter' " and other places and documents often closed to the news media in the past.

Years ago, Judge Learned Hand described his career on the bench as "shoveling smoke." In 1979, the Supreme Court unlimbered its smoke generator in the infamous *Gannett* case, ruling by a 5–4 margin that the public and the press did not have a right to attend pre-trial proceedings in criminal cases. Some of the Justices' language billowed beyond pre-trial matters. As noted, Justice Potter Stewart's plurality opinion announcing the Court's judgment in *Gannett* declared that rights guaranteed by the Sixth Amendment did not reach to the public or to the press. Those rights, said Stewart, " * * * are personal to the accused. * * * We hold that members of the public [and thus the press] have no constitutional right to attend criminal trials."[266]

Four members of the Court later made public statements professing shock about the way *Gannett* had been "misinterpreted," and that wholesale closings had not been endorsed by a majority of the Court. Howls of protest arose from the media. Goodale, then executive vice president of the *New York Times,* wrote in 1979 that only a small fraction—perhaps 10 per cent—of all criminal cases reach the trial stage. The real courtroom for most criminal proceedings is the pre-trial hearing.[267]

In the wake of *Gannett,* many pretrial *and* trial proceedings were closed. As a study by The Reporters Committee for Freedom of the Press showed, in the 10 months between the *Gannett* decision of July 2, 1979

---

[263] Editorial, "Wiping the Graffiti Off the Courtroom," *New York Times,* July 3, 1980.

[264] Opinion of Mr. Justice Stevens, 448 U.S. 555, 581, 100 S.Ct. 2814, 2830 (1980).

[265] Lewis, loc. cit.

[266] *Gannett Co., Inc. v. DePasquale,* 443 U.S. 368, 99 S.Ct. 2898 (1979).

[267] Goodale, loc. cit.

and April 30, 1980, there were at least 220 attempts to close criminal justice proceedings. More than half were successful. Jack C. Landau, director of The Reporters Committee, wrote that "[j]udges are closing pre-indictment, trial, and post-trial proceedings, in addition to pre-trial proceedings."[268] *Newsweek* reported that in the year after *Gannett,* 155 proceedings were closed, including 30 actual trials. Four hundred attempts were made to close courtrooms between July, 1979, and May, 1981.[269]

The *Richmond* case arose when Baltimore resident John Paul Stevenson was convicted of second-degree murder in the slaying of a Hanover County, Virginia, motel manager. In late 1977, however, the Virginia Supreme Court reversed Stevenson's conviction, concluding that a bloodstained shirt belonging to Stevenson had been admitted improperly as evidence.[270] Subsequently, two additional jury trials of Stevenson ended in mistrials, one when a juror had to be excused and the other because a prospective juror may have read about the defendant's previous trials and may have told other jurors about the case before the retrial began.

On Sept. 11, 1978, the same court—for the fourth time—attempted to try Stevenson. Reporters Tim Wheeler of the *Richmond Times-Dispatch* and Kevin McCarthy of the *Richmond News-Leader,* along with all other members of the public, were barred from the courtroom by Hanover County Circuit Court Judge Richard H.C. Taylor, after defense counsel said:[271]

> "[T]here was this woman that was with the family of the deceased when we were here before. She had sat in the Courtroom. I would like to ask that everybody be excluded from the Courtroom because I don't want any information being shuffled back and forth when we have a recess as to what—who testified to what."

Trial Judge Taylor had presided after two of the previous three trials of Stevenson. After hearing that the prosecution had no objection to the closure, excluded all parties from the trial except witnesses when they testified.[272] Since no one—including reporters Wheeler and McCarthy—had objected to closure, the order was made. Later that same day, however, the Richmond newspapers and their reporters asked for a hearing on a motion to vacate the closure order. Reporters were not

---

[268] The Reporters Committee for Freedom of the Press, Court Watch Summary, May, 1980; *Southern Newspaper Publishers Association Bulletin,* Aug. 10, 1981.

[269] *Newsweek,* July 14, 1980.

[270] *Stevenson v. Commonwealth,* 218 Va. 462, 237 S.E.2d 779 (1977).

[271] Opinion of Chief Justice Burger, *Richmond Newspapers, Inc. v. Virginia,* 448 U.S. 555, 559, 100 S.Ct. 2814, 2818 (1980).

[272] Virginia Code § 19.2–2.66, which provided that courts may, in their discretion, exclude any persons from the trial whose presence would impair the trial's conduct, provided that the right of an accused to a fair trial shall not be violated.

allowed to attend the hearing on that order, however, since Judge Taylor ruled that it was a part of the trial. The closure order remained in force.

On the trial's second day, Judge Taylor—after excusing the jury—declared that Stevenson was not guilty of murder, and the defendant was allowed to leave. The Richmond Newspapers then appealed the court closing, unsuccessfully petitioning the Virginia Supreme Court for writs of mandamus and prohibition. The Supreme Court of the United States granted certiorari.

CHIEF JUSTICE BURGER'S OPINION

Chief Justice Warren Burger reiterated his view, as stated in *Gannett v. DePasquale*, that while pre-trial hearings need not be open, trials should be open. In this case, he did not take the Sixth Amendment (right to fair trial) route of the majority in *DePasquale*.[273] Instead, he emphasized that the question in *Richmond Newspapers*[274] was whether the First and Fourteenth Amendments guarantee a right of the public (including the press) to attend trials.

He said that in prior cases, the Court has dealt with questions involving conflicts between publicity and defendants' rights to a fair trial, including *Nebraska Press Association v. Stuart*,[275] *Sheppard v. Maxwell*,[276] and *Estes v. Texas*.[277] But this case, in his view, was a "first:" the Court was asked to decide whether a criminal trial itself may be closed to the public on the defendant's request alone, with no showing that closure is required to protect the right to a fair trial.

After having thus stated the issue, the Chief Justice traced Anglo-American judicial history back to the days before the Norman Conquest and forward through the American colonial experience.[278] In addition to this historical ammunition, Burger quoted Dean Wigmore, who wrote long ago that " '[t]he publicity of a judicial proceeding is a requirement of much broader bearing than its mere effect on the quality of testimony.' " The Chief Justice also found a "significant community therapeutic value" in public trials. He then became expansive about the role of the press as a stand-in for the public, a role often claimed by the press but one which had received little judicial support.[279]

> Looking back, we see that when the ancient "town meeting" form of trial became too cumbersome, twelve members of the

---

[273] *Gannett Co., Inc. v. DePasquale*, 443 U.S. 368, 99 S.Ct. 2898 (1979).

[274] *Richmond Newspapers, Inc. v. Virginia*, 448 U.S. 555, 564, 100 S.Ct. 2814, 2821 (1980).

[275] *Nebraska Press Association v. Stuart*, 427 U.S. 539, 96 S.Ct. 2791 (1976).

[276] *Sheppard v. Maxwell*, 384 U.S. 333, 86 S.Ct. 1507 (1966).

[277] *Estes v. Texas*, 381 U.S. 532, 85 S.Ct. 1628 (1965). The Chief Justice also cited *Murphy v. Florida*, 421 U.S. 794, 95 S.Ct. 2031 (1975), in which Jack (Murph the Surf) Murphy, unsuccessfully pleaded that prejudicial pre-trial publicity had deprived him of a fair day in court.

[278] *Richmond Newspapers, Inc. v. Virginia*, 448 U.S. 555, 100 S.Ct. 2814 (1980).

[279] Ibid. at 572, 2825,

> community were delegated to act as surrogates, but the community did not surrender its right to observe the conduct of trials. The people retained a "right of visitation" which enabled them to satisfy themselves that justice was in fact being done.
>
> People in an open society do not demand infallibility from their institutions, but it is difficult for them to accept what they are prohibited from observing.
>
> * * *
>
> In earlier times, both in England and America, attendance at court was a common mode of "passing the time." * * * With the press, cinema and electronic media now supplying the representations of reality of the real life drama once available only in the courtroom, attendance at court is no longer a widespread pastime. * * * Instead of acquiring information about trials by firsthand observation or by word of mouth from those who attended, people now acquire it chiefly through the print and electronic media. In a sense, this validates the media claim of functioning as surrogates for the public. While media representatives enjoy the same right of access as the public, they often are provided special seating and priority of entry so that they may report what people in attendance have seen and heard. This "contribute[s] to public understanding of the rule of law and to comprehension of the functioning of the entire criminal justice system. * * * " *Nebraska Press Ass'n v. Stuart*, 427 U.S. 539, 587, 96 S.Ct. 2791, 2816 (1976) (Brennan, J., concurring).

Burger then disposed of the State of Virginia's arguments that neither the constitution nor the Bill of Rights contains guarantees of a public right to attend trials. He responded that the Court has recognized that "certain unarticulated rights" are implicit in the Bill of Rights, including the rights of association, privacy, and the right to attend criminal trials. He then inserted footnote 17, which became important in the future: "Whether the public has a right to attend trials of civil cases is a question not by this case, but we note that historically *both civil and criminal trials* have been presumptively open."[280]

Despite the sweep of Burger's words, he was not saying that all criminal trials must be open to the press and public. Instead, he criticized the conduct of the court in the murder trial of John Paul Stevenson. There, despite its being the fourth trial of the defendant, the judge " * * * made no findings to support closure; no inquiry was made as to whether alternative solutions [such as sequestration of the jury] would have met the need to insure fairness; there was no recognition of any right under the Constitution for the public or press to attend the trial." He concluded: "Absent an overriding interest articulated in findings, the trial of a

[280] Ibid. at 581, 2829, at footnote 17. Emphasis added.

criminal case must be open to the public. Accordingly, the judgment under review is reversed."[281]

Note that Justice Powell took no part in the consideration or decision of this case. And remember that Powell declared, concurring in *Gannett v. DePasquale,* that reporters had a *limited* First Amendment right to attend pre-trial hearings. And Justices Blackmun, Brennan, White, and Marshall all agreed that public and press had a right, either under the First or the Sixth Amendment, to attend both pre-trial hearings and trials. Thus, although the First Amendment is not an absolute, it appears that the breadth of the language in *Richmond Newspapers* about *trials* has once again made attendance at *pre-trial* proceedings an open question.

In his concurring opinion, Justice Stevens said:[282]

> * * * I agree that the First Amendment protects the public and the press from abridgment of their rights of access to information about the operation of their government, including the judicial branch; given the total absence of any record justification for the closure order entered in this case, that order violated the First Amendment.

Justice Brennan, joined by Justice Marshall, presented a marvelously complex concurrence, speaking of the structural value of public access in various circumstances. "But the First Amendment embodies more than a commitment to free expression and communicative interchange for their own sakes; it has a *structural* role to play in securing and fostering our republican form of self-government." He added:[283]

> Open trials assure the public that procedural rights are respected, and that justice is afforded equally. Closed trials breed suspicion of prejudice and arbitrariness, which in turn spawns disrespect for the law. Public access is essential, therefore, if trial adjudication is to achieve the objective of maintaining public confidence in the administration of justice.

Note also that Justice Rehnquist, seeming unconcerned by possible threats of secret judicial proceedings to society, was the only member of the court in both the *Gannett* and *Richmond* cases who could find no support for a right of public and press to attend judicial proceedings under either a Sixth Amendment or First Amendment rationale.[284]

---

[281] Ibid. at 581, 2830.

[282] Ibid. at 584, 2829.

[283] Ibid. at 595, 2833, 2837.

[284] Ibid. at 606, 2843.

ACCESS RIGHTS NEED DEFENSE

Although *Richmond Newspapers* has a much nicer ring *than Gannett v. DePasquale*, it did leave unanswered questions about the right to cover pre-trial matters, the matters which make up the bulk of our criminal justice process. During the dark days of 1979 and '80, after *Gannett v. DePasquale* was decided, reporters covering the judicial process began carrying their "Gannett cards." Various organizations made up statements for reporters to read in court when they were about to be ousted from pre-trial or trial proceedings. In fact, a Gannett card—literally from the Gannett organization—said:[285]

> "Your honor, I am ___, a reporter for ___, and I would like to object on behalf of my employer and the public to this proposed closing. Our attorney is prepared to make a number of arguments against closings such as this one, and we respectfully ask the Court for a hearing on those issues. I believe our attorney can be here relatively quickly for the Court's convenience and he will be able to demonstrate that closure in this case will violate the First Amendment, and possibly state statutory and constitutional provisions as well. I cannot make the arguments myself, but our attorney can point out several issues for your consideration. If it pleases the Court, we request the opportunity to be heard through counsel."

Reporters, then, should hang on to their "Gannett Cards" and be ready to read them should a judge decide—on application from counsel—to give them the heave-ho from a judicial (including pre-trial) proceedings. After all, as attorney James C. Goodale has written, even the *Gannett* case required three conditions before closure of a pre-trial hearing:[286]

> (1) there would be irreparable damage to the defendant's fair trial rights,
>
> (2) there were no alternative means to deal with the publicity and
>
> (3) the closure would be effective, i.e. no leaks.

In order to close a criminal trial, three things must be done by the court:

> (1) The court must make detailed findings.
>
> (2) The court must find a substantial probability of prejudice to a compelling interest of the defendant, government, or third party, which closure would prevent.

[285] Other news organizations, such as Knight-Ridder, had similar cards made for their reporters.

[286] James C. Goodale, "The Three-Part Open Door Test in Richmond Newspapers Case," *The National Law Journal*, Sept. 22, 1980.

(3) The court must have considered alternatives and choose the least restrictive means to protect the compelling interests identified.

If judicial proceedings are to remain open, reporters will have to stand ready to speak up, to protest closures. And their employers, obviously, will have to stand ready to go to court—to expend the money and energy to try to keep court proceedings open. Without protests and court tests, closures will simply occur. And when contested, closures can often be reversed. Reporters in courts—whether they like it or not—must sometimes be a first line of defense against secret court proceedings.[287]

The issue of closure remains a problem even today. In the fall of 2006, the *Fort Worth Star-Telegram* challenged a Texas judge's order banning the public and press from attending hearings in a criminal case and also reporting details from the case.[288] State District Judge Wayne Salvant barred access to pretrial hearings involving three former Texas Christian University student athletes charged with sexually assaulting another student. A lawyer for one of the student athletes had asked for the closure because she was concerned about the effect of publicity on her client's Sixth Amendment rights. A few days later, following widespread reporting on the action, the judge cancelled the order saying it was overly broad.[289]

ACCESS TO COURTS AFTER RICHMOND NEWSPAPERS

During the first few years after *Richmond Newspapers v. Virginia* (1980), the Supreme Court of the United States filled in some of that decision's promising outlines where coverage of the judicial process is concerned. Four key cases are:[290]

1. *Globe Newspaper Co. v. Superior Court* (1982)
2. *Press-Enterprise Co. v. Superior Court* (1984) ("*Press Enterprise I*")
3. *Waller v. Georgia* (1984)
4. *Press-Enterprise Co. v. Superior Court* (1986) "*Press-Enterprise II* (1986)"

---

[287] See James D. Spaniolo, Dan Paul, Parker D. Thomson and Richard Ovelman, "Access After *Richmond Newspapers,*" in James C. Goodale, chairman, *Communications Law 1980* (New York: Practising Law Institute, 1980), pp. 385–648, for an intensive discussion of and listing of recent cases involving access to judicial proceedings. See especially pp. 452–456, dealing with access to judicial records.

[288] Melody McDonald, "Star-Telegram challenging judge's order in case of former TCU athletes," *Fort Worth Star-Telegram*, Oct. 28, 2006.

[289] Max B. Baker, "Gag order lifted in rape case," *Fort Worth Star-Telegram*, Nov. 2, 2006.

[290] *Globe Newspaper Co. v. Superior Court for Norfolk County*, 457 U.S. 596, 102 S.Ct. 2613 (1982). 1689; *Press-Enterprise Co. v. Superior Court of California*, 464 U.S. 501, 104 S.Ct. 819 (1984). 1161; *Waller v. Georgia*, 467 U.S. 39, 104 S.Ct. 2210 (1984); *Press-Enterprise Company v. Superior Court*, 478 U.S. 1, 106 S.Ct. 2735 (1986).

GLOBE NEWSPAPER CO. V. SUPERIOR COURT

The Boston Globe challenged the constitutionality of a Massachusetts statute providing for the exclusion of the public from trials of certain sex offenses involving victims under the age of 18. *Globe* reporters had tried unsuccessfully to get access to a rape trial in the Superior Court for the County of Norfolk, Massachusetts. Charges against the defendant in the trial involved forcible rape and forced unnatural rape of three girls who were minors at the time of the trial—two were 16 and one was 17. Writing for the Court, Justice Brennan held that the Massachusetts statute providing for mandatory closure of such cases violated the First Amendment of access to criminal trials. He said:[291]

> The Court's recent decision in Richmond Newspapers firmly established for the first time that the press and the general public have a constitutional right of access to criminal trials. Although there was no opinion of the Court in that case, seven Justices recognized that this right of access is embodied in the First Amendment, and applied to the States through the Fourteenth Amendment.
>
> * * *
>
> * * * [T]he right of access to criminal trials plays a particularly significant role in the functioning of the judicial process and the government as a whole. Public scrutiny of a criminal trial enhances the quality and safeguards the integrity of the fact-finding process, with benefits to both the defendant and to society as a whole.
>
> * * *
>
> We agree * * * that the first interest—safeguarding the physical and psychological well being of a minor is a compelling one. But as compelling as that is, it does not justify a mandatory closure rule, for it is clear that the circumstances of the particular case may affect the significance of the interest. A trial court can determine on a case-by-case basis whether closure is necessary to protect the welfare of a minor victim.

Chief Justice Burger and Justice Rehnquist dissented, complaining that Justice Brennan had ignored " * * * a long history of exclusion of the public from trials involving sexual assaults, particularly those against minors."[292]

---

[291] *Globe Newspaper Co. v. Superior Court for Norfolk County*, 457 U.S. 596, 603–607, 102 S.Ct. 2613, 2618–2620 (1982).

[292] Ibid. at 614, 2624. 8 Med.L.Rptr. at 1697.

PRESS-ENTERPRISE V. SUPERIOR COURT

The Riverside (California) Press-Enterprise was trying to cover a rape trial, and wanted its reporters present during the *voir dire* proceedings, the in-depth questioning of prospective jurors. The newspaper moved that the *voir dire* be open to public and press. The State of California opposed the motion, arguing that with the public and press present, jurors' responses would not be candid, and that this would endanger the entire trial.

Writing for a unanimous Supreme Court, Chief Justice Burger wrote that the roots of open trials reach back to the days before the Norman Conquest in England, and related to that was a "presumptive openness" in the jury selection process.[293] He added:

> No right ranks higher than the right of the accused to a fair trial. But the primacy of the accused's right is difficult to separate; from the right of everyone in the community to attend the *voir dire* which promotes fairness.

This fact situation was made harsher by the trial judge's keeping six weeks of the *voir dire* proceedings closed (although three days were open). Media requests for transcripts of the *voir dire* were refused; the California court argued that Sixth Amendment (defendant's right to a fair trial) and juror privacy rights coalesced to support closure of the proceeding. The Supreme Court disagreed. Chief Justice Burger wrote:[294]

> The judge at this trial closed an incredible six weeks of *voir dire* without considering alternatives to closure. Later the court declined to release a transcript of the voir dire even while stating that most of the material in the transcript was "dull and boring." * * * Those parts of the transcript reasonably entitled to privacy could have been sealed without such a sweeping order; a trial judge should explain why the material is entitled to privacy.

Students and practitioners who consider the matter resolved should note the trial of Martha Stewart in 2004. Presiding Judge Miriam Goldberg Cedarbaum barred the media from attending the voir dire. The media appealed. A panel of the 2nd Circuit vacated the order.[295] Because of the high profile nature of the case, the judge and the prosecution and defense created a two-part system of jury selection. Prospective jurors were given questionnaires and the individuals who made it through that screening process would be interviewed separately in the judge's robing room. Reporters sought information about access to the interviews and asked to attend or to have a press pool attend the process.

---

[293] *Press-Enterprise Co. v. Superior Court of California*, 464 U.S. 501, 104 S.Ct. 819, 823 (1984).

[294] Ibid. at 513, 825.

[295] *ABC, Inc. v. Stewart*, 360 F.3d 90 (2d Cir. 2004).

Judge Cedarbaum decided instead to bar the media from the interviews and instead provide them with transcripts, minus the names and other personal information about the jurors. The media appealed the order and the 2nd Circuit panel took up the case. Citing *Press-Enterprise* and its progeny, the panel said that closure of the voir dire process violated a right of access. The availability of a transcript was not an adequate substitute, the panel said, notwithstanding the government's argument that the only loss to the media was the "color and texture" of the proceedings.[296] "The ability to see and to hear a proceeding as it unfolds is a vital component of the First Amendment right of access—not, as the government describes, an incremental benefit."

WALLER V. GEORGIA

Waller was a defendant charged with violation of Georgia's Racketeer Influenced and Corrupt Organizations (RICO) Act. A pre-trial suppression hearing was held, in which Waller and other defendants asked that wiretap evidence and evidence seized during searches be suppressed—that is, disallowed or declared inadmissible.

The prosecuting attorney asked that the suppression hearing be closed, contending that if the evidence were presented in open court and published, it might become "tainted" and therefore unusable, especially in future prosecutions. The court ordered the suppression hearing closed to all persons except witnesses, the defendants, and lawyers and court personnel. Defendant Waller, however, wanted the hearings to be open.

Writing for the Court, Justice Lewis Powell cited *Press Enterprise I* approvingly, noting that even though the suppression hearing had been closed for its entire seven days, there was less than two and one-half hours' worth of wiretap evidence tapes played in the court.[297]

"PRESS-ENTERPRISE II" [PRESS-ENTERPRISE V. RIVERSIDE COUNTY SUPERIOR COURT]

In 1986, the Supreme Court of the United States continued to back away from its much-criticized decision in *Gannett v. DePasquale* (1979), which held that pre-trial hearings could be closed to press and public. *De Pasquale*, decided under the Sixth (fair trial) amendment, now seems to have been overruled by "*Press Enterprise II*, decided under the First Amendment."

In that case, Robert Diaz—a nurse suspected of murdering a dozen hospital patients by lethal injections of huge amounts of the heart drug lidocaine—was to have a hearing to see whether there was probable cause to hold him for trial. The magistrate excluded the press from the

[296] Ibid. at 99.

[297] *Waller v. Georgia*, 467 U.S. 39, 42, 104 S.Ct. 2210, 2213 (1984).

hearing, which dragged on for 41 days. The magistrate ordered a trial for Diaz.[298]

The California Supreme Court upheld the exclusion order, on the ground that there is no general First Amendment right of access to preliminary hearings, not if a judge found there was "a reasonable likelihood of substantial prejudice."[299]

The U.S. Supreme Court overturned that view, stating that the California rule called for a lesser burden of proof than is required under the First Amendment: there should be a "substantial probability" of prejudice before closure could be allowed.[300]

Chief Justice Burger, writing for a total of seven Justices (Stevens and Rehnquist dissented), declared that the interest of free press and of fair trial are not necessarily inconsistent. He added, "[O]ne of the important means of assuring a fair trial is that the process is open to neutral observers." Finally:[301]

> The considerations that led the Court to apply the First Amendment right of access to criminal trials in *Richmond Newspapers* and the selection of jurors in *Press-Enterprise I* lead us to conclude that the right of access applies to preliminary hearings as conducted in California.

SEALED RECORDS IN THE "ZOO MAN" CRIMINAL CASE

In Tennessee, the *Knoxville News-Sentinel* tried in 1997 to get access to records of taxpayers' money paid to court-appointed attorneys and time sheets for expert witnesses working on behalf of accused serial killer Thomas "Zoo Man" Huskey. The *News-Sentinel* got half a loaf when Criminal Judge Richard Baumgartner ordered release of the total amount paid up to July, 1997, in expenses and expert witness fees. As if public interest would not be high enough in the trial of a man accused of serial murders, the case became even more newsworthy when the defendant, accused of killing prostitutes near the Knoxville Zoo, claimed multiple personalities and asked for a separate lawyer for each personality.

Attorneys' time sheets were withheld from the newspaper, but in October, 1998, John North, then a reporter with the *News-Sentinel*, told a Huskey defense attorney that he had received copies of the sealed time records from a confidential source and was preparing a story. Huskey's defense team quickly petitioned Judge Baumgartner, who issued a temporary restraining order against the newspaper. The newspaper

---

[298] *Press-Enterprise Company v. Superior Court*, 478 U.S. 1, 106 S.Ct. 2735 (1986).

[299] Ibid. at 5, 2739.

[300] Ibid. at 14, 2743.

[301] Ibid. at 10, 2741.

ignored the order and published a story revealing information in the sealed records.

In November, 1998, Judge Baumgartner recast the temporary restraining order as a temporary injunction, and early in 1999—the Tennessee Court of Criminal Appeals—claiming an incomplete record and that it lacked copies of the time sheets reporter North had obtained—dismissed the newspaper's appeal against the restrictive order.

Meanwhile, thanks to the controversy stirred up by the *News-Sentinel*, the Tennessee legislature amended a Tennessee openness statute to provide that in criminal trials, total payments made to court-appointed defense attorneys are a public record. The statutory devil was in the details, however, because the statute also provided that *detailed* attorney fee records and expense records could be sealed and kept from the public until a criminal trial is completed. The victory for openness came in that total payments expended on court-appointed criminal case defenses could be reported as trials progressed.[302]

In June, 1999, Judge Baumgartner released all but three items of the sealed fee claims to the newspaper. Huskey's attorneys again appealed to the Court of Criminal Appeals and received a temporary stay. Later, that court upheld Judge Baumgartner's decision to release most of the records.

Thanks to his confidential source, reporter John North was able to write a story telling the *News-Sentinel*'s readers that the defense of convicted multiple rapist and accused serial killer Thomas D. Huskey had cost more than $250,000 in taxpayers' money, one of the highest taxpayer-funded cases in Tennessee history. Since the Huskey case resulted in a hung jury—meaning that Huskey would be tried again—taxpayer expenditures in the case were by no means complete.[303]

ACCESS TO CIVIL MATTERS

Coverage of the justice system overwhelmingly focuses on criminal cases. A person who has "seemed pretty quiet and never bothered anybody" is charged with multiple murders. The case immediately involves the defendant, victims and the families and acquaintances of all concerned. But apart from Timothy McVeigh and the 9-11 attackers, how many defendants have been involved in the deaths or injuries of hundreds? Yet the scale of manufacturing and marketing means that a single product injected into the stream of commerce has the ability to affect hundreds or thousands of lives with sometimes deadly results.

Although civil trial coverage may not appear as important or sexy as criminal trials to journalists and civil libertarians, all of the judicial process—criminal or civil, or in law or equity—needs to be open to the

302 The *News Media & the Law*, Spring, 1999, pp. 8–9.

303 John North, "Judge lifts order that hid cost of Huskey defense," *Knoxville News-Sentinel*, June 8, 1999.

public. Public funds pay for the courts and judges, whether the cases involved be criminal or civil. Furthermore, when the judicial process is closed or otherwise hidden from public view, the likelihood is great that private rather than public welfare is being served.

Ford became known as the American automaker that made dangerously defective automobiles in the 1970s when the media focused on the Pinto and its rear-mounted gas tank. What most Americans did not know, was that General Motors had a similar design that was responsible for a number of fires and explosions.

> * * * General Motors built cars with designs similar to Ford's and GM cars were involved in numerous accidents in which persons were severely injured or killed because of gas-tank fires and explosions.
>
> The difference between the publicity the two received lay in General Motors' savvy use of the court system to throw up a shield of secrecy over its legal problems * * *[304]

In a series published in 1988, the *Washington Post* reported on GM's strategies in keeping its name out of the press. "Over the last five years, in defending itself against scores of lawsuits filed by victims of fiery car crashes, General Motors Corp. has used court secrecy procedures throughout the nation to keep closely held and controversial documents about auto safety from becoming public."[305]

GM had good reason to keep its secrets. While Ford was losing major lawsuits and suffered declining sales linked to the news about the Pinto, GM's reputation was largely intact despite the similarities between the companies' car-making techniques and safety analyses.

In 1970, GM officials were told of risks associated with the rear placement of its gas tanks. In 1971, GM considered moving its gas tanks from behind the axle where they were vulnerable, to a position in front of the rear axle where they would be more protected. To do so would result in the loss of some trunk space and cost between $8.59 and $11.59 per car. GM decided not to make the change. Two years later, the company considered the risks from the rear gas tank placement. A June 29, 1973 memo, titled "Value Analysis," looked at the problem, the *Washington Post* reported.

"A GM engineer, Edward C. Ivey, assigned a $200,000 value to each human life and assumed that a maximum of 500 people died annually in GM cars 'where the bodies were burnt.' "

Then, in a two-stage calculation relating to new GM cars, Ivey determined what level of expenditure could be justified to try to avoid fiery deaths in the 5 million cars GM was producing annually. "This

---

[304] Bill Loving, "Media Access to Civil Court Records," paper presented to the Law Division, Association for Education in Journalism and Mass Communication, Boston, MA, Aug. 1991.

[305] "Court Secrecy Masks Safety Issues," *Washington Post*, Oct. 21, 1988, p. A1–22.

analysis indicates that for GM it would be worth approximately $2.20 per new auto to prevent a fuel fed fire in all accidents."[306]

Ford did not keep information about its suits or its documents secret. Ford had allowed a similar Ford analysis to become public. That document also placed a value of $200,000 per human life lost in a fiery accident. In February of 1978, Ford lost a California case involving a Pinto. The jury awarded the plaintiffs $128.5 million. A few days later, GM lost one of the few fuel tank cases it was forced to go to trial on. GM lost and the plaintiffs were awarded $2.5 million. GM appealed saying the jury had been influenced by the publicity about the Pinto. GM settled the case for less than the amount of the judgment and entered into a confidentiality agreement with the plaintiffs.

Other instances of secrecy involving products include defective mechanical heart valves, children's playground equipment, prescription painkillers, cigarette lighters while other cases involve claims of medical and legal malpractice. The common thread is the use of settlements and confidentiality orders to keep news of the injuries and suits out of the public eye. The means of achieving this secrecy include:

Protective Orders: This in effect gags persons who receive information from the defendant, thus keeping information damaging to the defendant away from the public, the press, or other litigants.

Confidentiality Agreements: Defendants and plaintiffs often agree to keep details of the lawsuit, including causes of injuries or amounts of settlements, secret.

Sealed Files: When a lawsuit is settled out of court, sealing the files will keep everyone else—the public, environmental health officials, the news media—from knowing just what kind of deal has been cut.

In an adversarial system with opposing counsel and the supervision of a judge, how can corporations manage to keep things quiet? It is a combination of factors in which all the participants can find themselves working together for the purpose of limiting publicity. Lawyers, parties and the courts take their parts in this.

Lawyers are required to serve their clients with the utmost devotion. The Canons of Professional Ethics, Canon 15, states:

> "The lawyer owes 'entire devotion to the interests of his client, warm zeal to the maintenance and defense of his rights and the exertion of his utmost learning and ability' to the end that nothing be taken or withheld from him, save by the rules of law, legally applied."

That means defense lawyers must serve their clients and if that means keeping things confidential, so be it. Confidentiality is an important consideration. For example, a person buys a widget from the Widget Co. She is severely injured because of a design and manufacture

[306] Ibid.

defect. The person may attribute her injury to bad luck or some other external factor. Without publicity about the defective widget, the injured party may not even realize that she has a claim to pursue. If a lawyer can prevent a lawsuit from being filed, he has saved his client great expense. If an injured party does suspect a design and manufacturing defect, the defense lawyer has the job of trying to eliminate the suit before it can generate publicity and put other injured persons on notice that their injuries might have been caused by the Widget Co. thus generating more suits. That can mean offers of settlement that include extra money in return for confidentiality agreements.

Plaintiff's attorneys likewise have strong pressures to go along with secrecy. Just like defense lawyers, plaintiff's attorneys have a duty to their clients. They are required to inform their clients about settlement offers even when those offers may seem to be against the greater public good. James Gilbert, an attorney in Arvada, Colorado. told *Newsday* that he settled a case involving a "dangerous vehicle." But because of the settlement agreement's secrecy terms, Gilbert, "can't say whether the vehicle is a car or truck. I can't say who makes it. I can't even say which part of the vehicle is involved. And it bothers me because that vehicle is still on the road."[307]

If the client wants to take the settlement offer and sign a secrecy agreement, the lawyer must comply. Defendants may pay more than the injury is worth to avoid dangerous publicity. Sometimes, though the plaintiff's attorney will see a compelling need for confidentiality. Premature disclosure of a suit could lead to hundreds more being filed by other, similar victims. A flood of suits could bankrupt the defendant and prevent recovery for anyone. That was the case for the A.H. Robins Co., the company that produced the Dalkon Shield I.U.D. "Hundreds of women who filed claims against the company went unpaid after the company sought bankruptcy protection in the face of the legal onslaught."[308] Secrecy therefore protects the plaintiff and her lawyer must see to that need first.

Judges are caught in the middle. The courts are clogged with cases and any settlement means one less case that needs to be tried. If lawyers for both sides come to chambers with a signed settlement agreement, judges are likely to approve. After all, the opposing sides are in agreement so why should the court object. Many times the settlement agreements are brought during court recesses, on lunch breaks, or get squeezed into spaces between appointments. The *Washington Post* learned that some judges who sign settlement and confidentiality agreements have little idea of what they are approving. There are simply too many pages in too many controversies for the judge to examine all of the details. Judges who oppose secrecy face problems from savvy litigators. In one case, GM attorneys sought a confidentiality order on all

[307] "System Thwarts Sharing Data on Unsafe Products," *Newsday*, April 24, 1988.

[308] "Legal Merry-Go-Round," *Newsday*, June 5, 1988.

of the documents the car maker was turning over to the plaintiff's attorney. When Judge David Peeples expressed his reluctance to grant a sweeping order, the GM attorney said he would ask for a hearing on each document. There were 15,000 documents. Judge Peeples granted the GM request.[309]

Paul McMasters, Freedom of Information chair for the Society of Professional Journalists in 1990, put the issue of civil litigation secrecy in sharp focus:[310]

> We're not talking about irrelevant facts left in the files of the litigants. We're talking about documents and decisions involving unsafe products, dangerous drugs, toxic wastes, all with potentially devastating effects on people unaware of that danger.

Such records secrecy in civil litigation has long been routine in most jurisdictions. In Texas, however, Justice Lloyd Doggett of the Texas Supreme Court led the fight which resulted in a new standard in that state for sealing court records, saying explicitly that records may not be removed from (civil) court files except as allowed by statute or court rule. Such records are presumed open, and may be closed only upon a showing of a substantial interest outweighing the presumption of openness and any probable adverse effect that sealing records might have on public health or safety. This presumption of openness in Texas does include settlement agreements "that seek to restrict disclosure of information concerning matters that have a probable adverse effect upon general public health or safety * * * ."[311]

Similarly, in 1990, Florida passed its Sunshine in Litigation statute which demands that courts not enter secrecy orders or seal records which would prevent the public from being informed about hazardous products or public hazards in general. Nationwide attention is needed to provide public knowledge of all trials; information embedded in civil trials can be at least as important to the public as knowledge of criminal trials.

GM was not able to forestall publicity about another fuel-tank problem that arose in the early part of the 1990s. A Georgia family sued GM over the death of their son, who was killed in a GM pickup truck. Shannon Moseley's family sued, claiming that GM had defectively designed and manufactured trucks with side-saddle gas tanks, gas tanks placed outside of the rails of the frame. The Moseley family would not settle the case. They wanted their day in court. The controversy over the GM trucks also led to the NBC Dateline debacle in which Dateline ran a story about the GM trucks and illustrated the story with a crash test that

---

[309] Even so, GM lost in the Texas Supreme Court where the plaintiff's attorney fought the broad protective order.

[310] Quoted at Bill Loving, "Media Access to Civil Court Records," paper presented to the Law Division, Association for Education in Journalism and Mass Communication, Boston, MA, Aug. 1991.

[311] Quoted in Ibid.

included an overfilled gas tank, a wrong gas cap and toy rocket engines that were to ensure ignition of the gas. That video cost NBC a great deal of credibility and led to an on-air apology. If NBC had done its job differently it might have gotten a copy of GM's own crash testing showing the dangers of the fuel tanks.[312]

James Butler, Jr., was the Moseley's attorney. He had researched the GM truck and learned about secret crash tests, company memos and other evidence that pointed to GM's knowledge of the risks of the fuel-tank design. Shannon Moseley was 16 when his parents bought him the 1985 GMC Sierra pickup truck. The family had been loyal GM drivers and bought the truck because they believed it to be safe. On Oct. 21, 1989, Shannon Moseley's truck was struck on the side by another truck driven by a drunk driver. Moseley's truck skidded 150 feet. The fire started before the truck came to a halt. Moseley was not visibly injured. The autopsy concluded that he survived the crash and then burned to death.[313]

Butler found a disaffected, retired GM engineer who blew open the case for him. Ronald Elwell was, at one time, one of GM's star testifying experts. He explained fuel systems in GM cars for juries and was considered "an integral part of GM's product liability team."[314] One of Butler's partners, Bob Cheeley, tracked Elwell down and told him the story of Shannon Moseley. Elwell opened up and began talking about GM including the story that low-level engineers had expressed doubts about the fuel tank design but had been overruled by management.

> "Perhaps most important, Elwell told Cheeley about a highly sensitive series of 22 truck crash tests that GM had staged in the early '80s but had failed to disclose to any of the more than 100 plaintiffs who had sued the company over post-collision fuel-fed truck fires. Elwell said he had been in the dark about the tests until September 1983."[315]

Elwell said that he discovered the tests when the head of GM's engineering analysis division told him to check on some safety research at GM's facility in Milford, Michigan.

> "At the proving grounds, he later testified, he saw a row of pickup trucks that had been crash-tested, obviously for the purpose of exploring the performance of the outside-the-frame-rail fuel tanks. Virtually all the fuel systems had failed. ('They were badly smashed,' Elwell to the jury in Atlanta. 'There were holes in them as big as melons. They were split open.' ")[316]

---

[312] It turns out that the danger resulted not from the placement of the fuel tanks outside the rails of the frame, but rather from the use of metal straps to hold the tanks in place. The straps caused the fuel tank failures when they pierced the metal of the gas tanks.

[313] Terence Moran, "How GM Burned Itself," *Automotive News*, May 3, 1993.

[314] Ibid.

[315] Ibid.

[316] Ibid.

Elwell's deposition revealed GM strategies for dealing with discovery. Where tests supported GM claims, the company would produce many documents. If the tests reflected poorly on GM vehicles, the discovery requests were carefully parsed.

> " 'It was very, very constricted,' he said. 'So that if you had to give anything, you gave only one test, or maybe you would say that none (existed) because none (of the vehicles in the test) were painted red with white sidewalls (like the vehicle described in the request.)' "[317]

The jury returned a $105 million award against GM. GM settled with the Moseleys in 1995 for an undisclosed amount.

The *Los Angeles Times* reported in May 2003 that GM had settled 297 lawsuits and paid more than $495 million involving the 1973–1987 C/K pickup truck models.[318] The disclosure came in a 2000 case in Montana that later settled for an undisclosed amount. The story surfaced when the *Times* looked into an agreement between federal regulators and GM in which GM paid $51 million in return for an end to a safety investigation of its C/K pickup trucks. The *Los Angeles Times* reported that in the period following the agreement, at least 65 people burned to death in C/K pickup trucks.

---

[317] Ibid.

[318] Myron Levin, "GM paid $495 million in suits: The automaker settled 297 cases involving fiery pickup truck crashes, a court document reveals," *Los Angeles Times*, May 7, 2003.

CHAPTER 10

SHIELDING INFORMATION FROM DISCLOSURE

60. THE GOVERNMENT CONTEMPT POWER

Persons who disobey the orders of courts may be cited, tried and convicted for contempt of court, the coercive power that underlies the courts' authority. The legislative branch has similar power. Journalists most often have come in conflict with the contempt power when they have refused court orders to disclose confidential information.

The common law has long provided that relationships between certain people are so personal that their confidences deserve protection against legally compelled disclosure. The clergyman and penitent, the physician and patient, the attorney and client, the husband and wife all share information that in some circumstances warrants unbroken confidentiality. The law has resisted expanding the protection to other interpersonal relationships, and even in the few listed above it has carefully avoided establishing any never-failing or absolute protection against the general rule. When government requires a citizen's testimony in furthering its legitimate ends such as ensuring fair judicial process or making laws, it is the citizen's duty to appear and testify.[1]

Printers of the American colonial period universally provided many contributors with anonymity, and occasionally resisted demands of the legislative branch to reveal their names. Early in nationhood, journalists continued to refuse demands of Congress and legislatures to break confidences, and as the Nineteenth Century progressed, sought expansion of the common law's protection to their own craft. They argued that journalistic ethics and their own professional livelihood required that they keep confidences, especially in reporting corruption in government. The public interest required that the news be told and that sometimes the news could be told only if journalists promised their sources confidentiality. Their success was modest indeed, but by 1900, a start was made toward legal protection when the State of Maryland passed the nation's first "shield law" for journalists—a law that recognized a journalist's privilege to not reveal confidential sources.

---

1 8 J. Wigmore, *Evidence*, 2286, 2290, 2394 (J. McNaughton Rev.Ed.1961).

Within the next three or four decades, a few more states joined Maryland in establishing journalists' privilege by statute. Broad protection, however, did not emerge until the 1970s, when some expansive readings of the First Amendment, increased numbers of state statutes, and the federal common law were brought to bear on problems of confidentiality. But early in the Twenty-First Century, some federal courts expressed disbelief that a reporter's privilege shield existed, and showed increased willingness to jail journalists who kept their source confidentiality promises.

The contempt power provides government with its authority to compel testimony and to respond to persons'—including journalists'—refusal to obey subpoenas or answer questions under oath. Government may declare that refusals to testify are contempt of authority, and may punish the person in contempt with imprisonment. That contempt power can be employed in response to conduct in the course of a judicial proceeding.

Annette Buchanan wrote a story for her college newspaper, the University of Oregon *Daily Emerald,* about the use of marijuana among students at the university. She said that seven students, whom she did not name, gave her information. And when the district attorney asked her to name the sources of information to a grand jury that was investigating drug use, and subsequently a judge directed her to do so, she refused. A reporter should be privileged not to reveal her sources, she said, and not to break confidences. To betray a pledge of secrecy to a source, Buchanan added, would be a signal to many sources to "dry up." The judge, upheld on appeal by the Oregon Supreme Court, found her in contempt of court for refusing to obey the judge's order, and she was sentenced to a brief jail term.[2]

Buchanan's situation was a case of "direct" contempt. It took place in the presence of the judge. Thomas Goss, a television personality, was not within shouting distance of the court when on his program he attacked witnesses in a divorce case in which he was accused of adultery with the wife. For his attempt to prevent witnesses from giving testimony unfavorable to him by vilifying them, he was convicted of contempt which takes place away from the court, by publication, called indirect or "constructive" contempt.[3] On appeal, his conviction was overruled, the court holding that his broadcasts were no real danger to justice because while the targets might have been angered by his words, they had no reason to feel threatened in their testimony by them.[4]

In the *Goss* case of contempt by publication as in the *Buchanan* case of direct contempt, a judge ruled initially that the reporter's acts

---

[2] *State v. Buchanan,* 250 Or. 244, 436 P.2d 729 (1968), certiorari denied 392 U.S. 905, 88 S.Ct. 2055 (1968).

[3] *People v. Goss,* 10 Ill.2d 533, 141 N.E.2d 385, 390 (1957).

[4] *Goss v. State of Illinois,* 204 F.Supp. 268 (N.D.Ill.1962), reversed on other grounds 312 F.2d 257 (7th Cir.1963).

interfered with the administration of justice—that the acts were contemptuous of court. In each case, the judge convicted the reporter under a judge's inherent power to punish for the interference, punishment for contempt being the basis of all legal procedure and the means of courts' enforcing their judgments and orders.[5]

The cases brought differing results. Buchanan failed in her appeal, Goss succeeded in his. Indeed, the outcomes illustrate the varying fortunes of reporters in recent years in similar circumstances. Direct contempt is a current, serious problem for the press.

"Summary" procedure is the ordinary procedure in contempt. In a summary proceeding, a judge accuses, tries, and sentences in his or her own case without resort to trial by jury. It is often justified by reference to the British legal writer of the Eighteenth Century, Sir William Blackstone, who declared that rude or "contumelious" [insolent] behavior in front of a judge, or lying, or "any wilful disturbance whatever" in court could be grounds for punishment for contempt. Also punishable, to Blackstone, were:[6]

> disobeying or treating with disrespect the king's writ, or the rules of process of the court; by perverting such writ or process to the purposes of private malice, extortion, or injustice * * *
>
> The process of attachment for these and the like contempts must necessarily be as ancient as the laws themselves * * * .

In the United States, an act establishing the law of contempt in the federal courts, passed in 1831, is the basis of contempt proceedings before federal judges. State courts likewise possess the power to punish for contempt, under authority of a judicially proclaimed inherent power, by a statute, or both.[7] State courts have ignored or denied acts by state legislatures to limit this power.[8] For example, in *State v. Morrill* (1855) an Arkansas court was faced with a state statute limiting contempt proceedings to specified acts not including out-of-court publications. The court ruled that the statute was not binding upon the judiciary, for it must have power to enforce its own process, and the contempt power which provides this springs into existence upon the creation of the courts.[9] Without this authority, courts would be powerless to enforce their orders.

Attempts by Congress and state legislatures to limit contempt to certain specific classifications have not been universally successful. The legislative and judicial branches of government are equal in importance under the "separation of powers" doctrine that gives each branch of

---

5 Sir John C. Fox, *History of Contempt of Court* (Oxford, 1927), p. 1.

6 Blackstone, pp. 284, 285.

7 Act of Mar. 2, 1831, c. 99, 4 Stat. 487.

8 *State v. Morrill*, 16 Ark. 384 (1855) is an influential case mimicked by courts elsewhere to protect their "inherent" contempt powers from legislative limitations.

9 Ibid. at 384, 407.

government autonomy. While the legislative branch of any governmental unit has the power to make the law, the judicial branch has inherent rights to enforce courts' orders, rules, writs, or decrees. Even in states where there is a strict definition of what constitutes contempt, under special circumstances there is precedent for courts to consider their own inherent power as superior to a legislative enactment.[10]

Some object, arguing that American traditions are violated where a judge may sit as accuser, prosecutor, and judge in his own or a fellow judge's case: "It is abhorrent to Anglo-Saxon justice as applied in this country that one man, however lofty his station * * *, should have the power of taking another man's liberty from him."[11] There are flaws in the Blackstonian position that summary procedure is an "immemorial power" of judges in all contempt cases.[12] The United States Supreme Court addressed itself to that flawed argument in 1968 and said that the old rule did not justify denying defendants a jury trial in serious contempt cases. The Court ruled in *Bloom v. Illinois* that "If the right to a jury trial is a fundamental matter in other criminal cases, * * * it must also be extended to criminal contempt cases." Bloom's jail sentence for contempt was two years, which the Court found to be a "serious" penalty.[13]

LEGISLATIVE CONTEMPT AND THE PRESS

In addition to courts, legislative bodies are protective of their power to cite for contempt. Congressional and state legislative investigating committees sometimes seek the testimony of reporters who have special knowledge about subjects under the committees' official inquiry. Citations for contempt have occurred when reporters have refused to answer lawmakers' questions, and occasionally, over the last two centuries, journalists have been convicted.

The legislative power to cite for contempt derives its force from the power possessed by the English Parliament, on which both the legislatures and the Congress were modeled.[14] No limitations are imposed upon Congress in its punishment for either disorderly conduct or contempt, but in *Marshall v. Gordon* (1917),[15] it was held that the punishment imposed could not be extended beyond the session in which the contempt occurs.

---

10 For a more detailed description of this license renewal process and its flaws, see Don R. Le Duc, *Beyond Broadcasting: Patterns in Policy and Law* (White Plains, NY: Longman, 1987), pp. 43–56.

11 *Ballantyne v. United States*, 237 F.2d 657, 667 (5th Cir.1956); J. Edward Gerald, *The Press and the Constitution*, pp. 30–31.

12 Walter Nelles and Carol Weiss King, "Contempt by Publication in the United States," 28 *Columbia L.Rev.* 408 (1928).

13 *Bloom v. Illinois*, 391 U.S. 194, 208, 88 S.Ct. 1477, 1485 (1968).

14 Max Radin, *Anglo American Legal History*, pp. 63, 64.

15 *Marshall v. Gordon*, 243 U.S. 521, 37 S.Ct. 448 (1917).

The Supreme Court has conceded to Congress the power to punish nonmembers for contempt when there occurs "either physical obstruction of the legislative body in the discharge of its duties, or physical assault upon its members, for action taken or words spoken in the body, or obstruction of its officers in the performance of their official duties, or the prevention of members from attending so that their duties might be performed, or finally, for refusing with contumacy to obey orders, to produce documents or to give testimony which there was a right to compel."[16]

Reporters seldom go to jail for refusing to reveal a source of information to Congress, but it can happen. A 1966 case involved Z.L. White and Hiram J. Ramsdell, Washington correspondents of the *New York Tribune*. They published what they claimed was the "Treaty of Washington," a document being studied by the Senate in a closed session. They refused to say who gave them the copy, were tried and convicted of contempt by the Senate, and were committed to the custody of the Sergeant at Arms until the end of the Session.[17]

Congress has not in many decades chosen to try and convict for contempt. Instead, it has cited for contempt and certified the persons cited to the district attorney of the District of Columbia for prosecution under a law that gives the courts power to try such cases.[18]

It is uncertain how far the principles of freedom of the press protect reporters from contempt charges if they refuse to answer the questions of a Congressional committee. Journalists have argued that the First Amendment sharply limits Congress in questioning and investigating the press: Congress may investigate only the matters on which it may legislate, they point out, and the First Amendment says that "Congress shall make no law * * * abridging freedom of * * * the press."

"THE SELLING OF THE PENTAGON"

In 1971, a prize-winning television documentary by CBS, "The Selling of the Pentagon," raised a storm of protest against alleged bias in the film's portrayal of the American military's public information programs. Selective editing for the documentary, the military charged, distorted the intent, management and messages of the military. The House of Representatives Commerce Committee, under its chairman Rep. Harley O. Staggers, undertook an investigation of the matter, and CBS president Frank Stanton refused to furnish the committee parts of film edited out of the final version. In response to the subpoena ordering him to appear with the materials, he appeared but declared that

[16] Ibid.

[17] U.S. Senate, Subcommittee on Administrative Practice and Procedure of Committee on the Judiciary, The Newsman's Privilege, 89 Cong., 2 Sess., Oct. 1966, pp. 57–61. Nineteenth Century investigations of news media and reporters were not rare according to Kaminski, op.cit., p. 85.

[18] 2 U.S.C.A. §§ 192, 194.

furnishing materials would amount to a violation of freedom of the press. The Committee voted 25 to 13 to recommend to Congress a contempt citation. The House, however, turned down the recommendation, Rep. Emanuel Celler declaring that "The First Amendment towers over these proceedings like a colossus. No tenderness of one member for another should cause us to topple over this monument to our liberties."[19]

DANIEL SCHORR AND CONGRESS

In the 1970s, newsman Daniel Schorr, then of CBS, came under protracted investigation by Congress, and heavy fire from a segment of the media, for his refusal to testify. Schorr had obtained a copy of the Pike Committee (House Intelligence Committee) report on operations of the Central Intelligence Agency, which the House of Representatives had voted should be kept secret after heavy pressure not to disclose it from the federal administration. National security, the administration said, was at stake. Schorr broadcast some of the contents; passed the report to the *Village Voice* which published much of it; was investigated for several months during which he was suspended by CBS, and finally came before the House Ethics Committee.[20] Under a congressman's solemn admonition against publishers' taking it "upon themselves to publish secret and classified information against the will of Congress and the people,"[21] Schorr illuminated the rationale for a journalist's refusing to reveal sources, saying in part:[22]

> For a journalist, the most crucial kind of confidence is the identity of a source of information. To betray a confidential source would mean to dry up many future sources for many future reporters. The reporter and the news organization would be the immediate losers. The ultimate losers would be the American people and their free institutions.
>
> But, beyond all that, to betray a source would be to betray myself, my career, and my life. It is not as simple as saying that I refuse to do it. I cannot do it.

Unlike the committee that recommended on Stanton, the Ethics Committee did not recommend to the full House that Schorr be cited for contempt. He was released from subpoena without revealing his source.

The courts have not decided contempt of Congress cases on First Amendment grounds, one of them saying, "We shrink from this awesome task" of drawing lines between the investigative power of Congress and

[19] Congressional Record, 117:107, July 13, 1971, p. 6643.

[20] See Daniel Schorr, *Clearing the Air* (New York: Houghton Mifflin, 1977), passim; "The Daniel Schorr Investigation," *Freedom of Information Center Report*, #361, Oct. 1976.

[21] Anthony Lewis, "Congress Shall Make No Law * * * ," *New York Times*, Sept. 16, 1976, p. 39.

[22] I. William Hill, "Schorr Sticks to His Refusal to Name Source," *Editor & Publisher*, Sept. 25, 1976, p. 14. In 2007, National Public Radio (NPR) celebrated Schorr's 90th birthday—and his work as an NPR commentator—by naming its New York newsroom after him.

the First Amendment rights of a member of the press. Instead, the courts have found other reasons for reversing convictions of newsmen—such as faulty indictments—who were found in contempt of Congress for refusing to answer questions.[23]

Deja vu set in early in 1992, when reporters Nina Totenberg (National Public Radio) and Timothy Phelps (*Newsday*) balked at answering Senate questions. They faced subpoenas to reveal the sources of their reports of Professor Anita Hill's charges of sexual harassment against Supreme Court nominee—and ultimately Supreme Court Justice—Clarence Thomas.[24] The Senate soon dropped the inquiry.

61. REFUSING TO TESTIFY ABOUT SOURCES AND INFORMATION

Journalists' clashes with courts for refusing to testify as to sources and information were infrequent until the 1970s when the incidents multiplied manyfold. Qualified protection developed under the First Amendment, the common law, and state statutes.

Reporters' refusal to testify before grand juries and courts about confidential sources has become a familiar phenomenon since the 1970s. Subpoenas to appear and testify were for decades only an occasional problem for journalists whose stories suggested to officials that the reporters had information of use to government. There were probably fewer than 40 reported contempt cases before 1965 for refusal to testify when subpoenaed. But in 1969 and 1970 the sometime trickle of subpoenas changed to a flood, and across the nation hundreds of reporters faced demands that they appear and testify. No one was able to track down every subpoena issued during the early 1970s. But in a three-year period, 121 subpoenas for news material went to CBS and NBC in total, and more than 30 to Field Enterprises newspapers.[25]

In particular demand were reporters who had been reporting widespread social and political turmoil of the 1970s. Grand juries wanted these journalists to reveal their confidential sources as well as to surrender their unpublished notes and records, unused photographs, tape recordings and television film "out takes." To much of this, reporters responded "no" with intensity and solidarity.[26] Their unwritten code of

[23] *Shelton v. United States*, 117 U.S.App.D.C. 155, 327 F.2d 601 (1963); 89 Editor & Publisher 12, July 7, 1956. *Russell v. United States*, 369 U.S. 749, 767, 82 S.Ct. 1038, 1049 (1962).

[24] Neil A. Lewis, "Constitutional Test Is Seen in Inquiry in Leak to Press," *New York Times*, Feb. 3, 1992, p. A9.

[25] House of Rep. Committee on the Judiciary, Subcommittee No. 3, 92 Cong., 2d sess., "Newsmen's Privilege," Hearings, Oct. 4, 1972, p. 204; Sept. 27, 1972, p. 134.

[26] S. Res. 3552, 91 Cong., 2d Sess., 116 Cong.Rec. 4123–31, 1970; Noyes & Newbold, "The Subpoena Problem Today," *Am.Soc. Newspaper Editors Bull.*, Sept. 1970, pp. 7–8; *Editor & Publisher*, Feb. 7, 1970, p. 12. For several journalists' positions, see U.S. Congress, Senate,

ethics stood in the way of breaking confidences, they said. Even more important, if they broke confidences they would become known as untrustworthy and their sources would dry up, thereby harming or destroying their usefulness as news gatherers for the public, and their own status as professionals would be damaged. Moreover, some argued, compelling them to disclose their news sources was tantamount to making them agents of government investigation.

As for turning over unused film, files, photos and notes, some media adopted the policy of early destruction of unpublished materials after *Time, Life, Newsweek,* the *Chicago Sun-Times,* CBS, NBC and others were called by subpoena. Alternatively, in the name of cooperation with government, some subpoenaed news organizations provided overwhelming quantities of news materials.[27] According to Attorney General John Mitchell, who served under President Nixon, journalists' willingness to accept contempt convictions and jail terms rather than reveal confidences, along with their unyielding protests to government, made the controversy "one of the most difficult issues I have faced * * * ."[28] The storm of objection to subpoenas issuing from the Department of Justice led attorneys general to issue "Guidelines for Subpoenas to the News Media"—a set of instructions to Justice Department attorneys across the nation—that sought to resolve testimonial questions with reporters through negotiating rather than through subpoenas except in the last resort.

From the mid-1970s through the 1980s, there was growing protection shielding journalists from being compelled to testify about sources or otherwise to reveal confidences. The pattern was by no means uniform nationally, however, and there were indications in the 1990s that those hard-won, if spotty, protections were being whittled away.

THE CONSTITUTIONAL PROTECTION

Journalists who assumed or asserted that the First Amendment guarantee of freedom of the press has protected the craft historically against compelling testimony did not understand the course of court decisions. Privilege cases were adjudicated for most of a century under the common law or state statutes without the Constitution even entering the picture. Not until 1958, in *Garland v. Torre,*[29] was the first claim to First Amendment protection an issue in the reported cases.

Marie Torre, columnist for the *New York Herald Tribune,* attributed to an unnamed executive of a broadcasting company, certain statements which actress Judy Garland said libeled her. In the libel suit, Torre

---

Committee on the Judiciary, Newsmen's Privilege Hearings Before the Subcommittee on Constitutional Rights, 93rd Cong., 1st Sess., 1973, passim.

[27] *Columbia Journalism Rev.,* Spring 1970, pp. 2–3.

[28] *Editor & Publisher,* Aug. 15, 1970, pp. 9–10.

[29] *Garland v. Torre,* 259 F.2d 545 (2d Cir.1958), certiorari denied 358 U.S. 910, 79 S.Ct. 237 (1958).

refused to name the executive, asserting privilege under the First Amendment. She was cited for contempt and convicted, and the appeals court upheld the conviction. "The concept that it is the duty of a witness to testify in a court of law," the Second Circuit Court of Appeals said, "has roots fully as deep in our history as does the guarantee of a free press." It added that if freedom of the press was involved here, "we do not hesitate to conclude that it too must give place under the Constitution to a paramount public interest in the fair administration of justice."[30] Subsequent claims to constitutional protection also were denied in other cases.[31]

THE WILLIAM FARR CASE

In the early 1970s, William Farr, a reporter for the *Los Angeles Herald Examiner* and later the *Los Angeles Times*, was cited for contempt for refusing to reveal his source of information while reporting on the sensational murder trial of Charles Manson, murderer of Sharon Tate, the pregnant young wife of acclaimed movie director Roman Polanski. Farr learned that a woman had given a statement to a district attorney claiming that a Manson "family" member, Susan Atkins, had confessed to taking part in multiple crimes and told of the group's plans for other murders.

A judge in the case had ordered attorneys, witnesses, and court employees not to release to the public contents of any information on the content or nature of any testimony that might be given at the trial. Farr, however, obtained copies of the woman's statement from two attorneys When the judge learned that Farr had the statement, he refused to tell the court the names of his sources, and published a story carrying sensational details. Later, Farr identified a group of six attorneys as including the two. The judge queried them, and all denied being a source. Once more the court asked Farr for his sources, and he continued to refuse under the California's reporters' privilege law as it stood in 1970.[32] The court denied him protection under the statute and he appealed.

The appeals court upheld the conviction for contempt, essentially under the doctrine of the "inherent power" of courts to regulate judicial proceedings without interference from other branches, a principle reaching far back in the history of contempt. It said that courts' contempt power is inherent in their constitutional status, and no legislative act could declare that certain acts do not constitute contempt. If Farr received immunity from liability for refusing to testify, it would violate the principle of separation of powers among the three branches of government. Such a grant of immunity would interfere with the judicial

30 Ibid. at 548–549.

31 *In re Goodfader's Appeal*, 45 Haw. 317, 367 P.2d 472 (1961); *In re Taylor*, 412 Pa. 32, 193 A.2d 181 (1963); *State v. Buchanan*, 250 Or. 244, 436 P.2d 729 (1968), certiorari denied 392 U.S. 905, 88 S.Ct. 2055 (1968).

32 West's Ann.Cal.Evidence Code § 1070.

branch's powers to control its own officers.[33] An attorney participating in a trial is legally an "officer of the court."

Farr served 46 days in jail before he was released pending a further appeal. He lived for years with the possibility of indeterminate, unlimited imprisonment if his appeal failed and if he persisted in refusing to reveal his sources. That "coercive" contempt sentence was later ruled by the courts to have no further purpose. There was no likelihood that continuing it would induce Farr to testify. But it was still possible that he might have to serve a further "punitive" sentence for contempt. On Dec. 6, 1976—five years after the opening of the case against Farr, he finally was freed from the latter possibility by a California appeals court ruling.[34]

But Farr's ordeal was not over. Two of the six attorneys whom he identified brought a $24 million libel suit against him. The trial court and a California appellate court ruled that the shield law did not protect him from answering questions about the case.[35] The long contest ended in April, 1979, after the libel plaintiffs missed the five-year statute of limitations for bringing such an action. At long last, a judge dismissed the suit.[36]

Sixteen months later, Californians voted to elevate the state's shield for journalists to a better-fortified position than that of a statute. They passed ballot Proposition 5, which placed the shield directly into the California Constitution.[37]

THE BRANZBURG CASE (1972)

The United States Supreme Court in 1972 ruled for the first time on whether the First Amendment protects journalists from testifying about their confidential sources and information. The cases of three newsmen who had refused to testify before grand juries during 1970 and 1971 were decided together in *Branzburg v. Hayes*.[38] Paul Branzburg, a reporter for the *Louisville Courier-Journal,* had observed two people synthesizing hashish from marijuana and written about that and drug use, and had refused to answer the grand jury's questions about the matters. Paul Pappas, a television reporter of New Bedford, Massachusetts, had visited Black Panther headquarters during civil turmoil in July 1970, and

---

[33] *Farr v. Superior Court of Los Angeles County*, 22 Cal.App.3d 60, 99 Cal.Rptr. 342, 348 (1971). New Mexico's Supreme Court ruled similarly that the state's shield law was without effect where testimony before courts was concerned. See *Ammerman v. Hubbard Broadcasting, Inc.*, 89 N.M. 307, 551 P.2d 1354 (1976).

[34] *In re Farr*, 64 Cal.App.3d 605, 134 Cal.Rptr. 595 (1976); *Milwaukee Journal*, Dec. 7, 1976.

[35] *In re Farr*, 64 Cal.App.3d 605, 134 Cal.Rptr. 595 (1976). See also Quill, Nov. 1977, p. 14.

[36] "William Farr's Seven [sic] Year Fight to Protect Sources is Victorious," *News Media & the Law*, Aug./Sept. 1979, p. 22.

[37] "Californians Vote to Include a Newsman's Shield in the State Constitution," *Quill*, July/August 1980, p. 9; Calif. Const. § 2, subd. (b).

[38] *Branzburg v. Hayes*, 408 U.S. 665, 92 S.Ct. 2646 (1972), 1 Med.L.Rptr. 2617.

refused to tell a grand jury what he had seen there. Earl Caldwell, a black reporter for the *New York Times* in San Francisco, who had covered Black Panther activities regularly for some years, was called by a federal grand jury and had refused to appear or testify.

Only Caldwell received protection from the lower courts. The federal district court of California and the Ninth Circuit Court of Appeals ruled that the First Amendment provided a qualified privilege to newsmen and that it applied to Caldwell.[39] The Kentucky Court of Appeals refused Branzburg protection under either the Kentucky privilege statute, or the First Amendment interpretation of the *Caldwell* case.[40] And the Supreme Judicial Court of Massachusetts, where no privilege statute existed, rejected the idea of a First Amendment privilege.[41]

The Supreme Court of the United States found that none of the three men warranted First Amendment protection. It reversed the *Caldwell* decision of the lower federal court and upheld the *Kentucky* and *Massachusetts* decisions, in a 5–4 decision.[42] It said that the First Amendment would protect a reporter if grand jury investigations were not conducted in good faith, or if there were harassment of the press by officials who sought to disrupt a reporter's relationship with his news sources.[43] But it found neither of these conditions present here. The journalist's obligation is to respond to grand jury subpoenas as other citizens do and to answer questions relevant to commission of crime, it said.

The reporters had asserted that the First Amendment should take precedence over the grand jury's power of inquiry. The Supreme Court said that at common law, courts consistently refused to recognize a privilege in journalists to refuse to reveal confidential information, and that the First Amendment claim to privilege had been turned down uniformly in earlier cases, the courts having concluded "that the First Amendment interest asserted by the newsman was outweighed by the general obligation of a citizen to appear before a grand jury or at trial, pursuant to a subpoena, and give what information he possesses."[44] It said that the only constitutional privilege for unofficial witnesses before grand juries is the Fifth Amendment privilege against compelled self-incrimination, and the Court declined to create another.

The reporters argued that the flow of news would be diminished by compelling testimony from them. The Supreme Court said it was unconvinced, and "the evidence fails to demonstrate that there would be

---

[39] *Application of Caldwell*, 311 F.Supp. 358 (N.D.Cal.1970); *Caldwell v. United States*, 434 F.2d 1081 (9th Cir.1970).

[40] *Branzburg v. Pound*, 461 S.W.2d 345 (Ky.1970); *Branzburg v. Hayes*, 408 U.S. 665, 92 S.Ct. 2646 (1972).

[41] *In re Pappas*, 358 Mass. 604, 266 N.E.2d 297 (1971).

[42] *Branzburg v. Hayes*, 408 U.S. 665, 92 S.Ct. 2646 (1972).

[43] Ibid. at 706–709, 92 S.Ct. at 2669–2670.

[44] Ibid. at 684, 686, 92 S.Ct. at 2658, 2659.

a significant constriction of the flow of news to the public if the Court reaffirms the prior common law and constitutional rule regarding the testimonial obligations of newsmen."[45]

The reporters said the freedom of the press would be undermined. The Court said this is not the lesson that history teaches, for the press had operated and thrived without common law or constitutional privilege since the beginning of the nation.[46]

The Supreme Court said that while the Constitution did not provide the privilege sought, Congress and the state legislatures were free to fashion standards and rules protecting journalists from testifying by passing legislation.

Concurring, Justice Lewis F. Powell, Jr., expanded, in general terms, the possibilities for first Amendment protection for journalists subpoenaed to testify. "The Court," he said, "does not hold that newsmen * * * are without constitutional rights with respect to the gathering of news or in safe-guarding their sources. * * * [T]he courts will be available to newsmen under circumstances where legitimate First Amendment interests require protection." And where they claim protection, Powell said, "The asserted claim to privilege should be judged on its facts by the striking of a proper balance between freedom of the press and the obligation of all citizens to give relevant testimony * * * ."[47] His opinion was to become central to many subsequent cases.

The dissenting justices wrote two opinions. One was that of Justice William O. Douglas, who said that a reporter's immunity from testifying is "quite complete" under the First Amendment and a journalist "has an absolute right not to appear before a grand jury * * * ."[48]

Dissenting for himself and two others, Justice Potter Stewart argued for a qualified privilege. He called the majority's opinion a "crabbed view of the First Amendment" that reflected a disturbing insensitivity to the critical role of an independent press. And he said that in denying the protection, "The Court * * * invites state and federal authorities to undermine the historic independence of the press by attempting to annex the journalistic profession as an investigative arm of government." Justice Stewart said the protection was essential, not "for the purely private interests of the newsman or his informant, nor even, at bottom, for the First Amendment interests of either partner in the news-gathering relationship."[49]

> Rather it functions to insure nothing less than democratic decision making through the free flow of information to the public, and it serves, thereby, to honor the "profound national

[45] Ibid. at 692, 92 S.Ct. at 2663.

[46] Ibid. at 698, 92 S.Ct. at 2665.

[47] Ibid. at 708, 710, 92 S.Ct. at 2670, 2671.

[48] *United States v. Caldwell*, 408 U.S. 665, 712, 92 S.Ct. 2686, 2691 (1972).

[49] *Branzburg v. Hayes*, 408 U.S. 665, 737, 92 S.Ct. 2646, 2678 (1972).

commitment to the principle that debate on public issues should be uninhibited, robust, and wide-open."

Stewart indicated what the government should be required to show in overriding a constitutional privilege for the reporter:[50]

> * * * it is an essential prerequisite to the validity of an investigation which intrudes into the area of constitutionally protected rights of speech, press, association and petition that the State *show a substantial relation between the information sought and a subject of overriding and compelling state interest.*
>
> * * *
>
> Government officials must, therefore, demonstrate that the information sought is *clearly* relevant to a *precisely* defined subject of governmental inquiry. * * * They must demonstrate that it is reasonable to think the witness in question has that information. * * * And they must show that there is not any means of obtaining the information less destructive of First Amendment liberties.

These were essentially the requirements placed upon government by the lower courts in holding that Caldwell had been protected by the First Amendment, and Stewart endorsed that decision. He would have upheld the protection for Caldwell, and vacated and remanded the Branzburg and Pappas judgments.

Largely innocent of the history of the shield, reporters and editors expressed shock and dismay that the First Amendment did not protect the reporters in the Supreme Court's *Branzburg* decision.[51]

After the *Branzburg* decision, many journalists predicted doom for press freedom. Those predictions were premature: buried within *Branzburg* were statements which said the First Amendment could be used in confidentiality cases. There was Justice White's plurality opinion, which said that journalists would be protected against the harassment of bad-faith investigations. Justice Powell's concurrence said that courts would protect journalists "where legitimate First Amendment interests require protection." And Justice Stewart's dissent, as matters turned out, contained concepts that courts quickly came to use in subsequent cases to protect journalists. (See discussion on following pages.)

Then only months after *Branzburg* was decided, the U.S. Court of Appeals, Second Circuit, gave the doom-predictors a most welcome surprise. That court said that journalist Alfred Balk was *protected* by the First Amendment in his refusal to name a source. Balk had once written an article on discriminatory real estate practices—"block-busting"—for The Saturday Evening Post. Civil rights advocates, in a court action,

---

[50] Ibid. at 739–742, 92 S.Ct. at 2679–2680.

[51] See generally *Columbia Journalism Review*, 10:3, Sept.–Oct. 1972, for articles by Norman E. Isaacs, Benno C. Schmidt, Jr., and Fred W. Friendly. The only extensive history of journalists' privilege is Gordon, op.cit.

sought to have Balk reveal the identity of one of his confidential sources ("Vitchek," a pseudonym). Balk refused, on grounds that Vitchek gave him the information in confidence. The trial court ruled in Balk's favor, and the appeals court affirmed. The decision stood because the Supreme Court of the United States—for whatever reason—refused to grant certiorari.[52]

The court found that the identity of Vitchek did not go to the heart of the appellants' case, and that, anyway, there were other available sources that the appellants could have tried to reach and that might have disclosed Vitchek's identity (see Stewart's dissent in *Branzburg*). It said that the majority in *Branzburg* had applied traditional First Amendment doctrine, which teaches that First Amendment rights cannot be infringed absent a "compelling" or "paramount" state interest (once more, Stewart).[53] Even though the *Branzburg* majority emphasized public interest in grand jury investigation of crimes, this case found that

> "there are circumstances, at the very least in civil cases, in which the public interest in non-disclosure of a journalist's confidential sources outweighs the public and private interest in compelled testimony. The case before us is one where the First Amendment protection does not yield."

Here was a line of reasoning (one which took its departure from the widely damned *Branzburg* decision) that for three decades often gave protection to the journalist whose testimony was being demanded with increasing and truly disturbing frequency. In civil cases, the public's interest was likely to weigh with the journalist's refusal to name his sources, and thus the journalist's position would outweigh the private litigant's demand for disclosure. It was the start of courts' using *Branzburg* in both civil and criminal cases to establish a qualified privilege under the First Amendment for journalists who claimed protection not to reveal sources.

Quickly other courts brought the privilege into play.[54] In a case decided in 1973, the District Court for the District of Columbia ruled on a demand of the Committee for the Re-Election of the President (Nixon) for news materials.[55] The Committee was party to civil actions arising out of the break-in at the Watergate offices of the Democratic National Committee. It had obtained subpoenas for reporters or management of the *New York Times*, the *Washington Post*, the *Washington Star-News*, and *Time* magazine to appear and bring all papers and documents they had relating to the break-in. The media asked the court to quash the subpoenas.

---

[52] *Baker v. F and F Investment*, 470 F.2d 778 (2d Cir.1972), certiorari denied 411 U.S. 966, 93 S.Ct. 2147 (1973).

[53] Ibid. at 783–785. See also *United States v. Orsini*, 424 F.Supp. 229 (E.D.N.Y.1976).

[54] See Press Censorship Newsletter, IX, April–May 1976, pp. 46, 48–9; *Loadholtz v. Fields*, 389 F.Supp. 1299 (M.D.Fla.1975).

[55] *Democratic National Committee v. McCord*, 356 F.Supp. 1394 (D.D.C.1973).

Judge Richey defined the issue: Were the subpoenas valid under the First Amendment? He distinguished this case from *Branzburg,* noting that the re-election committee was not involved in criminal cases, but civil contempts. He declared, furthermore, that the cases were of staggering import: " * * * unprecedented in the annals of legal history." "What is ultimately involved in these cases * * * is the very integrity of the judicial and executive branches of our Government and our political processes in this country."[56]

Not only did the civil nature of the cases involving the re-election committee weigh for the media in Richey's opinion. He saw a chilling effect in the enforcement of the subpoenas upon the flow of information about Watergate to the press and thus to the public:[57]

> This court stands convinced that if it allows the discouragement of investigative reporting into the highest levels of Government no amount of legal theorizing could allay the public suspicions engendered by its actions and by the matters alleged in these lawsuits.

Richey then balanced competing interests. As Justice Powell had instructed in *Branzburg,* a reporter's claim to privilege should be judged " * * * 'on its facts by the striking of a proper balance between freedom of the press and the obligation of all citizens to give relevant testimony.' " Richey said that here, "The scales are heavily weighted in the * * * [media's] favor." For the Committee for the Re-Election of the President had made no showing that "alternative sources of information have been exhausted or even approached. Nor has there been any positive showing of the materiality of the documents and other materials sought by the subpoenas [i.e., that the materials sought 'go to the heart of the claim']."[58]

Even the legal proceeding which the lead opinion in *Branzburg* was so concerned to elevate above reporter's privilege—namely, the grand jury investigation—could in some circumstances give way to the journalist's claim.

This happened in the case of Lucy Ware Morgan, who for three years fought a 90-day contempt sentence for refusing to disclose her source, and finally won.[59] Her story in the *St. Petersburg (Florida) Times* brought two actions against her to compel her to say who told her of a grand jury's secret criticism of Police Chief Nixon. The Florida Supreme Court found the story innocuous. It overruled the lower court which had found that the mere preservation of secrecy in grand jury proceedings outweighed any First Amendment considerations. The high state court said "A

[56] Ibid. at 1395–1397.

[57] Ibid. at 1397.

[58] Ibid. at 1398. On exhausting the sources of information, see also *Connecticut State Board of Labor v. Fagin,* 33 Conn.Sup. 204, 370 A.2d 1095, 1097 (1976), 2 Med.L.Rptr. 1765, 1766; *Altemose Const. Co. v. Building & Const. Trades Council of Philadelphia and Vicinity,* 443 F.Supp. 489 (E.D.Pa.1977), 2 Med.L.Rptr. 1878.

[59] *Morgan v. State,* 337 So.2d 951 (Fla.1976).

nonspecific interest, even in keeping the inner workings of the Pentagon secret, has been held insufficient to override certain First Amendment values."[60] It found further that the proceedings against Morgan had an improper purpose—namely, "to force a newspaper reporter to disclose the source of published information, so that the authorities could silence the source." Then it called on the leading case in precedent:[61]

> The present case falls squarely within this language in the *Branzburg* plurality opinion: "Official harassment of the press undertaken not for purposes of law enforcement but to disrupt a reporter's relationship with his news sources would have no justification."

Thus with *Branzburg* supporting, First Amendment protection for the reporter's shield was being discovered.[62] No court conceded that the privilege under the First Amendment was an "absolute" protective shield for the journalist in all conceivable circumstances. In applying the First Amendment, courts widely started with Justice Powell's instruction in *Branzburg* ("striking a proper balance between freedom of the press and the obligation of all citizens to give relevant testimony"), and then used criteria such as those advocated by Justice Stewart in his *Branzburg* dissent (whether the testimony sought from reporters was clearly relevant, whether the subject was one of overriding state interest, whether all other means of obtaining the sought-after information had first been exhausted). In most cases in which the First Amendment was employed, the procedure worked out to provide protection.[63]

But the First Amendment shield sometimes dropped. For one thing, in balancing the journalist's right to a shield against the need of the state or a plaintiff, courts sometimes found that persons or institutions seeking testimony had a greater right. This could happen at trial or in pre-trial discovery procedure, as described in Chap. 4, Sec. 26.

First, consider the hurdles which the state in criminal cases, or the plaintiff in civil cases, would have to clear before overcoming the journalist's First Amendment qualified privilege. These have been expressed in several ways. During the 1970s and 1980s, frequently used rules[64] were that the party seeking the information from the journalist must show:

---

[60] Ibid. at 955.

[61] Ibid. at 956.

[62] Gora, p. 28. Gora's handbook, prepared for the American Civil Liberties Union, despite being dated, should be available to every reporter and editor. It covers true-to-life, practical problems in several fields of law that involve journalists, using a "Q" and "A" approach.

[63] *United States v. Hubbard*, 493 F.Supp. 202, 206, 209 (D.D.C.1979), 5 Med.L.Rptr. 1719; *Montezuma Realty Corp. v. Occidental Petroleum Corp.*, 494 F.Supp. 780 (S.D.N.Y.1980), 6 Med.L.Rptr. 1571; *Application of Consumers Union of United States, Inc.*, 495 F.Supp. 582 (S.D.N.Y.1980), 6 Med.L.Rptr. 1681; *Hart v. Playboy Enterprises* (D.Kan.1978), 4 Med.L.Rptr. 1616; *United States v. DePalma*, 466 F.Supp. 917 (S.D.N.Y.1979), 4 Med.L.Rptr. 2499; *Zelenka v. State*, 83 Wis.2d 601, 266 N.W.2d 279 (1978).

[64] Others have included: Plaintiff must show that the information "is necessary to prevent a miscarriage of justice" *Florida v. Taylor* (Fla.Cir.Ct.1982), 9 Med.L.Rptr. 1551; there is

- That the information sought can be obtained from no other source or by means less destructive of First Amendment interests:
- That the information is centrally relevant to the party's case ("goes to the heart of the claim," or is information for which the party has a "compelling need").
- That the subject is one of "overriding and compelling state interest."

As we saw on the preceding pages, the journalist could win because the plaintiffs failed to show that the materials sought "went to the heart of their claim," or that the information might not be available from an alternative source, other parties seeking information have been more successful in piercing the shield of the First Amendment. That was the case in *Winegard v. Oxberger*,[65] decided by the Iowa Supreme Court in 1977.

WINEGARD V. OXBERGER (1977)

Diane Graham, a reporter for the *Des Moines Register,* wrote articles about legal proceedings brought by Sally Ann Winegard to dissolve her claimed common-law marriage to John Winegard. The articles quoted Sally Winegard's attorney extensively. John Winegard, who denied that there had been a marriage, brought a libel suit and invasion of privacy action against the attorney. The attorney told John Winegard that he had spoken with reporter Graham, but denied uttering the alleged libel. Then John Winegard sought, through discovery proceedings before the trial, to obtain from Graham or the *Register* any information they had in connection with the preparation of the articles.

Graham was subpoenaed, and refused to answer questions about conversations with her sources or their identity, and about preparation and editing of the articles. She said that the First Amendment and the Iowa Constitution protected her. She and the *Register* applied to the court for an order quashing the subpoena; John Winegard moved to compel discovery; and Judge Oxberger ruled for Graham and the *Register*, saying that a qualified privilege under the First Amendment protected Graham.

John Winegard appealed to the Iowa Supreme Court, which reversed the trial court and said that Judge Oxberger had erred in denying John's motion to compel discovery from reporter Graham. The Supreme Court

"reasonable possibility that information sought would affect the verdict" *State v. Rinaldo*, 36 Wash.App. 86, 673 P.2d 614 (1983), 9 Med.L.Rptr. 1419; the action is not "facially frivolous or patently without merit" *Winegard v. Oxberger*, 258 N.W.2d 847, 852 (Iowa 1977).

[65] *Winegard v. Ocberger,* 258 N.W.2d 847 (Iowa 1977), certiorari denied 436 U.S. 905, 98 S.Ct. 2234 (1978), 3 Med.L.Rptr. 2409. See also *Goldfeld v. Post Pub. Co.* (Conn.Sup.1978), 4 Med.L.Rptr. 1167; *In re Powers* (Vt.Dist.1978), 4 Med.L.Rptr. 1600.

said that a First Amendment qualified privilege existed, but was lost to Graham upon the application of the Court's "three-pronged standard."[66]

First, it said that John's basic discovery objective "is necessary and critical to his cause of action" against the attorney; John Winegard "needs to know what was said to Graham and by whom." Second, the Court said, John's questioning of Sally Winegard's attorney resulted in the attorney's denying "having made statements attributed to him by Graham's articles. Under these circumstances we find John Winegard did reasonably exercise and exhaust other plausible avenues of information," and that "Graham is apparently the only remaining person who could conceivably provide the information essential to John Winegard's invasion of privacy and defamation action." And as for the last of the "three-prong standard," the Court said there was nothing in the record to suggest that John's action against the attorney was frivolous or without merit. For good measure, the unanimous opinion said that the Court found no cause to hold that John was abusing judicial process to force a "wholesale disclosure of a newspaper's confidential sources of news," nor that John Winegard was embarked upon a course "designed to annoy," embarrass or oppress Graham.[67] John Winegard won the case for compelled disclosure.

During the 1980s, some courts denied or doubted that any First Amendment protection exists. The Massachusetts Supreme Judicial Court did so in the case of Paul Pappas,[68] and reaffirmed that position in 1982.[69] A Connecticut Superior Court has said that the First Amendment gives no greater protection to the electronic media "than the same action by any other citizen," nor "any privilege to refuse to reveal information solely because the writers deem it confidential."[70] Idaho's Supreme Court once read *Branzburg v. Hayes*, the leading case,[71] to mean that "no newsman's privilege against disclosure of confidential sources exists * * * ."[72] In 1985, however, the Idaho Supreme Court recognized a reporter's right to protect source confidentiality in both criminal and civil cases.[73]

---

66 *Winegard v. Oxberger*, 258 N.W.2d 847, 852 (Iowa 1977).

67 The Iowa Court relied directly on the first of the shield cases in which a reporter claimed a First Amendment protection—*Garland v. Torre*, 259 F.2d 545 (2d Cir.1958), which continues to carry weight with courts in frequent citations. An example is *Silkwood v. Kerr-McGee Corp.*, 563 F.2d 433 (10th Cir.1977), 3 Med.L.Rptr. 1087, 1091.

68 *In the Matter of Pappas*, 358 Mass. 604, 266 N.E.2d 297 (1971).

69 *Corsetti v. Massachusetts*, 458 U.S. 1306, 103 S.Ct. 3 (1982), 8 Med.L.Rptr. 2117 and reporter's jail term for contempt commuted in 1982, 8 Med.L.Rptr. #28, 9/14/82, News Notes. In 1984, the Massachusetts Supreme Judicial Court was asked by a governor's task force to promulgate rules about journalists' privilege, and recommended details for protection of journalists asserting such, the Court having denied until then any recognition of privilege: 10 Med.L.Rptr. #41, 10/16/84, News Notes.

70 *Rubera v. Post-Newsweek* (1982), 8 Med.L.Rptr. 2293, 2295.

71 *Branzburg v. Hayes*, 408 U.S. 665, 92 S.Ct. 2646 (1972), 1 Med.L.Rptr. 2617.

72 *Caldero v. Tribune Pub. Co.*, 98 Idaho 288, 562 P.2d 791 (1977), 2 Med.L.Rptr. 1490, 1495.

73 *In re Contempt of Wright*, 108 Idaho 418, 700 P.2d 40 (1985).

For journalists, the best defense against subpoenas probably is a "good offense." That is, if a news organization is known to judges and prosecuting attorneys as one willing to fight against subpoenas—even to the point of having reporters and editors go to jail to resist yielding up confidential sources or information—chances of subpoenas being served might be lessened, although federal judges showed increased willingness to jail journalists protecting their sources after 2001.[74]

IN RE FARBER (1978)

A shield case which arose in New Jersey cost its media principals more than any other in the 1970s. It was the famous case called *In re Farber*.[75] Before it had run its course, in fines alone it had cost the *New York Times* approximately $285,000, at the rate of $5,000 per day in civil contempts plus a flat $101,000 in criminal contempts. Reporter Myron Farber was jailed for 40 days. Farber had written lengthy articles about deaths at a New Jersey hospital, and their possible connection with drugs. A grand jury probe of the matter resulted in the indictment of Dr. Mario Jascalevich for murder, and after he went to trial, Farber and the *Times* were subpoenaed to bring thousands of documents to the court for *in camera* inspection. The *Times* and Farber demanded a hearing before turning over materials. But the trial judge refused a hearing, saying he would have to examine the documents before deciding whether the shield law would protect them against disclosure to Jascalevich. Facing contempt citations, the *Times* and Farber appealed unsuccessfully; the contempt findings went into effect, with jail for Farber and the $5,000-a-day fine against the *Times* pending its bringing forth the materials.

Appealing once more, the newspaper and reporter reached the New Jersey Supreme Court. That court denied that the First Amendment provided any privilege to remain silent, interpreting *Branzburg v. Hayes* to be a flat rejection of that notion. In response to the journalists' claim to privilege, the New Jersey court said that U.S. Supreme Court Justice White, had "stated the issue and gave the Court's answer in the first paragraph of his opinion":[76]

> "The issue in these cases is whether requiring newsmen to appear and testify before state or federal grand juries abridges the freedom of speech and press guaranteed by the First Amendment. We hold that it does not."
>
> * * *

---

[74] See the discussion of the Valerie Plame Wilson case earlier in this text.

[75] *In re Farber*, 78 N.J. 259, 394 A.2d 330, 345 (1978), 4 Med.L.Rptr. 1360, 1362; see also Anon., "Lets Stand Contempts Against New York Times," *News Media & the Law*, Jan. 1979, 4–5. For a step-by-step account of the complex process applied to the *Times* and Farber, see Anon., "Reporter Jailed; N.Y.Times Fined," Ibid., Oct. 1978, 2–4. Farber and the *Times* were ultimately pardoned of the criminal contempt conviction by the Governor of New Jersey, and the $101,000 criminal contempt fine was returned: 7 Med.L.Rptr. #42, 2/2/82, News Notes.

[76] *In re Farber*, 78 N.J. 259, 266, 394 A.2d 330, 333 (1978), 4 Med.L.Rptr. 1360, 1362.

> Our conclusion that appellants cannot derive the protection they seek from the First Amendment rests upon the fact that the ruling in *Branzburg* is binding upon us and we interpret it as applicable to, and clearly including, the particular issue framed here. It follows that the obligation to appear at a criminal trial on behalf of a defendant who is enforcing his Sixth Amendment rights is at least as compelling as the duty to appear before a grand jury.

Having settled the First Amendment issue for New Jersey, the court held that the *Times* and Farber of course deserved a hearing such as they sought, but that they had aborted it by refusing to submit the material subpoenaed for the court to examine in private, and that such an examination is no invasion of the New Jersey shield statute. "Rather, it is a preliminary step to determine whether, and if so to what extent, the statutory privilege must yield to the defendant's constitutional rights."

It added, however, that in future similar cases there should be a preliminary determination before being compelled to submit materials to a trial judge—in which the party seeking the materials would show the relevancy of them to his defense, and that the information could not be obtained from any less intrusive source. This, it said, did not stem from any First Amendment right, but rather, it would seem necessary from the legislature's "very positively expressed" intent, in passing the shield law, to protect confidentiality of media sources.

Farber was released from jail in October 1978, following the acquittal of Jascalevich by a jury at the end of an eight-month trial. The New Jersey legislature began work on a bill to prevent a recurrence of the Farber incident, and on Feb. 28, 1981, Governor Byrne signed a law saying that a criminal defendant would have to prove at a subpoenaed journalist's hearing that the material sought was relevant and unavailable elsewhere, and that the hearing would be held before the start of the criminal trial.[77]

It should be clear that despite the language of shield laws or of court precedent erecting some sort of a "shield" for journalists, such shields often turn out to be of little help at crunch time. First Amendment attorney James C. Goodale, for example, looked at the *Farber* case and exclaimed about the persistent ineffectiveness of New Jersey's shield statute. He complained that Farber had been shipped off to jail without a hearing, even though there was a statute stating that Farber was totally protected against requests for confidential sources and even though there are scores of decisions upholding claims of privilege even in states where there is no shield statute.

Journalists need to keep up with the kaleidoscopically shifting patterns of shield protection. One way of managing this is to subscribe to

---

[77] *New York Times*, Feb. 28, 1981, p. 25. *Maressa v. New Jersey Monthly*, 89 N.J. 176, 445 A.2d 376 (1982), 8 Med.L.Rptr. 1473, 1475–1476.

The News Media & the Law, published four times a year by the Reporters Committee for Freedom of the Press, and which puts out periodic guides on the status of shield laws from jurisdiction to jurisdiction.[78]

CONFIDENTIALITY UNDER THE FEDERAL COMMON LAW

Some cases, such as *Riley v. Chester* (1979)[79] in the Third Circuit, found a First Amendment-supported reporter's privilege. In that case, reporter Geraldine Oliver was called as a witness in a case about the suspension and punishment of William Riley, a police officer who was running for mayor of Chester, Pennsylvania. When Riley sued claiming violation of his right to campaign, reporter Oliver refused a judge's order to identify the source of information for a story she wrote about the disciplining of the policeman, and was cited for civil contempt. On appeal, the Third Circuit reversed the contempt citation. The Third Circuit held that information on policeman/candidate Riley might have been available from other sources, including other reporters, that Riley had not shown that reporter Oliver possessed information relevant to Riley's case.

The Court then added:[80]

> The strong public policy which supports the unfettered communication to the public of information, comment and opinion and the Constitutional dimension of that policy, expressly recognized in *Branzburg v. Hayes*, leads us to conclude that journalists have a federal common law privilege, albeit qualified, to refuse to divulge their sources.

In two later federal common law cases in the Third Circuit, the reporter's shield was denied. In one, concerning a newspaper reporter's refusal to say whether she had conversations with a U.S. attorney in the "Abscam" prosecutions, ruled that the information was crucial to the defendant's case and that it could be obtained only from the reporter. The court followed standard judicial procedure in choosing to decide the case on common law instead of a First Amendment standard: " ' * * * [W]e ought not to pass on questions of constitutionality * * * unless such adjudication is unavoidable * * * .' "[81]

In the other case, a television network was ordered by a court to submit to a pre-trial, *in camera* [in private, in the judge's chambers] proceeding. In that proceeding film, audio tapes, and written transcripts were to be revealed concerning persons whom the government intended to call as witnesses in a trial. The TV network refused and appealed the order. But the order was upheld so far as it applied to the named persons

---

[78] The Reporters Committee on Freedom of the Press is located at 1101 Wilson Blvd., Suite 1100, Arlington, VA 22209. Email: rcfp@rcfp.org; Web site: http://www.rcfp.org/; Phones: (800) 366–4243 or (703) 807–2100.

[79] Ibid. at 713, 714.

[80] Ibid.

[81] *United States v. Criden*, 633 F.2d 346, 353 (3d Cir.1980).

whom the government intended to call, but was overturned as to other people, whose testimony was not relevant.[82]

JAMES RISEN FIGHTS FOR A REPORTER'S PRIVILEGE

Although no journalist has been prosecuted under the Espionage Act, the discussion continues since then-Attorney General Alberto Gonzalez raised the issue. That possibility became more ominous in a case involving an author writing a book on the CIA. Federal prosecutors had sought to force James Risen to provide information about sources for his 2006 book, State of War: The Secret History of the CIA and the Bush Administration.[83] A former CIA officer, Jeffrey A. Sterling was charged with leaking information about a failed effort to sabotage Iranian nuclear research in 2000. That effort, described in Risen's Chap. 9 "A Rogue Operation," was to have a former Russian scientist provide flawed plans for a nuclear weapon to Iran. While Risen refused to say who his source was, the chapter included details of two separate meetings. Sterling was the only person to have attended both meetings.

U.S. District Judge Leonie M. Brinkema ruled that government attorneys prosecuting Sterling could not force Risen to tell about the sources for his book. While that was welcome news, she also suggested that Risen might face prosecution himself. It might be a felony for him to have received classified information.[84]

Judge Brinkema's ruling rested on the possible outcome of Risen's testimony as to the source of information about the CIA operation. Telling a grand jury or prosecutors that he received classified information from a CIA officer could leave him open to prosecution.[85] "Risen's statements are adverse to his penal interest because receiving classified information without proper authorization is a federal felony under 18 U.S.C. 793(e)."

Judge Brinkema also held that Risen had a qualified privilege against testifying. The only way that the government could overcome the privilege would be to meet the three-part test that the Fourth Circuit established for reporters' claims of privilege in civil cases.

A panel of the circuit established the test in a case over a lawsuit and counterclaim involving political figure Lyndon LaRouche, National Broadcasting Co. and the Anti-Defamation League of B'Nai B'Rith.[86] The case arose over a defamation suit that LaRouche filed against the

[82] *United States v. Cuthbertson*, 630 F.2d 139 (3d Cir.1980), 6 Med.L.Rptr. 1545.

[83] Charles Savage, "An Opinion by Judge on Spy Law Creates a Stir," *New York Times*, Aug. 4, 2011.

[84] *U.S. v. Sterling*, 818 F.Supp.2d 945 (E.D.Va.,2011).

[85] Ibid. at 957.

[86] *LaRouche v. National Broadcasting Co., Inc.*, 780 F.2d 1134 (4th Cir. 1986).

network and the ADL over two separate stories, one on the *NBC Nightly News* and the second on a news magazine program, *First Camera*.[87]

> In the story, NBC published statements to the effect that LaRouche believes that Jews are responsible for all the evils in the world, that any serious investigation of the LaRouche organization by the IRS would lead to criminal indictment, and that LaRouche once proposed the assassination of President Carter and several of his aides.

NBC refused to identify confidential sources that it used in its stories about LaRouche and the trial court sided with the network. Judge Brinkema used the test applied by the Fourth Circuit to NBC's refusal. The Fourth Circuit applied a three-part test based on the Supreme Court's decision in *Branzburg v. Hayes*.[88]

> In determining whether the journalist's privilege will protect the source in a given situation, it is necessary for the district court to balance the interests involved. *Branzburg v. Hayes*, 408 U.S. 665, 710, 92 S.Ct. 2646, 2671, 33 L.Ed.2d 626 (1972) (Powell, J., concurring). To aid in the balancing of these interests, courts have developed a three-part test: (1) whether the information is relevant, (2) whether the information can be obtained by alternative means, and (3) whether there is a compelling interest in the information.

Judge Brinkema concluded that Risen had the same qualified privilege and that the government had not passed parts two and three of the test in that[89] "the Government had failed to demonstrate that the information was unavailable from other means and that it had a compelling interest in presenting it to the jury."

FOURTH CIRCUIT SAYS NO PRIVILEGE FOR RISEN

But a panel of the Fourth Circuit Court of Appeal hearing the government's appeal of Judge Brinkema's order, held that no privilege exists.[90]

> There is no First Amendment testimonial privilege, absolute or qualified, that protects a reporter from being compelled to testify by the prosecution or the defense in criminal proceedings about criminal conduct that the reporter personally witnessed or participated in, absent a showing of bad faith, harassment, or

---

[87] Ibid. at 1137.

[88] Ibid. at 1139. Citing *Miller v. Transamerican Press, Inc.*, 621 F.2d 721, modified, 628 F.2d 932 (5th Cir.1980), cert. denied 450 U.S. 1041, 101 S.Ct. 1759, 68 L.Ed.2d 238 (1981).

[89] *U.S. v. Risen*, 724 F.3d 482, 490 (4th Cir. 2013).

[90] Ibid. at 492. Citing *Branzburg v. Hayes*, 408 U.S. 665, 92 S.Ct. 2646, 33 L.Ed.2d 626 (1972), the Supreme Court "in no uncertain terms rejected the existence of such a privilege." *In re Grand Jury Subpoena, Judith Miller*, 438 F.3d 1141, 1146 (D.C.Cir.2006).

> other such non-legitimate motive, even though the reporter promised confidentiality to his source.

The Fourth Circuit panel rejected the application of the LaRouche test, created in a civil lawsuit, to a criminal case.[91]

> [O]ur circuit has already considered and rejected such "a qualified [reporter's] privilege, grounded on the First Amendment, against being compelled to testify in [a] criminal trial." *In re Shain*, 978 F.2d 850, 851 (4th Cir.1992) (emphasis added).
>
> The *Shain* reporters were held in contempt for their refusal to comply with subpoenas to testify in the criminal trial of a former state senator whom they had previously interviewed. At the time, two of our sister circuits had extended the three-part test that had been adopted in civil actions to criminal proceedings, albeit with little to no discussion of the *Branzburg* opinion. See *United States v. Caporale*, 806 F.2d 1487, 1503–04 (11th Cir.1986) (citing *Miller*, 621 F.2d at 726); *United States v. Burke*, 700 F.2d 70, 76–77 (2d Cir.1983) (citing *Zerilli*, 656 F.2d at 713–15).

The only protection that Risen could use would arise if there was evidence that the government was using its subpoena power to harass him or was acting in bad faith, the Fourth Circuit panel held.

SUPREME COURT REFUSES TO HEAR RISEN APPEAL

Risen appealed to the Supreme Court but his petition for a writ of certiorari was denied.[92] As the process continued, press organizations spoke up to support Risen.[93] The Department of Justice received petitions with more than 100,000 names on his behalf. Attorney General Eric Holder suggested in a meeting with journalists that Risen might not be punished.[94]

> "As long as I'm attorney general, no reporter will go to jail for doing his job," Holder told those in attendance.
>
> The department said that Holder wasn't speaking about any particular case but was reiterating a position he has long held. But his statement suggests that Risen won't face time in prison if he continues to withhold the name of his sources, as he has vowed to do, when the case goes back to the lower court.

---

[91] Ibid. at 497.

[92] *Risen v. U.S.*, 572 U.S. 1149, 134 S.Ct. 2696 (2014).

[93] Catherine Taibi, "Press Freedom Groups Ramp Up Campaign For James Risen," *Huffington Post*, Aug. 15, 2014.

[94] Sari Horwitz and Robert Barnes, "Supreme Court refuses to take reporter's case on revealing confidential source," *Washington Post*, June 2, 2014.

Ironically, as the *New York Times* noted, during the preceding week, Holder announced new guidelines to narrow the circumstances under which reporter's records could be obtained by government.

As it stands, the Obama administration holds the record for prosecutions for leaks with six cases brought. That compares with three prosecutions under all prior administrations.[95] Risen had pointed words for Obama.[96] *New York Times* columnist Maureen Dowd spoke with Risen and then dedicated a column to his case.[97]

> "How can he [Obama] use the Espionage Act to throw reporters and whistle-blowers in jail even as he defends the intelligence operatives who 'tortured some folks,' and coddles his CIA chief, John Brennan, who spied on the Senate and then lied to the senators he spied on about it?" Dowd wrote.
>
> Risen had one word to describe Obama's actions: "hypocritical."
>
> "A lot of people still think this is some kind of game or signal or spin," he told Dowd. "They don't want to believe that Obama wants to crack down on the press and whistle-blowers. But he does. He's the greatest enemy to press freedom in a generation."

Ultimately, the Risen affair ended without much of a bang. He was not called to testify in the case.[98] "At the last minute, under pressure from journalist groups and liberal advocates, Holder relented and did not force Mr. Risen to choose between revealing his source or going to jail." Nonetheless, Sterling was convicted.

Sterling was sentenced to three and a half years in prison. The Justice Department had suggested that Sterling could be sentenced to 20 years in prison. Still, Sterling's sentence and that of other mid-level former intelligence officers contrasted with the treatment given to high-ranking officers, the *Times* reported.[99]

> By comparison, the FBI investigated a decorated military leader, retired Gen. James E. Cartwright, after public reports described a highly classified wave of American cyberattacks against Iran. But that investigation has stalled because investigators considered the operation too sensitive to discuss at a public trial.
>
> Mr. [retired general] Petraeus, meanwhile, retains his status as an adviser to the Obama administration despite giving Paula Broadwell, his biographer, who was also his lover, notebooks

---

[95] Scott Shane and Charles Savage, "Administration Took Accidental Path to Setting Record for Leak Cases," *New York Times*, June 19, 2012.

[96] Katherine Fung, "James Risen: Obama Is 'Greatest Enemy To Press Freedom In A Generation,'" *Huffington Post*, Aug. 17, 2014.

[97] Maureen Dowd, "Where's the Justice at Justice?" *New York Times*, Aug. 16, 2014.

[98] Matt Apuzzomay, "Ex-CIA Officer Sentenced in Lead Case Tied to Times Reporter," *New York Times*, May, 11, 2015.

[99] Ibid.

> containing handwritten classified notes about official meetings, war strategy, intelligence capabilities and the names of covert officers. Ms. Broadwell had a security clearance but was not authorized to receive the information.

Mr. Petraeus also admitted lying to the FBI, and the leniency of his plea deal infuriated many prosecutors and agents.

RECURRING NEWS MEDIA/FEDERAL GRAND JURY STRUGGLES

Wartime—including undeclared war situations such as the "War on Terrorism"—is not healthy for civil liberties or for the right to report on government. Reporting on or criticism of illegal actions by the government early in the Twenty-First Century led to contempt citations against news media when journalists sought to protect their sources from federal grand juries. But national security was not the only issue involving reporter's privilege in the first decade of the Twenty-First Century.

For example, one notable reporter's privilege case stemmed from federal grand jury testimony leaked from an investigation of steroid use by major league baseball players including home run record-holder Barry Bonds. *San Francisco Chronicle* reporters Mark Fainaru-Wada and Lance Williams had appealed 18-month contempt sentences for their reporting—grand jury proceedings are secret until their results are made public—of the Balco steroids case. Fainaru-Wada and Williams escaped punishment when an attorney revealed that he had leaked the grand jury testimony to the reporters.[100]

In another case, the refusal by blogger/free-lance videographer Joshua Wolf of San Francisco to provide out-takes of his video footage cost Wolf seven and one-half months in jail. Wolf posted some footage of a police car being set afire, and was released from jail only after he agreed to posting his out-takes on the Web. Josh Wolf was told that prosecutors reserved the option of subpoenaing him again.[101]

THE VALERIE PLAME WILSON CASE

During the "War on Terrorism," the administration of President George W. Bush was embarrassed when exposed for being, as the British phrase goes, "economical with the truth." During the run-up to the Iraqi War, the Bush administration made erroneous claims about the existence of Iraqi WMDs (weapons of mass destruction) including manufacture of nuclear weapons. Ambassador Joseph Wilson IV

---

[100] *In re Grand Jury Subpoenas to Mark Fainaru-Wada and Lance Williams*, 438 F.Supp.2d 1111 (N.D.Cal.2006).

[101] *In re Grand Jury Subpoena, Joshua Wolf*, 201 Fed.Appx. 430 (9th Cir. 2006); Gene Policinski, "Now-Freed Josh Wolf went to jail . . . why?" http://www.firstamendmentcenter.org/after-226-days-freelancer-josh-wolf-released-from-jail. A federal grand jury was involved because federal funds had contributed to the purchase of the San Francisco police car.

challenged President Bush's Jan. 28, 2003 assertion that Iraqi dictator Saddam Hussein "sought to obtain significant quantities of uranium from Africa." Wilson, who had been sent by the CIA to Africa in 2002 to investigate such claims, wrote an op-ed piece published in the *New York Times*, saying presidential assertions about purchase of Nigerian "yellow cake uranium" by Iraq were not true.

Shortly after Wilson challenged President Bush, columnist Robert Novak wrote that "two senior administration officials" had said Wilson was sent to Africa to investigate the claims because his wife, Valerie Plame, "an agency operative on weapons of mass destruction" had suggested him. Identifying deep-cover such as Valerie Plame Wilson is illegal. As noted in Chap. 2, a 1982 statute passed following the public outing of CIA agents by Philip Agee makes it a felony to name a covert intelligence agent.[102]

Subsequent news reports revealed that Wilson had been targeted by the Bush administration before his wife was designated an undercover CIA operative. A federal grand jury investigating the matter subpoenaed telephone records for Air Force One as well as records of staff contacts about reporters who wrote stories about Wilson, the uranium claims, and Wilson's wife. Some of the subpoenaed reporters said that the Bush administration had tried to discredit Wilson by saying that he was sent to Africa to check out the uranium story because of his wife's influence. Ambassador Wilson and Valerie Plame Wilson maintained that her career was ruined in retaliation against Wilson.

Because identifying deep-cover CIA agents is a crime, Special Prosecutor Patrick Fitzgerald was appointed to lead a grand jury investigation to learn who had outed Valerie Plame Wilson. Columnist Robert Novak claimed that his sources were two administration officials and did not say whether he had been subpoenaed. Two *Washington Post* reporters, Glenn Kessler and Walter Pincus, testified after their sources gave approval for the reporters to testify.

Judith Miller, who later left the *New York Times*, gathered information on Valerie Plame Wilson and was subpoenaed even though she never wrote a story on the matter. She refused to testify to the grand jury about who gave her information about Valerie Plame's status as a CIA operative and spent 85 days in jail. She finally testified after her source, I. Lewis (Scooter) Libby, chief of staff to Vice President Dick Cheney, signed a waiver giving her permission to speak and was released from jail. Libby, was sentenced to 30 months in jail and fined $250,000 for perjury, obstruction of justice, and lying to investigators This jail sentence, however, was commuted by President George W. Bush The commutation left the conviction on Libby's record, although President Bush might later give him full pardon. The fine was left standing

[102] See Chap. 2, and *Haig v. Agee*, 453 U.S. 280, 101 S.Ct. 2766 (1981).

(presumably be paid by White House loyalists who organized a Lewis Libby Legal Defense Fund).[103]

Matthew Cooper of *Time* magazine had written two stories on Valerie Plame, which put him in the sights of Special Prosecutor Patrick Fitzgerald. Cooper said that he tried to explain to his small son why Daddy might have to go to jail. Cooper's intention to refuse to identify his source or sources, however, was undercut by *Time's* publisher at the time, Norman Pearlstine, who said that the magazine would not disobey an order from a federal judge. Deprived of support from his employer, Cooper testified before the grand jury.

It was unclear how much damage the Valerie Plame Wilson situation did to the concept of reporter's privilege. Supposedly chasing down leads on the leaker or leakers of CIA deep cover operative Wilson's identity, Special Prosecutor Patrick Fitzgerald also subpoenaed not only Wilson and Matthew Cooper but also NBC's Tim Russert. All were coerced by the contempt power to testify about confidential sources. Given the array of investigative resources available to a federal special prosecutor—including the FBI—using the contempt power against reporters seems perilously close to harassment of the press warned about by Justice Potter Stewart in the landmark case of *Branzburg v. Hayes.*

THE WEN HO LEE CASE: PROTECTING CONFIDENTIALITY . . . AT A PRICE

On Dec. 30, 1998, a House select committee reported that China had gotten secret American technology, including information about nuclear weapon design.[104] The report covered 20 years of Chinese acquisition of American technology and included revelations of a pattern of nuclear weapons design technology from U.S. military labs. The committee made a number of suggestions, including several aimed at tightening security at weapons labs.

In 1995, the federal government began to suspect that China had acquired nuclear weapons information from Los Alamos. Wen Ho Lee, a Taiwanese-born naturalized American citizen became a subject of the investigation. The first news report about the investigation into a Los Alamos scientist appeared in the *Wall Street Journal* in January 1999. Widespread public attention into the investigation did not come until an article appeared in the *New York Times* some two months later. In that article, *Times* reporters James Risen and Jeff Gerth wrote about the chief suspect and wrote about his employment history, personal finances and what were said to be the results of the suspect's polygraph examinations.[105] Two days later, the federal government fired a scientist

[103] http://www.scooterlibby.com/.

[104] Jeff Gerth and Eric Schmitt, "Report: China got sensitive data; Military gains, thefts happened under Democratic, GOP leaders," *Austin American-Statesman*, Dec. 31, 1998.

[105] *Lee v. Department of Justice*, 287 F.Supp.2d 15, 19 (D.D.C. 2003).

for what were called "serious security violations" and identified him as Lee.

Eventually, Lee was arrested on 59 counts of mishandling classified information to benefit a foreign power. At least 39 of the charges carried the possibility of life in prison. Lee was released after pleading guilty to a single charge of copying files to an unsecured cassette tape. The presiding judge apologized to Lee in the hearing, saying, "I sincerely apologize to you, Dr. Lee, for the unfair manner in which you were held in custody by the executive branch."[106]

Lee filed suit against the Department of Justice, Department of Energy and FBI for violating the Privacy Act of 1974 (in Chap. 8) for disclosing government information about him and for failing to ensure that the information was correct. Central to his case was establishing that officials in the three departments gave information to the press. No government official admitted giving the information to reporters, so Lee sought subpoenas for the reporters who had written the stories with that detailed information. He named James Risen and Jeff Gerth of the *New York Times*; Robert Drogin of the *Los Angeles Times*; Josef Hebert of the Associated Press; and Pierre Thomas of CNN.

The reporters and their news organizations challenged the subpoenas but in October, 2003, Judge Thomas Penfield Jackson ordered them to comply and testify about their sources. Citing *Branzburg* and two D.C. Circuit cases involving claims of privilege against testimony, Judge Jackson concluded that Lee had established the necessary prerequisites to compel the testimony, that is the centrality of the information to the case, the lack of alternative sources and a compelling interest.[107]

Judge Jackson concluded that Lee had exhausted all other reasonable sources for the information having looked to (1) the answers of the defendants to the initial complaint, (2) the production of documents from the defendants in the discovery process that would show whether the defendants had given the information, (3) answers to interrogatories that addressed the question of who the defendants talked to and what they said, (4) replies to requests for admissions that the defendants gave the information and (5) depositions in which defendants and their officers and agents were asked about the leaks. None of those worked, leaving the journalists as the remaining source.[108]

A final requirement, that there be an overriding and compelling interest in requiring testimony, was satisfied by the existence of the Privacy statute, which provides both civil and criminal penalties for unlawful disclosure. "[T]he Court has some doubt that a truly worthy

---

[106] James Sterngold, "Nuclear scientist set free after plea in secrets case; Judge attacks U.S. conduct," *New York Times*, Sept. 13, 2000.

[107] *Lee v. Department of Justice*, 287 F.Supp.2d 15, 20 (D.D.C. 2003).

[108] Ibid. at 22.

First Amendment interest resides in protecting the identity of government personnel who disclose to the press information that the Privacy Act says they may not reveal."[109] As the authors have discussed in Chap. 2, the First Amendment does not trump laws of general applicability. Judge Jackson, in ordering the journalist to testify, reached the same conclusion.

On Nov. 2, 2005, the D.C. Circuit refused to rehear the journalists' appeal en banc. On June 5, 2006, the Supreme Court declined to grant certiorari in the case, leaving reporters with the choice between testifying about the sources of the information about Lee or facing contempt citations.[110] Wen Ho Lee's case against Justice, Energy and FBI came to an end when he agreed to a settlement of $1.6 million. The *Los Angeles Times*, the *Washington Post*, the Associated Press and ABC News contributed a total of $750,000 to the settlement. None of the media companies had been defendants in Lee's lawsuit. Their participation in the settlement talks and contributions to the settlement amount was a way to avoid having to reveal reporters' sources.[111]

USA TODAY'S TONI LOCY AND DR. STEVEN J. HATFILL

Toni Locy, a former reporter for *USA Today*, was held in contempt of court for refusing to reveal her confidential sources in a civil lawsuit by Dr. Steven J. Hatfill who sued the federal government.[112] Judge Reggie B. Walton took the unusual step of imposing fines beginning at $500 a day for seven days, then escalating to $1,000 a day for seven days, then $5,000 a day for seven days.[113] Judge Walton said after that he would consider other options which could include jail time.

Hatfill was a bioterrorism expert for the Army who sued the FBI and the Department of Justice, for violating the Privacy Act, saying his reputation was ruined by leaks to the news media from law enforcement officials linking him to the 2002 anthrax attacks which killed five people and remains unsolved.[114]

Locy refused to identify any of her sources arguing a reporter's privilege under the First Amendment and federal common law.[115] Beyond that, Locy could not identify the specific sources Hatfill was seeking. She said she routinely spoke with as many as a dozen sources in the Justice Department and the FBI. Typically she would run through a

---

[109] Ibid. at 23.

[110] *Drogin v. Wen Ho Lee*, 547 U.S. 1187, 126 S.Ct. 2351 (2006).

[111] Ibid.

[112] Eric Lichtblau, "Reporter Held in Contempt in Anthrax Case," *New York Times*, February 20, 2008.

[113] Ibid.

[114] Ibid.

[115] *Hatfill v. Mukasey*, 539 F. Supp. 2d 96, 97, 2008 U.S. Dist. LEXIS 17756 (United States District Court for the District of Columbia, (March 7, 2008, Filed), *available at* https://advance-lexis-com.proxy.lib.utk.edu/api/document?collection=cases&id=urn:contentItem:4S1C-DX30-TXFP-H216-00000-00&context=1516831.

litany of questions for each one. Now she can't remember exactly what information she got from each particular source.[116] "I have no notes to refresh my recollections," Locy said. "I was taught always discard my notes."[117] "I cannot match up the information in that story to a particular source out of the larger pool of sources," she said. "If Hatfill's lawyers get all those names, several people who had nothing whatsoever to do with the story will be burned."[118]

Locy was facing personal bankruptcy because the judge ruled that she must personally bear the burden of paying the fines and may not receive any monetary assistance from *USA Today*. "While her reporting was conducted in the scope of her employment at *USA Today*, her contempt was not."[119]

In 2008, the Justice Department settled the lawsuit with Hatfill for $4.6 million.[120] That settlement provided relief for Locy because the U.S. Court of Appeals for the District of Columbia ruled her contempt citation was moot since Hatfill settled and he no longer needed the identity of her sources.[121]

FBI SEEKS FILES FROM JACK ANDERSON'S HEIRS

Even after his death in 2005, muckraking reporter Jack Anderson, was at the heart of controversy involving classified documents. The FBI sought to search nearly 200 boxes containing Anderson's files to see whether they contained any classified documents. During Anderson's career, he exposed CIA plans to assassinate Fidel Castro, reported on the Iran-Contra scandal, and feuded with the FBI about excesses in that agency.[122]

Anderson's son refused to allow the search. Kevin Anderson said, "The government has always and continues to this day to abuse the secrecy stamp. My father's view was that the public is the employer of government employees and has a right to know what they're up to."[123]

---

[116] Aimee Edmondson, "Toni Locy Keynote," National Freedom of Information Coalition (May 2008), https://www.nfoic.org/toni-locy-keynote.

[117] Ibid.

[118] Thomas Mitchell, "Time is Running Out for Toni Locy," *Las Vegas Review-Journal*, May 18, 2008.

[119] *Hatfill v. Mukasey*, at 107.

[120] Scott Shane and Eric Lichtblau, "Scientist is Paid Millions by U.S. in Anthrax Suit," *New York Times*, June 28, 2008.

[121] *Hatfill v. Mukasey*, 2008 U.S. App. LEXIS 23804 (United States Court of Appeals for the District of Columbia Circuit (November 17, 2008, Filed), *available at* https://advance-lexis-com.proxy.lib.utk.edu/api/document?collection=cases&id=urn:contentItem:4TYH-S7B0-TXFX-H3DN-00000-00&context=1516831.

[122] Scott Shane, "FBI Is Seeking to Search Papers of Dead Reporter," *New York Times*, April 18, 2006.

[123] Ibid.

CONFIDENTIALITY UNDER STATE STATUTES AND IN STATE COURTS

The mixed results for confidentiality under the First Amendment and the federal common law, meanwhile, were characteristic of developments under state shield statutes and state court decisions. Media Attorney Robert Sack has said that shield laws are like insurance policies, in that "they cover absolutely everything except what happens to you."[124] Probably more reporters were going to jail in in the first years of the Twenty-First Century for refusal to reveal sources than for any offense since 1798–1800 and the Alien and Sedition Acts. The interpretations of the legitimacy (or illegitimacy) of journalists' privilege under state laws and rulings contributed heavily to fact. Even so, it has been plain that the large majority of state (and federal) jurisdictions had recognized qualified shield protection.

In 2000, University of Minnesota law professor Jane Kirtley complained that subpoenas were " 'going through the roof' in California" despite the state's shield law.[125] In California and elsewhere, judges showed willingness to order reporters to testify about confidential information, shield law or no shield law, under pain of going to jail for contempt of court if they refused to comply.

Although more states have shield laws than ever before, there continues to be no guarantee that judges will honor them. Note, for example, that the Supreme Court's landmark decision in *Branzburg v. Hayes*[126] involved a Kentucky reporter who probably thought he was protected against being compelled to testify by that state's shield statute.

Shield laws have varied in usefulness from state to state. In Tennessee, for example, the shield law is believed to be helpful because up to 2008, not journalist had been compelled to testify about confidential sources or information. In other states, the shield statutes sometimes get swept aside by judges who balance such legislation against other values, primarily the Sixth Amendment right to a fair trial. On the other hand, courts in states without shield statutes have at times held that journalists or even individuals producing material for publication or broadcast have a qualified First Amendment right not to reveal confidential sources or information.

Despite this checkered record, journalists tend to believe that it is better to have a shield law than not to have one. Small newspapers may have very real financial problems in fighting subpoenas. Legal costs are burdensome, and, with small-staff operations, pulling a reporter off

---

[124] 9 Med.L.Rptr. #7, 3/15/83, News Notes.

[125] Maureen Dolan, "Reporters Facing Greater Pressure to Reveal Sources," *Los Angeles Times*, March 10, 2000, p. A1.

[126] *Branzburg v. Hayes*, 408 U.S. 665, 92 S.Ct. 2646 (1972).

stories to testify can be problematic. Also, never underestimate the hostility that some officials have for the news media.

MILLER V. SUPERIOR COURT (CALIF., 2000)

In March, 2000, the *Los Angeles Times* interviewed San Joaquin County Deputy District Attorney Dorothy B. Klishevich, who was said to have suggested, "If the media do not want to be hauled into court, reporters should refrain from gathering sensitive material in criminal cases." She said, "I don't know why it is the news media should be talking to suspects anyway."[127]

That could be sour grapes because Klishevich was on the losing side in a November, 1999, California Supreme Court decision called *Miller v. Superior Court.*[128] Klishevich had gone to court in 1996 to force Sacramento TV station KOVR to hand over out-takes of a jailhouse interview with a murder suspect she was prosecuting, Anthony Lee DeSoto. After hearing that DeSoto had confessed to killing a cell-mate, KOVR reporter Tom Layson videotaped an interview with DeSoto. Portions of that interview were broadcast over KOVR in March, 1996.

KOVR was subpoenaed to produce the entire interview, but submitted only those parts of the interview that had been broadcast, invoking California's shield law. KOVR then asked that the subpoena be quashed, but provided an alternative.[129]

> " 'If the court should determine that the District Attorney has established and produced evidence of a colorable [having the appearance of truth] interest in this matter, KOVR requests that the court review in camera [in secret, before only the judge or, in this case, before the judge and defense counsel] those portions of the videotape claimed to be essential to protecting the interests of the People.' "

In reply, the prosecution argued that under California's shield law, only confidential or sensitive information was protected, and that KOVR had not contended that the out-takes were confidential or sensitive. After "in camera" inspection, the court ordered that an unedited copy of the interview be provided to the prosecution. KOVR tried to appeal.

But then, the California Court of Appeal, 4th District, ordered the Superior Court to tell KOVR to disclose the disputed material or be held in contempt. KOVR news director Ellen Miller was ordered to turn the

---

[127] Maura Dola, "Reporters Facing Greater Pressure to Reveal Sources," *Los Angeles Times*, March 10, 2000, p.A1.

[128] *Miller v. Superior Court*, 21 Cal.4th 883, 89 Cal.Rptr.2d 834, 986 P.2d 170 (1999), 28 Med.L.Rptr. 1161. Although prosecutor Klishevich was not named in the decision, she was so identified in Maura Dolan's story for the *Los Angeles Times*.

[129] 28 Med.L.Rptr. at 1162, citing Art. I § 2, California State Constitution, and Evidence Code § 1070. See 1162, n. 2: "The shield law is found in almost identical versions in both the state Constitution and the Evidence Code."

unedited videotape over to the prosecution. She refused, and was told that the shield law would not protect her from contempt.

California's Supreme Court, however, came to the rescue of Ellen Miller and KOVR. It upheld the state's shield law and declared that under it, reporters have an absolute privilege to keep in confidence unpublished information gathered through news gathering.[130]

VARIATIONS IN SHIELD PROTECTION AMONG FEDERAL CIRCUITS

As noted in the discussion of the Valerie Plame Wilson case, federal prosecutors and grand juries can be relentless in trying to coerce reporters' to testify about sources or information. If, as in *Branzburg v. Hayes* (1972), a reporter refuses to divulge information about commission of a crime or a situation threatening the public welfare, a "balancing test" will be used to weigh First Amendment concerns against Sixth Amendment administration of justice or fair trial concerns. It appears that a reporter's privilege argument, in general, may fare better in matters involving civil trials rather than criminal proceedings.

As James C. Goodale and colleagues wrote in Communications Law 2007, "The weight afforded the privilege in the Second Circuit depends upon whether the reporter is relying on the First Amendment or a state shield law; whether the information sought is confidential or nonconfidential, and whether the underlying case is criminal or civil."[131] In general, most federal circuits have recognized a qualified reporter's privilege, often interpreted via a "balancing" test taking into account the specifics of each fact situation involved, and weighing First Amendment versus Sixth Amendment concerns, plus other considerations such as the availability of the information from sources other than the news media.

GONZALES V. NATIONAL BROADCASTING CO. (1999)

The Second Circuit held, in *Gonzales v. National Broadcasting Company* that journalists' nonconfidential materials—including video out-takes and unpublished photos—may also be protected by a qualified or limited privilege. But because the privilege was *qualified,* NBC ultimately was forced to divulge the out-takes.[132]

Albert and Mary Gonzales were suing a Louisiana deputy sheriff for stopping them on Interstate 10 without any probable cause and, they charged, detaining them because they were Hispanic. Mr. and Mrs. Gonzales sought to see out-takes (never broadcast) from an NBC "Dateline" program aired early in 1997 which showed the same Louisiana deputy who stopped them pulling over a car driven by an NBC employee.

---

[130] Ibid. See also The *News Media & the Law,* Winter, 2000, pp. 15–16.

[131] James C. Goodale, et. al., "Reporter's Privilege Overview," *Communications Law 2007,* Vol. III (New York: Practising Law Institute, 2007), at p. 89.

[132] *Gonzales v. National Broadcasting Co.,* 194 F.3d 29, 27 Med.L.Rptr. 2459 (2d Cir.1999), reconsidering 26 Med.L.Rptr. 2300 (2d Cir.1998).

In the Dateline broadcast, the NBC employee who was pulled over by Deputy Darrell Pierce had not been speeding or driving erratically. In fact, his car was set on cruise control just below the legal speed limit, and NBC had the videotape to prove it. Dateline described widespread abuses by Louisiana law enforcement officers, including harassment and seizure of property.

NBC objected to the subpoenas on grounds that they were protected by journalists' qualified privilege. The U.S. Court of Appeals, 2nd Circuit, concluded, however, that these out-takes were vital to the cases of both the Gonzaleses and Deputy Pierce because they were not available from other sources.[133] Judge Pierre Leval wrote:[134]

> Where a civil litigant seeks nonconfidential materials from a nonparty press entity, the litigant is entitled to the requested discovery notwithstanding a valid assertion of the journalists privilege if he can show that the materials at issue are of likely relevance to a significant issue in the case, and are not reasonably obtainable from other reliable sources.

While there is a citizen's tendency to applaud the court's helping the Gonzales family pursue its lawsuit against an officer who may have been misusing his authority and violating civil rights, there is a practical reason why news organizations are unwilling to be cooperative and yield up out-takes. If news organizations become known as sources for information to help people pursue lawsuits or to help police authorities apprehend criminals through a videotape of a riot scene, then the meaningful separation between authorities and the news media will have been breached. Furthermore, camera operators for the news media will be placed in jeopardy if their employers become known as shills for authorities.

STATE SHIELD LAWS

The Supreme Court in *Branzburg* made it plain that either Congress or the states or both might pass laws providing a shield. Attempts in state legislatures to adopt shield laws (15 preceded *Branzburg*) were sometimes successful in following years, the total of old and new reaching 40 states plus the District of Columbia.[135] Many state courts have adopted a qualified privilege in case decisions, while a few rejected the privilege.[136]

---

[133] 27 Med.L.Rptr. 2459, 2462 (2d Cir.1999).

[134] Ibid. at 2465.

[135] *Reporters Privilege Compendium*, Reporters Committee for Freedom of the Press, https://www.rcfp.org/reporters-privilege/.

[136] See the remarkably useful overview, "Reporter's Privilege," by James C. Goodale, John S. Kiernan, Jeremy Feigelson, and Susan A. McMahon, in Goodale, chairman, *Communications Law* 2007, Vol. II, pp. 757–7765, and Vol. III, pp. 9–510 (New York: Practising Law Institute, 2007). A state-by-state listing summarizes the status of Reporter's Privilege, including summaries of state statutes and decisions. Also provided are relevant decisions of federal courts, Circuit by Circuit.

Some statutes provided a privilege that appeared "absolute," while others qualified the protection in various ways. Alabama's was one of those that, on the surface, seemed absolute—as long as a person could claim to be with a journalistic organization:[137]

> No person engaged in, connected with, or employed on any newspaper, or radio broadcasting station or television station, while engaged in a news gathering capacity shall be compelled to disclose in any legal proceeding or trial, before any court or before a grand jury of any court, before the presiding officer of any tribunal or his agent or agents or before any committee of the legislature or elsewhere the sources of any information procured or obtained by him and published in the newspaper, broadcast by any broadcasting station or televised by any television station on which he is engaged, connected with or employed.

Presumably, under Alabama law—and the law of numerous other states—a free-lancer or an Internet journalist "not connected with * * * or employed on any newspaper, or radio broadcasting station, or television station * * * " would be out of luck unless, when asked to reveal confidential information, encountered a judge who would find a First Amendment privilege to protect that non-employee of a traditional media outlet.

IS A BLOGGER A JOURNALIST?

A California appellate court extended protections enjoyed by reporters under California's privilege law in a trade secret case brought by Apple Computer. In November, 2004, O'Grady's Powerpage and Apple Insider carried stories about new Apple products bearing the development names of "asteroid" or "Q97." The new product would allow users to create digital live recordings on Apple computers.[138]

Apple filed a trade secret action against the two websites and sought discovery to identify the sources for the stories. It subpoenaed a third site, Thinksecret.com., in an effort to pinpoint sources of the disclosures.

The three Web operators fought the subpoenas, arguing that they were entitled to the protections afforded other journalists. Apple responded that the privilege did not apply in trade secret cases and that the defendants did not qualify for the privilege because they were not, in fact, journalists.

Justice Conrad Rushing of California's 6th District Court of Appeal concluded that the Web sites were publications as defined by California's privilege statute. "News-oriented Web sites like petitioners' are surely

[137] Ala. Code § 12–21–142 (Cum.Supp. 1988). See Jacqueline L. Jackson, "Shield Laws Vary Widely," *Presstime*, May, 1981; see also a New Jersey decision, *Maressa v. New Jersey* Monthly, 89 N.J. 176, 445 A.2d 376 (1982), 8 Med.L.Rptr. 1473.

[138] "Apple loses court bid to identify its sources," *Associated Press*, May 26, 2006.

'like' a newspaper or magazine for these purposes."[139] The lower (trial) court in this case had assumed that the defendants were journalists but did not apply the California shield law because of questions about the legality of the acquisition of the information.[140]

APPLYING VARYING STATUTES: IS INFORMATION RELEVANT? ABSOLUTE OR QUALIFIED BY PRIVILEGED?

Among states that hedged the privilege, Illinois, for example, said that a person seeking the reporter's information could apply for an order divesting the reporter of the privilege. The application would have to state the specific information sought, its relevancy to the proceedings, and a specific public interest which would be adversely affected if the information sought were not disclosed. And the court would have to find, before taking away the privilege, that all other available sources of information had been exhausted and that disclosure of the information was essential to the protection of the public interest involved.[141]

But absolute or qualified, state laws might contain loopholes through which, under certain conditions, journalists could lose the privilege. Branzburg, before seeking constitutional protection, had failed to receive protection under Kentucky's statute. The statute gave him a firm shield, as a newspaper employee, against disclosing before a court or grand jury, the source of information procured by him and published in a newspaper. But the Kentucky court held that he himself was the source of information for a story reporting his observation of the manufacture of hashish by others. He would have to give the identity of the manufacturer—to identify those whom he saw breaking the law. It was contempt for him to refuse to do so.[142]

New York's shield law, long termed "absolute" in its protection, but that only applies to information taken in confidence.[143] So, back in 1984, CBS was not protected against producing, under subpoena, video and audio takes and out takes not made under promises of confidentiality.[144] California's constitution immunizes against contempt convictions for refusing to testify, but not against various other sanctions[145] nor does it

---

[139] *O'Grady v. Superior Court*, 139 Cal.App.4th 1423, 1460, 44 Cal.Rptr.3d 72, 99 (Cal.App. 6th Dist.2006).

[140] Ibid. at 1438, 81.

[141] Ill.Legis.H.Bill 1756, 1971, Gen. Assembly.

[142] *Branzburg v. Pound*, 461 S.W.2d 345 (Ky.1970). For a similar position under New York's statute, see *People v. Dupree*, 88 Misc.2d 791, 388 N.Y.S.2d 1000 (1976); for Texas, *Ex parte Grothe*, 687 S.W.2d 736 (Tex.Cr.App.1984), 10 Med.L.Rptr. 2009.

[143] N.Y. Civ. Rights Law § 79–h (1996); *Beach v. Shanley*, 62 N.Y.2d 241, 476 N.Y.S.2d 765, 465 N.E.2d 304 (1984).

[144] *People v. Korkala*, 99 A.D.2d 161, 472 N.Y.S.2d 310 (1984), 10 Med.L.Rptr. 1355; see also *Knight-Ridder Broadcasting, Inc. v. Greenberg*, 70 N.Y.2d 151, 518 N.Y.S.2d 595, 511 N.E.2d 1116 (1987), 14 Med.L.Rptr. 1299.

[145] *KSDO v. Superior Court Riverside County*, 136 Cal.App.3d 375, 186 Cal.Rptr. 211 (1982), 8 Med.L.Rptr. 2360. Also New York: *Oak Beach Inn Corp. v. Babylon Beacon*, 62 N.Y.2d 158, 476 N.Y.S.2d 269, 464 N.E.2d 967 (1984), 10 Med.L.Rptr. 1761; see Calif. Constitution Art. I, § 2, subd. (b).

protect certain free-lance authors. California's shield statute protects unpublished or "out-take" materials.[146] Ohio's shield law protects against disclosure only of the source of the information, not against disclosure of information in notes, tapes, and records from the source.[147] Under Tennessee's statute, both confidential and nonconfidential information is protected, which has the effect of shielding notes, tapes, or video out-takes from courts or grand juries.[148]

In 1982, one test demonstrating the limitation of the new California shield *in the state's constitution* came when Riverside (California) policemen brought a libel suit against KSDO radio and its reporter, Hal Brown, for a story that implicated police in drug traffic. They demanded Brown's notes and memoranda.[149] And while Brown and KSDO won in their refusal to yield the material, they did so under *First Amendment* protection, said the court of appeal. The police had failed to show that the information was not available from any other source, or that the desired material went to the heart of their case.[150]

But so far as California's constitutional shield was concerned, said the court, decades of assumptions about its protective reach were mistaken: All it does is protect a journalist from contempt conviction. It does not stop courts from taking other actions in a libel case, as here, where journalists themselves are defendants: Their refusal to testify about information needed by the plaintiff could result in the court's striking their defense, or even awarding the plaintiff a default judgment. The court said that the shield law[151]

> * * * does not create a privilege for newspeople, rather, it provides an immunity from being adjudged in contempt. This rather basic distinction has been misstated and apparently misunderstood by members of the news media and our courts as well.

Though vulnerable under any law, journalists occasionally got more protection from their states' courts than the statutes suggested might be available. And sometimes they got less protection than expected. One loophole in several "absolute" statutes was the lack of provision protecting the reporter from revealing *information* that he had gathered, even though it protected him from revealing the *source* of that information. Robert L. Taylor, president and general manager, and Earl Selby, city editor of the *Philadelphia Bulletin,* were convicted of contempt

---

[146] *In re Van Ness* (Cal.Super.1982), 8 Med.L.Rptr. 2563; Evidence Code of Calif. (§ 1070).

[147] *Ohio v. Geis,* 2 Ohio App.3d 258, 441 N.E.2d 803 (1981), 7 Med.L.Rptr. 1675.

[148] Dorothy A. Bowles, Media Law in Tennessee. 2d ed. (Stillwater, OK: New Forums Press, 1999), discusses Tennessee Code Ann.24–1–208 at pages 106–107, and *Austin v. Memphis Publishing Co.,* 655 S.W.2d 146 (Tenn.1983) and *State ex rel. Gerbitz v. Curriden,* 738 S.W.2d 192 (Tenn.1987).

[149] *KSDO v. Superior Court of Riverside County,* 136 Cal.App.3d 375, 186 Cal.Rptr. 211 (1982), 8 Med.L.Rptr. 2360.

[150] Ibid. at 217, 8 Med.L.Rptr. at 2366.

[151] Ibid. at 213, 8 Med.L.Rptr. at 2362.

of court for refusing to produce documents in a grand jury investigation of possible corruption in city government. Both were fined $1,000 and given five-day prison terms. They appealed, relying on the Pennsylvania statute stating that no newsman could be "required to disclose the source of any information" that he had obtained. "Source" they said, means "documents" as well as "personal informants." The Pennsylvania Supreme Court, reversing the conviction, agreed. The court said that the legislature, in passing the act, declared the gathering of news and protection of the source of news as of greater importance to the public interest than the disclosure of the alleged crime or criminal.[152]

SHIELD LAWS AND LIBEL

Consider the issue of whether a shield against testifying is justified where a newspaper and reporter are sued for libel. If a reporter refuses to reveal an unnamed source who had allegedly libeled the plaintiff, may the plaintiff be foreclosed from discovering and confronting his accuser? Who, besides the reporter, can identify the accuser? Conversely, if the sources must be revealed, then is it not possible "for someone to file a libel suit as a pretext to discover the reporters' sources and subject them to harassment"?[153] This line of actions, of course, produced the suit which, perhaps more than any other, alerted the news world to the possibilities of danger in required testimony—*Garland v. Torre*, of 1958. As Marie Torre in that case, most other reporters since then who have been sued for libel have argued fruitlessly that they should not be required to name the source.

Shield statutes of Oregon, Rhode Island, Oklahoma and Tennessee provide expressly that the privilege is not available to persons sued for libel.[154] Supreme Courts of Massachusetts[155] and Idaho, which have no shield statutes, reject reporters' claims that there is an alternative First Amendment protection against the requiring of testimony—including testimony about sources of alleged libel. An Idaho decision, in which certiorari was denied by the United States Supreme Court, confirmed a 30-day jail sentence for reporter-editor Jay Shelledy.[156] He had quoted a "police expert" as criticizing state narcotics agent Michael Caldero who had been involved in a shooting incident. He was sued for libel by the agent, and, refusing to reveal the name of the expert, was held in contempt. The trial judge decided not to press the contempt citation, however, finding that another course of action would be more helpful to

[152] *In re Taylor*, 412 Pa. 32, 193 A.2d 181, 185 (1963). The Reporters Committee 1990 Guide, "Confidential Sources of Information," lists "absolute" and "qualified privilege" states as to both confidential sources *and* information.

[153] Gora, p. 40.

[154] Gora, p. 247. See Kaufman, op. cit., at footnote 84, above, *passim*, for comments on state shield statutes.

[155] *Dow Jones & Co., Inc. v. Superior Court*, 364 Mass. 317, 303 N.E.2d 847 (1973).

[156] *Caldero v. Tribune Pub. Co.*, 98 Idaho 288, 562 P.2d 791 (1977), certiorari denied 434 U.S. 930, 98 S.Ct. 418 (1977).

Caldero: The court would treat Shelledy's failure to identify the police expert "as an admission by the defendant Shelledy that no such 'police expert' exists, and the jury shall be so instructed."[157] The trial proceeded; the jury was instructed, and in place of the shield that he had hoped to raise, the jury came to the rescue: It brought in the verdict that Shelledy's article was not libelous.

The Caldero trial judge's ruling that Shelledy "had no source" was unusual but not unique. Only months before, a decision by the New Hampshire Supreme Court dealt with a claim by a former police chief who sued for libel after a newspaper cast doubt on his truthfulness. The newspaper had claimed the police chief had failed polygraph tests. Newspaper staffers refused to reveal the sources of the accusation. The court, after determining that the sought-after testimony was "essential to the material issue in dispute," and "not available from any source other than the press," granted the chief's motion to compel disclosure. The newspaper appealed, and the New Hampshire Supreme Court held that there was a better way to enforce the trial court's order than by holding the newspaper in contempt.[158]

> We are aware * * * that most media personnel have refused to obey court orders to disclose, electing to go to jail instead. Confining newsmen to jail in no way aids the plaintiff in proving his case. Although we do not say that contempt power should not be exercised, we do say that something more is required to protect the rights of a libel plaintiff. Therefore, we hold that when a defendant in a libel action, brought by a plaintiff who is required to prove actual malice under *New York Times,* refuses to disclose his sources of information upon a valid order of the court, there shall arise a presumption that the defendant had no source. The presumption may be removed by a disclosure of the sources a reasonable time before trial.

See also *DeRoburt v. Gannett*[159] and *Miller v. Transamerican Press*[160] for additional case law holding for the plaintiff's right to uncover confidential sources. In *Miller,* the 5th Circuit holding that disclosure can be compelled when the plaintiff has no other means to establish actual malice.

---

157 Anon., "Lewiston reporter Wins Jury Verdict in Libel Case," *News Media & the Law,* Oct./Nov.1980, 10–11, *Downing v. Monitor Pub. Co. Inc.,* 120 N.H. 383, 415 A.2d 683 (1980), 6 Med.L.Rptr. 1193.

158 *Downing v. Monitor Pub. Co. Inc.,* 120 N.H. 383, 415 A.2d 683, 686 (1980), 6 Med.L.Rptr. 1193, 1195; see also *Sprague v. Walter,* 518 Pa. 425, 543 A.2d 1078, 1086 (1988), in which the Pennsylvania Supreme Court held that a reporter-defendant in a libel case could invoke the state's shield law to protect the identity of sources. And the jury was to draw "*no inference either favorable or adverse*" from the invoking of the shield law as to the reliability of an unidentified source.

159 *DeRoburt v. Gannett Co.,* 507 F.Supp. 880 (D.Hawaii 1981).

160 *Miller v. Transamerican Press,* 621 F.2d 721 (5th Cir.1980).

The frequent success of the claim to the shield (usually where plaintiffs fail to show necessity, relevancy, and unavailability of the information) occasionally can extend to the libel situation, where the reporter is so likely to be vulnerable because he is the only source of the information sought. Before Marie Torre ever pleaded for protection in a libel case, a decision under the shield law of Alabama had furnished it to a reporter who refused to reveal sources of a story on prison conditions.[161] New York, New Jersey, and Pennsylvania protect, in varying degree, confidentiality in libel cases.[162]

Even in Idaho (which has no shield law and whose Supreme Court has interpreted *Branzburg* to provide no First Amendment protection), the appeal process brought relief to journalists who unsuccessfully sought a shield in discovery proceedings in a libel case. Sierra Life Insurance Co. demanded the names of confidential sources for a series of stories about the firm's financial difficulties, written by reporters for the *Twin Falls Times-News*.[163] Through complex legal processes, the reporters and the newspaper alleged that their stories were true and refused to name sources. In response, the trial judge ruled that Idaho provided no protection for them, struck all their defenses, and entered a "default" judgment against them for $1.9 million.

But the Idaho Supreme Court reversed the trial court. It did not believe that the refusal to testify should stand in the way of the newspaper's employing defenses—truth and lack of a connection between the stories and the damages suffered. Striking defenses in this case, it agreed, amounted to unwarranted punishment of the newspaper. And it said that Sierra had failed to show that its inability to discover the sources damaged its ability to prove the news stories false, which would be necessary to its case. It remanded the case, with "guidance" to the trial judge which included the Supreme Court's suggestion that the confidential sources' identity might not be relevant.[164]

SUMMARIZING ISSUES IN CONFIDENTIALITY

After the *Branzburg* decision hedged the constitutional protection that the news world sought, the media turned to lobbying for statutes at the state and federal levels, and to strengthening existing state statutes.

---

[161] *Ex parte Sparrow*, 14 F.R.D. 351 (N.D.Ala.1953). Federal courts have provided protection in some libel cases also: *Mize v. McGraw-Hill, Inc.*, 82 F.R.D. 475 (S.D.Tex.1979), 5 Med.L.Rptr. 1156; *Bruno & Stillman, Inc. v. Globe Newspaper Co.*, 633 F.2d 583 (1st Cir.1980), 6 Med.L.Rptr. 2057.

[162] Respectively, *Oak Beach Inn Corp. v. Babylon Beacon, Inc.*, 62 N.Y.2d 158, 476 N.Y.S.2d 269, 464 N.E.2d 967 (1984), 10 Med.L.Rptr. 1761; *Maressa v. New Jersey Monthly*, 89 N.J. 176, 445 A.2d 376 (1982), 8 Med.L.Rptr. 1473; *D'Alfonso v. A.S. Abell Co.*, 765 F.2d 138 (4th Cir.1985), 11 Med.L.Rptr. 2117; and *Hatchard v. Westinghouse Broadcasting Co.*, 516 Pa. 184, 532 A.2d 346 (1987): Reporters have to yield up evidence in a libel suit when it does not reveal identify of sources of confidential information.

[163] *Sierra Life Insurance Co. v. Magic Valley Newspapers, Inc.*, 101 Idaho 795, 623 P.2d 103 (1980), 6 Med.L.Rptr. 1769.

[164] Ibid. at 109, 6 Med.L.Rptr. at 1773.

Repeated efforts by news organizations in the last three decades of the Twentieth Century to get passage of a federal shield statute, however, found no success. For example, it was estimated in 1973 that more than 50 shield bills had been introduced into Congress and more appeared in subsequent years.[165]

(1) What are the competing social values in granting or denying journalists an immunity from testifying? The reporter's ethic of not betraying sources, and his property right in not losing his effectiveness and value as a reporter through losing his sources, had long been asserted unsuccessfully in cases under the common law. Now he was grounding his claim in society's loss of his service if he lost his sources through betraying them.

Earl Caldwell was one of a tiny number of reporters who had gained the confidence of the Black Panthers at a time when society had a real need to know about this alienated group. The Ninth Circuit Court of Appeals accepted Caldwell's argument that he would lose the Panthers' confidence if he even entered the secret grand jury chambers, for this extremely sensitive group would not know what he might say under the compulsion of the legal agency.[166] And if Caldwell could not report on the Panthers, society was the real loser. This situation illustrated the difference between the values served in the case of privilege for the journalist and that for the doctor, lawyer, or clergyman:[167]

> "* * * the doctor-patient privilege is there to make it possible for patients to get better medical care. A journalist's privilege should be there not only to make it possible for a journalist to get better stories, but to contribute to the public's right to know. So in that sense it is a more critical privilege than some of these other privileges, which are based primarily on the relationship between two people."

Asserting an equal service in the cause of the "public's right to know" was the position that in many circumstances, government-as-the-public sought information from reporters vital to the public welfare. In *State v. Knops,*[168] an "underground" newspaper editor refused to tell a grand jury the names of people to whom he had talked about the bombing of a university building that killed a researcher, and about alleged arson of another university building. "[T]he appellant's information could lead to the apprehension and conviction of the person or persons who committed a major criminal offense resulting in the death of an innocent person," said the Wisconsin Supreme Court in denying privilege to editor Mark

---

165 Thomas Collins, "Congress Grapples with Press Bill," *Milwaukee Journal,* March 25, 1973.

166 *Caldwell v. United States,* 434 F.2d 1081, 1088 (9th Cir.1970).

167 House of Rep. Committee on the Judiciary, Subcommittee No. 3, 92 Cong., 2d Sess., "Newsmen's Privilege," Hearings, Testimony of Victor Navasky, Oct. 5, 1972, p. 236.

168 *State v. Knops,* 49 Wis.2d 647, 183 N.W.2d 93 (1971).

Knops.[169] Here government was saying that the journalist was practicing secrecy similar to that which he so often criticized in government, and that government was trying to serve the public's right to know about a major crime.

THE JANET COOKE DEBACLE

A few reporters, meanwhile, rejected the notion that the privilege was either needed by or appropriate to the journalist. They said that most journalists of the nation had done their work for decades without a shield. And they worried about unethical reporters using a shield law to hide behind in dishonest reporting. Keeping in mind the respect, or lack of respect with which journalists are held from the chapters on defamation, unethical activities only serve to reinforce positions holding that a privilege is undeserved.

Directly on point was the episode—dismaying to journalists everywhere—of the fabricated story of rookie reporter Janet Cooke of the *Washington Post* in 1981. Her account of an unnamed eight-year-old heroin addict, whose identity she refused to disclose to her editors out of alleged fear of death from the child's "supplier," was awarded a Pulitzer Prize. But the award was scarcely announced when a standing challenge to the story's accuracy by city officials (resisted by *Post* editors who had insisted on shielding their reporter from disclosure of her sources), took strength from the revelation that Cooke had falsified her biographical resume in applying for a position at the *Post*. Faced with the dual challenge, she confessed that she had made up the story and resigned. The *Post* returned the Pulitzer Award with agonized apologies to readers, the city, and the field of journalism. No law court, no threat of contempt was involved, but the parallels were too close for comfort. The integrity of a shield claimed by a reporter and afforded by editors had been shattered; and so, too, in some measure, had that of a great newspaper, and the fact-gathering principle of special treatment—privilege—for the journalist.[170]

(2) Can the news gathering function be protected by a qualified immunity, or must it be absolute? Hard positions for absolute shields were taken by many journalists and their organizations including the directors of the American Newspaper Publishers Association and those of the American Society of Newspaper Editors.[171]

Yet "absolute" protection was an illusion, as we have seen in the previous section.[172] And a federal statute of any kind became a more and

---

[169] Ibid. at 99.

[170] Jerry Chaney, "Level With Us, Just How Sacred Is Your Source?", *Quill*, March 1979, 28; *Quill*, 61:4, April 1973, 38. Paul Magnusson, "Reporter's Lies Undermine Paper, Profession," *Wisconsin State Journal*, April 19, 1981, Sec. 4, p. 6; Robert H. Spiegel, "Notes from Pulitzer Juror," *Wisconsin State Journal*, April 21, 1981, Sec. 1, p. 6.

[171] *Quill*, 61:1, Jan. 1973, 29.

[172] AP Log, Sept. 3–9, 1973, pp. 1, 4.

more remote possibility as years of drafting, committee work, and lobbying failed.[173]

(3) Also at issue was the question: Who deserves the shield? and following that: Would not defining "reporter" in effect be to license journalists and thus bring them under state control? The United States Supreme Court in denying Paul Branzburg protection summarized the question and found that deciding it would bring practical and conceptual difficulties of a high order:[174]

> Sooner or later, it would be necessary to define those categories of newsmen who qualified for the privilege, a questionable procedure in light of the traditional doctrine that liberty of the press is the right of the lonely pamphleteer who uses carbon paper or a mimeograph just as much as of the large metropolitan publisher who utilizes the latest photo-composition methods * * * . Freedom of the press is a "fundamental personal right" which "is not confined to newspapers and periodicals." It necessarily embraces pamphlets and leaflets * * * . Almost any author may quite accurately assert that he is contributing to the flow of information to the public, that he relies on confidential sources of information, and that these sources will be silenced if he is forced to make disclosures before a grand jury.

Troubling as the question was, it did not deter states as they adopted statutes from 1970 onward. New York's 1970 law defined "professional journalist" and "newscaster" in its law that protected only those agencies normally considered "mass media"—newspaper, magazine, news agency, press association, wire service, radio or television transmission station or network.[175] Illinois, in its 1971 statute, defined "reporter" as one who worked for similar media.[176] Neither included books among the media immunized; neither included scholars and researchers among the persons immunized. In two cases, courts have ruled that state statutes which gave protection specifically to newspapers did not protect magazines.[177] But in late 1977, the U.S. Court of Appeals, Tenth Circuit, ruled that Arthur (Buzz) Hirsch, a film maker engaged in preparing a documentary on Karen Silkwood who had died mysteriously in a puzzling auto accident in Oklahoma, was indeed protected by the First Amendment in refusing to disclose confidential information concerning his investigation. This was the case despite the fact that the Oklahoma

---

173 Press Censorship Newsletter No. IX, April–May 1976, p. 53.

174 *Branzburg v. Hayes*, 408 U.S. 665, 702, 92 S.Ct. 2646, 2668 (1972).

175 McKinney's N.Y.Civ.Rights Law § 79–h (Supp.1971). In *People v. LeGrand*, 67 A.D.2d 446, 415 N.Y.S.2d 252 (1979), 4 Med.L.Rptr. 2524, the law was held not to apply to a book author, because the law specifies that only professional journalists and newscasters are shielded.

176 Ill.Legis.H.Bill 1756, 1971 Gen.Assembly.

177 *Cepeda v. Cohane*, 233 F.Supp. 465 (S.D.N.Y.1964); *Deltec, Inc. v. Dun & Bradstreet, Inc.*, 187 F.Supp. 788 (N.D.Ohio 1960).

shield law gave protection only to those "regularly engaged in obtaining, writing, reviewing, editing or otherwise preparing news."[178]

The Second Circuit reached a different conclusion with respect to a reluctant witness in the civil case of *von Bulow v. von Bulow*[179] The children of Martha "Sunny" von Bulow sued Claus von Bulow alleging that Claus von Bulow put Sunny von Bulow into a permanent coma with a surreptitious injection of insulin. In the course of discovery, the plaintiffs sought notes taken by Andrea Reynolds, an intimate friend of von Bulow. Reynolds was his companion in his trial on charges of assault to murder his wife. The plaintiffs also sought investigative reports into the von Bulow matter that Reynolds had commissioned and a manuscript of an unpublished book that Reynolds described as "the manuscript of my story of the von Bulow affair."[180]

Reynolds submitted the notes and investigative reports but kept her manuscript. The district court ruled that all the materials were discoverable and ordered them turned over. Reynolds asserted a journalist's privilege and refused to comply.[181] The district court found her in contempt and Reynolds appealed. The issue for the Second Circuit was whether Reynolds deserved to assert the privilege. (It should be noted that Reynolds' conduct during this controversy did little to help her position.) She failed to comply with the first subpoena, denied the existence of any of the subpoenaed documents other than her manuscript and in her deposition without benefit of counsel claimed the journalist's privilege as well as "any other privilege that exists under the sun."[182]

The district court looked to Reynolds' journalistic pedigree. Reynolds offered the court a press card from Polish Radio and Television that had been issued in 1979. She also said she had "drafted" an article about von Bulow for the German magazine *Stern*, had an agreement with a German publishing agency for serialization of her completed work, and said she had a press pass for the *von Bulow* trial from the *New York Post* along with a letter from a *Post* editor asking her to cover the trial.

That list might appear to justify a claim to being a journalist, but the district court looked further into her materials. It found that Reynolds never published anything herself, that she had not managed to come to an agreement with the *Post* for coverage, that the *Post* had never published anything by Reynolds, that the article in *Stern* magazine she claimed credit for had been carried her husband's name on the byline. She also said that the manuscript she was working on had not been

---

[178] *Silkwood v. Kerr-McGee*, see "Court Protects Film Maker's Sources," *News Media & the Law*, 1:1 (Oct.1977), p. 26.

[179] 811 F.2d 136 (2d Cir.1987), see also *von Bulow v. von Bulow*, 634 F.Supp. 1284 (S.D.N.Y.1986).

[180] 811 F.2d 136, 139 (2d Cir.1987).

[181] Reynolds later asserted an attorney-client privilege saying that she was a "paralegal" for the defense team during the trial. That issue is not dealt with here.

[182] 811 F.2d 136, 139 (2d Cir.1987).

prepared under contractual obligation to any publisher and "that her relationship with the publisher of her proposed book 'has nothing to do with my privileges as a journalist.' "[183] The district court found Reynolds did not qualify for the journalist's privilege because persons who claim the privilege must be actively involved in the gathering and dissemination of news to do so.

In its review of the district court's findings, the Second Circuit panel laid out the requirements for asserting the journalist's privilege.

> First, the process of news gathering is a protected right under the First Amendment, albeit a qualified one. This qualified right, which results in the journalist's privilege, emanates from the strong public policy supporting the unfettered communication of information by the journalist to the public. Second, whether a person is a journalist, and thus protected by the privilege, must be determined by the person's intent at the inception of the information-gathering process. Third, an individual successfully may assert the journalist's privilege if he is involved in activities traditionally associated with the gathering and dissemination of news, even though he may not ordinarily be a member of the institutionalized press. Fourth, the relationship between the journalist and his source may be confidential or nonconfidential for purposes of the privilege. Fifth, unpublished resource material likewise may be protected.[184]

The court then examined the New York shield law which, in a previous case, did not serve to protect the author of a book because the author was found to fall outside the definition of a "professional journalist" as laid out in the statute.[185] Finding the state law and the federal approach to be similar because of their similar interests in protecting the press, the court then applied its standard to Reynolds' case. "We hold that the individual claiming the privilege must demonstrate, through competent evidence, the intent to use material—sought, gathered or received—to disseminate information to the public and that such intent existed at the inception of the news gathering process."[186] Such a test, the court said, would require the district court to look into the intent element. The Second Circuit did not put limits on how the "journalist" would have to disseminate his news. The court said it could be through every sort of medium. The court also said that while prior journalistic experience would be helpful, it was not going to require that every person asserting the privilege to have had such a background.

---

[183] Ibid.

[184] Ibid. at 142.

[185] *People v. LeGrand*, 67 A.D.2d 446, 415 N.Y.S.2d 252 (2d Dep't 1979), although the case left the door open for such a finding with a future author under different facts.

[186] 811 F.2d 136, 144.

The court looked at Reynolds' claim and the testimony she provided explaining how and why she engaged in her information gathering. The investigative reports focused on Sunny von Bulow's children to check on their credibility and for her primary concern of vindicating Claus von Bulow. Reynolds said her notes from the case were "worthless doodles." Her manuscript contained either material in the public domain or the notes and investigative reports. The public domain information was already known and the court concluded that the notes and reports were not the result of any journalistic endeavor when they were created. As such, the court affirmed the contempt order.

The *Reynolds* court may seem troubling with the finding by the court that she was not entitled to assert the journalist's privilege. But the court's analysis makes clear that it intended to prevent a misuse of the label journalist. The court noted the Tenth Circuit's decision regarding Silkwood film maker Arthur "Buzz" Hirsch.[187] The Second Circuit found a journalistic intent in that case that agreed with its own test. The Second Circuit explicitly said that even authors who have not published or are just beginning could assert the privilege if the requisite intent existed and was proven. "The burden indeed may be sustained by one who is a novice in the field."[188]

PROTECTING AN INVESTIGATIVE AUTHOR: SHOEN V. SHOEN (1993, 1995)

A wealthy family's internal struggles for control over the U-Haul Co. are part of the background for a defamation/author's privilege actions known as *Shoen v. Shoen.* Leonard Shoen, a major owner of U-Haul, cooperated with investigative author Ronald Watkins, helping him to write a book titled *Birthright.* This book dealt with members of the family jousting for control of the company.

In 1990, the wife of Shoen's oldest son, Sam, was the victim of an unsolved murder. In interviews with the news media, Leonard Shoen said he suspected two other sons, Mark and Edward Shoen, of having indirect ties to the murder.[189]

Mark and Edward Shoen sued their father for defamation. Seeking information for their lawsuit, they subpoenaed book author Watkins to produce any information he had about the murdered woman, Eva Berg Shoen. District Court Judge Roger C. Strand refused Watkins' order for a protective order to protect him from a subpoena on grounds that a state court had interpreted Arizona's state law as excluding book authors.[190]

---

[187] *Silkwood v. Kerr-McGee Corp.*, 563 F.2d 433 (10th Cir.1977).

[188] 811 F.2d 136, 144.

[189] *Shoen v. Shoen*, 5 F.3d 1289 (9th Cir.1993), 21 Med.L.Rptr. 1961; *News Media & the Law*, Fall, 1993, pp. 28–29.

[190] *News Media & The Law*, Fall, 1993, p. 28.

Held in contempt for refusing to testify, Watkins appealed to the U.S. Court of Appeals for the Ninth Circuit. Watkins contended that a First Amendment privilege should be available to protect not only regularly employed establishment journalists but also independent authors such as himself. He also argued that if forced to testify, that would discourage his sources from providing information. Perhaps most telling, the point was made that the persons subpoenaing Watkins had not exhausted other sources.[191]

The Ninth Circuit held that Watkins, as an investigative journalist, could invoke the shield privilege: "The journalist's privilege is designed to protect investigative reporting, regardless of the medium used to report news to the public. * * * What makes journalism is not its format but its content." Further, even if Watkins did not gain access to his material under a confidentiality agreement, the shield privilege still should protect him.

The district court again found Watkins in contempt for refusing to obey a discovery subpoena, and Watkins again appealed.[192] But in a 2–1 decision, the Ninth Circuit again found in Watkins' favor held that when a civil litigant's discovery efforts run into a valid assertion of journalist's privilege by a non-party (in this case a writer who was no directly involved in the matter as a litigant), substantial deference should be given to that privilege. The Ninth Circuit held that in a civil suit, a litigant could overcome the journalist's privilege.

However, the Ninth Circuit held that the plaintiffs had not made the necessary showing to overcome the journalist's privilege. Notes or tapes Watkins had compiled in interviewing the father, Leonard Shoen, appeared to the Ninth Circuit to be superfluous. The sons' defamation suit against their father already contained substantial evidence of the father's ill will toward them. In fact, in a deposition the elder Shoen referred repeatedly to one of his sons as "Hitler" and said he believed his sons were sociopaths.

Source confidentiality has sharp issues for journalists and investigative authors. Advice from the late Clark R. Mollenhoff, a Pulitzer-Prize winner: "You'd better know what you're getting into."[193] In other words, journalists should be reluctant to pledge confidentiality. They may find that if they wish to stay "on the record," sources often will talk to them anyhow. And if confidentiality is pledged, for how long? Until the moon no longer shines? Or for some lesser period? Promises of confidentiality are not to be made lightly.

---

[191] *Shoen v. Shoen*, 5 F.3d 1289 (9th Cir.1993), 21 Med.L.Rptr. 1961.

[192] *Shoen II* (*Shoen v. Shoen*), 48 F.3d 412 (9th Cir.1995), 23 Med.L.Rptr. 1522; *Shoen I* (*Shoen v. Shoen*), 5 F.3d 1289 (9th Cir.1993), 21 Med.L.Rptr. 1961.

[193] *Quill*, March 1979, p. 27, for Mollenhoff's rules.

62. PROTECTING NEWSROOMS FROM SEARCH AND TELEPHONE RECORDS FROM DISCLOSURE

Courts have not granted First Amendment protection against officials' searches of newsrooms, but Congress and several states have passed laws providing protection. Confidentiality of journalists' telephone-call records that are on file at telephone companies has not been recognized.

When the United States Supreme Court rejects a claim to First Amendment protection, Congress and state legislatures may be able to furnish protection by passing laws. The news world's drive for a statutory privilege against revealing sources—after the Supreme Court in *Branzburg v. Hayes* seemed to journalists to restrict protection under the First Amendment to a shadow—succeeded in a few states by dint of long, hard work, and failed in others. The effort to get a law through Congress ground to a frustrated halt in 1976 and 1977 as we saw above.

But another aspect of confidentiality denied First Amendment protection by the Supreme Court—shielding news rooms and offices against official searches and seizures of news material—got an early remedy in the form of state legislation and a national law—the Privacy Protection Act of 1980.[194] It was passed less than three years after a Supreme Court decision of May 1978 sent the news media into a reaction of alarm and denunciation; the very security of their news rooms and files was at stake. Journalists' outrage over the decision was widespread at what they saw as the Court's approval of a "right to rummage" in their offices, a breach of custom and understanding.

By a 5–3 margin, the Court said in 1978's *Zurcher v. Stanford Daily* that newspapers (and all citizens, for that matter) may be the subjects of unannounced searches as long as those searches are approved beforehand by a court's issuance of a search warrant.[195] They need not be suspected of any crime themselves; but as "third parties" who may hold information helpful to law enforcement, their property may be searched. A particular issue in this case was a question of how to interpret the words of the Fourth Amendment to the Constitution. That amendment says:

> The right of the people to be secure in their persons, houses, papers, and effects, against unreasonable searches and seizures, shall not be violated, and no Warrants shall issue, but upon probable cause, supported by Oath or affirmation, and particularly describing the place to be searched, and the persons or things to be seized.

---

[194] Pub.Law #96–440, 94 Stat. 1879, approved Oct. 13, 1980, 6 Med.L.Rptr. 2255. For summary and discussion of the law and the state actions, see Anon., "Newsroom Searches," *News Media & the Law*, Oct./Nov. 1980, 3–5.

[195] *Zurcher v. Stanford Daily*, 436 U.S. 547, 98 S.Ct. 1970 (1978) 3 Med.L.Rptr. 2377.

The *Zurcher* case arose during violent demonstrations at Stanford University on April 9, 1971. Two days later, the *Stanford Daily* carried articles and photographs about the clash between demonstrators and police. It appeared to authorities from that coverage that a *Daily* photographer had been in a position to photograph fighting between students and police. As a result, a search warrant was secured from a municipal court. The warrant was issued:[196]

> on a finding of "just, probable and reasonable cause for believing that: Negatives and photographs and films, evidence material and relevant to the identification of the perpetrators of felonies, to wit, Battery on a Peace Officer, and Assault with a Deadly Weapon, will be located [on the premises of the Daily]."

Later that day, the newspaper office was searched by four police officers, with some newspaper staffers present. The search turned up only the photographs already published in the *Daily*, so no materials were removed from the newspaper's office. In May of 1971, the *Daily* and some of its staffers sued James Zurcher, the Palo Alto chief of police, the officers who conducted the search, and the county's district attorney.

A federal district court held that the search was illegal. It declared that the Fourth and Fourteenth Amendments forbade the issuance of a warrant to search for materials in possession of a person not suspected of a crime unless there was probable cause to believe, based on a sworn affidavit, that a subpoena *duces tecum* would be impractical.

Some translation is needed here. As *New York Times* reporter Warren Weaver, Jr. noted, a subpoena *duces tecum* (that's Latin for "bring it with you") "can be enforced by a judge only after a hearing in which the holder of the evidence has the opportunity to present arguments why the material should not be given to the government." That process means, of course, that the holder of the documents sought would have some warning and perhaps even a chance to "clean up" files. (But if one does tamper with evidence under subpoena—and if that tampering is revealed, it is surely punishable as contempt.) If investigators have a search warrant, on the other hand, the holder of the documents "has no more warning than a knock on the door."[197] In finding in favor of the *Stanford Daily*, District Judge Robert F. Peckham wrote:[198]

> It should be apparent that means less drastic than a search warrant do exist for obtaining materials from a third party. A subpoena duces tecum, obviously, is much less intrusive than a search warrant: the police do not go rummaging through one's house, office, or desk armed only with a subpoena. And, perhaps

[196] Ibid. at 551, 98 S.Ct. at 1974.

[197] Warren Weaver, Jr., "High Court Bars Newspaper Plea Against Search," *New York Times*, June 1, 1978, pp. Al ff, at p. B6.

[198] *Stanford Daily v. Zurcher*, 353 F.Supp. 124, 130 (N.D.Cal.1972).

> equally important, there is no opportunity to challenge the search warrant prior to the intrusion, whereas one can always move to quash the subpoena before producing the sought-after materials. * * * In view of the difference in degree of intrusion and the opportunity to challenge possible mistakes, the subpoena should always be preferred to the search warrant, for non-suspects.

The *Daily*'s lawsuit thus was upheld by a U.S. district court and, five years later, by a U.S. Court of Appeals.[199] The Supreme Court of the United States, however, in a decision announced by Justice White, declared that newspapers are subject to such unannounced "third party" searches as the one involving the *Stanford Daily*. Justice White's majority opinion said:[200]

> It is an understatement to say that there is no direct authority in this or any other federal court for the District Court's sweeping revision of the Fourth Amendment. Under existing law, valid warrants may be issued to search *any* property, whether or not occupied by a third party, at which there is probable reason to believe that fruits, instrumentalities, or evidence of a crime will be found.
>
> * * *
>
> The critical element in a reasonable search is not that the owner of the property is suspected of a crime but that there is reasonable cause to believe that the specific "things" to be searched for and seized are located on the property to which entry is sought.

The Court enumerated—and rejected—the following arguments that additional First Amendment factors would forbid use of search warrants and permit only the subpoena *duces tecum*—arguments which held that searches of newspaper offices for evidence of crime would threaten the ability of the press to do its job.[201]

> This is said to be true for several reasons: first, searches will be physically disruptive to such an extent that timely publication will be impeded. Second, confidential sources of information will dry up, and the press will also lose opportunities to cover various events because of fears of the participants that press files will be readily available to the authorities. Third, reporters will be deterred from recording and preserving their recollections for future use if such information is subject to seizure. Fourth, the processing of news and its dissemination will be chilled by the prospects that searches will disclose internal editorial deliberations. Fifth, the press will resort to self-censorship to

[199] 550 F.2d 464 (9th Cir.1977).

[200] *Zurcher v. Stanford Daily*, 436 U.S. 547, 554–556, 98 S.Ct. 1970, 1975–1977 (1978).

[201] Ibid. at 561–566, 1977–1982.

> conceal its possession of information of potential interest to the police.

Justice White's majority opinion brushed aside such arguments and expressed confidence that judges could guard against searches which would be so intrusive as to interfere with publishing newspapers.

Justice Potter Stewart, joined by Justice Thurgood Marshall, dissented, arguing that in place of the unannounced "knock-on-the-door" intrusion, "a subpoena would afford the newspaper itself an opportunity to locate whatever material might be requested and produce it." Then, as did his dissent in *Branzburg v. Hayes*, his argument hammered at society's need for confidentiality of the journalist's information, and for its constitutional protection.[202]

> Perhaps as a matter of abstract policy a newspaper office should receive no more protection from unannounced police searches than, say, the office of a doctor or the office of a bank. But we are here to uphold a Constitution. And our Constitution does not explicitly protect the practice of medicine or the business of banking from all abridgment by government. It does explicitly protect the freedom of the press.

Justice John Paul Stevens' dissent focused not on First Amendment matters, but on the justification needed to issue a search warrant without running afoul of the Fourth Amendment. Stevens wrote that every private citizen—not only the media—should be protected.[203]

Students of the problem questioned Justice White's reliance on "neutral magistrates" to protect media from harassment, and to issue warrants only upon reasonable requests whose propriety they could gauge on the basis of probable cause to believe that evidence would be found on the premises to be searched. For one thing, between the 1971 raid on the *Stanford Daily* offices and the Supreme Court decision in 1978, there were at least 14 other searches of media properties. And in addition:[204]

> Journalists should perhaps be forgiven if they regard the protection of "neutral magistrates" as illusory. First, most, if not all, journalists tend to believe the folklore item about police walking around with fill-in-the-blank search warrants already signed by a complacent magistrate. Even if that is rankest slander of the judiciary, statistics on the issuance of search warrants compel the belief that the preconditions for warrant issuance are often improperly administered. "From 1969 through 1976, police sought 5,563 applications for search warrants under the 1968 Omnibus Crime Control Act. Only 15

---

202 Ibid. at 576, 1987.

203 Ibid. at 581–583, 1990–1991.

204 Dwight L. Teeter and Singer, S. Griffin, "Search Warrants in Newsrooms," 67 *Ky.L.Journ.* 847, 858 (1978–79).

of these applications were denied." Bluntly, the general rule seems to be that a search warrant sought equals a search warrant granted.

The legislation that Congress passed in 1980 in reaction to the *Zurcher* decision took effect in 1981. It provides a subpoena procedure, and a hearing for those subpoenaed. It prohibits "knock-on-the-door," search-warrant raids of news media offices and those of authors and researchers, by federal, state, and local law enforcement agencies, except in three unusual circumstances. These are: where there is cause to believe that the reporter himself is involved in a crime, where the information sought relates to the national defense or classified information, or where there is reason to believe that immediate action through search warrant is needed to prevent bodily harm or death to a human being.[205]

The Privacy Protection Act was amended in 1996 to allow law enforcement personnel to conduct searches of newsroom for additional types of materials. The law, sponsored by Sen. Orrin Hatch (R-Utah), allows searches for materials linked to child pornography and other child exploitation offenses. Hatch said the amendment was needed to protect law enforcement officers from being sued over searches conducted in connection with child pornography cases.[206]

SAN FRANCISCO POLICE AND BRYAN CARMODY

San Francisco Police sought a search warrant seeking to find out who leaked a confidential police report to freelance journalist Bryan Carmody concerning the death of San Francisco Public Defender Jeff Adachi.[207] Officers showed up at Carmody's door and used a crowbar to enter his home office and seized equipment and notes. Carmody was protected by the Privacy Protection Act and the California Shield Law and should have been served with a subpoena rather than a search warrant.

Adachi was a vocal opponent of police misconduct and some city officials believed a member of the police department leaked the report to smear Adachi. The report noted that he was with a woman who was not his wife when he died.[208]

San Francisco County Superior Court Judge Rochelle East, who initially issued the search warrant, quashed it after she found out Carmody was a journalist and barred investigators from using any of the

[205] Pub.Law 96–440, 94 Stat. 1879; 6 Med.L.Rptr. 2255, 2256 (1981). And see "Carter Signs Newsroom Raid Ban," *News Media & the Law*, Oct./Nov. 1980, 3–5.

[206] "Amendments to Privacy Protection Act Become Law," *News Media and the Law*, Fall 1996.

[207] Matt Hamilton, "When a Journalist Would Not Betray His Source, Police Came to His Home With Guns and a Sledgehammer," *Los Angeles Times*, May 11, 2019.

[208] Megan Cassidy, "Jeff Adachi Case: Judge Quashes SFPD Warrant," *San Francisco Chronicle*, July 18, 2019.

evidence that was obtained from that order.[209] Judge East said that police investigators did not tell her Carmody was a journalist when they asked for the search warrant.[210]

JOURNALISTS' TELEPHONE RECORDS

Searches of newsrooms slowed after adoption of the Privacy Protection Act of 1980, but occasional police or FBI searches may occur.[211] And there are other intrusions. In 1976, the Reporters Committee for Freedom of the Press and other journalists lost a case in federal district court to compel AT & T to inform media when government subpoenas were issued for media phone records. The court of appeals also turned down the media, saying that no right of privacy under the First Amendment existed because the records belonged to the telephone company and not the media.[212] In an unsuccessful appeal to the United States Supreme Court to review the decision, the journalists stated the heart of their case for protection of their telephone records:[213]

> When government investigators obtain a reporter's toll records * * * they learn the identity of (his) sources. And they also learn * * * much about the pattern of his investigative activities—whom he called, when and in what order he makes calls to develop his leads, what subjects he is looking into and how actively he is exploring these subjects.

In the fall of 1980, it was reported that phone records of the Atlanta bureau of the *New York Times,* as well as those of its bureau chief, Howell Raines, had been subpoenaed in June by the Justice Department. The telephone company had waited 90 days, at the request of the Justice Department, before telling the *Times*. Shortly thereafter, Attorney General Benjamin Civiletti announced new rules for issuing subpoenas for phone records—essentially, that no subpoena is to be issued to media people for their toll phone records without "express authorization" of the Attorney General.[214] This was the extent of protection that the media found.

So in this setting, journalists were asserting that secrecy—anathema when employed by the government—was essential to the highest performance of their own craft. Journalists argue, however, that without the ability to keep their records and sources away from the long reach of government, their traditional role of "watchdogs" over

---

[209] Ibid.

[210] Dan Noyes and Khaled Sayed, "Journalist Bryan Carmody Has Victory in Court Over San Francisco Police in Jeff Adachi Death Investigation," *ABC7News*, July 19, 2019, https://abc7news.com/journalist-has-victory-in-court-over-sf-police-in-adachi-death-investigation/5404833/.

[211] "Police Raid Newspaper Printing Office," *News Media & the Law*, Aug./Sept. 1980, 25.

[212] *Reporters Committee for Freedom of Press v. American Tel. & Tel. Co.*, 593 F.2d 1030 (D.C.Cir.1978), certiorari denied 440 U.S. 949, 99 S.Ct. 1431 (1979), 4 Med.L.Rptr. 2536.

[213] Quoted in *News Media & the Law*, Oct./Nov. 1980, p. 6.

[214] *New York Times*, Nov. 13, 1980, A30; 28 C.F.R. § 50.10.

government and other powerful institutions would be hampered. The goal of journalists is to inform the members of an open society about their world.

Growing technological sophistication for government (and private) surveillance of and listening to "persons of interest" should tell Twenty-First Century journalists that telephones, whether wired or wireless, are not private or secure. After the attacks on the World Trade Center and the Pentagon on Sept. 11, 2001, federal investigative agencies at times chose not to get legally required court-authorized warrants before intercepting communications.[215] Shortly after the attacks, however, and before passage of the USA PATRIOT ACT eased restrictions on investigators,[216] the Oct. 1, 2001 *New York Times* published a story co-authored by Judith Miller and Philip Shenon about planned federal searches of and asset freezes of organizations suspected of raising money for terrorists. The federal government planned to freeze the assets and/or search the premises of the Holy Land Foundation [HLF] and the Global Relief Foundation [GRF]. A federal grand jury was told how the *Times* reporters learned of the planned searches and asset freezes and phoned the HLF and GRF seeking comments from them about the planned searches *before* they were carried out.[217]

The government, believing the reporters' calls not only alerted the HLF and GRF and allowed "them to take steps mitigating the effects of the freeze and searches" and endangered the agents executing the searches. Under federal statutes, if a government agent makes an unauthorized disclosure of impending law enforcement actions, that could be prosecuted as a crime. The government sought the newspaper's phone records to identify reporter's sources who broke the law by leaking secret information.[218]

Circuit Judge Winter noted that the *Times*' Oct. 1, 2001 story by Miller and Shenon asserted that the government was considering adding the GRF to a list of organizations suspected of ties to terrorism. Miller said she received this information from "confidential sources." Miller called an HLF representative on Dec. 3, 2001, seeking a reaction to the government's planned seizure of assets. This information was published on a *New York Times* website and in its late edition papers on Dec. 3, the day before the search was carried out. Similarly, *Times* reporter Philip Shenon contacted the GRF on Dec. 13, 2001, seeking a reaction to the government's intention to freeze its assets. When the FBI search took place on Dec. 14, it was found that the GRF was " 'expecting them and

---

[215] *American Civil Liberties Union v. U.S.*, 493 F.3d 644 (6th Cir. 2007).

[216] See the discussion of the USA Patriot Act.

[217] *New York Times Company v. Alberto Gonzales*, 459 F.3d 160, 162–164 (2d Cir. 2006).

[218] Ibid. at 163. See 18 U.S.C. § 793(d) "(prohibiting communication of national defense information to persons not entitled to receive it), including the felony of obstruction of justice, 18 U.S.C. § 1503(a)."

already had a significant opportunity to remove items.' " The day after the FBI search of GRF offices, the times published Shenon's article.[219]

When he learned government's plans to search GRF had been leaked, Patrick J. Fitzgerald, U.S. Attorney for the Northern District of Illinois, began an investigation to identify the government employees who leaked the information to reporters. Fitzgerald asked the *Times* to voluntarily provide its telephone records from Sept. 24 to Oct. 2, 2001, and from Dec. 7 to 15, 2001. Fitzgerald's letter to the *Times* said "that the First Amendment did not protect the 'potentially criminal conduct' of Shenon's source or Shenon's ' "decision . . . to provide a tip to the subject of a terrorist fundraising activity." ' The *New York Times* refused the request, stating that the First Amendment protects the press from ' "having to disclose confidential source information to the government." ' "[220]

In Oct. 27, 2004, U.S. District Judge Sweet finally granted the *Times's* motion for summary judgment on its claims that telephone records of reporters Miller and Shenon were protected by two First Amendment qualified privileges against a newspaper's compelled disclosure of confidential sources. One privilege came from federal common law under Federal Rule of Evidence 501. The other privilege stemmed from the First Amendment.[221]

Considering this fact situation, the Second Circuit of the U.S. Court of Appeals held that a First Amendment reporter's privilege, if indeed it existed under *Branzburg v. Hayes*,[222] was not applicable. Circuit Judge Winter wrote that whatever standard was used (highly material and relevant, necessary or critical to the maintenance of the claim, and not obtainable from other available sources), "the privilege has been overcome as a matter of law."[223]

In dissent, Circuit Judge Robert Sack contended that reporters should be able to obtain declaratory judgments to protect the identity of their sources.[224]

Judge Sack proposed a test to protect both reporters and society when information leaks are investigated. If telephone companies provide calling records identifying sources, prosecutors could identify journalists' confidential sources virtually at will. Reporters would be placed in the position of contacting their confidential sources much as drug dealers do, "by use of clandestine cell phones and meetings in darkened doorways." He added, "Ordinary use of the telephone could become a threat to

---

[219] Ibid. at 164.

[220] Ibid. at 165.

[221] Ibid., citing Judge Sweet's decision in *New York Times Co. v. Gonzales*, 382 F.Supp. 2d 457 (S.D.N.Y.2005), at 492, 508.

[222] See discussion of *Branzburg v. Hayes*. Above.

[223] *New York Times Company v. Alberto Gonzales*, 459 F.3d 160, 170 (2d Cir. 2006).

[224] Dissent of Circuit Judge Sack. At 175.

journalists and source alike. It is difficult to see in whose best interest such a regime would operate."

Judge Sack contended that courts should evaluate whether " . . . nondisclosure of the information would be contrary to the public interest, taking into account both the public interest in newsgathering and the maintaining a free flow of information to citizens."[225]

KIRIAKOU, AP PHONE RECORDS AND THE OBAMA ADMINISTRATION'S SEARCH FOR LEAKERS

As *New York Timesman* James Reston once wrote, "A government is the only vessel that leaks from the top." Government also leaks, of course, from the middle or from the bottom. And it should be noted, one person's lawbreaking leaker is another person's heroic whistleblower. The obsession of the administration of President Barack Obama with plugging leaks to bottle up news the public arguably needs to know seems unprecedented. In 2013, the president who pledged "greater transparency" in the federal government came under a drumfire of criticism. President Obama, the former University of Chicago constitutional law professor, seemed to have forgotten much about the First Amendment and allied topics including access to government information and the public's right to know what government is doing. Obama, to journalists, seemed to have reverted to the narrow view of the late Justice Potter Stewart. Stewart wrote in 1975:[226]

> "So far as the Constitution goes, the autonomous press may publish what it knows, and may seek to learn what it can.
>
> "But this autonomy cuts both ways. The press is free to do battle against secrecy and deception in government. But the press cannot expect from the Constitution any guarantee that it will succeed. There is no constitutional right to have access to particular government information, or to require openness from the bureaucracy. The public's interest in knowing about government is protected by a guarantee of a Free Press, but the protection is indirect. The Constitution itself is neither a Freedom of Information Act nor an Official Secrets Act.
>
> "The Constitution, in other words, establishes the contest, not its resolution. Congress may provide a resolution, at least in some instances, through carefully drawn legislation. For the rest, we must rely, as so often in our system we must, on the tug and pull of the political forces in American society."

John Kiriakou, 49, became the 2012–2013 symbol of the Obama administration's determined campaign to root out the identities of leakers/whistleblowers. He became the first CIA officer to go to prison for disclosing classified information to a reporter. While with the CIA,

---

[225] Ibid.

[226] Potter Stewart, "Or of the Press," 26 *Hastings L.J.* (1975).

Kiriakou was honored for his willingness to go in harm's way and for his effectiveness in gathering important information in Iraq and Iran during the Second Gulf War. But by 2004, when he resigned from the CIA after nearly 15 years of service to become—what else?—a security consultant, his former employer viewed him as a "loose cannon." In 2007, after leaving the CIA, Kiriakou became the first CIA officer to publicly confirm and describe the "interrogation technique" of waterboarding. He did so in an interview with ABC-TV correspondent Brian Ross. Waterboarding, involving strapping down a subject and pouring water over his mouth and nose give the sensation of drowning, understandably is often denounced as a form of torture.

BEWARE OF YOUR EMAIL!

The interview with Brian Ross evidently put Kiriakou, figuratively speaking, in the CIA's crosshairs. The outgoing and flamboyant Kiriakou lunched with a friend—a freelance reporter doing a book on American intelligence activities. Kiriakou—who should have known better given his background as a spy, emailed the name of a covert CIA operative as a potential source for the journalist. The operative's name was never made public, and the journalist was referred to in Kiriakou's indictment only as "Journalist B."[227]

In a major profile of Kiriakou for the *New York Times*, Scott Shane wrote that his supporters see a particular injustice in his imprisonment. After all, in Kiriakou's first appearance on ABC News in 2007, he defended extreme measures by the CIA. But, Shane wrote, Kiriakou said "he had come to believe that waterboarding was torture and should no longer be used in American interrogations." Waterboarding, Shane explained, was considered a notorious torture method since the Inquisition, but declared legal in secret memoranda by the Justice Department in secret opinions that were later withdrawn.[228]

Shane quoted Bruce Riedel, a now-retired CIA officer who conducted an Afghan war review for President Obama, said Kiriakou was a fine CIA officer who did not deserve prison. Riedel noted that Kiriakou became " 'the first CIA officer ever to go to jail over torture' " even though he denounced torture publicly. Riedel added, " '[I]t's deeply ironic under the Democratic president who ended torture.' "[229]

Nevertheless, Kiriakou was charged with felonies under the Espionage Act and under the Intelligence Identities Protection Act. Kiriakou, who spent more than $1 million in legal fees defending himself, was able to dodge an Espionage Act prosecution through a plea bargain with the Department of Justice. He admitted to a single count of violating the Intelligence Identities Protection Act because he had revealed the

---

[227] Scott Shane, "From Spy to Convict: Former C.I.A. Officer is the First to Face Prison for a Classified Leak," *New York Times*, January 6, 2013, pp. 1ff.

[228] Ibid. at 22.

[229] Ibid.

name of a CIA covert agent. His guilty plea in January, 2013 meant that Kiriakou began serving a 30-month prison sentence at the Federal Correctional Institution, Loretto, Pennsylvania, on Feb. 28, 2013.

ASSOCIATED PRESS PHONE RECORDS GRABBED BY DEPARTMENT OF JUSTICE

Despite President Barack Obama's 2008 campaign pledges of greater transparency in the federal government and his repeated statements of support for a free and vibrant press, Obama administration actions say something different. The search for information leakers within government cast a shadow over perceptions of and professions favoring news media freedom.

Exhibit A against the administration is a 2012 Department of Justice action, secretly obtaining more than two months of telephone records.[230] While President Obama may talk about the role of the press as a watchdog, the secret Department of Justice subpoenas getting into AP phone records showed a distinct preference for a lapdog press. On May 13, 2013, White House spokesman Jay Carney's words offered a mixed message. Carney said that the president respects the news media's need to do investigative reporting. But on the other hand, Carney said the president recognizes " 'the need for the Justice Department to investigate alleged criminal activities without undue influence.' "[231]

The claimed justification for the Department of Justice's seizure of phone records of 20 AP reporters and editors over a two-month period involved the search for leakers in what Attorney General Eric Holder called one of the most serious security breaches in his memory. The investigation was triggered by a May, 2012 AP report about a thwarted al-Qaida plot in Yemen to blow up an airliner headed for the United States. A House of Representatives panel inquiring about the government snooping into AP phone records expressed concern. The action, panel members said, inflicted serious damage on AP's efforts to report important news. " 'It seems to me that the damage to a free press has been substantial,' " said Rep. Zoe Lofgren (D-Calif.). Rep. John Conyers (D-Mich.), said he was deeply troubled that the United States government would " 'secretly pursue such a broad array of phone records over such a long period of time.' "[232]

HOW LARGE A NET WAS CAST BY THE U.S. LEAK INQUIRIES?

The *New York Times* reported that even before the FBI seized phone records of Associated Press reporters and interviewed 550 officials trying to locate leakers who provided information for a 2012 article on foiling a Yemen bomb plot, agents were seeking the same reporters' sources for

[230] Aamer Madhani and Kevin Johnson, "Obama team defends war on leaks," *USA Today* news analysis, May 15, 2013, p. 3A.

[231] Ibid.

[232] Kevin Johnson, "Holder offers how, why in the AP flap," *USA Today*, May 16, 2013.

two articles about terrorism.[233] That same article noted that in a separate situation, the FBI sought phone and email records of a *Times* reporter covering computer attacks on Iran.

Access to information clearly is paying a high price for this search for leakers. Ethan Bronner, Charlie Savage and Scott Shane reported:[234] Some officials are now declining to take calls from certain reporters, concerned that any contact may lead to investigation. Some complain of being taken from their offices to endure uncomfortable questioning. And the government officials typically must pay for lawyers themselves, unlike reporters for large news organizations whose companies provide legal representation.

That article also contended that the administration is using the full extent of its power to try to intimidate journalists. Fox News's James Rosen's email records were seized under a warrant in 2009. The warrant used language terming Rosen "an aider, abettor and/or co-conspirator," labeling that could set Rosen up for prosecution under the Espionage Act. Then-Attorney General Eric Holder signed off on that particular warrant.

JUSTICE DEPARTMENT REVIEWS ITS POLICY ON SURVEILLANCE OF JOURNALISTS

In July, 2013, following the revelations about surveillance of Associated Press and Fox News reporters, the Justice Department issued a report on the methods it would use when dealing with members of the news media. The Department of Justice Report on Review of News Media Policies, laid out significant changes that would prevent surreptitious investigation of reporters. Before readers go out to get the champagne and party hats, be aware that each one of the new policies include exceptions that would allow the Justice Department to go after information about journalists and their records in secret.

The Justice Department reported that it would change its presumption regarding giving notice to journalists and news organizations about efforts to obtain their records. Under policies in place at the time of the AP and Fox investigation, the Justice Department would only give notice and try to negotiate with news media when the[235] "responsible Assistant Attorney General determines that such negotiations would not pose a substantial threat to the integrity of the investigation." The new policy has the Department notifying journalists and news organizations ahead of time and negotiating for the information unless[236] "advance notice and negotiations would pose a

[233] Ethan Bronner, Charlie Savage and Scott Shane, "Sweeping Leak Inquiries Reveal How Wide a Net U.S. Has Cast," *New York Times*, May 16, 2013.

[234] Ibid.

[235] Department of Justice Report on Review of News Media Policies, July 12, 2013. Italics retained.

[236] Ibid.

clear and substantial threat to the integrity of the investigation, risk grave harm to national security, or present an imminent risk of death or serious bodily harm." That language parallels that of the Privacy Protection Act of 1980 (discussed earlier in this chapter).

The Justice Department will create a News Media Review Committee to advise the attorney general when the department considers gathering information in secret. That committee will[237] "include senior Department officials, including but not limited to the Department's Director of the Office of Public Affairs and the Department's Chief Privacy and Civil Liberties Officer." There is no mention of a press representative or academic in the composition of the committee advising the attorney general.

The policy incorporates the Privacy Protection Act's exception for search warrants when the journalist is a suspect in the investigation. Under the revision, the Department will apply that exception,[238] only when the member of the news media is the focus of a criminal investigation for conduct not connected to ordinary newsgathering activities. Under this revised policy, the Department would not seek search warrants under the PPA's suspect exception if the sole purpose is the investigation of a person other than the member of the news media.

The policy requires that the attorney general approve of search warrants with the advice of the new committee. The attorney general also would have to have the director of national intelligence weigh in on investigations into news media in cases involving national security. The director would have to certify[239] "the significance of the harm that could have been caused by the unauthorized disclosure and reaffirm the intelligence community's continued support for the investigation and prosecution before the Attorney General authorizes the Department to seek media-related records in such investigations."

MAY, 2013: OBAMA ADMINISTRATION SEEKS FEDERAL SHIELD STATUTE

Clearly stung by the AP phone records controversy, the Obama administration tried to toss an olive branch to the news media. On May 15, 2013, the White House asked Congress to resurrect shield law legislation. White House aide Ed Pagano contacted the office of Senator Charles E. Schumer (D-NY), asking him to resubmit a 2009 bill known as the Free Flow of Information Act. As of May, 2013, there was no federal media shield law to provide partial protections to reporters in keeping their sources and communications confidential. A majority of states, however, has some protections for journalists who refuse to name confidential sources in law enforcement proceedings. In 2010 proposed

[237] Department of Justice Report on Review of News Media Policies, July 12, 2013. Italics retained.

[238] Ibid.

[239] Ibid.

shield legislation in Congress never received a vote. It was caught in the backwash of the WikiLeaks scandal, when archives of secret government documents were released to the Internet.[240]

NEWSROOM CONFIDENTIALITY: A CONTINUING STRUGGLE

Despite passage of the federal Privacy Act of 1980, aimed at protecting newsrooms from searches under most circumstances,[241] the late 1980s saw a number of efforts to search newsrooms. The searches showed that law is not self-executing, and that reporters need a working understanding of the law—with preparation from knowledgeable attorneys—when a search is attempted. Searches became sufficiently bothersome in 1988 that the National Association of Broadcasters (NAB) issued a memo urging broadcast stations to review procedures with their attorneys for fending off a search.[242]

When a police department or sheriff asks a judge for a search warrant, there is some likelihood that the judge won't know that the Privacy Protection Act of 1980 forbids searches of newsrooms except in limited situations as noted above, at footnote 205. Despite this statute and despite similar legislation in at least nine states, occasional searches have continued. The *News Media & The Law* reported in the fall of 1988 that four newsroom searches had taken place between December, 1986, and mid-August of 1988, in Minneapolis and Golden Valley, Minnesota, and in Palm Springs and Los Angeles, California. No searches have been reported in recent years. The most recent occurred during the Gizmodo episode in 2010 when police searched the home of the owner of the site looking for a missing iPhone.[243]

The *News Media & The Law* emphasized that the Privacy Protection Act of 1980 made it illegal for the seizure of either the "work product" or "documentary materials" from persons who are creating newspapers, books or broadcasts.[244] That magazine recommended:

First, journalists in the newsroom should object to the search and, if possible, should stall long enough for the company's lawyer and upper-level management to arrive.

---

[240] Charlie Savage, "Criticized on Seizure of Records, White House Pushes Media Shield Law," *New York Times*, May 16, 2013, p. A17. For WikiLeaks background, see Textbook, pp. 44–46, 504–507.

[241] See discussion above. Those limited occasions in which a federal or state judge may issue a warrant for a newsroom search include a reasonable showing that newsroom personnel are involved in commission of a crime, in possession of contraband or classified or national defense information, or where there is reason to believe that information in a newsroom is needed by authorities to protect human life.

[242] Jane E. Kirtley, Counsel Memo: "Dealing With Newsroom Searches," N.A.B. Info-Pak, October/November, 1988.

[243] https://bits.blogs.nytimes.com/2010/04/27/can-gizmodo-win-the-iphone-legal-battle/?_r=0.

[244] *News Media & The Law*, Fall, 1988, pp. 4–5.

Second, journalists should not interfere with the search, but they do not have to assist in it. The search should be limited by the terms of the warrant to certain areas and to specific materials.

Third, *News Media & The Law* recommended that a videotape or photographic record be made if the search proceeds.

Finally, once a search has taken place, a lawyer should be consulted about the possibility of suing the governmental agency carrying out the search. If the search is found illegal under the terms of the Privacy Protection Act of 1980, the journalist whose office was searched can collect $1,000 in damages (plus reimbursement for any actual harm done in the search) plus lawyer's fees.[245] It should be apparent that most search warrants issued against newsrooms are illegal and invalid, and journalists should be prepared to fight back. Lawsuits are not the only weapons, however. Publicity about governmental units acting illegally may be the media's strongest weapon in protecting newsrooms from searches.

Obviously, journalists should remain vigilant, ready to contend—by all lawful means—against newsroom subpoenas or searches. News processes should remain separate from government. As the late Justice Potter Stewart wrote in dissent in *Branzburg v. Hayes*, the historic independence of the press is important, and should not be undermined "by attempting to annex the journalistic profession as an investigative arm of government." Democratic decision-making relies on the free flow of information to the public, in keeping with the " 'profound national commitment to the principle that debate on public issues should be uninhibited, robust, and wide-open.' "[246]

LAW ENFORCEMENT CALLS ON CELL PHONE SERVICE PROVIDERS

The risks for reporters are part of a general erosion of privacy rights in a connected world. Cell phone companies told Congress that they had received 1.3 million demands from law enforcement in 2011 for subscriber information.[247]

A staple of television police dramas, the cell phone information was sought by local, state and federal agencies in connection with investigations from everything from street crimes to intelligence operations. Sprint reported the highest rate of inquiries telling Congress that it received an average of 1,500 data requests a day.

---

245 Ibid. at 6; See also Kirtley, op. cit.

246 Justice Stewart's dissent in *Branzburg v. Hayes*, 408 U.S. 665, 737, 92 S.Ct. 2646, 2691 (1972), quoting *New York Times Co. v. Sullivan*, 376 U.S. 254, 84 S.Ct. 710 (1964).

247 Eric Lichtblau, "More Demands on Cell Carriers in Surveillance," *New York Times*, July 8, 2012.

FDA MONITORS EMAILS FROM ENEMIES LIST

The Food and Drug Administration made headlines in the summer of 2012 when a surveillance operation it conducted on its own scientists went public. The operation captured emails that FDA staffers sent privately to members of Congress, lawyers, labor officials, journalists and even President Obama.[248]

The operation began during a dispute between some FDA scientists and administrators over the agency's approval of some mammogram and colonoscopy devices that, the scientists argued, exposed patients to dangerous levels of radiation.[249]

A confidential government review in May by the Office of Special Counsel, which deals with the grievances of government workers, found that the scientists' medical claims were valid enough to warrant a full investigation into what it termed "a substantial and specific danger to public safety."

Some officials working for the medical imaging companies complained to the FDA that proprietary information was being leaked to reporters and consumer advocacy groups. The FDA then began to check the emails of five scientists. But the surveillance grew as the agency focused on a list of opponents.[250]

Moving to quell what one memorandum called the "collaboration" of the FDA's opponents, the surveillance operation identified 21 agency employees, congressional officials, outside medical researchers and journalists thought to be working together to put out negative and "defamatory" information about the agency.

The surveillance operation used software used by employers to monitor worker computer usage. The spying recorded keystrokes as employees used laptops at work and at home. It took screenshots, intercepted emails and copied documents on the scientists' thumb drives.

The FDA's activities became public because of a mistake. A private document handling company that does contract work for the agency posted the documents on a website. The documents included[251] "confidential letters to at least a half-dozen congressional offices and oversight committees, drafts of legal filings and grievances, and personal e-mails. . . . Drafts and final copies of letters the scientists sent to Mr. Obama about their safety concerns were also included."

Two FDA scientists who had written emails about taking a complaint to the Office of Special Council were let go and a third suspended, the *Times* reported. The surveillance may have been

---

[248] Eric Lichtblau and Scott Shane, "Vast F.D.A. Effort Tracked E-Mails of Its Scientists," *New York Times*, July 14, 2012.

[249] Ibid.

[250] Ibid.

[251] Ibid.

improper under rules that protect communications between attorneys and their clients, whistleblowers and grievances.

CONTROLLING ACCESS TO INFORMATION THE PUBLIC NEEDS TO KNOW: EDWARD SNOWDEN, GLENN GREENWALD AND NSA SECRETS (AND CIA, AND FBI)

On June 14, 2013, the *Guardian* newspaper in Britain reported on a secret American court order enabling the NSA to require a Verizon subsidiary to provide all of its customers' records for a three-month time span. The National Security Agency (NSA)—the mammoth, super-secretive electronic spying arm of the United States government—wanted to do this data mining. This program, classified Top Secret, had already been underway for at least seven years. As in the case of Pfc. Chelsea (born Bradley Manning in 1987) Manning to WikiLeaks in 2010, there had been a massive, embarrassing leak of classified information. The Manning leaks of State Department cables, however, generally were at a lower security classification—Secret rather than the Top Secret revelations in the *Guardian*.

Edward Snowden, then 29, was a civilian contractor employed by Booz Allen Hamilton, a defense contractor headquartered in McLean, Virginia. The computer-adept Snowden, lived with his girlfriend at his home in Hawaii. He had a high-paying job and a Top Secret clearance for handling some of the most sensitive defense materials for the United States government. Snowden became a fugitive by stealing NSA secrets and by working with Glenn Greenwald of the *Guardian*, an accomplished and aggressive reporter who works on U.S. and British defense stories.[252]

After lifting a huge but undetermined number of Top Secret electronic files, Snowden disappeared. He wound up keeping an extremely low profile in a Hong Kong hotel, and contacted the award-winning investigative reporter Greenwald through a series of cloak-and-dagger maneuvers including encryption of email messages. Greenwald's book about his work with Snowden—aptly titled "*No Place to Hide*"—is a cautionary tale about the perils of trying to break a major story that the government wants to keep under wraps. For example, the NSA has the capability to track people who are carrying cellphones. As a result, Greenwald was told by Snowden to be sure to remove the battery from his phone to try to thwart NSA tracking of him as an individual.[253] And both Snowden and the documentary filmmaker Laura Poitras, who encouraged Greenwald to follow this important story about NSA's unfettered spying, had to resort to elaborately encrypted emails in order to communicate. Also, Greenwald purchased a laptop to use but not to be connected with the Internet. He called it his "air gapped machine." He

---

[252] Siobhan Goran, Evan Perez, and Janet Hook, "U.S. Collects Vast Data Trove," *Wall Street Journal*, June 7, 2013.

[253] Glenn Greenwald, *No Place to Hide: Edward Snowden, the NSA, and the U.S. Surveillance State* (New York: Metropolitan Books, 2014), pp. 8–9.

explained, "It is much more difficult to subject an Internet-free computer to surveillance."[254]

Ultimately, Greenwald—who resides in Rio de Janiero, Brazil—went to Hong Kong to meet with Snowden and Poitras.[255] Although the NSA and other government security agencies fell back on their "we're protecting you from terrorists" gambit, it required a leak by a young NSA contract employer to reveal the enormity of NSA intrusions into individual's privacy, both domestic and international. The traditional press evidently was clueless about the vast extent of NSA snooping.

Greenwald wrote that as Snowden instructed him to go to Hong Kong immediately, he said:[256]

> "I want to spark a worldwide debate about privacy, Internet freedom, and the dangers of state surveillance. I'm not afraid of what will happen to me," he said. "I've accepted that my life will likely be over from my doing this. I am at peace with that. I know it's the right thing to do."

Greenwald wrote that his agreement with the *Guardian* gave him full editorial independence, but still had to clear initial scrutiny from editors and from *Guardian* lawyers as he struggled to break a now-legendary expose' of NSA activities. Early in this process, Greenwald read thousands of documents taken by Snowden. Among them, the reporter found a Foreign Intelligence Surveillance Act (FISA) court order. The FISA court's orders are secret warrants to authorize government eavesdropping through electronic surveillance. Despite the command of the Sixth Amendment that courts shall be open to the public, "All of its rulings are automatically designated Top Secret, and only a handful of people are authorized to access its documents," Greenwald wrote. He noted that he had never seen a FISA court order before, but then,[257] "Almost nobody had." The order in question held that wholesale and indiscriminate collection of American telephone records was justified by Sec. 215 of the USA Patriot Act.

Other documents acquired by Edward Snowden showed the NSA program ominously called BOUNDLESS INFORMANT to have collected more than three billion pieces of data from U.S. communication systems alone in a 30-day period early in 2013. Greenwald compared that with an answer by U.S. Director of National Intelligence James Clapper to a question asked by Sen. Ron Wyden of Oregon. Sen. Wyden asked whether NSA collected any data whatsoever on millions or hundreds of millions of Americans. (Snowden wanted it made public that Clapper lied to Congress.) Clapper's answer:[258] "No, sir." Clapper's definition of PRISM?

---

[254] Ibid. at 22.

[255] Peter Maass, "How Laura Poitras Helped Snowden Spill His Secrets," *New York Times Magazine*, Aug. 13, 2013.

[256] Greenwald, *No Place to Hide*, p. 18.

[257] Ibid. at p. 27.

[258] Ibid. at p. 30.

He termed it[259] " 'an internal government classification system used to facilitate the government's statutorily authorized collection of foreign intelligence information from electronic communication service providers under court supervision.' "[260]

One of Snowden's leaks involved the sealed Foreign Intelligence Surveillance Agency (FISA) court's standing order directing Verizon to hand over records to the NSA. Verizon not alone in receiving many NSA requests. AT&T and Nextel, in spring, 2013, were subject to standing court orders too. Evidently just skimming the surface, Sen. Edward Markey (D-MA) said that four major carriers complied with tens of thousands of court orders each year. The *Wall Street Journal* reported Verizon alone "received 260,000 requests for customer data in 2011.[261] These records, known as metadata, involve telephone numbers, call duration, and at times, call locations. These FISA Court authorizations, renewable every three months, do not allow eavesdropping on the content of calls.

Greenwald was critical of a practice of leading American newspapers—the *New York Times* and the *Washington Post*—in delaying reporting of important stories if asked by government to do so. Greenwald declared that on occasion newsworthy information gets suppressed. That, Greenwald wrote, is what happened to a *Washington Post* story on illegal overseas CIA torture sites by concealing the names of those countries where the torture-enabling prisons were based.

During a 10-day period in Hong Kong with Snowden, Greenwald and Poitras chose which stories to report, and in what order. First up in the Greenwald reports based on documents supplied by Snowden: the Top Secret program known as PRISM. NSA collected data from nine of the largest internet companies, including Google, Facebook, Verizon, Skype, and Yahoo!!.[262]

Law Professor Jonathan Turley of Georgetown University commented in 2013 that President Barack Obama was asking for supporters to back him in spying on every American, "fundamentally altering our society. Indeed, he and congressional allies are trying to convince Americans that they can free themselves from fear only by redefining privacy in a way that allows ubiquitous surveillance.[263] Supporters of the program argue that collecting metadata does not really

[259] Ibid. at pp. 54–55.

[260] Authors' Note: Pay attention to the words "foreign intelligence."

[261] Danny Yadron, Spencer E. Ante, and Anton Troianovski, "When NSA Calls, Companies Answer," *Wall Street Journal*, June 7, 2013, p. A4.

[262] Greenwald, pp. 20–21, 63–64, 75–76.

[263] Jonathan Turley, "Creeping surveillance state, creepy conclusions: Who, when and where reveal too much," *USA Today*, June 10, 2013, p. 6A.

invade personal privacy and does not reveal the contents, for example, of telephone conversations.[264]

Turley and others have warned, however, that if an individual's phone calls and email records are available, much can be learned about a person. Emails to a medical marijuana resource line? Repeated calls to an abortion clinic? To an Alcoholics Anonymous hotline? When government promises to protect Americans if they will "temporarily" give up some liberties, a benign government can protect them. Turley declared that Obama was repeating "the siren call of all authoritarian figures throughout history. . . ." Turley reiterated Benjamin Franklin's warning,[265] "[T]hose who would give up essential liberty to purchase a little temporary safety deserve neither liberty nor safety."

Because of Edward Snowden's disclosures, published initially through the *Guardian* newspaper, both conservatives and liberals in the United States now know—and are alarmed by—NSA's overreaching spying activities. And as this text goes to press, Snowden, traitor or patriot, is now in Vladimir Putin's grimly authoritarian Russia. He has spoken of a desire to return home and even serve some time. But Snowden is adamant that he will not become a poster boy for national security by coming home to be sent to prison for life.

WHAT HAPPENED TO THE "INALIENABLE RIGHTS" OF THE FOURTH AND SIXTH AMENDMENTS?

On June 23, 2013, legendary *New York Timesman* Max Frankel raised this question in that paper's *Sunday Review* section. "Where Did our 'Inalienable Rights' go?" Frankel, *Times* editorial page editor from 1977 to 1986 and executive editor from 1986 to 1994, wrote that "the issue . . . is not how we balance personal privacy with police efficiency." He provided historical context involving the famed "Pentagon Papers" leaks and the 1971 U.S. Supreme Court decision in *New York Times v. United States* allowing publication of news stories based on a leaked Top Secret study about involvement in the Vietnam War.[266]

> Frankel wrote,[267] "As those of us who had to defend the 1971 publication of the secret Pentagon Papers about the Vietnam War have been arguing ever since, there can be no mature discussion of national security policies without the disclosure—authorized or not—of the government's hoard of secrets."

Although the Obama administration has argued strenuously that aggregating vast troves of data does not really imperil the privacy of ordinary individuals, that reassurance rings hollowly for those who recall

---

[264] Kathleen Hennessey, "Obama defends data collection," *Los Angeles Times*, June 9, 2013, p. A1.

[265] Turley, op. cit.

[266] Max Frankel, "Where Did Our 'Inalienable Rights' Go?", *New York Times Sunday Review*, p 1, June 23, 2013.

[267] Ibid.

or who have researched misuse of FBI-gathered information to smear reputations, or who know about Sen. Joseph R. McCarthy's fanciful and unproven 1950s accusations of disloyalty that ruined a number of careers. Presidents Lyndon B. Johnson and, especially, Richard M. Nixon used secret files from the Internal Revenue Service to harass political opponents.

As Frankel pointed out, even though reporters had been getting pieces of the story about National Security Agency (NSA) data vacuuming, the enormity of the NSA's data net—aided and abetted by for-profit firms receiving NSA's outsourced largesse—did not become clear until 2013. The catalyst for this frightening clarity? Leaker Edward J. Snowden, a 29-year-old computer expert working for security consultants Booz Allen Hamilton, an NSA contractor. Until Snowden went public, government was denying the very existence of the top secret "Prism" program indiscriminately amassing phone and Internet messages. The searches are routinely approved (see "rubber-stamped") by the secret Foreign Intelligence Surveillance Court (FISC). The FISA court has 11 judges, and their identities are, of course, secret.[268]

Snowden, a fugitive from the United States as of July, 2013, was charged in absentia under the Espionage Act on June 22, 2013. Charges against him involved violating the Espionage Act, stealing government property, and disclosing secret information to the *Guardian* of London and to the *Washington Post*. Each of the three charges carries sentences up to 10 years, to a maximum of 30 years. Additional counts were believed likely.[269]

WHAT HAPPENED TO THE FOURTH AND SIXTH AMENDMENTS?

War or fear of terrorism trumps civil liberties in the United States and, indeed, in every nation.[270] Consider the wording of the Fourth and Sixth Amendments to the Constitution of the United States:

Amendment IV

The right of the people to be secure in their persons, houses, papers, and effects, against unreasonable searches and seizures, shall not be violated, and no Warrants shall issue, but upon probable cause, supported by Oath or affirmation, and particularly describing the place to be searched, and the persons or things to be seized.

Amendment VI

In all criminal prosecutions, the accused shall enjoy the right to a speedy and public trial, by an impartial jury of the State and district wherein the crime shall have been committed, which district shall have

---

[268] Ibid. FISC was established by the Foreign Intelligence Surveillance Act (FISA) of 1978.

[269] Scott Shane, "Leaker Charged With Violating Espionage Act," *New York Times*, June 22, 2013.

[270] See Geoffrey R. Stone, *War and Liberty: An American Dilemma; 1790 to the Present* (New York: W.W. Norton & Co., 2007), pp. 145–146, 152–153 and passim.

been previously ascertained by law, and to be informed of the nature and cause of the accusation; to be confronted with the witnesses against him; to have compulsory process for obtaining witnesses in his favor, and to have the Assistance of Counsel for his defense.

Either oblivious to or uncaring about the Fourth and Sixth Amendments, the Obama administration defends the NSA searches as reasonable because they protect Americans by helping to identify potential terrorists. For ordinary Americans, it is argued, their daily lives and communication patterns should not make them NSA "persons of interest" because the initial NSA data gathering does not get person-specific without some triggering cues or clues.

The NSA data gathering may indeed be indiscriminate, but technocrats can mine to isolate specific data with great rapidity. According to a June 9, 2013, *New York Times* article by James Risen and Eric Lichtblau, the U.S. intelligence community has turned to the private sector to help fathom the secrets of "Big Data." For example, the U.S. has hired Palantir Technologies, Inc., headquartered in Palo Alto, California. Palantir, founded in 2004 by some inventors who developed PayPal, developed software capable of exponentially faster data mining. Palantir has offices in other key locations, including McLean, Virginia, and Abu Dhabi.

Pulitzer Prize-winner Eric Lichtblau's reporting on the ever-expanding powers of the NSA ought to trigger a push-back against U.S. security. He reported:[271] In more than a dozen classified rulings, the nation's surveillance court [the FISC or the FISA court] has created a secret body of law giving the NSA the power to amass vast collections of data on Americans while pursuing not only terrorism suspects, but also people possibly involved in nuclear proliferation, espionage and cyberspace attacks, officials say.

Lichtblau wrote that the FISA court formerly concentrated on case-by-case surveillance or wiretapping orders, but legislative changes have enabled it to become "almost a parallel Supreme Court," with the final say on surveillance matters.

The FISA court, Lichtblau reported, has created a "special needs" doctrine establishing "an exception to the Fourth Amendment's requirement of a warrant for searches and seizures."

Lichtblau quoted unnamed officials, and thus may become, once again, a target for a federal recriminations if not investigation. Remember that Lichtblau, along with James Risen, won a Pulitzer Prize for reporting in 2005 that the NSA had been indulging in vast amounts of warrantless wiretapping, not even bothering to go through the surveillance-friendly FISA court. Hawkish Vice President Dick Cheney

---

[271] Eric Lichtblau, "In Secret, Court Vastly Broadens Powers of N.S.A., *New York Times*, July 7, 2013, p. 1.

called the Risen-Lichtblau story disloyal and unworthy of the Pulitzer Prize it received.

CHAPTER 11

OBLIGATIONS ON BROADCASTING AND CABLE

63. LICENSING BROADCASTERS

The licensing process has provided both the legal authority and the procedures essential for the regulation of broadcast service in the United States.

The Radio Act of 1927 marked both the beginning of broadcast regulation in the United States and the end of that era when use of the airwaves was an inherent right of every citizen, limited only by the availability of spectrum space.[1] Sec. 11 of the Radio Act diminished this *right* to the status of a *privilege*, to be granted by the Federal Radio Commission (FRC) only in circumstances where the agency found that issuing or renewing a broadcast license would serve the "public interest".[2] This same regulatory approach was followed by the Communications Act of 1934 that created the Federal Communications Commission (FCC) to replace the FRC.[3]

Because these governmental bodies were viewed as bestowing a *privilege* upon those they permitted to broadcast, the United States Supreme Court upheld their authority as regulatory agencies to impose conditions on the private use of this public resource of broadcast spectrum space, including a requirement that broadcast programming serve the interests of the public.[4] As a later Supreme Court decision

---

1 Sec. 2 of the Radio Act of 1912 required the Secretary of Commerce to issue licenses upon request, allowing conditions to be imposed upon a license only in instances where its operation might interfere with those of other licensed stations.

2 Sec. 11, Radio Act of 1927, "If upon examination of any application for a station license or for the renewal or modification of a station license the licensing authority shall determine that public interest, convenience or necessity would be served by the granting thereof, it shall authorize the issuance, renewal or modification thereof in accordance with such finding."

3 Communications Act of 1934, Public Law 416, 73d Congress, Secs. 307–309.

4 *National Broadcasting Company, et al. v. United States, et al.*, 319 U.S. 190, 63 S.Ct. 997 (1943). See also, Chap. 3, Sec. 14 of this text for a more extensive discussion of this decision.

would declare in even stronger terms, such government program standards were viewed as enhancing, rather than repressing broadcast freedom of expression because,

> When there are substantially more individuals who want to broadcast than there are frequencies to allocate, it is idle to posit an unabridgeable First Amendment right to broadcast comparable to the right of individuals to speak, write or publish * * * the people as a whole retain their interest in free speech and their collective right to have the medium function consistently with the ends and purposes of the First Amendment.[5]

It is this broadcast licensing power, then, that has furnished the federal government with both the legal authority essential to regulate American broadcast service and that administrative process necessary to enforce its regulatory policies during the past eight decades.

The licensing process itself has always been more a matter of form than of substance. Applications for a construction permit, a broadcast license or renewal of a license each require the completion of countless forms, all filed in multiple copies with the FCC in Washington, D.C. There a small desk-bound staff of less than two dozen civil servants process this paperwork to determine whether each application should be approved.[6]

The forms themselves are generally prepared for the broadcaster by one of the major communication law firms in Washington, D.C. that specializes in dealings with the FCC. These attorneys, often former FCC employees, are in daily contact with the Commission staff to resolve any problems that might arise from their clients' broadcast filings. In nearly all cases, the end result of the process is that the application for the permit, license or license renewal is eventually granted.[7]

However, in that very small percentage of cases where a broadcast license application cannot be approved because, "a substantial and material question of fact is presented, or the Commission for any reason is unable to make the finding specified," the applicant is notified of the Commission's intention to hold a hearing before deciding what action should be taken.[8]

---

5 *Red Lion Broadcasting Co. v. FCC*, 395 U.S. 367, 89 S.Ct. 1794 (1969).

6 For an excellent description of this administrative process, see Barry Cole and Mal Oettinger, *Reluctant Regulators: The FCC and the Broadcast Audience* (Reading, MA: Addison-Wesley, 1978).

7 In 1976, for example, the FCC processed 2,995 applications for renewal of broadcast licenses of which just 23 were designated for hearing, and only 8 ultimately denied. In other words, 99.2 percent of all renewal applicants were approved without hearing and only 3/10 of 1 percent were eventually denied. Cole, Oettinger, op. cit., p. 147.

8 U.S.C.A. Title 47, § 309(e). Recently, one of the few comparative standards the FCC had been using in deciding among competing candidates for a broadcast license was overturned by the court in *Bechtel v. FCC*, 957 F.2d 873 (D.C.Cir.1992). The court questioned the validity of the "integrated ownership" standard the Commission claimed to have been following since 1965, asking the FCC to produce one case during those years in which an applicant who received

In most instances, a broadcaster unsuccessful at the informal hearing level still has the right to have this administrative finding reviewed both within the FCC itself and then by the Court of Appeals for the District of Columbia before being forced to accept an adverse Commission decision.[9]

The FCC does not monitor broadcast transmissions and so at time of renewal, it has always had to rely upon the records or "logs" of programming maintained by each station in determining whether the broadcaster had complied with the program proposals the station filed with the Commission when the license was last renewed.[10] During the 1980s the agency reduced this level of supervision even further, releasing broadcasters from the obligation to submit program logs to the Commission at the time of a station's license renewal.[11]

In 1991, however, the Commission decided to begin enforcing certain basic broadcast rules more aggressively, using its forfeiture power to impose monetary fines on licensees violating these rules. This tactic allowed the FCC to react to these violations much more quickly and efficiently than if it threatened a broadcaster's license, because many of the procedural safeguards of the licensing process did not apply in cases where the Commission sought only a monetary penalty.

After adopting a comprehensive *Table of Forfeitures* which for the first time specified the specific monetary amount that would be levied for each type of rule violation, the agency started almost immediately to invoke its new sanctions.[12] In the first six months of 2006, the FCC imposed fines of $3.93 million for broadcast indecency.[13] In addition, the agency imposed additional fines for slamming (changing a telephone service without the permission of the customer), broadcasting telephone conversations, faded paint on broadcast towers and failing to comply with V-chip requirements.

---

a license after pledging to personally manage a station had actually done so. Rather than respond to this challenge, the agency decided in April 1992 to review its entire comparative licensing process. See Reexamination of the Policy Statement on Comparative Broadcast Hearings, 7 FCC Rcd 2664 (1992); see also, Anchor Broadcasting, 72 R.R.2d 98 (1993).

[9] U.S.C.A. Title 47, § 402(b). Although a broadcaster may also seek U.S. Supreme Court review of an adverse Court of Appeals decision, the Supreme Court agrees to review, or accept certiorari only in a very limited number of appeal situations each year.

[10] H.J. Kenner, *The Fight for Truth in Advertising* (1936) pp. 13–14; Alfred McClung Lee, *The Daily Newspaper in America* (1937), p. 328.

[11] Revision of Applications of Renewals of License of Commercial and Non-Commercial AM, and Television Licensees, 50 R.R.2d 704 (1981).

[12] *In re Standards for Assessing Forfeitures*, 69 R.R.2d 823 (1991), affirmed on reconsideration 70 R.R.2d 11206 (1992). In July 1994, the U.S. Court of Appeals for the D.C. District upheld a U.S. Telephone Association challenge of this new uniform forfeiture schedule, holding that the FCC had failed to give those broadcasters, cable operators and telephone company licensees it affected adequate opportunity to comment on the new schedule before it was adopted. The Court did not find the concept of uniform fines to be unacceptable in itself but did question the equity of this particular schedule of fines that seemed to be overly severe in punishing telephone company regulatory violations.

[13] https://apps.fcc.gov/edocs_public/attachmatch/FCC-95-24A1.pdf.

For the most part, though, broadcasters have tended to conform to Commission regulatory policies not because of any fear of forfeiture, or concern about what the licensing process might reveal about their programming practices, but rather because even the slightest threat to a station's license is a risk worth avoiding at virtually any cost.

This type of indirect rule worked particularly well during an era when the Commission could decide for itself when its understaffed Broadcast Bureau was capable of using the license renewal process to enforce certain specific FCC regulatory standards. Until the mid 1960s, only a competing broadcaster could compel the FCC to conduct a comparative hearing before awarding or renewing a broadcast license of another station in that market, and then only if the evidence clearly indicated that the award could cause intolerable transmission interference or severe economic injury to the complaining broadcaster.[14]

In all other situations, the Commission had sole authority to decide whether the public interest demanded that it conduct an elaborate and time consuming hearing before renewing a broadcast license. Not surprisingly, it rarely did.

In 1966, however, a federal court found that the FCC had been wrong in assuming that because the Commission was created to protect the interests of the public, members of the public themselves had no right to become involved in a broadcast licensing proceeding.[15] This decision, authorizing members of a community to challenge in federal court any license renewal granted by the Commission without adequate evidence of the local station's effective past performance, set off such a massive barrage of "citizen group" license challenges that the entire structure of American broadcast regulation seemed imperiled for a time.

Licensing has become an even more important issue with the rise in the number of station licenses that any one entity may own.

RENEWING THE BROADCAST LICENSE

Recognizing the right of citizen groups to challenge the renewal of a broadcast license created new constraints upon broadcast freedom of expression.

During the period from 1970 to 1977, the FCC received a total of 447 citizen petitions or objections involving the licenses of 936 broadcast stations; almost 10 percent of all the commercial broadcasters then being licensed by the Commission.[16] Many in the broadcast industry felt that they had been betrayed by the courts, and abandoned by a Commission no longer capable of protecting them from private pressures. After

[14] Title 47, U.S.C.A. § 316(b).

[15] *Office of Communication of the United Church of Christ v. FCC*, 359 F.2d 994 (D.C.Cir.1966).

[16] Comptroller General, Report to the Congress, "Selected FCC Regulatory Policies and Consequences for Commercial Radio and Television," CED 79–62, 4 June 1979, p. 17.

complying with FCC rules for almost a half century with the understanding that the agency posed the only threat to their licenses, they were now suddenly being forced to defend themselves from citizen challenges as well, attacks upon an unprotected flank that left them vulnerable to interest group demands.

The FCC tried to end this siege of license renewal challenges in 1970 by proposing rules that made it virtually impossible to deny license renewal to an existing broadcast station, but a federal court refused to allow these rules to be adopted.[17] As the 1970s drew to a close, this "citizen group" movement lost its momentum, frustrated by the Commission's skilled use of procedural delay to deny them the hearings they sought. But this chaotic era of widespread license challenge had convinced the broadcast industry that it could no longer rely upon the FCC or the Communications Act of 1934 to protect their broadcast licenses from challenge.

Instead, the primary political objective for broadcasters during the 1980s became convincing Congress to adopt new legislation capable of sheltering existing broadcast station licenses from citizen group attack much more effectively at time of renewal. In 1981, Congress did act to reduce the dimensions of the license renewal problem to some extent by increasing the length of each television station license from three years to five, and lengthening each radio license period from three years to seven.[18] In 1997, the term was extended to eight years.[19]

The Commission's decision to attempt to protect broadcasters from citizen organized license challenges is based upon the belief that such private pressure can pose a greater, if more subtle threat to broadcast freedom of expression that any federal regulatory policy may have posed in the past. Although the First Amendment shields broadcasting from government censorship, it provides no legal protection against private pressure. In addition, while government regulation is a public process, open for all to observe, interest group negotiations typically are conducted in secret, with concessions being granted without public knowledge or consent.

Ironically, then, the same FCC that was once viewed by the industry as the enemy of broadcast free speech is now the industry's only ally in the struggle to safeguard those free speech rights from the influence of self-styled "citizen groups."

But why should broadcast industry be so susceptible to such private pressure, particularly since any "citizen group" license challenge will

---

[17] The FCC rules were proposed in "Policy Statement Concerning Comparative Hearings Involving Regular Renewal Applicants," 22 FCC2d 424 (1970). The rules were rescinded when challenged by a public service law firm in *Citizens Communications Center v. FCC*, 447 F.2d 1201 (D.C.Cir.1971).

[18] Omnibus Reconciliation Act of 1981, 95 Stat. 736–37, as amended by Public Law 97–259.

[19] https://transition.fcc.gov/Bureaus/Mass_Media/News_Releases/1997/nrmm7002.txt.

ultimately be brought to the FCC for resolution? Those who champion the First Amendment rights of broadcasting are often critical of stations or networks willing to negotiate their programming practices with these interest groups, arguing that such broadcast organizations have the financial resources to protect, rather than bargain away their precious freedom of expression.

What these critics fail to realize is that while a media organization may have such resources, the decision to fight rather than negotiate a license challenge must be made by some highly paid executive within this organization, generally the station manager, whose dependence upon that generous salary to meet monthly mortgage payments and other financial obligations makes this employee far more vulnerable to such private pressure than any abstract concept of broadcast free speech would suggest.

Continuing controversy over station programming practices tends to disrupt normal business operations, is likely to damage a station's public image in the area it serves, and is almost certain to be viewed with alarm and displeasure at the corporate headquarters of the station's group owner. In addition, even a successful defense of a station's license may result in uncompensated legal expenses ranging from $100,000 to $500,000.[20] With these facts in mind, then, it may be easier to understand why a number of broadcast stations have yielded to the programming demands of well organized, politically sophisticated pressure groups, and why both the industry and the FCC view such privately negotiated programming concessions with such concern.

The FCC was finally able to adopt a revised set of license renewal rules in 1989, designed to discourage the challenging of a broadcast license merely to profit from a subsequent payment by the licensee to withdraw the challenge.[21] The new rules require that the Commission approve in advance all negotiated settlements between the license holder and a challenger or competing applicant. No settlement will be approved if payments to the challenger exceed what the FCC finds to be the "legitimate and prudent" expenses actually incurred by the challenger during the proceeding.

In addition, other forms of indirect compensation are now also presumed to violate the agency's settlement standards, such as an agreement by the station to hire or retain any member of the challenging organization, or to schedule specific programming produced or provided by that organization.

---

[20] For example, WBBM-TV Chicago viewed it as a "victory" when they were able to settle a license challenge brought by Center City for *only* $187,000; reimbursement of Center City's legal expenses in filing the challenge. See "Settlement Reached in WBBM-TV Chicago Challenge," *Broadcasting*, July 18, 1988, p. 33.

[21] Broadcast Renewal Process, 66 R.R.2d 708 (1989); petition for reconsideration denied, 67 R.R.2d 1515 (1990) also see 67 R.R.2d 1526 (1990) for the adoption of similar standards for citizen petitions to deny applications for new stations, license modifications and transfer applications.

A survey of renewal proceedings conducted soon after the new rules were adopted disclosed a significant decrease in the number of challenges being filed, suggesting that these new procedural safeguards were achieving their desired policy objectives. Encouraged by these results, the FCC decided in May 1990 to impose similar settlement payment restrictions on all future comparative hearings involving new broadcast license applications as well.

After two decades of rulemaking and litigation, the Commission finally appears to have developed renewal standards capable of discouraging the filing of improperly motivated license challenges, while at the same time continuing to permit legitimate challenges to be evaluated fairly and impartially. Although the broadcast industry might have hoped for an even more elaborate set of regulatory safeguards to shelter licensees from the threat of other types of unjustified challenges, this appears to be the most extensive protection of a broadcaster licensee's renewal rights that the FCC, as an agency of Congress, has the legal authority to provide.

There are some things to keep in mind regarding renewal. If a station is sold, the renewal process will only concern itself with the performance of the current licensee. This can be a benefit or a detriment. To the good, a new licensee will not be saddled with the poor performance of the predecessor and to the bad the new licensee will have little time to create a record sufficient to withstand a challenge.

In addition to complying with general public service requirements, television stations also need to show evidence of compliance with the Children's Television Act. The Act requires stations to broadcast three hours of educational programming for children 16 years old and younger. The programing must advance their cognitive, social and emotional development. That tosses out broadcasts of "The Jetsons," "The Flintstones," and "G.I. Joe." In the early years of the Children's Television Act, broadcasters had tried to argue that "The Jetsons" prepared children for life in the Twenty-Second Century, "The Flintstones" taught children about prehistoric times (apparently the failure of hominids and dinosaur co-existence from that time is a valuable lesson that children need to learn for present co-existence with endangered species), and "G.I. Joe" provided the much needed lesson that good or evil can live together as long as they keep missing each other as they blow up each other's stuff.

New, much stricter rules went into effect Sept. 1, 1997. Broadcasters will now have to label their educational and information shows. The programming must be shown between 7 a.m. and 10 p.m., though broadcasters may show additional hours of children's programming at other times. The new requirements mean that broadcasters must identify their qualifying programming and designate a station employee to serve as a liaison and file annual reports with the FCC. Failure to comply will be a consideration in license renewal.

OWNERSHIP RULES

The Telecommunications Act of 1996 provided for major changes in the rules governing station ownership. These changes reflect the changing market in which fewer media conglomerates own more media outlets. The FCC reviewed the ownership rules in 2003 and retained the 1996 ownership limits. Ownership in radio is now subject only to limits related to markets themselves. Where there are 45 or more commercial stations in a particular market, an entity may own a maximum of eight stations. Of those eight stations, a maximum of five are permitted in either service. That is to say that an owner could own five FM stations at most. The rest would have to be AM stations, or vice versa. If the market had between 30 and 44 commercial stations, ownership would be limited to seven with a maximum of four in one service. In markets of 15 to 29 stations, the limit is six with a maximum of four in one service. Where there are fewer than 15 stations, the limits are governed by two rules: owners may own up to five stations, but if owning five would constitute more than 50 percent of the stations in the market, that number would be reduced. No single owner can own more than 50 percent of a market's stations. Owners are limited to three stations in one service for this smallest category.[22]

Television ownership rules also changed (see The FCC, Congress and the 39 Percent Solution later in this chapter). As with radio there is no limit as to the number of television stations that one entity can own. The limitation deals with coverage, how much of the total viewership a corporation's stations reach. The Telecommunication Act of 1996 retained the television duopoly rule that limited entities to owning a single television station per market. But the Act also granted the FCC the power to waive the duopoly rule where the agency finds compelling circumstances. This waiver provision applies to the top 50 markets.[23]

ELIMINATING THE DUOPOLY RULE

In a vote that followed party lines, the FCC voted on Dec. 18, 2007, to eliminated the Newspaper/Broadcast Cross-Ownership rule that prohibited a company from owning both a newspaper and a television or radio station in the same market.[24] The change in the rule, in existence since 1975, was controversial with the Senate Commerce Committee voicing unanimous opposition, strong arguments from the Democratic

---

[22] Peter D. O'Connell, "Summary of FCC Multiple Ownership Rules and Policies," presented to American Bar Association Forum on Communications Law, Representing Your Local Broadcaster, April 6, 1997, Las Vegas, Nev.

[23] Leon T. Knauer, Ronald K. Machtley, and Thomas Lynch, *Telecommunications Act Handbook* (Rockville, Md., Government Institutes Inc., 1996, p. 63.).

[24] "FCC Adopts Revision to Newspaper/Broadcast Cross-Ownership Rule," *FCC News*, Dec. 18, 2007.

members of the commission and protests from groups who said the change would reduce the number of voices in local media.[25]

The vote led the House Energy and Commerce Committee to begin a probe into whether the decision by the Commission had been "fair, open and transparent." A legal challenge was expected and Democratic senators pledged to reverse the move.

The change was explained as a move to further the public interest in helping newspapers fight revenue losses from declining readership and falling advertising revenues.[26]

> Under the new approach, the Commission presumes a proposed newspaper/broadcast transaction is in the public interest if it meets the following test:
>
> (1) the market at issue is one of the 20 largest Nielsen Designated Market Areas ("DMAs");
>
> (2) the transaction involves the combination of only one major daily newspaper and only one television or radio station;
>
> (3) if the transaction involves a television station, at least eight independently owned and operating major media voices (defined to include major newspapers and full-power TV stations) would remain in the DMA following the transaction; and
>
> (4) if the transaction involves a television station, that station is not among the top four ranked stations in the DMA.

The Act also permits common ownership of broadcast networks and cable systems. It also allows cross ownership of cable and wireless cable services, subject to the requirement that the cable operator continues to exist in a competitive environment. In addition to changing the Cross-Ownership Rule, the FCC limited ownership of cable systems in its December 2007 meeting. The commissioners voted to impose a new rule limiting ownership of cable systems to a maximum of 30 percent of the national market, a tighter control than the rule on broadcast ownership. A similar move was struck down by the federal courts.[27]

A portion of the ownership rules bars ownership of an American broadcast license by a foreign government or alien. This extends to both direct station ownership and ownership through a parent corporation. Sec. 310 (a) and (b) says that aliens may not own more than 20 percent of an individual station and no more than 25 percent of a corporation that holds a license. In 1995, Australian-born media magnate Rupert Murdoch won permission to retain his ownership of six television stations that helped form the Fox Network. Although Murdoch himself became

[25] Frank Ahrens, "FCC's Contested Cross-Ownership Rule Set for Vote," *Washington Post*, Dec. 18, 2007.

[26] "FCC Adopts Revision to Newspaper/Broadcast Cross-Ownership Rule," *FCC News*, Dec. 18, 2007.

[27] Frank Ahrens, "Divided FCC Enacts Rules On Media Ownership," *Washington Post*, Dec. 19, 2007.

an American citizen to comply with the law, his holding company was based in Australia. That holding company put up nearly all the money to pay for the stations. In granting Murdoch permission to keep the stations, the FCC said it would not serve the public interest to punish his company * * * Murdoch acted in the public interest by creating the Fox Network, a competitor for the three major networks, the FCC said.[28]

Digital and High Definition TV (HDTV) broadcasting issues have been largely resolved. Stations were permitted to continue to use their analog frequencies while they started their digital services. On Feb. 17, 2009, the date that analog television stopped in the U.S., the stations had to return their analog frequencies to the government.[29]

THE FCC, CONGRESS AND THE 39 PERCENT SOLUTION

Sometimes the FCC gets only part of what it wants. By a 3–2 vote along party lines, the Federal Communications Commission made it clear that the Miltonian principle of diversity—called the "marketplace of ideas"[30] was subordinated by Republican "free market" ideology and by media conglomerates thirsting to get even bigger. The FCC's new rules would have meant that one company could own TV stations reaching 45 percent of U.S. households, replacing the 35 percent ceiling set by the Communications Act of 1996. Also, the new rules wiped out the prohibition against a company or person owning both a TV station and a newspaper in the same city (except in small markets with three or fewer TV stations).[31]

Under severe pressure from the public, Congress balked, legislatively setting, at 39 percent, the percentage of U.S. households that any one owner of TV stations may reach. The 39 percent figure was reached after closed-door bargaining between the then-Republican leadership of Congress and White House aides.[32] Meanwhile, FCC Chairman Michael K. Powell and the Republican majority on the Commission held to the assertion that because of new media carriers, including proliferating cable channels and news Web sites, new rules were demanded.

The courts stepped in as well. A panel of the Third Circuit held that the FCC's decision on ownership raising the limit to 45 percent and its

---

[28] "U.S. Allows Murdoch to Keep TV Stations," *Wall Street Journal*, July 31, 1995.

[29] Richard Wiley, "Media and Telecommunications," in Volume 2 *Communications Law 2007*, 612 (James Goodale ed. 2007).

[30] See this textbook's references to Miltonian theory in Chap. 1, including especially Justice Holmes's dissent in *Abrams v. United States* (1919).

[31] David Ho, "Media ownership rules loosened," AP story in the Knoxville *News Sentinel*, June 3, 2003, p. C-1.

[32] David B. Caruso, "FCC Defends Media Ownership Rules Changes," *BizReport*, Feb. 11, 2004.

change in rules to replace the newspaper/broadcast ownership prohibition were not adequately justified by the FCC.[33]

Did then-Chairman Powell—son of Secretary of State Colin Powell—have his judgment affected by too-cozy relationships with big media? The Center for Public Integrity reported that the 50 largest media companies spent $111.3 million to influence Congress and the Executive Branch between 1996 and 2000, paying for 1,460 all-expense-paid trips for FCC bureaucrats and 315 junkets by members of the Congress and their staff.[34] Furthermore, Chairman Powell could not be bothered with public hearings. According to the Nader Page, FCC Chairman Michael Powell refused to hold more than one public hearing on this rule-making procedure outside of Washington, D.C. So two other FCC Commissioners—Democrats Michael Copps and Jonathan Adelstein—held more than one dozen unofficial public hearings, including one in Washington, D.C., none of which were attended by Chairman Powell.[35]

Despite the controversy over FCC ownership rules for television, radio behemoth Clear Channel Communications has become a poster boy for the dangers of concentration of ownership. Clear Channel, with more than 1,200 radio station—up from just 43 in 1994—has taken flak for its intolerance for any views but those of its management. And Clear Channel is *huge*. In 2003, there were 1,214 Clear Channel stations with a total weekly audience of 104.6 million; the next largest chain in listener ship, Infinity, had 183 stations reaching 61.1 million of listeners weekly. Disney, third largest with 63 stations and 13.7 million listeners weekly, and Cox Broadcasting fourth, with 75 stations and 13 million listeners per week.[36]

Glenn Beck, a radio talk show host syndicated by Clear Channel subsidiary Premiere Radio Networks, has organized pro-military rallies, apparently to answer anti-war comments by celebrities. Lead singer Natalie Maines of the Dixie Chicks said at a concert in England that "We're ashamed that the president of the United States is from Texas." Some Clear Channel country music stations then stopped playing Dixie Chicks' records.[37]

The effects of Clear Channel's concentrated ownership—with more than 1,200 of roughly 11,000 radio stations in the United States—can perhaps be seen most clearly in a poignant story out of Minot, North Dakota. Minot, population 37,000, is the state's fourth-largest city. In North Dakota, where there are about 80 commercial radio stations, with Clear Channel owning 23 of them, radio signals are more relied upon daily than in more populous areas—for weather updates, farm

[33] *Prometheus Radio Project v. F.C.C.*, 373 F.3d 372 (3d Cir. 2004).

[34] Sharon Perlowin, "FCC set to pave way for media monopolies," 5/23/03 http://www.publicintegrity.org/2000/09/27/3266/media-firms-buy-their-way-political-access.

[35] http://www.publicintegrity.org/2003/05/29/6034/behind-closed-doors.

[36] Ibid.

[37] Ibid.

commodity prices, neighborly talk and news of births and deaths, and warnings about the occasional onrushing tornado. Through some quirk in FCC rules and decision-making, all six commercial radio stations in Minot are owned by Clear Channel.

In January, 2002, a train derailment let loose an enormous white cloud of anhydrous ammonia fertilizer. One person died from exposure to the fumes. The *New York Times* reported that police could not reach anyone by phone at KCJB, Minot's designated emergency broadcasting station. Station employees had to be located and brought to the station, causing a substantial delay in warning the citizens.[38]

Jennifer 8. Lee reported for the *Times* that the communication breakdown occurred because Clear Channel was piping a satellite feed in from elsewhere, making a human presence at the station "dispensable." She wrote that Clear Channel said that someone was always on duty at night, but "busy phone lines and technological misunderstandings resulted in the emergency failure."[39]

As a result, Minot Police Chief Fred Debowey commented, " 'We very seldom hear local news anymore.' " *Minot Daily News* reporter Ken Crites complained about the lack of local radio news: " 'I get up in the morning and it's a disc jockey reading A.P. copy,' he said. 'The Canadians could come over the border, and we would never know it.' "[40]

FCC REJECTS AD-SHARING SCHEME FOR LOCAL STATIONS

Although FCC regulations still ban single ownership of multiple stations in broadcasting markets, clever broadcast executives figured out a way to merge local stations through advertising sales. A single station's ad firm would enter into an advertising contract and then split up the ad buy among multiple stations. Although there would still be separate individual owners for each station, the "joint sales agreements" would make them operate like a single economic entity.

In March of 2014, the FCC banned the practice saying that the partnerships threatened diversity and competition.[41] The commission adopted rules that when one station bought at least 15 percent of another station's advertising, it would be considered to have an ownership interest in the other station. That would violate the commission's rules on multiple station ownership in single markets.

---

[38] Jennifer 8. Lee, "On Minot, N.D., Radio, A Single Corporate Voice," *New York Times*, March 31, 2003, p. C7.

[39] Ibid.

[40] Ibid.

[41] Cecelia Kang, "FCC bans local TV stations from forming advertising partnership," *Washington Post*, March 31, 2014.

64. CONTROLLING CABLE

In truth, the emergence of cable TV was simply an historical accident, caused by a noble but flawed policy effort of the FCC to design a system of "community oriented" local television in the United States.

The FCC television allocation plan of 1952 provided for more than 2000 television stations to serve some 1300 different communities throughout the nation.[42] The engineering staff of the Commission had based its television service projections on just such a fully operational system. Unfortunately, only 530 of these 2000 stations were actually in operation at the end of that decade, even though nearly 85 percent of all American homes already were television households.[43]

What the FCC planners had failed to foresee was that no one would apply for a television license in any of those communities too small to generate enough advertising revenues to interest a television network in providing the station with programming. As a result, instead of establishing a nationwide system of local television stations, the Commission succeeded only in creating conditions that would allow a new, more effective system of television program distribution to develop.

COMMUNITY ANTENNAS

Originally "community antennas," as cable systems were then called, were exactly that; shared master antenna hookups that allowed a cluster of homes located just beyond the coverage area of the nearest television station to receive a marginally acceptable picture.[44] During the early 1950s these primitive aerials were viewed as being nothing more than a temporary solution to an immediate problem, destined to disappear in time as newly licensed stations began filling in each of the many gaps remaining in national network television coverage.

Within a few years, however, it became clear the Commission would not abandon its original television station allocation policy despite the plan's obvious limitations. As late as 1958, some 34 percent of America's television households still could receive only one television channel.[45] Located in less populous markets without an audience base large enough to support additional affiliate television stations, these viewers had

---

[42] 6th Report and Order, 17 Reg. 3905–4100 (May 2, 1952) allocated 2,053 television stations to 1,291 different communities in the United States, many with populations of less than 50,000.

[43] U.S. Congress, Senate, Committee on Interstate and Foreign Commerce, Television Inquiry: Television Allocations 86th Cong. 2nd sess. 1960, p. 4587.

[44] As in the early days of radio, many of these first community antenna operators were actually appliance stores, trying to stimulate demand for the TV receivers they wanted to sell by providing television reception to households that otherwise would have been unable to receive a broadcast television signal.

[45] U.S. Congress, Senate, Committee on Interstate and Foreign Commerce, "VHF Boosters and Community Antenna Legislation"; Hearings on S. 1739 * * * 86th Congress, 1st sess. 1959, p. 455.

access to only one of those three sources of network fare they were eager to watch each evening.

During this era an enterprising community antenna operator asked the FCC's Common Carrier Bureau for permission to use a microwave system to deliver to his system the network programming not available in his area from nearby network affiliate stations.[46] Because communication common carrier regulation at that time involved nothing more than a review of the reasonableness of the charges for service, his request was routinely granted.[47]

THE CATV ERA

Microwave relays opened an entirely new domain for CATV operators, allowing them for the first time to enter larger communities where some television service was already available. Until this time, a cable system could only improve the quality of existing over-the-air television service.

Now, however, cable TV could attract far more subscribers by offering them channels of network programs they were unable to receive over-the-air. Although those affiliate stations whose network programs were being exported by CATV systems without payment or permission were the first to complain about this usage, they really sustained no economic injury through this unauthorized carriage of their signals.[48] Few of the programs being exported by CATV were actually owned by these stations, and the wider circulation each station's advertising messages gained through cable dissemination actually increased rather than diminished their potential to earn revenues.

Instead, the damage was being inflicted upon small market television stations located in those communities where the CATV systems were operating. Until this time, station managers had generally been pleased with the community antenna systems that sprang up along the edges of their coverage contours, for they extended a station's effective transmission range at no cost to the broadcaster.

Now, however, these CATV systems were providing competing television channels to subscribers in the broadcaster's own market, substantially reducing the number of viewers watching the local station's programs. What had been a symbiotic relationship between the station

---

[46] FCC 54–58; *In the Matter of J.E. Belnap*. For a discussion of the impact this decision had upon cable TV development and regulation in the 1950s and 1960s, see Don R. Le Duc, *Cable Television and the FCC* (Philadelphia):(Temple University Press, 1973) pp. 74–77.

[47] In a 1961 case, *Federal Power Com'n v. Transcontinental Gas Pipe Line Corp.*, 365 U.S. 1, 81 S.Ct. 435, the Supreme Court approved the common carrier regulatory approach of looking beyond simple authorization of a service to determine whether the ultimate result of its use would be in the public interest. It was this decision that gave the FCC authority to begin denying cable TV its microwave relay requests in *Carter Mountain Transmission Corp. v. FCC*, 321 F.2d 359 (D.C.Cir.1963).

[48] *Intermountain Broadcasting & Television Corp. v. Idaho Microwave, Inc.*, 196 F.Supp. 315 (D.Idaho 1961).

and community antenna had been transformed into a parasitic one, for CATV was preying on small one-station markets in the weakest financial condition. Yet, ironically, it was the marginal nature of these markets that sheltered CATV from immediate federal regulatory reaction.

LOCAL CABLE TV CONTROLS

Because the federal government had not claimed exclusive control over cable TV, local governments began to exert their own legal authority to impose program service obligations upon cable operators who wanted to construct cable systems in their communities. They were able to do this without unconstitutionally abridging the free speech rights of the cable operator because of one special characteristic of cable TV operation.

It was virtually impossible to construct a cable system without first obtaining a public *easement*, the property right a cable operator needed from local government to permit the system's cable to be strung across the municipality's streets and other public rights-of-way. Within a short time, however, local governments began to realize if a cable operator expected to benefit from this use of public property, the citizens of the community to be served also had a right to benefit from this use of their land.

The contract that local governments offered an operator interested in providing cable TV service became known as the *franchise agreement*, offering the operator the privilege of a "public easement" to construct the cable system in return for an annual lease payment, called the *franchise fee,* and other regulatory requirements imposed on the system for the benefit of the citizens of that community who were the rightful owners of this municipal property.

As large corporations began buying groups of small CATV systems in the early 1960s, they started to exert strong influence upon the industry's trade group, the National Cable Television Association (NCTA), to *support*, rather than oppose federal regulation of cable TV. These new corporate cable owners found it extremely inconvenient to manage cable systems operating under vastly different local franchise agreements, and so they favored the broadest possible federal preemption of cable control to reduce the degree of diversity among these local cable laws.

FEDERAL CABLE MICROWAVE CONSTRAINTS

Although the FCC had no legal authority to regulate cable, it did have such authority over the microwave relay services essential to deliver the additional television signals cable TV needed to attract subscribers in major markets.[49] In 1963, the Commission had actually

[49] To attract paying subscribers in major markets, cable TV had to offer viewers more service than those three network channels virtually all households in urban area could already receive with a simple antenna. This meant that programming from non-network stations in

begun, on a case-by-case basis, to decide whether approving an application for a particular cable microwave relay would lessen the financial capacity of local television stations in the cable system's area to provide effective broadcast service.

When the FCC began to deny microwave applications on this basis, a federal court upheld the agency's right to use this power to protect the public's interest in maintaining the quality of broadcast television.[50] Then in 1965 the FCC declared that it would no longer authorize *any* applications to microwave television programs into a "top 100" broadcast market until the agency was able to adopt permanent cable microwave rules.[51] In the end, this "temporary" freeze on microwave applications would actually remain in force for more than seven years, effectively denying the cable TV industry any growth opportunities in the nation's most profitable broadcast markets from 1965 to 1972.

Although the Commission has been widely criticized for suppressing cable industry expansion during this extended period of time, it is only fair to point out that Congress was at least equally to blame for the agency's conduct. The FCC was convinced that it would not be in the public interest to allow the cable industry to undermine the economic stability of television stations, while at the same time offering the public virtually no programming of its own and contributing nothing to the production costs of those television programs it carried.

Cable TV was free to take and distribute whatever broadcast programming it wanted without permission or payment simply because the only legally recognized property rights in these programs were defined by the Copyright Act of 1909, a law adopted before the birth of radio broadcasting. Because it had been written in the era of vaudeville and the musical hall, the Act of 1909 protected copyrighted material from infringement only if it was being "performed" without permission. In 1968, the Supreme Court affirmed earlier decisions by several lower federal courts that mere delivery of a television program by a cable TV system was not a "performance" of that program, and therefore that television programming was not protected by the Copyright Act of 1909 from unauthorized cable TV usage.[52]

Congress had begun efforts to revise the copyright law to include cable TV carriage of broadcast programming in 1965, but it took more

---

distant markets had to be imported as well, offering different film packages, syndicated programs and sports than local stations provided. Until 1975, when the first communication satellites began operation, there was no other means for delivering television signals from one market to another except by microwave network.

[50] *Carter Mountain Transmission Corp. v. FCC*, 321 F.2d 359 (D.C.Cir.1963), cert. denied 375 U.S. 951, 84 S.Ct. 442 (1963).

[51] "Proposed Rulemaking in Docket 15971", 1 FCC2d 463 (1965). By making this an interim or temporary rule, the FCC protected it from being challenged in federal court, because the court, except in an exceptional case, will not hear an appeal from an order until the action is final.

[52] *Fortnightly Corp. v. United Artists Television, Inc.*, 392 U.S. 390, 88 S.Ct. 2084 (1968).

than a decade to accomplish this task and cable TV would not actually come under the provisions of the new Copyright Act of 1976 until January 1, 1978.[53] During this entire era, the FCC stood as the broadcast industry's only legal defense against cable TV's unauthorized use of television programming.

In 1968 the Supreme Court affirmed for the first time the Commission's use of its microwave relay authority to discourage cable TV from entering major broadcast markets.[54] At that point the FCC announced its intention to launch a series of full scale hearings to develop rules and long range policy for the development of cable TV service in the United States. Four years later the agency completed these deliberations, and in March 1972, it issued these new rules, declaring that the era of modern cable TV service in the United States had finally begun.[55]

In reality, the FCC would continue to make it virtually impossible for cable TV systems to serve the 50 largest broadcast markets, where 75 percent of the television audience was located, until the Copyright Act of 1976 came into force. However, from 1972 onward, the cable TV industry would at least be regulated by rules designed for its systems, rather than solely for the protection of its broadcast industry competitor.

Cable TV had sprung up like a weed in a carefully cultivated garden. In attempting to create favorable conditions for the growth of locally oriented television service, the FCC had succeeded only in providing fertile opportunities for a rival distribution system to take root.

In this environment cable TV was the intruder, the electronic medium to be restrained in order to encourage more useful growth. Viewed from this perspective, it is easier to understand why the FCC simply suppressed cable TV, rather than trying to incorporate its systems within plans to provide more effective distribution of the nation's television services. Unfortunately, the damage caused by this repression would become all too apparent in the near future, when the cable industry did not have the financial capacity necessary to fulfill the promises it made to citizens in a number of American cities.

FEDERAL CABLE TV REGULATION

The 1972 FCC cable rules required every new system being constructed in one of the largest 100 broadcast markets to provide its subscribers with a minimum of 20 channels, and to set aside specific channels for educational, governmental, leased and public access programming. While the FCC denied local governments any regulatory authority over cable TV's television signal carriage or program

[53] Title 17, United States Code, "Copyright Act of 1909" was rescinded and replaced by the new Title 17, as enacted by Public Law No. 94–553, 94th Stat. 2541 (1976).

[54] *United States v. Southwestern Cable Co.*, 392 U.S. 157, 88 S.Ct. 1994 (1968), in which the high court affirmed the FCC's authority to regulate cable TV's use of television signals as being a reasonable ancillary of its power to regulate broadcasting in the public interest.

[55] "Third Report and Order on Docket 18397", 24 RR2d 1501 (1972).

origination practices, it permitted municipal or state cable regulators to continue to establish franchise boundaries, select cable operators, determine terms of service and decide upon the amount to be collected as a franchise fee, although each of these powers now had to be exercised within standards set by the federal government.

It was difficult for the Commission to regulate cable TV effectively, because the agency had no constitutional authority to deny these non-spectrum communication systems permission to operate. Instead, the agency could only deny those cable systems in violation of its rules the right to carry broadcast signals, and if necessary, to enforce this denial through a federal court order. However, since the effect of this order would be to prevent the system's subscribers from receiving those services for which they were willing to pay, it was an action the Commission was obviously reluctant to take.

Initially, the FCC imposed an extremely elaborate system of restrictions upon the importation of television signals to major market cable systems, but after the Copyright Act of 1976 established a system compensating broadcasters and program suppliers for cable TV carriage, the Commission rescinded most of these restraints. By 1983, the only major FCC rule remaining in this field was "must carry", requiring cable TV systems to provide channel space for all local television stations their subscribers could receive over-the-air.

Even though the new copyright law did require cable TV systems to begin paying for the television programming they were importing, the terms and conditions of payment reflected a clear legislative victory for the cable industry. Cable was granted a *compulsory license* by the Copyright Act, compelling television stations and program suppliers to allow cable TV to carry their programs in return for a program use fee to be determined by a government body, the Copyright Royalty Tribunal. The Tribunal was empowered by the Act to collect from each cable system a percentage of that system's gross subscriber revenues to be used to compensate these television program suppliers.[56]

In gaining the "compulsory license," the cable industry was able to avoid having to pay the marketplace value for the programs it used. When the first distribution was made from this cable copyright pool, program suppliers complained bitterly that payments they received from the Tribunal were not only far less than the actual value of these programs, but even less than the financial damage they sustained because of this cable TV usage.[57]

---

56 This "secondary transmission" cable copyright payment procedure is described in Title 17, U.S.C.A. §§ 801–810.

57 The Tribunal collected $15 million from cable systems during 1978, the first year this system was in operation. The distribution formula granted 75 percent of this money to program and movie syndicators, 12 percent to sports organizations and only 3.5 percent to television stations. This allocation was approved by the courts in *National Ass'n of Broadcasters v. Copyright Royalty Tribunal*, 675 F.2d 367 (D.C.Cir.1982).

In 1982 the Tribunal instituted new proceedings to adjust the amount of subscriber revenues each system would be required to pay into the copyright revenue pool. Until that time, cable systems paid only 0.625 percent of their annual revenues to import one distant television signal, and another 0.425 percent for each additional distant signal imported. Program suppliers urged the Tribunal to increase this fee substantially, because by bringing major feature films packages and popular series programming into areas where they had not yet been sold to local stations, cable TV was significantly diminishing the value, and thus the price of these features as "first run" attractions for television stations in that market where the cable system was located.[58]

After lengthy deliberations the Tribunal finally decided upon new rates for cable systems to pay for each distant television signal imported, almost 10 times higher than the base percentages established only four years before.[59] Although the cable industry complained bitterly about this massive increase in its copyright fee payments, the actual economic impact of these higher copyright rates upon cable systems was not very severe, simply because cable operators were by this time far less dependent upon broadcast stations for cable system programming.[60]

CABLE SATELLITE NETWORKS

Between 1975 and 1980, satellite delivered pay-TV services, superstations, and advertising-supported cable networks not only reduced cable TV's dependence on the broadcast industry for programming, but also furnished cable systems with new sources of revenue. Home Box Office (HBO) launched the first cable pay-TV service in 1975, offering system owners the opportunity to earn profits from a vacant channel by devoting it to the delivery of the HBO service.

In 1977, USA, the first advertising-supported cable TV network, began operation. It sought, at least initially, to cover its costs and generate profits solely on the basis of the commercials it could place in its programming. Although cable operators receive no payment from these advertising-supported channels, and in most cases are now charged a monthly per subscriber fee for the privilege of carriage, systems can earn money from placing local advertising in network time slots provided,

---

[58] This problem became more severe in 1980 when the FCC rescinded its "syndicated exclusivity" rules, that until this time had forced cable TV to "black out" programs on those channels it imported that local stations held exclusive rights to broadcast in that market.

[59] CRT 1982 "Distribution Proceeding and Partial Distribution of Fees" 48 Fed.Reg. 46412 (Oct. 12, 1983). This determination was sustained by the courts in *National Cable Television Ass'n v. Copyright Royalty Tribunal*, 689 F.2d 1077 (D.C.Cir.1982).

[60] In December 1993, Congress abolished the Copyright Royalty Tribunal, replacing this tax-supported agency with ad hoc arbitration panels chosen by the Librarian of Congress and working in consultation with the Register of Copyrights. Copyright owners will now be required to provide the funding for these panels that will decide how to allocate the compulsory license payments that cable systems and juke box owners make annually to those who own the programs and music they use.

and are likely to attract a greater number of subscribers because of offering these additional channels of programming.

So-called "superstation" cable service began in 1976, when Ted Turner, owner of a small UHF station in Atlanta, started delivering his station's programming by satellite to cable systems throughout the nation. Turner, whose ownership of the Atlanta Braves and part-ownership of the Atlanta Hawks allowed him to offer professional sports as well as the usual assortment of older syndicated series programs, generated his revenues through the higher advertising rates he could charge sponsors for his vastly expanded national cable viewing audience. By the mid-1980s, his service was already reaching more than 12.5 million American homes, or roughly one-sixth of all television households in the United States.

By 1980, cable TV system operators could choose among five competing pay-TV services, six "superstations" and more than 40 advertising-supported cable networks, such as Entertainment and Sports Network (ESPN), Cable Satellite Public Affairs Network (C-SPAN), Cable News Network (CNN) and a host of other general and specialized program services to fill their systems' channels.

Ironically, this explosive growth in new satellite delivered services that transformed cable TV from a passive relay system for broadcast services into a truly unique and independent electronic medium was also the unanticipated by-product of an FCC major policy decision involving a different form of communication.

When the FCC authorized domestic communication satellite service in 1972, no one could foresee how its competitive "open skies" satellite policy would affect future cable TV service in the United States.[61] Until this time AT&T had held a virtual monopoly over the national distribution of television programming. Broadcast networks were charged a relatively low rate to deliver their programs to affiliate stations, because they were willing to pay for 24 hour a day usage of special AT&T television circuits set aside specifically for this purpose. When other television distributors tried to lease similar circuits from AT&T on an occasional use basis, however, the charge for this service was prohibitively high, because AT&T was forced to reroute thousands of telephone circuits to find the space necessary to deliver a full-sized television channel.

The Commission's policy decision to encourage competition by opening the communication satellite field to any organization meeting basic qualifications standards was not designed with the intention of ending this AT&T monopoly over national television delivery, but rather in the hope of reducing AT&T's domination over nationwide distribution

[61] "Domestic Communication Satellite Facilities," 35 FCC2d 844 (1972).

of telephonic, telegraphic and other personal and business messages.[62] However, when Western Union's Westar I and RCA's Americom were finally launched in the mid-1970s, these new satellite system owners were eager to lease their unused delivery channels to video program organizations at rates far lower than AT&T had been charging.

The other factor that had inhibited the growth of new nationwide television services had been the absence of local outlets to distribute these programs. Most broadcast markets had only three television stations, each already affiliated with a major network. As cable TV began to expand during the mid-1970s, however, with the 20-channel system capacity required by the FCC rules, virtually all operators had vacant channels available to serve as those local outlets that national satellite delivered program services required.

Thus, through another fortunate historical accident, the emergence of privately owned, competitively priced national domestic satellite system service happened to coincide with the growing demand of urban multi-channeled cable systems for additional programming to result in the establishment of a much more independent and prosperous cable industry.

THE URBAN CABLE SYSTEM ERA

Unfortunately, though, extensive campaigns launched by each of the major cable ownership groups to capture as many urban cable franchises as possible once the FCC signal importation restrictions had been lifted, left most of these multiple system owners (MSOs) in a very precarious financial position as the 1980s began. In their eagerness to win franchise agreements from major city governments, each applicant tried to outbid all other competitors by offering an impressive range of communication services without carefully considering the operational costs involved. Adding to their difficulties was the fact that as many of these urban systems were being built in 1978 and 1979, interest rates on the substantial investment needed for cable construction soared to more than 20 percent.[63]

If the cable industry had been allowed by the FCC to expand gradually in urban markets through the years, it seems reasonable to assume that this period of frantic franchise speculation would have been avoided. Instead, the net result of all this destructive bidding was simply a trail of broken cable franchise promises, denying subscribers those benefits that had earned the MSO its franchise.

During the late 1970s, cable growth came to a virtual halt as financially overextended MSOs sought the additional funding essential

[62] The FCC Common Carrier Bureau had begun this policy effort to reduce the AT&T-Bell domination of American personal and business communication services in 1959 by allowing carriers other than AT&T to operate microwave relay networks.

[63] For a detailed summary of many of these urban market problems, see "Cable Franchising Update," *Broadcasting.*

to complete those systems they were already committed to build. The timing couldn't have been more unfortunate for the cable industry, because, ironically, that very satellite delivered programming that could have made cable TV successful in major television markets was now seen by direct broadcast satellite (DBS), multi-channel, multi-point, distribution system (MMDS) and low power television (LPTV) promoters as being the program services that would allow them to invade these markets and claim that urban audience cable TV was still struggling to reach.[64]

Cable TV had been the first of the "new media." What made cable TV different from broadcasting was its program delivery function. Each radio or television station must depend upon a single channel of communication to entertain and inform its audience and earn its advertising revenues. In contrast, a cable system serves as a broadcast spectrum for its subscribers, allowing them to select from among those various channels of programming it provides.

This difference gave cable TV a tremendous competitive advantage over the individual television station. The cable system did not have to displace a popular, profitable program in order to provide more specialized features for particular segments of the audience. Instead, popular and specialized programs could be distributed simultaneously, attracting as paying subscribers not only those seeking mass appeal features, but also viewers especially interested in sports, politics, religion, culture, news or any of the many other cable delivered services. In fact, cable systems soon began packaging groups of these program channels in various priced "tiers" of subscriber fees, allowing operators to profit to an even greater extent from the diversity of services the system offered.

Yet, although cable TV was able to exploit this multi-channel distribution system advantage when competing with broadcasting, its massively expensive coaxial distribution system made it vulnerable to challenge from newer multi-channeled systems far less expensive to build, and capable of beginning service much more rapidly than cable.

Until this point, the cable industry had been totally committed to the principle of free competition in a marketplace environment to determine which form of electronic media service should prevail. During the 1980s, that commitment became somewhat less than total.

65. CONTENT CONTROL

Broadcast program requirements have always been stated in general terms to avoid encroaching unnecessarily upon the

---

[64] As late as 1981, more than 60 percent of all American cable TV systems still had no more than a 12 channel delivery capacity, a capacity reduced even further by franchise and FCC signal carriage rules. Sydney Head and Christopher Sterling, *Broadcasting in America* 4th ed. (Boston: Houghton Mifflin, 1982) p. 296.

free speech rights of the broadcast licensee. But both broadcast and cable must comply with certain minimum standards regarding their content.

In 1929, only two years after it began regulating broadcast service in the United States, the FRC issued its first comprehensive description of federal broadcast program policy. Beginning a regulatory tradition that would endure until the 1980s, the agency pointed out in this earliest public programming statement that it would not establish any list of *preferred* program categories. Instead, the FRC simply directed each station to offer its audience a balanced schedule of different types of programs capable of serving the needs of every segment of the station's audience. The Commission described its program policy objectives in this way:

> The tastes, needs and desires of all substantial groups among the public should be met, in fair proportion, by a well-rounded program schedule, in which entertainment, religion, education and instruction, important public events, discussions of public questions, weather, market reports, news and matters of interest to all members of the family find a place.[65]

NETWORK PROGRAM CONTROL

The FRC soon discovered, however, that it was difficult to achieve even these rather basic and generalized programming goals because stations had begun to rely upon national broadcast networks to provide a substantial portion of their daily program schedule. Network broadcasting had existed since 1924, but it was not until 1929 that NBC and the newly formed CBS became the dominant national programming and advertising forces in American radio.[66]

Stations were eager to affiliate with one of the major broadcast networks because they offered the type of popular, professionally produced entertainment shows no local station could hope to duplicate. To become a network affiliate, however, a station had to agree to carry a substantial number of network programs each week, and to reserve other portions of its broadcast schedule to be used for whatever programs the network chose to provide.

Both the FRC and the FCC saw the networks as distorting that balance in the various forms of programming these regulatory bodies had sought to encourage; furnishing affiliate stations with a vast array of light entertainment shows while offering virtually no public affairs, educational or children's' programming.

---

[65] *In the matter of the application of Great Lakes Broadcasting*, 3 FRC Annual Reports 32 (1929).

[66] NBC actually operated two separate radio networks until 1941, the "Red" network which it retained, and the "Blue" network sold in 1941 and renamed the American Broadcasting Company in 1945.

Yet neither agency had authority to regulate the networks *directly*, because networks did not use the broadcast spectrum to distribute their programs, delivering them instead to their affiliated stations through privately leased telephone lines. Since the networks required no broadcast license to operate these non-spectrum programming services, there was no legal basis for imposing any public interest standards upon the shows they provided their affiliate stations.[67]

Unable to regulate network program practices directly, the FCC began during the late 1930s to use its licensing authority instead to force the network affiliate stations themselves to reclaim from their national network the right to program a larger proportion of their own daily broadcast schedule. In 1940, the Commission adopted rules that established severe restrictions on the amount of broadcast time any station could devote to network programming, including an enforcement provision that allowed the Commission to revoke the broadcast license of any station exceeding these network time limitations.[68]

In 1970, the Commission tried a somewhat similar tactic in television, restricting network affiliate television stations in major markets to only three hours of network supplied prime-time programming each evening.[69] This "Prime Time Access Rule", modified and amended several times to make it more effective, was designed to stimulate local station production during the most popular viewing period of the day, or at the very least to provide non-network program suppliers with access to major market television audiences.

Neither of these efforts was particularly successful. The Commission's vision of a locally oriented broadcast service, offering a broad and balanced assortment of public affairs, educational and other programs overlooked those powerful economic incentives that propelled the broadcast industry towards nationwide delivery of popular entertainment financed by national advertising.

Through the years, however, the FCC and the broadcast networks managed to develop a rather close working relationship on most regulatory issues. The FCC was useful to the networks, because by regulating broadcasting, it shielded the industry from other, more powerful political pressures, and furnished broadcasting with a stable and predictable legal environment in which the networks could prosper. On the other hand, the FCC had to rely upon the networks to carry out

---

[67] Each network did own and operate broadcast stations itself, (O & O stations) but the tactic of trying to influence national network program practices through regulations imposed upon these network owned stations never worked successfully.

[68] FCC rules CFR § 47. 3.101–3.108. The *NBC v. US* Supreme Court opinion that approved these rules is discussed in Chap. 3, Sec. 14.

[69] 23 FCC2d 282 (1970); modified by 44 FCC2d 1081, and further modified by 46 FCC2d 829.

programming reforms the Commission did not have the legal authority to achieve on its own.[70]

ABOLISHING FORMAT REQUIREMENTS

Although the Commission was constantly involved in efforts to improve the quality of network broadcast service, it was generally reluctant to interfere in any way with the programming practices of individual broadcast stations. As long as stations were not violating any specific FCC programming rule, the agency was willing to allow broadcasters the widest possible discretion in selecting their own format or schedule.

Thus, in 1970, when a classical music station was being sold to investors who intended to change its musical format, the Commission routinely approved the sale, even though a citizens' group had petitioned the FCC to deny the license transfer. Upon appeal, the court reversed the Commission decision, ordering the FCC to conduct a hearing to determine whether the sale would result in depriving the audience in that broadcast market of its only source of this type of programming.[71] In response to the FCC's argument that it was not authorized to act as a "national arbiter of taste," the court declared,

> The Commission is not dictating tastes when it seeks to discover what they presently are, and to consider what assignment of channels is feasible and fair in terms of their gratification.[72]

Four years later the Commission was faced with another sale of a classical music station to a group eager to convert it into a "top 40" outlet, and once again the agency approved the sale without permitting the local citizens' group the hearing they had requested to oppose the license transfer and change of format. The court again reversed the *FCC* decision, this time with the observation that,

> We think it axiomatic that preservation of a format that would otherwise disappear; although economically and technologically viable and preferred by a significant number of listeners, is generally in the public interest.[73]

At this point the Commission decided to conduct a public policy hearing to determine what its future role in such program format controversies should be. At the conclusion of these deliberations, the FCC adopted the rather daring stance that despite any instructions it had received from the federal court of appeals, it would no longer allow itself

[70] For one example of such close FCC-network cooperation, see the "Family Viewing" opinion in *Writers Guild of America, West, Inc. v. FCC*, 423 F.Supp. 1064 (C.D.Cal.1976).

[71] *Citizens Committee to Preserve the Voice of Arts in Atlanta v. FCC*, 436 F.2d 263 (D.C.Cir.1970).

[72] Ibid. at 272 n. 7.

[73] *Citizens Committee to Save WEFM v. FCC*, 506 F.2d 246 (D.C.Cir.1973).

to be involved in any regulation of broadcast station formats because, as the Commission explained it,

> Our reflection * * * has fortified our conviction that our regulation of entertainment formats as an aspect of the public interest would produce an unnecessary and menacing entanglement in matters that Congress meant to leave to private discretion.[74]

A citizens' group immediately appealed this FCC policy decision, but after it had been reversed at the Court of Appeals level, the Supreme Court decided to consider this format regulation issue itself for the first time. In *Federal Communications Commission v. WNCN Listeners Guild*[75] the Commission's position was upheld by the court, on the basis that the FCC's format policy reflected a reasonable balance between, "promoting diversity in programming and * * * avoiding unnecessary restrictions upon licensee discretion."

MUST CARRY

In 1997, the Supreme Court became involved in a content-related case that tested the ability of the federal government to force cable operators to support over-the-air television. In *Turner Broadcasting System v. F.C.C.*,[76] cable operators sued claiming that the "Must Carry" provisions of the Cable Television Consumer Protection and Competition Act were unconstitutional.

In the Cable Act of 1992, television broadcasters were given a choice in their treatment by cable operators. The TV broadcasters could choose to negotiate for payment for the carriage of their signals on cable systems under the "Retransmission Consent" agreement or they could require cable operators to include them in their service under the "Must Carry" rules. As part of the "Must Carry" provision, the Cable Act required cable operators with more than 12 channels to set aside one-third of their channel capacity for local broadcasters.

The cable industry challenged the "Must Carry" provisions and in a series of lawsuits and appeals reached the Supreme Court twice. In the first Supreme Court appearance, the case was remanded to the lower courts for additional fact-finding. After 18 months of fact gathering, the district court found for the government. When the case returned in 1997, the Court ruled by a 5–4 margin that the "Must Carry" provisions were constitutional. The provisions were the government's way to ensure the continued existence of speakers, here local television stations.

Delivering the majority opinion for the Court, Justice Kennedy found that the "Must Carry" provisions served three interconnected and important government interests: "preserving benefits of free, over-the-air

---

[74] "Changes in the Entertainment Formats of Broadcast Stations," 37 R.R.2d 1679, 1976.

[75] *FCC v. WNCN Listeners Guild*, 450 U.S. 582, 101 S.Ct. 1266 (1981).

[76] *Turner Broadcasting System v. FCC*, 520 U.S. 180, 117 S.Ct. 1174 (1997).

local broadcast television; promoting widespread dissemination of information from multiplicity of sources; and promoting fair competition in market for television programming."[77]

Kennedy said that the government had a legitimate interest in protecting the broadcast station that would rely on "Must Carry" to reach the audiences they needed to remain viable. Kennedy said that Congress could constitutionally conclude there was a need to protect local broadcasters. There was a substantial body of evidence that

> "[A] broadcast station's viability depends to a material extent on its ability to secure cable carriage and thereby to increase its audience size and revenues; broadcast stations had fallen into bankruptcy, curtailed their operations, and suffered serious reductions in operating revenues as a result of adverse carriage decisions by cable systems; stations without carriage encountered severe difficulties obtaining financing for operations; and the potentially adverse impact of losing carriage was increasing as the growth of 'clustering'—i.e., the acquisition of as many cable systems in a given market as possible—gave multiple system operators centralized control over more local markets."[78]

The need to preserve the over-the-air stations was important because some 40 percent of U.S. households still relied on broadcast stations for their television programming. In his analysis of the relationship between broadcast stations and cable operators, Justice Kennedy pointed to legislative findings of Congress as it developed the Cable Act. Included were data showing that cable operators enjoyed monopolies in the communities they served. Only 1 percent of communities were served by more than one cable operation. Congress also found that cable operators had economic incentives, through relationships with programmers, to favor those affiliated programming services over broadcasters. Further, cable operators were in direct competition with broadcasters because the incentive to subscribe to cable is lower in markets with many over-the-air viewing options. If broadcasters failed, cable operators were more likely to get more subscribers.

Justice Kennedy also took into consideration the serious problems encountered by over-the-air broadcasters when they were dropped from cable service or not picked up at all by cable operators.

"Documents produced on remand reflect that internal cable studies 'clearly establish the importance of cable television to broadcast television stations. Because viewership equals ratings and in turn ratings equate to revenues, it is unlikely that broadcast stations could

[77] Ibid.

[78] Ibid. at 1182.

afford to be off the cable system's line-up for an extended period of time.' "[79]

Justice Kennedy found further support for his position with an FCC-sponsored study showing a denial of carriage for broadcast stations when a previous "Must Carry" requirement was struck by a lower court. In that study, 280 out of 912 stations responding to the survey reported they had been denied carriage. The "Must Carry" rules meant that broadcast stations would be preserved with little impact on cable operators.

> "[S]ignificant evidence adduced on remand indicates the vast majority of cable operators have not been affected in a significant manner. This includes evidence that: such operators have satisfied their Must Carry obligations 87 percent of the time using previously unused channel capacity; 94.5 percent of the cable systems nationwide have not had to drop any programming; the remaining 5.5 percent have had to drop an average of only 1.22 services from their programming; operators nationwide carry 99.8 percent of the programming they carried before Must Carry; and broadcast stations gained carriage on only 5,880 cable channels as a result of Must Carry. The burden imposed by Must Carry is congruent to the benefits it affords because, as appellants concede, most of those 5,880 stations would be dropped in its absence. Must Carry therefore is narrowly tailored to preserve a multiplicity of broadcast stations for the 40 percent of American households without cable."[80]

The dissent, led by Justice O'Connor, focused on the standard of review applied by the majority, an "intermediate scrutiny" approach. The proper standard, Justice O'Connor argued, was a "strict scrutiny" analysis because the case dealt with the content of speech and as such, should have to pass a more demanding test. Justice O'Connor was not persuaded by the findings that Justice Kennedy cited as he explained his conclusion. The fact that some broadcast stations would fail without the "Must Carry" rule was not enough to justify the imposition of the requirement on cable operators because of their anti-competitive pressures.

"I fully agree that promoting fair competition is a legitimate and substantial Government goal. But the Court nowhere examines whether the breadth of the 'Must Carry' provisions comports with a goal of preventing anti-competitive harms."[81] Instead, Justice O'Connor argued, the majority simply assumed that broadcasters would be harmed by the cable operators decisions not to carry them.

---

[79] Quoting "Memorandum from F. Lopez to T. Baxter re: Adlink's Presentations on Retransmission Consent," dated June 14, 1993, (App. 2118), in Turner, at 1196.

[80] *Turner Broadcasting v. FCC*, 520 U.S. 180, 117 S.Ct. at 1182 (1997).

[81] Ibid. at 1206–1207.

"The Court provides some raw data on adverse carriage decisions, but it never connects that data to markets and viewership. Instead, the Court proceeds from the assumption that adverse carriage decisions nationwide will affect broadcast markets in proportion to their size; and that all broadcast programming is watched by all viewers. Neither assumption is logical or has any factual basis in the record."[82]

INDECENT PROGRAMMING

Yet, even though the Commission has been reluctant to become involved in most phases of local station programming, one specific type of programming has been singled out recently by the FCC for close supervision. Both the Radio Act of 1927 and the Communications Act of 1934 contained regulatory provisions authorizing the imposition of fines and possible revocation of the license of any station broadcasting obscene, indecent or profane language.[83]

As discussed earlier, punishing "indecent" broadcast language presented no constitutional problem for either federal regulatory agency, because speech or conduct found to be obscene is not recognized by American law as meriting First Amendment protection.[84] "Indecent" or "profane" speech, on the other hand, is constitutionally protected, and so regulatory efforts to discourage such utterances or to penalize stations for scheduling an "indecent" or "profane" program impose greater constraints upon the broadcast medium than upon any other form of American mass communication.

In reality, though, the broadcast networks and their industry association, the National Association of Broadcasters (NAB), were able to shield the FRC and FCC from the problem of tasteless broadcast content until the early 1970s. Each of the networks demanded that their affiliated stations follow NAB program standards far more restrictive in areas of public taste than any regulatory agency could have required, and while independent stations were not bound by these agreements, they hesitated to isolate themselves in this way from the protection of the NAB.

As the 1970s began, however, a number of smaller, typically urban market FM stations saw an opportunity to attract a larger audience with a new format called "topless radio," featuring sexually oriented talk shows to capitalize upon the so-called new morality of that era. By 1973, stations adopting the "topless" format had become top-rated during their

---

[82] Ibid. at 1207.

[83] In 1948, Congress transferred these statutory provisions to the U.S. Criminal Code, Title 18, U.S.C.A. § 1464, because they also contained criminal penalties (imprisonment of up to 5 years) that could be enforced more effectively by the U.S. Justice Department. However, the FCC was granted continuing authority to penalize broadcasters under the new code section.

[84] See *FCC v. Pacifica Foundation*, 438 U.S. 726, 98 S.Ct. 3026 (1978).

sex talk segments in several major markets, as letters of complaint from outraged listeners began flooding the FCC.[85]

In that same year the FCC imposed a $2,000 fine upon a station that had presented a particularly explicit discussion of oral sex techniques, pointing out,

> We are emphatically not saying that sex per se is a forbidden subject on the broadcast medium * * * sex and obscenity are not the same things.[86]

but holding that because the program had been broadcast at a time when a substantial number of children could be presumed to be listening, the station had disregarded its public interest responsibilities towards that special segment of its audience.

A citizens' group petitioned for a hearing to challenge the Commission's decision, but a federal appeals court upheld both the FCC action and its right to reject such a petition.[87]

In that same year, another station, in a mid-afternoon program, featured an excerpt from a comedy album of George Carlin, his "Filthy Words" routine, discussing in detail the nuances of several of the seven four-letter words he said couldn't be mentioned on radio or television. The FCC issued a declaratory ruling against the station, this time defining its position on indecency with even greater clarity. According to the Commission, "indecent" programming was that which,

> * * * describes, in terms patently offensive as measured by contemporary community standards for the broadcast medium, sexual or excretory activities and organs, at times of the day where there is reasonable risk that children may be in the audience.[88]

The FCC's newly established indecency standard was overturned almost immediately by a federal appeals court, but at that point the Supreme Court intervened to consider whether more stringent restrictions could legally be imposed upon broadcast free speech than other forms of media expression.

A majority of the Justices affirmed the Commission's position, basing their affirmation of the FCC's right to hold broadcasting to a higher standard of care in this area of speech on two special characteristics of the medium, its pervasiveness and its unique

---

85 The FCC received more than 2,000 letters from listeners complaining about these programs in 1972; in 1974, they received more than 20,000 letters of complaint. "Programming of Violent, Indecent or Obscene Material", Broadcast Management/Engineering, June 1975, pp. 22–24.

86 *Sonderling Broadcasting*, 27 RR2d 285 (1973).

87 *Illinois Citizens Committee for Broadcasting v. FCC*, 515 F.2d 397 (D.C.Cir.1974).

88 *Pacifica Foundation*, 56 FCC2d 94 (1975).

accessibility to children.[89] In addition, the crucial factor in the view of the court was that the FCC was not attempting to ban the broadcasting of indecent programs, but only to require that such programs be scheduled at times when they were not likely to reach a large youthful audience.

Although a divided Court had affirmed the right of the Commission to treat indecent programming as a nuisance, "channeling" it away from younger viewers or listeners, the new "marketplace" oriented FCC of the 1980s seemed reluctant to exercise this power. Despite complaints from various citizen groups about the explicit nature of certain new "shock" radio formats, the agency decided initially to restrict its definition of "indecent" only to broadcasts containing one or more of those famous seven words George Carlin had uttered in the monologue that led to the *Pacifica* action.[90]

In 1987, however, the Commission, under pressure from Congress, began to assert that authority the Supreme Court had authorized almost a decade earlier. The FCC sent public notices to two broadcast stations the agency found to be in violation of the rule, and declared its intention to adopt rules reestablishing the broader definition of indecency it had followed during the 1970s.

CHANNELING INDECENCY TO A SAFE HARBOR

Following the "channeling" approach the Supreme Court had approved in *Pacifica,* the FCC declared that indecent programming would be punished only if were scheduled at a time when there was "reasonable risk that children might be in the audience."[91] Originally the Commission had stated that programs scheduled after 10 p.m. could be aired without concern for their accessibility to children. However, when audience research revealed that a substantial number of children were still listening or viewing at 10 p.m. each evening, the FCC narrowed its "safe harbor;" making the period from midnight to 6 a.m. the only appropriate time for such "adult" programming.

This new campaign by the Commission to shield young viewers and listeners from indecent broadcast programming was immediately attacked by a coalition of public interest and trade organizations.[92] Upon

[89] *FCC v. Pacifica Foundation*, 438 U.S. 726, 98 S.Ct. 3026 (1978). It's important to note, however, that the FCC's indecency definition was upheld by a narrow 5–4 vote, suggesting quite clearly that its authority to enforce this type of content control would be narrowly construed.

[90] The "shock" radio format goes one step beyond "topless," trying to offend the sensibilities of as many different groups in our society as possible by using racial jokes, ethnic slurs and other forms of base humor to attract an audience.

[91] *New Indecency Enforcement Standards*, 62 RR2d 1218 (1987).

[92] *Action for Children's Television v. FCC*, 852 F.2d 1332 (D.C.Cir.1988). It is interesting to note that this legal challenge was spearheaded by the nation's largest and most influential advocacy group for the broadcast programming rights of young viewers and listeners. Through the years ACT has constantly campaigned for more extensive government restrictions on broadcast commercials to protect American youth from the damaging effects of advertising, but its leaders apparently saw no similar need to protect young viewers from the damaging effects of indecent programming, defined by the FCC as "describing or depicting sexual or excretory activities in a patently offensive manner." ACT has explained that it opposes any governmental

review, the D.C. Court of Appeals affirmed the fundamental right of the FCC to restrict indecent programming to those hours of the day when children were least likely to be present in the broadcast audience. In this instance, however, the Court held that the Commission had not adequately documented its claim that the midnight to 6 a.m. period it selected as a "safe harbor" for such programming was actually the most narrowly drawn one capable of realizing this policy objective.

As the FCC was preparing to justify its six hour indecency "harbor" as being the least extensive time period required to achieve its goal, Congress acted to make the agency's already difficult legal position virtually impossible to defend. In October 1988 Congress passed legislation that compelled the Commission to enforce an absolute *ban* on indecent broadcast programming on a *24-hour-a-day basis*.[93] The FCC had no choice but to comply with this Congressional directive, even though it meant that the agency would now be required to *prohibit* a constitutionally protected form of expression it had sought only to channel within a "safe harbor" of time.

When the Commission announced its intention to begin enforcing a total ban on indecent programming in January 1989, the same coalition of media and public interest groups was able to obtain an order from the D.C. Court of Appeals preventing the Commission from implementing this new rule until its validity could be determined by the Court. In doing so, however, the Court granted the FCC permission to continue the enforcement of its indecency standards on a provisional basis in order to gather further documentation relating to the nature of this indecent programming it could submit when the case was ultimately heard by the Court.

After completing its review in July 1990, the Commission voted unanimously to adopt a report supporting a 24-hour-a-day ban of both indecent radio and television program content, arguing that because at least some portion of the broadcast audience was likely to be composed of children at all times of the day and night, anything less than a total ban of such programming would not achieve the objectives of the regulation.[94]

---

restrictions on "indecent" broadcasts because indecency is expression protected by the First Amendment. The only problem with that explanation is that commercial speech is also expression protected by the First Amendment.

[93] Public Law 100–459, § 608 (1988). Two months later the FCC adopted an order enforcing this ban. See 67 RR2d 1714.

[94] 67 RR2d 1714 (1990). To understand more clearly the type of content that triggered the FCC action, and that had motivated the more than 6,000 indecency complaints the FCC had been receiving annually since the mid 1980s, here are a few excerpts from some of those programs broadcast during a time of day when a substantial number of children could be expected to be in the broadcast audience: WLUP Chicago, " * * * went down on that other woman and oh God, you had your tongue in her vagina. It was fabulous * * * "; KSJO, San Jose, "I'd love to lick the matzo balls right off your butt * * * I'd like to have a smorgasbord in your butt. I'd like to have matzos in there with borscht, everything. I'd just have a buffet * * * "; WLLZ Detroit, "He puts Penthouse on his desk/he's got big muscles in his wrist/he holds his organ in his fist/He gives his pink dolphin a mighty twist * * * All the girls in the office they say, 'Hard-on, hard-on,

In April 1991 the U.S. Court of Appeals struck down the 24-hour-a-day ban of indecent broadcast programming, but directed the FCC to consider once again the possibility of establishing a reasonable defined "safe harbor" for indecent content capable of channeling such programs away from children without unduly restricting adult access to them.[95]

Freed by the Court of its Congressionally imposed burden to *ban* indecent broadcasting from the airwaves, the FCC tried initially to enlarge its "safe harbor" from six to ten hours a day, permitting such programs to be aired at any time between 8 p.m. and 6 a.m. But when Congress attached a 12 p.m. to 6 a.m. "safe harbor" provision to the Public Broadcasting funding bill of 1992, the FCC was forced to revert to a uniform midnight to 6 a.m. "harbor" for all its licensees, aware that it could not justify punishing one group of broadcasters for scheduling indecent program material during a time period when another group was free to schedule such programming without penalty.[96]

The Public Telecommunications Act of 1992 contained a provision requiring the FCC to adopt new (30b) regulations prohibiting the transmission of indecent programming between the hours of 6 a.m. and midnight, thereby restricting such programs to a midnight to 6 a.m. "safe harbor." However, the same legislation allowed public broadcast stations that signed off before midnight to air such programming after 10 p.m.[97]

The rules adopted by the FCC in response to this Congressional directive faced their customary challenges from Action for Children's Television (ACT), perennial champion of the right of children to have access to a wide spectrum of programming on a 24-hour-a-day basis. A three-judge panel of the Court of Appeals for the District of Columbia upheld the ACT challenge and the court voted the hear the case, *en banc*.[98]

In a 7–4 decision, the full court affirmed the FCC's legal authority to adopt such indecency regulations, although it expanded the agency's indecency "safe harbor" to an eight-hour period from 10 p.m. to 6 a.m. to avoid what the full court found to be an unjustifiably different set of standards on commercial and public stations.

In what is now known as the "ACT III" decision, the majority found that the government did have a compelling interest in protecting children under 18 years of age from indecent program content, and that the channeling of such programs to a period of time when minors were least likely to have access to them did not unduly burden the First Amendment rights of broadcasters or the public.

---

beg my pardon.' Walk with an erection"; WMCA New York, "When you can't call welfare people 'sluts' and 'whores,' 'cocksuckers' or 'freeloaders,' then our English language serves no purpose."

[95] *ACT v. FCC*, 932 F.2d 1504 (D.C.Cir.1991), cert. denied 503 U.S. 913, 112 S.Ct. 1281 (1992).

[96] Public Telecommunications Act of 1992, Pub. Law 102–356. § 16(a), 106 Stat. 949, 954.

[97] Pub. L. 102–356, § 16(a), 106 Stat. 949, 954.

[98] *ACT v. FCC*, 11 F.3d 170 (D.C.Cir.1993).

Writing for the majority, Judge Buckley described this compelling interest as being a dual obligation on the part of the government to protect the well-being of children and to support parental efforts to supervise the viewing and listening choices of their children. In terms of "least restrictive means," Judge Buckley deferred to the judgment of Congress. He declared that the judiciary should not reject a Congressional decision involving the particular period of time that would best serve its policy objective as long as there was sufficient evidence to support that legislative determination.

In his dissent, Chief Judge Edwards argued that the government had not demonstrated any compelling need for such restrictive regulation. He wrote that even if some form of constraint were required, less sweeping alternatives such as scrambling devices or blocking chips could achieve the same objective without infringing on the free speech rights of broadcasters.[99] In a separate dissent, joined by Judges Rogers and Tatel, Judge Wald attacked the majority's decision as granting government virtually unharnessed power to censor. She wrote that the majority ruling permitted a government agency to suppress free speech without offering a scintilla of evidence to establish the degree of potential harm involved to the children its regulations claimed to be protecting.

In July, 1995, the FCC won another victory in this area when the D.C. Court of Appeals—in what is called the "ACT IV" decision—found that the Commission was properly administering its own indecency policy.[100] The court, responding to ACT's appeal against several indecency forfeitures previously imposed by the FCC, held that the Commission had not infringed on the rights of broadcasters, even though some indecency cases had remained unresolved for as long as seven years.[101]

In January, 1996, the Supreme Court refused to review the D.C. Court of Appeals' "ACT III" decision. That allowed the FCC to continue enforcing its current indecency policy with a 10 p.m. to 6 a.m. "safe harbor." The following week, the Supreme Court also refused to review the "ACT IV" case, making the FCC's victory in the field of broadcast indecency complete.

A result of the Janet Jackson "wardrobe malfunction," during the 2004 Super Bowl halftime show, was the passage of higher indecency fines. The new maximum fine is $325,000 per incident, 10 times the previous limit.[102]

The FCC went to work shortly after the fines were raised, seeking copies of tapes from broadcasts of live sporting events.[103]

---

[99] *Action for Children's Television v. FCC*, 58 F.3d 654 (D.C.Cir. *en banc* 1995).

[100] *Action for Children's Television v. FCC*, 59 F.3d 1249 (D.C.Cir. *en banc*.1995).

[101] "High Court Stands by Indecency Ban," *Variety*, Jan. 15, 1995, p. 43.

[102] Brooks Boliek, "FCC combing air tapes for dirty words," Reuters, July 12, 2006.

[103] Ibid.

> Tapes requested by the commission include live broadcasts of football games and NASCAR races where the participants or the crowds let loose with an expletive.

A broadcast executive said that the agency was seeking tapes from programs featuring crowd noise.

SUPREME COURT UPHOLDS FCC'S REVISED FLEETING EXPLETIVE RULE

Late in April, 2009, the Supreme Court by a 5–4 vote upheld the FCC's right to interpret 18 U.S.C. § 1464 banning any "indecent, obscene or profane language" in broadcasts.[104] The case began with an appearance by Bono at the Golden Globes in 2004 where he referred to winning a Golden Globe as being "really, really fucking brilliant."[105] The FCC ruled that the use of the F-word was indecent because it is "one of the most vulgar, graphic and explicit definitions of sexual activity."[106]

It was a change from prior FCC enforcement in that the Commission and its staff had taken the position through prior staff rulings and Commission dicta that fleeting or isolated use of the F-word in broadcasts would not be treated as broadcast indecency. The FCC then turned to two Fox Television broadcasts of the Billboard Awards. In the 2002 and 2003 broadcasts, Cher and Nicole Richie used the F-word and Richie used the S-word. Mindful of the impact of indecency on minors, the FCC noted that an estimated 2.5 million minors had seen each of the Billboard Awards shows.

When Fox and its fellow broadcasters challenged the FCC finding of liability for indecency, a three-judge panel of the 2nd Circuit ruled that the change in FCC policy was not proper under the Administrative Procedure Act. The Act requires that decisions by federal agencies be the result of reasoned thinking and not arbitrary or capricious.

The Supreme Court, in a majority opinion by Justice Scalia, held that the FCC properly exercised its power to change the fleeting expletive rule. Justice Scalia rejected the 2nd Circuit panel's conclusion that the FCC had to provide a clear or substantial explanation for changing its policy for it to comply with the APA. Justice Scalia concluded that agencies only need show that they are aware of the change in policy.[107]

> And of course the agency must show that there are good reasons for the new policy. But it need not demonstrate to a court's satisfaction that the reasons for the new policy are *better* than the reasons for the old one; it suffices that the new policy is

---

[104] *Federal Communications Commission v. Fox Television Stations*, 556 U.S. 502, 129 S.Ct. 1800 (2009).

[105] *Fox Television Stations v. Federal Communications Commission*, 489 F.3d 444 (2d Cir. 2007).

[106] Ibid.

[107] Ibid.

> permissible under the statute, that there are good reasons for it, and that the agency *believes* it to be better, which the conscious change of course adequately indicates.

In dissent, Justice Breyer, joined by Justices Stevens, Souter and Ginsburg, argued that the FCC policy change was arbitrary, capricious and an abuse of discretion. The change in a policy that was a quarter century old without a reasoned explanation was a violation of the APA, Justice Breyer wrote. The majority's approach of allowing the FCC to simply declare a preference in making the change would create a system in which no agency decision could be subject to review.[108]

> After all, if it is *always* legally sufficient for the agency to reply to the question "why change?" with the answer "we prefer the new policy" (even when the agency *has not considered* the major factors that led it to adopt its old policy), then why bother asking the agency to focus on the fact of change?

The Supreme Court did not address the question of whether the First Amendment would prevent the FCC from applying its changed policy regarding fleeting expletives. As Justice Scalia wrote, "This Court, however, is one of final review, "not of first view." citing *Cutter v. Wilkinson*, 544 U. S. 709, 718, n. 7 (2005).

The case was remanded to the 2nd Circuit where the constitutional question could be considered and, perhaps, returned to the Supreme Court.

On remand, the 2nd Circuit found the fleeting expletives rule to be unconstitutional because it was vague, that is to say it did not provide adequate notice of what was proscribed and could be penalized.[109]

> We now hold that the FCC's policy violates the First Amendment because it is unconstitutionally vague, creating a chilling effect that goes far beyond the fleeting expletives at issue here. Thus, we grant the petition for review and vacate the FCC's order and the indecency policy underlying it.

The opinion points to the difficulties for broadcasters to know what would be accepted by the FCC and what would be subject to penalties. The police drama "NYPD Blue," poster child for the pushing of the broadcast envelope illustrated the problem. Judge Rosemary Pooler wrote:[110]

> The first problem arises in the FCC's determination as to which words or expressions are patently offensive. For instance, while the FCC concluded that "bullshit" in a "NYPD Blue" episode was patently offensive, it concluded that "dick" and "dickhead" were

---

[108] Ibid.

[109] *Fox Television Stations, Inc. v. F.C.C.*, 613 F.3d 317, 318, 38 Media L. Rep. 1993, 50 Communications Reg. (P & F) 1365 (2d Cir.2010).

[110] Ibid. at 332.

> not. * * * Other expletives such as "pissed off," "up yours," "kiss my ass," and "wiping his ass" were also not found to be patently offensive. * * * The Commission argues that its three-factor "patently offensive" test gives broadcasters fair notice of what it will find indecent. However, in each of these cases, the Commission's reasoning consisted of repetition of one or more of the factors without any discussion of how it applied them. Thus, the word "bullshit" is indecent because it is "vulgar, graphic and explicit" while the words "dickhead" was not indecent because it was "not sufficiently vulgar, explicit, or graphic." This hardly gives broadcasters notice of how the Commission will apply the factors in the future.

Judge Pooler wrote that networks declined to air some broadcasts because of the uncertainty about the FCC's enforcement of its content rules. Some CBS affiliates refused to broadcast the Peabody Award winning documentary "9/11" because expletives uttered by firefighters at the site of the World Trade Center. Other instances where stations refused to show content for fear of FCC penalties included the funeral of Pat Tillman and a local candidate debate.[111]

The chilling effect of the uncertainty of the FCC rule was enough to render it unconstitutional. The 2nd Circuit said it was not declaring every indecency rule unconstitutional, just the one the FCC had adopted.

SUPREME COURT RESOLVES FOX, ABC INDECENCY CASE ON NARROW GROUNDS

The continuing issue of broadcast indecency took a step, though not firmly in any direction, in 2012 when the Supreme Court ruled in the Fox TV indecency case. For all the anticipation, the decision was limited.[112]

The Court, in an opinion by Justice Kennedy and joined by all the justices except for Justice Ginsburg and excluding Justice Sotomayor who did not participate in the case, held that the Fox and ABC networks had not been given sufficient notice of the FCCs new policy on fleeting expletives and brief nudity.

The case turned on the FCC's decision to penalize "fleeting expletives" involving the use of the word "fuck" and the seven-second showing on the ABC drama "NYPD Blue" of a female character's buttocks and a momentary glimpse of the side of her breast.

While the FCC had long penalized extended indecency, it had a different policy on momentary expletives. In the *Pacifica* case (discussed earlier in this chapter), the FCC had focused on the extended nature of Carlin's monologue.[113]

---

[111] Ibid. at 334.

[112] *FCC v. Fox Television Stations*, 567 U.S. 239, 132 S.Ct. 2307 (2012).

[113] Ibid. at 2313.

> In the context of expletives, the Commission determined "deliberate and repetitive use in a patently offensive manner is a requisite to a finding of indecency."

At the same time, the FCC said that just because a prohibited word was not repeated did not mean that it would not be treated as an indecent broadcast. The FCC's order in the *Pacifica* case came in 1975. In 2001, the FCC issued guidance on the issue of indecency.[114] The FCC takes action when material describes or depicts sexual or excretory organs or activities. The FCC also uses a patent offensiveness test.

> [T]he *explicitness or graphic nature* of the description or depiction of sexual or excretory organs or activities; (2) whether the material *dwells on or repeats at length* descriptions of sexual or excretory organs or activities; (3) *whether the material appears to pander or is used to titillate, or whether the material appears to have been presented for its shock value.*[115]

In its explanation of the factors and how they had been applied in indecency actions by the FCC, the commission said,[116]

> Repetition of and persistent focus on sexual or excretory material have been cited consistently as factors that exacerbate the potential offensiveness of broadcasts. In contrast, where sexual or excretory references have been made once or have been passing or fleeting in nature, this characteristic has tended to weigh against a finding of indecency.

Broadcasters relied on this fleeting expletive approach. In the case of Fox and ABC, the FCC changed its policy in the indecency finding over Bono's use of the F-word in his acceptance speech. *In re Complaints Against Various Broadcast Licensees Regarding Their Airing of the "Golden Globe Awards" Program*, 19 FCC Rcd. 4975 (discussed earlier in this chapter), the FCC,[117]

> * * * reversed prior rulings that had found fleeting expletives not indecent. The Commission held "the mere fact that specific words or phrases are not sustained or repeated does not mandate a finding that material that is otherwise patently offensive to the broadcast medium is not indecent."

Justice Kennedy wrote that the FCC applied its new policy to Fox and ABC even though their broadcasts took place before it ruled in the Golden Globes complaint. The fact that the two networks were sanctioned before the FCC made the rule public meant that the networks

---

[114] *In re Industry Guidance on Commission's Case Law Interpreting 18 U.S.C. Sec. 1464 and Enforcement Policies Regarding Broadcast Indecency*, 16.

[115] Italics retained.

[116] Ibid. at 8008.

[117] *In re Complaints Against Various Broadcast Licensees Regarding Their Airing of the "Golden Globe Awards" Program*, 19 FCC Rcd. 4975, 4980.

were not given adequate notice that their broadcasts would result in FCC sanctions. That was at the heart of Justice Kennedy's opinion.[118]

A fundamental principle in our legal system is that laws which regulate persons or entities must give fair notice of conduct that is forbidden or required. See *Connally v. General Constr. Co.*, 269 U.S. 385, 391, 46 S.Ct. 126, 70 L.Ed. 322 (1926) ("[A] statute which either forbids or requires the doing of an act in terms so vague that men of common intelligence must necessarily guess at its meaning and differ as to its application, violates the first essential of due process of law").

And so, instead of a broad opinion setting a clear frame around indecency, the Court focused on the facts of the case. The FCC continues to wrestle with the issue of indecency.

THE FCC AND CABLE INDECENCY

The Telecommunications Act provides guidelines for cable operators in the area of indecent and obscene communications. The Act provides for fines of up to $100,000 for transmitting obscene material over cable TV; requires, at the subscriber's request, the scrambling or blockage of audio and video of programming a subscriber has chosen not to buy; and to block the audio and video content of sexually explicit channels so that subscribers who do not buy them do not see them.

In 1997, the Supreme Court upheld a lower court's ruling on a portion of the Act requiring blockage of signals of sexually explicit channels. The *Playboy* and *Spice* channels had sued over that portion of the Act when cable operators decided to black out the two channels' programming from 6 a.m. to 10 p.m. The cable operators took that action because of a technical problem in blocking channel signals. A phenomenon called "signal bleed" allowed some distorted and undistorted signal to be picked up by nonsubscribers. Cable operators had the option of installing expensive scrambling or blocking technologies or simply dropping the adult programming until late night hours. They chose the less expensive black-out option. A lower federal court ruled against *Playboy* and *Spice* and the Supreme Court, without commenting, issued an order upholding the lower court decision.[119] But, as we will see shortly, the Supreme Court would revisit the issue with a decidedly different result.

Government regulation of adult cable content was limited in *Denver Area Educational Telecommunications Consortium v. FCC*.[120] In *Denver*, providers of content on public, educational and governmental (PEG) channels challenged a portion of federal regulation requiring cable operators to block "patently offensive" programming offered on leased

[118] *FCC v. Fox Television Stations*, 567 U.S. 239, 252, 132 S.Ct. 2307, 2317 (2012).

[119] Lyle Denniston, "Cable TV's Adult Fare May Be Limited," *Baltimore Sun*, March 25, 1997.

[120] 518 U.S. 727, 116 S.Ct. 2374, 135 L.Ed.2d 888 (1996).

channels or to place all indecent programs on a single channel and block it at subscribers' requests. In a highly splintered ruling, the Court allowed cable operators to decline to show such material on leased channels. But the Court upheld protections for PEG channels. Opponents of the regulation said it could serve to ban programs on AIDS, abortion or human reproduction.[121]

The *Playboy* and *Spice* Channels made their way back to the Supreme Court late in 1999. And on May 22, 2000, the Court ruled that the section of the Telecommunications Act of 1996 that required scrambling or complete blockage of sexually oriented channels was unconstitutional.[122]

Sec. 505 of the Telecommunications Act of 1996 required "fully scrambled or otherwise fully blocked" transmission of those channels or limit on their transmission to hours when children are unlikely to be viewing. The Act set those hours at between 10 p.m. and 6 a.m.

As stated earlier, signal bleed was a problem. As the Court noted, "[w]ith imperfect scrambling, viewers who have not paid to receive *Playboy's* channels may happen across discernible images of a sexually explicit nature."[123]

So the Act had the effect of requiring that the sexually oriented content be relegated to the eight hours out of a day when children weren't expected to be watching cable TV. *Playboy*, which operates the *Playboy* and *Spice* channels, challenged Sec. 505 and a district court agreed saying the Act was a content-based restriction on speech. Instead, the district court reasoned, cable operators could simply give subscribers the ability to block out not only the channels that *Playboy* and *Spice* were shown on, but the other channels where signal bleed would take place.

The Supreme Court agreed that Sec. 505 singled out channels like *Playboy* and *Spice*, that feature primarily sexually oriented programming and noted the constitutional problems with that kind of focus. "Laws designed or intended to suppress or restrict the expression of specific speakers contradict basic First Amendment principles. Sec. 505 limited *Playboy's* market as a penalty for its programming choice, though other channels capable of transmitting like material are altogether exempt."[124]

Premium cable channels like HBO or Cinemax present adult-oriented and adult-themed content but were not affected by Sec. 505, whose sponsors named the *Playboy* and *Spice* channels during the creation of the Act. The *Playboy* and *Spice* channels were entitled to First

---

[121] "Justices Overturn Cable TV Smut Law," *Capital Times* [Madison, Wisconsin], June 28, 1996.

[122] *United States v. Playboy Entertainment Group*, 529 U.S. 803, 120 S.Ct. 1878 (2000).

[123] Ibid. at 1884.

[124] Ibid. at 1887.

Amendment protection because their programming was, by definition, indecent rather than obscene.

And so, the Court reasoned, "[t]he effect of the federal statute on the protected speech is now apparent. It is evident that the only reasonable way for a substantial number of cable operators to comply with the letter of Sec. 505 is to time channel, which silences the protected speech for two-thirds of the day in every home in a cable service area, regardless of the presence or likely presence of children or of the wishes of the viewers."[125]

Because Sec. 505 restricted protected First Amendment speech, it was required to pass the strict scrutiny test, that is to say the government must show a compelling interest and it must choose the least restrictive means of achieving that interest. The application of Sec. 505 did not use the least restrictive means available as the Supreme Court had reasoned and the district court had concluded. The Act was therefore unconstitutional and could not be enforced.

"Our precedents teach these principles. Where the designed benefit of a content-based speech restriction is to shield the sensibilities of listeners, the general rule is that the right of expression prevails, even where no less restrictive alternative exists. We are expected to protect our own sensibilities 'simply by averting [our] eyes.' *Cohen v. California*, 403 U.S. 15, 21, 91 S.Ct. 1780, 29 L.Ed.2d 284 (1971); accord, *Erznoznik v. Jacksonville*, 422 U.S. 205, 210–211, 95 S.Ct. 2268, 45 L.Ed.2d 125 (1975)."[126]

THE V-CHIP AND TELEVISION RATINGS

One of the provisions of the Telecommunications Act of 1996 was the inclusion of a requirement that all television sets produced after a particular date have an additional piece of technology called the "V-Chip." The V-Chip was the creation of Canadian Tim Collings[127] and would allow set owners to decide the level of violence, language and sex they watched. Explained most simply, broadcasters would send a signal out along with their programs. The signal would carry three separate indicators for violence, language and sex. When any one of the indicators reached the maximum amount determined by the viewer, the V-Chip would block the television broadcast and leave the viewer with a dark and silent screen. The V-Chip is adjustable and would let viewers choose to see more violence and less sex and rough language or more sex and less violence and language.

The FCC announced its technical standards for the V-Chip in the fall of 1997. The Commission said it expected that all television sets with

---

[125] Ibid.

[126] Ibid.

[127] Collings stepped into the pages of media law history when he said at the press conference announcing the V-Chip, "In Canada, Thank God, there is no First Amendment."

screens at least 13 inches, manufactured starting in July of 1999 to have the chip.[128] In order for the V-Chip to work, broadcasters will have to employ ratings codes for their program that will continuously monitor the targeted categories. The categories released by the FCC are: S for sex, V for violence, L for foul language, D for suggestive dialogue and FV for fantasy violence for use on children's shows.[129]

A study by the University of Pennsylvania's Annenberg Public Policy Center of the V-Chip showed that two in five parents have the V-Chip or other means of blocking out objectionable programming on their TVs. But only half of those parents actually use the devices.[130]

Congressional committees considered measures to require the FCC to study the effectiveness of the V-Chip and to consider the creation of a safe harbor for violent programming if the agency finds that the V-Chip was not effective in limiting television violence.[131] The violence safe harbor proposal was modeled after the indecency safe harbor restricting indecent broadcast material to a period between 10 p.m. and 6 a.m.

BROADCAST HOAXES

From 1938 onward, when Orson Welles's *Mercury Theater* adaptation of H.G. Well's *War of the Worlds* caused panic among thousands of Americans who were convinced by the broadcast program that Mars had attacked the United States, the FCC has never been amused by any effort, however clever or humorous, to tease or frighten a broadcast audience.[132]

In 1992 the Commission reacted to complaints about a series of broadcast hoaxes that had aired during the previous two years by adopting new rules authorizing it to fine stations a maximum of $25,000 for knowingly broadcasting

> * * * information or other material it knows to be false if it is foreseeable that broadcast of the information could cause substantial public harm, and if the broadcast of the information does in fact directly cause substantial public harm.[133]

Recent hoax broadcasts have included a news report asserting that the United States was under nuclear attack, another claiming that a popular radio personality had just been shot and a third involving a talk

---

[128] Bloomberg News, "FCC Releases its Plan for Phasing in Television V-Chip Broadcasting," *Los Angeles Times*, Sept. 26, 1997.

[129] Ibid.

[130] Deborah Belgum, "Why Don't V-Chips Work? Parents Don't Understand System," *Los Angeles Business Journal*, Sept. 25, 2000.

[131] Brooks Boliek, "Senators push safe-harbor bill," *Hollywood Reporter*, Feb. 16, 2001.

[132] For a vivid description of some of the public hysteria caused by this broadcast, see "Radio Listens in Panic, Taking War Drama As Fact," *New York Times*, October 31, 1938, p. 1.

[133] Amendment of Part 73 Regarding Broadcast Hoaxes.

show host who had arranged for a caller to confess falsely on air to having just committed a murder.[134]

The agency considers such harm to be "foreseeable" if the broadcaster could reasonably expect that public harm will occur. In this context, the FCC pointed out that an April Fools Day newscast claiming that a local football team had just traded one of its stars would not come under this rule, because while it might distress some fans, it would not create that degree of harm or damage contemplated by the rule.

A VICTORY, OF SORTS, IN THE NET NEUTRALITY BATTLE

The FCC faced three losses from the D.C. Circuit in its attempt to come up with rules for net neutrality. Net neutrality is generally defined as requiring Internet Service Providers to treat all content and content providers equally. That means the ISPs cannot give preference to clients or even its own content providers. They must remain neutral. ISPs have argued that outside, independent content providers, particularly those that offer content like movies, consume so much of the bandwidth that service is slowed down for even its own or client content. As such, ISPs have sought to block these outside providers, called Edge Providers, or require customers to pay higher fees to maintain access to the independent sources. Edge providers include entities like Amazon and Google that provide services and content to consumers.

Opponents say that without Net Neutrality, ISPs could freeze out diversity and make it more difficult to compete with the ISPs' own content or content that the ISPs have contracted to carry. The FCC has taken the position that ISPs should provide equal access.

Comcast was discovered to be providing preferential treatment to some of its high-speed Internet subscribers.[135] The first loss came when the FCC claimed it had the authority to regulate an Internet service provider's network management practices and issued an order for Comcast to stop interfering with some subscribers use of peer-to-peer networking applications.[136] In other words, the Commission could mandate net neutrality, through its ancillary powers—powers that are not expressly authorized by statute, but under sec. 4(1) of the Communications Act of 1934, has the authority to "perform any and all acts, make such rules and regulations, and issue such orders * * * , as

---

[134] Nuclear attack; Emmis Broadcasting, KSHE-FM, 69 R.R. 2d 195 (1991); false report of a shooting, Letter to Frank Battaglia, President, North American Broadcasting Co. 70 R.R. 2d 1329 (1992); false report of a murder; General Manager, Radio Station KROQ-FM, 6 F.C.C. R. 7262 (1991).

[135] Peter Svensson, "Comcast Blocks Some Internet Traffic," *Associated Press*, Oct. 19, 2007.

[136] *Comcast Corp. v. FCC*, 600 F.3d 642, 644, 390 U.S. App. D.C. 111, 2010 U.S. App. LEXIS 7039, 49 Comm. Reg. (P & F) 1226 (United States Court of Appeals for the District of Columbia Circuit April 6, 2010, Decided), available at https://advance-lexis-com.proxy.lib.utk.edu/api/document?collection=cases&id=urn:contentItem:7Y5V-9B40-YB0V-T01K-00000-00&context=1516831.

may be necessary in the execution of this function."[137] The D.C. Circuit disagreed and found that the FCC failed to tie its assertions of ancillary authority to any statutorily mandated responsibility and vacated the order.[138]

In 2014, the D.C. Circuit handed the FCC its second loss in its continuing effort to come up with rules on net neutrality.[139] In *Verizon v. FCC*, a panel of the D.C. Circuit examined a challenge to the Open Internet Order, which imposes disclosure, anti-blocking, and anti-discrimination requirements on broadband providers.

The D.C. Circuit previously held that the FCC's earlier attempt to preserve net neutrality exceeded its regulatory authority. This time, the panel found authority for the FCC in secs. 706(a) and (b) of the 1996 Telecommunications Act.[140] In his opinion, Judge David Tatel, agreed with the FCC that the Act first gave it oversight and the power to act.[141]

> It further provides that should the Commission find that "advanced telecommunications capability is [not] being deployed to all Americans in a reasonable and timely fashion," it "shall take immediate action to accelerate deployment of such capability by removing barriers to infrastructure investment and by promoting competition in the telecommunications market."

FCC lawyers argued that Internet service providers could limit access to the "edge providers." Judge Tatel wrote that the record supported the FCC's claim that providers had, in fact, restricted access to the Internet.[142]

> In support of its conclusion that broadband providers could and would act to limit Internet openness, the Commission pointed to four prior instances in which they had done just that. These involved a mobile broadband provider blocking online payment services after entering into a contract with a competing service; a mobile broadband provider restricting the availability of competing VoIP and streaming video services; a fixed broadband provider blocking VoIP applications; and, of course, Comcast's impairment of peer-to-peer file sharing that was the subject of the Comcast Order.

But even though the statutory authority existed for the FCC to work to ensure openness and access to the Internet, the method it used was specifically forbidden to it, Judge Tatel wrote. The FCC treated the

---

137 Ibid.

138 Ibid. at 661.

139 *Verizon v. FCC*, 740 F.3d 623 (D.C.Cir. 2014).

140 47 U.S.C. § 1302(a). Secs. 706(a), 706(b).

141 *Verizon v. FCC*, 740 F.3d 623, 635 (D.C.Cir. 2014).

142 Ibid. at 648.

providers much like common carriers.[143] The problem for the FCC was that its authority to do so was specifically excluded under the Telecommunications Act of 1996.[144]

> We think it obvious that the Commission would violate the Communications Act were it to regulate broadband providers as common carriers. Given the Commission's still-binding decision to classify broadband providers not as providers of "telecommunications services" but instead as providers of "information services," see supra at 630–31, such treatment would run afoul of section 153(51): "A telecommunications carrier shall be treated as a common carrier under this [Act] only to the extent that it is engaged in providing telecommunications services." 47 U.S.C. § 153(51)

Even though the D.C. Circuit overturned the regulatory scheme that the FCC created, the commission won the important recognition that it had authority to regulate the Internet in its pursuit of net neutrality.

That led to the FCC's third attempt to craft rules to provide Net Neutrality.

NET NEUTRALITY

The FCC faced another test of its Net Neutrality rules as a panel of the D.C. Circuit Court of Appeals heard another challenge to its attempts to maintain open access to the Internet.[145] After proposing new rules and taking more than 4 million public comments, the FCC rolled out its third version.

The Commission invoked its Title II authority to reclassify fixed and mobile broadband Internet access service (BIAS) as a telecommunications service.[146]

> [T]he Commission defined BIAS as "a mass-market retail service by wire or radio that provides the capability to transmit data to and receive data from all or substantially all Internet endpoints, including any capabilities that are incidental to and enable the operation of the communications service, but excluding dial-up Internet access service." The Commission adopted three "bright-line" rules applicable to both fixed and mobile BIAS that prohibit blocking, throttling, and paid prioritization.

---

[143] Common carrier comes from trade and transportation. Common carriers, like railroads, would carry passengers or goods indifferently, that is to say without regard to who or what it carries.

[144] *Verizon v. FCC*, 740 F.3d 623, 635, 650 (D.C. Cir. 2014).

[145] Sam Thielman, "Net neutrality has its day in court—with lawyers, Christians and the Cheshire Cat," *Guardian*, Dec. 5, 2015.

[146] *In the Matter of Protecting and Promoting the Open Internet*, 30 FCC Rcd. 4681 (F.C.C.), 30 F.C.C.R. 4681, 2015 WL 2195245.

The rule is possible because of the Commission's act of defining the broadband providers as entities engaged in mass market retailing. As such, the Commission would have the authority to create its rules. The most significant of them is the open Internet conduct rule that prevents BIAS providers from unreasonably restricting their subscribers from being able to choose content or services or restricting the ability of Edge Providers from offering and providing content or services.[147]

> As the Commission explained in the Order, "[b]ased on our findings that broadband providers have the incentive and ability to discriminate in their handling of network traffic in ways that can harm the virtuous cycle of innovation, increased end-user demand for broadband access, and increased investment in broadband network infrastructure and technologies, we conclude that a no-unreasonable interference/ disadvantage standard to protect the open nature of the Internet is necessary."

In their petition to halt the FCC's action, broadband providers[148] argued that the Commission could not define their services as being a common carrier and thus subject to FCC regulation. They pointed to the FCC's decision in 2002 to classify broadband cable modem services as "information services" and not "telecommunications services."[149] The National Cable & Telecommunications Association challenged that classification in *National Cable & Telecommunications Ass'n v. Brand X Internet Services* and the case made its way to the Supreme Court where the FCC won. The opinion, written by Justice Clarence Thomas, held that the Commission's action was a lawful interpretation of the Communications Act.

Defining the broadband services as common carriers conflicted with the *Brand X* case, they argued. The FCC replied that things had changed. The Supreme Court deferred to the Commission's finding that,[150]

> * * * cable modem service was a functionally integrated offering of an information service as a permissible (although perhaps not the best) interpretation of the Act. Notably, Brand X also explained that " '[A]n initial agency interpretation is not instantly carved in stone. On the contrary, the agency . . . must consider varying interpretations and the wisdom of its policy on a continuing basis, for example, in response to changed factual circumstances. . . .' " Thus, consistent with Brand X, the Commission has now properly revisited its prior interpretation

---

[147] Ibid.

[148] United States Telecom Association, CTIA—The Wireless Association, AT&T Inc., Wireless Internet Service Providers Association, CenturyLink; 1, American Cable Association and the National Cable & Telecommunications Association.

[149] *National Cable & Telecommunications Ass'n v. Brand X Internet Services*, 545 U.S. 967, 125 S.Ct. 2688 (2005).

[150] *In the Matter of Protecting and Promoting the Open Internet*, 30 FCC Rcd. 4681 (F.C.C.), 30 F.C.C.R. 4681, 2015 WL 2195245.

of these ambiguous statutory terms, and on the basis of the current record, reasonably concluded that the specific service that is BIAS is best understood as "offering" a telecommunications service.

The third attempt was successful. The panel of the D.C. Circuit upheld the FCC's 2015 Order Internet Order.[151]

In 2017, Ajit Pai, the FCC chairman installed by President Donald Trump, dismantled the 2015 Order and did away with Net Neutrality arguing that unregulated business will eventually yield to innovation and help the economy.[152]

66. POLITICAL ACCESS RULES

Despite deregulation, Congress still requires the FCC to enforce all equal access broadcast requirements.

The "equal time", or more accurately the "equal opportunities" requirement for political candidates has been an obligation imposed upon broadcasting since the Radio Act of 1927 was adopted. Sec. 18 of the Radio Act became the well known Sec. 315 of the Communications Act of 1934, stating,

> If any licensee shall permit any person who is a legally qualified candidate for any political office to use a broadcasting station, he shall afford equal opportunities to all other such candidates for that office in the use of such broadcasting station * * *

This section also denied the broadcaster any authority to censor political candidates exercising their rights of access under the terms of Sec. 315.

In 1959, a political candidate used this access to make defamatory remarks about his opponent. The opponent sued the broadcast station for airing these defamatory statements, but in *Farmers Educational & Cooperative Union of America v. WDAY, Inc.*,[153] the Supreme Court held that in establishing the terms and conditions for such political broadcast access, Congress had preempted state defamation law and created an absolute privilege that shielded the broadcast station from legal liability for statements made by such candidates.

During this same era, television news coverage of public events began raising a question Congress had no reason to consider when Sec. 315 was adopted. If a political candidate could be seen by viewers in film

---

[151] *United States Telecom Ass'n v. FCC*, 825 F.3d 674, 423 U.S. App. D.C. 183, 2016 U.S. App. LEXIS 10716, 64 Comm. Reg. (P & F) 1663, 2016 WL 3251234 (United States Court of Appeals for the District of Columbia Circuit June 14, 2016, Decided), available at https://advance-lexis-com.proxy.lib.utk.edu/api/document?collection=cases&id=urn:contentItem:5K0Y-9VG1-F04K-Y08C-00000-00&context=1516831.

[152] Cecilia Kang, "F.C.C. Repeals Net Neutrality Rules," *New York Times*, Dec. 14, 2017; Federal Communication Commission, "Restoring Internet Freedom," https://www.fcc.gov/restoring-internet-freedom.

[153] *Farmers Educ. & Co-op. Union v. WDAY*, 360 U.S. 525, 79 S.Ct. 1302 (1959).

clips of a news event broadcast by a television station, was such an appearance a "use" of broadcast facilities requiring the station to offer all opponents of that candidate equal access to television time?

The Commission decided in 1959 that such an appearance did constitute a "use" under the Act, even though broadcast journalists had pointed out that if each televised glimpse of a candidate triggered an obligation by a station to make free time available to all opponents, it would be virtually impossible for a television station to provide its viewers with adequate local news coverage during an election campaign.[154]

Congress reacted promptly by amending Sec. 315 to exempt from its equal opportunities requirement any appearance by a legally qualified candidate on a

(1) bona fide newscast

(2) bona fide news interview

(3) bona fide documentary (if the appearance of the candidate is incidental to the presentation of the subject or subjects covered by the news documentary), or

(4) on-the-spot coverage of bona fide news events (including but not limited to political conventions and activities incidental thereto) * * *

This amendment offered broadcast journalists the protection from equal access obligations necessary to cover most news events, but in special situations not fitting neatly into one of these four exempted categories of coverage, the FCC has been reluctant to extend the scope of such exemptions. In 1960, for example, Congress was forced to suspend the application of Sec. 315 to presidential candidates to permit the three television networks to broadcast the famous Kennedy-Nixon debates without being required to provide an equal amount of free network broadcast time to all minor party presidential candidates.

In 1975, however, the Commission reversed its earlier position that neither broadcast coverage of political candidate debates nor candidate press conferences came within the exemption Congress had granted for on-the-spot coverage of bona fide news events.[155] It now held that debates were exempt from Sec. 315 requirements if they were controlled by someone other than the candidates or the broadcaster, and also exempted coverage of press conferences if they were "newsworthy and subject to on-the-spot coverage."[156]

---

[154] *Columbia Broadcasting System,* 26 FCC2d 715 (1970).

[155] *Petition of Aspen Institute and CBS,* 35 RR2d 49 (1975). In *Petition of Henry Geller, et al.,* 54 R.R.2d 1246 (1983) the FCC relaxed its political candidates' debates rules still further, allowing broadcasters themselves to sponsor debates between political candidates without being required by Sec. 315 to extend this right of debate to all candidates for the office in question.

[156] This change in FCC policy was sustained by the court of appeals in *Chisholm v. FCC,* 538 F.2d 349 (D.C.Cir.1976), cert. denied 429 U.S. 890, 97 S.Ct. 247 (1976). Senator Kennedy

The League of Women Voters acted as the independent host of these presidential debates for the television networks in 1976 and 1980. Since 1984, however, the Commission no longer has required the presence of an outside sponsoring organization in order to exempt political debates from 315 requirements, finding no basis for its previous belief that such an independent group was needed to insure impartial coverage of such debates.[157]

In 1991 the Commission relaxed its equal access requirements still further, expanding the "spot news" exemption of Sec. 315 to permit the broadcasting of candidate-prepared campaign statements and interviews limited to the two major presidential candidates without obligating a station to offer lesser candidates equal access.[158]

Through the years the FCC has also extended its category of broadcast programs exempted from political access requirements to include entertainment shows that provide news or current event coverage as regularly scheduled segments of the program. In this way, not only "Today", "Good Morning America" and "This Morning" but even "Donahue", "Entertainment Tonight" and "Entertainment This Week" have been able to invite political candidates to discuss public issues without exposing the network or station carrying them to "equal time" demands by rival candidates.[159]

On the other hand, the Commission has held rigidly to its position that any "use" of station time by a political candidate not expressly exempted by Sec. 315 creates an obligation for equal access. For example, the FCC declared that any station broadcasting a Ronald Reagan film during any campaign period in which he was a political candidate would

---

challenged the new press conference exemption, claiming that President Carter had used such a conference to attack Kennedy, then a competing presidential candidate. The FCC's position was upheld in *Kennedy for President Committee v. FCC*, 636 F.2d 432 (D.C.Cir.1980).

[157] The FCC's position was affirmed in *League of Women Voters Educ. Fund v. FCC*, 731 F.2d 995 (D.C. Cir.1984).

[158] *Request of King Broadcasting Company Licensee of KING-TV, Seattle, Washington for a Declaratory Ruling*, 69 R.R.2d 1017 (1991). However, in reversing earlier decisions denying these exemptions in *Request for Declaratory Ruling by WEBE, 108 Radio Co.*, 63 R.R.2d 1748 (1987) rev'd and remanded sub nom. *King Broadcasting Co. v. FCC*, 860 F.2d 465 (D.C.Cir.1988), the Commission did caution broadcasters that failure to include a major third-party presidential candidate in their news coverage might risk the loss of the spot news exemption the agency had granted.

[159] Although the Donahue exemption was originally denied by the FCC, it was subsequently granted in 1984 despite the show's rather sporadic commitment to coverage of significant political events or issues. See *Multimedia Entertainment*, 56 RR2d 143 (1984). In justifying its exemption for show business promotional programs such as "Entertainment Tonight," the FCC observed that the news exemption to Sec. 315 is not based on "the subject matter reported" but only on whether a program "reports news of some area of current events". In addition, the agency pointed out that if it began deciding in each case whether the information provided by a particular program was sufficiently important or significant to justify an exemption, it could be involving itself more deeply in the evaluation of broadcast program content than the First Amendment would permit. *Request for Declaratory Ruling by Paramount Pictures Corp.* (1988).

obligate that station to offer all his legally qualified opponents the same degree of access to its audience.[160]

In 1991 the agency did modify this policy significantly, declaring that an appearance by a political candidate would be considered a "use" only when the candidate's voice or picture was authorized or sponsored by the candidate or the candidate's campaign committee.[161] Recognizing the increasingly common practice in negative campaign commercials to include audio clips or video footage of a candidate's opponent, the FCC wanted to clarify its position that unauthorized use of a political opponent's voice or image would not then entitle the candidate who produced such ads to claim air time on the basis of this "appearance" by the opponent.

Under this new standard, then, the broadcast of an old feature film of a candidate such as Ronald Reagan would no longer provide his political opponents with a right of equal access unless Reagan or his campaign committee had actually approved or authorized the scheduling of the film.

At the same time, though, the Commission refused to alter its policy regarding typical broadcast employees, a policy that still effectively denies any broadcast performer the right to run for political office. The FCC has defined "use" of broadcast facilities to include virtually any type of on-air performance, including working under an assumed name as the radio host of a weekly dance show.[162] Under this strict interpretation of the rules, as soon as a broadcast performer becomes a political candidate, each subsequent on-air performance obligates the station to provide a similar amount of free air time to each of the employee's political opponents.

In one recent case, station management estimated that it would be required to provide more than 33 hours of free broadcast response time if a television reporter went ahead with his plans to become a candidate for a town council position.[163] Not surprisingly, the reporter was ordered by the station to make an immediate choice between a career in politics and one in broadcasting.

Yet, it would be unfair to blame the FCC too severely for this unfortunate result, because Congress has allowed the Commission virtually no discretion in the enforcement of this broadcast "use" standard. Despite the fact that both the NAB and the Radio Television News Directors Association (RTNDA) have on several occasions urged that Congress amend Sec. 315 to allow broadcast employees to exercise

---

[160] *In re Adrian Weiss*, 36 R.R.2d 292 (1976). See also *In re Pat Paulsen*, 33 R.R.2d 835 (1972), affirmed 491 F.2d 887 (9th Cir.1974).

[161] *Codification of the Commission's Political Programming Policies*, 70 R.R. 2d 239 (1991).

[162] See Letter to WUGN, 40 FCC2d 293 (1958).

[163] *Branch v. FCC*, 824 F.2d 37 (D.C. Cir.1987), 14 Med.L.Rptr. 1465.

this basic right of citizenship, Congressional leaders have seemed content to continue treating broadcasting as a less legally privileged medium.

Nowhere is that attitude of Congress more clearly reflected than in legislation it enacted in 1971 to take advantage of broadcasting's status as a federally regulated medium. In that year the Communications Act was amended by Congress to compel each broadcast station to provide candidates for federal office a reasonable amount of broadcast time, and to furnish time for purchase by federal candidates at the lowest rate charged regular advertisers for that same time period.[164] In essence, members of Congress had decided to combat the rising costs of federal election campaigns by imposing upon broadcasting, the only medium controlled by government, requirements designed to reduce their own campaign costs at the broadcast industry's expense.

The first major test of this new legislation occurred in 1980, when the Carter-Mondale Committee sought to purchase a half hour of prime time from each network to present a documentary portraying President Carter's first term accomplishments just after Carter's formal announcement of his intention to seek a second term. When none of the networks were willing to provide the full 30 minutes of time the Committee demanded, the group filed a complaint with the FCC.[165] The Commission found the networks in violation of the "reasonable access" rule, and on appeal, the Supreme Court, in a 5–4 decision, narrowly affirmed this finding.[166]

In 1990, an extensive FCC audit revealed that more than two-thirds of the 30 radio and televisions stations the agency had investigated were not charging political candidates the lowest advertising rates required by federal law.[167] The Commission also discovered that a substantial number of these stations had not fully informed candidates of the availability of lower priced packages of advertising for which they qualified. As a result of this audit the FCC adopted new rules requiring stations to make full disclosure to political candidates of all advertising unit rates offered to any of the station's regular commercial accounts.[168]

However, when several politicians who had been candidates during the 1990 election campaign sued broadcast stations to recover what they claimed were excessive charges for political commercials, the FCC quickly intervened to shield broadcasters from such litigation, asserting

[164] The "reasonable access" amendment created sec. 312(a)(7) of the Communications Act, and the "lowest rate" provision became sec. 315(b).

[165] Networks were reluctant to sell a large block of prime time for a political program during a non-election year, aware that inserting such a political documentary into a regular evening lineup of shows would substantially reduce the audience for all programs following the political program the evening it was scheduled. CBS offered a 5 minute prime time segment, and ABC a full 30 minute prime time slot during a non-rating period in January, but the Committee refused these offers.

[166] *CBS, Inc. v. FCC*, 453 U.S. 367, 101 S.Ct. 2813 (1981).

[167] Political Program Audit, 68 R.R. 2d 113 (1990).

[168] Codification of the Commission's Political Programming Policies, 70 R.R. 2d 219 (1991).

that the Commission had sole authority to decide when a station was in violation of federal political broadcast advertising laws.[169] Instead of permitting such controversies to be decided by the courts, the agency offered candidates two options for resolving future broadcast advertising rate disputes; either to submit them to a neutral arbitrator for a binding decision, or to ask the Commission to determine the proper charges through the agency's complaint process.

Considering the advantages that politicians currently obtain from the "equal opportunities," "lowest advertising rate" and "reasonable access" provisions of the Communications Act of 1934, it seems highly unlikely that Congress will ever be eager to release broadcasting from the constraints of regulation so long as these benefits continue to result from such control.[170]

The *Citizens United* and *McCutcheon* cases paved the way for massive campaign spending. Television continues to draw the lion's share of campaign ad dollars. The "lowest unit rate" that candidates enjoy do not apply to the SuperPACs trying to influence elections.

THE CONTENT OF POLITICAL ADS

The Federal Communications Commission does not engage in censorship of political broadcasts, in most cases. Sec. 315, which provides candidates with equal access at lowest rates, also denies stations from censoring the "use" of political advertising time by a bona fide candidate. This doctrine has led to some painful decisions by the FCC and the courts when dealing with political language and messages that are shocking.

In Re Complaint by Julian Bond,[171] the FCC ruled that it could not ban the use of the word, "nigger" by a legally qualified candidate for the governorship of Georgia. J.B. Stoner, running for the Georgia governorship had used the offending word in his radio and television spots. The FCC replied that "in light of Section 315, we may not prevent a candidate from utilizing that word during his 'use' of a licensee's broadcast facilities."[172] Bond and the Atlanta NAACP sought in the alternative to have the word declared obscene or indecent and added to the list of proscribed words from *Pacifica*. The FCC declined saying that the word did not fall into the narrow category of words from *Pacifica*, words that were patently offensive and dealing with sex or excretion.

---

169 Exclusive Jurisdiction with Respect to Potential Violations of the Lowest Unit Charge Requirements of Sec. 315(b), Communications Act, 70 R.R.2d 1 (1991).

170 Congress has always favored the "equal opportunities" provision of Sec. 315, because while virtually every incumbent can gain constant broadcast access to constituents between elections through news items most local stations are eager to carry, any challenger is restricted by § 315 during the campaign period to access under the same terms and conditions as the incumbent, thus protecting the incumbent's pre-election advantage.

171 69 F.C.C.2d 943 (1978).

172 Ibid.

The issue arose again in the 1980 presidential race when Citizens Party candidates used the word "bullshit" in a political ad transmitted by NBC.[173] NBC initially rejected the ad but relented, although it preceded the transmission of the ad to its affiliates with an advisory about "offensive language." The FCC ruled that the advisory to the NBC affiliates, many of which did not run the ad with the offending words, did not constitute censorship, although it said, "[t]he initial reactions of the NBC staff in rejecting the spot and urging its modification were clearly in error. NBC needs to take additional steps to assure that its staff is fully aware of the no-censorship requirements of the law, and we expect it to take such steps."[174]

It took Larry Flynt to make the FCC take a step back from its expansive protection of political ads. The FCC ruled in 1984 that stations were not required to broadcast obscene or indecent material as part of a political advertisement. The issue arose when Flynt, publisher of Hustler Magazine, showed some ads from his 1984 bid for the presidency. Flynt intended to use clips from adult movies to illustrate his campaign ads. Lawmakers sprang into action and sought a ruling from the FCC. Then FCC Chairman Mark Fowler wrote to Rep. Thomas Luken (D-Ohio) to tell him that the anti-censorship provision of Sec. 315 had not been tested against a situation in which a candidate aired obscene materials. But an FCC staffer said that laws should not be read to lead to unreasonable results.

> "Because the purpose of fostering political debate is untainted by subjecting broadcasters to the prohibitions against obscenity and indecency (which by definition lack serious political value), it is concluded that it would be unreasonable to exempt broadcasters from (the law's) criminal prohibitions," Fowler wrote to Luken.[175]

Flynt left the issue unresolved when he withdrew from the race for the Republican nomination. The question of content arose again when a congressional candidate sought protection for his political ads that featured graphic images of aborted fetuses. The FCC had granted stations permission to review Becker's ads and channel them to "safe harbor" because of their intense and graphic nature. But in *Becker v. FCC*,[176] the D.C. Circuit Court of Appeals ruled that the FCC's order violated the rule against censorship of political advertising.

---

[173] *In re Complaint of Barry Commoner and LaDonna Harris*, 87 F.C.C.2d 1 (1980). The ad contained the following lines:

Man: Bullshit.

Woman: What?

Man: Carter, Reagan and Anderson. It's all such bullshit.

[174] Ibid.

[175] "Stations Needn't Show Political Ads with Obscenities," *Wall Street Journal*, Jan. 25, 1984.

[176] 95 F.3d 75 (D.C.Cir.1996).

As the court noted, "the 1992 election campaign witnessed the advent of political advertisements depicting the aftermath of abortions. * * * At 7:58 p.m. on July 19, Station WAGA-TV aired, at Mr. Becker's request, a campaign advertisement that included photographs of aborted fetuses. WAGA-TV received numerous complaints from viewers who saw the advertisement."[177]

Anticipating that Becker would want to repeat his commercials, WAGA, an Atlanta station, sought a ruling from the FCC that would permit the station to channel Becker's ads to a "safe harbor." A number of other broadcasters also sought a ruling from the Commission that they would not have to air political advertisements that presented, "graphic depictions or descriptions of aborted fetuses or any other similar graphic depictions of excised or bloody fetal tissue, where there is * * * the good-faith judgment of the licensee, a reasonable risk that children may be in the audience."[178] The stations asked the FCC to declare such advertisements indecent. The FCC viewed the ads and concluded they were not indecent and said that the station could not censor them.

Becker returned to the station and tried to buy time for a 30-minute political commercial, "Abortion in America: The Real Story," which he wanted to air after a televised professional football game. The station refused claiming the program would violate the indecency rules. The FCC then issued a notice saying that until it ruled, stations could decline to broadcast material they believed were indecent. The FCC later ruled that while Becker's ads were not indecent, they posed a threat of psychological damage to children who saw them. The Commission ruled, "that nothing in 312(a)(7)[179] precludes a broadcaster's exercise of some discretion with respect to placement of political advertisements so as to protect children * * * and channeling would not violate the no-censorship of section 315(a)."[180]

But the D.C. Circuit Court of Appeals ruled that the FCC's order violated Becker's rights under the reasonable access rules. The court also said that in issuing its order, the FCC was giving permission for broadcasters to discriminate against political advertisers on the basis of content, which violated the no censorship and equal opportunity sections of the Telecommunications Act.

> "As we explain below, by permitting a licensee to channel political advertisements that it believes may harm children, the Declaratory Ruling frustrates what the Commission itself has identified as Congress's primary purpose in enacting Section 312(a) (7); namely to ensure 'candidate access to the time

177 Ibid. at 76–77.

178 Ibid.

179 Sec. 312 provides that a station license may be revoked for willful or repeated failure to allow reasonable access by qualified political candidates.

180 95 F.3d 75, 78 (D.C.Cir.1996).

> periods with the greatest audience potential * * * ' Licensee Responsibility, 47 F.C.C.2d at 517"[181]

The court said that it would be impossible for the FCC to meet that responsibility and also channel the advertisement to a safe harbor where no children might be harmed. It acknowledged the conflicting interests of protecting children from "images that are not indecent but may nevertheless prove harmful," and the candidate's interest in reaching the largest audience he can. If the FCC were permitted to grant discretion to stations, the risk would be that candidates would lose access to potential supporters. Merely requiring that the station's judgment be "reasonable" would open the door to questionable decisions that might mean the difference in an election.

> "These are slippery standards, and it is of small solace to a losing candidate that an appellate court might eventually find the Commission's approval of a licensee's channeling decision was an abuse of discretion or contrary to law. Moreover, the acceptance of a subjective standard renders it impossible to determine whether it was the advertisement's message rather than its images that the licensee found too shocking for tender minds."[182]

For some messages, like that of the abortion opponents, the message is inextricably entwined with image, the court said. Candidates might well tone down their ads for fear of being denied carriage and so result in self-censorship. If a candidate did not change an ad, a station might channel it to "safe harbor" while continuing to show an opponent's ads in prime time. If a station chose to be fair and channel both candidates' ads, the second and non-offensive candidate would suffer for the excesses of another and be denied the fair access guaranteed under the law.

The court did not address Becker's First Amendment claim because it had disposed of the case based on the Telecommunications Act.

67. FAIRNESS DOCTRINE OBLIGATIONS

Although the FCC has repealed the Fairness Doctrine, it has never been declared unconstitutional by the courts and could be reinstituted by Congress or the Commission.

In contrast, the fairness doctrine, the other major public issue oriented principle of broadcast regulation, has never been as directly related to Congressional self-interest. In fact, Congress never bothered to formally codify the doctrine, simply declaring when amending the "equal opportunities" provision of Sec. 315 in 1959 that it had no intention of relieving broadcasters,

---

[181] 95 F.3d 75, 80.

[182] Ibid. at 81.

> * * * from the obligations imposed upon them under this Act to operate in the public interest and to afford reasonable opportunity for the discussion of conflicting views on issues of public importance.[183]

The concept of broadcast "fairness" emerged instead from years of specific decisions made by the FRC and FCC in determining the exact extent of a licensee's obligation to provide the public with balanced coverage of controversial matters of public importance. In 1949, the FCC issued the first formal description of this doctrine, declaring,

> One of the most vital questions of mass communications in a democracy is the development of an informed public opinion through the public dissemination of news and ideas concerning the vital public issues of the day.[184]

Elaborating on this concept, the Commission established a twofold obligation for every broadcaster; to devote a reasonable amount of time to the coverage of important public issues, and to provide this coverage in a fair and balanced manner.

In 1969, the Supreme Court had its first opportunity to consider the First Amendment issues raised by the fairness doctrine. Although only one narrow portion of the doctrine, its personal attack rule, was truly at issue, the consolidation of this case with an action brought by a group of broadcast news directors allowed the court to consider the broader constitutional implications of this Commission policy.

Justice White, speaking for a unanimous court, declared in affirming the doctrine that the federal government did have the constitutional authority to require broadcasters to furnish their audiences with balanced coverage of controversial issues of public importance because,

> It is the purpose of the First Amendment to preserve an uninhibited marketplace of ideas in which truth will ultimately prevail, rather than to countenance monopolization of that market, whether it be by the Government itself or a private licensee * * * It is the right of the viewers and listeners, not the right of the broadcasters, which is paramount.[185]

In 1967 the Commission had taken the position that in accepting cigarette advertising, a station obligated itself under the fairness doctrine to present programming or public service announcements balancing the advocacy of smoking with information describing the threat that cigarette smoking posed to health.[186] By establishing this precedent, the FCC soon found itself under pressure from a wide range of interest groups demanding that this "counter advertising" broadcast

---

[183] Public Law No. 274, 86th Congress 1959.

[184] Editorializing by Broadcast Licensees, 13 FCC 1246 (1949).

[185] *Red Lion Broadcasting Co. v. FCC*, 395 U.S. 367, 89 S.Ct. 1794 (1969).

[186] *Banzhaf v. FCC*, 405 F.2d 1082 (D.C. Cir.1968).

obligation be extended to require informational messages criticizing virtually every product advertised on television or radio.

Expanding the scope of the fairness doctrine in this way would have made it extremely difficult for broadcasters to continue to compete with newspapers or magazines for advertising revenues, since few advertisers would be likely to use a medium that was obligated by law to provide free air time to those who wished to criticize the products they had paid to promote. As a result, when the Federal Trade Commission (FTC) filed a brief with the FCC in 1972 that urged the Commission adopt broadcast counter advertising rules as a "suitable approach to some of the present failings of advertising which are beyond the FTC's capacity," the FCC realized that it was being maneuvered into a regulatory position that would undercut the financial base of the entire broadcast industry.[187]

In 1974 the Commission rejected this FTC proposal and issued a policy statement effectively removing all product advertising from the requirements of the fairness doctrine, except in situations where the advertising itself expressly raised a controversial issue of public importance.[188] In this same policy statement the FCC also tried to clarify basic broadcast obligations under the doctrine, concluding that broadcasters needed only to devote a reasonable amount of time to the coverage of public issues, and through this coverage, to provide opportunities for the presentation of contrasting points of view relating to these issues.

Citizen groups viewed this effort at clarification as an attempt to retreat from regulatory guidelines that in the past had been construed by the agency itself as requiring broadcasters actively to seek out controversial issues of public importance and to assume primary responsibility for providing balanced coverage of these issues. Eventually, however, the FCC's new, more limited definition of broadcast fairness doctrine obligations was sustained by the courts.[189]

As the 1980s began, even this more narrowly defined set of fairness obligations soon appeared too repressive of free speech for an FCC now fully committed to a policy of deregulation. In 1981, the Commission asked Congress to repeal the fairness doctrine, pointing to what it felt was an ever increasing inequity between the programming requirements broadcasters had to accept, and the much less extensive programming obligations the agency could legally impose upon all other forms of competing electronic media service.[190]

---

[187] FTC Docket 19.260.

[188] *In the Matter of Handling of Public Issues under the Fairness Doctrine*, 48 FCC2d 1 (1974).

[189] *National Citizens Committee for Broadcasting v. FCC*, 567 F.2d 1095 (D.C.Cir.1977), cert. denied 436 U.S. 926, 98 S.Ct. 2820 (1978).

[190] FCC Report No. 5068, Setting Forth Proposals for Amending the Communications Act (Sept. 17, 1981).

When Congress failed to respond to the FCC's request, the agency launched its own extensive investigation of the doctrine's effects on broadcast free speech. In 1985, the Commission released its report based on this investigation, concluding the fairness doctrine no longer served the public interest.[191] This was true, according to the report, because a rapid expansion in the number of information services available to American audiences made them far less dependent upon broadcasting to be informed than they had been when the doctrine was adopted. In the absence of such continuing dependence, further intrusion by government in this area of broadcast free speech was not only unwarranted, in the Commission's view, but also dangerous, because it provided too many opportunities for political pressure to affect broadcast coverage of public issues.

Congress reacted to this FCC report by ordering the agency *not* to alter any of its existing fairness doctrine enforcement policies for a two-year period ending in August 1987. Instead, the Commission was directed to complete, within this two-year period, a detailed assessment of various alternative methods the agency might recommend for continuing to protect the public's interest in balanced treatment of controversial issues without unnecessarily infringing upon a broadcaster's editorial discretion.

During the preparation of its 1985 Fairness Doctrine report, the FCC had actually enforced its provisions for the first time in nearly a decade. In 1984 the Commission found that *Meredith Broadcasting*, owner of a television station in Syracuse, New York violated the doctrine's provisions by refusing to balance editorial advertisements supporting the building of a nuclear power plant with anti-nuclear energy public service announcements pointing out the drawbacks of this source of energy.[192]

Perhaps it was only coincidental that the Commission had decided to begin enforcing the doctrine again at this particular time, but there certainly was a clear tactical advantage in doing so. As long as Congress remained unwilling to relieve the FCC of its statutory obligation to enforce the fairness doctrine, the only avenue open for the Commission to escape this responsibility was to give the D.C. Court of Appeals the opportunity to declare its efforts to punish an alleged fairness doctrine violator to be unconstitutional and therefore unenforceable; exactly the situation that the *Meredith* case just happened to present.

But whatever the FCC's intentions, the Court of Appeals acted instead in *Telecommunications Research and Action Center (TRAC) v. FCC* to free the Commission from its legal obligation to enforce the fairness doctrine without considering the constitutionality of the doctrine itself.[193] In this relatively obscure case decided just prior to *Meredith*, the

191 Fairness Report, 102 FCC 2d 143 (1985).

192 *In re Syracuse Peace Council*, 57 R.R.2d 519 (1984).

193 801 F.2d 501 (D.C.Cir.1986).

Court held that the FCC was not obligated to make broadcast teletext services conform to fairness doctrine standards because, contrary to the prevailing view, the attempt of Congress in 1959 to incorporate the doctrine into the Communication Act had not been clear or specific enough to actually *codify* it into law.

As a result, when the Court returned the *Meredith* case to the Commission, it instructed the FCC to resolve the controversy simply on the basis of whether the agency *itself* believed the fairness doctrine served the public interest, because in its *TRAC* decision the Court had already released the Commission from any Congressional imposed obligation to enforce the doctrine.[194]

As the year 1987 began, members of Congress who wanted to preserve the doctrine realized that they would soon have to add a new, more clearly stated "fairness" clause to the Communications Act in order to prevent the FCC from exercising the freedom the Appeals Court had just given it to rescind the doctrine on its own. Congressional leaders succeeded in marshaling new "fairness" legislation through both houses of Congress during the spring of 1987 and a bill codifying the doctrine was presented to President Reagan by mid-June.[195]

During this period of feverish legislative activity, the NAB decided not to oppose this attempt to codify the fairness doctrine, fearing that such opposition might antagonize members of Congress whose support was needed for more important comparative renewal legislation.[196] Yet, even though the broadcast industry had been unwilling to campaign publicly to extend its right of freedom of expression under these circumstances, President Reagan decided on his own to veto the bill, a veto Congress lacked the votes to override.

After this veto, the FCC stood alone in the political spotlight. The Court of Appeals had found no language in the Communications Act compelling the Commission to continue to enforce the doctrine, and Congress had failed in its efforts to insert a new fairness doctrine provision in the Act.

At the time the agency was still bound by instructions from Congress not to abandon its enforcement of the doctrine prior to August 1987, when it was to provide Congress with a list of alternative methods for achieving the same objectives of balance in the broadcast coverage of controversial issues. On Aug. 4, 1987, it issued this study Congress had requested.[197]

---

[194] *Meredith Corp. v. FCC*, 809 F.2d 863 (D.C.Cir.1987). Because the Supreme Court had found that the fairness doctrine did not infringe upon broadcaster First Amendment rights in the *Red Lion* case, the lower court obviously preferred to avoid basing its decision on constitutional grounds.

[195] S. 742 was passed by the Senate on April 21 and H.R. 1934 was passed by the House in May. The reconciled bill was vetoed by President Reagan on June 19, 1987, and unable to override the veto, the legislation was returned to committee without action.

[196] "CBS's Bob McConnell and the Story Behind the Veto," *Broadcasting*, July 6, 1987, p. 33.

[197] Fairness Alternatives, 63 R.R.2d 488 (1987).

At the same time, however, the agency released its decision in the *Meredith* case, rescinding all broadcast fairness doctrine requirements, except those rules relating to "personal attack" and "political editorializing".[198]

Supporters of the doctrine in Congress reacted angrily to the Commission's action, drafting new fairness legislation while seeking some approach that could shelter it from presidential veto. But despite their best efforts, this second attempt to make the fairness doctrine part of the Communications Act also failed to survive President Reagan's veto in December 1987.

On review, the FCC's decision to rescind the Fairness Doctrine was upheld by a divided three-judge panel.[199] The Court found that the Commission had not acted in an arbitrary or capricious manner in abolishing both of the Doctrine's requirements; to seek out controversial issues of public importance and to cover them in a balanced, impartial fashion. In essence, the majority decision accepted the FCC's conclusions that the Fairness Doctrine tended to discourage broadcast coverage of controversial public issues and also tended to encourage too great a degree of governmental interference in areas of broadcast freedom of expression.

Each judge wrote a separate opinion. Judge Starr, while concurring in the result, argued that the constitutionality of the Doctrine itself was so closely interwoven into the Commission's action that its validity under the First Amendment needed to be considered independently by the court before reaching its decision. On the other hand, Judge Wald in his dissent contended that although no independent consideration of First Amendment issues was necessary, the FCC had not adequately demonstrated the need to repeal the "first prong" of the Doctrine, the requirement "to seek out controversial issues" when finding that the second or "balance" prong no longer serves the public interest.

At this point, then, the Commission's decision to repeal the basic requirements of the Fairness Doctrine has been sustained by the D.C. Court of Appeals, but because of the Court's refusal to base its decision on constitutional grounds, Congress has not been precluded from adopting legislation in the future that would once again require the FCC to enforce its requirements.

In the meantime the FCC continues to reduce the range of its fairness doctrine obligations, deciding by a 3–2 vote in 1992 that it will no longer enforce one of the doctrine's corollaries, the requirement of

---

198 *In re Complaint of Syracuse Peace Council Against WVTH, Memorandum Opinion and Order*, 63 RR2d 542 (1987). See also "The Decline and Fall of the Fairness Doctrine: Fairness Held Unfair," Broadcasting, Aug. 19, 1987, p. 27.

199 *Syracuse Peace Council v. FCC*, 867 F.2d 654 (D.C.Cir.1989). See also the FCC reconsideration of its *Meredith Broadcasting* decision that formed the basis for this appeal in *Syracuse Peace Council*, 64 R.R.2d 1073 (1988).

fairness in broadcast coverage of elections or ballot issues.[200] In a 7–5 vote affirming the Commission's decision, a federal appeals court agreed that the agency was not obligated to enforce any element of the doctrine unless Congress enacted legislation that required it to do so.[201]

68. THE END OF THE PERSONAL ATTACK AND POLITICAL EDITORIAL RULES

When a broadcast attacked the integrity or character of a person or group, or an editorial supports or opposes a political candidate, stations were required to promptly notify the person attacked or opposed, furnishing that person with the content of the attack, and offering air time to respond. A panel of the D.C. Circuit Court of Appeals ordered the FCC to repeal these two surviving elements of the Fairness Doctrine.

When the FCC issued its Fairness Report in 1985, concluding that the doctrine was inconsistent with the public interest and First Amendment because of the growth of new and alternate media outlets, it left standing the Personal Attack and Political Editorial rules. In part, this was because the FCC had made the rules, originally attachments to the Fairness Doctrine, as rules in their own right.[202]

The rules required that:[203]

> When, during the presentation of views on a controversial issue of public importance, an attack is made upon the honesty, character, integrity, or like personal qualities of an identified person or group, the licensee shall * * * transmit to the persons or group attacked * * * [the substance of the attack] and an offer of a reasonable opportunity to respond over the licensee's facilities.

In the case of political editorials, the rule provided that when licensees endorsed or opposed a legally qualified candidate, the station had to give the candidate notice of the time and date of the editorial, a copy of the script or tape of the editorial and an offer of a reasonable opportunity for the candidate or spokesman to respond on the air.[204]

The rules were to provide protections for people who were not wealthy or powerful enough to be able to afford a broadcast station. As the Supreme Court said in *Red Lion Broadcasting Co. v. FCC*,[205] given the scarcity of broadcast spectrum relative to interested users, the

---

200 *Arkansas AFL-CIO v. KARK-TV*, 70 R.R.2d 369 (1992).

201 *Arkansas AFL-CIO v. FCC*, 980 F.2d 1190 (8th Cir.1992).

202 Amendment of Part 73 of the Rules to Provide Procedures in the Event of a Personal Attack or Where a Station Editorializes as to Political Candidates, 8 F.C.C.2d 721 (1967).

203 47 C.F.R. § 73.1920(a) (1998).

204 47 C.F.R. § 73.1930(a).

205 *Red Lion Broadcasting v. FCC*, 395 U.S. 367, 89 S.Ct. 1794 (1969).

victims of personal attacks and editorials might be "unable without government assistance to gain access to * * * [broadcast media] * * * for expression of their views."[206] And so, in the *Red Lion* case, the Supreme Court upheld the constitutionality of the Fairness Doctrine and its attendant Personal Attack and Political Editorial rules.

At the same time, though the Supreme Court acknowledged that the Fairness Doctrine might well be reconsidered if, as the doctrine was enforced, there was a demonstration that instead of enhancing communication, the doctrine instead reduced it. The FCC concluded in its 1985 report that the Fairness Doctrine had that opposite effect and so repealed it in 1987. The D.C. Circuit upheld the constitutionality of the repeal although it should be noted that *Red Lion* remains good law. The FCC could find compelling reasons to reimpose it should conditions warrant.

The FCC also began to look at the Personal Attack and Editorial rules in 1983, issuing a Notice of Proposed Rule Making (NPRM) regarding the two rules. In doing so, the FCC acknowledged that broadcasters had made a "compelling case that the personal attack and political editorial rules do not serve the public interest."[207] When the FCC issued its Fairness Report in 1985, it did not mention the Personal Attack and Political Editorial rules. When the agency repealed the Fairness Doctrine, it did nothing to those two rules.

Broadcasters and other interested parties sought action and filed a petition for expedited rulemaking in 1987 and again in 1990. The 1990 petition argued that the two rules were obsolete and should have been repealed along with the Fairness Doctrine. The Radio-Television News Directors Association filed a petition with the federal courts to get the FCC to move on its rulemaking process. The court declined to order the FCC to act but left open the door for the broadcasters to try again.

Seven years later, the FCC announced that it was deadlocked. Two commissioners favored repeal and two others said they wanted to look into the matter further. The broadcasters went to court again in a second mandamus action. While this was occurring, two commissioners were replaced on the FCC but the result was a continuing deadlock. Then FCC Chairman William Kennard recused himself from the proceedings. In May of 1998, the federal court considering the mandamus action, ruled that the deadlock constituted the FCC's final word on the matter and moved forward.[208]

The broadcasters argued that the Fairness Doctrine's repeal and subsequent endorsement of that repeal by the federal court amounted to a rescission of the two rules because they were, after all, based on the

---

[206] Id. at 400.

[207] *Repeal of Modification of the Personal Attack and Political Editorial Rules*, 48 Fed.Reg. 28,295, 28,301 (1983).

[208] *Radio-Television News Directors Association v. FCC*, 184 F.3d 872 (D.C.Cir.1999).

Fairness Doctrine. But while it acknowledged the death of the Fairness Doctrine and the doctrine's parentage of the two rules, the FCC denied that the two rules ended when the Fairness Doctrine died.

The D.C. Circuit Court of Appeals took up the matter and considered whether the repeal of the Fairness Doctrine and its subsequent legal endorsement meant that the Personal Attack and Political Editorial rules were similarly dead. The appellate court noted that Syracuse Peace Council,[209] the case in which the D.C. Circuit endorse the end of Fairness, did not address the two rules. And, the appellate panel reasoned:[210]

> The challenged rules are substantially narrower and more refined than the fairness doctrine, which covered all public issues, rather than a subset of attacks and editorials. A broad rule can be flawed for reasons that do not affect its narrower adjuncts. Thus, it could be theoretically consistent for the FCC to have concluded that the public interest did not require fairness to all views all of the time, but that fairness to particular views in particular circumstances remained desirable.

The appellate panel looked at the history of the debate within the FCC and the First Amendment arguments raised by the broadcasters who maintained that the increasing number of channels of communication available to the public reduced the obligation on broadcast license holders. It weighed the interveners' arguments who brought up the continuing scarcity of access, the rationale for the rules in the first place, and the importance of assuring balanced coverage of local political issues.

In the end, the appellate panel sent the issue back to the FCC, but with an admonition to act quickly.[211]

> Accordingly, we grant the petitions for review and remand the case to afford the FCC an opportunity to provide an adequate justification for retaining the personal attack and political editorial rules, and for such proceedings as the FCC may determine are appropriate to implement this mandate. Given its prior delay in this proceeding, the FCC need act expeditiously.

The FCC did not do so. Instead, the FCC merely suspended the two rules for 60 days. The FCC said it would use the time to "obtain a better records on which to review the rules."[212] The Commission said it intended to examine what occurred during the fall 2000 political campaign to see the effect of the rules. And, the Commission said, the suspension, "will

---

[209] *Syracuse Peace Council v. FCC*, 867 F.2d 654 (D.C.Cir.1989).

[210] *Radio-Television News Directors Association v. FCC*, 184 F.3d 872, 879 (D.C. Cir.1999).

[211] Id. at 889.

[212] *In the Matter of Repeal or Modification of the Personal Attack and Political Editorial Rules*, 15 F.C.C.R. 19,973, 15 FCC Rcd 19,973 (FCC 2000).

allow us to work from a relatively clean slate," as the court suggested.[213] The Commission invited broadcasters to submit evidence in favor of a repeal 60 days after the end of the suspension. One of the pieces of evidence that the Commission sought was proof of a contention by broadcasters that there would be a dramatic increase in the number of political editorials that broadcasters would present if there were no Political Editorial Rule.[214]

> Suspension of the rule will permit us to test that prediction, and we request the Broadcasters to supply us with the information necessary to do so. More specifically, we will want information on the number of political editorials run during the suspension of the rules and comparative information concerning the number of editorials run during prior election cycles.

The Commission also wanted broadcasters to show the effect of the suspension of the Personal Attack Rule, comparing the number and character of the complaints about personal attacks made during the 60-day suspension compared with a similar 60-day period while the rule was in effect. In addition, the Commission asked groups that sought to preserve the two rules to provide their own evidence.

That did not sit well with the D.C. Circuit panel and on Oct. 11, 2000, a week after the FCC suspended the rules, the panel ordered the FCC to repeal both the Personal Attack and Political Editorial rules.[215] The appellate panel noted the delays in resolving the two rules.[216]

> The court has previously recounted the chronology of events, now exceeding twenty years when in response to a 1980 petition to vacate the rules, nothing happened for long periods of time.

The appellate panel noted that it had ordered the FCC to come up with justifications for retaining the two rules, not engage in further research. Further, the panel said, the results of the 60-day experiment were questionable at best.[217]

> * * * not only does the Order provide short notice for broadcasters to change their plans, but their conduct will in any event be affected by the fact that the rules will be reinstated on December 3, 2000. In short, the October 4th Order compounds the problems, affording no relief to petitioners and no assurance that final action is imminent, much less to be expeditiously accomplished. The petition to vacate the rules has been pending since 1980, and less stalwart petitioners might have abandoned their effort to obtain relief long ago. If these circumstances do

---

213 Ibid.

214 Ibid.

215 *Radio-Television News Directors Association v. FCC*, 229 F.3d 269 (D.C. Cir.2000), 28 Med.L.Rptr. 2465.

216 Id. at 270.

217 Id. at 271–272.

> not constitute agency action unreasonably delayed, it is difficult to imagine circumstances that would.

The court then issued its writ of mandamus compelling the FCC to immediately repeal the Personal Attack and Political Editorial rules. The repeal order did not mean the end for the two rules, the appellate court, noting the continued validity of *Red Lion* and the inherent power of the FCC to regular broadcasters.[218]

> Of course, the Commission may institute a new rule-making proceeding to determine whether, consistent with constitutional constraints, the public interest requires the personal attack and political editorial rules. These are issues that the court has yet to decide.

And while many commentators consider the two rules as moribund as the Fairness Doctrine, the possibility exists for them and the Fairness Doctrine itself to be resurrected in response to evidence that broadcasters, increasingly in the hands of a shrinking number of owners, are not serving the public interest.

69. PUBLIC BROADCASTING

Created to offer an alternative to commercial radio and television, public broadcasting has been sheltered from direct FCC control by a separate set of regulations.

Unlike most other Western industrial nations, no special provisions were made for non-commercial broadcasting when broadcast regulation began in the United States. Those college and university radio stations that had already received a broadcast license from the Commerce Department during the early 1920s were permitted to remain on the air, but no spectrum space was specifically set aside by either the Radio Act of 1927 or the Communications Act of 1934 to encourage the development of a nationwide educational or cultural broadcasting service.[219]

Reworking broadcast frequency assignments in 1945, the FCC—at the urging of Commissioner Frieda Hennock—allotted 10 percent of the new FM spectrum space to non-commercial applicants. In 1952, it allotted 10 percent of the TV spectrum for non-commercial stations.[220]

---

[218] Id. at 272.

[219] Many of the earliest radio stations had been experimental projects of some college physics or engineering department. Yet as late as 1927, when the FRC began issuing broadcast licenses, most of the more than 200 noncommercial stations it licensed were still operated by educational institutions. Within the decade however, their number had dwindled to less than 30, victims of both a Depression era economy and the absence of any clearly defined educational broadcasting objectives. Most were purchased by commercial broadcasters, eager to obtain their valuable frequency assignments. Sec. 307(C) of the Act of 1934 did require the FCC to report to Congress on the advisability of allocated fixed percentages of radio broadcasting facilities to various types of non-commercial broadcasters but the Commission reported back to Congress in 1935 that existing commercial stations were providing sufficient cultural and education programming to make any special non-commercial allocations unnecessary.

[220] The first FCC attempt to reserve space for non-commercial FM broadcasting actually occurred in 1940, but World War II suspended efforts to implement this allocation plan and it

This late recognition of non-commercial broadcasting—opposed by the National Association of Broadcasters—did little to stimulate educational broadcasting's growth. By 1960, for example, there were only 162 educational FM stations throughout the U.S., and only 44 educational TV stations.

What these educational television stations lacked in particular was any major source of funding capable of underwriting the massive production costs demanded by even a relatively modest television program schedule. In 1962 the federal government passed the first significant piece of legislation offering financial support for educational television, the Educational Television Facilities Act.

Five years later an extremely influential report issued by the Carnegie Commission on Educational Television resulted in Congress enacting the Public Broadcasting Act of 1967. This Act created the Corporation for Public Broadcasting (CPB), a non-profit, non-governmental organization charged with funding all forms of educational broadcasting in the United States.[221]

To protect this new non-commercial service from being dominated by a centralized bureaucracy in Washington, CPB was denied the right to provide any type of broadcast service of its own to the general public. Instead, it was directed to work with existing public broadcast stations to develop new forms of culturally or educationally oriented radio and television programming.

In 1970 CPB and a coalition of public broadcast stations formed the Public Broadcast Service (PBS) and National Public Radio (NPR), organizations established to distribute public radio and television programs to member stations. Four years later CPB and its member television stations created the Station Program Cooperative (SPC) plan, further decentralizing public television operation by making local stations primarily responsible for deciding which specific proposed television series productions will be funded.

When Congress established the Corporation for Public Broadcasting in 1967, it inserted new regulatory language in the Communications Act of 1934 specially designed to govern its functions.[222] The question soon arose whether by creating a separate set of regulatory requirements for

---

was substantially modified when reintroduced in 1945. Radio broadcast licenses have always been issued nationwide on a first-come, first-serve basis, only conditioned on an applicant being able to establish that transmission on the frequencies assigned will not interfere with other existing radio broadcast signals. In contrast, the FCC's FM and TV license allocation programs have assigned each specific authorized FM or TV channel to a particular locality in the United States, and designed a specified segment of the FM band and a specific proportion of all TV channels for non-commercial use.

[221] The Carnegie Commission had recommended the term "public" rather than "educational" to describe the new non-commercial broadcast services it proposed, contended that to label them as "educational" would unduly restrict their role as alternatives to commercial broadcasting.

[222] Statutory provisions of the Communications Act of 1934 that relate to CPB and public broadcasting are found in Sec. 390–399 of the Act of 1934.

public broadcasting, Congress had thereby exempted these stations from all other obligations imposed on broadcasters by the Communications Act.

In *Accuracy in Media, Inc. v. FCC* a federal court found that because Congress had included specific language in the Act of 1967 requiring public broadcasters to provide balanced and objective programming, it was Congress rather than the FCC that should be primarily responsible for supervising compliance with its directive.[223]

This special regulatory language governing non-commercial broadcasting had also denied those stations receiving funding from CPB the right to editorialize. In a 5–4 decision, the U.S. Supreme Court struck down this ban as an unconstitutional abridgement of broadcast free speech.[224]

In *Muir v. Alabama Educational Television Commission*, a majority of the huge en banc panel of 22 federal judges held that public broadcast stations had the same degree of editorial freedom in selecting and scheduling their programming as all other broadcasters.[225] Viewers challenging the refusal of two public broadcast stations to carry a controversial PBS documentary had argued that their tax supported status transformed them into "public forums" with less discretion to ignore the demands of the citizens who provided their funding, but the majority opinion rejected this distinction between commercial and non-commercial public interest standards.

Although most non-commercial licenses in the United States are held by public broadcast stations operated by state or local governments, universities, or school districts, other non-profit organizations are also licensed to broadcast by the FCC. Religious groups or institutions do not qualify for a reserved educational broadcast channel unless the primary emphasis of their programming is on education, but they as well as other community supported broadcasters such as "Pacifica" are authorized to receive a non-commercial broadcast license.

Periodic campaigns have been waged to deny religious broadcasters spectrum space because their opponents contend they are too narrowly oriented to serve the interests of the general public.[226] The FCC has never

---

[223] 521 F.2d 288 (D.C.Cir.1975), cert. denied 425 U.S. 934, 96 S.Ct. 1664 (1976). The court was particularly impressed by the argument that Congress had sought to shelter public broadcasting as much as possible from federal interference, and FCC regulation in the area of program content would operate to undercut that objective.

[224] *FCC v. League of Women Voters of California*, 468 U.S. 364, 104 S.Ct. 3106 (1984). In this instance, the station editorializing was not a public broadcaster but rather a non-commercial station that had accepted funding from CPB and therefore came under the federal statute.

[225] 688 F.2d 1033 (5th Cir.1982). The large panel of judges resulted from the consolidation of appeals from two conflicting lower court actions resulting from the refusal of two public broadcast stations to carry the controversial documentary "Death of a Princess" that portrayed Saudi Arabian society as being primitive and barbaric.

[226] See Multiple and Religious Ownership of Educational Stations, 34 R.R.2d 1217 (1975). The Commission rejected this argument, but does employ the "fair break" principle first

accepted this argument, however, maintaining that religious and other non-commercial broadcasters perform a useful service by enhancing that degree of diversity available to American broadcast audiences.

described in *Noe v. FCC*, 260 F.2d 739 (D.C.Cir.1958), requiring a broadcast licensee to give all listeners reasonable access to views opposing those held by the broadcaster.

CHAPTER 12

REGULATION OF ADVERTISING

70. FROM CAVEAT EMPTOR TO CONSUMER PROTECTION

The history of advertising in the United States has seen a gradual change away from the motto of caveat emptor ("let the buyer beware").

It is hardly news that advertising is both a necessity and a nuisance in American society. It encourages and advances the nation's economy by providing information to the public about goods and services. Although its economic role in supporting the news media has been criticized, advertising has paid the bills for most of the news and various entertainment which we receive. Historically, we owe advertising another debt. The rise of advertising in the Nineteenth Century did much to free the press from excessive reliance on political parties or government printing contracts—which tended to color news columns with their bias.

Advertising also played a major role in the growth of the Internet. Because the Internet was not owned by any one, single entity, it relied on individuals, institutions and businesses for its development. Various models for funding Internet access, services and sites were introduced as means of providing revenues to operate and grow. The free nature of the Internet was, however, harmful to legacy media, which relied on advertising that has since moved to free sites. Newspaper classified advertising,[1] once a major source of income from local and national sources, has declined significantly in the current decade from $19.6

[1] Classified advertising takes its name from the fact that the advertising is put into different classifications such as "Autos," "Antiques" or "Sporting Goods."

billion in 2000 to $4.7 billion in 2012[2] and trend models continue to predict declines.

Local television advertising revenue saw a benefit from the Supreme Court's *Citizens United* case that eliminated a system of campaign finance limits. Television political advertising spending was expected to hit $4.4 billion in the 2016 presidential election year.[3] TV political ad spending in the 2012 presidential election year was $3 billion.[4] The bulk of political advertising is spent in markets that cover swing states or important congressional districts.

Eventually though, advertising dominated the business model of the Internet with advertisers initially paying sites based on the number of visitors who might see their ads. As the Internet became more sophisticated, new models that required consumer interactivity, such as the click-through ad, gave advertisers proof of consumer contact. While advertising revenues were anemic in the early days of the Internet,[5] they have grown and Internet advertising is a significant part of most companies' advertising strategy. In 2014, the Internet generated $50.7 billion dollars, including mobile advertising.[6] Digital advertising now makes up more than a quarter of all media advertising.[7]

But, despite advertising's undeniably worthwhile contributions, this chapter unavoidably must emphasize the seamy side of American salesmanship. It will concentrate to a great extent upon issues raised by cheats and rascals. There can be little question that all too much advertising has been—and is—inexact, if not spurious and deceitful. Better units of the communications media now operate their advertising as a business with a definite obligation to the public. The realization evidently has dawned on some advertisers that unless their messages are both truthful and useful, the public may react unfavorably.

Advertising in the United States today has grown up from a colorful if sometimes sordid past. From the first days of the nation throughout the Nineteenth Century, the philosophy motivating advertising was largely *laissez faire.* Too much advertising, in spirit if not to the letter, resembled this 1777 advertisement for "Dr. RYAN's *incomparable* WORM *destroying* SUGAR PLUMBS, *Necessary to be kept in all* FAMILIES:"[8]

---

[2] Michael Barthel, Newspapers Fact Sheet: State of the Media 2015, Pew Research Center, April 29, 2015.

[3] Peter Overby, "Political TV Advertising Expected To Cost $4.4 Billion In 2016," *NPR*, July 24, 2015.

[4] Ibid.

[5] The Internet Advertising Bureau reported in February of 1999 that Internet advertising for the first nine months of 1998 was $1.3 billion. The Bureau reported in November of 2007 that revenue for the first nine months of 2007 was $15.2 billion.

[6] Kenneth Olmstead and Kristine Lu, Digital News-Revenue Fact Sheet, State of the News Media 2015, Pew Research Center, April 29, 2015.

[7] Ibid.

[8] *Pennsylvania Gazette*, March 12, 1777.

> The plumb is a great diuretic, cleaning the veins of slime; it expels wind, and is a sovereign medicine in the cholic and griping of the guts. It allays and carries off vapours which occasion many disorders of the head. It opens all obstructions in the stomach, lungs, liver, veins, and bladder; causes a good appetite, and helps digestion.

Such exploitation of the *laissez faire* philosophy went unpunished for more than a century of the nation's existence. There was little or no regulation; what would be termed unreliable or even fraudulent advertising was published by some of the most respected newspapers and periodicals. The general principle seemed to be that advertising columns were an open business forum with space for sale to all who applied.

Before 1900, advertising had little established ethical basis. The liar and the cheat capitalized on glorious claims for dishonest, shoddy merchandise. The faker lured the ill and suffering to build hopes on pills and tonics of questionable composition. Cures were promised by the bottle. Fortunes were painted for those who invested in mining companies of dubious reliability. Foods often were adulterated.

Exposés of frauds and fraud promoters who were using advertising to ensnare new prospects were important early in the Twentieth Century. Mark Sullivan exposed medical fakes and frauds in the *Ladies Home Journal* in 1904. Upton Sinclair's novel, *"The Jungle,"* revolted readers with its description of filthy conditions in meat-packing plants. Spurred by such exposés, Congress passed the Pure Food and Drug Act in 1906. Despite being a truth-in-labeling measure the 1906 statute did nothing to insure truth in advertising.[9]

Campaigning against advertising chicanery, many magazines and newspapers exposed fraudulent practices.[10] Some newspapers of this period, including the *Cleveland Press* and other Scripps-McRae League papers, monitored advertisements, refusing those which appeared to be fraudulent or misleading. A Scripps-McRae official asserted that the newspaper group turned away approximately $500,000 in advertising revenue in one year by rejecting advertisements.

Such self-regulation has grown considerably over the years, and legal restraints have grown, too. People working in advertising come under all the laws which affect other branches of mass communications, including libel, invasion of privacy, copyright infringement, and obscenity. In addition, there are batteries of statutes and regulatory powers aimed at advertising *in addition to* the laws which affect, for example, the editorial side of a newspaper. There's the Food and Drug Administration (FDA), the Securities Exchange Commission (SEC), the Federal Communications Commission (FCC), and quite an alphabet soup of other federal agencies which get into the advertising regulation act.

9 Ibid.

10 Ibid.

Beyond that, there is increasing activity at the state level to attempt to control false or deceptive advertising. This chapter, then, can be only a sparse survey of advertising regulatory structures.

In addition to regulation of advertising, this chapter takes up issues relating to trademarks, those distinctive symbols that let us know that up there, in the distance, is a place where we can get a cheeseburger and fries. The golden arches gleaming in the distance on the interstate are a mark that tells us with confidence all that we need to know, for good or ill, about the food, service and cleanliness of the restaurant. Trade and service marks are important to the advertiser who seeks to build consumer confidence and loyalty. Companies zealously guard those marks as they are the lifeblood of continued business.

71. ADVERTISING AND THE CONSTITUTION

Beginning in 1975, some commercial advertising began to receive protection under the First Amendment.

Commercial speech often is referred to as a stepchild of the First Amendment. Over the years, commercial speech—or advertising, to use an everyday term—was denied freedoms of speech and press granted to unconventional religious minorities,[11] to persons accused of blasphemy,[12] to free-love advocates,[13] and to persons sued for defaming public officials or public figures.[14] During the 1970s and 1980s, the Supreme Court—however grudgingly and qualifiedly—held that just because a message is disseminated as paid-for advertising does not wipe out all First Amendment protection for that message.[15] By the late 1990s, however, Supreme Court backing for constitutional support for advertising evidently was wobbling.[16]

Back in 1942, evidently with little reflection or receiving of evidence, the Supreme Court of the United States denied advertising First Amendment protection in *Valentine v. Chrestensen*.[17] In 1940, F.J. Chrestensen owned a World War I submarine moored at an East River pier in New York City. As World War II threatened to engulf the U.S., Chrestensen was trying to make money by charging for tours of a "U-

---

11 *Minersville School Dist. v. Gobitis*, 310 U.S. 586, 60 S.Ct. 1010 (1940).

12 *Joseph Burstyn, Inc. v. Wilson*, 343 U.S. 495, 72 S.Ct. 777 (1952).

13 *Kingsley Intern. Pictures Corp. v. Regents of N.Y.U.*, 360 U.S. 684, 688–689, 79 S.Ct. 1362, 1365 (1959).

14 See *New York Times Co. v. Sullivan*, 376 U.S. 254, 84 S.Ct. 710 (1964) and later cases, including *Rosenblatt v. Baer*, 383 U.S. 75, 86 S.Ct. 669 (1966); *Curtis Pub. Co. v. Butts, Associated Press v. Walker*, 388 U.S. 130, 87 S.Ct. 1975 (1967), and *St. Amant v. Thompson*, 390 U.S. 727, 88 S.Ct. 1323 (1968).

15 *Bigelow v. Virginia*, 421 U.S. 809, 95 S.Ct. 2222 (1975); *Virginia State Board of Pharmacy v. Virginia Citizens Consumer Council*, 425 U.S. 748, 96 S.Ct. 1817 (1976).

16 See *Posadas de Puerto Rico v. Tourism Co.*, 478 U.S. 328, 106 S.Ct. 2968 (1986); *Board of Trustees of the State University of New York v. Fox*, 492 U.S. 469, 109 S.Ct. 3028 (1989), and *Austin v. Michigan Chamber of Commerce*, 494 U.S. 652, 110 S.Ct. 1391 (1990).

17 *Valentine v. Chrestensen*, 316 U.S. 52, 62 S.Ct. 920 (1942).

Boat." New York City officials, however, ordered him not to distribute handbills advertising the submarine. Chrestensen's handbill listed an admission fee. New York City Police Commissioner Lewis J. Valentine said that the city's Sanitary Code forbade distributing commercial advertising matter in the streets.[18]

Chrestensen changed his handbill. One side then consisted of a notice about the submarine, but reference to the admission fee was deleted. The other side of the redone handbill was used to protest against city policies he disliked. Police officials then told Chrestensen he could distribute a handbill criticizing the city, but that invitation to visit the submarine was a commercial ad and was not permitted. In 1942, the Supreme Court held unanimously that although streets may be used to communicate information and disseminate opinion, the Constitution does not restrain government from controlling "purely commercial advertising," and that it is not entitled to First Amendment protection.[19]

The 1942 *Valentine v. Chrestensen* decision stated the law for some years to come. In 1959, in a now-famous concurring opinion in *Cammarano v. United States*, Justice William O. Douglas complained that the *Chrestensen* decision was "casual, almost offhand. And it has not survived reflection." Cammarano, a beer distributor, had tried to deduct, as a business expense, a contribution to a fund used to buy political ads to oppose a ballot measure which would have turned all wine and beer sales over to a state agency. Although he concurred in the decision denying Cammarano the IRS deduction, Justice Douglas wrote: " * * * I find it impossible to say that the owners of the * * * business who were fighting for their lives in opposing these initiative [ballot] measures were not exercising First Amendment rights."[20]

N.Y. TIMES V. SULLIVAN AND ADVERTISING

Ironically, the "breakthrough" case in protecting advertising under the Constitution is little thought of as a "commercial speech case." In part, however, that's exactly what the landmark 1964 libel decision of *New York Times v. Sullivan*[21] was. In *Sullivan*, the Supreme Court granted First Amendment protection for advertisements which deal with important political or social matters.

The Supreme Court held that such a reliance on *Chrestensen* to deny First Amendment protection to all advertising was "wholly misplaced." Writing for the *Sullivan* majority, Justice William J. Brennan, Jr. declared:[22]

---

18 Ibid. at 54, 921.

19 Ibid.

20 *Cammarano v. U.S.*, 358 U.S. 498, 79 S.Ct. 524 (1959).

21 *New York Times v. Sullivan*, 376 U.S. 254, 84 S.Ct. 710 (1964).

22 Ibid. at 266, 718.

> The publication here [in *Times v. Sullivan*] was not a "commercial" advertisement in the sense in which the word was used in *Chrestensen*. It communicated information, expressed opinion, recited grievances, protested claimed abuses, and sought financial support on behalf of a [civil rights] movement whose existence and objectives are matters of the highest public concern. * * * That the *Times* was paid for publishing the advertisement is as immaterial in this connection as is the fact that newspapers and books are sold.

What advertising, then, was protected by the First Amendment after *New York Times v. Sullivan*? Not all advertising—and especially, not advertising for an illegal activity—the Supreme Court said in *Pittsburgh Press Co. v. Pittsburgh Commission on Human Relations*. A Pittsburgh ordinance empowered the city's human relations commission to issue cease and desist orders against discriminatory hiring practices. The *Pittsburgh Press* ran "Help Wanted" ads in columns labeled "Jobs—Male Interest," and "Jobs—Female Interest." The city commission sought—and won—a cease and desist order against the *Pittsburgh Press* to prevent it from publishing illegal advertisements.[23]

Writing for the Court's five-member majority, Justice Lewis Powell held that discrimination in employment is an illegal commercial activity under the Pittsburgh ordinance. Justice Powell rejected the argument of attorneys for the *Pittsburgh Press* that the order violated the First Amendment by tampering with the newspaper's editorial judgment in accepting and placing ads. "We have no doubt," Justice Powell wrote, "that a newspaper constitutionally could be forbidden to publish a want ad proposing sale of narcotics or soliciting prostitution."[24] The principle here is that advertising of an illegal activity is not protected by the First Amendment.

BIGELOW V. VIRGINIA

It should be emphasized that the Court, in *New York Times v. Sullivan*, drew a distinction between "commercial advertising" which attempted to sell products or services and other kinds of expression. This distinction, however, was too simple. Some products or services—by their very nature—are matters of public debate or controversy, and advertisements for those products or services may have the characteristics and importance of political speech. A 1975 Virginia case involving advertising about the availability and legality of abortions in New York—the case called *Bigelow v. Virginia*—showed that "commercial speech" can have some degree of constitutional protection.

---

[23] *Pittsburgh Press Co. v. Pittsburgh Commission on Human Relations*, 413 U.S. 376, 377, 93 S.Ct. 2553, 2555 (1973).

[24] Ibid. at 387, 2560.

Early in 1971, an advertisement for a New York-based abortion service—saying only that there were no residency requirements and offering to provide information and counseling—was published in the *Virginia Weekly*, a newspaper focusing its coverage on the University of Virginia. Jeffrey C. Bigelow was managing editor and a director of the newspaper when it published the ad.[25]

A Virginia court convicted Bigelow of violating a section of the Virginia Code: "If any person, by publication, lecture, advertisement, or by the sale or circulation of any publication, or in any other manner, shall encourage or prompt the procuring of an abortion or miscarriage, he shall be guilty of a misdemeanor."[26] The Virginia Supreme Court affirmed Bigelow's conviction, declaring that because the ad involved was a "commercial advertisement," Bigelow's First Amendment claim was not valid. Such an advertisement, said the Virginia Supreme Court, " 'may be constitutionally prohibited by the state, particularly where, as here, the advertising relates to the medical-health field.' "[27]

The Supreme Court overruled the Virginia Supreme Court. Writing for a 7–2 majority, Justice Harry Blackmun concluded that Virginia courts erred in assuming that advertising is not entitled to First Amendment protection. Justice Blackmun distinguished the Virginia case from *Chrestensen*. He wrote that the handbill ad involved in *Chrestensen* did no more than propose a purely commercial transaction, while The *Virginia Weekly's* advertisement about abortions "contained factual material of clear 'public interest.' "[28]

A State, Justice Blackmun wrote, "may not * * * bar a citizen of another State from disseminating information about an activity that is legal in another State." Although advertising "may be subject to reasonable regulation that serves a legitimate public interest," some commercial speech is still worthy of constitutional protection. "The relationship of speech to the marketplace of products or services does not make it valueless in the marketplace of ideas."[29]

VIRGINIA STATE BOARD OF PHARMACY V. VIRGINIA CITIZENS CONSUMER COUNCIL, INC.

What the Supreme Court started in 1975 with the *Bigelow* case continued the next year with the decision in the *Virginia State Board of Pharmacy v. Virginia Citizens Consumer Council, Inc.*, case. In fact, an excellent study of advertising law emphasized—as of 1991—that *Virginia State Board of Pharmacy* represented the decision in which the

---

[25] *Bigelow v. Virginia*, 421 U.S. 809, 95 S.Ct. 2222 (1975).

[26] Ibid. at 813, 2228.

[27] *Bigelow v. Virginia*, 421 U.S. 809, 814, 95 S.Ct. 2222, 2229 (1975), quoting *Bigelow v. Commonwealth*, 213 Va. 191, 193–195, 191 S.E.2d 173, 174–176 (1972).

[28] Ibid. at 819, 2231.

[29] Ibid. at 826, 2235.

Supreme Court gave broadest First Amendment protection for commercial advertising.[30]

The *Virginia State Board of Pharmacy v. Virginia Citizens Consumer Council, Inc.,* dealt with a matter of price advertising. It arose because a Virginia statute forbade "the advertising of the price for any prescription drug." This statute was challenged in a lawsuit by two consumer organizations and by a Virginia citizen who had to take prescription drugs on a daily basis. The plaintiffs claimed that the First Amendment entitled users of prescription drugs to receive information from pharmacists—through advertisements or other promotional means—about the price of those drugs.[31]

By a 7–1 vote expressed via Justice Blackmun's majority opinion in *Virginia State Board of Pharmacy,* the Court overturned the state's ban on advertising of prescription drug prices.[32] The Supreme Court declared that the consumer had a great interest in the free flow of commercial information—perhaps a greater interest than in the day's most important political debate. The individuals hardest hit by the suppression of prescription price information, wrote Justice Blackmun, were the poor, the sick and the old.[33]

Subsequent cases indicated that commercial speech could receive constitutional protection in a variety of areas. Later in 1976, for example, the *Horner-Rausch Optical Co.* case, decided by a Tennessee court, declared an administrative regulation against price ads for eyeglasses to be unconstitutional.[34] And in 1977, the U.S. Supreme Court decided the now famous "lawyer ad case," *Bates v. State Bar of Arizona.*[35] By a 5–4 margin, the Court held that lawyers have a constitutional right to advertise their prices for their various services.

Justice Blackmun's majority opinion in *Bates* said, "[I]t is entirely possible that advertising will serve to reduce, not to advance, the cost of legal services to the consumer." In this case, the consumer's need for information about the cost of legal services was held to outweigh the legal profession's interest in having a regulated self-restraint against virtually all kinds of advertising by attorneys. The majority opinion added that the time, place and manner of advertising may be regulated, and that false or misleading advertising by lawyers may be forbidden.[36]

---

[30] For an excellent discussion of the *Virginia Board of Pharmacy* case and, indeed, of the key cases involving advertising and the First Amendment to 1991, see Richard T. Kaplar, *Advertising Rights, The Neglected Freedom: Toward a New Doctrine of Commercial Speech* (Washington, D.C.: The Media Institute, 1991).

[31] *Virginia State Board of Pharmacy v. Virginia Citizens Consumer Council, Inc.*, 425 U.S. 748, 96 S.Ct. 1817 (1976).

[32] Ibid. at 759–761, 1824–1825.

[33] Ibid. at 763, 1826.

[34] *Horner-Rausch Optical Co. v. Ashley*, 547 S.W.2d 577 (Tenn.App.1976).

[35] *Bates v. State Bar of Arizona*, 433 U.S. 350, 97 S.Ct. 2691 (1977).

[36] Ibid. at 383–384, 2706–2709. Advertising by attorneys can go too far, however, when it includes a lawyer's visiting the family of a person injured in an auto accident, and even visiting

THE BELLOTTI CASE: PROTECTING CORPORATE SPEECH

If abortion clinics, pharmacists, and lawyers have some First Amendment protection for their ads, what about corporations right to exercise political speech? In *First National Bank of Boston v. Bellotti*,[37] the U.S. Supreme Court invalidated a Massachusetts statute forbidding business corporations from making contributions or expenditures " 'for the purpose of * * * influencing or affecting the vote on any question submitted to the voters, other than one materially affecting the property, business, or assets of the corporation.' " That statute provided that a corporation violating its provisions could be fined $50,000 and that its officers could be fined up to $10,000, imprisoned for up to one year, or both.

The U.S. Supreme Court, however, found the Massachusetts statute unconstitutional. Writing for the Court, Justice Lewis Powell declared that the political argument the bank wished to make "is at the heart of the First Amendment's protection." He added, "[t]he question in this case, simply put, is whether the corporate identity of the speaker deprives the proposed speech of what otherwise would be its clear entitlement to protection."[38]

Justice Powell cited the Court's 1970s commercial speech cases—including *Virginia State Board of Pharmacy*—as illustrating "that the First Amendment goes beyond protection of the press and the self-expression of individuals to prohibit government from limiting the stock of information from which members of the public may draw." Thus corporations' political speech was entitled to First Amendment protection.[39] *Bellotti* was limited by subsequent court decisions until *Citizens United.*

CENTRAL HUDSON AND A FOUR-PART TEST

In 1980, the Supreme Court of the United States created an important test to try to outline just when advertising might be deemed worthy of constitutional protection. This case, *Central Hudson Gas & Electric Corp. v. Public Service Commission of New York*, involved a commission order that the utility stop promoting consumption of electricity. This order was promulgated during an energy shortage, under the assumption that cutting Central Hudson's "buy appliances" advertising might assist in energy conservation. The U.S. Supreme Court, however, invalidated New York's ban on promotional advertising

---

with the driver herself in her hospital room. Personal solicitation of that nature (bedpan chasing?) is unreasonable. See *Ohralik v. Ohio State Bar Ass'n*, 436 U.S. 447, 98 S.Ct. 1912 (1978). If lawyer advertising is fundamentally misleading, it will not be tolerated: See *Peel v. Attorney Registration and Disciplinary Com'n of Illinois*, 496 U.S. 91, 110 S.Ct. 2281 (1990).

[37] *First National Bank of Boston v. Bellotti*, 435 U.S. 765, 98 S.Ct. 1407 (1978).

[38] Ibid. at 778, 1416 (1978).

[39] Ibid. at 783, 1409 (1978).

by electric utilities. Justice Powell, writing for an 8–1 Court, laid out a four-part test:[40]

> In commercial speech cases, then, a four-part analysis has developed. At the outset, we must determine [1] whether the expression is protected by the First Amendment. For commercial speech to come within that provision, it at least must concern lawful activity and not be misleading. [2] Next, we ask whether the asserted governmental interest is substantial. If both inquiries yield positive answers, we must determine [3] whether the regulation directly advances the governmental interest asserted, and [4] whether it is not more extensive than necessary to serve that interest.

Because advertising promoting use of electricity was seen as protected by the First Amendment, and because the ad was neither misleading nor "unlawful," the New York regulation was overturned as unconstitutional. Although the state had a substantial interest in energy conservation, the state's regulation was more extensive than necessary. No demonstration was made that the state's interest in energy conservation could not have been served adequately by a more limited restriction on the content of promotional advertisements.[41]

NARROWING CONSTITUTIONAL PROTECTION: POSADAS DE PUERTO RICO V. TOURISM COMPANY

For eleven years after deciding the abortion advertising case of *Bigelow v. Virginia* (1975),[42] the U.S. Supreme Court held that if a product or service was legal and was the subject of public or corporate interest, truthful ads for that product or service had First Amendment protection.[43] As noted earlier in this section, this protection covered ads for abortion referral services, prices of prescription drugs, eyeglasses, lawyers, banks' political stances, promotions by a public utility during an energy shortage.

This expansiveness came to a halt in 1986, when the Supreme Court ruled that government may forbid truthful ads for some products or services, even though they are legal for sale. Not surprisingly, this decision—involving Puerto Rico's regulations against *local* ads

---

[40] *Central Hudson Gas & Electric Corp. v. Public Service Com'n of New York,* 447 U.S. 557, 100 S.Ct. 2343 (1980).

[41] Ibid. See also a related case, *Consolidated Edison Co. of New York, Inc. v. Public Service Commission of New York,* 447 U.S. 530, 100 S.Ct. 2326 (1980), 6 Med.L.Rptr. 1518. There, the Court struck down an order forbidding the utility's including in mailings statements of "Con Ed's" views on public policy controversies. Powell, quoting *First National Bank of Boston v. Bellotti,* 435 U.S. 765, 98 S.Ct. 1407 (1978), wrote for the Court that the Commission's censorship attempt "strikes at the heart of the freedom to speak."

[42] *Bigelow v. Virginia,* 421 U.S. 809, 95 S.Ct. 2222 (1975).

[43] See also *New York Times Co. v. Sullivan,* 376 U.S. 254, 84 S.Ct. 710 (1964), the pivotal libel case extending First Amendment protection to ads dealing with major social or political concerns.

promoting gambling in Puerto Rico's legal casinos—alarmed the tobacco and liquor industries in the United States.[44]

When, in *Posadas de Puerto Rico v. Tourism Company*,[45] a hotel-casino challenged the advertising regulations as unconstitutional, it did seem to have plenty to complain about. The regulations were sweepingly broad. For example, consider this Tourism Company memo:[46]

> "This prohibition includes the use of the word 'casino' in matchbooks, lighters, envelopes, inter-office and/or external correspondence, invoices, napkins, brochures, menus, elevators, glasses, plates, lobbies, banners, flyers, paper holders, pencils, telephone books, directories, bulletin boards or in any hotel dependency or object which may be accessible to the public in Puerto Rico."

When the case reached the U.S. Supreme Court, Justice (subsequently Chief Justice) William H. Rehnquist wrote for the Court's five-member majority. He said the issue was whether the Puerto Rico statute and regulations "impermissibly suppressed commercial speech in violation of the First Amendment and the equal protection and due process guarantees of the United States Constitution."[47]

Justice Rehnquist said that this case involved " * * * the restriction of pure commercial speech which does 'no more than propose a commercial transaction.' "[48] That meant, he wrote, that First Amendment discussion of this case was controlled by the four-part analysis set forth in the *Central Hudson Gas & Electric Corp.* case discussed earlier.

The Court's majority opinion concluded that advertising of casino gambling in Puerto Rico "concerns a lawful activity and is not misleading or fraudulent, at least in the abstract."[49] Even so, Justice Rehnquist's majority opinion deferred to Puerto Rico's legislative judgment: It was not an unreasonable policy choice to believe that excessive casino gambling by Puerto Rico's residents would produce great harm to citizens welfare. The Court's majority concluded that the hotel/casino's First Amendment claims had been rejected properly.

He wrote acidly that even though products or activities including cigarettes, alcoholic beverages, and prostitution had been legalized for sale in some jurisdictions did not mean that their advertising could not be limited.[50]

---

[44] Stuart Taylor, Jr., "High Court, 5–4, Sharply Limits Constitutional Protection for Ads," The *New York Times*, July 2, 1986, p. 2 (National Edition).

[45] *Posadas de Puerto Rico v. Tourism Company*, 478 U.S. 328, 106 S.Ct. at 2968.

[46] Ibid. at 333, 2972–2973.

[47] Ibid. at 328, 2970.

[48] Ibid. at 340, 2976.

[49] Ibid. at 340–341, 2975.

[50] Ibid. at 346, 2977.

The *Posadas* decision promised to make it more difficult to overturn State laws that constrain commercial free speech. The *Central Hudson* test Justice Rehnquist claimed to be applying in the *Posadas* case had permitted States to use only the "least restrictive means" available in regulating advertising messages. In fact, however, *Posadas* simply required a State to demonstrate that any advertising laws it adopts are "reasonable" ones, in effect diluting the four-part test from *Central Hudson* and making First Amendment protection for advertising seem less secure.[51]

Posadas would be rejected in *44 Liquormart, Inc. v. Rhode Island*, 517 U.S. 484, 116 S.Ct. 1495 (1996) which follows below. For a time, though, it exercised some influence on commercial speech cases.

RETHINKING POSADAS: EDENFIELD V. FANE (1993), RUBIN V. COORS AND FLORIDA BAR V. WENT FOR IT INC.

As noted earlier in this chapter, the four-part test from *Central Hudson Gas & Electric Corp. v. Public Service Commission of New York* (1980) laid out a routine for determining whether commercial speech qualified for First Amendment protection.[52] Following that four-part test, and until *Posadas de Puerto Rico v. Tourism Commission* (1986), it seemed that if advertising was not misleading and was about a lawful service or product, it had First Amendment protection. In *Posadas*, however the Supreme Court of the United States upheld efforts to protect Puerto Ricans from the lure of *legalized* casino gambling through sweeping local advertising regulations.[53]

Back in 1986, *Posadas* was seen as shrinking hard-won gains for constitutional protection for advertising. This decision made it more difficult to overturn state laws constraining commercial speech. The *Central Hudson* test Justice Rehnquist claimed to be applying in *Posadas* had permitted states to use only the "least restrictive means" in regulating advertising. In fact, however, *Posadas* simply required a State to demonstrate that any advertising laws it adopted were "reasonable." In 1993, however, the judicial pendulum moved back toward reestablishing protections eroded by the *Posadas* decision in a decision about regulating advertising by accountants.

---

[51] See Denise M. Trauth and John L. Huffman, "The Commercial Speech Doctrine: Posadas Revisionism," *Communication and the Law* (Feb. 1988), pp. 43–56. For an example of a case strengthening state regulation of advertising, see *Board of Trustees of State University of New York v. Fox*, 492 U.S. 469, 109 S.Ct. 3028 (1989).

[52] *Central Hudson Gas & Electric Corp. v. Public Service Comm'n of New York*, 447 U.S. 557, 100 S.Ct. 2343 (1980).

[53] *Posadas de Puerto Rico v. Tourism Company of Puerto Rico*, 478 U.S. 328, 333, 106 S.Ct. 2968, 2973 (1986).

EDENFIELD V. FANE

Scott Fane, a certified public accountant (CPA) licensed in Florida, sued the Florida Board of Accountancy to prevent the Board from enforcing one of its rules. That rule prohibited CPAs from " 'direct, in-person, uninvited solicitation' "to get new clients. A U.S. district court enjoined the rule's enforcement, and the Court of Appeals, 11th Circuit, upheld the injunction. Writing for an 8–1 Supreme Court, Justice Kennedy ruled that as applied to CPA advertising, "Florida's prohibition is inconsistent with the free-speech guarantees of the First and Fourteenth Amendments." Using language far more supportive of commercial speech than that used in *Posadas,* Justice Kennedy wrote for the Court:[54]

> The commercial marketplace * * * provides a forum where ideas and information flourish. Some of these ideas and information are vital, some of slight worth. But the general rule is that the speaker and the audience, not the government, assess the value of the information presented. Thus even a communication that does no more than propose a commercial transaction is entitled to the coverage of the First Amendment.

RUBIN V. COORS

If *Edenfield* sounded supportive of commercial speech, consider the U.S. Supreme Court's specific downplaying of *Posadas* and reaffirmation of the *Central Hudson* test in *Rubin, Secretary of the Treasury v. Coors Brewing Company* (1995). Coors brought an action for a declaratory judgment that the Federal Alcohol Administration Act (FAAA) section forbidding use of beer labels listing alcohol content violated the First Amendment. Upholding a Tenth Circuit ruling, the U.S. Supreme Court agreed 9–0 that the FAAA had overstepped itself in trying to control brewers "strength war" advertising.

Writing for the unanimous court, Justice Clarence Thomas agreed with the Tenth Circuit's conclusion that no relationship had been shown between factual information about alcohol content and competition based on that information. Justice Thomas relied on language from *Central Hudson* asking " 'whether the regulation advances the governmental interest asserted, and whether it is not more extensive than is necessary to serve that interest.' "[55] The court relied on federalism, a faith in state powers, holding that states have sufficient authority to ban the disclosure of alcohol content if they chose to do so. Then, citing *Edenfield,* Justice Thomas concluded that the FAA Act " * * * would not withstand First Amendment scrutiny because the Government's regulation of

[54] *Edenfield v. Fane,* 507 U.S. 761, 113 S.Ct. 1792, 1798 (1993).

[55] *Rubin, Secretary of the Treasury v. Coors Brewing Company,* 514 U.S. 476, 486, 115 S.Ct. 1585, 1591 (1995). The FAAA subsection under scrutiny was § 5 (3) 2.

speech is not sufficiently tailored to its goal."[56] Therefore, the Court found that the statute section forbidding advertising of alcohol strength on malt beverage labels flunked the *Central Hudson* test.

Relying on federalism, a faith in state powers, Justice Thomas concluded that the federal government's interest in preserving its authority in the alcohol labeling area is not exclusive. " * * * [O]ne state's decision to permit brewers to disclose alcohol content will not preclude neighboring States from effectively banning such disclosure of information within their borders."[57]

FLORIDA BAR V. WENT FOR IT, INC.

First Amendment lawyers found the outcome of *Rubin*, discussed above, to be a welcome return to heightened protection for commercial speech. However, in the *Went For It* decision, the U.S. Supreme Court—by a vote of 5–4—found it could bend the *Central Hudson* test to uphold a Florida State Bar rule forbidding lawyers from sending direct mail solicitations to disaster victims for 30 days after harm had befallen them or their loved ones.[58]

Writing for the Court, Justice Sandra Day O'Connor paid specific attention to a survey done by the Florida Bar, showing substantial public opposition to direct mail from attorneys. Again, commercial speech had lesser standing in the majority opinion's phrasing about " 'its limited measure of protection, commensurate with its subordinate protection in the scale of First Amendment values.' "[59]

Curiously, the four-part *Central Hudson* test discussed earlier was here termed a "three-part test" by the Court. The first part of the *Central Hudson* test—that the commercial speech must be neither false nor misleading and must be for a legal product or activity—was used as a preamble for the rest of the test. As renumbered, that changed the test to:[60]

(1) Does government have a substantial interest in restricting this particular commercial speech?

(2) Does the regulation directly advance that governmental interest?

---

[56] Ibid. at 1591–1592.

[57] Ibid. at 1591. Here, Justice Thomas distinguished *Rubin* from *United States v. Edge Broadcasting Co.*, 509 U.S. 418, 113 S.Ct. 2696 (1993). In *Edge*, the U.S. Supreme Court upheld a federal law prohibiting lottery advertising on broadcast stations located in states that did not operate lotteries.

[58] *Florida Bar v. Went For It, Inc.*, 515 U.S. 618, 622, 115 S.Ct. 2371, 2375 (1995).

[59] Ibid. at 623, 2376, 1803, quoting *Board of Trustees of the State University of New York v. Fox*, 492 U.S. 469, 477, 109 S.Ct. 3028 (1989) quoting *Ohralik v. Ohio State Bar Assn.*, 436 U.S. 447, 456, 98 S.Ct. 1912, 1918 (1978).

[60] Ibid. at 624, 2376.

(3) Is the regulation more extensive than needed to serve that governmental interest?

In her majority opinion, Justice O'Connor wrote "[W]e have consistently recognized that 'the State's interest in protecting the well-being, tranquility, and privacy of the home is certainly of the highest order in a free and civilized society.'" They also expressed concern about protecting the integrity of the legal profession.[61] The majority also found that the Florida Bar's rule against direct mail solicitation of disaster victims directly advanced an important government interest and was not too extensive in serving that interest.[62]

This led to some acrimony on the Court, with Justice Kennedy (joined by Justices Stevens, Souter, and Ginsburg) arguing in dissent that commercial speech has a higher constitutional value than admitted to by the majority. Justice Kennedy declared that the Court "today undercuts this guaranty in an important class of cases and unsettles leading First Amendment precedents, at the expense of those victims most in need of legal assistance."[63]

But by a margin of one vote, Justice O'Connor and the majority upheld the Florida Bar Rule against direct mail solicitation of disaster victims during their first 30 days after being injured or suffering a loss. It may be that she quoted, in passing a better rule on how to protect free expression and deal with direct mail. In another direct mail case, the Supreme Court advised that the " 'short, though regular, journey from mail box to trash can * * * is an acceptable burden, at least so far as the Constitution is concerned.' "[64]

SWOOSH! IS A NIKE PR CAMPAIGN POLITICAL OR COMMERCIAL SPEECH?

Nike v. Kasky had all the earmarks of a landmark freedom of speech decision by the Supreme Court of the United States. Does public relations speech have full First-Amendment protection as political speech, or does it have only the more limited First Amendment protection of "commercial speech" doctrine? Was this the case that would dismantle part or all of commercial speech landmark case known as "*Central Hudson*?"

This case arose when San Franciscan Marc Kasky was outraged by a *New York Times* story containing claims that Nike abused its employees. Nike was trying to counter bad publicity with news releases,

[61] Ibid. at 624–625, 2381–2382.

[62] Ibid. at 635, 2381.

[63] Ibid. at 635–636, 2381, 180, quoting *Shapero v. Kentucky Bar Assn.*, 486 U.S. 466, 108 S.Ct. 1916 (1988).

[64] Ibid. 115 S.Ct. at 2379, 23 Med.L.Rptr. at 1806 (1995), with Justice O'Connor quoting *Bolger v. Youngs Drug Products Corp.*, 463 U.S. 60, 72, 103 S.Ct. 2875, 2883 (1983), quoting *Lamont v. Commissioner of Motor Vehicles*, 269 F.Supp. 880, 883 (S.D.N.Y.1967), affirmed 386 F.2d 449 (2d Cir.1967).

letters to editors and to university presidents and athletic directors.[65] Kasky sued Nike under a California consumer protection statute allowing individuals or groups to act as "private attorneys general," suing to stop businesses from communicating in a way that might have a tendency to confuse a California consumer.[66]

The California Supreme Court ruled that Nike's messages were commercial speech " 'because the messages in question were directed by a commercial speaker to a commercial audience, and because they made representations of fact about the speaker's own business operations for the purpose of promoting its sales and its products, * * * [the] messages are commercial speech.' "[67]

The Supreme Court took the unusual step of granting certiorari in a case in which there was no final resolution in a lower court.[68]

Reflecting the high corporate stakes involved in *Nike v. Kasky*, advocates sent a blizzard of *amicus curiae* briefs to the Supreme Court, with Nike getting support of advertising, PR, and publishing industries plus the American Civil Liberties Union, the AFL-CIO, and the Bush administration. Ralph Nader's Public Citizen, environmental and anti-globalization groups, and 17 states filed briefs supporting Mr. Kasky.[69]

Just when a decision was expected from the Court, *Nike v. Kasky* was sent back to the California courts for further proceedings. The Court changed its mind, ruling on June 26, 2003 that its granting of Nike's writ of certiorari was "improvidently granted." For one thing, the California Supreme Court had never entered a final judgment.[70]

Jeff Milchen, director of ReclaimDemocracy.org, an anti-globalization group, hailed the Court's rejection of the Nike appeal. Milchen said it was " 'a relief to hear that the court was not prepared to consider even more extreme judicial activism on behalf of corporate America and against U.S. citizens by creating a corporate right to lie.' "[71]

---

[65] Ankur Bahr, brief of *Nike, Inc. v. Kasky*, "On the Docket—Medill School of Journalism," p. 1.

[66] Thomas H. Clarke, Jr. and Peter Clarke, "Op-Ed: Will Nike v Kasky ignite Corporate Social Responsibility Trade Wars between the U.S. and European Union?," (no longer online but available through author).

[67] Concurring opinion of Justice Stevens in *Nike v. Kasky*, 539 U.S. 654, 123 S.Ct. 2554 (2003), quoting the California Supreme Court in the *Kasky* case, 27 Cal.4th 939, 119 Cal.Rptr.2d 296, 45 P.3d 243, 247 (2002).

[68] Linda Greenhouse, "Supreme Court to Review Case on Nike's Right to Speech," *New York Times*, Jan. 10, 2003.

[69] Greenhouse, loc. cit.; Ankur Bahr, brief of *Nike, Inc. v. Kasky*, Ankur Bahr, "On the Docket—Medill School of Journalism," pp. 5–8.

[70] *Nike, Inc. v. Kasky*, 539 U.S. 654, 123 S.Ct. 2554 (2003), 67 U.S.P.Q.2d 1001, 2003 Daily Journal D.A.R., 16 Fla. L.Weekly Fed.S 470; Linda Greenhouse, "The Supreme Court: Advertising; Nike Free Speech Case Unexpectedly Returned to California," *New York Times*, June 27, 2003. The Court granted Nike's writ of certiorari in January, 2003, and heard oral arguments in the case on April 23, 2003.

[71] Greenhouse, Ibid.

Requiring corporations to prove "truth" of their statements may put them on a slippery slope under commercial speech doctrine, which is less protected than political speech. Compare the broader protections for political speech as spelled out in the great libel decision in *New York Times v. Sullivan*. There, the Supreme Court held that public official plaintiffs must prove that defamatory falsehoods published about them were published with knowing falsity or with reckless disregard for the truth. With political or socially significant speech, even falsehoods will be tolerated, unless published with "actual malice."[72] Commercial speech is far less protected than political or social speech. Under Part I of the *Central Hudson* test, if a commercial communication is to be protected under the First Amendment, "it at least must concern lawful activity and not be misleading."[73]

In his concurring opinion in favor of sending *Nike v. Kasky* back to the California courts, Justice Stevens wrote that certiorari originally had been granted[74]

> * * * to decide two questions: (1) whether a corporation participating in a public debate may "be subjected to liability for factual inaccuracies on the theory that its statements are 'commercial speech' * * * ; and (2) Even assuming the California Supreme Court properly characterized such statements as commercial speech, whether the First Amendment, as applied to the states through the Fourteenth Amendment, permit[s] subjecting speakers to the legal regime approved by that court in the decision below."

Attorney Thomas H. Clarke, Jr. wrote that under California law, a resident of that state "can file suit against a company and force it to defend its advertising materials, PR announcements, brochures, web sites, business cards, letterhead and news conference content." The plaintiff can also seek any profits earned via such communications. California has gained notoriety for such suits, including one against the California Milk Board's advertising about "Happy Cows," cows that plaintiffs claimed really suffered.[75]

Activist Marc Kasky's lawsuit returned to the California courts. But the case settled, leaving open whether Nike's claims about treating and paying its overseas workers well were misleading examples of commercial speech and thus actionable.

---

[72] *New York Times v. Sullivan*, 376 U.S. 254, 84 S.Ct. 710 (1964), discussed extensively in this textbook in Chap. 5, "Constitutional Defense Against Libel Suits."

[73] *Central Hudson Gas & Electric Co. v. Public Service Commission of New York*, 447 U.S. 557, 100 S.Ct. 2343 (1980).

[74] Stevens opinion, Ibid.

[75] Clarke, at 1–2.

The real-world potential had this lawsuit proceeded under California law was that Nike would have submitted to discovery and revealed what the corporation actually was paying its workers in its overseas factories.

44 LIQUORMART, INC. V. RHODE ISLAND

This decision echoed the Supreme Court's insistence in *Rubin* (see above) that advertising is protected by the First Amendment. The *44 Liquormart, Inc. v. Rhode Island* case grew out of Rhode Island's banning price advertising for alcoholic beverages. The Court without a dissenting vote—held that the ban on price advertising for a lawful product was not permitted by the First Amendment.[76]

> When a State regulates commercial messages to protect consumers from misleading, deceptive, or aggressive sales practices, or requires the disclosure of beneficial consumer information, the purpose of its regulation is consistent with the consistent with the reasons for according constitutional protection to commercial speech and therefore justifies less than strict review. However, when a State entirely prohibits the dissemination of truthful, nonmisleading commercial messages for reasons unrelated to the preservation of a fair bargaining process, there is far less reason to depart from the rigorous review that the First Amendment generally demands.

Justice Stevens also took pains to renounce the narrower view of First Amendment protection for advertising expressed in *Posadas*.[77]

> [O]n reflection, we are now persuaded that *Posadas* erroneously performed the First Amendment analysis. The casino advertising ban was designed to keep truthful, misleading speech from members of the public for fear that they would be more likely to gamble if they received it * * *
>
> * * *
>
> The *Posadas* majority's conclusion cannot be reconciled with the unbroken line of prior cases striking down similarly broad regulations on truthful, nonmisleading advertising when non-speech alternatives were available. See *Posadas*, [478 U.S. 328,] at 350, 106 S.Ct. at 2981–9882 (Brennan, J., dissenting) * * * ; Kurland, *Posadas de Puerto Rico v. Tourism Company*: " 'Twas Strange, 'Twas Passing Strange; 'Twas Pitiful, 'Twas Wondrous Pitiful," 1986 S.Ct. Rev. 1, 12–15.

[76] *44 Liquormart, Inc. v. Rhode Island*, 517 U.S. 484, 116 S.Ct. 1495, 1498 (1996). Justice Stevens was joined in this part of his opinion by Justices Ginsburg and Kennedy. *Liquormart*, although decided without a dissenting vote, was more a collection of complementary opinions than a "unanimous" judgment.

[77] Ibid. at 1498. Justice Stevens was joined by Justices Kennedy, Souter, and Ginsburg in this portion of his opinion.

Finally, *44 Liquormart*—in abandoning the weaker protection for commercial speech as expressed in *Posadas*—breathed new life into the four-part *Central Hudson* test for evaluating the constitutionality of advertising regulations.

TINKERING WITH COMMERCIAL SPEECH PROTECTION: LORILLARD TOBACCO CO. V. REILLY

In 2001 and 2002, the Supreme Court of the United States continued to wrestle with the extent of First Amendment protection for commercial speech. In its 2001 decision in *Lorillard Tobacco Co. v. Reilly,*[78] the Court decided a challenge to Massachusetts' extensive regulations of tobacco product sales. The regulations included prohibitions against outdoor and point-of-sale advertising of smokeless tobacco and cigars within 1,00 feet of a school or playground and also specified point-of-sale practices for indoor advertising (e.g., displays no lower than five feet from the floor). The impulse by Massachusetts authorities to protect children from tobacco ads thus collided with tobacco manufacturers' notions about constitutional protections for their advertising.

The Supreme Court held that the Federal Cigarette Labeling and Advertising Act, 15 U.S.C. § 1333, pre-empted Massachusetts regulations involving outdoor advertising and point-of-sale advertising of tobacco products. For one thing, the Court held, the State had failed to show that its regulations were no more extensive than necessary to serve the state's interest in protecting minors. That requirement, that the regulations not be more extensive than necessary, comes from *Central Hudson* (discussed above) in which the Court crafted a four-part test for regulation of commercial speech.[79]

The parties disposed of the first two parts of the test in their pleadings and the Court found that there was ample evidence of the advancement of the government interest regarding minors' consumption of tobacco products. The Court held that whatever evidence the Massachusetts attorney general had [linking adolescent tobacco use to various kinds of advertising], " * * * the regulations do not satisfy *Central Hudson's* fourth step."

Some of the Massachusetts point-of-sale regulations, however, were upheld. A state rule requiring that tobacco products be kept behind counters and that customers receive tobacco products from salespersons

[78] *Lorillard Tobacco Co. v. Reilly, Attorney General of Massachusetts,* 533 U.S. 525, 121 S.Ct. 2404, 29 Med.L.Rptr. 2121 (2001).

[79] The test's four parts are: (1) whether the expression is not misleading and thus acceptable under the First Amendment; (2) whether the asserted government interest is substantial; (3) whether the regulation directly advances the government interest asserted, and (4) whether the regulation is more extensive than necessary to serve that interest. This test is applied where the commercial speech concerns a lawful product or service.

was upheld as a way of controlling access to tobacco by minors and unrelated to expression.[80]

F.E.C. v. WISCONSIN RIGHT TO LIFE: DECIMATING THE 2002 MCCAIN-FEINGOLD LAW REGULATION OF PRE-ELECTION BROADCAST ADVERTISING

Passed in 2002, the McCain-Feingold law—the Bipartisan Campaign Reform Act (BCRA)—forbade attacking candidates by name in broadcast advertising 30 days before a primary and 60 days before a general election. This legislation, bearing the names of Senator John McCain (R-AZ) and Senator Russ Feingold (D-WI), was an attempt to rein in spending for and running of attack ads by special interest groups, unions, and corporations just before elections. McCain-Feingold was upheld generally as constitutional in 2003 in *McConnell v. Federal Election Commission*.[81]

In *McConnell*, the McCain-Feingold law survived a First Amendment challenge to its provisions. Provisions upheld included McCain-Feingold's forbidding not only of political advocacy seeking a candidate's election or defeat and also "issue advocacy" about public issues that also mentioned a candidate.[82]

In mid-2007, however, the U.S. Supreme Court punched a hole in McCain-Feingold in *Federal Election Commission (FEC) v. Wisconsin Right to Life*.[83] In 2007, new members of the Court—Chief Justice John Roberts and Justice Samuel Alito—made a great difference in the outcome as they invalidated much of the 2002 statute. Denouncing the decision, Michael Waldman of the Brennan Center called the 2007 decision a "huge setback to democracy * * * Any adman with a computer mouse and a modicum of creativity will be able to steer millions of dollars of special interest money into campaigns."[84]

The controversy triggering this case began on July 24, 2004, when Wisconsin Right to Life (WRTL) broadcast advertisements saying that a group of Senators was filibustering to delay or block confirmation of federal judge nominees. The ad asked voters to contact Wisconsin Senators Feingold and Herb Kohl (D-WI) to ask them to oppose the filibuster. WRTL, realized, however, that on August 15, 2004–30 days before the Wisconsin primary—that the ads it wished to continue

[80] Ibid. at 2140.

[81] *McConnell v. Federal Election Commission*, 540 U.S. 93, 124 S.Ct. 619 (2003).

[82] BCRA, 2 U.S.C. § 434(f) (3) (A), specified broadcasts referring to candidates for federal office aired within 30 days of a federal primary election or within 60 days of a federal general election. BCRA § 441b(b)(2) made it a crime for a corporation to use its general treasury funds to pay for an "electioneering communication."

[83] *FEC v. Wisconsin Right to Life*, 551 U.S. 449, 127 S.Ct. 2652 (2007).

[84] "Brennan Center Statement on Ruling in *FEC v. Wisconsin Right to Life*," https://www.brennancenter.org/our-work/research-reports/summary-supreme-court-decision-fec-v-wisconsin-right-life.

broadcasting conflicted the McCain-Feingold law. WRTL, believing it had a First Amendment right to broadcast such "electioneering communication" ads despite § 203 of the BCRA, sued the Federal Election Commission.[85]

In 2006, a U.S. district court found in favor of Wisconsin Right to Life in a second proceeding on the matter, holding that the ads were genuine issue ads, not express advocacy against a political candidate.[86] And in 2007, the U.S. Supreme Court affirmed that decision in *FEC v. Wisconsin Right to Life, Inc.*

One of the three ads run by WRTL was a radio message titled "Wedding." The transcript of "Wedding" follows:[87]

> " 'PASTOR: And who gives this woman to be married to this man?
>
> "BRIDE'S FATHER: Well, as father of the bride, I certainly could.
>
> But instead, I'd like to share a few tips on how to properly install drywall. Now you put the drywall up * * *
>
> " 'VOICE-OVER: Sometimes it's just not fair to delay an important decision.
>
> " 'But in Washington, it's happening. A group of Senators is using the filibuster delay tactic to block federal judicial appointees from a simple "yes" or "no" vote. So qualified candidates don't get a chance to serve.
>
> " 'It's politics at work, causing gridlock and backing up some of our courts to a state of emergency.
>
> " 'Contact Senators Feingold and Kohl and tell them to oppose the filibuster.
>
> " 'Visit: BeFair.org.
>
> " 'Paid for by Wisconsin Right to Life (befair.org), which is responsible for the content of this advertising and not authorized by any candidate or candidate's committee.' "466 F.Supp. 2d 195, 198, n. 3 (DC 2006).

Writing for the Supreme Court, Chief Justice John G. Roberts, Jr., wrote that in 2006, the Court had rejected an "as-applied challenge" to § 203 of the BCRA in Wisconsin Right to Life's first challenge against the legislation.[88] But in 2007, Chief Justice Roberts wrote,[89]

---

[85] *FEC v. Wisconsin Right to Life, Inc.*, 551 U.S. 449, 460, 127 S.Ct. 2652, 2661 (2007).

[86] *Wisconsin Right to Life, Inc. v. FEC*, 466 F.Supp.2d 195 (D.D.C.2006).

[87] *FEC v. Wisconsin Right to Life*, 551 U.S. 449, 458, 127 S.Ct. 2652, 2660 (2007).

[88] Ibid. at 2654 (2007), citing "WRTL I," *Wisconsin Right to Life v. Federal Election Comm'n*, 546 U.S. 410, 411–412, 126 S.Ct. 1016, 1018 (2006) (*per curiam*).

[89] Ibid. at 2659.

> We have long recognized that the distinction between campaign advocacy and issue advocacy "may often dissolve in practical application. Candidates, especially incumbents, are intimately tied to public issues involving legislative proposals and governmental actions." *Buckley v. Valeo*, 424 U.S. 1, 42 (1976) (*per curiam*).

Development of the law in that area, Roberts wrote, required the Court to draw a line between campaign speech (or its " 'functional equivalent' ") and issue advocacy.[90]

> In drawing that line, the First Amendment requires us to err on the side of protecting political speech rather than suppressing it. We conclude that the speech at issue in this as-applied challenge is not the "functional equivalent" of express campaign speech. We further conclude that the interests held to justify restricting corporate issue advocacy do not justify restricting issue advocacy, and accordingly, we hold that BCRA § 203 is unconstitutional as applied to the advertisements at issue in these cases.

Chief Justice Roberts declared, " 'Where the First Amendment is implicated, the tie goes to the speaker.' " Tony Mauro, First Amendment Center legal correspondent, seized on those ringing words. Mauro, a long-time observer of the Supreme Court, wrote that this is a quote that will live on in history books and legal briefs of First Amendment litigants. But, Mauro observed, "The star power of Roberts' quote may be tempered . . . by its appearing in the only case of the term where the clear winner was over a government adversary."[91]

Justice Samuel Alito concurred separately, as did Justice Antonin Scalia, joined by Justices Anthony Kennedy and Clarence Thomas.

Justice David H. Souter dissented vigorously, and was joined by Justices John Paul Stevens, Ruth Bader Ginsburg and Stephen Breyer. Justice Souter declared:[92]

> The significance and effect of today's judgment * * * turn on three things: the demand for campaign money in huge amounts from large contributors, whose power has produced a cynical electorate; the congressional recognition of the ensuing threat to democratic integrity as reflected in a century of legislation restricting the electoral leverage of concentrations of money in corporate and union treasuries; and *McConnell v. Federal Election Comm'n*, 540 U.S. 93 (2003), declaring the facial validity of the most recent Act of Congress in that tradition, a decision that is effectively, and unjustifiably, overruled today.

---

[90] Ibid. at 2659.

[91] Tony Mauro, "Rhetoric aside, most First Amendment claimants lose," http://www.firstamendmentcenter.org/rhetoric-aside-most-first-amendment-claimants-lose.

[92] *FEC v. Wisconsin Right to Life*, 551 U.S. 449, 504, 127 S.Ct. 2652, 2687 (2007).

Justice Souter argued that the majority was wrong in terming the Wisconsin Right to Life ads "issue" ads. He noted that during the 2004 senatorial campaign, WRTL's Political Action Committee (PA) issued press releases saying that its " 'Top Election Priorities' were to 'Re-elect George W. Bush' and to 'Send Feingold Packing.' * * * In one of these, the Chair of WRTL's PAC was quoted as saying, 'We do not want Russ Feingold to continue to have the ability to thwart President Bush's judicial nominees.' " Furthermore, the WRTL PAC's quarterly magazine said " 'the defeat of Feingold must be uppermost in the minds of Wisconsin's pro-life community in the 2004 elections.' "[93]

Justice Breyer targeted WRTL's coded messages, which didn't directly call for the electoral defeat of Senator Feingold, but instead urged voters to contact Feingold to ask him to oppose filibusters on judicial nominees. Breyer wrote,[94]

> In sum, any Wisconsin voter who paid attention would have known that Democratic Senator Feingold supported filibusters against Republican presidential judicial nominees, that the propriety of the filibusters was a major issue in the senatorial campaign, and that WRTL along with the Senator's Republican challengers opposed his reelection because of his position on the filibusters. Any alert voters who heard or saw WRTL's ads would have understood that WRTL was telling them that the Senator's position on the filibusters should be grounds to vote against him."

Breyer expressed concern about further jeopardizing the integrity of democratic government. "After today," wrote Breyer, "the ban on contributions by corporations and unions and the limitation on their corrosive spending when they enter the political arena are open to easy circumvention, and the possibilities for regulating corporate and union campaign money are unclear."[95]

72. FEDERAL ADMINISTRATIVE CONTROLS: THE FEDERAL TRADE COMMISSION

The most important federal government controls over advertising have been exercised by the Federal Trade Commission, which has experienced considerable controversy.

THE FEDERAL TRADE COMMISSION

During the Twentieth Century, the Federal Trade Commission became more important than other official controls over advertising. The

[93] Ibid. at 2697.

[94] Ibid. at 2698.

[95] Ibid. at 2705.

FTC Act was passed in 1914 to supplement sanctions against unfair competition which had been provided by the Sherman Anti-Trust Act of 1890 and by the Clayton Act of 1914.[96] In its early days, trial and intermediate appellate courts sought to limit the power of the FTC to regulate only unfair competition. Consumer interests were left waiting. Gradually though with favorable holdings in the Supreme Court, the FTC grew in power and assumed an increasingly important place in regulating advertising.

The Federal Trade Commission is an example of administrative rule- and law-making authority delegated by Congress. Five Federal Trade Commissioners are appointed by the President and confirmed by the Senate for five-year terms. No more than three of the five commissioners may be from the same political party. The strength of the FTC as a regulatory agency has varied greatly over the years, changing with the level of congressional support and with the variable political attitudes toward the effectiveness of government efforts to control unfair competition.

The FTC machinery—which is described later at some length—is set up to enforce Sec. 5 of the Federal Trade Commission Act, which says: "Unfair methods of competition in commerce, and unfair or deceptive practices in commerce, are declared unlawful."[97]

Early FTC cases which came before the courts cast doubt on the Commission's powers over advertising.[98] And when in 1921 the FTC tried to stop an underwear manufacturer from mislabeling with terms such as "Natural Merino" or "Australian Wool," a U.S. Court of Appeals held that the FTC was powerless to prevent misleading labels.[99] The Supreme Court of the United States, however, upheld the FTC in language broad enough to support the Commission's power to control false labeling and advertising as unfair methods of competition. That was the emphasis: harm to competitors, *not* harm to consumers, although Justice Louis D. Brandeis at least mentioned consumers. Speaking for the Court, Justice Brandeis declared that the FTC was justified in regarding misbranded goods as a fraud diverting customers from the producers of truthfully marked goods.[100]

Despite the efforts of the Federal Trade Commission, the general idea of consumer protection had little support from the courts until well into the Twentieth Century.[101]

---

[96] Sherman Act, 26 Stat. 209 (1890), 15 U.S.C.A. § 1; Clayton Act, 38 Stat. 730 (1914), 15 U.S.C.A. § 12.

[97] 5 U.S.C.A. § 45(a)(1).

[98] *Federal Trade Commission v. Gratz*, 253 U.S. 421, 40 S.Ct. 572 (1920); *L.B. Silver Co. v. Federal Trade Commission of America*, 289 Fed. 985 (6th Cir.1923).

[99] *Winsted Hosiery Company v. Federal Trade Commission*, 272 Fed. 957 (2d Cir.1921).

[100] *Federal Trade Commission v. Winsted Hosiery Co.*, 258 U.S. 483, 493–494, 42 S.Ct. 384, 385–386 (1922).

[101] See *Federal Trade Commission v. Raladam Co.*, 283 U.S. 643, 51 S.Ct. 587 (1931). The Supreme Court of the United States held that Sec. 5 of the FTC Act did not forbid deceiving

The FTC's authority over advertising grew slowly. As late as 1936—when the FTC had existed for 22 years—the famed Judge Learned Hand of the Second Circuit Court of Appeals decided a case against the FTC and in favor of an advertising scheme for encyclopedias which involved a false representation that purchasers of encyclopedias would receive additional free volumes (the "free" volumes were part of the package that all buyers received).[102] "Such trivial niceties are too impalpable for practical affairs, they are will-o'-the-wisps, which divert attention from substantial evils," Judge Hand declared.

When the *Standard Education* case reached the Supreme Court, Justice Hugo L. Black reacted indignantly, saying the sales method used to peddle the encyclopedia "successfully deceived and deluded its victims."[103] In overturning Judge Hand's "let the buyer beware" ruling in the lower court, Justice Black added:[104]

> The fact that a false statement may be obviously false to those who are trained and experienced does not change its character, nor take away its power to deceive others less experienced. There is no duty resting upon a citizen to suspect the honesty of those with whom he transacts business. Laws are made to protect the trusting as well as the suspicious.

In 1938, the year after the Supreme Court endorsed the concept of consumer protection from advertising excesses, Congress acted to give the FTC greater authority over deceptive advertising. The 1938 Wheeler-Lea Amendment changed Sec. 5 of the Federal Trade Commission Act to read: "Unfair methods of competition *in commerce,* and unfair or deceptive acts or practices in commerce, are hereby declared unlawful."[105] Note the italicized phrase. The words were added by the Wheeler-Lea Amendment, and this seemingly minor change in phrasing proved to be of great importance. No longer would the FTC have to prove that a misleading advertisement harmed a competing business. Thereafter, if an advertisement deceived consumers—who like businesses also were involved "in commerce"—the FTC's enforcement powers could be put into effect.[106]

---

customers unless it could be shown that deceptive advertising injured competing businesses. Raladam Co. was unscrupulously selling an "obesity cure" made of "desiccated thyroid" as safe and effective when it doubtless was extremely dangerous to health when ingested.

[102] *Federal Trade Commission v. Standard Educ. Society,* 302 U.S. 112, 116, 58 S.Ct. 113, 115 (1937), quoting Judge Hand's opinion in the same case in the Circuit Court, 86 F.2d 692, 695 (2d Cir.1936). The scheme had several elements but the key was this: Buyers who purchased the current year supplement for $69.50 under the special offer received a free set of encyclopedias. In reality, the normal price for the set of encyclopedias, including the supplement, was $69.50. There was no "deal" for consumers to take advantage of.

[103] Ibid. at 117, 115.

[104] Ibid. at 116, 115.

[105] 52 Stat. 111 (1938); 15 U.S.C.A. § 45. Italics added.

[106] Ibid.; Earl W. Kintner, "Federal Trade Commission Regulation of Advertising," *Michigan Law Review* Vol. 64:7 (May, 1966) pp. 1269–1284, at pp. 1275–1276, 1276n.

Aiming at false advertising, the Wheeler-Lea Amendment also inserted Secs. 12 and 15(a) into the Federal Trade Commission Act. Sec. 12 provides:[107]

> It shall be unlawful for any person, partnership, or corporation to disseminate, or cause to be disseminated, any false advertisement—(1) by United States mails, or in [interstate] commerce by any means, for the purpose of inducing, or which is likely to induce, directly or indirectly, the purchase in commerce of food, drugs, devices or cosmetics.

Sec. 15(a) of the FTC Act says:

> The term "false advertising" means an advertisement, other than labeling, which is misleading in a material respect; and in determining whether any advertisement is misleading, there shall be taken into account (among other things) not only representations made or suggested by statement, word, design, device, sound, or any combination thereof, but also the extent to which the advertisement fails to reveal facts material in the light of such representations or material with respect to consequences which may result from the use of the commodity * * *.

Such statutory changes gave the FTC some of the power it sought to protect consumers. As FTC Commissioners Everette MacIntyre and Paul Rand Dixon wrote in the 1960s, the Wheeler-Lea "amendment put the consumer on a par with the businessman from the standpoint of deceptive practices."[108]

Even so, this commission was often called "toothless" and other less flattering things. The delays which have dogged FTC enforcement procedures—especially those involving lengthy court battles—became legendary. An often cited example was the famed "Carter's Little Liver Pills" case. In 1943, the FTC decided that the word "liver" was misleading, and a classic and lengthy battle was on. Carter's Little Liver Pills had been a well known laxative product for 75 years. It took the FTC a total of 16 years—from 1943 to 1959—to win its point before the courts and get "liver" deleted.[109]

In addition, the FTC could not hope to regulate all advertising in (or affecting) interstate commerce—it could merely regulate by example, by pursuing a relatively small number of advertisers who appeared to operate in a deceptive fashion, in hopes that this would encourage others to tone down their advertising claims. It has been objected that during most of the FTC's history, it had tended to go after "little guys" or

---

[107] Sec. 12, 52 Stat. 114 (1938), 15 U.S.C.A. § 52; Sec. 15(a), 52 Stat. 114 (1938), 15 U.S.C.A. § 55(a).

[108] Everette MacIntyre and Paul Rand Dixon, "The Federal Trade Commission After 50 Years," *Federal Bar Journal* Vol.24:4 (Fall, 1964) pp. 377–424, at p. 416.

[109] *Carter Products, Inc. v. Federal Trade Commission*, 268 F.2d 461 (9th Cir.1959), certiorari denied 361 U.S. 884, 80 S.Ct. 155 (1959).

unimportant issues, too often ignoring misdeeds by big and powerful corporations which tied into important issues.

STRENGTHENING THE FTC: THE 1970S

Strengthening of the FTC's regulatory powers came in 1973 in a sneaky fashion. While an energy crisis had the attention of Congress in 1973, a rider to the Trans-Alaska Pipeline Act gave the FTC powers it had sought for many years.[110] Thanks to that rider, the FTC was given the power to go to a federal court and seek an injunction against an advertisement which the FTC believes to be clearly in violation of federal law prohibiting false and misleading advertising. This injunctive sanction is little used because it is drastic. However, an injunction could, in critical instances, put a stop to ads which might otherwise continue to run through their campaign cycle—be it three months or six months or longer—before the FTC could take action.

The FTC was further strengthened in 1975 with the Moss-Magnuson Act.[111] Before the Moss-Magnuson Act, jurisdiction of the FTC was limited to advertising in interstate commerce, but under Moss-Magnuson, the FTC was given the power, in effect, to say that all commerce affects interstate commerce, and therefore is under FTC jurisdiction.[112]

Also, the Moss-Magnuson Act gave the FTC power to get beyond "regulation by example." That is, the FTC no longer had to be content with issuing a "cease and desist" order against a shave cream manufacturer using a misleading advertising campaign. Moss-Magnuson gave the FTC the ability to issue Trade Regulation Rules with the force of law. Fines for violation of a Trade Regulation Rule through misleading advertising can draw fines of up to $11,000 per instance, so the FTC was given the clout to make advertisers pay attention.

WEAKENING THE FTC: THE 1980S

Although the Magnuson-Moss Act strengthened FTC powers, the activist stance of the FTC during the late 1970s brought a counterattack from business plus legislation to weaken the FTC. Although the Great Sugar Controversy—an abortive FTC rulemaking to regulate sugar in cereals heavily advertised to children—was by no means the only source

---

[110] 15 U.S.C.A. § 53. See Note, " 'Corrective Advertising' Orders of the Federal Trade Commission," 85 *Harvard Law Review* (Dec., 1971), pp. 485–486. The FTC has injunctive powers to deal with advertising for products which could pose an immediate health threat to consumers, including foods, drugs, cosmetics, and medical devices.

[111] Pub.L. 93–637, 88 Stat. 2183 (1975). The official title of the statute was the Consumer Product Warranties and Federal Trade Commission Improvements Act, providing disclosure standards for written consumer product warranties.

[112] The Moss-Magnuson Act overcame a 1941 Supreme Court decision which held that an Illinois company limiting its sales only to wholesalers in that state was not in interstate commerce, and therefore was beyond FTC control. See *Federal Trade Commission v. Bunte Bros.*, 312 U.S. 349, 61 S.Ct. 580 (1941).

of the FTC's troubles in the 1980s, it is an example of Commission behavior that drew fire from business and industry. In 1977 and 1978,[113]

> [t]he FTC staff proposed rules that would have resulted in a ban of most children's television advertising. The FTC primarily premised its far-reaching rulemaking proceeding on "unfairness," a standard with few legal precedents, rather than on "deception," a well-established standard with more confining limits.

Issues involving regulation of children's advertising—including an FTC hearing on whether some sugary foods should be banned—resulted in strenuous attacks on the commission. FTC Chairman Michael Pertschuk, in particular, was accused of unfairness and asked by the Kellogg Company and by the Association of National Advertisers to disqualify himself from any hearing on sugary cereals. Pertschuk had incurred wrath by saying, among other things, that, " 'Advertisers seize on the child's trust and exploit it as a weakness for their gain. * * * Cumulatively, commercials directed at children tend to distort the role of food.' "[114]

THE FTC IMPROVEMENTS ACT OF 1980

Under severe political leverage and with millions of dollars in campaign contributions at stake, Congress folded like a $5 umbrella. Congress passed the ironically named Federal Trade Commission Improvements Act of 1980.[115] This legislation removed "unfairness" as a basis for regulation of commercial advertising. Instead of being to forbid "unfair" ads, the FTC had to show out-and-out deception, which is harder to prove. Also, the 1980 act removed FTC powers to make rules on children's advertising and on the funeral industry, another target of FTC activism for preying on the grief-stricken. In addition, the so-called "FTC Improvements Act" gave the FTC the problem of having Congress breathing down its neck. A 90-day review period was established by Congress for any proposed FTC Trade Regulation Rules. If both Houses of Congress pass a resolution objecting to an FTC rulemaking, the rule is overturned. This was sometimes called the "two-House legislative veto."[116]

---

[113] Foote and Mnookin, op. cit., p. 90.

[114] The *News Media & the Law*, Vol. 3: No. 2 (May/June, 1979), p.18. The Court of Appeals for the D.C. Circuit ruled that Chairman Pertschuk's mind was not unalterably closed during the proceeding on children's advertising, refusing to disqualify him. *Association of National Advertisers v. FTC*, 627 F.2d 1151 (D.C.Cir.1979). Even so, Pertschuk withdrew from that administrative rulemaking procedure.

[115] Pub.L.No. 96–252, 94 State. 374 (1980); Foote and Mnookin, op. cit., pp. 90–91.

[116] Pub.L.No. 96–252, 94 Stat. 374 (1980), § 21, discussed in Earl W. Kintner, Christopher Smith, and David B. Goldston, "The Effect of the Federal Trade Commission Improvements Act of 1980 on the FTC's Rulemaking and Enforcement Authority," 58 *Washington University Law Quarterly* No. 4 (Winter, 1980), pp. 847–859, at 853.

"UNFAIRNESS" IN THE 1990S AND BEYOND

Remember that the key provision of the Federal Trade Commission Act is Sec. 5, which reads: "Unfair methods of competition in commerce, and unfair or deceptive practices in commerce, are declared unlawful." In 1994, Congress again tinkered with the operational meaning of "unfairness" as that term is to be interpreted by the FTC. The 1994 amendment to Sec. 5 added this language: Before an act can be found unlawful by the FTC on grounds of "unfairness," the Commission must show that "the act or practice causes or is likely to cause substantial injury to consumers which is not reasonably avoidable by consumers themselves and not outweighed by countervailing benefits to consumers or to competition."[117]

In other words, the FTC can't assume harm to consumers. The Commission must show, at the least, a likelihood that an advertisement will cause "substantial injury." At best, this can be a set of minor procedural hurdles for the FTC. At worst, Sec. 5, as amended, could stifle efforts to head off real harm to consumers.

FTC ORGANIZATION AND ADVERTISING REGULATION

The Federal Trade Commission looks formidable on a table of organization. Then, one realizes that the FTC's entire budget for handling both antitrust matters and protecting consumers (including regulation of advertising) was less than $300 million in 2015. American advertising spending was expected to grow to $189 billion in 2015 some 630 times the regulatory budget.[118]

This is a classic overmatch. It is on the scale of a little league baseball team taking on the New York Yankees.

The FTC has three Bureaus,[119] two of which do not deal directly with advertising regulation:

* The Bureau of Competition, the FTC's antitrust arm.

* The Bureau of Economics, which aids the FTC in predicting the economic consequences of its actions.

* The Bureau of Consumer Protection, which has a broad mandate to protect consumers against unfair, fraudulent or deceptive practices.

The Bureau of Consumer Protection includes **The Division of Advertising Practices**, which will be discussed at some length, below. The Advertising Practices unit enforces truth-in-advertising laws,

[117] Sec. 5 of the FTC Act, 15 U.S.C. § 45ff.

[118] "Advertisers Will Spend Nearly $600 Billion Worldwide in 2015," *Media Buying*, Dec. 10, 2014. http://www.emarketer.com/Article/Advertisers–Will–Spend–Nearly–600–Billion–Worldwide–2015/1011691#sthash.UleEzMuy.dpuf.

[119] The other two elements are the Office of General Counsel; https://www.ftc.gov/about-ftc/bureaus-offices/office-general-counsel; and Office of the Executive Director. https://www.ftc.gov/about-ftc/bureaus-offices/office-executive-director.

emphasizing food claims, over-the-counter drugs, dietary supplements, alcohol and tobacco. Some concerns involve high-tech products and the Internet, including the implanting of spyware. There are six other Divisions in the Bureau of Consumer Protection.[120]

* Consumer and Business Education. The objective of this division is to give consumers tools needed to make informed decisions—and businesses the tools needed to comply with the law.

* Enforcement. This division litigates civil contempt and civil penalty actions to enforce FTC federal court injunctions ("cease and desist orders"), litigates civil actions against those who defraud customers, and develops and enforces consumer protection rules. Enforcement also works with law enforcement agencies when it appears that criminal laws have been broken.

* Financial Practices. This division acts on deceptive or unfair financial practices, including predatory or discriminatory lending. The staff targets firms that make deceptive offers to assist consumers in reducing or renegotiating debt, including mortgage, car and credit card debt. Unfair and abusive debt collection practices and predatory payday lending also come under the authority of Financial Practices.

* Marketing Practices. The division enforces the FTC Act and other federal consumer protection laws, filing FTC actions in federal district court for immediate and permanent orders to stop scams; preventing criminals from perpetrating frauds, freezing assets of those who victimize consumers; and getting compensation for scam victims. It also covers the Do Not Call and Can-Spam (Controlling the Assault of Non-Solicited Pornography and Marketing) rules.

* Advertising Practices. It protects consumers from unfair or deceptive advertising and marketing practices that can cause economic, health and safety harms. It brings law enforcement actions in federal district court to halt advertising fraud. The division coordinates with federal and international law enforcement agencies. It also brings administrative lawsuits to stop unfair and deceptive advertising.

* Privacy and Identity Protection, the newest division, oversees consumer privacy, credit reporting, identity theft, and information security. It enforces the Fair Credit Reporting Act requiring credit bureaus to maintain accurate information about consumers and protecting the privacy of that information. Privacy and Identity Protection also enforces the Children's

[120] Federal Trade Commission, https://www.ftc.gov/about-ftc/bureaus-offices/bureau-consumer-protection/about-bureau-consumer-protection.

Online Privacy Protection Act. The Act is aimed at giving parents control over information collected by online businesses.

THE DIVISION OF ADVERTISING PRACTICES

FTC literature summarizes the scope of the Division of Advertising Practices' law enforcement priorities in this fashion:[121]

* Combating deceptive advertising of fraudulent cure-all claims for dietary supplements and weight loss products.

* Monitoring and stopping deceptive Internet marketing practices that develop in response to public health issues.

* Monitoring and developing effective enforcement strategies for new advertising techniques and media, such as word-of-mouth marketing.

* Monitoring and reporting on the advertising of food to children, including the impact of practices by food companies and the media on childhood obesity.

* Monitoring and reporting on industry practices regarding the marketing of violent movies, music, and electronic games to children.

* Monitoring and reporting on alcohol and tobacco marketing practices.

"WEAPONS" OF THE FTC

The FTC has several weapons to use against misleading advertising; "getting the FTC's attention" is accomplished in a variety of ways. Letters from consumers or businesses, inquiries from Congress, or articles on consumer issues all may trigger FTC actions:[122]

(1) "Voluntary Compliance" (Consent Orders): When the FTC suspects that a violation of law occurred, it will begin an investigation. Typically, such investigations are nonpublic, the FTC says, "in order to protect both the investigation and the company" being investigated. When the FTC and the company reach terms, the agreement is made public in order to let people comment. One mechanism available to the Commission is to try to get what is termed "voluntary compliance" by negotiating a "consent order" with the company. "A company that signs a consent order need not admit that it violated the law, but must agree

[121] https://www.ftc.gov/about-ftc/bureaus-offices/bureau-consumer-protection/our-divisions/division-advertising-practices.

[122] Ibid. at 19.

to stop the disputed practices * * * " as outlined by the FTC in a complaint.[123]

A lot of the consent orders arise from ads for products or services that most people see on a daily basis. *In the Matter of Network Solutions, LLC*[124], the FTC settled an administrative complaint against an Internet company through a consent order. Network Solutions offered domain registration and Web hosting services. Prices vary with the term of the Web hosting agreement that customers choose. Network Solutions offered a 30-day money back guarantee. The offer, which it started in 2008, appeared to be a way for customers to try out a website without risking any money. Network Solutions charged $120 a year for its most basic Web hosting services. Its second tier of service was $160 a year and its "Premium Web Hosting" cost $350 a year.

The logo was straightforward 30 Day Money Back Guarantee. But Network Solutions did not refund the customers' entire fee. Depending on the length of the Web hosting contract, Network Solutions charged a cancellation fee. For a one-year contract, the fee could be as much as $34.99 or as little as $29.95. Network Solutions did not provide notice of its cancellation fee when it advertised the money-back guarantee. On the pages that contained the offer, Network Solutions put in a much smaller font the following:[125]

> See Terms and Conditions for," followed by several hyperlinks, including one that reads: "30-day Money Back Guarantee." Respondent did not disclose the existence of the cancellation fee in these notes. Respondent sometimes placed the hyperlink in blue text against a black background. The placement, wording, size, and color of these hyperlinks made it unlikely that customers would notice them * * *

The failure to inform customers of the cancellation fee was enough to trigger FTC action under § 5(a) of the Federal Trade Commission Act that prohibits unfair or deceptive practices.[126]

> * * * Respondent has failed to disclose adequately that it withholds part of the refund from customers who: (1) purchase an annual or multi-year web hosting package, (2) register the included domain name, and (3) cancel within thirty days. This fact would be material to consumers in deciding whether to purchase web hosting services from Respondent.

The FTC and Network Solutions reached an agreement and entered into a "consent order." As happens with settlements, instead of matters taken to trial, Network Solutions neither admitted or denied the FTC's allegations. It did agree to comply with the FTC's order, though. That

---

[123] Ibid. Rosden & Rosden, op. cit., Vol. II, § 25.06.

[124] *Network Solutions*, FTC No. 132–3084.

[125] Ibid.

[126] Ibid.

order requires that the company not take customers' billing information (credit card or other payment system) without first disclosing[127] "the material terms of any applicable money back guarantee, including but not limited to the existence and amount of any service charges or other fees applicable to any such money back guarantee."

The order also forbids Network Solutions from keeping any money in a refund unless it has "clearly and conspicuously" posted its service charges and other fees where the money-back guarantee is displayed. The company will be subject to the order for 20 years and in that time must provide the FTC with copies of all advertising that includes its money-back guarantee. It also has to turn over accounting records showing fees and refunds.

Not all consumer complaints are resolved so easily and in those cases, the FTC moves to the next level.

(2) Administrative Complaints: If a consent agreement is not reached, the FTC may issue an administrative complaint. As the "Guide to the Federal Trade Commission" says, "If an administrative complaint is issued, a formal proceeding before an administrative law judge begins that is much like a court trial: evidence is submitted; testimony is heard; and witnesses are examined and cross-examined. If a law violation is found, a cease and desist order * * * may be issued. Initial decisions by administrative law judges [Civil Service employees independent of the FTC] may be appealed to the full Commission." Appeals from a final FTC decision may be made to a U.S. Court of Appeals and, ultimately, to the U.S. Supreme Court. Violation of such an order is punishable by a civil penalty of $10,000 a day for each offense.

Advertisements for Sensa, a weight loss product, were one example. The ads were appealing. The makers of Sensa said sprinkle their powder on your favorite food and it would make the foods taste and smell so good that you would feel full faster and, thus, eat less. That would lead to weight loss without having to go on a diet.[128]

The FTC said it was too good to be true and it filed an administrative complaint against the company. The feel-full-and-eat-less claim was appealing. Sensa sold its powder in 12 flavors. The company marketed the powder on cable TV, with ads and infomercials on Home Shopping Network and ShopNBC. It ran radio and print advertisements and through retail chains including Costco and GNC. The company charged $59 plus shipping and handling for a one-month supply. U.S. sales of Sensa between 2008 and 2012 totaled more than $364 million, the complaint alleged.

[127] Ibid.

[128] "Sensa and Three Other Marketers of Fad Weight-Loss Products Settle FTC Charges in Crackdown on Deceptive Advertising" FTC Press Release, Jan. 7, 2014. https://www.ftc.gov/news-events/press-releases/2014/01/sensa-three-other-marketers-fad-weight-loss-products-settle-ftc.

The FTC complaint also named CEO Adam Goldenberg, and Sensa creator and endorser and Sensa Products part-owner Dr. Alan Hirsch. Hirsch conducted two studies showing the effectiveness of the powder and wrote a promotional book that included his "scientific evidence."

Sensa settled with the FTC before the case made it through to the administrative law proceeding. Under the terms of the settlement, the company was fined $46.5 million but was ordered to pay $26.5 million for customer refunds because it did not have the money. In addition, the defendants were prohibited from making claims about drugs, dietary supplements or foods relating to weight loss unless they had competent scientific evidence.[129]

> "Dr. Hirsch is also barred under the order from providing expert endorsements unless he relies on both competent and reliable scientific evidence and his own expertise. And he is barred from providing to others studies, promotional materials, endorsements, or other means for deceiving consumers."

The administrative complaint also named two other companies making weight loss claims. A settlement with L'Occitane, Inc. means the company will no longer make claims that its Almond Beautiful Shape and Almond Shaping Delight skin creams can result in a slimmer body. L'Occitane claimed that it had conducted clinical studies that proved the effectiveness of its creams. The company charged $48 for 7 ounces of Almond Shaping Delight and $44 for 6.7 ounces of Almond Beautiful Shape.

HCG Diet Direct, and its director Clint Ethington, entered into a settlement with the FTC to stop making claims that HGC Diet Direct Drops would promote weight loss.[130]

> The defendants sold HCG Diet Direct Drops, a diluted liquid form of human chorionic gonadotropin—a hormone produced by the human placenta that has been falsely promoted for decades as a weight-loss supplement.

The FTC complaint included an FDA advisory that the HCG Diet Direct Drops were "mislabeled drugs" under the FDA Act.

(3) Other FTC Sanctions: In situations where substantial harm to consumers, as in cases of suspected fraud, "the FTC can go directly to court to obtain an injunction, civil penalties, or consumer redress * * * 'By going directly to court, the FTC can stop the fraud' * * * to try to minimize the number of consumers injured."

In *FTC v. Sameer Lakhany*, The Credit Shop, Fidelity Legal Services, et. al,[131] the FTC went to federal court in the Central District

---

129 Ibid.

130 Ibid.

131 *FTC v. Sameer Lakhany, The Credit Shop, Fidelity Legal Services, et. al,* SACV 12–00337-CJC(JPR) (C.D.Calif. 2012).

of California in March of 2012 seeking a restraining order against several individuals and companies targeting homeowners who were having problems paying their mortgages.

Lakhany and the companies took advantage of hundreds of homeowners promising a legal solution to their mortgage problems.[132]

> In one scam, the FTC claims the defendants masqueraded as a specialty law firm, Precision Law Center, and sent out direct mail resembling a class action settlement notice, holding out the false promise to consumers that if they sued their lenders along with other homeowners in so-called "mass joinder" lawsuits, they could obtain favorable mortgage concessions from their lenders or stop the foreclosure process.

The law firm was a sham, the FTC alleged. Attorneys were hired briefly to file the lawsuits but then were let go. The suits were dismissed by the courts or the companies simply neglected to pursue them. The companies charged the homeowners $6,000 to $10,000 in advance each, but failed to get promised results, the FTC claimed. After the initial filing, the FTC added two other companies that it said were engaged in mortgage relief fraud.

Lakhany and defendants The Credit Shop, LLC, Fidelity Legal Services LLC, and Titanium Realty, Inc., represented themselves as nonprofits and charged homeowners between $795 and $1,595 for a so-called "forensic loan audit," the FTC alleged.[133]

> They told consumers the loan audits would find lender violations 90 percent of the time or more, and that this would force lenders to give them better mortgage terms. In fact, the complaint alleged that consumers rarely if ever obtained better mortgage terms as a result of these "forensic loan audits."

Federal District Judge Cormac Carney granted the restraining order halting the fraud. Carney then approved a preliminary injunction, appointing a receiver to take control of the defendants' assets that would be used to provide relief for the homeowners who had been victimized.

(4) Publicity: The FTC publicizes complaints and cease and desist orders which it promulgates. News releases on such subjects are issued regularly to the media, and publicity has proven to be one of the strongest weapons at the FTC's disposal.[134] The FTC routinely sends out press

[132] Ibid.

[133] Ibid.

[134] Federal Trade Commission, Your FTC: What It Is and What It Does, p. 19.

releases updating the status of cases and announcing new enforcement actions.

OTHER TOOLS

The FTC also operates three major programs to provide information and guidance to companies and consumers. They are:

(1) Industry Guides: This program involved issuing interpretations of the rules of the Commission to its staff. These guides are made available to the public, and are aimed at certain significant practices of a particular industry, especially those involved in advertising and labeling. The guides can be issued by the Commission as its interpretation of the law without a conference or hearings, and, therefore, in a minimum of time.

The FTC posted a guide for native advertising in 2015.[135] Native advertising is content that is sponsored by an advertiser. It may be a selection of stories, resembling in some ways, the editorial content of a website. The Commission warns that it will consider native advertising deceptive if the advertising suggests to consumers, either expressly or through implication, that the content is impartial or independent or from a source other than the advertiser.[136]

> In evaluating whether an ad is deceptive, the FTC considers the net impression the ad conveys to consumers. Because ads can communicate information through a variety of means—text, images, sounds, etc.—the FTC will look to the overall context of the interaction, not just to elements of the ad in isolation. Put another way, both what the ad says and the format it uses to convey that information will be relevant. Any clarifying information necessary to prevent deception must be disclosed clearly and prominently to overcome any misleading impression * * *
>
> The FTC also provides examples of what would be considered deceptive and what is acceptable. It also provides methods that advertisers should use to avoid deceptiveness.

(2) Advisory Opinions: In 1962, the FTC began giving advisory opinions in response to industry questions about the legality of a proposed industry action. Advisory opinions generally predict the FTC's

---

[135] https://www.ftc.gov/tips-advice/business-center/guidance/native-advertising-guide-businesses.

[136] Ibid.

response, although the Commission reserves the right to reconsider its advice if the public interest so requires.[137]

In a June 2015 opinion letter, the FTC responded to a question about a practice in a funeral home.[138]

> You have questioned whether a funeral provider violates the Funeral Rule by placing a consumer in its casket display room to wait to speak with a funeral director without first showing the consumer a casket price list ("CPL").

Readers who are familiar with Jessica Mitford's "*The American Way of Death*," published in 1963 would find the FTC question is a familiar one. As a review on Amazon.com described the book, "Jessica Mitford's exposé of the funeral industry, a number one bestseller upon first publication, is a model of muckraking—an almost incredible description of how undertakers in the U.S. assault people's souls and wallets."—Michael Joseph Gross.

Some funeral home operators would have the survivors wait in a casket display room showing more expensive models. As Mitford wrote in her book, the bereaved could ask about less expensive caskets only to be shown an obviously cheaply made box. The comparison often would drive the grieving family members to choose one of the much more expensive caskets they first saw.

> [T]he Commission deliberately sought to ensure that cost disclosure would be made "before showing the caskets." Significantly, the required price disclosure does not apply only to those caskets the provider chooses to display. It also requires the provider to list the cost of other caskets it offers. [Funeral Rule, 12 (FTC April 2015) https://www.ftc.gov/tips-advice/business-center/guidance/complying-funeral-rule.]
>
> This enables consumers to identify the least expensive options as they consider the favorable qualities of displayed models. The absence of a funeral director from the room is not relevant to whether the consumer can review her purchase options. Accordingly, it is staff's opinion that a funeral provider violates the rule when placing a consumer in its casket display or other arrangement room containing such items to wait for a funeral director without first showing the consumer a CPL.

(3) Trade Regulation Rules: The FTC publishes a notice before issuing a Trade Regulation Rule on a specific practice. Industry

---

[137] Rosden and Rosden, Law of Advertising, III, § 32.04.

[138] https://www.ftc.gov/policy/advisory-opinions/opinion-15-1-.

representatives may then comment on the proposed Trade Regulation before the rule is adopted and put into effect.[139]

The FTC approved changes in its Energy Labeling Rule[140] in October, 2015. The amendments to the Rule added items that the rule would apply to and addressed the issue of consumer notice, making sure that buyers could see the average energy costs of appliances and comparisons with other appliances.[141] "The Rule requires manufacturers to attach yellow EnergyGuide labels for many of the covered products and prohibits retailers from removing the labels or rendering them illegible."

Over the years, the FTC became much more active in challenging nutritional claims made for various food products, especially important in a weight-conscious society. The Commission has developed standards to be used to determine when a processed food can be called "lite" or "light," and has challenged the right of those marketing products with a substantial amount of saturated fat from claiming they are "cholesterol free." The FTC, along with the FDA and Department of Agriculture, regulates statements made about foods, including daily values, amounts and percentages of fats, sodium, proteins and carbohydrates.

In 2014, the FDA proposed changes in nutrition facts labels to more accurately reflect the calories that consumers actually eat. The *New York Times* reported on the changes that would require more realistic serving sizes.[142]

> [T]he proposed label will highlight the number of calories in the amounts of food most people consume at a sitting. Though an official "serving" of a soft drink might be eight ounces, for example, people may habitually consume the entire 12-ounce can or 20-ounce bottle; if so, the calories in that amount would be featured on the label.

The FDA created the Nutrition Facts label in 1993. It based its serving size, called Reference Amounts Customarily Consumed or RACCS, on eating and drinking habits of Americans from 1977–1978 and 1987–1988. Those numbers are out of date and don't reflect how much people consume.

Labels often list the calories in a bag of chips as X number per serving with two servings in a bag. But Americans don't stop at the one serving portion. They eat the whole bag. The changes would list the calories for what is now a single serving, the whole bag.

---

139 Ibid. § 32.05.

140 https://www.ftc.gov/policy/federal-register-notices/16–cfr-part–305–energy-labeling-rule-final-rule-expands-coverage.

141 https://www.ftc.gov/system/files/documents/federal_register_notices/2015/11/151102 energylabelingfrn.pdf.

142 Jane R. Brody, "Revised Food Labels Still Won't Tell Whole Story," *New York Times*, Oct. 26, 2014.

The changes are intended to make clear just what shoppers are deciding to buy, perhaps in the frozen food aisle.[143]

> Labels on ice cream, too, now list one-half cup as a serving. That would increase to one cup on the new label, bringing a serving of Haagen-Dazs Chocolate Peanut Butter Ice Cream, for example, to a whopping 680 calories.
>
> With that amount prominently displayed on the carton, a shopper might instead choose Edy's Slow Churned Double Fudge Brownie Ice Cream—just 240 calories a cup.

The proposal also includes movie theaters which would have to post the calorie count for their different sizes of popcorn (with or without butter) and restaurants that have more than 20 locations. With a general recommendation that people consume about 2,000 calories a day, the new information will make menu choices more informed ones.[144]

> During a drive-through visit to McDonald's, for instance, an individual must determine whether she can afford to add a sweet tea (150 calories) and an order of French fries (230 calories) to her crispy chicken club sandwich (670 calories) and still wrap up her day consuming 2,000 calories or fewer. In the process, she might also ponder whether she can, in fact, maintain a stable weight while consuming 2,000 calories a day—a total that may be low for a teenage athlete and high for a post-menopausal office worker.

In addition to covering the nutrition content of foods, the Federal Trade Commission established guidelines in 1992 requiring documentation of advertising claims that use of a particular product benefits the environment. The FTC standards allow an advertiser to claim that a product is "ozone safe," "biodegradable" or "compostable" only if the manufacturer can produce evidence that the ecological benefits of the product are substantial.[145] The Commission publishes the "FTC's Guides for the Use of Environmental Marketing Claims (the Green Guides)" giving advertisers the meanings of environmental terms and acceptable advertising claims.

---

[143] Ibid.

[144] Melissa Healy, "FDA unveils new national calorie-posting rules," *Los Angeles Times*, Nov. 25, 2014.

[145] The FTC sent letters to the makers of dog waste bags in 2015 warning them that their claims of the biodegradability or compostability might be deceptive. The FTC warned that simply putting the label "biodegradable" on the packaging without providing more information could be misleading, "such a claim without any qualification generally means to consumers that the product will completely break down into its natural components within one year after customary disposal. Most waste bags, however, end up in landfills where no plastic biodegrades in anywhere close to one year, if it biodegrades at all." The Commission warned of similar deception regarding claims of compostability. FTC Staff Warns Marketers and Sellers of Dog Waste Bags That Their Biodegradable and Compostable Claims May Be Deceptive, February 3, 2015, https://www.ftc.gov/news-events/press-releases/2015/02/ftc-staff-warns-marketers-sellers-dog-waste-bags-their.

73. DECEPTIVENESS: THE FTC'S DEFINITION

Even literally true statements may cause an advertiser difficulty if those statements are part of a deceptive advertisement.

Since the mid-1980s, the Federal Trade Commission has defined deceptive advertising as "a material representation, omission, or practice that is likely to mislead a consumer acting reasonably under the circumstances." Taking this definition apart, "material representation" may be taken to mean an important or decision-influencing statement in an advertisement. Also, the consumer who is to be protected is not naive or foolish, but a reasonable person who is acting sensibly.

Note that the definition does not refer to "false advertising." As noted advertising law scholar Ivan L. Preston has noted, many people will say regulators regulate "false advertising." He cautions:[146]

> That's fine for ordinary usage, but technically it's better to use the term deceptive advertising. By strict definition, false means only claims that are explicitly, literally false. However, ads also make claims [often by omission of key facts] that are explicitly true but produce false meanings.

DECEPTION BY OMISSION

In some advertisements, what is not said may be more important—and deceptive—than what is said. Omitted material, in other words, may make an implied claim which is misleading. The case of *Bristol-Myers v. FTC* involved various Young & Rubicam advertising campaigns for Bufferin, the well known pain reliever. For a time, Bufferin ads claimed that "doctors recommended Bufferin more than any other 'leading brand' of OTC [over-the-counter] internal analgesic." The FTC found it was true that from 1967 through 1971, Bufferin was recommended by doctors more often than Bayer, Excedrin, and Anacin—all, like Bufferin, aspirin-based pain relievers. Upholding an FTC finding of deceptiveness against Bristol-Myers, the Second Circuit stated:[147]

> [T]he Commission found that the ads conveyed the message that physicians recommend Bufferin more than any other OTC internal analgesic, and not just the three other leading brands of aspirin-based products. Since in fact doctors recommend Tylenol, Ascriptin and generic aspirin more often than Bufferin, the FTC found the message conveyed by the ads false and misleading.

Similarly, an over-reaching claim in an advertisement can cause difficulties for the advertiser. In the 1973 case of *Firestone Tire & Rubber Co. v. FTC*, the Commission took exception to ads with the slogan,

[146] Ivan L. Preston, *The Tangled Web They Weave: Truth, Falsity and Advertisers* (Madison: University of Wisconsin Press, 1994), p. 9.

[147] *Bristol-Myers Company v. FTC*, 738 F.2d 554, 563 (2d Cir.1984).

" 'When you buy a Firestone tire—no matter how much or how little you pay—you get a safe tire.' " Note that the advertisement made no overt claim that all Firestone tires are safe, but the FTC ruled that the ad's language contained an implied message that all Firestone tires are absolutely safe. A U.S. Court of Appeals upheld the FTC's cease-and-desist order against Firestone.[148]

TELEVISION AD MOCK-UPS

To what extent can "reality" be suspended during the filming of a television commercial without producing an ad that improperly misleads the public? Products such as butter and ice cream that would melt under the hot studio lights of yesteryear had to be replaced, often by mashed potatoes, in commercials. New cars are parked under powerful floodlights to accentuate the sheen of their finishes, and the complexions of many of those breathtakingly beautiful models shown in cosmetic ads have been artfully retouched on the computer. Do such common practices actually deceive consumers and cause them to buy goods they would otherwise refuse to purchase?

In the early days of television, cameras required a substantial amount of light for their image receptors to be able to capture images. That meant lots of lights and those lights created a lot of heat. As a result, live shots for commercials for ice creams amounted to a race between the time the cameras came on and the time it took for a scoop of ice cream to melt into a puddle. Because of that, advertisers were allowed to substitute mock ups for the original. In the case of ice cream, advertisers used mashed potatoes, suitably colored to simulate chocolate, strawberry and vanilla.

But the FTC drew a line. Advertisers could not use a mock up when they were demonstrating the feature that consumers are interested in. Using a mock up would constitute deception.

Some of the cases were based on a literal understanding of the content of the commercials. The Commission found one television commercial used to depict the protective qualities of Colgate Dental Cream with Gardol to be deceptive.[149] The ad positioned an announcer on a tropical island. As he spoke, an actor in the commercial threw a coconut at him. The coconut hit "an invisible shield" protecting the announcer. Colgate's Dental Cream with Gardol protected teeth the same way.[150]

> The visual innuendo was intended, and was conveyed to the viewer, that decay cannot get to the teeth of a person brushing

[148] *Firestone Tire & Rubber Co. v. FTC*, 481 F.2d 246, 249 (6th Cir.1973), cert. denied 414 U.S. 1112, 94 S.Ct. 841 (1973).

[149] *In the Matter of Colgate-Palmolive Company*, Docket 7660. Complaint, Nov. 1959-Decision, ll–Ia1. 9, 1961.

[150] Ibid.

> with Colgate Dental Cream with Gardol. This representation was and is false, misleading and deceptive. It deceives and misleads the public concerning the properties and the caries prevention value, if any, of Colgate Dental Cream with Gardol.

The FTC targeted a number of television ads in the 1960s with one of the most celebrated cases involving shaving cream and sandpaper.[151]

Colgate-Palmolive Company, the manufacturer and seller of Rapid Shave, commissioned the Ted Bates advertising agency to produce a series of television commercials dramatizing the superior qualities of its shaving cream. Realizing that all shaving creams were pretty much alike, some creative genius at the agency came up with the idea of demonstrating on camera that Rapid Shave could not only soften tough beards but even soften the roughest type of sandpaper.

But when the agency tried to film the commercial, the shaving cream wet the sandpaper, causing it to rip as it was being shaved. Rather than abandon the idea, the agency decided instead to coat a piece of plastic with sand to make it look like sandpaper, and use the plastic replica in its Rapid Shave campaign.

As the "sandpaper" was shown being shaved in the commercial, an announcer intoned, "To prove RAPID SHAVE'S super-moisturizing power, we put it right from the can onto this tough dry sandpaper. It was applied * * * soak * * * and off in a stroke."[152]

One hopes that few consumers rushed out to buy Rapid Shave to see whether they could shave sandpaper. The FTC issued a complaint contending that the ad constituted a deceptive advertising practice. However, when an FTC hearing examiner discovered that sandpaper actually could be shaved with Rapid Shave after it had soaked to the paper for an hour or so, he dismissed the complaint.[153] William L. Pack, the hearing examiner, noted the differences between the commercial in which Rapid Shave was applied to what appeared to be a dry sheet of sandpaper and then shaved before the 60-second commercial ended. Because sandpaper did not look like sandpaper on the television screen, the use of the mockup was acceptable, he concluded.[154]

But the FTC reversed the hearing examiner's finding concluding that the issue was not whether Rapid Shave could eventually soften sandpaper but what was depicted on the television screen. The ad contained two representations:[155]

---

[151] *Federal Trade Commission v. Colgate-Palmolive Co.*, 380 U.S. 374, 85 S.Ct. 1035 (1965). For an amusing account of this case, see Daniel Seligman, "The Great Sandpaper Shave: A Real-Life Story of Truth in Advertising," *Fortune* (Dec.1964) pp. 131–133ff.

[152] 380 U.S. 374, 376, 85 S.Ct. 1035, 1038 (1965).

[153] 380 U.S. 374, 376–377, 85 S.Ct. 1035, 1038 (1965).

[154] *In the Matter of Colgate-Palmolive Company, et al.*, 59 F.T.C. 1452, 1961.

[155] Ibid.

> (1) When applied to coarse, gritty sandpaper, 'Rapid Shave' will so moisturize the sandpaper that, immediately upon lathering, it can be cleanly shaved.
>
> (2) As proof of that fact, the viewers need not take respondents' word for it; they can see with their own eyes a test or demonstration of how 'Rapid Shave' actually shaves such sandpaper.

The commercial showed a split screen with a well-known football player on one side and the "sandpaper" on the other. Rapid Shave was applied to the player's beard and the sandpaper and then the screen showed the player on one side and a hand wielding a razor on the other making a downward stroke. The fact that Colgate-Palmolive did not disclose the time needed to soak sandpaper made the commercial deceptive, the FTC concluded. In its cease and desist order to Colgate and the Bates advertising agency, the Commission ordered it to stop using "pictures, depictions, or demonstrations are not in fact genuine or accurate representations, depictions, or demonstrations of, or do not prove the quality or merits of, any such product."

Colgate appealed and the case was taken up by the First Circuit.[156] There, Chief Judge Bailey Aldrich held that the FTC was correct in its conclusion that the ad was deceptive.[157] But the FTC's order that Colgate-Palmolive and the Bates advertising agency never use a mock up again went too far, Aldrich wrote. The case was sent back to the FTC to come up with a different order.

The FTC amended its order and Colgate appealed. The case wound up in front of Judge Aldrich again. The FTC's new order essentially repeated its Colgate's use of mock ups in ordering the company to not:[158]

> Unfairly or deceptively advertising any such product by presenting a test, experiment or demonstration that (1) is represented to the public as actual proof of a claim made for the product which is material to inducing its sale, and (2) is not in fact a genuine test, experiment or demonstration being conducted as represented and does not in fact constitute actual proof of the claim, because of the undisclosed use and substitution of a mock-up or prop instead of the product, article, or substance represented to be used therein.'

Judge Aldrich's opinion sent the case back to the FTC. The FTC appealed to the Supreme Court which took up the matter.[159] In ruling for the FTC, Chief Justice Earl Warren concluded that "the undisclosed use of plexiglass in the present commercials was a material deceptive

---

[156] *Colgate-Palmolive Co. v. FTC*, 310 F.2d 89 (1st Cir. 1962).

[157] Judge Aldrich called the matter "a rather trivial case." Ibid. at 92.

[158] Ibid. at 520.

[159] *Federal Trade Commission v. Colgate-Palmolive Co.*, 380 U.S. 374, 85 S.Ct. 1035 (1965).

practice, independent and separate from the other misrepresentation found."[160]

Because the commercial invited the viewer to see how Rapid Shave could even make sandpaper shaveable, it constituted a misrepresentation. The viewer and potential buyer was not seeing an actual demonstration or test of the product, Chief Justice Warren said. The FTC's order applied to that use of mock ups, he concluded. Colgate and the advertising agency would not be under an unbearable burden if the order were upheld.[161]

> In commercials where the emphasis is on the seller's word, and not on the viewer's own perception, the respondents need not fear that an undisclosed use of props is prohibited by the present order. On the other hand, when the commercial not only makes a claim, but also invites the viewer to rely on his own perception, for demonstrative proof of the claim, the respondents will be aware that the use of undisclosed props in strategic places might be a material deception.

The final example of misrepresentation came in a Campbell Soup commercial. The company slipped over the fine line between "demonstration" and "deception," at least in the eyes of the Federal Trade Commission.[162] Campbell Soup wanted to show just how chock full of good ingredients its vegetable soup was. The problem was that the vegetables always sank to the bottom of the bowl. Campbell's then put clear glass marbles in the bottom of the bowl so that the vegetables sat on them and were visible in its commercials.

The FTC filed a complaint and entered into a consent order with Campbell in which the company agreed to stop using the marbles.[163]

74. CORRECTIVE ADVERTISING ORDERS OF THE FTC

The Federal Trade Commission has attempted to enforce truth in advertising by requiring some advertisers to correct past misstatements.

When the FTC orders a company to run corrective advertising, it does so because the earlier, deceptive advertising has created a false impression among consumers and reinforced that belief through its continuing advertising. Corrective advertising, paid for by the company, is needed to correct that mistaken belief.

---

[160] Ibid. at 390, 1045.

[161] Ibid. at 393, 1047.

[162] *Campbell Soup Co.*, 77 F.T.C. 664 (1970).

[163] *Campbell Soup Co.*, 3 Trade Reg.Rep. Para. 19,261 (FTC, 1970).

In ordering one company to run corrective advertising, Robert Pitofsky, chairman of the Commission said,[164]

> It is important for advertisers to know that it is not enough just to discontinue a deceptive ad, and that they can be held responsible for the lingering misimpressions created by deceptive advertising.

Corporate defendants in cases where the FTC has sought to obtain corrective advertising include Coca Cola, for claims made about nutrient and vitamin content of its Hi-C fruit drinks,[165] and ITT Continental Baking Company, for ads implying that eating Profile Bread could help people to lose weight. The FTC charged that Profile was different from other bread only in being more thinly sliced, meaning that there were seven fewer calories per slice. ITT Continental Baking Company consented to a cease and desist order which did two things: first, it prohibited all further claims of weight-reducing attributes for Profile Bread, and second, the company had to devote 25 per cent of its Profile advertising for one year to disclosing that the bread was not effective for weight reduction.[166]

Similarly, the FTC ordered in 1972 that Warner-Lambert make this disclosure in its advertisements for some months: "Contrary to prior advertising, Listerine will not help prevent colds or sore throats or lessen their severity." Hearing the case on appeal, the Court of Appeals for the Fifth Circuit affirmed the order, but dropped the phrase "Contrary to Prior Advertising."[167] Writing for the court in 1977, Circuit Judge J. Skelly Wright found persuasive scientific testimony that gargling Listerine could not help a sore throat because its active ingredients could not penetrate tissue cells to reach viruses.[168] In this case the Warner-Lambert Company was not playing for small monetary stakes. The FTC required the corrective advertising statement to appear in Listerine advertising until about $10 million had been spent on touting the mouthwash.

The Court of Appeals thus approved the Commission's standard for imposing corrective advertising. The FTC standard said if a deceptive advertisement played a substantial role in creating or reinforcing "in the public's mind a false and material belief which lives on after the false advertising ceases," then there is clear harm to competitors and to the consuming public. Since merely ceasing the ad cannot avert injury to the public, the FTC said it could require corrective ads: "affirmative action

---

[164] Doan's Pills Must Run Corrective Advertising: FTC Ads Claiming Doan's Is Superior In Treating Back Pain Were Unsubstantiated May 27, 1999. https://www.ftc.gov/news-events/press-releases/1999/05/doans-pills-must-run-corrective-advertising-ftc-ads-claiming.

[165] 3 Trade Reg.Rep. Para. 19,351 (FTC, 1970).

[166] 3 Trade Reg.Rep. Para. 19,780 (FTC, Aug. 17, 1971); Note, " 'Corrective Advertising' Orders of the Federal Trade Commission," 85 *Harvard Law Review* (December, 1971), p. 478.

[167] *Warner-Lambert Co. v. FTC,* 562 F.2d 749, 762 (D.C.Cir.1977).

[168] Ibid. at 754.

designed to terminate the otherwise continuing ill effects of the advertisement."[169]

The most recent instance of FTC ordering corrective advertising came in 1999 when it ordered the makers of Doan's Pills to run the following language:[170]"Although Doan's is an effective pain reliever, there is no evidence that Doan's is more effective than other pain relievers for back pain." Doan's was the subject of a marketing campaign that focused on the pill's efficacy in treating back pain.[171]

> The new advertisements characterized Doan's as a remedy effective specifically for back pain and as containing a special ingredient (magnesium salicylate) not found in other over-the-counter analgesics. At least some of the advertisements displayed images of competing over-the-counter pain remedies.

The Commission issued a complaint about Doan's advertising finding that its advertising claims suggesting that Doan's was more effective than other pain relievers for back pain was not substantiated by scientific evidence. Its order required Novartis Corporation and Novartis Consumer Health, Inc., the marketers of Doan's, to run corrective advertising for one year and until Novartis had spent as much money as was spent on that ad campaign. Novartis petitioned the D.C. Circuit Court of Appeals to review and overturn the order.

Circuit Judge Karen LeCraft Henderson upheld the order and rejected the petition. Novartis argued that its claims about comparative effectiveness was not a material fact that needed correction. But, Judge Henderson rejected that argument pointing to the FTC's approach to what was material in consumer beliefs.[172]

> The Commission has historically presumed materiality for certain categories of claims: (1) all express claims, (2) intentional implied claims and (3) claims that "significantly involve health, safety, or other areas with which the reasonable consumer would be concerned," including a claim that "concerns the purpose, safety, efficacy, or cost of the product or service," its "durability, performance, warranties or quality" or "a finding by another agency regarding the product."

Judge Henderson quoted the *Warner-Lambert* decision in upholding the corrective advertising order. The FTC used Doan's own market research in which two studies, one done before the campaign and the other six months after the campaign ended.[173]

---

[169] Ibid. at 762.

[170] Doan's Pills Must Run Corrective Advertising: FTC Ads Claiming Doan's Is Superior In Treating Back Pain Were Unsubstantiated May 27, 1999. https://www.ftc.gov/news-events/press-releases/1999/05/doans-pills-must-run-corrective-advertising-ftc-ads-claiming.

[171] *Novartis Corp. v. FTC*, 223 F.3d 783 (D.C.Cir. 2000).

[172] Ibid. at 787.

[173] Ibid. at 788.

> [I]n 1996, a disproportionately high percentage of Doan's users and aware non-users believed that Doan's was more effective than other OTC pain relievers for back pain relief."

Because an interest in correcting mistaken beliefs by consumers was a significant government interest, that is remedying deception, Judge Henderson upheld the FTC's findings and its order for corrective advertising.

COMPARATIVE ADVERTISING

People reading or viewing advertising sometimes see claims made that Product A is "better," "more effective," etc. than Product B. This is what is known as "comparative advertising" and has been encouraged by the Federal Trade Commission in the belief that this will assist consumers in getting more needed information about products.

FTC policies say that comparative advertising should make use of competitor's trademarks and identity to help consumers make more informed choices. In a case involving the maker of Werther's Original butter cream hard candies and Nabisco, a Seventh Circuit panel rejected a trademark infringement claim on the grounds that using the Werther's name in Nabisco candy label advertising for a competing product complied with the FTC policy.[174]

> Both the FTC and the FDA encourage product comparisons. The FTC believes that consumers gain from comparative advertising, and to make the comparison vivid the Commission "encourages the naming of, or reference to competitors". 16 C.F.R. § 14.15(b). A "comparison" to a mystery rival is just puffery; it is not falsifiable and therefore is not informative.

This comparative advertising, however, must be susceptible of substantiation; false and misleading comparative statements will draw legal consequences.

For example, consider *American Home Products* [makers of Anacin] *v. Johnson and Johnson* [makers of Tylenol]. Anacin ads based on the theme "Your Body Knows" contended that Anacin was superior to Tylenol, that it was more effective in reducing inflammation, and that it worked faster than Tylenol. Johnson and Johnson [Tylenol] complained to the three television networks that the Anacin advertising was deceptive and misleading. American Home Products [Anacin] countered by suing Johnson and Johnson, claiming that the makers of Tylenol violated the Lanham Trademark Act by disparaging a competitor's product,[175] seeking an injunction against Tylenol advertising.[176]

---

174 *August Storck K.G. v. Nabisco, Inc.*, 59 F.3d 616, 618 (7th Cir. 1995).

175 Lanham Trademark Act, 44 Fed.Reg. 4738 § 43(a).

176 *American Home Products Corp. v. Johnson and Johnson*, 436 F.Supp. 785 (S.D.N.Y.1977), affirmed 577 F.2d 160 (2d Cir.1978).

This lawsuit backfired, however, because a federal district court dismissed the American Home Products [Anacin] suit and instead slapped a permanent injunction on American Home Products forbidding publishing of a misleading advertisement.[177]

ADVERTISING SUBSTANTIATION

Since the early 1970s, the FTC has set down requirements that advertisers make available proof—"substantiation," in FTC terminology—to back up their claims. At the start of its substantiation efforts, the Commission demanded of entire industries—e.g. soap and detergents, air conditioners, deodorant manufacturers—that they come forward to back up their claims. An early case in the substantiation area was the FTC proceeding, *In re Pfizer, Inc.*, decided in 1972. Pfizer, a chemical/drug manufacturing concern, had advertised its "Un-Burn" product with claims that its application would stop the discomfort of sunburn by tuning out nerve endings. The FTC told Pfizer that unless it could prove such a claim, that would be considered an unfair (and therefore illegal) trade practice. That meant an advertiser should have "a reasonable basis [for its claims] before disseminating an ad."[178] As FTC Associate Director for Advertising Practices Wallace S. Snyder wrote in 1984, " * * * ads for objective claims imply that the advertiser has a prior reasonable basis for making the claim. In light of the implied representation of substantiation, therefore, a performance claim that lacks a reasonable basis is deceptive."[179]

THE FTC AND INTERNET COMMERCE

The Internet provides growing business opportunities for "e-commerce," but the Federal Trade Commission is struggling to deal with its downside, multiplying uses of the Internet to defraud consumers.

In 2000, the FTC published a book, *"Dot Com Disclosures: Information About Online Advertising,"* urging the business community to play fair. In 2015, the FTC had more than 6,000 hits for the search term "online advertising." As online advertising continues to grow, the FTC increases its efforts to deal with traditional marketing issues as well as those that are unique to the online environment.

Essentially, the FTC applies all of its rules to the Internet, as it does any other medium of communication. The Act is not medium specific. That said, there are some features of the Internet that give rise to special consideration. Spam, the electronic message and not the trademark of

---

177 Ibid.

178 Wallace S. Snyder, "Advertising Substantiation Program," in Christopher Smith and Christian S. White, chairmen, *The FTC 1984* (New York: Practising Law Institute, 1984), p. 121; *In re Pfizer Inc.*, 81 FTC 23 (1972).

179 Snyder, loc. cit., citing *National Dynamics Corp.*, 82 FTC 488 (1973), and also *Firestone Tire & Rubber Co.*, 81 FTC 398 (1972), affirmed 481 F.2d 246 (6th Cir.1973), certiorari denied 414 U.S. 1112, 94 S.Ct. 841 (1973).

the Hormel Co., is governed by the FTC. Any misleading message that would cause a reasonable consumer to be misled falls under the purview of the FTC. The FTC also has jurisdiction over website advertising.

Advertising agencies or website designers are responsible for reviewing the information used to substantiate ad claims. They may not simply rely on an advertiser's assurance that the ad claims are substantiated. In determining whether an ad agency should be held liable, the FTC looks at the extent of the agency's participation in the preparation of the challenged ad, and whether the agency knew or should have known that the ad included false and deceptive claims.

The FTC also provides consumers with information about chain emails, e-payments, "free" sites and search engines. It may come as news to some Web surfers, but some search engines will raise the rankings for some sites during searches based on whether the site has paid the search engine company.

The FTC has stepped up its enforcement of rules regarding false claims about sharing data with third parties, failure to provide appropriate security for sensitive consumer data, use of invasive spyware or invisible tracking mechanisms, and unwanted spam[180] and telemarketing.

EFFORTS TO CONTROL SPAM

Many who use email would equate spam with litter. Anecdotal information puts the time lost in reading and deleting spam at hours every work week, although more sophisticated filtering software has substantially cut down on that time.[181] There have been any number of attempts to halt spam, either through filters and blocks or the courts, with varying degrees of success.

Spam, defined as unsought and unwelcome email, came about as the result of technology. The ability of an advertiser to contact millions of consumers at little cost has driven the rise of spam. Even if only a fraction of 1 percent of recipients reply and buy the product or service, it is cost effective. This compares with the cost of printing solicitations and the expense of postage. The *Financial Times* of London predicted that by the end of the summer of 2003, that half of all email would be spam.[182] Various online sources put the percentage of spam worldwide at between 60 and 50 percent in 2015.

---

[180] Is it a non sequitur to write "unwanted spam"?

[181] Now, of course, there is the need to canvass the spam folder to find emails from legitimate contacts.

[182] Chris Nuttall, "Warning that one in two e-mails will soon be junk messages," *Financial Times*, July 3, 2003.

In what is believed to be the largest civil award in a spam case, yet, a federal judge awarded more than $1 billion to an email service provider against three defendants in an anti-spam case.[183]

The suit was brought by an Iowa Internet service provider that serves about 5,000 subscribers. The company sued about 300 spammers who allegedly sent more than 10 million spam emails a day in 2000. The plaintiff's attorney said the company did not expect to collect the judgment.

The CAN SPAM Act[184] provides some protections and tools to help in the fight against spam. The Act provides for lawsuits by the FTC and states' attorneys general. Action by the individual states is governed by whether the federal statute has pre-empted state authority. A 2009 case[185] illustrates the operation of the Act. In *Gordon v. Virtmundo,* a private citizen brought a number of suits against an online marketing business. James Gordon's case was dismissed by a federal district court and he appealed to the Ninth Circuit Court of Appeals. There, Circuit Court Judge Richard Tallman wrote an opinion affirming the lower court's dismissal. As he did, he went through the elements of CAN-SPAM.[186]

> The Act does not ban spam outright, but rather provides a code of conduct to regulate commercial e-mail messaging practices. Stated in general terms, the CAN-SPAM Act prohibits such practices as transmitting messages with "deceptive subject headings" or "header information that is materially false or materially misleading.

The Act allows for some private party actions. Internet Service Providers who are harmed by spam may sue in federal court. Successful litigants can get injunctions against the spam provider or may seek damages. If a party chooses damages, they can be, either, the actual damages caused by the spam or a statutory amount as much as $300 per email at the discretion of the court. But apart from Internet Access Service Providers, there are no provisions for private party lawsuits.

Gordon sought to sue as an Internet Service Provider. He and his company operate on server space that they leased from GoDaddy, a domain registrar and web hosting company. GoDaddy also provides software and services. After he registered gordonworks.com Gordon created additional email accounts through the domain for about a half dozen clients, his friends and family members. He monitored the accounts and found email solicitations from Virtmundo and other online marketers. Eventually, he brought suit.

---

183 "Judge Awards ISP $1 Billion in Spam Suit," The Associated Press, Dec. 21, 2004.

184 15 U.S.C.A. Chap. 103-Controlling the Assault of Non-Solicited Pornography and Marketing Act of 2003.

185 *Gordon v. Virtmundo, Inc.*, 575 F.3d 1040 (9th Cir. 2009).

186 Ibid. at 1047–48.

A key question in the case was Gordon's status. Was he a private party or an Internet Service Provider. Gordon said he was, arguing that he gave users access to Internet content and email through gordonworks.com. But Gordon did not either control or access the hardware used to connect to the Internet, Judge Tallman wrote. That control and the hardware belong to GoDaddy.[187]

> Verizon enables his online access. GoDaddy provides the service that enables ordinary consumers to create e-mail accounts, register domain names, and build personalized web pages. Gordon has simply utilized that service for himself and on behalf of others. It matters not that he entered the keystrokes or clicked the mouse. Nor is it relevant that he created gordonworks.com e-mail addresses for family and friends, and not merely himself. While Verizon and GoDaddy might have a compelling argument that they are IAS providers within the meaning of the CAN-SPAM Act, Gordon's claim that he holds such elite status is unconvincing.

PROTECTING CHILDREN'S PRIVACY

The Children's Online Privacy Protection Act (COPPA) requires Web sites to comply with specific precautions to protect privacy rights of children under 13. The Act is aimed at commercial websites or online services directed at those children. In addition, general audience Web site operators who have actual knowledge that they are collecting information from children under 13 must comply.

These sites must get parental permission before collecting personal information from children. In one of the first actions brought under COPPA, the FTC went after Ohio Art Co., the company that makes Etch-A-Sketch.[188]

> The FTC alleged that the company's Web site collected the names, mailing addresses, e-mail addresses, age, and date of birth from children who wanted to qualify to win an Etch-A-Sketch toy on their birthday. The FTC charged that the company merely directed children to "get your parent or guardian's permission first" and then collected the information without first obtaining parental consent as required by COPPA. In addition, the FTC alleged the company collected more information from children than was reasonably necessary for children to participate in this "birthday club" activity.

The company and the FTC settled the dispute and Ohio Art agreed to pay a $35,000 penalty, delete the information it had gathered, put a

---

187 Ibid. at 1052.

188 William Savino, "Protecting Online Privacy," *Marketing Management*, Sept. 1, 2002.

link to the FTC site on its own Web page and report on its compliance with COPPA.

The social networking site Xanga.com agreed to pay a $1 million fine for violating COPPA after the FTC said the site accepted personal information from children under 13 without the consent of their parents. Xanga said that it had accepted registrations from persons who were under 13.[189]

In the summer of 2014, the FTC filed suit against Amazon because the company made it too easy for children to make purchases, without their parent's knowledge or permission, while playing games.[190]

> The Federal Trade Commission said Amazon charged parents millions of dollars of unauthorized payments for what's known as "in-app purchases," typically make-believe items popularly offered within mobile games such as Candy Crush Saga that enhance a game or allow a user to advance levels.

Critics, including child development experts, said that children purchasing things like gold coins or acorns were real-world transactions that their parents would have to pay.

In one cautionary tale, *Gizmodo* reported on an English boy, Danny Kitchen age 5, who managed to put $2,500 on his parents' credit card in 10 minutes while playing Zombie v. Ninja.[191] The boy's parents allowed him to use their iPad and access to their password to get the free-to-download game. They let him play.[192]

> Danny then went in-app purchase crazy, buying stacks of the $100 in-game keys and weapon packs, and racking up an enormous credit card bill for his mom. "I was worried and I felt sad," said Danny, when he found out, adding: "I'm banned from the iPad now."

The FTC continues to publish Industry Guides to help businesses follow the terms of the Act.

STATE REGULATION OF ADVERTISING

In the 1980s, a time in which "deregulation" was a major theme of the Reagan Administration, one effect was a continued scaling back of the aggressiveness of the nation's prime governmental regulator of advertising, the Federal Trade Commission. But from the mid-1980s on, occasional comments were heard from leaders in the advertising business

---

[189] Yuki Noguchi, "Xanga to Pay $1 Million in Children's Privacy Case," *Washington Post*, Sept. 8, 2006.

[190] Cecelia Kang, "FTC sues Amazon over children's in-app purchases," *Washington Post*, July 10, 2014.

[191] Gary Cutlack, "This Kid Blew $2,500 on In-Game Purchases in Just 10 Minutes," *Gizmodo* UK, March 1, 2013. http://gizmodo.com/5987799/this-kid-blew-2500-on-in-game-purchases-in-just-10-minutes.

[192] Ibid.

to the effect that deregulation had its problems, too. Although "getting government off the back of business and the public" was good for political mileage, when FTC regulation diminished, regulatory efforts in some states to some extent moved into the void. Perhaps it might be said that regulators, like nature, abhor a vacuum.

Advertising executives had reason to worry as state ad regulation became more insistent. Whatever their feelings about the FTC, state-to-state regulatory differences in the 1980s threatened to assemble a crazy-quilt pattern of regulations. A number of state statutes addressed that issue by relying on FTC definitions of what constituted unfair or deceptive advertising. In one California case, a state appellate court referred to federal standards. "No California court has yet defined in this setting the parameters of the term 'unfair business practice.' There are, however, guidelines set by the Federal Trade Commission and sanctioned by the United States Supreme Court * * * "[193]

Part of the rise of more aggressive state regulation of advertising may be found in the National Association of Attorneys' General. In February, 1988, Daniel Oliver, then chairman of the Federal Trade Commission, expressed some doubts about the states' consumer-protection, saying the state attorneys general were exceeding their authority. Oliver added, "Obviously, deregulation gives the opportunity for the most restrictive of attorneys general to bring cases that will have national effect, and that's not what the American consumer needs."[194]

THE NATIONAL ASSOCIATION OF ATTORNEYS GENERAL (NAAG): ENLISTING IN THE "TOBACCO WARS" OF THE LATE 1990S

During the 1990s the organization of state attorneys general became even more active. The issue: regulation of sales and advertising tobacco. By mid-1997, Big Tobacco—Philip Morris, RJR Nabisco Holdings Corp., B.A.T. Industries, Brown & Williamson and Loew's Corp's. Lorillard—was ready to compromise with regulators and critics. There had been a drumfire of criticism from Dr. David Kessler, Commissioner of the Food and Drug Administration and from former Surgeon General C. Everett Koop, and they sang along in a chorus with public health organizations including the American Cancer Society and the American Heart Association. This common-sense chorus was assisted by scores of lawsuits filed by cancer victims or their survivors, and by lawsuits filed by state attorneys general seeking billings in damages to reimburse states for healthcare costs caused by smoking. Those lawsuits, not incidentally, smoked out documents giving the lie to tobacco executives'

[193] *People v. Casa Blanca Convalescent Homes, Inc.*, 159 Cal.App.3d 509, 530, 206 Cal.Rptr. 164.

[194] M.D. Hinds, "States Are Taking Lead on Consumer Protection," *New York Times*, Feb. 8, 1988, p. 12.

claims that they had doubts that tobacco was a carcinogen or that nicotine was addictive.

The $50 billion-a-year tobacco industry reached an agreement with 46 states in which the four largest American tobacco companies agreed to make $200 billion in payments to the states and restrict their marketing efforts.

PRIVATE SUITS SUPPLEMENT GOVERNMENT ACTION

Consumers and businesses, the groups that feel the sting of uncompetitive behaviors and marketplace deception also play a part in the regulation of commercial speech. In *POM Wonderful v. Coca Cola,*[195] a distributor of pomegranate juices sued a division of the Coca Cola company over a label on a juice drink. Coca Cola objected to the suit and it was up to the Supreme Court to decide who could sue. The Court, in an opinion by Justice Anthony Kennedy, held that private parties could sue.

The case began when POM took notice of a competing juice sold by the Minute Maid division of Coca Cola. Minute Maid marketed three different "enhanced juice" drinks. One was labeled "Natural Energy," another "Antioxidants" and the third "Help Nourish Your Brain." The "Help Nourish Your Brain" drink featured the words "Pomegranate" and "Blueberry" in capital letters above a smaller set of words reading "flavored blend of juices."

Concerned about the competition and loss of its own pomegranate juice drinks, POM took a look at the Minute Maid juices, specifically the pomegranate/blueberry blend. The blend contained 0.3 percent pomegranate juice and 0.2 percent blueberry juice. The juice also contained 0.1 percent raspberry juice. The remainder of the blend was a combination of apple and grape juice.[196] POM sued under the Lanham Act.[197]

> POM alleged that the name, label, marketing, and advertising of Coca-Cola's juice blend mislead consumers into believing the product consists predominantly of pomegranate and blueberry juice when it in fact consists predominantly of less expensive apple and grape juices. Id., at 27a. That confusion, POM complained, causes it to lose sales. Id., at 28a. POM sought damages and injunctive relief. Id., at 32a–33a.

The district court granted partial summary judgment to Coca Cola reasoning that the Federal Food, Drug, and Cosmetic Act (FDCA) precluded a private suit. The FDCA prohibits the mislabeling of food. Coca Cola argued that POM could not sue because it was the sole responsibility of the federal government to deal with mislabeling

---

[195] *POM Wonderful v. Coca-Cola Co.*, 573 U.S. 102, 134 S.Ct. 2228 (2014).

[196] Ibid. at 2235.

[197] Ibid.

cases.[198] The Ninth Circuit Court of Appeals agreed with the district court and the case was accepted by the Supreme Court. Justice Kennedy took little time in correcting the lower courts.[199]

> The ruling that POM's Lanham Act cause of action is precluded by the FDCA was incorrect. There is no statutory text or established interpretive principle to support the contention that the FDCA precludes Lanham Act suits like the one brought by POM in this case. Nothing in the text, history, or structure of the FDCA or the Lanham Act shows the congressional purpose or design to forbid these suits. Quite to the contrary, the FDCA and the Lanham Act complement each other in the federal regulation of misleading food and beverage labels. Competitors, in their own interest, may bring Lanham Act claims like POM's that challenge food and beverage labels that are regulated by the FDCA.

The Lanham Act, with its emphasis on preventing unfair competition, was made for competitors. The Act allows competitors to sue but consumers can not. Justice Kennedy looked at the language of both acts but could not find any reference to the FDCA barring Lanham Act claims, he wrote.[200]

> This absence is of special significance because the Lanham Act and the FDCA have coexisted since the passage of the Lanham Act in 1946. 60 Stat. 427 (1946); ch. 675, 52 Stat. 1040 (1938). If Congress had concluded, in light of experience, that Lanham Act suits could interfere with the FDCA, it might well have enacted a provision addressing the issue during these 70 years.

In fact, competitors are in a better position to see unfair practices than federal regulators, Justice Kennedy wrote. The FDA does not pre-approve labels and instead relies on enforcement to police the market. Even then, the FDA does not take action in every instance where a label is claimed to be objectionable. Justice Kennedy sent the case back to the lower courts to take action consistent with the opinion of the Court.

POM was set to go to trial against Coca Cola in 2016.[201]

---

[198] *POM Wonderful v. Coca Cola Co.*, 727 F.Supp.2d 849 (C.D.Calif. 2010). In a number of areas of the law, federal statutes preclude anyone else from acting. This is a part of pre-emption. Under pre-emption, the federal government has decided that a subject or controversy is national in nature, that is it needs to be dealt with at the national or federal government level. As such, the states are pre-empted from regulating on these topics.

[199] *Pom Wonderful LLC v. The Coca Cola Co.*, 573 U.S. 102, 106, 134 S.Ct. 2228, 2233 (2014).

[200] Ibid. at 2237.

[201] POM had marketing problems of its own. The FTC issued a cease-and-desist order against the company after concluding that POM had engaged in false, misleading and unsubstantiated claims in its advertising that daily consumption of its products could treat, prevent, or reduce the risk of various ailments, including heart disease, prostate cancer, and erectile dysfunction. POM appealed and the D.C. Circuit Court of Appeals upheld the FTC. *POM Wonderful v. FTC*, 777 F.3d 478 (D.C.Cir 2015).

In 2011, a California woman sued Ferrero, the company that makes and markets Nutella, alleging that it had misled consumers about the health benefits of the spread. Nutella's ads which declared that Nutella was part of a "good kids' breakfast."[202]

> In the U.S., the ads featured a mother and her active children, sitting down in a sun-filled kitchen for some hearty toast with Nutella spread. The commercial suggests Nutella is a great way to get kids to eat a healthy breakfast. It just neglected to point out Nutella would be the least healthy part of it.

Ferrero entered into a settlement agreement in which it agreed to change its label, revise marketing statements and create new TV ads. In addition, the company set aside $2.5 million to pay claims from consumers who bought the spread between January 2008 and February 2012.

Patrick Hendricks, another Californian, sued StarKist alleging that the company was short-filling its canned tuna, *Consumer Reports* reported in 2015. StarKist settled the case offering cash or vouchers to consumers who filed claims (the claim period ended in November, 2015.).[203] *Consumer Reports* talked to a Northern California prosecutor about other claims over short-filling.[204]

> Larry Barlly, supervising deputy district attorney in Yolo County, Calif., told us that since 2009, 27 slack-fill cases have been settled in civil penalties against companies including Coty, CVS, Hershey, Johnson & Johnson, Mars, and Walgreens. As part of the settlements, the companies were also compelled to redesign their packaging.

Other cases are pending against other companies over the practice, Consumer Reports reported.

75. OTHER FEDERAL ADMINISTRATIVE CONTROLS

In addition to the Federal Trade Commission, many other federal agencies—including the Food and Drug Administration, the Federal Communications Commission, and the United States Postal Service—exert controls over advertising in interstate commerce.

Although of paramount importance as an advertising regulator, the FTC does not stand alone among federal agencies in its fight against suspect advertising. Federal agencies which have powers over advertising include:

---

[202] Carly Rothman, "In Nutella lawsuit over false health claims, a two-fold lesson," *Star-Ledger*, April 27, 2012.

[203] "Package Downsizing Proves That Less Is Not More," *Consumer Reports*, Sept. 24, 2015. http://www.consumerreports.org/cro/magazine/2015/09/packaging-downsizing-less-is-not-more/index.htm.

[204] Ibid.

(1) The Food and Drug Administration

(2) The United States Postal Service

(3) The Securities and Exchange Commission

(4) The Alcohol and Tobacco Tax Division of the Internal Revenue Service

Such a list by no means exhausts the number of federal agencies which, tangentially at least, can exert some form of control over advertising. Bodies such as the Federal Aeronautics Administration and the Interstate Commerce Commission and the Federal Power Commission have power to curtail advertising abuses connected with matters under each agency's jurisdiction.[205]

THE FOOD AND DRUG ADMINISTRATION AND TOBACCO SMOKE

The Food and Drug Administration's (FDA) activities in controlling labeling and misbranding overlap the powers of the FTC to a considerable degree. The Pure Food and Drug Act gives the FDA jurisdiction over misbranding and mislabeling of foods, drugs, and cosmetics.[206] The FTC, however, was likewise given jurisdiction over foods, drugs, and cosmetics by the Wheeler-Lea Amendment.[207] It used to be said that the FTC and the FDA have agreed upon a division of labor whereby FTC concentrates on false advertising and the FDA focuses attention on false labeling.[208] However, this division of labor is quite inexact. Pamphlets or literature distributed with a product have been held to be "labels" for purposes of FDA enforcement.[209]

Unlike the five-commissioner FTC—with no more than three individuals from one political party—the FDA is headed by one individual. That can add up to more aggressive approaches to high-profile controversies by the FDA than the FTC will take on. The high-energy Dr. David Kessler, a physician and a lawyer, quickly made his mark when he became FDA Commissioner in 1991. In the early to mid-1990s, the FDA was handed increased responsibility for blood safety and drugs from aspirin to AIDS medications. As science writer Herbert Burkholz wrote, "25 cents out of every dollar spent by the American consumer goes for products regulated by the FDA."

[205] See Note, "The Regulation of Advertising," *Columbia Law Review* Vol. 56:7 (Nov. 1956) pp. 1019–1111, at p. 1054, citing 24 Stat. 378 (1887), 49 U.S.C.A. § 1 (ICC); 41 Stat. 1063 (1920), 16 U.S.C.A. § 791(a) (FTC); 52 Stat. 1003 (1938), as amended, 49 U.S.C.A. § 491.

[206] 52 Stat. 1040 (1938), 21 U.S.C.A. § 301.

[207] See "The Wheeler Lea Amendment" to the Federal Trade Commission Act, 52 Stat. 111 (1938), as amended, 15 U.S.C.A. § 45(a)(1).

[208] See, for example, 2 CCH Trade Reg.Rep. (10th ed.), Paragraph 8540, p. 17,081 (1954).

[209] See *United States v. Kordel*, 164 F.2d 913 (7th Cir.1947); *United States v. Article of Device Labeled in Part "110 V Vapozone,"* 194 F.Supp. 332 (N.D.Cal.1961).

The FDA also has responsibility for inspection of fish and meat and food products, under the 1938 Federal Food, Drug, and Cosmetic Act. Dr. Kessler faced daunting challenges, but set about streamlining FDA investigations and enforcement, and was much in the headlines in 1994 as he took on tobacco industry claims that nicotine is not addictive. Among Dr. Kessler's suggestions to Congress was the possibility of regulating nicotine as a drug (to be sold by prescriptions at pharmacies?) and restricting cigarette advertising to protect children from intentional or unintentional encouragement to smoke.[210] As the FDA confronted the tobacco industry, the FTC decided not to take on the "Joe Camel" billboards and magazine ads criticized on the theory they were aimed at making cigarette smoking attractive to children. The crusading Dr. Kessler, however, resigned from the FDA in 1997.

LABELING RULES GET BACKING OF THE D.C. CIRCUIT: REYNOLDS OVERTURNED

Background: In the landmark libel decision in *New York Times v. Sullivan* (1964), advertising for the first time received limited protection under the First Amendment. Since then, protection for advertising ("commercial speech") has grown, restricting some government regulatory efforts. In general, if an advertisement touts a legal product and is not misleading, government regulation may be curtailed. In such cases, under the *Central Hudson* precedent, government must show that its regulatory efforts are not overly extensive and that regulations will create the good effect sought by government.[211] In addition, there are precedents in advertising law where advertisers have been forced by the Federal Trade Commission to put "corrective" statements on their messages if previous ads contained false or misleading statements.[212]

In 2009, Congress passed the Family Smoking Prevention and Tobacco Control Act[213] intended to reduce the number of young people who smoke. The Food and Drug Administration was given the task and approached it in a number or ways including more regulation of sales, advertising and package labeling.

The FDA approached the task of warning people about the dangers of cigarettes with graphic warning labels that showed explicitly the possible health consequences of smoking. They included labels featuring a diseased lung, the corpse of a smoker and cigarette smoke coming from a tracheotomy tube. The FDA announced its plans in 2011 and the

---

[210] Philip J. Hilts, "Ban on Cigarettes Could be Avoided, FDA Chief Says," *New York Times*, June 29, 1994, pp. A1, A10.

[211] *Central Hudson Gas & Electric Co. v. Public Service Commission of New York*, 447 U.S. 557, 100 S.Ct. 2343 (1980), discussed in this textbook at pp. 863–864.

[212] See, e.g., *Warner-Lambert Co. v. FTC*, 562 F.2d 749, 762 (D.C.Cir. 1977); see also Note, Corrective Advertising Orders of the Federal Trade Commission, 85 *Harvard Law Review* (December, 1971), p. 478.

[213] 111 P.L. 31; 123 Stat. 1776.

nation's largest tobacco companies, including R.J. Reynolds and Lorillard sued.

In *R.J. Reynolds Tobacco Company et al. v. United States Food and Drug Administration,* Judge Richard J. Leon granted a preliminary injunction against the FDA campaign.[214] Judge Leon wrote, "... [P]laintiffs raise for the first time in our Circuit the question of whether the FDA's new and mandatory graphic images, when combined with certain textual warnings on cigarette packaging, are unconstitutional under the First Amendment." The judge concluded that the plaintiffs had demonstrated a "substantial likelihood that they will prevail on the merits of their position that these images unconstitutionally compel speech and that they will suffer irreparable harm absent injunctive relief pending judicial review of the constitutionality of the FDA's Rule."

The D.C. Circuit Court of Appeals heard the FDA's appeal but upheld the circuit court.[215] The D.C. Circuit panel concluded in a 2–1 decision that an intermediate scrutiny test[216] should be applied. Under the test, the state must show that the law advances a substantial state interest and must be substantially related to achieving those purposes. In an Opinion by Judge Janice Brown, the two-judge majority concluded that the FDA had not met the burden of showing evidence of the effects of such advertising.[217]

> FDA has not provided a shred of evidence—much less the "substantial evidence" required by the APA[218]—showing that the graphic warnings will "directly advance" its interest in reducing the number of Americans who smoke. FDA makes much of the "international consensus" surrounding the effectiveness of large graphic warnings, but offers no evidence showing that such warnings have directly caused a material decrease in smoking rates in any of the countries that now require them.

Judge Brown's opinion noted the FDA's offer of studies conducted in Canada and Australia, but rejected their relevance to the narrow interpretation of the intent of the graphic warnings.[219]

> While studies of Canadian and Australian youth smokers showed that the warnings on cigarette packs caused a substantial number of survey participants to think—or think more—about quitting smoking, Proposed Rule at 69,532, and

[214] *R.J. Reynolds Tobacco Company, et al. v. United States Food and Drug Administration*, Civil Case No. 11–1482 (RJL), Memorandum Opinion, November 7, 2011 [Dkt.#11], pp. 1–2.

[215] *R.J. Reynolds Tobacco Co. v. FDA*, 696 F.3d 1205 (4thCir. 2012).

[216] See Appendix B.

[217] *R.J. Reynolds Tobacco Co. v. FDA*, 696 F.3d 1205, 1219 (4thCir. 2012).

[218] The analysis was governed by the Administrative Procedure Act. "The APA requires us to 'hold unlawful and set aside agency action, findings, and conclusions found to be ... unsupported by substantial evidence.' 5 U.S.C. § 706(2)." At 1218.

[219] *R.J. Reynolds Tobacco Co. v. FDA*, 696 F.3d 1205, 1219 (4thCir. 2012).

> FDA might be correct that intentions are a "necessary precursor" to behavior change, Final Rule at 36,642, it is mere speculation to suggest that respondents who report increased thoughts about quitting smoking will actually follow through on their intentions. And at no point did these studies attempt to evaluate whether the increased thoughts about smoking cessation led participants to actually quit. Another Australian study reported increased quit attempts by survey participants after that country enacted large graphic warnings, but found "no association with short-term quit success."

Following the loss in the Circuit Court of Appeals, the FDA abandoned its efforts to require the graphic warnings.[220] The FDA faced a deadline to file an appeal to the Supreme Court and Attorney General Eric Holder said that consultations among the Justice Department, the Department of Health and Human Services and the FDA came to the conclusion that the government would not seek Supreme Court review. As for the FDA, the agency said it would take another try to implement the Tobacco Control Act.[221]

> The FDA said in a statement Tuesday that it will go back to the drawing board and "undertake research to support a new rulemaking consistent with the Tobacco Control Act," the 2009 law that requires the agency to find ways to reduce the estimated 440,000 annual deaths attributable to tobacco use.

But in the summer of 2014, the D.C. Circuit overturned the decision in *R.J. Reynolds*.[222] In *American Meat Institute v. Department of Agriculture*, meat producers challenged a government requirement that meat products show the country of origin for the meat. A district court in the District of Columbia rejected the American Meat Institute's (AMI) request for an injunction against the regulations. A three-judge panel of the D.C. Circuit affirmed the district court and the case was resubmitted to the whole of the D.C. Circuit en banc[223].

> The regulation required specificity in the labeling of all aspects of the meat business.[224]

> For example, meat derived from an animal born in Canada and raised and slaughtered in the United States, which formerly could have been labeled "Product of the United States and Canada," would now have to be labeled "Born in Canada, Raised and Slaughtered in the United States."

---

[220] Brady Dennis, "Government quits legal battle over graphic cigarette warnings," *Washington Post*, March 19, 2013.

[221] Ibid.

[222] *American Meat Institute v. U.S. Dept. of Agriculture*, 2014 WL 3732697 (D.C. Cir. 2014).

[223] See Appendix B.

[224] *American Meat Institute v. U.S. Dept. of Agriculture*, 2014 WL 3732697 (D.C. Cir. 2014).

In his opinion for the Circuit, Senior Judge Stephen Williams held that the test for government regulation of commercial speech would allow for the new requirement. Judge Williams applied a test for government regulation that came from a Supreme Court case involving the regulation of attorney advertising.[225] In *Zauderer v. Office of Disciplinary Counsel*, the Supreme Court dealt with an Ohio state bar rule regarding attorney advertising.[226] The Supreme Court held that some of Zauderer's attorney advertisements were protected as commercial speech but that other parts could be regulated by the state bar. Justice Byron White, writing the opinion for the Court noted the development of the commercial speech doctrine, the principles that rule the government's ability to control or punish speech.[227]

> Our general approach to restrictions on commercial speech is also by now well settled. The States and the Federal Government are free to prevent the dissemination of commercial speech that is false, deceptive, or misleading, see *Friedman v. Rogers*, 440 U.S. 1, 99 S.Ct. 887, 59 L.Ed.2d 100 (1979), or that proposes an illegal transaction, see *Pittsburgh Press Co. v. Human Relations Comm'n*, 413 U.S. 376, 93 S.Ct. 2553, 37 L.Ed.2d 669 (1973). Commercial speech that is not false or deceptive and does not concern unlawful activities, however, may be restricted only in the service of a substantial governmental interest, and only through means that directly advance that interest. *Central Hudson Gas & Electric*, supra, 447 U.S., at 566, 100 S.Ct., at 2351.

The Fourth Circuit had applied the *Central Hudson* test to the FDA's proposal to require graphic warning labels on cigarette packs. Because the FDA had not shown that the warning labels would, in fact, advance the interest in reducing the number of people smoking, that regulation was not constitutional.

But in the *American Meat* case, the Fourth Circuit decided to use the *Zauderer* test. *Zauderer* permitted the government to regulate speech by requiring additional information.[228]

> We do not suggest that disclosure requirements do not implicate the advertiser's First Amendment rights at all. We recognize that unjustified or unduly burdensome disclosure requirements might offend the First Amendment by chilling protected commercial speech. But we hold that an advertiser's rights are adequately protected as long as disclosure requirements are

[225] *Zauderer v. Office of Disciplinary Counsel of the Supreme Court of Ohio*, 471 U.S. 626, 105 S.Ct. 2265 (1985).

[226] State bar associations have long been concerned with the image of the legal profession and so have regulated the style and content of attorney advertising, punishing advertising that would lessen the public's image of the profession of law and demean the dignity of the practice.

[227] *Zauderer v. Office of Disciplinary Counsel of the Supreme Court of Ohio*, 471 U.S. 626, 638, 105 S.Ct. 2265, 2275 (1985).

[228] Ibid. at 2282.

> reasonably related to the State's interest in preventing deception of consumers.

The Meat Institute argued that there was not substantial interest for the government to require disclosure of the country of origin of the meat products.[229] AMI disparages the government's interest as simply being that of satisfying consumers' "idle curiosity."

But Judge Williams found substantially more consumer interest in the origins of meat products.[230]

> But here we think several aspects of the government's interest in country-of-origin labeling for food combine to make the interest substantial: the context and long history of country-of-origin disclosures to enable consumers to choose American-made products; the demonstrated consumer interest in extending country-of-origin labeling to food products; and the individual health concerns and market impacts that can arise in the event of a food-borne illness outbreak. Because the interest motivating the 2013 rule is a substantial one, we need not decide whether a lesser interest could suffice under Zauderer.
>
> Country-of-origin information has an historical pedigree that lifts it well above "idle curiosity."

Along with affirming the three-judge panel and the district court, the D.C. Circuit specifically overruled the *Reynolds* decision that required the FDA to produce evidence that its graphic warning labels would, in fact, reduce smoking and smoking-related illnesses and deaths.

THE U.S. POSTAL SERVICE

Postal controls over advertising can be severe. Congress was provided with lawmaking power to operate the postal system under Article I, Sec. 8 of the Constitution. This power was long delegated by Congress to a Postmaster General and his Post Office Department. It has long been established that the mails could not be used to carry things which, in the judgment of Congress, were socially harmful.[231] The Postmaster General had the power to exclude articles or substances which Congress has proscribed as non-mailable. With the passage of the Postal Reorganization Act of 1970, the Post Office Department was abolished as a Cabinet-level agency, and was replaced by the United States Postal Service, a subdivision of the Executive branch.[232]

Perhaps the Postal Service's greatest deterrent to false advertising is contained in the power to halt delivery of materials suspected of being

---

[229] *American Meat Institute v. U.S. Dept. of Agriculture,* 760 F.3d 18 (D.C. Cir. 2014).

[230] Ibid.

[231] See, for example *Public Clearing House v. Coyne,* 194 U.S. 497, 24 S.Ct. 789 (1904).

[232] 39 U.S.C.A. § 3003.

designed to defraud mail recipients.[233] The Postal Service can order nondelivery of mail, and can impound suspected mail matter.[234]

The administrative fraud order is not the only kind of mail fraud action available to the Postal Service. Instead of administrative procedure through the Service, a *criminal* mail fraud case may be started. Criminal cases are prosecuted by a U.S. attorney in a United States District Court. Conviction under the federal mail fraud statute can result in a fine of up to $1,000, imprisonment for up to 5 years, or both.[235] Criminal fraud orders are used when the U.S. Postal Service wishes to operate in a punitive fashion. The administrative fraud orders, on the other hand, are more preventive in nature.

THE SECURITIES AND EXCHANGE COMMISSION

Securities markets are attractive to fast-buck artists, so the sale and publicizing of securities are kept under a watchful governmental eye. Most states have "Blue Sky" laws which enable a state agency to halt the circulation of false or misleading information about the sale of stocks, bonds or the like.[236] The work of the Securities and Exchange Commission, however, is far more important in protecting the public.

After the stock market debacle of 1929, strong regulations were instituted at the federal level to prevent deceptive statements about securities. Taken together, the Securities Act of 1933[237] and the Securities Exchange Act of 1934[238] gave the SEC great power over the sale and issuance of securities.

Sale of securities to investors cannot proceed until complete and accurate information has been given, registering the certificates with the SEC.[239] A briefer version of the registration statement is used in the "prospectus" circulated among prospective investors before the stock or bond can be offered for sale.[240] If misleading statements have been made about a security "in any material respect" in either registration documents or in the prospectus, the Commission may issue a "stop order" which removes the right to sell the security.[241] Furthermore, unless a security is properly registered and its prospectus accurate, it is a criminal offense to use the mails to sell it or to advertise it for sale.[242]

---

233 Ibid. III, § 50.02.

234 Ibid. Rosden & Rosden II, § 18.02, n. 17.

235 18 U.S.C.A. § 1341; Ague, Ibid. at 61.

236 See Note, "The Regulation of Advertising," *Columbia Law Review* op. cit. p. 1065.

237 48 Stat. 74 (1933), 15 U.S.C.A. § 77.

238 48 Stat. 881 (1934), as amended, 15 U.S.C.A. §§ 78(a)–78(jj).

239 48 Stat. 77 (1933), as amended, 15 U.S.C.A. § 77(f).

240 48 Stat. 78 (1933), 15 U.S.C.A. § 77(j).

241 48 Stat. 79 (1933), as amended, 15 U.S.C.A. § 77(h)(b) and (d). For an example of litigation charging false statements in the sale of corporate bonds, see *Escott v. BarChris Construction*, 283 F.Supp. 643 (S.D.N.Y.1968).

242 48 Stat. 84 (1933), as amended, 15 U.S.C.A. § 77(e).

An unscrupulous seller of securities has more to fear than just the SEC. Under a provision of the United States Code, a person who has lost money because he was tricked by a misleading prospectus may sue a number of individuals, including persons who signed the SEC registration statement and every director, officer, or partner in the firm issuing the security.[243]

THE ALCOHOL AND TOBACCO TAX DIVISION, INTERNAL REVENUE SERVICE

Ever since this nation's unsuccessful experiment with prohibition, the federal government has kept a close eye on liquor advertising. The responsible agency is the Alcohol and Tobacco Tax Division of the Internal Revenue Service.[244] Liquor advertising may not include false or misleading statements, and may not disparage competing products. False statements may include misrepresenting the age of a liquor, or claiming that its alcoholic content is higher than it is in reality.[245]

The Alcohol and Tobacco Tax Division has harsh sanctions at its disposal. If an advertiser violates a regulation of the Division, he is subject to a fine, and could even be put out of business if his federal liquor license is revoked.[246]

The FTC and other federal agencies by no means provide the whole picture of controls over advertising. There are many state regulations affecting political advertising and legal advertising by government bodies, but they cannot be treated here. States also regulate the size and location of billboards, but space does not permit discussion of these statutes. We now turn to consideration of some of the ways in which states have regulated commercial advertising in the mass media.

76. THE PRINTERS' INK STATUTE

Most states have adopted some version of the model statute which makes fraudulent and misleading advertising a misdemeanor.

One of the best known restraints upon advertising exists at the state level in the various forms of the Printers' Ink statute adopted in 48 states. *Printer's Ink*, magazine, in 1911, advocated that states adopt a model statute which would make false advertising a misdemeanor. Leaders in the advertising and publishing world realized the difficulty in securing prosecutions for false advertising under the usual state fraud statutes. Considerable initiative in gaining state enactment of Printers' Ink

243 48 Stat. 82 (1933), 15 U.S.C.A. § 77(k).

244 27 U.S.C.A. § 205.

245 Ibid.

246 Ibid.

statutes was generated through the Better Business Bureau and through various advertising clubs and associations.

Although the Printers' Ink statute is famous, its fame is greater than its present-day usefulness as a control over advertising. Relatively few relevant cases exist which indicate that the statute has seen little use in bringing cheating advertisers to court. The Printers' Ink statute may still be useful as a guideline, or in providing a sanction which local Better Business Bureaus may threaten to invoke even if they seldom do so.[247]

The Printers' Ink statute is aimed and enforced primarily against advertisers rather than against units of the mass media which may have no knowledge that an ad is false or misleading.[248] This statute was widely adopted, apparently because the common law simply did not provide adequate remedies against false advertising, especially in an economy which has grown so explosively.

77. LOTTERIES

Federal and state prohibitions on advertising or publicizing of lotteries are changing as many states have started lotteries as revenue measures.

The theory of laws forbidding advertising or publicizing lotteries is that the public needed to be protected from gambling.[249] In recent years, however, the desperate search for revenues led to creation of government-run lotteries in many states, making federal efforts to silence advertising or publicity hopelessly outdated.

What then, is a lottery? There are three elements:

(1) *Consideration*—This usually means money paid to purchase a lottery ticket or a chance on an auto or some other item which a service organization is offering to raise money. But in some states, consideration need not be money paid. Just the effort required to enter a contest, as going to a store to get an entry blank or having to mail a product label, at times has been termed "consideration."[250]

(2) *Prize*—A prize in a lottery is something of value, and generally of greater worth than the consideration invested.

(3) *Chance*—The element of chance—the gambling element—is what led Victorian-era Congressmen to pass the first federal statutes against lotteries in 1890. There can, however, be an element of certainty accompanying the buying of chances in a lottery. For example, if a woman buys

---

[247] Note, "The Regulation of Advertising," op. cit. p. 1057.

[248] Ibid. at 1059–1060; *State v. Beacon Pub. Co.*, 141 Kan. 734, 42 P.2d 960 (1935).

[249] 18 U.S.C.A. § 1304 forbade ads or information about lotteries, and 39 U.S.C.A. § 3005 prohibited mailing information giving publicity to lotteries.

[250] *Brooklyn Daily Eagle v. Voorhies*, 181 Fed. 579 (C.C.E.D.N.Y.1910).

> a newspaper subscription she is certain to receive the newspaper which includes a chance in a prize contest, but—many years ago—one court termed that promotion a lottery.[251]

In May 1990, a new federal law, the "Charity Games Clarification Act," went into effect, permitting print or broadcast promotion and advertising of lotteries conducted by non-profit organizations and of all official state lotteries in any state conducting such lotteries.[252] The new law also allows commercial corporations to advertise occasional lotteries as long as such a promotional activity is not related to the corporation's usual course of business.

Originally, congressional lottery legislation was aimed at helping states to control that form of gambling. In general, federal law made broadcasting of a lottery advertisement a crime. However, an exception was made to allow broadcasters to carry ads for state-run lotteries on those stations licensed in states which themselves have lotteries.[253]

Radio and television broadcasts, however, don't stop at state lines. This was the underlying problem confronting the U.S. Supreme Court involving a North Carolina radio station owned by Edge Broadcasting Co. That broadcaster was located in the, then, non-lottery state of North Carolina. The radio station, however, is only three miles from the Virginia state line, and Virginia does have a state lottery. More than 90% of the radio station's audience lives in Virginia.

The radio station challenged the federal ban on broadcasting lottery ads, and a federal district court and a U.S. Court of Appeals held that the ban was unconstitutional. The Court of Appeals held 2–1 that there was no reasonable fit between the goal of protecting North Carolina listeners and the means chosen to achieve it. The reason? About 10% of the listeners in North Carolina could get the same lottery information from Virginia media.[254]

The U.S. Supreme Court, however, reversed the appellate court by a margin of 7–2. Writing for the Court, Justice Byron White found that despite its minimal impact in this case, the federal statute was sufficiently effective in advancing a state's legitimate governmental aim of restricting dissemination of gambling ads. This upheld the constitutionality of the federal ban on advertising lotteries over stations which are not physically located in states having state lotteries.[255]

---

[251] *Brooklyn Daily Eagle v. Voorhies*, 181 Fed. 579 (C.C.E.D.N.Y.1910).

[252] Public Law 100–667, 132, amending Sec. 43(a) Title 15 USC 1125(a).

[253] 18 U.S.C.A. § 1307.

[254] *Edge Broadcasting Co. v. United States*, 956 F.2d 263 (4th Cir.1992).

[255] *United States v. Edge Broadcasting Co.*, 509 U.S. 418, 113 S.Ct. 2696 (1993), 21 Med.L.Rptr. 1577.

GREATER NEW ORLEANS BROADCASTING ASSN. V. UNITED STATES

It turned out that *United States v. Edge Broadcasting* (1993) did not have much power to extend its conclusions by analogy from efforts to regulate lottery ads to controlling advertisements of casino gambling. As noted above, the *Edge Broadcasting* decision upheld the constitutionality of 18 U.S.C. § 1304, the federal statute which was applied to prevent broadcast advertising of the Virginia Lottery by a radio station located in North Carolina.[256]

In 1999, however, the Supreme Court voted unanimously in *Greater New Orleans Broadcasting Association v. United States* that § 1304 could not be applied to ads for private casino gambling broadcast by radio and TV stations in Louisiana, where casino gambling is legal. This was the holding even though signals from Louisiana broadcasting stations reach far into both Texas and Arkansas, where private casino gambling is unlawful.[257]

The statute in question, captioned "Broadcast Lottery Information," prohibits broadcasting over licensed stations of " 'information concerning any lottery, gift, enterprise, or similar scheme, offering prizes dependent in whole or in part upon lot or chance * * * ' " Each day's violation of this statute by licensed broadcaster called for a criminal penalty of a fine and imprisonment for not more than a year, or both. But even though those criminal sanctions existed, the Federal Communications Commission generally dealt with violations of § 1304 with administrative sanctions against the offending radio or TV station.[258]

Writing for the Court, Justice John Paul Stevens noted that § 1304 was passed in 1934 when there was a uniform policy, before states and Indian tribes had legalized gambling operations.

Greater New Orleans Broadcasting Association (GNOBA) brought a claim against the United States and the Federal Communications Commission that the enforcement of § 1304 and related FCC regulations violate the First Amendment. Interpreting the four-part *Central Hudson* test,[259] both a U.S. district court and the Fifth Circuit Court of Appeals upheld the government's right to prohibit advertising of gaming.[260]

The district and circuit courts held that the restrictions sufficiently supported government's " 'substantial interest (1) in protecting the interest of nonlottery states and (2) in reducing participation in gambling and thereby minimizing the social costs associated therewith.' " The district court pointed out that not all broadcast advertising about casinos

---

[256] Ibid.

[257] *Greater New Orleans Broadcasting Association v. United States*, 527 U.S. 173, 119 S.Ct. 1923, 1926 (1999).

[258] 527 U.S. 173, 119 S.Ct. 1923, 1926 (1999).

[259] The *Central Hudson* test is discussed above.

[260] Ibid. at 1927–1928.

was prohibited. Advertising "promoting a casino's amenities rather than its 'gaming aspects' " not only was permissible. Further, it was observed that advertising of casinos in Louisiana and Mississippi was actually abundant.[261]

Following the *Central Hudson* test's Part 1, the broadcast ads were not misleading and concerned the lawful activity of legal casino gambling. Under Part 2, the government was characterized by the Supreme Court as having a substantial interest in preventing societal ills associated with gambling. Even so, Congress—with its legislation sanctioning casino gambling for Indian tribes and exempting state-run lotteries and casinos from anti-gambling statutes sent a mixed message. As Justice Stevens wrote, "Whatever its character in 1934 when § 1304 was adopted, the federal policy of discouraging gambling in general and casino gambling in particular is now decidedly equivocal."[262]

Part 3 of the *Central Hudson* test—"whether the speech restriction directly and materially advances the asserted governmental interest"—and Part 4—"whether the speech restriction is not more extensive than necessary"—did not pass muster in the context of the regulations as applied to Louisiana broadcasters. Justice Stevens wrote that the " * * * operation of § 1304 and its attendant regulatory regime is so pierced by exemptions and inconsistencies that the Government cannot hope to exonerate it." He noted that a broadcaster may not carry advertising about privately operated casino gambling,[263]

> regardless of the location of the station or the casino. * * * On the other hand, advertisements for tribal casino gambling authorized by state compacts—whether operated by the tribe or by a private party pursuant to management contract—are subject to no such broadcast ban, even if the broadcaster is located in or broadcasts to a jurisdiction with the strictest of antigambling policies * * *

Lifting the prohibition of advertising private casino gambling from Louisiana broadcasters, Justice Stevens wrote:[264]

> Had the Federal Government adopted a more coherent policy, or accommodated the rights of speakers in States that have legalized the underlying conduct, see *Edge*, 509 U.S. at 428, 113 S.Ct. 2696, this might be a different case. But under current federal law, as applied to * * * [the broadcasters] and the messages they wish to convey, the broadcast prohibition in 18

[261] Ibid. at 1919, quoting 866 F.Supp. 974, 979 (E.D.La.1994). The government's prohibitions of advertising gaming in this case were upheld twice by the Fifth Circuit, at 69 F.3d 1296, 1298 (1995), affirming a grant of summary judgment for the government, and again, after remand, at 149 F.3d 334 (1998).

[262] Ibid. at 1931–1932.

[263] Ibid. at 1933.

[264] Ibid. at 1935–1936.

U.S.C. § 1304 and 47 CFR § 73.1211 violates the First Amendment.

78. SELF-REGULATION

Leading communications companies have developed standards to govern their acceptance or rejection of advertising.

Publishers and broadcasters must know the legal status of advertising. If it can be proved that they knew that an advertisement is fraudulent, they may be held responsible for that ad along with the person or company who placed it in the publication. Advertising departments on many newspapers, moreover, often serve as a kind of advertising agency. In this capacity, the advertising staff must be able to give knowledgeable counsel and technical advice to advertisers.

In general, publishers are not liable to the individual consumer for advertising which causes financial loss or other damage unless the publisher or his employees knew that such advertising was fraudulent or misleading. The absence of liability for damage, however, does not mean that there is an absence of responsibility to the public generally and to individual readers of a publication.

The newspaper or broadcast station which permits dishonest or fraudulent advertising hurts its standing with both its readers and its advertisers. Publishers and broadcasters, who perceive psychological and economic advantages in refusing dishonest advertising, also appear to be becoming more cognizant that they have a moral duty to protect the public.

Responsible media units go to great lengths to ensure that advertising which they publish or broadcast is honest. Some newspapers' advertising acceptance statements, such as the one used by the *Dallas Morning News*, are very specific, spelling out advertisements which will not be accepted for publication. For example, the *Dallas Morning News* says it will not accept "bait and switch" ads: "Advertisements describing goods not available and not intended to be sold on request, but used as 'bait' to lure customers." Other newspapers provide long lists of ads that are not acceptable; some include fortune tellers, palm readers, and faith healers, along with forbidding publication of ads for illegal or harmful activities or substances.[265]

THE NATIONAL ADVERTISING DIVISION/NATIONAL ADVERTISING REVIEW BOARD

In addition to self-regulation by individual media units, a broader voluntary alternative exists in the National Advertising Division of the Council of Better Business Bureau and the National Advertising Review

---

[265] *Dallas Morning News* Standards, 1983; R.L. Moore, R.T. Farrar & E.L. Collins, *Advertising and Public Relations Law* (Mahwah, NJ, 1998) 319–324.

Board (NAD/NARB). These organizations serve as unofficial channels to try to resolve advertising disputes. Established in the 1970s by the Council of Better Business Bureaus and major advertising associations,[266] the NAD receives questions and complaints about national advertising, and conducts preliminary discussions with advertisers. Its purview is strictly national advertising which is suspected of deception. The NAD takes complaints from individuals and companies and also generates some of its own "cases" by monitoring national advertising in print and electronic mass media.

If an advertiser and the NAD cannot agree after initial discussions, NAD publishes a report outlining the issues for referral to the NARB.[267] Later, the NARB will produce its own report on the specific controversy. For example, the NAD in 1992 investigated Norelco's 950 RX electric razor, in response to an inquiry about how accurately a TV animation depicted "the action of the lift and cut system." After Norelco produced copies of six United States patents plus microphotography showing the lift and cut system actually in operation, the NAD concluded that the animated claim in the TV ad was substantiated. Findings such as these—including some which are adverse to advertisers and then referred to the NARB for further review—are published in NAD Reports. The reports contain the disclaimer that if an advertisement is changed or stopped, that "is not be taken as an admission of impropriety on any advertiser's part."

Nevertheless, some advertisers who face NAD questions do discontinue or modify ads, or provide substantiation before running the ads again. Take the case of a consumer who complained that the U.S. Postal Service had not lived up to its TV ads claiming "Two, Two, Two, Two-day Priority Mail. Two. That's delivery in just two days of up to two pounds for just $2.90." The ad did have a disclaimer, "Some restrictions Apply." In fact, a consumer who mailed documents from Michigan to Connecticut discovered that his shipment took 10 days, not two. This NAD inquiry resulted in the Postal Service agreeing to add a statement telling customers to consult their local post office for details.[268]

79. THE RIGHT TO REFUSE SERVICE

A newspaper or magazine is not a public utility and, in general, may choose those with whom it cares to do business. The right, however, is not absolute when media use advertising refusal as an unfair competitive weapon.

---

[266] The American Advertising Federation, the American Association of Advertising Agencies, and the Association of National Advertisers.

[267] NAD Case Reports, Feb. 17, 1992.

[268] Ibid.

The general rule: A newspaper or magazine is a private enterprise and may carry on business transactions with whom it pleases. An old but important case decided in 1931 declared:[269]

> If a newspaper were required to accept an advertisement, it could be compelled to publish a news item. If some good lady gave a tea, and submitted to the newspaper a proper account of the tea, and the editor of the newspaper refused to publish it * * * she, it seems to us, would have as much right to compel the newspaper to publish the account as would a person engaged in business to compel a newspaper to publish an advertisement * * *
>
> Thus, as a newspaper is strictly a private enterprise, the publishers thereof have a right to publish whatever advertisements they desire and to refuse to publish whatever advertisements they do not desire to publish.

THE RESIDENT PARTICIPATION CASE

One of the most eloquent pleas for forced access to advertising space was seen in an air pollution dispute in Denver, Colorado. The setting in Denver should be idyllic—a city ringed by the magnificent Rocky Mountains. But not all was well in the late 1960s. On some days, Denver residents suffered from eye-burning smog.

When news arrived that Pepcol, Inc., a subsidiary of the giant conglomerate Beatrice Foods, was going to build a rendering plant within the Denver city limits, protests resulted. A citizens group calling itself Resident Participation of Denver, spurred by visions of a smelly plant processing "dead animals, guts, and blood" and producing "disgusting garbage,"[270] attempted to place advertisements in Denver's competing dailies, the *Denver Post* and the *Rocky Mountain News*. The newspapers rejected the ads on the ground that the proposed wording called for a boycott of Beatrice Foods products, and boycott advertising was forbidden by Colorado statute.[271]

The Resident Participation group then re-worded its advertising without reference to boycott, but listed Beatrice Foods products such as Meadow Gold milk, cheese, and ice cream. The ad, as rewritten, included suggested letters. Readers were asked to clip out, sign, and mail the letters, protesting the rendering plant project to city and state officials. Both newspapers again refused to print the advertisements.[272]

---

[269] *Shuck v. Carroll Daily Herald*, 215 Iowa 1276, 1281, 247 N.W. 813, 815 (1933). See also *Miami Herald Pub. Co. v. Tornillo*, 418 U.S. 241, 94 S.Ct. 2831 (1974).

[270] Plaintiffs Exhibit "A," Resident Participation, Inc. Newsletter quoted in brief of Resident Participation of *Denver, Inc. v. Love*, 322 F.Supp. 1100 (D.Colo.1971). Thanks to Thomas A. Stacey for his help.

[271] Colo.Rev.Stat.Ann. § 80–11–12.

[272] *Resident Participation of Denver, Inc. v. Love*, 322 F.Supp. 1100, 1101 (D.Colo.1971).

Resident Participation then sought a court order under the First Amendment to force the newspapers to publish the advertisements. The newspapers countered with arguments that the First Amendment forbids only government abridgements of free speech, not private rejections, and this was an argument the ecology group could not overcome. Nevertheless, Resident Participation argued to have newspapers declared to be official or state action, on grounds that the newspapers "enjoy monopoly control in a vital area of public concern" and because Colorado statutes required publication of legal notices in newspapers of general circulation.[273] Other provisions said to make newspapers a public entities included a statute exempting editors and reporters form jury service and a Denver ordinance allowing newspaper vending machines on public property, including sidewalks.[274]

A three-judge federal district court rejected these arguments, saying it could find nothing "remotely suggesting that these measures are sufficient to justify labeling the newspapers' conduct state action."[275]

OTHER ALLOWABLE ADVERTISING REFUSALS

In California, Times-Mirror Co.—publishers of the *Los Angeles Times*—was sued by the Adult Film Association of America, distributors of sex films. The film producers and distributors claimed that refusals to publish their ads created a business tort. A California court disagreed, saying that a newspaper's advertisements, like a newspaper's editorial policy, fix the newspaper's image in readers' minds. The newspaper, in other words, had a right to protect itself from public disfavor by *not* accepting some ads.[276]

The *Milwaukee Journal*, which had published a series of articles critical of nursing homes, was sued by the Wisconsin Association of Nursing Homes after the newspaper refused to carry an advertisement responding to the newspaper's reporting. A Wisconsin appellate court held that under the First Amendment, the newspaper's executives had the discretion to refuse such advertising.[277]

FINANCIAL INTERESTS MAY LIMIT AD REFUSALS

If a publication has a financial conflict of interest with a would-be advertiser, that can put a dent in the otherwise sweeping right to refuse advertisements. A United States Court of Appeals case—*Home*

---

[273] Ibid. at 1102.

[274] Colo.Rev.Stat.Ann. § 7801.3 (1963); Denver Municipal Code, §§ 339G, 334.1–2.

[275] 322 F.Supp. 1100, 1103 (D.C.Colo.1971).

[276] *Adult Film Association of America v. Times Mirror Co.*, 3 Med.L.Rptr. 2292 (Cal.Super.Ct.1978), affirmed 97 Cal.App.3d 77, 158 Cal.Rptr. 547 (1979), 5 Med.L.Rptr. 1865.

[277] *Wisconsin Association of Nursing Homes v. Journal Co.*, 92 Wis.2d 709, 285 N.W.2d 891 (App.1979).

Placement Company v. Providence Journal (1982)[278]—gives an illustration of that scenario. After the newspaper refused classified advertising from a rental referral company, this was held to run afoul of federal antitrust law.

The court noted that the *Providence Journal* not only had monopoly power as the only metropolitan daily in its area, it also was competing with Home Placement Company for real estate advertisements. This refusal to run advertising was viewed as an illegally anticompetitive refusal to do business under the Sherman Antitrust Act.[279] Thus, under unusual circumstances where a media unit has a financial conflict, advice from an antitrust law specialist could make good sense before rejecting an ad which is somehow in competition with the media unit itself.

One other situation where an ad refusal could bring legal trouble involves contract law. If a newspaper, for example, has entered into a contract to carry advertising and then refuses to do so, that could be a problem. That's the message from a 1982 Indiana case, *Herald Telephone v. Fatouros*. That case involved a political ad which was accepted by a newspaper—as was payment for the ad—then the message was refused because it might be "inflammatory." The Indiana Court of Appeals, Fourth District, said:[280]

> * * * we agree * * * that a newspaper has a right to publish or reject advertising as its judgment dictates. However, once a newspaper forms a contract to publish an advertisement, it has given up the right to publish nor not publish * * *

In usual situations, however, the media are free to refuse ads, as in *Person v. New York Post Corp.* (1977). The plaintiff asked a court order to prevent a newspaper from refusing to carry a "tombstone" ad on a financial matter. Instead, the federal district court declared that it is a newspaper's prerogative to accept or to reject advertisements as it sees fit.[281]

"STATE ACTION" LIMITS RIGHT OF AD REFUSAL

Non-private entities such as transit authorities or state-owned publications cannot refuse advertising with impunity. Back during the troubled 1960s, a California case involved a group called Women for

---

[278] *Home Placement Service v. Providence Journal*, 682 F.2d 274, 8 Med.L.Rptr. 1881 (1st Cir.1982), cert. denied 460 U.S. 1028, 103 S.Ct. 1279 (1983).

[279] Ibid. finding that §§ 1 and 2 of the Sherman Antitrust Act, 15 U.S.C §§ 1, 2 were violated.

[280] *Herald Telephone v. Fatouros*, 431 N.E.2d 171 (Ind.App.4th Dist.1982), 8 Med.L.Rptr. 1230, 1231.

[281] *Person v. New York Post Corporation*, 427 F.Supp. 1297 (E.D.N.Y.1977), affirmed 573 F.2d 1294 (2d Cir.1977).

Peace. That group sought to place advertising placards in buses owned by the Alameda-Contra Costa Transit District. The placards said:[282]

> "Mankind must put an end to war or war will put an end to mankind." President John F. Kennedy.
>
> "Write to President Johnson: Negotiate Vietnam. Women for Peace, P.O. Box 944, Berkeley."

The private advertising agency which managed advertising for the transit district rejected the placards. It was declared that "political advertising and advertising on controversial subjects are not acceptable unless approved by the [transit] district, and that advertising objectionable to the district shall be removed * * * "After a trial and two appeals, Women for Peace won their case before the California Supreme Court. The court said that the ad was protected under the First Amendment and that once a public facility is opened for use of the general public, arbitrary conditions cannot be imposed upon the use of that facility.[283]

The theme of state action also ruled the outcome of a number of other cases in which courts held that publications must accept advertisements. When the official campus newspaper at Wisconsin State University-Whitewater refused to accept "editorial advertisements," ads expressing political views. U.S. District Court Judge James Doyle ruled that the newspaper's restrictive advertising policy—"enforced under color of state law—is a denial of free speech and expression."[284]

ADVERTISING BOYCOTTS AND ANTITRUST LAW

At times, anger against a media units becomes so extreme that an advertising boycott results. Under certain circumstances, that may bring antitrust law—either federal or state—into play on the side of a publisher or broadcaster. P. Cameron DeVore and Robert D. Sack cited *Mims v. Kemp* (1977), a case in which a jury, under federal antitrust law, awarded treble damages to a newspaper suffering losses from an advertising boycott.[285]

---

[282] *Wirta v. Alameda-Contra Costa Transit District*, 68 Cal.2d 51, 64 Cal.Rptr. 430, 432, 434 P.2d 982, 984.

[283] 68 Cal.2d 51, 64 Cal.Rptr. 430, 433, 434 P.2d 982, 985 (1967).

[284] *Lee v. Board of Regents of State Colleges*, 306 F.Supp. 1097, 1101 (W.D.Wis.1969).

[285] P. Cameron DeVore and Robert D. Sack, "Advertising and Commercial Speech," in James C. Goodale, chairman, *Communications Law 1996*, Vol. III (New York: Practising Law Institute), p. 534, citing *Mims v. Kemp*, No. 72–627 (D.S.C. 1977). They added, however, that if the ad boycott is political rather than economic, it may be protected. See *Environmental Planning & Information Council v. Superior Court*, 36 Cal.3d 188, 203 Cal.Rptr. 127, 680 P.2d 1086 (1984), 10 Med.L.Rptr. 2055.

NEWSPAPER LIABILITY FOR ALLEGEDLY DISCRIMINATORY ADS?

Sometimes, despite the quest for revenue, newspapers might be better off if they would refuse some advertisements. *Ragin v. New York Times*[286] and *Housing Opportunities Made Equal v. Cincinnati Enquirer*[287] both addressed the question of whether a newspaper is liable for publishing advertising that may violate the standards of the Federal Fair Housing Act. Based on conflicting outcomes, the answer seemed to depend on the federal circuit where the newspaper is located.

The *New York Times* was sued by a group of African Americans who asserted that the newspaper's real estate ad section over two decades rarely displayed pictures of blacks as prospective homeowners or renters, an omission constituting a racial preference in violation of federal law. The Second Federal Circuit refused to dismiss the action, holding that a jury might reasonably conclude that such a pattern over a long period of time was not protected commercial speech because it would be an illegal activity.[288]

On the other hand, the Sixth Federal Circuit Court of Appeals dismissed similar allegations brought against the *Cincinnati Enquirer*, finding that a series of housing ads depicting only whites constituted legally protected commercial free speech. Further, the Sixth Circuit held that the newspaper should not be required to serve as an arm of government reviewing all housing advertisements it accepted to make sure that they reflected a proper mixture of races.[289]

IS AN ADVERTISING OFFER A CONTRACT?

Students frequently ask why government agencies get involved in regulating advertising. They suggest that consumers are able to protect themselves by suing businesses that engage in false advertising. But, American courts traditionally have not wanted to get into the business of governing business, especially when dealing with the area of offers and promises and contracts that arise under advertising.

An old case—*Craft v. Elder & Johnston Co.* (1941)—still states the law as it is in most jurisdictions. Craft looked in a newspaper one day and saw an advertisement by the Elder & Johnston Co., offering for sale an "all-electric sewing machine" for the sum of $26 as a "Thursday Only Special." Ms. Craft went to the store that Thursday and tried to pay $26 for the sewing machine. The store refused to sell.

---

[286] *Ragin v. New York Times*, 923 F.2d 995 (2d Cir.1991).

[287] *Housing Opportunities Made Equal v. Cincinnati Enquirer*, 943 F.2d 644 (6th Cir.1991).

[288] *Ragin v. New York Times*, 923 F.2d 995 (2d Cir.1991), cert. denied 502 U.S. 821, 112 S.Ct. 81 (1991).

[289] *Housing Opportunities Made Equal v. Cincinnati Enquirer*, 943 F.2d 644 (6th Cir.1991).

She sued for the normal value of the machine $149 (less the $26 she would have paid). The trial court dismissed her case saying the ad was not an offer which could be accepted to form a contract. Her case went to an Ohio Court of Appeals, which said, "It is clear that in the absence of special circumstances an ordinary newspaper advertisement is not an offer, but is an offer to negotiate—an offer to receive offers * * * "[290] The court gave an example:[291]

> "A clothing merchant advertises coats of a certain kind for sale at $50. This is not an offer but an invitation to the public to come and purchase.
>
> "Thus, if goods are advertised for sale at a certain price, it is not an offer and no contract is formed by the statement of an intending purchaser that he will take a specified quantity of goods at that price.
>
> "[Advertisements] are merely invitations to all persons who may read them that the advertiser is ready to receive offers for the goods at the price stated."

Consumer advocates learned from cases such as this that they could not use contract law to force businesses to live up to the ads they had published. So, they instead turned to rules regulating advertising. In *Geismar v. Abraham & Strauss* (1981), a New York case, a consumer sued a department store. The store had advertised china that normally sold for $280 for only $39.95. Judith Geismar went to the store and tried to pay $39.95, but the store wouldn't take the money. She sued for breach of contract but lost under the principles of the *Craft v. Elder & Johnston Co.* case discussed above.

Ms. Geismar didn't walk away completely empty-handed, because the court allowed recovery under a New York statute providing that if anyone is injured by a misleading ad, they can collect up to $50. However, a cost-benefit analysis for consumers might suggest that suing over misleading ads—especially when major corporations are involved—is a situation of diminishing returns. Major corporations, of course, have legal departments that can tie the single plaintiff in knots.[292]

80. BROADCAST ADVERTISING

Broadcasters also have the right to refuse to accept advertising messages, except for federal political candidate ads during an election period.

In *Columbia Broadcasting System Inc. v. Democratic National Committee*, the Supreme Court held that radio and television stations are

[290] *Craft v. Elder & Johnston Co.*, 38 N.E.2d 416, 419 (Oh.Ct.App.2d Dist. Montgomery County 1941).

[291] Ibid.

[292] *Geismar v. Abraham & Strauss*, 439 N.Y.S.2d 1005, 109 Misc.2d 495, 439 N.Y.S.2d 1005 (Dist.Ct., Suffolk County, 1981).

not legally required to broadcast any advertisements they do not want to accept.[293] By a 7–2 vote, the Court recognized a right for broadcasting similar to the print media's "right to refuse service".

This case dealt with the efforts of a political party and an anti-war group to get airtime for their respective viewpoints. Business Executives' Move for a Vietnam Peace (BEM) was the anti-war group that filed a complaint with the Federal Communications Commission alleging that a radio station in Washington, D.C., WTOP had violated the fairness doctrine by refusing to sell the group time to broadcast a series of one-minute spot announcements against the Vietnam conflict. (The fairness doctrine, which held that broadcasters should make reasonable time available for differing sides of public issues, was repealed by the FCC in 1987.)[294] WTOP refused, saying it already had presented full and fair coverage of all important viewpoints concerning U.S. policy in Southeast Asia.

A few months later, the Democratic National Committee (DNC) sought a declaratory ruling from the FCC on this statement:

> That under the First Amendment * * * and the Communications Act, a broadcaster may not, as a general policy, refuse to sell time to responsible entities * * * for comment on public issues.

The Commission rejected the demands of both DNC and BEM, but the Court of Appeals reversed the FCC, declaring that a flat ban on paid public-issue announcements was "in violation of the First Amendment, at least when other types of paid announcements are accepted."[295]

The Supreme Court, however, upheld the FCC's decision by a margin of 7 to 2. Chief Justice Burger's plurality opinion—he was joined by Justices Rehnquist and Stewart—concluded that broadcast licensees were not common carriers.

He compared a newspaper's right of editorial judgment with that of a broadcast licensee, finding that the broadcaster's degree of freedom was somewhat less extensive than that of the newspaper publisher. Broadcasters are supervised—and periodically licensed—by the FCC which must "oversee without censoring."[296] Even so, the opinion declared, government control over broadcast licensees is not broad enough to transform their stations into "common carriers" or "public utilities", compelled to accept and deliver whatever message any individual might be willing to pay to have transmitted.

---

[293] *CBS, Inc. v. Democratic Nat. Committee*, 412 U.S. 94, 93 S.Ct. 2080 (1973).

[294] The fairness doctrine, although not in force through the 1990s, could be reinstated if both Congress and the President agreed that it is good policy. The fairness doctrine was upheld as constitutional by the Supreme Court of the United States in *Red Lion Broadcasting Co. v. FCC*, 395 U.S. 367, 89 S.Ct. 1794 (1969).

[295] *Business Executives' Move for Vietnam Peace v. FCC, Democratic National Committee v. FCC*, 450 F.2d 642 (D.C.Cir.1971) overturning *Business Executives*, 24 FCC2d 242 (1970) and *Democratic National Committee*, 25 FCC2d 216 (1970).

[296] 412 U.S. 94, 93 S.Ct. 2080 (1973).

Based upon this decision, then, a broadcaster has the judicially recognized right to refuse to sell commercial time to anyone except those within that one specific category guaranteed advertising access by Congress: legally qualified candidates for federal elective offices.[297]

ADVERTISING AND CHILDREN

Action for Children's Television (ACT), a citizens' group, had been pressuring the FCC since the early 1970s to reduce the amount of commercialism in television programs produced for children. In 1986, the Commission eliminated the commercial guidelines it had established for television broadcast licensees, including limitations on the number of commercial minutes per hour of programs designed for children.[298] ACT challenged this FCC action, and the Court of Appeals, D.C. Circuit, sustained the challenge, declaring that the Commission had not presented adequate justification for its assumption that the marketplace would operate to prevent over-commercialization of children's programs.[299]

In October 1988, a consensus children's television advertising bill, reflecting the compromise agreement the NAB had negotiated with various interest groups, was enacted by Congress but vetoed by President Reagan.[300]

Two years later Congress passed new legislation with many of the same provisions contained in the earlier compromise agreement. This time, however, President Bush's failure to veto the "Children's Television Act" allowed it to become law in October 1990.[301] The Act limited advertising contained in weekday television or cable TV programs intended for children to 10½ minutes per hour, while allowing 12 minutes per hour on the weekend.

---

[297] Title 47 Sec. 312(a)(7) provides that station licenses may be revoked for refusing to allow reasonable access or to allow the purchase of reasonable amounts of time by legally qualified candidates for federal elective offices. For a more detailed discussion of this requirement, see Chap. 11.

[298] Programming Commercialization Policies, 60 R.R.2d 526 (1986).

[299] *Action for Children's Television v. FCC*, 821 F.2d 741 (D.C.Cir.1987). For more than a half century, the National Association of Broadcasters had been actively involved in limiting the amount of commercialization in programs designed for children, working with the networks to voluntarily limit the number of commercial minutes per hour. In 1982, however, the Justice Department decided to bring an antitrust action against the NAB, charging that its commercial codes were in constraint of trade. At that point, the NAB was forced to enter into a consent agreement to abandon all efforts to negotiate for further limitations upon broadcast advertising. See *United States v. National Association of Broadcasters*, 536 F.Supp. 149 (D.D.C.1982). As a result, the FCC's rescission of its commercial time limitations in 1986 left broadcasters free of any regulatory or self regulatory constraints upon commercialization.

[300] "Congress, in Overtime, Passes TVRO, Children's Ad Bills," *Broadcasting*, October 24, 1988, p. 27.

[301] Children's TV Act of 1990, PL 101–437, 47 U.S.C.A. §§ 303a, 303b, 394. Implemented by the FCC, In the Matter of Policies and Rules Concerning Children's Television Programming, 68 R.R.2d 1615 (1991). See also, "President's Pocket Unveto Allows Children's Bill to Become Law," *Broadcasting*, October 22, 1990, p. 35.

In addition, the law also requires broadcasters to meet the educational needs of children or face possible license revocation by the FCC, and established a federal endowment to fund the production of educational programs for children. At the insistence of Action for Children's Television, the bill also directed the FCC to determine whether certain "super-hero" cartoon strips based on toy characters merchandised by the advertiser constitute "program-length" commercials, and therefore automatically violate the law by exceeding maximum advertising time standards for such programs.

In January, 1992, the FCC began an audit of broadcast stations to determine the degree of compliance with the rules the Commission adopted to enforce the Children's Television Act of 1990. The audit revealed seven stations and three cable systems in apparent violation of one or more provisions of the Act. Only one of the stations cited by the FCC was able to provide a satisfactory explanation of its programming practices. The others were either fined or admonished. One TV station, KWHE, Honolulu, was fined $20,000 for its violations and two other stations, WFTS Tampa and WTTA St. Petersburg were each fined $10,000.[302]

Continuing its effort to get compliance with the Act, the FCC decided in February, 1993, to delay renewing the licenses of seven TV stations in Ohio and Michigan until the stations demonstrated they were meeting the educational needs of children.[303]

The Commission also issued a notice of inquiry to determine whether it was proper for broadcasters to log entertainment shows for children as programs meeting their informational needs, and whether short "educational" inserts could properly be considered as fulfilling broadcasters' obligations to children.[304]

Although the National Association of Broadcasters supported the legislation, its constitutionality was challenged by the Radio-Television News Directors Association. The RTNDA claimed the bill violated the First Amendment rights of broadcasters by requiring them, "to provide programming and supporting advertising material as the federal government demands."[305]

Even if such legislation is upheld as constitutionally valid, its value in protecting children from the hazards of over-commercialization may turn out to be less significant than hoped. Studies of children's viewing behavior in the early 1990s revealed a continuing downward trend in the

---

302 Harry Jessell, "Six TV's Hit for Violating Kids TV Rules," *Broadcasting*, Jan. 18, 1993, p. 95.

303 "FCC Means Business," *Broadcasting*, Feb. 1, 1993, p. 36.

304 Policies and Rules Concerning Children's Television Programming, 58 Fed. Reg. 14367 (1993).

305 "Media Groups Challenge Kidvid Bill Constitutionality," *Variety* January 28, 1991, p. 44.

amount of time spent watching broadcast television each day.[306] These studies do not suggest that children are actually viewing less video entertainment each year, but rather that they were spending more of their time watching rented cassettes on the family VCRs where they can expose themselves to program-length commercials like "The Care Bears Battle the Freeze Machine," "Transformers: The Ultimate Doom" or "Mutant Ninja Turtles" to their hearts' content without interference from any well-intentioned adult interest group.

81. TRADEMARKS: THE SIGNS OF QUALITY, SOURCE AND CONSUMER CHOICE

Companies protect their names, trademarks and trade dress in order to retain the confidence of consumers, tell buyers the source of the product or service and inspire confidence in the purchase.

When consumers see the Golden Arches or the distinctive Swoosh mark on a pair of athletic shoes, they know what they are looking at. McDonald's and Nike have put considerable effort and spent a lot of money creating an image of their products and services that are conjured up whenever consumers see their trademarks. Their marks are an assurance of the quality of their products and a way to appeal to the goodwill they have built up with consumers. But what if any hamburger joint could stick the Golden Arches on its roof or put the name McDonald's on its doors? Soon, McDonald's would not mean anything. The Golden Arches would not be a promise of a particular kind of burger and fries. Going into a "McDonald's" would be a gamble and many consumers would not choose that bet. The result would be the death of the McDonald's chain of restaurants. The same for Nike and its Swoosh mark. People would not spend hundreds of dollars for a "Nike" shoe if they were not confident of the quality of the shoe or its source.

Consumer knowledge and confidence in the goods they buy and services they use is at the heart of trademark law. In *Scandia Down Corp. v. Euroquilt, Inc.* Seventh Circuit Judge Frank Easterbrook explained the nature of trademark.[307]

> Trademarks help consumers to select goods. By identifying the source of the goods, they convey valuable information to consumers at lower costs. Easily identified trademarks reduce the costs consumers incur in searching for what they desire, and the lower the costs of search the more competitive the market. A trademark also may induce the supplier of goods to make higher quality products and to adhere to a consistent level of quality. The trademark is a valuable asset, part of the "goodwill" of a business. If the seller provides an inconsistent level of

[306] See, for example, Nielsen 1990, Report on Television.

[307] *Scandia Down Corp. v. Euroquilt, Inc.*, 772 F.2d 1423, 1429–30 (7th Cir. 1985).

> quality, or reduces quality below what consumers expect from earlier experience, that reduces the value of the trademark. The value of a trademark is in a sense a "hostage" of consumers; if the seller disappoints the consumers, they respond by devaluing the trademark. The existence of this hostage gives the seller another incentive to afford consumers the quality of goods they prefer and expect.

Companies defend their marks. No business wants a competitor to use its trademark and sell shoddy goods or provide poor service. That would erode consumer confidence and lead to a loss of customers.

Trademarks first were protected under the common law. Later, states crafted their own statutes on trademarks and, finally, the Congress passed The Lanham Act, the federal trademark law.

TRADE MARKS, SERVICE MARKS, TRADE NAMES AND COLLECTIVE/CERTIFICATION MARKS

Under the Lanham Act, trademarks can take a number of forms:[308] A word, name, symbol, or device, or any combination thereof, can serve as a trademark. Other things can be trademarks as well. Shapes (the distinctive shape of the Coca Cola bottle), numbers (7-Eleven), slogans (When You're in Good Hands), sounds (The MGM lion's roar) and even a fragrance/smell (one company uses a distinctive peppermint scent) can serve as trademarks.

Products have trademarks and services have service marks. Citibank provides banking services so "Citibank" is its service mark. Greyhound offers transportation services so its service mark is "Greyhound." Service marks are protected like trademarks. Trade names are the names that businesses use to identify themselves. Say the name McDonald's and most people will think of the fast food chain.

Collective marks are those identifiers of group membership. "Realtor" is the collective mark for people who deal in real estate and who have passed the requirements for membership in the National Association of Realtors. Not everyone who works in real estate is a Realtor. A certification mark is one that certifies that a product or service has certain characteristics such as manufacture in a particular geographic region or production by union labor. Certifying entities do not produce products or provide services, they certify the characteristic of the product or service. A Good Housekeeping Seal means that a product or service meets a particular set of standards. Good Housekeeping certifies but does not manufacture goods.

---

[308] Lanham Act http://www.uspto.gov/sites/default/files/documents/tmlaw.pdf 15 U.S.C. § 1127.

CREATING A TRADEMARK

Getting a trademark means doing business. The Patent and Trademark office will not register a trademark unless it has been used in business. As the trademark exists to provide consumers with important information, a trademark has no reason to exist outside of trade. In 1918, Justice Mahlon Pitney wrote for the court in a case over which company could use the word "Rex" as a trademark for its medicines. The case turned on whether the second business to use "Rex" had used it continuously in the part of the country where the first business had not yet entered in trade.[309]

> The law of trade-marks is but a part of the broader law of unfair competition; the right to a particular mark grows out of its use, not its mere adoption; its function is simply to designate the goods as the product of a particular trader and to protect his good will against the sale of another's product as his; and it is not the subject of property except in connection with an existing business. *Hanover Milling Co. v. Metcalf,* 240 U. S. 403, 412–414, 36 Sup. Ct. 357, 60 L. Ed. 713.

The Court held that the continuous use by the latter business gave it right to the trademark in the part of the country where it had done business. The case illustrates one of the rules of trademark, that it be in continuous use. It means people cannot simply create a trademark and then wait for a company to buy it. Trademarks must be legitimate in order to be valid. They must actually be used in commerce and they must have a consumer identification, that is to say that consumers must identify the trademark with a particular product. Registrants cannot simply create a trademark in the hopes that some product might, in the future, fit its use.

Whether a trademark get protection of the trademark registration system depends on a number of factors, the first of which is the strength of the mark. The strength of a trademark is its ability to be associated with a particular product or service. Marks that cannot command that association cannot be trademarked.

Proposed trademarks are classified into four categories, from weakest, incapable of association with one product or service, to strongest, marks that almost automatically bring forth the product or service.

1. **Generic**—a common name for a product. Because the term is common, it can refer to any number of products or services. A tire company that called itself, "Tires" would not have a trademark because tires is the name for the product no matter where it is purchased.

2. **Descriptive**—a description for the product or service. In an appeal of the denial of trademark protection for the proposed "GasBadge"

[309] *United Drug Co. v. Theodore Rectanus Co.,* 248 U.S. 90, 97, 39 S.Ct. 48, 51 (1918).

trademark, the Court of Customs and Patent Appeals upheld the denial of the mark by the Patent, Trademark Office.[310] The Abcor Development Company developed a wearable device, a badge, to measure exposure to "gaseous pollutants." Judge Howard Markey explained the reason that "GasBadge" could not be used as a trademark, citing the descriptive nature of the name.[311]

> The major reasons for not protecting such marks are: (1) to prevent the owner of a mark from inhibiting competition in the sale of particular goods; and (2) to maintain freedom of the public to use the language involved, thus avoiding the possibility of harassing infringement suits by the registrant against others who use the mark when advertising or describing their own products. *Armour & Co. v. Organon* Inc., 245 F.2d 495, 498 and 500, 44 Cust.Pat.App. 1010, 1014 and 1016, 114 USPQ 334, 337 and 338 (1957).

There is a last examination of descriptive terms that must be done before they are rejected. Has the term acquired a "secondary meaning?"[312]

> A descriptive term is subject to protection under section 43(a) only if the proponent of protection demonstrates that, in addition to the ordinary common meaning of the word or words, the term has acquired a secondary meaning in its particular market—that the consuming public primarily associates the term with a particular source.

3. Suggestive—a term or symbol that "suggests" what the product or service is. Examples include Spray 'n Wash, a laundry pre-treater, Citibank, a bank, and Lube 'n Go, a drive through oil change business.

In *Bristol-Myers Squibb v. McNeill-P.P.C.*,[313] Bristol-Myers, the maker of Excedrin PM, sued McNeill to prevent that company from using "PM" in Tylenol PM. Bristol-Myers lost on the use of "PM" but won on the similarity of the packaging in the trial court and the case made its way to the Second Circuit Court of Appeals.

Chief Judge Thomas J. Meskill's opinion found that "PM" was not suggestive, as Bristol-Myers had argued. A mark is suggestive if it suggests to the consumer whose product it is. The consumer must add additional information in order to arrive at the conclusion that it is X product, made by X Co.[314] "A term is suggestive " 'if it requires imagination, thought and perception to reach a conclusion as to the

---

[310] *In re Abcor Development Corp.*, 588 F.2d 811 (C.C.P.A.1978).

[311] Ibid. at 814.

[312] *Bristol-Myers Squibb Co. v. McNeil-P.P.C., Inc.*, 973 F.2d 1033, 1040 (2d Cir. 1992).

[313] Ibid.

[314] Ibid.

nature of goods.' " *Abercrombie & Fitch*, 537 F.2d at 11 (citation omitted)."

Judge Meskill concluded that the trial court judge was correct that "PM" was descriptive rather than suggestive.[315]

> the conclusion that "PM" describes rather than suggests a nighttime product was not clearly erroneous. Once the consumer arrives at an awareness that the product is useful at nighttime, the "purpose or utility" of the product has been conveyed, even though the consumer is not aware of why the product is useful at night.

Bristol-Myers having lost, the consuming public can buy any number of nighttime pain relievers with "PM" on the box.

Suggestive might be better understood in the context of a trademark case between Abercrombie & Fitch and Hunting World[316] over the use of the word "Safari" in trademarks for clothing and outdoor gear.

Before A&F became known as a shop for hip teens and notorious for its bare-chested and otherwise briefly clothed models, it was known as a shop to outfit explorers. It featured clothing that explorers, or the well-to-do, might buy in anticipation of a night on the veldt. Second Circuit Judge Henry Friendly looked at A&F's trademarks across its catalog. While some of the uses of "Safari" were descriptive and not protectible without proof of secondary meaning, the term was suggestive for others.

> The generic term for A&F's 'safari cloth Bermuda shorts', for example, is 'Bermuda shorts', not 'safari'; indeed one would suppose this garment to be almost ideally unsuited for the forest or the jungle and there is no evidence that it has entered into the family for which 'Safari' has become a generic adjective. The same analysis holds for luggage, portable grills, and the rest of the suburban paraphernalia, from swimtrunks and raincoats to belts and scarves, included in these registrations. * * *
>
> * * *
>
> * * * 'Safari' as applied to ice chests, axes, tents and smoking tobacco does not describe such items. Rather it is a way of conveying to affluent patrons of A&F a romantic notion of high style, coupled with an attractive foreign allusion * * *

"Safari" suggests that the product would be something used on a safari but a consumer would have to give it more thought to make the connection with A&F.

4. **Arbitrary/Fanciful**—Arbitrary trademarks are words that already exist in language. They achieve arbitrary status when they are used to identify a product or service not normally connected with them.

---

[315] Ibid. at 1041.

[316] *Abercrombie & Fitch v. Hunting World*, 537 F.2d 4 (2d Cir. 1976).

Pigeon would be arbitrary when used as a trademark for a bicycle.[317] The same applies to Shell gasoline and Ivory soap.

Fanciful names are those created out of whole cloth for a product or service. Exxon did not appear in any dictionary until it was created for the oil company. Rolex came into being as the trademark name for the watch.

Whether the Trademark Office accepts a trademark depends on consideration of which of the four categories the name falls into. Judge Thomas Meskill found a telling explanation of the four categories in *Bristol-Myers v. McNeill.*[318]

> "[T]he word 'apple' would be arbitrary when used on personal computers, suggestive when used in 'Apple-A-day' on vitamin tablets, descriptive when used in 'Tomapple' for combination tomato-apple juice and generic when used on apples." 1 J.T. McCarthy, Trademarks and Unfair Competition § 11:22, at 498–99 (2d ed. 1984).

OTHER BARS TO REGISTRATION

Even if the mark is strong, it can still be rejected by the Register of Trademarks. Trademarks are not given to national symbols or insignia, such as a coat of arms or flag. The Register of Trademarks also will not grant trademark registration to immoral, deceptive, or scandalous or that may disparage or falsely suggest a connection with persons, institutions, beliefs.

THE WASHINGTON REDSKINS

The controversy over the Washington Redskins trademark lasted nearly 25 years, but was resolved after a Supreme Court decision involving the name of an Asian rock band (see below) found that a key section of federal law banning trademarks that "may disparage" people was a violation of the First Amendment.[319]

Daniel Snyder, owner and operator of the team, appealed a decision of a federal court upholding a decision by the Trademark Trial and Appeal Board to cancel its trademark registration.[320]

The decision by the Board was the latest in a decades-long controversy. The team began in Boston in 1933 with the Redskins name chosen by its first owner, George Preston Marshall. The name was picked to avoid confusion with Boston's professional baseball team, the

---

[317] Flying Pigeon is the name of a Chinese bicycle company.

[318] *Bristol-Myers Squibb Co. v. McNeil-P.P.C., Inc.*, 973 F.2d 1033, 1043 (2d Cir. 1992).

[319] Ian Shapira & Ann E. Marimov, "Washington Redskins Win Trademark Fight Over the Team's Name," *Washington Post,* June 29, 2017.

[320] *Pro-Football, Inc. v. Amanda Blackhorse*, 2015 WL 4096277 (E.D.Va. 2015).

Braves.[321] The Redskins was trademarked in 1967. The controversy grew in the late 1960s and early 1970s.[322]

> [I]n 1972, Leon Cook, President of the National Congress of American Indians ("NCAI"), among others, met with Edward Bennett Williams, the president of PFI, to explain that the team name was a slur; Williams reported the meeting to the NFL Commissioner the following day.

Susan Harjo and six other Native Americans petitioned to cancel the registrations[323] of the Redskins Marks in 1992. In 1999, the Trademark Trial and Appeal Board ruled that the Redskins Marks "may disparage" Native Americans. It ordered the cancellation of the registrations.[324] The case was appealed to federal district court where the judge concluded that disparagement had not been proven and that the petitioners had waited too long to take action. The D.C. Circuit upheld the lower court on the delay grounds. It did not address the disparagement issue.

In 2006, while the *Harjo* case was still on appeal Amanda Blackhorse, Marcus BriggsCloud, Phillip Cover, Jillian Pappan, and Courtney Tsotigh filed a petition to cancel the same six registrations of the Redskins Marks. The Trademark Trial and Appeal Board delayed consideration until the *Harjo* case was decided.[325]

> On June 18, 2014, the TTAB scheduled the cancellation of the registrations of the Redskins Marks under Section 2(a) of the Lanham Act, 15 U.S.C. § 1052(a), finding that at the time of their registrations the marks consisted of matter that both "may disparage" a substantial composite of Native Americans and bring them into contempt or disrepute. See *Blackhorse v. Pro-Football, Inc.*, 111 U.S.P.Q.2d 1080, 2014 WL 2757516 (T.T.A.B.2014).

The Redskins petitioned the federal district court to overturn the Board's action. Judge Gerald Bruce Lee denied the petition and the case has been appealed to the D.C. Circuit. While the Redskins generated significant media attention with an appellate filing that noted that the Patent and Trademark Office had granted trademark registration to beer, clothing, porn and sex devices with names that are offensive.[326]

> "By way of example only, the following marks are registered today: Take Yo Panties Off clothing; Dangerous Negro shirts . . . Midget-Man condoms and inflatable sex dolls," the Redskins lawyers wrote in their opening brief filed Friday with the U.S.

---

[321] Ibid.

[322] Ibid.

[323] The owners of the team registered a half dozen trademarks using Redskins or a variation thereof.

[324] *Harjo v. Pro-Football, Inc.*, 50 U.S.P.Q.2d 1705, 1999 WL 375907 (T.T.A.B.1999).

[325] *Pro-Football, Inc. v. Amanda Blackhorse*, 2015 WL 4096277 (E.D.Va. 2015).

[326] Ian Shapira, " 'Take Yo Panties Off' defense: Redskins cite other protected products in trademark appeal," *Washington Post*, Nov. 3, 2015.

> Court of Appeals for the 4th Circuit, based in Richmond. The lawyers later added a footnote with 31 more trademark registrations, many of them unprintable in *The Washington Post*. On the list: "Party With Sluts . . . Redneck Army apparel . . . Booty Call sex aids . . . Dumb Blonde hair products."

The Redskins attorneys have two major elements in their appeal. Their first is based on the registrations for the arguably offensive trademarks. The second, and one that likely has more legal appeal, is one that claims that cancelling the Redskins trademark violates First Amendment rights.

The second argument appears to have gotten a significant boost from the full Federal Circuit Court of Appeals in a case involving an Asian-American band. The band wanted to register its name, The Slants, and the Patent and Trademark Office rejected the application citing § 2(a) of the Lanham Act, barring registration for marks that disparage groups. Trademark examiners look to see:[327]

> (1) What is the likely meaning of the matter in question, taking into account not only dictionary definitions, but also the relationship of the matter to the other elements in the mark, the nature of the goods or services, and the manner in which the mark is used in the marketplace in connection with the goods or services; and
>
> (2) If that meaning is found to refer to identifiable persons, institutions, beliefs or national symbols, whether that meaning may be disparaging to a substantial composite of the referenced group.
>
> Trademark Manual of Exam. Proc. ("TMEP") § 1203.03(b)(i) (Jan.2015 ed.)

The Redskins case was before the Fourth Circuit Court of Appeals when the Supreme Court heard the Slants case (see below). In the aftermath of the Supreme Court's decision in *Tam*, the Court of Appeals for the Fourth Circuit vacated the district court's order that granted the cancellation of the Redskin's trademarks consistent with the ruling in *Tam*.[328]

Simon Shiao Tam, the front man for the Slants,[329] "named his band The Slants to "reclaim" and "take ownership" of Asian stereotypes. J.A. 129–30." But when Tam filed the final part of the application for the trademark, he was turned down.[330]

> The examiner refused to register Mr. Tam's mark, finding it likely disparaging to "persons of Asian descent" under § 2(a).

[327] *In re Simon Shiao Tam*, 2015 WL 9287035 (Fed. Cir. 2015).

[328] *Pro-Football, Inc. v. Blackhorse*, 709 Fed. Apps. 182, 183, 2018 U.S. App, Lexis 1186**, 2018 WL 460653, Jan. 18, 2018.

[329] Ibid.

[330] Ibid.

> The examiner found that the mark likely referred to people of Asian descent in a disparaging way, explaining that the term "slants" had "a long history of being used to deride and mock a physical feature" of people of Asian descent. J.A. 42. And even though Mr. Tam may have chosen the mark to "reappropriate the disparaging term," the examiner found that a substantial composite of persons of Asian descent would find the term offensive. J.A. 43.

Tam appealed the ruling to the Trademark Trial and Appeal Board and continued his appeal to the Federal Circuit Court of Appeals after the Board upheld the examiner's decision. The three-judge panel upheld the Board, but the case was heard en banc and a majority of the judges found for Tam and against the Board.

Judge Kimberly Ann Moore, writing for the en banc majority, found Sec. 2(a) and its application to Tam's registration unconstitutional under a Strict Scrutiny analysis (Strict Scrutiny is addressed earlier in this text).[331]

> Strict scrutiny is used to review any governmental regulation that burdens private speech based on disapproval of the message conveyed. Section 2(a), which denies important legal rights to private speech on that basis, is such a regulation. It is therefore subject to strict scrutiny. It is undisputed that it cannot survive strict scrutiny.

The examiner's conclusion that the band's name would be disparaging to Asian-Americans and the language of Sec. 2(a) defining the kind of trademark that would be rejected, set up a collision between the statute and the First Amendment, inviting a close examination by the circuit judges.[332]

> Viewpoint-based regulations, targeting the substance of the viewpoint expressed, are even more suspect. They are recognized as a particularly "egregious form of content discrimination," id., though they have sometimes been discussed without being cleanly separated from topic discrimination, see, e.g., *Mosley*, 408 U.S. at 95. Such measures "raise[ ] the specter that the government may effectively drive certain ideas or viewpoints from the marketplace." *Simon & Schuster, Inc. v. Members of N.Y. State Crime Victims Bd.*, 502 U.S. 105, 116, 112 S.Ct. 501, 116 L.Ed.2d 476 (1991); see also *Sorrell v. IMS Health Inc.*, 131 S.Ct. 2653, 2667, 180 L.Ed.2d 544 (2011); *Rosenberger v. Rector & Visitors of Univ. of Va.*, 515 U.S. 819, 828, 115 S.Ct. 2510, 132 L.Ed.2d 700 (1995)

Tam named his band The Slants in a confrontation with racial stereotypes to "take ownership" of them. The Slants have been in the

---

331 Ibid.

332 Ibid.

heart of political and cultural discussions about race and society, Judge Moore wrote.[333]

> This case exemplifies how marks often have an expressive aspect over and above their commercial-speech aspect. Mr. Tam explicitly selected his mark to create a dialogue on controversial political and social issues. With his band name, Mr. Tam makes a statement about racial and ethnic identity. He seeks to shift the meaning of, and thereby reclaim, an emotionally charged word. He advocates for social change and challenges perceptions of people of Asian descent. His band name pushes people. It offends. Despite this—indeed, because of it—Mr. Tam's band name is expressive speech.

When Sec. 2(a) denied that expression, it stepped beyond the bounds of simple commercial speech and into the preserve of the First Amendment. It's content-based judgment means the section and the actions taken under are presumptively unconstitutional, Judge Moore wrote.

The majority was not endorsing the mark, Judge Moore wrote, acknowledging that some Asian-Americans might be offended. The panel, instead, was weighing in on the First Amendment.[334]

> Whatever our personal feelings about the mark at issue here, or other disparaging marks, the First Amendment forbids government regulators to deny registration because they find the speech likely to offend others. Even when speech "inflict[s] great pain," our Constitution protects it "to ensure that we do not stifle public debate." *Snyder*, 562 U.S. at 461. The First Amendment protects Mr. Tam's speech, and the speech of other trademark applicants.
>
> We hold that the disparagement provision of § 2(a) is unconstitutional because it violates the First Amendment. We vacate the Board's holding that Mr. Tam's mark is unregistrable, and remand this case to the Board for further proceedings.

The government appealed to the Supreme Court to determine if the disparagement clause is "facially invalid under the Free Speech Clause of the First Amendment."[335]

The government argued that trademarks are commercial speech and should be subject to relaxed scrutiny outlined in the four-part *Central Hudson* test.[336] Tam's attorneys argued that trademarks have an expressive component that goes beyond identifying a product or service, but points to a broader issue. In this instance the name The Slants not

---

[333] Ibid.

[334] Ibid.

[335] *Matal v. Tam,* 582 U.S. ___, 137 S. Ct. 1744 (2017).

[336] Ibid. at 1763.

only identifies the band, but expresses a view about social issues.[337] The Court declined to resolve this issue, because the disparagement clause cannot even withstand even *Central Hudson* review. The Court found that there is a

> deeper problem with the argument that commercial speech may be cleansed of any expression likely to cause offense. The commercial market is well stocked with merchandise that disparages prominent figures and groups, and the line between commercial and non-commercial speech is not always clear, as this case illustrates. If affixing the commercial label permits the suppression of any speech that may lead to political or social "volatility," free speech would be endangered.[338]

Justice Samuel A. Alito, writing for the Court found that the disparagement clause violates the Free Speech Clause of the First Amendment.[339]

That was not the end of the Patent and Trademark Office's attempt to ban trademarks it found offensive. Eric Brunetti started a clothing line that uses the trademark FUCT. According to Brunetti, the brand is pronounced as four letters, one after the other F-U-C-T, but one might not read it that way and see it as a form of a well-known profanity.[340]

In *Tam*, the Court found the prohibition of disparaging any person, living or dead, was viewpoint based and thus unconstitutional. In *Brunetti*, the court was asked to address a neighboring provision of the Lanham Act—one that prohibits "immoral or scandalous" trademarks.

Justice Elena Kagan, writing for the Court in *Brunetti* referred to *Tam* and found that this case also violated the First Amendment stating that the "immoral or scandalous" bar was substantially overbroad.[341]

PRESERVING THE TRADEMARK

Because of the value of a trademark, companies work to protect them. They sue when another company or person uses their marks without permission. Unauthorized use comes in multiple forms. Sometimes it is to sell products or provide services, deceiving consumers into believing they are getting the genuine article. Other times, an unauthorized user will use a mark to show an association with a legitimate business or to suggest an endorsement. Some unauthorized uses aren't even for business purposes. Trademarks are often used to make social commentary or criticism. Finally, trademarks are used by ordinary consumers to refer to generic products.

---

[337] Ibid. at 1764.

[338] Ibid. at 1770.

[339] Ibid. at 1771.

[340] *Iancu v. Brunetti*, 588 U.S. ___, ___, 139 S. Ct. 2294, 2296 (2019).

[341] Ibid. at 2302.

When trademark holders do not defend their marks, they run the risk of losing them. Once lost, the trademark can be used by anyone and the company will have lost its identity in the marketplace. Aspirin was once a trademark of the Bayer Company. It is now a generic term for pain reliever. Refrigerator was the Leonard Company's trademark for its electric food storage and cooling appliance. Now, it means whatever stands in the kitchen keeping the milk cold. Companies engage in campaigns to prevent their valuable trademarks from becoming a generic term for a thing. If you publish an article that refers to xeroxing copies, you will get a letter from the Xerox thanking you for thinking of Xerox brand photocopiers but warning you that Xerox is a trademark and should not be used to refer to anything but a Xerox brand photocopier,

Unlike names (look in the phone book for how many Smiths there are), trademarks cannot be used by more than one company in the same geographic area. A trademark is the sole property of the company that creates and uses it. And once a business has created a valid trademark, it has the right to its exclusive use, even worldwide. The United States signed the Trademark Law Treaty in 1999 and joined a global effort to simplify trademark law and enforcement. Under the treaty, valid trademarks in one country are protected in other signatory countries, thus creating an international monopoly for trademarks.

THE LANHAM ACT (SEC. 43a): PROTECTING RIGHTS

The Lanham Trademark Act is another lever to be used with the FTC Act to discourage deceptive advertising or promotional activities. Sec. 43(a) of the Lanham Act, as amended in 1988, makes it possible for persons who believe they are injured by deceptive advertising to sue for damages. P. Cameron DeVore and Robert D. Sack have written that the present Sec. 43(a) is intended to operate as a commercial defamation act. That portion of the Lanham Act says that individuals who misrepresent "the nature, characteristics, qualities or geographical origins of his or hers or another person's goods, services, or commercial activities shall be liable in a civil action [brought] by any person who believes that he or she is likely to be damaged by such act."[342]

Although the language of the Lanham Act uses the word "persons," that term was largely limited to competitors by a 1993 decision of the 3rd Circuit United States Court of Appeals. In *Serbin v. Ziebart International Corporation,*[343] it was held that the Lanham Act was written by Congress to protect competing firms, not consumers. In that case, consumers had sued claiming that misleading advertising had induced them to purchase insurance against auto rust. The 3rd Circuit said the consumers did not have standing to sue under § 43(a) of the Lanham Act. Consumers have

[342] P. Cameron DeVore and Robert D. Sack, "Advertising and Commercial Speech," in James C. Goodale, chairman, *Communications Law 1993* (New York: Practising Law Institute, 1993), p. 175, see Lanham Act as amended in 1987, Sec. 43(a), 15 U.S.C.A. Sec. 1125(a) (1988).

[343] 11 F.3d 1163 (3d Cir. 1993).

the FTC, state consumer protection laws and individual lawsuits to preserve their rights and remedy wrongs.

DILUTION

Trademark holders also must deal with uses of their marks by persons other than direct competitors. The unauthorized use of the mark can have the effect of blurring the connection between the mark and the product or service in the minds of consumers. Say, for example, that you hold the trademark for Honda cars. If someone starts selling Honda chewing gum, the trademark will not be as pure. This is referred to as dilution and trademark holders can bring action under the Lanham Act to stop such uses of their marks.

A second form of dilution can occur in noncommercial uses of a mark. If the maker of a video about, say ISIL/S, and has them all wearing Nike shoes, the apparent connection between the mark and a widely hated group can tarnish the mark. Dilution by tarnishing can occur in less extreme circumstances. Trademark holders do not generally allow the makers of video games to put their marks in games for fear that game play or characters might, by association, tarnish their marks.

THE ANTICYBERSQUATTING CONSUMER PROTECTION ACT

The ACPA, 15 U.S.C.A.§ 1125(d), denies registrants domain names where it has been proven that a registrant has registered a domain name in bad faith with the intent to profit from an ultimate sale to the holder of the same trademarked name. The other essential elements of calling the Act into use are that a registrant has registered a name that is so similar that it would create confusion in the minds of consumers and that the registrant has no real interest in using the domain name.

The National Football League has used the ACPA to reclaim domain name "NFLToday.com" and celebrities including Madonna, Nicole Kidman and Julia Roberts have reclaimed domain names based on their names. The NFL sent a cease-and-desist letter to New York doctor Lee Schulman who registered "www.nfldraft.com" for $70 and set up a Web site with a picture of a small dog and the title, "World of Yorkies" and "Yorkshire Terriers of the World." The domain name no longer shows yorkies, is still for sale and now redirects to www.soccertickets.net. The doctor said that he happens to buy domain names, figure someone, somewhere, would give me something for it. "I'm not a bad guy." Schulman said he also has registered buyinsurance.com, viagraonline.com, and homeownersinsurance.com.[344]

The ACPA is based on the Lanham Act antidilution provisions that prevent outsiders from using trademarks in a fashion that lessens the significance of the mark. The ACPA was employed in the case of *Virtual*

---

[344] Greg Couch, "Draft day is going to the cyberdogs, Web squatter gets under NFL's skin," *Chicago Sun-Times*, April 11, 2001.

Works, Inc. v. Volkswagen of America, Inc.[345] over the domain name "vw.net." In that case, Volkswagen sued under the ACPA over Virtual's registration, claiming that it was done in bad faith and for the purpose of selling the name to Volkswagen.

In finding for Volkswagen, the court concluded that Virtual Works registered the name with the idea of selling the site "for a lot of money" to Volkswagen. The court noted that under the ACPA, persons are cybersquatters if they have bad faith intent to profit from the mark, register a mark that is distinctive where the mark is identical or confusingly similar to another's trademark or dilutes that trademark.[346]

The Act allows courts to consider a number of factors in determining whether a domain registrant is acting in bad faith. As spelled out at 15 U.S.C. § 1125(d)(1)(A), those factors include:

> (I) the trademark or other intellectual property rights of the person, if any, in the domain name;
>
> (II) the extent to which the domain name consists of the legal name of the person or a name that is otherwise commonly used to identify that person;
>
> (III) the person's prior use, if any, of the domain name in connection with the bona fide offering of any goods or services;
>
> (IV) the person's bona fide noncommercial or fair use of the mark in a site accessible under the domain name;
>
> (V) the person's intent to divert consumers from the mark owner's online location to a site * * * that could harm the goodwill represented by the mark, either for commercial gain or with the intent to tarnish or disparage the mark * * * ;
>
> (VI) the person's offer to transfer, sell, or otherwise assign the domain name to the mark owner or any third party for financial gain without having used * * * the domain name in the bona fide offering of any goods or services * * * ;
>
> (VII) the person's provision of material and misleading false contact information when applying for the registration of the domain name * * * ;
>
> (VIII) the person's registration or acquisition of multiple domain names which the person knows are identical or confusingly similar to the marks of others * * * ; and
>
> (IX) the extent to which the mark incorporated in the person's domain name registration is nor is not distinctive and famous * * *

Courts are allowed to look at the circumstances of each dispute to determine whether a domain registrant is a cybersquatter and are not

---

[345] *Virtual Works, Inc. v. Volkswagen of America, Inc.* [238 F.3d 264 (4th Cir. 2001)].

[346] Ibid. at 267–268.

limited to the nine factors listed above. There is a safe harbor under the ACPA which protects people who believe that their use of the domain name was a fair use or otherwise lawful. Violations of the ACPA that took place after the Nov. 29, 1999 enactment date are subject to both a transfer of the domain name to the trademark holder and monetary damages. For pre-enactment violations, the remedy is merely the transfer of the domain name.

FIGHTING TRADEMARK POACHING IN OTHERS' DOMAIN NAMES

Traditional legal rules that specify where people can file lawsuits limited the application of the ACPA in a case involving Mattel, Inc., the company that make Barbie and Hot Wheels. In 2002, Mattel sued the owners of 52 domain names that featured Mattel trademarks and trade names.[347] Mattel brought suit in federal district court in the Southern District of New York. Four of the holders of the domain names registered those names in the federal district. Most had registered in Virginia, California and Maryland.

The owner of captainbarbie.com,[348] one of the out-of-district defendants, challenged the suit and the district court dismissed that portion of the case as well as cases against the other defendants who were not in the judicial district.

The district court reached this conclusion by determining that the ACPA does not allow *in rem* jurisdiction "except in the judicial district in which the domain name registry, registrar, or other domain name authority is located."[349]

Mattel appealed the decision to the 2nd Circuit, which upheld the district court. It is important to note that the lack of jurisdiction needed to be raised by the defendant or it would not have been waived.

Persons who believe that their names have been hijacked can turn for relief to other forums. "Jurassic Park" author Michael Crichton won his claim against a Canadian Internet group in a proceeding before the World Intellectual Property Organization (WIPO). The WIPO Arbitration and Mediation Center previously had ruled in favor of actor Kevin Spacey and "Bridget Jones" author Helen Fielding in other domain name cases.

Another part of Sec. 43(a) of the Lanham Act allows an individual or company to sue for damages for confusion created by an advertisement misrepresenting a product. That is precisely what singer Tom Waits did when a singer imitating Waits was used in a Frito-Lay commercial to tout a new product. Holding that Waits has a recognizable product (his voice), the Court of Appeals for the 9th Circuit upheld a $2.375 million

---

[347] *Mattel v. Barbie-Club.com*, 310 F.3d 293 (2d Cir. 2002).

[348] captainbarbie.com operated in Australia.

[349] Mattel v. Barbie-Club.com, loc. cit.

judgment for Waits for linking his identity to a commercial product without his permission.[350]

Comparative advertising cases can involve both ad regulation and copyright law. Triangle Publications—when publishers of *TV Guide*—sued Knight-Ridder Newspapers, publishers of *The Miami Herald*. The newspaper had started a television program guide as a Sunday supplement.

The *TV Guide* complaint stemmed from the newspaper's use of a copyrighted cover in a promotional ad. Ultimately, it was held that *The Herald*'s use of the *TV Guide* cover in the context of a truthful comparative advertisement was indeed a "fair use".[351] (See Copyright, Chap. 13, on the defense of "fair use.")

---

[350] *Waits v. Frito-Lay, Inc.*, 978 F.2d 1093, 1101–1105 (9th Cir.1992).

[351] *Triangle Publications, Inc. v. Knight-Ridder Newspapers, Inc.*, 626 F.2d 1171 (5th Cir.1980), affirming 445 F.Supp. 875 (S.D.Fla.1978), 3 Med.L.Rptr. 2086; see also DeVore and Sack, op. cit., p. 476.

CHAPTER 13

COPYRIGHT: PROTECTION AND CONSTRAINT

82. THE RATIONALE OF COPYRIGHT LAW

Copyright law provides a financial incentive for creativity while ensuring that the public will eventually gain full access to the copyrighted work.

"Imitation is not the sincerest form of flattery—a big royalty check is!"[1]

Copyright is the legal protection for works of creativity. Literally, it is the legal right to copy. More generally, it is the right to exploit an original work of creativity. After going through chapters on the worth of freedom, the protection of media in reporting and the restrictions on prior restraint, we come to an area of the law that restricts the free use of works. It may seem counterintuitive, but copyright law works to ensure the free flow of creativity that ultimately benefits society. Just as with trademark protections from the prior chapter, copyright is intended to provide incentives, in this case to creative persons, for them to create works that have value.

Suppose that you are a publisher. In order to ensure that you have a continuing flow of popular, and profitable, books, you encourage new authors. You pay advance royalties on a dozen books, most of which do not sell enough to cover the costs of production. Finally, one of your authors comes up with a book that will be a best seller. Your profits from that one book must help cover the cost of doing business for your whole publishing company. You must pay royalties to your new star author. But

1 Author unknown, though believed to have been inspired by Robert Heinlein.

the money you make also must go to recouping the cost for the authors of the other 11 books.

But, a competitor, seeing the potential for profits, buys a copy of your new book. He scans the pages into a computer and produces his own version of the book that he can sell for less than you can, either as an e-book or in paper form. After all, he is not paying to support the unsuccessful authors of the other 11 books. He is not paying royalties to the author. He didn't even invest in the new typeface you commissioned for the book. He undercuts your sales. You fail to make enough profit to remain in business.

The result of the scenario is the failure of your publishing business and all other publishers who do business in traditional ways. Without publishers to fund new authors, little to no literature is created. Authors, denied the ability to earn something from their creativity, will choose other pursuits that will put food on the table. The end result is that society is denied the product of the creativity of artists, composers, writers, game makers, app creators, film makers—all those creative people who add to the sum and substance of life.

THE HISTORY OF COPYRIGHT

The value of copyrights has been evident since the time of the invention of moveable type, coupled with new press technology in Europe.[2] Johannes Gutenberg's invention of metal type in the form of individual letters allowed printers to assemble text piecemeal instead of waiting for a woodblock of the entire text to be carved.[3] Printers were able to duplicate books and other writing much faster than copyists who worked by hand. This ability to distribute information was significant to the Renaissance. Knowledge could be shared and, tested independently, by readers far removed from the original author.

Governments recognized that new ideas could bring increased commerce and the ability to innovate. The printing trade would be important to the development of centers of learning in Renaissance Europe. The biggest obstacle to spreading knowledge was the limited number of printers. Governments needed to attract printers or their apprentices to set up printing houses. The Republic of Venice was the most successful at doing so and enjoyed power and prominence, in part, because of its printing presses. Venice was home to the largest number

---

[2] Chinese printer Pi Sheng created ceramic moveable type in the Eleventh Century. His work was made difficult by the number of characters in Chinese. Chinese uses characters instead of letters. The characters are based on pictures of the concepts. There are about 80,000 characters in the language, though persons can get by knowing only about 3,500. Pi Sheng would have had to create massive character bins instead of the hundred or so needed by early printers in Europe.

[3] Gutenberg apprenticed as a goldsmith and the experience taught him about working with metals. While some printers had tried to create type using wood, the small size of the letters made it difficult to carve from wood, which tended to break, and wood did not have the durability needed to make a sharp reproduction through the printing process because of wear.

of typographers in Italy with 267. Rome had 41, Milan, 63, Naples 27 and Florence 37.[4]

Venice also created the first state protections of printers' rights to be the sole producers of books and other writings.[5]

> On Sept. 1, 1486, the College bestowed upon Marc' Antonio Sabellico, historiographer to the Republic, the sole right to authorize the publication of his *Decades rerum Ventarum*, under a penalty of five hundred ducats. This is the earliest instance in which the government recognized an author's literary proprietorship in his own work.

Sabellilco's first "copyright"[6] took the form of a privilege, a private right granted by the authorities. The College, or Cabinet, of the Republic also created a right to make copies for printers. The printer's right consisted of a right to copy certain works. The printer did not have to have written the work. The printer received the right to print the specific works of others.[7]

> The first example of a copyright to an editor, which is recorded in the minutes of the College, is that granted to Joannes Dominicus Nigro for his edition of *Haliaba* and of Xantis de Pisauro, *De Venenis*. The formula is still the same as in the case of copyright to author, no one may print the editions *excepto dumtaxat illo impressore quem prefatus dominus Joanes Dominicus duxerit eligendum*.[8]

Without copyrights, the authors and printers would run the risk of competitors printing popular works at lower cost and then underselling the copyright holders, threatening their businesses. The Republic, working in its own self-interest, began to protect its own printing industry. Here, the benefit to the greater entity, the nation itself, was more important than the rights of authors.

Much of American law came from the British colonial experience and after the colonies gained their independence, American courts often looked at English statutory and case law for direction. Parliament passed the Statute of Anne 8 in 1709 (it took effect in 1710), creating statutory protection for intellectual property, "an Act for the Encouragement of

---

[4] Horatio Brown, *The Venetian Printing Press*, (New York: G.F. Putnam's Sons,1891).

[5] Ibid. at 11.

[6] John of Speyer is referred to as the first printer to receive a copyright. The Republic of Venice, eager to attract its first printer, granted him a 5-year monopoly on all of printing, rather than a right to print specific works. The monopoly would have prevented other printers and typographers from doing business in Venice, but John of Speyer fell ill and died after one year and the door was opened to other printers. After that, the Republic of Venice granted rights to makes copies of specific works to printers.

[7] Horatio Brown, *The Venetian Printing Press*, (New York: G.F. Putnam's Sons,1891). At 54.

[8] "Save only that the printer has the aforementioned John Dominic marry choices."

Learning, by Vesting the Copies of Printed Books in the Authors or Purchasers of such Copies, during the Times therein mentioned."

In language similar to the scenario in the introduction, the Statute of Anne pointed to harms that befell authors whose works were printed without their permission.[9]

> Whereas Printers, Booksellers, and other Persons, have of late frequently taken the Liberty of Printing, Reprinting, and Publishing, or causing to be Printed, Reprinted, and Published Books, and other Writings, without the Consent of the Authors or Proprietors of such Books and Writings, to their very great Detriment, and too often to the Ruin of them and their Families:

The statute gave the authors and proprietors[10] "sole Right and Liberty of Printing such Book and Books" for a limited number of years. The rights to published works ran for 21 years with the term beginning April 10, 1710. Unpublished works enjoyed a 14-year term starting on the date the work was first published.

THE AMERICAN EXPERIENCE

American copyright arises directly from the U.S. Constitution in Article I, Sec. 8.

> The Congress shall have power * * * to promote the Progress of Science and useful Arts by securing for limited Times to Authors and Inventors the exclusive Right to their respective Writings and Discoveries.

Passage of the first federal copyright statute in 1790, a year before the Bill of Rights, indicates that America's Post-Revolutionary generation had a lively concern about the need for copyright protection. Additional copyright statutes were enacted during the Nineteenth Century[11] and the copyright statute was rewritten and added to several times during the Twentieth Century.

As in the Republic of Venice and Great Britain, American copyright law makes clear that the copyright monopoly's purpose is to benefit society.[12]

> The copyright law, like the patent statute, makes reward to the owner a secondary consideration. The sole interest of the United States and the primary objective in conferring the monopoly lies in the general benefits derived by the public from the labors of authors.

---

[9] 8 Anne, c. 19 (1710).

[10] Ibid.

[11] Thorvald Solberg, *Copyright Enactments of the United States*, 1783–1906. Washington, 1906.

[12] *Fox Film Corp. v. Doyal*, 286 U.S. 123, 127, 52 S.Ct. 546, 547 (1932).

83. THE NATURE OF COPYRIGHT

Reflecting an awareness that new technologies continue to emerge and that human ingenuity will devise new forms of expression, the language of the copyright statute is sweeping in listing the sorts of things that may be copyrighted. Sec. 102 says:[13]

(a) Copyright protection subsists, in accordance with this title, in original works of authorship fixed in any tangible medium of expression, now known or later developed, from which they can be perceived, reproduced, or otherwise communicated, either directly or with the aid of a machine or device. Works of authorship include the following categories:

(1) literary works;

(2) musical works, including any accompanying words;

(3) dramatic works, including any accompanying music;

(4) pantomimes and choreographic works;[14]

(5) pictorial, graphic, and sculptural works;

(6) motion pictures and other audiovisual works;

(7) sound recordings; and

(8) architectural works.

(b) In no case does copyright protection for an original work of authorship extend to any idea, procedure, process, system, method of operation, concept, principle, or discovery, regardless of the form in which it is described, explained, illustrated, or embodied in such work.

The reasons for denying copyright in ideas, systems, processes, concepts, principles or discovery is clear when considering the effects of granting someone the copyright to "1 + 1 = 2." That copyright holder would soon be richer than Bill Gates as every first grader and elementary math text publisher had to pay royalties to use that system. There are additional restrictions on copyright dealing with the requirement that a work must be sufficiently original and have a certain minimal level of creativity.

In a 2007 case, a federal court in Utah explained long-standing doctrine that prohibits granting copyrights to ideas. In *Close to My Heart v. Enthusiast Media*,[15] the trial court looked at a copyright infringement claim regarding scrapbooking. Scrapbooking is a multi-billion dollar industry and Close to My Heart sued Enthusiast for copyright and trademark infringement and sought a preliminary injunction to prevent

---

[13] 17 U.S.C.A. § 102.

[14] Choreography was not mentioned in the copyright statute until it was included in the 1976 Act. Before that, it was only as a "dramatic composition."

[15] *Close to My Heart v. Enthusiast Media*, 508 F.Supp.2d 963 (D. Utah 2007).

Enthusiast from selling products that contained instructions and layouts that infringed Close to My Heart's copyrights.

Judge Tena Campbell denied the request, explaining that the materials Close to My Heart wanted to protect through copyright were not protectable.[16]

> Copyright law only protects the original expressions of ideas, not the ideas themselves; the concepts underlying expression, remain free for anyone's taking. See Melville B. Nimmer & David Nimmer, 4 Nimmer on Copyright, ("Nimmer") § 2.03[D]; *Autoskill Inc. v. National Educational Support Systems, Inc.*, 994 F.2d 1476, 1491 (10th Cir.1993) (stating that one of the fundamentals of copyright law is that a copyright does not protect an idea, but only the expression of the idea). "The sine qua non of copyright is originality." *Feist Pubs., Inc. v. Rural Tel. Serv. Co.*, 499 U.S. 340, 345, 111 S.Ct. 1282, 113 L.Ed.2d 358 (1991).

In *Baker v. Selden*,[17] the Supreme Court held that an author's book on bookkeeping that included lines and forms could not be copyrighted because that would give him a monopoly on the practice of bookkeeping.

> [I]t is contended that the ruled lines and headings, given to illustrate the system, are a part of the book, and, as such, are secured by the copyright; and that no one can make or use similar ruled lines and headings, or ruled lines and headings made and arranged on substantially the same system, without violating the copyright. * * *
>
> A treatise on the composition and use of medicines, be they old or new; on the construction and use of ploughs, or watches, or churns; or on the mixture and application of colors for painting or dyeing; or on the mode of drawing lines to produce the effect of perspective,-would be the subject of copyright; but no one would contend that the copyright of the treatise would give the exclusive right to the art or manufacture described therein.

Justice Joseph P. Bradley's opinion explained that the creation of a new method or invention would be protected by patent instead of copyright.

> Take the case of medicines. Certain mixtures are found to be of great value in the healing art. If the discoverer writes and publishes a book on the subject (as regular physicians generally do), he gains no exclusive right to the manufacture and sale of the medicine; he gives that to the public. If he desires to acquire such exclusive right, he must obtain a patent for the mixture as a new art, manufacture, or composition of matter. He may

---

16 Ibid. at 967.

17 *Baker v. Selden*, 101 U.S. 99 (1879).

> copyright his book, if he pleases; but that only secures to him the exclusive right of printing and publishing his book. So of all other inventions or discoveries.

FIVE KEYS TO UNDERSTANDING COPYRIGHT

(1) Copyright applies to original works of creativity.

Copyright is separate from protections for useful articles like fuel injectors, video monitors and cellular telephones. Those items are protected by patent laws. Copyright also does not apply to those symbols that represent corporations or businesses. Those marks are protected by trademark laws. Instead, copyright protects original creativity expressed in an artistic manner. As such, it applies to the literary style of an article, news story, book, or other intellectual creation. It does not apply to the themes, ideas, or facts contained in the copyrighted material. Anyone may write about any subject. Copyright's protection extends only to the particular manner or style of expression. What is "copyrightable" in text, for example, is the order and selection of words, phrases, clauses, sentences, and the arrangement of paragraphs.

(a) Creativity

The requirement that works have a minimal amount of creativity in order to gain the protection of copyright is one that, like many other areas of law, has no bright lines to guide us. Indeed, the courts have referred to the fact that "minimal standards apply."[18] In *John Muller & Co. v. New York Arrows Soccer Team*,[19] a panel of the 8th Circuit Court of Appeals affirmed a lower court decision that a logo design for a soccer team did not have enough creativity to qualify for a copyright. "The logo consisted of four angled lines which form an arrow and the word 'Arrows' in cursive script below the arrow."[20] The panel, citing earlier cases from both the circuit and authoritative treatises, affirmed the district court's ruling.[21]

> If, as here, the creator seeks to register the item as a "work of art" or "pictorial, graphic or sculptural work, the work must embody some creative authorship in its delineation or form." There is no simple way to draw the line between "some creative authorship" and not enough creative authorship * * *

This minimal requirement for creativity explains why titles of works and short phrases may not be copyrighted. In *Domsalla v. Stephens*,[22] a Texas record company brought an infringement suit against a band over the

---

[18] *Gardenia Flowers v. Joseph Markovits*, 280 F.Supp. 776, 782 (S.D.N.Y. 1968).

[19] *John Muller & Company, Inc. v. New York Arrows Soccer Team, Inc.*, 802 F.2d 989 (8th Cir.1986).

[20] Ibid. at 990. Persons interested in looking at the logo can find it in the middle of the page at http://www.oursportscentral.com/misl/arrows.php.

[21] Ibid.

[22] *Domsalla v. Stephens*, 2001 WL 493157, 2001 Copr.L.Dec. P 28,280 (N.D.Tex. 2001).

use of the phrase "Texas Thunder." The federal district court dismissed the claim on the grounds that the plaintiff could not hold a copyright in that short phrase.[23] In *Dobson v. NBA Properties*,[24] Maxie Dobson offered to sell a promotional project, that included the registered phrase[25] "Chicago Bulls Repeat Threepeat," to the NBA for $250,000. The NBA turned Dobson down, but later authorized the use of the promotional project, but without paying him. Dobson sued but the district court dismissed his claim because his "repeat threepeat" was merely a phrase and thus incapable of copyright.

The holding that short titles are not capable of being copyrighted means that people are sometimes surprised when they look for a movie or book of a particular title and find a different work with the same title. Cinephiles looking for the 2014 film "*Fury*" will wind up with four other films of the same name, including a 1936 film about a man who escapes a lynch mob and then tries to frame the participants for his murder, a 1973 movie about a peasant revolt in pre-revolutionary Russia, a 1923 silent movie about a son who seeks out his mother who abandoned his father, a 1970 movie about a North Korean agent who turns against his countrymen after learning that North Korea killed his parents and six other films that have a different original title but also were advertised as "*Fury*." In a play on the rule, humorist Robert Benchley, famous in the 1930s, once published a book with the title *"20,000 Leagues Under the Sea or David Copperfield."*

The creativity requirement also applies to works that are more substantial than those in *Domsalla* and *Dobson*. Rural Telephone, a small Kansas phone company, had invested a substantial amount of time compiling a directory that listed the names and addresses of its subscribers in several different communities.

When Feist Publications, a competitor for advertising, sought to publish a regional phone directory, Rural refused to give Feist permission to include Rural's copyrighted white pages. Feist went ahead and incorporated Rural's listings, altering some of the information to conform to its own directory format, but publishing many of the listings exactly as they appeared in the Rural telephone directory.

The case made it to the Supreme Court where all nine justices sided with Feist. Justice Sandra Day O'Connor, writing for the Court, explained that although both the Copyright Act of 1909 and 1976

---

[23] In addition, the court noted, the phrase lacked the required originality for copyright protection having been used by a motor speedway, at least three bands, a girls' fast-pitch softball team and 41 other entities.

[24] *Dobson v. NBA Properties, Inc.*, 1999 WL 97901, 254 Copr.L.Dec. P. 27891 (S.D.N.Y. 1999).

[25] Dobson filed a copy of his registration certificate with the court but did not provide a copyright certificate of registration. In any event, courts may, and are often asked to, invalidate a grant of copyright by the Register of Copyright if the facts and law require that. The Register, which must deal with all copyright applications by all creative persons does not have the resources to examine the nature and background of all copyright applications.

recognized the right of a compiler to claim copyright protection for a collection of facts, a subsequent compiler was free to use those same facts in preparing a competing work so long as the new work did not follow exactly the same selection and arrangement of those facts.[26]

Here the Court found that although *Rural* had devoted sufficient effort to make its white pages useful, it had not done so in a sufficiently creative way to make the work original. As the Court itself had explained this crucial distinction between effort and originality almost a century ago,[27]

> The right thus secured by the copyright act is not a right to the use of certain words, because they are the common property of the human race, and are as little susceptible of private appropriation as air or sunlight; nor is it the right to ideas alone, since in the absence of means of communicating them they are of value to no one but the author. But the right is to that arrangement of words which the author has selected to express his ideas * * *

We can look to two other important Supreme Court cases to understand the concept of creativity as applied to works other than in mere words. *Burrow-Giles Lithographic Co. v. Sarony*[28] and *Bleistein v. Donaldson Lithographing Co.*[29] provide insight into the analysis of originality. *Sarony* dealt with the, then, relatively new issue of whether photographs were works of sufficient creativity to qualify for copyright. *Bleistein* dealt with the concept of protection of drawings and engravings that were made of actual persons in real life.

Napoleon Sarony, a photographer, sued Burrow-Giles Lithographic over the copying of a photograph of Oscar Wilde.[30] Burrow-Giles had obtained a copy of the photograph and made 85,000 copies. Burrow-Giles argued that while it had made the copies, it had not violated Sarony's copyright because photographs were not capable of copyrightability. Photographs, the lithographer argued, were mere reproductions of the exact features of objects or persons. As such, they did not amount to works of creativity. Further, photographs were not listed in the sorts of works protected by copyright when the statute was created. Justice Samuel Miller's opinion for a unanimous Supreme Court disposed of this argument by simply noting that the Constitution could stretch to cover photographs "as far as they are representatives of original intellectual conceptions of the author."[31]

---

[26] *Feist Publications, Inc. v. Rural Telephone Service Co.*, 499 U.S. 340, 111 S.Ct 1282 (1991).

[27] *Holmes v. Hurst*, 174 U.S. 82, 86, 19 S.Ct. 606, 607 (1899).

[28] *Burrow-Giles v. Sarony*, 111 U.S. 53, 4 S.Ct. 279 (1884).

[29] *Bleistein v. Donaldson*, 188 U.S. 239, 23 S.Ct. 298 (1903).

[30] A copy of the portrait is available at: https://commons.wikimedia.org/wiki/File:Oscar_Wilde_portrait_by_Napoleon_Sarony_-_albumen.jpg.

[31] 111 U.S. 53, 58, 4 S.Ct. 279, 281 (1884).

The Court then turned to the question of the creativity of photographs. Engravings, prints and paintings were original works of creativity because they represented the creativity of their creators with all the novelty, invention and originality that involved. Photographs, on the other hand, were mechanical and chemical reproductions of the physical features of objects or people. They were the result of the reaction of chemicals to light allowed to strike the photographic plate. Development and printing are mere steps in a mechanical process. But the Court looked beyond that recitation of the process of photography and noted the findings of the lower court that the picture was,[32]

> "a new, harmonious, characteristic, and graceful picture, and that said plaintiff made the same * * * entirely from his own original mental conception, to which he gave visible form by posing the said Oscar Wilde in front of the camera, selecting and arranging the costume, draperies, and other various accessories in said photograph, arranging the subject so as to present graceful outlines, arranging and disposing the light and shade, suggesting and evoking the desired expression * * * "

For those reasons, the Supreme Court concluded that Sarony's photograph was a work of original creativity that deserved copyright protection.[33]

THE MONKEY'S TALE: WHO GETS THE COPYRIGHT?

The monkey, here a crested black macaque (Macaca nigra) in an Indonesian forest, happened upon British photographer David Slater's cameras in 2011.

One day, Slater said, he set up a tripod and walked away for a few moments. When he returned, he discovered that the monkeys had grabbed his camera and started snapping pictures. Thus, the monkey-selfie was created.

The story and the photos took off in media reports. The most iconic of the images was featured by the *Guardian*, the *Telegraph* and *Huffington Post*, among others.

Soon enough, it showed up on Wikipedia—first on the page for the species of monkey, then on Wikimedia Commons, which hosts images in the public domain. Slater asked Wikimedia to take down the image to honor his claim of copyright in the photo. He also got into a dispute with the tech blog Techdirt which argued that Slater could not have the copyright in a post.[34]

---

[32] Ibid. at 54, 4 S.Ct. at 279.

[33] French law did not protect ordinary snapshots for many years, The French copyright law of 1957 only protected works that were artistic or documentary. The French copyright law changed in 1985 to extend protections to other works, provided that they met a requirement of originality that showed the photographer had stamped his personality through the work.

[34] Mike Masnick, "Monkeys Don't Do Fair Use; News Agency Tells Techdirt To Remove Photos," *Techdirt*, July 12, 2011.

> The whole post was about whether or not anyone had a legitimate copyright claim on the photos, noting that the photographer, David Slater, almost certainly did not have a claim, seeing as he did not take the photos, and even admits that the images were an accident from monkeys who found the camera (i.e., he has stated publicly that he did not "set up" the shot and let the monkeys take it). And yet, Caters News Agency has a copyright notice on two of the images, claiming to hold the rights to them. We doubted that the monkeys—who might have the best "claim" to copyright on these photos, if there is one, had licensed the images.

The U.S. Copyright office weighed in with a policy statement soon after the story about the copyright dispute spread. "The Office will not register works produced by nature, animals, or plants," the office said in a draft of its compendium of U.S. copyright office practices. "Likewise, the Office cannot register a work purportedly created by divine or supernatural beings, although the Office may register a work where the application or the deposit copy(ies) state that the work was inspired by a divine spirit."

So much for the famous paintings made by Asian elephants in tourist attractions in Thailand. And, incidentally, the Shakespeare works would be incapable of being copywritten as they passed into the public domain hundreds of years ago.

On the other hand, if Slater had set up the photograph, arranging the other elements of the composition and attending to the lighting and other elements, he would have had a better claim. Had the animal only triggered the shot that Slater put together, the photograph would still have been "created" by Slater.

In *Bleistein*,[35] the Supreme Court dealt with a copyright claim arising over the preparation of advertising posters for a circus. The posters featured portraits that purported to represent drawings of the circus performers engaged in their acts. "One of the designs was of an ordinary ballet, one of a number of men and women, described as the Stirk family performing on bicycles, and one group of men and women whitened to represent statues."[36] Bleistein and his company, the Courier Lithographic Co., had made the chromolithographies (colored lithographs) which Donaldson Lithographing had used to make the advertising posters.

The trial court ruled that the lithographs did not deserve the protection of the copyright law and the court of appeals sustained the verdict. The Supreme Court reversed on a 7–2 vote. Justice Holmes took up and quickly disposed of the issue of the subject matter of the

[35] *Bleistein v. Donaldson Lithographic Co.*, 188 U.S. 239, 23 S.Ct. 298 (1903).

[36] Ibid. at 248, 299.

lithographs. They appeared to be representations of actual performers engaged in performance.

> [T]he plaintiff's case is not affected by the fact, if it be one, that the pictures represent actual groups—visible things. They seem from the testimony to have been composed from hints or description, not from sight of a performance. But even if they had been drawn from life, that fact would not deprive them of protection. The opposite proposition would mean that a portrait by Velasquez or Whistler was common property because others might try their hand on the same face.[37]

Holmes then turned to an issue raised by the trial court that the degree of artistic accomplishment as an actual depiction or "copy" of the actual performers and the use of the work in an advertisement meant it did not deserve copyright protection. The trial court reserved copyright protection to the fine arts and not to such works as this. "That the picture which represents a dozen or more figures of women in tights, with bare arms, and with much of the shoulder displayed, and by means of which it is designed to lure men to a circus, is in any sense a work of the fine arts or a pictorial illustration in the sense of the statute, I do not believe."[38]

Holmes replies that the test is not the degree of sophistication of the work or its usefulness in trade. "A picture is none the less a picture, and none the less a subject of copyright, that it is used for an advertisement."[39]

Copyright also requires that the work be original. Copies don't get copyright. Otherwise, someone would copy over Shakespeare's plays and charge people for putting on *Romeo and Juliet* or *Richard III.*

(b) Originality

Originality is a fundamental principle of copyright; originality implies that the author or artist created the work through his own skill, labor, and judgment. The concept of originality means that the particular work must be firsthand, pristine; not copied or imitated. Originality, however, does not mean that the work must be necessarily novel or unique, or that it have any value as literature or art. What constitutes originality was explained in an old but frequently quoted case, *Emerson v. Davies.* The famed Justice Joseph Story of Massachusetts wrote in 1845:[40]

> In truth, in literature, in science and in art, there are, and can be, few, if any, things, which, in an abstract sense, are strictly new and original throughout. Every book in literature, science,

---

37 Ibid. at 249, 299.

38 *Bleistein v. Donaldson Lithographing Co.*, 98 Fed. 608 (C.C.D.Ky.1899).

39 *Bleistein v. Donaldson Lithographing Co.*, 188 U.S. 239, 251, 23 S.Ct. 298, 300 (1903).

40 *Emerson v. Davies*, 8 Fed. Cas. 615 (C.D.D. Mass 1845).

and art, borrows, and must necessarily borrow, and use much which was well known and used before.

The question of originality seems clear in concept but this quality of composition is not always easy to separate and identify in particular cases. This is true especially when different authors have conceived like expressions or based their compositions upon commonly accepted ideas, terms, or descriptions in sequence. It must be borne in mind that an idea as such cannot be the subject of copyright; to be eligible for copyright, ideas must have particular physical expressions, as signs, symbols, or words. As was stated in *Kaeser & Blair, Inc. v. Merchants' Association, Inc.*,[41] "copyright law does not afford protection against the use of an idea, but only as to the means by which the idea is expressed."

The originality requirement will even protect similar expression, that is, when that similar expression is the product of independent creation. In this way, copyright is unlike patent, which gives the patent holder all rights against similar or identical devices no matter how they came into being. Therefore, a work might be identical but protectable if an original and uncopied work. As Judge Learned Hand explained in *Sheldon v. Metro-Goldwyn Pictures*,[42] an infringement case involving the unauthorized copying of a stage play in move form, while the law of copyright does not protect the copier, it will stand for the person who, however coincidentally, creates the same expression. "Borrowed the work indeed not be, for a plagiarist is not himself pro tanto an 'author'; but if by some magic a man who had never known it were to compose Keats's *"Ode on a Grecian Urn,"* he would be an 'author,' and, if he copyrighted it, others might not copy that poem, though they might of course copy Keats's."

Sometimes, that originality comes in the form of a creative addition to an older work. While the older, original work cannot be copyrighted again, the addition can be if it satisfies the creative and originality requirements.

In *Italian Book Co. v. Rossi*,[43] a federal district court in New York found in favor of a Sicilian sailor's additions to an old folk song in an infringement case over the sailor's new version. Paolo Citorello, the Sicilian sailor, played his guitar and sang folk songs he remembered from his youth. He could not read music, so his singing was based on his memory alone. Where he could not remember the words, he created new ones. Citorello played and sang his song for Italian Book Co., a music publisher. The publisher had an arranger write down the score and words and Citorello obtained a copyright which he assigned to Italian Book.

---

[41] *Kaesar & Blair v. Merchants' Ass'n.*, 64 F.2d 575 (6thCir. 1933). The case revolved around an infringement claim over stationery catalogs.

[42] *Sheldon v. Metro-Goldwyn Pictures*, 309 U.S. 390, 60 S.Ct. 681 (1940).

[43] *Italian Book Co. v. Rossi*, 27 F.2d 1014 (S.D.N.Y. 1928).

Rossi, another song publishing company, copied the song and, after changing some of the words, filed for its own copyright. Italian Book Co. sued for copyright infringement and Rossi defended on the grounds that Citorello's song was really an old Sicilian folk song that had been published in 1871 and so he could not copyright it.

The trial court agreed that the song had its origins in Sicily years before. But, Citorello's contribution was an original creation and deserved protection.[44]

> How much of Citorello's composition was subconscious repetition of this old song, as he had heard it sung, and how much of it was original with him, no one can say. No doubt he had heard some variation of the old song and was trying to remember it, but the product differed in words and music from any version of it that has been proved although the theme was the same and the music quite similar. To the extent of such difference he was the author of the new arrangement of the words and music of an old song.

District Court Judge Thomas Thacher wrote that Rossi could make copies of the original Sicilian folk song. Or, they could create their own version, but he wrote, they could not "copy Citorello's variation." Citorello's copyright existed in his contributions. He created what is known as a derivative work, a work that is derived from an original. Derivative works are covered later in this chapter.

Originality was another key element in the *Feist* case.[45] When Rural sued over Feist's use of its white pages, it was asserting a copyright in the listing of names, addresses and telephone numbers. That, Justice O'Connor wrote did not satisfy the threshold requirement that a work be original to qualify for copyright.[46]

> Original, as the term is used in copyright, means only that the work was independently created by the author (as opposed to copied from other works), and that it possesses at least some minimal degree of creativity. 1 M. Nimmer & D. Nimmer, Copyright §§ 2.01[A], [B] (1990).

Rural did not create the listings, it merely recorded them, O'Connor wrote.[47] The names, addresses and numbers of telephone subscribers

---

[44] Ibid.

[45] *Feist Publications, Inc. v. Rural Telephone Service Co., Inc.*, 499 U.S. 340, 111 S.Ct. 1282 (1991).

[46] Ibid. at 345, 1287.

[47] Ibid. at 347, 1288.

existed before Rural compiled the facts.[48] Rural did not create the information and so it did not originate them.[49]

> "No one may claim originality as to facts." * * * * This is because facts do not owe their origin to an act of authorship. The distinction is one between creation and discovery: The first person to find and report a particular fact has not created the fact; he or she has merely discovered its existence.

Now, some compilations of facts can be copyrighted. But it is not the facts that are considered to be original, only the words used to put the facts together, the compilation. Box scores of baseball games are compilations of facts and, so, cannot be copyrighted. A story about the game will have the facts, but is copyrightable because of the words used to describe the events that were recorded in the box score. Justice O'Connor explained the difference between protecting the facts and the expression.[50]

> [I]f the compilation author clothes facts with an original collocation of words, he or she may be able to claim a copyright in this written expression. Others may copy the underlying facts from the publication, but not the precise words used to present them.

Some compilations can meet the originality requirement if the selection and arrangement of the facts are original, that is to say, the author is the first person to select and arrange that way.[51] In any event, the facts still may be used.

(2) Copyright is both a protection for and a restriction of the communications media.

Copyright protects the media by preventing the wholesale taking of the form of materials, without permission, from one person or unit of the media for publication by another person or unit of the media. Despite the guaranty of freedom of the press in the First Amendment, newspapers and other communications media must acquire permission to publish material that is protected by copyright.

---

[48] Some clever student will no doubt point out that Rural assigned the telephone numbers to its subscribers and thereby created that "original" information. But a string of 10 numbers is a short phrase and not entitled to copyright protection.

[49] *Feist Publications, Inc. v. Rural Telephone Service Co., Inc.*, 499 U.S. 340, 347, 111 S.Ct. 1282, 1288 (1991).

[50] Ibid. at 348, 1289.

[51] To complicate matters, a legal doctrine called "merger" can deny copyright protection for an original work of creativity if there are only a very few ways to express that idea. This is covered in defenses to infringement.

(c) Protections

Copyright gives the person who creates an original work certain rights. One of the most important is getting to decide if and when to share that work with the world.[52]

In *Harper & Row v. Nation Enterprises,*[53] the Supreme Court noted that one of the rights that copyright holders have is to decide when, or whether, to publish. In the *Harper* case, *Nation* magazine published excerpts of former President Gerald Ford's memoir, "*A Time to Heal,*" dealing with his pardon of former President Richard Nixon for any and all crimes associated with the Watergate burglary and subsequent coverup.

Harper & Row sued Nation for copyright infringement. *Nation* countered that the publication was protected under "Fair Use," a part of the copyright statute that allows for use of copyrighted works without permission of the copyright holder (We will cover that in defenses to infringement claims). The Supreme Court, in a 6–3 decision, held that *Nation* magazine had violated President Ford's copyright. Justice Sandra Day O'Connor's opinion addressed the rights of first publication.[54]

> Publication of an author's expression before he has authorized its dissemination seriously infringes the author's right to decide when and whether it will be made public * * * The right of first publication implicates a threshold decision by the author whether and in what form to release his work. First publication is inherently different from other § 106 rights in that only one person can be the first publisher * * *

But once a copyright holder decides to share a work with the world, a menu of uses comes into play. This is known as the "Bundle of Rights" that covers the multiple ways a copyrighted work can be exploited.

THE BUNDLE OF RIGHTS

A copyright grants to its holder certain exclusive rights that involve the exploitation of the work. They are:[55]

1. reproduction of the work in copies or phono records;

---

[52] Before 1976, copyright was divided into protection for published works and unpublished works. Giving the copyright holders of unpublished works the right to choose when or if to publish was a significant issue before the copyright began to treat all works the same generally. If a work was published without complying with the registration and deposit requirements, it would lose its copyrightability and become a work in the public domain. Because of that, many cases turned on whether an author had, in fact, published a work. Martin Luther King's "I Have a Dream" speech wound up before a federal circuit court of appeals in a case where the court had to decide whether his delivery of the speech to a national audience amounted to publication that would cause him to lose his copyright. The appeals court held that it did not and King and his estate retained the copyright allowing them to control its use. *King v. Mister Maestro,* 224 F.Supp. 101 (S.D.New York, 1963).

[53] *Harper & Row v. Nation Ent.,* 471 U.S. 539, 105 S.Ct. 2218 (1985).

[54] Ibid. at 552–553, 2226–2227.

[55] 17 U.S.C.A. § 106.

2. preparation of derivative works based on the work itself;

3. distribution by rent, lease, loan, sale or other transfer of ownership of copies or phono records of the copyrighted work;

4. public performance of literary, musical, dramatic, choreographic works, pantomimes, motion pictures and other audiovisual work;

5. public display of pictorial, graphic, sculptural, literary, musical, dramatic, choreographic works, pantomimes, and individual images of motion pictures and other audiovisual works; and

6. public performance of sound recordings by means of digital audio transmission.

The copyright holder can hold onto or sell each of the individual parts of the bundle of rights.[56] A copyright holder also can license one or more of the rights. Licensing is a written contract[57] that gives a licensee a right to exploit an aspect of a copyrighted work. For example, a novelist could license the novel to be turned into a graphic novel by one licensee and license turning the novel into a movie by another licensee. The copyright holder can further subdivide licenses so that one licensee could have the rights to turn the novel into a television in Europe and another the right to turn the novel into a television movie in Asia.

(3) As a form of literary property, copyright belongs to that class of personal property including patents, trade-marks, trade names, trade secrets and good will.

As personal property, copyrights can be sold, transferred, bequeathed or left in a person's estate. The rules for transferring copyrights follows in the section after the duration of copyrights.

(4) Copyright, it must be emphasized, is quite different from creativity.

Copyright is created at the moment that an original work of creativity is fixed in tangible form. The creator has the copyright from the act of creation, generally. But, unlike the artistic spark of creativity, copyright can be held by someone other than the creator. If sold or otherwise transferred, the copyright will belong to someone else. If the work is a work for hire (a term of legal art), then the copyright will belong to the hiring party even at the moment of fixation in tangible form.

---

[56] Early copyright contemplated copyright as a single thing that covered all possible uses. Copyright holders simply sold their "copyright," and all their rights. As time passed, the law of copyright recognized the multiple components of works. Today, copyright holders have the option to sell individual bits of their copyrights. Copyright holders can license parts of their copyrights and, of course, they can always sell the whole thing and not have to worry about which parts to keep.

[57] The copyright statute requires that all transfers of copyright be in writing and signed by the parties.

The section on Works for Hire lays out the sorts of relationships that show that a creator of an original work of creativity was an employee whose work belongs to the employer.

(5) Copyright is distinct from the tangible thing created.

A letter, for example, may be copyrighted. The recipient of the letter is said to own the physical letter—the ink and paper—but the copyright remains with the author. The author has the exclusive right to decide whether or how to exploit what was said in the letter. If you buy a painting, unless you have purchased the copyright, you do not have the right to make and sell copies.

In *Salinger v. Random House*,[58] the 2nd Circuit held that the receipt and physical possession of a work did not give the recipient a copyright. J.D. Salinger was a highly regarded novelist and short story writer, best known for his novel, "The Catcher in the Rye." His last work was published in 1965, and since that time until his death tried to avoid any publicity about himself, refusing to grant interviews or to respond to any inquiries about his private life. Ian Hamilton, a respected literary critic for the *London Sunday Times,* contacted the reclusive author in 1983 to tell him that he intended to write a biography about Salinger to be published by Random House. Although Salinger responded that he did not want to have his biography written during his lifetime, Hamilton spent the next three years completing the work, titled *"J.D. Salinger: A Writing Life."*

Lacking any cooperation from Salinger himself, Hamilton relied heavily upon information contained in letters Salinger had written to various friends during his early years as a writer. These letters had been donated by their recipients to several university libraries, but Salinger was apparently unaware that they would be available to Hamilton.

When Salinger read the galley proofs of the book Random House planned to publish, he notified the publisher that he would attempt to block its publication unless all direct quotations from these private letters he had written his friends were deleted.

Responding to these objections, Hamilton revised his work, omitting most of the direct quotations from Salinger's letters, but still paraphrasing very closely some 59 passages from this correspondence. As Random House was about to publish this revised version of the biography, Salinger sued to prevent publication, claiming among other things that such extensive reliance upon passages from his unpublished letters exceeded the reasonable bounds of fair use.

After originally granting Salinger's request for a preliminary injunction, a lower federal court had decided to lift the injunction and

---

[58] *Salinger v. Random House*, 811 F.2d 90 (2d Cir.1987).

allow publication when a U.S. Court of Appeals intervened, ordering that this ban on publication be made permanent.[59]

The opinion, by Judge Jon O. Newman, explained Salinger's right as well as the rights of the recipients of his letters to have deposited them with the libraries.[60]

> The author of letters is entitled to a copyright in the letters, as with any other work of literary authorship. See *Meeropol v. Nizer*, 560 F.2d 1061, 1069 (2d Cir.), cert. denied, 434 U.S. 1013, 98 S.Ct. 727, 54 L.Ed.2d 756 (1977); *Folsom v. Marsh*, 2 Story 100, 9 F.Cas. 342, 346 (C.C.D.Mass.1841) (No. 4,901); 1 Nimmer on Copyright § 5.04 (1986); W. Patry, Latman's The Copyright Law 130 (6th ed. 1986). * * * The copyright owner owns the literary property rights, including the right to complain of infringing copying, while the recipient of the letter retains ownership of "the tangible physical property of the letter itself." * * * Having ownership of the physical document, the recipient (or his representative) is entitled to deposit it with a library and contract for the terms of access to it.

DURATION OF COPYRIGHT

The Statute of Anne 8 granted copyright for 14 years to creators of new works. The first American copyright statute granted a 14-year copyright with a right to renew for another 14 years. The 1831 Act made it 28 years with a renewal for another 14. The 1909 Act made it 28 years with a renewal for another 28 years. The 1976 Act made copyright for the life of the author plus 50 years. In 1998, President Bill Clinton signed the Sonny Bono Copyright Term Extension Act which extended the life of copyright to the lifetime of the creator plus 70 years.[61] This is an extension of 20 years over the term provided for in the 1976 Act.[62] The Act was the latest in a series of copyright revisions granting more time for copyright holders to benefit from their works.

The renewal process that existed before the 1976 Act took effect was extensively criticized and copyright case law is full of cautionary tales about the complexities of renewal and examples of valuable copyrights lost because of simple clerical mistakes in the process.

---

[59] *Salinger v. Random House*, 811 F.2d 90 (2d Cir.1987). The Supreme Court has declined to review this decision, so the ban on the publication of the book remains permanent. "Supreme Court Refuses to Review Salinger Ruling," New York Times, October 6, 1987, p. 11. On the other hand, in *Maheu v. CBS*, 201 Cal.App.3d 662, 247 Cal.Rptr. 304 (1988), a California court refused to allow an action for copyright infringement by an assistant of Howard Hughes for the unauthorized use of correspondence he received from Hughes because of his failure to obtain copyright protection for this unpublished correspondence that was copyrightable.

[60] Ibid. at 95.

[61] Pub.L.No. 105–298, 12 Stat. 2827.

[62] In 2006, most countries in the European Union set copyright duration at life of the author plus 70 years.

One such case involved the movie "*It's a Wonderful Life.*" In 1973, Republic Pictures, which had owned the copyright, failed to file the needed renewal papers and the movie fell into the public domain. That led to hundreds of showings of the Frank Capra holiday classic by television stations that no longer had to get permission from the copyright owner or pay royalties. Some distributors added color to the black-and-white film laying on color overlays that created a "garish" end result.[63] [64]

The Bono Act extended the copyright protection for works for hire and also works created before the 1976 Act went into effect (The 1976 Act actually began to apply to copyright on Jan. 1, 1978,). Works created before the 1976 Act went into effect were known as pre-1978 works. Those works had their copyright durations extended to a set 95 years. Works for hire had their copyrights extended for the shorter of either 75 years from publication or 100 years from the date of creation. The reason for this set period of years is to simplify the treatment of all of these works. As the 1976 Act did away with renewal, it was necessary to figure out a way that would give these works protection in what would have been their renewal term.

The extension was more generous than the original 28-and 28-year terms would have been. An oft-cited example of this is the Disney cartoon, "Steamboat Willie," the cartoon in which Mickey Mouse (though his name was Mortimer in this work) appeared for the first time. The cartoon got its first copyright in 1928. It was created under the 1909 Act and so with its single renewal, "Steamboat Willie" would have passed into the public domain in 1984, available for anyone to use without permission. When the 1976 Act went into effect it gave all pre-1978 works protection until 2004. But the extension under the Bono Act now provides copyright protection for "Steamboat Willie" to 2023, 95 years from its creation. Even then, Disney will still be able to protect Mickey Mouse under trademark law (see Chap. 12) even after the copyright in "Steamboat Willie" finally expires.

So works created today will have copyright durations that will vary from work to work as they are arise from creator to creator. The chief difference: the life span of the artistic creator. The term is not drawn from the life of the copyright holder, which can be different from the author or creator. If the copyright duration was decided by the life of the copyright holder, one could make copyright perpetual by assigning the copyright to an infant every 70 or 80 years.

---

[63] http://www.rogerebert.com/reviews.

[64] Republic need not be pitied for too long. It managed to regain control of the film by acquiring the rights to the music. It already held the rights to the underlying short story. Republic's savvy move is discussed in the section on derivative works.

Copyright terms today are:[65]

(a) single creator—life of the creator, plus 70 years

(b) joint works—life of the last living creator, plus 70 years

(c) anonymous works, works created under a pseudonym and works made for hire—95 years from first publication or 120 years from the date of its creation, whichever expires first. If the identity of the anonymous or pseudonymous creator is discovered before the end of the copyright term, then either (a) or (b) apply.

Can you extend the duration of copyright by making it a joint work by attaching the names of several newborns to a copyright registration form? You can, but if challenged, it might be hard to explain how an infant contributed to the work. Another problem is that any of the joint authors can exploit the work meaning that the infant joint authors could make use of the work in ways the initial author did not like. The only restriction on the joint author's use is that the profits must be accounted for with the other joint authors.

UPHOLDING THE BONO ACT: ELDRED V. ASHCROFT

The Sonny Bono Copyright Term Extension Act was upheld in 2003 in *Eric Eldred v. John D. Ashcroft, Attorney General of the U.S.*[66] A group of publishers who make use of public domain materials challenged the statute. The publishers had counted on a number of works passing into the public domain when the copyright term under the previous law expired. Many of their projects were halted by the extension of the copyright term. In their petition, they noted that Dover Publications had planned to publish several famous works from the 1920s and 1930s, including *"The Prophet"* by Kahlil Gibran and *"The Harp-Weaver"* by Edna St. Vincent Millay.[67] The lead plaintiff, Eric Eldred, was editor at Eldritch Press, a publisher of free books on the Web.

The plaintiffs built their case chiefly on the grounds that Congress did not have the right to extend the length of copyright protection and that the extension conflicted with the First Amendment.

The challengers focused on the phrase, "securing for limited times to authors and inventors the exclusive right to their respective Writings and Discoveries," from Article I, Sec. 8, the copyright clause of the Constitution of the United States: They argued that Congress regularly escaped the restriction of "limited times" by repeatedly extending the terms of existing copyrights—11 times in the past 40 years.

The challengers also countered the longstanding interpretation of many courts that copyrights trump First Amendment rights. In *Harper*

65 17 U.S.C.A. § 302 (a), (b) and (c).

66 *Eldred v. Ashcroft*, 537 U.S. 186, 123 S.Ct. 769 (2003).

67 Ibid.

& Row v. Nation Magazine (discussed in the textbook earlier and later in this chapter), the Supreme Court ruled that the copyright rights of a book publisher took precedence over a magazine's First Amendment right to publish excerpts from former President Gerald Ford's memoirs. The passages in question dealt with Ford's role in the final days of the Watergate scandal and his decision to pardon former President Richard Nixon, who had resigned in disgrace. *Nation* magazine got an unauthorized copy of the memoir before Harper & Row could publish it in book form and published parts of it in its own magazine story.

Nation's defense against a copyright infringement claim, cited the public's interest in knowing what Ford had written about that key moment in American history. But the Supreme Court rejected the claim by a 6–3 decision, that held that the First Amendment defense had to give way to Harper & Row, which was going to publish the memoir. Circuit courts of appeal have taken their direction from the Supreme Court decision in that case and consistently have ruled that the First Amendment does not take precedence over copyrights.[68]

The challengers to the Bono Act argued that the decision in *Harper & Row* did not apply to their case. Unlike the *Nation* case in which the magazine argued for a right to use material during a valid copyright period, the Bono Act was an unconstitutional extension of the time period in which others were denied the right to make use of the copyrighted content.[69]

The challengers argued that the Supreme Court could use the First Amendment to decide whether the extension of the ban on use violated principles of free expression.

The government's reply was relatively simple, based on the language of the Bono Act and the Supreme Court's cases on the issues raised by the challengers. First, the government rejected the challengers' contention that the extension violated the "constitutional" requirement that copyright terms be of limited duration.[70]

> "Since the CTEA's [Copyright Term Extension Act's] term of life-plus—70 years is not unlimited or perpetual, it satisfies the constitutional mandate that copyrights last only for 'limited times.' "

---

[68] *Roy Export Co. Establishment v. Columbia Broadcasting System, Inc.*, 672 F.2d 1095 (2d Cir.), cert. den., 459 U.S. 826, 103 S.Ct. 60, 74 L.Ed.2d 63 (1982), ruling that CBS did not have a Fair Use/First Amendment right to use copyrighted films to report on Charlie Chaplin's death. See also *New Era Publications Intern., APS v. Henry Holt Co.*, 884 F.2d 659 (2d Cir.), cert. den. 493 U.S. 1094, 110 S.Ct. 1168 (Mem.), in which the publisher of an unauthorized biography of L.Ron Hubbard lost a copyright infringement suit despite the claim of the publisher that the infringing material the claim of the publisher that the infringing material had compelling public interest.

[69] Pub.L.No. 105–298, 12 Stat. 2827. 2002 WL 1041928 (U.S.Dist.Col.Pet. Brief) at 34–35 *Eldred v. Ashcroft*, 534 U.S. 1160, 122 S.Ct. 1170 (Mem.) (2002).

[70] 2002 WL 1836720 (U.S.Dist.Col.Resp. Brief) at 7; *Eldred v. Ashcroft*, 534 U.S. 1160, 122 S.Ct. 1170 (2002).

Writing for the Court, Justice Ruth Bader Ginsburg concluded that the Bono CTEA " * * * is a rational enactment; we are not at liberty to second-guess congressional determinations and policy judgments of this order, however debatable and arguably unwise they may be." She concluded that the CTEA was a permissible exercise of congressional power under the Constitution's Copyright Clause.[71] She also rejected Eldred's argument that CTEA's 20-year extension resulted in "perpetual" copyrights.

Dissenting, Justice Stevens complained that allowing Congress to extend existing monopoly privileges *ad infinitum* means that The Court was " * * * failing to protect the public interest in free access to the products of inventive and artistic genius."[72]

Similarly, Justice Breyer saw the extended copyright period as "virtually perpetual." The Bono CTEA, he noted, " * * * extends the terms of most existing copyrights to 95 years and that of many new copyrights to 70 years after the author's death." He wrote that 20 years amounted to "the longest blanket extension since the founding of the nation."[73]

Justice Breyer asserted that the CTEA,[74]

> "Will likely restrict traditional dissemination of copyrighted works. It will likely inhibit new forms of dissemination through the use of new technology. It threatens to interfere with efforts to preserve our Nation's historical and cultural heritage * * * It is easy to understand how the statute might benefit the private financial interests of corporations or heirs who own existing copyrights. But I cannot find any constitutionally legitimate copyright-related way in which the statute will benefit the public.

84. SECURING A COPYRIGHT

Essentials in acquiring a copyright include notice of copyright, application, deposit of copies in the Library of Congress, and payment of the required fee.

THE FORMALITIES

Copyright registration can be accomplished online at: https://eco.copyright.gov/eService_enu/start.swe?SWECmd=Start&SWEHo=eco.copyright.gov or by filling out a form obtainable from: http://copyright.gov/eco/ or by mail from Register of Copyrights, Library of Congress, Washington, D.C. 20559.

---

71 *Eldred v. Ashcroft*, 537 U.S. 186, 123 S.Ct. 769, at 772 (2003).

72 Ibid. at 801.

73 Ibid.

74 Ibid. at 813.

The Register of Copyrights will require (with some exceptions specified by the Copyright Office), that material deposited for registration shall include two complete copies of the best edition.[75] These copies are to be deposited within three months after publication, along with a completed form as prescribed by the Register of Copyrights.[76]

The online registration fee for a single work with a single creator where the work is not a work for hire, is $35. All other online registrations are $55. When the registrant wants to file a paper form, the fee is $85.[77] It should be noted that registration is required before any action for copyright infringement can be started.[78]

THE COPYRIGHT NOTICE

Notice in copyright exists to let people know whose copyrighted work they are hoping to use. It identifies the owner of the copyright so that arrangements can be made to use the work.

Sec. 401 makes the following general requirement about placing copyright notices on "visually perceptible copies."[79]

> Whenever a work protected under this title [Title 17, United States Code, the copyright statute] is published in the United States or elsewhere by authority of the copyright owner, a notice of copyright in this section shall be placed on all publicly distributed copies from which the work can be visually perceived, either directly or with the aid of a machine or device.
>
> The copyright notice shall consist of these three elements:[80]
>
> (1) the symbol © (the letter C in a circle), or the word "Copyright" or the abbreviation "Copr."; and
>
> (2) the year of first publication of the work; in the case of compilations or derivative works incorporating previously published material, the year date of the first publication of the compilation or derivative work is sufficient. The year date may be omitted where a pictorial, graphic, or sculptural work, with accompanying text matter, if any, is reproduced in or on greeting cards, postcards, stationery, jewelry, dolls, toys, or any useful articles; and
>
> (3) the name of the owner of copyright abbreviation by which the name can be recognized or a generally known alternative designation of the owner.

---

[75] 17 U.S.C.A. § 407.

[76] Ibid. Useful circulars which may be pulled down from the Copyright Office website, http://www.copyright.gov/circs/.

[77] http://copyright.gov/about/fees.html. Payment of fees is specified by 17 U.S.C.A. § 708.

[78] 17 U.S.C.A. § 411; see also 17 U.S.C.A. § 205.

[79] 17 U.S.C.A. § 401(a).

[80] 17 U.S.C.A. § 401(b).

If a sound recording is being copyrighted, the notice takes a different form. The notice shall consist of the following three elements:[81]

(1) the symbol ©; and

(2) the year of first publication of the sound recording; and

(3) the name of the owner of copyright in the sound recording, or an abbreviation by which the name can be recognized, or a generally known alternative designation of the owner; if the producer of the sound recording is named on the phono record labels or containers, and if no other name appears in conjunction with the notice, the producer's name shall be considered a part of the notice.

The copyright statute adopts one of the former law's basic principles: in the case of works made for hire, the employer is considered the author of the work (and therefore the initial copyright owner) unless there has been an agreement to the contrary. The statute requires that any agreement under which the employee will own rights be in writing and signed by both the employee and the employer.[82]

The copyright notice shall be placed on the copies "in such manner and location as to give reasonable notice of the claim of copyright." Special methods of this "affixation" of the copyright notice and positions for notices on various kinds of works will be prescribed by regulations to be issued by the Register of Copyrights.[83]

Under the 1909 Act, a failure to properly give notice of the copyright meant a loss of the copyright. The 1976 Act provided some protection where copyright notice was not put on a work provided the omission was on a limited number of copies or if a reasonable attempt was made to fix the omission within five years or if the omission was a mistake on the part of the distributor where the copyright holder had expressly called for the distributor to put the proper notice on the works.

For works published on or after March 1, 1989, copyright notice is no longer a requirement for keeping a copyright, though it is helpful for copyright holders to let consumers know that a work is copyrighted so that unintended infringement does not occur. Copyright registration also is a pre-requisite for filing an infringement suit.

Even though the lack of a proper copyright notice no longer bars a claim for copyright infringement, it is still important to provide proper notice in order to prevent someone who has used a copyrighted work without permission from escaping statutory penalties by claiming to be unaware that the work was copyrighted. The lack of a copyright notice can play into a mitigation of penalties for "innocent" infringers.

---

[81] 17 U.S.C.A. § 402(b), (c).

[82] 17 U.S.C.A. § 201(b); see discussion of this section in House of Representatives Report No. 94–1476, "Copyright Law Revision."

[83] 17 U.S.C.A. § 401(c).

Use of a "bluff copyright"—that is, a copyright notice on a work at the time of publication without going through the formalities can result in criminal prosecution and imposition of a fine of up to $2,500.[84] At the same time, the fraudulent removal of a copyright notice on an analog work can result in a fine of $2,500.[85] The reference to analog work is important in that the law provides different treatment to digital works.

The Digital Millennium Copyright Act[86] provides protections for digital content. Its provisions make it a crime to provide false copyright management information or to remove copyright management information. The CMI includes the name of the creator of the work, the name of the copyright holder and all of the information in the copyright notice.

COPYRIGHT OWNERSHIP AND TRANSFER

Copyright comes into being at the moment of fixation in tangible form and belongs to the copyright holder. In most cases that will be the creative person who has put words or music on paper, paint to canvas, chisel to stone, light to photographic emulsion or photosensitive electronic or input code. Sometimes, it will be to the person who has hired the creative personality under the concept of "work for hire." Once in existence, copyright may be disposed of like other forms of property under the special rules of copyright law and practice.

WORKS FOR HIRE

When a person creates a work as a part of his or her job, the rules provide for a different treatment. Sec. 101 of the 1976 Act defines a "work made for hire" as: (1) a work prepared by an employee within the scope of his or her employment; or (2) a work specially ordered or commissioned for use as a contribution to a collective work, as part of a motion picture or other audiovisual work, as a translation, as a supplementary work, as a compilation, as an instructional text, as a test, as answer material for a test, or as an atlas, if the parties expressly agree in a written instrument signed by them that the work shall be considered a "work made for hire."

An unpublished case that arose in the wake of the bombing of the Alfred P. Murrah Federal Building in Oklahoma City demonstrates the application of Sec. 101.[87] Lester LaRue, a safety coordinator for Oklahoma Natural Gas, was in his office the morning that Timothy

---

[84] 17 U.S.C.A. § 506(c).

[85] 17 U.S.C.A. § 506(d).

[86] Digital Millennium Copyright Act, Pub. L. No. 105–304, 112 Stat. 2860, 2887 (title IV amending § 108, § 112, § 114, chap. 7 and chap. 8, title 17, United States Code), enacted Oct. 28, 1998.

[87] *Oklahoma Natural Gas Co. v. Larue*, 156 F.3d 1244 (10th Cir. 1998).

McVeigh and Ed Nichols detonated their bomb that damaged the Murrah Building and killed 168 men, women and children.

Part of LaRue's job was to investigate natural gas explosions, examining the scene and taking photographs. After the bomb went off, LaRue went to downtown Oklahoma City thinking that the explosion might have been caused by a natural gas leak. Larue took along a camera and film supplied by the gas company. At the scene, LaRue took photos, assisted gas company crews, located and shut off gas mains and stayed in touch with company headquarters.[88]

> At one point, while preparing to photograph a company crew going into a basement area to rescue victims, Mr. LaRue noticed a firefighter cradling an injured infant. He took a photograph of the two, which became the well-known "firefighter and baby" photograph at the heart of this dispute.

The next day, *Newsweek* magazine approached Larue asking to publish his photographs. *Newsweek* published two of LaRue's photos, including the firefighter and baby picture. Then, LaRue signed a contract to market his photos.[89]

> On April 25, 1995, Mr. LaRue entered into a contract with Sygma, a clearinghouse for photographs, granting it worldwide syndication rights to the photographs. According to the contract, the photographs were to be distributed with the credit "Lester (Bob) LaRue/Sygma." The Company did not initially object to Mr. LaRue's sale of the photographs; however, it did claim ownership of them on May 18, 1995. The "firefighter and baby" photograph continues to be widely used as a result of Mr. LaRue's contract with Sygma.

The gas company gave Larue time to acknowledge that it owned the copyright and hand over the money he had made from the photographs. LaRue refused and was fired. The gas company then sued in federal district court to establish its copyright. The trial court ruled for the gas company and LaRue appealed to the 10th Circuit Court of Appeals.

Judge Wade Brorby's opinion disposed of LaRue's appeal quickly, pointing to the trial court's application of the work for hire section of the copyright statute.[90]

> Overwhelming evidence demonstrates Mr. LaRue was acting within the scope of his employment as he took the photographs in question, including: taking photographs was part of his job; it was during work hours; he used a company camera and film; the Company paid to develop the film; he reported in to the Company throughout the day; and he never told anyone he was

[88] Ibid. at 1244.

[89] Ibid. at 1245.

[90] Ibid. at 1247.

taking personal time. The district court properly focused on application of the work made for hire doctrine, through which the Company was entitled to ownership of the copyrights.

The issue becomes complicated where there is no clearly defined servant-master relationship. That occurs when a company goes outside its ranks, often because a project requires special skills or artistic talent. In order for someone other than the artist or artisan to claim the copyright ownership, there must be an express written agreement signed by the parties. Any agreements must be made before the work is being created. Because copyright comes into existence once a work is created, ownership can become an issue. Any agreement covering ownership after fixation would be a transfer and not a definition of rights under the "work made for hire" provision of the Act. Where there is no agreement, the artist retains the copyright. For (2) to apply, the work must fall into one of the categories laid out in the definition. But what about (1)? When is an artist considered an employee and what creative activity falls within the "scope of his or her employment?" Does anyone lose her copyright just because she is employed by someone else?

The Supreme Court took up the question in *Community for Creative Non-Violence v. Reid.*[91] The case arose over a dispute between the Community for Creative Non-Violence (CCNV), a group dedicated to aiding the homeless, and a sculptor. The homeless group asked James Reid to create a sculpture to show the plight of the homeless. "[I]n lieu of the traditional Holy Family, the two adult figures and the infant would appear as contemporary homeless people huddled on a street side steam grate" with the legend, "and still there is no room at the inn."[92] It was to be shown during the 1985 Christmas pageant in Washington.

On several occasions during the creation of the work, members of CCNV visited Reid to both check on his progress and make preparations for the construction of the base of the sculpture which CCNV was to make. The CCNV visitors commented and, as the Court reported in its syllabus of the case, "Reid accepted most of CCNV's suggestions and directions as to the sculpture's configuration and appearance."[93] Once the project was completed and paid for, CCNV and Reid installed the sculpture on the base and put it on display. Then, a dispute developed over CCNV's plans to take the sculpture on tour. Reid, who had possession of the sculpture, and CCNV then independently filed for copyright. The district court ruled that CCNV owned the copyright because it was a "work made for hire." The court of appeals reversed saying that the work did not fall under "work for hire" because Reid was not an employee. He was, instead, an independent contractor. Because sculpture was not on the list of "commissioned or specially ordered"

---

91 *Community for Creative Non-Violence v. Reid*, 490 U.S. 730, 109 S.Ct. 2166 (1989).

92 Ibid. at 733, 2169.

93 Ibid. at 730, 2167.

works, it could not be considered a work for hire, especially since there was no written agreement making it a work for hire.

The Supreme Court agreed with the appellate court that the sculpture did not fit into the list of works under § 101(2) that would qualify it as a work for hire. The Court then turned to the question of whether Reid was an employee under § 101(1). The justices had little direct guidance from the Copyright Act. Unlike many other terms, it does not define employee or scope of employment and the lower courts had come up with several different and conflicting approaches. One approach looked at the degree of actual control exercised over the creative person. A second test rested on whether the hiring party retained the right to control regardless of whether the hiring party actually exercised that control. A third approach would limit "employee" status only to those people who were "formal, salaried employees."

The Supreme Court rejected those approaches and settled on a straightforward approach that relied on traditional ways to defining who is what. "In the past when Congress has used the term 'employee' without defining it, we have concluded that Congress intended to describe the conventional master-servant relationship as understood by common-law agency doctrine * * * "[94] The Court then laid out the rule that would apply to determine when a work belonged to the hiring party or the actual creator.

> In determining whether a hired party is an employee under the general common law of agency, we consider the hiring party's right to control the manner and means by which the product is accomplished. Among the other factors relevant to this inquiry are the skill required; the source of the instrumentalities and tools; the location of the work; the duration of the relationship between the parties; whether the hiring party has the right to assign additional projects to the hiring party; the extent of the hired party's discretion over when and how long to work; the method of payment; the hired party's role in hiring and paying assistants; whether the hiring party is in business; the provision of employee benefits; and the tax treatment of the hired party. * * * No one of these factors is determinative.[95]

In *Reid*, the Court determined that consideration of these factors led to a conclusion that Reid was not an employee and that his work was not a work for hire. Among other things, Reid was a highly skilled artist, he supplied his own tools, worked for CCNV for a brief period, made his own decisions in hiring his assistants, he was paid in a manner consistent with independent contractors and did not have Social Security or payroll taxes paid by CCNV. Therefore, CCNV was not the copyright owner under "work for hire." However, the Court did not make Reid the

---

[94] Ibid. at 739–740, 2172.

[95] Ibid. at 751, 2178–2179.

copyright owner either. Because of the contributions that CCNV made in the process of creating the sculpture, a lower court had raised the issue of whether it was a joint work. The Supreme Court sent the case back down to the lower courts for a disposition of the issue.

Perhaps following the lawyer's maxim: "Better a slim settlement than a fat lawsuit," CCNV and Reid entered into a consent agreement to end the suit. In an unreported opinion, the D.C. district court entered an order in which the two parties each took part of the copyright.[96]

Reid was recognized as the sole author of the sculpture while CCNV was declared the sole owner of the original sculpture itself. Reid received the rights to three-dimensional copies of the sculpture while Reid and CCNV shared ownership of the rights to two-dimensional reproductions.

Reporters, PR practitioners, coders, software and web designers and other media professionals will be treated as employees in the normal course of their work. Free-lance journalists will most likely sell the copyrights to their works. Students working in the classroom may be considered to be under the direction of their schools. Most universities have policies that establish intellectual property rights of students, staff and faculty. Generally speaking, universities follow the work for hire section of the copyright statute. Staff and students who create works as part of their employment by the university, are not entitled to copyrights. Where faculty have received extraordinary support, universities will sometimes claim a portion of the copyright. Otherwise, universities generally recognize the copyrights of faculty, staff and students. It is best, though, to review the copyright policies of the university or any employer for that matter.

Sound recording artists found themselves on the wrong side of the works for hire equation after Congress passed the Satellite Home Viewer Improvement Act of 1999. A little-known but significant provision of the Act made sound recordings works for hire. That had the effect of giving copyrights to record companies when artists made records.

Before the change, recording artists would license their sound recordings to the record companies for a period of 35 years. After the end of the period, artists could reclaim their copyrights and exploit their sound recordings themselves. After the bill became law, artists protested and began a move to repeal the law. The repeal came in October of 2000 with President Clinton's signature on the Works Made for Hire and Copyright Corrections Act. The law returned sound recordings to their original status taking them out of the "works for hire" category. Even with the repeal, the controversy over the status of recording artists and their rights to the songs they record remains largely unsettled. Artists and record companies are still sparring over who owns the rights to sound recordings.

---

96 *Community for Creative Non-Violence v. Reid*, 1991 WL 415523 (D.D.C. 1991).

THE TURTLES AND RIGHTS IN RECORDS

The 1909 Act, which predated commercial radio broadcasting, did not include sound recordings. Congress decided against granting that right following the Supreme Court case of *White-Smith Music Publishing Co. v. Apollo Co.*[97] In that case, the copyright owner of musical compositions sued the manufacturer of piano rolls.[98] Sheet music had already been granted copyright protections but this advance in technology had not come before the Court before. In *White-Smith*, the Court held that the owner of a musical composition did not own any rights to the piano rolls. The piano rolls were not equivalent to sheet music, Justice William R. Day wrote:[99]

> After all, what is the perforated roll? The fact is clearly established in the testimony in this case that even those skilled in the making of these rolls are unable to read them as musical compositions, as those in staff notations are read by the performer. It is true that there is some testimony to the effect that great skill and patience might enable the operator to read this record as he could a piece of music written in staff notation. But the weight of the testimony is emphatically the other way, and they are not intended to be read as an ordinary piece of sheet music, which, to those skilled in the art, conveys, by reading, in playing or singing, definite impressions of the melody.
>
> These perforated rolls are parts of a machine which, when duly applied and properly operated in connection with the mechanism to which they are adapted, produce musical tones in harmonious combination. But we cannot think that they are copies within the meaning of the copyright act.

Congress did not include sound recordings as copyrighted works until 1971 when it revised the statute to include sound recordings made after Feb. 15, 1972. The sound recordings made before that date had copyright protections for the music itself. The composers and lyricists had the copyright from when they created the work. They received royalties when the song was sold and then again from the public performance such as on the radio or being played in a music venue. The performing artists had no separate rights under federal copyright law. But, individual state laws on copyright might give the artists rights.

The state-law based rights allowed the performers to assert copyrights in the recordings. Howard Kaylan and Mark Volman, two of the original members of The Turtles, bought the rights to the sound

[97] *White-Smith Music Publishing Co. v. Apollo Co.*, 209 U.S. 1, 28 S.Ct. 319, 52 L.Ed. 655 (1908).

[98] Piano rolls were the "software" used in player pianos. The rolls had perforations that allowed air to pass through them, actuating the keys and producing the song played by specially built pianos or pianos with special attachments.

[99] *White-Smith Music Publishing Co. v. Apollo Co.*, 209 U.S. 1, 17, 28 S.Ct. 319, 323 (1908).

recordings of their hit songs from their former band members. They sued Sirius XM Radio for copyright infringement for playing those hits without getting permission bringing suits in California, New York and Florida.

Three separate federal district courts ruled on the matter. The New York court denied Sirius' motion for summary judgment and in its analysis using New York state law laid out why Kaylan and Volman would prevail.[100] The only sticking point was whether Kaylan and Volman would be able to continue the case as a class action. Ostensibly, class action certification would allow the case to resolve the rights of many more of the artists whose pre-1972 recordings were being performed without permission or royalty payments.

The California federal court granted Kaylan and Volman summary judgment on their claims arising from the public performance of their pre-1972 recordings.[101] Judge Philip Gutierrez applied California state law invoking specific language about the recordings:[102]

> California's copyright statute contains a provision that directly addresses pre-1972 sound recordings. See Cal. Civ.Code § 980(a)(2). Section 980(a)(2) provides:
>
> The author of an original work of authorship consisting of a sound recording initially fixed prior to Feb. 15, 1972, has an exclusive ownership therein until Feb. 15, 2047 * * *

Forbes reported in 2015 that Kaylan and Volman had won class action status in their California suit.[103] Forbes reported that Judge Gutierez made his ruling to allow other artists whose records fell into the pre-1972 category to work together in order to press their claims.[104]

Judge Gutierrez argued that a class distinction was needed, precisely because of smaller claimants, stating that, "given SiriusXM's aggressive litigation tactics thus far, its public statements about intent to appeal adverse decisions, and its decision to continue to perform pre-1972 recordings without authorization, it may be cost-prohibitive for owners with smaller value claims to pursue their claims against SiriusXM in this environment."

The federal district court in Florida, applying that state's intellectual property laws reached the opposite conclusion, granting summary judgment to Sirius.[105]

---

[100] *Flo & Eddie, Inc. v. Sirius XM Radio, Inc.*, 80 F.Supp.3d 535 (S.D.N.Y. 2015).

[101] *Flo & Eddie, Inc. v. Sirius XM Radio, et al.*, 2014 WL 4725382 (C.D.Calif. 2014).

[102] Ibid. at 4.

[103] Nomi Prins, "The Turtles Win Class Action Certification In Sirius XM Copyright Lawsuit, Opening Door For Others," Forbes, May 28, 2015. http://www.forbes.com/sites/nomiprins/2015/05/28/the-turtles-win-class-action-certification-in-siriusxm-copyright-lawsuit-opening-door-for-others/#4fb30b1f1663.

[104] Ibid.

[105] *Flo & Eddie, Inc. v. Sirius XM Radio, Inc.*, 2015 WL 3852692 (S.D.Fla. 2015).

Several record labels, including Sony, Universal and Warner reached an agreement with Sirius in 2015 in which Sirius paid $210 million to come to an agreement to play pre-1972 recordings.[106]

JOINT WORKS

"Success has a thousand fathers, while failure is an orphan."

Sometimes, a creative work is the product of a collaboration between two people. Sec. 101 of the Copyright Act defines a "joint work" as "a work prepared by two or more authors with the intention that their contributions be merged into inseparable or interdependent parts of a unitary whole." Joint work can create problems if the language is read literally. An editor will make contributions to an article or book and those contributions are intended to be merged into the work as a whole. A research assistant will prepare a summary of the materials found which may be included verbatim in the final research project. A songwriter, looking for just the right word to complete a lyric may ask an acquaintance for help. Does the editing, research summary or single word turn the work into a joint work? This can be particularly troubling when dealing with works that have many contributors, such as team projects. Joint works are valuable to the copyright owners. Each may exploit the work, with or without the consent of the other owner, and is only required to account for the profits to the other owner.

The 2nd Circuit Court of Appeal has helped refine the concept. In *Childress v. Taylor*[107] the 2nd Circuit dealt with a case arising over conflicting copyright claims by a playwright and actress. *Childress* arose over a play about the life of the legendary comedienne Jackie "Moms" Mabley. Actress Clarice Taylor had portrayed "Moms" Mabley in an off-Broadway production in the 1980s. After the experience, Taylor began collecting material about the comedienne and interviewing friends and family. In 1985, Taylor contacted Alice Childress, an award-winning playwright about writing a play based on "Moms" Mabley.

After an initial rejection, Childress agreed to take on the project, although the two did not enter into any firm arrangements about the play at the time. The theater chosen for the production required that the work be completed in six weeks. Taylor turned her research material over to Childress and conducted additional research at Childress' request. Childress was the author, though Taylor provided insights into the character of "Moms" Mabley, suggested scenes and proposed the inclusion of additional characters. In all, Childress identified eight major contributions to the play made by Taylor. As the court wrote, "Essentially, Taylor contributed facts and details about 'Moms' Mabley's

---

[106] Ryan Faughnder, "Sirius XM to pay $210 million to labels over pre-1972 recordings," *Los Angeles Times*, June 26, 2015.

[107] *Childress v. Taylor*, 945 F.2d 500 (2d Cir.1991).

life and discussed some of them with Childress. However, Childress was responsible for the actual structure of the play and the dialogue."[108]

Childress finished the play in time for the production. Taylor paid her $2,500 and produced the work. Childress filed for and received the copyright in the play. Taylor then prepared for a second production. In the course of the writing of the play and during the two productions, Taylor sought to establish through her agent that both she and Childress would own the play together. Childress responded through her agent that she was "claiming originality for her words only in said script." The two exchanged draft contracts but could not come to terms. Eventually Childress sued Taylor for copyright infringement. Taylor responded that she was a joint author and had an equal right to the play.

The district court granted summary judgment to Childress saying that the facts were clear enough that Childress, who had written the play, was the sole owner and that trial was not necessary. Taylor appealed and the court of appeals took over from there dealing with the issues of copyrightability as a requirement of co-authorship and the intent question. At the time, a significant issue in joint authorship was whether the contribution of the second author had to be copyrightable itself. Various lower courts had reasoned that if the contribution could not stand alone as a copyrightable work, it could not lead to a joint copyright. The appellate court criticized the copyrightability test.

> The Act surely does not say that each contribution to a joint work must be copyrightable, and the specification that there be "authors" does not necessarily require a copyrightable contribution. "Author" is not defined in the Act and appears to be used only in its ordinary sense of an originator. The "author" of an uncopyrightable idea is nonetheless its author even though, for perfectly valid reasons, the law properly denies him a copyright on the result of his creativity. * * * It has not been supposed that the statutory grant of "authorship" status to the employer of a work for hire exceeds the Constitution, through the employer has shown skill only in selecting employees, not in creating protectable expression.[109]

But even though it voiced the criticism the appellate court decided to adopt the copyrightability test. It may seem counterintuitive that it did, but the court explained that to decline to require that the claimed contribution be copyrightable would be to open the doors to false claims by people who could not point to a concrete contribution, but who nonetheless could still say they had inspired or in some other way helped along the way. The court said that the copyrightability requirement struck a balance between the provinces of copyright and contract law. Where two or more authors contribute copyrightable material, copyright

[108] Ibid. at 502.

[109] Ibid. at 506.

protects relative interests. Where one party hires an author, contract law will establish the relationship and the "work for hire" rules will assign the copyright where it belongs. Where a contributor does not have a copyrightable contribution, a contract can set out the rights of the parties even down to an assignment of part of the copyright. "It seems more consistent with the spirit of copyright law to oblige all joint authors to make copyrightable contributions, leaving those with non-copyrightable contributions to protect their rights through contract."[110]

The 2nd Circuit then turned to the intent test for joint works. The intent test that the 2nd Circuit focuses on goes beyond the simple "intention that their contributions be merged into inseparable or interdependent parts of a unitary whole" laid out in the Act. The 2nd Circuit concluded that a simple application of that intent test would create unintended and unwanted consequences.

> For example, a writer frequently works with an editor who makes numerous useful revisions to the first draft, some of which will consist of additions of copyrightable expressions. Both intend their contributions to be merged into inseparable parts of a unitary whole, yet few editors and even fewer writers would expect the editor to be accorded the status of joint author, enjoying an undivided half interest in the copyright in the published work. Similarly, research assistants may on occasion contribute to an author some material as would be entitled to copyright, yet not be entitled to be regarded as a joint author of the work in which the contributed material appears. What distinguishes the writer-editor and the writer-researcher from the true joint author relationship is the lack of intent of both participants in the venture to regard themselves as joint authors.[111]

In *Childress*, the 2nd Circuit noted that the trial court found no such intent on Childress' part. "As Judge Haight observed, whatever thought of co-authorship might have existed in Taylor's mind 'was emphatically not shared by the purported co-author.' There is no evidence that Childress ever contemplated, much less would have accepted, crediting the play as 'written by Alice Childress and Clarice Taylor.' "[112]

Contributors who wish to preserve their rights then must make sure that what they bring to a project first qualifies as copyrightable material and then firmly establish that joint authorship is what all contributing authors had in mind. Evidence can take the form of declarations of the authors *at the time the work is created,* jointly approved promotional material or solicitations that clearly state the co-authorship relationship

110 Ibid. at 507.

111 Ibid.

112 Ibid. at 509.

and representations, by the author who later claims sole authorship, of his intent at the time, to be involved in a joint work.

TRANSFER OF RIGHTS

As with many works of creativity, the truest test of admiration of a work is the willingness of someone else to part with cash for it. In copyright, the value of a work may be tested by a buyer's willingness to pay for the right to exploit the work. In this segment, we talk about the process of transferring the various rights of the copyright bundle to buyers.

The rights that accrue to the copyright holder are laid out in the segment on "The Bundle of Rights." In this segment we deal with the ways a copyright holder can transfer some or all of her rights in the copyrighted work. During the term of the copyright, addressed in the section on duration, the copyright holder has the right to transfer all or part of her rights. On her death, if the rights have not been transferred, they may pass by descent to her heirs who then have the right to transfer the rights until the remainder of the copyright term expires.

Under the 1909 statute, a *single* legal title was held by a "proprietor" to any writing or artistic creation. Typically if an author sold the right to publish a work, it meant that *all* rights then belonged to the purchaser.[113] Under the current statute, authors can sell *some* rights or *all* rights as they wish. Sec. 201(d)(2) says that, "Any of the exclusive rights comprised in a copyright, including any subdivision of any of the rights specified by section 106 may be transferred and owned separately." In that way, a writer may sell "one-time rights"—for use of the work only once—and then will keep other rights to re-sell the same work. For example, a magazine article—such as "*The Urban Cowboy*," published in *Esquire* magazine—became the basis for a smash motion picture of the same name. Under § 201 of the revised copyright act, an author retains ownership in anything that author has written unless those rights are *expressly* granted to a publisher.[114]

The Copyright Act defines transfers as "an assignment, mortgage, exclusive license, or any other conveyance, alienation, or hypothecation of a copyright or of any of the exclusive rights comprised in a copyright, whether or not it is limited in time or place of effect, but not including a nonexclusive license."[115] In plain English, this means that there are any number of ways to move the rights from the original copyright holder to someone else. When authors are beginning their careers, they often start

---

[113] Harry G. Henn, "Ownership of Copyright, Transfer of Ownership," in James C. Goodale, chairman, *Communications Law 1979* (New York: Practising Law Institute, 1979), pp. 709–711.

[114] 17 U.S.C.A. § 201. Beginning writers should note that publishers have, for many decades, used their economic power to get authors, especially new authors, to part with most or all of their copyrights. Established and popular authors have the clout to retain more of their copyrights.

[115] Ibid.

out in weak bargaining positions and when publishers take a chance on them, they may ask for an assignment of all rights. That means that if the work is a success, the publisher will be able to recoup the expenses of developing new authors. Periodicals may seek the exclusive rights for North American publication, becoming the party able to control publication in that geographical area. Other times, parties may seek to purchase serialization rights, the right to publish in a series of articles. Movie rights are the holy grail for many new writers. Movie production companies may seek to purchase all rights to a work. They may also seek, for substantially less money, a license for a period of time in which to develop a movie. If the movie is made the license will continue, if not the license will expire and the writer is free to seek new producers.

Copyright holders should take care to protect the bundle of rights and to sell only what they want to sell at a particular time. One of the ways to help protect copyright holders come in the requirement that copyright transfers be in writing and signed by the owner.[116] That formality makes the transfer one that is not lightly undertaking. Transfers may be recorded with the Register of Copyrights and that will provide the transferee with a constructive (understood rather than actual) notice of his rights. Even without that recordation, the transfer is effective when the owner of the copyright or the owner's agent has signed a document that transfers the copyright. All transfers of copyrights must be in writing and signed.

The writing and signature requirements apply to digital content. Because actual signatures are not generally available in online agreements,[117] both Congress and the courts have provided for electronic transfers through the Electronic Signatures in Global and National Commerce Act.

In *Metropolitan Regional Information Systems, Inc. v. American Home Realty Network, Inc.*,[118] the Fourth Circuit Court of Appeals resolved a copyright infringement case involving the ownership of copyrights in photographs uploaded to a website. The defendant, American Home Realty, challenged a preliminary injunction preventing it from using photographs of homes for sale contained in the Metropolitan Regional database. A ruling in favor of Metropolitan would indicate that the appellate panel agreed with its claim of copyright ownership.

---

[116] The requirement that transfers be in writing is important in all transactions, but especially so in copyright. Take the example of Captain America. Marvel Enterprises settled a 4-year-old legal dispute over the rights to Captain America with comics creator Joe Simon in Sept. 2003. Captain America was created in 1940 and the dispute arose over terms of a verbal agreement between Simon and Timely Comics, a predecessor to Marvel. "We're talking about an arrangement that was never committed to paper and took place 63 years ago," said Ross Charap, a copyright attorney who represented Simon for three years.—Alan Wax, "Marvel, comics creator reach deal," *Bloomberg News*, Sept. 30, 2003.

[117] The Electronic Signatures in Global and National Commerce Act 15 U.S.C. § 7001 et seq. provides for the use of e-signatures through agreement between parties.

[118] *Metropolitan Regional Information Systems, Inc. v. American Home Realty Network, Inc.*, 722 D.3d 591 (4th Cir. 2013).

American Home argued that Metropolitan could not have the copyrights to the photographs because the original copyright holders had not signed an express transfer of copyright. The transfer language only needs to show that the copyright holder intended to transfer the ownership.[119]

> Courts have elaborated that a qualifying writing under Section 204(a) need not contain an elaborate explanation nor any particular "magic words," *Radio Television Espanola S.A. v. New World Entm't, Ltd.*, 183 F.3d 922, 927 (9th Cir.1999), but must simply "show an agreement to transfer copyright." *Lyrick Studios*, 420 F.3d at 392 (citation omitted).

The Fourth Circuit panel then applied the only existing case regarding an electronic transfer of copyright.[120]

> the Southern District of Florida held that the conveyance of a copyright interest by e-mail was valid. See *Vergara Hermosilla v. Coca-Cola Co.*, 2011 WL 744098, at *3 (S.D.Fla. Feb. 23, 2011), aff'd by per curiam opinion, 446 Fed.Appx. 201 (11th Cir.2011). In its brief analysis of the issue, that court relied on the purpose of Section 204, which is to "resolve disputes between copyright owners and transferees and to protect copyright holders from persons mistakenly or fraudulently claiming oral licenses or copyright ownership," not to be "unduly burdensome" or to "necessitate[ ] protracted negotiations nor substantial expense." Id. (citations and internal quotations omitted). The court reasoned that allowing the transfer of copyright ownership via e-mail pursuant to the E-Sign Act accorded with, rather than conflicted with, this purpose.

With that precedent, the 4th Circuit panel concluded that clicking an agreement to abide by the terms of service, TOS, the original copyright holders had transferred ownership to Metropolitan.[121]

> To invalidate copyright transfer agreements solely because they were made electronically would thwart the clear congressional intent embodied in the E-Sign Act. We therefore hold that an electronic agreement may effect a valid transfer of copyright interests under Section 204 of the Copyright Act. Accordingly, we agree with the district court that MRIS is likely to succeed against AHRN in establishing its ownership of copyright interests in the copied photographs.

The *Metropolitan* and *Vergara Hermosilla* cases are important as the creators of content, from photographs through videos to poetry and songs

---

[119] Ibid. at 600.

[120] Ibid. at 602.

[121] Ibid. at 602–603.

are at risk of losing their copyrights if they click agree to terms of service that give the copyright to the website or service they use.

A case on copyright transfer made international headlines in September of 2015 when a federal court ruled that the copyright in the English language's most popular song, *"Happy Birthday to You,"*[122] was invalid because there had never been a transfer of the copyright.[123] The case started when film makers, making a documentary about the song, challenged its copyright. Rupa Marya, Robert Siegel, Good Morning to You Productions Corp., and Majar Productions, LLC, sued Warner/ Chappell Music, Inc. and Summy-Birchard, Inc.'s.

The song brought in about $2 million in licensing fees[124] annually from its performance in movies and television shows. The plaintiffs argued that Warner/Chappell, a subsidiary of Warner Music Group, did not have a valid copyright and that it should refund all the license fees it had collected over the years.

Schoolteacher Patty Smith Hill and her sister Mildred Hill wrote a song, *"Good Morning to You,"* sometime around 1893. One of the verses was *"Happy Birthday."* The Hill sisters assigned their rights in the manuscript to Clayton Summy in 1893. In the challenge to the copyright, the plaintiffs argued that it was not clear (1) who wrote *"Happy Birthday"*, (2) whether the copyright had been lost through publication without notice, and, (3) whether the copyright properly had been transferred to Clayton Summy or The Clayton F. Summy Co. Judge George H. King noted that the song had been published a number of times without reference to the Hills as authors.[125]

> References to the lyrics (without full publication) appeared in 1901 and 1909. The words were fully published in 1911, 1912, 1915, 1922, 1924, and 1928. The song was performed in several movies in the early to mid-1930s. Furthermore, though none of these publications explicitly credited anyone with authoring the *Happy Birthday* lyrics, several of them were copyrighted, and the certificates of registration listed other authors. For instance, The Elementary Worker and His Work, which was published in 1911 and contained the full *Happy Birthday* lyrics, listed Alice Jacobs and Ermina Chester Lincoln as its authors in the copyright certificate.

---

[122] Eriq Gardner, " 'Happy Birthday' Song Copyright Ruled to Be Invalid," *Billboard*, Sept. 22, 2015. http://www.billboard.com/articles/news/6706919/happy-birthday-song-public-domain-warner-chappel.

[123] *Marya, et al. v. Warner/Chappell Music*, 131 F.Supp.3d 975, 2015 WL 5568497, 2015 Copr.L.Dec. P 30,823, 116 U.S.P.Q.2d 1563 (C.D.Calif. 2015).

[124] Ben Sisariosept, " 'Happy Birthday' Copyright Invalidated by Judge," *New York Times*, Sept. 22, 2015. http://www.nytimes.com/2015/09/23/business/media/happy-birthday-copyright-invalidated-by-judge.html.

[125] *Marya, et al. v. Warner/Chappell Music*, 131 F.Supp.3d 975, 2015 WL 5568497, 2015 Copr.L.Dec. P 30,823, 116 U.S.P.Q.2d 1563 (C.D.Calif. 2015). At 8.

Judge King concluded that the authorship of *"Happy Birthday"* could be found to be either the Hills or someone else. Judge King concluded that it was still an open question as to whether the Hills, if the real authors, had lost their copyright through the publication of the song in songbooks from 1911 through 1928 and through performance in movies and stage plays.

Judge King then turned to the question of copyright transfer. He found compelling, if complicated, facts from a lawsuit that the Hills filed against the Clayton F. Summy Co. in 1942. In that case, the Hills sued because Summy had been licensing *"Happy Birthday"* for use in sound motion pictures. When the Hills entered into its agreement with Summy, movies with sound had not become commercial so the grant agreement could not have included such licensing.[126]

> And yet, according to the Amended Complaint, that was precisely what Summy Co. had been doing: "secretly enter[ing] into various agreements with the producers of sound motion pictures and of stage or dramatic performances . . . for the sound and dialogue rights for the use of the song 'HAPPY BIRTHDAY TO YOU' and purport[ing] to hold itself out as having the right to grant licenses or sub-licenses in respect to the use of the aforesaid song." * * * This conduct, the Hill Foundation alleged, was "in violation of the rights conferred upon" the Hill sisters and the Hill Foundation "by the copyright laws of the United States of America."

The fact that the Warner/Chappel and Summy-Birchard could not produce direct evidence of a transfer from the Hills to Summy led to the grant of summary judgment for the plaintiffs. The question of repaying the royalties was left for separate consideration.

85. PROTECTING THE BUNDLE OF RIGHTS

It is one thing to own the exclusive rights that involve the exploitation of the work. The rights have no value if the owner cannot protect them:

1. reproduction of the work in copies or phono records;
2. preparation of derivative works based on the work itself;
3. distribution by rent, lease, loan, sale or other transfer of ownership of copies or phono records of the copyrighted work;
4. public performance of literary, musical, dramatic, choreographic works, pantomimes, motion pictures and other audiovisual work;
5. public display of pictorial, graphic, sculptural, literary, musical, dramatic, choreographic works, pantomimes, and

[126] Ibid. at 14.

individual images of motion pictures and other audiovisual works; and

6. public performance of sound recordings by means of digital audio transmission.[127]

REPRODUCTION OF THE WORK

Reproduction of the work is just that—making copies. The Copyright holder (and here we will presume that the copyright holder is also the author), having given birth through the creative process, has the right to decide when or even if his creativity will be copied. This is the most basic of the rights regarding the exploitation of creative works. In *NBC v. Sonneborn*[128] a federal district court found that a firm that made and sold reprints of audiovisual works had infringed NBC's copyright to a kinescope (precursor of today's videotape) of "*Peter Pan*," shown by the network on Dec. 8, 1960. The network lost track of several of the kinescopes after its broadcast. One of the copies apparently made it to the East Brunswick, New Jersey, library. In 1979 Joel Sonneborn, president of Reel Images, was told by someone at the library that the library had a copy of the "*Peter Pan*" kinescope. Sonneborn offered to repair the kinescope, which was damaged, in return for being able to copy and sell videotaped copies of "*Peter Pan*." In 1980, NBC applied for copyright registration for "*Peter Pan*" and obtained an injunction against Sonneborn. As mentioned above, NBC had to go through the formalities of registration before it could go to court. The district court found that once it had the valid copyright registration, NBC could exercise its rights under § 106(1) to prevent Sonneborn from making copies.

PREPARATION OF DERIVATIVE

Preparation of derivative works goes to the adaptation of a work. Take a novel. A play based on the novel will be derived from that literary work. A movie made of the play will be derived from the play and the novel both. A multimedia presentation made from the movie will be derived from the movie, play and novel. As long as a work is taken from the creative expression of a previous work, it is considered a derivative. This right is particularly valuable as movie rights can command impressive sums.

An interesting point about derivative rights is that each subsequent version of the original work will have a copyright all its own for the original content created in the derivative work. *Ricordi & Co. v. Paramount Pictures*[129] illustrates the point. The case deals with the rights of the original author of the novel "*Madame Butterfly*," the author of a stage play made from the novel and the authors of an opera made

[127] 17 U.S.C.A. § 106.

[128] *NBC v. Sonneborn*, 630 F.Supp. 524 (D.Conn.1985).

[129] *Ricordi v. Paramount*, 189 F.2d 469 (2d Cir.1951).

from play and novel. John Luther Long, the author of the novel, wrote his work in 1897. In 1900, David Belasco wrote his play with Long's permission. In 1904, Ricordi obtained the rights to make a libretto for an opera based on Belasco's play, which was based on Long's novel. In 1932, the administrator of Long's estate granted Paramount the right to make a movie based on the novel. Both sides claimed the rights to make the movie—Ricordi, because it owned the rights to the libretto; Paramount, because it had obtained the movie rights to the novel. Each side asserted its right to what it owned. The result was a standoff. Paramount could not make a movie without the dramatic elements from the opera. Ricordi could not make a movie without the underlying story (The court ended its work with the finding of the respective rights. It left matters up to Ricordi and Paramount to resolve the issue.).[130]

The issue of derivative rights came into play over the Frank Capra movie, "*It's a Wonderful Life.*" Republic Pictures owned the copyright to the 1947 movie. In 1973, Republic failed to file the necessary papers to renew its copyright (This was under the 1909 Act which created an initial copyright term and a second renewal term). The movie fell into the public domain and anyone and everyone could exploit it without getting permission from or paying fees to Republic. But a 1990 case involving another movie that ran afoul of the complexities of the renewal process gave Republic a means of reasserting control.

That case, *Stewart v. Abend*[131] dealt with the movie "*Rear Window.*" "*Rear Window*" was based on a short story, "*It Had to Be Murder*" written by Cornell Woolrich. Woolrich sold the movie rights to "*It Had to Be Murder*" and five other stories. He agreed to renew those rights when he renewed his copyright. But Woolrich died before he could do that. He had renewed his copyright in the story and that went into his estate. Abend bought the rights from the executor of Woolrich's estate for $650 plus 10 percent of the proceeds he generated from the story. The Supreme Court held that Abend had the rights to the underlying work and those rights controlled the uses of the derivative work movie.

Republic owned the rights to the story. It obtained the rights to the music used in the picture and then announced a crackdown on the unauthorized display, distribution and sales of "*It's a Wonderful Life.*"[132] In addition to halting the multiple showings of the movie, Republic's actions also served to take out of circulation unauthorized colorized versions of the movie. Executive vice president of Republic Pictures Steven Beeks said that Republic had taken steps to ensure the quality of the copies of the movie available to the public. "People have hacked it up

[130] Ibid. at the risk of making this even more complicated, Belasco did not renew his copyright in his play and it passed into the public domain, which meant that anyone could use it, that is the elements he added to the novel. The copyright in the novel was renewed so the elements of the novel incorporated into the play could not be used without permission.

[131] *Stewart v. Abend*, 495 U.S. 207, 110 S.Ct. 1750 (1990).

[132] Chris Koseluk Entertainment News Service, "Not a 'Wonderful' Year Now We'll Discover What Life is Like Without George Bailey," *Chicago Tribune*, Dec. 1993.

* * * people have these scratched up negatives * * * the picture isn't given its due."[133]

Derivative rights include other media and works as well. In *Mirage Editions v. Albuquerque A.R.T.*,[134] the courts dealt with a company that was taking artworks and creating ceramic decorative tiles out of them. Albuquerque A.R.T. had taken a commemorative book of the artwork of Patrick Nagel, removed selected pages and mounted them on ceramic tiles which it then sold. The trial court found that the transformation from book form to decorative tile amounted to the creation of derivative works and that Albuquerque did not have permission from the copyright holder to do so. The district court granted summary judgment to Mirage and the 9th Circuit affirmed.

Persons engaged in multimedia production should take note of derivative works rights for two reasons: (1) the use of a copyrighted work in a multimedia production may infringe a copyright holder's exclusive right to make derivative works, and (2) multimedia producers may not be protected even if they obtain a right from a single party to use a derivative work, such as a movie, because that license may not cover all potential plaintiffs.

> The copyright holder in an original literary work turned into a motion picture holds the underlying copyright. The screenwriter can hold a derivative copyright in the photo play for those elements she has added to the original. The songwriter holds the copyright in the music for the score, the choreographer can hold the copyright in the choreography and the motion picture company holds the copyright for the work as a whole.[135]

As advertisers use elements from popular culture to sell their products and services, they often run into problems involving the creation of derivative works using those copyrighted pieces of pop culture. Rapper Eminem's publishing company sued Apple Computer in February of 2004 after the computer maker used the song "*Lose Yourself*" in its ads for its new iTunes pay-per-download music software. The commercial was a derivative work that improperly used Eminem's song.[136]

It may seem counterintuitive, but a derivative work can be created when someone takes something out of a copyrighted work. A CleanFlicks franchise sued 16 movie directors seeking declaratory judgment that the company could edit Hollywood films to remove violence, nudity and foul language as a First Amendment right. Not surprisingly, the directors disagreed. They filed a countersuit alleging, among other things,

---

[133] *Stewart v. Abend*, 495 U.S. 207, 110 S.Ct. 1750 (1990).

[134] *Mirage Editions v. Albuquerque A.R.T.*, 856 F.2d 1341 (9th Cir.1988).

[135] Bill Loving, "Teaching Multimedia in the Law Class," *Feedback*, Volume 37, Number 4, Fall 1996.

[136] Bill Zwecker, "Ad has Eminem aiming to core Apple in court," *Chicago Sun Times*, Feb. 26, 2004.

copyright infringement and Lanham Act violations (the Lanham Act is discussed in the previous chapter).[137] While the owner of a video may be able to do what he wishes with the physical thing, the creation of a "new" version which then is injected into commerce violates the rights of copyright holders.

Clean Flicks came out on the losing end in 2006 when Judge Richard Matsch issued an injunction against the creation and distribution of the edited movies.[138] Clean Flicks argued that its edited versions constituted a fair use derivative work. The company pointed out that consumers had no other means of obtaining movies without profanity, nudity, sex or violent content. But Judge Matsch replied that the law of copyright governed the outcome of the case.[139]

> The accused parties make much of their public policy argument and have submitted many communications from viewers expressing their appreciation for the opportunity to view movies in the setting of the family home without concern for any harmful effects on their children. This argument is inconsequential to copyright law and is addressed in the wrong forum. This Court is not free to determine the social value of copyrighted works. What is protected are the creator's rights to protect its creation in the form in which it was created.

Consumers are not without recourse, though. In 2005, Congress passed the Family Movie Act.[140] That law allows a member of a household to edit a movie to remove objectionable material. It does not, however, create a right for commercial enterprises to do the same.

Judge Matsch looked to the four factors governing fair use and concluded that Clean Flicks was making use of substantial portions of the directors' and studios' works, that the company was doing so for commercial gain and that the creation of the works violated the copyright holders' rights to choose if and when to make edited versions of their movies.

DISTRIBUTION OF COPIES

Distribution of copies through sale, lease, loan, etc., to the public encompasses a large part of the economic heart of copyright. Best sellers mean high volume sales and each sale generates income for the copyright holder. In most cases, though, the creator of the work will have transferred the bundle of copyrights to a publisher who will exploit the work and reap the income.

---

[137] Shannon Starr, "New Business offers 'sanitized movies'; the owner of the video rental store says he has the right to edit out objectionable content," *Riverside Press-Enterprise*, Aug. 30, 2003.

[138] *Clean Flicks of Colorado, LLC v. Soderbergh*, 433 F.Supp.2d 1236 (D.Colo. 2006).

[139] Ibid. at 1240.

[140] Pub.L. No. 109–9, 119 Stat. 218.

In *Columbia Pictures, et al. v. Landa*,[141] thirteen movie and video production companies took three owners of video rental stores to court over their copying and distribution of more than 200 movies. An undercover investigator for the Motion Picture Association of America (MPAA) swore by affidavit that he purchased or rented 35 illegally duplicated videocassettes from the three stores. Deputy U.S. Marshals, on orders of the court, seized more than 4,000 videocassettes from the defendants' stores and seven duplicating machines and supplies to make copies from co-defendant Jason Frank's home. In granting summary judgment to the plaintiffs, the court noted that the movie companies had not granted copying or distribution rights to Landa and the other defendants, that Frank admitted copying and distribution and that the videocassettes themselves failed to show the marks that would prove they were authorized copies. That meant that Landa and his co-defendants were liable for infringement two ways:

> [T]he uncontradicted evidence reveals that Defendant Landa, without proper authorization, illegally distributed to the public copyrighted material owned by Plaintiff. Thus, whether the Court draws the inference that Landa copied the protected material or finds that Landa distributed illegally duplicated videocassettes, does not change the result; Landa is liable for copyright infringement pursuant to 17 U.S.C. § 106.[142]

A federal judge ruled in late February 2003 that a software company that made a product enabling people copy DVDs violated copyright law.[143] Judge Susan Illston ordered 321 Studios to stop selling its DVD Copy Plus and DVD X COPY software which contained a feature that let it defeat the security software protecting DVDs.

PUBLIC PERFORMANCE OF WORKS

Public performance of works covers the economic exploitation through the process of letting the people come see the work as expressed by performers. Friday and Saturday nights we see this in action as people line up at the MegaCineOmniPlexOdeon to watch the latest Hollywood blockbuster. It also covers concerts, stage plays and even night clubs. The genesis of the public performance right began in the mid-to-late 1800s when the right of public performance was granted to the copyright owners of dramatic and musical works. Things were relatively quiet on that front until the composer Victor Herbert sued the Shanley Company over the performance of one of Herbert's songs in the dining room of the Vanderbilt Hotel.

At the time composers benefitted from their copyrighted compositions through royalties they earned on the sale of their sheet

---

141 *Columbia Pictures v. Landa*, 974 F.Supp. 1 (C.D.Ill.1997).

142 Ibid. at 13.

143 "DVD copying software seen banned despite stay plea," Reuters, Feb. 23, 2004.

music. Herbert, though, believed that others were gaining an advantage by being able to play his compositions. He wanted to be compensated for this exploitation and he brought suit. The district court agreed with Herbert and decided he should be paid for this public performance. The circuit court of appeals reversed, saying that the Shanley Company's performance in the hotel dining room was not a performance for profit. Herbert would be entitled to compensation if the hotel were selling tickets to a concert, the circuit court said. "We construed the language of the act giving to the copyright proprietor the exclusive right 'to perform the copyrighted work publicly for profit, if it be a musical composition,' to be limited to performances where an admission fee or some direct pecuniary charge is made."[144] That set the stage for the Supreme Court to rule. Justice Holmes delivered the opinion of the court in which he concluded that the 2nd Circuit's analysis was incorrect.

> If the rights under the copyright are infringed only by a performance where money is taken at the door, they are very imperfectly protected.
>
> * * *
>
> The defendants' performances are not eleemosynary. They are part of a total for which the public pays, and the fact that the price of the whole is attributed to a particular item which those present are expected to order is not important. It is true that the music is not the sole object, but neither is the food, which probably could be got cheaper elsewhere. The object is a repast in surroundings that to people having limited powers of conversation, or disliking rival noise, give a luxurious pleasure not to be had from eating a silent meal. If music did not pay, it would be given up.[145]

The principle in *Herbert* applies today to businesses that install sound systems to create a more pleasing atmosphere for their customers. It also requires that television stations, radio stations, movie companies pay royalties to the copyright owners of musical compositions (See Sec. 95. Broadcast Music Licensing Rights and the subsection on Webcasting for treatment of this issue.). As it is difficult for the individual to promote, distribute and oversee the use of her works, this right will often be sold to a corporation that specializes in public entertainment or a voluntary association that will represent all its member copyright holders for purposes of negotiation and collection of their just due (Broadcast Music Licensing Rights are dealt with later in this chapter.).

With the advent of commercial radio broadcasts, the courts and later Congress had to deal with the treatment of music played in commercial establishments through radio receivers. In *Buck v. Jewell-La Salle*

---

[144] *Herbert v. Shanley*, 229 Fed. 340 (2d Cir.1916).

[145] *Herbert v. Shanley*, 242 U.S. 591, 594–595, 37 S.Ct. 232, 233 (1917).

Realty,[146] the Supreme Court concluded that a hotel that had wired its guests' room with radio speakers was publicly performing the works and had to compensate the copyright holders.[147]

The issues posed by the case were both clarified and muddied in *Twentieth Century Music Corp. v. Aiken*[148]. In *Aiken* the court was faced with a case in which a business was playing the plaintiff's copyrighted works through four speakers connected to a radio receiver. George Aiken owned George Aiken's Chicken, a small fast-food restaurant in Pittsburgh, Pennsylvania. It was a small restaurant and much of the business was carry-out trade. The evidence suggested that the primary benefit of having the radio and speakers was to keep the restaurant staff entertained on the job. The few patrons who ate at Aiken's Chicken did so quickly and left without whiling away the time listening to the radio. The plaintiff sued Aiken alleging that his radio reception of a Pittsburgh radio station amounted to public performance. The Supreme Court disagreed saying that it would be impossible to keep track of all the small businesses that keep radios on their premises. Further, the Court said, holding that tuning in to a radio broadcast amounted to public performance would mean that small business owners would have to monitor the songs to be sure that only those compositions for which they had licenses were heard. Finally, the Court said, giving copyright holders the right to force listeners to pay would exceed the logic of the system of copyright protections.

> [T]o hold that all in Aiken's position "performed" these musical compositions would be to authorize the sale of an untold number of licenses for what is basically a single public rendition of a copyrighted work. The exaction of such multiple tribute would go far beyond what is required for the economic protection of copyright owners * * *[149]

When Congress wrote the 1976 Copyright Act, it looked at *Aiken*. The House committee sponsoring the Act referred to the case and said that *Aiken* represented the "outer limit" of the exemption to the public performance right. That exemption allowed small businesses with unsophisticated sound systems to receive radio broadcasts. The committee said that larger establishments and better sound systems could be equated to commercial music services. In 1981, the federal courts had the opportunity to apply that to a case involving copyright holders and the business community.

---

[146] *Buck v. Jewell-La Salle Realty*, 283 U.S. 191, 51 S.Ct. 410 (1931).

[147] In this case, the radio station had failed to secure a permission to publicly perform the songs as well. The station also was forced to make payments. The case left open the question of whether the hotel would have had to pay if the radio station had already obtained permission to publicly perform the works. That would be answered in the next case.

[148] *Twentieth Century Music v. Aiken*, 422 U.S. 151, 95 S.Ct. 2040 (1975).

[149] Ibid. at 162–163, 2047.

In *Sailor Music v. Gap*,[150] a federal district court dealt with the public performance rights in music played through radio broadcasts used in a retail setting. A group of music companies sued The Gap Stores for playing their copyrighted songs over sound systems in two Gap stores in New York City. One Gap store encompassed 2,769 square feet of customer space and the second had 4,690 square feet. That compared with Aiken's Chicken's 620 square feet. The smaller Gap store had four speakers mounted in the ceiling and the larger had seven, all placed to provide music in the customer areas. Aiken's had four located in the kitchen area. The Gap sought the protection of Sec. 110(5)[151] which lays out exemptions to the exclusive rights granted under Sec. 106. Subsection 5 provides that it is not an infringement to communicate a radio broadcast provided that the broadcast is received on a single receiver "of a kind commonly used in private homes." But even if the broadcasts are relayed through such a receiver it still can be an infringement if: "(A) a direct charge is made to see or hear the transmission; or (B) the transmission received is further transmitted to the public."[152]

The presiding judge explained that the exemption would serve those "small commercial establishments whose proprietors merely bring onto their premises small standard radio or television equipment and turn it on for their customers' enjoyment * * *"[153] But the Gap store sound systems went beyond the simple home systems that were intended to be protected by Sec. 110(5), the judge said. The Gap's set up amounted to a retransmission of the copyrighted songs to the public through its use of its loudspeaker music system which carried the radio broadcasts.

The public performance issue became a public relations hot potato from 1995 through 1997 when the American Society of Composers, Authors and Publishers (ASCAP) approached the American Camping Association in 1995 and said it wanted to settle the matter of public performance fees.[154] Campers were singing songs covered by copyrights held by ASCAP members and their singing, "where a substantial number of persons outside of a normal circle of a family and its social acquaintances is gathered."[155] ASCAP offered to discount its site fees and the camping association agreed. But later in 1995, the camping group sent a newsletter to its members warning that ASCAP could charge for singing around the campfire. ASCAP was dealing with an attack on the public performance fees it collected under the Copyright Act.[156] Small

---

[150] *Sailor Music v. Gap*, 516 F.Supp. 923 (S.D.N.Y.1981), *affirmed* 668 F.2d 84 (2d Cir.1981), *cert. denied* 456 U.S. 945, 102 S.Ct. 2012 (1982).

[151] 17 U.S.C. § 110(5).

[152] Ibid.

[153] *Sailor Music v. Gap*, 516 F.Supp. 923, 925 (S.D.N.Y.1981).

[154] Elisabeth Bumiller, *New York Times* News Service, "Campfire Royalties Burn ASCAP," *Cleveland Plain Dealer*, Dec. 22, 1996.

[155] 17 U.S.C. § 101.

[156] Lou Carlozo, "The Sound of Money," *Chicago Tribune*, Aug. 12, 1996.

businesses and religious groups were in front of Congress seeking an exemption from the fees. *Bloomberg Business News* reported that the Girls Scouts were facing fees for singing around the campfire and the national media seized the story with both hands culminating in a scene in which a group of Elves, Girl Scout helpers, danced the *Macarena* in silence for reporters. ASCAP eventually reached an agreement with the camping association in which the association would pay $1 per camp per year for the right to publicly perform ASCAP-licensed music.

The Fairness in Music Licensing Act of 1998 gave relief to retailers and restaurant owners by exempting them from paying public performance fees for their small-size businesses. The Act exempts retailers with less than 2,000 square feet of business space and restaurants with less than 3,750 square feet from music performance fees.[157]

Larger retail businesses and restaurants can be exempted based on the systems they use to play the music or show the video. Like the analysis in *Twentieth Century Music v. Aiken*,[158] these larger businesses must restrict themselves to a fairly modest system. In order to avoid paying the public performance fees, these larger businesses must limit themselves to a maximum of six speakers and four television screens. In addition to the restriction on the total number, the Act permits no more than four speakers or one television screen per room. The television screens are limited to 55 inches.[159]

THOUSANDS OF TINY ANTENNA AND ONE SUPREME COURT DECISION

Barry Diller, the man who created the Fox network, caused a big stir back in 2012 when he announced Aereo. The service would allow consumers to stop relying on cable, satellite or over-the-air broadcasts to watch TV.[160] Aereo would put up thousands of antennas "—each the size of a thumbprint[161]—so that each subscriber has an assigned antenna." Aereo subscribers could watch broadcast programming on their computers, mobile devices or laptops using Aereo's Internet-based connection. Subscribers could watch on the TV sets only if they had a device that could access the Internet.

---

[157] In order to qualify for the exemption, the businesses and restaurants must not charge an admission fee or retransmit the music outside the business or beyond the area where the customers are served.

[158] *Twentieth Century Music v. Aiken*, 422 U.S. 151, 95 S.Ct. 2040 (1975).

[159] Sometime after the law went into effect, news reports told of Irish musical groups suffering because most of the bars their music was played in qualified for the exemption and the groups were not receiving royalties on their songs.

[160] Brian Stelter, "New Service Will Stream Local TV Stations in New York," *New York Times*, Feb. 14, 2012.

[161] The trial court would later describe these as "dime-sized."

Chet Kanojia, founder and chief executive of Aereo, told reporters presciently at the time that he and his company expected there might be some legal issues.[162]

> [T]he company is bracing for possible legal challenges from TV stations. "We understand that when you try to take something meaningful on, you have to be prepared for challenges," Mr. Kanojia said.

ABC led a suit that challenged Aereo's business model alleging that the company was illegally performing the programs broadcast by the major networks.[163] The TV audience can watch free over-the-air programs with the broadcasters paid by the commercials that run with the shows. Alternatively, viewers can watch on cable or satellite. In those cases, the broadcasters get royalties from the cable and satellite providers.[164]

Aereo did not pay anything to the broadcasters. Instead it collected monthly fees from its subscribers of between $8 and $12. The broadcasters were not getting any payments from Aereo's "public performance" of the television shows and they filed suit. Sec. 106(4) of the Copyright Act of 1976 makes clear that the copyright holder gets to decide when, if, or where a work is publicly performed. ABC and the other entities that held copyrights to works carried by Aereo said that they had not agreed to Aereo's pubic performance of their works.

ABC and the other plaintiffs sought a preliminary injunction.[165] District Court Judge Alison J. Nathan rejected the request concluding that the broadcasters were not likely to succeed in their copyright infringement suit. Judge Nathan laid out the particulars of the Aereo system.

Subscribers would log into Aereo's website and pick programming to watch or record. Aereo would then send the subscriber a Web page containing the broadcast content. Subscribers would be watching the program stream as it was processed through the Aereo site. Programs could be paused or the program saved.[166]

> [F]rom the user's perspective, Aereo's system is similar in operation to that of a digital video recorder ("DVR") (See, e.g., Hrg. Tr. 290:11–291:10, 298:16–23, 305:9–306:12), particularly a remotely located DVR, although Aereo users access their

---

[162] Ibid.

[163] *American Broadcasting Companies, et al., v. Aereo, WNET, et al., v. Aereo,* 874 F.Supp.2d 373 (S.D.N.Y. 2012).

[164] Those royalties were set up in the 1976 Copyright Act. Sec. 111 creates a complex, highly detailed compulsory licensing scheme that sets out the conditions, including the payment of compulsory fees, under which cable systems may retransmit broadcasts.

[165] *American Broadcasting Companies, et al., v. Aereo, WNET, et al., v. Aereo,* 874 F.Supp.2d 373 (S.D.N.Y. 2012).

[166] Ibid. at 377.

programming over the internet rather than through a cable connection.

Judge Nathan looked at the likelihood that the plaintiffs would win their infringement case through the lens of the 2nd Circuit's decision in *Cartoon Network v. CSC Holdings and Cablevision.*[167] In that case, known generally as *Cablevision*, Cartoon Network and major television content creators sued Cablevision over its remote storage system, RS-DVR. The plaintiffs argued that the remote video recorder created an infringing copy of their works and, later through playback, created an infringing public performance of the programming. The 2nd Circuit panel concluded that Cablevision's remote video recorder was being used by subscribers and that it was subscribers who caused the copying of the programming and also caused the later playback.[168]

> Because each RS-DVR playback transmission is made to a single subscriber using a single unique copy produced by that subscriber, we conclude that such transmissions are not performances "to the public," and therefore do not infringe any exclusive right of public performance.

Judge Nathan concluded that the Aereo system operated much like the RS-DVR in the *Cablevision* case. Customers initiated the collection of the programming and the unique copy of the program was delivered to the individual customers.[169]

> Aereo's use of single antennas does, however, reinforce the conclusion that the copies created by Aereo's system are unique and accessible only to a particular user, as they indicate that the copies are created using wholly distinct signal paths. Moreover, Aereo's antennas also reinforce the dividing line between the over-the-air signal the Aereo antennas receive and the transmissions Aereo's system makes to its users. * * * Aereo's antennas thus reinforce the significance of the copies its system creates and aid the Court in finding that Aereo does not create mere facilitating copies.

A 2nd Circuit panel affirmed the trial court in a majority decision and the case then made its way to the Supreme Court.[170] At the Supreme Court, Justice Stephen Breyer concluded that Aereo was more like a cable television system rather than a digital video recorder. Based on that, Aereo was subject to the public performance sections of the Copyright Act.

Aereo argued that its new technology made it unlike cable television systems. Its subscribers chose which programs to watch and in doing so,

---

[167] *Cartoon Network, et al. v. CSC Holdings and Cablevision*, 536 F.3d 121 (2d. Cir. 2008).

[168] Ibid. at 139.

[169] *American Broadcasting Companies, et al., v. Aereo, WNET, et al., v. Aereo*, 874 F.Supp.2d 373, 397 (S.D.N.Y. 2012).

[170] *American Broadcasting Companies v. Aereo*, 573 U.S. 431, 134 S.Ct. 2498 (2014).

used a single antenna. Cable systems, on the other hand, carried programs to everyone connected to the system. The difference in audiences made Aereo different and exempt from application of the cable system rules. Justice Breyer disposed of the argument declining to enter a technological analysis.[171]

> In terms of the Act's purposes, these differences do not distinguish Aereo's system from cable systems, which do perform "publicly." Viewed in terms of Congress' regulatory objectives, why should any of these technological differences matter? They concern the behind-the-scenes way in which Aereo delivers television programming to its viewers' screens. They do not render Aereo's commercial objective any different from that of cable companies.

Justice Breyer was careful to limit the analysis to the Aereo, stating specifically that cloud, remote storage DVRs and other technological innovations would have to wait until cases involving those particular developments came before the Court. On remand, Judge Nathan granted the preliminary injunction against Aereo.

Aereo shut down, refunding subscribers the last month's fees. The company then applied to the Copyright Office to a license to carry over-the-air television signals in the same way that cable companies operate. But Aereo was rejected. The Copyright Office said that because Aereo was an online distributor, it did not meet the definition of a cable system. Because it wasn't a cable system, the portions of the Copyright Act that gives cable systems a license did not apply.

The Copyright Office left Aereo in a sort of limbo. Aereo's filings would not be refused, but rather accepted on a provisional basis until the Congress changed the law, the courts ruled differently or the FCC defined Aereo as the equivalent of a cable system.

Some five months after the Supreme Court decision, Aereo filed for bankruptcy.[172] The company said long before the case that it had no "Plan B"[173] should it lose in court.

THE RIGHT OF PUBLIC DISPLAY

The right of public display covers those works that generally are considered to be in the fine arts. It also applies to individual images from movies or other audiovisual works. Persons familiar with college campuses will note that bands often create promotional material by using still photos from movies. Such uses can run afoul of Sec. 106(5).

---

[171] Ibid. at 2508.

[172] Emily Steel, "Aereo Concedes Defeat and Files for Bankruptcy," *New York Times*, Nov. 21, 2014.

[173] Ibid.

SEC. 106(6)

Sec. 106(6) deals with the rights of copyright holders when their works are transmitted by means of digital audio transmission. Simply put, this covers the field of specialized music services, including interactive "music on demand" services that have arisen as technology has provided the means to offer personalized information, data and entertainment services.

The division of the copyright into these six areas came with the implementation of the 1976 Copyright Act. This bundle of rights has benefitted copyright holders by allowing them to sell or license them individually and thus more effectively exploit the works. As Professor Kent R. Middleton has pointed out, authors' ownership of rights under the old statute was precarious indeed. "One change," Middleton wrote, "which makes copyright divisible, gives the author greater flexibility in selling his work to different media. The other, vesting initial ownership with the creator of a work, makes the author's title more secure."[174]

Technology has added complexity to the issue of sale of rights and royalties. In 1993, Jonathon Tasini and nine other freelance writers sued the *New York Times, Time* magazine, the *Atlantic* magazine, Mead Data Central and University Microfilms.[175] Tasini and his co-plaintiffs sued over the defendants' use of their articles in electronic databases and CD ROMs. The writers had sold their articles to the periodicals. After printing the articles on paper, the publishers then published them on their websites, databases and CD-ROMs. The case was significant because many of the contracts used by publishers did not mention electronic publishing.

The Supreme Court agreed to hear the case following two conflicting lower court decisions. Initially, the district court ruled that the publishers were entitled to publish in both paper and electronic forms without having to get additional permissions from the freelance writers.[176] The 2nd Circuit Court of Appeals reversed, saying that the copyright statute did not give publishers the right to take the freelancers' articles and put them into the new collective work.[177]

The case turned on § 201I of the Copyright Statute. That section allows the purchaser of an article to use it in revisions of publications. In large measure, § 201(c) is a matter of common sense. News occurs during the publishing cycle and a newspaper may put out as many as a half dozen editions in the course of a day. Magazines may alter the content of an issue to market to particular regions. If the publishers had to negotiate and purchase new publication rights for each edition, they

---

[174] Kent R. Middleton, "Copyright and the Journalist: New Powers for the Free-Lancer," *Journalism Quarterly* 56:1 (Spring, 1979), p. 39.

[175] *Tasini v. New York Times*, 972 F.Supp. 804 (S.D.N.Y.1997).

[176] Ibid.

[177] *Tasini v. New York Times*, 206 F.3d 161, 166 (2d Cir.2000).

would be paralyzed, unable to go to press for lack of a freelancer's permission.

The controlling question was whether including the articles from the pages of the newspaper or magazine in the online data base or CD-ROM constituted a revision of the collection of stories that made up the original editions of the newspaper or magazine or were new collective works that would require a new purchase of publishing rights from the authors.

Justice Ruth Bader Ginzburg, writing for the 7–2 majority of the Court, concluded that the databases and CD-ROMS were not revisions of the publications. That meant that Tasini and fellow writers owned the rights to the use of their work in those later compilations.

Justice Ginzburg noted that there were significant differences between the freelance articles appearing in the periodicals and the articles in the data bases. Unlike microfilms, which are photographed pages of the periodical, the articles were presented as part of an electronic whole made up of millions of individual articles. They are presented on screen in a format unlike the original publication and without the whole of the content of the original edition.[178]

> In that compendium, each edition of each periodical represents only a minuscule fraction of the ever-expanding Database. The Database no more constitutes a "revision" of each constituent edition than a 400-page novel quoting a sonnet in passing would represent a "revision" of that poem.

The publishers claimed that a ruling for the freelance authors would have a tremendous and negative impact on research. They predicted that the publishers of the on-line and CD-ROM databases would have to chop away massive portions of their libraries to avoid infringement. But Justice Ginsburg was not moved by the warnings, including some by noted historians, saying:[179]

> Notwithstanding the dire predictions from some quarters, it hardly follows from today's decision that an injunction against the inclusion of these articles in the Databases (much less all freelance articles in any databases) must issue. * * * The parties (Authors and Publishers) may enter into an agreement allowing continued electronic reproduction of the Authors' works; they, and if necessary the courts and Congress, may draw on numerous models for distributing copy-righted works and remunerating authors for their distribution. In any event, speculation about future harms is no basis for this Court to shrink authorial rights Congress established in § 201(c).

Even before the Supreme Court heard the case, many of the publications had taken steps to preserve their rights regarding freelancer

---

[178] *New York Times v. Tasini*, 533 U.S. 483, 121 S.Ct. 2381 (2001).

[179] Ibid.

work. Many companies revised their freelancer agreements so that freelancers would transfer the right to include their articles in database form after initial publication in the periodical.

86. DEVELOPMENTS IN TECHNOLOGY

Violation of copyright includes such use or copying of an author's work that his or her profit is lessened.

Anyone who violates any of the exclusive rights spelled out by Secs. 106 through 108 of the copyright statute is an infringer. As such, infringers bear liability to the copyright holder for lost profits, actual losses and the damage created by the taking. Infringement can even result in criminal penalties. The following cases illustrate infringement in different categories of work. The principles involved should serve as a cautionary tale for users of new forms of communication.

For technology continues to evolve and each new innovation has led to infringement of copyrights and forced, first, the courts and then Congress to adapt the copyright statute. When movable type made it possible to mass produce what had previously been hand copied it created opportunities to pirate popular works. Contemporary printing makes it even easier to churn out multiple of copies of copyrighted works. Universities and copy shops became defendants when the publishers of academic and literary works found infringing course packs.

Motion picture versions of plays and books led to court cases as to the legality of such uses in that new technology. The VCR raised questions that would eventually be settled by the Supreme Court (see the Sony case later in this chapter) as did DAT, the digital audio tape recorder that now seems an evolutionary dead end.

As we continue through the Twenty-First Century, the Internet and proliferation of digital devices have generated new forms of infringement. FTP, file transfer protocols, Torrent and whatever new form of digital sharing that allow users to share works peer-to-peer create new ways to infringe digital copies of copyrighted works.

THE DIGITAL MILLENNIUM COPYRIGHT ACT

Recognizing the need to foster the development of the Internet, Congress passed the Digital Millennium Copyright Act[180] The Act has five parts. Only the first two titles concern the audience for this textbook:

> Title I. WIPO[181] Copyright and Performances and Phonograms Treaties Implementation Act of 1998.
>
> Title II. Online Copyright Infringement Liability Limitation Act.

[180] Pub. L. No. 105–304. 112 Stat. 2860 (1998).

[181] World Intellectual Property Organization.

Title I includes rules that ban the use of technologies to overcome anti-copying protections. It also includes a section making the removal of Copyright Management Information a crime (discussed earlier in this chapter in the section on copyright notice).

Title II provides protections for Internet Service Providers from copyright claims. This section is known at the "Safe Harbor" provision. This immunity for ISPs requires them to do four things to help preserve the rights of copyright holders. ISPs must put into place policies to:

(1) create a working notification system to receive notices of copyright infringement (these generally are referred to as "take-down" notices),

(2) deal with notifications from copyright holders

(3) not stand in the way of copyright holders in gathering information in order to report infringement, and

(4) adopt and reasonably implement a policy of terminating in appropriate circumstances the accounts of subscribers who are repeat infringers;

Adhering to the four policies has kept ISPs from winding up on the losing end of infringement cases. YouTube (discussed below) won a multi-year infringement suit by Viacom because of its adherence to the policies.

Cox Communications made headlines in 2015 when it lost a $25 million jury award for contributory infringement.[182] BMG, which controls rights to music from artists including David Bowie, sued Cox alleging that the ISP failed to implement the policies required in order to be protected by the "Safe Harbor."

U.S. District Judge Liam O'Grady allowed a jury to consider Cox Communications' liability after denying the company's motion for summary judgment. In allowing the suit to get to the jury, O'Grady noted the conduct of the company with regard to DMCA take-down notices and its actions when its subscribers were the subjects of multiple complaints of copyright infringement.

O'Grady noted Cox's policies on the take-down notices:[183]

> Three features of the CATS system are worth mentioning. First, when Cox receives multiple complaints in one day for a single account, the tickets are "rolled up," meaning Cox counts only the first ticket. Id. ¶ 8 & n.4; Zabek Decl. ¶ 9; Theodore Decl. Ex. 1 at 155–56. Second, Cox imposes a "hard limit" on the number of complaints a complainant can submit that will receive customer-facing action. Beck Decl. ¶ 8. If a complainant exceeds the hard limit, CATS automatically sends an e-mail informing the complainant that the daily limit has been reached and the

---

[182] *BMG Rights Management and Round Hill Music v. Cox Communications*, 2015 WL 7756130 (E.D. Va. 2015).

[183] Ibid. at 2.

> tickets created from those e-mails are automatically closed. Theodore Decl. Ex. 42 at 7. The default limit is 200 complaints per complainant per day, but Cox says it will work with a complainant to set a reasonable number. Id.; Zabek Decl. ¶ 30.

Cox sends notices to subscribers when it does take complaints but only on the 10th complaint (which means complaints on 10 different days because of the Cox "roll up" policy) does Cox deactivate the subscriber's service. When Cox receives a 14th complaint in an "Abuse Cycle," a 180-day period, it considers terminating the subscriber's account. Termination is at the discretion of Cox employees. The failure of Cox to actually terminate subscribers was sufficient to deny it a Safe Harbor, O'Grady wrote.[184]

> The record conclusively establishes that before the fall of 2012 Cox did not implement its repeat infringer policy. Instead, Cox publicly purported to comply with its policy, while privately disparaging and intentionally circumventing the DMCA's requirements. Cox employees followed an unwritten policy put in place by senior members of Cox's abuse group by which accounts used to repeatedly infringe copyrights would be nominally terminated, only to be reactivated upon request. Once these accounts were reactivated, customers were given clean slates, meaning the next notice of infringement Cox received linked to those accounts would be considered the first in Cox's graduate response procedure.

O'Grady quoted language from a number of Cox internal emails about subscribers who were the subjects of complaints about infringement. Time after time, he noted, Cox reactivated subscriber accounts. One March 2011 email was especially telling.[185]

> a representative emailed Zabek[186]: "Here is another example of a customer that I consider a[ ] habitual abuser. In a year was terminated twice and turned back on. I suspended him again since no email address and according to procedure he start over [sic] in the process." Id. Ex. 45 (emphasis added). Zabek responded, "It is fine. We need the customers."

The subscribers also had their own liability for their illegal copying. Cox Communications' responsibility was for its practices that allowed the infringement. The *Hollywood Reporter* published a story about the case that included a reference to Cox Communications' insurer bringing its own suit.[187]

---

[184] Ibid. at 14.

[185] Ibid. at 16.

[186] Jason Zabek, Cox's Manager of Customer Abuse Operations.

[187] Eriq Gardner, "Music Publisher Gets $25 Million Jury Verdict Against Cox in Trailblazing Piracy Case," *Hollywood Reporter*, Dec. 17, 2015.

Cox is also facing a lawsuit from its insurer aiming to escape the tab in this BMG case due to "Cox's business policy and practice of ignoring and failing to forward infringement notices and refusing to terminate or block infringing customers' accounts."

INTERNET VIDEO AND FILM

Just as movies created copyright issues regarding the presentation of books and stage plays on the silver screen, technological changes have raised new issues regarding permissible uses of movie and television content on the Web.

While Napster and MP3 gained headlines, another Web entity was dealing with copyright questions regarding multimedia and movies. Five students from UCLA founded Scour.com in 1997. It was a media file sharing operation. It developed into Scour Exchange a peer-to-peer exchange program that allowed users to do more than simply trade music. It permitted users to share music videos, television shows and full-length movies.

The Motion Picture Association of America and the Recording Industry Association of America filed suit in July of 2000 alleging copyright infringement. Scour filed for Chapter 11 bankruptcy in October and shut down the Scour Exchange the next month.[188]

RecordTV.com and iCraveTV.com, two Canadian Internet entities that allowed users to download television programs shut down after being sued for copyright infringement by television producers and networks.[189] Television content copyright holders are quick to act against anyone making and distributing copies of their property without permission.

A California computer programmer, who tried to please his 8-year-old daughter by copying episodes of the "*Pokemon*" cartoon program, ran into a $10 million lawsuit.[190] David Simon of Agoura Hills, California, began copying the episodes of the cartoon on his family computer when his VCRs proved unreliable. When his daughter's friends found out about the computer copies, Simon began providing the episodes on a Web site where they all could access the show. Simon decided to expand the operation into a business that would let computer users log onto a Web site to see television shows. He started a company and almost immediately drew the multi-million dollar infringement suit.

While it is technically feasible to copy, compress and send files containing television programs and movies, the underlying legal rights

---

188 David S. Stolzar (*Harvard Crimson*, Harvard U.), "Two companies hope to revive Scour, uncertain about video file-sharing," U-Wire, Nov. 30, 2000.

189 Susanne Craig, "Music, TV copyright issues rein in Wild Wild Web," *Globe and Mail*, July 10, 2000.

190 Associated Press, "Man who posts TV shows online is now target of industry lawsuits," July 5, 2000.

of copyright holders to control when and if copies are made, make that ability a dangerous one to exercise.

YouTube, the online video source, uses filtering software to keep copyrighted material off its site.[191] It also responds quickly to take-down notices from copyright holders. Viacom Inc. and movie and television production companies sued YouTube for $1 billion for showing thousands of clips that the New York-based company owned."[192] The case dragged on for seven years with the trial and appellate courts siding with YouTube based upon its practices of taking down videos once it received a take-down notice.

MUSIC, MP3 AND NAPSTER

These cases had their beginnings with the creation of the Internet. Sharing, and coincidentally illegally distributing songs, took a leap forward in 1987 when the Moving Pictures Expert Group set out a standard file format for the storing of audio recordings in digital format. The format was called MPEG-3 and later shortened in general use as "MP3." This formatting system allows computer users to take an audio compact disk and place its contents into their computers' memories. The compression of the audio files also allows for "relatively" fast transmission of these digitized audio files from one computer to another.

The changing technology allowed the courts to continue to put "old wine in new bottles" as traditional copyright principles were applied to new media. In the case of *UMG Recordings v. MP3.com*,[193] a federal court ruled that MP3's music service infringed the copyrights of record companies.

As the U.S. district court described the service in a copyright infringement suit:[194]

> MP3.com, on or around January 12, 2000, launched its "My MP3.com" service, which is advertised as permitting subscribers to store, customize and listen to the recordings contained in their CDS from any place where they have an Internet connection.

In order to get the music, subscribers had to demonstrate that they owned a particular piece of music. They would load their CDs into their computers and log into the MP3 site. The MP3 computer would verify the CD and then add that CD title to the list of CDs available to that subscriber. Instead of having to play their CDs on a CD player, subscribers could retrieve their songs from MP3's server.

---

[191] Michael Liedtke, "YouTube unveils anti-piracy filters," Associated Press, Oct. 16, 2007.

[192] Ibid.

[193] *UMG Recordings v. MP3.Com*, 92 F.Supp.2d 349 (S.D.N.Y.2000).

[194] Ibid.

MP3 got into trouble because it had to make copies of the CDs to create master files that subscribers could download from. MP3's conduct amounted to an infringement of the copyright holders' exclusive rights to make those copies.

MP3 tried to argue that its service was a fair use under the copyright law but a federal judge ruled that the copying of the original CDs and the replaying of the CDs in the music service fell outside the boundaries of fair use.[195]

> Although defendant seeks to portray its service as the "functional equivalent" of storing its subscribers' CDs, in actuality defendant is re-playing for the subscribers converted versions of the recordings it copied, without authorization, from plaintiffs' copyrighted CDs. On its face, this makes out a presumptive case of infringement under the Copyright Act of 1976.

That cleared the way for the record companies and the copyright holders, notably ASCAP, BMI and SESAC to move ahead. MP3 voluntarily shut down its subscriber service, though it continued other services for which it had licensing agreements, most notably a classical music service as it negotiated licensing agreements with the major record labels.

Napster, the brainchild of Shawn Fanning, allowed computer users to search the hard drives of other computer users and share MP3 files through the Napster system. The result was that millions of persons were able to share CD-quality music with each other. This freed them from having to buy music from commercial music sellers and, as would be expected, upset most recording companies and many recording artists who saw their sales, profits and royalties disappearing.

Interestingly enough, despite the focus of most news stories about college students making use of Napster to get free music, the majority of Napster users were older than 30. "It's a misconception that this is just a bunch of kids in dorm rooms," Napster CEO Hank Barry told *Cleveland Plain Dealer* Music Critic John Soeder.[196] But no matter who was using Napster, record companies and music stores complained that their sales were declining because of the illegal copying.

And so, A & M Records, Geffen Records, Interscope Records, Sony Music Entertainment, MCA Records, Atlantic Recording Corp., Island Records, Motown Records, Capitol Records, La Face Records, BMG Music, Universal Records, Elektra Entertainment Group, Arista Records, Sire Records Group, Virgin Records, America and Warner Bros.

---

[195] Ibid. at 350.

[196] John Soeder, "Adults Top Group Swapping Tunes Driving the Napster Bandwagon," *Cleveland Plain Dealer*, Oct. 22, 2000.

Records, Dr. Dre and Metallica sued Napster for copyright infringement.[197]

> The record supports the district court's determination that "as much as 87 percent of the files available on Napster may be copyrighted and more than 70 percent may be owned or administered by plaintiffs."

The plaintiffs argued and the district court agreed that the downloading of the copyrighted works infringed the copyright holders rights. Napster spent little time denying that conclusion.[198]

> The district court also noted that "it is pretty much acknowledged * * * by Napster that this is infringement." We agree that plaintiffs have shown that Napster users infringe at least two of the copyright holders' exclusive rights: the right of reproduction 106(1); and distribution § 106(3). Napster users who upload file names to the search index for others to copy, violate plaintiffs' distribution rights. Napster users who download files containing copyrighted music violate plaintiffs' reproduction rights.

Napster defended itself saying that its users were protected under the "fair use" exception to copyright infringement. Both the district court and the 9th Circuit panel disagreed with Napster on the fair use defense and that will be taken up in the section on fair use later in this chapter. Having disposed of Napster's defense, the 9th Circuit then sent the case back to the district court to fine tune its injunction against Napster to ensure that the company only permitted songs in the public domain to be traded. Napster and its users also need to pay attention to the No Electronic Theft Act, which provides for prosecutions even when copiers are not uploading and downloading for money. The NET Act, discussed in the Penalties section makes copiers liable if they, either, get unauthorized copies in return, or, upload works that exceed a certain monetary value.

AIMSTER AND OTHER FILE SHARING CASES

Napster was followed by a number of other peer-to-peer file sharing cases. In *In re Aimster Copyright Litigation*[199] a federal district court in the Northern District of Illinois granted a preliminary injunction to prevent Aimster from contributorily or vicariously infringing copyrighted music. The case was a consolidation of 11 different infringement suits brought against the Internet company.[200] Aimster used Instant Messaging to let its members identify large numbers of other users who they could exchange files with. The district court described Aimster as "a

---

[197] *A & M Records, et al. v. Napster, Inc.*, 239 F.3d 1004, 1013 (9th Cir.2001).

[198] Ibid. at 1014.

[199] *In re Aimster Copyright Litigation*, 2002 WL 31443236 (N.D.Ill. 2002).

[200] *In re Aimster Copyright Litigation*, 252 F.Supp.2d 634 (N.D. Ill. 2002).

service whose very *raison d'etre* appears to be the facilitation of and contribution to copyright infringement on a massive scale."[201]

Movie studios and record companies, led by Metro-Goldwyn-Mayer,[202] sued Grokster, Ltd., Streamcast and others alleging that the defendants were contributory infringers by distributing software that permitted users to share music files. The *Grokster* case is one of three recent Internet infringement cases brought by copyright holders. Morpheus and Kazaa, along with Grokster, were targeted for providing peer-to-peer file sharing software.[203]

MGM lost on a motion for summary judgment filed by the defendants. Judge Stephen Wilson found that the principles from the Sony[204] case applied. Just as Sony won its case because the video tape recorder had substantial noninfringing use, Judge Wilson granted summary judgment to Grokster and the other defendants because their file-sharing software was being used for legitimate sharing of works.[205]

The MGM case was distinct from the *Napster* case in the important area of knowledge of infringement taking place.[206]

> [L]iability for contributory infringement accrues where a defendant has actual—not merely constructive knowledge of the infringement at a time during which the defendant materially contributes to the infringement.

It turned out that one of Napster's founders wrote a memo in which he pointed out the need to "remain ignorant of users' real names and IP addresses 'since they are exchanging pirated music,' "[207] and Napster had been told that there were thousands of infringing files in the Napster system. Grokster merely provided software that infringers used. MGM appealed the grant of summary judgment to the 9th Circuit Court of Appeals.

In addition to pursuing the companies that enable people to illegally copy their intellectual property, copyright holders have expanded the

---

[201] Ibid. at 1.

[202] *Metro-Goldwyn-Mayer Studios, Inc. v. Grokster, Ltd.*, 259 F.Supp.2d 1029 (C.D.Cal. 2003).

[203] Jason Fry, "What comes after Napster? Vincent Falco may have the answer," *The Wall Street Journal*, Sept. 16, 2002. In December 2003, the Dutch Supreme Court ruled that Kazaa's operation in the Netherland could not be held liable for copyright infringement for works shared using the company's software. "Court: Kazaa not responsible for swapping," The Associated Press, Dec. 2003. Kazaa faced infringement claims in Australian courts. Jamie Tarabay, "U.S. proceedings shouldn't affect Australian case against file-swapping company," Associated Press, Feb. 20, 2004.

[204] *Sony Corporation of America v. Universal City Studios, Inc.*, 464 U.S. 417, 104 S.Ct. 774 (1984).

[205] Some of the legitimate uses included the distribution of movie trailers, free songs, public domain works, government documents and other works that owners permit distribution of * * *.

[206] Quoting *A & M Records, et. al. v. Napster, Inc.*, 239 F.3d 1004, 1020 (9th Cir.2001). *Metro-Goldwyn-Mayer Studios, Inc. v. Grokster, Ltd.*, 259 F.Supp.2d 1029, 1034 (C.D.Cal. 2003).

[207] *A & M Records, et. al. v. Napster, Inc.*, 239 F.3d 1004, 1020 (9th Cir.2001).

scope of their suits to include the copiers. In the *In re Verizon Internet Services, Inc. Enforcement Matter*,[208] the Recording Industry Association of America (RIAA) sought the identity of a subscriber to the Verizon Internet Service.

The Verizon subscriber was reported to reside in the Pittsburgh area and the RIAA claimed that the subscriber has shared hundreds of songs.[209] Verizon resisted the subpoena on the grounds that the Digital Millennium Copyright Act protects Internet service providers when they have no knowledge of or participation in infringement. Verizon argued that because the infringement took place through Kazaa and by its subscriber, it is not responsible and the music association has no legal power to compel it to reveal the information.[210]

Even so, a federal court issued two subpoenas against Verizon. But a three-judge panel of the D.C. Circuit reversed saying that DMCA did not give the RIAA the power to get the Internet Service Provider's records.[211] Judge Douglas Ginsburg ruled for Verizon holding that DMCA only gives copyright holders subpoena power when an Internet Service Provider actually stores infringing material on its servers. Because Verizon, like other Internet Service Providers, serves only as a conduit for data and the actual storage of infringing material takes place in the computers of the file sharers, Verizon is exempt from the subpoena power of DMCA. Judge Ginsburg also held that Verizon would not come under the "notice and take-down" provisions of DMCA.[212]

> No matter what information the copyright owner may provide, the ISP can neither "remove" nor "disable access to" the infringing material because that material is not stored on the ISP's servers. Verizon can not remove or disable one user's access to infringing material resident on another user's computer because Verizon does not control the content on its subscribers' computers.

Even without the ability to compel ISPs to reveal the identifies of their subscribers, the recording industry has been able to find peer-to-peer sharers to sue. In the fall of 2003, the Recording Industry Association of America filed suits against more than 400 persons it said were illegally copying songs.[213] The RIAA sued in two batches, going after 261 persons in September and another 204 in October. The RIAA

---

[208] *In re Verizon Internet Services, Inc. Subpoena Enforcement Matter*, Civ.No. 1:02MSOO323 (D.D.C. enforcement motion).

[209] Brooks Boliek, "Music biz pressures court to make Verizon provide ID," *Hollywood Reporter*, Oct. 7, 2002.

[210] Ibid.

[211] *Recording Industry Ass'n of America, Inc. v. Verizon Internet*, 351 F.3d 1229 (D.C.Cir. 2003).

[212] Ibid. at 1235.

[213] John Schwartz, "Record industry warns 204 before suing on swapping," *New York Times*, Oct. 18, 2003.

reported in October that it had settled with more than 60 defendants for an average of $3,000 each.

News of the lawsuits, including four targeting college students operating large-scale music sharing sites, prompted a number of file sharers to discontinue their efforts.[214] But a few months later, the Associated Press reported that music sharing was on the rise again.[215]

The recording industry also offered amnesty for file sharers in the fall of 2003.[216] In return for signatures on notarized affidavits and the deletion of all illegally copied songs, the Recording Industry Association of America would agree not to sue. Amnesty participants who renege and resume copying could expect to face prosecution for willful infringement.

The RIAA had filed some 20,000 infringement lawsuits by the summer of 2007.[217] Most cases settled out of court for a premium price. In one notable case, a single-mother of two in Minnesota lost an infringement suit.[218] Jammie Thomas decided to fight in court claiming that she had not downloaded music. Evidence linked Thomas' computer to illegal downloads. The jury ordered Jammie Thomas to pay $222,000 for willfully copying 24 songs. The Thomas case was the first of the RIAA's lawsuits to go to trial.[219]

Music and movie companies continue to work successfully with colleges and universities that provide their students, faculty, and staff with access to the Internet as a Pitzer College student in Claremont, California, discovered in the fall of 2002.

Alex Honigman was searching the Web when he came to a site and clocked open a file that happened to contain scenes from the Clint

---

[214] Amy Harmon, "Recording industry goes after students over music sharing," *New York Times*, April 23, 2003. One student, identified only as Jason, a computer science major, shut down his popular Web site within hours of learning of the suits. "I don't think I was doing anything wrong * * * But who wants to face a $98 billion debt for the rest of their lives? I was scared.".

[215] "Illegal music downloading climbs," Associated Press, Jan. 15, 2004.

[216] "Amnesty offered for repentant downloaders," Reuters, Sept. 5, 2003.

[217] David Kravets, "Happy Anniversary Pirates: 20,000 Copyright Lawsuits and Counting," *Wired*, Aug. 29, 2007.

[218] Joseph Menn, "File-sharing verdict a triumph for record labels," *Los Angeles Times*, Oct. 5, 2007.

[219] The verdict in Ms. Thomas' infringement case was the third in three separate jury trials. In each case, the jury found Ms. Thomas had infringed and returned judgments of $1.9 million, $1.5 million and finally $222,000. Ms. Thomas denied illegal downloading and variously said that any downloads might have been done by her children or a boyfriend or someone else. Investigators found that a user, "tereastarr," had downloaded songs through Kazaa. At trial, Thomas-Rasset conceded that "tereastarr" is a username that she uses regularly for Internet and computer accounts. She admitted familiarity with and interest in some of the artists of works found in the tereastarr KaZaA account. She also acknowledged that she wrote a case study during college on the legality of Napster—another peer-to-peer file sharing program—and knew that Napster was shut down because it was illegal. Nonetheless, Thomas-Rasset testified that she had never heard of KaZaA before this case, did not have KaZaA on her computer, and did not use KaZaA to download files. The jury also heard evidence from a forensic investigator that Thomas-Rasset removed and replaced the hard drive on her computer with a new hard drive after investigators notified her of her potential infringement. The new hard drive did not contain the infringing files.

Eastwood movie, *Blood Work*. When he opened the file, he activated an alarm system at moviemaker Warner Bros. The company then notified Honigman's school.[220]

> In no time, Honigman, 20, was suspended briefly from the campus computer network and required to write a letter of apology to the Hollywood studio. Pitzer administrators also warned him that a second offense could bring a year's suspension from the network.

The entertainment companies rely on elements of the Digital Millennium Copyright Act (DMCA) to get colleges and universities to help stem the flood of copyright piracy. In addition, the MPAA has lobbied Congress for a new law that would require universities to cooperate in the discovery of campus pirates. That effort was undercut in early 2008 when the MPAA admitted that it had made a mistake in a 2005 study attributing the percentage of movie piracy to students.[221] Originally, the MPAA said that students were responsible for 45 percent of piracy. The actual figure was 15 percent. Under terms of the DMCA, Internet service providers have immunity from copyright infringement suits provided that they, among other things, act quickly to remove infringing content once they are notified of the piracy. Failure to act can result in a loss of the immunity from copyright infringement suit. As a result, college administrators are taking an active role to stamp out infringement by their system users.

The colleges and universities are having to act because of the problems caused by the volume of downloading songs, movies, games, and software. The sheer volume is slowing down or clogging their campus computer networks. At one California university, faculty members complained that they could not make use of the Internet in their evening classes.

The RIAA sent letters to 13 universities in early 2007 asking if the university would turn over the identities of students illegally downloading music.[222] The association was prepared to provide student IP addresses so that the universities could provide identities. The association would then offer the downloaders the chance to settle suits at a "substantial discount" over the typical settlement offer.

File sharing lawsuits continue and with the release of any new film, cases pop up. The Academy Award winning *Dallas Buyers Club*, was the subject of more than a dozen infringement suits in 2014 and 2015. [223]Dallas Buyers Club LLC sued a Tyler Madsen in a Washington (state

[220] Rebecca Trounson, "Pirated Files Clog College Networks, Student Downloads Flood Systems and Draw Complaints from Entertainment Firms," *Los Angeles Times*, Dec. 2, 2002.

[221] "MPAA Admits Mistake on Downloading Study," Associated Press, Jan. 23, 2008.

[222] Eliot Van Buskirk: "A Poison Pen from the RIAA," *Wired*, Feb. 28,

[223] *Dallas Buyers Club, LLC v. Tyler Madsen*, 2015 WL 6680260 (W.D.Washington 2015).

not D.C.) federal court alleging that Madsen illegally downloaded parts of the film *Dallas Buyers Club*.

Because Madsen did not respond to the suit, the plaintiffs sought a default judgment.[224] To win, Dallas Buyers Club had to show that it owned the copyright in the movie and that Madsen had made an illegal copy. A copy of the copyright registration was enough to prove the first element. The second element was a little trickier.[225]

> Plaintiff has also alleged that Mr. Madsen copied pieces of Dallas Buyers Club. See id. ¶¶ 18, 32, 42. More specifically, Plaintiff has alleged and presented evidence that the IP address assigned to Mr. Madsen copied and distributed pieces of the film. See id. ¶ 18; see also Dkt. #47 (Lowe Decl.) Ex. A at 10.
>
> * * *
>
> The Court acknowledges that a dispute may arise concerning material facts, including whether Mr. Madsen is the actual infringer. See *In re BitTorrent Adult Film Copyright Infringement Cases*, 296 F.R.D. 80, 84 (E.D.N.Y.2012) (finding that "it is no more likely that the subscriber to an IP address carried out a particular computer function . . . than to say an individual who pays the telephone bill made a specific telephone call."). Nevertheless, the Court finds that such a possibility is insufficient to outweigh the other factors weighing in favor of granting default judgment.

Judge Richard A. Jones eventually awarded Dallas Buyers Club $750 in actual damages, attorneys fees of $2,099.80 and costs in the amount of $170.

87. INFRINGEMENT

In order to win a lawsuit for copyright infringement, a plaintiff must establish two separate facts, as the late Circuit Judge Jerome N. Frank wrote some years ago: "(a) that the alleged infringer copied from plaintiff's work, and (b) that, if copying is proved, it was so 'material' or substantial as to constitute unlawful appropriation."[226] Of course, the plaintiff must prove to the court that it has standing to sue, ownership or an interest in the copyrighted work.

Even so, the material copied need not be extensive or "lengthy" in order to be infringement. "In an appropriate case," Judge Frank noted, "copyright infringement might be demonstrated, with no proof or weak

---

[224] A key thing to remember is that if you are sued and you think it is a mistake, you still need to get representation and respond to the suit. If you don't the plaintiff may seek a default judgment, sort of a you forfeit because you did not show up for the game. That can lead to the award of damages, attorneys fees and court costs.

[225] Ibid. at 2.

[226] *Heim v. Universal Pictures Co.*, 154 F.2d 480, 487 (2d Cir.1946).

proof of access, by showing that a simple brief phrase, contained in both pieces, was so idiosyncratic in its treatment as to preclude coincidence."[227] Judge Frank also noted that even a great, famous author or artist might be found guilty of copyright infringement. He wrote, "we do not accept the aphorism, when a great composer steals, he is 'influenced'; when an unknown steals, he is 'infringing'."[228]

The Baltimore Ravens found out the hard way about the impact of similarity in infringement. Frederick Bouchat, a building security guard and an amateur artist in Baltimore, created a team logo in anticipation of the arrival of the city's new football team. He sent copies of his drawings to the official who won the franchise for the city. The team later came out with its logo and it was remarkably similar to Bouchat's. Bouchat sued and his victory was upheld by the 4th Circuit.[229] Despite his victory on the infringement part of his suit, Bouchat lost in his claim for $10 million, the amount of profits that he alleged that the Baltimore Ravens generated from the use of his logo (the damages portion of the case is discussed later in this chapter).

That principle, which forms the basis for the requirement that the plaintiff in a copyright case show both similarity and access, came into play in *Selle v. Gibb*,[230] an infringement case brought by a Chicago musician against the brothers Gibb, otherwise known as the Bee Gees. Selle had written a song, "*Let It End*," in the fall of 1975. He obtained copyright the same fall. He played the song several times with his band in the Chicago area and then sent a demo tape and sheet music of the song to 11 different recording and publishing companies. Eight companies returned the materials and three did not. Other than that, Selle did not publicize his song. In 1978, Selle heard the Bee Gees' song, "*How Deep Is Your Love*," and recognized it as his own "*Let It End*." Selle sued for infringement. Time magazine writer Michael Walsh described the case in an essay on musical infringement: "For Selle's suit against the Bee Gees, four bars of the two scores were blown up to display a suspiciously exact correspondence of notes; on the witness stand, even Bee Gees Maurice Gibb couldn't tell the two songs apart."[231]

The Bee Gees, their manager and two musicians testified about the creation of "*How Deep Is Your Love*?" in a recording studio near Paris in 1977. They introduced a work tape that showed how the song came into being. The court of appeals described the creative process, saying that "[a]lthough the tape does not seem to preserve the very beginning of the process of creation, it does depict the process by which ideas, notes, lyrics and bits of the tune were gradually put together."[232] Only one expert

---

227 Ibid. at 488.

228 Ibid.

229 *Bouchat v. Baltimore Ravens Football Club, Inc.*, 346 F.3d 514 (4th Cir. 2003).

230 *Selle v. Gibb*, 741 F.2d 896 (7th Cir.1984).

231 Michael Walsh, "Has Somebody Stolen Their Song?" *Time*, Oct. 19, 1987, p. 86.

232 *Selle v. Gibb*, 741 F.2d 896, 899 (7th Cir.1984).

witness testified, a professor of music at Northwestern University, who analyzed the two songs and said, "the two songs had such striking similarities that they could not have been written independent of one another."[233] Even the Time reporter noted the similarities, writing,[234]

> The similarities between the Bee Gees' hit from Saturday Night Fever and the unpublished Let It End are amusing; it seems to defy chance that two composers could have hit upon the same ugly tune.

The jury agreed and found for Selle.

But the judge overruled the jury, granting the Gibb brothers a judgment notwithstanding the verdict (the judge here substituted his own decision for that of the jury). The judge focused on the fact that Selle had not established that the Gibbs had access to his song and had failed to refute the testimony regarding the Gibbs' independent creation of the work. The 7th Circuit affirmed the district court, rejecting Selle's contention that the jury could infer access by the striking degree of similarity between the two songs. But the court rejected that saying that access was an essential element. "Proof of copying is crucial to any claim of copyright infringement because no matter how similar the two works may be (even to the point of identity), if the defendant did not copy the accused work, there is no infringement."[235]

Other cases have turned on the defendant's ability to show that what he copied was not the plaintiff's work, but rather another work altogether, one that already has fallen into the public domain and thus can be used by anyone. In these cases, it is up to the plaintiff to prove that the defendant copied his original and not someone else's. Sometimes, the defendant can prove that the material in question is not copyrightable, such as a collection of facts incorporated into a copyrighted work.

The U.S. Court of Appeals, 2nd Circuit ruled that A. A. Hoehling could not collect damages from Universal City Studios in a dispute involving the motion picture, *The Hindenburg.* Back in 1962, Hoehling—after substantial research—published a copyrighted book, *"Who Destroyed the Hindenburg?"* That book advanced the theory that a disgruntled crew member of The Graf Zeppelin had planted a crude bomb in one of its gas cells.

Ten years later, after consulting Hoehling's book plus many other sources, Michael MacDonald Mooney published his own book, *"The Hindenburg."* Mooney's book put forward a similar cause for the airship's destruction, but there was also evidence that other authors before

---

[233] Ibid. Quoting trial transcript.

[234] Michael Walsh, "Has Somebody Stolen Their Song?" *Time*, Oct. 19, 1987, p. 86.

[235] *Selle v. Gibb*, 741 F.2d 896, 901 (7th Cir.1984).

Hoehling had suggested the same cause for the explosion. Circuit Judge Kaufman said for the court:[236]

> All of Hoehling's allegations of copying, therefore, encompass material that is non-copyrightable as a matter of law * * *
>
> * * *
>
> * * * in granting * * * summary judgment for defendants, courts should assure themselves that the works before them are not virtually identical. In this case, it is clear that all three authors relate the story of the Hindenburg differently.
>
> In works devoted to historical subjects, it is our view that a second author may make significant use of prior work, so long as he does not bodily appropriate the expression of another. *Rosemont Enterprises, Inc.,* 366 F.2d at 310. This principle is justified by the fundamental policy undergirding the copyright laws—the encouragement of contributions to recorded knowledge * * * Knowledge is expanded as well, by granting new authors of historical works a relatively free hand to build upon the work of their predecessors.

Alex Haley, author of the best-seller *"Roots,"* was sued for both copyright infringement and unfair competition by Margaret Walker Alexander. Ms. Alexander claimed that Haley's book, published in 1976, was drawn substantially from her novel, *Jubilee,* published in 1966, and a pamphlet, *"How I Wrote Jubilee,"* published in 1972. A federal district court granted Haley a summary judgment, finding that no copyright infringement had occurred. The court said:[237]

> Many of the claimed similarities are based on matters of historical or contemporary fact. No claim of copyright protection can arise from the fact that plaintiff has written about such historical and factual items, even if we were to assume that Haley was alerted to the facts in question by reading *"Jubilee."* * * *
>
> Another major category of items consists of material traceable to common sources, the public domain, or folk custom. Thus, a number of claimed infringements are embodiments of the cultural history of black Americans, or of both black and white Americans planning out the cruel tragedy of white-imposed slavery. Where common sources exist for the alleged similarities, or the material that is similar is otherwise not original with the plaintiff, there is no infringement. * * * This group of asserted infringements can no more be the subject of copyright protection than the cause of a date or the name of a president or a more conventional piece of historical information.

---

[236] *Hoehling v. Universal City Studios, Inc.*, 618 F.2d 972, 979–980 (2d Cir.1980).

[237] *Alexander v. Haley*, 460 F.Supp. 40, 44–45 (S.D.N.Y.1978).

There are numerous cases where copyright claims have failed because the plaintiff cannot show that his work was reproduced in the allegedly infringing work. The similarity test has been a tough obstacle for many who believe that their creations have been pirated.

In *Litchfield v. Spielberg*, the U.S. Court of Appeals for the 9th Circuit decided in 1984 that a copyright infringement/unfair competition lawsuit involving the movie *E.T.—The Extraterrestrial* was—if not out of this world—at least legally insupportable. Lisa Litchfield claimed that her copyrighted one-act musical play, *Lokey from Maldemar*, had been infringed upon by *E.T.*, the box-office smash hit. As the appeals court put it, the issue, in addition to that of infringement, was whether the lower court had acted properly in granting defendants a summary judgment.[238] After independently reviewing the facts, the court of appeals held:[239]

> There is no substantial similarity * * * between the sequences of events, mood, dialogue and characters of the two works. Any similarities in plot exist only at the general level for which plaintiff cannot claim copyright protection.
>
> * * *
>
> As is too often the case, Litchfield's action was premised "partly upon a wholly erroneous understanding of the extent of copyright protection; and partly upon that obsessive conviction, so common among authors and composers, that all similarities between their works and any others to appear later must be ascribed to plagiarism." *Dellar v. Samuel Goldwyn, Inc.*, 150 F.2d 612 (2d Cir.1945).

Copyright cases involving music have proved to be difficult. The evidence in such cases is largely circumstantial, resting upon similarities between songs. The issue in such a case, as one court expressed it, is whether "so much of what is pleasing to the ears of lay listeners, who comprise the audience for whom such popular music is composed, that defendant wrongfully appropriated something which belongs to the plaintiff."[240]

More than "lay listeners" often get involved in such cases, however. Expert witnesses sometimes testify in copyright infringement cases involving music. But it can happen that the plaintiffs who feel that their musical compositions have been stolen, and the defendants as well, will *both* bring their own expert witnesses into court, where these witnesses expertly disagree with each other.[241]

In proving a case of copyright infringement—and not just for those cases dealing with music—it is often useful if plaintiffs can show that the

---

[238] *Litchfield v. Spielberg; MCA, Inc., Universal City Studios, Inc., Extra-Terrestrial Productions, Kennedy, Tanen, and Mathison*, 736 F.2d 1352 (9th Cir.1984).

[239] Ibid. at 1355.

[240] *Arnstein v. Porter*, 154 F.2d 464, 473 (2d Cir.1946).

[241] Ibid.

alleged infringement had "access" to the original work from which the copy was supposed to have been made. Such "access" needs to be proved by the plaintiff, if only by the circumstantial evidence of similarity between two works.

During the 1940s, songwriter Ira B. Arnstein tried to show that the noted composer, Cole Porter, not only had access to his work, but that Porter had taken freely from Arnstein.

Arnstein began a copyright infringement lawsuit against Cole Porter in a federal district court. Arnstein charged that Porter's "*Begin the Beguine*" was a plagiarism from Arnstein's "the *Lord is My Shepherd*" and "*A Mother's Prayer*." He also claimed that Porter's "*My Heart Belongs to Daddy*" had been lifted from Arnstein's "*A Mother's Prayer.*"

On the question of access, plaintiff Arnstein testified that his apartment had been burglarized and accused Porter of receiving the stolen manuscripts from the burglars. Arnstein declared that Porter's "*Night and Day*" had been stolen from Arnstein's "*I Love You Madly*," which had never been published but which had been performed once over the radio. Technically, this meant that Arnstein's "*I Love You Madly*" had never been published.

In reply, Porter swore that he had never seen or heard any of Arnstein's compositions, and that he did not know the persons said to have stolen them. Even so, Arnstein's lawsuit asked for a judgment against Porter of "at least one million dollars out of the millions this defendant has earned and is earning out of all the plagiarism."[242]

At the original trial, the district court directed the jury to bring in a summary verdict in favor of Porter. Arnstein then appealed to a U.S. Circuit Court of Appeals, where Judge Jerome Frank explained what the appellate court had done. The Circuit Court of Appeals had listened to phonograph records of Cole Porter's songs and compared them to records of Arnstein's songs. As he sent the case back to a district court jury, Judge Frank wrote:

> * * * we find similarities, but we hold that unquestionably, standing alone, they do not compel the conclusion, or permit the inference, that defendant copied. The similarities, however, are sufficient so that, if there is enough evidence of access to permit the case to go to the jury, the jury may properly infer that the similarities did not result from coincidence.

The jury then found that Cole Porter's "*Begin the Beguine*" had indeed been written by Cole Porter. The courts declared that Porter had not infringed upon any common law or statutory copyrights held by Arnstein. Porter's victory in the courts was hard-won, however.

Stephen King found himself in similar straits after publication of his book, "*Misery.*" King was named in a copyright infringement case by a

[242] Ibid., 474.

New Jersey woman who complained that King had stolen the work from her in two ways. The woman claimed that King had burglarized her home and taken poems that he used as the basis for *"Misery." The National Law Journal* reported on Nov. 16, 1992, that,[243]

> [t]he same woman, Anne Hiltner, had previously claimed that Mr. King had eavesdropped on her while flying in an airplane over her home. Ms. Hiltner's 1991 copyright infringement and conspiracy suit, filed in federal court in Washington, D.C., named several federal officials as co-defendants, in addition to Mr. King. Among these were, then-Senate Majority leader George Mitchell, Speaker of the House Tom Foley and then-vice chairman of the Senate Intelligence Committee, Sen. William Cohen.

Ms. Hiltner reportedly claimed that the defendants placed her under surveillance in order that she might serve as the "living character" of King's novel. The suit was dismissed.

As noted earlier in this chapter, facts or ideas are not copyrightable, only the style in which they are expressed. An additional gloss was put on this by a 1978 case, *Miller v. Universal City Studios*, which raised the question whether the research effort put into gathering facts is copyrightable.

Pulitzer Prize-winning reporter Gene Miller of the *Miami Herald* collaborated on writing a book with Barbara Mackle about her ordeal in a famous kidnaping incident. Ms. Mackle was held for ransom while literally buried alive in a box with seven days' life-sustaining capacity. She was rescued from the box on the fifth day. Miller worked an estimated 2,500 hours in researching and writing this book.

A Universal Studios executive, William Frye, then offered Miller $15,000 for rights to use the Miller-Mackle account in a television "docudrama." Miller refused, asking for $200,000. At this point, negotiations between Miller and the studio collapsed, but the studio proceeded to produce and air a docudrama titled "*The Longest Night*." This production had obvious similarities to the Miller-Mackle book, and Miller sued for copyright infringement.[244]

The script writer had proceeded to write "*The Longest Night*" on the assumption that his studios had closed a deal with Miller for rights to the book and that he could proceed to write the script on that basis. Even so, Universal City Studios argued that no matter how hard Miller had worked to research the facts in the Mackle kidnaping case, he "may not monopolize those facts because they are historical facts and everyone has

---

[243] Stan Soocher, "His Tales of Horror," *National Law Journal*, Nov. 16, 1992, p. 1.

[244] *Miller v. Universal City Studios, Inc.*, 460 F.Supp. 984, 985–986 (S.D.Fla.1978).

the right to write about them and communicate them to the public." The court disagreed with Universal City Studios' argument, saying:[245]

> To this court it doesn't square with reason or common sense to believe that Gene Miller would have undertaken the research involved in writing of *83 Hours Till Dawn* (or to cite a more famous example, that Truman Capote would have undertaken the research required to write *In Cold Blood*) if the author thought that upon completion of the book a movie producer or television network could simply come along and take the profits of the books and his research from him.

On appeal, however, Universal City Studios won a reversal of the judgment. The U.S. Court of Appeals, 5th Circuit, ruled that Universal should have a new trial " * * * because the case was presented and argued to the jury on a false premise: that the labor of research by an author is protected by copyright." The Court of Appeals added that its decision was difficult to reach because there was " * * * sufficient evidence to support a finding of infringement * * * under correct theories of copyright law." In sum, the Court of Appeals did not believe that *research* itself is copyrightable, only the manner in which it is *presented.* "It is well settled that copyright protection extends only to an author's expression of facts and not to the facts themselves."[246]

DAMAGES

A plaintiff in an infringement suit also may opt to ask for "statutory damages" rather than actual damage and profits:[247] The damage limits were raised with the passage and signing of the Digital Theft Deterrence and Copyright Damages Act of 1999 (the changes are reflected in the text below).

> (1) * * * the copyright owner may elect, at any time before final judgment is rendered, to recover, instead of actual damages and profits, an award of statutory damages for all infringements involved in the action, with respect to any one work, for which any one infringer is liable individually, or for which any two or more infringers are liable jointly and severally, in a sum of not less than $750 or more than $30,000 as the court considers just. * * *
>
> (2) In a case where the copyright owner sustains the burden of proving, and the court finds, that infringement was committed willfully, the court in its discretion may increase the award of statutory damages to a sum of not more than $150,000. In a case where the infringer sustains the burden of proving, and the court finds, that such infringer was not

---

245 Ibid., p. 987 n. 988.

246 *Miller v. Universal City Studios, Inc.*, 650 F.2d 1365, 1368 (5th Cir.1981).

247 17 U.S.C.A. § 504(c)(1), (2).

> aware and had no reason to believe that his acts constituted an infringement of copyright, the court in its discretion may reduce the award of statutory damages to a sum of not less than $200.

If you own a copyright and it is infringed upon, you have an impressive arsenal of remedies or weapons under the 1976 copyright statute. A court may, in its discretion, award full court costs plus a "reasonable attorney's fee" to the winning party in a copyright lawsuit.[248]

For openers, if you know that someone is infringing on your copyright or you can prove is about to do so, a federal court has the power to issue temporary and permanent injunctions "on such terms as it may deem reasonable to prevent or restrain injunctions."[249] Furthermore, this injunction may be served on the suspected copyright infringer anywhere in the United States.[250] That's a form, in other words, of prior restraint at the disposal of an affronted copyright owner.

A copyright owner may also apply to a federal court to get an order to impound "on such terms as it may deem reasonable, * * * all copies or phono records claimed to have been made or used in violation of the copyright owner's exclusive rights."[251] And, if a court orders it as part of a final judgment or decree, the articles made in violation of the copyright owner's exclusive rights may be destroyed or otherwise disposed of.[252]

A copyright infringer, generally speaking, is liable for either of two things: (1) the copyright owner's actual damages and any additional profits of the infringer * * * or (2) statutory damages.[253]

ACTUAL DAMAGES AND PROFITS

Consider the statute's language on "actual damages and profits":[254]

> The copyright owner is entitled to recover the actual damages suffered by him or her as a result of the infringement, and any profits of the infringer that are attributable to the infringement and are not taken into account in computing actual damages. In establishing the infringer's profits, the copyright owner is required to present proof only of the infringer's gross revenue, and the infringer is required to prove his or her deductible expenses and the elements of profit attributable to factors other than the copyrighted work.

---

[248] 17 U.S.C.A. § 505.

[249] 17 U.S.C.A. § 502(a). For an example of an unsuccessful attempt to get an injunction, see *Belushi v. Woodward*, 598 F.Supp. 36 (D.D.C.1984). The case involved widow of actor John Belushi asking that author Bob Woodward and publisher Simon & Schuster be enjoined from publishing book because of allegedly unauthorized use of her copyrighted photo.

[250] 17 U.S.C.A. § 502(b).

[251] 17 U.S.C.A. § 503(a).

[252] 17 U.S.C.A. § 503(b).

[253] 17 U.S.C.A. § 504(a).

[254] 17 U.S.C.A. § 504(b).

The damages are awarded to compensate the copyright owner for losses from the infringement, and profits are awarded to prevent the infringer from unfairly benefitting from a wrongful act.

In seeking to recover profits from a copyright infringer, the burden of proof falls upon the plaintiff to show the gross sales or profits arising from the infringement. The copyright infringer is permitted to deduct any legitimate costs or expenses which he can prove were incurred during publication of the stolen work. The winner of a suit to recover profits under copyright law can receive only the *net profits* resulting from an infringement. As the Supreme Court of the United States has declared, "The infringer is liable for actual, not for possible, gains."[255]

Net profits can run to a great deal of money, especially when the work is a commercial success as a book or motion picture. Edward Sheldon sued Metro-Goldwyn Pictures Corp. and others for infringing on his play, "*Dishonored Lady*" through the production of the Metro-Goldwyn film, "*Letty Lynton*." A federal district court, after an accounting had been ordered, found that Metro-Goldwyn had received net profits of $585,604.37 from their exhibitions of the motion picture.[256]

Mr. Sheldon did not get *all* of Metro-Goldwyn's net profits from the movie, however. On appeal, it was held that Sheldon should not benefit from the profits that motion picture stars had made for the picture by their talent and box-office appeal. Sheldon, after his case had been heard by both a United States Court of Appeals and the Supreme Court of the United States, came out with only 20 percent of the net profits, or roughly $118,000. It still would have been much cheaper for Metro-Goldwyn simply to have bought Sheldon's script. Negotiations with Sheldon for his play had been started by Metro-Goldwyn, but were never completed. The asking price for movie rights to the Sheldon play was evidently to be about $30,000, or slightly more than one-fourth of the amount the courts awarded to the playwright.[257]

Sometimes, in dealing with a major Hollywood film studio, establishing infringement is actually less difficult than forcing the studio to make an honest disclosure of a film's earnings. Although it is not a copyright case, it does show the difficulties in finding out how much an infringer has profited. Humorist Art Buchwald sold a screen *treatment* (a story outline) to Paramount in 1983 for a movie featuring Eddie Murphy. Paramount later made "*Coming to America*" following the general plot line of Buchwald's treatment, but refused to honor its contract to pay Buchwald the $250,000 and 19 percent of the film's net profits specified by the agreement.

---

[255] *Sheldon v. Metro-Goldwyn Pictures Corp.*, 309 U.S. 390, 400–401, 60 S.Ct. 681, 683 (1940); *Golding v. R.K.O. Pictures*, 35 Cal.2d 690, 221 P.2d 95 (1950).

[256] *Sheldon v. Metro-Goldwyn Pictures Corp.*, 26 F.Supp. 134, 136 (S.D.N.Y.1938), 81 F.2d 49 (2d Cir.1936), 106 F.2d 45 (2d Cir.1939).

[257] *Sheldon v. Metro-Goldwyn Pictures Corp.*, 309 U.S. 390, 398, 407, 60 S.Ct. 681, 683, 687 (1940); see Nimmer, op. cit., § 14.03 fn. 30 (1988).

Although Paramount contended that the Buchwald screen treatment was only one of several the studio had used in preparing a shooting script, and that three other writers were claiming similar rights in the picture, the Court found that a substantial number of obvious parallels between Buchwald's treatment and the actual screen play justified a holding that the movie was based primarily upon his work and that the contract had been fulfilled.[258]

However, when Buchwald sought to claim his share of the film's profits, Paramount's accountants maintained that even though the film had grossed more than $125 million in all media sales worldwide, there were no profits to share with him because the studio's account books still showed a net loss for the film of $18 million.[259] The judge was not impressed by studio bookkeeping that appeared to be far more creative than the film itself, and insisted on an independent analysis of the accounting procedures employed by Paramount before making his final award to Buchwald. On the basis of that analysis, the Court awarded Buchwald and his partner a $900,000 judgment.[260]

Frederick Bouchat's infringement case against the Baltimore Ravens Football Club (see above) did not include a claim for actual or statutory damages. Instead, he sued for the profits that he alleged were attributable to the use of his logo. That totaled $10 million, he argued.

While the jury found that the Ravens did, in fact, use his logo,[261] infringing his copyright. The damages portion of the case left Bouchat with only the profits from the sale of t-shirts, caps, souvenir cups, and other items bearing the Flying B logo. The Ravens presented evidence that people bought the t-shirts, caps, cups and the other items with the logo, not because of the logo, but because of people's interest in football and the team.[262]

CRIMINAL PENALTIES

There can be *criminal* penalties for copyright infringement. Changes in the Copyright Act upped the ante where phono record or movie pirates are concerned. Sec. 506 provides:[263]

> *(a) Criminal Infringement.—Any person who infringes a copyright willfully either—*

---

[258] *Buchwald v. Paramount Pictures Corp.* (Cal.1990).

[259] "Par to Buchwald; We're $18-Mil in Hole," *Variety*, February 28, 1990, p. 5.

[260] Dan Cox, "Paramount Finally Files Buchwald Appeal," *Variety*, April 11, 1994, p. 32.

[261] It turned out that Bouchat's Ravens logo had been used by mistake. Someone thought that the drawing had been created for the team. *Bouchat v. Baltimore Ravens Football Club, Inc.*, 346 F.3d 514, 517 (4th Cir. 2003).

[262] Ibid. at 526.

[263] 17 U.S.C.A. § 506. See also § 507, which orders a three-year statute of limitations for both criminal prosecutions and civil proceedings under the Copyright Statute.

> (1) *for purposes of commercial advantage or private financial gain, or*
>
> (2) *by the reproduction or distribution, including by electronic means, during any 180-day period, of 1 or more copies or phonorecords of 1 or more copyrighted works, which have a total retail value of more than $1,000, shall be punished as provided under section 2319 of title 18, United States Code.*

U.S.C. 18 § 2319 provides for prison terms of up to five years for persons who infringe for commercial advantage or private financial gain under Sec. 506(a)(1) above. If someone is convicted for a second offense under the section the penalty goes up to 10 years in prison.

A person convicted under Sec. 506(a)(2) faces a maximum prison term of three years and fine. The maximum prison sentence is six years for a subsequent conviction. And fines of up to $2,500 await any person who, "with fraudulent intent," places on any article a notice of copyright that is known to be false. Similar fines may be levied against individuals who fraudulently remove a copyright notice, or who knowingly make misstatements in copyright applications or related written statements.[264]

The term "for private financial gain" from Sec. 506(a)(1) includes the receipt of copyrighted work so persons who exchange pirated software or music are at risk under this section of the Copyright Act. The change was made to deal with persons who would copy and distribute works without asking for anything in return. These infringers, in many cases acting on a philosophy that works should be free to all users, were difficult to deal with under the old section because they weren't infringing to make money. The exchange provision and the provision triggering prosecution because of the value of the works copied were tailored to address that.

Digital infringement, either on individual computers or on the Internet has become a risky business with amendments to the No Electronic Theft (NET) Act of 1997. Under the Act, infringements of digital works is a federal crime. Willful reproductions of digital works can result in fine and prison term. If the copied material is valued at $2,500 or more, a convicted copier can be fined up to $250,000 and sentenced to as many as five years in prison. Software piracy is estimated to cost the software industry an estimated $13 billion a year in losses.[265]

The first conviction under the NET came at the end of 1999 with the guilty plea of University of Oregon senior Jeffrey Levy. Levy had posted an estimated $70,000 worth of movies, music and software on his Web site. Although he didn't get paid for making the copyrighted works available to the people who visited his site, he still violated the Act

[264] 17 U.S.C.A. § 506(c), (d) and (e).

[265] Darry Van Duch, "Eyes on 'Pirates' trial in Chicago," *The National Law Journal*, March 26, 2001, B-1.

because of the value of the works copied. Levy was given probation and his Internet use subject to monitoring by law enforcement agencies.

A student at Ohio University was charged with violating the NET Act for making copies of Nintendo games and putting them on his Web site. The U.S. Attorney's office in Seattle, where Nintendo has its American headquarters said that Ryan Carey fell under the statute because of the value and number of copies he posted.[266]

The NET Act isn't just for college students with computers. Federal prosecutors went after a group of 17 people, including former employees of Microsoft and Intel, who called themselves Pirates with Attitude. The group, according to published reports, believes that software in Cyberspace should be free. The group is blamed for the free distribution of a pre-release version of Microsoft Windows 2000 and other software. Prosecutors called the group the "oldest and most sophisticated" band of software pirates ever to operate on the Internet.[267]

88. COPYRIGHT, UNFAIR COMPETITION AND THE NEWS

The news element of a story is not subject to copyright, although the style in which an individual story is written may be protected from infringement. Reporters, in short, should do their own reporting.

Any unauthorized and unfair use of a copyrighted news story constitutes an infringement which will support either lawsuits for damages or an action in equity to get an injunction against further publication. Although a news story—or even an entire issue of a newspaper—may be copyrighted, the *news element* in a newspaper story is not subject to copyright. News is *publici juris*—the history of the day—as was well said by Justice Mahlon Pitney in the important 1918 case of *International News Service v. Associated Press*. Justice Pitney wrote:[268]

> A News article, as a literary production, is the subject of copyright. But the news element—the information respecting current events in the literary production, is not the creation of the writer, but is a report of matters that ordinarily are publici juris; it is the history of the day. It is not to be supposed that the framers of the Constitution, when they empowered Congress to promote the progress of science and useful arts, by securing for limited times to authors and inventors the exclusive rights to their respective writings and discoveries (Const. Art. 1, § 8, par. 8), intended to confer upon one who might happen to be first to

[266] "Ohio U Student Charged with Online Nintendo Piracy," MMWire, *Warren Communications News, Inc.*, March 7, 2001.

[267] Darry Van Duch, "Eyes on 'Pirates' trial in Chicago," *The National Law Journal*, March 26, 2001, B–1.

[268] *INS v. AP*, 248 U.S. 215, 234, 39 S.Ct. 68, 71 (1918).

report an historic event the exclusive right for any period to spread the knowledge of it.

The Associated Press had complained of news pirating by a rival news-gathering agency, International News Service. The Supreme Court upheld an injunction granted to the Associated Press against the appropriation, by INS, of non-copyrighted AP stories while the news was still fresh enough to be saleable. This was true even though in that era, and until the Copyright Act of 1976, material was not copyrighted unless it carried the © symbol and notice at the time of publication. "The peculiar value of news," Justice Pitney declared, "is in the spreading of it while it is fresh; and it is evident that a valuable property interest in the news, as news, cannot be maintained by keeping it secret."

Justice Pitney also denounced the taking, by INS, of AP stories, either by quoting or paraphrasing. Justice Pitney wrote that INS, "in appropriating * * * news and selling it as its own is endeavoring to reap where it has not sown, and by disposing of it to newspapers that are competitors * * * of AP members is appropriating to itself the harvest of those who have sown."[269]

What, then, can a newspaper or other communications medium do when it has been "beaten" to a story by its competition? It must be emphasized that the historic case of *International News Service v. Associated Press* did *not* say that the "beaten" news medium must sit idly by. "Pirating" news, of course, is to be avoided: pirating has been defined as "the bodily appropriation of a statement of fact or a news article, with or without rewriting, but without independent investigation or expense."[270]

However, first-published news items may be used as "tips." When one newspaper discovers an event, such as the arrest of a kidnaper, its particular news presentation of the facts may be protected by copyright. Even so, such a first story may serve as a tip for other newspapers or press associations. After the first edition by the copyrighting news organization, other organizations may independently investigate and present their own stories about the arrest of the kidnaper. In such a case, the time element between the appearance of the first edition of the copyrighting newspaper and the appearance of a second or third edition by a competing newspaper might be negligible as far as the general public is concerned; only a few hours. If other newspapers or press associations make their own investigations and obtain their own stories, they do not violate copyright.

But, to copy a copyrighted news story—or to copy or paraphrase substantially from the original story—may lead to court action, as shown in the 1921 case of *Chicago Record-Herald Co. v. Tribune Association.* This case arose when the *New York Tribune* copyrighted a special news

---

[269] 248 U.S. 215, 239–240, 39 S.Ct. 68, 71–72 (1918).

[270] *International News Service v. Associated Press,* 248 U.S. 215, 243, 39 S.Ct. 68, 74 (1918).

story on Germany's reliance upon submarines. This story, printed in the *New York Tribune* on Feb. 3, 1917, was offered for sale for exclusive publication in the *Chicago Herald.* The *Herald* declined this opportunity, and the *Chicago Daily News* then purchased the Chicago rights to the story.

With full knowledge that the *Tribune's* story on the German submarine campaign was copyrighted, the *Herald* nevertheless ran a version of the same story featuring identical paragraph after identical paragraph on the morning of Feb. 3.

The *Chicago Daily News* then refused to publish the story or to pay the *New York Tribune* for it. The *Daily News,* having agreed to purchase an exclusive story, had the right to refuse a story already published in its market. The publishers of the *New York Tribune* successfully sued the *Chicago Herald* for infringement.

The judge declared that the *New York Tribune's* original story "involves authorship and literary quality and style, apart from the bare recital of the facts or statement of news." So, although facts are not copyrightable, the style in which they are expressed is protected by law.

As noted in *International News Service v. Associated Press* (1918), the AP won its case despite the fact that the news stories it telegraphed to its members were not copyrighted. There, the Supreme Court of the United States held that the AP had a "quasi property" right in the news stories it produced, even after their publication. Once the Supreme Court found that such a "quasi property" right existed, it then declared that appropriation of such stories by INS amounted to unfair competition and could be stopped by a court-issued injunction against INS.[271]

A newspaper—the (Pottstown, Pennsylvania) *Mercury*—won an unfair competition suit against a Pottstown radio station, WPAZ, getting an injunction which prevented WPAZ, "from any further appropriation of the newspaper's local news without its permission or authorization."[272] The broadcaster was charged with taking the news from the day's newspaper and turning it into its own newscast.

Adopting the rather cynical view that news coverage was simply a function newspapers and broadcasters employed to attract advertisers, the Pennsylvania Supreme Court held that the radio station had unfairly competed with the *Mercury* for these advertisers through its unauthorized taking of the newspaper's new stories. The court said:[273]

> * * * for the purpose of an action of unfair competition the specialized treatment of news items as a service the newspaper provides for advertisers gives the News Company [publishers of

---

[271] See reference to this case at footnote 268, above. The case of *International News Service v. Associated Press* was cited as important by the more recent case of *Pottstown Daily News Pub. Co. v. Pottstown Broadcasting Co.,* 411 Pa. 383, 192 A.2d 657, 662 (1963).

[272] Ibid.

[273] 411 Pa. 383, 192 A.2d 657, 663–664 (1963).

> the Pottstown *Mercury*] a limited property right which the law will guard and protect against wrongful invasion by a competitor * * *

The limited property right in news is to some extent waived by member organizations of the Associated Press. All AP members are entitled to all *spontaneous* news from areas served by other AP member newspapers or broadcasting stations. Membership in the Associated Press includes agreement to follow this condition as stated in Article VII of the AP bylaws:

> Sec. 3. Each member shall promptly furnish to the [AP] Corporation all the news of such member's district, the area of which shall be determined by the Board of Directors. No news furnished to the Corporation by a member shall be furnished by the Corporation to any other member within such member's district.
>
> Sec. 4. The news which a member shall furnish to the Corporation shall be all news that is spontaneous in origin, but shall not include news that is not spontaneous in its origin, or which has originated through deliberate and individual enterprise on the part of such member.

AP member newspapers or broadcasting stations are expected to furnish spontaneous or "spot" news stories to the Associated Press for dissemination to other members throughout the nation. However, Sec. 3 of the AP By-Laws (above) will protect the news medium originating such a story within its district.

Even if a newspaper copyrights a spot news story, other AP members could use the story despite the copyright. By signing the AP By-Laws, the originating newspaper has given its consent in advance for all AP members to use news stories of *spontaneous* origin. On the other hand, if a newspaper copyrights a story based on that newspaper's individual enterprise and initiative, the other AP members could not use the story without permission from the copyrighting newspaper.

INS-STYLE APPROPRIATION DEAD BUT NOT

In *Barclays Capital, Inc. v. TheFlyOnTheWall.com, Inc.*,[274] the 2nd Circuit Court of Appeals took up the question of whether copyright law would still protect the "hot news" collected and published by financial firms from being taken and reproduced on the Internet by a news aggregator.

Barclays and the other plaintiffs are multinational financial firms providing services to investors and other business customers. They offer investment information as part of their services to their clients. A

---

[274] *Barclays Capital, et.al. v. TheFlyOnTheWall.com, Inc.*, 650 F.3d 876 (2d Cir. 2011).

significant part of the investment information consists of reports on companies that are publicly traded.[275]

> The reports, which vary in format, range from a single page to hundreds of pages in length. They typically include data analysis, qualitative discussion, and the recommendation. In the process of producing and disseminating the reports, the Firms employ hundreds of research analysts and spend hundreds of millions of dollars annually.

The firms publish[276] " 'Recommendations,' a term which the district court defined as 'actionable reports,' i.e., Firm research reports' likely to spur any investor into making an immediate trading decision."

Investors who do not have accounts with the plaintiffs are still interested in the reports and recommendations. Those investors will pay for early access to the information. As a result, several aggregators have gone into the business of gathering and selling access to the plaintiffs' reports and recommendations, TheFlyOnTheWall is one such company.[277]

> The cornerstone of Fly's offerings is its online newsfeed, which it continually updates between 5:00 a.m. and 7:00 p.m. during days on which the New York Stock Exchange is open. The newsfeed typically streams more than 600 headlines a day in ten different categories * * * One such category is recommendations." There, Fly posts the recommendations (but not the underlying research reports or supporting analysis) produced by sixty-five investment firms' analysts, including those at the plaintiff Firms. A typical Recommendation headline from 2009, for example, reads "EQIX: Equinox initiated with a Buy at BofA/Merrill. Target $110."

The Recommendations are valuable to investors who have early access to them. That information gives them an advantage over other investors who do not get the plaintiffs' Recommendations.[278]

> The Firms' ability to generate revenue from the reports and Recommendations therefore directly relates to the informational advantage they can provide to their clients. This in turn is related to the Firms' ability to control the distribution of the reports and Recommendations so that the Firms' clients have access to and can take action on the reports and Recommendations before the general public can.

But if investors can get the same information by paying significantly less to an aggregator, such as TheFlyOnTheWall, they are less likely to become or remain a client of the plaintiffs. Barclays and its co-plaintiffs

---

[275] Ibid. at 880–881.

[276] Ibid. at 881.

[277] Ibid. at 883.

[278] Ibid.

complained to TheFlyOnTheWall about its practices and warned about lawsuits but TheFlyOnTheWall continued its practices.

Barclays and the other plaintiffs then filed a lawsuit claiming that TheFlyOnTheWall infringed by publishing excerpts of multiple research reports and engaged in "hot news" misappropriation through its continuing Internet publication of their Recommendations. The federal district court ruled for Barclays on the copyright infringement claim and entered an order against TheFlyOnTheWall requiring it to wait from 30 minutes to two hours.

The 2nd Circuit reversed and Judge Robert Sack's analysis and discussion made clear that *INS* was no longer valid.[279]

> INS itself is no longer good law. Purporting to establish a principal of federal common law, the law established by INS was abolished by *Erie Railroad Co. v. Tompkins*, 304 U.S. 64, 58 S.Ct. 817, 82 L.Ed. 1188 (1938), which largely abandoned federal common law.

Preemption means that federal law has replaced earlier state or common law. As *INS* was based on a common law theory, its rationale no longer applied, having been superseded by federal statute, the 1976 Copyright Act.[280]

Still, the "Ghost of INS" remains. In a prior 2nd Circuit case involving a claim by the NBA[281] that Motorola was appropriating real-time information about its games for a pager service, a different panel concluded that *INS* had in some form survived.

In the *NBA* case, the plaintiffs argued that Motorola's live pager information service both infringed the NBA's copyright on its games and also amounted to appropriation as the service sent out live updates as the game was played. The opinion, written by Judge Ralph Winger, disposed of the copyright claim concluding that the information about the game was not copyrightable even if the live broadcast was. Copyright law protects the broadcast but not the underlying event, Judge Winter wrote.

Judge Winter then turned to the appropriation claim based on *INS*.[282]

> Courts are generally agreed that some form of such a claim survives preemption. *Financial Information, Inc. v. Moody's Investors Service, Inc.*, 808 F.2d 204, 208 (2d Cir.1986), cert. denied, 484 U.S. 820, 108 S.Ct. 79, 98 L.Ed.2d 42 (1987) ("FII").

---

[279] Ibid. at 894.

[280] The 1976 amendments also contained provisions preempting state law claims that enforced rights "equivalent" to exclusive copyright protections when the work to which the state claim was being applied fell within the area of copyright protection. See 17 U.S.C. § 301. *National Basketball Association v. Motorola*, 105 F.3d 841, 843 (2d Cir. 1997).

[281] *National Basketball Association v. Motorola*, 105 F.3d 841 (2d Cir. 1997).

[282] Ibid. at 850.

This conclusion is based in part on the legislative history of the 1976 amendments. The House Report stated:

> "Misappropriation" is not necessarily synonymous with copyright infringement, and thus a cause of action labeled as "misappropriation" is not preempted if it is in fact based neither on a right within the general scope of copyright as specified by sec. 106 nor on a right equivalent thereto. For example, state law should have the flexibility to afford a remedy (under traditional principles of equity) against a consistent pattern of unauthorized appropriation by a competitor of the facts (i.e., not the literary expression) constituting "hot" news, whether in the traditional mold of *International News Service v. Associated Press*, 248 U.S. 215 [39 S.Ct. 68, 63 L.Ed. 211] (1918), or in the newer form of data updates from scientific, business, or financial data bases.

Judge Winter turned to the general principle of copyright, that the right is granted to benefit the public. If, as in *INS*, a competitor could make use of the news that the AP collected, the AP would stop collecting. The public would lose because the AP would not be collecting news, including "hot news" and the competitor would have nothing to appropriate as its own. Judge Winter then looked to those factors that made misappropriating still valid.[283]

> We therefore find the extra elements—those in addition to the elements of copyright infringement—that allow a "hotnews" claim to survive preemption are: (i) the time-sensitive value of factual information, (ii) the free-riding by a defendant, and (iii) the threat to the very existence of the product or service provided by the plaintiff.

Motorola was not free-riding, Judge Winter concluded. It had its own staff to collect live information about the games, it operated its own network and created its own reports. There was no threat to the NBA's existence because no one considered the Motorola service a substitute or the equivalent of going to a game. In fact, the NBA was developing its own live update service. The NBA had not shown the necessary elements for a misappropriation claim.

Judge Sack, in the *Barclays* case, found similar efforts on the part of FlyOnTheWall. It had a staff of 28 collecting information, including the plaintiffs' recommendations, summarizing them and producing a newsfeed. All of those showed that FlyOnTheWall was not free-riding. Because FlyOnTheWall had not appealed the copyright infringement claim, that decision remained.

ROY EXPORT COMPANY V. CBS

Eagerness to present the news as effectively as possible in pressure situations may sometimes lead to disregard of ownership rights. Evident

---

283 Ibid. at 853.

lack of concern about such rights cost the Columbia Broadcasting System $717,000[284] in copyright and unfair competition damages for missteps making a documentary on the occasion of the death of film legend Charlie Chaplin.

In 1977, CBS broadcast a film biography of Chaplin, including film clips from six Chaplin-motion pictures. Exclusive rights in those films were held by several parties, including the first-named plaintiff in this case, *Roy Export Company Establishment of Vaduz, Liechtenstein*.[285]

The events leading to this lawsuit are traceable to 1972, when the Academy of Motion Picture Arts and Sciences (AMPAS) arranged to have a film tribute made from highlights of Chaplin's films. This tribute was broadcast by NBC-TV in connection with an appearance by Chaplin at the 1972 Academy Awards ceremonies. It was understood that excerpts compiled in that tribute were to be used only on that one occasion.[286]

In 1973, CBS started work on a retrospective of Chaplin's life, to be used as a broadcast obituary when Chaplin died. CBS made repeated requests for permission to use excerpts from Chaplin's films, but was rebuffed. CBS was told that the copyright owners were involved in producing their own film biography of Chaplin titled "*The Gentleman Tramp*." That production used some of the same footage used in the Academy Awards show compilation, but did not use that compilation itself. CBS, meanwhile, made a "rough cut" of a Chaplin obituary/ biography. The network was offered a chance to purchase rights to show "*The Gentleman Tramp*" in 1976 and 1977, but did not do so.

Chaplin died on Christmas day, 1977. CBS had its "rough cut" biography ready to use, but instead used a copy of the 1972 Academy Award show compilation which CBS had obtained from NBC. CBS put together a new biography, depending heavily "on what CBS knew to be copyrighted material." This hastily assembled new biography was broadcast on Dec. 26, 1977.[287]

Roy Export Company and other copyright owners of Chaplin films then sued CBS for copyright infringement and for unfair competition. The latter claim said the CBS broadcast competed unfairly with the copyright owners' own Chaplin retrospective, "*The Gentleman Tramp*." A

---

[284] *Roy Export Co. Establishment of Vaduz, Liechtenstein v. CBS*, 672 F.2d 1095, 1097 (2d Cir.1982). See footnote 6: "Of the compensatory total, $7,280 was for statutory copyright infringement, $1 was for common-law copyright infringement, and $300,000 was for unfair competition. The punitive damages were divided between the common-law claims: $300,000 for common-law copyright infringement and $110,000 for unfair competition."

[285] *Roy Export Co. Establishment of Vaduz, Liechtenstein v. CBS*, 672 F.2d 1095 (2d Cir.1982), cert. denied 459 U.S. 826, 103 S.Ct. 60 (1982). This case was complicated, Circuit Judge Newman said, by troublesome questions coming from pre-1978 common law protection for intellectual property, plus challenges to statutory copyrights, "on the ground that the work lost its common copyright prior to January 1, 1978, entered the public domain, and therefore was not eligible for statutory copyright." Judge Newman cited M. Nimmer, *Nimmer on Copyright*, Sec. 4.01 [B].

[286] Ibid. at 1098.

[287] Ibid.

jury trial in a U.S. district court found CBS liable to the plaintiffs for $307,281 compensatory and $410,000 punitive damages.

In its appeal, CBS asserted that the First Amendment provides a general privilege to report newsworthy events such as Chaplin's death, and that this privilege shielded the network from liability. CBS claimed that the main reason for Chaplin's fame was his films, and that it would be meaningless to try to provide a full account of his life without making use of his films. Circuit Judge Newman summed up the network's First Amendment argument:[288]

> In CBS's view, the 1972 Academy Awards ceremony, at which the Compilation received its single public showing, was an "irreducible single news event" to which the showing of the Compilation was integral. The significance of the ceremony, CBS contends, was not simply that Chaplin appeared after a twenty-year exile provoked by Senator [Joseph] McCarthy's investigations, but that a collection of his work was shown, thereby bringing home to the American people both what they had been deprived of by McCarthyism and how ludicrous had been the attempt to find subversion and political innuendo in Chaplin's films. CBS concludes that the plaintiff's claims for infringement of the copyright in the films and the compilation must give way to an asserted First Amendment news-reporting privilege.

The Court of Appeals found CBS's First Amendment arguments "unpersuasive," resting on a theory that someday, some way, there might be an inseparability of news value and copyrighted work to the extent that copyright would have to yield. Judge Newman wrote, however: "No Circuit that has considered the question * * * has ever held that the First Amendment provides a privilege in the copyright field distinct from the accommodation embodied in the 'fair use' doctrine." And in a footnote he added,[289]

> Fair use balances the public interest in the free flow of ideas and information with the copyright holder's interest in exclusive proprietary control of his work. It permits use of the copyrighted matter "in a reasonable manner without [the copyright owner's] consent, notwithstanding the monopoly granted to the owner." *Rosemont Enterprises, Inc. v. Random House, Inc.*, 366 F.2d 303 (2d Cir.1966), cert. denied 385 U.S. 1009, 87 S.Ct. 714 * * * (1967) * * * .

THE ROY EXPORT CASE AND UNFAIR COMPETITION

CBS also argued that the plaintiffs could not maintain a claim that the network's Dec. 26, 1977, broadcast unfairly competed with the

[288] Ibid. at 1099.

[289] Ibid. at 1099.

plaintiffs' rights in "*The Gentleman Tramp.*" CBS asserted the unfair competition claim rested on "misappropriation" of films under New York state law, " * * * and that a state law claim based on misappropriation of federally copyrighted materials is pre-empted * * * "[290] The Court of Appeals replied:

> An unfair competition claim involving misappropriation usually concerns the taking and use of the plaintiff's property to compete against the plaintiff's use of the same property, e.g. *International News Service v. Associated Press* * * * [248 U.S. 215, 39 S.Ct. 68 (1918)]. By contrast, in this case the Compilation was taken and used to compete unfairly with a different property, "*The Gentleman Tramp.*" Despite the unusual facts, we are satisfied that the plaintiffs have established an unfair competition tort under New York law.
>
> * * *
>
> CBS unquestionably appropriated the "skill, expenditures and labor" of the plaintiffs to its own commercial advantage. Its actions, in apparent violation of its own and the industry's guidelines, were arguably a form of "commercial immorality." We are confident that the New York courts would call that conduct unfair competition.

The Court of Appeals ruled that the damages of more than $700,000 against CBS should stand, including the punitive damage awards totaling $410,000. Judge Newman wrote, "The deterrent potential of an award of $410,000 must be measured by its likely effect on a national television network with 1977 earnings of some $217,000,000 * * * ".[291]

LINKING ISSUES RAISED IN GATEHOUSE MEDIA V. NEW YORK TIMES CO. (SETTLED 2009)

"News aggregators"—persons or organizations collecting and re-disseminating news collected by others—raise many copyright questions. In *GateHouse Media v. New York Times Co.*, GateHouse sued on Dec. 22, 2008 in a Massachusetts federal court, claiming copyright infringement by the *Times*-owned *Boston Globe* and the Boston.com website. Thorny copyright issues raised were postponed when the parties settled on the eve of the trial in January, 2009. The *Times* agreed to stop its practice, removing headlines and text excerpts from GateHouse newspapers' stories posted earlier on Boston.com.[292]

Under attack was a basic business model of Web news and aggregators, up to and including the massive Google.com. If what

[290] Ibid. at 1104–1105.

[291] Ibid. at 1107.

[292] Wendy Davis, "GateHouse, New York Times, Co. Settle Copyright Dispute," *Online Media Daily*, Jan. 27, 2009, https://www.mediapost.com/publications/article/98929/gatehouse-new-york-times-co-settle-copyright-sui.html.

Boston.com was doing was not defensible as fair use—and attorney Sarah Bird argues that it was—then a common web-linking practice could be in serious and labyrinthine legal trouble. "If this practice is not fair use and the *New York Times* actually is in the wrong, then the Internet, as we know it, could drastically change."[293]

Boston.com was copying headlines verbatim, repeating the first sentence from the articles, then adding links to full articles in newspapers across Massachusetts published by GateHouse Media, Inc. The GateHouse group, headquartered in Fairport, New York, owns 125 papers across Massachusetts, including dailies, paid weeklies, and free-circulation weeklies. The question of whether or not the *Times*-owned media properties were legally wrong in their linking practices now will have to wait for a definitive court decision.

The swift settlement by the New York Times Co. could have occurred because lawsuits are money pits and the *Times*, like all major metropolitan newspapers, is under financial stress during the recession of 2008–2009, and also feels the effects of new technologies siphoning away readers.

SAMPLING AND THE "8-BAR/30-SECOND MYTHS"

Another copyright issue deals with taking of music through sampling. There are any number of myths about copyright and what people freely can take. Some believe that taking 30 seconds of any song is permitted while other believe that eight bars falls within the rights of the public. There is no such rule and court rulings make clear that even small snippets of songs can be protectable.

In one of the first cases to deal with sampling, a federal district court in New York declared quite simply, "Thou shalt not steal." *In Grand Upright Music v. Warner Brothers Records*,[294] the court was faced with a case involving the taking of three words from a copyrighted song. The case was relatively simple. Rap artist Biz Markie was recording a song for Cold Chillin' Records called "*Alone Again.*" That song took portions of the previously recorded and copyrighted song "*Alone Again Naturally*," written by Gilbert O'Sullivan. After the song was recorded, but before it was released, Markie and his recording company sought permission to use the song. They were denied but decided to go ahead with the release, as part of the album "*I Need a Haircut.*"

The copyright holders learned of the action and went to federal court to prevent the release of the album. The court agreed. The portion taken from the O'Sullivan song were three words and a portion of the music. That was enough to constitute unlawful use of the recording. The court focused on the record company's attempt to sell the record without the required license for use of the song. In the analysis, the court is critical

---

[293] Ibid.

[294] In *Grand Upright Music v. Warner Brothers Records*, 780 F.Supp. 182 (S.D.N.Y.1991).

of the record company's conduct and motivation. "From all the evidence produced at the hearing, it is clear that the defendants knew that they were violating the plaintiff's rights as well as the rights of others. Their only aim was to sell thousands upon thousands of records. This callous disregard for the law and for the rights of others requires not only the preliminary injunction sought by the plaintiff but also sterner measures."[295]

In a later case, *Jarvis v. A & M Records*,[296] a federal district court looked to the use of "ooh," "moves," and "free your body" in terms of copyright infringement. In that case, the defendants had sampled portions of a previous work written by Boyd Jarvis. A significant issue was whether the taking of the words and phrase would constitute infringement. Other cases have held that where copying of material that does not rise to the level of copyrightability, there is no infringement. The material must be sufficiently original and novel to get copyright protection. If it is not, there is no infringement. In this case, the court held that the use of the words and music riff were significant.

> "There is no question that the combined phrase 'ooh ooh ooh ooh * * * move * * * free your body' is an expression of an idea that was copyrightable. Moreover, the keyboard line that was copied represents a distinctive melody/rhythm that sets it far apart from the ordinary cliched phrases held not copyrightable. It, too, is an idea, and is capable of being infringed."[297]

The conclusion then is that multimedia or song artists must think twice about "borrowing" bits and pieces of existing works. It may be that the material taken will support an infringement claim. It is mostly a matter of common sense. If a piece is taken because it appeals to the user, its theft shows its distinctiveness and value to the infringer.

COPYRIGHT TURNABOUT: CORPORATIONS TAKE FROM CREATIVE INDIVIDUALS

Ordinary people who posted photographs on the Web are finding that their works are appearing in ads and on sites run by major corporations. In one case, Tracey Gaughran-Perez, a Baltimore woman, saw a picture of her pet pug, dressed in a Santa outfit, in a holiday promo from Fox Sports.[298]

> "It's not like the picture was some golden chalice of Internet wonder. It's a picture of a stupid dog," says the Baltimore mom. "But it's *my* dog and it's my photo!"

---

[295] Ibid. at 185.

[296] *Jarvis v. A & M Records*, 827 F.Supp. 282 (D.N.J.1993).

[297] Ibid. at 292.

[298] Monica Hesse, "Hey, Isn't That . . . People Are Doing Double-Takes, And Taking Action, As Web Snapshots Are Nabbed for Commercial Uses," *Washington Post*, January 9, 2008.

> Supreme irony: "Every commercial break there would be a warning from Fox saying, 'This telecast may not be reproduced,'" she says. "I guess copyright pertains only to them."

A Dallas teen found her picture, taken at a church carwash, in a national campaign for Virgin Mobile in Australia. The teen and a friend, who took the picture, have filed suit against Virgin. Web sites and advertisers, looking for "authentic" people and scenes have used copyrighted materials without getting permissions and more home photographers are turning to the courts to hold the infringers accountable.

89. THE DEFENSE OF FAIR USE

The fair use doctrine—invented by courts to allow some use of others' works—was made explicit by the Copyright Act of 1976. Major cases—such as Sony and The Nation magazine—continue to add to the definition of fair use in a piecemeal fashion.

The copyright law phrase "fair use" made a good deal of news since the mid-1980s. Its growth in importance is quite remarkable, stemming as it does from judicial wriggling many years ago. Its growth may be understood as being fueled, in a major way, by onrushing technological changes. Recent examples of important fair use cases decided by the Supreme Court—and which are taken up later in this section—are *Sony Corporation of America v. Universal City Studios, Inc.*,[299] and *Harper & Row, Publishers, Inc. v. Nation Enterprises.*[300]

The old 1909 copyright statute gave each copyright holder an exclusive right to "print, reprint, publish, copy and vend the copyrighted * * * ." As stated in that Act, it was an *absolute* right; the wording was put in terms so absolute that even pencil-and-paper copying was a violation of the U.S. Copyright Act.[301] Because the 1909 statute's terms were so stringent, if enforced to the letter, it could have prevented anyone except the copyright holder from making any copy of any copyrighted work.

Such a statute was clearly against public policy favoring dissemination of information and knowledge and was plainly unenforceable. As a result, courts responded by developing the doctrine called "fair use."

---

[299] *Sony Corporation of America v. Universal City Studios, Inc.*, 464 U.S. 417, 104 S.Ct. 774 (1984).

[300] *Harper & Row, Publishers, Inc. v. Nation Enterprises*, 471 U.S. 539, 105 S.Ct. 2218 (1985).

[301] See 17 U.S.C.A. § 10 of the statute which preceded the Copyright Statute of 1976: Verner W. Clapp, "Library Photocopying and Copyright: Recent Developments," *Law Library Journal* 55:1 (Feb., 1962) p. 12.

American courts assumed—in creating a judge-made exception to the absolute language of the 1909 copyright statute—that "the law implies the consent of the copyright owner to a fair use of his publication for the advancement of science or art."[302] The fair use doctrine, although a rather elastic yardstick, was a needed improvement. The 1976 copyright statute has distilled the old common law copyright doctrine into some statutory guidelines. Factors to be considered by courts in determining whether the use made of a work in any particular case is a fair use include:[303]

(1) the purpose and character of the use, including whether such use is of a commercial nature or is for nonprofit educational purposes;

(2) the nature of the copyrighted work;

(3) the amount and substantiality of the portion used in relation to the copyrighted work as a whole; and

(4) the effect of the use upon the potential market for or value of the copyrighted work.

What, then, is fair use? In 1964, one expert asserted that fair use of someone's copyrightable materials exists "somewhere in the hinterlands between the broad avenue of independent creation and the jungle of unmitigated plagiarism."[304] No easy or automatic formula can be presented which will draw a safe line between fair use and infringement. Fifty words taken from a magazine article might be held to be fair use, while taking one line from a short poem might be labeled infringement by a court. The House of Representatives Committee on the Judiciary said this in its report on the 1976 copyright statute:[305]

General intention behind the provision

> The statement of the fair use doctrine in section 107 offers some guidance to users in determining when the principles of the doctrine apply. However, the endless variety of situations and combinations of circumstances that can rise in particular cases precludes the formulation of exact rules in the statute. The bill endorses the purpose and general scope of the judicial doctrine of fair use, but there is no disposition to freeze the doctrine in the statute, especially during a period of rapid technological change. Beyond a very broad statutory explanation of what fair use is and some of the criteria applicable to it, the courts must be free to adapt the doctrine to particular situations on a case-by-case basis. Section 107 is intended to restate the present

---

[302] Wittenberg, op. cit., p. 148, offers a good non-technical description of fair use before it was expanded in 1967.

[303] 17 U.S.C.A. § 107.

[304] Arthur N. Bishop, "Fair Use of Copyrighted Books," *Houston Law Review*, 2:2 (Fall, 1964) at p. 207.

[305] H.R. Report No. 94–1476, discussing the fair use provisions of 17 U.S.C.A. § 107.

judicial doctrine of fair use, not to change, narrow, or enlarge it in any way.

Generally speaking, courts have been quite lenient with quotations used in scholarly works or critical reviews. However, courts have been less friendly toward use of copyrighted materials for commercial purposes, or in works which compete with the original copyrighted piece.[306] The problems surrounding the phrase "fair use" have often arisen in connection with scientific, legal, or scholarly materials. With such works, it is to be expected that there will be similar treatment given to similar subject matters.[307] A crucial question, obviously, is whether the writer makes use of an earlier writer's work without doing substantial independent work.

Wholesale copying is *not* fair use.[308] Even if a writer had no intention of making unfair use of someone else's work, that writer still could be found liable for copyright infringement.[309] The idea of independent investigation is of great importance here. Copyrighted materials may be used as a *guide* for the purpose of gathering information, provided that the researcher then performs an original investigation and expresses the results of such work in the researcher's own language.[310]

FAIR USE AND PUBLIC INTEREST

Although many earlier cases expressed a narrow, restrictive view of the doctrine of fair use, some important decisions since the mid-1960s have emphasized the idea of *public* interest. This changed approach is of great importance to journalists and scholars, for where there are matters which are newsworthy or otherwise of interest to the public, courts will consider such factors in determining whether a fair use was made of copyrighted materials.

A key case here is the 1967 decision known as *Rosemont Enterprises, Inc. v. Random House, Inc. and John Keats*. This case arose because Howard Hughes, a giant in America's aviation, oil and motion picture industries had a passionate desire to remain anonymously out of the public eye. A brief chronology will illustrate how this copyright infringement action came about:

- January and February, 1954: Look magazine, owned by Cowles Communications, Inc., published a series of three

---

[306] *Eisenschiml v. Fawcett Publications, Inc.*, 246 F.2d 598 (7th Cir.1957); *Benny v. Loew's Inc.*, 239 F.2d 532 (9th Cir.1956), affirmed 356 U.S. 43, 78 S.Ct. 667 (1958), rehearing denied 356 U.S. 934, 78 S.Ct. 770 (1958); Pilpel and Zavin, op. cit., pp. 160–161.

[307] *Eisenschiml v. Fawcett Publications, Inc.*, 246 F.2d 598 (7th Cir.1957), certiorari denied 355 U.S. 907, 78 S.Ct. 334 (1957).

[308] *Benny v. Loew's Inc.*, 239 F.2d 532 (9th Cir.1956), affirmed 356 U.S. 43, 78 S.Ct. 667 (1958), rehearing denied 356 U.S. 934, 78 S.Ct. 770 (1958).

[309] *Wihtol v. Crow*, 309 F.2d 777 (8th Cir.1962).

[310] *Jeweler's Circular Pub. Co. v. Keystone Pub. Co.*, 281 Fed. 83 (2d Cir.1922), certiorari denied 259 U.S. 581, 42 S.Ct. 464 (1922).

articles by Stanley White, titled "The Howard Hughes Story."

- In 1962, Random House, Inc., hired Thomas Thompson, a journalist employed by Life magazine, to prepare a book-length biography of Hughes. Later, either Hughes or his attorneys learned of the forthcoming Random House book. An attorney employed by Hughes warned Random House that Hughes did not want this biography and "would make trouble if the book was published." Thompson resigned from the project, and Random House then hired John Keats to complete the biography.
- Rosemont Enterprises, Inc., was organized in September, 1965 by Hughes' attorney and by two officers of his wholly-owned Hughes Tool Company.
- On May 20, 1966, Rosemont Enterprises purchased copyrights to the Look articles, advised Random House of this, and five days later brought a copyright infringement suit in New York. Attorneys for Rosemont somehow had gained possession of Random House galley proofs of the Random House biography of Hughes then being published: "*Howard Hughes: a Biography by John Keats*."[311]

Rosemont Enterprises sought an injunction to restrain Random House from selling, publishing, or distributing copies of its biography of Hughes because the book amounted to a prima facie case of copyright infringement. With his five-day-old ownership of the copyrights for the 1954 *Look* magazine articles, Hughes was indeed in a position to "cause trouble" for Random House.

The trial court agreed with the Rosemont Enterprises argument that infringement had occurred, and granted the injunction against Random House, holding up distribution of the book. The trial court rejected Random House's claims of fair use of the *Look* articles, saying that the privilege of fair use was confined to "materials used for purposes of criticism or comment or in scholarly works of scientific or educational value." This district court took the view that if something was published "for commercial purposes"—that is, if it was designed for the popular market—the doctrine of fair use could not be employed to lessen the severity of the copyright law.[312] The district court found that the Hughes biography by Keats was for the popular market and therefore the fair use privilege could not be invoked by Random House.[313]

Circuit Judge Leonard P. Moore, speaking for the Circuit Court of Appeals, took another view. First of all, he noted that the three Look

---

[311] *Rosemont Enterprises, Inc. v. Random House, Inc. and John Keats*, 366 F.2d 303, 304–305 (2d Cir.1966).

[312] Ibid. at 304, citing the trial court, 256 F.Supp. 55 (S.D.N.Y.1966).

[313] Ibid.

articles, taken together, totaled only 13,500 words, or between 35 and 39 pages if published in book form. Keats' 1966 biography on the other hand, had 166,000 words, or 304 pages in book form. Furthermore, Judge Moore stated that the *Look* articles did not purport to be a biography, but were merely accounts of a number of interesting incidents in Hughes' life. Judge Moore declared:[314]

> * * * there can be little doubt that portions of the Look article were copied. Two direct quotations and one eight-line paraphrase were attributed to Stephen White, the author of the articles. A mere reading of the *Look* articles, however, indicates that there is considerable doubt as to whether the copied and paraphrased matter constitutes a material and substantial portion of those articles.
>
> Furthermore, while the mode of expression employed by White is entitled to copyright protection, he could not acquire by copyright a monopoly in the narration of historical events.

In any case, the Keats book should fall within the doctrine of fair use. Quoting a treatise on copyright, Judge Moore stated: "Fair use is a privilege in others than the owner of a copyright to use the copyrighted material in a reasonable manner without his consent, notwithstanding the monopoly granted to the owner * * * ."[315]

Judge Moore demanded that public interest considerations—the public's interest in knowing about prominent and powerful men—be taken into account. He wrote that "public interest should prevail over possible damage to the copyright owner." He complained that the district court's preliminary injunction against Random House deprived the public of the opportunity to become acquainted with the life of a man of extraordinary talents in a number of fields: "A narration of Hughes' initiative, ingenuity, determination and tireless work to achieve his concept of perfection in whatever he did ought to be available to a reading public."[316]

THE ZAPRUDER CASE

A stunning event—the assassination of President John F. Kennedy—gave rise to a copyright case which added luster to the defense of fair use in infringement actions. On Nov. 22, 1963, dress manufacturer Abraham Zapruder of Dallas stationed himself along the route of the President's motorcade, planning to take home movie pictures with his 8 millimeter camera. As the procession came into sight, Zapruder started his camera. Seconds later, the assassin's shots fatally wounded the

---

314 Ibid. at 306–307, certiorari denied 385 U.S. 1009, 87 S.Ct. 714 (1967).

315 Ibid. at 306, quoting Ball, *Copyright and Literary Property*, p. 260 (1944).

316 Ibid., p. 309. And, at p. 311, Judge Moore discussed Rosemont's claim that it was planning to publish a book: "One can only speculate when, if ever, Rosemont will produce Hughes' authorized biography."

President and Zapruder's color film caught the reactions of those in the President's car.

On that same day, Zapruder had his film developed and three color copies were made from the original film. He turned over two copies to the Secret Service, stipulating that these were strictly for governmental use and not to be shown to newspapers or magazines because Zapruder expected to sell the film.

Three days later, Zapruder negotiated a written agreement with Life magazine, which bought the original and all three copies of the film (including the two in possession of the Secret Service). Under that agreement, Zapruder was to be paid $150,000, in yearly installments of $25,000. *Life,* in its Nov. 29, 1963, issue then featured thirty of Zapruder's frames. Life subsequently ran more of the Zapruder pictures. *Life* gave the Commission appointed by President Lyndon B. Johnson to investigate the killing of President Kennedy permission to use the Zapruder film and to reproduce it in the report.[317]

In May of 1967, *Life* registered the entire Zapruder film in the Copyright office as an unpublished "motion picture other than a photo play." Three issues of *Life* magazine in which the Zapruder frames had been published had earlier been registered in the Copyright office as periodicals.[318] This meant that *Life* had a valid copyright in the Zapruder pictures when Bernard Geis Associates sought permission from *Life* magazine to publish the pictures in Josiah Thompson's book, *"Six Seconds in Dallas,"* a serious, thoughtful study of the assassination. The firm of Bernard Geis Associates offered to pay *Life* a royalty equal to the profits from publication of the book in return for permission to use specified Zapruder frames in the book. *Life* refused this offer.

Having failed to secure permission from *Life* to use the Zapruder pictures, author Josiah Thompson and his publisher decided to copy certain frames anyway. They did not reproduce the Zapruder frames photographically, but instead paid an artist $1,550 to make charcoal sketch copies. Thompson's book was then published, relying heavily on the sketches, in mid-November of 1967. Significant parts of 22 copyrighted frames were reproduced in the book.[319]

The court ruled that *Life* had a valid copyright in the Zapruder film, and added that "the so-called 'sketches' in the book are in fact copies of the copyrighted film. That they were done by an 'artist' is of no moment." The Court then quoted copyright expert Melville B. Nimmer:[320]

[317] *Time Inc. v. Bernard Geis Associates,* 293 F.Supp. 130, 131–134 (S.D.N.Y.1968). Although the Commission received permission from *Time,* Inc. to reproduce the photos, the Commission was told that it was expected to give the usual copyright notice. That proviso evidently was disregarded by the Commission.

[318] Ibid at137.

[319] Ibid. at 138–139.

[320] Ibid. at 144, citing *Nimmer on Copyright,* p. 98.

"It is of course, fundamental, that copyright in a work protects against unauthorized copying not only in the original medium in which the work was produced, but also in any other medium as well. Thus copyright in a photograph will preclude unauthorized copying by drawing or in any other form, as well as by photographic reproduction."

The court then ruled that the use of the photos in Thompson's book was a copyright infringement, "unless the use of the copyrighted material in the Book is a 'fair use' outside the limits of copyright protection."[321] This led the court to a consideration of fair use, the issue which is " 'the most troublesome in the whole law of copyright.' "[322] The court then found in favor of Bernard Geis Associates and author Thompson, holding that the utilization of the Zapruder pictures was a "fair use."[323] The court said:

> There is an initial reluctance to find any fair use by defendants because of the conduct of Thompson in making his copies and because of the deliberate appropriation in the Book, in defiance of the copyright owner. Fair use presupposes "good faith and fair dealing." * * * On the other hand, it was not the nighttime activities of Thompson which enabled defendants to reproduce copies of Zapruder frames in the Book. They could have secured such frames from the National Archives, or they could have used the reproductions in the Warren Report [on the assassination of President Kennedy] or in the issues of *Life* itself. Moreover, while hope by a defendant for commercial gain is not a significant factor in this Circuit, there is a strong point for defendants in their offer to surrender to *Life* all profits of Associates from the Book as royalty payment for a license to use the copyrighted Zapruder frames. It is also a fair inference from the facts that defendants acted with the advice of counsel.
>
> In determining the issue of fair use, the balance seems to be in favor of defendants.
>
> There is a public interest in having the fullest information available on the murder of President Kennedy. Thompson did serious work on the subject and has a theory entitled to public consideration. While doubtless the theory could be explained with sketches * * * [not copied from copyrighted pictures] * * * the explanation actually made in the Book with copies [of the Zapruder pictures] is easier to understand. The Book is not bought because it contained the Zapruder pictures; the Book is bought because of the theory of Thompson and its explanation, supported by the Zapruder pictures.

---

[321] Ibid. at 144.

[322] Ibid., quoting from *Dellar v. Samuel Goldwyn, Inc.*, 104 F.2d 661 (2d Cir.1939).

[323] Ibid. at 146.

> There seems little, if any, injury to plaintiff, the copyright owner. There is no competition between plaintiff and defendants. Plaintiff does not sell the Zapruder pictures as such and no market for the copyrighted work appears to be affected. Defendants do not publish a magazine. There are projects for use by plaintiff of the film in the future as a motion picture or in books, but the effect of the use of certain frames in the Book on such projects is speculative. It seems more reasonable to speculate that the Book would, if anything, enhance the value of the copyrighted work; it is difficult to see any decrease in its value.

HARPER & ROW V. NATION ENTERPRISES (REDUX)

The defense of fair use, often helpful in fending off lawsuits for copyright infringement, can be pushed too far. The Supreme Court of the United States served notice in 1985 that the fair use doctrine at times may not prevent liability for unauthorized publishing, even if the material involved is highly newsworthy.

Nation magazine—reputedly America's longest continuously published weekly magazine—in 1979 received an unauthorized copy of former President Gerald R. Ford's memoirs. *Nation* Editor Victor Navasky received the draft from an undisclosed source; this writing was the result of a collaboration between Ford and Trevor Armbrister, a senior editor of *Reader's Digest*.[324]

Nation magazine carried an article developed by Navasky from the unauthorized copy, published in its issue of April 3, 1979, and was just over 2,000 words long. Harper & Row and The Reader's Digest Association, Inc., sued for copyright infringement. At the trial court level, U.S. District Judge Owen found that Navasky knew that the memoirs were soon to be published in book form by Harper & Row and *Reader's Digest*, with some advance publication rights assigned to *Time* magazine. Judge Owen wrote:[325]

> However, believing that the draft contained "a real hot news story" concerning Ford's pardon of President Nixon * * * Navasky spent overnight or perhaps the next twenty-four hour period quoting and paraphrasing from a number of sections of the memoirs. Navasky added no comment of his own. He did not check the material. As he later testified, "I wasn't reporting on the truth or falsity of the account; I was reporting the fact that Ford reported this * * * ." Part of Navasky's rush apparently was caused by the fact that he had to get the draft back to his "source" with some speed.

---

[324] *Harper & Row, Publishers, Inc. and Reader's Digest Ass'n, Inc. v. Nation Enterprises and Nation Associates*, 557 F.Supp. 1067, 1069 (S.D.N.Y.1983).

[325] Ibid.

The *Nation's* article was about 2,250 words long, of which 300 to 400 words were taken from the Ford memoirs manuscript. *Nation's* publication may be said to have skimmed some of the more newsworthy aspects from the manuscript, which Harper & Row and Reader's Digest Association, as copyright holders, were preparing to market. For one thing, the copyright owners had negotiated a pre-publication agreement in which *Time* magazine agreed to pay $25,000 ($12,500 in advance and the balance at the time of publication) for rights to excerpt 7,500 words from Mr. Ford's story of his pardon of President Nixon.

The Supreme Court of the United States said that the *Nation* had timed its publication to "scoop" Time magazine's planned article. As a result of *Nation's* publication, Time canceled its article and refused to pay the remaining $12,500 to Harper & Row and to Reader's Digest Association.[326] Writing for the Court, Justice Sandra Day O'Connor found that *Nation's* publication was not covered by the fair use defense:[327]

> * * * The *Nation* has admitted to lifting verbatim quotes of the author's original language totaling between 300 and 400 words and constituting some 13 percent of the *Nation* article. In using generous verbatim excerpts of Mr. Ford's unpublished manuscript to lend authenticity to its account of the forthcoming memoirs, The *Nation* effectively arrogated to itself the right of first publication, an important marketable subsidiary right. * * * [W]e find that use of the copyrighted manuscript, even stripped to the verbatim quotes conceded by the *Nation* to be copyrightable expression, was not a fair use within the meaning of the Copyright Act.

Justice O'Connor examined the tension between racing to publish news first and copyright:[328]

> In our haste to disseminate news, it should not be forgotten that the Framers intended copyright itself to be the engine of free expression. By establishing a marketable right to the use of one's expression, copyright supplies the economic incentive to create and disseminate ideas.

Further, she held that a writer's public figure status did not create a waiver of the copyright laws:[329]

> In view of the First Amendment protections already embodied in the Copyright Act's distinction between copyrightable expression and uncopyrightable facts and ideas, and the latitude for scholarship and comment traditionally afforded by

---

[326] *Harper & Row Publishers, Inc. v. Nation Enterprises,* 471 U.S. 539, 105 S.Ct. 2218 (1985).

[327] Ibid. at 549, 2225.

[328] Ibid. at 559, 2230.

[329] Ibid. at 559–560, 2230–2231.

fair use, we see no warrant for expanding the doctrine of fair use to create what amounts to a public figure exception to copyright. Whether verbatim copying from a public figure's manuscript in a given case is or is not fair must be judged according to the traditional equities of fair use.

The Court's majority opinion marched through the Copyright Statute's list of four factors to be considered in determining whether a use is "fair":

(1) *The Nature and Purpose of the Use*—Justice O'Connor said the general purpose of the *Nation's* use was "general reporting." Part of this, however, was the *Nation's* stated purpose of scooping the forthcoming hardcover books and the excerpts to be published in *Time* magazine. This, Justice O'Connor said, had " * * * the intended purpose of supplanting the copyright holder's commercially valuable right of first publication."[330]

(2) *Nature of the Copyrighted Work*—Justice O'Connor wrote that President Ford's narrative, "*A Time to Heal*" was "an unpublished historical narrative or autobiography." She said the unpublished nature of the work was critical to considering whether use of it by the *Nation* was fair. Although substantial quotes might qualify as fair use in a review or discussion of a published work, "the author's right to control the first public appearance of his expression weighs against such use of the work before its release."[331]

(3) *Amount and Substantiality of the Copying*—"Stripped of the verbatim quotes, the direct takings from the unpublished manuscript constitute at least 13 percent of the infringing article. * * * the *Nation* article is structured around the quoted excerpts which serve as its dramatic focal points."

(4) *Effect on the Market*—Noting that *Time* magazine had canceled its projected serialization of the Ford memoirs and had refused to pay $12,500, Justice O'Connor said those occurrences were direct results from the infringement. "Rarely will a case of copyright infringement present such clear cut evidence of damage."[332]

Thus a six-member majority concluded that the *Nation's* use of the Ford memoirs was not a fair use. This meant that a Court of Appeals finding that the *Nation's* publication was overturned, and that the *Nation* was liable to pay the $12,500 in damages, matching the amount

[330] Ibid. at 563, 2232.

[331] Ibid.

[332] Ibid. at 564, 2233.

which *Time* magazine had refused to pay the copyright holders after the unauthorized publication.

Justice William J. Brennan, Jr.—who was joined by Justices Byron White and Thurgood Marshall—dissented. "The Court holds that the *Nation's* quotation of 300 words from the unpublished 200,000-word manuscript of President Gerald R. Ford infringed the copyright," wrote Brennan. He said the Court's majority reached this finding even though the quotations related to a historical event of undoubted significance—the resignation and pardon of President Richard M. Nixon. Brennan added that "this zealous defense of the copyright owner's prerogative will, I fear, stifle the broad dissemination of ideas and information copyright is intended to nurture."[333]

Brennan concluded,[334]

> The Court's exceedingly narrow approach to fair use permits Harper & Row to monopolize information. This holding "effect[s] an important extension of property rights and a corresponding curtailment in the free use of knowledge and of ideas." *International News Service v. Associated Press*, 248 U.S. at 263 (Brandeis, J., dissenting). The Court has perhaps advanced the ability of the historian—or at least the public official who has recently left office—to capture the full economic value of information in his or her possession. But the Court does so only by "risking the robust debate of public issues * * * ."

PUBLICATION OF ANOTHER'S PRIVATE LETTERS HELD NOT A "FAIR USE"

The *Salinger* case (discussed above) also dealt with the defense of "fair use." As noted above, the 2nd Circuit Court of Appeals held that Salinger had a copyright in the letters he sent to others. When Ian Hamilton tried to use those letters, Salinger sued. Having established that Salinger had a copyright, the 2nd Circuit turned to whether Hamilton's use of them was protected as a "fair use."

Salinger claimed that Hamilton's extensive reliance upon passages from his unpublished letters exceeded the reasonable bounds of fair use.

After originally granting Salinger's request for a preliminary injunction, a lower federal court had decided to lift the injunction and allow publication when the 2nd Circuit intervened, ordering that the ban on publication be made permanent.[335] In its attempt to follow the

---

[333] Ibid. at 578, 2240.

[334] Ibid. at 604, 2254.

[335] *Salinger v. Random House*, 811 F.2d 90 (2d Cir.1987).The Supreme Court declined to review this decision, so the ban on the publication of the book remains permanent. "Supreme Court Refuses to Review Salinger Ruling," *New York Times*, Oct. 6, 1987, p. 11. On the other hand, in *Maheu v. CBS*, 201 Cal.App.3d 662, 247 Cal.Rptr. 304 (1988), a California court refused to allow an action for copyright infringement by an assistant of Howard Hughes for the

Supreme Court's concept of fair use as defined in the *Harper & Row* case, the Court of Appeals decision placed special emphasis upon the fact these letters of Salinger's were unpublished.

That Supreme Court opinion had declared that "the scope of fair use is narrower with respect to unpublished works." Following this argument, the court found that because an author's privilege to incorporate unpublished material of another in his own work was a relatively limited one, and because Hamilton had relied so heavily upon the unpublished letters of Salinger in his biography, he had clearly exceeded the reasonable boundaries of permissible fair use.

In essence, then, the "nature of the copyrighted work" and "the amount and substantiality of the portion used" were the two elements of the *Harper & Row* decision that this court emphasized in finding that Hamilton's biography of Salinger had failed the test and was not a "fair use."

GIGI HADID AND FAIR USE

Model Gigi Hadid was sued by a paparazzi agency called Xclusive-Lee for posting a photo to her Instagram account which has 48.7 million followers. The agency claimed that Hadid did not have the right to one of its photos and sued for copyright infringement. Hadid's lawyers argue she has the rights to the photo because she contributed to it by the way she posed and smiled for the camera, she chose her outfit for the day and cropped the picture before posting it.[336]

U.S. District Judge Pamela Chen dismissed the claim because the paparazzi agency had not received a copyright registration by the time it filed the lawsuit.[337] Hadid's claim of fair use, if successful, had the potential to threaten photographers copyright protections.

TECHNOLOGY AND FAIR USE: THE SONY "BETAMAX" DECISION

When videocassette recorders became available to the general public in the early 1980s, it was clear that technology was once again moving beyond the scope of existing copyright law. The public had rejected RCA's efforts to market a videodisc player with no ability to record video programs, but was eager to buy Sony's new Betamax machines that

unauthorized use of correspondence he received from Hughes because of his failure to obtain copyright protection for this unpublished correspondence that was copyrightable.

[336] Paige Leeskin, "The Copyright Lawsuit Accusing Gigi Hadid of Posting a Paparazzi Photo She Didn't Have the Rights to Has Been Thrown Out," *Business Insider*, July 18, 2019, https://www.businessinsider.com/gigi-hadid-copyright-infringement-lawsuit-over-instagram-paparazzi-photo-dismissed-2019-7.

[337] *Xclusive-lee, Inc. v. Jenela Noura "Gigi" Hadid*, No. 19-CV-520 (PKC)(CLP), (E.D.N.Y. July 18, 2019).

allowed them to record and duplicate those broadcast programs and films that copyright owners had only expected them to view off-air.[338]

Because Congress proved itself incapable of amending the Copyright Act of 1976 to establish what rights copyright owners had to prevent such unauthorized copying of their works, the courts were soon forced to interpret an already out-dated Act in some manner that would bring this new form of usage within its provisions.

In January, 1984, the Supreme Court decided 5–4 that video recorders were legal for sale and home use under the Copyright Statute and the doctrine of fair use.[339] This case arose when Universal City Studios and Walt Disney productions sued Sony, claiming that use of Sony Betamax VCRs in homes by private individuals constituted copyright infringement.

In 1979, a federal district court held off-the-air copying for private, non-commercial use to be a "fair use." Plaintiffs had not proved to the court's satisfaction that harm to copyrighted properties was being done by such taping.[340] But in 1981, the United States Court of Appeals for the 9th Circuit overturned that ruling, holding that makers and distributors of home video recorders were liable for damages if the machines were used to tape programs broadcast over-the-air.[341]

The Supreme Court agreed in mid-1982 to hear Sony's appeal from the Court of Appeals holding. The Court, however, held the case over into a second term, and had it argued a second time in October, 1983.[342] Writing for a five-Justice majority, Justice John Paul Stevens said that most people use a VCR principally to record a program they cannot see as it is being telecast, and then use the home recording to watch the program at another time. This "time-shifting" practice, Justice Stevens said, enlarges the viewing audience:[343]

> * * * [A] significant amount of television programming may be used in this manner without objection from the owners of the copyrights on the programs. For the same reason, even the two respondents in this case, who do assert objections to time-

---

[338] For a concise description of both RCA's marketing failure and Sony's marketing success, see, "RCA Calls It Quits With Videodisks," *Broadcasting*, April 4, 1984, p. 39. By the time the Supreme Court decided the Sony case in 1984, more than 13 million VCRs had already been sold. "3-d Quarter VCR U.S. Population Pegged at 13 Mil," *Variety*, October 23, 1984, p. 1.

[339] *Sony Corporation of America v. Universal City Studios, Inc.*, 464 U.S. 417, 104 S.Ct. 774 (1984). Ironically, although Sony had won this legal battle, its "Beta" format lost out in the marketing war to its "VHS" format competitors. By 1988 Sony was abandoning "Beta" and producing its own VHS format VCRs. See, "Sony Adds VHS to VCR Format," *Variety*, January 12, 1988, p. 1.

[340] *Universal City Studios, et. al. v. Sony Corporation*, 480 F.Supp. 429, 452–453 (D.Cal.1979).

[341] *Universal City Studios, Inc. v. Sony Corporation*, 659 F.2d 963 (9th Cir.1981).

[342] *Sony Corporation v. Universal City Studios, et. al*, 464 U.S. 417, 418, 104 S.Ct. 774, 777 (1984); Wermeil, loc. cit.

[343] *Sony Corporation v. Universal City Studios, et. al*, 464 U.S. 417, 421, 104 S.Ct. 774, 778 (1984).

> shifting * * * were unable to prove that the practice has impaired the commercial value of their copyrights * * *

Justice Stevens noted that Universal and Disney studios were not seeking damages from individual Betamax users whom they claimed infringed their copyrights. Instead, they charged Sony with "contributory infringement." To prevail, this required them to prove that Sony encouraged those who purchased its Betamax machines to unlawfully copy feature films produced by studios such as Universal and Disney.[344] Justice Stevens added,[345]

> If vicarious liability is to be imposed on * * * [Sony] * * * , it must rest on the fact that they have sold equipment with constructive knowledge of the fact that their consumers may use that equipment to make unauthorized copies of copyrighted material. There is no precedent in the law of copyright for the imposition of vicarious liability on such a theory.

The Betamax decision was limited to noncommercial home uses. "If the Betamax were used to make copies for a commercial or profit-making purpose, such use would be presumptively unfair," Justice Stevens said.[346] Thus the *Sony* case is clearly distinguishable from a situation where off-the-air taping is being done for commercial reasons.[347]

Importantly, Justice Stevens concluded that the home use of VCRs for noncommercial purposes was a fair use.[348]

> * * * [To] the extent that time-shifting expands public access to freely broadcast television programs, it yields societal benefits. Earlier this year, in *Community Television of Southern California v. Gottfried*, 103 S.Ct. 885, 891–892, 74 L.Ed.2d 705 (1983), we acknowledged the public interest in making television broadcasting more available. Concededly, that interest is not unlimited. But it supports an interpretation of the concept of "fair use" that requires the copyright holder to demonstrate some likelihood of harm before he may condemn a private act of time-shifting as a violation of federal law.

Justice Stevens concluded the opinion of the Court with a summary of findings and with an invitation to Congress to provide legislative guidance in this case:[349]

---

[344] Ibid. at 434, 785.

[345] Ibid. at 438, 787.

[346] Ibid. at 449, 792.

[347] Melville B. Nimmer, *Nimmer on Copyright*, Vol. 3, § 13.5[F] (New York: Matthew Bender, 1963, 1980), citing *Elektra Records Co. v. Gem Electronic Distributors, Inc.*, 360 F.Supp. 821 (E.D.N.Y.1973) (taping of copyrighted records for commercial redistribution ruled infringing) and *Walt Disney Productions v. Alaska Television Network, Inc.*, 310 F.Supp. 1073 (W.D.Wash.1969) (videotaping for commercial use).

[348] *Sony Corporation v. Universal Studios, et. al.*, 464 U.S. 417, 454, 104 S.Ct. 774, 795 (1984).

[349] Ibid. at 456, 796.

> In summary, the record and findings of the District Court lead us to two conclusions. First, Sony demonstrated a significant likelihood that substantial numbers of copyright holders who license their works for broadcast on free television would not object to having their broadcasts time-shifted by private viewers. And second, respondents failed to demonstrate that time-shifting would cause any likelihood of nominal harm to the potential market for, or the value of, their copyrighted works. The Betamax is, therefore, capable of substantial noninfringing uses. Sony's sale of such equipment to the general public does not constitute contributory infringement of respondent's copyrights.
>
> * * *
>
> One may search the copyright act in vain for any sign that the elected representatives of the millions of people who watch television every day have made it unlawful to copy a program for later viewing at home, or have enacted a flat prohibition against the sale of machines that make such copying possible.
>
> It may well be that Congress will take a fresh look at this new technology, just as it so often has examined other innovations in the past. But it is not our job to apply laws that have not yet been written. Applying the copyright statute, as it now reads, to the facts as they have been developed in this case, the judgment of the Court of Appeals must be reversed.

Justice Blackmun, joined by Justices Marshall, Powell, and Rehnquist, dissented.[350]

> It is apparent from the record and from the findings of the District Court that time-shifting does have a substantial adverse effect upon the "potential market for" the Studios' copyrighted works. Accordingly, even under the formulation of the fair use doctrine advanced by Sony, time-shifting cannot be deemed a fair use.

Justice Blackmun added that the case should have been sent back to District Court for additional findings of fact on the matter of infringement and contributory infringement.[351]

MP3 AND NAPSTER'S FAILED FAIR USE DEFENSES

Sony was able to defend itself on the basis of fair use. The video tape recorder could be used to simply time shift the copyrighted programs of the plaintiffs. There were also a number of program producers who wanted their works to be copied freely. But in the cases of MP3 and Napster, fair use failed. MP3 and Napster argued that many artists

[350] Ibid. at 485, 811.

[351] Ibid. at 493, 815.

wanted their works to be distributed, that users were merely space shifting, moving songs from their CD players to their computers and allowing consumers to sample music.

MP3 argued in its failed defense that it had a fair use defense because of the nature of its service. After all, MP3 said, subscribers were only accessing CDs they already owned. In order to gain access to the copy at the MP3 site, subscribers had to load their CDs into their computers. The MP3 computer would then add that CD title to the list of CDs available to the subscriber.

But the federal court ruled that the act of copying the CD onto the MP3 site constituted infringement on its face. The court weighed the four factors that determine whether a use is a fair use. The court found that MP3 was a commercial entity operated for profit, a conclusion weighing against fair use. MP3 also was copying creative works. Traditionally, courts have found that creative, fictional works get greater protection than factual, nonfiction works. MP3 copied entire CDs. This amount and substantiality test worked against a fair use finding. Finally, the court looked at the effect of MP3's copying on the market rights of copyright holders.

MP3 said that it had no effect on the sales of CDs because subscribers had to obtain CDs and show proof that they had them in order to access the MP3 copy. MP3 also said its listening service encouraged sales. And, MP3 argued, none of the copyright holders had entered the business of licensing their works for services like MP3's.[352]

> Any allegedly positive impact of defendant's activities on plaintiffs' prior market in no way frees defendant to usurp a further market that directly derives from reproduction of the plaintiffs' copyrighted works. This would be so even if the copyright holder had not yet entered the new market in issue, for a copyright holder's "exclusive" rights, derived from the Constitution and the Copyright Act, include the right, within broad limits, to curb the development of such a derivative market by refusing to license a copyrighted work or by doing so only on terms the copyright owner finds acceptable. Here, moreover, plaintiffs have adduced substantial evidence that they have in fact taken steps to enter that market by entering into various licensing agreements.

> Both MP3 and Napster argued that they were engaged in space shifting, that is allowing users to enjoy their own CDs in different form. In fact, the issue had been raised in *Recording Industry of America v. Diamond Multimedia Systems*,[353] the case over the Rio. The Rio, was a handheld device that could

[352] *UMG Recordings v. MP3.Com*, 92 F.Supp.2d 349, 352 (S.D.N.Y.2000).

[353] *Recording Industry Ass'n of America v. Diamond Multimedia Systems*, 29 F.Supp.2d 624 (C.D.Cal.1998).

receive, store and play back digital audio files. The audio files could be downloaded from computers.

The recording industry sued on the basis that Rio's ability to store and playback files constituted illegal copying. The industry sought to prevent the sale and distribution of Rio devices. A quick look at electronics stores and their inventories of digital audio players shows the failure of that effort. The district court found that, like the Sony video tape recorder, the Rio was capable of non-infringing uses. Because it had that legitimate use, the Rio could not be banned.[354]

MP3 failed in its space-shifting arguments because it had engaged in wholesale copying of copyrighted works. It was a far cry from an individual consumer making a duplicate of music for personal use.[355]

> Here, although defendant recites that My.MP3.com provides a transformative "space shift" by which subscribers can enjoy the sound recordings contained on their CDs without lugging around the physical discs themselves, this is simply another way of saying that the unauthorized copies are being retransmitted in another medium—an insufficient basis for any legitimate claim of transformation.

There also were differences between the *Rio* case and *Napster*. The 9th Circuit panel said that *Napster* differed from *Rio* and *Sony* in that those shifting did not involve the simultaneous distribution of copyrighted material. The Rio took the music from files already on the owner's computer. The majority of users of video tape recorders merely time-shifted programs and enjoyed them themselves rather than distributing them. Napster, on the other hand, involved sharing of copyrighted works.[356]

> [I]t is obvious that once a user lists a copy of music he already owns on the Napster system in order to access the music from another location, the song becomes "available to millions of other individuals," not just the original CD owner.

Napster also said that it was, in fact, helping the market for sound recordings by allowing consumers to sample works before buying. But the district court found that even that use of Napster ran afoul of the copyrights of the music industry. Record companies charged fees for downloading of their works, restricted samples to 30 or 60 seconds of music or provided "time out" protection for entire songs ("time out" meant that the songs would remain on a user's computer for only a brief time). Napster provided entire works that would remain permanently and Napster's sampling had a negative effect on the music market.[357]

---

[354] Ultimately, it was competition from the iPod that put the RIO into the dustbin of digital audio players.

[355] *UMG Recordings v. MP3.Com*, 92 F.Supp.2d 349, 351 (S.D.N.Y.2000).

[356] *A & M Records, et al. v. Napster, Inc.*, 239 F.3d 1004, 1019 (9th Cir.2001).

[357] Ibid. at 1018.

> The record supports the district court's preliminary determination that: (1) the more music that sampling users download, the less likely they are to eventually purchase the recordings on audio CD; and (2) even if the audio CD market is not harmed, Napster has adverse effects on the developing digital download market.

Like Sony's video tape recorder, Napster was capable of helping to spread works whose owners wanted free distribution. The recording companies did not seek to prevent that copying and focused their suit on the copying of their own works.

Napster also argued that it was doing nothing more than enabling individuals to make copies of music. Copying of sound recordings was nothing new. In fact the Home Recording Copyright Act of 1986 allowed persons to make copies of sound recordings they purchased for their own personal use. That Act has been replaced by the Audio Home Recording Act of 1992[358] which allows for the use of recording devices for the noncommercial use by consumers in making copies of sound recordings.

But Napster's involvement did not fall under the protections of the home recording act. The fact that Napster users downloaded onto their computers placed them outside the statutory protections. The Audio Home Recording Act states:[359]

> No action may be brought under this title alleging infringement or copyright based on the manufacture, importation, or distribution of a digital audio recording device, a digital audio recording medium, an analog recording device, or an analog recording medium, or based on the noncommercial use by a consumer of such a device or medium for making digital music recordings or analog musical recordings.

The district court and 9th Circuit panel explained that home computers do not qualify as recording devices because "their primary purpose is not to make digital audio copied recordings."[360]

Napster has turned to Congress to seek a mandatory licensing system that would allow it to continue to allow users to exchange music files upon payment of a set fee. Internet copying still persists, though. Gnutella and FreeNet have distributed programs similar to Napster's, but that do not require that sharing pass through a central system like Napster's.

GROKSTER AND THE CONTINUING LEGACY OF SONY

In June, 2005, the Supreme Court took up the issue of file sharing technology in a case that pitted movie companies, songwriters and music

---

[358] Audio Home Recording Act of 1992, 17 U.S.C. § 1008.

[359] Ibid.

[360] *A & M Records, et al. v. Napster, Inc.*, 239 F.3d 1004, 1024 (9th Cir.2001).

publishers against Grokster and StreamCast Networks, Inc., distributors of file sharing software.[361] Before the decision was released, many commentators suggested that the case would signal the end of the Sony doctrine. But Justice Souter's opinion made clear that Sony remains good law in cases where companies sell or distribute products or software capable of infringement as long as those companies do not promote copyright infringement.

Metro-Goldwyn-Mayer and the other plaintiffs sued Grokster and StreamCast alleging that the companies distributed their software in order for computer users to make illegal copies of copyrighted works.

Unlike the *Napster* case, Grokster involved peer-to-peer file sharing that did not require users to send files through a central computer. Instead, the software provided by Grokster and StreamCast allowed computer users to make their own connections with other computer users to share materials. The problem was the computer users were sharing copyrighted materials at an astronomical rate.[362] "Discovery revealed that billions of files are shared across peer-to-peer networks each month."

The district court and 9th Circuit Court of Appeals ruled for Grokster and StreamCast. Those courts noted that the two companies were not actually making the illegal copies, but merely provided software to other persons who infringed the copyrights. As such, Grokster and StreamCast could only be found liable if they were found to have contributorily infringed, that is to have made a substantial contribution to the actual infringement. The 9th Circuit reasoned that under Sony, the only way Grokster and StreamCast could have been held liable would be if both companies knew of actual infringement and did nothing about it.

But, Justice Souter noted in his opinion for the court, even though Grokster and StreamCast had no direct way of knowing which files were being copied, users often informed them when asking about copying copyrighted works. As Justice Souter's opinion made clear,[363]

> Respondents are not merely passive recipients of information about infringement. The record is replete with evidence that when they began to distribute their free software, each of them clearly voiced the objective that recipients use the software to download copyrighted works and took active steps to encourage infringement. After the notorious file-sharing service, Napster, was sued by copyright holders for facilitating copyright infringement, both respondents promoted and marketed themselves as Napster alternatives.

---

[361] *Metro-Goldwyn-Mayer Studios, Inc. v. Grokster Ltd.*, 545 U.S. 913, 125 S.Ct. 2764 (2005).

[362] Ibid. at 917, 2767.

[363] Ibid. at 913, 2766.

As with Sony's videocassette recorder, the software from Grokster and Streamcast could be used for noninfringing uses. That was the basis of 9th Circuit's decision against MGM as the court concluded that where there was a substantial noninfringing use, there could be no liability.

But that was incorrect, Justice Souter wrote,[364] "This view of Sony, however, was error, converting the case from one about liability resting on imputed intent to one about liability on any theory."

The record showing the two companies' inducement and aid in infringing was enough to support a finding of liability, Souter wrote.[365]

> Evidence of "active steps * * * taken to encourage direct infringement," *Oak Industries, Inc. v. Zenith Electronics Corp.*, 697 F.Supp. 988, 992 (N.D.Ill.1988), such as advertising an infringing use or instructing how to engage in an infringing use, show an affirmative intent that the product be used to infringe, and a showing that infringement was encouraged overcomes the law's reluctance to find liability when a defendant merely sells a commercial product suitable for some lawful use

Souter acknowledged the difficulties that the court's holding might have on the development of technology. But, he said, the protections afforded by Sony remained and would protect companies that made devices that could be used by infringers.[366]

> We are, of course, mindful of the need to keep from trenching on regular commerce or discouraging the development of technologies with lawful and unlawful potential. Accordingly, just as Sony did not find intentional inducement despite the knowledge of the VCR manufacturer that its device could be used to infringe, 464 U.S., at 439, n. 19, 104 S.Ct. 774, mere knowledge of infringing potential or of actual infringing uses would not be enough here to subject a distributor to liability.

The decision makes clear that persons developing new technologies or applications still have protection from contributory infringement claims under the Sony doctrine.

ORACLE V. GOOGLE GOES BEFORE THE SUPREME COURT

Oracle filed a lawsuit claiming that Google used 11,500 lines of code from Oracle's Java programing language for use in its Android mobile operating system. Google originally approached Oracle about licensing Java for Android after it failed to write its own code. Negotiations stalled and Google simply copied the code anyway. Oracle sued Google in 2010

---

364 Ibid. at 934, 2778.

365 Ibid. at 936, 2779.

366 Ibid. at 937, 2780.

alleging a violation of copyright law. Google argues the use of the code falls under the "fair use" doctrine.[367]

The Supreme Court has granted certiorari and is expected to hear oral argument in March 2020 and a decision by June.[368]

DIGITIZING LIBRARIES A FAIR USE

The 2nd Circuit Court of Appeals advanced the ball in the continuing controversy over the digitizing of the world's library. In *Authors Guild v. Hathi,*[369] a three-judge panel held that it was a fair use for an organization of universities to turn the contents of their libraries into digital copies.

The case had its inception in 2004 when the University of Michigan, the University of California at Berkeley, Cornell University, the University of Indiana and others entered into an agreement allowing Google to scan the books in their libraries. The universities created an entity called the HathiTrust to operate the Hathi Digital Library (HDL). By 2014, the HathiTrust had 80 member institutions and a library of more than 10 million works.

Hathi provides three separate services based on it digital compilation of the works. The first is a search service that allows the public to search all the works in the digital library for particular terms or words. That search is limited.[370]

> Unless the copyright holder authorizes broader use, the search results show only the page numbers on which the search term is found within the work and the number of times the term appears on each page. The HDL does not display to the user any text from the underlying copyrighted work (either in "snippet" form or otherwise). Consequently, the user is not able to view either the page on which the term appears or any other portion of the book.

Hathi's second service provides access to persons with certified print disabilities. Print disabilities include blindness and the inability to hold a book or to turn its pages. The final service preserves the works held by the institutions.

Third, by preserving the copyrighted books in digital form, the HDL permits members to create a replacement copy of the work, if the member already owned an original copy, the member's original copy is lost,

---

[367] Rachel Brovard, "The Supreme Court Must Not Let Google's Theft of Intellectual Property Stand," *National Review*, Dec. 17, 2019, https://www.nationalreview.com/2019/12/supreme-court-must-punish-google.

[368] Electronic Frontier Foundation, "Oracle v. Google," https://www.nationalreview.com/2019/12/supreme-court-must-punish-google.

[369] *Authors Guild v. HathiTrust*, 755 F.3d 87 (2d Cir. 2014).

[370] Ibid. at 90.

destroyed, or stolen, and a replacement copy is unobtainable at a "fair" price elsewhere.[371]

The Authors Guild and about 20 individual authors and international organizations representing authors sued claiming copyright infringement in the creation and distribution of the digital copies. The U.S. District Court for the Southern District of New York granted summary judgment for Hathi. District Judge Harold Baer, Jr., also held that the Authors Guild and the other organizations representing authors did not have standing[372] to participate in the case.[373]

[A]s we have previously explained, § 501 of "the Copyright Act does not permit copyright holders to choose third parties to bring suits on their behalf." *ABKCO Music, Inc. v. Harrisongs Music, Ltd.*, 944 F.2d 971, 980 (2d Cir.1991); see also *Itar-Tass Russian News Agency v. Russian Kurier, Inc.*, 153 F.3d 82, 92 (2d Cir.1998) ("United States law permits suit only by owners of 'an exclusive right under a copyright'. . . ." (quoting 17 U.S.C. § 501(b))).

Sec. 107 provides a four-factor test to determine whether a use of a copyrighted work is a "fair use" and therefore protected from suit by a copyright holder. The factors (covered above) include consideration of whether the subsequent use is "transformative." Merely republishing or copying the original copyrighted work is not transformative. More must be done, Circuit Judge Barrington D. Parker wrote:[374]

> The inquiry is whether the work "adds something new, with a further purpose or different character, altering the first with new expression, meaning or message. . . ." *Campbell*, 510 U.S. at 579, 114 S.Ct. 1164 (citing *Leval*, 103 Harv. L. Rev. at 1111). "[T]he more transformative the new work, the less will be the significance of other factors . . . that may weigh against a finding of fair use." Id.

The creation of the searchable library was a transformative use, Judge Parker concluded. The transformation occurred because the library search could not provide the full text of the work, unless the author already had granted permission. Hathi was not making any of the text of the books available to the searcher. It merely told the searcher how many times the search term appeared and which pages the term was on.[375]

---

[371] Ibid. at 92.

[372] Standing means that a party has a legally recognizable interest in the controversy. If a person or entity has no standing, it cannot take part in the case because it has nothing to win or lose. The Authors Guild, though representing authors in some matters, did not own any of the copyrights being sued over. As such, it had no standing and could be dismissed from the case.

[373] *Authors Guild v. HathiTrust,* 755 F.3d 87, 94 (2d Cir. 2014).

[374] Ibid. at 96.

[375] Ibid. at 97.

> Consequently, in providing this service, the HDL does not add into circulation any new, human-readable copies of any books. Instead, the HDL simply permits users to "word search"—that is, to locate where specific words or phrases appear in the digitized books. Applying the relevant factors, we conclude that this use is a fair use.

The Fourth Circuit panel gave great deference to the fourth factor in the fair use analysis: the effect of the use upon the potential market for or value of the copyrighted work. Copyright holders have to prove, in the fourth test, a real harm.[376]

> To defeat a claim of fair use, the copyright holder must point to market harm that results because the secondary use serves as a substitute for the original work. See *Campbell*, 510 U.S. at 591, 114 S.Ct. 1164 ("cognizable market harm" is limited to "market substitution"); see also *NXIVM Corp. v. Ross Inst.*, 364 F.3d 471, 481–82 (2d Cir.2004).

Judge Parker concluded that instead of replacing the copyrighted works, the searchable library added to the value of the original works. The plaintiffs argued that the creation of the digital library could cause them harm because there might be a market for digitally copying their works sometime in the future. The existence of a search service would not prevent authors from selling the right to digitally copy their works to a publisher who wanted to sell copies of their works, Judge Parker said. The search library did not provide users with a full or partial text of the works.

The plaintiffs also lost their claim that making copies of their works for persons who have print disabilities. That right was built into the legislative history of the Copyright Act itself, Judge Parker wrote.[377]

First, the Supreme Court has already said so. As Justice Stevens wrote for the Court: "Making a copy of a copyrighted work for the convenience of a blind person is expressly identified by the House Committee Report as an example of fair use, with no suggestion that anything more than a purpose to entertain or to inform need motivate the copying." *Sony Corp. of Am.*, 464 U.S. at 455 n. 40, 104 S.Ct. 774.

The 4th Circuit panel sent the part of the case dealing with the preservation of the works digitally for the individual libraries back to the district court to determine whether the remaining plaintiffs had a recognizable claim.

PARODY AND FAIR USE

Can a parody be fair use? The "*Saturday Night Live*" television program did a skit poking fun at New York City's public relations

---

[376] Ibid.

[377] Ibid. at 102.

campaign and its theme song. In this four-minute skit, the town fathers of Sodom discussed a plan to improve their city's image. This satire ended with the singing of "*I Love Sodom*" to the tune of "*I Love New York*." In a per curiam opinion, the U.S. Court of Appeals, 2nd Circuit rejected the complaint of Elsmere Record Co., owner of copyright to "*I Love New York*." "Believing that, in today's world of often unrelieved solemnity, copyright law should be hospitable to the humor of parody," the Court of Appeals approved District Judge Gerard Louis Goettel's decision granting the defendant National Broadcasting Company a summary judgment on ground that the parody was a fair use.[378]

Judge Goettel's opinion said, in words useful for understanding both the concept of fair use and its application to parodies charged with copyright infringement:[379]

> In its entirety, the original song *"I Love New York"* is composed of a 45 word lyric and 100 measures. Of this only four notes, D C D E (in that sequence), and the words "*I Love*" were taken in the Saturday Night Live sketch (although they were repeated 3 or 4 times). As a result, the defendant now argues that the use it made was insufficient to constitute copyright infringement.
>
> This court does not agree. Although it is clear that, on its face, the taking involved in this action is relatively slight, on closer examination it becomes apparent that this portion of the piece, the musical phrase that the lyrics "*I Love New York*" accompanies, is the heart of the composition. * * * Accordingly, such taking is capable of rising to the level of a copyright infringement.
>
> Having so determined, the Court must next address the question of whether the defendant's copying of the plaintiff's jingle constituted a fair use which would exempt it from liability under the Copyright Act. Fair use has been defined as a "privilege in others than the owner of the copyright to use the copyrighted material in a reasonable manner without his consent, notwithstanding the monopoly granted to the owner of the copyright".

Judge Goettel then reviewed the four criteria set out by the 1976 copyright revision, 17 U.S.C.A. § 107 [quoted at the beginning of this section], and compared those criteria to relevant cases on the fair use doctrine. He quoted copyright specialist Melville B. Nimmer, who has said, "short of * * * [a] complete identity of content, the disparity of functions between a serious work and a satire based upon it, may justify the defense of fair use even where substantial similarity exists."[380]

---

[378] *Elsmere Music, Inc. v. NBC*, 623 F.2d 252 (2d Cir.1980).

[379] *Elsmere Music, Inc. v. NBC*, 482 F.Supp. 741, 742 (S.D.N.Y.1980).

[380] *Nimmer on Copyright*, 13.05[C], at 13–60–61 (1979), quoted by Judge Goettel at 482 F.Supp. 741 at 745 (S.D.N.Y.1980).

Plaintiff Elsmere Records argued that "*I Love Sodom*" was not a valid parody of "*I Love New York*." Elsmere pointed to two raunchy cases in which copyright infringement was found because use of copyrighted material was not parodying the material itself, but was instead using someone's intellectual property, without permission, to make statements essentially irrelevant to the original work.[381] *Elsmere Records cited MCA, Inc. v. Wilson*, in which the song "*Cunnilingus Champion of Company C*" was held to infringe the copyright of "*Boogie Woogie Bugle Boy of Company B*."[382] And in *Walt Disney Productions v. Mature Pictures Corporation*, the court held that using the copyrighted "*Mickey Mouse March*" as background for a teen-age group sex scene in a "*Happy Hooker*" movie was not fair use.[383]

However, Judge Goettel found that the *Saturday Night Live* sketch validly parodied the plaintiff's jingle and the "*I Love New York*" ad campaign. Also, he ruled that the parody did not interfere with the marketability of a copyrighted work. Therefore, he held that the sketch was a fair use, and that no copyright violation had occurred.

CAMPBELL A.K.A. SKYYWALKER V. ACUFF-ROSE MUSIC, INC.

In 1992 Acuff-Rose Music, Inc. sued 2 Live Crew, contending that the Crew's song "*Pretty Woman*" infringed the Acuff-Rose copyright of Roy Orbison's rock ballad, "*Oh Pretty Woman*." The District Court granted summary judgement for 2 Live Crew, holding that its song was a parody that made *fair use* of the original ballad.[384]

The Court of Appeals overturned the lower court decision, deciding that the parody's commercial nature, coupled with what the court found as a matter of law to be its too extensive use of the original song in the parody, presented issues that could result in a finding of copyright infringement against 2 Live Crew.[385]

A unanimous Supreme Court reversed the Court of Appeals.[386] Justice Souter, speaking for the Court, stated that the key in determining whether the parody of a copyrighted work infringes on the original is not its commercial or non-commercial nature, but the extent it alters the original through new expression, message or meaning. Thus, as Souter expressed it, the more "transformative" the parody, the less significant

---

[381] *Elsmere Music, Inc. v. NBC*, 482 F.Supp. 741, 745 (S.D.N.Y.1980).

[382] *MCA, Inc. v. Wilson*, 425 F.Supp. 443 (S.D.N.Y.1976).

[383] 389 F.Supp. 1397 (S.D.N.Y.1975). Similarly, in *Fisher v. Dees*, 794 F.2d 432 (9th Cir.1986), a U.S. Court of Appeals Court found that a parody of the plaintiff composers' song "*When Sunny Gets Blue*," performed as "*When Sunny Sniffs Glue*," took no more from the copyrighted song than was necessary to reasonably accomplish its purpose. It was neither obscene nor immoral in nature, and was parody entitled to fair use protection.

[384] *Acuff-Rose Music, Inc. v. Campbell*, 754 F.Supp. 1150 (M.D.Tenn.1991).

[385] *Acuff-Rose Music, Inc. v. Campbell, a.k.a. Skyywalker*, 972 F.2d 1429 (6th Cir.1992).

[386] *Campbell v. Acuff-Rose Music, Inc.*, 510 U.S. 569, 114 S.Ct. 1164 (1994).

the other factors—(the commercial/non-commercial nature of the use; the amount used; its impact on the market value of the original).

This transformative element might well have been the reason why the 11th Circuit decided to lift an injunction against the publication of "*The Wind Done Gone*," a parody of Margaret Mitchell's "*Gone With the Wind*."

The 11th Circuit reversed an order entered by the district court for the Northern District of Georgia against the publication of the book. The trustees for Mitchell's estate sought the injunction claiming that the work was a sequel rather than a true parody. The district court found that the book had transformative elements but took too much from the original. The appeals court ruled that the injunction was an abuse of the court's discretion and amounted to a prior restraint.

90. BROADCAST MUSIC LICENSING RIGHTS

Electronic media must obtain copyright clearance for the music they use through private agreements with organizations that represent the composers and publishers of this music.

In 1923 the National Association of Broadcasters (NAB) was founded primarily to negotiate an agreement with the American Society of Composers and Publishers (ASCAP) to allow radio stations to broadcast the copyrighted music of the society's composers and music publishers.

ASCAP had been formed in 1914 as a performing rights, copyright licensing agency for a group of music publishers and their composers whose works were being performed in music halls and in Vaudeville theaters without permission or payment.[387] When radio stations began broadcasting recorded music of ASCAP's composers and publishers during the early 1920s, the organization demanded copyright royalties for this program use.

During this pioneering era of broadcasting, stations were not yet permitted to sell commercial time and so until the early 1930s these radio station music licensing payments were little more than token contributions. By 1932, however, as radio was emerging as one of the few profitable industries during the Great Depression, ASCAP suddenly demanded a 300 percent increase in its broadcast music licensing fees.

For a time the NAB was able to convince its member stations to fill their schedules with the few public domain compositions they had on record, but when ASCAP offered a lower rate to newspaper owned stations, opposition collapsed and broadcasters agreed to this massive rate hike.

[387] During this era, sheet music was still the primary source of income for the music industry. Publishing companies would either hire composers and lyricists to write the songs that would be published and sold to the public or purchase songs from established composers. Today a music publisher simply promotes and produces musical recordings.

In 1937 the broadcast industry attempted to dilute ASCAP's absolute power over broadcast music rights by encouraging the formation of a rival group, Broadcast Music Incorporated (BMI), hoping that competition for broadcast business would force ASCAP to reduce its fees. The tactic worked for a short time, but soon BMI began bargaining as aggressively as ASCAP during each renegotiation of its licensing agreements.

When television began to emerge during the 1950s as the dominant electronic medium in the United States, the "blanket license" approach that both ASCAP and BMI used to grant broadcast use of their music was challenged by the television industry. Most radio stations had been willing to accept this type of license that granted them full broadcast use of music from ASCAP and BMI composers in return for a payment of less than 1 percent of their annual advertising revenues. For television stations, however, with their far larger advertising revenues, and their far less extensive use of music, neither the blanket license nor the per-use alternative offered by ASCAP or BMI seemed reasonably related to the actual value a station owner received from such music usage.

Beginning in 1950, the All-Industry Television Station Music License Committee, negotiating on behalf of its member stations, sought some other type of arrangement with the music licensing groups that would reflect more accurately the minimal benefits the blanket license offered television stations. Although each new round of negotiations resulted in a further reduction of the percentage of advertising revenues to be charged during the subsequent license period, neither ASCAP nor BMI was willing to abandon a licensing structure that by 1970 was providing an estimated 20–25 percent of their annual music rights revenue.[388]

After failing to reach agreement with the music licensing organizations on a satisfactory alternative to the blanket license, CBS, acting on behalf of the television networks, began an antitrust action against ASCAP and BMI in 1969. CBS alleged that these organizations had acted in concert to prevent the composers and publishers they represented from dealing directly with the television networks or its producers who sought to purchase broadcast music rights from the parties who held title to them, in restraint of trade and in direct violation of sec. 1 of the Sherman Antitrust Laws.[389]

In 1981, the U.S. Supreme Court held that the blanket license was not a per se violation of the Act, and on remand the Court of Appeals then dismissed the action.[390] In 1978 a group of local television stations began their own antitrust action against ASCAP and BMI, alleging the same type of anticompetitive practices. Unlike CBS, however, these local

388 "Broadcasters Press On Against ASCAP, BMI," *Variety* January 8, 1986, p. 209.

389 *CBS v. ASCAP*, 620 F.2d 930 (2d Cir.1980).

390 *BMI v. CBS*, 441 U.S. 1, 99 S.Ct. 1551 (1979).

stations were successful in convincing a lower court that the blanket music licensing agreements did constitute an illegal restraint of trade.[391]

According to the opinion, what made the conduct of ASCAP and BMI anti-competitive was their concerted effort to discourage program producers from obtaining directly from composers complete copyright clearance for broadcast usage of the programs they produced. The court found that, unlike the television networks, individual stations did not have sufficient bargaining power to force music licensing organizations to alter their practices, and therefore they required the protection the law provided in order to be capable of bargaining with ASCAP and BMI on equal footing.

ASCAP and BMI challenged this federal trial court decision, and a federal appeals court reversed the lower court holding, finding that the difference in the degree of bargaining power exercised by the stations and the networks was not substantial enough to require a finding that the music licensing organizations were acting in restraint of trade.[392]

When the U.S. Supreme Court refused to review this appellate court decision, broadcasting turned immediately to Congress to obtain through legislation what it had been unable to gain through litigation. During recent years the NAB has been attempting during each session of Congress to obtain passage of a law that would legally obligate every television producer to acquire full musical broadcast performance rights to all programs to be distributed for television broadcast. Although none of these "source licensing" bills have been adopted by Congress, the NAB continues in its lobbying efforts because it believes that such "source licensing" would clear at least 90 percent of the musical content now broadcast by television stations throughout the United States, making it possible for networks and most television stations to avoid the need of a "blanket" music license from ASCAP or BMI.

In 1990, the cable industry charged these music licensing organizations with anti-competitive practices under the Sherman antitrust act, challenging the refusal of these groups to offer cable TV networks a blanket music license. The industry eventually prevailed, obtaining agreements from both organizations to accept license payments from each cable network and a single annual fee from each cable system.[393]

Because payment arrangements for electronic media usage of copyrighted music are not established by the statutory provisions of the Copyright Act, all terms and conditions of usage must be negotiated between the music licensing organizations and representatives of

---

[391] *Buffalo Broadcasting Co. v. ASCAP*, 546 F.Supp. 274 (S.D.N.Y.1982).

[392] *Buffalo Broadcasting Co. v. ASCAP*, 744 F.2d 917 (2d Cir.1984).

[393] *National Cable Television Assn. v. Broadcast Music Inc.*, 772 F.Supp. 614 (D.D.C.1991). *U.S. v. American Society of Composers, Authors and Publishers (ASCAP)*, 782 F.Supp. 778 (S.D.N.Y.1991), affirmed per curiam 956 F.2d 21 (2d Cir.1992), cert. denied 504 U.S. 914, 112 S.Ct. 1950 (1992).

electronic media. Considering the amount of money involved, it is not surprising that so many of these efforts have ended up in litigation, requiring the courts to define for the parties the reasonable value of the music rights involved.

Recently, pay-TV organizations have begun to have their day in court. Early in 1991, HBO negotiated an interim settlement with BMI, agreeing to pay the broadcast music performing rights organization a monthly fee for use of BMI music until a federal court determines whether BMI can rightfully demand music rights payments both from a pay-TV service that is providing programming and each cable system that is distributing it.[394] One week later ASCAP, the other major broadcast music licensing organization, negotiated a similar interim settlement with Showtime.[395]

This entire electronic media music performing rights controversy is yet another illustration of technology complicating the process of effectively compensating the creative artist for the use of that individual's intellectual property. Paying some arbitrarily determined amount of money to a licensing organization to be divided in almost as arbitrarily a fashion among that group of artists it represents is certainly far less efficient or cost effective than direct negotiations between the purchaser and the artist.[396]

Unfortunately, though, such direct negotiations for the use of music are seldom possible in this modern era. At the beginning of the Twentieth Century a vaudeville or music hall producer could purchase from a publisher the performing rights to a complete musical score for a stage show that might run for several years. Today, however, it would be virtually impossible for the typical radio station to negotiate for the rights to each of fifteen to twenty different musical compositions it schedules on each hour's Playlist.

91. MERGER AND TRANSFORMATIVE USE

The doctrines of merger and transformative use can serve as a defense to an infringement suit. Merger means that an expression cannot be copyrighted because the idea can only be expressed in one or a few ways. Giving someone a copyright to that idea would be giving a monopoly.

Although it seems that merger might be considered in the copyrightability of the infringed work, most courts have used merger in

---

394 "BMI Makes Deal with HBO; Lawsuit Dropped," *Variety*, Jan. 14, 1991, p. 121.

395 "ASCAP, Showtime Settle on Fees," *Variety*, Jan. 21, 1991, p. 90.

396 Cable TV's compulsory license to allow it to pay a percentage of its subscriber revenues into a pool to compensate those who own the TV programs the system has imported from a distant broadcast market operates in basically the same fashion as the broadcast music licensing agreement, but in cable TV's situation the pooling arrangement is created by federal law.

an infringement analysis. This means that even slight differences will serve to clear a subsequent work of being infringing.[397]

> If the idea and the author's particular way of expressing that idea cannot be separated, under the concept of merger only identical copying of the expression is barred. See *Krofft*, 562 F.2d at 167–68.
>
> * * *
>
> Merger means there is practically only one way to express an idea. But if technical or conceptual constraints limit the available ways to express an idea, even though there is more than one avenue of expression available, copyright law will abhor only a virtually-identical copy of the original. *Telemarketing Resources v. Symantec Corp.*, 12 USPQ2d 1991, 1989 WL 200350 (N.D.Cal.1989), aff'd in part as *Brown Bag Software v. Symantec Corp.*, 960 F.2d 1465 (9th Cir.1992).

The concept of idea/expression unity was laid out in an infringement suit over a jeweled pin in the shape of a bee.[398] Judge James Robert Browning wrote for a panel of the 9th Circuit that the idea of a bee-shaped jeweled pin was so particular that any subsequent bee-shaped jeweled pin might infringe the original. That, Judge Browning wrote, could not work under the copyright law.[399]

> When the 'idea' and its 'expression' are thus inseparable, copying the 'expression' will not be barred, since protecting the 'expression' in such circumstances would confer a monopoly of the 'idea' upon the copyright owner free of the conditions and limitations imposed by the patent law. *Baker v. Selden*, 101 U.S. 99, 103, 25 L.Ed. 841 (1879); *Morrissey v. Procter & Gamble Co.*, 379 F.2d 675, 678–679 (1st Cir. 1967); *Crume v. Pacific Mut. Life Ins. Co.*, 140 F.2d 182, 184 (7th Cir. 1944). See also *Continental Cas. Co. v. Beardsley*, 253 F.2d 702, 705–706 (2d Cir. 1958).

Transformative use refers to the change in a copyrighted work into a new thing with a new message or meaning. The doctrine of transformative use advanced with the case of photographer Patrick Cariou against appropriation artist Richard Prince.[400] Cariou had spent six years living with Rastafarians in Jamaica. He produced a book of photographic portraits and landscapes called "*Yes Rasta*" in 2000. Prince is an appropriation artist, someone who takes an object or existing work of art to create a new artwork.

[397] *Apple Computer v. Microsoft Corp.*, 799 F.Supp 1006, 1021 (N.D.Calif. 1992).

[398] *Herbert Rosenthal Jewelry Corp. v. Kalpakian*, 446 F.2d 738 (9th Cir. 1971).

[399] Ibid. at 742.

[400] *Cariou v. Prince*, 714 F.3d 694 (2d Cir. 2013). The 2nd Circuit, along with the 9th Circuit, is one of the two most important circuit courts dealing with intellectual property. Traditional publishing houses and broadcast network headquarters are located in the 2nd Circuit and Hollywood and television production facilities are in the 9th Circuit.

As Circuit Judge Barrington D. Parker wrote,[401] Prince's work, going back to the mid-1970s, has involved taking photographs and other images that others have produced and incorporating them into paintings and collages that he then presents, in a different context, as his own. Prince found a copy of Cariou's book in 2005. He tore out 35 photographs and incorporated them into a collage that was part of art show that he held in December 2007 through February 2008. In that art show, Prince painted over the eyes, noses and mouths of many of the faces in the portraits. Later in 2008, Prince bought three additional copies of "*Yes Rasta*" and created a new art show in which 29 of the 30 pieces used elements from the book. In one piece, Prince took the headshots from Cariou's portraiture and put them on images that he took from a different artist and stuck the assemblage onto a canvas that he had painted.

Cariou did now know of Prince's use of his work. He did look into doing a show of his "*Yes Rasta*" work but the gallery owner he had been in contact with decided against it because a Rasta show already had been done, by Prince. The gallery owner later told Cariou about Prince's work and Cariou filed an infringement suit.

The trial judge, using the analysis from the "*Pretty Woman*," 2 Live Crew, suit above, ruled for Cariou concluding that Prince had not intended to provide commentary on the photographs and so did not meet the test for transformative use.

The 2nd Circuit panel noted the commentary aspect of fair use in the "*Pretty Woman*" case.[402]

> Certainly, many types of fair use, such as satire and parody, invariably comment on an original work and/or on popular culture. For example, the rap group 2 Live Crew's parody of Roy Orbison's "Oh, Pretty Woman" "was clearly intended to ridicule the white-bread original." *Campbell*, 510 U.S. at 582, 114 S.Ct. 1164 (quotation marks omitted). Much of Andy Warhol's work, including work incorporating appropriated images of Campbell's soup cans or of Marilyn Monroe, comments on consumer culture and explores the relationship between celebrity culture and advertising.

Judge Parker, citing the "*Pretty Woman*" case, explained that[403] "to qualify as a fair use, a new work generally must alter the original with 'new expression, meaning, or message.' " At least 25 of Prince's work met that requirement.[404]

> Where Cariou's serene and deliberately composed portraits and landscape photographs depict the natural beauty of Rastafarians and their surrounding environs, Prince's crude

[401] Ibid. at 699.

[402] Ibid. at 706.

[403] Ibid.

[404] Ibid.

> and jarring works, on the other hand, are hectic and provocative. Cariou's black-and-white photographs were printed in a 9 1/2" x 12" book. Prince has created collages on canvas that incorporate color, feature distorted human and other forms and settings, and measure between ten and nearly a hundred times the size of the photographs. Prince's composition, presentation, scale, color palette, and media are fundamentally different and new compared to the photographs, as is the expressive nature of Prince's work.

Five other works that used Cariou's photographs did not clearly fit into the transformative category, Judge Parker wrote.[405]

> Although the minimal alterations that Prince made in those instances moved the work in a different direction from Cariou's classical portraiture and landscape photos, we can not say with certainty at this point whether those artworks present a "new expression, meaning, or message."

The 2nd Circuit panel sent the case back to the trial court so that it could decide whether those five works were infringing.

And for those who regularly post to Instagram, keep in mind that putting photographs on the Internet provides opportunities for other people to take and make use of them. The *Washington Post* reported in 2015 about an artist who took photographs from the Internet and transformed them into artworks that sold for $90,000 apiece.[406]

Richard Prince, the appropriation artist from the last case, made the news when his "New Portraits" collection was shown in New York. The pieces were taken from Instagram.[407]

> The collection, "New Portraits," is primarily made up of pictures of women, many in sexually charged poses. They are not paintings, but screenshots that have been enlarged to 6-foot-tall inkjet prints. According to Vulture, nearly every piece sold for $90,000 each.

The *Post* reporter, Jessica Contrera, reported that Prince appears able to take the works by making changes, just as he did with the photographs of Patrick Cariou.[408]

> Although he did not alter the usernames or the photos themselves, he removed captions. He then added odd comments on each photo, such as "DVD workshops. Button down. I fit in one leg now. Will it work? Leap of faith" from the account "richardprince1234."

---

[405] Ibid. at 711.

[406] Jessica Contrera, "A reminder that your Instagram photos aren't really yours: Someone else can sell them for $90,000," *Washington Post*, May 25, 2015.

[407] Ibid.

[408] Ibid.

Prince's own account has 10,200 followers. But visitors will not turn up a single picture of Prince himself.

ANDY WARHOL FOUNDATION AND LYNN GOLDSMITH'S PHOTO OF PRINCE

Lynne Goldsmith photographed Prince on assignment for *Newsweek* magazine in December of 1981, but the photos were never published. In 1984, *Vanity Fair* licensed one of the black and white photographs for $400, to be used as an artist's reference and commissioned Andy Warhol to create an illustration for an article about the musician.[409] Goldsmith did not know that the photograph was licensed to be used as an artist's reference. Her photo agency submitted the photograph to *Vanity Fair*.

The article in *Vanity Fair* said it featured a special portrait by Andy Warhol and included a copyright attribution credit for the portrait that cited a "source photograph" by Goldsmith.[410] Based on Goldsmith's Prince photograph, Warhold created the Prince series of 16 distinct pieces of artwork.[411]

United States District Judge John G. Koetl, found that the Andy Warhol's pieces did not constitute copyright infringement of Goldsmith's photograph, rather they were transformative. Judge Koetl wrote, they "have a different character, * * * and employ new aesthetics with creative and communicative results distinct from [Goldsmith's]."[412]

---

[409] Sarah Cascone, "The Warhol Foundation Has Won Out Against a Photographer Who Claimed the Pop Artist Pilfered Her Portrait of Prince," *artnetnews*, April 11, 2017, https://news.artnet.com/art-world/warhol-foundation-strikes-first-photographer-complains-copyright-922025.

[410] Associated Press, Andy Warhol's 'Prince Series' Is Fair Use, Court Rules," *New York Times*, July 2, 2019, https://www.nytimes.com/2019/07/02/arts/design/andy-warhol-prince-fair-use.html.

[411] *Andy Warhol Found. for the Visual Arts, Inc. v. Goldsmith*, 382 F. Supp. 3d 312, 319, 2019 U.S. Dist. LEXIS 110086, 2019 U.S.P.Q.2D (BNA) 244359, 2019 WL 2723521 (S.D.N.Y. July 1, 2019, Filed), available at https://advance-lexis-com.proxy.lib.utk.edu/api/document?collection=cases&id=urn:contentItem:5WG7-R4D1-K054-G00G-00000-00&context=1516831.

[412] Ibid. at 326.

APPENDIX A

ABBREVIATIONS

A.	Atlantic Reporter.
A.2d	Atlantic Reporter, Second Series.
A.C.	Appeal Cases.
A.L.R.	American Law Reports.
Aff.	Affirmed; affirming.
Ala.	Alabama; Alabama Supreme Court Reports.
Am.Dec.	American Decisions.
Am.Jur.	American Jurisprudence, a legal encyclopedia.
Am.Rep.	American Reports.
Am.St.Rep.	American State Reports.
Ann.Cas.	American Annotated Cases.
App.D.C.	Court of Appeals, District of Columbia.
App.Div.	New York Supreme Court, Appellate Divisions, Reports.
Ariz.	Arizona; Arizona Supreme Court Reports.
Ark.	Arkansas; Arkansas Supreme Court Reports.
Bing.	Bingham, New Cases, Common Pleas (England).
C.D.	Copyright Decision.
C.F.R.	Code of Federal Regulations.
C.J.	Corpus Juris, a legal encyclopedia.
C.J.S.	Corpus Juris Secundum, a legal encyclopedia.
Cal.	California; California Supreme Court Reports.
Can.Sup.Ct.	Canada Supreme Court Reports.
Cert.	Certiorari, a legal writ by which a cause is removed from an inferior to a superior court.
Colo.	Colorado; Colorado Supreme Court Reports.
Conn.	Connecticut; Connecticut Supreme Court of Errors Reports.
Cranch	Cranch, United States Supreme Court Reports; United States Circuit Court Reports.
Cush.	Cushing (Massachusetts).
D.C.App.	District of Columbia Court of Appeals Reports.

Dall, Dal.	Dallas, United States Supreme Court Reports; Pennsylvania Reports.
Del.	Delaware; Delaware Supreme Court Reports.
Edw.	Edward; refers to a particular king of England; which king of that name is indicated by the date; used to identify an act of Parliament.
Eng.Rep.	English Reports (reprint).
F.	Federal Reporter.
F.2d	Federal Reporter, Second Series.
F.3d	Federal Reporter, Third Series.
F.C.C.	Federal Communications Commission Reports.
F.R.D.	Federal Rules Decisions.
F.Supp.	Federal Supplement.
F.Supp.2d	Federal Supplement, Second Series.
Fed.Cas. or F.Cas.	Reports of United States Circuit and District Courts, 1789–1879.
Fla.	Florida; Florida Supreme Court Reports.
Ga.	Georgia; Georgia Supreme Court Reports.
Ga.App.	Georgia Appeals Reports.
How.St.Tr.	Howell's State Trials.
Hun	Hun, New York Supreme Court Reports.
Ibid.	Ibidem, the same, in the same volume, or on the same page.
Ill.	Illinois; Illinois Supreme Court Reports.
Ill.App.	Illinois Appellate Court Reports.
Ind.	Indiana; Indiana Supreme Court Reports.
Ind.App.	Indiana Appellate Court Reports.
Johns.Cas.	Johnson's Cases (New York).
K.B.	King's Bench Reports (England).
Kan.	Kansas; Kansas Supreme Court Reports.
Ky.	Kentucky; Kentucky Court of Appeals Reports.
L.J.	Law Journal (England).
L.R.A.	Lawyers Reports Annotated.
L.R.A.,N.S.,	Lawyers Reports Annotated, New Series.
L.R.Ex.	Law Reports, Exchequer (England).
L.R.Q.B.	Law Reports, Queen's Bench (England).
L.T.	The Law Times (England).

La.	Louisiana; Louisiana Supreme Court Reports.
La.Ann.	Louisiana Annual Reports.
Mass.	Massachusetts; Massachusetts Supreme Judicial Court Reports.
Md.	Maryland; Maryland Court of Appeals Reports.
Me.	Maine; Maine Supreme Judicial Court Reports.
Mich.	Michigan; Michigan Supreme Court Reports.
Minn.	Minnesota; Minnesota Supreme Court Reports.
Miss.	Mississippi; Mississippi Supreme Court Reports.
Mo.	Missouri; Missouri Supreme Court Reports.
Mo.App.	Missouri Appeals Reports.
Mont.	Montana; Montana Supreme Court Reports.
N.C.	North Carolina; North Carolina Supreme Court Reports.
N.D.	North Dakota; North Dakota Supreme Court Reports.
N.E.	Northeastern Reporter.
N.E.2d	Northeastern Reporter, Second Series.
N.H.	New Hampshire; New Hampshire Supreme Court Reports.
N.J.	New Jersey; New Jersey Court of Errors and Appeals Reports.
N.J.L.	New Jersey Law Reports.
N.M.	New Mexico; New Mexico Supreme Court Reports.
N.W.	Northwestern Reporter.
N.W.2d	Northwestern Reporter, Second Series.
N.Y.	New York; New York Court of Appeals Reports.
N.Y.S.	New York Supplement Reports.
Neb.	Nebraska; Nebraska Supreme Court Reports.
Nev.	Nevada; Nevada Supreme Court Reports.
Ohio App.	Ohio Appeals Reports.
Ohio St.	Ohio State Reports.
Okl.	Oklahoma; Oklahoma Supreme Court Reports.
Ops.	Opinions, as of Attorney General of the United States, or a state.
Or., Ore., Oreg.	Oregon; Oregon Supreme Court Reports.
P.	Pacific Reporter.

P.2d	Pacific Reporter, Second Series.
P.L. & R.	Postal Laws and Regulations (1948 ed.).
Pa.	Pennsylvania District and County Court Reports.
Pa.D. & C.	Pennsylvania District and County Court Reports.
Pa.Super.	Pennsylvania Superior Court Reports.
Paige	Paige, New York Chancery Reports.
Phila. (Pa).	Philadelphia Reports.
Pick.	Pickering, Massachusetts Reports.
Q.B.	Queen's Bench.
R.	Rex, king; Regina, queen.
R.C.L.	Ruling Case Law.
R.C.P.	Rules of Civil Procedure.
R.I.	Rhode Island; Rhode Island Supreme Court Reports.
R.R.	Pike & Fisher Radio Regulations.
S.C.	South Carolina; South Carolina Supreme Court Reports.
S.Ct.	Supreme Court Reporter.
S.D.	South Dakota; South Dakota Supreme Court Reports.
S.E.	Southeastern Reporter.
S.E.2d	Southeastern Reporter, Second Series.
S.W.	Southwestern Reporter.
S.W.2d	Southwestern Reporter, Second Series.
Sandf.	Sandford, New York Superior Court Reports.
Sec.	Section.
So.	Southern Reporter.
So.2d	Southern Reporter, Second Series.
Stark.	Starkie, English Reports.
T.L.R.	Times Law Reports (England).
Tenn.	Tennessee; Tennessee Supreme Court Reports.
Tex.	Texas; Texas Supreme Court (and the Commission of Appeals) Reports.
Tex.Civ.App.	Texas Civil Appeals Reports.
Tex.Cr.R.	Texas Court of Criminal Appeals Reports.
U.S.C.	United States Code.
U.S.C.A.	United States Code Annotated.
U.S.P.Q.	United States Patents Quarterly.

V.	Volume.
Va.	Virginia; Virginia Supreme Court of Appeals Reports.
Vt.	Vermont; Vermont Supreme Court Reports.
W.Va.	West Virginia; West Virginia Supreme Court of Appeals Reports.
Wash.	Washington; Washington Supreme Court Reports.
Wash.L.Rep.	Washington Law Reporter, Washington, D.C.
Whart.	Wharton (Pa.).
Wheat.	Wheaton (U.S.).
Wis.	Wisconsin; Wisconsin Supreme Court Reports.
Wyo.	Wyoming; Wyoming Supreme Court Reports.

APPENDIX B

Selected Court and Pleading Terms

Action

A formal legal demand of one's rights made in a court of law.

Actionable per quod

Words not actionable on their face but are defamatory when understood in the context of extrinsic facts.

Actionable per se

Words that need no explanation in order to determine their defamatory effect.

Amicus curiae

A friend of the court or one who interposes and volunteers information upon some matter of law.

Answer

The pleading of a defendant against whom a complaint has been filed.

Appeal

An application by an appellant to a higher court to change the order or judgment of the court below.

Appellant

The person or party appealing a decision or judgment to a higher court.

Appellee

The party against whom an appeal is taken.

Bind over

To hold on bail for trial.

Brief

A written or printed document prepared by counsel to file in court, normally providing both facts and law in support of the case.

Cause of action

The particular facts on which an action is based.

Certiorari

A writ commanding judges of a lower court to transfer to a higher court records of a case so that judicial review may take place.

Change of venue

Removing a civil suit or criminal action from one county or district to another county or district for trial. This is done to preserve a party's rights to a fair trial.

Civil action (suit, trial)

Court action brought to enforce, redress, or protect private rights, as distinguished from a Criminal action (q.v.).

Code

A compilation or system of laws, arranged into chapters, and promulgated by legislative authority.

Common law

The law of the decided cases, derived from the judgments and decrees of courts. Also called "case law." Originally, meant law which derived its authority from the ancient usages or customs of the land.

Complaint

The initial proceeding by a complainant, or plaintiff, in a civil action.

Contempt of court

Any act calculated to embarrass, hinder, or obstruct a court in the administration of justice, or calculated to lessen its dignity or authority.

Courts of record

Those whose proceedings are permanently recorded, and which have the power to fine or imprison for contempt. Courts not of record are those of lesser authority whose proceedings are not permanently recorded.

Criminal action (trial)

An action undertaken to punish a violation of criminal laws, as distinguished from a Civil action (q.v.).

Damages

Monetary compensation which may be recovered in court by a person who has suffered loss, detriment, or injury to his person, property, rights, or business, through the unlawful or negligent act of another person or party.

De novo

Anew, afresh. A trial de novo is a retrial of a case.

Dictum (pl. Dicta; also, Obiter Dictum)

An observation made by a judge, in an opinion on a case, that does not go to the main issue—a saying "by the way". The judge may comment without the comment having the actual force of law or of a legal holding. These can be influential on later cases.

Discovery

A party's pre-trial devices used, in preparation for trial, to obtain facts from the other party. It includes depositions (testimony under oath), interrogatories (written questions), admissions (a party admits that some facts are true) and production (a party has to produce things for examination by the other side).

Due process

Law in its regular course of administration through the courts of justice. The guarantee of due process requires that every person have the protection of a fair trial.

En banc

A session where the entire membership of a court, instead of one or a few, participates in the decision of an important case. ("Banc" means the judge's "bench" or place to sit.)

Equity

That system of jurisprudence which gives relief when there is no full, complete and adequate remedy at law; based originally upon the custom of appealing to the King or chancellor when the formality of the common law did not give means for relief.

Estoppel

An admission which prevents a person from using evidence which proves or tends to prove the contrary.

Executive session

A meeting of a board or governmental body that is closed to the public.

Ex parte

By or concerning only one party. This implies an examination in the presence of one party in a proceeding and the absence of the opposing party.

Ex post facto

After the fact.

Habeas corpus

Latin for "you have the body." A writ issued to an officer holding a person in detention or under arrest to bring that person before a court to determine the legality of the detention.

In camera

In the judge's private chambers or in a courtroom from which all spectators have been excluded.

Indictment

A written accusation of a crime prepared by a prosecuting attorney and presented for the consideration of a grand jury.

Information

A formal, written accusation of a crime prepared by a competent law officer of the government, such as a district or prosecuting attorney.

Injunction

A judicial order in equity directed against a person or organization directing that an act be performed or that the person or organization refrain from doing a particular act.

Intermediate scrutiny

A standard of review used to determine the constitutionality of a law. This is the middle of three bases for review. A law that does not, on its face, impinge on constitutional rights but nevertheless creates some constitutional problems in its enforcement will be examined under intermediate scrutiny. Under the test, the state must show that the law advances a substantial state interest and must be substantially related to achieving those purposes. See also Strict Scrutiny and Rational Basis.

Judgment

The decision of a court of law.

Jury

A group of a certain number of persons, selected according to law and sworn to inquire into certain matters of fact, and to declare the truth from evidence brought before them. A *grand jury* hears complaints and accusations in criminal cases, and issues bills of indictment in cases where the jurors believe that there is enough evidence to bring a case to trial. A *petit jury* consists of 12 (or fewer) persons who hear the trial of a civil or criminal case.

Mandamus

An extraordinary legal writ issued from a court to a corporation or its officers, to a public official, or to an inferior court commanding the doing of an act which the person, corporation, or lower court is under a duty to perform.

Motion to dismiss

A formal application by a litigant or his counsel addressed to the court for an order to dismiss the case.

Nol pros, nolle prosequi

A formal notification of unwillingness to prosecute which is entered upon the court record.

N.O.V. ("non obstante veredicto")

A judgment by the court in favor of one party notwithstanding a verdict that has been given to the other party. The jury verdict is tossed out and the judge's decision substituted.

Per se

In itself or by itself, as in libelous *per se*.

Plaintiff

The person (including an organization or business) who initiates a legal action.

Pleading

The process in which parties to a lawsuit or legal action alternately file with a court written statements of their contentions. By this process of statement and counterstatement, legal issues are framed and narrowed. These statements are often termed "pleadings."

Preliminary hearing, preliminary examination

A person charged with a crime is given a preliminary examination or hearing before a magistrate or judge to determine whether there is sufficient evidence to hold that person for trial.

Prima facie (pron.: prīma fā shē)

"At first sight" or "on the face of it." So far as can be judged from the first disclosure.

Rational basis

A standard of review used to determine the constitutionality of a law. This is the least challenging basis for review. The government only need show that the law has a reasonable foundation and purpose. See also Strict Scrutiny and Intermediate Scrutiny.

Reply

The pleading of plaintiff in response to the "answer" of the defendant.

Res adjudicata or res judicata

A thing decided.

Respondent

A party who gives an answer to a bill in equity; also, one who opposes a party who has taken a case to a higher court.

Stare decisis

To stand by the decisions, or to maintain precedent. This legal doctrine holds that settled points of law will not be disturbed.

Strict Scrutiny

A standard of review used by the courts whenever a law infringes on a constitutional right. This is the highest-level of review for laws and the government is required to show that is has a compelling interest to justify the law and that the law is narrowly tailored, that is there is no less restrictive means available. See also Intermediate Scrutiny and Rational Basis.

Subpoena

A command to appear at a place and time and to give testimony. "Subpoena-duces tecum" is a command to produce some document or paper at a trial.

Summary

Connoting "without a full trial." A summary judgment is a judge's rule that one party in a lawsuit wins before the conclusion of a full trial.

Venue

The particular county, city, or geographical area in which a court with jurisdiction may hear and decide a case.

Verdict

The decision of a jury as reported to the court.

Voir dire

Denotes the preliminary examination which the court may make of one presented as a witness or juror, where his competency or interest is objected to.

Writ

A legal instrument in the judicial process to enforce compliance with orders and sentences of a court.

APPENDIX C

SOME NOTES ON THE LEGAL PROCESS

During the first chapter of this book you were introduced rather rapidly to a wide assortment of legal terms. At that point, you probably did nothing more than to try to memorize as many of these terms as possible, expecting to find one or more of them lurking somewhere on your mid-term exam.

In reality, though, the most effective way of understanding what each of these legal terms actually means is to see how it operates in an actual case situation. Here, for example, are how the terms "criminal," "civil," "common" and "constitutional" law apply to various elements of a case discussed in Chap. 5 of this text. Although the right of the press to publish public information has been extended to some extent since *Cox Broadcasting v. Cohn*[1] was decided in 1975, the case still serves as a useful illustration of how the legal process operates.

A. Criminal, Civil and Common Law

In *Cox Broadcasting v. Cohn* a reporter disclosed the name of a rape victim during a television broadcast. The State of Georgia, where the broadcast originated, had enacted a provision in its criminal code that made it a crime for,

> any news media or other person to print, publish, broadcast, televise or disseminate through any other medium . . . the name or identity of any female who may have been raped.

If that official responsible for prosecuting those in that locality violating Georgia's "criminal law," (generally called the "District Attorney") believed that a reporter had violated this statute and thus committed a crime as defined by the criminal code of Georgia, the District Attorney would file a complaint describing the nature of the crime and charging the reporter with having committed it.[2] If the reporter entered a plea of "guilty" to this charge, the criminal court judge would then have the authority to impose any penalties provided by the law for this offense. However, if the reporter should enter a plea of "not guilty," the state would be required to prove "beyond a reasonable doubt" that *each*

[1] 420 U.S. 469, 95 S.Ct. 1029 (1975). This protection was extended to include information gathered from a police report in *Florida Star v. B.J.F.*, 491 U.S. 524, 109 S.Ct. 2603 (1989). Also see *Smith v. Daily Mail*, 443 U.S. 97, 99 S.Ct. 2667 (1979).

[2] Criminal law in most states classifies each crime as being either a "misdemeanor" or a "felony". A misdemeanor is a less serious crime, generally providing for a maximum jail term of less than one year, while a felony is a more serious crime, carrying a prison sentence in excess of one year. In this instance, disclosing the name of a rape victim was classified as being a misdemeanor crime.

element of the crime had occurred—in this case that (1) that the defendant reporter had knowingly disclosed the name of a woman (2) who may in fact have been a rape victim (3) and that the reporter's disclosure was disseminated by broadcasting or some other communications medium to the general public. Unless the state can establish beyond a reasonable doubt that each element of the criminal charge has taken place, the defendant reporter must be found "not guilty."

Here, for instance, if the District Attorney could not prove that this disclosure had actually been broadcast or disseminated to the public through some other medium, the charge against the defendant would have had to be dismissed "with prejudice," meaning that the State could not try this reporter again for this same offense.

But even if the reporter had been tried and found not guilty of any criminal offense, he could still be required by "civil law" to compensate anyone damaged because of the disclosure. In other words, even though not guilty of violating a criminal law designed to protect society in general, a reporter could still be required by civil law to pay money damages to any specific individual actually injured by this same act.

Civil law actions can be based either upon statutory rights granted individuals by State legislation or upon traditional rights granted by Anglo Saxon "common law." In the *Cox* case the father of the deceased rape victim used a "common law" right of "invasion of privacy" as the basis for a legal action claiming damages from the reporter and his television station employer.[3] Although the state of Georgia had not enacted a law granting an individual the right to sue for invasion of privacy, the Georgia courts did recognize a historic right of privacy developed by past judicial decisions that allowed those damaged by public disclosure of private information to be compensated for their embarrassment or humiliation.[4]

As this civil action to recover damages for invasion of privacy was about to begin, however, an issue of "constitutional law" was raised, delaying the trial until this question could be resolved.

The defendant broadcast station claimed that the rape victim's name had already been revealed to the public before it was disclosed during the television news program, because she had been identified by name in the criminal proceedings used to charge her assailants. Under these circumstances, the defendant argued that to compel a broadcast station to pay damages for disclosing a fact that any member of the public could have discovered in the files of the local courthouse improperly penalized

[3] Even though the reporter may have been the one primarily responsible for any damages the father of the deceased rape victim sustained, law suits of this type always attempt to include the media organization as a co-defendant, because juries tend to be far more generous in awarding damages when they are taking them from a giant corporation, rather than an individual.

[4] At common law, this type of right is called a "tort", meaning that the law allows a party injured by the act of another to recover damages caused by that act.

a communications medium for exercising its free speech right to disseminate public information.

In essence then, the defendant broadcast station was claiming that no matter how much anguish or embarrassment it might have caused, there should be no civil trial to determine what monetary compensation it should pay for these damages. Instead, the defendant demanded that the case be dismissed immediately without awarding any damages, because to punish a station for reporting information already a matter of public record would improperly inhibit its right of freedom of expression protected by the First and Fourteenth Amendments.

B. The Judicial Process

The Supreme Court of Georgia rejected this constitutional argument, finding nothing in either the Georgia state constitution or the federal constitution that guaranteed a broadcaster an absolute right to reveal the identity of an individual whose privacy was expressly protected by Georgia law. This decision meant that the civil action to decide whether the defendants were actually liable for damages caused by their news report could now begin.

Here, however, the Supreme Court of the United States intervened to grant *certiorari*, meaning that it would review the Georgia court's decision to determine if the State court had correctly interpreted the constitutionally protected free speech rights of the broadcast medium under these circumstances. Once again, then, the trial had to be postponed until the Supreme Court was able to decide whether the defendant broadcast station could be held liable for invasion of privacy damages without illegally infringing upon its right of freedom of expression.

Eventually, as you may recall, a majority of the Supreme Court Justices joined in a decision that shielded the broadcast defendant from civil liability for any damages caused by the disclosure of information already a matter of public record, finding that to allow a communications medium to be penalized for disseminating facts available to every citizen would "invite timidity and self-censorship and very likely lead to the suppression of many items . . . that should be made available to the public".[5]

Thus in *Cox*, as in many of the other cases discussed in this book, there was never any exciting conflict in open court; no trial with its fascinating array of witnesses, caustic cross examinations, angry objections or eloquent closing statements. Instead, clashes between attorneys representing the embittered family of the rape victim and those protecting the free speech rights of the broadcasters occurred in the hushed atmosphere of an appeals court, defined by carefully researched

---

[5] *Cox Broadcasting v. Cohn*, 420 U.S. 469, 95 S.Ct. 1029 (1975).

legal arguments in written documents called "briefs", and explained by these attorneys in polite, precisely reasoned statements to the court.

After considering these briefs and arguments, an appeals court determines how to resolve the issue or issues of law raised by the appeal, writing an opinion to explain the legal basis for this decision, and to point out to those lower trial courts under its authority how they should resolve the same legal issue if it should arise again during any legal proceeding in the future.

But what if the trial in the *Cox* case had already taken place before the defense attorneys raised any questions about its constitutionality, and the jury had found that this news broadcast did invade the privacy of the plaintiff, entering a verdict granting the injured party a massive award of monetary damages? In that case, the attorneys for the defendants would have the right to appeal this verdict, asking the court with review authority over the trial judge to consider any material legal issues the appealing attorney claims were not considered, or were decided erroneously at during the trial, resulting in the appealing party losing the case.

In our *Cox* case example, the reviewing court judge would then accept briefs and hear arguments on only that single issue raised on appeal, determining whether the free speech safeguards of the First and Fourteenth amendments protect a broadcast station from being held liable for monetary damages caused by disclosure of information already a matter of public record.

This appeals court generally has three options available to it after considering the legal issues it has reviewed. The first option is to *affirm* the lower court decision, indicating that the lower court was correct in its interpretation of the legal issue raised on appeal. The second option is to *reverse and remand* with instructions, finding the lower court to be in error and sending the case back for a new trial or "retrial" in which the judge will follow the guidance of the review court to avoid those errors that caused the first trial to be invalid. In this situation, the third option would be to *vacate* the judgement, declaring that law suit should not have been tried in the first place because the plaintiff had no legal right to bring the action.

Unfortunately, this is seldom the end of the litigation process. The party losing at this appeal court level generally has the right to seek a review of the appeal court decision by a higher level appellate court or the state Supreme Court, and if as in the *Cox* case, an important federal issue has been raised by the litigation, the entire matter can be removed to federal court, where the proceedings begins anew.

A process this slow, expensive and risky is one that provides every incentive for out-of-court settlements and explains why one legal scholar described litigation as being the "pathology" of the law. In reality, then, those appeal court opinions published and discussed in this book can be understood most accurately not as typical cases in communication law, but rather the unusual ones that were considered so important by the parties involved that they were willing to accept the delays, costs and risks of litigation in order to establish that point of law described in the opinion.

C. Administrative Law and the Courts

The FCC is an administrative agency, created by Congress to enforce the provisions of the Communications Act of 1934. As a regulatory body, the Commission has been granted authority by Congress to adopt "administrative law" rules to define more clearly those generalized broadcast public interest standards contained in the Communications Act. In addition, the FCC has been empowered by Congress to hold hearings to determine whether a broadcast licensee may have violated Commission rules, or the provisions of the Communications Act, and to impose penalties upon those licensees not conforming to these regulatory standards.

At the same time, Congress has established the Court of Appeals for the District of Columbia as the federal court responsible for reviewing FCC decisions. In a case such as *CBS v. FCC*, described in Chap. 11 of your text, an administrative law judge held a hearing to determine whether the refusal of CBS to provide air time for the broadcast of a political documentary represented a violation of the reasonable access requirements of section 312(a) of the Communications Act.

As administrative law has been structured by Congress, this hearing is considered to be a "trial court" proceeding, establishing a legal record for the decision that can later be reviewed on appeal by the Court of Appeals for the District of Columbia, and ultimately by the United States Supreme Court if it should decide to accept certiorari.

The finding of the administrative law judge that CBS had violated the access requirements of section 312(a) was reviewed initially within the FCC by review board created expressly for this purpose. When this decision was affirmed by the board, and finally approved by a 4–3 vote of the FCC Commissioners, the network petitioned the D.C. Court of Appeals to review those errors in law alleged to have caused the Commission to improperly interpret the legal requirements of this section of the Act.

As in the *Cox* case, the Court of Appeals had the option of affirming the Commission decision, remanding it for a new hearing on issues it overlooked or improperly decided at the original hearing, or vacating the decision if the appeals court could find no legal basis for the *FCC*'s determination.

In this example, after the appeals court affirmed the *FCC* decision, the Supreme Court agreed to review the case and eventually also affirmed the Commission's decision by a 6–3 margin, with Justice Burger writing the majority opinion explaining that such a reasonable political access requirement did not improperly infringe upon the free speech rights of the broadcaster because there was "nothing in the First Amendment which prevents Government from requiring a licensee to share his frequency with others . . . "[6]

Understanding these basic legal terms in the context of that system of law in which they operate should help you to become more fully aware of the actual legal effects of those communication law decisions contained in this book. But if you'd be interested in finding and actually reading these or other important communication law opinions on your own, no area of study is organized more logically or indexed more effectively than the field of American law.

D. Locating Judicial Source Material

All decisions of the United States Supreme Court are published by two commercial publishers in series called *Supreme Court Reporter* (West Publishing) and another called *U.S. Supreme Court Reports, Lawyer's Edition* (Lawyers' Cooperative Publishing Company). Each of these series contains every opinion of the Supreme Court, but West and Lawyers' Cooperative provide additional reference and indexing material as part of their total system of legal publications for lawyers.

Decisions of the federal Courts of Appeal are published in the *Federal Reporter*, and most federal District Court decisions are found in the *Federal Supplement*, both West Publishing series. All reported decisions of state courts are contained in West Publishing's National Reporter System, divided geographically into seven different regional series; the *Atlantic, Pacific, Southern, Southwestern, Southeastern, Northwestern* and *Northeastern*. To locate a particular judicial opinion, all you need to do is to follow the instructions provided by its citation. For example, to find the famous *United Church of Christ v. FCC* case, cited as 359 F.2d 994, that recognized the right of citizen groups to challenge the renewal of a broadcast license, you would open the 359th volume of the *Federal Reporter*, 2nd series, and turn to page 994 where the opinion begins.

If your university library doesn't have these legal publications among its holdings, they can all be found in the library of your nearest county courthouse. In addition, you should find a service called *Shepard's Citators* there that allows you, by using its various judicial indexing books, to discover whether any later decisions have had any effect upon those legal principles defined by that judicial opinion you've just been reading.

This brief survey of communication law research literature is not intended to do anything more than illustrate how simple the process of legal research can really be. There is no reason to provide an elaborate description of a wide variety of communication law research techniques here, because there are so many excellent books and studies already

[6] *CBS v. FCC*, 453 U.S. 367, 101 S.Ct. 2813 (1981).

covering every aspect of this topic in great detail. For further guidance, any of the following books and articles are highly recommended:

1. Cohen, M.L. *How to Find the Law* St. Paul, Minn., West Publishing. (often updated with new editions).

2. Cohen, M.L. *Legal Research in a Nutshell* St. Paul, Minn., West Publishing, (frequently updated).

3. Foley, J.M. "Broadcast Regulation Research: A Primer for Non-Lawyers," *Journal of Broadcasting* 17/2 (Summer 1973) pp. 147–159.

4. Goehlert, R. *Congress and Law Making: Researching the Legislative Process* Santa Barbara, CA Clio Books, 1979.

5. Honigsburg, P.J. *Cluing Into Legal Research* Berkeley, CA Golden Rain Press, 1979.

6. Jacobstein J.M. and R. M. Mersky, *Fundamentals of Legal Research* Mineola, NY Foundation Press, 1992.

7. Le Duc, D.R. "Broadcast Legal Documentation: A Four-Dimensional Guide," *Journal of Broadcasting* 17/2 (Summer 1973) pp. 131–146.

8. Pauwels, C.K, in J.R. Bittner, *Broadcast Law and Regulation* Englewood Cliffs NJ Prentice Hall 1982 pp. 397–411.

9. Price, M.O. and H. Bittner, *Effective Legal Research* Boston Little Brown (1979).

APPENDIX D

BIBLIOGRAPHY

Adler, Allan Robert, Litigation Under the Federal Open Government Act, 18th ed., Washington, D.C., 1993.

Adler, Renata, Reckless Disregard, New York, 1986.

Altschull, Herbert, From Milton to McLuhan: The Ideas Behind American Journalism. New York, 1990.

American Law Institute, Restatement of the Law: Torts. 2d ed. St. Paul, 1977.

Bagdikian, Ben, The Media Monopoly, 7th ed., Boston, 2004.

Baker, C. Edwin, Human Liberty and Freedom of Speech. New York. 1989.

Balkin, Jack, and Reva B. Siegel, eds., The Constitution in 2020. New York, 2009.

Barnouw, Erik, A History of Broadcasting in the United States, 3 vols. (N.Y., 1966–1972).

Barron, Jerome, Freedom of the Press for Whom? Bloomington, Ind., 1973.

Berns, Walter, The First Amendment and the Future of American Democracy. New York, 1976.

Bezanson, Randall P., Gilbert Cranberg, and John Soloski, Libel Law and The Press: Myth and Reality, New York, 1987.

Bittner, John R., Law and Regulation of Electronic Media (2nd ed.) New Jersey, 1994.

Blackstone, William, Commentaries on the Law of England, IV, adapted by Robert Malcom Kerr, Boston, 1952.

Blasi, Vincent, The Checking Value in First Amendment Theory, American Bar Foundation Research Journal, 1977, #3.

Bok, Sissela, Secrets. New York, 1983.

Brant, Irving, The Bill of Rights: Its Origin and Meaning. New York, 1965.

Brown, Cynthia, ed., Lost Liberties: Ashcroft and the Assault on Personal Freedom New York, The New Press, 2003.

Chafee, Zechariah, Jr., Free Speech in the United States. Boston, 1941.

_______, Government and Mass Communications, 2 vols. Chicago, 1947.

Chamberlin, Bill F., and Charlene Brown, The First Amendment Reconsidered. Chapel Hill, 1981.

Churchill, Winston S., A History of the English-Speaking Peoples. New York, 1963.

Cole, David, Enemy Aliens: Double Standards and Constitutional Freedoms in the War on Terrorism New York, The New Press, 2003.

Cooley, Thomas M., Constitutional Limitations. (8th ed.). Boston, 1927.

Cooper, Thomas, The Law of Libel and the Liberty of the Press. New York, 1830.

Cross, Harold L., The People's Right to Know. New York, 1953.

Dadge, David, Casualty of War: The Bush Administration's Assault on a Free Press Amherst, N.Y., Prometheus Books, 2004.

Denniston, Lyle, The Reporter and the Law. New York, 1980.

Dienes, C. Thomas, Lee Levine, and Robert C. Lind, Newsgathering and the Law, Charlottesville, Virginia, 1997.

Duniway, Clyde A., The Development of Freedom of the Press in Massachusetts. Cambridge, 1906.

Emerson, Thomas I., The System of Freedom of Expression. New York, 1970.

Emery, Walter B., Broadcasting and Government: Responsibilities and Regulations. East Lansing, Mich., 1961.

Folkerts, Jean, Dwight L. Teeter, Jr., and Edward Caudill, Voices of a Nation: A History of the Mass Media in the United States, 5th ed., Boston, 2009.

Fox, Sir John C., The History of Contempt of Court. Oxford, 1927.

Friendly, Fred, Minnesota Rag. New York, 1981.

Fueroghne, Dean K., Law & Advertising: Current Legal Issues for Agencies, Advertisers and Attorneys. Chicago, 1995.

Gellhorn, Walter, Security, Loyalty, and Science. Ithaca, New York, 1950.

Gerald, J. Edward, The Press and the Constitution, 1931–1947. Minneapolis, 1948.

Gillmor, Donald M., Free Press and Fair Trial. Washington, D.C., 1966.

Goldfarb, Ronald L., The Contempt Power. New York, 1963.

Goodale, James, C., chairman, Communications Law 2007, 3 vols. New York, 2007.

Goodman, Mark, Law of the Student Press (2nd ed.) Washington, D.C., SPLC, 1994.

Gora, Joel M., The Rights of Reporters. New York, 1974.

Griswold, Erwin, The First Amendment Today. Cambridge, 1955.

Hachten, William A., The Supreme Court on Freedom of the Press: Decisions and Dissents. Ames, Iowa, 1968.

Haight, Anne Lyon, Banned Books (rev. 2d ed.). New York, 1955.

Hallin, Daniel C., "The Uncensored War:" The Media and Vietnam. Berkeley, 1986.

Havick, John J., Communications Policy and the Political Process. Westport, Conn., 1983.

Head, Sydney W. and Christopher Sterling, Broadcasting in America. (5th ed.). Boston, 1987.

Hentoff, Nat, History of Freedom of the Press in America. New York, 1980.

_______, The War on the Bill of Rights And the Gathering Resistance New York, Seven Stories Press, 2003.

Heymann, Phillip B., Terrorism, Freedom and Security: Winning Without War Cambridge, MA, MIT Press, 2003.

Hocking, William E., Freedom of the Press. Chicago, 1947.

Holmes, Oliver Wendell Jr., The Common Law. Boston, 1881.

Hopkins, W. Wat, Mr. Justice Brennan and Freedom of Expression. New York, 1991.

Hurst, James Willard, Law and Conditions of Freedom. New York, 1962.

Jolliffe, John, The Constitutional History of Medieval England (2d ed.). London, 1947.

Jones, William, Cases and Materials on Electronic Mass Media. Mineola, N.Y., 1977.

Kahn, F.J., ed., Documents of American Broadcasting, 4th ed. New York, 1984.

Katz, Stanley Nider, A Brief Narrative of the Case and Trial of John Peter Zenger. Cambridge, Mass., 1963.

Kaufman, Henry R., ed., LDRC 50-State Survey 1984, III. New York, 1984.

Kinsley, Philip, Liberty and the Press. Chicago, 1944.

Konvitz, Milton R., First Amendment Freedoms. Ithaca, 1963.

Kovach, Bill and Tom Rosenstiel, Warp Speed: America in the Age of Mixed Media. New York, 1999.

Le Duc, Don R., Beyond Broadcasting: Patterns in Policy and Law. (New York, 1987).

Leone, Richard C. and Greg Anrig, Jr., eds., Liberty Under Attack: Reclaiming Our Freedoms in an Age of Terror, New York, 2007.

Levy, Leonard W., Emergence of a Free Press. New York, 1985.

______, ed., Freedom of the Press from Zenger to Jefferson. Indianapolis, 1966.

______, Legacy of Suppression: Freedom of Speech and Press in Early American History. Cambridge, 1960.

Lewis, Anthony, Make No Law: The Sullivan Case and the First Amendment. New York, 1991.

Lockhart, William B., and Robert C. McClure, Censorship of Obscenity: the Developing Constitutional Standards, 45 Minnesota Law Review 5 (Nov. 1960).

______, Literature, the Law of Obscenity, and the Constitution, 38 Minnesota Law Review (March 1954).

Lofton, John, The Press as a Defender of the First Amendment. Columbia, S.C., 1980.

Main, Jackson Turner, The Antifederalists: Critics of the Constitution. Chapel Hill, 1961.

McChesney, Robert, Rich Media, Poor Democracy. Urbana, IL, 1999.

McCormick, Robert R., The Freedom of the Press. New York, 1936.

Media Law Resource Center (MLRC), ed., 50-State Survey, Media Libel Law 2010–2011,

Meiklejohn, Alexander, Free Speech and Its Relation to Self Government. New York, 1948.

Miller, Arthur, The Assault on Privacy. Ann Arbor, 1971.

Miller, Charles, The Supreme Court and the Uses of History. Cambridge, Mass., 1969.

Moore, Roy L., Ronald T. Farrar and Erik L. Collins, Advertising and Public Relations Law. Mahwah, NJ, 1998.

Murphy, Paul, World War I and the Origins of Civil Liberties in the United States. New York, 1979.

Nelson, Harold L., ed., Freedom of the Press from Hamilton to the Warren Court. Indianapolis, 1967.

Newman, Roger K., ed., The Yale Biographical Dictionary of American Law, New Haven & London, 2009.

Nimmer, Melville B., Nimmer on Copyright, 4 vols. New York, 1963–1988.

Nye, Russel Blaine, Fettered Freedom. East Lansing, Mich., 1951.

Owen, Bruce M., Economics and Freedom of Expression. Cambridge, 1975.

Parenti, Christian, The Soft Cage: Surveillance in America from Slavery to the War on Terror New York, Basic Books, 2003.

Parsons, Patrick, Cable Television and the First Amendment. Lexington, MA, 1987.

Paul, James C.N., and Murray L. Schwartz, Federal Censorship: Obscenity in the Mail. New York, 1961.

Pember, Don R., Privacy and the Press. Seattle, 1972.

Peterson, H.C., and Gilbert C. Fite, Opponents of War, 1917–1918. Madison, 1957.

Phelps, Robert H. and E. Douglas Hamilton, Libel: Rights, Risks, Responsibilities. New York, 1966.

Pilpel, Harriet, and Theodora Zavin, Rights and Writers. New York, 1960.

Plucknett, Theodore F.T., A Concise History of the Common Law. London, 1948.

Pool, Ithiel de Sola, Technologies of Freedom. Cambridge, Mass., 1983.

Powe, Lucas A., Jr., American Broadcasting and the First Amendment, Berkeley, 1987.

_______, The Fourth Estate and the Constitution. Berkeley, 1991.

Preston, Ivan, The Tangled Web They Weave: Truth, Falsity and Advertisers. Madison, 1994.

Preston, William, Jr., Aliens and Dissenters. Cambridge, 1963.

Prosser, William L., The Law of Torts. 4th ed. St. Paul, 1971.

Rabban, David M., Free Speech in its Forgotten Years. Cambridge, England, 1997.

Roberts, Gene, ed., Thomas Kunkel & Charles Layton, general eds., Leaving Readers Behind: The Age of Corporate Newspapering, Fayetteville, AR, 2001.

Rosden, George Eric and Peter Eric, The Law of Advertising, 4 vols. (New York, 1963—present).

Rosen, Jeffrey, The Naked Crowd: Reclaiming Security and Freedom in an Anxious Age New York, Random House, 2003.

Rosenberg, Norman L., Protecting the Best Men: An Interpretive History of Libel, Chapel Hill, 1986.

Rourke, Francis E., Secrecy and Publicity. Baltimore, 1961.

Sack, Robert D., and Sandra S. Baron, Libel, Slander, and Related Problems, 2nd ed. New York, 1994.

Sanford, Bruce, The Law of Libel and the Right of Privacy. New York, 1984.

Schlesinger, Arthur M., Prelude to Independence: The Newspaper War on Britain, 1763–1776. New York, 1958.

Schmidt, Benno C., Jr., Freedom of the Press vs. Public Access. New York, 1976.

Seldes, George, Freedom of the Press. Cleveland, 1935.

Shapiro, Martin, Freedom of Speech: The Supreme Court and Judicial Review. Englewood Cliffs, N.J., 1966.

Siebert, Fredrick S., Freedom of the Press in England, 1476–1776. Urbana, 1952.

Simmons, Steven J., The Fairness Doctrine and the Media. Berkeley, 1978.

Simon, Morton J., Public Relations Law. New York, 1969.

Smith, James Morton, Freedom's Fetters: the Alien and Sedition Laws and American Civil Liberties. Ithaca, 1956.

Smith, Jeffery A, War and Press Freedom: The Problem of Prerogative Power, New York, 1999.

Smolla, Rodney, Jerry Falwell v. Larry Flynt, Urbana, 1988.

_______, Law of Defamation.

_______, Suing the Press. New York, 1986.

Stansbury, Arthur J., Report of the Trial of James H. Peck. Boston, 1833.

Sterling, Christopher, and John Michael Kittross, Stay Tuned: A Concise History of American Broadcasting, 3rd ed. New York, 2002.

Stevens, John D., Shaping the First Amendment: The Development of Freedom of Expression. Beverly Hills, 1982.

Stone, Geoffrey R., Perilous Times: Free Speech in Wartime from the Sedition Act of 1798 to the War on Terrorism. New York, 2004.

Sullivan, Harold W., Contempts by Publication. New Haven, 1940.

_______, Trial by Newspaper. Hyannis, Mass., 1961.

Toobin, Jeffrey, The Nine: Inside the Secret World of the Supreme Court. New York, 2007.

Warren, Samuel D., and Louis D. Brandeis, The Right to Privacy, 4 Harvard Law Review 193 (1890).

Weiner, Tim, Legacy of Ashes: A History of the CIA. New York, 2007.

Westin, Alan, Privacy and Freedom. New York, 1967.

Winfield, Richard N., New York Times v. Sullivan, the Next Twenty Years (New York, Practising Law Institute, 1984).

Wolff, Robert Paul, Barrington Moore and Herbert Marcuse, A Critique of Pure Tolerance. Boston, 1965.

Wortman, Tunis, Treatise Concerning Political Enquiry, and the Liberty of the Press. New York, 1800.

Yudof, Mark G., When Government Speaks. Berkeley, 1983.

Additional Resources

American Digest System, Decennial Digests, valuable for lists of cases and points adjudicated.

American Jurisprudence, a legal encyclopedia.

Annotated Report System, selected reports and annotations, with summaries of arguments of counsel.

Compilations of Laws Affecting Publications, particularly those put out by various states. Consult managers of various state press associations.

Corpus Juris Secundum, a legal encyclopedia.

Freedom of Information Center, University of Missouri, issues frequent Reports, the FOI Digest (bi-monthly newsletter), and occasional studies covering a wide variety of media-and-law-subjects. Invaluable for state laws on meetings and records.

Law Dictionaries, including Black's, Ballentine's, and Bouvier's.

Law Reviews. Among the outstanding law reviews published under the direction of law schools are Columbia Law Review, Cornell Law Quarterly, the Federal Communications Law Journal, Harvard Law Review, Illinois Law Review, Michigan Law Review, Texas Law Review, Wisconsin Law Review, and Yale Law Journal. See also Communication Law & Policy, a publication of the Law and Policy Division of the Association for Education in Journalism and Mass Communication.

Libel Defense Resource Center, LDRC 50-State Survey 1996–97: Media Libel Law (New York, 1996) *and* LDRC 50-State Survey 1996–97: Media Libel Law (New York, 1996).

Media Law Reporter. Bureau of National Affairs, Inc., Washington, D.C. This looseleaf service provides up-to-date coverage of court decisions (full texts) and news notes in communication law, beginning in 1976.

Media Libel Law 2009–2010, Media Law Resource Center 50-State Survey, New York, 2010.

National Reporter System, giving texts of appellate court decisions in various jurisdictions of the nation.

News Media and the Law, publication of the Reporters Committee for Freedom of the Press (formerly Press Censorship Newsletter). Washington, D.C.

Westlaw, a computerized search and reference service.

Words and Phrases, a legal encyclopedia based on definitions of terms as used in statutes and by the courts.

APPENDIX E

WEBSITES OF CODES OF ETHICS AND PRINCIPLES OF THE SPJ, ASNE, RTDNA AND PRSA

As the distinguished observer of the United States Supreme Court Lyle Denniston has said, if journalists paid more attention to their ethics, they'd spend less time talking to lawyers and judges. Reproduced below are web addresses for ethical guidelines of some of the leading organizations of mass communication practitioners. These codes of ethics or principles do not have the force of law, although on occasion, arguments about what is ethical sometimes get involved in libel and privacy lawsuits. Teachers may wish to ask their students to download these codes and study them. It may be instructive to ponder how many of the court decisions discussed in this textbook might not have arisen if more attention had been paid—before publication or broadcast—to such ethical precepts. All of these codes were accessed on April 2020.

- The Society of Professional Journalists Code of Ethics:

  http://www.spj.org/ethicscode.asp

- American Society of News Editors Ethics Forum:

  http://asne.org/content.asp?contentid=236

- Code of Ethics and Professional Conduct Radio Television Digital News Association:

  http://www.rtdna.org/content/rtdna_code_of_ethics

[The Radio Television Digital News Association was named the Radio Television News Directors Association until October 13, 2009.]

- Public Relations Society of America Member Code of Ethics:

  http://www.prsa.org/AboutPRSA/Ethics/CodeEnglish/

- National Press Photographers Association [NPPA] Code of Ethics:

  https://nppa.org/code_of_ethics

INDEX

References are to Pages